AMERICAN Chronicle

Six decades in American life 1920–1980

AMERICAN Chronicle

Six decades in American life 1920–1980

Lois Gordon
Alan Gordon

ATHENEUM   NEW YORK

Atheneum
Macmillan Publishing Company
866 Third Avenue, New York, N.Y. 10022
Collier Macmillan Canada, Inc.

Library of Congress Cataloging-in-Publication Data

Gordon, Lois G.
    American chronicle.

    1. United States—Civilization—20th century—
Chronology. 2. United States—Civilization—20th century
—Miscellanea. I. Gordon, Alan, 1936-   .II. Title.
E169.1G665   1987   973.9   86-20621
ISBN 0-689-11899-6
ISBN 0-689-11901-1 (pbk.)

Macmillan books are available at special discounts for bulk
purchases for sales promotions, premiums, fund-raising, or
educational use.
For details contact:

        Special Sales Director
        Macmillan Publishing Company
        866 Third Avenue
        New York, N.Y. 10022

10 9 8 7 6 5 4 3 2

Printed in the United States of America

Contents

Preface

"America was designed by Providence for the theatre on which man was to make his true figure, on which science, virtue, liberty, happiness, and glory were to exist in peace." This was the hope of John Adams before the Revolution, and it remains the dream of continuing generations. We, like most Americans, feel blessed to live in this country and to share this dream, which predicates not only that liberty is the inalienable right of all people, but that it grants them the greatest opportunity for fulfilling their talents.

The years chronicled in this book represent an important era in the history of the dream. The six decades between 1920 and 1980 were immensely rich and varied—a time of great energy and productivity, as well as often fierce struggle for the ideals of human liberty. This was an era of American ascendancy, when the United States took a leading role on the world stage and also staked its claim to preeminence in the various arenas of human endeavor. The period 1920–80 also covers roughly three generations, and is therefore within the recollection of most Americans or their immediate forebears, accessible through individual recall or from family history. Although we originally planned to extend this book to the present, the material lent itself to a decade structure. We therefore conclude in 1979, in order to cover each decade in its entirety, as well as to allow some distance for reflection.

The book thus has two purposes. First, it tries to document the flowering of modern America and offer the student of American culture a useful and comprehensive reference work that is a collation of the myriad surfaces of the American scene. In many of the areas—music, art, theater, film, fashion, sports, science—this is the first such extensive year-by-year compilation.

Second, it tries, through the accretion of information, to re-create each particular year. Our intention was to provide the stuff of contemporary memory, to evoke, enrich, and expand the contexts in which most people, their parents, and their grandparents have lived their lives. In a sense, we have hoped to furnish the reader with background material for his or her own autobiography.

"The earth did shake when I was born," proclaims Shakespeare's mighty but vain Glendower. While we could not declare the same for ourselves, we have been fascinated, in researching the book, to discover multiple resonances and a certain inner coherence that have tended to give not just our birth years but each year a unique personality. Although at one time the span of years tended to blur in each of our memories, we have, through the data of this book, had the pleasure of reexperiencing and imagining them with clearer definition and understanding. Our greatest wish is to provide the reader with a similar experience. Facts, it is our final observation, serve not only to inform and satisfy intellectual curiosity, but they also serve as symbols that evoke one's personal and public heritage.

> Other echoes
> Inhabit the garden. Shall we follow?
> —T.S. Eliot, *Burnt Norton*

New York City

Lois Gordon
Alan Gordon

Acknowledgments

We wish to thank the following librarians and curators for their generous assistance: Ruth Schwartz, Mary McMahon, Judy Katz, Laila Rogers, Judy Barrett, Michelle Fanelli, Eileen McIlvaine, Rita Kecheissen, Mikki Carpenter, Maya Falaco, Franklin Riehlman, Marian Weston, Patrick Hardish, Joyce Goulet, William L. Bird, May Castleberry, Anita Duquette, Beth Diefendorf, and Roxanna Deane. John Kelly, at the Library of Congress, was of immeasurable assistance. We also express special thanks to a number of people who commented upon our material in the various areas of their expertise: Warren French, David Shapiro, Oleg Kerensky, Mary Ann Farese, Jacqueline Rettig, David Sarturen, Bernard Dick, Michael T. Garodnitz, and, especially, Gene Barnett, whose sustained interest and general knowledgeability were invaluable. For their encouragement and assistance in any number of ways, we thank Lowell Gibbs, Alberto Caputo, Lois Spatz, Doris Auerbach, Susan Shapiro, Vernon Schonert, Peggy Anderson, Hugh Johnson, Roger Whitehouse, Pauline Klaw, Josephine Mangiaracina, Marty Feely, David Protomastro, Shepard Goldfein, and Ricardo Quintana. Finally, for the extraordinary care, skill, and enthusiasm with which they worked on this book, along with their meticulous attention to detail, we thank Michael Sims, Carole Rollins, and Cecile Watters at G. K. Hall. To our general editor, Janice Meagher, for her initial interest in this project and her ongoing support and many helpful suggestions, we express our deepest gratitude. To Lawrence McIntyre, our editor at Atheneum, for the competence and thoughtfulness with which he handled the final stages of production, we also express our sincere appreciation. To our son, Robert, we offer a very special thanks for reasons he well knows.

To the Reader

Reference materials and photos were collected from a number of institutions, including the Library of Congress; the Smithsonian divisions of Political History, Domestic Life, Community Life, and Social and Cultural Life; the National Air and Space Museum; the National Archives; the U.S. Department of the Navy; Martin Luther King Library (Washington, D.C.); New York Public Library; Museum of the City of New York; Metropolitan Museum of Art; National Gallery; Philadelphia Museum of Art; Museum of Modern Art; Whitney Museum; Guggenheim Museum; Juilliard School of Music; Fashion Institute of Technology; Fairleigh Dickinson University; and Columbia University. Sources include a wide variety of primary and secondary materials—newspapers, magazines, government documents, and the reference texts, encyclopedias, and general and specific historical and critical studies appropriate to the subject areas and time periods.

It would be unwieldy to detail the specific sources for the many areas surveyed in this book. The broad rubric of music, for example, involved collecting data on first performances of significant works throughout the country, performers' debuts, important events (of major conductors, symphony orchestras, and virtuosos), the dating of major compositions, the openings of major concert facilities; operatic debuts and performances of major works and stars in companies throughout the country; ballet history of the major classic and modern dance companies; and popular music ranging from top songs, records, and albums (from swing to country and soul) to jazz developments and the formation of big bands, along with major awards within each category.

Our overall goals and general methodology are easier to explain. In certain areas, such as Theater, Critically Acclaimed Books, and Movies, we tried to present a spectrum of what was popular or considered important at the time, along with what has come to have retrospective significance. With Quotes, Ads, and Kaleidoscope, we tried to emphasize the preoccupations and sensibility of each year—in a manner of speaking, its unique personality. Our single imperative was to be thorough, and as we read through the extensive sources, our aim remained the collection of material of significant historical or topical importance.

Different categories required different emphases. For the Quotes, Ads, Facts and Figures, Fashion, and Kaleidoscope, we concentrated on primary materials. On the other hand, awards listings, like Pulitzer Prizes, because self defined, involved little in the way of choice. Where popularity was concerned, we tried to crosscheck our data with multiple sources. We consulted, for example, attendance tallies and sales charts to verify our lists of, say, plays, movies, records, and fashion. We tried similarly to validate "important," if not popular, works and events by extensive reading of critical and scholarly reviews and studies written both during the period and subsequently. Finally, we consulted experts in each field in order to minimize errors, omissions, and eccentricities in choice. Responsibility for the final content of the text, needless to say, remains ours. We realize that someone else studying the rich history and culture of America over these sixty years might have designed the project differently, with other categories and other listings.

The following is intended to give further details of methodology and format relating to the various individual areas. It also includes those sources not indicated in the text from which we obtained specific awards listings.

The materials in the section **In the News** have been written in the form of headlines in an attempt to recapture their immediacy. In keeping with our overview, they include the major current events of each year that captured public interest, as well as national and international events of manifest historical significance.

Vital, economic, social, and consumer statistics are represented at the opening of each decade to provide a perspective on the country's changing demographic profile. **Facts and Figures,** given yearly, include an economic profile, followed by a list of statistics organized in a repetitive pattern according to the digit with which the year ends, such that the first entries after **Economic Profile** for 192*1*, 193*1*, 194*1*, for example, furnish similar data in each decade (except in the decade year). Prices were selected from newspapers throughout the country, and they cover a range of items from household goods to luxury products; fads and technological innovations are incorporated in the years in which they appeared. Where possible, prices were selected from familiar stores like F. W. Woolworth, Sears, or Saks Fifth Avenue. The lists of **Deaths** for each year does not include persons whose deaths are mentioned elsewhere, such as in the headlines.

Radio is covered consistently until the fifties, when it became a local medium. **TV** is listed extensively from 1946, the time of its commercial emergence. **Movies** were selected on the basis of their critical importance or popular success, either at their time of release or subsequently. Film dating is often controversial; some authorities use the date of general release, others the New York release, or the date films were screened here or abroad to qualify for a variety of awards. We have placed them according to the year they received general U.S. distribution. On occasion, the release and Academy Award dates differ—for example, for *Casablanca* (1942 and 1943). The **Stars of Tomorrow** and **Top Box-Office Stars** were recorded from the Quigley surveys, which began in 1932 and 1941, respectively; material listed before these dates reflects a consensus of data reported in contemporary magazines and newspapers.

Hit Songs are listed according to copyright dates or, on rare occasions, the year the copyright was renewed and the song gained its first popularity. **Top Records** and **Top Performers,** under **Jazz and Big Bands,** include top sellers and performers reported by *Billboard, Downbeat, Cashbox,* and the various industry data sheets that tallied this information before these publications began. Because of space limitations, Top Records are not repeated under Hit Songs. **Theater** includes long runs, as well as shows of contemporary or retrospective importance. **Pulitzer Prizes** and **Tony Awards** are listed in the years they were awarded, which is, at times, the year following the production's premiere. **Classics and Revivals On and Off Broadway** also includes new Off-Broadway plays.

Other than those in New York, Washington, and Philadelphia, **Art** exhibitions are listed by city, rather than museum. Unless otherwise specified, exhibitions were held at the following museums in these cities: Art Institute of Chicago, Chicago; Museum of Fine Arts, Boston; Albright Art Gallery (more recently Albright-Knox), Buffalo; Baltimore Museum of Art, Baltimore; Carnegie Institute, Pittsburgh; County Museum of Art, Los Angeles; Wadsworth Atheneum, Hartford; Cleveland Museum of Art, Cleveland; Detroit Institute of Arts, Detroit; Walker Art Center, Minneapolis; Nelson Art Gallery, Kansas City; and the Toledo Museum of Art, Toledo.

Best-Sellers lists hardcover fiction and nonfiction, as tallied by *Publisher's Weekly.* The additional books listed under **Critics' Choice** were selected on the basis of their importance or interest at their time of publication or subsequently. Owing to space limitations, Best-Sellers are not repeated under Critics' Choice. **Pulitzer Prizes** are listed in the year of the book's publication. Books preceded by the symbol ❧ represent the American publication of influential foreign works.

Items in **Science and Technology** preceded by the symbol ❧ are important foreign scientific events. In **Sports,** in the **Winners** section, the following data are based on selections by the indicated organizations: Baseball's MVPs: *Sporting News* (until 1929) and Baseball Writers of America thereafter; Pro football MVP: Joe F. Carr Trophy (1938–45) and Jim Thorpe Trophy (since 1955); top college football team: Citizens Savings Athletic Foundation (1920–35), Associated Press (1936–50), AP and United Press (1950–58), and AP and UPI thereafter; top college basketball team: Helms Foundation (1920–39), NCAA and NIT (1939–50), and NCAA (1950–present).

Men's **Fashion** is not included with regularity until the late fifties, since innovation tended to be less frequent until then. Italicized items in the section reflect dramatic stylistic changes that, while worn by a limited population, gained wide attention or influenced future fashion. **Kaleidoscope** highlights the events, personalities, and trends that were part of the general public awareness each year; it also amplifies or complements the material in other areas. Comparable material is placed in the particular areas of Art, Popular and Classical Music, and Sports, where it seemed that a more specialized appeal was indicated. It is in Kaleidoscope, as in **Quotes** and **Ads,** that we particularly attempted to convey the unique imprint of each year. **First Appearances** presents a range of entries from popular comic strips and well-known products to technological advances not mentioned in Science and Technology.

To Robert

THE Twenties

Women registering to vote in Los Angeles. *General Research Division. The New York Public Library. Astor, Lenox and Tilden Foundations.*

Statistics

Vital

Population: 106,491,000
   Urban/Rural: 54/52
   Farm: 30%
Life expectancy
   Male: 53.6
   Female: 54.6
Births/1,000: 27.7
Marriages/1,000: 12.0
Divorces/1,000: 1.6
Deaths/1,000: 13.0
   per 100,000
      Heart: 370
      Cancer: 83
      Tuberculosis: 113
      Car accidents: 11

Economic

Unemployed: 2,132,000
GNP: $91.5 billion
Federal budget: $6.4 billion
National debt: $23.7 billion
Union membership: 5 million
Strikes: 3,411
Prime rate: 5.4%
Car sales: 1,905,500
Average salary: $1,236

Social

Homicides/100,000: 6.8
Suicides/100,000: 10.2
Lynchings: 61
Labor force, male/female: 4/1
Public education: $1.04 billion
College degrees
   Bachelors'
      Male: 32,000
      Female: 17,000
   Doctorates
      Male: 522
      Female: 93
Attendance
   Movies (weekly): 33 million
   Baseball (yearly): 9.3
   million

Consumer

Consumer Price Index
   (1967 = 100): 60
Eggs: 68¢ (doz.)
Milk: 17¢ (qt.)
Bread: 12¢ (loaf)
Butter: 70¢ (lb.)
Bacon: 52¢ (lb.)
Round steak: 42¢ (lb.)
Oranges: 63¢ (doz.)
Coffee: 47¢ (lb.)

When America entered the Great War in 1917, it became, as British prime minister Lloyd George said, "a world power in a sense [it] never was before." Led by the idealism of Woodrow Wilson, the United States sent troops into battle for the first time on European soil in an effort to aid England and France in their bloody stalemate with the German Empire. This was the war "to make the world safe for democracy," and with American assistance, the war finally ended. When Wilson went to the Peace Conference at Versailles, the French greeted him as a savior. America had moved to the forefront of the world stage, its ideals and might triumphant. In the same year that America entered the war, a sealed train sped Lenin across Germany to the Finland Station. Within a few months, the Bolsheviks seized control of the Russian Revolution, and Marxism-Leninism found its first national home.

Profound changes were also taking place in science and technology. Max Planck and Albert Einstein were formulating discoveries that challenged the divine order of Newtonian physics. Sigmund Freud was proposing theories that questioned the prim rectitude and proud self-mastery of Victorian society. Technology was rapidly advancing with the advent of wireless communication, the airplane, auto, movie, and phonograph; indeed, airplanes were used as a military weapon for the first time during World War I, and truck transport played a role at the Battle of the Marne. As the new technology and ideas of time, space, matter, energy, and human behavior were harbingers of modernity, the immense carnage of World War I appeared to many a Last Judgment on nineteenth-century positivism.

The immediate postwar period was a time of disappointment for Wilson and America. Widespread strikes, along with fears of "Reds" and terrorist bombs, frightened the public and gave rise to stern police action. Inflation, unemployment, and the Prohibition Amendment, passed in 1918, further unsettled a triumphant America. As the contentiousness and disarray of the postwar world become apparent, many questioned whether the noble aims for which the war had been fought and for which so many had died could be achieved. The final blow was the Peace Conference in France, where it soon became clear that the European victors wanted their material spoils more than a just, international order.

Feeling betrayed, America recoiled from Europe and from Wilson's League of Nations and, in 1920, elected a little-known, handsome, and well-spoken Ohio senator, Warren Harding, who promised "not revolution but restoration." Politically, the subsequent decade was marked by a turning away from the activism of Teddy Roosevelt (1900–1908) and Woodrow Wilson (1912–20), both of whom had

sought a powerful role for government. Elected by wide margins, the laissez-faire Republican presidents and Congresses of the twenties legislated less, taxed less, and reduced armaments. Although the United States was not a member of the league, its leaders nonetheless convened disarmament conferences, mediated when necessary for the hopelessly combative Europeans, and supported international treaties settling boundaries and outlawing war. The active leadership in the world that Wilson had sought was thus restricted to a more ceremonial role.

In 1920, America turned from the world into itself with unparalleled economic, social, and intellectual energy, and until the Crash in 1929, public excitement soared. During this time, many of the bold features of the face of modern America were drawn, and many of the heroes of the American pantheon were born. The economy underwent a transformation that was virtually an industrial revolution. Henry Ford's ideas—the mass production of lower cost luxuries and the payment of higher wages to workers which increased their buying power—became the model for industry. Simultaneously, aggressive new advertising methods accelerated sales and enlarged markets. The economy took off in 1921 on eight years of sustained flight, during which the GNP grew 40 percent with little inflation. As wages rose and working hours moderated, consumers had more leisure time for recreational pursuits, as well as more income for self-indulgence, self-improvement, and invidious consumption. The upwardly mobile consumer society developed. A forthright spiritual glorification of business took place. Calvin Coolidge likened factories to places of worship, and Bruce Barton, an advertising pioneer, wrote best-sellers that portrayed Christ as the archetypal entrepreneur in a scheme that compared business to salvation, advertising to the Gospel, and salesmen to the apostles. Universities, in growing numbers, sought to develop a more scientific, if no less enthusiastic, approach to business.

While not a time of social reform, the booming economy, combined with the new technology, both enlarged the middle class and had a democratizing effect. Radio gave everyone a common reservoir of diverse entertainment (varying from "Amos 'n' Andy" to live theater, from sporting events to concerts, jazz, and popular evangelists), as well as a common and immediate awareness of important events (from presidential speeches, like Harding's inaugural, to first flights, like those of the Graf Zeppelin and Lindbergh); the global village was in its inception. Recordings similarly exposed everyone to the same music—the Ipana Troubadours, the New York Philharmonic-Symphony Orchestra, Enrico Caruso, Paul Whiteman, Al Jolson, and Bessie

Smith. Movies provided common fantasies and idols, from the Sheik, Rudolph Valentino, and the "It Girl," Clara Bow, to the innocent Mary Pickford and vamp Theda Bara. Charlie Chaplin, Buster Keaton, and Harold Lloyd provided a shared comic imagery. The new advertising industry, in its mission to reach the largest possible audience, presented role models often based on common culture heroes; the pleasures, conveniences, and status symbols of the wealthy were also presented as attainable in some version to everyone. The well-to-do and less well-off began to look more alike.

Stirred by competition from the new media and aided by improved communications and the rapidly growing appetite for news, excitement, and heroes, journalists were on the spot everywhere, producing mountains of type to fill tabloid front pages. They covered everything from news of sports figures and trials to movie stars, divorces, and natural disasters. Adultery-murder trials like the Hall-Mills and Snyder-Gray cases received greater coverage than the Great War. The nation waited with bated breath to learn the fate of Floyd Collins, trapped in a mine for 18 days, the delivery of diphtheria vaccine in Alaska by the husky dog Baltho, and the whereabouts of the sexy evangelist Aimee Semple McPherson. Figures like Charles Atlas, the new Miss America, Texas Guinan, and Helen Morgan, and events like the Teapot Dome scandal and St. Valentine's Day Massacre, along with new modifications in manners, such as Emily Post's *Etiquette* and Trojan contraceptives, also received great attention.

Some of the heroes matched the mountains of type—the sports figures Babe Ruth, Red Grange, Jack Dempsey, Gene Tunney, Bill Tilden, Bobby Jones, Helen Wills, Johnny Weismuller, and Gertrude Ederle; public figures Clarence Darrow, William Jennings Bryan, Margaret Sanger, Billy Mitchell, and Adm. Richard Byrd; and performing and creative artists Isadora Duncan, Bessie Smith, and George Gershwin. Most honored of the twenties' heroes was Charles Lindbergh, the modest, courageous farm boy who flew solo across the Atlantic.

Extensive coverage was also given to the most unusual and colorful of the decade's businesses, those created in response to the Eighteenth Amendment—bootlegging and speakeasies. Prohibition, the "noble" experiment in moral betterment, by edict, was widely ignored, and for the first time, a vast mass of Americans of all classes openly and knowingly patronized crime. This made gangsters into public servants of sorts, and Al Capone, the most enterprising of all, was a popular and oft-quoted personality.

The interplay of economic and social forces produced other dramatic changes. As economic opportunities drew people to the cities, urban dwelling became the increasingly predominant mode of American life. Bigger office and apartment buildings were constructed, including the many art deco masterpieces of the late twenties. The car became an achievable staple in everyman's American dream; more roads were paved, and as congestion increased, more traffic lights and no-parking signs appeared. The city began to take on the look of today, as did the countryside, where gas stations and motels multipled.

In the freedom of the city, in the atmosphere of the speakeasy, in the wake of postwar disillusion and the advent of popular Freudianism, the music of the Jazz Age and the dancing of the Charleston flourished. Victorian manners and morals were shed, along with their cumbersome over- and undergarments, and the flapper appeared. There was a thrust for female emancipation sartorially, sexually, and intellectually. Business also contributed to the new liberation, as it sought customers for everything from baked bread to vacuum cleaners, all of which were promoted as emancipators from household drudgery. Women, first allowed to vote nationally in 1920, were thus encouraged to the higher life, which could and did include, in increasing numbers, college and employment and, in unknown numbers, free love.

All these social changes were not without powerful resistance. Intense controversy developed over women smoking, skirt and hair lengths, contraception, and "loose" morals in films; the latter culminated in a film code limiting sexual material. Early in the decade there was strong political reaction. Alleged radicals were incarcerated without evidence, strikes were brutally suppressed, the KKK was revived, and immigration was restricted on ethnically discriminatory lines. In the two great and closely followed trials of the decade, a Tennessee teacher (Scopes) was convicted of teaching scientific material that conflicted with religious fundamentalism, and two Italian immigrant anarchists (Sacco and Vanzetti) were convicted and executed for murder, although many thought their "crime" was their political ideology and foreign origin.

Reaction came as well from the intellectuals, as many despaired of hollow materialism, forsaken idealism, and small-town provincialism. F. Scott Fitzgerald's *The Great Gatsby* portrayed the "meretricious [American] dream"; Ernest Hemingway's *The Sun Also Rises* told of the "lost generation"; William Faulkner's *The Sound and the Fury* detailed the moral decay of the South; Sinclair Lewis indicted the bourgeoise of midwestern America, and H. L. Mencken relentlessly assailed the "booboisie." His focus less social than

As the sale of alcohol becomes illegal, prohibitionists in Norfolk, Virginia, gleefully bury the bottle. *D. Ouellette Collection.*

psychological, Eugene O'Neill devised experimental forms to portray the perennial conflicts that arise from the disparity between dream and reality. T. S. Eliot's *The Waste Land* remains the ultimate indictment of the modern world's loss of personal, moral, and spiritual values.

But the hope and excitement of the new predominated. America seemed to be acting on the motto of Emil Coué's best-selling self-help book, "Every day, in every way, I am getting better and better." As the decade progressed, the possibilities for everyone seemed boundless, and get-rich-quick schemes proliferated. The Florida land rush of the mid-twenties drew large numbers eager for instant profit, and although latecomers bought swamp, the speculative spirit remained undampened. The greatest and most surefire possibility of rapid wealth

was provided by the Great Bull Market of the late twenties. As a *New York Times* headline of 1929 reported, a "speculative fever" gripped the nation.

In 1928, American elected yet another rugged individualist to the White House; by far the best qualified of the three presidents of the decade, Herbert Hoover foresaw the end of poverty in America. Then, just two months before the end of the decade, the Great Bull Market expired. A shock of disbelief met the Crash. Those in power attempted to deny its reality or importance—it was just another swing in the boom-depression cycle. But the "up" in American life had lasted so long that people had forgotten the "downs"; the Great Depression that followed was to equal in magnitude that great sweeping exaltation that was the twenties.

1920

Facts and Figures

Economic Profile
Dow-Jones: ↓
   High 100–Low 67
GNP: +9%
Inflation: +8.2%
Unemployment: 5.2%
Maxwell: $885
Chandler: $1,895
Cadillac: $2,885
Russian pony coat: $169.50
Tweed coat (Hart Schaffner
  & Marx): $37.50
Jackal mink coat: $1,750–
  $2,750
E-Z ladies' garters: 40¢–60¢
Waltham wristwatch: $5
Women's silk stockings:
  $1.65–$3.65
Sloane's vacuum cleaner: $48
Grafonola: $300–$2,100
Phonograph (Sears &
  Roebuck): $115
Player piano: $475
Baby stroller: $12.50–$25
Miloviolet scented, gold-
  tipped cigarettes: 10¢
  (pack)

Deaths

Reginald DeKoven, William
  C. Gorgas, William Dean
  Howells, Amedeo
  Modigliani, Robert E.
  Peary, John Reed.

In the News

ATTORNEY GENERAL A. MITCHELL PALMER DIRECTS NEW YEAR'S DAY RAIDS ON REDS . . . PROHIBITION AMENDMENT TAKES EFFECT . . . SECRETARY OF STATE ROBERT LANSING IS FORCED TO RESIGN FOR HOLDING UNAUTHORIZED CABINET MEETINGS . . . FIVE ELECTED SOCIALISTS ARE BARRED FROM N.Y. ASSEMBLY . . . LEAGUE OF NATIONS OPENS IN PARIS . . . WOODROW WILSON REFUSES SENATE COMPROMISE ON LEAGUE, SENATE DEFEATS U.S. MEMBERSHIP . . . POLES UNDER JOSEF PILSUDSKI INVADE RUSSIA . . . DEMOCRATS NOMINATE W. W. COX FOR PRESIDENT ON 44TH BALLOT, FRANKLIN D. ROOSEVELT FOR VICE PRESIDENT . . . WARREN HARDING IS CHOSEN BY GOP, CALVIN COOLIDGE IS POPULAR CHOICE AS RUNNING MATE . . . EUGENE V. DEBS, IN PRISON, IS SOCIALIST CANDIDATE . . . NICOLA SACCO AND BARTOLOMEO VANZETTI, ANARCHIST LABORERS, ARE ARRESTED FOR PAYROLL MURDERS IN BRAINTREE, MASS. . . . MARCUS GARVEY'S UNIVERSAL NEGRO IMPROVEMENT ASSOCIATION MEETS IN NEW YORK, 25,000 ATTEND . . . FAMINE SWEEPS RUSSIA, LENIN ASKS AMERICAN COMMUNIST PARTY FOR INFORMATION ON U.S. AGRICULTURAL METHODS . . . BRITAIN GETS LEAGUE MANDATE FOR PALESTINE . . . EIGHT CHICAGO WHITE SOX ARE INDICTED FOR 1919 WORLD SERIES FIX . . . BOMB EXPLODES ON WALL STREET KILLING 20 . . . WOMEN VOTE FOR FIRST TIME IN NATIONAL ELECTION . . . HARDING WINS WITH 16 MILLION VOTES, COX GAINS 9 MILLION, DEBS, 919 THOUSAND . . . ENGLAND GRANTS NORTH AND SOUTH IRELAND SEPARATE PARLIAMENTS . . . CALIFORNIA PASSES LAW LIMITING JAPANESE LAND HOLDINGS.

Quotes

"The great creators of the government . . . thought of America as a light to the world, as created to lead the world in the assertion of the right of peoples and the rights of free nations."

— Woodrow Wilson, in defense of the League of Nations

"America's present need is not heroics but healing; not nostrums but normalcy; not revolution but restoration; not surgery but serenity."

— Warren G. Harding

"The Department of Justice has undertaken to tear out the radical seeds that have entangled American ideas, . . . the IWW's, the most radical socialists, the misguided anarchists, . . . the moral perverts and the hysterical neurasthenic women who abound in communism."

— Attorney General A. Mitchell Palmer

"My candle burns at both ends; / It will not last the night; / But ah, my foes, and, oh, my friends— / It gives a lovely light."   — Edna St. Vincent Millay

"If our world is ever . . . to be destroyed, the problems are that its destruction will come from outside of our own solar system. Accordingly, we should probably have plenty of time to await such a possible disaster."   — *Munsey's* magazine

"If Mr. Einstein doesn't like the natural laws of this universe, let him go back to where he came from."

— Robert Benchley

"Here was a new generation, . . . dedicated more than the last to the fear of poverty and the worship of success; grown up to find all gods dead, all wars fought, all faiths in man shaken.

— F. Scott Fitzgerald, *This Side of Paradise*

Ads

Bathing beauties with a Columbia Six sportscar. The decade begins with more cars and less body covering. *Library of Congress.*

Radio

Dr. Frank Conrad, director of Westinghouse's station, KDKA, Pittsburgh, plays music records for radio hams; he terms these events *broadcasts* • On November 2, KDKA makes the first scheduled broadcast, the Harding-Cox election • Thirty radio licenses are issued.

Fourth of July parade in Boise, Idaho. While Woodrow Wilson tours the country proseletyzing for the League of Nations, America is busy cultivating its own traditions. *Library of Congress.*

Movies

THE OFFICIAL REPUBLICAN CAMPAIGN SONG

HARDING
You're The Man For Us

WARREN G. HARDING
Republican Candidate for President

CALVIN COOLIDGE
Republican Candidate for Vice President

Words and Music by

AL JOLSON

30

Campaign song for the candidates of "Law and Order" and "America First." *La Salle Collection. Smithsonian Institution.*

Openings

Dr. Jekyll and Mr. Hyde (John S. Robertson), John Barrymore, Nita Naldi

The Idol Dancer (D. W. Griffith), Clarine Seymour, Richard Barthelmess

Copperhead (Charles Maigne), Lionel Barrymore

The Golem (Paul Wegener), Paul Wegener, Albert Steinruck

Huckleberry Finn (William Desmond Taylor), Gordon Griffith

Humoresque (Frank Borzage), Vera Gordon, Dore Davidson

The Love Flower (D. W. Griffith), Carol Dempster, Richard Barthelmess

Way Down East (D. W. Griffith), Lillian Gish, Richard Barthelmess

Madame X (Frank Lloyd), Pauline Frederick, William Courtleigh

Mark of Zorro (Fred Niblo), Douglas Fairbanks, Noah Beery

One Week (Buster Keaton), Buster Keaton

Passion (Ernst Lubitsch), Pola Negri

Pollyanna (Paul Powell), Mary Pickford

The Cabinet of Dr. Caligari (Robert Wiene), Conrad Veidt

Top Box-Office Stars

Wallace Reid, Marguerite Clark, Roscoe ("Fatty") Arbuckle, Douglas Fairbanks, Mary Pickford, Charles Chaplin, Tom Mix, William S. Hart, Alla Nazimova, Gloria Swanson, Dorothy Gish, Lillian Gish, Constance Talmadge, Norma Talmadge, Mary Miles Minter, Mabel Normand, Thomas Meighan, Charles Ray

Popular Music

Hit Songs
"Avalon"
"I'll Be with You in Apple
Blossom Time"
"When My Baby Smiles at Me"
"Whispering"
"Look for the Silver Lining"
"I Never Knew I Could Love
Anyone Like You"
"My Mammy"
"Daddy, You've Been a Mother to
Me"
"Hiawatha's Melody of Love"

"When the Moon Shines on the
Moonshine"
"Who Ate Napoleons with
Josephine when Bonaparte Was
Away?"

Top Records
Crazy Blues (Mamie Smith), first
blues recording; *Wang Wang Blues*
(Harry Busse); *Dardanella* (Ben
Selvin Orchestra); *Japanese
Sandman* (Paul Whiteman); *I'll*

See You in C-U-B-A (Ted Lewis
Orchestra); *After You Get What
You Want, You Don't Want It* (Van
and Schenck); *Margie* (Original
Dixieland Jazz Band)

Jazz and Big Bands
Paul Whiteman tours Europe, and
interest in jazz booms. Louis
Armstrong, 20, plays cornet on a
Mississippi River steamboat.

Theater

Broadway Openings

Plays
The Emperor Jones (Eugene O'Neill), Charles S.
Gilpin
Beyond the Horizon (Eugene O'Neill), Richard
Bennett
Miss Lulu Bett (Zona Gale), Carroll McComas
The Bat (Mary Roberts Rinehart, Avery Hopwood),
Effie Ellsler
Enter Madame (Gilda Varesi, Dolly Byrne), Gilda
Varesi
Rollo's Wild Oat (Clare Kummer), Roland Young
Bab (Edward Childs Carpenter), Helen Hayes
Ladies Night (Avery Hopwood, Charlton Andrews),
John Cumberland, Judith Vosselli, Charles
Ruggles
The First Year (Frank Craven), Frank Craven
Heartbreak House (George Bernard Shaw), Effie
Shannon, Lucile Watson, Dudley Digges
The Wonderful Thing (Lillian Trimble Bradley),
Jeanne Eagels
The Skin Game (John Galsworthy), Marsh Allen
Poldekin (Booth Tarkington), George Arliss

Musicals
Sally (Jerome Kern, Victor Herbert, Clifford Grey),
Marilyn Miller, Leon Errol
Ziegfeld Follies of 1920 (Victor Herbert, Irving
Berlin), Fannie Brice, W. C. Fields
The Night Boat (Jerome Kern, Anne Caldwell),
Louise Groody, John E. Hazzard
Tickle Me (Herbert Stothart, Otto Harbach, Oscar
Hammerstein II), Frank Tinney

John Barrymore, "the
great profile," stars on
stage in *Richard III*
(left) and in the movie
*Dr. Jekyll and Mr.
Hyde. Billy Rose
Theatre Collection. The
New York Public
Library at Lincoln
Center. Astor, Lenox,
and Tilden
Foundations.*

The Passing Show (Jean Schwartz, Harold
Atteridge), Janet Adair, Marie Dressler, Willie
Howard, Eugene Howard
Honeydew (Efrem Zimbalist, Joseph Herbert),
Ethelind Terry, Mlle. Marguerite, Hal Forde
Mary (Lou Hirsch, Otto Harbach, Frank Mandel),
Jack McGowan, Janet Velie
George White Scandals (George Gershwin, Arthur
Jackson), Ann Pennington, Lou Holtz
Poor Little Ritz Girl (Sigmund Romberg, Richard
Rodgers, Alex Gerber, Lorenz Hart), Lulu
McConnell, Charles Purcell

Classics and Revivals On and Off Broadway
Richard III (John Barrymore, Shakespeare debut);
Medea (Euripides), Ellen Von Volkenberg; *The
Power of Darkness* (Tolstoy); *Deirdre of the Sorrows,
Cathleen ni Houlihan* (William Butler Yeats); *The
Beggar's Opera* (John Gay); *An Enemy of the People*
(Ibsen)

Pulitzer Prize
Beyond the Horizon, Eugene O'Neill

Classical Music _____

Compositions
Edgard Varèse, *Amériques*
Aaron Copland, Keyboard Sonatas 1–3
Carl Ruggles, *Men and Angels*

Important Events
The Cleveland Institute and Juilliard are founded.

Notable Performances: Damrosch Series (History of the Symphony); Harold Bauer, Ossip Gabrilowitsch, Olga Samarov, Concerto for Three Pianos (Bach-Stokowski); Festivals: 71st Armory Regiment, New York, the largest musical event in 40 years; London String Quartet, complete Beethoven Quartets (New York); Efrem Zimbalist and Henry Cowell, Beethoven, opus 96, Brahms, opus 108, and works of Cowell (Berkshire Festival)

Major Recitals: Sergei Rachmaninoff, Josef Hofmann, Josef Lhévinne, Guiomar Novaes, Jascha Heifetz, Pablo Casals, Fritz Kreisler, Alfred Cortot, Luisa Tetrazzini, Mrs. Ernestine Schumann-Heink

Major Conductors: Walter Damrosch (New York Symphony); Joseph Stransky (Philharmonic, New York); Artur Bodanzky (National, New York); Pierre Monteux (Boston); Leopold Stokowski (Philadelphia); Eugène Ysaye (Cincinnati); Ossip Gabrilowitsch (Detroit)

Debuts: Louis Kentner, Joseph Fuchs

First Performances
Edward Elgar, *Enigma Variations* (Philadelphia); Jean Sibelius, *Finlandia* (New York); Gustav Holst, *The Planets* (Chicago); Rachmaninoff, *The Bells* (Philadelphia); Ralph Vaughan Williams, *London Symphony* (New York); John Alden Carpenter, *A Pilgrim Vision* (Mayflower Centennial, Philadelphia); Sergei Prokofiev, *Overture on Hebrew Themes* (New York); Frank S. Converse, Symphony no. 1 (Chicago), Symphony no. 4 (Boston); Ernest Bloch, Suite for Viola and Orchestra (New York)

Opera

Metropolitan: 172 performances of 36 works by 25 composers. Most frequently performed: Geraldine Farrar, *Zaza* (Ruggiero Leoncavallo). Most popular: *Monsieur Beaucaire* (André Messager). Premieres: Madame Chrysanthème (Messager); *Cleopatra's*

Sergei Rachmaninoff, premiering his own works in America. *Library of Congress.*

Night (Henry Hadley); *Parsifal* (in English); *Eugene Onègin* (in Italian). Debuts: Beniamino Gigli, Frances Peralta (*Mefistofele*); Ann Roselle (*La bohème*); Giusseppe Danise (*Aïda*); Mario Chamlee (*Tosca*); Florence Easton (*Madama Butterfly*).

Chicago: Mary Garden, *L'amore dei tre re* (Italo Montemezzi). Premieres: *L'heure espagnole* (Ravel); *Edipo ré* (Leoncavallo); *Rip Van Winkle* (Henry De Koven)

San Diego: *The Sunset Trail* (Charles Wakefield Cadman, premiere)

Cincinnati: *Martha* (company's inaugural performance)

Music Notes
New York replaces Berlin as the mecca for musical hopefuls • Three orchestras compete with Beethoven performances (for the 150th anniversary) and experimental pieces like Francesco Malipiero's *Impressions* • Visiting Willem Mengelberg tries to convert hostile New York audiences to Gustav Mahler • The New York Symphony is the first American orchestra to tour Europe • Arturo Toscanini brings the La Scala Orchestra to New York • Enrico Caruso collapses on stage in *I pagliacci;* he bursts a blood vessel in *L'elisir d'amore;* his last performance is *La Juive.*

Art

Painting

John Marin, *Lower Manhattan*

Marsden Hartley, *Lilies in a Vase*

Charles Demuth, *Stairs, Providence, Machinery, End of the Parade, Box of Tricks, The Tower*

Georgia O'Keeffe, *Red Cannas*

Thomas Hart Benton, *Portrait of Josie West*

Lyonel Feininger, *Church, Viaduct*

Charles Burchfield, *February Thaw, The Interurban Line, Railroad Gantry, Peppin House*

George Bellows, *Elinor, Jean and Anna*

Joseph Stella, *Flowers, Portrait of Walt Whitman*

Important Exhibitions

Museums

New York: *Metropolitan:* Fiftieth anniversary exhibition (the most important in American history) includes loans from private collections of arms, Byzantine ivories, glass, modern masters; other shows: Renoir, van Gogh, Gauguin, Dürer; Flemish tapestries of the sixteenth century

Sculpture

Jo Davidson, *Gertrude Stein*

Paul Manship, *J. Pierpont Morgan Memorial* (cornerstone tablet in the Great Hall, Metropolitan Museum of Art, New York)

Lorado Taft, *Fountain of Time* (Chicago Art Institute)

Architecture

Field Museum, Chicago (Graham, Anderson, Probst, and White)

Amphitheater, U.S. National Cemetery, Arlington, Virginia (Carrère and Hastings)

Barnsdall House, Hollywood (Frank Lloyd Wright)

Philadelphia: Italian paintings of the fourteenth and sixteenth centuries

Boston: Colonial objects; Japanese prints

Chicago: Thirty-third annual exhibit of American art: Frederick Frieseke and George Luks win top prizes. Museum purchases Redon prints and etchings.

Pittsburgh: Carnegie International resumes after the war years.

Individual shows

New York: Maurice Prendergast, James A. MacNeill Whistler, William Glackens, Frederick Detwiller, Mary Cassatt, George Bellows, Winslow Homer; Jo Davidson and Mahonri Young (war sculptures)

Art Briefs

Marcel Duchamp, Man Ray, and Katherine Dreier found the N.Y. Société Anonyme to promote modern art • Man Ray photographs Duchamp in his female disguise as Rrose Sélavy • Duchamp builds his first motor-driven constructions • Joseph Pennell's widely discussed letter to the *New York Times* urges that the Metropolitan Museum of Art exhibit works of living artists.

Dance

The Pavley-Oukrainsky Ballet debuts. It is the first American ballet company and the official ballet of the Chicago Civic Opera.

The innovative Isadora Duncan, shortly before departing for Moscow to open a school of dance. *Library of Congress.*

Books

Fiction

Critics' Choice
Main Street, Sinclair Lewis
Poor White, Sherwood Anderson
This Side of Paradise, F. Scott Fitzgerald
Flappers and Philosophers, F. Scott Fitzgerald
Youth and the Bright Medusa, Willa Cather
Master Eustace, Henry James (posthumous)
The Vacation of the Kelwyns, William Dean Howells
Miss Lulu Bett, Zona Gale
One Man's Initiation, John Dos Passos
Moon-Calf, Floyd Dell
🡪 *Women in Love*, D. H. Lawrence
🡪 *Guermantes' Way*, Marcel Proust

Best-Sellers
The Man of the Forest, Zane Grey
Kindred of the Dust, Peter B. Kyne
The Re-Creation of Brian Kent, Harold Bell Wright
The River's End, James Oliver Curwood
A Man for the Ages, Irving Bacheller
Mary-Marie, Eleanor H. Porter
The Great Impersonation, E. Phillips Oppenheim

Harriet and the Piper, Kathleen Norris
The Lamp in the Desert, Ethel M. Dell
The Portygee, Joseph C. Lincoln

Nonfiction

Critics' Choice
Character and Opinion in the U.S., George Santayana
Ancient Man, Hendrik Willem Van Loon
Darkwater, W. E. B. Du Bois
The Ordeal of Mark Twain, Van Wyck Brooks
Recreations of a Psychologist, G. S. Hall
Autobiography, Andrew Carnegie
Reconstruction in Philosophy, John Dewey
🡪 *The Concept of Nature*, Alfred North Whitehead
🡪 *Relativity*, Albert Einstein
🡪 *A General Introduction to Psychoanalysis*, Sigmund Freud

Best-Sellers
Now It Can Be Told, Philip Gibbs
The Economic Consequences of the Peace, J. M. Keynes
Roosevelt's Letters to His Children, ed. Joseph B. Bishop
Theodore Roosevelt, William Roscoe Thayer

White Shadows in the South Seas, Frederick O'Brien
An American Idyll, Cornelia Stratton Parker
The Years Between, Rudyard Kipling
Bolshevism, John Spargo
Belgium, Brand Whitlock

Poetry
T. S. Eliot, *Poems*
Ezra Pound, *Umbra, Hugh Selwyn Mauberley*
William Carlos Williams, *Kora in Hell*
Edna St. Vincent Millay, *A Few Figs from Thistles*
Edwin Arlington Robinson, *Lancelot, The Three Taverns*
Conrad Aiken, *The House of Dust*
Carl Sandburg, *Smoke and Steel*
H. D., *Poems by a Little Girl*
Edgar Lee Masters, *Domesday Book*

Pulitzer Prizes
The Age of Innocence, Edith Wharton (novel)
The Victory at Sea, William S. Sims, with Burton J. Hendrick (U.S. history)
The Americanization of Edward Bok, Edward Bok (biography)
No prize is awarded in poetry.

Science and Technology

A. A. Michelson and Francis Pease, at the Mt. Wilson Observatory, California, measure the diameter of a star, Betelgeuse, at 240 million miles.

Public radio begins with Pittsburgh's KDKA broadcast of the Harding-Cox election returns.

The first regular commercial airline service in the United States begins; it connects Key West and Havana and takes approximately one hour.

William G. Harkins, of the University of Chicago, postulates the existence of a subatomic particle, the neutron, a heavy particle of no electric charge.

The Smithsonian Institution announces Robert Goddard's work with rockets, which, it says, will eventually fly people to the moon.

The tommy gun is patented by retired army officer John T. Thompson.

The Duesenberg car introduces hydraulic brakes.

Specialized scientific journals begin to flourish.

Babe Ruth's 54 home runs break the previous record by 25. *Library of Congress.*

Sports

Baseball

The Boston Red Sox sell Babe Ruth to the New York Yankees for $100,000, plus a $385,000 loan. Ruth hits 54 home runs and asks that his salary be doubled to $20,000. The Yankees draw a record 1,289,422. Ruth's slugging percentage is .847.

A young boy approaches Shoeless Joe Jackson, one of the eight White Sox players accused of throwing the 1919 World Series, and pleads: "Say it ain't so, Joe."

In the longest game ever, 26 innings, the Brooklyn Dodgers and Boston Braves tie, 1–1.

Bill Wambsganss, Cleveland second baseman, makes the first unassisted triple play in a World Series.

Champions

Batting	Pitching
Rogers Hornsby (St. Louis, NL), .370	Burleigh Grimes (Brooklyn, NL), 23–11
George Sisler (St. Louis, AL), .407	Jim Bagby (Cleveland, AL), 31–12
	Home Runs
	Babe Ruth (New York, AL), 54

Football

The American Professional Football Association, the first organized pro league, is formed in Canton, Ohio, with Jim Thorpe as president. Franchises are $100. George Halas buys the Decatur Staleys and moves them to Chicago. Games are poorly attended.

Pro Stars: Paddy Driscoll (Racine), Joe Guyon (Canton)

College All-Americans: George Gipp (FB), Notre Dame; Donald Lourie (QB), Princeton; Timothy Callahan (C), Yale

Rose Bowl (Jan. 1, 1921): California 28–Ohio State 0

Olympics

The Olympics are held at Antwerp, Belgium. American gold medal winners include Charles Paddock (100m, 10.8 s.), Alan Woodring (200m, 22.0s), Dick Landon (high jump, 6'3"), Frank Foss (pole vault, 13'5"), John Kelly (single and double skulls), Duke Kahanamoku (100m, swimming), Ethelda Bleibtrey (100m, 200m, and relay swimming).

Other Sports

Tennis: Bill Tilden is the first American to win at Wimbledon.

Horse Racing: Man O'War wins in all his 11 races, including the Preakness and Belmont, and is retired after the season.

Winners

World Series	Stanley Cup
Cleveland (AL) 5	Ottawa
Brooklyn (NL) 2	*U.S. Tennis Open*
American Professional Football Association	Men: William Tilden II
	Women: Molla Mallory
Akron Pros	*U.S. Golf Association Open*
College Football	Ted Ray
California	*Kentucky Derby*
College Basketball	Paul Jones (T. Rice, jockey)
Penn	
Player of the Year	
Howard McCann, N.Y.U.	

Fashion

For Women: Release of war tensions and the new emancipation liberate "bachelor girls" from heavy corsetry, hoops, and bustles (the hourglass look) for loose, easy-fitting, casual clothes. Hand-embroidered silk or crepe de chine lingerie flattens the bosom, waist, and hips into a body cylinder. The flapper age, in its infancy, introduces barrel-shaped skirts above the ankle with the waistline dropped to the hip. Bobbed and waved hair is brought forward to the cheeks; the bun is discarded. Edwardian feathers and flowers begin to disappear; black stockings and high-laced shoes give way to natural-colored hose that exposes the well-turned leg in low pumps. The increasing emphasis on the flat, boyish look and greater angularity is paralleled through the decade by shorter hair and skirts. Soon to appear are ready-made clothes and the fashion industry, "style" (clothing obsolescence), and fashion magazines.

High-fashion notes: The caftan; Chanel's transparent overdresses.

Kaleidoscope

- "Good-bye, John. You were God's worst enemy," chant 10,000 Virginia Prohibitionists, as they bury a 20-foot, horse-drawn coffin symbolizing John Barleycorn.
- Speakeasies open almost as fast as saloons close.
- As women enter speakeasies, many check their old-fashioned corsets in the powder room, order the new "cocktail" ("Between the Sheets"), smoke, and discuss current topics like sex and the new psychology.
- Places to hide the "hooch" or "giggle water" include canes, hot-water bottles, and satin garters.
- Margaret Sanger campaigns for birth control and advocates women's personal and economic freedom.
- The General Federation of Women's Clubs attempts to stamp out popular songs because of their "influence on our young people"; it will endorse only old standards like "Keep the Home Fires Burning" and "The Long, Long Trail."
- A large whiskey still is found on the farm of Texas senator Morris Sheppard, a leading proponent of the Eighteenth Amendment.
- Portable stills are available in hardware stores for $6.
- The high cost of living is a predominant national complaint as a result of postwar inflation.
- Financier Charles Ponzi receives $15 million from 40,000 people by claiming rapid profits from foreign exchange manipulations; after the pyramid scheme fails and his arrest, investors recover 12 cents on the dollar.
- Advertising expands, and the public is warned about acid teeth, B.O., cigarette throat, and wallflowerism. Aiming as well at children, advertisers market Santa Claus, in low favor over the past five years.
- Installment buying gains popularity; a vacuum cleaner costs $40—$2 down, $4 monthly.
- Cars on the market include the Templar, Stanley Steamer, Stephens, Salient, Overland, Stutz, Hupmobile, Maxwell, Pierce-Arrow, Milburn Electric, Chalmers, Franklin, Liberty, Peerless, Ford, Chevrolet, Hudson, Packard, Cadillac, Mercedes, and Rolls-Royce.
- Women are urged by the Fleischmann Company to buy, not bake, bread.
- Sales of coffee, tea, soft drinks, and ice-cream sodas increase with the advent of Prohibition.
- A postwar interest develops in nutrition, caloric consumption, and physical vitality.
- Coco Chanel introduces a new perfume, Chanel No. 5.
- The Algonquin Hotel in New York hosts "Round Table" gatherings with writers such as Dorothy Parker, Robert Benchley, George S. Kaufman, Alexander Woollcott, Heywood Broun, and Robert E. Sherwood. They meet in the Rose Room and call themselves the "Vicious Circle."
- Mary Pickford and Douglas Fairbanks marry, and their home, Pickfair, becomes a center of Hollywood social life.

- Newly married Scott and Zelda Fitzgerald achieve renown as uninhibited New York partygoers whose escapades include riding taxitops down Fifth Avenue and diving into fountains at Union Square and in front of the Plaza Hotel.
- Six thousand people are arrested on January 1, as alleged Communists; 2,000 are arrested the next day; few charges are substantiated.
- After Chicago gangster and restaurateur Big Jim Colossimo is shot to death, his gangland funeral, the first of its kind, is attended by movie and opera stars, judges, aldermen, and his suspected assassin, Johnny Torrio ("We was like brothers").
- The illiteracy rate reaches a new low of 6 percent.
- Of nearly 3 million miles of rural highways, over 90 percent are for horse travel.
- Two-thirds of the world's oil originates in the United States.
- The greatest national celebration of the year is the Tercentenary of the Pilgrim landing at Plymouth.

New Words and Usages: Pep, jazz, profiteer, addict, fabricated, sundae, tank, repression, Freudian slip, nonmonogamous love, fetish, and fixation

First Appearances: Trojan contraceptives, two-pants suits, Hilton Hotel Corporation, pogo sticks, Sunkist trademark, Frigidaire, Kellogg's All-Bran, La Choy, Hercule Poirot (in *The Mysterious Affair at Styles,* Agatha Christie), Pitney Bowes postage meter, ITT, water skiing, boysenberries (a cross between blackberries, raspberries, logenberries), Brillo, Assorted Charms candy, Campfire marshmallows, Underwood sardines, Baby Ruth (named after Grover Cleveland's daughter), "Call for Philip Morris . . ."

Gangster Big Jim Colossimo and his girlfriend, Dale Winter. *Library of Congress.*

1921

A divided public considered Sacco and Vanzetti (*center*) either red anarchists or victims of official persecution. *Library of Congress.*

Facts and Figures

Economic Profile
  Dow-Jones: ↓ High 81–
    Low 65
  GNP: −24%
  Inflation: −6.4%
  Unemployment: 11.7%
Median age, first marriage:
  Male: 24.6, Female: 21.2
Average household size: 4.6
Population over 65: 4.6%
Population under 10: 23%
Beaver teddy bear: $5
Shah of Persia soap: 3/$1
Scotch linen knickers: $11
Alaskan seal coat: $600–$750
Dress oxford shoes (Saks):
  $7.75
Meat prices per pound
  leg of lamb: 38¢
  chicken: 47¢
  salmon steak: 35¢
  butterfish: 22¢
Chocolate bonbons: 2/$1

Enrico Caruso. *Library of Congress.*

Deaths

Enrico Caruso, Engelbert
  Humperdinck, Camille
  Saint-Saëns, Barrett
  Wendell.

In the News

U.S. STEEL REDUCES WAGES FOR THE THIRD TIME AS ECONOMY FALTERS . . . WARREN HARDING IS INAUGURATED, HIS SPEECH IS BROADCAST ON RADIO . . . U.S. REJECTS SOVIET PLEA FOR TRADE . . . NEBRASKA LAW FORBIDS ALIENS FROM HOLDING LAND . . . EMERGENCY QUOTA ACT RESTRICTS IMMIGRATION TO 3% OF 1910 CENSUS . . . SAMUEL GOMPERS DEFEATS JOHN L. LEWIS FOR AFL PRESIDENCY . . . FORMER PRESIDENT W. H. TAFT IS APPOINTED CHIEF JUSTICE, SUPREME COURT . . . UNEMPLOYMENT CONFERENCE BEGINS UNDER HERBERT HOOVER, 3.5 MILLION ARE OUT OF WORK . . . FAMINE RELIEF ACT AUTHORIZES $20 MILLION IN GRAIN, CORN, MILK, FOR RUSSIA . . . BRITAIN GRANTS SOUTH IRELAND DOMINION STATUS . . . BILLY MITCHELL DESTROYS GERMAN BATTLESHIP WITH AIR BOMBS . . . GENERAL ACCOUNTING OFFICE IS CREATED TO MONITOR FEDERAL SPENDING . . . CONGRESS PASSES OIL DEPLETION ALLOWANCE . . . HOOVER ORGANIZES RELIEF FOR RUSSIAN FAMINE . . . SACCO AND VANZETTI ARE SENTENCED TO DEATH . . . ARKANSAS RIVER OVERFLOWS, KILLING 1,500 . . . EUGENE DEBS'S PRISON SENTENCE IS COMMUTED BY HARDING . . . CONGRESS DECLARES OFFICIAL END TO WAR WITH GERMANY . . . FATTY ARBUCKLE IS ACCUSED OF STARLET MURDER . . . GREEKS DEFY LEAGUE OF NATIONS AND DECLARE WAR WITH TURKEY . . . FASCISTS GAIN FIRST SEATS IN ITALIAN PARLIAMENT . . . ARMISTICE DAY IS PROCLAIMED, THE FIRST CEREMONY HELD FOR THE UNKNOWN SOLDIER . . . WASHINGTON ARMS LIMITATION CONFERENCE BEGINS, BRITAIN, FRANCE, ITALY, JAPAN ATTEND . . . PERSIA EXPELS RUSSIANS . . . KLAN BURNINGS MULTIPLY IN SOUTH AND MIDWEST.

Quotes

"We seek no part in directing the destinies of the world."

— Warren G. Harding

"Since the Crusades I do not know of any enterprise which has done more honor to men than the intervention of America in the War."

— C. de Wiert, prime minister of Belgium

"The cost of modern warfare is so colossal that wars can no longer be waged at a profit."

— Hudson Maxim, "Shall America Disarm?" *Current Opinion*

"The future of the white race relies on driving out the twin evils of liquor and prostitution."

— Charles W. Eliot, president emeritus, Harvard

"Fads run their course through the mob like the measles. . . . One of the latest is psychoanalysis."

— Dr. Frank Crane, *Current Opinion*

"An economist asks what England gets out of Ireland. The question isn't what, but when."

— *Cleveland News*

"The future work of the business man is to teach the

The handsome and genial Warren Harding was fond of White House gatherings in order to meet his constituents. *Library of Congress.*

teacher, preach to the preacher, admonish the parent, advise the doctor, justify the lawyer, superintend the statesman, fructify the farmer, stabilize the banker, harness the dreamer, and reform the reformer."

— Edward E. Purinton, *Independent*

"From drugstore to drugstore is the shortest distance between two pints."

— *Life*

Ads

FOOD UP 85%
One cent buys . . . but a bite of meat or a bit of fish; ⅕ of an egg, or a small potato; a slice of bacon or a single muffin.

One cent buys a big dish of Quaker Oats.

(Quaker Oats)

Yes, Frigidaire, the electrical home refrigerator, actually freezes your own favorite drinking water into cubes for table use.

(Frigidaire)

HOW MANY WORDS DO
YOU KNOW?
Roosevelt knew
125,000 words
Lloyd George knows
100,000 words
Shakespeare knew
24,000 words
(Funk and Wagnalls Course in Practical English and Mental Efficiency)

The Greatest Living Authors Are Now Writing with Paramount . . . Sir James M. Barrie, . . . Joseph Conrad, Arnold Bennett, . . . E. Phillips Oppenheim, . . . Elinor Glyn, . . . W. Somerset Maugham.

(Paramount Pictures)

"Aren't you sometimes tempted to swear a little when you have tire trouble, Parson?" "—Well, I might be, but you see I avoid the temptation by using Kelly-Springfields."

(Kelly-Springfield Tires)

Williams' Shaving Cream
Covers a Multitude of Chins
(Williams' Shaving Cream)

Radio

Firsts

Church broadcast (Calvary Episcopalian Church, Pittsburgh)
Band concert (T. J. Vastine)
Farm news (Sioux City, Ia.)
Stock report (New York)
Boxing match (Johnny Ray vs. Johnny Dundee, with Florent Gibson as announcer)
World Series (New York Giants vs. New York Yankees)

Of Note

President Harding delivers the Armistice Day address from the Tomb of the Unknown Soldier at Arlington National Cemetery • Vincent Lopez, radio's first bandleader, starts his broadcast from the Hotel Taft, New York, with "Lopez speaking . . ." • WWJ, Detroit, begins with the first news broadcast • WJZ originates from the Westinghouse factory roof, Newark, with announcer Thomas H. Cowan • Westinghouse produces the first popular-priced home receiver; it sells for $60.

Movies

Openings

The Kid (Charles Chaplin), Charles Chaplin, Jackie Coogan (debut)
Dream Street (D. W. Griffith), Carol Dempster, Ralph Graves
The Sheik (George Melford), Rudolph Valentino, Patsy Ruth Miller
Tol'able David (Henry King), Richard Barthelmess, Lassie
The Saphead (Buster Keaton), Buster Keaton, Beula Booker
The Four Horsemen of the Apocalpyse (Rex Ingram), Rudolph Valentino, Alice Terry
Deception (Ernst Lubitsch), Henry Porten
Gypsy Blood (Ernst Lubitsch), Pola Negri
One Arabian Night (Ernst Lubitsch), Pola Negri, Ernst Lubitsch

Little Lord Fauntleroy (Alfred E. Green), Mary Pickford
Peck's Bad Boy (Sam Wood), Jackie Cooper, Charles Hatton, Queenie (a dog)
The Passion Flower (Herbert Brenon), Norma Talmadge
Miss Lulu Bett (William de Mille), Lois Wilson, Milton Sills

Top Box-Office Stars

Mary Pickford, Douglas Fairbanks, Wallace Reid, Charles Ray, Norma Talmadge, Constance Talmadge, Thomas Meighan, Eugene O'Brien, Anita Stewart, Dorothy Gish, William S. Hart, William Faversham, Clara Kimball Young, Gloria Swanson

Far left: Rudolph Valentino, as the exotic lover in *The Sheik,* drove women to faint in the aisles and men to slick down their hair. *Movie Star News.*

Left: Charles Chaplin with Jackie Coogan in *The Kid.* By this time, Chaplin's portrayal of "the little fellow" or "the tramp" has made him the world's most famous movie star. *Movie Star News.*

Popular Music

Hit Songs
"Second Hand Rose"
"Make Believe"
"I'm Nobody's Baby"
"Ain't We Got Fun?"
"I'm Just Wild about Harry"
"The Sheik of Araby"
"Ma—He's Making Eyes at Me"
"Shuffle Along"
"Whip-poor-will"
"Say It with Music"
"Eve Cost Adam Just One Bone"
"When Buddha Smiles"
"Don't Send Your Wife to the Country"
"Big Chief Wally Ho Woo (He'd Wiggle His Way to Her Wigwam)"

Top Records
Wabash Blues (Isham Jones); *Make Believe* (Nora Bayes); *Bandana Days* (Eubie Blake); *April Showers* (Al Jolson); *I Love You Sunday* (Ted Lewis); *Aunt Hagar's Blues* (Ladd's Black Aces); *The Harlem Strut* (James P. Johnson)

Jazz and Big Bands
The New Orleans Rhythm Kings play at the Friars' Inn, Chicago. James P. Johnson makes his first solo jazz piano session for Okeh records.

Theater

Broadway Openings

Plays
Anna Christie (Eugene O'Neill), Pauline Lord
Diff'rent (Eugene O'Neill), Mary Blair, James Light
Gold (Eugene O'Neill), Willard Mack
The Straw (Eugene O'Neill), Margola Gilmore, Otto Kruger
Liliom (Ferenc Molnár), Eva Le Gallienne, Joseph Schildkraut
A Bill of Divorcement (Clemence Dane), Katharine Cornell
Dulcy (George S. Kaufman, Marc Connolly), Lynn Fontanne, Elliott Nugent
The Green Goddess (William Archer), George Arliss
Getting Gerty's Garter (Wilson Collison, Avery Hopwood), Hazel Dawn
The Wren (Booth Tarkington), Helen Hayes, Leslie Howard
Blood and Sand (Tom Cushing), Otis Skinner, Cornelia Skinner
Bluebeard's Eighth Wife (Alfred Savoir), Ina Claire
The Circle (Somerset Maugham), Mrs. Leslie Carter, John Drew
The Intimate Strangers (Booth Tarkington), Billie Burke, Alfred Lunt
The Playboy of the Western World (John Synge), Thomas Mitchell
The Trial of Joan of Arc (Emile Moreau), Margaret Anglin

Musicals
Shuffle Along (Noble Sissle, Eubie Blake), Josephine Baker, Noble Sissle (first Broadway musical acted, directed, and written by blacks)
Blossom Time (Sigmund Romberg, Dorothy Donnelly), Bertram Peacock, Olga Cook
Bombo (Sigmund Romberg, Harold Atteridge), Al Jolson, Janet Adair
Music Box Review (Irving Berlin), Ethelind Terry, Joseph Santley
The Perfect Fool (Ed Wynn), Ed Wynn, Janet Velie
Tangerine (Carlo Sanders, Howard Johnston), Julia Sanderson, Joseph Cawthorn
Greenwich Village Follies (Carey Morgan, Arthur Swanstron), Irene Franklin, Joe E. Brown
Two Little Girls in Blue (Vincent Youmans, Arthur Francis), Fairbanks Twins, Oscar Shaw

Classics and Revivals On and Off Broadway
Macbeth, Lionel Barrymore, Walter Hampden; *The Taming of the Shrew*, E. H. Sothern; *Twelfth Night*, Julia Marlowe; *Iphigenia in Aulis* (Euripides), Margaret Anglin

Regional
Cleveland Playhouse, begun in 1915, becomes the first resident professional theater in the United States.

Pulitzer Prize
Miss Lulu Bett, Zona Gale

Classical Music _____

Compositions

Carlos Salzedo, *Four Preludes to the Afternoon of a Telephone*
George Antheil, *Zingareska*
Arthur Farwell, *Music for the Pilgrimage Play*
Charles Ives, Thirty-four Songs for Voice and Piano
John Powell, *Virginia*
Percy Grainger, *Molly on the Shore*
Howard Hanson, Concerto for Organ, Strings, and Harp

Important Events

The New York National and Philharmonic symphonies merge into the Philharmonic-Symphony Orchestra of New York. The Cleveland Orchestra, under Nikolai Sokoloff, tours Washington, Boston, and New York. The Eastman School opens, Rochester, N.Y. Isadora Duncan opens her Moscow school for the dance. Edgard Varèse founds the International Composers Guild to champion contemporary music.

Debuts: Artur Schnabel, Erica Morini

First Performances

John Alden Carpenter, *Krazy Kat* (Chicago); Sergei Prokofiev, pianist, Piano Concerto no. 3 (Chicago); Henry F. Gilbert, *Indian Sketches* (Boston); Henry Hadley, conducting, *The Ocean* (New York)

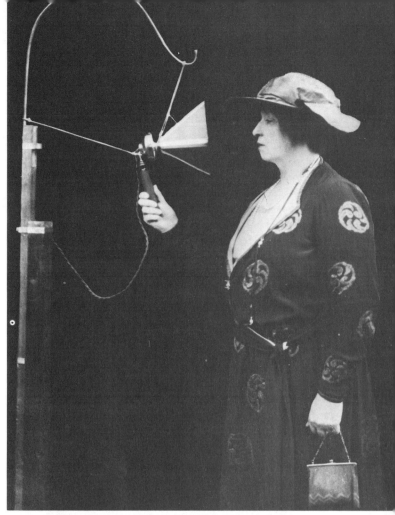

Nellie Melba's broadcasts over the wireless contribute to the popular interest in opera and classical music. *Library of Congress.*

Teenage Josephine Baker and Noble Sissle (*center*) in *Shuffle Along*. Billy Rose Theatre Collection. *The New York Public Library at Lincoln Center. Astor, Lenox, and Tilden Foundations.*

Opera

Metropolitan: Amelita Galli-Curci, *La traviata;* Maria Jeritza, *Die tote Stadt, Tosca;* Feodor Chaliapin, *Boris Godunov;* Leon Rothier, *Louise; L'oracolo, Mefistofele*

Chicago: Mary Garden: *Le jongleur de Notre-Dame; The Love for Three Oranges* (Prokofiev, also conducting, world premiere)

Music Notes

Aaron Copland studies in Paris with the famed Nadia Boulanger • Howard Hanson wins the Prix de Rome • "Organized audience plans" (music series) begin • Antheil provokes an international scandal with his violent compositions and piano performances • The futurists play concerts of noise instruments to reproduce the machine age • Mary Garden's realistic performance of *Salomé* creates a scandal in Chicago • Radio and record sales spur a great interest in classical music.

Art

Painting

Stuart Davis, *Lucky Strike, Bull Durham*
Niles Spencer, *City Walls*
Charles Demuth, *Business, Assassin and Nicolette, Incense of a New Church, Roofs and Steeples*
Arthur G. Dove, *Thunderstorm*
John Marin, *Off Stonington*
Joseph Stella, *Collage #11*
Max Weber, *Still Life*
Lyonel Feininger, *Gelmeroda, VIII*

Sculpture

Alexander Archipenko, *Turning Torso*
Robert Laurent, *Flirtation*
William Zorach, *Figure of a Child*
Elie Nadelman, *Dancer*
Man Ray, *Cadeau*

Architecture

Wrigley Building, Chicago (Graham, Anderson, Probst, and White)
Harkness Quadrangle, New York (James Gamble Rogers)

Important Exhibitions

Museums

New York: *Metropolitan:* "Paintings of the Peace Conference: American and Allied Leaders on View"; early Oriental rugs and carpets; modern Japanese paintings; "Impressionism and Postimpressionism"; children's art. *Public Library:* Manet prints. *Société Anonyme:* Alexander Archipenko

Individual Shows

Alfred Stieglitz, art photos; Stuart Davis, John Sloan, Robert Henri, Reynolds Peal (Society of Independent Artists)

Art Briefs

The Phillips Gallery in Washington, D.C., opens, the first American modern art museum • George Bellows and Franklin DeHaven win national art prizes • The Impressionism and Postimpressionism show at the Metropolitan begins a controversy: an anonymous pamphlet that attacks the show is called KKK propaganda; a long debate follows on the virtues of showing living American artists rather than older foreign masters • Henry E. Huntington buys Gainsborough's *The Blue Boy* and Reynolds's *Portrait of Mrs. Siddons* for $1 million • Raibolini's *Virgin and Child,* discovered in a New York restaurant and wrapped in a newspaper, is returned to the Bologna Museum.

Lyonel Feininger, *Gelmeroda VIII,* 1921. Oil. 39 1/4 × 31 1/4″. *Collection of Whitney Museum of American Art. Purchase.*

The fascination with flight continues, and interest grows in using the plane for mail service. Right: "The Goddess of Flight." *Library of Congress.*

Books

Fiction

Critics' Choice

Three Soldiers, John Dos Passos
The Triumph of the Egg, Sherwood Anderson
Carter and Other People, Don Marquis
Erik Dorn, Ben Hecht
Figures of Earth, James Branch Cabell
The Big Town, Ring Lardner

Best-Sellers

Main Street, Sinclair Lewis
The Brimming Cup, Dorothy Canfield
The Mysterious Rider, Zane Grey
The Age of Innocence, Edith Wharton
The Valley of Silent Men, James Oliver Curwood
The Sheik, Edith M. Hull
A Poor Wise Man, Mary Roberts Rinehart
Her Father's Daughter, Gene Stratton Porter
The Sisters-in-Law, Gertrude Atherton
The Kingdom Round the Corner, Coningsby Dawson

Nonfiction

Critics' Choice

The American Novel, Carl Van Doren
Notes and Reviews, Henry James (posthumous)
Symptoms of Being Thirty-Five, Ring Lardner
Representative Government, William H. Taft
Our Common Country, Warren Harding
America and the Young Intellectual, Harold Stearns
The Engineers and the Price System, Thorstein Veblen
Of All Things, Robert Benchley
🕭 *Dream Psychology*, Sigmund Freud
🕭 *Tractatus Logico-Philosophicus*, Ludwig Wittgenstein

Best-Sellers

The Outline of History, H. G. Wells
The Mirrors of Downing Street, by a Gentleman with a Duster (Harold Begbie)
Mystic Isles of the South Seas, Frederick O'Brien
White Shadows in the South Seas, Frederick O'Brien
Peace Negotiations, Robert Lansing

The Theater, the Drama, the Girls, George Jean Nathan
Miracle Mongers and Their Methods, Harry Houdini
The Story of Mankind, Hendrik Willem Van Loon
Queen Victoria, Lytton Strachey
The Autobiography of Margot Asquith, Margot Asquith

Poetry

Ezra Pound, *Poems 1918–1921, Cantos I–IV*
Edwin Arlington Robinson, *Avon's Harvest*
Edna St. Vincent Millay, *Second April, Renascence, The Lamp and the Bell*
Amy Lowell, *Legends*
Marianne Moore, *Poems*
William Carlos Williams, *Sour Grapes*

Pulitzer Prizes

Alice Adams, Booth Tarkington (novel)
The Founding of New England, James Truslow Adams (U.S. history)
A Daughter of the Middle Border, Hamlin Garland (biography)
Collected Poems, Edwin Arlington Robinson (poetry)

Science and Technology

The antiknock properties of tetraethyl lead, which facilitate premium gasoline, are discovered by Thomas Midgeley.
Newly developed quartz crystals stabilize fluctuating radio signals.
Herbert McLean Evans discovers vitamin E, an antisterility substance.
Elmer V. McCollum discovers vitamin D, a substance in cod liver oil, which prevents rickets.
The Mayo Clinic pioneers dye techniques to outline the kidneys on X rays.
Ear microsurgery is introduced.

Edward Murray East and George Harrison Schull develop a hybrid corn for higher crop yields.
Theories of atomic structure and absorption are proposed by Irving Langmuir.
🕭 The "ink-blot" test is devised by Hermann Rorschach.

Sports

Baseball

Kenesaw Mountain Landis is appointed commissioner of baseball following the "Black Sox Scandal," with a mandate to maintain the integrity of the game.

Babe Ruth (New York, AL) hits 59 home runs, bats .378, and drives in 170 runs.

Eight Chicago White Sox are found not guilty when grand jury testimony disappears; Commissioner Landis bans them from baseball.

Champions

Batting	Pitching
Rogers Hornsby (St. Louis, NL), .397	Art Nehf (New York, NL), 20–10
Harry Heilmann (Detroit, AL), .394	Carl Mays (New York, AL), 27–9
	Home runs
	Babe Ruth (New York, AL), 59

Football

Joseph Carr takes over the American Professional Fooball League; franchises are reduced to $50; the Chicago–New York game draws 80 people.

Pro Stars: George Halas (Chicago), Jim Thorpe (Cleveland)

College All-Americans: Glenn Killinger (HB), Penn State; Malcolm Aldridge (HB), Yale

Rose Bowl (Jan. 1, 1922): Washington & Jefferson 0–California 0

Basketball

The New York Whirlwinds, with Nat Holman, play the New York Original Celtics with Pete Barry and Johnny Whitty in a "World Series." Holman later joins the Original Celtics.

Other Sports

Boxing: Jack Dempsey KO's Georges Carpentier in the fourth round for the heavyweight title; this is the first fight gate of over $1 million.

Winners

World Series
New York (NL) 5
New York (AL) 3
American Professional Football Association
Chicago Staleys
College Football
Cornell
College Basketball
Penn
Player of the Year
George Williams, Mo.
Stanley Cup
Ottawa
U.S. Tennis Open
Men: William Tilden II
Women: Molla Mallory
U.S. Golf Association Open
James M. Barnes
Kentucky Derby
Behave Yourself (C. Thompson, jockey)

Fashion

For Men: The Prince of Wales style is popular: padded shoulders, narrow lapels, a tight fit over the hips, "working-class" brown shoes, bright red ties, colored pocket handkerchiefs. Dress becomes less formal—for example, with butterfly bow ties or long ties with sailor knots. Oxford shoes replace high-buttoned styles; wristwatches replace the pocket watch and fob. The new sports look focuses on the belted Norfolk jacket with knickers or Oxford "bags" (pants with unusually wide trousers, sometimes 25 inches around the knees). Formal wear is also more relaxed, the matching frock coat and cutaway now challenged by the single- or double-breasted dark jacket with striped trousers and soft, medium-wing collars. Shirts are white, with silver gray, black, or white ties. High hats, if worn, are placed at a rakish angle. Spats are linen or canvas in white, biscuit, or gray. Accessories consist of chesterfield coats with mufflers knotted at the neck, and crooked-handle or straight-shaft malacca canes.

High-fashion note: Reboux's straw hats

Kaleidoscope

- A bill is proposed in Utah to imprison any woman who wears her skirt higher than three inches above the ankle.
- The American Medical Association continues to endorse whiskey prescriptions; 2.5-gallon quantities of beer are prescribed for a variety of complaints.
- President Harding pleads for a "Ban by Civilization on War."
- Harding pardons the ailing socialist Eugene Debs and invites him to the White House: "I have heard so damned much about you, Mr. Debs, that I am very glad to meet you personally."
- "Here rests in honored glory an American soldier, known but to God" is inscribed on the Tomb of the Unknown Soldier at Arlington National Cemetery.
- A silver quarter is minted with "Peace" under the figure of an eagle and the liberty head on the reverse side.
- A *New York Times* editorial speculates that Robert Goddard's rockets will not work, since there is nothing in outer space for a rocket's exhaust to push against.
- Prof. Albert Einstein arrives in New York, delivers a lecture at Columbia University on relativity, and introduces "time as the fourth dimension."
- Literature dealing with contraception is banned; a New York physician is convicted of selling *Married Love*.
- Conditions of work for children under 14 are regulated by the Education Act.

- Cigarette consumption rises to 43 billion annually, despite its illegality in 14 states; college girls are often expelled if caught smoking; Iowa legalizes cigarette sales to adults.
- Disillusioned with American values, Ernest Hemingway, William Carlos Williams, Ezra Pound, Glenway Wescott, Katherine Anne Porter, and F. Scott Fitzgerald, among many others, depart for Europe.
- The Chicago Crime Commission records that during the year 10,000 criminals have stolen $12 million.
- Universities whose business schools expand include California, Chicago, Dartmouth, New York, Boston, Harvard, Northwestern, Cincinnati, Syracuse, Ohio State, Michigan, Wisconsin, and Stanford.
- Boston bans *Birth of a Nation*.
- Because threats have been made to people who propose to produce German opera in its original language, the Metropolitan and Chicago opera companies boldly advertise all operas "IN ENGLISH."
- A rage to visit Harlem and see black entertainment is stimulated by the show *Shuffle Along*.
- Plastic surgery becomes heavily advertised in trade union journals in terms of the "WONDERS" it has performed on actors' faces.
- Rudolph Valentino skyrockets to fame in *The Four Horsemen of the Apocalpyse*.
- Hollywood star types include the sweet, innocent girl (Mary Pickford); strong, silent cowboy (William S. Hart); exuberant, boyish athlete (Douglas Fairbanks); lonely, funny tramp (Charles Chaplin); vamp (Theda Bara); and exotic, foreign lover (Rudolph Valentino).
- For the first time, heart disease ranks as the number one cause of death.
- Former U.S. secretary of the navy Franklin D. Roosevelt, 39, is stricken with poliomyelitis.

First Appearances: Mounds bar, Eskimo Pie (replacing I-Scream bar), Betty Crocker, Bel Paese cheese, Wise potato chips, Wrigley's chewing gum, iodized salt, Band-Aids, table tennis, Miss America pageant in Atlantic City (and one-piece form-fitting bathing suits), Sardi's, Lindy's, Arrow shirts and the "Sanforizing Process," starchless but stiff collars (Van Heusen), artificial or "cultured" pearls, "Tillie the Toiler," "Smitty," American Birth Control League (Margaret Sanger), Emmett Kelley's career with Barnum and Bailey, Austin 7, Lincoln auto, Electrolux vacuum cleaner, Drano, coin bearing a living person's portrait (Alabama centennial commemorative half-dollar with image of Governor T. E. Kilby), helium-filled balloons, coast-to-coast telephone service

The well-dressed man wearing knickers, oxford shoes, and a hip-hugging coat. *D. Ouellette Collection.*

1922

Secretary of Interior Albert P. Fall, whose secret leases of oil on public lands have come under investigation. *Library of Congress.*

Facts and Figures

Economic Profile
  Dow-Jones: ↑ High 78– Low 65
  GNP: +6%
  Inflation: −3.4%
  Unemployment: 6.7%
Radios manufactured: 100,000
AM stations: 30
Households with telephones: 35%
Toll rate, New York–San Francisco: $13.50
Advertising expenditures: $2.6 billion
Girls' high-laced winter shoes (Franklin Simon): $6.50
London Character men's oxford shoes: $7.50
Children's winter coat (Altman's): $14.50–$16.50
Ladies' Aquascutum camel's hair coat: $58
Warner's wrap-around girdle: $4 and up
Waterman Lifetime pen: $2.50–$5
Sloane's linoleum: 95¢– $3/yard
Ice skates: $9.95
Vanity puff: 50¢–$1

Deaths

Alexander Graham Bell, W. H. Hudson, William H. ("Wee Willie") Keeler, Marcel Proust, William Rockefeller, Lillian Russell.

In the News

FIRST IRISH GOVERNMENT IS FORMED UNDER MICHAEL COLLINS, THE SINN FEIN REBEL . . . U.S., BRITAIN, JAPAN, FRANCE, ITALY AGREE ON NAVAL LIMITATIONS TREATY AND AFFIRM CHINESE "OPEN DOOR" . . . MAHATMA GANDHI IS SENTENCED TO SIX YEARS FOR CIVIL DISOBEDIENCE . . . HARDING ORDERS U.S. TROOPS HOME FROM RHINELAND . . . OIL IS DISCOVERED IN VENEZUELA . . . COAL MINERS AND STRIKE BREAKERS CLASH AT HERRIN, ILLINOIS, 26 DIE . . . SECRETARY OF INTERIOR ALBERT FALL IS QUESTIONED ON TEAPOT DOME LAND LEASES . . . U.S. REFUSES TO FORGIVE EUROPEAN ALLIES' DEBT . . . WASHINGTON, D.C., KNICKERBOCKER THEATER ROOF COLLAPSES, 98 ARE KILLED . . . REBECCA L. FELTON, GEORGIA, IS FIRST WOMAN APPOINTED TO THE SENATE . . . MUSSOLINI LEADS MARCH ON ROME . . . MICHAEL COLLINS IS ASSASSINATED BY I.R.A. . . . KEMAL PASHA PROCLAIMS TURKISH REPUBLIC, ENDING SULTANATE . . . ECONOMY REVIVES, AUTOS LEAD THE WAY . . . JAMES DOOLITTLE MAKES FIRST ONE-DAY TRANSCONTINENTAL FLIGHT, 21 HOURS, 28 MINUTES . . . TOMB OF KING TUTANKHAMEN IS OPENED BY AMERICAN HOWARD CARTER AND BRITISH LORD CARNARVON . . . CONGRESS PASSES RESOLUTION FAVORING PALESTINE AS JEWISH HOMELAND . . . CLERGYMAN EDWARD HALL AND CHOIR MEMBER ELEANOR MILLS ARE FOUND SHOT TO DEATH IN N.Y. SUBURB, HALL IS HUSBAND OF JOHNSON & JOHNSON HEIRESS . . . INDEPENDENT MONARCHY IS PROCLAIMED IN EGYPT, BRITISH PROTECTORATE ENDS.

Quotes

"I do not like women who know too much."
— Rudolph Valentino

"[There has been] a change for the worse during the past year in feminine dress, dancing, manners, and general moral standards. [One should] realize the serious ethical consequences of immodesty in girls' dress."
— *Pittsburgh Observer*

"Day by day, in every way, I am getting better and better."
— Coué motto for widely successful self-improvement course

"The real hope of the world lies in putting as painstaking thought into the business of mating as we do into other big businesses."
— Margaret Sanger

"His motor car was poetry, tragedy, love and heroism."
— Sinclair Lewis, *Babbitt*

"An imposed peace was made at Paris. There was left out every element of justice and hope for brotherhood which [Woodrow] Wilson had. . . . The allies thought vengeance was theirs. . . . The fruits are bitter."
— Frank A. Vanderlip

"Eugenics [is] the science of race betterment, . . . the segregation of the insane and feeble-minded, . . . the prevention of all obvious degenerates from having children."
— Essay on Lothrop Stoddard's *The Revolt against Civilization,* in *Current Opinion*

"The picture is so essentially Spanish that I want everyone in the theater . . . to eat garlic during the performance."
— Fred Niblo, discussing his film *Blood and Sand*

Margaret Sanger, founder of the American Birth Control League, persuades an American manufacturer to produce diaphragms. *Library of Congress.*

Ads

Radio

Premieres
"Broadway Broadcasting," Miss Bertha Brainard
(play reviews)
"Lucky Strike Radio Show"
"New York Philharmonic-Orchestra"
"Paul Whiteman"

Specials
Warren Harding's opening speech to Congress; "The Perfect Fool," Ed Wynn (first comedic play); first presidential news conference; "The Great Commoner" (sermon by William Jennings Bryan); "Will Rogers and the Ziegfeld Follies Girls"

Of Note
The first radio commercial is for apartments in Jackson Heights, N.Y. • With 314 stations, a federal legislative authority is established.

Movies

Openings
Orphans of the Storm (D. W. Griffith), Lillian Gish,
Dorothy Gish, Joseph Schildkraut
Foolish Wives (Erich von Stroheim), Eric von
Stroheim, Miss Dupont
Prisoner of Zenda (Rex Ingram), Lewis Stone, Alice
Terry
Blood and Sand (Fred Niblo), Rudolph Valentino,
Lila Lee, Nita Naldi
Grandma's Boy (Fred Newmeyer), Harold Lloyd
Robin Hood (Allan Dwan), Douglas Fairbanks,
Wallace Beery
When Knighthood Was in Flower (Robert G.
Vignola), Marion Davies, Ernest Glendinning
Sherlock Holmes (Albert Parker), John Barrymore,
Carol Dempster, Hedda Hopper, Roland Young

One Glorious Day (James Cruze), Will Rogers, Lila
Lee, Alan Hale
Oliver Twist (Frank Lloyd), Jackie Coogan, Lon
Chaney
A Doll's House (Charles Bryant), Alla Nazimova
Nanook of the North (Robert Flaherty) (first
documentary)
Salomé (Charles Bryant), Alla Nazimova
Nosferatu (F. W. Murnau), Max Schreck

Top Box-Office Stars
Mary Pickford, Douglas Fairbanks. *Also popular:* Norma Talmadge, Constance Talmadge, Tom Mix, Buck Jones, John Gilbert, Ramon Novarro, Charles Chaplin, Ben Turpin, Lon Chaney

Far left: after two hung juries, a third trial exonerates "Fatty" Arbuckle of murder. *Movie Star News.*

Lillian and Dorothy Gish play endangered innocents in *Orphans of the Storm,* D. W. Griffith's epic of the French Revolution. *Movie Star News.*

Popular Music

Hit Songs
"I Wish I Could Shimmy Like My Sister Kate"
"Georgia"
"Ain't It a Shame"
"Chicago—That Toddling Town"
" 'Way Down Yonder in New Orleans"
"L'Amour—Toujours—L'Amour"
"Rose of the Rio Grande"
"Do It Again"
"Somebody Stole My Gal"
"Lovin' Sam, the Sheik of Alabam' "
"Ooo Ernest—Are You Earnest with Me?"
"You Remind Me of My Mother"

Top Records
Dreamy Melody (Art Landry and Call of the North Orchestra); *Sing Song Man* (Nora Bayes); *I Love Her, She Loves Me* (Eddie Cantor); *Mister Gallagher and Mister Shean* (Gallagher and Shean); *Hot Lips* (Cotton Pickers); *Lonesome Mama Blues* (Mamie Smith); *Birmingham Blues* (Fats Waller)

Jazz and Big Bands
Paul Whiteman plays at the Palais Royale. Louis Armstrong joins King Oliver's Creole Jazz Band in Chicago.

First Recordings: Coleman Hawkins with Mamie Smith; Kid Ory with Spike's Seven Pods of Pepper Orchestra in Los Angeles

New Bands: Red Nichols, New York; Miff Mole, with the Original Memphis Five.

Theater

Broadway Openings

Plays
Rain (John Colton, Clemence Randolph), Jeanne Eagels
Merton of the Movies (George Kaufman, Marc Connelly), Glenn Hunter
Abie's Irish Rose (Anne Nichols), Robert Williams, Marie Carroll, John Cope
Loyalties (John Galsworthy), James Dale
Back to Methusela (George Bernard Shaw), George Gaul, Margaret Wycherly
The Hairy Ape (Eugene O'Neill), Louis Wolheim
R.U.R. (Karel Čapek), Basil Sydney
The World We Live In (Joseph and Karel Čapek), May Hopkins, Kenneth MacKenna
The Cat and the Canary (John Willard), Florence Eldridge, Henry Hull
The Old Soak (Don Marquis), Harry Beresford
Seventh Heaven (Austin Strong), Helen Menken, George Gaul
The Tidings Brought to Mary (Paul Claudel), Jeanne de Casalis
Six Characters in Search of an Author (Luigi Pirandello), Margaret Wycherly, Florence Eldridge
He Who Gets Slapped (Leonid Andreyev), Richard Bennett
Fashions for Men (Ferenc Molnár), Helen Gahagan

Musicals
Ziegfeld Follies (Louis A. Hirsch, Ring Lardner), Will Rogers, Gallagher and Shean, Olsen and Johnson
The Gingham Girl (Albert Von Tilzer, Neville Fleeson), Eddie Buzzell, Helen Ford
Sally, Irene and Mary (J. Fred Coots, Raymond Klages), Eddie Dowling, Hal Van Rensselaer
Greenwich Village Follies (George V. Hobart, Louis A. Hirsch), John E. Hazzard, Savoy and Brennan
Little Nellie Kelly (George M. Cohan), Elizabeth Hines, Robert Pitkin
The Blushing Bride (Sigmund Romberg, Cyrus Wood), Cleo Mayfield
The Blue Kitten (Rudolph Friml, Otto Harbach), Joseph Cawthorn, Lillian Lorraine
Orange Blossoms (Victor Herbert, B. G. DeSylva), Queenie Smith, Edith Day, Hal Skelly
Make It Snappy (Jean Schwartz, Harold Atteridge), Eddie Cantor, Lew Hearn
Chauve-Souris, Nikita Baliuff's revue of Russian folk songs, dances, and burlesque skits.

Classics and Revivals On and Off Broadway
Hamlet, John Barrymore; *The Merchant of Venice,* David Warfield, Glenn Hunter; *Julius Caesar,* Fritz Lieber; *Macbeth, Romeo and Juliet,* both with Ethel Barrymore; *The Rivals* (Sheridan), Robert Warwick

Pulitzer Prize
Anna Christie, Eugene O'Neill

Classical Music _____

Compositions

Douglas Moore, *Four Museum Pieces*
George Antheil, *Airplane Sonata* for Piano, *Sonata Sauvage, Death of the Machines,* Jazz Sonata, Symphony no. 1
Howard Hanson, Symphony no. 1
Edgard Varèse, *Offrandes*
Aaron Copland, Passacaglia for Piano
Edward Hill, *Stevensoniana* Suite
Arthur Farwell, *Symbolistic Study* no. 3

Important Events

A record $7 million is earned in an extraordinary New York season; four orchestras give 100 concerts at Carnegie Hall. At an unusual benefit in New York, five conductors in a single concert lead their specialties for the Damrosch Fellows in Rome (conductors: Joseph Stranksy, Artur Bodanzky, Albert Coates, Willem Mengelberg, Leopold Stokowski). In another benefit, 15 pianists perform in unison to raise $15,000 for Moritz Moszkowski (pianists include Harold Bauer, Ossip Gabrilowitsch, Percy Grainger, Josef Lhévinne). 108 music festivals include the Berkshire, Sing Sing Prison, and Columbia University festivals, the visiting Berlin State Opera *Ring,* the Philadelphia Orchestra's 80th anniversary celebration, and the New York String Quartet Festival.

Notable Performances: Richard Strauss, Sergei Rachmaninoff, Geraldine Farrar, Pablo Casals, Josef Hofmann, Vincent d'Indy, Fritz Kreisler, Albert Coates

Debut: Myra Hess

First Performances

Ernest Schelling, *A Victory Ball* (Philadelphia); Ernest Bloch, Quintet for Piano and String Quartet (New York); Leo Sowerby, Symphony no. 1 (New York)

Opera

Metropolitan: Titta Ruffo, Amelita Galli-Curci, *Il barbiere di Siviglia;* Elisabeth Rethberg (debut), *Aïda;* premiere: *Cosi fan tutte; Le roi d'Ys*

Chicago: Mary Garden, *Thaïs*

San Francisco: Premieres, in Russian: *Boris Godunov, Eugene Onègin; The Czar's Bride* (Nikolai Rimsky-Korsakov)

Los Angeles: *Snegourotchka* (Rimsky-Korsakov)

Music Notes

Richard Strauss hires the Philadelphia Orchestra to play four concerts of his work in New York, one in Philadelphia • George Antheil goes to Paris to join Ezra Pound, James Joyce, Sylvia Beach, and Virgil Thomson • The New York Philharmonic Orchestra, with Willem Mengelberg conducting, records the *Coriolan Overture* on two 12-inch, single-faced discs for Victor Company, the orchestra's first recording.

Gertrude Stein, one of the leading Americans abroad, entertained Hemingway, William Carlos Williams, and Sherwood Anderson, among others, at her Paris home. *Library of Congress.*

Art

Painting

George Bellows, *The White House*
Maurice Prendergast, *Acadia*
John Marin, *Lower Manhattan II, Maine Islands*
William Zorach, *Sailing by Moonlight*
Joseph Stella, *Skyscrapers*
Arthur G. Dove, *Gear*
Charles Demuth, *Still Life, No. 1*

Sculpture

Gaston Lachaise, *Walking Woman*
John Storrs, *Male Nude*
William Zorach, *Floating Figure*
Saul Baizerman, *Road Builder's Horse*

Architecture

Institute of Fine Arts, Detroit (Paul Phillippe Cret)
Lincoln Memorial, Washington, D.C. (Henry Bacon)
William Randolph Hearst's San Simeon, Calif., house (Julia Morgan).

Important Exhibitions

Museums

New York: *Metropolitan:* Duncan Phyfe furniture; Japanese sword fittings; Chinese funerary portraits

Milwaukee: Wisconsin painters and sculptures

Chicago: Second international watercolor show

Cleveland: Renaissance art

Pittsburgh: Carnegie International First Prize: George Bellows's *Elinor, Jean, and Anna*

Art Briefs

The Baltimore Museum of Art opens • William Jennings Bryan learns that his so-called copy of Gilbert Stuart's *George Washington* is an original • Public debate occurs over the exhibition of George Bellows's *Nude Girl with a Shawl*.

The World We Live In (or *The Insect Comedy*) and *R. U. R.* (which introduces the term "robot") express the Capeks' fear of the dehumanizing effects of technological advances. *Billy Rose Theatre Collection. The New York Public Library at Lincoln Center. Astor, Lenox, and Tilden Foundations.*

Left: popular brother-and-sister dance team Fred and Adele Astaire. *Movie Star News.*

Books

Fiction

Critics' Choice

The Beautiful and Damned, F. Scott Fitzgerald
Tales of the Jazz Age, F. Scott Fitzgerald
Babbitt, Sinclair Lewis
The Enormous Room, E. E. Cummings
The Glimpses of the Moon, Edith Wharton
One Man in His Time, Ellen Glasgow
☙ *Ulysses*, James Joyce
☙ *The Garden Party*, Katherine Mansfield
☙ *The Forsythe Saga* (completed), John Galsworthy

Best-Sellers

If Winter Comes, A. S. M. Hutchinson
The Sheik, Edith M. Hull
Gentle Julia, Booth Tarkington
The Head of the House of Coombe, F. H. Burnett
Simon Called Peter, Robert Keable
The Breaking Point, Mary Roberts Rinehart
This Freedom, A. S. M. Hutchinson
Maria Chapdelaine, Louis Hémon
To the Last Man, Zane Grey

Nonfiction

Critics' Choice

The Economic Basis of Politics. Charles and Mary Beard
Public Opinion, Walter Lippmann
The Argument about Co-Education, C. Pestalozzi
Human Nature and Conduct, John Dewey
Peter Wiffle, Carl Van Vechten
American Individualism, Herbert Hoover
Geography and Plays, Gertrude Stein
All in a Life-Time, Henry Morgenthau
Prejudices, H. L. Mencken
☙ *Methodology of the Social Sciences*, Max Weber
☙ *Decline of the West*, Oswald Spengler

Best-Sellers

The Outline of History, H. G. Wells
The Story of Mankind Hendrik Willem Van Loon
The Americanization of Edward Bok, Edward Bok
Diet and Health, Lulu Hunt Peters
The Mind in the Making, James Harvey Robinson
The Outline of Science, J. Arthur Thomson

Outwitting Our Nerves, Josephine A. Jackson, Helen M. Salisbury
Queen Victoria, Lytton Strachey
Mirrors of Washington, Anonymous (Clinton W. Gilbert)
In Defense of Woman, H. L. Mencken

Poetry

T. S. Eliot, *The Waste Land*
Conrad Aiken, *Priapus and the Pool*
Carl Sandburg, *Slabs of the Sunburnt West*
John Hall Wheelock, *The Black Panther*
☙ W. B. Yeats, *Later Poems*

Pulitzer Prizes

One of Ours, Willa Cather (novel)
The Supreme Court in United States History, Charles Warren (U.S. history)
The Life and Letters of Walter H. Page, Burton J. Hendrick (biography)
The Ballad of the Harp-Weaver, A Few Figs from Thistles, 8 Sonnets in American Poetry, 1922, A Miscellany, Edna St. Vincent Millay (poetry)

Science and Technology

Ur, the ancient Sumerian city on the Euphrates, 2600 B.C., is unearthed by Charles Woolley of the British Museum and a University of Pennsylvania team.

Numerous well-preserved artifacts are discovered in the 1350 B.C. tomb of King Tutankhamen, in the Valley of the Kings, at Luxor, Egypt.

New devices are developed for chiseling vibrations into wax that improve the quality of records.

The first mechanical telephone switchboard is installed, in New York (its exchange is Pennsylvania).

The beneficial effect of calves' liver on hemoglobin production is demonstrated by George Hoyt Whipple.

Herbert McLean Evans discovers the substance that promotes human growth, a hormone from the anterior lobe of the pituitary gland.

A converted cargo ship becomes the first U.S. aircraft carrier, the U.S.S. *Langley*.

☙ Insulin, which regulates the use of sugar by cells, is extracted and first used to treat diabetes by Frederick Banting and Herbert Best.

Sports

Jim Thorpe. *Pro Football Hall of Fame.*

Baseball

Babe Ruth is suspended by Commissioner Landis for 40 days for barnstorming; Ruth's salary increases to $56,000.

A record 49 runs is scored in one game: Chicago 26–Philadelphia 23 (NL).

Champions

Batting	Pitching
Rogers Hornsby (St. Louis, NL), .401	Pete Donohue (Cincinnati, NL), 18–9
George Sisler (St. Louis, AL), .420	Joe Bush (New York, AL), 26–7
(Ty Cobb, Detroit, AL, also bats over .400, at .401)	*Home Runs*
	Rogers Hornsby (St. Louis, AL), 42

Football

The American Professional Football Association is renamed the National Football League; Green Bay joins the league. Jim Thorpe organizes an all-Indian pro team, the Oorang Indians.

Pro Stars: Pete Henry (Canton), Curly Lambeau (Green Bay)

College All-Americans: Harold Kipke (HB), Michigan; Edward Kaw (HB), Cornell; Cal Hubbard (G), Harvard

Rose Bowl (Jan. 1, 1923): Southern California 0–Penn State 0

Basketball

Jim Furey reorganizes the Original Celtics to play in the New York Armory, with salaries instead of per-game pay; Celtics include Johnny Beckman, Tom Furey, Dutch Dehnert, Johnny Witte, and Joe Lapchik, most from New York's Hell's Kitchen. They win 194 of 204 games. The Renaissance Rens, a black team, is organized.

Other Sports

Golf: Gene Sarazen wins the PGA title.

Winners

World Series	Player of the Year
New York (NL) 4	Charles Carney, Ill.
New York (AL) 0	*Stanley Cup*
MVP	Toronto
NL–Not chosen	*U.S. Tennis Open*
AL–George Sisler, St. Louis	Men: William Tilden II
	Women: Molla Mallory
NFL	*USGA Open*
Canton Bulldogs	Gene Sarazen
College Football	*Kentucky Derby*
Cornell	Morvich (A. Johnson, jockey)
College Basketball	
Kansas	

Fashion

For Women: Edwardian laces and feathers are rejected for epicene fashions: "men's" lounging robes and blazers, shirts with ties and cuff links, fitted suits. Hair is cropped short at the ears with waves. Antoine de Paris's mannish shingle bob appears, despite Irene Castle's lingering 1914 bob. With the emphasis on youth, little makeup is worn. The focus is on the flat, angular look; every curve of the body is suppressed by long, cylindrical corsets or hip belts and bust bodices (the "foundation garment") to create the hipless and bosomless appearance. Underwear, now called "undies," is more practical and hygienic: cotton replaces silk in cream, beige, soft pastels, and "ivory" (surplus khaki dye added to white). The "thin voman" of Greenwich Village, like her Left Bank counterpart, gains attention in harem pantaloons and skirts above the ankle (in black hose), Dutch-boy hairdos, berets, asexual smocks, unconventional colors (chartreuse, henna, puce, magenta), and African jewelry of bangles and bone, wood, shell, mock jade (by Chanel).

High-fashion notes: Silk, velvet masks for the flirtatious vamp to peek through; gauntlet gloves with art deco lines; onyx and crystal hat pins; low-strapped pumps with chunky heels and perforated detailing; Chanel's Balkan embroideries; Vuitton luggage.

Kaleidoscope

- Clara Bow, 17, wins a fan magazine contest for "The Most Beautiful Girl in the World"; Charles Atlas wins the "World's Most Perfectly Developed Man" contest.
- Describing the new "flapper," *Vanity Fair* reports: "[She] will never . . . knit you a necktie, but she'll go skiing with you. . . . She may quote poetry to you, not Indian love lyrics but something about the peace conference or theology."
- Radio becomes a national obsession, and many stay up half the night listening to concerts, sermons, "Red Menace" news, and sports. Those without home radios gather around crystal sets in public places like the post office.
- $5,000-a-week star Roscoe "Fatty" Arbuckle, exonerated of starlet Virginia Rappe's murder following an alleged sexual episode, changes his name to William Goodrich but is still blacklisted.
- Actresses Mabel Normand, Mary Miles Minter, and Mary Pickford are romantically linked with murdered actor-director William Desmond Taylor; only Pickford's career remains unharmed.
- One-time actor-idol Wallace Reid, addicted to rum and morphine, dies in a sanitarium; Hollywood has recently placed his name first on a blacklist of 117 "unsafe" persons.
- Although the Hollywood morals code is established with William H. Hays as its chief enforcer, studios continue to advertise films with "red kisses," "white kisses," and "pleasure-mad daughters [and] sensation-craving mothers."
- The two-year ban on James Branch Cabell's *Jurgen* is lifted.
- Protestant Episcopal bishops vote to erase *obey* from the marriage ceremony.

- Women married to aliens are no longer required to relinquish their citizenship.
- *Reader's Digest* starts a wave of magazine book digests.
- Attorney General Harry Daugherty persuades Harding that government control of railroads would be "a conspiracy worthy of Lenin" and then obtains an injunction barring all union activity.
- H. L. Mencken defends the American husband against current charges of infidelity, calling him "fundamentally moral," if only because he "lacks . . . courage . . . [and] money."
- Boston mayor Curley bans Isadora Duncan from the stage when she wears a transparent Greek dress and publicly praises the Soviet regime.
- Syracuse University bans dancing.
- Florenz Ziegfeld forbids his stars to work on radio because it "cheapens them."
- The manager of radio station WEAF rejects the first toothpaste commercial because "care of the teeth" is too delicate a subject for the air.
- At the Washington Arms Limitation Conference presided over by Secretary of State Charles Evans Hughes, the first agreement in history is made to reduce already existing armaments of major powers.
- The U.S. Post Office burns 500 copies of James Joyce's *Ulysses*.
- Henry Ford, who earns over $264,000 a day, is declared a "billionaire" by the Associated Press.

Fads: Radio, college football, Eskimo Pies, the three o'clock raisin break, collecting tabloids

First Appearances: Self-winding wristwatch, Checker Cab, State Farm Mutual auto insurance, commercially prepared baby food (Clapp's vegetable soup), Canada Dry ginger ale, cruise ship circumnavigating the world, Federal Narcotics Board, New York City curfew (2 A.M.) on dancing, skywriting, push-button elevators, Maytag Gyrofoam washing machine, soybean processing plant, Thom McAn, microfilm machine, *New York Daily Mirror, Better Homes and Gardens, True Confessions, New York Times Book Review* (as a separate section), transcontinental dirigible flight, parachuting from a disabled flight, the expression "Pike's Peak or Bust," woman automotive engineer, Strongheart (first leading dog movie star)

Commercial flights, like the "Highball Express" to Bimini, are frequently short hops between small cities. *Library of Congress.*

1923

In the News

PRESIDENT HARDING SHAKES 10,000 SHRINER HANDS AT WHITE HOUSE . . . SECRETARY OF STATE CHARLES EVANS HUGHES REJECTS U.S. RECOGNITION OF U.S.S.R. UNTIL FOREIGN DEBTS ARE HONORED . . . FRANCE AND BELGIUM OCCUPY THE RUHR TO FORCE GERMAN REPARATIONS PAYMENT, GERMANY ORGANIZES PASSIVE RESISTANCE . . . WASHINGTON, D.C., MINIMUM WAGE FOR WOMEN AND CHILDREN IS DECLARED UNCONSTITUTIONAL . . . WARREN HARDING DIES OF CEREBRAL APOPLEXY IN SAN FRANCISCO AFTER HECTIC ALASKAN JOURNEY . . . CALVIN COOLIDGE TAKES OFFICE, SWORN IN BY FATHER, VERMONT JUSTICE OF THE PEACE . . . ECONOMY SOARS, UNEMPLOYMENT FALLS . . . U.S. OFFERS TO MEDIATE GERMAN DEBT PROBLEM, FRANCE REFUSES . . . OKLAHOMA GOVERNOR DECLARES MARTIAL LAW TO COMBAT KKK OUTRAGES, STATE SENATE MOVES TO IMPEACH HIM . . . FEDERAL TAX DISCLOSURE LAW IS PASSED, JOHN D. ROCKEFELLER, SR., PAYS $124,000, ROCKEFELLER, JR., $7.4 MILLION . . . U.S. STEEL FIGHTS REDUCTION OF 12-HOUR DAY . . . EARTHQUAKE DESTROYS TOKYO AND YOKAHAMA, U.S. OFFERS AID . . . KKK CONVENTION AT KOKOMO, IND., DRAWS 200,000 . . . HUNG JURY FREES COMMUNIST WILLIAM Z. FOSTER, TRIED FOR PREACHING VIOLENT REVOLUTION . . . OILMAN HARRY SINCLAIR PLANS TO VISIT RUSSIA TO BUY SIBERIAN OIL FIELDS . . . PANCHO VILLA IS ASSASSINATED . . . LAST-MINUTE SETTLEMENT AVERTS COAL STRIKE . . . GERMAN CURRENCY GOES TO ONE TRILLION MARKS PER DOLLAR . . . ADOLF HITLER FAILS IN ATTEMPT TO OVERTHROW GERMAN GOVERNMENT FROM MUNICH BEER GARDEN . . . SENATE WALSH COMMITTEE STARTS TEAPOT DOME INVESTIGATION . . . U.S. STEEL AGREES TO 8-HOUR DAY.

Quotes

"My soul yearns for peace. My passion is for justice over force. My hope is in the Great Court. If in our search for everlasting peace, we . . . follow humbly but dauntlessly the 'kindly light' of divine inspiration, . . . God will not let us fail."
— President Warren G. Harding, on the World Court

"My God, this is a hell of a job! I have no trouble with my enemies. I can take care of my enemies all right. But my damn friends, my God-damn friends. . . . They're the ones that keep me walking the floor nights!"
— President Warren G. Harding (quoted in William Allen White, *Autobiography*)

"Men nowadays are tired of liberty. . . . These masses like rule by the few. . . . Fascismo . . . will pass again without the slightest hesitation over the more or less decomposed body of the goddess of liberty."

— Benito Mussolini

"[It is resolved] that war between nations should be outlawed as an instrument of settlement of international controversies by making it a public crime."

— Senator Hiram Borah, Senate resolution

"The height of folly is to imagine that the cutting of armaments would ensure peace. World peace is best maintained when nations are armed to the hilt."
— Japanese general Kenichi Oshimi

"If this nation is to obtain its destiny, there will have to be a harmonious assimilation [which] three powerful elements will defy: . . . the Negro, . . . alarmingly vitiated by venereal infection, . . . the Jew, . . . not American, . . . [and] the illiterate Catholic."
— Imperial Wizard H. W. Evans, keynote speaker, KKK State Fair, Texas

"[Evolution theory is a] program of infidelity masquerading under the name of science."
— William Jennings Bryan

"No woman is justified in being supported in idleness by any man. The most womanly woman today is the woman who works."
— Mrs. Carrie Chapman Catt, suffragist

Library of Congress.

Ads

One Year Married and All Talked Out . . .
Is there anything that would brighten their evenings?
. . . How can they turn their silent, lonely hours into real human companionship?
(*Dr. Eliot's Five-Foot Shelf of Books*)

The truth is—the Playboy was built for her. Built for the lass whose face is brown with the sun when the day is done of revel and romp and race.
(*Car named after Synge's* The Playboy of the Western World)

She Who Prizes Beauty Must Obey Nature's Law!
Faulty Elimination is the greatest enemy that beauty knows. It plays havoc with the complexion, brings sallow skin, dull and listless eyes.
Everybody / Everyday / Eat POST's Bran Flakes, as an ounce of Prevention.

(*Post's Bran Flakes*)

The King and Queen Might Eat Thereof / And Noblemen Besides.

(*JELL-O*)

At thirty every woman reaches a crossroads. Will she develop—or merely age?
(*Boncilla Beautifier, the Clasmic Clay*)

Try the "Daily Dozen" Muscle Build to Music.
(*Daily Dozen*)

What is the great story of the War? Is it . . . Joffre at the first Marne or . . . Foch at the second? Or . . . "They shall not pass" at Verdun? Is it . . . the first gas attack at Ypres? . . . Or . . . the Lost Battalion? . . . A different sort of story stands comparison with these . . . of a fight by the soldiers . . . against a countless and implacable foe.

(*Zonite Antiseptic*)

Radio

Premieres
"Eveready Hour" (variety)
"The Happiness Boys," Billy Jones, Ernie Hare
     (first comedy series)
"Roxy and His Gang"
"Dr. Walter Damrosch" (lecture-recital)
"Joseph M. White, 'The Silver-Masked Tenor' "
"A & P Gypsies," Harry Orlich Orchestra

Specials
"The Laughing Lady" (Ethel Barrymore, first radio
     drama)

Of Note
Sponsors take over the air waves: Cliquot Club
Eskimos, Ipana Troubadours, A & P Gypsies,
Rheingold Quartet, Lucky Strike Show • Announcer
Graham McNamee gains wide popularity with news
"editorializing."

Movies

Openings
The Ten Commandments (Cecil B. DeMille), Richard
     Dix, Rod La Rocque
Anna Christie (John Griffith Wray), Blanche Sweet,
     William Russell
The Covered Wagon (James Cruze), Lois Wilson, J.
     Warren Kerrigan
Peg O'My Heart (King Vidor), Laurette Taylor
The Green Goddess (Sidney Olcott), George Arliss,
     Alice Joyce
The Hunchback of Notre Dame (Wallace Worsley),
     Lon Chaney, Ernest Torrence
Our Hospitality (Buster Keaton), Buster Keaton
Main Street (Harry Beaumont), Monte Blue, Noah
     Beery, Robert Gordon
Peter the Great (Dimitri Buchowetzski), Dagni
     Servais, Emil Jannings
The Pilgrim (Charles Chaplin), Charles Chaplin,
     Edna Purviance

Rosita (Ernst Lubitsch), Mary Pickford, Holbrook
     Blinn
Safety Last (Fred Newmeyer), Harold Lloyd,
     Mildred Davis
Scaramouche (Rex Ingram), Ramon Novarro, Alice
     Terry
White Sister (Henry King), Lillian Gish, Ronald
     Colman
A Woman of Paris (Charles Chaplin), Edna
     Purviance, Adolphe Menjou

Top Box-Office Stars
Norma Talmadge, Thomas Meighan

Stars of Tomorrow
Jean Arthur, Clara Bow, Norma Shearer, Ronald
Colman

Rin Tin Tin, a German
shepherd saved by an
American soldier in
World War I, becomes
a film star. *Movie Star
News.*

Far left: the shy Harold
Lloyd character
performs daredevil
stunts in *Safety Last* in
order to win his girl.
Movie Star News.

Popular Music

Hit Songs
"Yes! We Have No Bananas"
"Who's Sorry Now?"
"Charleston"
"Mexicali Rose"
"It Ain't Gonna Rain No Mo' "
"That Old Gang of Mine"
"You've Got to See Mamma Ev'ry Night—or You Can't See Mamma at All"

Top Records
Three O'Clock in the Morning (Paul Whiteman); *Somebody Stole My Gal* (Ted Williams); *Barney Google* (Jones and Hare); *I Won't Say I Will* (Irene Bordoni); *Linger Awhile* (Paul Whiteman); *Twelve O'Clock at Night* (Sophie Tucker)

Jazz and Big Bands
Roseland replaces society dance orchestras with Fletcher Henderson's jazz band. Henderson also brings a ten-piece band to the Club Alabam, New York. Newly organized bands include Bix Beiderbecke, King Oliver (with Louis Armstrong), Jelly Roll Morton's Red Hot Peppers, Jabbo Smith's Rhythm Aces, and the Reuben Reeves River Boys. Bessie Smith's *Downhearted Blues* sells a record 2 million copies. Other popular blues singers include Ma Rainey and Ida Cox.

Other New Bands: Horace Heidt, Oakland; Ted Weems, Philadelphia

Theater

Broadway Openings

Plays
St. Joan (George Bernard Shaw), Winifred Lenihan
The Swan (Ferenc Molnár), Eva Le Gallienne, Basil Rathbone
Icebound (Owen Davis), Edna May Oliver, Willard Robertson
The Shame Woman (Lula Vollmer), Florence Rittenhouse
The Adding Machine (Elmer Rice), Dudley Digges, Margaret Wycherly
White Cargo (Leon Gordon), Richard Stevenson
Tweedles (Booth Tarkington, Harry Wilson), Ruth Gordon
Spring Cleaning (Frederick Lonsdale), Violet Heming, Estelle Winwood
Meet the Wife (Lynn Starling), Mary Boland, Clifton Webb
Laugh, Clown, Laugh (David Belasco, Tom Cushing), Lionel Barrymore

Musicals
Kid Boots (Harry Tierney, Joseph McArthur), Eddie Cantor, Mary Eaton
Wildflower (Herbert Stothart, Vincent Youmans, Oscar Hammerstein II), Edith Day, Guy Robertson
Ziegfeld Follies (Victor Herbert et al., Gene Buck), Fannie Brice, Eddie Cantor, Ann Pennington
Poppy (Stephen Jones, Arthur Samuels), W. C. Fields, Madge Kennedy
Battling Butler (Walter Rosemont), Charles Ruggles, Marie Saxon, William Kent
Earl Carroll's Vanities (Earl Carroll), Joe Cook, Peggy Hopkins Joyce
Runnin' Wild (James Johnson, Cecil Mack), Miller and Lyles, all-black cast

Classics and Revivals On and Off Broadway
The Devil's Disciple (George Bernard Shaw), Basil Sydney, Roland Young; *The Lady from the Sea, Ghosts* (Ibsen), Eleonora Duse; *Romeo and Juliet,* Jane Cowl; *Pelleas and Melisande* (Maeterlinck), Jane Cowl; *Cymbeline,* E. H. Sothern, Julia Marlowe; *The School for Scandal* (Sheridan), John Drew, Ethel Barrymore; *Oedipus Rex* (Sophocles), John Martin Harvey; *Cyrano de Bergerac* (Rostand), Walter Hampton; *Hamlet,* John Barrymore

Regional

Founded: Hedgerow Theatre, near Philadelphia, by Jasper Deeter

Pulitzer Prize
Icebound, Owen Davis

Classical Music

Compositions

Ernest Schelling, *A Victory Ball*
George Antheil, Violin Sonata no. 1
Wallingford Riegger, *La belle Dame sans merci*
Howard Hanson, *North and West, Lux Aeterna*
Roger Sessions, *The Black Maskers*
Aaron Copland, *As It Fell upon a Day*
Arthur Farwell, Symphonic Song on "Old Black Joe"
Charles Loeffler, *Music for Four String Instruments*

Important Events

Notable Concerts: Darius Milhaud conducts and plays the piano with the City Symphony (New York); George Enesco conducts the New York Philharmonic; Fritz Kreisler gives a farewell concert in Hollywood; the San Francisco Orchestra features the new English school of composers: Eugene Goossens, Ralph Vaughan Williams, Arthur Bliss, Frederick Delius, Gustav Holst

Major Recitals: Ignace Paderewski, Efrem Zimbalist, Pierre Monteux, Artur Rubinstein, Mrs. Ernestine Schumann-Heink, Ossip Gabrilowitsch, Mr. and Mrs. Pablo Casals, Mr. and Mrs. Josef Lhévinne, Myra Hess, Alexander Cortot, Moriz Rosenthal, Josef Hofmann, Jascha Heifetz

Guest Conductors Visiting the United States: Willem Mengelberg, Eugene Goossens, Albert Coates, Bruno Walter, Darius Milhaud

Debuts: Wanda Landowska, Claudio Arrau

First Performances

Edgard Varèse, *Hyperprism* (New York); Frank S. Converse, *Scarecrow Sketches* (Boston)

Opera

Metropolitan: The company enjoys the largest subscription to date; audiences also expand as the company travels to Brooklyn and Philadelphia. Productions: Maria Jeritza, Feodor Chaliapin, *Boris Godunov;* Lucrezia Bori, *Anima allegra* (Franco Vittadini, premiere); Richard Crooks, *Manon;* Beniamino Gigli, Frances Alda, *Martha;* Lawrence Tibbett (debut), *Faust.* Six major revivals include *Don Carlo, Roméo et Juliette, Faust, Tannhaüser, Der Rosenkavalier* (in German for the first time since the war)

Chicago: Claudia Muzio, Alexander Kipnis, *La forza del destino*

Los Angeles: Inaugural productions: Giovanni Martinelli, *La bohème;* and *I pagliacci.* First full production: *Il trittico* (Giacomo Puccini)

Music Notes

Josef Hofmann gives a benefit recital for Robert Schumann's daughters • Arnold Schoenberg's *Kammersymphonie* is met with public hissing • John McCormack sings in darkness as his audience demands more encores • 3,256 people perform in Cincinnati's golden jubilee production of *Elijah* • Geraldine Farrar is banned from singing in two Atlanta churches • Boston bans Richard Strauss's *Salomé* • Richard Wagner's wife, in a state of poverty, sells her late husband's artifacts.

The comedy hit *Abie's Irish Rose* deals with religious intermarriage. Billy Rose Theatre Collection. *The New York Public Library of Lincoln Center. Astor, Lenox and Tilden Foundations.*

Art

Painting

George Bellows, *Between Rounds*

John Marin, *Ship, Sea and Sky Forms, Impression*

Marsden Hartley, *New Mexico Recollections, Color Analogy*

Charles Sheeler, *Bucks County Barn, Self-Portrait*

Rockwell Kent, *Shadows of Evening* (1921–23), *The Kathleen*

Preston Dickinson, *Industry*

Sculpture

James Earle Fraser, *Head of a Faun*

Lorado Taft, *Mask from the Fountain of Time*

Gertrude V. Whitney, *Chinoise*

Important Exhibitions

Museums

New York: *Metropolitan:* "Tut-ankh-Amen Discoveries"; American handicrafts; art of the Italian Renaissance; George Fuller centennial; women painters and sculptors; John Singer Sargent, Winslow Homer, Childe Hassam, John Marin, Paul Dougherty. *Public Library:* James A. McNeill Whistler

Boston, Washington, Pittsburgh, Minneapolis: Spanish art

Boston: Indian art

Chicago: Artists of Chicago and vicinity

Cleveland: Cleveland arts and craftsmen

Gallery Shows

New York: Naum Gabo constructions; Jacob Epstein's female portraits and bust of Joseph Conrad; Gaston Lachaise's *Egyptian Head*. Bellows's

Architecture

St. Bartholomew's Church, New York (Bertram Goodhue)

Millard House, Pasadena, Calif. (Frank Lloyd Wright)

Bowery Savings Bank, New York (York and Sawyer)

Standard Oil Building, New York (Carrère and Hastings)

Skyscraper in Black Glass and Aluminum project, Los Angeles (Rudolph Schindler)

Crucifixion of Christ dominates the fifth New York Society of Artists Annual Exhibition. The Grand Central Palace opens with a Russian art show.

Art Briefs

Gainsborough's *The Blue Boy* tours • National attention is given to Alfred Stieglitz's photographs • Interest grows in war subjects—Sargent's *Marching Soldiers, The Duke of York, Death and Victory*—and in animal sculpture—Robert Laurent, Herbert Haseltine • Dr. A. C. Barnes plans a gallery in Merion, Pa., to house his $3 million collection.

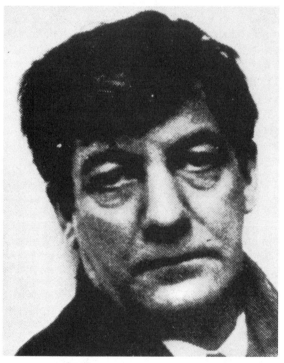

Sherwood Anderson. *D. Ouellette Collection.*

Dance

Mikhail Mordkin, formerly with the Bolshoi and partner of Pavlova, forms a dance company that performs in the *Greenwich Village Follies;* Martha Graham joins.

Books

Fiction

Critics' Choice
A Lost Lady, Willa Cather
The Shadowy Third and Other Stories, Ellen Glasgow
Streets of Night, John Dos Passos
Three Stories and Ten Poems, Ernest Hemingway
Many Marriages, Sherwood Anderson
Four of a Kind, John Marquand
Cane, Jean Toomer
The High Place, James Branch Cabell
&◗ *Antic Hay*, Aldous Huxley
&◗ *The Good Soldier Schweik*, Jaroslav Hašek

Best-Sellers
Black Oxen, Gertrude Atherton
His Children's Children, Arthur Train
The Enchanted April, "Elizabeth"
Babbitt, Sinclair Lewis
The Dim Lantern, Temple Bailey
The Sea-Hawk, Rafael Sabatini
This Freedom, A. S. M. Hutchinson
The Mine with the Iron Door, Harold Bell Wright
The Wanderer of the Wasteland, Zane Grey
Flaming Youth, Warner Fabian

Nonfiction

Critics' Choice
Money, Credit and Commerce, Alfred Marshall
Unemployment, W. A. Appleton
My Life and Loves, Frank Harris
Indiscretions, Ezra Pound
Science and Life, Robert Millikan
Skepticism and Animal Faith, George Santayana
Absentee Ownership and Business Enterprise in Recent Times, Thorstein Veblen
&◗ *The Ego and the Id*, Sigmund Freud
&◗ *Psychological Types*, Carl Jung
&◗ *I and Thou*, Martin Buber

Best-Sellers
Etiquette, Emily Post
The Life of Christ, Giovanni Papini
The Life and Letters of Walter H. Page, ed. Burton J. Hendrick
The Mind in the Making, James Harvey Robinson
The Outline of History, H. G. Wells
Diet and Health, Lulu Hunt Peters
Self-Mastery through Conscious Auto-Suggestion, Emile Coué
The Americanization of Edward Bok, Edward Bok
The Story of Mankind, Hendrik Willem Van Loon
A Man from Maine, Edward Bok

Poetry
Wallace Stevens, *Harmonium*
E. E. Cummings, *Tulips and Chimneys*
William Carlos Williams, *Spring and All*
Vachel Lindsay, *Collected Poems*
Elinor Wylie, *Black Armour*
Louise Bogan, *Body of This Death*
&◗ Kahil Gibran, *The Prophet*

Pulitzer Prizes
The Able McLaughlins, Margaret Wilson (novel)
The American Revolution—A Constitutional Interpretation, Charles Howard McIlwain (U.S. history)
From Immigrant to Inventor, Michael I. Pupin (biography)
New Hampshire: A Poem with Notes and Grace Notes, Robert Frost (poetry)

Science and Technology

Astronomers' measurements of the bending of the sun's rays during an eclipse are in accord with Einstein's theory of relativity.

Lee De Forest devises a method of recording sound directly on film—fonofilm.

The iconoscope, the first electronic television camera, is patented by Vladimir Zworykin.

The first American helium-filled rigid airship, the *Shenandoah*, is launched at Lakehurst, N.J.

Harry Steenbock, at the University of Wisconsin, discovers that radiating food with ultraviolet light adds vitamin D.

A whooping cough (pertussis) vaccine is developed.

Scopolamine, previously used as a childbirth anesthetic, is reported to be a "truth" serum after tests on convicts at San Quentin Prison.

Surgeons debate the virtues of the Steinach sex-gland rejuvenation transplants.

&◗ Tetanus toxoid is developed by Gaston Ramon.

Nobel Prize
Robert A. Millikan wins the prize in physics for his work on photoelectric phenomena.

Sports ———————————

Baseball

Yankee Stadium opens, the "house that Ruth built." Ruth hits .398 with 41 home runs. Casey Stengel's home runs win two World Series games, 1–0.

Champions ———————————

Batting
Rogers Hornsby (St. Louis, NL), .403
Harry Heilmann (Detroit, AL), .401
Pitching
Adolfo Luque (Cincinnati, NL), 27–8
Herb Pennock (New York, AL), 19–6

Home runs
Babe Ruth (New York, AL), 41
Fred Williams (Philadelphia, NL), 41

Football

Red Grange begins his college career at Illinois.

Pro Stars: Guy Chamberlin (Canton), Jim Conzelman (Rock Island).

College All-Americans: Red Grange (HB), Illinois; Cal Hubbard (G), Harvard.

Rose Bowl (Jan. 1, 1924): Navy 14–Washington 14

Basketball

The Original Celtics' game at Cleveland draws a record 22,000.

Other Sports

Tennis: Helen Wills, 17 ("Little Miss Poker Face"), wins the U.S. Open Singles. Bill Tilden wins his third straight U.S. Open Singles.

Golf: Gene Sarazen wins his second straight PGA title. Bobby Jones wins his first USGA Open.

Boxing: Jack Dempsey KO's "Wild Bull of the Pampas" Luis Firpo in the second round, after being knocked out of the ring in the first.

Swimming: Johnny Weismuller swims 200 yards free style in a record 1 minute, 59 ⅕ seconds.

Amateur Bobby Jones, who won the National Open on the 18th hole. *Library of Congress.*

Winners ———————————

World Series
New York (AL) 4
New York (NL) 2
MVP
NL–Not chosen
AL–Babe Ruth (New York)
NFL
Canton Bulldogs
College Football
Illinois
College Basketball
Kansas

Player of the Year
Paul Endacott, Kansas
Stanley Cup
Ottawa
U.S. Tennis Open
Men: William Tilden II
Women: Helen Wills
USGA Open
Robert T. Jones, Jr.
Kentucky Derby
Zev (E. Sande, jockey)

Fashion ———————————

For Women: Boyish bobbed hair transforms into the shingle cut, flat and close to the head, with a center or side part. A single curl at each ear is pulled forward onto the face. New felt cloche (helmet-shaped) hats appear with little or no decoration in colors that match the day's dress. Hats are pulled down to the eyes, and their brims are turned up in the front or back. Eccentric hairstyles also gain popularity, for example, curled and brushed to a peak resembling a rooster's comb. In clothing, the straight line still emphasizes the boyish look, but fabrics are now embroidered, striped, printed, and painted, influenced by Chinese, Russian, Japanese, and Egyptian art. The Tutankhamen discoveries set off a rage for oriental fringed scarves, slave bangles, and long earrings. Artificial silk stockings, later called rayon, are stronger and less expensive than real silk ones, although they are shiny. The new seamless stocking, despite its wrinkling, also makes the leg look naked. At bedtime, girls wear boyish pajama bottoms, halter tops, and boudoir caps to protect their new hairdos.

High-fashion notes: Poirot's oriental dress; Lanvin's "robe de style"

Kaleidoscope

- The nation mourns President Harding as his cortege travels from San Francisco to Washington; the public's response is "the most remarkable expression of affection, respect and reverence in U.S. history" (*New York Times*).
- Prescription liquor remains unlimited.
- Secretary of Interior Albert Fall's affluence comes under scrutiny during the Senate Walsh committee's investigation of federal oil leases; Fall has purchased a costly ranch in New Mexico with hundred-dollar bills.
- Marcus Garvey, leader of the Universal Negro Improvement Association, is convicted of mail fraud in raising money for his Black Star shipping line.
- Two of Harding's appointees suspected of graft commit suicide.
- An interest in psychology and self-healing continues to capture the nation; Emile Coué's mind-over-matter prescriptions attract thousands.
- Evangelist Aimee Semple McPherson opens a $1.5 million Angelus Temple in Los Angeles; it includes a "miracle room" for discarded crutches and wheelchairs and a rotating, illuminated cross visible for 50 miles.
- Clarence Darrow and William Jennings Bryan debate evolution versus fundamentalism in the *Chicago Tribune*.
- "It won't be Long now" becomes the popular slogan directed against Huey Long in the Louisiana gubernatorial race.
- Nicola Sacco goes on a 30-day hunger strike.
- President Coolidge, as a matter of budget and character, sleeps in a train berth rather than a Pullman.
- After the public's hostile response toward his 6 A.M. "matutinal" exercises, Coolidge turns to horseback riding.
- When his daughter is mailed *Women in Love*, Boston justice Ford prosecutes the offending circulating library; a "Clean Books League" forms to judge new and old books, and a long debate over D. H. Lawrence begins.
- Arthur Schwartz's Broadway show *Artists and Models*, with its bare-breasted chorus, sets off a censorship drive.
- Ida Rosenthal introduces Maidenform bras by giving them away to unshapely flappers who patronize her dress shop.
- In a record-setting dance marathon—90 hours, 10 minutes—Homer Morehouse, 27, drops dead in the 87th hour.
- Tennessee flappers are banned from public schools until they roll their stockings back up over their knees.
- Chicago racketeer Johnny Torrio goes into the bootleg business and makes $25,000 a week.
- Rudolph Valentino attacks Adolph Zukor on the radio with "language waves so hot" he is cut off the air. Valentino pans the motion picture "trust" for producing "nothing but cheap trash."

- The vast improvement in recording electronics eradicates screeches and howls.
- ASCAP wins a court decision requiring broadcasters to pay for the right to play copyrighted music on the air.
- Montana and Nevada are the first states to introduce old-age pensions.
- A HOLLYWOODLAND sign (now HOLLYWOOD) is erected in Los Angeles, each letter measuring 30 by 50 feet.
- A German Shepherd, Rin Tin Tin, becomes a top movie star.
- An air speed record of 243.67 m.p.h. is set in a Curtiss monoplane by former New York Giants pitcher Lt. A. I. Williams.
- Montana grasshoppers devour all plants in an area 300 miles long, 100 miles wide, and a half mile in altitude.
- $250 million is invested in the construction of 300 hotels; the largest is the $8 million Shelton in New York with 1,200 rooms.

Fads: Marathon dancing; flagpole sitting; spiritualism; ouija boards; mah-jongg (1.5 million sets sold); and the King Tut craze, extending to hats, rings, home decorations, jewelry, dress patterns, hair accessories, and newborn babies' names

First Appearances: Rubber diaphragm, Pan American World Airlines, Zenith, Milky Way, Butterfinger, Sanka, *Time, American Mercury,* Pet milk, Libby's tomato soup, Welch's grape jelly, Russell Stover, the name *Popsicle* (changed from *epsicle*), Birds Eye, "Moon Mullins," neon tube advertising sign, chinchilla farm, "Junior Year Abroad," oven thermostat, photoelectric eye, Schick electric razor patent, Du Pont cellophane, Hertz Drive-Ur-Self, eggbeater and wooden bowl patent, 2¢ commemorative stamp of President Harding, White House Christmas tree lights, birth control clinic (New York)

Easter-egg rolling at the White House. *Library of Congress.*

1924

Facts and Figures

Economic Profile

Dow-Jones:—High 120– Low 89

GNP: 0%

Inflation: +0.1%

Unemployment: 5.0%

Expenditures

Recreation: $2.7 billion

Spectator sports: $47 million

European travel: $2.3 million

Golf courses: 131

Bowlers: 60,000

Willys-Knight: $1,450

Chrysler: $1,395

Steinway: $875 (upright), $1,425 (grand)

Mah-jongg set: $3

Ouiji board: 87¢

Gorham silver spoon: $8.50

Hand-tailored wool tuxedo: $55

Man's collar pin, 14k gold, 1¾": $1

Sulka silk cravat: $6

Deaths

Frances Hodgson Burnett, Ferruccio Busoni, Joseph Conrad, Gabriel Fauré, Anatole France, Victor Herbert, Franz Kafka, Maurice Prendergast, Giacomo Puccini, Louis Sullivan, Woodrow Wilson.

In the News

CONGRESS PASSES SOLDIERS' BONUS BILL OVER COOLIDGE VETO . . . LENIN DIES, JOSEPH STALIN, LEV KAMENEV, GRIGORY ZINOVIEV TAKE OVER . . . U.S. MARINES LEAVE NICARAGUA . . . SECRETARY OF INTERIOR ALBERT FALL, NAVY SECRETARY EDWIN DENBY, AND ATTORNEY GENERAL HARRY DAUGHERTY RESIGN IN TEAPOT DOME SCANDAL . . . 171 ARE KILLED IN CASTLE GATE, UTAH, COAL MINE DISASTER . . . NEW IMMIGRATION LAW TAKES EFFECT: 2% OF 1890 CENSUS AND NO JAPANESE . . . BRITAIN RECOGNIZES U.S.S.R. . . . U.S. BANKER CHARLES DAWES PROPOSES PLAN FOR GERMAN REPARATIONS . . . GOP NOMINATES COOLIDGE, DEMOCRATS NOMINATE JOHN DAVIS ON 103RD BALLOT . . . CONGRESS DECLARES NATIVE-BORN INDIANS CITIZENS . . . N.Y. REPEALS ITS STATE PROHIBITION ENFORCEMENT LAW . . . ITALIAN SOCIALIST DEPUTY GIACOMO MATTEOTI IS MURDERED, FASCISTS DENY RESPONSIBILITY . . . TWO WELL-TO-DO YOUTHS, NATHAN LEOPOLD AND RICHARD LOEB, ARE ACCUSED OF MURDERING 14-YEAR-OLD BOBBY FRANKS . . . ADOLF HITLER IS SENTENCED TO FIVE YEARS FOR MUNICH PUTSCH . . . JAPANESE CONDEMN IMMIGRATION HUMILIATION IN "HATE AMERICA" RALLIES . . . DAWES'S PLAN FOR GERMAN REPARATIONS IS ACCEPTED . . . FRANCE AGREES TO LEAVE RUHR . . . GERMAN MARK STABILIZES . . . J. EDGAR HOOVER IS APPOINTED HEAD OF BUREAU OF INVESTIGATION . . . ZINOVIEV LETTER URGING COMMUNIST INFILTRATION HELPS BRITISH CONSERVATIVES RECAPTURE GOVERNMENT . . . COOLIDGE WINS LARGE VICTORY FOR PRESIDENT, ROBERT M. LA FOLLETTE, THIRD-PARTY CANDIDATE, RECEIVES 17% . . . CLARENCE DARROW PLEA AVERTS DEATH PENALTY FOR LEOPOLD AND LOEB.

Quotes

"I can picture them awakened in the gray light of morning, furnished a suit of clothes by the State, led to the scaffold, . . . black caps down over their heads, . . . the hangman pressing a spring. . . . I can see them fall through space."

— Clarence Darrow's courtroom appeal against the death penalty for Leopold and Loeb

"The United States once went on the notion that all men are created equal, and admitted everybody. . . . But we found we were becoming an insane asylum. . . . Unless the U.S. adopts this biologic principle [of racial differences] they will be flooded over by people of inferior stock because of their greater fecundity."

— Dr. Harry H. Laughlin for the secretary of labor, on the new exclusionary immigration law

"He would be a national advertiser today, I am sure, as He was a great advertiser in His own day. He thought of His life as business."

— Bruce Barton, speaking of Christ

"Ford has saved America from a social crisis. . . . When alcohol was taken [away], . . . the flivver was needed to replace it."

— Samuel M. Vaudain, labor leader

"I am making this statement of my own free will and spending my own money . . . to assure well-meaning friends, who have been incessantly telephoning me and expressing their condolences, . . . that I'm satisfied."

— Fannie Brice, in defense of the plastic surgeon who reconstructed her nose

"We are leaning too much on government. If our forefathers did not make enough money, they worked harder, and did not run to the government for a bonus. The American stock is changing."

— Sen. David Reed (R-Pa.)

An ad for mineral water in which the tastes of the upper class appear accessible to all. *Library of Congress.*

Ads

Calvin Coolidge and his sons. "This is a business country, and it wants a business government," affirmed the president during a campaign speech. *Library of Congress.*

Radio

Premieres
"Spike Shannon" (early-morning physical culture)
Political convention coverage (Republican, Cleveland; Democratic, New York)

Of Note
Many actresses, like Olga Petrova, stand before a microphone in full costume • Debates continue over whether industry, government, or voluntary contributions should subsidize radio • Questions of licensing are also raised, as well as whether performers should be salaried • News and sports stations begin to expand • Radio sales rise from $60 million (1923) to $350 million.

Movies

Openings
America (D. W. Griffith), Carol Dempster, Lionel Barrymore
Babbitt (Harry Beaumont), Willard Louis, Mary Alden
Beau Brummel (Harry Beaumont), John Barrymore, Mary Astor
The Eternal City (George Fitzmaurice), Barbara La Marr, Bert Lytell
Girl Shy (Fred Newmeyer, Sam Taylor), Harold Lloyd, Jobyna Ralston
Greed (Erich von Stroheim), ZaSu Pitts, Gibson Gowland, Jean Hersholt (42 reels)
He Who Gets Slapped (Victor Seastrom), Lon Chaney
The Last Laugh (F. W. Murnau), Emil Jannings
The Iron Horse (John Ford), George O'Brien, Madge Bellamy
The Marriage Circle (Ernst Lubitsch), Marie Prevost, Florence Vidor, Adolphe Menjou
Merton of the Movies (James Cruze), Glenn Hunter, Charles Sellon
Monsieur Beaucaire (Sidney Olcott), Rudolph Valentino, Bebe Daniels
Isn't Life Wonderful? (D. W. Griffith), Carol Dempster, Neil Hamilton
The Thief of Bagdad (Raoul Walsh), Douglas Fairbanks, Anna May Wong

The dashing acrobatic Douglas Fairbanks in *The Thief of Bagdad,* which he also wrote under the pseudonym Elton Thomas. *Movie Star News.*

Sherlock Holmes (Buster Keaton), Buster Keaton, Kathryn McGuire
Le ballet mécanique (Fernand Léger, designer)

Top Box-Office Stars
Norma Talmadge, Rudolph Valentino. *Also popular:* Thomas Meighan, Lionel Barrymore, Jackie Coogan, Harold Lloyd, Tom Mix, Pola Negri, Mary Pickford, Rin Tin Tin

Popular Music

Hit Songs
"Somebody Loves Me"
"Lady, Be Good"
"Indian Love Call"
"Rose Marie"
"I'll See You in My Dreams"
"Deep in My Heart, Dear"
"I Want to Be Happy"
"California, Here I Come"
"All Alone"
"The Drinking Song"
"Mandalay"
"Fascinating Rhythm"
"The Man I Love"
"Does the Spearmint Lose Its Flavor on the Bedpost over Night?"

Top Records
The Prisoner's Song (Vernon Dalhart); *The Sinking of the "Titanic"* (Ernest Van "Pop" Stoneman); *Charley My Boy* (Eddie Cantor); *What'll I Do?* (Lewis Hames), *June Night* (Waring's Pennsylvanians); *There's Yes Yes in Your Eyes* (Paul Whiteman); *Tea Pot Dome Blues* (Fletcher Henderson)

Jazz and Big Bands
Paul Whiteman introduces *Rhapsody in Blue* at Aeolian Hall, New York. Fletcher Henderson lures Louis Armstrong away from King Oliver. Bix Beiderbecke records with the First Wolverine Orchestra.

New Band: Earl Hines, Chicago

Theater

Broadway Openings

Plays
Desire under the Elms (Eugene O'Neill), Walter Huston, Mary Morris, Walter Abel
S. S. Glencairn (Eugene O'Neill), Walter Abel, James Meighan
All God's Chillun Got Wings (Eugene O'Neill), Paul Robeson
Hell-Bent fer Heaven (Hatcher Hughes), Glenn Anders
They Knew What They Wanted (Sidney Howard), Pauline Lord, Richard Bennett, Glenn Anders
What Price Glory? (Maxwell Anderson, Laurence Stallings), Louis Wolheim, William Boyd
The Show-Off (George Kelly), Louis John Bartels
Minick (George S. Kaufman, Edna Ferber), Phyllis Povah, O. P. Heggie
Outward Bound (Sutton Vane), Alfred Lunt, Leslie Howard
Beggar on Horseback (George S. Kaufman, Marc Connelly), Roland Young, Osgood Perkins, Spring Byington
Dancing Mothers (Edgar Selwyn, Edmund Goulding), Helen Hayes
A Right to Dream (Irving Kaye Davis), Ralph Shirley, Bertha Broad
The Guardsman (Ferenc Molnár), Alfred Lunt, Lynn Fontanne
The Firebrand (Edwin Justus Mayer), Joseph Schildkraut, Edward G. Robinson
Old English (John Galsworthy), George Arliss
The Miracle (Max Reinhardt, Karl Vollmoeller), Lady Diana Manners

Musicals
The Student Prince (Sigmund Romberg, Dorothy Donnelly), Ilse Marvenga, Howard Marsh (biggest money-maker in history)
Rose Marie (Rudolph Friml, Otto Harbach), Dennis King, Mary Ellis, William Kent
Ziegfeld Follies (Victor Herbert et al., Gene Buck), Will Rogers, Ann Pennington, W. C. Fields
Lady Be Good (George Gershwin, Ira Gershwin), Fred and Adele Astaire
I'll Say She Is (Tom Johnstone, Will Johnstone), Marx Brothers, Lotta Miles
George White's Scandals (George Gershwin, B. G. DeSylva), Winnie Lightner, Lester Allen
Music Box Review of 1924 (Irving Berlin), Fannie Brice, Clark and McCullough, Grace Moore, Claire Luce
André Charlot Review of 1924 (Noel Coward), Beatrice Lillie, Gertrude Lawrence

Classics and Revivals On and Off Broadway
Antony and Cleopatra, Jane Cowl, Rollo Peters; *The Second Mrs. Tanqueray* (Pinero), Ethel Barrymore; *Hedda Gabler* (Ibsen), Clare Eames; *Peter Pan* (James M. Barrie), Marilyn Miller

Pulitzer Prize
Hell-Bent fer Heaven, Hatcher Hughes

Classical Music _____

Compositions
George Antheil, *Ballet mécanique*
George Gershwin, *Rhapsody in Blue*
Ferde Grofé, *Mississippi Suite*
Charles Wakefield Cadman, *The Witch of Salem*
Edgard Varèse, *Octandre*
Carl Ruggles, *Men and Mountains*
Henry Cowell, *Vestiges*
Charles Ives, Three Pieces for Two Pianos
Aaron Copland, Symphony for Organ and Orchestra
John Alden Carpenter, *Skyscrapers*

Important Events
The Piano Festival at the Metropolitan for the
Association for Improving the Condition of the Poor
includes Harold Bauer, Alexander Brailowsky, Ossip
Gabrilowitsch, Myra Hess, Josef Lhévinne, Guiomar
Novaes, and Ernest Schelling.

Major Recitals: Efrem Zimbalist, Wanda
Landowska, Moritz Rosenthal, Siegfried Wagner,
Maria Jeritza

New Appointments: Howard Hanson becomes
director of the Eastman Symphony, Serge
Koussevitsky, of the Boston Symphony.

Debut: Alexander Brailowsky

First Performances
Ralph Vaughan Williams, Violin Concerto
(Minneapolis); Deems Taylor, *Alice through the
Looking Glass* (Philadelphia); Henry Hadley, *Ocean
Symphony* (Boston); Igor Stravinsky, *Histoire du
Soldat* (League of Composers, New York); *Le chant
du rossignol* (New York); Frederick Jacobi,
Symphony No. 1 (San Francisco); Arthur Honegger,
Pacific 231 (New York)

Opera

Metropolitan: Antonio Scotti celebrates his twenty-
fifth anniversary with *Tosca;* Giacomo Lauri-Volpi,
Le roi de Lahore; Karin Branzell, *Die Walküre;*
Friedrich Schorr (debut), *Tannhaüser;* premiere: *I
compagnacci* (Primo Riccitelli); *Le coq d'or; La
habanera* (Raoul Laparra)

Chicago: *The White Bird* (Ernest Carter, premiere)

San Francisco: Beniamino Gigli, Giuseppe De Luca,
Claudia Muzio, *Andrea Chenier*

Dallas: Mary Garden, *Salomé*

Music Notes
The St. Louis and Curtis Institutes open • Siegfried
Wagner makes his first U.S. visit to raise $200,000
for the Bayreuth Festival • Nellie Melba bids one of
many farewells • Ernest Schelling begins the
Children's Concerts with the New York
Philharmonic.

George Bellows, *Dempsey and Firpo.*
1924. Oil. 51 × 63 1/4 inches. *Collection
of Whitney Museum of American Art.*

Art

Painting

Arthur G. Dove, *Portrait of Ralph Dusenberry*
George Bellows, *Dempsey and Firpo*
Georgia O'Keeffe, *Dark Abstraction*
Max Weber, *Still Life with Chinese Teapot*
Peter Blume, *Fruit*
Yasuo Kuniyoshi, *Sleeping Beauty*

Sculpture

Malvina Hoffman, *Mask of Anna Pavlova*
Alexander Calder, *The Horse*
Gaston Lachaise, *Dolphin Fountain*
Alexander Archipenko, *Archipenturo*

Architecture

American Radiator Building, New York (Hood, Godley, and Fouilhoux)
National Academy of Science and Research Council, Washington, D.C. (Bertram C. Goodhue)
Cathedral of St. John the Divine, New York, renewed construction (Heins and LaFargue, Cram)
Federal Reserve Building, Cleveland (Walker and Weeks)

Arthur G. Dove, *Portrait of Ralph Dusenberry*, 1924. Oil. 22 × 18". *The Metropolitan Museum of Art, The Alfred Steiglitz Collection.*

Art Briefs

The third traveling exhibit leaves the Metropolitan Museum of Art to tour the United States with works by Chase, Colman, Dabo, J. G. Brown, Hicks, Hopner, Nicol, Wyant, and Van der Velde • Stanford White's Madison Square Garden is razed; its Saint-Gaudens tower, "Diana," is to be reerected at University Heights, New York University.

Important Exhibitions

Museums

New York: *Metropolitan:* Arts of the book; J. Alden Weir; Chinese color prints; European drawings; Art of the American home (displayed in the new American wing). *Société Anonyme:* Paul Klee's first U.S. show. *Whitney:* American folk art: Kuniyoshi, Sheeler, Demuth

Cleveland: Winslow Homer

Detroit: American art, featuring Maurice Prendergast's *Landscape with Figures*

Chicago: Works by Chicago artists

Buffalo: Selected American paintings and sculpture

Washington: *Corcoran:* Contemporary American painting, featuring Childe Hassam and Charles Webster Hawthorne

Individual and Group Shows: Wassily Kandinsky, Aristide Maillol, Jo Davidson, John Marin, George Bellows, Dürer, Matisse, and Sargent; Whistler and Alfred Stieglitz continue to draw much attention; Russian lapidary work is popular.

Dance

Michel Fokine, with Vera Fokina, organizes the American Ballet.

Books

Fiction

Critics' Choice

In Our Time, Ernest Hemingway
Old New York, Edith Wharton
How To Write Short Stories (with Samples), Ring Lardner
The Apple of the Eye, Glenway Wescott
The Green Bay Tree, Louis Bromfield
Balisand, Joseph Hergesheimer
🞂 *Strait Is the Gate*, André Gide
🞂 *Death in Venice*, Thomas Mann
🞂 *A Passage to India*, E. M. Forster

Best-Sellers

So Big, Edna Ferber
The Plastic Age, Percy Marks
The Little French Girl, Anne Douglas Sedgwick
The Heirs Apparent, Philip Gibbs
A Gentleman of Courage, James Oliver Curwood
The Call of the Canyon, Zane Grey
The Midlander, Booth Tarkington
The Coast of Folly, Coningsby Dawson
Mistress Wilding, Rafael Sabatini
Hopalong Cassidy Returns, Clarence Mulford

Nonfiction

Critics' Choice

A Story Teller's Story, Sherwood Anderson
The Seven Lively Arts, Gilbert Seldes
Antheil and the Treatise on Harmony, Ezra Pound
Sticks and Stones, Louis Mumford
State of the Nation, A. J. Beveridge
Democracy and Leadership, Irving Babbitt
Lawrence in Arabia, Lowell J. Thomas
The Gift of Black Folk, W. E. B. Du Bois
🞂 *Manifesto of Surrealism*, André Breton
🞂 *Beyond the Pleasure Principle*, Sigmund Freud

Best-Sellers

Diet and Health, Lulu Hunt Peters
The Life of Christ, Giovanni Papini
The Boston Cooking School Cookbook, new ed., Fannie Farmer
Etiquette, Emily Post

Ariel, André Maurois
The Cross Word Puzzle Books, Prosper Buranelli et al.
Mark Twain's Autobiography, Mark Twain
Saint Joan, George Bernard Shaw
The New Decalogue of Science, Albert E. Wiggam
The Americanization of Edward Bok, Edward Bok

Poetry

John Crowe Ransom, *Chills and Fever*
Marianne Moore, *Observations*
Edgar Lee Masters, *The New Spoon River Anthology*
Robinson Jeffers, *Tamar and Other Poems*

Pulitzer Prizes

So Big, Edna Ferber (novel)
A History of the American Frontier, Frederic L. Paxson (U.S. history)
Barrett Wendell and His Letters, M. A. DeWolfe Howe (biography)
The Man Who Died Twice, Edwin Arlington Robinson (poetry)

Science and Technology

Edwin Hubble, at Mt. Wilson Observatory, California, demonstrates that spiral nebulae are composed of stars like our own galaxy; this is the first indication of the immense size of the universe; Hubble also begins measuring the distances of stars from the earth.

Two Douglas world cruisers—the *Chicago*, piloted by Lowell Smith and Alva Harvey, and the *New Orleans*, by Erick Nelson and John Harding—complete round-the-world flights.

RCA transmits a wireless photo from London to New York in 25 minutes.

A radio message is transmitted to and from Japan in 1 minute, 45 seconds.

Liver is shown to prevent pernicious anemia by Boston physicians George Minot and William Murphy.

George and Gladys Dick demonstrate that streptococcus is the cause of scarlet fever.

Dye techniques for gall bladder X rays are devised by Ewart Graham and Lewis Cole.

Malaria, or "fever therapy," shows promise as a treatment for third-stage syphilis.

🞂 Hans Berger develops the electroencephalogram (EEG) for recording brain waves.

Sports

Baseball

Bucky Harris, 24, becomes the "boy wonder" manager of the Washington Senators (AL); the team wins the pennant and the World Series.

Champions

Batting
Rogers Hornsby (St. Louis, NL), .424
Babe Ruth (New York, AL), .378

Pitching
Dazzy Vance (Brooklyn, NL), 28–6
Walter Johnson (Washington, AL), 28–7
Home runs
Babe Ruth (New York, AL), 46

Football

Red Grange, Illinois, runs 95, 67, 56, and 44 yards the first four times he handles the ball against Michigan. Sportswriter Grantland Rice calls him the "Galloping Ghost." Notre Dame upsets Army 13–7; Rice calls the ND backfield the "Four Horsemen of the Apocalypse": Stuldreyer, Miller, Crowley, and Layden.

Pro Stars: Jim Thorpe (Rock Island), Ernie Hamer (Frankford)

College All-Americans: Red Grange (HB), Illinois; Walter Koppisch (HB), Columbia

Rose Bowl (Jan. 1, 1925): Notre Dame 27–Stanford 10

Olympics

In the summer games at Paris U.S. winners include Jackson Scholz (200m, 21.6s), D. C. Kinsey (100 mh, 15.0s), F. Morgan Taylor (400 mh, 52.6s), Harold Osborn (high jump, 6′5 5/16″), Delfort Hubbard (broad jump, 24′5 1/8″ and decathlon), Johnny Weismuller (swimming, 100m and 400m), A. C. White (2 in diving), Ethel Lackie (swimming, 100m), Martha Norelius (swimming, 400m). Harold Abrahams and Eric Liddell of Great Britain and Paavo Nurmi of Finland are other gold medal winners.

Other Sports

Horse Racing: Exterminator retires with a record 50 wins and $252,996 earnings.

Tennis: The Forest Hills Tennis Stadium opens.

Winners

World Series
Washington (AL), 4–New York (NL), 3
MVP
NL–Arthur Vance, Brooklyn
AL–Walter Johnson, Washington
NFL
Cleveland Bulldogs
College Football
Notre Dame
College Basketball
North Carolina

Player of the Year
Charles Black, Kansas
Stanley Cup
Montreal
U.S. Tennis Open
Men: William Tilden II
Women: Helen Wills
USGA Open
Cyril Walker
Kentucky Derby
Black Gold (J. D. Mahoney, jockey)

Fashion

For Women: Still stylish is the straight, knee-length skirt, gathered slightly or cut with two front pleats, and long sleeveless tops, middies, or Peter Pan blouses. Coats, broadly cut at the shoulder and tapered to the knee, are fastened with a single button at the hip and have honey beige or dyed ermine fur on the collar and cuffs. The cloche hat covers the eyes. Enormous interest grows in masklike makeup (orange lips and rouge are also popular) and accessories (strings of pearls trail from the shoulder or are knotted at the neck and thrown over the right shoulder and under the arm). Silver bracelets are worn on the upper arm.

High-fashion notes: The chinchilla wraparound; Lanvin's black georgette crepe dress with steel discs and slashed sleeves.

For Men: Interest grows in the F. Scott Fitzgerald look and narrower torso: the blue blazer with sport or school badge and shorter and less padded jacket and Oxford bags—high-waisted and pleated but loose in the hips. Shoes have round toes and laces; socks are patterned. Top coats, with loose raglan sleeves and wide collars, fall well below the knee. More formal dress includes bow ties in striped, paisley, and spotted patterns, bowlers, spats, double-breasted suits, and vests.

Kaleidoscope _____

- In his two-day plea against the death penalty for Leopold and Loeb, Clarence Darrow introduces into the courtroom the concept of mental illness, quotes poetry, and weeps as he begs for mercy.
- "Galloping Ghost" Red Grange is so popular that college football surpasses boxing as a national pastime; Grange is wooed by Hollywood, big business, and a variety of political groups.
- The Charleston, carried north from Charleston, South Carolina and incorporated into the all-black show *Shuffle Along,* is picked up by white dancers at Texas Guinan's El Fey Club and Silver Slipper.
- Newest places to hide liquor include shoe heels, flasks form-fitted to women's thighs, folds of coats, and perfume bottles.
- Whether a woman should work outside the home becomes a major topic of discussion.
- Commercial laundry use increases 57 percent (since 1914); bakery production, 60 percent; 90 percent of all homes have electric irons.
- The Methodist Episcopal General Conference lifts its ban on theatergoing and dancing.
- "America's Most Beautiful Suburb" is the catchphrase of the Florida get-rich-quick ads, and thousands flock south to buy land with small down payments (binders), which they can then quickly sell for profit.
- Gangland king Dion O'Banion is buried in a $10,000 bronze casket; 40,000 call at the funeral chapel and 20,000 attend the funeral. Although Catholic rites are denied him, a priest-friend says three Hail Marys and the Lord's Prayer.
- Former Rutgers football player Paul Robeson, acting as a black man married to a white woman in *All God's Chillun Got Wings,* is threatened by the KKK; police officers stand guard in the theater.
- Whether or not to specifically condemn the KKK is a major concern at both presidential conventions; neither issues an outright condemnation.
- News takes a prominent position on radio, challenging the popularity of dance music.
- The U.S. Supreme Court declares unconstitutional an Oregon law requiring all grammar school children to attend school.
- A popular GOP convention drink is the "Keep Cool with Coolidge" highball, consisting of raw eggs and fruit juice.
- Alvin "Shipwreck" Kelly sits on top of a flagpole for 13 hours and 13 minutes.
- Henry Ford pays $2,467,946 in income tax.
- Half a million people write Henry Ford begging for money.
- Pulps—dime magazines of 150 pages like *Detective Story* and *Western Story*—increase in circulation to half a million.
- Five violinists at one of Herbert Bayard Swope's famous Long Island parties engage in an endurance contest by repeating Paganini's *Moto Perpetuo;* Josef Fuchs lasts 21 minutes, defeating Jascha Heifetz,

Efrem Zimbalist, Paul Kochaniski, and Albert Spalding.
- John Barrymore earns from Warner's $76,250 per picture, plus $7,625 over seven weeks and all expenses.
- Walt Disney begins creating cartoons with "Alice's Wonderland."
- Lillian Leitzel, Ringling Brothers and Barnum and Bailey star, sets a record of 239 planges (swinging in circular revolutions by throwing the lower part of her body over her shoulder while hanging from a rope).
- Ernest Hemingway leads fellow writers Donald Ogden Stewart and John Dos Passos in a running of the bulls at Pamplona, Spain, and gains esteem at home and abroad.

Fads: Richard L. Simon and Max L. Schuster begin the Plaza Publishing Company with the *Cross Word Puzzle Book* (pencils are attached). Crossword puzzles and mah-jongg are the year's most popular fads. The B & O Railroad stocks dictionaries for its passengers.

First Appearances: Ice-cream-cone rolling machine, chrome-plating process, the permanent wave, contact lenses (imported), MGM, Columbia Pictures, two perfect games rolled by a bowler, U.S. Foreign Service, Chrysler, IBM, Kleenex ("Celluwipes"), airmail service (New York to San Francisco), spiral-bound notebook, spin dryer, deadbolt lock, college marriage course (University of North Carolina, Chapel Hill), Beech-Nut Coffee, Wheaties, Stouffer's chain, corn-husking championship, "Little Orphan Annie," Barney's, Macy's Thanksgiving Day Parade down Central Park West, New York

The Mack Sennett girls from the studio of the "King of Comedy," whose movies include *Boobs in the Woods* and *The Wild Goose Chasers. Movie Star News.*

1925

Facts and Figures

Economic Profile
  Dow-Jones: ↑ High 157–
    Low 115
  GNP: +10%
  Inflation: +1.3%
  Unemployment: 3.2%
Infant mortality/1,000: 71
Maternal mortality/10,000: 65
Physicians: 147,812
Dentists: 64,481
Hospital beds: 802,265
Gas range: $49.50
Frigidaire: $190–$245
Seth Thomas chiming clock:
  $56
Radiola with loudspeaker:
  $269
Wardrobe trunk: $50–$75
Kraft cheese: 38¢ (lb.)
Doughnuts: 19¢ (doz.)
Sar-a-Lee spread: 19¢–38¢
Spanish olives: 52¢ (32 oz.)
Soap chips: $3.63 (25 lbs.)

Above: Clarence Darrow and
Williams Jennings Bryan,
opposing lawyers at the
Monkey Trial. *Library of
Congress.*

Deaths

George Bellows, William
  Jennings Bryan, Walter
  Camp, Robert M. La
  Follette, Amy Lowell,
  John Singer Sargent, Erik
  Satie, Sun Yat-sen.

In the News _____

NELLIE ROSS, WYOMING, BECOMES FIRST WOMAN GOVERNOR . . .
"MA" FERGUSON, TEXAS, BECOMES SECOND WOMAN GOVERNOR . . .
LEON TROTSKY IS DEMOTED, JOSEPH STALIN EXTENDS HIS POWER
. . . CORRUPT PRACTICES ACT OUTLAWS DIRECT CORPORATE
CONTRIBUTIONS IN ELECTIONS . . . FRENCH TROOPS BEGIN RUHR
EVACUATION . . . FLOYD COLLINS, TRAPPED IN COAL MINE, DIES
AFTER 18 DAYS . . . COLONEL BILLY MITCHELL ACCUSES NATIONAL
AIR BOARD OF INCOMPETENCE . . . COOLIDGE ARBITRATES PERU-
CHILE BORDER DISPUTE . . . DRUZES REVOLT IN SYRIA, THE FRENCH
BOMB DAMASCUS . . . WORLD POWERS SIGN TREATY TO OUTLAW
POISON GAS . . . MASSIVE COAL STRIKE HITS W. VA. . . . FLA.
PASSES LAW REQUIRING DAILY BIBLE READING . . . DIRIGIBLE
SHENANDOAH IS TORN BY STORM, 14 DIE . . . LOCARNO TREATIES
BETWEEN WORLD WAR FOES SETTLE GERMAN BOUNDARIES . . . JOHN
SCOPES GOES ON TRIAL IN DAYTON, TENN., FOR TEACHING
EVOLUTION, CLARENCE DARROW DEFENDS SCOPES . . . BRITISH
SOLDIERS KILL CHINESE STUDENTS IN SHANGHAI RIOT . . . 40,000
KKK MARCH IN WASHINGTON, D.C. . . . CARL ROGERS FLIES
SEAPLANE NONSTOP FROM SAN FRANCISCO TO HONOLULU . . . JOHN
SCOPES IS CONVICTED AND FINED $100, WILLIAM JENNINGS BRYAN,
PROSECUTOR, DIES OF HEART ATTACK . . . GREECE INVADES
BULGARIA, LEAGUE OF NATIONS SETTLES DISPUTE . . . BILLY
MITCHELL IS COURT-MARTIALED FOR INSUBORDINATION . . . FLORIDA
LAND SCAMS ARE EXPOSED, UNDERWATER LOTS WERE SOLD.

Quotes

"Our defense planes are the worst of any country I know. . . . Our pilots know they are going to be killed in the old floating coffins that we are still flying."
— Col. Billy Mitchell

"The business of America is business."
— Calvin Coolidge

"This is the way the world ends
Not with a bang but a whimper."
— T. S. Eliot, "The Hollow Men"

"[In New York] I saw 7,000,000 two-legged animals penned in an evil smelling cage, . . . streets as unkempt as a Russian steppe, . . . rubbish, waste paper, cigar butts. . . . One glance and you know no master hand directs."
— Article in *Pravda*

"Shoot them in the head,
Shoot them in the feet,
Shoot them in the dinner bucket;
How are they going to eat?"
— Coal miners' song during West Virginia strike

Bryan: I believe that everything in the Bible should be accepted as it is given there.
Darrow: But when you read that Jonah swallowed the whale—or that the whale swallowed Jonah—do you literally interpret it?
Bryan: Yes sir. . . . If the Bible said so.
— Clarence Darrow's cross-examination of William Jennings Bryan in the Scopes trial

"If a young man at the age of twenty-three can write a symphony like that, in five years he will be ready to commit murder."
— Walter Damrosch, conducting Aaron Copland's Symphony for Organ and Orchestra

Ads

New scientific discoveries like radium are marketed for commercial use. *Library of Congress.*

Radio

Premieres
"Atwater Kent Audition," Graham McNamee
"Gold Dust Twins"
"Goodrich Silvertown Orchestra"
"EWSM Barn Dance" ("Grand Ole Opry")
"Sam and Henry" ("Amos 'n' Andy"), Freeman
    Gosden, Charles Correll

Of Note
NBC, the first nationwide network, is established •
New catchphrase: "I'm goin' back to the wagon,
boys. These shoes are killin' me" ("Grand Ole
Opry") • "NEAF Grand Opera Company" begins
weekly opera performances.

The radio audience is estimated at 50 million. *Library of Congress.*

Movies

Openings
The Gold Rush (Charles Chaplin), Charles Chaplin,
    Mack Swain
The Big Parade (King Vidor), John Gilbert
The Merry Widow (Erich von Stroheim), Mae
    Murray, John Gilbert
The Dark Angel (George Fitzmaurice), Ronald
    Colman, Vilma Banky
Stella Dallas (Henry King), Ronald Colman, Belle
    Bennett
Ben-Hur (Fred Niblo), Ramon Novarro, Francis X.
    Bushman

Potemkin (Sergei Eisenstein), A. Antonov
The Salvation Hunters (Josef von Sternberg), George
    K. Arthur
Lord Jim (Victor Fleming), Percy Marmont, Noah
    Beery
The Golden Bed (Cecil B. DeMille), Lillian Rich,
    Rod La Rocque
Madame Sans-Gene (Léonce Perret), Gloria
    Swanson, Charles De Roche
The Phantom of the Opera (Rupert Julian), Lon
    Chaney
The Freshman (Fred Newmeyer), Harold Lloyd,
    Jobyna Ralston
The Vanishing American (George B. Seitz), Noah
    Beery, Richard Dix
The Eagle (Clarence Brown), Rudolph Valentino,
    Vilma Banky

Top Box-Office Stars
Rudolph Valentino, Norma Talmadge. *Also popular:*
Douglas Fairbanks, Mary Pickford, Charles Chaplin,
Harold Lloyd, Gloria Swanson, Pola Negri,
Constance Talmadge, Dorothy Gish, Lillian Gish

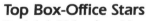
"Stoneface" Buster Keaton in *Go West. Movie Star News.*

Popular Music _____

Hit Songs
"If You Knew Suzy"
"I'm Sitting on Top of the World"
"Sweet Georgia Brown"
"Sleepy Time Gal"
"Dinah"
"Manhattan"
"If You Were the Only Girl"
"Keep Your Skirts Down, Mary
    Ann"
"Always"

Top Records
Yes Sir, That's My Baby (Gene
Austin); *Poor Little Rich Girl*
(Gertrude Lawrence); *Carolina*

Shout (James P. Johnson); *Sleepy-
Time Gal* (Jesse Crawford); *Five
Foot Two* (Art Landry); *Sugar
Foot Stomp* (Fletcher Henderson);
Death of Floyd Collins (Vernon
Dalhart); *Song of the Vagabonds*
(Vincent Lopez)

Jazz and Big Bands
Popular stars include Louis
Armstrong, Tennessee Tooters,
Cotton Pickers, Halfway House
Orchestra, Bix Beiderbecke and
his Rhythms Jugglers, Lanin's
Redheads

First Recordings: Louis
Armstrong Five; Duke Ellington
Washingtonians

Blues Singers: Bessie Smith,
Edith Wilson, Ethel Waters,
Lucille Hegamin, Alberta Hunter,
Mary Stafford

Jazz Piano: Hersal Thomas,
Meade Lux Lewis, Clarence
"Pinetop" Smith, Charles "Cow
Cow" Davenport

New Band: Lawrence Welk,
North Dakota

Theater _____

Broadway Openings

Plays
The Vortex (Noel Coward), Noel Coward, Lillian
    Braithwaite
Hay Fever (Noel Coward), Laura Hope Crews
Easy Virtue (Noel Coward), Jane Cowl
Craig's Wife (George Kelly), Josephine Hull
The Enemy (Channing Pollock), Fay Bainter
The Green Hat (Michael Arlen), Katharine Cornell,
    Leslie Howard
The Jazz Singer (Samson Raphaelson), George Jessel
The Cradle Snatchers (Russell Medcroft, Norma
    Mitchell), Mary Boland, Edna May Oliver,
    Humphrey Bogart
The Last of Mrs. Cheyney (Frederick Lonsdale), Ina
    Claire, Roland Young
The Butter and Egg Man (George S. Kaufman),
    Gregory Kelly
The Dove (Djuna Barnes), Judith Anderson

Musicals
Sunny (Jerome Kern, Otto Harbach, Oscar
    Hammerstein II), Marilyn Miller, Clifton Webb,
    Jack Donahue
The Vagabond King (Rudolf Friml, Brian Hooker),
    Dennis King
Artists and Models (J. Fred Coots, Clifford Grey),
    Walter Woolf, Lulu McConnell
Earl Carroll's Vanities (Clarence Gaskill, William A.
    Grew), Julius Tannen, Ted and Betty Healy

Garrick Gaieties (Richard Rodgers, Lorenz Hart),
    Sterling Holloway, Libby Holman
The Cocoanuts (Irving Berlin), Marx Brothers,
    Frances Williams
George White's Scandals (Ray Henderson, B. G.
    DeSylva), Helen Morgan, Tom Patricola
Ziegfeld Follies (Sigmund Romberg et al.), W. C.
    Fields, Ray Dooley

Classics and Revivals On and Off Broadway
Caesar and Cleopatra, Helen Hayes, Lionel Atwill;
Candida, Peggy Wood, *Androcles and the Lion*,
Henry Travers, and *Arms and the Man* (George
Bernard Shaw), Alfred Lunt, Lynn Fontanne;
Merchant of Venice, (Walter Hampden, Ethel
Barrymore; *Hamlet*, Basil Sydney, in modern dress;
Othello, Walter Hampden; *The Wild Duck* (Ibsen),
Blanche Yurka; *Lysistrata* (Aristophanes; music by
Glière), Moscow Art Theatre

Regional

Founded: Goodman Theatre, Chicago, by the
Kenneth Sawyer Goodman family

Pulitzer Prize
They Knew What They Wanted, Sidney Howard

Classical Music

Compositions

Aaron Copland, *Music for the Theater, Grogh, Dance Symphony*
Howard Hanson, *The Lament of Beowulf*
Edgard Varèse, *Intégrales*
John Powell, *At the Fair*
Wallingford Riegger, Rhapsody for Orchestra
Henry Cowell, *The Banshee*
John Alden Carpenter, Jazz Orchestra Pieces
Ernest Bloch, Concerto Grosso

Important Events

Ignace Paderewski, Fritz Kreisler, and Igor Stravinsky triumph in their U.S. appearances. Stravinsky plays *Song of the Volga Boatmen* with the New York Philharmonic and Concerto for Piano and Winds with the Boston Symphony.
Paul Whiteman performs George Gershwin's *Twenty Minute Grand Opera* and *135th Street* and Deems Taylor's *Circus Day* at Carnegie Hall.
The New York Philharmonic celebrates its 2,000th concert with a portion of its first, December 1842, program: Beethoven's Symphony no. 5 and Johann Kalliwoda's New Overture in D.

Debut: Paul Robeson

First Performances

George Gershwin, playing, Concerto in F for Piano and Orchestra (New York); Leo Sowerby, *Monotony, Syncopation* (Chicago); Aaron Copland, Symphony for Organ and Orchestra (New York)

Opera

Metropolitan: Rosa Ponselle, *La Gioconda;* Giovanni Martinelli, *Tosca;* Maria Jeritza, Beniamino Gigli, *Fedora;* Jeritza, *Turandot;* Lucrezia Bori, *L'heure espagnole;* Lawrence Tibbett, *Falstaff*

Chicago: Mary Garden, *Resurrection* (Franco Alfano); *Carmen*

San Francisco: Tito Schipa, *Manon*

Music Notes

For the first Festival of Chamber Music, at the Library of Congress, work is commissioned from Charles Loeffler, Frederick Stock, and Frederick Jacobi • In honor of Leopold Auer, 80, celebrated violin teacher, a benefit concert is given in New York by Efrem Zimbalist, Jascha Heifetz, Josef Hofmann, Sergei Rachmaninoff, and Ossip Gabrilowitsch; $25,000 is raised for Auer • Copland wins the first Guggenheim Fellowship.

Exercising on the beach—part of the national trend toward slimness and physical fitness. *Library of Congress.*

Art

Painting

Edward Hopper, *House by the Railroad*
Stuart Davis, *Italian Landscape*
Charles Demuth, *Apples and Bananas*
Lyonel Feininger, *Tower*
Arthur G. Dove, *Portrait of Alfred Stieglitz*
Yasuo Kuniyoshi, *Waitresses from Sparhawk*
Man Ray, *Sugar Loaves*

Sculpture

Malvina Hoffman, *England*
Herbert Haseltine, *Percheron Mare and Foal*
John Storrs, *Seated Gendarme*
Paul Manship, *Flight of Europa*

Architecture

Chicago Tribune Tower, Chicago (Hood and Howells)
New York Telephone Building, New York City (McKenzie, Vorhees, and Gmelin)
Powell Symphony Hall, St. Louis (Rapp and Rapp)
Warren and Wetmore receive the Fifth Avenue Association Gold Award for Steinway Hall.
Horace Trumbauer completes the Gothic design plan for Duke University.

Important Exhibitions

Museums

New York: *Metropolitan:* Greek athletes; objects from the International Exposition of Modern Decorative Art; telephotographs; George Bellows memorial; American historical portraits

Boston: Mural decorations by John Singer Sargent; Eleanor Norcross memorial

St. Louis: 100 paintings by 100 American artists; Ivan Mestrovic

Philadelphia: American Sculpture Prizes are awarded to Walker Hancock, William James, and George Bellows

Art Briefs

"The Blue Four" gain a following after their New York show: Alexei Von Jawlensky, Wassily Kandinsky, Paul Klee, and Lyonel Feininger • John D. Rockefeller makes possible the purchase of medieval art and property for what will become the

F. Scott Fitzgerald's *The Great Gatsby* portrays the "Jazz Age" and the problematical nature of the American dream. *Scribners.*

Cloisters • Henry E. Huntington bequeaths 188 paintings to the Metropolitan, which also records the largest attendance in its history—1,156,102 visitors.

Dance

Mikhail Mordkin organizes his Russian Ballet Company with Vera Nemchinova, Hilda Butsova, and Pierre Vladimiroff.

Books

Fiction

Critics' Choice

The Great Gatsby, F. Scott Fitzgerald
In Our Time (revised), Ernest Hemingway
The Professor's House, Willa Cather
An American Tragedy, Theodore Dreiser
Manhattan Transfer, John Dos Passos
Drums, James Boyd
Barren Ground, Ellen Glasgow
Porgy, DuBose Heyward
&. *Mrs. Dalloway*, Virginia Woolf
&. *No More Parades*, Ford Madox Ford

Best-Sellers

Soundings, A. Hamilton Gibbs
The Constant Nymph, Margaret Kennedy
The Keeper of the Bees, Gene Stratton Porter
Glorious Apollo, E. Barrington
The Perennial Bachelor, Anne Parish
Arrowsmith, Sinclair Lewis
Gentlemen Prefer Blondes, Anita Loos
The Green Hat, Michael Arlen
One Increasing Purpose, A. S. M. Hutchinson
The Carolinian, Rafael Sabatini

Nonfiction

Critics' Choice

The Tragedy of Waste, Stuart Chase
In the American Grain, William Carlos Williams
The New Negro: An Interpretation, Alain Locke
Seventy Years of Life and Labor, Samuel Gompers
Experience and Nature, John Dewey
The Phantom Public, Walter Lippmann
The Book of American Negro Spirituals, ed. James Weldon Johnson
The Diaries of George Washington, ed. John C. Fitzpatrick
Our Debt and Duty to the Farmer, Henry Wallace
Calvin Coolidge, William Allen White
My Disillusionment in Russia, Emma Goldman
&. *Mein Kampf*, Adolph Hitler
&. *Science and the Modern World*, Alfred North Whitehead

Best-Sellers

Diet and Health, Lulu Hunt Peters
The Boston Cooking School Cook Book, new ed., Fannie Farmer
When We Were Very Young, A. A. Milne
The Man Nobody Knows, Bruce Barton
Twice Thirty, Edward Bok
Twenty-Five Years, Lord Grey
Jungle Days, William Beebe
Anatole France Himself, J. J. Brousson
The Life of Christ, Giovanni Papini
Ariel, André Maurois

Poetry

T. S. Eliot, *Poems, 1909–1925*
Ezra Pound, *A Draft of XVI Cantos*
H. D., *Collected Poems*
E. E. Cummings, *XLI Poems*, &
Robinson Jeffers, *Roan Stallion*
Edwin Arlington Robinson, *Dionysus in Doubt*
Countee Cullen, *Color*

Pulitzer Prizes

Arrowsmith, Sinclair Lewis (novel)
The History of the United States, Edward Channing (U.S. history)
The Life of Sir William Osler, Harvey Cushing (biography)
What's O'Clock, Amy Lowell (poetry)

Science and Technology

An all-electric radio mechanism is developed that eliminates the need for bulky batteries and crystal sets with earphones.
Charles David Jenkins produces a working television set.
The all-electric phonograph is developed.
The Menninger Clinic, which emphasizes a "total environment approach," opens on a farm in Topeka, Kansas.
James B. Collip isolates the parathyroid hormone.

Alfred Sturdevant, Columbia University, demonstrates that developmental effects of genes are influenced by neighboring genes.
John Abel isolates insulin.
Vitamin A deficiency is shown to cause night blindness.
W. W. Coblentz's measurements of temperature conditions on Mars indicate it may be suitable for life.
&. John Baird, in London, transmits the first television image, a ventriloquist's dummy named Bill.

Sports

Baseball

Lou Gehrig (New York, AL), former Columbia University star, takes over first base from Wally Pipp. Rogers Hornsby wins the triple crown and leads the majors with 39 home runs.

Champions

Batting
Rogers Hornsby (St. Louis, NL), .403
Harry Heilmann (Detroit, AL), .393

Pitching
Dazzy Vance (Brooklyn, NL), 22–9
Stan Covaleskie (Washington, AL), 23–7
Home runs
Rogers Hornsby (St. Louis, NL), 39

Football

Red Grange, Illinois, gains 363 yards against Pennsylvania, quits college, and tours with an all-star team organized by C.C. ("Cash and Carry") Pyle; he earns $80,000 on tour and then joins the Chicago Bears; 73,000 attend in New York to see Grange. Tim Mara buys the N.Y. Giants for $500; Jim Thorpe plays for the Giants.

Pro Stars: George Trafton (Chicago), Walter French (Pottsville)

College All-Americans: Red Grange (HB), Illinois; Ernie Nevers (F), Stanford

Rose Bowl (Jan. 1, 1926): Alabama 20–Washington 19

Basketball

The American Basketball League is organized, the first "national" pro league with teams from Fort Wayne to New York.

Other Sports

Tennis: Bill Tilden wins his fifth straight U.S. Open Singles; Helen Wills wins her third straight U.S. Open Singles

Golf: Bobby Jones wins his second straight USGA Open.

Red Grange brings his college fame to pro football, drawing unprecedented crowds as he plays 10 games in 17 days. *Pro Football Hall of Fame.*

Winners

World Series
  Pittsburgh (NL) 4
  Washington (AL) 3
MVP
  NL–Rogers Hornsby, St. Louis
  AL–Roger Peckinpaugh, Washington
NFL
  Chicago Cardinals
College Football
  Alabama
College Basketball
  Princeton

Player of the Year
  Earl Mueller, Colorado College
Stanley Cup
  Victoria
U.S. Tennis Open
  Men: William Tilden II
  Women: Helen Wills
USGA Open
  Willie Macfarlane
Kentucky Derby
  Flying Ebony (E. Sande, jockey)

Fashion

For Women: Fashion turns to the "little girl look" in "little girl frocks": curled or shingled hair, saucer eyes, the turned-up nose, bee-stung mouth, and obliterated eyebrows, which emphasize facial beauty; shirt dresses have huge Peter Pan collars or floppy bow ties and are worn with ankle-strap shoes with Cuban heels and an occasional buckle. Underwear is fashionable in both light colors and black, and is decorated with flowers and butterflies. With the cult of youth and the new spirit of equality come the camisole knickers and the cami-knickers; also fashionable is no underwear at all. Along with the rage for drastic slimming, women still strive to flatten their breasts and obliterate their hips; the waistline remains ignored. The cult of the tan begins; lotions to prevent burning and promote tanning appear on the market; skin stains are also manufactured, along with Elizabeth Arden and Helena Rubinstein moisturizers, tonics, cream rouges, eye shadows, and more varied lipstick shades. Women use two pounds of powder yearly.

High-fashion note: Vionnet's shimmy dress

Kaleidoscope

- President Coolidge cuts the White House budget $12,500; he replaces paper cups with glasses, reduces the number of towels supplied in the lavatories from 175 to 88, orders that manila envelopes be reused, and rations food in the kitchen.
- Bootleg prices appear regularly at the end of the "Talk of the Town" section of the *New Yorker.*
- Cars appear for the first time in such colors as Florentine cream and Versailles violet; bodies are lower with balloon tires; a new interest in line and style appears.
- As prosperity increases with 40 percent of the population earning at least $2,000 a year, the mass market increases for items like cars, radios, refrigerators, and vacuum cleaners.
- Bruce Barton's best-selling *The Man Nobody Knows* insists that "selling" continues Christ's mission: "Jesus . . . picked up twelve men from the bottom ranks of business and forged them into an organization that conquered the world."
- John Scopes reads to his class Hunter's *Civil Biology:* "We have now learned that animal forms may be arranged so as to begin with the simple one-celled forms and culminate with a group which includes man himself."
- The nation's press and numerous evangelists gather in rural Tennessee to watch Clarence Darrow "show up fundamentalism" and William Jennings Bryan "protect the word of God against the greatest atheist and agnostic in the United States."
- The credibility of the KKK is greatly impaired when Grand Dragon Davis Stevenson, convicted of his secretary's murder, makes revelations that damage the reputations of major pro-Klan Indiana politicians.
- Chicago mayor William Hale ("Big Bill") Thompson is the congenial associate of gangsters Johnny Torrio and Al Capone.
- Prohibition agents Izzy Einstein and Moe Smith—who, through various disguises, confiscated an estimated 5 million bottles of bootleg liquor in five years—are fired. Many speculate that their superiors were jealous of their fame.
- Delaware sheriffs and deputy constables are permitted to whip criminals: 60 lashes for poisoning attempts, 30 for wife beating, and 6 for setting fire to the courthouse.
- The nightclub business booms with stars like Paul Whiteman, Roger Wolfe, Texas Guinan, and Joe E. Lewis.
- The top burlesque star is Carrie Finnel, who twirls tassels from her breasts and buttocks.
- Detroit wages for a bartender average $75 a week, with $50 additional for each arrest; if the arrest occurs over a Sunday and no bail can be arranged, a $75 bonus is added.
- "Yellow-Drive-It-Yourself-Systems" become popular: 12¢ a mile for a Ford and 22¢ for a 6-cylinder car.
- Courtship trends change, as the car replaces the parlor.

- The last fire engine drawn by a span of three horses, in Washington, D.C., is retired.
- President Coolidge buys a mechanical hobbyhorse to exercise on in the White House.
- After surviving an attempt on his life, Chicago gangland boss John Torrio turns his entire crime empire over to his former bodyguard Al Capone and retires to Italy with $10–$30 million.
- Floyd Collins's entrapment and death in a Kentucky cave is much publicized as an example of man's fight against nature.
- One of the year's best-covered events involves the half-breed malamute dog Balto, as it leads a team to Nome, Alaska, with life-saving antidiphtheria serum.
- The police dog becomes a house pet after the film success of Rin Tin Tin.
- Joseph Schenck, of United Artists, hires Lucille LeSueur, who is then named Joan Crawford by a fan-magazine contest.
- The top-grossing film to date is *The Big Parade* ($22 million), the most expensive, *Ben-Hur* ($3.95 million).
- In a Metropolitan performance of *Siegfried,* tenor Curt Taucher plunges 25 feet through a trap door, breaks his finger, staggers back on stage, and finishes his performance.
- Of the New York season's new plays (244 productions: 194 plays, 50 musicals), 75 percent fail.
- Blacks continue to move North as manufacturers tour the South and promise good jobs and pay. Black Harlem, with its "Negro Renaissance," joins midtown Manhattan and Greenwich Village as a major cultural center.
- Trinity College changes its name to Duke University when James B. Duke contributes $40 million.
- Earl Wise's potato chips are so successful that he moves his business from a remodeled garage to a concrete plant in Berwick, Pa.
- While on a Caribbean tour, Harold S. Vanderbilt invents contract bridge.

Fads: Limerick contests, baseball cards, athlete hero worship (Babe Ruth, Dempsey, Tunney, Bobby Jones, Helen Wills, Weismuller, Grange), marathons (flagpole sitting, dancing, talking, eating, drinking)

First Appearances: National Spelling Bee (organized by a Louisville newspaper), the motel, dry ice, covered vacuum flasks, automatic potato-peeling machine, Wesson oil, Caterpillar tractors, automatic and self-lubricating GE refrigerator, Lux soap, Woman's world's fair, compulsory auto insurance, embossed and inlaid linoleum, outdoor museum (Tuxedo Park, N.Y.), University of Miami, Charlie Chan (*The House without a Key,* Der Biggers), *New Yorker, Cosmopolitan, Parents'* magazine, Simmons Beautyrest mattress, high-vacuum radio tube patent, electrical records, Lucky Strike, Old Gold

1926

Economic Profile
  Dow-Jones: ↑ High 162–
    Low 145
  GNP: +4%
  Inflation: 0.0%
  Unemployment: 1.8%
Male/female ratio: 53/51
High school graduates
  entering college: 12%
Four-year colleges: 1,224
Public/private school ratio:
  10/1
Cunard four-month around-
  the-world cruise, $1,250
  and up
Tripler linen jacket, knickers:
  $18
Linenlike collars: 3/$1
Rayon-pigskin garters: 50¢
Mon Boudoir (Houbigant)
  perfume: $12–$20 (oz.)
Kent toothbrush: 75¢
Cocker spaniel (from kennel):
  $35
Toy Pomeranian (from
  kennel): $50
Marlboro cigarettes: 20¢
  (pack)
Cocoa chocolate (Huyler's):
  $1.50 (lb.)

Deaths

Luther Burbank, Mary
  Cassatt, Emile Coué,
  Eugene V. Debs, Charles
  Eliot, Claude Monet,
  Annie Oakley, Joseph
  Pennell, Rainer Maria
  Rilke.

In the News

BILLY MITCHELL IS CONVICTED OF INSUBORDINATION AND SUSPENDED FROM SERVICE . . . U.S. ACCEPTS WORLD COURT, WITH CONDITIONS . . . CAPONE HEADQUARTERS ARE MACHINE-GUNNED FROM A FILE OF CARS . . . FIRST TRANSATLANTIC PHONE CALL IS MADE . . . PEACHES, 16, SUES MILLIONAIRE "DADDY" BROWNING, 53, FOR DIVORCE . . . ARMY AIR CORPS IS ESTABLISHED . . . GERTRUDE EDERLE SWIMS ENGLISH CHANNEL IN RECORD TIME . . . CHIANG KAI-SHEK BECOMES HEAD OF CHINESE REVOLUTIONARY PARTY, KUOMINTANG . . . ADM. RICHARD BYRD AND FLOYD BENNETT MAKE FIRST FLIGHT OVER NORTH POLE . . . RUDOLPH VALENTINO DIES, 100,000 ATTEND FUNERAL . . . HIROHITO BECOMES JAPANESE EMPEROR . . . U.S. TROOPS RETURN TO NICARAGUA TO QUELL REVOLT . . . SUPREME COURT OVERRULES 1878 LAW AND DECLARES PRESIDENT CAN REMOVE CABINET OFFICERS . . . HEIRESS FRANCES STEPHENS HALL IS ACQUITTED IN MURDER OF HUSBAND AND CHOIR-GIRL MISTRESS . . . GENE TUNNEY BEATS JACK DEMPSEY FOR HEAVYWEIGHT TITLE . . . LEON TROTSKY AND GRIGORY ZINOVIEV ARE EXPELLED FROM POLITBURO, STALIN RULES ALONE . . . HARRY HOUDINI DIES FROM STOMACH PUNCH LEADING TO PERITONITIS . . . FRANCE PROCLAIMS LEBANON A REPUBLIC . . . WORLD COURT REJECTS U.S. CONDITIONS . . . NEW YORKERS CHALLENGE LAW ALLOWING RELIGIOUS INSTRUCTION IN SCHOOLS.

Col. Billy Mitchell, convicted of insubordination, after accusing the army of negligence in the care of its aircraft. *Library of Congress.*

Quotes

"Applesauce" / "So's your anchovie" / "banana oil"/ "Chew to the line" / "Let the hips fall where they will"
— A "lady's" retorts to "uncouth" advances, quoted in *Life* magazine

"The very thing that made us stands in the way of our development as a civilized people. . . . The machine [has caused] the herding of men into towns and cities, the age of the factory. . . . Men all began to dress alike, eat the same foods, read the same kind of newspapers and books. Minds began to be standardized as were the clothes men wore."
— Sherwood Anderson, on America's 150th birthday

"The smell of money in Florida attracts men as the smell of blood attracts a wild animal."
— G. M. Shelby, on the "Florida Frenzy," *Harper's*

"You are all a lost generation."
— Gertrude Stein, quoted in Ernest Hemingway's *The Sun Also Rises*

"The restlessness approached hysteria. The parties were bigger. The shows were bigger. The pace was faster, . . . the buildings higher, the morals looser."
— F. Scott Fitzgerald

FIVE DEFINITIONS OF "THE IDEAL WOMAN"

"When in my company, she never admires other men."—Charles Chaplin

"(1) Lockjaw, (2) Hereditary obesity, (3) Absolutely fireproof, (4) Day and night elevator service."
—Ring Lardner

"Fidelity . . . [and] courage."   —Rudolph Valentino

"Native refinement . . . the quality of glory, . . . as definite yet intangible as the perfume of flowers."
—Florenz Ziegfeld

"She may weigh four hundred pounds, if her heart is of gold. [Also] the gift of stretching a can of sardines into a banquet."—Al Jolson
— *Vanity Fair*

Ads

Radio _____

Premieres
"Allen's Alley"
"Betty Crocker" (recipes)

Of Note
New voices on the air include Alice Brady, Father
Charles E. Coughlin, Eddie Cantor, George Burns
and Gracie Allen, Al Jolson, Jack Benny, Groucho
Marx, Bing Crosby, and Jimmy Durante.

Movies _____

Openings
Don Juan (Alan Crosland), John Barrymore, Mary
　　Astor
Beau Geste (Herbert Brenon), Ronald Colman, Noah
　　Beery
What Price Glory? (Raoul Walsh), Victor McLaglen,
　　Edmund Lowe
Metropolis (Fritz Lang), Alfred Abel, Gustav
　　Froelich
The Scarlet Letter (Victor Seastrom), Lillian Gish,
　　Lars Hanson
Moana (Robert Flaherty), documentary
So This Is Paris (Ernst Lubitsch), Monte Blue
The Black Pirate (Albert Parker), Douglas Fairbanks,
　　Billie Dove
Tramp, Tramp, Tramp (Harry Edwards), Harry
　　Langdon, Joan Crawford
Up in Mabel's Room (E. Mason Hopper), Marie
　　Prevost
Kid Boots (Frank Tuttle), Eddie Cantor, Clara Bow
The Son of the Sheik (George Fitzmaurice), Rudolph
　　Valentino, Vilma Banky
The Torrent (Monta Bell), Greta Garbo (American
　　debut), Ricardo Cortez
The Great Gatsby (Herbert Brenon), Warner Baxter,
　　Lois Wilson
The Sorrows of Satan (D. W. Griffith), Adolphe
　　Menjou, Lya de Putti

Top Box-Office Stars
Colleen Moore, Tom Mix

New Faces
Greta Garbo, Janet Gaynor, Charles "Buddy"
Rogers, Delores Del Rio, Walter Pidgeon, Myrna
Loy, James Hall, Ralph Forbes, Basil Rathbone, Fay
Wray

Helen Morgan, the original torch singer. *Movie Star News.*

Sex symbol Clara Bow, the "It" girl. *Movie Star News.*

Popular Music

Hit Songs
"One Alone"
"The Blue Room"
"If I Could Be with You One Hour To-Night"
"Bye Bye Blackbird"
"After I Say I'm Sorry"
"Breezin' Along with the Breeze"
"The Birth of the Blues"
"Baby Face"
"La Cumparsita"
"In a Little Spanish Town"
"Someone to Watch over Me"
"When the Red, Red Robin Comes Bob, Bob, Bobbin' Along"
"There's a New Star in Heaven Tonight" (written for Valentino's death)

Top Records
Some of These Days (Sophie Tucker); *Two Black Crows* (Moran and Mack); *You Made Me Love You* and *Heebie Jeebies* (Louis Armstrong); *I Wonder What's Become of Joe* (Goofus Five); *Black Bottom Stomp* (Morton's Red Hot Peppers); *Tootin' in Tennessee* (Ipana Troubadours)

Jazz and Big Bands
Duke Ellington plays at the Kentucky Club, New York

First Recordings: Jelly Roll Morton's Red Hot Peppers on Victor; Red Nichols's Five Pennies; Jean Goldkette

New Bands: Gus Arnheim, Los Angeles; Ben Pollack, Los Angeles (with Benny Goodman, age 16)

Theater

Broadway Openings

Plays
The Great God Brown (Eugene O'Neill), William Harrigan
Caponsacchi (Arthur Goodrich, Rose A. Palmer), Walter Hampden
The Play's the Thing (Ferenc Molnár), Holbrook Blinn, Reginald Owen
The Silver Cord (Sidney Howard), Laura Hope Crews, Vernon Steele
In Abraham's Bosom (Paul Green), Rose McClendon
Gentlemen Prefer Blondes (Anita Loos, John Emerson), June Walker, Frank Morgan
An American Tragedy (Philip Dunning, George Abbott), Miriam Hopkins, Morgan Farley
The Noose (Willard Mack), Barbara Stanwyck
The Constant Wife (W. Somerset Maugham), Ethel Barrymore
The Goat Song (Franz Werfel), Alfred Lunt, Lynn Fontanne, Edward G. Robinson
The Great Gatsby (Owen Davis), James Rennie
Yellow (Margaret Vernon), Spencer Tracy, Chester Morris
Sex (Jane Mast), Mae West (who goes to jail for one day when it is closed down)
Juno and the Paycock (Sean O'Casey), Augustan Duncan, Louise Randolph

Musicals
The Desert Song (Sigmund Romberg, Otto Harbach, Oscar Hammerstein II), Robert Halliday, Vivienne Segal
Oh Kay! (George Gershwin, Ira Gershwin), Victor Moore, Gertrude Lawrence
Countess Maritza (Emmerich Kalman, Julius Brammer), Yvonne D'Arle, Odette Myrtil, Walter Woolf
Great Temptations (Maurice Rubens, Clifford Grey), Hazel Dawn, Jack Benny
Earl Carroll's Vanities (Morris Hamilton, Grace Henry), Julius Tannen, Moran and Mack, Smith and Dale
Americana (Con Conrad, Ira Gershwin, George Gershwin), Helen Morgan
Honeymoon Lane (Eddie Dowling, James Hanley), Eddie Dowling, Kate Smith
Tip Toes (George Gershwin, Ira Gershwin), Queenie Smith, Jeanette MacDonald

Classics and Revivals On and Off Broadway
Pygmalion (George Bernard Shaw), Lynn Fontanne; *What Every Woman Knows* (James M. Barry), Helen Hayes; *Ghosts* (Ibsen), Lucile Watson. *Founded:* The Civic Repertory Theater by Eva Le Gallienne

Regional
Goodman Theatre, Chicago: *The Game of Love and Death* (Romain Rolland), premiere

Pulitzer Prize
Craig's Wife, George Kelly

Classical Music

Compositions

Aaron Copland, Piano Concerto, Jazz Symphoniette
    for 22 Instruments
Carl Ruggles, *Portals*
Edgard Varèse, *American Arcana*
George Gershwin, Three Preludes for Piano
Ernest Bloch, *America*
Virgil Thomson, *Sonata da Chiesa*
William Grant Still, *From the Black Belt*
Howard Hanson, *Pan and the Priest,* Concerto for
    Organ and Orchestra
Roy Harris, *Impressions of a Rainy Day*

Important Events

The United States continues to lead the world in the magnitude of orchestral events. A renewed interest in the old masters is marked by numerous performances of Bach's *Brandenburg Concertos* and Mozart's *Eine kleine Nachtmusik.* Also much performed are Sibelius's Symphony no. 7 and *Tapiola,* Respighi's *Pines of Rome,* Stravinsky's Two Suites for Orchestra, and Ralph Vaughan Williams's *Fantasia on a Theme by Thomas Tallis.*

For the American sesquicentennial, the Philadelphia Orchestra plays two concerts a week for 16 weeks with conductors Willem Van Hoogstraten, Nikolai Sokoloff, Artur Rodzinski, and Leopold Stokowski.

Major Recitals: violinists Albert Spalding, Josef Szigeti, Paul Kochanski, Efrem Zimbalist, Fritz Kreisler; pianists Ossip Gabrilowitsch, Harold Bauer, Alexander Cortot, Alfredo Casella, Darius Milhaud; harpsichordist Wanda Landowska; cellists Pablo Casals, Felix Salmont; and joint artists Josef and Rosina Lhévinne, Albert Spalding and Efrem Zimbalist

Guest Conductors: Arturo Toscanini (premiering Respighi's *Pines of Rome,* New York Philharmonic Society), Otto Klemperer (New York Symphonic Society), Georges Enesco (New York Philharmonic)

Debut: Walter Gieseking

First Performances

Darius Milhaud, playing *Carnival d'Aix* (New York); George Antheil, *Amériques* (Philadelphia); Douglas Moore, *Pageant of P. T. Barnum* (Cleveland); Louis Gruenberg, *The Creation* (New York); William Grant Still, *Darker Avenue* (New York); Emerson Whitehorne, *New York Days and Nights* (Philadelphia)

Opera

Twenty cities actively produce opera; especially popular are *The Witch of Salem* (Charles Wakefield Cadman) and *Hansel and Gretel* (Englebert Humperdinck). The 100th anniversary of Italian opera and 25th anniversary of Verdi's death are widely celebrated.

Metropolitan: Ezio Pinza (debut), Rosa Ponselle, *La vestale;* Lauritz Melchior (debut), *Tannhaüser.* Premieres: *Skyscraper* (John Alden Carpenter); *La vida breve* (Manuel de Falla); Maria Jeritza, *Le rossignol* and *Turandot* (American premieres); Mrs. Ernestine Schumann-Heink returns. Free opera is performed at the Polo Grounds and Starlight Park (Coney Island).

Chicago: *A Light from St. Agnes* (W. Franke Harling); *Judith* (Arthur Honegger)

Philadelphia: *Deep River* (W. Franke Harling); *Tannhaüser* (in English)

Northampton, Mass.:   *L'incoronazione di Poppea*

San Francisco: *Pique dame* (Tchaikovsky); *Fra Diavolo* (Auber)

Music Notes

The Pittsburgh Symphony Orchestra, disbanded in 1910, reorganizes under Richard Hageman • Plans continue to construct a new Metropolitan Opera House • Leopold Stokowski tries the daring experiment of conducting in a dark hall with the podium alone lighted; his performance raises great indignation.

Art

Painting

Thomas Hart Benton,
*The Lord Is My
Shepherd, The Path
Finder*
Charles Demuth,
*Eggplant and
Tomatoes*
Edward Hopper, *Mrs.
Acorn's Parlor*
Georgia O'Keeffe, *Black
Iris, Abstraction*
Raphael Soyer, *Reading
from Left to Right*
Walt Kuhn, *Dressing
Room*
John Marin, *Fir Tree,
Deer Isle, Maine*
Glenn O. Coleman,
Downtown Street
Guy Pène du Bois,
Opera Box

Sculpture

William Zorach, *Child
with Cat*
Mahonri M. Young,
Groggy
Paul Manship, *Indian
Hunter*

Architecture

Sunnyside Gardens, New
York City (Clarence
Stein, Henry Wright)
Philip Lovell Beach
House, Newport
Beach, Calif. (Rudolph
Schindler)
Liberty Memorial,
Kansas City, Mo. (H.
Van Buren Magonigle)

Important Exhibitions

Museums

New York: *Metropolitan:* John Singer Sargent;
Joseph Pennell; modern decorative arts; the K Wing
opens to house the Altman Collection. *Brooklyn:*
"International Exhibition of Modern Art" (307 works
from 23 countries)

Chicago: Modern painting, with prizes to George
Luks, Charles Hopkinson, Eugene Speicher

Washington: *Corcoran:* Tenth exhibit of
contemporary paintings, with awards to Charles W.
Hawthorne and W. Elmer Schofield

Los Angeles: Painters of the West

Hispanic Society of America: Paintings of the
provinces of Spain by Joachim Sorolla y Bastida
(opening show)

Traveling Exhibitions: The American Federation of
Arts sponsors 40 to 50 shows that reach all but four
states.

Art Briefs

The Toledo Museum receives a $14 million
endowment, and Kansas City receives $8 million for
the Nelson Gallery • Also expanding are museums in
St. Louis, Cincinnati, Baltimore, Newark, Houston,
and Providence; Des Moines purchases land for a
museum site • Alexander Calder holds his first
exhibition of paintings at the Artist's Gallery in New
York.

Dance

Martha Graham debuts in New York as a
choreographer and dancer in *Three Gopi Maidens*
and *A Study in Lacquer.*

Miriam Hopkins and Morgan Farley in *An American
Tragedy* (adapted from Theodore Dreiser's novel), an
attack on contemporary social and business morality. *Billy
Rose Theatre Collection. The New York Public Library at
Lincoln Center. Astor, Lenox and Tilden Foundations.*

Books

Fiction

Critics' Choice

The Sun Also Rises, Ernest Hemingway
The Torrents of Spring, Ernest Hemingway
Soldier's Pay, William Faulkner
The Silver Stallion, James Branch Cabell
My Mortal Enemy, Willa Cather
The Love Nest, Ring Lardner
All the Sad Young Men, F. Scott Fitzgerald
The Cabala, Thornton Wilder
Preface to a Life, Zona Gale

Best Sellers

The Private Life of Helen of Troy, John Erskine
Gentlemen Prefer Blondes, Anita Loos
Sorrell and Son, Warwick Deeping
The Hounds of Spring, Sylvia Thompson
Beau Sabreur, P. C. Wren
The Silver Spoon, John Galsworthy
Beau Geste, P. C. Wren
Show Boat, Edna Ferber
After Noon, Susan Ertz
The Blue Window, Temple Bailey

Nonfiction

Critics' Choice

Dictionary of American Usage, H. W. Fowler
The Physical Significance of the Quantum Theory, F. Lindemann
The Outlook for American Prose, Joseph Warren Beach
Art through the Ages, Helen Gardner
The Making of the Modern Mind, Herman Randall
Microbe Hunters, Paul de Kruif
Notes on Democracy, H. L. Mencken
The Mauve Decade, Thomas Beer
Abraham Lincoln: The Prairie Years, Carl Sandburg
Tar: A Midwest Childhood, Sherwood Anderson
🙤 *Religion and the Rise of Capitalism*, R. H. Tawney
🙤 *The End of Laissez-Faire*, J. M. Keynes

Best-Sellers

The Man Nobody Knows, Bruce Barton
Why We Behave Like Human Beings, George A. Dorsey
Diet and Health, Lulu Hunt Peters
Our Times, vol. I, Mark Sullivan
The Boston Cooking School Cook Book, new ed., Fannie Farmer
Auction Bridge Complete, Milton C. Work
The Book Nobody Knows, Bruce Barton

Ernest Hemingway, whose *The Sun Also Rises* portrays the "lost generation" of American expatriots in postwar Europe. *Library of Congress.*

The Story of Philosophy, Will Durant
The Light of Faith, Edgar A. Guest
Jefferson and Hamilton, Claude G. Bowers

Poetry

E. E. Cummings, *Is 5*
Hart Crane, *White Buildings*
Langston Hughes, *The Weary Blues*
Laura Riding, *The Close Couplet*
Sara Teasdale, *Dark of the Moon*

Pulitzer Prizes

Early Autumn, Louis Bromfield (novel)
Pinckney's Treaty, Samuel Flagg Bemis (U.S. history)
Whitman, Emory Holloway (biography)
Fiddler's Farewell, Leonora Speyer

Science and Technology

Robert Goddard fires the first liquid fuel–propelled rocket, and it rises 41 feet at 60 m.p.h.

The first movie with sound is demonstrated, a comedy short with Chic Sale.

A three-engine, all-metal Stout airplane is developed by Henry Ford for the purpose of improved passenger service.

Thomas Hunt Morgan, in *Theory of the Gene*, presents his theories of heredity developed at his Drosophila (fruit fly) workshop, Columbia University.

Thomas M. Rivers defines distinctions between viruses and bacteria, establishing virology as a separate discipline.

James B. Sumner isolates the metabolic enzyme urease.

The semiautomatic .30 MI rifle is patented by John Garand.

Auto antifreeze for radiators permits year-round motoring.

🙤 Oscar Barnack develops the 35mm camera.

Sports

Baseball

Babe Ruth hits three home runs in a World Series game. Aging Grover Alexander (St. Louis, NL), in relief, strikes out Tony Lazzeri (New York, AL) with the bases loaded to save the seventh game.

Champions

Batting	Pitching
Eugene Hargrave (Cincinnati, NL), .353	Ray Kremer (Pittsburgh, NL), 20–6
Heinie Manush (Detroit, AL), .378	George Uhke (Cleveland, AL), 27–11
	Home runs
	Babe Ruth (New York, AL), 47

Football

"Cash and Carry" Pyle starts the American Football League with Red Grange; the league is a financial failure. The NFL rules that college players are ineligible until their classes graduate.

Pro Stars: Elbert Bloodgood (Kansas City), Ernie Nevers (Duluth).

College All-Americans: Bennie Friedman (Q), Michigan; Victor Hanson (E), Syracuse.

Rose Bowl (Jan. 1, 1927): Alabama 7–Stanford 7.

Basketball

New York's Original Celtics are broken up to keep the ABL competitive; their overall record is 1,320–66.

Gertrude (Trudy) Ederle, during her record-breaking swim from Dover, England, to Gris-Nez, France. *Library of Congress.*

Other Sports

Swimming: Bronx-born Gertrude Ederle swims the English Channel in 14 hours and 31 minutes, breaking the previous record by 2 hours.

Boxing: Gene Tunney, a Shakespeare fan ("I worship at his shrine"), beats Jack Dempsey by a decision for the heavyweight title in Philadelphia; the gate is a record $1.9 million.

Tennis: Suzanne Lenglen beats Helen Wills in the "Match of the Century" at Cannes. Wills suffers appendicitis after the match. C. C. Pyle tours the United States with Lenglen, pays her $50,000, and draws large crowds.

Winners

World Series	*Player of the Year*
St. Louis (NL) 4	John Cobb, North Carolina
New York (AL) 3	*Stanley Cup*
MVP	Montreal Maroons
NL–Robert O'Farrell, St. Louis	*U.S. Tennis Open*
AL–George Burns, Cleveland	Men: René Lacoste
	Women: Molla Mallory
NFL	*USGA Open*
Frankford Yellow Jackets	Robert T. Jones, Jr.
College Football	*Kentucky Derby*
Stanford	Bubbling Over (A. Johnson, jockey)
College Basketball	
Syracuse	

Fashion

For Women: Skirts, shortest of the decade, stop just below the knee with flounces, pleats, and circular gores that extend from the hip; they are worn with horizontal-striped sweaters and long necklaces. Short and colorful evening dresses have elaborate embroidery, fringes, futuristic designs, beads, and appliques. The cocktail dress is born, and Clara Bow's "look" replaces Mary Pickford's. The new sex appeal extends from the bee-stung mouth and touseled hair to a new focus on legs, with silk stockings rolled around garters at rouged knees. The "debutante slouch" emerges: hips thrown forward, as the woman grips a cigarette holder between her teeth. Mothers and daughters are flappers, many nearly nude beneath the new, lighter clothing. Epicene fashions peak in a final statement of emancipation; also stylish is the odd earring, a pearl stud in one ear and dangling paste from the other.

High-fashion notes: Callot's beaded sheath; Chanel's simple two-piece jersey; gold and silver baguette bracelets; Premet's "garçonne dress"

Kaleidoscope

- Elinor Glyn uses the term "It Girl" to describe Clara Bow and the new sex appeal: the "same as before but more of it showing" and "a little more available." "Flaming youth" is coined for the younger generation.
- The popular "Charleston flare dress" sells at Gimbels for $1.58.
- Stars like Pola Negri and Marion Kay compete at Rudolph Valentino's funeral to show their devotion to him; a widely publicized photo of Valentino meeting Caruso in heaven appears in the *Evening Graphic*.
- The Supreme Court upholds the law limiting the medical prescription of whiskey to one pint every ten days.
- 2,000 people die of poisoned liquor; the illegal liquor trade nets $3.5 billion a year; prices for bootleg Scotch are $48 a case; rye, $85; champagne, $95; beer, $30.
- Over 14,500 movie houses show 400 films a year, as movies become America's favorite entertainment. *The Black Pirate* is the first in technicolor.
- Many top movie stars—John Gilbert, Greta Garbo, Emile Jannings, Pola Negri, Conrad Veidt—are forced to learn English with the advent of the Vitaphone sound system; some will retire because of the poor quality of their recorded voices.
- Greta Garbo's salary goes from $350 to $5,000 a week at MGM. Football star Red Grange is paid $300,000 for a film (*One Minute to Play*).

- The U.S. sesquicentennial is celebrated.
- Gertrude Ederle loses her hearing after swimming the English Channel.
- After his victory over Dempsey, Gene Tunney lectures on Shakespeare at Yale and then visits Europe with Thornton Wilder.
- Evangelist Aimee Semple McPherson's fame turns to notoriety as her so-called kidnapping is suspected by some to have been a romantic interlude with her radio operator.
- After "Daddy" Browning divorces her, Peaches loses 40 pounds and earns $8,000 a week in vaudeville.
- New faces on the Broadway stage include Barbara Stanwyck, Paul Muni, Spencer Tracy, Chester Morris, and Claudette Colbert.
- In one of his last feats, Houdini stays underwater 91 minutes with only 5 to 6 minutes of air.
- The New York Public Library starts its "Ten Worst Books Contest."
- The public eagerly follows the Hall-Mills murder case and is especially interested in their love letters: "I just want to crush you for two hours" (Hall).
- *Vanities'* producer Earl Carroll offers 17-year-old Joyce Hawley $1,000 to sit naked in a bathtub of champagne at a party he is hosting; she begins to cry when the guests appear.
- The tabloid market expands; Bernarr Macfadden's *True Story* gains a circulation of 2 million with stories such as "The Diamond Bracelet She Thought Her Husband Didn't Know About"; many call the *Evening Graphic* the "Porno-Graphic."
- Sinclair Lewis refuses the Pulitzer Prize because it makes the writer "safe, polite, obedient, and sterile."
- To fight the depression in the auto industry, Henry Ford introduces the eight-hour day and five-day week.
- Advocated by Secretary of the Treasury Andrew Mellon, a bill to reduce taxes on incomes of $1 million or more from 66 percent to 20 percent is passed by Congress.

First Appearances: Distinguished Flying Cross, Scotch tape, zippers, pop-up electric toaster, John Powers model agency, Hotel Carlyle (New York), Mark Hopkins hotel (San Francisco), Inter-Greyhound Racing Association, plastic surgery professorship, coin bearing the portrait of a living president (Calvin Coolidge), Chrysler Imperial, Prestone, safety glass and windshields, Pontiac, Du Pont waterproof cellophane, Safeway stores, First National, Trans World Airways, flavored yogurt, Book-of-the-Month Club (40,000 subscribers), Long Island University, Sarah Lawrence College, senator unseated after a recount (S. W. Brookhart), 16mm film (Kodak)

High School basketball team, Englewood, New Jersey. *I. Goldfein.*

1927

Facts and Figures

Economic Profile

Dow-Jones: ↑ High 202–
Low 152

GNP: −2%

Inflation: −0.5%

Unemployment: 3.3%

Average salary: $1,312

Teacher: $1,277

Lawyer: $5,205

Physician: $5,150

Factory worker: $1,502

Pillowcases, sheets: $1

Wool blankets, 70″ by 80″:
$9.95

Face towels: $7.50–$10.50
(doz.)

Liggett's Drugs

Phillips milk of magnesia:
50¢

Listerine, Lavoris: $1

Kolynos, Pepsodent: 50¢

Odorona: 60¢; Mum: 25¢

Wampole's cod liver oil: $1

Ivory soap: 8¢

In the News

COOLIDGE CALLS FOR NAVAL DISARMAMENT CONFERENCE, BRITAIN AND JAPAN ATTEND, FRANCE AND ITALY DECLINE . . . FRENCH MINISTER ARISTIDE BRIAND SUGGESTS OUTLAWING WAR, SECRETARY OF STATE FRANK KELLOGG ENDORSES BRIAND . . . TEAPOT DOME LEASE IS INVALIDATED BY SUPREME COURT . . . CHIANG KAI-SHEK AND COMMUNIST FORCES DEFEAT WARLORDS IN SHANGHAI, CANTON, NANKING . . . REGULAR TRANSATLANTIC PHONE SERVICE BEGINS . . . GERMAN ECONOMY COLLAPSES ON "BLACK FRIDAY" . . . GIANT FEDERAL RELIEF EFFORT UNDER HERBERT HOOVER AIDS FLOODED MISSISSIPPI VALLEY . . . LAST APPEALS FAIL, SACCO AND VANZETTI ARE EXECUTED, WORLDWIDE PROTESTS OCCUR . . . CHARLES LINDBERGH FLIES SOLO, NONSTOP, FROM NEW YORK TO PARIS, 3,610 MILES IN 33 ⅓ HOURS, 100,000 FRENCH CHEER LINDBERGH'S ARRIVAL . . . COOLIDGE SAYS: "I CHOOSE NOT TO RUN" IN '28 . . . HOUSEWIFE RUTH SNYDER AND ART DIRECTOR HENRY GRAY ARE CONVICTED OF HUSBAND'S MURDER . . . GENE TUNNEY, DOWN FOR THE "LONG COUNT," RISES TO DECISION JACK DEMPSEY BEFORE 104,943 IN CHICAGO . . . BRITAIN BREAKS DIPLOMATIC RELATIONS WITH RUSSIA, CLAIMING SOVIET INTRIGUE . . . SUPREME COURT RULES ILLEGAL INCOME IS TAXABLE . . . 40 MEN DIE IN SUB S-4 AFTER RESCUE EFFORTS FAIL.

Deaths

Lizzie Borden, Georg
Brandes, John Dillon, John
Drew.

Quotes

"Isn't it nice thåt Calvin is President? You know we really never had room before for a dog."
— Mrs. Coolidge

"I am going to St. Petersburg, Florida, tomorrow. Let the worthy citizens of Chicago get their liquor the best they can. I'm sick of the job—it's a thankless one and full of grief. I've been spending the best years of my life as a public benefactor."
— Al Capone

Question: In other words, you want the jury to believe that you were a perfect lady? . . . You did nothing to make your husband unhappy?
Reply: Not that he knew about.
— Testimony of housewife Ruth Snyder, accused of murder

"I am innocent. I am suffering because I am a radical . . . an Italian . . . more for my family and for my beloved than for myself, but I am so convinced to be right that if you could execute me two times, and I could be reborn two other times, I would live again to do what I have done already."
— Bartolomeo Vanzetti

"This man [Vanzetti], although he may not actually have committed the crime . . . is . . . the enemy of our existing institutions. . . . The defendant's ideals are cognate with crime."
— Webster Thayer, presiding judge at the Sacco-Vanzetti trial

"I am Charles A. Lindbergh," he said, when he arrived in Paris. *Library of Congress.*

"There was a closet in the anteroom, evidently a place for hats and coats. . . . We repaired there many times in the course of my visits to the White House . . . and there the President [Harding] and his adoring sweetheart made love."
— Nan Britton's autobiography, *The President's Daughter*

"Lindbergh . . . has shown us that we are *not* rotten at the core, but morally sound and sweet and good!"
— Mary B. Mullet, "The Biggest Thing that Lindbergh Has Done," *American* magazine

Ads

Radio

Premieres

"The Two Black Crows," George Moran, Charles Mack

"The Cities Service Concert" (opera from the Chicago Civic Auditorium)

"Ida Bailey Allen and Her Cooking School"

"The Palmolive Hour"

"Duke Ellington" (from the Cotton Club)

"Rose Bowl" (first coast-to-coast program)

Specials

Lindbergh's landing, announced by Graham McNamee; Dempsey-Tunney fight; Floyd Bennett's funeral service from Arlington; Herbert Hoover accepting the Republican nomination in Palo Alto; Ted Husing announcing the arrival of the Graf Zeppelin at Lakehurst, N.J.

Of Note

The Federal Radio Commission is appointed.

Movies

Openings

The Jazz Singer (Alan Crosland), Al Jolson (first successful full-length talkie)

Wings (William A. Wellman), Clara Bow, Buddy Rogers, Gary Cooper

Napoleon (Abel Gance), Albert Dieudonne

The King of Kings (Cecil B. DeMille), Joseph Schildkraut, Rudolph Schildkraut, H. B. Warner

Flesh and the Devil (Clarence Brown), Greta Garbo, John Gilbert

Underworld (Josef von Sternberg), Evelyn Brent, George Bancroft

The Night of Love (George Fitzmaurice), Ronald Colman, Vilma Banky, Montagu Love

Camille (Fred Niblo), Gilbert Roland, Norma Talmadge

The Way of All Flesh (Victor Fleming), Emil Jannings

The Ten Days that Shook the World (Sergei Eisenstein), V. Nikandrov, N. Popov

Sunrise (F. W. Murnau), Janet Gaynor, George Brien

Seventh Heaven (Frank Borzage), Janet Gaynor, Charles Farrell

Love (Edmund Goulding), Greta Garbo, John Gilbert

The Unknown (Tod Browning), Lon Chaney, Joan Crawford

The General (Buster Keaton, Clyde Bruckman), Buster Keaton

Top Box-Office Stars

Tom Mix, Colleen Moore, John Gilbert, Greta Garbo

Al Jolson's limited dialogue in *The Jazz Singer* includes "You ain't seen nothin' yet." *Movie Star News.*

Popular Music

Hit Songs
"Ol' Man River"
"Bill"
"Can't Help Lovin' Dat Man"
"Why Do I Love You?"
"I'm Looking over a Four-Leaf Clover"
"S'Wonderful"
"Let a Smile Be Your Umbrella"
"Blue Skies"
"My Heart Stood Still"
"The Best Things in Life Are Free"
"East of the Moon, West of the Stars"
"Jealousy"
"Me and My Shadow"
"Ramona"
"Thou Swell"
"Henry's Made a Lady out of Lizzie"

Top Records
The Song Is Ended, It All Depends on You (Ruth Etting); *Side by Side* (Ipana Troubadours); *Rio Rita* (The Knickerbockers); *Highways Are Happy Ways* (Ted Weems); *Hear My Prayer* (Ernest Lough); *Ida, Sweet as Apple Cider* (Red Nichols); *The Soldier's Sweetheart* (Jimmie Rodgers); *My Blue Heaven* (Gene Austin)

Jazz and Big Bands
Earl Hines joins Louis Armstrong. Duke Ellington opens at the Cotton Club, New York, where he begins radio broadcasting. Wayne King plays at Chicago's Aragon Ballroom.

First Recordings: Adelaide Hall's *Creole Love Call* with Duke Ellington (the first use of voice as orchestral instrument); Red McKenzie and Eddie Condon (the first classic Chicago jazz session)

New Bands: Jack Teagarden, New York; Jimmy Lunceford, Memphis

Theater

Broadway Openings

Plays
Paris Bound (Philip Barry), Madge Kennedy
The Royal Family (George S. Kaufman, Edna Ferber), Otto Kruger
Saturday's Children (Maxwell Anderson), Ruth Gordon, Roger Pryer
The Road to Rome (Robert E. Sherwood), Jane Cowl
Coquette (George Abbott, Anna Preston Bridges), Helen Hayes
The Barker (Kenyon Nicholson), Claudette Colbert
Her Cardboard Lover (Jacques Deval), Jeanne Eagels, Leslie Howard
Burlesque (Arthur Hopkins), Barbara Stanwyck, Oscar Levant
The Trial of Mary Dugan (Bayard Veiller), Ann Harding, Rex Cherryman, Robert Cummings
The Letter (W. Somerset Maugham), Katharine Cornell
Crime (Samuel Shipman, John B. Hymer), Sylvia Sidney, Chester Morris
Dracula (Hamilton Deane, John Balderston), Bela Lugosi
Porgy (Dorothy Heyward, DuBose Heyward), Rose McClendon, Frank Wilson
Baby Mine (Margaret Mayo), Roscoe Arbuckle, Humphrey Bogart

Musicals
Good News (Ray Henderson, B. G. DeSylva), John Price Jones, Mary Lawlor
Ziegfeld Follies (Irving Berlin), Eddie Cantor, Ruth Etting, Claire Luce
A Connecticut Yankee (Richard Rodgers, Lorenz Hart), William Gaxton, Constance Carpenter
Show Boat (Jerome Kern, Oscar Hammerstein II), Helen Morgan, Charles Winninger, Edna May Oliver
Hit the Deck (Vincent Youmans, Leo Robin), Louise Groody, Charles King, Brian Donlevy
Funny Face (George Gershwin, Ira Gershwin), Fred and Adele Astaire
The Merry Malones (George M. Cohan), George M. Cohan, Polly Walker
Padlocks of 1927 (Henry H. Tobias, Billy Rose), Texas Guinan, Lillian Roth
Sidewalks of New York (Eddie Dowling, Jimmy Hanley), Ruby Keeler, Ray Dooley

Classics and Revivals On and Off Broadway
Electra (Sophocles), Margaret Anglin; *The Doctor's Dilemma* (George Bernard Shaw), Alfred Lunt, Lynn Fontanne; *Trelawney of the Wells* (Pinero), John Drew, Pauline Lord; *An Enemy of the People* (Ibsen), Walter Hampden; *A Midsummer Night's Dream*, Lili Darvis; *The Plough and the Stars* (Sean O'Casey), Arthur Sinclair; *Escape* (John Galsworthy), Leslie Howard

Pulitzer Prize
In Abraham's Bosom, Paul Green

Classical Music

Compositions

Virgil Thomson, *La valse grégorienne*
Roy Harris, Concerto for Piano, Clarinet and String Quartet
Wallingford Riegger, Study in Sonority for Nineteen Violins and Any Multiple of Ten

Important Events

An unusual amount of modern music is performed, and works of Gershwin, Copland, Varèse, and Antheil receive wide acclaim. Bartók's and Antheil's appearances in New York receive unprecedented publicity.

New Appointment: Georg Schneevoight becomes conductor of the Los Angeles Philharmonic.

Debut: Yehudi Menuhin, age 10

First Performances

Igor Stravinsky, Octet (International Composers League, New York); Carlos Salzedo, Concerto for Harp and Seven Woodwinds (New York); Aaron Copland, playing, Concerto for Piano and Orchestra (Boston); Roger Sessions, Symphony in E minor (Boston); George Antheil, *Ballet mécanique* (New York); Sergei Rachmaninoff, playing, Piano Concerto no. 4 (Philadelphia); Frank S. Converse, *Flivver 10,000,000* (Boston); Edgard Varèse, *Arcane* (New York); Leoš Janáček, *Sinfonietta* (New York); Ruth Crawford, Violin Sonata (New York); James Dunn, *WE* (celebrating Lindbergh's flight, New York); Béla Bartók, *The Miraculous Mandarin* (Cincinnati); Albert Roussel, Suite (Boston); Alfredo Casella, *Scarlattiana* (New York); Charles Ives, Symphony no. 4 (New York); Emerson Whitehorne, *Aeroplane* (Cleveland)

Opera

Metropolitan: Rosa Ponselle, *Norma;* Edward Johnson, *Roméo et Juliette;* Richard Mayr, Grete Stückgold, *Die Meistersinger.* Premieres: *The King's Henchman* (Deems Taylor, Edna St. Vincent Millay); *Violanta* (Erich Korngold)

Chicago: *Judith* (Arthur Honegger, premiere)

Philadelphia: *Boris Godunov* (original score)

San Francisco: Antonio Scotti, *Falstaff; La cena della Beffe* (Giordano)

Music Notes

Ernest Bloch's *America* wins the $3,000 "Musical America" prize • The Pittsburgh Symphony is founded • During Hungarian Week in New York, Zoltán Kodály performs Béla Bartók and Imre Weisshaus • Cleveland audiences are shocked by the orchestra's performances of Bax and Scriabin • Radio scheduling begins to include contemporary music, as well as the old masters.

Ziegfeld Follies' star Ruth Etting. *Movie Star News.*

Art

Painting

Alfred Maurer, *Self-Portrait*

Lyonel Feininger, *The Steamer Odin, Village*

Guy Pène du Bois, *Americans in Paris*

Edward Hopper, *Manhattan Bridge, Lighthouse Hill*

Georgia O'Keeffe, *Radiator Building, New York*

Charles Demuth, *My Egypt, Eggplant and Squash*

Thomas Hart Benton, *Lonesome Road*

Stuart Davis, *Egg Beater, No. 2*

Arthur G. Dove, *Hand Sewing Machine*

Gerald Murphy, *Wasp and Pear*

Sculpture

Mahonri Young, *Right with the Jaw*

Gaston Lachaise, *Georgia O'Keeffe, Floating Figure, Standing Woman* (also called *Elevation*)

John Storrs, *Study in Form #1*

Reuben Nakian, *The Lap Dog, Young Calf*

Elie Nadelman, *Man in a Top Hat*

Architecture

Dymaxion House, 4-D house model (Buckminster Fuller)

Heath House, Los Angeles (Richard Neutra)

Ocotillo Camp design (Frank Lloyd Wright)

Grauman's Chinese Theatre, Hollywood, Calif. (Meyer and Holler)

Important Exhibitions

Museums

New York: *Metropolitan:* American miniatures, 1720–1850; Swedish contemporary decorative arts; painted and printed fabrics

Chicago: Chinese Buddhist art of the Wei Dynasty

Boston: Claude Monet; Tricentennial exhibition of the Society of Arts and Crafts

Art Briefs

Highlights of the Alexander Archipenko show in New York include *Two Women, Woman Walking,* and *Torso* • Gutzon Borglum begins a five-year, $437,500 project on Mt. Rushmore in South Dakota: 465-foot figures of Washington, Jefferson, Lincoln, and Roosevelt • An estimated 10,000 professional artists live in the United States • The influx of European art dealers gains public attention • The Fogg Museum at Harvard opens.

Dance

Martha Graham founds the Martha Graham School of Contemporary Dance.

John Storrs, *Forms in Space*, 1927. Stainless steel and copper. 20½ × 25". *The Metropolitan Museum of Art, Bequest Fund, 1967.*

Books

Fiction

Critics' Choice

Mosquitos, William Faulkner
Death Comes for the Archbishop, Willa Cather
The Grandmothers, Glenway Wescott
Men without Women, Ernest Hemingway
Blue Voyage, Conrad Aiken
Giants in the Earth, Ole Rölvaag
Oil! Upton Sinclair
&. *To the Lighthouse*, Virginia Woolf
&. *The Magic Mountain*, Thomas Mann

Best-Sellers

Elmer Gantry, Sinclair Lewis
The Plutocrat, Booth Tarkington
Doomsday, Warwick Deeping
Sorrell and Son, Warwick Deeping
Jalna, Mazo de la Roche
Lost Ecstasy, Mary Roberts Rinehart
Twilight Sleep, Edith Wharton
Tomorrow Morning, Anne Parrish
The Old Countess, Anne Douglas Sedgwick
A Good Woman, Louis Bromfield

Nonfiction

Critics' Choice

The Story of a Wonder Man, Ring Lardner
The Main Stream, Stuart Pratt Sherman
The American Songbag, Carl Sandburg
The Rise of American Civilization, Charles Beard, Mary Beard
The Emergence of Modern America, Allan Nevins
Platonism and the Spiritual Life, George Santayana
Evolution in Science and Religion, Robert Millikan
My Religion, Helen Keller
What about Advertising? Kenneth Goode, Harford Powel, Jr.

Best-Sellers

The Story of Philosophy, Will Durant
Napoleon, Emil Ludwig
Revolt in the Desert, T. E. Lawrence
Trader Horn, vol. 1, Alfred Aloysius Horn, Ethelreda Lewis
We, Charles A. Lindbergh
Ask Me Another, Julian Spafford, Lucien Esty
The Royal Road to Romance, Richard Halliburton
Why We Behave Like Human Beings, George A. Dorsey
Mother India, Katherine Mayo
The Glorious Adventure, Richard Halliburton

Poetry

Laura Riding, *Voltaire*
Robinson Jeffers, *The Women at Point Sur*
John Crowe Ransom, *Two Gentlemen in Bonds*
Amy Lowell (posthumous), *Ballads for Sale*
Countee Cullen, *Copper Sun, The Ballad of the Brown Girl*
Don Marquis, *archy and mehitabel*

Pulitzer Prizes

The Bridge of San Luis Rey, Thornton Wilder (novel)
Main Currents in American Thought, Vernon Louis Parrington (U.S. history)
The American Orchestra and Theodore Thomas, Charles Edward Russell (biography)
Tristram, Edwin Arlington Robinson

Science and Technology

Physicists Clinton Davisson and Lester Germer, of Bell Telephone Laboratories, confirm de Broglie's theory that electrons behave as "matter waves."

A. A. Michelson, at Mt. Wilson Observatory in California, begins experiments to measure the speed of light.

Philo T. Farnsworth constructs the first all-electronic television set.

The first national radio beacon to inform pilots when they are off course is implemented.

Philip Drinker, at Harvard, devises the iron lung, a respirator for people who cannot breathe on their own.

Thyroxine, a thyroid hormone, is prepared synthetically, enabling cretinism to be treated.

An adrenal cortical extract, cortin, prepared by F. A. Hartman, is used to treat once-fatal Addison's disease.

Karl Landsteiner and Philip Levine, of the Rockefeller Institute, discover blood groups M, N, and P.

The Holland Tunnel is the first vehicular route across the Hudson River between New York and New Jersey.

&. Fossil remains of Pithecanthropus pekinensis, "Peking man," 300,000–400,000 B.C., are discovered by Davidson Black.

&. Werner Heisenberg propounds the Uncertainty Principle.

Nobel Prize

Arthur H. Compton wins the prize in physics for his discovery of wave-length change in diffused X rays.

Sports ━━━━━━━━━━━━━━━━━━━━━━

Baseball

Babe Ruth (New York, AL) hits a record 60 home runs. Lou Gehrig (New York, AL) bats .378 with 175 runs batted in and 47 home runs. The Yankees win a record 110 games with "Murderers' Row"—Ruth; Gehrig; Earle Coombs, .356; Bob Meusel, .336; and Tony Lazzeri, .309.

Walter Johnson retires with a record 113 shutouts and 3,497 strikeouts.

Champions ━━━━━━━━━━━━━━━━━

Batting
  Paul Waner (Pittsburgh, NL), .380
  Harry Heilmann (Detroit, AL), .398

Pitching
  Jessie Haynes (St. Louis, NL), 24–10
  Waite Hoyt (New York, AL), 22–7
Home runs
  Babe Ruth (New York, AL), 60

Football

The NFL goes from 32 to 12 teams.

Pro Stars: Steve Owens, Cal Hubbard (New York)

College All-Americans: Bennie Oosterban (Q), Michigan; Chris Cagle (H), Army

Rose Bowl (Jan. 1, 1928): Alabama 7–Pittsburgh 6

Basketball

The Harlem Globetrotters, a black team, is organized by Abe Saperstein.
Brooklyn, with most of the Original Celtics, wins the ABL.

The Rens, a black team, splits an exhibition series with Brooklyn.

Other Sports

Boxing: Jack Dempsey fails to go to a neutral corner when he knocks Gene Tunney down; the length of the count is disputed; the gate at Soldier's Field, Chicago, is a record $2.65 million. The Golden Gloves is inaugurated by the *New York Daily News*.

Swimming: Johnny Weismuller swims 100 yards in a record 51 seconds.

Tennis: Helen Wills returns and wins the Wimbledon Singles.

Golf: Walter Hagen wins his fourth straight PGA title.

Winners ━━━━━━━━━━━━━━━━━

World Series
  New York (AL) 4
  Pittsburgh (NL) 3
MVP
  NL–Paul Waner, Pittsburgh
  AL–Lou Gehrig, New York
NFL
  New York Giants
College Football
  Illinois
College Basketball
  Notre Dame

Player of the Year
  Victor Hanson, Syracuse
Stanley Cup
  Ottawa
U.S. Tennis Open
  Men: Rene Lacoste
  Women: Helen Wills
USGA Open
  Tommy Armour
Kentucky Derby
  Whiskery (L. McAtee, jockey)

Fashion ━━━━━━━━━━━━━━━━━━━━━

For Men: September *Vanity Fair* reports the "sartorial practices" of "a certain flamboyant youth," the Harvard, Yale, or Princeton collegian who moves "like a darting elephant": he wears gray sagging Oxford pants, drooping socks over square-toed, barely visible saddle shoes with crepe or rubber soles, and a single-breasted, gray Oxford overcoat. A felt hat, battered, bent, twisted, or folded, falls over his nose, or a cap is pushed to the back of his head.

Knickers or white denims, overalls, and jackets are sometimes worn, as well as the double-breasted lounge jacket and soft white shirt with attached collar (inserted with a simple pin), tweed worsteds, and chemises. Two- or three-button single-breasted sack coats are most stylish; ties are knitted. Clothes are made only by local, New York, or London tailors; they appear better pressed at Yale.

U.S. delegates at the Geneva Disarmament Conference. Left to right: George V. Strong, H. C. Train, J. N. Greely, Frank B. Kellogg, J. T. Marriner, A. T. Long. *Library of Congress.*

- Eighteen hundred tons of ticker tape and shredded newspaper and phone books contribute to the Lindbergh parade in New York; it costs the city $16,000 to sweep up.
- Lindbergh receives 3.5 million letters containing $100,000 in return postage, 100,000 wires, and 7,000 job offers; a dance, the "Lindy Hop" is named for him.
- Edna St. Vincent Millay is arrested outside the Boston courthouse during the deathwatch for Sacco and Vanzetti. Others defending them include three-fourths of the Harvard Law School graduating class, Felix Frankfurter, Heywood Broun, Dorothy Parker, Robert Benchley, John Dos Passos, Albert Einstein, G. B. Shaw, H. G. Wells, Anatole France, Rabbi Stephen Wise, Jane Addams, Romain Rolland, and John Galsworthy.
- The bootleg best-seller *The President's Daughter* by Nan Britton tells of Britton's love affair with President Harding and their illegitimate daughter.
- Babe Ruth's record home run pace elicits such epithets as the Sultan of Swat, Behemoth of Swing, and Colossus of Clout.
- Film producers add sound sequences to silent films and call them "part-talkies."
- The Ford Model A appears in four colors (including Arabian Sand) with a self-starter and other gadgetry, a rumble seat, and shatterproof windshield. Ford has sold 15 million Model Ts since 1908.
- The Hays list of do's and don'ts for Hollywood films prohibits "any licentious or suggestive nudity," "miscegenation," "ridicule of clergy," and "inference of sexual perversion"; it also urges care on themes such as "the sale of women."
- A survey reports a "loosening" in manners and morals. Mrs. Bertrand Russell defends "free love," and Judge Lindsay advocates "companionate [trial] marriage."
- Restaurants hire detective-waiters to search customers for hip flasks and bottles before serving ice and ginger ale; Prohibition agents can arrest clients on the basis of "a good smell."
- Because lethal ingredients are added to industrial alcohol, the wets accuse the government of murder.
- Since diguised government agents are allowed to shoot to kill, a number of innocent people die.
- The Al Capone gang nets $100 million in the liquor trade, $30 million in protection money, $25 million in gambling, $10 million in vice, and $10 million in the "rackets" (a new word).

Kaleidoscope

- The influence of the *American Mercury* is so powerful that *Harper's, Forum, Atlantic,* and *Scribner's* begin to similarly attack the "Christian" glorification of business, moral conformity, and the "booboisie" (Mencken's word).
- The Scripps-Howard and Hearst news empires expand as public interest increases in scandals and gossip.
- Henry Ford publicly apologizes for his *Dearborn Independent* newspaper remarks against Jews.
- The latest topics in Bernarr Macfadden's confessional magazines include feminism and the various ways of carousing.
- Alexander Kerensky, head of the provisional government during the 1917 Russian Revolution, settles in New York.
- Black leader Marcus Garvey, convicted of mail fraud in 1923, has his sentence commuted and is deported to the West Indies by President Coolidge.
- Isadora Duncan dies of a broken neck when her scarf is tangled in the wheel of a moving car.
- President Coolidge urges that the nation pray more.
- Strong language, like *lousy, damn,* and *hell,* enters the popular arts and replaces words like *grand* and *swell.*
- Broadway presents a record 268 plays. Florenz Ziegfeld opens a theater with his name and presents *Show Boat* and *Rio Rita.*
- The "clean book" bill is defeated in the Senate; forty leading authors form the Committee for the Suppression of Irresponsible Censorship.
- The postwar education boom peaks, along with a variety of outline and how-to books.
- Fifteen million Sears & Roebuck catalogs are distributed to U.S. homes.
- One of the nation's best-dressed men, President Coolidge wears $125–$140 suits, which are double-breasted and cuffless; he dislikes soft collars, prefers black to brown shoes, and wears only one ring; he always carries three cigars, even in his formal wear, and never wears a fob.

First Appearances: All-electric juke box, cyclone rollercoaster (Coney Island), lightweight brick, electric sign flasher, car radio, Federal Radio Commission, commercial armored car hold-up, pilot license granted a woman, phonograph with automatic record changer, drive-up mailbox (Houston), Yeshiva College, Super Suds, Borden's homogenized milk, the slow fox-trot, the "Varsity Drag," Volvo, carbonated grape Welch-Ade, wall-mounted can opener, B&M Brick Oven baked beans, Literary Guild of America, Remington Rand, Hostess cakes, Sherry Netherland Hotel (New York), Delmonico's, A & W root beer, Lender bagel factory, Gerber baby food, *Ile de France,* GE refrigerator with "monitor top," simultaneous television-phone transmission, Movietone News

1928

Facts and Figures

Economic Profile
Dow-Jones: ↑ High 300–
 Low 194
GNP: +2%
Inflation: −0.7%
Unemployment: 4.2%
Balance of international
 payments: + $1.1 billion
Military on duty: 250,907
Voter participation:
 57% (1928)
 49% (1924)
 49% (1920)
Women's clothing (Best &
 Co.):
 Lisle mesh sport shirt:
  $2.95
 Wool jersey shirt and skirt
  outfit: $17.50
 Suede leather sport jacket:
  $32.50
 Feather boas: $8.50–$30
 Voile underwear: $1
Men's clothing:
 Arrow broadcloth shirt:
  $1.95
 Calfskin gloves: $5
 Ties: 95¢–$2.45
 BVD suit: $1.30

Deaths

Roald Amundsen, Vicente
 Blasco-Ibáñez, Holbrook
 Blinn, William Du Pont,
 Henry F. Gilbert, George
 Goethals, Thomas Hardy,
 Leoš Janáček, Robert
 Lansing, Ellen Terry.

In the News

COOLIDGE OPENS INTER-AMERICAN CONFERENCE IN HAVANA . . . 25TH ANNIVERSARY OF KITTY HAWK IS CELEBRATED, LINDBERGH RECEIVES AWARD . . . SOCIALIST PARTY NOMINATES NORMAN THOMAS FOR PRESIDENT, COMMUNISTS NOMINATE WILLIAM Z. FOSTER . . . TURKEY DECLARES ISLAM NO LONGER STATE RELIGION . . . ST. FRANCIS DAM, IN CALIFORNIA, COLLAPSES, 450 ARE KILLED . . . GOP NOMINATES HERBERT HOOVER, DEMOCRATS NOMINATE AL SMITH . . . CHIANG KAI-SHEK BECOMES CHINESE PRESIDENT . . . AMELIA EARHART IS FIRST WOMAN TO FLY ATLANTIC . . . U.S. SIGNS KELLOGG-BRIAND PACT TO OUTLAW WAR, BRITAIN, FRANCE, GERMANY, AND RUSSIA ALSO SIGN . . . ALBANIA BECOMES KINGDOM UNDER ZOG I . . . ADMIRAL RICHARD BYRD DEPARTS ON ANTARCTIC EXPEDITION . . . BRITISH WOMEN GAIN THE VOTE . . . U.S. AND CHINA AGREE TO COMMERCE TREATY . . . INTERNATIONAL CONFERENCE ON ECONOMIC STATISTICS MEETS IN GENEVA . . . RUSSIA ANNOUNCES FIVE-YEAR PLAN TO COLLECTIVIZE AGRICULTURE . . . PAN-AMERICAN CONFERENCE MEETS TO PROVIDE FOR ARBITRATION IN INTERNATIONAL DISPUTES . . . MEXICAN PRESIDENT ALVARO OBREGON IS ASSASSINATED . . . HOOVER DEFEATS SMITH 21 TO 15 MILLION, THOMAS RECEIVES 260,000 VOTES, FOSTER, 21,000 . . . FDR WINS N.Y. GUBERNATORIAL RACE . . . CLARK MEMO STATES U.S. WILL NOT PLAY "COP" IN LATIN DISPUTES . . . BOULDER DAM ACT PASSES, GOVERNMENT WILL PARTICIPATE IN HYDROELECTRIC POWER.

Quotes

"We in America today are nearer to the final triumph over poverty than ever before in the history of any land. The poor-house is vanishing from among us."
— Herbert Hoover

"Here were the imponderable processes and forces of the cosmos, harmonious and soundless. Harmony, that was it! . . . The universe was a cosmos, not a chaos; man was as rightfully a part of that cosmos as were the day and night."
— Adm. Richard E. Byrd, on flying over the North Pole

"It is very difficult and expensive to undo after you are married the things that your mother and father did to you while you were putting your first six birthdays behind you."
— from a study prepared by the Bureau of Social Hygiene

"Moving pictures need sound as much as Beethoven symphonies need lyrics."
— Charles Chaplin

"After twenty years of being only in its infancy, the moving picture which gave some promise of an interesting adult life has suddenly gone senile—and garrulous. It is talking at the top of its voice, talking to itself, talking in its sleep. Terrified of . . . radio broadcasting, it has incorporated radio itself."
— Gilbert Seldes, "The Movies Commit Suicide," *Vanity Fair*

"Wall Street's brokerages were overflowing with a new type of speculator, . . . the inexperienced—the "suckers," . . . men who had been attracted by newspaper stories of the big, easy profits to be made in a tremendous bull market."
— *Nation*

"I say it's spinach and I say the hell with it."
— *New Yorker* cartoon of child refusing to eat the "new" Italian vegetable, broccoli

Ads

An ad demonstrating both fashion and art deco design.

Radio

Premieres

"Real Folks, Main Street" (first drama series)
"Chase and Sanborn Hour," Maurice Chevalier
"The Voice of Firestone"
"National Farm and Home Hour," Don Ameche
"Music Appreciation Hour," Walter Damrosch
"True Story with Mary and Bob"
"National Radio Pulpit"
"Shell Chateau," Al Jolson
"Uncle Don," Don Carney

Of Note

Maurice Chevalier is paid $5,000 a week by Chase and Sanborn • Al Smith's pronunciation of "raddio" is much parodied • NBC is organized into two semi-independent networks, the Red and Blue • Popular singer Vaughn de Leath, "the Radio Girl," develops the new style of singing called "crooning" to deal with the limitations of radio technology.

Movies

Openings

The Last Command (Josef von Sternberg), Emil Jannings, Evelyn Brent, William Powell
The Racket (Lewis Milestone), Thomas Meighan, Marie Prevost
The Crowd (King Vidor), Emil Jannings, Marlene Dietrich
Sadie Thompson (Raoul Walsh), Gloria Swanson, Lionel Barrymore
Abie's Irish Rose (Victor Fleming), Charles Rogers
Our Dancing Daughters (Harry Beaumont), Joan Crawford
Steamboat Bill, Jr. (Charles F. Reisner), Buster Keaton
Street Angel (Frank Borzage), Janet Gaynor, Charles Farrell
The Singing Fool (Lloyd Bacon), Al Jolson
The Mysterious Lady (Fred Niblo), Greta Garbo
The Passion of Joan of Arc (Carl Dreyer), Marie Falconetti, Antonin Artaud
The Circus (Charles Chaplin), Charles Chaplin, Merna Kennedy
The Docks of New York (Josef von Sternberg), George Bancroft, Betty Compson
Sorrell and Son (Herbert Brenon), H. B. Warner

Academy Awards (1927–28)

First year of presentations.

Best Picture: *Wings*
Best Director: Frank Borzage (*Seventh Heaven*)
Best Comedy Director: Lewis Milestone (*Two Arabian Knights*)
Best Actress: Janet Gaynor (*Street Angel, Seventh Heaven, Sunrise*)
Best Actor: Emil Jannings (*The Way of All Flesh, The Last Command*)
Special Awards: Charles Chaplin (*The Circus*), Warner Brothers (*The Jazz Singer*)

Top Box-Office Stars

Clara Bow, Lon Chaney. *Also popular:* Greta Garbo, Emil Jannings, Harold Lloyd, John Gilbert

Joan Crawford, Clara Bow's rival as the prototype of flaming youth, in *Our Dancing Daughters*. *Movie Star News.*

Popular Music

Hit Songs

"She's Funny That Way"
"Lover, Come Back to Me"
"You're the Cream in My Coffee"
"Crazy Rhythm"
"Button Up Your Overcoat"
"Love Me or Leave Me"
"Makin' Whoopee!"
"Sweet Lorraine"
"I'll Get By"
"I Can't Give You Anything but Love"
"Short'nin' Bread"
"Stout-Hearted Men"

Top Records

Sonny Boy (Al Jolson); *Ramona* (Gene Austin); *My Yiddishe Momme* (Sophie Tucker); *Was It a Dream?* (Dorsey Brothers Orchestra); *Laugh Clown, Laugh* (Ted Lewis); *Maybe My Maybe Don't Mean Maybe* (Paul Whiteman); *The Mooche* (Duke Ellington); *Blue Yodel* (Jimmie Rodgers)

Jazz and Big Bands

Soloists gain importance: Coleman Hawkins, Benny Goodman, Gene Krupa, Fats Waller, Teddy Wilson, Johnny Hodges, Roy Eldridge, Bunny Berigan. Johnny Hodges joins Duke Ellington; Count Basie joins Walter Page's Blue Devils. Luis Russell plays at the Savoy Ballroom, Harlem.

First Recordings: Benny Goodman, as leader; Pinetop Smith's *Boogie Woogie,* Chicago

New Bands: Cab Calloway, Chicago; Rudy Vallee, New York

Theater

Broadway Openings

Plays

Strange Interlude (Eugene O'Neill), Lynn Fontanne, Glenn Anders, Tom Powers
Holiday (Philip Barry), Hope Williams
Marco Millions (Eugene O'Neill), Alfred Lunt, Morris Carnovsky, Dudley Digges
The Front Page (Ben Hecht, Charles MacArthur), Lee Tracy, Osgood Perkins, Dorothy Stickney
Machinal (Sophie Treadwell), Clark Gable
The Age of Innocence (Margaret Ayer Barnes), Katharine Cornell, Franchot Tone, Rollo Peters
The Kingdom of God (G. Martinez Sierra), Ethel Barrymore
The Big Fight (Milton Herbert Gropper), Estelle Taylor, Jack Dempsey (Mr. and Mrs. Dempsey)
The Patriot (Alfred Neumann), Lyn Harding, John Gielgud (U.S. debut)
Brothers (Herbert Ashton, Jr.), Bert Lytell (dual role)
Diamond Lil (Mae West), Mae West (closed by police)
Maya (Simon Gantillon), Aline MacMahon (closed by police)

Musicals

The New Moon (Sigmund Romberg, Oscar Hammerstein II), Evelyn Herbert, Robert Halliday
Blackbirds of 1928 (Jimmy McHugh, Dorothy Fields), Bill Robinson, Adelaide Hall, The Plantation Orchestra
Animal Crackers (Harry Ruby, Bert Kalmar), Marx Brothers, Margaret Dumont
Whoopee (Walter Donaldson, Gus Kahn), Eddie Cantor, Ruth Etting
The Three Musketeers (Rudolph Friml, P. G. Wodehouse, Clifford Grey), Dennis King, Vivienne Segal
Rosalie (George Gershwin, Sigmund Romberg, P. G. Wodehouse, Ira Gershwin), Marilyn Miller, Frank Morgan, Jack Donahue
Earl Carroll's Vanities (Morris Hamilton), W. C. Fields, Lillian Roth, Vincent Lopez Orchestra
Present Arms (Richard Rodgers, Lorenz Hart), Charles King, Busby Berkeley, Flora LeBreton

Classics and Revivals On and Off Broadway

Volpone (Ben Jonson), Alfred Lunt, Dudley Digges; *The Cherry Orchard* (Chekhov), Alla Nazimova; *The Merry Wives of Windsor,* Mrs. Fiske, Otis Skinner; *The Merchant of Venice,* George Arliss, Peggy Wood; *She Stoops to Conquer* (Goldsmith), Fay Bainter

Pulitzer Prize

Strange Interlude, Eugene O'Neill

Classical Music

Compositions
Virgil Thomson, *Symphony on a Hymn Tune, Four Saints in Three Acts*
Frank S. Converse, *California*
Douglas Moore, *Moby Dick*
Roy Harris, Piano Sonata
John Alden Carpenter, String Quartet

Important Events
Albert Stoessel and the Oratorio Society debut at Carnegie Hall with the Bach B minor Mass.
The New York and Philharmonic Symphonies merge; Arturo Toscanini become director of the New York Philharmonic. Béla Bartók is soloist in the first New York performance of his Piano Concerto no. 1. Frequently performed are works by Carlos Chávez (New York, San Francisco, Chicago); Adolph Weiss and Charles Ives (New York, San Francisco); Nicolas Slonimsky (Boston): Igor Stravinsky (*Oedipus Rex,* Boston, New York); Bloch's *America* is performed by 20 orchestras.

Theodore Dreiser. *Library of Congress.*

Guest conductors
Guest conductors at the Philadelphia Orchestra: Fritz Reiner, Ossip Gabrilowitch, Willem Mengelberg, Frederick Stock, Thomas Beecham, Pierre Monteux. Under Reiner, Bartók performs his Rhapsody for Piano and Orchestra.

Debuts: Thomas Beecham, Andrés Segovia, Maurice Ravel, José Iturbi, Ruggiero Ricci. Vladimir Horowitz, 23, debuts at Carnegie Hall; he and Sir Thomas Beecham perform the Tchaikovsky B-flat minor concerto at tempos different from each other.

First Performances
Walter Piston, *Symphonic Piece* (Boston); George Gershwin, playing, *An American in Paris* (New York); Randall Thompson, *Jazz Poem* (Rochester, N.Y.); David Mason, *Chanticleer Overture* (Cincinnati)

Opera

Metropolitan: Lucrezia Bori, *La rondine* (Puccini, premiere); Maria Jeritza, *Die aegyptische Helena* (Richard Strauss, premiere); *Carmen*; Elisabeth Rethberg, Giovanni Martinelli, *La campana sommersa* (Respighi, premiere); Beniamino Gigli, *Manon;* Grace Moore, *La Bohème*

Jolson Theater, New York: *L'histoire du soldat* (Igor Stravinsky, premiere)

Chicago, Ravinia: *Marouf* (Henri Rabaud, premiere)

Philadelphia: *Ariadne auf Naxos* (Richard Strauss, American premiere)

San Francisco: Ezio Pinza, *L'amore dei tre re*

Music Notes
The "Leaderless Orchestra" in New York debuts, in which each member "can express himself" • The Beethoven Symphony disbands • Artur Bodanzky resigns • Percy Grainger marries a Swedish woman in a public ceremony at the Hollywood Bowl. They stand at a lighted cross atop the mountain, and then he conducts "To a Nordic Princess" before 22,000 people.

Art

Painting

Charles Demuth, *I Saw the Figure Five in Gold*
Charles Sheeler, *River Rouge Industrial Plant*
Thomas Hart Benton, *Loading Louisiana Rice Fields*
Kenneth Hayes Miller, *Shopper*
John Steuart Curry, *Baptism in Kansas*
Edward Hopper, *From Williamsburg Bridge*
John Sloan, *Sixth Avenue Elevated at Third Street*
Max Weber, *Tranquility*
John Kane, *Fourth of July Parade*
Georgia O'Keeffe, *New York Night*
Arshile Gorky, *Composition, Horse and Figures*
Edwin Dickinson, *The Fossil Hunters*
Marsden Hartley, *The Window*

Sculpture

Gaston Lachaise, *Dancer, John Marin*
Alexander Calder, *The Horse, Sow, The Hostess, Elephant Chain with Lamp, Soda Fountain*

Architecture

New York Life Insurance Company, New York (Cass Gilbert)
Radburn, N.J., plan (Clarence Stein and Henry Wright)
House of 2089 project (William Lescaze)
Merchandise Mart, Chicago (Graham, Anderson, Probst, and White)
Fisher Building, Detroit (Albert Kahn)
333 North Michigan Building, Chicago (Holabird and Root)
Grant's Tomb, New York, design (Duncan and Pope)

Charles Demuth, *I Saw the Figure Five in Gold*, 1928. Oil. 36 × 29¾". *The Metropolitan Museum of Art, The Alfred Stieglitz Collection.*

Important Exhibitions

Museums

New York: *Metropolitan:* French Gothic tapestries; Spanish paintings from El Greco to Goya; international ceramic arts

Chicago: George Inness

Philadelphia: Portraits of the seventeenth through the nineteenth centuries

Washington: *Corcoran:* Contemporary American art, including Bernard Karfiol, Henry Lee McFee, Frederick C. Frieseke, Eugene Speicher

San Francisco: Comprehensive sculpture exhibit with 1,500 works

Boston: Decorative arts of Europe and America (on display in its new wing)

San Antonio: Texas wild flowers, ranch life

Pittsburgh: Carnegie International First Prize: Henri Matisse

Art Briefs

Giorgio de Chirico holds his first American one-man show in New York • Alexander Calder has his first one-man show of wire animals and caricatures in New York • Department stores, such as New York's Macy's, Abraham and Strauss, and Lord and Taylor, hold public exhibits of modernist art • After a long trial, a customs court determines that Constantin Brancusi's *Bird in Space* can enter the United States as a duty-free work of art rather than a manufactured object, despite its nonrepresentational nature.

Dance

Le sacre du printemps (Léonide Massine, Stravinsky) is staged in Philadelphia and New York with the Philadelphia Symphony Orchestra and Martha Graham in the lead role.

Books

Fiction

Critics' Choice

The Children, Edith Wharton
Good-bye, Wisconsin, Glenway Wescott
The Island Within, Ludwig Lewisohn
The Bishop's Wife, Robert Nathan
Nothing Is Sacred, Josephine Herbst
Strange Fugitive, Morley Callaghan
🍂 *Lady Chatterley's Lover*, D. H. Lawrence, expurgated ed.
🍂 *Swann's Way, The Past Regained*, Marcel Proust
🍂 *Point Counterpoint*, Aldous Huxley

Best-Sellers

The Bridge of San Luis Rey, Thornton Wilder
Wintersmoon, Hugh Walpole
Swan Song, John Galsworthy
The Greene Murder Case, S. S. Van Dine
Bad Girl, Viña Delmar
Claire Ambler, Booth Tarkington
Old Pybus, Warwick Deeping
All Kneeling, Anne Parrish
Jalna, Mazo de la Roche
The Strange Case of Miss Annie Spragg, Louis Bromfield
Strange Interlude (play), Eugene O'Neill

Nonfiction

Critics' Choice

Coming of Age in Samoa, Margaret Mead
The Happy Warrior, Alfred E. Smith
The New Russia, Theodore Dreiser
The Rediscovery of America, Waldo Frank
Anthropology and Modern Life, Franz Boaz
Life of Lincoln, Albert J. Beveridge
The Art of the Dance, Isadora Duncan (posthumous)
Psychological Care of Infant and Child, John B. Watson
🍂 *The Nature of the Physical World*, A. S. Eddington

Best-Sellers

Disraeli, André Maurois
Mother India, Katherine Mayo
Trader Horn, vol I, Alfred Aloysius Horn, Ethelreda Lewis
Napoleon, Emil Ludwig
We, Charles A. Lindbergh
Count Luckner, the Sea Devil, Lowell Thomas
Goethe, Emil Ludwig
Skyward, Richard E. Byrd

The Intelligent Woman's Guide to Socialism and Capitalism, George Bernard Shaw

Poetry

Edwin Arlington Robinson, *Sonnets 1889–1927*
Robert Frost, *West-Running Brook*
Archibald MacLeish, *The Hamlet of A. MacLeish*
Allen Tate, *Mr. Pope and Other Poems*
Ezra Pound, *A Draft of Cantos XVII to XXVII*
Robinson Jeffers, *Cawdor and Other Poems*
Edna St. Vincent Millay, *The Buck in the Snow*
🍂 W. B. Yeats, *The Tower*

Pulitzer Prizes

Scarlet Sister Mary, Julia Peterkin (novel)
The Organization and Administration of the Union Army, 1861–1865, Fred A. Shannon (U.S. history)
The Training of an American, The Earlier Life and Letters of Walter H. Page, Burton J. Hendrick (biography)
John Brown's Body, Stephen Vincent Benét (poetry)

Science-Technology

Milton Humason begins to measure the speed of stars, at the 100-inch Mt. Palomar telescope.

Margaret Mead's anthropological study of Samoans indicates that more tolerant attitudes about sex among the islanders have beneficial social effects.

E. Herzfeld discovers Pagarsardae, the Persian capital prior to Persepolis.

George Papanicolau develops a test for early detection of uterine cancer, the "Pap" test.

Oscar Riddle discovers the pituitary (postpartum) milk-releasing hormone.

GE and RCA hold the first public demonstration of home television sets in Schenectady, N.Y.;

W2XCW, Schenectady, becomes the first regularly broadcasting station.

Vladimir Zworykin perfects the kinescope, a television receiver.

The first animated electric sign, on the *New York Times* building, begins operation.

🍂 Alexander Fleming observes a mold, penicillin, that destroys bacteria.

🍂 Albert Szent-Györgi isolates vitamin C.

🍂 The Ascheim-Zondek urine pregnancy test is developed.

Meetings between heroes of different sports captivate the public. Left: Johnny Weismuller gives swimming advice to Jack Dempsey. *Library of Congress.*

Baseball

Ty Cobb retires with lifetime records of 4,191 hits, .367 BA, and 892 stolen bases. Babe Ruth bats a record .625 in the World Series.

Champions

Batting	Pitching
Rogers Hornsby (St. Louis, NL), .387	L. Benton (New York, NL), 25–9
Goose Goslin (Washington, AL), .397	Lefty Grove (Philadelphia, AL), 20–6
	Alvin Crowder (St. Louis, AL), 21–5
	Home runs
	Babe Ruth (New York, AL), 54

Football

Pro Stars: Jim Conzelman (Providence), Ben Friedman (Detroit)

College All-Americans: Ken Strong (F), New York University; Chris Cagle (H), Army

Rose Bowl (Jan. 1, 1929): Georgia Tech 8–California 7

Basketball

The Brooklyn Celtics win the ABL for the second year.

Sports

Olympics

The Olympics are held in Amsterdam. U.S. winners include Ray Barbuti (400m, 47.8s), Edward Hamm (broad jump, 25′4 ¾″), Sabin Carr (pole vault, 13′9 ¾″), John Kuck (shot put, 52′ 11/16″), Clarence Howser (discus, 155′ 2 ⅘″), Elizabeth Robinson (100m, 12.2s), Johnny Weismuller (swimming, 400m), Albina Osipowich (swimming, 100m), Martha Norelius (swimming, 400m).

Other Sports

Boxing: Gene Tunney beats Tom Heeney in a title defense, gains a $525,000 purse, retires, and marries an heiress.

Swimming: Johnny Weismuller retires, having set 67 world records and won three Olympic gold medals.

Hockey: Les Patrick, 44-year-old New York Rangers coach, plays goalie in one Stanley Cup game.

Winners

World Series	*Player of the Year*
New York (AL) 4	Vic Holt, Oklahoma
St. Louis (NL) 0	*Stanley Cup*
MVP	New York Rangers
NL–Jim Bottomly, St. Louis	*U.S. Tennis Open*
AL–Gordon Cochrane, Philadelphia	Men: Henri Cochet
	Women: Helen Wills
NFL	*USGA Open*
Providence Steamrollers	Johnny Farrell
College Football	*Kentucky Derby*
Georgia Tech	Reigh Count (E. Lang, jockey)
College Basketball	
Pittsburgh	

Fashion

For Men: The Chaplin mustache is replaced by the John Gilbert pencil-line style with waxed tips. Valentino sideburns are now rarely seen as men part their hair in the middle and apply pomades. The more mature man, in his square-cut jacket, wears bold, checked patterns, and his silhouette complements that of his escort, whose loose, shapeless chemise emphasizes the broad-shouldered, slim-hipped line. The gentleman's formal dress consists of an Oxford gray morning coat with squared collar of natural width, notched lapels, and one button. For slightly less formal occasions he wears a morning coat with ribbed silk and silk-covered buttons, and pleatless trousers with a slight break over the instep. The well-dressed man has at least six pairs of shoes (*Esquire*), including two-tone saddles for the active sports look; blue, dark gray, or lightweight brown shoes for country wear; plain brown shoes for informal business and travel; dark reddish brown, patterned shoes for conservative suits; and spectators for flannels and washable fabrics.

High-fashion note: Worth tweeds

Kaleidoscope _____

- The continuing veneration of business is apparent in the noticeable growth of college business courses and service clubs, such as Rotary and Kiwanis.
- Speakeasies host a new mix of people: women in the carriage trade, alongside women in the skin trade.
- By the end of the year, 78 percent of the world's motor vehicles—21,630,000 cars and 3,120,000 trucks—are on U.S. roads.
- Real wages (adjusted for inflation) are up 33 percent from 1914.
- The Methodist Board of Temperance, Prohibition, and Public Morals reports that high school and college students are drinking at parties and dances and in hotels and parked cars.
- Various devices that provide entrance to speakeasies include ringing bells, sliding door panels, cabalistic signatures, and passwords like "Joe sent me."
- Al Smith's wet attitudes and Catholicism are major election issues.
- Hoover, "the great engineer," promises a chicken in every pot and two cars in every garage.
- Five states of the solid South vote Republican.
- Of the 231 members of the Academy Awards selection body, only Mary Pickford, Douglas Fairbanks, Louis B. Mayer, Sid Grauman, and Joe Schenck vote. "Oscar" is designed by Cedric Gibbons.
- Broadway stars who leave for Hollywood include Claudette Colbert, Clark Gable, Barbara Stanwyck, Cary Grant, Paul Muni, Chester Morris, Lee Tracy, and Miriam Hopkins.
- Walt Disney produces *Galloping Gaucho* and *Steamboat Willie,* the first cartoons with sound.
- Personal loans are initiated by National City Bank of New York.
- Brokers' loans to stock market margin investors reach a record $4 billion.
- Three car mergers take place: Chrysler and Dodge, Studebaker and Pierce-Arrow, Chandler and Cleveland.

- Five women employed in a New Jersey factory are poisoned by radium and are awarded $10,000, medical costs, and their pension.
- Dutch Schultz gives up bartending to join the mob in beer running; he begins his association with the Maddens, Costellos, and "Legs" Diamond.
- The Feds and Coast Guard arrest 75,000 people a year for Prohibition violations.
- The Treasury Department fires 706 Prohibition agents and prosecutes 257 for taking bribes.
- Speakeasies, like Texas Guinan's and Helen Morgan's, feature torch singers who sit on top of pianos; Helen Morgan popularizes "Can't Help Lovin' Dat Man" and "Why Was I Born?"
- Al Jolson's "Sonny Boy" sells 12 million copies in four weeks.
- Eleven-year-old Yehudi Menuhin goes East from California and astonishes audiences with his performances of the Beethoven and Tchaikovsky violin concertos.
- *Abie's Irish Rose,* the most popular play in Broadway history, closes after 2,400 performances.
- Crooner Rudy Vallee opens at New York's Heigh-Ho Club with a megaphone to amplify his voice.
- North Carolina governor May O. Gardner blames dieting women for the drop in farm prices.
- A thousand crew members gather on the USS *Utah* and sing "Let Me Call You Sweetheart," as President-Elect and Mrs. Hoover return from a Christmas cruise.
- An Ohio University study catalogs undergraduate words that refer to an unpopular girl; expressions include *pill, pickle, priss, drag, rag, oilcan, flat tire,* and *nutcracker.* A popular girl is a *peach, whiz, sweet patootie, pippin, choice bit of calico,* and *snappy piece of work.*

Fads: Ninety-one couples last three weeks in the $5,000 "Dance Derby of the Century"; after 482 hours, it is closed down. Other fads include talkathons and travel. Steeplejack and flagpole sitter Howard Williams ties for first place in a talk marathon, a "Noun and Verb Rodeo" that lasts 81 hours and 45 minutes.

First Appearances: Peter Pan peanut butter, peanut butter cracker sandwiches, Rice Krispies, Nehi, adhesive tape, *Modern Mechanics,* Barricini candy, shredded wheat, Philco radios, quartz clock, Frog-Jumping Jubilee, Mickey Mouse, diesel electric freight locomotives, night coaches (Yelloway), someone going over Niagara Falls in a rubber ball, fully automated film developing machinery, *Oxford English Dictionary,* Bryce Canyon National Park, Newark airport, Plymouth, DeSoto, Marcel Breuer chair

Walt Disney's popular rodent debuts in *Steamboat Willie,* with Disney himself recording Mickey's voice. *Movie Star News.*

1929

Economic Profile
  Dow-Jones: ↑↓ High
    381–Low 198
  GNP: +6%
  Inflation: 0.0%
  Unemployment: 3.2%
Police expenditures, federal,
  state, and local: $320
  million
Prisoners, federal and state:
  120,000
Executions: 155
Paroles, federal and state:
  24,008
Furniture (W&J Sloane):
  Upholstered armchair:
    $24.50–$50
  Martha Washington serving
    table: $19.50
  Windsor chair: $7.75–$40
  Persian rug: $44–$55
Furniture (Wanamaker):
  Dining room suite: $110–
    $330
  Lounging chair: $200–$333
Isphahan rug (Stern's): $289
Flower bulbs, hyacinths: 68¢
  (doz.)

Deaths
David Buick, Georges
  Clemenceau, Sergei
  Diaghilev, Jeanne Eagels,
  Joseph Goldberger, Robert
  Henri, Hugo von
  Hofmannsthal, Lillie
  Langtry, Thorstein Veblen.

In the News —————

FEDERAL RESERVE HALTS LOANS FOR MARGIN SPECULATION . . .
CRUISER ACT AUTHORIZES NEW WARSHIPS . . . SEVEN "BUGS"
MORAN ASSOCIATES ARE MACHINE-GUNNED TO DEATH ON ST.
VALENTINE'S DAY . . . CONGRESS PASSES SEVERE PENALTIES FOR
VOLSTEAD VIOLATIONS . . . ALBERT FALL, FORMER SECRETARY OF
INTERIOR, IS CONVICTED FOR TEAPOT DOME FRAUD . . . LEON
TROTSKY IS EXPELLED FROM U.S.S.R. . . . AGRICULTURAL
MARKETING ACT ALLOCATES $500 MILLION FOR PRICE SUPPORTS . . .
KELLOGG-BRIAND PACT IS RATIFIED BY SENATE, OUTLAWRY OF WAR
IS PROCLAIMED . . . MISSISSIPPI LYNCH MOB OF 2,000 BURNS
ACCUSED NEGRO . . . CHARLES LINDBERGH MARRIES DIPLOMAT'S
DAUGHTER, ANNE MORROW . . . THREE DIE IN STRIKE AT GASTONIA
MILLS, SOUTH CAROLINA . . . STOCK MARKET REACHES ALL-TIME
HIGH, 381 . . . CHARLES MITCHELL, OF FIRST NATIONAL CITY BANK,
DECLARES ECONOMY SOUND . . . STOCK MARKET PLUMMETS, 19
MILLION SHARES ARE SOLD . . . MARKET CRASHES, SELLING PANIC
CONTINUES, BILLIONS ARE LOST OVERNIGHT . . . HOOVER AFFIRMS
CONFIDENCE IN AMERICAN BUSINESS . . . ADMIRAL BYRD FLIES OVER
SOUTH POLE.

Wall Street
hysteria began on
Black Thursday,
October 24th
(*left*), and peaked
on Black
Tuesday, October
29th. *Library of
Congress.*

Quotes _____

Before the Crash

"[This] has been a twelvemonth of unprecedented advance, of wonderful prosperity. . . . If there is any way of judging the future by the past, this new year may well be one of felicitation and hopefulness."
— Herbert Hoover

"If a man saves $15 a week and invests in good common stocks, . . . at the end of 20 years, he will have at least $80,000 and . . . $400 a month. He will be rich. And because income can do that, I am firm in my belief that anyone not only can be rich, but ought to be rich."
— John T. Raskob, former top executive, General Motors, and chairman, Democratic National Committee

After the Crash

"Any lack of confidence in the economic future of the basic strength of business in the United States is foolish."
— Herbert Hoover

"[There is just] a little distress selling on the Stock Exchange."
— Financier Thomas Lamont, after leaving the offices of J. P. Morgan

John D. Rockefeller says, during the Crash: "[I see] nothing to warrant the destruction of values. . . . My son and I have . . . been purchasing sound common stocks." *Library of Congress.*

*

"Nobody shot me."
— Dying Moran gang member, St. Valentine's Day

"[Women] must pay for everything. . . . They do get more glory than men for comparable feats. But, also, women get more notoriety when they crash."
— Amelia Earhart

"The report has gotten out that Miss [Marion] Davies has a pronounced lisp, which may have caused the scrapping of the talkie version."
— *Photoplay,* discussing *The Five O'Clock Girl*

"The hope [college students] . . . cherish is not that of ingesting in culture, but that of increasing in efficiency."
— Editorial, *American Mercury*

"The legitimate theatre is in a panic . . . [with] talking pictures . . . [and] all their seats at the same price. . . . Get it? The rich man stands in line with the poor."
— Lloyd Lewis, *New Republic*

Ads _____

Radio

Premieres

"The Back Home Hour" (Billy Sunday)

"Fleischmann Hour," Rudy Vallee (first radio variety)

"La Palma Smokers' Program" (with leading entertainers)

"H. V. Kaltenborn News"

"The Rise of the Goldbergs," Gertrude Berg

"Headline Hunters," Floyd Gibbons, Lowell Thomas

"The Hour of Charm," Phil Spitalny and His All-Girl Orchestra, Arlene Frances (emcee)

"Blackstone Plantation," Frank Crumit, Julia Sanderson

"First Nighter," Charles P. Hughes (host), Don Ameche, June Meredith (drama)

"Amos 'n' Andy," Freeman Gosden, Charles Correll (network)

Specials

"Symphonic Music from Queen's Hall" (first shortwave broadcast from London); "Over and Under New York" (airplane broadcast, parachutist describing his descent); "Leopold Stokowski conducts *Sacre du printemps*" (Philadelphia Orchestra).

Of Note

CBS is founded by William S. Paley, age 27 • Rudy Vallee, the "Vagabond Lover," opens each show with "Heigh-Ho, everybody" and closes with "Your Time Is My Time" • Arthur Godfrey debuts on a Baltimore amateur hour.

New Catchphrases: "I'se regusted!" "Holy mackerel, Andy!" "Now ain't that sumpin'!" (Amos 'n' Andy, of the Mystic Knights of the Sea Lodge)

Movies

Openings

The Broadway Melody (Harry Beaumont), Anita Page, Bessie Love, Charles King

In Old Arizona (Raoul Walsh), Warner Baxter, Edmund Lowe

Pandora's Box (G. W. Pabst), Louise Brooks

Blackmail (Alfred Hitchcock), Anny Ondra, Sara Allgood

Coquette (Sam Taylor), Mary Pickford

The Last of Mrs. Cheyney (Sidney Franklin), Norma Shearer, Basil Rathbone, Hedda Hopper

Madame X (Lionel Barrymore), Ruth Chatterton, Lewis Stone, Sidney Toler

Rio Rita (Luther Reed), John Boles, Bebe Daniels

Sunny Side Up (David Butler), Janet Gaynor, Charles Farrell, Joe Brown

The Four Feathers (Merian C. Cooper, Ernest Schoedsack), Richard Arlen, Fay Wray, William Powell

The Love Parade (Ernst Lubitsch), Maurice Chevalier, Jeanette MacDonald, Lillian Roth

Hallelujah! (King Vidor), Daniel L. Haynes

The Taming of the Shrew (Sam Taylor), Douglas Fairbanks, Mary Pickford

Bulldog Drummond (F. Richard Jones), Ronald Colman, Joan Bennett

The Virginian (Victor Fleming), Gary Cooper, Walter Huston

The Letter (Jean De Limur), Jeanne Eagels, Reginald Owen, Herbert Marshall

Academy Awards (1928–29)

Best Picture: *The Broadway Melody*

Best Director: Frank Lloyd (*The Divine Lady*)

Best Actor: Warner Baxter (*In Old Arizona*)

Best Actress: Mary Pickford (*Coquette*)

Top Box-Office Stars

Clara Bow, Lon Chaney

The Marx Brothers—Zeppo, Groucho, Chico, and Harpo— film their first movie, *The Cocoanuts* (*above*), while starring on Broadway in *Animal Crackers*. *Movie Star News*.

Popular Music

Hit Songs
"Tiptoe through the Tulips"
"Singin' in the Rain"
"Honeysuckle Rose"
"Am I Blue?"
"More than You Know"
"Happy Days Are Here Again"
"I'm Just a Vagabond Lover"
"With a Song in My Heart"
"Ain't Misbehavin' "
"You Do Something to Me"
"Without a Song"
"Stardust"
"That Old Gang of Mine"

Top Records
Piccolo Pete (Ted Weems); *I Get the Blues When It Rains* (Guy Lombardo); *Why Was I Born?* and *Don't Ever Leave Me* (Helen Morgan); *My Kinda Love* and *Till We Meet Again* (Bing Crosby); *I'll Always Be in Love with You* (Morton Downey)

Jazz and Big Bands
The "golden era" of recording includes Armstrong's Hot Five and Hot Seven; Jelly Roll Morton and his Red Hot Peppers; Nichols and the Pennies; Bix and Trumbauer; Venuti and Lang.

New Bands: Shep Fields, New York; Glen Gray and the Casa Loma Orchestra

Popular Bands: Austin High Gang, Chicago; Duke Ellington, New York; Andy Kirk, Kansas City: Earl Hines, Chicago; Jimmy Lunceford, Memphis

Theater

Broadway Openings

Plays
Street Scene (Elmer Rice), Erin O'Brien-Moore, Mary Servoss, Beulah Bondi
Murder on the Second Floor (Frank Vasper), Laurence Olivier (first American role)
Journey's End (R. C. Sherriff), Leon Quartermaine, Colin Keith-Johnstone, Derek Williams
The First Mrs. Fraser (St. John Ervine), Grace George, A. E. Matthews
Young Sinners (Elmer Harris), Raymon Guion (Gene Raymond)
Death Takes a Holiday (Alberto Casella), Philip Merivale, Rose Hobart
Meteor (S. N. Behrman), Alfred Lunt, Lynn Fontanne
Candle Light (Siegfried Geyer), Leslie Howard, Gertrude Lawrence, Reginald Owen
Broken Dishes (Martin Flavin), Bette Davis
Serena Blandish (S. N. Behrman), Ruth Gordon
Dynamo (Eugene O'Neill), Claudette Colbert
Gypsy (Maxwell Anderson), Louis Calhern
Berkeley Square (John Balderston), Leslie Howard
June Moon (Ring Lardner, George S. Kaufman), Frank Otto, Jean Dixon

Musicals
Earl Carroll's Sketch Book (E. Y. Harburg, Jay Gorney), Will Mahoney, Patsy Kelly, William Demarest
Sons-O-Guns (J. Fred Coots, Arthur Swanstrom, Benny Davis), Jack Donahue, Lily Damita, William Frawley
Fifty Million Frenchmen (Cole Porter), William Gaxton, Genevieve Tobin, Betty Compton
Sweet Adeline (Jerome Kern, Oscar Hammerstein II), Helen Morgan, Irene Franklin, Charles Butterworth
Hot Chocolates (Thomas Waller, Harry Brooks), Jazz Lips Richardson, Jimmy Baskette, Louis Armstrong
The Street Singer (John Gilbert, Graham Johns), Queenie Smith, Guy Robertson
The Show Girl (George Gershwin, Ira Gershwin), Ruby Keeler, Jimmy Durante, Duke Ellington Orchestra

Classics and Revivals On and Off Broadway
Mrs. Bumpstead-Leigh (Henry James Smith), Mrs. Fiske; *The Lady from the Sea* (Ibsen), Blanche Yurka; *The Seagull* (Chekhov), Jacob Ben-Ami

Pulitzer Prize
Street Scene, Elmer Rice

Speakeasy queen Texas Guinan (*center*), who starred in Hollywood westerns before coming to New York. *Movie Star News*.

President Herbert Hoover. *Library of Congress*.

Classical Music

Compositions

Aaron Copland, *Dance Symphony, Vitebsk, Symphonic Ode*
Frank S. Converse, *American Sketches*
Samuel Barber, Serenade for String Quartet
Walter Piston, Viola Concerto
Roy Harris, Piano Sonata, *American Portraits*
George Antheil, *Transatlantic*

Important Events

Alexander Glazunov, on his first U.S. visit, conducts his symphony no. 6 in Detroit. Twenty-four perform at Carnegie Hall in the "Musicians' Gambol" for the MacDowell Colony.

Major Recitals: Andrés Segovia, José Iturbi, Walter Gieseking, Paul Robeson, Arthur Honneger, Alexander Glazunov, Vladimir Horowitz

Debuts: Nathan Milstein, Gregor Piatigorsky

First Performances

Leo Sowerby, Symphony no. 2 (Chicago, Alexander Glazunov conducting); Symphony no. 6 (Detroit); Anton Webern, *Symphonie* (New York); Frederick Stock, Cello Concerto (Chicago); Arnold Bax, Symphony No. 2 (Boston); Louis Gruenberg, *Jazz Suite* (Cincinnati)

Opera

Metropolitan: Gladys Swarthout (debut), *La Gioconda, Carmen;* return of Ernestine Schumann-Heink, 68, *Das Rheingold;* Ezio Pinza and Elisabeth Rethberg, *Don Giovanni;* Lauritz Melchior, *Tristan und Isolde*

Chicago: In new Opera House, Edith Mason, *Iris* (Mascagni); Rosa Raisa, *Otello*

Music Notes

Stravinsky's *Les noces* draws a $25,000 audience at the Met • Eugene Goossens leads the Rochester Civic Orchestra.

Art

Painting
Edward Hopper, *The Lighthouse at Two Lights*
Georgia O'Keeffe, *Blue Cross, Late George Window*
John Kane, *Self-Portrait*
Charles Sheeler, *Upper Deck*
Arshile Gorky, *The Artist and His Mother*
Charles Demuth, *Poppies, Corn and Peaches*
Grant Wood, *Woman with Plants, John B. Turner, Pioneer*
Lyonel Feininger, *Sailing Boats*
Thomas Hart Benton, *Georgia Cotton Pickers*
Guy Pène du Bois, *Woman with Cigarette*
Arthur G. Dove, *Distraction, Foghorns*

Sculpture
Alexander Calder, *Circus* (1927–29), *The Cow, The Brass Family, Josephine Baker*
Saul Baizerman, *Hod Carrier*
Isamu Noguchi, *Head of Martha Graham*
Paul Manship is commissioned to do an equestrian statue of General Grant.

Architecture
Lovell (Heath) House, Los Angeles (Richard Neutra)
Williamsburgh Savings Bank, New York (Halsey, McCormack, and Helmer)
Folger Shakespeare Library, Washington, D.C. (Paul Phillippe Cret)
Palmolive Building, Chicago (Holabird and Root)

Important Exhibitions

Museums

New York: *Metropolitan:* Chinese paintings of the Sung and Ming periods; the print collection; art deco; the architect and the industrial arts. *Museum of Modern Art:* A loan exhibit of the works of Cézanne, Seurat, Gauguin, van Gogh, and 19 living Americans (opening show)

Washington, Chicago, UCLA: Stuart Davis

Philadelphia, Minneapolis: American modernist art

San Francisco: American sculpture show (1,300 works)

Art Briefs
Modigliani has his first one-man show in New York • Gertrude Vanderbilt announces the founding of her museum, the Whitney Museum of American Art, which will be temporarily housed at 8 and 10 West 8th Street, New York • The American Artists' Professional League tries unsuccessfully to legislate a protective tariff on contemporary foreign art.

Dance

Atlanta Ballet starts as the Dorothy Alexander Concert Group. Martha Graham dances in *Heretic.*

Edward Hopper, *The Lighthouse at Two Lights,* 1929. Oil on canvas. 29½ × 43¼". *The Metropolitan Museum of Art Purchase, Hugo Rastor Fund, 1962.*

Horn and Hardart cafeteria in art deco style, Philadelphia. *Smithsonian Institution.*

Books

Fiction

Critics' Choice

The Sound and the Fury, William Faulkner
Sartoris, William Faulkner
A Farewell to Arms, Ernest Hemingway
Look Homeward, Angel, Thomas Wolfe
Hudson River Bracketed, Edith Wharton
The Way of Ecben, James Branch Cabell
Round Up, Ring Lardner
Cup of Gold, John Steinbeck
I Thought of Daisy, Edmund Wilson
Bottom Dogs, Edward Dahlberg
❯ *Lady Chatterley's Lover*, D. H. Lawrence, unabridged ed.

Best-Sellers

All Quiet on the Western Front, Erich Maria Remarque
Dodsworth, Sinclair Lewis
Dark Hester, Anne Douglas Sedgwick
The Bishop Murder Case, S. S. Van Dine
Roper's Row, Warwick Deeping
Peder Victorious, O. E. Rölvaag
Mamba's Daughters, DuBose Heyward
The Galaxy, Susan Ertz
Scarlet Sister Mary, Julia Peterkin
Joseph and His Brethren, H. W. Freeman

Nonfiction

Critics' Choice

The Modern Temper, Joseph Wood Krutch
Midstream: My Later Life, Helen Keller
The International Jurisdiction, Henry Morgenthau
Middletown, Robert Lynd, Helen Lynd
Is Sex Necessary? E. B. White, James Thurber
A Quest for Certainty, John Dewey
Men and Machines, Stuart Chase
Are We Civilized? R. H. Lowie
❯ *What Is Philosophy?* Martin Heidegger
❯ *Marriage and Morals*, Bertrand Russell

Best-Sellers

The Art of Thinking, Ernest Dimnet
Henry the Eighth, Francis Hackett
The Cradle of the Deep, Joan Lowell
Elizabeth and Essex, Lytton Strachey
The Specialist, Chic Sale
A Preface to Morals, Walter Lippmann
Believe It or Not, Robert L. Ripley
John Brown's Body (poetry), Stephen Vincent Benét
The Mansions of Philosophy, Will Durant
The Tragic Era, Claude G. Bowers

Poetry

Vachel Lindsay, *Every Soul Is a Circus*
Robinson Jeffers, *Dear Judas*
Edgar Lee Masters, *The Fate of the Jury*
Louise Bogan, *Dark Summer*
Countée Cullen, *The Black Christ*
Eleanor Wylie, *Angels and Earthly Creatures*
Edwin Arlington Robinson, *Cavender's House, The Prodigal Son*
Emily Dickinson, *Further Poems* (posthumous)

Pulitzer Prizes

Laughing Boy, Oliver La Farge (novel)
The War of Independence, Claude H. Van Tyne (U.S. history)
The Raven, Marquis James (biography)
Selected Poems, Conrad Aiken (poetry)

Science and Technology

Robert and Helen Lynd apply anthropological methods to the study of a small American city, Muncie, Indiana, in *Middletown*.
Edward Doisy isolates the female sex hormone estrogen in pure form.
George W. Corner, Rochester, isolates the female hormone progesterone.
Hypertension and heart disease are shown to be related by Samuel Levine, Harvard.
Manfred Sakel reports that overdoses of insulin in order to produce coma are successful in the treatment of schizophrenia.

Lt. James Doolittle pilots a plane solely on instruments.
Dunlop Rubber Company produces foam rubber—latex whipped with liquid soap.
❯ Alexander Fleming treats a skin infection successfully with penicillin, its first clinical trial; the absence of a pure, concentrated form makes use of the substance limited.
❯ Albert Einstein proposes the unified field theory.

Sports

Baseball

Babe Ruth (New York, AL) hits his 500th home run. Lefty O'Doul (Philadelphia, NL) gets a record 254 hits.

Champions

Batting	Pitching
Lefty O'Doul (Philadelphia, NL), .398	Charles Root (Chicago, NL), 19–6
Lew Fonseca (Cleveland, AL), .369	Lefty Grove (Philadelphia, AL), 20–6
	Home runs
	Babe Ruth (New York, AL), 46

Football

Ernie Nevers (FB) scores all 40 points in the Chicago Cardinal 40–0 defeat of the Chicago Bears.
The Rose Bowl at Pasadena draws 101,000. Roy Riegels, California center, runs 60 yards the wrong way with a fumble.

Pro Stars: Blood McNally, Verne Lewellen (Green Bay)

College All-Americans: Frank Carideo (Q), Notre Dame; Bronko Nagurski (T), Minnesota

Rose Bowl (Jan. 1, 1930): Southern California 47–Pittsburgh 7

Basketball

The Cleveland Rosenblums win the ABL with the Original Celtics' Joe Lapchik, Pete Barry, and Dutch Dehnert on the team.

Tennis star Bill Tilden wins his seventh U.S. Open. *Movie Star News.*

Other Sports

Tennis: Helen Wills wins the U.S. Open and Wimbledon, each for the third consecutive time.

Winners

World Series	*Player of the Year*
Philadelphia (AL) 4	J. A. Thompson, Montana State
Chicago (NL) 1	
MVP	*Stanley Cup*
NL–Rogers Hornsby, St. Louis	Boston
AL–Al Simmons, Philadelphia	*U.S. Tennis Open*
	Men: William Tilden II
NFL	Women: Helen Wills
Green Bay Packers	*USGA Open*
College Football	Robert T. Jones, Jr.
Notre Dame	*Kentucky Derby*
College Basketball	Clyde Van Dusen (L. McAtee, jockey)
Montana State	

Fashion

For Women: The flapper look passes as hems begin to fall and more body curves appear. Jean Patou drops the evening hem to the floor; backless, sleeveless frocks with panels or drapes lengthen to the ankle; all have a V neck. Undergarments change: flowery slips with bra tops appear, some with a shaped band at the waist and attached knickers. The bosom also makes its reappearance in the corset with "breast pockets." In addition to the unisex "sun tan bathing suits" (black, one piece, with buttons up the back), women buy the new backless style, cut in front with an X halter, or the racy white or orange jersey-top suit with black taffeta trunks. Beauty shops open for facials and pomades; face lifting is popularized. Women use, yearly, one pound of powder, eight rouge compacts, and countless face creams and lipsticks, like Mme. Rubinstein's crushed rose leaves (geranium) "for the convervative woman" and "Georgine Lachtee" if "muscles droop."

High-fashion note: Boulanger chiffon evening dress.

For Men: The ice-cream suit in husky diagonal tweeds for Ivy Leaguers.

Kaleidoscope

- On September 3, the big bull market peaks; on November 13, it reaches bottom; within a few weeks of "Black Tuesday," unemployment rises from 700,000 to 3.1 million.
- An estimated 4.5 million people put money into "investment trusts," brokerage offerings that speculate for them; there are 70,950 stockbrokers in the United States (26,609 in 1920).
- Frank Billings Kellogg receives the Nobel Peace Prize for the Kellogg-Briand Pact outlawing war.
- Commenting on contemporary mores, two prominent authors write: "If love has come to be less often a sin, it has also come to be less often a supreme privilege" (Joseph Wood Krutch, *The Modern Temper*), and "If you start with the belief that love is a pleasure of a moment, is it really surprising that it yields only a momentary pleasure?" (Walter Lippmann, *A Preface to Morals*).
- "Come on, suckers," begins Texas Guinan's famous invitation, "open up and spend some jack."
- At least 32,000 speakeasies thrive in New York City; especially popular are Jack and Charlie's, Texas Guinan's Three Hundred, and Belle Livingston's Country Club, all of which promise no danger from "jake foot," the disguised authorities. The Midwest has corresponding "beer flats," blind pigs," and "shock houses."
- Calvin Coolidge is elected director of the New York Life Insurance Company.
- The "Age of the Car" is manifest throughout the country in the marked increase in red and green lights, one-way streets, stop signs, parking regulations, and traffic.
- Several men, dressed like police, tell the Bugs Moran gang to "put your noses to the wall," then they spray them with bullets (St. Valentine's Day Massacre).
- Al Capone serves a year in Philadelphia on a weapons-carrying charge; it is widely believed that he governs his crime empire from his cell.
- The sister of Charles Lindbergh's fiancée, Constance Morrow, like others prominent in the news, is threatened with kidnapping; Lindbergh flies the family to Maine.
- "Air Way Limited" provides coast-to-coast commercial travel in only 48 hours by a combination of plane and overnight train.
- The Museum of Modern Art is founded by Abby Aldrich Rockefeller, Lizzie P. Bliss, and Mary Sullivan at 730 Fifth Avenue, New York.
- Because of the zeppelin's success, plans for the Empire State Building include a mooring mast as a dirigible way station 1,300 feet above the ground.
- Commander Richard E. Byrd plants a U.S. flag on the South Pole.
- President Hoover becomes a Tenderfoot Boy Scout; he also dresses like a cowboy and an Indian.
- "Amos 'n' Andy" is so popular that at resorts like Atlantic City, loudspeakers broadcast the show.
- Of the 20,500 movie theaters in the United States, the

With typical public charm, Al Capone (*left*) greets the respected Chicago chief of detectives, John Stege. *Library of Congress.*

number with sound facilities increases during the year from 1,300 to 9,000.
- Following the Crash, New York mayor Jimmy Walker urges movie houses to show cheerful pictures.
- Al Jolson tries to help his wife, Ruby Keeler, in her first role in *Show Girl* by appearing nightly in the aisle and singing "Liza" as she tap dances.
- Admission to New York theaters ranges from 35¢ to $2.50.
- Movie musicals are in vogue, such as *Broadway Melody, The Golddiggers of Broadway, Desert Song,* and *The Singing Fool.*
- Archie Leach (Cary Grant) stars in two Broadway musicals, *A Wonder Night* and *Boom Boom.* Guy Lombardo and the Royal Canadians open at the Hotel Roosevelt, New York.
- German Kurt Barthel sets up in New Jersey the first American nudist colony with three married couples.
- Goucher College girls are permitted to smoke.
- Robert Maynard Hutchins, 30, becomes president of the University of Chicago.
- A Baltimore survey discovers rickets in 30 percent of its children.

First Appearances: Paper money of the present size, American League for Physical Culture (nudist organization), automatic electric stock-quotation board, high-speed telegraph ticker, John Reed Club, Blue Cross Health Insurance (Dallas), Convention Hall in Atlantic City, New York Central, Bendix, Chicago Union Carbide, Riverside Church (New York), Temple Emanuel (New York), Temple Rodeph Sholom (New York), Herblock, "Popeye," Oscar Meyer wieners trademark, auto sun roof, Delta, Chevrolet 6 cylinder, Ford station wagon with boxed wood panels, mobile home trailer (Hudson), aluminum furniture, front-wheel drive (Auburn), gas range, electric food disposal, *Business Week,* 7-Up ("Lithiated Lemon"), Nestlé Colorinse in ten shades, auto radio (Motorola), Federated Department Stores, Conoco

THE *Thirties*

"Hoovervilles" in New York's Central Park, shantytowns built in the shadow of luxury. *Museum of the City of New York.*

Statistics

Vital
Population: 123,188,000
  Urban/Rural: 69/54
  Farm: 24.9%
Life expectancy
  Male: 58.1
  Female: 61.6
Births/1,000: 21.3
Marriages/1,000: 9.2
Divorces/1,000: 1.6
Deaths/1,000: 11.3
  per 100,000
    Heart: 414
    Cancer: 97
    Tuberculosis: 71
    Car accidents: 26.7

Economic
Unemployed: 4,340,000
GNP: $90.4 billion
Federal budget: $5.46 billion
National debt: $16.9 billion
Union membership: 3.6
  million
Strikes: 637
Prime rate: 3.6%
Car sales: 2,787,400
Average salary: $1,368

Social
Homicides/100,000: 8.8
Suicides/100,000: 15.6
Lynchings: 21
Labor force, male/female:
  3.7/1
Social welfare: $4.09 billion
Public education: $2.32 billion
College degrees
  Bachelors'
    Male: 73,600
    Female: 48,800
  Doctorates
    Male: 1,946
    Female: 353
Attendance
  Movies (weekly): 90 million
  Baseball (yearly): 10.2
    million

Consumer
Consumer Price Index
  (1967 = 100): 50.0
Eggs: 44¢ (doz.)
Milk: 14¢ (qt.)
Bread: 9¢ (loaf)
Butter: 46¢ (lb.)
Bacon: 42¢ (lb.)
Round steak: 42¢ (lb.)
Oranges: 57¢ (doz.)
Coffee: 39¢ (lb.)

The thirties, with the Great Depression and rise of fascism in Europe and Asia, were a period of profound trial in American life—not just of personal and material survival but of democracy and capitalism, the fundamental systems of the American way. The beginning of the decade was a time of increasing hardship and despair. After a brief rise in the market in 1930, the economic decline returned. Everything was falling: industrial output, employment, wages, prices, and, not least of all, human spirits. Banks began to fail and cities to default. Apple sellers appeared on street corners, breadlines at soup kitchens lengthened, and people slept on park benches. Large numbers of the homeless began to wander to the edges of towns, to other cities—anywhere—only to find more of the same. The farmer, beset by his unsellable produce and mortgage foreclosure, and the city dweller, unable to find work at retrenching factories and fearful that even his savings were not safe, shared the woe.

The government, as usual, depended on private charity and public optimism while it waited for the invisible hand of the free market to lift the economy. In some intellectual circles, the fulfillment of Marxist prophecy was thought to be at hand: the inevitable demise of capitalism had arrived. For most, a sense of numb shock, fear, and perhaps self-failure pervaded. There was remarkably little agitation. The most noted example of protest, the Bonus March of 1932, was comprised of 12,000 veterans who sought early payment of a promised bonus—nothing more. Since the twenties, people had believed in the endless potential of the system and of themselves. They could not just blame the system when all fell down.

Franklin Delano Roosevelt, the Democratic nominee in 1932, seemed to understand what the nation needed—recognition of its despair and a determined active government. An optimistic and gregarious patrician, FDR lifted the nation's spirits as he spoke of the "forgotten man." The country gave him a landslide victory over a somber Herbert Hoover, who warned that grass would grow in the streets of the cities if FDR won. In his inaugural address, Roosevelt pledged "a new deal," and then, using radio in an innovative manner to directly communicate with the people, he began his widely listened-to fireside chats.

The rest of the decade is the story of the New Deal with its three Rs: relief, recovery, and reform. With an overwhelming public mandate, Roosevelt kept Congress in session for a hundred days after his inauguration and enacted an encompassing legislative program affecting major areas of the American economic polity. Measures were passed concerning banking, securities, industry, and agriculture. To meet the immediate crisis, federal relief was provided in unprecedented amounts, and vast government work projects were authorized. The National Recovery Administration (NRA) was created to coordinate and regulate activities in all industries. Its emblem, the Blue Eagle, appeared in shops and factories everywhere as a symbol of labor and management's willingness to cooperate for the general well-being. A litany of initials for other new agencies multiplied, and the nation recited them with hope, as government took on a unique role in the direct regulation of the economy and provision of its people. Many of the early regulatory reforms were clearly necessary and beneficial. Those such as the Federal Deposit Insurance Corporation (FDIC) and the Securities Exchange Commission remain today, as does government responsibility to intervene in times of economic crisis and to directly aid the needy. Later legislation, such as Social Security, the minimum wage, and labor's right to collective bargaining, have also become part of American life.

Recovery proceeded more slowly. Industrial output and the market rose during the remainder of Roosevelt's first term, although unemployment remained high, and direct and work relief remained a necessity for millions. Opposition to FDR grew. Business leaders initially supportive of the president now took a public beating in congressional hearings, as their dubious twenties' business practices were exposed; by 1935 they had regrouped in such forums as the Liberty League and attacked "that man," FDR, as a dangerous radical. Charismatic demagogues and one-time supporters, like the radio priest Father Coughlin and Louisiana senator Huey Long, also denounced the president. Still others portrayed him as the kind of fascist now taking over in Europe. The Supreme Court began overturning major legislation, most notably the National Industrial Recovery Act.

In 1936, the nation gave Roosevelt the largest electoral majority in history, but early in his second term, his attempt to "pack" the Supreme Court in order to circumvent its opposition alienated many supporters. In 1937–38, the economy fell again; large-scale unemployment ended only with World War II. During the last half of the decade, nonetheless, many of the roads, bridges, public buildings, dams, and trees that cover the nation were set in place by federally employed workers. Other WPA projects included the arts, and these provided a remarkable opportunity for expression and acculturation for artists and public alike. The Federal Music Project, for example, presented thousands of low-cost or free concerts and premieres of such composers as Samuel Barber and Walter Piston. The Federal Theatre Project employed 1,300 and reached 25 million people with over 1,200 productions. The Federal Writers' Program hired such writers as Saul Bellow, Ralph

Ellison, and Nelson Algren. The Federal Art Project produced tens of thousands of paintings, along with hundreds of murals that still decorate post offices, statehouses, and other public buildings throughout the country. One of the most important art forms to emerge from these projects was the great photographic documentary of Walker Evans, Dorothea Lange, and Margaret Bourke-White.

In their hour of trial, the American people were entertained, of necessity, inexpensively. In the popular arts, escape was the order of the day. People sang "Life Is Just a Bowl of Cherries" and "I've Got My Love to Keep Me Warm." Radio matured as a mass medium. Comedians Jack Benny and Fred Allen carried on a decade-long feud over the quality of Benny's violin playing. Fibber McGee and Molly, Burns and Allen, and Bob Hope also gathered faithful audiences. Soap opera—serial melodrama sponsored by detergent makers—captured large followings with heroines such as "Oxydol's own Ma Perkins," "Backstage Wife" Mary Noble, and Helen Trent. The Lone Ranger, Buck Rogers in the 25th Century, and Jack Armstrong (the "All-American Boy") provided male heroes. Commentators like Gabriel Heatter, H. V. Kaltenborn, and Walter Winchell offered hard and soft news in breathless tones. Sales of magazines like *True Story* and *Screenland* skyrocketed. Media gave extensive coverage to the "G-men" tracking of "Public Enemies" such as John Dillinger, Bonnie and Clyde, and Ma Barker and her sons.

Movies also provided escape. Sound had dramatically enhanced the medium's possibilities, and Hollywood drew many talents from Broadway. There were Busby Berkeley extravaganzas, Cary Grant screwball comedies, and James Cagney and Edward G. Robinson gangster epics. Stalwart, confident heroes, like Clark Gable, Errol Flynn, James Stewart, and Gary Cooper, made love and war triumphantly. Blondes like Mae West and Jean Harlow were the popular sex symbols. Jeanette MacDonald and Nelson Eddy, and Fred Astaire and Ginger Rogers, sang and danced their way into everyone's heart, as did child stars like Shirley Temple and Mickey Rooney. Donald Duck and Snow White debuted. The casting of Rhett Butler and Scarlett O'Hara in the film version of Margaret Mitchell's best-selling *Gone with the Wind* was of major public interest.

Big bands played the land, and swing was king. Jazz, for the first time, became the predominant popular musical form, with Duke Ellington, Benny Goodman, and later Glenn Miller, among the popular bandleaders. Sidemen, like Count Basie, were also stars, and their moves from band to band were closely followed. The Italian musician Arturo Toscanini was recruited by NBC to lead a new symphony orchestra, and, like another classical conductor, Leopold Stokowski, he too became a star of radio and film.

Although spectator sports declined, softball became a popular hobby, and many people played golf when private links went public. Night baseball and the NFL championship began. A black athlete, Jesse Owens, won four gold medals at Berlin (with Hitler in attendance), and the "Brown Bomber," Joe Louis, beat another Aryan for the heavyweight title. Candid photography, backgammon, and contract bridge gained many enthusiasts, and fads included bingo and marathon dancing; the Charleston gave way to the jitterbug, big apple, shag, rhumba, samba, and congo.

Elsewhere, others sought to portray and confront the problems of the depression. James Farrell wrote of the hard times in the city. Steinbeck immortalized the farmer's plight through the decade of droughts, floods, and dust storms in his tale of the Okies' migration westward. John Dos Passos continued his moral dissection of America, and Clifford Odets, who sought to politically engage his audience, questioned the viability of capitalism and the validity of the American dream. Lillian Hellman portrayed the venality of the apparently proper, and *Tobacco Road,* the long-running hit of the decade, drew laughter from the encroachment of the modern world on the rural South. In the visual arts, controversial left-wing murals portrayed the plight of the masses, ironically, in such capitalist palaces as Rockefeller Center and Dartmouth College. It is interesting that some of the nation's greatest landmarks and skyscrapers, like the Empire State Building, the Chrysler Building, and Rockefeller Center, were built in the early 1930s; they had been planned in better times.

Needless to say, personal commitments and ideologies accommodated to the troubled times. On the one hand, the viability of capitalism and representative government came into question. There were those who thought that the age of rugged individualism was over and that a new ideology was needed. As militaristic, fascist governments grew more powerful abroad and the Western democracies struggled with economic problems and pacifist sentiments, Russia and its system appeared to some the only viable alternative. Many of the writers, intellectuals, and entertainers who became fellow travelers or Communists and, in some instances, spies were recruited in this atmosphere. On the other hand, populist movements gained a less educated but more substantial following. Leaders like Huey Long and Father Coughlin expressed a more fascistic ideology.

Most Americans, however, while disillusioned with the worship of business and eager to see a

John Barrymore and Greta Garbo in *Grand Hotel*. *Movie Star News*.

Russell Lee, *Daughter of Sharecropper; New Madrid County, Mo. Library of Congress*.

larger, more caring government role, retained their faith in the American system. During these difficult times, they shared a remarkable solidarity and sense of community with their fellow Americans; their accommodations to the troubled times were less political than practical. They married later, had fewer children, and divorced less. Extended families lived under one roof; college students were in no hurry to graduate. Whenever possible, women worked, and civil service jobs, looked upon as limited opportunities in prosperous times, became highly prized for the security they provided. If moving upward (affluence) was the common goal of the twenties, maintaining one's position (survival) was the main hope of the thirties.

It was thus only with aloof concern that America, preoccupied with its own troubles, heard the news of Japan's invasion of China, Hitler's remilitarization of the Rhine, and Italy's conquest of Ethiopia. While condemning aggressive conquest, the United States maintained an official policy of neutrality. The Spanish Civil War, nevertheless, stirred intense feelings in many who saw it as a test of democracy's will to resist fascism, and some, such

as the Lincoln Brigade, went illegally to fight with the Loyalists.

America's awareness of the fascist menace crystallized with Hitler's territorial threats against the Czechs. The nation listened closely to radio reports from the Munich Conference, which ended with Czechoslovakia's dismemberment and Chamberlain's improbable prediction of "peace for our time." America watched, still torn between its natural, emotional support of Britain and its strong fear of involvement in foreign war. FDR offered moral and, later, material support to the European democracies, but isolationist sentiment remained strong among the people and the Congress. Respected figures, such as Charles Lindbergh and Herbert Hoover, warned against American entanglement. By February 1939, Franco had won the Spanish Civil War, and in May, the world was stunned by the announcement of Germany's nonaggression pact with Russia. As the twenties had ended in a cataclysm foreshadowing prolonged suffering, so did the thirties. In September 1939, Hitler's armies invaded Poland, and Europe went to war.

1930

In the News

GRAIN, COTTON, COPPER PRICES FALL . . . UNEMPLOYMENT RISES SHARPLY . . . MAHATMA GANDHI REJECTS DOMINION STATUS AND DEMANDS INDEPENDENCE . . . HAILE SELASSIE BECOMES EMPEROR OF ETHIOPIA . . . U.S. JOINS FRANCE, BRITAIN, JAPAN, GERMANY, AND ITALY AT LONDON DISARMAMENT CONFERENCE . . . SMOOT-HAWLEY LAW RAISES IMPORT DUTIES, 1,000 ECONOMISTS PETITION AGAINST NEW TARIFFS . . . UNEMPLOYMENT PASSES FOUR MILLION . . . LAST ALLIED TROOPS LEAVE RHINELAND AND SAAR . . . BRITISH WHITE PAPER CALLS FOR HALT TO JEWISH IMMIGRATION TO PALESTINE . . . $230 MILLION PUBLIC BUILDINGS ACT IS PASSED . . . DOW-JONES RISES, UP NEARLY 30% SINCE '29 DROP . . . HOOVER APPOINTS COMMISSION FOR UNEMPLOYMENT RELIEF . . . N.Y. JUDGE CRATER DISAPPEARS, LAST SEEN HAILING TAXI . . . SUPREME COURT RULES PURCHASE OF LIQUOR IS NOT VIOLATION OF 18TH AMENDMENT . . . POLL SHOWS MAJORITY FAVOR REPEAL OF PROHIBITION . . . DROUGHT DEVASTATES WESTERN U.S. . . . CONGRESS PASSES RELIEF LAW . . . FIRE IN OHIO STATE PENITENTIARY KILLS 320 INMATES . . . EMERGENCY PUBLIC WORKS ACT PROVIDES $116 MILLION . . . MILITARY LEADS REVOLUTION IN ARGENTINA . . . POLICE RAID MARGARET SANGER CLINIC IN N.Y.C. . . . GETÚLIO VARGAS LEADS REVOLUTION IN BRAZIL . . . CHICAGO BOOTLEG CRACKDOWN INDICTS 31 CORPORATIONS AND 158 MEN . . . DEMOCRATS WIN FIRST CONTROL IN CONGRESS SINCE 1916 . . . BANK OF U.S. CLOSES ALL 60 BRANCHES . . . ONE MILLION ON RADIO HEAR KING GEORGE PROCLAIM SUCCESS OF LONDON DISARMAMENT CONFERENCE . . . FRANCE BEGINS CONSTRUCTION OF MAGINOT LINE.

Quotes

"I see nothing in the present situation that is either menacing or warrants pessimism. During the winter months there may be some slackness or unemployment, but hardly more than at this season each year."

— Secretary of Treasury Andrew W. Mellon

"While the crash only took place six months ago, I am convinced we have passed the worst."

— Herbert Hoover

"These really are good times but only a few know it."

— Henry Ford

"Probably no nation in modern times has suffered so frequently or so greatly as the United States from recurrent periods of exaggerated optimism and unrealistic interpretation of its economic situation."

— Virgil Jordan, *North American Review*

"This year, when we all needed something to take our minds off our troubles, miniature golf did it. . . . If we cannot find bread, we are satisfied with the circus."

— Elmer Davis, *Harper's*

"The woman who doesn't want to make a home is undermining our nation."

— Mrs. Thomas A. Edison (radio talk show)

Making, rather than buying, becomes popular. *Library of Congress.*

Far left: Al Capone's free soup kitchen in Chicago. *Library of Congress.*

Ads

Exhibition of Old Spanish Painting from the Collection of Count Contini Bonacossi In Aid of the Fascist Institute of Culture . . . to be held from April to June, 1930 at The Royal Gallery of Modern Art, Rome under the Patronage of His Excellency BENITO MUSSOLINI
(in Art News, *May 3)*

—It's Playtime in Havana Now.
(El Encanto, "Cuba's largest and smartest Department Store")

GARBO TALKS!
(Anna Christie)

Today the discriminating family finds it absolutely necessary to own two or more motor cars.
(Buick)

To give is to flatter, to excite and to leave all of a flutter! and to flatter, do not forget that in all the world there is nothing so close to the heart of a woman as her opinion of her own good taste. Then when that opinion is an opinion justified there is no gift like a Guerlain perfume!
(Guerlain)

If SIDNEY CARTON were alive to-day he could, on trying "King George IV," truthfully say—"It is a far, far better thing I do, than I have ever done before."
(King George IV Old Scotch Whiskey)

Participating in almost anything for an excessive period of time—and for money—remains in vogue. Left: a dance marathon in Chicago. *Library of Congress.*

Radio

Premieres

"The Adventures of Helen and Mary" ("Let's Pretend"), Bill Adams
"Lum and Abner," Chester Lauck, Norris Goff
"Singin' Sam, the Barbasol Man," Harry Frankel
"Tony Wons' Scrapbook" (poetry reading to women)
"Easy Aces," Goodman Ace
"Lady Esther Serenade," Wayne King Orchestra
"Believe It or Not" (Robert L. Ripley)
"Death Valley Days" (Tim Frawley)
"American School of the Air," Dr. Lyman Bryson

"Walter Winchell"
"Town Crier," Alexander Woollcott (mixture of gossip and literature)
"Father Charles E. Coughlin"

Specials

Two-way conversations between Adm. Richard E. Byrd in New Zealand and NBC; first broadcast from ship at sea; arrival of Albert Einstein in New York.

Of Note

Most popular shows include "Amos 'n' Andy," "Headline Hunters," "The Goldbergs," "Cities Service Concert," "The National Farm and Home Hour," "The Fleischmann Hour."

New Catchphrases: "So long . . . until tomorrow" (Lowell Thomas); "There will be a brief pause . . . while we throw at you Mrs. Pennyfeather's Personal Service for Perturbed People . . ." ("The Cuckoo Hour").

TV

W2XBS, the CBS pioneer experimental station, begins operation. First telecast: "Felix the Cat."

Movies

Openings

All Quiet on the Western Front (Lewis Milestone), Lew Ayres, Louis Wolheim
The Big House (George Hill), Robert Montgomery, Chester Morris
The Divorcee (Robert Z. Leonard), Norma Shearer, Chester Morris, Robert Montgomery
Disraeli (Alfred E. Green), George Arliss, Joan Bennett
Animal Crackers (Victor Heerman), Marx Brothers, Margaret Dumont
Abraham Lincoln (D. W. Griffith), Walter Huston, Una Merkel
The Blue Angel (Josef von Sternberg), Marlene Dietrich, Emil Jannings
Liliom (Frank Borzage), Charles Farrell, Rose Hobart
Monte Carlo (Ernst Lubitsch), Jeanette MacDonald, Jack Buchanan
Hell's Angels (Howard Hughes), Jean Harlow, Ben Lyon
Morocco (Josef von Sternberg), Marlene Dietrich, Adolphe Menjou

The Big Trail (Raoul Walsh), John Wayne, Marguerite Churchill
Little Caesar (Mervyn Leroy), Edward G. Robinson, Douglas Fairbanks, Jr., Glenda Farrell
Min and Bill (George Hill), Marie Dressler, Wallace Beery
Brats (James Parrott), Stan Laurel, Oliver Hardy
Dawn Patrol (Howard Hawks), Richard Barthelmess, Douglass Fairbanks, Jr.
Anna Christie (Clarence Brown), Greta Garbo, Charles Bickford, Marie Dressler

Academy Awards (1929–30)

Best Picture: *All Quiet on the Western Front*
Best Director: Lewis Milestone (*All Quiet on the Western Front*)
Best Actress: Norma Shearer (*The Divorcee*)
Best Actor: George Arliss (*Disraeli*)

Top Box-Office Stars

Joan Crawford, William Haines

Popular Music

Hit Songs
"Body and Soul"
"Georgia on My Mind"
"The Battle of Jericho"
"Beyond the Blue Horizon"
"What Is This Thing Called
    Love?"
"Walkin' My Baby Back Home"
"Embraceable You"
"I Got Rhythm"
"Bidin' My Time"
"Little White Lies"
"On the Sunny Side of the Street"
"Love for Sale"
"St. James Infirmary"

Top Records
Tiger Rag (Mills Brothers); *You Brought a New Kind of Love to Me* (Maurice Chevalier); *Ten Cents a Dance* (Ruth Etting); *Let Me Sing and I'm Happy* (Al Jolson); *Three Little Words* (Ipana Troubadours); *Puttin' on the Ritz* (Leo Reisman); *Kansas City Kitty* (Rudy Vallee); *Sing You Sinners* (Smith Ballew)

Jazz and Big Bands
Duke Ellington records *Mood Indigo.* Paul Whiteman is still called the "King of Jazz"; also popular is the Nichols Band with Benny Goodman, Gene Krupa, Tommy Dorsey, Glenn Miller, and Jack Teagarden.

First Recordings: Lionel Hampton, with Louis Armstrong

Theater

Broadway Openings

Plays
The Green Pastures (Marc Connelly), Richard B. Harrison, all-black cast
Hotel Universe (Philip Barry), Ruth Gordon, Franchot Tone, Morris Carnovsky
Elizabeth the Queen (Maxwell Anderson), Alfred Lunt, Lynn Fontanne
Bad Girl (Vina Delmar), Sylvia Sidney, Paul Kelly
Grand Hotel (Vicki Baum), Eugenie Leontovich, Henry Hull, Sam Jaffe
Once in a Lifetime (Moss Hart, George S. Kaufman), Spring Byington, Hugh O'Connell, Jean Dixon
A Farewell to Arms (Laurence Stallings), Elissa Landi, Glenn Anders
Courtesan (Irving Kaye Davis), Elsa Shelley
Tonight or Never (Lili Hatvany), Helen Gahagan, Melvyn Douglas
Penny Arcade (Marie Baumer), James Cagney, Joan Blondell
Scarlet Sister Mary (Daniel Reed), Ethel Barrymore, Estelle Winwood (in black face)
The Vinegar Tree (Paul Osborn), Mary Boland
Alison's House (Susan Glaspell), Eva Le Gallienne, Howard da Silva
Art and Mrs. Bottle (Benn W. Levy), Katharine Hepburn, Jane Cowl

Musicals
Brown Buddies (Joe Jordan, Millard Thomas), Bill Robinson, Adelaide Hall, all-black cast
Flying High (Ray Henderson, B. G. DeSylva), Oscar Shaw, Bert Lahr, Kate Smith
Garrick Gaieties of 1930 (Vernon Duke et al.), Edith Meiser, Sterling Holloway, Imogene Coca
Girl Crazy (George Gershwin, Ira Gershwin), Allen Kearns, Willie Howard, Ethel Merman, Ginger Rogers
The New Yorkers (Cole Porter), Clayton, Jackson, and Durante, Hope Williams
Simple Simon (Richard Rodgers, Lorenz Hart), Ed Wynn, Ruth Etting
Smiles (Vincent Youmans, Clifford Grey), Marilyn Miller, Fred and Adele Astaire, Eddie Foy, Jr., Bob Hope
Strike Up the Band (George Gershwin, Ira Gershwin), Clark and McCullough, Blanche Ring
Sweet and Low (Billy Rose), Fannie Brice, George Jessel, James Barton, Arthur Treacher

Classics and Revivals On and Off Broadway
A Month in the Country (Turgenev), Nazimova; *Uncle Vanya* (Chekhov), Lillian Gish, Osgood Perkins; *The Inspector General* (Gogol), Dorothy Gish; *Twelfth Night*, Jane Cowl. *Founded:* Group Theatre by Harold Clurman, Lee Strasberg, Morris Carnovsky, Stella Adler, and Sanford Meisner

Pulitzer Prize
The Green Pastures, Marc Connelly

Classical Music _____

Compositions
Ferde Grofé, *Grand Canyon Suite*
Walter Piston, Flute Sonata
Henry Cowell, *Synchrony*
Roy Harris, String Quartet no. 1
Aaron Copland, Piano Variations
Roger Sessions, Piano Sonata no. 1
Sergei Rachmaninoff (in U.S.), Three Russian Folk-
Songs

Important Events
Jacques Thiabaud, Pablo Casals, and Alexander
Cortot form a trio. Arthur Fiedler becomes
conductor of the Boston Pops. Ferdinand Schaefer
leads the Indianapolis Symphony Orchestra in its
first program. Bach's unknown Clavier Concerto in C
minor is discovered. CBS begins to broadcast Sunday
performances of the New York Philharmonic. *Fidelio*
is broadcast to the United States from Dresden.

First Performances
Roger Sessions, *Black Maskers* (Cincinnati); Charles
Sanford Skilton, *The Sun Bride* (New York); E. B.
Hill, Symphony no. 2 (Boston); Daniel Gregory
Mason, Symphony no. 2 (Cincinnati). For the fiftieth
anniversary of the Boston Symphony: Ottorino
Respighi's *Metamorphosis;* Sergei Prokofiev's
Symphony no. 4; Howard Hanson's Symphony no. 2;
Stravinsky's *Symphony of Psalms;* Albert Roussel's
Symphony in G minor; Walter Piston's Suite for
Orchestra (he conducts), and Paul Hindemith's
Concerto for Viola

Opera

Metropolitan: Rosa Ponselle, *Don Giovanni;*
Frederick Jagel, *Norma;* Friedrich Schorr, *Die
Meistersinger;* Ezio Pinza, *Il barbiere di Siviglia;*
Sadko (Nicolai Rimsky-Korsakov, American
premiere); Elisabeth Ohms (debut),
Götterdämmerung.

Chicago: Mary Garden, *Camille* (Hamilton Forrest,
premiere); Lotte Lehmann, *Die Walküre;* John
Charles Thomas, *I pagliacci*

San Francisco: Maria Jeritza, *The Girl of the
Golden West; L'enfant et les sortilèges*

Music Notes
The Society of Contemporary Musicians names as
the "Most Important Works of the Year": Edgard
Varèse's *Arcane;* Aaron Copland's Concerto; Louis
Gruenberg's *Jazz Suite;* and Carl Ruggles's *Portraits*
• The League of Composers' "Greatest Works of the
Year" include Wallingford Riegger's *Sonarities* and
Carlos Salzedo's Harp and Chamber Concerto • The
Conductorless Symphony of New York is disbanded.

William Faulkner. *Library of Congress.*

Philip Barry's *Hotel Universe. Billy Rose Theatre
Collection. The New York Public Library at Lincoln Center.
Astor, Lenox and Tilden Foundations.*

Art _____

Painting

Grant Wood, *American Gothic*
Edward Hopper, *Early Sunday Morning*
Thomas Hart Benton, *The Old South, City Scenes*
Stuart Davis, *Egg Beater V*
Reginald Marsh, *Why Not Use the "L"?*
John Kane, *Creek Valley, No. 1*
Peter Blume, *Parade*
Charles Sheeler, *American Landscape*
Ivan Le Lorraine Albright, *Into the World There Came a Soul Called Ida*
George Luks, *Mrs. Gamley*
Georgia O'Keeffe, *Horse's Skull*
John Marin, *Storm over Taos*
Lyonel Feininger, *Ruin by the Sea*
Patrick Henry Bruce, *Painting*

Sculpture

William Zorach, *Mother and Child*
John B. Flannagan, *Elephant*
Alexander Calder, *Little Ball with Counterweight*
Chaim Gross, *Offspring*
Gaston Lachaise, *Torso*

Important Exhibitions

Museums

New York: *Metropolitan:* Egyptian wall paintings from tombs and palaces of the eighteenth and nineteenth dynasties, 1600–1200 B.C.; the Henry Havemeyer collection. *Museum of Modern Art:*

Architecture

Daily News Building, New York (Hood and Howells)
Chrysler Building, New York (William Van Alen)
Constitution Hall, Philadelphia (John Russell Pope)
Shopping center, Michigan Square Building, Chicago (Holabird and Root)
A "Radio City" is planned to cover three New York city blocks; it will include underground bus terminals, subterranean boulevards, surface fountains, sculpture, and broadcasting facilities; its estimated cost is $250 million.

Reginald Marsh, *Why Not Use the 'L'?*, 1930. Egg tempera. 36 × 48". *Collection of Whitney Museum of American Art. Geoffrey Clements.*

Early watercolors of Charles Burchfield; "46 Artists under 35 Years Old"; Corot and Daumier; Weber, Klee, Lehmbruck, Maillol, Homer, Eakins

Boston: Russian icons; Boston painters

Philadelphia, Washington (Corcoran): American moderns

Pittsburgh: Carnegie international prizes to Picasso (for *Madame Picasso*), Henry Lee McFee, Niles Spencer, Maurice Sterne

Chicago: Sculpture prize to Heinz Warneke; Delacroix

Art Briefs

Walker Evans's *Lehmbruck: Head of Man* is the first photo acquired for the Museum of Modern Art's photo collection • Diego Rivera completes the San Francisco Stock Exchange mural • The construction of period rooms peaks throughout U.S. museums • Interest grows in prints, especially lithographs and woodcuts • The director of the Detroit Institute pays $400 for an overpainted Titian valued at $150,000 • Arguments continue over whether U.S. dealers should sell European art.

Books

Fiction

Critics' Choice
As I Lay Dying, William Faulkner
The 42nd Parallel, John Dos Passos
Flowering Judas, Katherine Anne Porter
The Babe's Bed, Glenway Wescott
Arundel, Kenneth Roberts
Laments for the Living, Dorothy Parker
Mirthful Haven, Booth Tarkington
The Maltese Falcon, Dashiell Hammett
Pure Gold, O. E. Rölvaag
🐌 *The Castle,* Franz Kafka

Best Sellers
Cimarron, Edna Ferber
The Door, Mary Roberts Rinehart
Exile, Warwick Deeping
Years of Grace, Margaret Ayer Barnes
The Woman of Andros, Thornton Wilder
Angel Payment, J. B. Priestley
Rogue Herries, Hugh Walpole
Chances, A. Hamilton Gibbs
Twenty-Four Hours, Louis Bromfield
Young Man of Manhattan, Katharine Brush

Nonfiction

Critics' Choice
The American Leviathan, Charles and Mary Beard
The Realm of Matter, George Santayana
I'll Take My Stand, Robert Penn Warren
The Human Mind, Karl Menninger
The Second Twenty Years at Hull House, Jane Addams
Little America, Adm. Richard E. Byrd
Pre-War America, Mark Sullivan
The Crusades: Iron Men and Saints, Harold Lamb
The Story of a Friendship, Owen Wister
🐌 *Civilization and Its Discontents,* Sigmund Freud
🐌 *The Revolt of the Masses,* Ortega y Gasset

Best-Sellers
The Story of San Michele, Axel Munthe
The Strange Death of President Harding, Gaston B. Means, May Dixon Thacker
Byron, André Maurois
The Adams Family, James Truslow Adams
Lone Cowboy, Will James
The Story of Philosophy, Will Durant
The Outline of History, H. G. Wells
The Rise of American Civilization, Charles Beard, Mary Beard
Lincoln, Emil Ludwig
The Art of Thinking, Ernest Dimnet

Poetry
T. S. Eliot, *Ash-Wednesday*
Hart Crane, *The Bridge*
Ezra Pound, *The Cantos,* vol. 3
Archibald MacLeish, *New Found Land*
Richard Eberhart, *A Bravery of Earth*
Edgar Lee Masters, *Lichee Nuts*
Edwin Arlington Robinson, *The Glory of the Nightingales*
🐌 W. H. Auden, *Poems*

Pulitzer Prizes
Years of Grace, Margaret Ayer Barnes (novel)
The Coming of the War, Bernadotte E. Schmitt (U.S. history)
Henry James, Charles W. Eliot (biography)
Collected Poems, Robert Frost (poetry)

Nobel Prize
Sinclair Lewis

Science and Technology

Ernest O. Lawrence devises the cyclotron, a means of accelerating particles by magnetic resonance for the purpose of splitting atoms.

Pluto is identified by photos taken at Lowell Observatory, Arizona, by C. W. Tombaugh; its discovery confirms mathematical predictions.

Robert R. Williams determines the chemical structure of the vitamin thiamine.

John H. Northrup isolates the enzyme pepsin in crystalline form.

W. C. Rose, University of Illinois, shows that ten amino acids are "essential" for rats.

The first psychoanalytic institute for training analysts opens in Boston.

The first all-air commercial New York–Los Angeles transport is begun by Transcontinental and West Airlines.

Dr. William Beebe, in his bathysphere, descends to a record 1,426 feet underwater.

Artificial fabrics are made from an acetylene base by biochemist J. Walter Reppe.

Nobel Prize
Karl Landsteiner wins the prize in physiology and medicine for the discovery of human blood groups.

Sports

Baseball

Babe Ruth's salary is increased to $80,000; when told it exceeds the president's, he quips, "Well, I had a better year than he did." Ruth hit 49 home runs.

Champions

Batting
Bill Terry (New York, NL), .401
Al Simmons (Philadelphia, AL), .380

Pitching
Fred Fitzsimmons (New York, NL) 19–2
Lefty Grove (Philadelphia, AL) 28–5
Home runs
Hack Wilson (Chicago, NL), 56, NL record

Football

The New York Giants beat Notre Dame in a benefit game for the Unemployment Fund.

Pro Stars: Bronko Nagurski (Chicago Bears), Ernie Nevers (Chicago Cards).

College All-Americans: Frank Carideo (Q), Notre Dame; Leonard Macaluso (B), Colgate.

Rose Bowl (Jan. 1, 1931): Alabama 24–Washington State 0

Other Sports

Golf: Bobby Jones, still an amateur, wins the Grand Slam and retires; 18,000 attend the U.S. Open at Marion, Ohio.

Horse Racing: Gallant Fox, ridden by jockey Earl Sande, wins the Triple Crown. The Irish Sweepstakes are organized.

Boxing: Max Schmeling beats Jack Sharkey for the heavyweight title on a foul before 75,000 spectators.

Winners

World Series
Philadelphia (AL) 4
St. Louis (NL) 3
MVP
NL–William Terry, New York
AL–Joseph Cronin, Washington
NFL
Green Bay Packers
College Football
Notre Dame
College Basketball
Pittsburgh

Player of the Year
Charles Hyatt, Pittsburgh
Stanley Cup
Montreal
U.S. Tennis Open
Men: John Doeg
Women: Betty Nuthall
USGA Open
Robert T. Jones, Jr.
Kentucky Derby
Gallant Fox (E. Sande, jockey)

A high school science teacher in Cleveland exhibits models of atomic structure, a subject of intense investigation in the scientific world. *Library of Congress.*

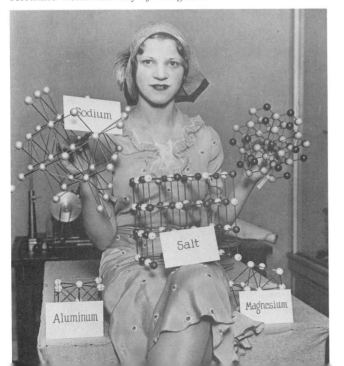

Fashion

For Women: With the Clara Bow flapper passé, the rage is for the sophisticated Garbo look. The silhouette is tall and slender, emphasizing broad shoulders, a small bosom, streamlined hips, and the normal waistline. Both hair and hems are longer; narrower skirts widen softly below the hip and then reach mid-calf. Several screen stars actually set the styles: Garbo and the windblown look (with hair parted at the side or middle); Crawford and puffed sleeves, which emphasize the small waist; Harlow's slinky halter tops and satin evening gowns; and Garbo and Dietrich's slacks. Thick, clinging fabrics are enormously popular. The gradual broadening and squaring of the shoulders leads to three-inch shoulder pads, even in nightgowns. Evening fashion consists of backless dresses with slightly bloused bodices and fox furs with heads and tails. Makeup emphasizes angularity. Every woman owns a magnifying mirror to pencil in well-plucked eyebrows and apply black mascara and eye shadow. Curling irons are popular.

Kaleidoscope _____

- Joke: "Have you heard the one about the two men who jumped hand in hand because they had a joint account?"
- The International Apple Shippers Association gives 6,000 jobless men surplus apples on credit to sell for 5¢ on street corners.
- More than 1,300 banks close by the end of the year.
- Early in the year, a Little Bull Market sees giants like U.S. Steel, General Motors, and General Electric regain ground, which leads to a wave of optimism among political and business leaders.
- The first federal census of unemployment appears in April and reports 3 million unemployed.
- William Randolph Hearst owns 33 newspapers with a total circulation of 11 million.
- In the last ten years the mileage of paved roads has doubled to 695,000; gas consumption rises to 16 billion gallons.
- The illiteracy rate falls to 4.3 percent.
- Ellen Church becomes the first airline stewardess (United Airlines). The job is created to allay passengers' fear of flying; requirements are that the applicant be female, single, at least 21 years old, no taller than 5'4", and under 115 pounds; she must also have a "pleasant personality."
- Operatic films are in vogue, such as *New Moon* with Grace Moore and Lawrence Tibbett.
- "The Lone Ranger," in Detroit, starts with the *William Tell* overture and "A fiery horse with the speed of light, a cloud of dust, and a hearty 'Hi-yo Silver'—the Lone Ranger Rides Again."
- The following want ad appears in the *New York Times:* "Bookkeeper and typist: Thoroughly experienced. Prefer someone with silk underwear."

- A well-publicized study reports that bright children are prone to bullying, perseverance, cruelty, and argumentativeness.
- A *Literary Digest* poll indicates that 40 percent favor Prohibition repeal, 29 percent favor modification.
- The new Institute for Advanced Studies at Princeton University is dedicated to the "usefulness of useless knowledge."
- Howard Hunt buys his first wildcat oil well for $40,000 in cash.
- "Gif me a viskey . . . and don't be stingy, baby," is Garbo's first line in *Anna Christie,* her first talkie.
- Jean Harlow becomes blonde for *Hell's Angels.*
- Busby Berkeley introduces his dizzying camera angle techniques into the filming of musical sequences.
- With the new, smaller and improved German cameras, spontaneous candid photography becomes popular.
- A federal law is passed requiring the labeling of substandard foods.
- Lloyd's of London begins to sell civilian commotion insurance in the U.S.
- *I'll Take My Stand,* a manifesto by Southern agrarian writers, supports the "Southern way of life against . . . the American or prevailing way."

New Words and Usages: *Hoovervilles* (slums), *Hoover blankets* (newspapers covering park-bench indigents), *Hoover flags* (pockets emptied and inside out), and *Hoover wagons* (mule-pulled trucks).

Fads: Tree sitting, contract bridge (overtaking whist), backgammon, "Sorry," and knitting

First Appearances: Hostess Twinkies, Snickers, sliced bread (Wonder), French's Worcestershire sauce, Mott's applesauce, Jiffy biscuits, supermarket (King Kullen), broiler chickens, dry ice, Birds Eye frozen vegetables, "freewheeling" drive (Studebaker), house trailers, windshield wipers, photoflash bulbs, plexiglass, "candid camera" (term), El Dorado (art deco apartment building, New York), Braniff, National, United, TWA, and American airlines, Brooklyn College, *Fortune, Daily Worker,* "Blondie," "Death Valley Days," Breck shampoo, Merthiolate, St. Moritz Hotel, Carlsbad Caverns National Park, mechanical operator for coal mines, windowless factory, Medical Rogues' Gallery, pinball machine, planetarium open to the public (Chicago), president buried in the National Cemetery at Arlington (Taft), benzedrine inhaler

With difficulties in prohibition enforcement and the decline in the economy, the "wet" movement gathers force. *Library of Congress.*

1931

Economic Profile
   Dow-Jones: ↓ High 194–
      Low 74
   GNP: −16%
   Inflation: −4.4%
   Unemployment: 15.9%
Median age, first marriage:
   Male: 24.3, Female: 21.3
Average household size: 4.11
Population over 65: 5%
Population under 10: 19%
Automobiles:
   Pierce-Arrow: $810
   Auburn: $945
   Buick: $1,025
   Cadillac: $2,695
Steinway: $875–$1,375
Lady's seal or caracul coat:
   $188
I. Miller shoes: $5.85
Rogers Peet wool coat: $20
Hart Schaffner & Marx suit:
   $29.50
Reading glasses: $3.50;
   bifocals: $4.95

Deaths

David Belasco, Arnold
   Bennett, Thomas Alva
   Edison, Daniel Chester
   French, Frank Harris,
   Vincent d'Indy, Vachel
   Lindsay, Nellie Melba,
   A. A. Michelson, Dwight
   Morrow, Anna Pavlova,
   Eugene Ysaye.

In the News

MASSACHUSETTS SENATE MAKES FIRST RESOLUTION TO REPEAL PROHIBITION . . . UNEMPLOYMENT NEARS 16% . . . BRITISH FREE GANDHI, ON HUNGER STRIKE, AND AGREE TO DISCUSS HIS DEMANDS . . . HOOVER'S WICKERSHAM COMMISSION FINDS PROHIBITION INEFFECTIVE . . . LARGEST VIENNA BANK GOES BANKRUPT . . . "LEGS" DIAMOND IS AMBUSHED OUTSIDE ALBANY ROOMING HOUSE . . . FEDERAL COUNCIL OF CHURCHES OF CHRIST AFFIRMS BIRTH CONTROL . . . JAPANESE INVADE MANCHURIA, CLAIM PROVOCATION AT MUKDEN . . . HOOVER PROPOSES MORATORIUM ON INTERNATIONAL DEBTS AND REPARATIONS . . . SPANISH KING ALFONSO IS DEPOSED, A REPUBLIC DECLARED . . . GRASSHOPPER PLAGUE HITS THE MIDWEST . . . MUSCLE SHOALS GOVERNMENT POWER PLANT IS VETOED BY HOOVER . . . STAR FAITHFULL, 25-YEAR-OLD BEAUTY, WASHES ASHORE ON LONG ISLAND, N.Y. . . . WILEY POST AND HAROLD GATTO FLY "WINNIE MAE" AROUND THE WORLD IN 8 DAYS . . . CHIANG KAI-SHEK'S NATIONALISTS CLASH WITH MAO TSE-TUNG'S COMMUNISTS . . . NINE NEGRO BOYS FROM SCOTTSBORO, CHARGED WITH RAPING TWO WHITE WOMEN ON A TRAIN, ARE SENTENCED TO DEATH . . . AMERICAN BAR ASSOCIATION APPROVES ELIHU ROOT FORMULA FOR U.S. TO ENTER WORLD COURT . . . BRITAIN LEAVES THE GOLD STANDARD, AMERICA AND FRANCE REMAIN . . . TWO OUT OF THREE WORKERS IN DETROIT ARE UNEMPLOYED . . . HUNGER MARCHERS ARE TURNED AWAY FROM WHITE HOUSE . . . AL CAPONE, GUILTY OF TAX EVASION, IS SENTENCED TO 11 YEARS . . . HOOVER ASKS FOR EMERGENCY RECONSTRUCTION FINANCE AND PUBLIC WORKS BILLS . . . STRIKING COAL MINERS BATTLE GUARDS IN HARLAN, KY., FOUR ARE KILLED . . . LEAGUE OF NATIONS ASKS U.S. TO SIT IN ON MANCHURIA MEETINGS, U.S. AGREES.

Quotes

"I should like to find out at what stage of your poverty other people realize or sense it, and pass you by as one no longer interesting or useful to them. . . . You realize that for the first time in your rather carefree, indifferent life you are worth more dead than alive—a good deal more."

— Frank G. Moorhead, *Nation*

"MIDDLETON, N.Y., Dec. 24—Attracted by smoke from the chimney of a supposedly empty summer cottage . . . in Sullivan County, [the] constable . . . found a young couple starving. Three days without food, the wife, who is 23 years old, was hardly able to walk. They went into the cottage, preferring to starve rather than beg."

— *Buffalo Evening News*

"More than 100,000 applications have been received at the [Soviet] Ambassador's . . . for the 6,000 jobs. . . . Because of the general knowledge that Russia is 'industrializing,' applicants usually are skilled workers."

— *New York Times*

"We are the first nation in the history of the world to go to the poorhouse in an automobile."

— Will Rogers

"I'm a small fish here in Washington. But I'm the Kingfish to the folks down in Louisiana."

— Huey Long

Ads

Commercial airlines provide new passenger comfort. *Library of Congress.*

Radio

Premieres

"The Ed Sullivan Show"
"The March of Time," Ted Husing
"The Eddie Cantor Show"
"Singing Lady," Irene Wicker
"Buck Rogers"
"Skippy," Franklin Adams, Jr.
"Little Orphan Annie," Shirley Bell
"Myrt and Marge," Myrtle Vail, Donna Damerel
    Fick
"Metropolitan Opera Broadcasts," Milton Cross
"The American Album of Familiar Music," Donald
    Dame

Specials

Mussolini broadcasts his peace goals; Pope Pius XI makes the first worldwide broadcast; Gertrude Ederle speaks from an aquaplane, William Beebe, from a bathysphere 2,200 feet below the sea.

Of Note

The longest running comedy is "Smith Brothers"; music, "Atwater Kent" and "Midweek Hymn Sing"; news, Frederick William Wile; religious-talk, "National Radio Pulpit"; and miscellaneous-talk, "Cook's Travelogue" and "Auction Bridge" • "The University of Chicago Round Table," with John Howe and George Probst, sends out transcripts of meetings; 21,000 subscribe • "Buck Rogers" fans can exchange Cocomalt box strips for "interplanetary maps" to become "solar scouts."

New Catchphrases: "Who's that little chatterbox? / The one with pretty auburn locks? / Who can it be? It's 'Little Orphan Annie'"; "Time . . . marches on! As it must to all men, death came this week to . . . ("The March of Time"); "How *do* you *do?*" ("The Eddie Cantor Show" with Bert Gordon as the Mad Russian)

Movies

Openings

The Struggle (D. W. Griffith, last film), Hal Skelly,
    Zita Johann
Cimarron (Wesley Ruggles), Richard Dix, Irene
    Dunne
The Front Page (Lewis Milestone), Pat O'Brien,
    Adolphe Menjou
Trader Horn (W. S. Van Dyke), Harry Carey
The Public Enemy (William A. Wellman), James
    Cagney, Jean Harlow
Monkey Business (Norman Z. McLeod), Marx
    Brothers
An American Tragedy (Josef von Sternberg), Sylvia
    Sidney, Phillips Holmes
A Nous la Liberté (René Clair), Raymond Cordy,
    Henri Marchand
The Champ (King Vidor), Wallace Beery, Jackie
    Cooper
City Lights (Charles Chaplin), Charles Chaplin,
    Virginia Cherrill
Dishonored (Josef von Sternberg), Marlene Dietrich,
    Victor McLaglen
Dracula (Tod Browning), Bela Lugosi
Frankenstein (James Whale), Boris Karloff, Colin
    Clive
Platinum Blonde (Frank Capra), Jean Harlow,
    Loretta Young

Laurel and Hardy are enormously successful in their displays of monumental ineptitude. Left: *Brats. Movie Star News.*

Street Scene (King Vidor), Sylvia Sidney
Tabu (F. W. Murnau, Robert Flaherty), Matahi, Reri,
    Hitu
A Free Soul (Clarence Brown), Norma Shearer,
    Lionel Barrymore, Clark Gable, Leslie Howard
The Guardsman (Sidney Franklin), Alfred Lunt,
    Lynn Fontanne
The Sin of Madelon Claudet (Edgar Selwyn), Helen
    Hayes, Lewis Stone, Robert Young
Skippy (Norman Taurog), Jackie Cooper

Academy Awards (1930–31)

Best Picture: *Cimarron*
Best Director: Norman Taurog (*Skippy*)
Best Actress: Marie Dressler (*Min and Bill*)
Best Actor: Lionel Barrymore (*A Free Soul*)

Top Box-Office Stars

Janet Gaynor, Charles Farrell

Popular Music

Hit Songs
"Life Is Just a Bowl of Cherries"
"Minnie, the Moocher"
"Mood Indigo"
"All of Me"
"Between the Devil and the Deep
   Blue Sea"
"Dancing in the Dark"
"Dream a Little Dream of Me"
"Of Thee I Sing"
"The Thrill Is Gone"
"Lady of Spain"
"Love Is Sweeping the Country"

Top Records
The Peanut Vendor (Don
Azpiazu); *Where the Blue of the
Night* (Bing Crosby); *Goodnight,
Sweetheart* (Ruth Etting); *When
the Moon Comes over the
Mountain* (Kate Smith); *You
Rascal You* (Jack Teagarden); *Just
a Gigolo* (Bing Crosby); *I Found a
Million-Dollar Baby* (Ben Pollack)

Jazz and Big Bands
Freddie Martin performs at the
Bossert Hotel in Brooklyn, N.Y.

First Recordings: Mildred Bailey;
Duke Ellington's extended *Creole
Rhapsody*

New Bands: Eddie Duchin, New
Jersey; Don Redman; Henry
Busse

Theater

Broadway Openings

Plays
Mourning Becomes Electra (Eugene O'Neill),
   Nazimova, Alice Brady
Tomorrow and Tomorrow (Philip Barry), Herbert
   Marshall, Osgood Perkins
Private Lives (Noel Coward), Noel Coward,
   Gertrude Lawrence
The Barretts of Wimpole Street (Rudolf Beiser),
   Katharine Cornell, Brian Aherne
Counsellor-at-Law (Elmer Rice), Paul Muni
Reunion in Vienna (Robert E. Sherwood), Alfred
   Lunt, Lynn Fontanne
Springtime for Henry (Benn W. Levy), Leslie Banks
The House of Connelly (Paul Green), Franchot Tone,
   Luther Adler, Stella Adler, Clifford Odets,
   Morris Carnovsky
As You Desire Me (Luigi Pirandello), Judith
   Anderson
The Left Bank (Elmer Rice), Katherine Alexander,
   Horace Braham

Musicals
America's Sweetheart (Richard Rodgers, Lorenz
   Hart), Harriette Lake (Ann Sothern), Jack
   Whiting
The Bandwagon (Arthur Schwartz, Howard Dietz),
   Fred and Adele Astaire, Frank Morgan
The Cat and the Fiddle (Jerome Kern, Otto
   Harbach), Eddie Foy, Jr., Bettina Hall
Earl Carroll's Vanities of 1931 (Harold Adamson,
   Burton Lane), William Demarest, Lillian Roth
George White's Scandals (Ray Henderson), Ethel
   Merman, Rudy Vallee, Alice Faye
Rhapsody in Black (Jimmy McHugh, Dorothy
   Fields), Ethel Waters, all-black cast

Stage and screen star Alla Nazimova (seated), in *Mourning
Becomes Electra,* Eugene O'Neill's retelling of Aeschylus's
Oresteia in a Civil War setting. *Billy Rose Theatre
Collection. The New York Public Library at Lincoln Center.
Astor, Lenox and Tilden Foundations.*

Of Thee I Sing (George Gershwin, Ira Gershwin),
   Victor Moore, William Gaxton, Lois Moran

Classics and Revivals On and Off Broadway
The Merchant of Venice, Otis Skinner, Maude
Adams; *Hamlet,* Raymond Massey, Celia Johnson;
The School for Scandal (Sheridan), Ethel Barrymore;
The Father (Strindberg), Robert Loraine; *Camille*
(Dumas), Eva Le Gallienne

Pulitzer Prize
Alison's House, Susan Glaspell

Auto Show in Detroit: handsome machines without buyers. *Library of Congress.*

With government relief limited, bread lines, like this one beneath the Brooklyn Bridge, form throughout the nation. *Library of Congress.*

Classical Music

Compositions

Samuel Barber, *School for Scandal, Dover Beach*
Virgil Thomson, Symphony no. 2, Serenade for Flute and Violin, *Stabat Mater*
John Powell, *Natchez on the Hill*
Henry Cowell, *Two Appositions*
Douglas Moore, *Overtures on an American Tune*
Walter Piston, Suite for Oboe and Piano
Gian Carlo Menotti, *Variation on a Theme of Schumann*

Important Events

The National and St. Louis symphonies are organized. Interest in American music grows abroad. Nicolas Slonimsky travels to Paris, Berlin, Vienna, Prague, and Stockholm, and plays Gershwin, Sessions, Copland, Gruenberg, and Ruggles. European publishers begin to publish living American composers.

Debuts: Isaac Stern, Milstein-Piatigorsky-Horowitz Trio

First Performances

Roy Harris, Andante (Los Angeles); Charles Ives, *Three Places in New England* (New York); Igor Stravinsky, *Symphony of Psalms* (Boston); Ferde Grofé, *Grand Canyon Suite* (Chicago); Arthur Honegger, Symphony no. 1 (Boston); Paul Hindemith, *Konzertmusik* (Boston); William Grant Still, *Afro-American Symphony* (Rochester); Ottorino Respighi, *Five Picture Studies* (Boston)

Opera

Metropolitan: Lucrezia Bori, Edward Johnson, *Peter Ibbetson* (premiere); Lily Pons (debut), *Lucia di Lammermoor, Rigoletto;* Elisabeth Rethberg, *Iris.* Premieres: *Schwanda* (Jaromir Weinberger); *La notte di Zoraima* (Montemezzi)

Philadelphia: *Oedipus Rex, Wozzeck* (premieres)

Chicago: René Maison, *Parsifal*

Music Notes

The Bruckner Society is organized "to develop in the public an appreciation of the music of Bruckner, Mahler, and other moderns" • "The Star Spangled Banner," written by lawyer Francis Scott Key (1814) and based on an English drinking tune, officially becomes the national anthem • Severence Hall in Cleveland opens • The first full-length opera from the Metropolitan is broadcast (*Hansel and Gretel*).

Art _____

Painting

Georgia O'Keeffe, *The White Flower, Cow's Skull, Red, White and Blue*

Walt Kuhn, *The Blue Clown*

Charles Sheeler, *Classic Landscape (River Rouge Plant)*

Edward Hopper, *Route 6, Eastham*

Arthur G. Dove, *Ferry Boat Wreck*

John Kane, *Panther Hollow*

Willem de Kooning, *Untitled*

Stuart Davis, *Salt Shaker, House and Street, Trees and El*

Reginald Marsh, *Swinging Carousel*

John Steuart Curry, *Spring Shower*

Grant Wood, *Midnight Ride of Paul Revere*

Charles Demuth, *Buildings Abstraction*

Sculpture

Isamu Noguchi, *The Queen*

Gloria Vanderbilt Whitney, *Titanic Memorial*

Ibram Lassaw, *Torso*

Architecture

McGraw-Hill Building, New York (Hood and Fouilhoux)

George Washington Bridge, New York and New Jersey (Othmar Ammann)

Arthur Peck house, Paoli, Pa. (William Lescaze)

Rockefeller Center construction begins (Reinhard & Hofmeister, Hood, Godley, and Fouilhoux, Corbett, Harrison, and MacMurray).

The Empire State Building (Shreve, Lamb, and Harmon) is completed, 102 stories and 1,250 feet high, the tallest building to date.

Georgia O'Keeffe, *The White Calico Flower,* 1931. *Oil. 30 × 36". Collection of Whitney Museum of American Art. Geoffrey Clements.*

Important Exhibitions

Museums

New York: *Metropolitan:* European arms and armor; Russian icons from the twelfth to the nineteenth centuries; early New York silver; Chinese court robes and accessories; ceramic art of the Near East; Robert Henri memorial; contemporary industrial art. *Museum of Modern Art:* Murals of Diego Rivera; German art—Beckmann, Grosz; Redon, Toulouse-Lautrec, Matisse retrospective. *Whitney:* George Bellows, Arthur B. Davies, William Glackens, George Luks, Maurice Prendergast, Robert Henri

Pittsburgh: Franklin C. Watkins receives the Carnegie International first prize for *Suicide in Costume.*

Hartford: *Wadsworth Atheneum:* "Newer Super-Realism: Ernst, Masson, Miró, Picasso, de Chirico, Dali"

Dance _____

Martha Graham dances in *Primitive Mysteries.*

Art Briefs

The Whitney opens with a permanent collection of 500 works, the first museum of American art • New galleries include the Addison (Andover, Mass.) and Jocelyn (Omaha) • Arshile Gorky holds his first one-man show in Philadelphia.

Books

Fiction

Critics' Choice

Sanctuary, William Faulkner
These Thirteen: Stories, William Faulkner
The Dream Life of Balso Snell, Nathanael West
S.S. San Pedro, James Gould Cozzens
Sparks Fly Upward, Oliver La Farge
Their Father's God, Ole Rölvaag
The Harbourmaster, William McFee
The Forge, T. S. Stribling
⌘ *The Son Avenger,* Sigrid Undset

Best-Sellers

The Good Earth, Pearl S. Buck
Grand Hotel, Vicki Baum
Shadows on the Rock, Willa Cather
The Road Back, E. M. Remarque
Back Street, Fannie Hurst
Maid in Waiting, John Galsworthy
The Bridge of Desire, Warwick Deeping
A White Bird Flying, Bess Streeter Aldrich
Years of Grace, Margaret Ayer Barnes
Finch's Fortune, Mazo de la Roche

Nonfiction

Critics' Choice

Axel's Castle, Edmund Wilson
Autobiography, Lincoln Steffens
Philosophy and Civilization, John Dewey
Only Yesterday, William Lewis Allen
The Brown Decades, Louis Mumford
The Genteel Tradition at Bay, George Santayana
The Owl in the Attic and Other Perplexities, James Thurber
Can Europe Keep the Peace? Frank Simonds
Tragic America, Theodore Dreiser
Living My Life, Emma Goldman
The Literary Mind, Max Eastman

Best-Sellers

Education of a Princess, Grand Duchess Marie
Washington Merry-Go-Round, Anonymous (Drew Pearson and Robert S. Allen)
Fatal Interview (poetry), Edna St. Vincent Millay
Culbertson's Summary, Ely Culbertson
The Story of San Michele, Axel Munthe

Contract Bridge Blue Book, Ely Culbertson
The Epic of America, James Truslow Adams
New Russia's Primer, M. Ilin
Mexico, Stuart Chase
Boners

Poetry

Conrad Aiken, *Preludes for Memnon*
Edwin Arlington Robinson, *Matthias at the Door*
Edgar Lee Masters, *Godbey*
Robinson Jeffers, *Descent to the Dead*
Langston Hughes, *Dear Lovely Death*
H. D., *Red Roses for Bronze*

Pulitzer Prizes

The Good Earth, Pearl S. Buck (novel)
My Experiences in the World War, John J. Pershing (U.S. history)
Theodore Roosevelt, Henry F. Pringle (biography)
The Flowering Stone, George Dillon (poetry)

Science and Technology

Karl Jansky, at Bell Telephone Laboratories, begins the science of radio astronomy as he observes interference in the form of hissing sounds coming from beyond the earth's atmosphere.

Harold Urey, Columbia University, discovers heavy water, water that contains deuterium, a rare hydrogen isotope.

Robert J. de Graaff constructs a subatomic particle accelerator that uses static electricity.

Lt. Robert Hyland, Washington, D.C., observes that planes can be detected by means of their reflection of radio beams.

Growth hormone is used clinically for the first time.

An electron microscope is developed by Vladimir Zworykin and James Hillier.

The enzyme trypsin is isolated in crystalline form by John H. Northrup and Moses Kunitz.

Clyde Pangborn and Hugh Herndon make the first nonstop flight across the Pacific, 4,860 miles in 41 hours.

The George Washington Bridge, the longest suspension bridge in the world, is built.

Sports _____

Baseball

Pepper Martin (St. Louis, NL) bats .500 as he leads
the "Gashouse Gang" to a World Series victory;
Herbert Hoover throws out the first ball and is
booed.

Champions _____

Batting
  Chuck Hafey (St. Louis,
  NL), .349
  Al Simmons (Philadelphia,
  AL), .390
Pitching
  Paul Derringer (St. Louis,
  NL), 18–8
  Lefty Grove (Philadelphia,
  AL), 31–4

Home runs
  Babe Ruth (New York, AL),
  46
  Lou Gehrig (New York,
  AL), 46

Football

Knute Rockne, Notre Dame coach, dies in a plane
crash. He had coached Notre Dame since 1918; his
record was 105 wins, 12 losses, and 5 ties.
Chicago, Green Bay, and Portsmouth are fined $1,000
for using players whose college class has not
graduated.

Pro Stars: Bronko Nagurski, Link Lyman (Chicago
Bears)

College All-Americans: Marchmont Schwartz (B),
Notre Dame; Paul Schwegler (T), Washington

Rose Bowl (Jan. 1, 1932): Southern California 21–
Tulane 12

Basketball

The ABL disbands because of financial problems.

Walter Hagen (left) demonstrating a sport that is growing
more and more egalitarian. *Library of Congress.*

Other Sports

Boxing: Max Schmeling is stripped of his
heavyweight crown by New York officials for his
refusal to fight Jack Sharkey.

Winners _____

World Series
  St. Louis (NL) 4
  Philadelphia (AL) 3
MVP
  NL–Frank Frisch, St. Louis
  AL–Robert Grove,
  Philadelphia
NFL
  Green Bay Packers
College Football
  USC
College Basketball
  Northwestern

Player of the Year
  Bart Carlton, Ada Teachers
Stanley Cup
  Montreal
U.S. Tennis Open
  Men: Ellsworth Vines, Jr.
  Women: Helen Wills Moody
USGA Open
  Billy Burke
Kentucky Derby
  Twenty Grand (C.
  Kurtsinger, jockey)

Fashion _____

For Women: New accessories include suede gloves
with matching bag and shoes, a red or gray fox fur
flung over one shoulder, batik or fine silk scarves,
heavy finger rings, and watches set with gems. Hats
are deep and close-fitting with large and small brims,
and they dip over one eye. Hair is longer and loosely
waved with a side part; a roll is sometimes combed in
the back. Fashionable shoes include the black silk
style with ankle strap and the white suede style with
T strap.

*High-fashion note: Reveillon's white satin pajama
suit.*

For Men: Hair is short and natural, parted on the
side; water replaces pomade for the Charles Farrell
or Buddy Rogers look; mustaches remain on the
older sophisticate, whose "essential accessories"
include cigarette case, wallet, signet ring, cuff links,
and two handkerchiefs, one in the breast pocket, the
other, for use, tucked up the coat sleeve. The hearty,
"tough" look appears with the double-breasted
darker suit and the hat brought down over the face.

Kaleidoscope _____

- National income is down 33 percent since 1929; payrolls drop 40 percent; department store clerks earn $5–$10 a week and secretaries, $15; many working women earn 25¢ an hour.
- Hundreds of the unemployed dig clams in New England and sell them door to door for 25¢ a peck.
- Double features begin; they provide a place for the unemployed to go.
- Gangster and horror films increase in popularity.
- Lectures and books on Russia become more popular as interest in the "Soviet experiment" increases.
- John Reed clubs, named after the American Communist who died in Moscow, form in many cities.
- For the first time, emigration exceeds immigration.
- Sales of glass jars increase dramatically, while sales of canned goods decline.
- The National Education Association reports that 75 percent of all cities ban the employment of wives.
- The rate of admissions to state mental hospitals for 1930–31 is triple that of 1922–30.
- To generate income, Nevada legalizes both gambling and the six-month divorce.
- The remains of Miles Standish, leader of the Mayflower, are transported and buried at Duxbury, Mass.
- Hattie T. Caraway (Arkansas) becomes the first woman elected to the U.S. Senate.
- Nearly 6,000 cases of infantile paralysis strike New York, which is placed in a state of partial quarantine.
- Farmers, to no avail, use electrified fences and other devices to inhibit the horde of grasshoppers that destroys 160,000 miles of America's finest farmlands.
- Lucky Luciano organizes the Mafia into federated families.
- Animal trainer Clyde Beatty debuts with Ringling Brothers and Barnum and Bailey.
- A popular joke: "But surely," cried Jean, "you didn't tell him straight out that you loved him?" "Goodness, no," Mary said calmly, "he had to squeeze it out of me" *(Buffalo News).*
- Ethel Merman steals the show in *George White's Scandals* with "Life Is Just a Bowl of Cherries."
- Ethel Waters, in *Rufus Jones for President,* is upstaged by five-year-old Sammy Davis, Jr.

Gangster films, like *The Public Enemy,* with Jean Harlow and James Cagney, surpass westerns at the box office; this is one of the first to portray gangsters as the spawn of social problems. *Movie Star News.*

- Silent film extra Clark Gable appears in *A Free Soul,* slaps Norma Shearer, and wins instant stardom; Bing Crosby croons in his debut in Max Sennett shorts.
- Universal recruits Bette Davis who, one agent reports, has "as much sex appeal as Slim Summerville."
- Kate Smith sets a record run of eleven weeks at the Palace.
- When the *New York World* ceases publication, Walter Lippmann goes to the *New York Herald Tribune,* becomes nationally syndicated, and achieves great popularity.
- Offended by his political remarks, Theodore Dreiser slaps Sinclair Lewis's face twice at a dinner of American writers at the Metropolitan Club, New York.
- Lucky Strike outsells its rival, Camel, for the first time.
- Charles Lindbergh builds a house, widely called a "Nest for the Lone Eagle," in a secluded area of New Jersey.
- Investigations into the death of Star Faithfull indicate that she was sexually abused as a teenager by a member of a distinguished Back Bay Boston family.
- *Oh, Yeah,* a series of optimistic statements by bankers and politicians about the depression, is a popular source of grim humor.
- Jane Addams and Nicholas Murray Butler win the Nobel Peace Prize.

First Appearances: Bahai House of Worship (Wilmette, Ill.), coaxial cable, moving picture of a grand opera *(I pagliacci),* Nobel Prize to an American woman (Addams), photoelectric cell installed commercially, infrared photograph, air conditioner, electric dry shaver (Schick), absolute monarch visiting the United States (King Prajadhipok, Siam), stockings in transparent mesh, Beech-Nut baby food, Hotel Bar butter, Wyler's bouillon cubes, Bisquick biscuit mix, Clairol hair dye, Black Muslims, Jehovah's Witnesses (the name), Starch Rating (public polling method), "Dick Tracy," Alka Seltzer (from Dr. Miles' Nervine Tonic), New School for Social Research, Waldorf Astoria, *New York World Telegram*

Catching bank robbers in N.Y.C. with machine guns and tear gas. *General Research Division. The New York Public Library. Astor, Lenox and Tilden Foundations.*

1932

Facts and Figures

Economic Profile
  Dow-Jones: ↓ High 88– Low 41
  GNP: −23%
  Inflation: −4.7%
  Unemployment: 23.6%
Radios produced: 2,446,000
AM stations: 604
Household telephones: 31%
Toll rate, New York–San Francisco: $7.50
Advertising expenditures: $1.5 billion
Mattress, box spring: $19.75
Gimbel's glider sofa: $8.94
Macy's coffee table: $9.94
Cut crystal stemware (dozen): $3.95
Eight-piece enameled pot set: $1
Dental filling: $1
Cigarettes: 15¢
Loft's candy, per pound:
  Chocolates: 49¢
  Chocolate, vanilla kisses, peanut brittle: 19¢

Above: Aviatrix Amelia Earhart. *Library of Congress.*

Deaths

Aristide Briand, William Burns, Hart Crane, George Eastman, Alfred Maurer, John Philip Sousa, G. Lytton Strachey, William Wrigley, Jr., Florenz Ziegfeld.

In the News

UNEMPLOYMENT REACHES 24% . . . SECRETARY OF STATE HENRY STIMSON SAYS U.S. WILL RECOGNIZE NO TERRITORIAL ACQUISITIONS BY AGGRESSION . . . JAPANESE PROCLAIM NEW STATE IN FORMER MANCHURIA AND ATTACK SHANGHAI . . . RECONSTRUCTION FINANCE CORPORATION LAW IS PASSED TO AID AGRICULTURE AND INDUSTRY . . . AUTO SALES ARE DOWN 80% FROM 1929 . . . GERMANS AGREE TO FINAL REPARATIONS PAYMENT . . . GLASS-STEAGALL BILL INCREASES FEDERAL RESERVE CREDIT . . . ADOLF HITLER GETS 32% OF GERMAN VOTE FOR PRESIDENT . . . NORRIS-LAGUARDIA BILL PROHIBITS EASY INJUNCTIONS AGAINST UNIONS . . . LINDBERGH BABY IS KIDNAPPED, ABDUCTED FROM N.J. HOME . . . LINDBERGH BABY IS FOUND DEAD . . . HOOVER IS RENOMINATED BY GOP, FRANKLIN DELANO ROOSEVELT, N.Y. GOVERNOR, IS NOMINATED BY THE DEMOCRATS ON FOURTH BALLOT . . . FDR TALKS TO THE "FORGOTTEN MAN" . . . SCOTTSBORO BOYS GAIN RETRIAL BASED ON ABSENCE OF COUNSEL . . . EMERGENCY RELIEF CONSTRUCTION ACT IS PASSED . . . HOUSE PASSES BUT SENATE DEFEATS BONUS BILL FOR VETERANS . . . RED CROSS DISTRIBUTES WHEAT GIVEN BY FEDERAL FARM BUREAU . . . AMELIA EARHART IS FIRST WOMAN TO FLY TRANSATLANTIC SOLO . . . NEW YORK MAYOR JIMMY WALKER RESIGNS IN CORRUPTION SCANDAL . . . 12,000 VETERANS PROTEST DEFEAT OF BONUS BILL AND MARCH ON WASHINGTON, D.C. . . . TROOPS UNDER GEN. DOUGLAS MACARTHUR DRIVE OUT BONUS MARCHERS . . . TWO STATES DECLARE MORATORIUM ON FIRST MORTGAGE FORECLOSURES . . . FDR IS ELECTED WITH 22 MILLION VOTES, HOOVER RECEIVES 15 MILLION, SOCIALIST NORMAN THOMAS, 880,000 . . . HITLER REJECTS CHANCELLORSHIP IN COALITION . . . JAPAN IS BRANDED AGGRESSOR IN CHINA BY LEAGUE OF NATIONS.

Quotes

"Brother, Can You Spare a Dime?"
— Gorney and Harburg song

"Men who lost their jobs dropped out of sight. They were quiet, and you had to know just when and where to find them: at night, for instance, on the edge of town huddling for warmth around a bonfire, or even the municipal incinerator; at dawn, picking over the garbage dump for scraps of food or salvageable clothing."
— *Fortune*

"It is obvious that relief is of the scantiest kind and in some districts entirely nonexistent. In one camp the women talked brokenheartedly of a bowel disease which they called 'Flux' that had proved fatal to some of the children and was the result of prolonged underfeeding and efforts to stay the pangs of hunger by devouring chunks of raw cabbage or anything at all which they could lay hands on."
— Jennie Lee, describing a Kentucky mine camp

"CHICAGO, June 18— . . . A check-up of the city schools revealed today that 11,000 hungry children are being fed by teachers . . . [who themselves] are seriously handicapped by the failure of the Board of Education to pay them."
— Report by the chief of the Children's Bureau, Department of Labor, in the *New York Times*

"[A] descent from respectability . . . must be numbered in the millions. This is what we have accomplished with our bread lines and soup kitchens, . . . defeated, discouraged, hopeless men and women cringing and bowing as they come to ask for public

On President Hoover's orders, General Douglas MacArthur commands his troops and tanks to disperse the Bonus Marchers. *Library of Congress.*

aid. . . . It is a spectacle of national degeneration. That is the fundamental tragedy for America."
— Joseph L. Heffernan, *Atlantic Monthly*

"The breakdown in which we are living is the breakdown of the particular romance known as business, . . . the revelation that the elated excitement of the romantic adventure has to be paid for with an equal depression."
— John Dewey

"Very well, we strike hands with our true comrades, the Communist Party."
— Edmund Wilson

"Ever since I could remember I'd wished I'd been lucky enough to be alive at a great time—when something big was going on, like the crucifixion. And suddenly I realized I was."
— Ben Shahn

"I pledge you, I pledge myself, to a new deal, for the American people. Let us all here assembled constitute ourselves prophets of a new order of competence and courage. This is more than a political campaign; it is a call to arms."
— FDR's acceptance of the presidential nomination

Ads

Do you inhale? Of course you do! Lucky Strike has dared to raise this vital question *because* certain impurities concealed in even the finest, mildest tobacco leaves are removed by Luckies' famous purifying process.

(*Lucky Strike Cigarettes*)

American markets today are being invaded with inferior foreign imitations, . . . shoddy products. Buy American! Help a worker hold his job.

(*Hygrade Sylvania Corp.*)

4 Out of 5 Democrats
Contain harmful Acids
—Insist on Hoover
Accept no Substitute
(*Political ad*)

Now you can have a Roosevelt
in your White House at Surprisingly Low Cost
the Candidate with the Monitor Top
Protected from either Dryness or Wetness
Silent—no Whirring Noises about Prohibition.
Keep Regular with Roosevelt

(*Political ad*)

Radio

Premieres
"Music That Satisfies," Ruth Etting, Boswell Sisters, Arthur Tracy ("The Street Singer")
"Kaltenmeyer's Kindergarten," Bruce Kamman
"The George Burns and Gracie Allen Show"
"Just Plain Bill," Arthur Hughes
"Yours for a Song," Jane Froman
"One Man's Family," J. Anthony Smythe
"Clara Lu'n" (first daytime serial)
"Today's Children," Helen Kane
"National Barn Dance"
"The Jack Benny Program," Jack Benny (age 38)
"The Fred Allen Show"
"Tom Mix," Artells Dickson
"The Fire Chief" (Ed Wynn)

Specials
"Tosca" (San Francisco Opera); Floyd Gibbons from the Manchurian battlefields; the World Disarmament Conference, Geneva

Of Note
Jack Benny debuts on "The Ed Sullivan Show" • Hourly bulletins follow the Lindbergh baby kidnapping • Ed Wynn insists upon a live audience for his "Fire Chief" program • The first broadcast from Radio City, November 11, includes a 400-piece symphony orchestra, Jane Cowl, Jessica Dragonette, John McCormack, Maria Jeritza, Rudy Vallee, Will Rogers, "Amos 'n' Andy," Paul Whiteman, and the Schola Cantorum Choir • Segments on "The Fred Allen Show" include the Mighty Allen Art Players, the Average Man's Round Table, and Allen's Alley, with Senator Claghorn, Titus Moody, and Ajax Cassidy.

New Catchphrases: "Good evening, Mr. and Mrs. America, and all the ships at sea" (Walter Winchell); "Now, cut that out," "Wait a minute," "Anaheim, Azusa, and Cu-ca-monga" (Jack Benny)

Movies

Openings
Grand Hotel (Edmund Goulding), John Barrymore Lionel Barrymore, Wallace Beery, Joan Crawford, Greta Garbo
Shanghai Express (Josef von Sternberg), Clive Brook, Marlene Dietrich
I Am a Fugitive from a Chain Gang (Mervyn LeRoy), Paul Muni
M (Fritz Lang), Peter Lorre
What Price Hollywood? (George Cukor), Constance Bennett (original of *A Star Is Born*)
The Sign of the Cross (Cecil B. DeMille), Claudette Colbert, Fredric March
Tarzan, the Ape Man (W. S. Van Dyke), Johnny Weismuller, Maureen O'Sullivan
A Farewell to Arms (Frank Borzage), Gary Cooper, Helen Hayes
Dr. Jekyll and Mr. Hyde (Rouben Mamoulian), Fredric March, Miriam Hopkins
Rain (Lewis Milestone), Joan Crawford, Walter Huston
Red-Headed Woman (Jack Conway), Jean Harlow, Charles Boyer
Blonde Venus (Josef von Sternberg), Marlene Dietrich, Cary Grant

Bill of Divorcement (George Cukor), John Barrymore, Katharine Hepburn
Trouble in Paradise (Ernst Lubitsch), Miriam Hopkins, Herbert Marshall
Mata Hari (George Fitzmaurice), Greta Garbo, Ramon Novarro
Scarface (Howard Hawks), Paul Muni, George Raft
Freaks (Tod Browning), Leila Hyams, Olga Baclanova

Academy Awards (1931–32)
Best Picture: *Grand Hotel*
Best Director: Frank Borzage (*Bad Girl*)
Best Actress: Helen Hayes (*The Sin of Madelon Claudet*)
Best Actor: Wallace Beery (*The Champ*), Fredric March (*Dr. Jekyll and Mr. Hyde*)
Special Award: Mickey Mouse

Top Box-Office Stars
Marie Dressler, Janet Gaynor, Joan Crawford, Charles Farrell, Greta Garbo, Norma Shearer, Wallace Beery, Clark Gable, Will Rogers, Joe E. Brown

Popular Music

Composer-performer Duke Ellington.

Hit Songs
"Night and Day"
"April in Paris"
"I'm Getting Sentimental over
  You"
"In a Shanty in Old Shanty Town"
"Shuffle Off to Buffalo"
"I Told Every Little Star"
"How Deep Is the Ocean?"
"Granada"
"You're an Old Smoothie"
"Forty-Second Street"
"You're Getting to Be a Habit
  with Me"

Top Records
New Tiger Rag (Louis
Armstrong); *Reefer Man* and *The
Man from Harlem* (Cab
Calloway); *If You Were the Only
Girl* (Rudy Vallee); *It Don't Mean
a Thing If It Ain't Got That Swing*
(Duke Ellington)

Jazz and Big Bands
Louis Armstrong makes his first
trip abroad. Fats Waller performs
at Adelaide Hall, New York.

New Band: Fats Waller, New
York

Theater

Broadway Openings

Plays
Another Language (Rose Franken), Glenn Anders,
  Margaret Wycherly
Autumn Crocus (C. L. Anthony), Dorothy Gish,
  Francis Lederer, Patricia Collinge
The Animal Kingdon (Philip Barry), Leslie Howard
The Late Christopher Bean (Sidney Howard), Pauline
  Lord, Walter Connolly
Criminal at Large (Edgar Wallace), Emlyn Williams,
  William Harrigan
Dangerous Corner (J. B. Priestley), Jean Dixon,
  Colin Keith-Johnston
When Ladies Meet (Rachel Crothers), Frieda
  Inescort, Walter Abel, Spring Byington
Dinner at Eight (George S. Kaufman, Edna Ferber),
  Ann Andrews, Cesar Romero, Sam Levene
Too True to Be Good (George Bernard Shaw),
  Beatrice Lillie, Leo G. Carroll
Biography (S. N. Behrman), Ina Claire
Twentieth Century (Ben Hecht, Charles MacArthur),
  Eugenie Leontovich

Musicals
Earl Carroll's Vanities of 1932 (Harold Arlen, Ted
  Koehler), Milton Berle, Lillian Roth
Flying Colors (Arthur Schwartz, Howard Dietz),
  Clifton Webb, Patsy Kelly, Buddy and Velma
  Ebsen, Imogene Coca, Larry Adler

Gay Divorce (Cole Porter), Fred Astaire, Luella
  Gear, Claire Luce
Hot-Cha (Ray Henderson, Lew Brown), Lupe Velez,
  Bert Lahr, Eleanor Powell
Music in the Air (Jerome Kern, Oscar Hammerstein
  II), Al Shean, Walter Slezak, Katherine
  Carrington
Take a Chance (Herb Brown, B. G. DeSylva), Ethel
  Merman, Jack Haley
Face the Music (Irving Berlin, Moss Hart), Andrew
  Tombes, Mary Boland

Classics and Revivals On and Off Broadway
Liliom (Molnár), Joseph Schildkraut; *Oedipus Rex,
The Rising of the Moon* (Lady Gregory), Abbey
Players

Regional

Founded: Barter Theatre, Abingdon, Va., by Robert
Porterfield

Pulitzer Prize
Of Thee I Sing, George S. Kaufman, Morrie
Ryskind, and Ira Gershwin

Classical Music

Compositions
Virgil Thomson, *Americana*
Samuel Barber, Sonata for Violoncello and Piano
Wallingford Riegger, *Dichotomy*
John Alden Carpenter, *Song of Faith*
Roy Harris, *From the Gayety and Sadness of the American Scene,* String Sextet, Fantasy, Chorale for Strings

Important Events
Because of the depression, many events are canceled, numerous musical organizations go bankrupt, and seasons are divided in half; sporadic concerts of the unemployed take place; "monster" concerts are played at the Roxy Theater, New York City; composers organize in protective organizations, such as ASCAP, the American Composers Alliance, and AGMA.

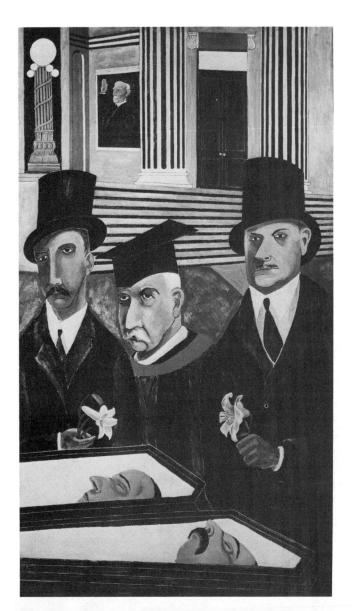

Guest Conductors: Ottorino Respighi and Bruno Walter, the New York Philharmonic

Debut: E. Power Biggs

First Performances
Respighi, conducting, *Maria Egiziaca* (New York); Ernest Bloch, *Helvetia* (Chicago); Arnold Bax, Symphony no. 4 (San Francisco); Aaron Copland, Symphonic Ode (Boston); George Gershwin, playing, *Second Rhapsody* (Boston); John Alden Carpenter, playing, *Patterns* (Boston)

Opera

Metropolitan: Lawrence Tibbett, *Simon Boccanegra* (Giuseppe Verdi, American premiere); Tito Schipa, *L'elisir d'amore, Don Giovanni;* Rose Bampton (debut), *La Gioconda;* Richard Bonelli, *Faust.* Premiere: *Il Signor Bruschino* (Gioacchino Rossini)

San Francisco: Lily Pons, Alfredo Gandolfi, *Tosca* (nationally broadcast); *The Fairy Queen* (Purcell, premiere)

Music Notes
The League of Composers performs Arnold Schoenberg's *Gurrelieder* • Aaron Copland organizes Yaddo (its name derived from a child's pronunciation of *shadow*) and the first Festival of Contemporary American music. Composer-performers include Copland, Piston, Thomson, Ives, Bowles, Bennett, Harris, Chávez, Riegger, Gruenberg, and Blitzstein • Leopold Stokowski publicly asks for compositions for radio performance and receives 400; he performs Powell, Gruenberg, Copland, Bennett, Piston, Cowell, and Cubensky • The Pan American Association of Composers continues to bring American music to European capitals. Most performed are Ives, Ruggles, Riegger, Harris, Crawford, and Cowell.

Ben Shahn, *The Passion of Sacco and Vanzetti,* 1931–32. Tempera. 84½ × 48". *Collection of Whitney Museum of American Art. Geoffrey Clements.*

Art

Painting

Raphael Soyer, *Mina*
Paul Cadmus, *Sailors and Floosies*
Georgia O'Keeffe, *Cross by the Sea*
Charles Sheeler, *Buck's County Barn, River Rouge Plant*
Grant Wood, *Daughters of the American Revolution*
Ben Shahn, *The Passion of Sacco and Vanzetti*
Clyfford Still, *Spring Landscape*
Peter Blume, *Light of the World*
Arshile Gorky, *Organization*
Reginald Marsh, *Tattoo and Haircut, Locomotive Watering*
Isabel Bishop, *On the Street*
John Marin, *Region of Brooklyn Bridge Fantasy*
John Kane, *From My Studio*

Sculpture

John Storrs, *Composition around Two Voids*
David Smith, *Head, Construction*
Theodore Roszak, *Airport Structure*
Gaston Lachaise, *Standing Woman*
William Zorach, *Torso*
Alexander Calder, *Motorized Mobile, Construction*
Elie Nadelman, *Construction Workers,* at the Fuller Building, New York

Architecture

Philadelphia Savings Fund Society, Philadelphia (Howe and Lescaze)
Travel and Transport Building, Century of Progress Exhibit, Chicago (Joseph Urban)
Pennsylvania Station, Philadelphia (Graham, Anderson, Probst and White)
Nebraska State Capitol Building, Lincoln (Bertram Goodhue)
U.S. Forest Products Laboratory, Madison, Wisc. (Holabird and Root)
Broadacre City model (Frank Lloyd Wright)

Important Exhibitions

Museums

New York: *Metropolitan:* "Favorite paintings of the Younger Generation: The Taste of Today in Masterpieces before 1900," Leonardo, Rembrandt, and Raphael, among others; the Washington Bicentennial; Costumes, 1750–1850; Samuel French Morse. *Museum of Modern Art:* American folk art, 1750–1900; "Art of the Common Man"; American painting and sculpture, 1862–1932; "Modern Architecture: International Exhibition"

Raphael Soyer, *Mina*, 1932. Oil on canvas. 28 × 26³⁄₁₆″. *The Metropolitan Museum of Art, Bequest of Margaret S. Lewisohn, 1954.*

Chicago: Drawings; modern paintings and watercolors; loan exhibit of Islamic bookbindings

Boston: Contemporary art

Pittsburgh: The Carnegie International is canceled because of the depression.

Art Briefs

Mural commissions are given to Diego Rivera, José Orozco, David Alfaro Siqueiros, and Frank Brangwyn for Rockefeller Center; to Dean Cornwall for the Los Angeles Public Library; to Thomas Hart Benton for the Whitney Museum; and to José Sert for the Waldorf Astoria • Max Ernst holds his first American show in New York • Depression arts are displayed in open-air marts, the first held in Washington Square, New York, where 970 of 1,700 works are sold; Chicago, Dallas, Cleveland, and Detroit also sponsor outdoor shows • Dealers hold shows where any painting costs $100 • Duchamp names Calder's mechanized constructions *mobiles*.

Books

Fiction

Critics' Choice

Light in August, William Faulkner
From Flushing to Calvary, Edward Dahlberg
The Unvanquished, Howard Fast
1919, John Dos Passos
The Gods Arrive, Edith Wharton
Year before Last, Kay Boyle
Young Lonigan, James Farrell
Tobacco Road, Erskine Caldwell
🔊 *Brave New World*, Aldous Huxley

Best-Sellers

The Good Earth, Pearl S. Buck
Sons, Pearl S. Buck
The Fountain, Charles Morgan
The Sheltered Life, Ellen Glasgow
Magnolia Street, Louis Golding
Old Wine and New, Warwick Deeping
Mary's Neck, Booth Tarkington
Inheritance, Phyllis Bentley
Magnificent Obsession, Lloyd Douglas
Three Loves, A. J. Cronin

Nonfiction

Critics' Choice

Death in the Afternoon, Ernest Hemingway
The Life of Emerson, Van Wyck Brooks
Mark Twain's America, Bernard De Voto
20,000 Years in Sing Sing, Warden Lewis E. Lawes
I Am a Fugitive from a Georgia Chain Gang, Robert E. Burns
Frank Lloyd Wright's Autobiography, Frank Lloyd Wright
The U.S. in World Affairs, Walter Lippmann
Moral Man and Immoral Society, Reinhold Niebuhr
A New Deal, Stuart Chase
The Age of Technocracy, Howard Scott
On Being Creative, Irving Babbitt
Anthropology and Modern Life, Franz Boaz

Best-Sellers

The Epic of America, James Truslow Adams
Only Yesterday, Frederick Lewis Allen
A Fortune to Share, Vash Young
Culbertson's Summary, Ely Culbertson
Van Loon's Geography, Hendrik Willem Van Loon
What We Live By, Ernest Dimnet
The March of Democracy, James Truslow Adams
Washington Merry-Go-Round, Anonymous (Drew Pearson, Robert S. Allen)
The Story of My Life, Clarence Darrow
More Merry-Go-Round, Anonymous (Drew Pearson, Robert S. Allen)

Poetry

T. S. Eliot, *Sweeney Agonistes*
Eleanor Wylie, *Collected Poems*
Robinson Jeffers, *Thurso's Landing*
Edwin Arlington Robinson, *Nicodemus*
Stephen Vincent Benét, *Rip Tide*
Allen Tate, *Poems 1928–1931*
🔊 W. H. Auden, *The Orators*

Pulitzer Prizes

The Store, T. S. Stribling (novel)
The Significance of Sections in American History, Frederick J. Turner (U.S. history)
Grover Cleveland, Allan Nevins (biography)
Conquistador, Archibald MacLeish (poetry)

Science and Technology

Carl David Anderson discovers the positron, a subatomic particle.
Edwin Land devises the first synthetic sheet light polarizer.
Dr. Arthur Holly Compton concludes that cosmic rays are electrons from the earth's upper atmosphere.
Adrenal cortex stimulating hormone, ACTH, is prepared by James C. Collip.
Dr. William Beebe, in his bathysphere, descends to a record 2,200 feet underwater.
The semiflexible gastroscope is introduced for internal viewing of the stomach.
James Chadwick discovers the neutron.
Ernest O. Lawrence constructs the first practical cyclotron. He splits the atom artificially two to three weeks after John Cockcroft and Ernest Walton in England use a beam of protons to split it; theirs is the first atomic transformation accomplished without a radioactive substance.
🔊 Prontosil, a sulfa red dye, is developed by Gerhard Domagk.
🔊 Albert Butenandt isolates the male sex hormone, testosterone.

Nobel Prizes

Edgar D. Adrian wins the prize in physiology and medicine for work on the function of the neuron.
Irving Langmuir wins in chemistry for research on surface chemistry.

Sports

Baseball

Babe Ruth (New York, AL), after being heckled from the Cubs' dugout, points "to the spot" and hits a home run off Charlie Root (Chicago, NL) in the World Series.

Lou Gehrig (New York, AL) hits four home runs in a nine-inning game.

Champions

Batting	Pitching
Lefty O'Doul (Philadelphia, NL), .368	Lon Warneke (Chicago, NL), 22–6
D. D. Alexander (Detroit-Boston, AL), .367	John Allen (New York, AL), 17–4
	Home runs
	James Foxx (Philadelphia, AL), 58

Football

NFL Season Leaders: Arnie Herber (Green Bay), passing; Bob Campiglio (Stapleton), rushing; Luke Johnsos (Chicago Bears), receiving.

College All-Americans: Harry Newman (Q), Michigan; William Corbus (G), Stanford

Bowls (Jan. 1, 1933)
Rose: Southern California 35–Pittsburgh 0
Orange: Miami 7–Manhattan 0

Basketball

A new college rule requires the ball to be brought over the midcourt line in 10 seconds.
Johnny Wooden, the "Indiana Rubber Man," is All-American, at Purdue, for the third time.

Olympics

The first Winter Games to be held in the United States are at Lake Placid, N.Y. John Shea (500m, 1500m) and Irving Jaffee (5000m, 10,000m) win gold medals in speed skating. In the Summer Games at Los Angeles, U.S. winners include Babe Didrikson (javelin, 143'4", and 80m hurdles, 11.7s), Eddie Tolan (100m, 10.3s and 200m, 21.1s), Edward Gordon (broad jump, 25' 4¾"), William Miller (pole vault, 14' 1⅞"), James Bausch (decathlon), Clarence "Buster" Crabbe (swimming, 400m), Helen Madison (100m and 400m), Eleanor Holm (100m backstroke).

Other Sports

Boxing: Jack Sharkey beats Max Schmeling to regain the heavyweight crown.

Tennis: Helen Wills Moody wins at Wimbledon.

Winners

World Series	Player of the Year
New York (AL) 4	John Wooden, Purdue
Chicago (NL) 0	*Stanley Cup*
MVP	Toronto
NL–Charles Klein, Philadelphia	*U.S. Tennis Open*
AL–James Foxx, Philadelphia	Men: Ellsworth Vines, Jr.
	Women: Helen Hull Jacobs
NFL	*USGA Open*
Chicago Bears	Gene Sarazen
College Football	*Kentucky Derby*
USC	Burgoo King (E. James, jockey)
College Basketball	
Purdue	

Fashion

For Women: With the growing vogue in slinky silks popularized through the movies, undergarments change dramatically. Though still embroidered and generally of one piece—in chemises, camisoles, vests, drawers, and slips—there is a new absence of seams, since they show through the tight or clinging clothing. Heavy corsetry soon appears on the market "to hold up the muscles," and a new interest emerges in the "uplift," provided by darts and hidden circular stitching. Artificial silks and zippers make clothing less expensive. A blue and white plaid rayon dress with sashed belt and bow collar is virtually ubiquitous. Fashionable hats range from the pillbox, toque, trimmed turban, and Basque beret (worn on the side like Dietrich), to summer styles trimmed with flowers, ribbons, and quills.

High-fashion notes: Mainbocher's molded sheath; Chanel's cotton evening dress

For Men: For the first time, wool, not silk, ties appear in solids, foulards, and stripes, or with small (often sports) figures.

Kaleidoscope _____

- Wages drop 60 percent since 1929; white-collar salaries are down 40 percent. Unemployment is over three times that of 1930. The suicide rate rises to 17.4 per 100,000 people, up 30 percent from 1920s levels; homicide levels remain stable.
- The Federal Reserve Board's index of production is down 55 percent from 1929.
- Indigents are barred from voting in Lewiston, Maine; a million nomads wander America with no voting rights in ten other states.
- Wages for picking figs are 10¢ per 50-pound box, $1.50 a day for 15 boxes; for picking peas, 14¢ a pound, $1.25 a day, $30 for the season.
- Twelve-thousand veterans encamp in Washington to demand their World War I bonus (due in 1945); Hoover calls out the army, headed by Douglas MacArthur and junior officers Dwight Eisenhower and George Patton, and the marchers are disbanded with tear gas and force of arms.
- On May 28, the Detroit Welfare Department announces that it owes $800,000 and has on hand only $8,000.
- News columnists assume great popular importance; joining Walter Lippmann are Westbrook Pegler, David Lawrence, Frank Kent, and Dorothy Thompson.
- Enormous public response to the Lindbergh kidnapping includes the AFL's offer of membership assistance and prayer by major religious figures.
- A new crime epidemic begins with Dillinger, "Baby Face" Nelson, "Machine Gun" Kelly, "Pretty Boy" Floyd, "Ma" Barker, and Bonnie and Clyde.
- The FBI publicizes a list of "Public Enemies."
- Sam Insull, the utilities magnate, escapes to Greece when he faces indictment for questionable business practices.
- Ivan Kreuger, the Swedish "match king" industrialist extensively financed by American banks, commits suicide as he faces charges of fraud.
- With depression audiences noticeably decreasing, theaters lower admissions and present low-budget productions.
- Radio City Music Hall, with 6,200 seats, opens, the world's largest movie theater.
- Nude statues by William Zorach, Gwen Lux, and Robert Laurent are barred from Radio City, creating a furor; after the ban is lifted, the situation is questioned as a publicity hoax.
- In Los Angeles, a David Siqueiros mural depicting a peasant's crucifixion under an American eagle is whitewashed.
- Two-a-day vaudeville closes on Broadway.
- In response to "Goodness, what beautiful diamonds!" Mae West, in her movie debut, *Night after Night,* replies, "Goodness had nothing to do with it."
- Ad executive Elmer Zilch is a featured character of *Ballyhoo,* a new satire magazine which soars to 2 million in circulation.
- New foreign actors in Hollywood include George Arliss, David Niven, Charles Laughton, Basil

Economically pressed veterans seek "bonus" payment for past service. *Library of Congress.*

Rathbone, Laurence Olivier, Maurice Chevalier, and Marlene Dietrich.
- Howard Scott gains a wide following with his "technocracy," which proposes the substitution of energy units, like ergs, for dollars and cents.
- The "Great I Am" movement, a mystic faith promising its followers wealth and power, gains 300,000 followers.
- New York physician Thomas Parran's attempt to fight venereal disease leads to the permissible use of the word *syphilis* in newspapers and other public media.
- In response to the depression, Hoover reduces his salary by 20 percent and asks the same of his vice president and nine cabinet members.
- On being questioned about a $26,000 stock gift, New York mayor Jimmy Walker replies that he has "many kind friends."
- Herbert Hoover declares that "grass will grow in the streets of 100 cities" if FDR is elected.
- Franklin Roosevelt breaks tradition and flies to address the Democratic National Convention immediately after he is nominated; "Happy Days Are Here Again" is the party's theme.
- FDR is aided by his brains trust, Columbia University Professors Raymond Moley, Rexford Tugwell, and Adolph Berle, Jr.
- With the recent discovery of the male hormone testosterone, animal gonad transplants provoke a great deal of interest.
- An interest in skiing is stimulated by the Winter Olympics at Lake Placid, N.Y.

Fads: New dances include the jitterbug and swing ("It don't mean a thing if it ain't got that swing," coined by Duke Ellington), the big apple, shag, boogie-woogie, Susie-Q, Lindy hop, and truckin'; Rudy Vallee becomes "the rage"; astrology.

First Appearances: Zippo lighter, Mounds (twin bars), Frito corn chips, Skippy peanut butter, Teachers College (Columbia), Folger Library (Washington), Revlon, Johnson Glo-Coat wax, International Experiment in Living, the name Saudi Arabia *(Hejas Nejd),* tax on gasoline, wooden money (Tacoma, Wash.), Route 66

1933

Facts and Figures

Economic Profile
  Dow-Jones: ↑ High 108–
    Low 50
  GNP: −4%
  Inflation: +1.3%
  Unemployment: 24.9%
Daily newspapers: 1,903
Books published: 8,092
Airmail postage: 8¢/oz.
Postcard: 1¢
IRS collections: $1.6 billion
Tuxedo (Saks Fifth Avenue):
  $39.50
Trousers (Brooks Brothers):
  $15–$18
Mark Cross gloves: $2.75
Four-course dinner: 60¢–
  $1.50 (Hotel Taft)
  Breakfast: 25¢
  Lunch: 40¢–50¢
Air fares:
  Chicago to Los Angeles:
    $207 (round trip)
  New York to Chicago:
    $86.31 (round trip)
Around-the-world cruise, 85
  days, 14 countries: $749
Kodak Brownie camera:
  $2.50

Above: FDR, at his
inauguration, asks for "broad
executive powers to wage a
war against the emergency."
Library of Congress.

Deaths

Roscoe "Fatty" Arbuckle,
  Irving Babbitt, Earl Derr
  Biggers, Calvin Coolidge,
  John Galsworthy, Stefan
  George, Ring Lardner,
  George B. Luks, George
  Moore, Frederick Henry
  Royce, Louis Comfort
  Tiffany.

In the News

HITLER BECOMES GERMAN CHANCELLOR . . . U.S. MARINES LEAVE NICARAGUA . . . GERMAN REICHSTAG BURNS DOWN, HITLER ASSUMES DICTATORIAL POWERS . . . ROOSEVELT ESCAPES FLORIDA ASSASSINATION ATTEMPT, CHICAGO MAYOR ANTON CERMAK IS SHOT TO DEATH . . . MICHIGAN GOVERNOR DECLARES EIGHT-DAY BANK HOLIDAY . . . N.Y. GOVERNOR DECLARES BANK HOLIDAY . . . FDR IS INAUGURATED . . . FDR DECLARES NATIONAL BANK HOLIDAY . . . 3.2% BEER AND WINE ARE AUTHORIZED BY CONGRESS . . . AGRICULTURAL ADJUSTMENT ACT IS PASSED TO RESTORE FARM PRICES . . . EMERGENCY BANK ACT GIVES PRESIDENT CONTROL OVER BANKING AND GOLD . . . FEDERAL DOLE BEGINS . . . ECONOMY ACT REDUCES VETERANS' PAY AND FEDERAL SALARIES . . . UNEMPLOYMENT RELIEF ACT CREATES CIVILIAN CONSERVATION CORPS . . . U.S. LEAVES GOLD STANDARD . . . SECURITIES ACT PROVIDES FOR CAREFUL REGULATION OF NEW SECURITIES . . . BANKS GIVE UP GOLD, GOLD CLAUSES IN CONTRACTS ARE VOIDED . . . TENNESSEE VALLEY AUTHORITY BILL IS PASSED ALLOWING GOVERNMENT TO PRODUCE ELECTRIC POWER . . . OIL IS STRUCK IN SAUDI ARABIA, SO-CAL OIL GETS CONCESSION . . . U.S. EMPLOYMENT AGENCY WILL COORDINATE UNEMPLOYMENT ACTIVITIES . . . JAPAN WITHDRAWS FROM LEAGUE OF NATIONS . . . NATIONAL INDUSTRIAL RECOVERY ACT PROVIDES CODES OF FAIR COMPETITION . . . FARM CREDIT ACT WILL CONSOLIDATE RURAL CREDIT AGENCIES . . . GLASS-STEAGALL BANK REFORM IS PASSED TO PROTECT DEPOSITS . . . GERMANY WITHDRAWS FROM LEAGUE OF NATIONS . . . CIVIL WORKS ADMINISTRATION WILL PROVIDE 400,000 EMERGENCY JOBS . . . ANTONIO SALAZAR BECOMES PORTUGUESE DICTATOR . . . U.S. RESUMES DIPLOMATIC TIES WITH U.S.S.R. . . . PROHIBITION REPEAL TAKES EFFECT.

Quotes _____

"We are at the end of our string. There is nothing more we can do."
— Herbert Hoover, on the eve of FDR's inauguration

"The only thing we have to fear is fear itself."
— FDR, inauguration speech

"I shall ask the Congress for the remaining instruments to meet the crisis—broad executive power to wage a war against the emergency, as great as the power that would be given me if we were invaded by a foreign foe."
— FDR

"In war in the gloom of night attack, soldiers wear a bright badge on their shoulders to be sure that comrades do not fire on comrades. On that principle, . . . we have provided a badge of honor [the blue eagle]. . . . It is essential to our purpose."
— FDR, fireside chat

"I can assure you that it is safer to keep your money in a reopened bank than under the mattress."
— FDR

"Professors are one of the chief curses of the country. They talk too much. Most professors are a bunch of cowards and meddlers. The sooner we get away from their influence the better."
— Frederick Henry Price, owner of 46 railroads

The blue eagle, emblem of the National Recovery Administration (NRA). *Smithsonian Institution.*

"Surely some professors are meddlers and busybodies, just as some financiers are crooks."
— Dean Ralph Emerson Heilman, Northwestern University

"There is no rule so sure as that one that the same mill that grinds out fortunes above a certain size at the top grinds out paupers at the bottom."
— Huey Long

"I will say one thing for this administration. It is the only time when the fellow with money is worrying more than the one without it."
— Will Rogers

Ads _____

[THESE ARE CHILDREN]
WHO NEVER KNEW WANT BEFORE
It's pretty hard to keep your chin up—as a man of 12 should—when your shoes are full of holes that keep getting bigger. And when you always, even right after breakfast, feel kind of funny and faint inside.—There are more than 200,000 small citizens trying to smile under just such conditions in New York.
(Emergency Unemployment Relief Committee)

So we can be ourselves once more! No need ever again to hide fiery bitterness with queer concoctions, . . . to apologize while filling a glass, . . . to force undesired draughts upon unhappy guests. We can toast fair ladies with HENNESSY once again.
(Hennessy Whiskey)

When you buy Camels you get fresh cigarettes. That's why women particularly prefer them.
(Camel Cigarettes)

The world's most pleasant alarm clock!
(Pillsbury Pancake Flour)

She's wearing Cherry Coke . . . one of Revlon's colors of the hour.
(Revlon)

Come, Lady Fair, and Dwell with me / Where enemies can't seize us; / Our cottage will a Palace Be / With Campbell's Soups to Please us!
(Campbell's Vegetable Soup)

Radio

Premieres
"The Romance of Helen Trent," Virginia Clark
"Jack Armstrong, the All-American Boy," St. John
    Terrell
"Don McNeill's Breakfast Club"
"The Lone Ranger," George Seaton, John Todd
"Ma Perkins," Virginia Payne
"The Jimmy Durante Show"

Specials
"Eleanor Roosevelt"; "Vatican City" (Pope Pius
opens the Holy Door of St. Peter's Basilica);
"George Bernard Shaw"

Of Note
Music offerings in a typical week might include the
Metropolitan Opera, New York Philharmonic, Boston
Symphony, Lily Pons, Lawrence Tibbett, and Josef
Hoffmann • Premiums offered for Wheaties' boxtops
include Jack Armstrong whistling rings, secret
decoders, and Norden "bombsights" • FDR begins

Radio stars Eddie Cantor, Al Jolson, Gracie Allen, and
George Burns, all of whom began in vaudeville. *Movie Star
News.*

his fireside chats • The largest radio audience to date
listens to FDR's plans to reopen the national banks •
The Federal Radio Commission becomes the FCC.

New Catchphrases: ". . . dedicated to the mothers
and fathers of the younger generation and their
bewildering offspring" ("One Man's Family");
". . . [the story of a woman] who sets out to prove
. . . romance can live . . . at thirty-five" ("The
Romance of Helen Trent"); "Be good to yourself!"
("Breakfast Club")

Movies

Openings
Cavalcade (Frank Lloyd), Diana Wynward, Clive
    Brook
Forty-second Street (Lloyd Bacon), Ruby Keeler,
    Dick Powell, Ginger Rogers, Bebe Daniels
The Private Life of Henry VIII (Alexander Korda),
    Charles Laughton, Elsa Lanchester
She Done Him Wrong (Lowell Sherman), Mae West,
    Cary Grant, Gilbert Roland
State Fair (Henry King), Janet Gaynor, Will Rogers,
    Lew Ayres
Dinner at Eight (George Cukor), John Barrymore,
    Lionel Barrymore, Marie Dressler, Jean Harlow
Little Women (George Cukor), Katharine Hepburn,
    Joan Bennett
The Invisible Man (James Whale), Claude Rains,
    Henry Travers
Gold Diggers of 1933 (Mervyn LeRoy), Dick Powell,
    Ruby Keeler, Joan Blondell, Aline MacMahon
Queen Christina (Rouben Mamoulian), Greta Garbo,
    John Gilbert
King Kong (Merian C. Cooper, Ernest Schoedsack),
    Fay Wray, Bruce Cabot
Flying Down to Rio (Thornton Freeland), Fred
    Astaire, Ginger Rogers, Dolores del Rio

Rasputin and the Empress (Richard Boleslawski),
    John Barrymore, Ethel Barrymore, Lionel
    Barrymore (only time all together on the screen)
Design for Living (Ernst Lubitsch), Gary Cooper,
    Fredric March, Miriam Hopkins
Duck Soup (Leo McCarey), Marx Brothers
Footlight Parade (Lloyd Bacon), James Cagney, Joan
    Blondell, Dick Powell, Ruby Keeler
Morning Glory (Lowell Sherman), Katharine
    Hepburn, Douglas Fairbanks, Sr.
Thunder over Mexico (Sergei Eisenstein, not
    completed)

Academy Awards
Best Picture: *Cavalcade*
Best Director: Frank Lloyd (*Cavalcade*)
Best Actress: Katharine Hepburn (*Morning Glory*)
Best Actor: Charles Laughton (*The Private Life of
    Henry VIII*)

Top Box-Office Stars
Marie Dressler, Will Rogers, Janet Gaynor, Eddie
Cantor, Wallace Beery, Jean Harlow, Clark Gable,
Mae West, Norma Shearer, Joan Crawford

Popular Music

Hit Songs

"It's Only a Paper Moon"
"Smoke Gets in Your Eyes"
"Lazy Bones"
"Easter Parade"
"Who's Afraid of the Big Bad
    Wolf?"
"Everything I Have Is Yours"
"Inka Dinka Doo"
"Lover"
"Let's Fall in Love"
"Temptation"

Top Records

Stormy Weather (Ethel Waters); *I Cover the Waterfront* (Eddy Duchin); *Forty-second Street* (Hal Kemp); *Gold Diggers' Song* (Dick Powell); *Honeymoon Hotel* (Freddy Martin); *Heartaches* (Ted Weems, with Elmo Tanner whistling); *Sophisticated Lady* (Duke Ellington)

Jazz and Big Bands

Duke Ellington and his band visit Europe. Charlie Barnet plays at the Paramount Grill, New York.

First Recordings: Billie Holiday, with Benny Goodman

New Band: Nemmu Carter (and Teddy Wilson)

Theater

Broadway Openings

Plays

Ah, Wilderness! (Eugene O'Neill), George M. Cohan, Gene Lockhart, Walter Vonnegut, Jr.
Tobacco Road (Jack Kirkland), Henry Hull, Margaret Wycherly, Dean Jagger
Both Your Houses (Maxwell Anderson), Walter C. Kelly, Sheppard Strudwick, Mary Philips
Men in White (Sidney S. Kingsley), Alexander Kirkland
Design for Living (Noel Coward), Alfred Lunt, Lynn Fontanne, Noel Coward
Alien Corn (Sidney Howard), Katharine Cornell, Luther Adler, James Rennie
The Lake (Dorothy Massingham, Murray MacDonald), Katharine Hepburn
Jezebel (Owen Davis), Miriam Hopkins, Joseph Cotten
The Green Bay Tree (Mordaunt Shairp), Laurence Olivier
Mary of Scotland (Maxwell Anderson), Helen Hayes

Musicals

As Thousands Cheer (Irving Berlin), Marilyn Miller, Clifton Webb, Ethel Waters
Champagne, Sec (Johann Strauss, Robert Simon), George Meader, Helen Ford, Peggy Wood, Kitty Carlisle
Let 'Em Eat Cake (George Gershwin, Ira Gershwin), William Gaxton, Victor Moore, Lois Moran
Murder at the Vanities (Herman Hupfield et al.), James Rennie, Bela Lugosi, Olga Baclanova
Roberta (Jerome Kern, Otto Harbach), Tamara, Ray Middleton, Bob Hope, Sydney Greenstreet, Fred MacMurray

The Golddiggers of 1933. Busby Berkeley's extravagant dance routines revolutionize the film musical. *Movie Star News.*

Strike Me Pink (Ray Henderson, Lew Brown), Jimmy Durante, Lupe Velez, Hope Williams

Classics and Revivals On and Off Broadway

Romeo and Juliet, Eva Le Gallienne; *The Cherry Orchard* (Chekhov), Nazimova, Eva Le Gallienne

Pulitzer Prize

Both Your Houses, Maxwell Anderson

Classical Music

Compositions
Roy Harris, Symphony no. 1, String Quartet no. 2
Walter Piston, Concerto for Orchestra, String
    Quartet no. 1
Howard Hanson, *Merry Mount*
Samuel Barber, *Music for a Scene from Shelley*
Aaron Copland, Short Symphony no. 2
John Cage, Sonata for Clarinet
Frank S. Converse, *American Sketches*
Henry Cowell, *Irish Suite*

Important Events
After Goebbels cancels Bruno Walter and forbids
Negro jazz, Jewish music, and Jewish musicians,
American musicians mail protest cables to Hitler.
Arnold Schoenberg, Walter, and Otto Klemperer
arrive in the United States. Nationalism increases
throughout the musical world. Societies of American
musicians form, and American music is performed
everywhere with a program that includes, typically,
Harris, Wallingford Riegger, Adolph Weiss, Edgard
Varèse, Piston, and Robert Russell Bennett.

New Appointment: Otto Klemperer becomes
conductor of the Los Angeles Philharmonic.

Debut: Rudolf Serkin

First Performances
Varèse, *Ionization* (New York); Leoš Janáček, *Taras
Bulba* (New York); William Walton, *Belshazzar's
Feast* (Boston); Werner Josten, *Concerto Sacro no. 1*
(Philadelphia); John Alden Carpenter, *Sea-Drift*
(Chicago); Rudolf Ganz, *Animal Pictures* (Chicago)

Opera

Metropolitan: Lawrence Tibbett, *The Emperor
Jones* (Louis Gruenberg, premiere); Frida Leider,
Tristan und Isolde; Richard Crooks, *Manon Lescaut;*
farewell: Antonio Scotti, *L'oracolo*

Chicago: Rosa Raisa, *Turandot*

Central City, Colo.: Gladys Swarthout, *The Merry
Widow*

Music Notes
Yehudi Menuhin, 15, tours.

Benny Goodman. *Movie Star News*.

Mae West in *I'm No Angel. Movie Star News*.

Art

Painting

Edward Hopper, *Cottages at Wellfleet*

William Gropper, *Farmers' Revolt*

Reginald Marsh, *The Park Bench, Belmont Hotel*

Niles Spencer, *Near Avenue A*

Florine Stettheimer, *Family Portrait*

Morris Kantor, *Skyrocket*

Thomas Hart Benton, *Civil War, Industry, and Agriculture*

John Steuart Curry, *Kansas Cornfield*

Sculpture

Gaston Lachaise, *Knees, The Conquest of Time and Space, Knowledge Combating Ignorance*

Paul Manship, Rainey Memorial Gate, New York Zoological Society

David Smith, *Chain Head*

John B. Flannagan, *Figure of Dignity— Irish Mountain Goat*

Malvina Hoffman's bronzes are placed in the Museum of Natural History, Chicago.

Architecture

Union Terminal, Cincinnati (Fellheimer and Wagner)

Oakland Bay Bridge, San Francisco (Pfleuger, Brown, and Donovan)

Seattle Art Museum (Bebb and Gould)

William Rockhill Nelson Gallery, Kansas City, Mo. (Wight and Kech)

Plans are completed for the U.S. Post Office and Court House, Philadelphia (Sternfeld).

Important Exhibitions

Museums

New York: *Metropolitan:* Plant forms in ornament; Islamic paintings and book illuminations; American japanned furniture. *Museum of Modern Art:* Sources of modern art; Edward Hopper; Maurice Sterne; photographs by Walker Evans. *Whitney:* Thomas Eakins

Pittsburgh: Carnegie Institute prizes: André Dunoyer, John Steuart Curry

Washington: Negro art

Chicago: *World's Fair:* "A Century of Progress," organized by the Art Institute, which simultaneously presents "Recent Art"

Portland: Mark Rothko

Philadelphia: European and American sculpture

Art Briefs

Salvador Dali has his first American one-man show in New York • José Orozco paints the largest mural to date, 3,000 square feet, at Dartmouth College • Ben Shahn joins the Diego Rivera group of artists working on the Rockefeller Center murals • Henri Cartier-Bresson has his first photo exhibit in New York.

Dance

Dancers in Colonel de Basil's Ballet Russe de Monte Carlo visit the United States and include teenagers Irina Baronova, Tamara Toumanova, and Tatiana Riabouchinska; choreographers include Léonide Massine, George Balanchine, and Mikhail Fokine. Balletomane Lincoln Kirstein meets ex-Diaghilev choreographer George Balanchine in Paris and invites him to New York.

The San Francisco Ballet is founded with Adolph Bolm as chief choreographer.

Prof. Albert Einstein, "the father of the theory of relativity," and Mrs. Einstein remain in the limelight. *Library of Congress.*

Books

Fiction

Critics' Choice

Miss Lonelyhearts, Nathanael West
God's Little Acre, Erskine Caldwell
Presenting Lily Mars, Booth Tarkington
The Disinherited, Jack Conroy
In Tragic Life, Vardis Fisher
Winner Take Nothing, Ernest Hemingway
To a God Unknown, John Steinbeck
❧ *Man's Fate*, André Malraux

Best-Sellers

Anthony Adverse, Hervey Allen
As the Earth Turns, Gladys Hasty Carroll
Ann Vickers, Sinclair Lewis
Magnificent Obsession, Lloyd C. Douglas
One More River, John Galsworthy
Forgive Us Our Trespasses, Lloyd C. Douglas
The Master of Jalna, Mazo de la Roche
Miss Bishop, Bess Streeter Aldrich
The Farm, Louis Bromfield
Little Man, What Now? Hans Fallada

Nonfiction

Critics' Choice

The Autobiography of Alice B. Toklas, Gertrude Stein
Mellon's Millions, Harvey O'Conner
Along This Way, James Weldon Johnson
The Brown Book of the Hitler Terror
Industrial Discipline, Rexford G. Tugwell
Principles of Harmonic Analysis, Walter Piston
Alice through the Cellophane, E. B. White
My Life and Hard Times, James Thurber
The Great Tradition, Granville Hicks
The Use of Poetry and the Use of Criticism, T. S. Eliot
Seeds of Revolt, Mauritz A. Hallgren
❧ *The Expanding Universe*, A. S. Eddington

Best-Sellers

Life Begins at Forty, Walter B. Pitkin
Marie Antoinette, Stefan Zweig
British Agent, R. H. Bruce Lockhart
100,000,000 Guinea Pigs, Arthur Kellet, F. J. Schlink
The House of Exile, Nora Waln
Van Loon's Geography, Hendrik Willem Van Loon
Looking Forward, Franklin D. Roosevelt
The March of Democracy, vol. 2, James Truslow Adams
Contract Bridge Blue Book of 1933, Ely Culbertson
The Arches of the Years, Halliday Sutherland

Poetry

Edwin Arlington Robinson, *Talifer*
Robinson Jeffers, *Give Your Heart to the Hawks*
Archibald MacLeish, *Frescoes for Mr. Rockefeller's City*
Sara Teasdale, *Last Poems*
Hart Crane, *Collected Poems*

Pulitzer Prizes

Lamb in His Bosom, Caroline Miller (novel)
The People's Choice, Herbert Agar (U.S. history)
John Hay, Tyler Dennett (biography)
Selected Verse, Robert Hillyer (poetry)

Science and Technology

Frequency modulation (FM) radio transmission is devised by Edwin Armstrong.

A. A. Michelson's work on the speed of light is completed posthumously by his coworkers; their finding is that light travels 186,264 miles per second.

Biochemist Roger J. Williams isolates pantothenic acid, an antiberiberi substance.

Theophilus S. Painter describes a new method of mapping out details of chromosome structure.

Maud Sly's research on rats indicates a genetic predisposition to cancer.

The use of electric shock to the heart to reverse potentially fatal ventricular fibrillation is developed by William Kouwenhoven and O. R. Langeworthy.

H. Trendley Dean begins studies relating fluoride and tooth decay.

Vitamin D-fortified milk is marketed.

The Douglas DC-1, which carries 12 passengers and travels 150 m.p.h., is introduced.

❧ The structure of vitamin C is determined by Albert Szent-Györgyi to be ascorbic acid.

Nobel Prize

Thomas H. Morgan wins the prize in physiology and medicine for work on the hereditary function of chromosomes.

Sports

Baseball

The first All-Star game is played in Comiskey Park, Chicago: AL 4–NL 2; Babe Ruth hits a home run.

Champions

Batting
Chuck Klein (Philadelphia, NL), .368
James Foxx (Philadelphia, AL), .356

Pitching
Lyle Tinning (Chicago, NL), 13–6
Lefty Grove (Philadelphia, AL), 24–8
Home runs
James Foxx (Philadelphia, AL), 48

Football

The first NFL championship game is played at Chicago: Chicago (Bears) 23–New York 21.
NFL franchises cost $10,000.
The Philadelphia Eagles, owned by Bert Bell, and the Pittsburgh Steelers, owned by Art Rooney, enter the NFL.
Goal posts in the pros are moved to the goal line.

NFL Season Leaders: Harry Newman (New York), passing; Cliff Battles (Boston), rushing; John Kelley (Brooklyn), receiving

College All-Americans: Beattie Feathers (B), Tennessee; Cotton Warburton (Q), USC.

Bowls (Jan. 1, 1934)
Rose: Columbia 7–Stanford 0
Orange: Duquesne 33–Miami 7

Basketball

The New York Renaissance (Rens), a black team, defeats the Celtics, 7–1, in a series. Rens' stars are Pappy Ricks, Fats Jenkins, Bruiser Saitch, Tarzan Cooper. Admission to the series is $1.
The ABL reopens, consisting of eastern teams within short distances of each other.

Other Sports

Boxing: Primo Carnera, "the Ambling Alp," KO's Jack Sharkey in the sixth for the heavyweight title.

Tennis: Helen Wills Moody wins her second straight Wimbledon title, her sixth Wimbledon to date.

Winners

World Series
New York (NL) 4
Washington (AL) 1
MVP
NL–Carl Hubbell, New York
AL–James Foxx, Philadelphia
NFL
Chicago (Bears) 23
New York 21
College Football
USC
College Basketball
Kentucky

Player of the Year
Forest Sale, Kentucky
Stanley Cup
New York Rangers
U.S. Tennis Open
Men: Fred Perry
Women: Helen Hull Jacobs
USGA Open
Johnny Goodman
Kentucky Derby
Broker's Tip (D. Meade, jockey)

Fashion

For Women: The stylish V shape, from wide shoulders to a small waist and flared skirt, places a new emphasis on corsetry—the two-way stretch and the new, all-in-one, full-length corset with Lastex bra and six suspenders to hold stockings. Bolero jackets and puff sleeves are also fashion news, as are short, fitted sweaters (sometimes in stripes) and buttons decorating pockets and belts. In the evening, necklines are frequently high in the front, and backs are bare; large brimmed hats reinforce the long, statuesque look. Women follow both Garbo in the new "man's" evening suit and Crawford in their makeup—bright lips, eye shadow, and artificial eyelashes (applied only in beauty salons; time: two hours).

High-fashion notes: Chanel's satin suit, Schiaparelli's exotic buttons; hair dusted with phosphorescent powder in bright colors; an evening shell-pink satin blouse wrapped and tied around a high-waisted black satin skirt (Lanvin).

Kaleidoscope _____

- Unemployment reaches 15 million, five times that in 1931. The marriage rate is down 40 percent from 1920s levels.
- During the week FDR declares that all banks must remain closed, the nation functions without readily available cash.
- *Esquire,* the first magazine for men, begins publication; it features women in scanty dress.
- Mae West's profile: she is from Brooklyn, N.Y., seldom drinks, smokes denicotinized cigarettes and is 5′5″, 120 pounds, 36–26–36; she likes diamonds, rare beefsteaks, and racehorses, and develops her body by lifting weights. The Central Association for Obstetricians and Gynecologists in Milwaukee congratulates her for popularizing the plump figure, "a boon to motherhood."
- Jack Benny becomes a radio sensation as a perpetual 39-year-old miser who owns an old Maxwell and keeps his money in a basement vault. His audience laughs longer than any in radio history when he replies to a gangster's "Your money or your life" with "I'm thinking it over."
- Movie star Baby LeRoy, 19 months old, works two hours a day in seven-minute periods; he especially likes baked potatoes, spinach, zweibach, and butter.
- Paul Getty earns $1,000 his first year in the oil business.
- The reputation of business falls with revelations such as First National City bank chairman Charles Mitchell's admission that he sold stocks at a loss to his family to cut his taxes and then bought them back the next year.
- The Federal Bureau of Investigation is expanded to become a "national Scotland Yard" in response to the "public enemies" threatening the nation.
- A survey estimates that illness is 40 percent higher among the jobless.
- To help raise farm prices by cutting supply, 6 million young pigs are killed and thousands of acres of cotton are plowed under.
- As part of the bargaining for American diplomatic recognition, Russia informally agrees not to interfere in American politics.
- "Don't shoot, G-Men," cries "Machine Gun" Kelly, who gives the FBI agents their nickname.
- A kidnapping wave strikes the United States; when two confessed kidnappers are lynched in San Francisco, California governor James Rolph praises the action as "the best lesson California ever had"; *rolphing* becomes a synonym for *lynching.*
- Diego Rivera is dismissed from the Rockefeller Center murals project when he refuses to erase a small head of Lenin; the mural is destroyed.
- Major attention is given Grant Wood's *American Gothic* at the Chicago World's Fair.
- In Judge Woolsey's opinion in favor of James Joyce's *Ulysses,* Woolsey comments: "[It is] in many places . . . emetic . . . nowhere aphrodisic."
- Frances Perkins becomes the first female cabinet

The end of prohibition, like its beginning 13 years ago, is widely celebrated. General Research Division. *The New York Public Library. Astor, Lenox and Tilden Foundations.*

member when FDR appoints her secretary of labor.
- Sally Rand is the star of the Chicago World's Fair in her fan dance with ostrich feathers.
- Mussolini sends 25 seaplanes to the Century of Progress Exposition at the fair.
- Calvin Coolidge leaves a $400,000 estate to his wife in a hand-written, 75-word will.
- The Federal Emergency Relief Administration (FERA) is set up under Harry Hopkins to distribute relief funds; Hopkins favors paid public work over a dole.
- The Public Works Administration (PWA), under Harold Ickes, utilizes private contractors for major public works, such as dams and bridges.
- The Civil Works Administration (CWA) authorizes employment for civic purposes, such as building and maintaining parks, roads, and schoolhouses.
- The National Industrial Recovery Act (NIRA) enables industry to regulate prices in return for guarantees on wages and hours; Section 7A affirms the right to collective bargaining.
- Eight states remain dry despite the repeal of Prohibition; all are southern except North Dakota and Kansas; 50 to 60 percent of the liquor consumed is still bootleg because it is readily available and less expensive.
- "The smallest woman in the world wants to meet the richest man in the world," says a circus midget, who sits in J. P. Morgan's lap during Senate hearings on banking practices.

First Appearances: Lame duck constitutional amendment, Sunsweet prune juice, Tree-sweet canned orange juice, blood banks, Sanka, Food-Fair margarine made from soybeans, Campbell's cream of mushroom and chicken noodle soup, Ritz crackers, "Liederkranz" cheese, mandatory death penalty for kidnapping (Kansas City, Mo.), drive-in (Camden, N.J.), Dy-Dee-Doll, Dreft, Windex, White House swimming pool, singing telegram, patent for invisible glass, walkie-talkies, *Newsweek, Catholic Worker,* "Smilin' Jack," Sheraton Corporation, Perry Mason (Erle Stanley Gardner)

1934

Facts and Figures

Economic Profile
  Dow-Jones:—High 110–
    Low 85
  GNP: +17%
  Inflation: 4.5%
  Unemployment: 21.7%
Expenditures:
  Recreation: $2.4 billion
  Spectator sports: $65
    million
  European travel: $1.78
    million
Golf courses: 343
Bowlers: 168,000
Original, signed etchings
  (including Curry, Hoffman,
  Ryder): $5
Elgin 17-jewel watch: $35
Barbizon Plaza Hotel, New
  York (1–2 rooms): $68 per
  month
Dinner:
  75¢ (Rosoff's, New York)
  $1.50 (Cavanaugh's)
Met opera (Saturday
  evening): $1.50–$4
Movie: 35¢–50¢
Madison Square Garden
  rodeo: $1
Fifty tulip bulbs: $2.19; ten
  daffodils: 79¢

Deaths

Marie Curie, Frederick
  Delius, Marie Dressler,
  Edward Elgar, Roger Fry,
  Cass Gilbert, Gustav
  Holst, Arthur Wing Pinero,
  Raymond Poincaré.

In the News

STORM TROOPER ERNST ROEHM AND 77 FOLLOWERS ARE KILLED BY HITLER . . . GOLD RESERVE ACT SETS VALUE OF GOLD TO DOLLAR . . . CIVIL WORKS EMERGENCY RELIEF AUTHORIZES $950 MILLION FOR WORK AND DIRECT RELIEF . . . RIOTS OCCUR IN FRANCE OVER STAVISKY STOCK FRAUD . . . CROP LOAN ACT WILL AID 4.7 MILLION ON RELIEF . . . COTTON CONTROL ACT PASSES . . . BONNIE PARKER AND CLYDE BARROW ARE GUNNED DOWN IN POLICE AMBUSH IN TEXAS . . . SUGAR IMPORT QUOTA ACT IS PASSED . . . DUST STORMS DENUDE LARGE PORTIONS OF MIDWEST . . . AUSTRIAN CHIEF DOLLFUSS IS ASSASSINATED BY LOCAL NAZIS . . . SECURITIES EXCHANGE COMMISSION IS ESTABLISHED . . . NATIONAL LABOR RELATIONS BOARD IS CREATED . . . CHINESE COMMUNISTS UNDER MAO TSE-TUNG BEGIN LONG RETREAT . . . PRESIDENT IS AUTHORIZED TO NATIONALIZE SILVER . . . FEDERAL COMMUNICATIONS COMMISSION IS CREATED . . . FRAZIER-LEMKE FARM BANKRUPTCY ACT RELIEVES FORECLOSURES . . . G-MEN KILL JOHN DILLINGER OUTSIDE CHICAGO THEATER . . . TAYLOR GRAZING ACT ENSURES SOIL CARE . . . RECIPROCAL TRADE ACT GIVES PRESIDENT SWEEPING POWER OVER TARIFFS . . . BRUNO HAUPTMANN IS ARRESTED FOR LINDBERGH KIDNAPPING . . . MIRONOVICH KIROV, STALIN ASSOCIATE, IS ASSASSINATED IN LENINGRAD . . . RUSSIA ENTERS LEAGUE OF NATIONS . . . JAPAN RENOUNCES WASHINGTON AND LONDON NAVAL LIMITATION TREATIES . . . FIRE ON CRUISE BOAT "MORRO CASTLE" OFF N.J. KILLS 130 . . . FIRST GENERAL STRIKE IN U.S. SLOWS SAN FRANCISCO . . . ITALY AND ETHIOPIA CLASH AT SOMALI BORDER.

Political cartoon. *Library of Congress.*

"The present depression is one of abundance, not of scarcity. . . . The cause of the trouble is that a small class has the wealth, while the rest have the debts. . . . The remedy is to give the workers access to the means of production, and let them produce for themselves, not for others, . . . the American way."
— Upton Sinclair, "The Epic Plan for California," *Nation*

Quotes

"She was sitting on the stoop. When I walked by, she crossed her legs showing her thighs and winked. I walked over to her. She said: 'How about it, hon?' I said: 'Christ, kid, if I had any dough I'd rather eat.'
— M. Shulimson, quoted in Albert Maltz, *New Masses*

"I am ready to concede that the capitalistic system is not fool-proof."
— John W. Davis of the Liberty League

"Puzzler: The average cost of a new automobile— $600—is almost as much as the average income."
— *Life*

"President Roosevelt is getting more like Huey P. Long every day."
— Huey P. Long

"I'm just dumb enough not to want to be a Tarzan all my life."
— Johnny Weismuller

"Everybody has a chance to become President of the United States. I'll sell mine for a quarter."
— Lawrence Lee

Ads

Fashion model.

Radio

Premieres
"Bob Becker: Talk about Paintings"
"Kraft Music Hall," Bing Crosby (host)
"The Bob Hope Show"
"Hollywood Hotel," Dick Powell, Louella Parsons
　　(hosts)
"The Palmolive Beauty Box Theatre," Jessica
　　Dragonette, Fannie Brice ("Baby Snooks")
"Heart Throbs of the Hills" (Mary Pickford drama)
"Major Bowes and His Original Amateur Hour"

Of Note
Popular comedian Joe Penner's "Wanna buy a
duck?" and "You *nasty* man" become part of
American lingo.

New Catchphrases: "The wheel of fortune goes
'round and 'round and where she stops nobody
knows" ("Major Bowes"); "Who's Yehoodi?"
"Greetings, Gate!" "Put something in the pot, boy"
("The Bob Hope Show," with Jerry Colonna)

Gossip columnist Louella Parsons and Dick Powell, hosts
of "Hollywood Hotel," which features movie stars in radio
dramas. *Movie Star News.*

Movies

Openings
It Happened One Night (Frank Capra), Claudette
　　Colbert, Clark Gable
The Thin Man (W. S. Van Dyke), William Powell,
　　Myrna Loy
Twentieth Century (Howard Hawks), John
　　Barrymore, Carole Lombard
The Gay Divorcée (Mark Sandrich), Ginger Rogers,
　　Fred Astaire
The House of Rothschild (Alfred L. Werker), George
　　Arliss, Loretta Young
Imitation of Life (John M. Stahl), Claudette Colbert,
　　Warren William
One Night of Love (Victor Shertzinger), Grace
　　Moore, Tullio Carminati
Viva Villa! (Jack Conway, Howard Hawks), Wallace
　　Beery, Stuart Erwin
The Lost Patrol (John Ford), Victor McLaglen, Boris
　　Karloff
Of Human Bondage (John Cromwell), Leslie
　　Howard, Bette Davis
Man of Aran (Robert Flaherty), Colman King
　　(documentary)
The Scarlet Pimpernel (Harold Young), Leslie
　　Howard, Merle Oberon

The Count of Monte Cristo (Rowland V. Lee), Robert
　　Donat, Elissa Landi
Cleopatra (Cecil B. DeMille), Claudette Colbert,
　　Henry Wilcox
Stand Up and Cheer (Hamilton MacFadden), Shirley
　　Temple, 6, Warner Baxter
It's a Gift (Norman Z. McLeod), W. C. Fields
The Scarlet Empress (Josef von Sternberg), Marlene
　　Dietrich, John Lodge (later governor of
　　Connecticut)
Treasure Island (Victor Fleming), Wallace Beery,
　　Freddie Bartholomew

Academy Awards
Best Picture: *It Happened One Night*
Best Director: Frank Capra (*It Happened One Night*)
Best Actress: Claudette Colbert (*It Happened One
　　Night*)
Best Actor: Clark Gable (*It Happened One Night*)

Top Box-Office Stars
Will Rogers, Clark Gable, Janet Gaynor, Wallace
Beery, Mae West, Joan Crawford, Bing Crosby,
Shirley Temple, Marie Dressler, Norma Shearer

Popular Music

Hit Songs
"Blue Moon"
"Anything Goes"
"Blow, Gabriel, Blow"
"I Only Have Eyes for You"
"Cocktails for Two"
"The Continental"
"What a Diff'rence a Day Made"
"Tumbling Tumbleweeds"
"On the Good Ship Lollipop"
"You and the Night and the
    Music"
"You're the Top"
"I Get a Kick out of You"
"Isle of Capri"
"The Very Thought of You"

Top Records
Honeysuckle Rose (Dorsey
Brothers); *Moonglow* (Duke
Ellington, Benny Goodman);
Limehouse Blues (Fletcher
Henderson); *Sweet Georgia Brown*
(Earl Hines); *Stars Fell on
Alabama* (Jack Teagarden); *Down
Yonder* (Gil Tanner); *The
Darktown Strutter's Ball* (Luis
Russell); *Let's Fall in Love* (Eddy
Duchin)

Jazz and Big Bands
Benny Goodman, 24, brings swing
to big audiences on his National
Biscuit radio series, "Let's
Dance." His band includes Bunny
Berigan, Jess Stacy, and Gene
Krupa, with arrangements by
Fletcher Henderson. *Downbeat* is
founded.

First Recordings: Jimmy
Lunceford

New Band: Dorsey Brothers

Theater

Broadway Openings

Plays
The Children's Hour (Lillian Hellman), Ann Revere,
    Katherine Emery
No More Ladies (A. E. Thomas), Melvyn Douglas,
    Lucile Watson, Ruth Weston
Dodsworth (Sidney Howard), Walter Huston, Fay
    Bainter
The Distaff Side (John Van Druten), Sybil
    Thorndike, Estelle Winwood
Personal Appearance (Lawrence Riley), Gladys
    George
Accent on Youth (Samson Raphaelson), Constance
    Cummings, Irene Purcell
They Shall Not Die (John Wexley), Ruth Gordon,
    Claude Rains
The Shining Hour (Keith Winter), Raymond Massey,
    Gladys Cooper
The Wind and the Rain (Merton Hodge), Mildred
    Natwick, Frank Lawton
The Farmer Takes a Wife (Frank B. Elser, Marc
    Connelly), Henry Fonda, June Walker
Dark Victory (George Brewer, Bertram Bloch),
    Tallulah Bankhead
Divided by Three (Margaret Leech, Beatrice
    Kaufman), Judith Anderson, James Stewart,
    Hedda Hopper
The Bride of Torozko (Otto Indig), Jean Arthur, Van
    Heflin
Within the Gates (Sean O'Casey), Moffat Johnston
Days without End (Eugene O'Neill), Earle
    Larrimore, Stanley Ridges

Yellow Jack (Sidney Howard), Robert Shayne,
    Geoffrey Kerr

Musicals
Anything Goes (Cole Porter), Ethel Merman, William
    Gaxton, Victor Moore
The Great Waltz (Johann Strauss, Sr. and Jr.,
    Desmond Carter), Guy Robertson, Marian Clare
Life Begins at 8:40 (Harold Arlen, Ira Gershwin),
    Bert Lahr, Ray Bolger, Brian Donlevy
New Faces of 1934 (Warburton Guilbert, Viola
    Shore), Hildegarde Halliday, Henry Fonda,
    Imogene Coca
Revenge with Music (Arthur Schwartz, Howard
    Dietz), Libby Holman, Georges Metaxa, Charles
    Winninger
Ziegfeld Follies of 1934 (Vernon Duke et al., E. Y.
    Yarburg), Fannie Brice, Willie Howard, Eugene
    Howard, Eve Arden, Jane Froman

Classics and Revivals On and Off Broadway
Romeo and Juliet, Katharine Cornell, Basil
Rathbone, Brian Aherne, Edith Evans; *L'Aiglon*
(Clemence Dane, Rostand), Eva Le Gallienne, Ethel
Barrymore; *The Plough and the Stars* (Sean
O'Casey), Barry Fitzgerald and *Playboy of the
Western World* (O'Casey), Abbey Players

Pulitzer Prize
Men in White, Sidney Kingsley

Classical Music

Compositions
Henry Cowell, *Four Continuations*
George Antheil, Symphony no. 3
Roy Harris, Symphony no. 2
Walter Piston, Prelude and Fugue
Ernest Bloch, *A Voice in the Wilderness*
William Schuman, *Choreographic Poem*
John Cage, Six Short Inventions for Seven
    Instruments
Arnold Schoenberg (in America), Suite in G for
    Strings

Important Events
Arnold Schoenberg makes his first appearance as a conductor, with the Boston Symphony Orchestra, in a concert of his early works.

Debut: Eugene List, Oscar Shumsky, Beveridge Webster

First Performances
Rachmaninoff, playing, *Rhapsody on a Theme by Paganini* (Philadelphia); Piston, Concerto for Orchestra (Boston); Harris, Symphony no. 5 (Boston); Louis Gruenberg, Symphony no. 1 (Boston); Ernest Toch, *Big Ben* (Boston); Edgard Varèse, *Ecuatorial* (New York)

Leading lady of the American stage Katharine Cornell and Basil Rathbone in *Romeo and Juliet. Billy Rose Theatre Collection. The New York Public Library at Lincoln Center. Astor, Lenox and Tilden Foundations.*

Clark Gable, "the King," and Claudette Colbert in *It Happened One Night.* Gable, at odds with MGM, was "demoted" to Columbia for this film, which won five major Academy Awards. *Movie Star News.*

Opera

Metropolitan: Elisabeth Rethberg, *Tannhaüser;* Rosa Ponselle, *La Gioconda;* Lotte Lehmann (debut) *Die Walküre;* Paul Althouse, *Tristan und Isolde;* return of Claudia Muzio, *La traviata; Merry Mount* (Harold Hanson, premiere)

Chicago: Giovanni Martinelli, *La forza del destino;* Ezio Pinza, *Don Giovanni*

Philadelphia: *Mavra* (Igor Stravinsky, premiere)

Hartford, Conn.: *Four Saints in Three Acts* (Virgil Thomson, Gertrude Stein, premiere, all black cast)

Music Notes
Albert Einstein makes his violin debut at the home of Adolph Lewisohn; for this benefit for Scientists in Nazified Berlin, Einstein plays the second violin in Bach's Concerto for Two Violins; he also plays in a Mozart quintet.

Art

Painting

Charles Burchfield, *November Evening*

Thomas Hart Benton, *Ploughing It Under*

Lyonel Feininger, *The Glassy Sea, Negroes on Rockaway Beach*

George Grosz, *Couple*

William Palmer, *Dust, Drought, and Destruction*

Ernest Lawson, *High Bridge*

Paul Cadmus, *Greenwich Village Cafeteria*

Jack Levine, *String Quartet*

Isabel Bishop, *Nude*

Sculpture

Joseph Cornell, *Object, Beehive*

Gaston Lachaise, *Torso*

Alexander Calder, *A Universe, Constellation with Red Object*

John Storrs, *Abstract Figure*

Architecture

Customs House, Philadelphia (Ritter and Shay)

Shusham Airport, New Orleans (Weiss, Dreyfous, and Seifforth)

North Dakota State Capitol Building, Bismarck (De Remer and Kurt, Holabird and Root)

Yale University School of Architecture plan, New Haven (Eero Saarinen)

Important Exhibitions

Museums

New York: *Metropolitan:* 300 Years of landscape painters, New York State furniture; Pennsylvania crafts; Lace and embroidered aprons. *Museum of Modern Art:* "Machine Art"; Otto Dix's war etchings; Whistler. *National Academy of Design:* Jo Davidson, Herbert Haseltine

Chicago: "A Century of Progress" (721 paintings from the Century of Progress Exhibit)

Pennsylvania Academy of Fine Arts: Henry Gottlieb, Yasuo Kuniyoshi; Raphael Soyer

Pittsburgh: Awards are given to Peter Blume (*South of Scranton*), Édouard Vuillard, André Derain, and Salvador Dali

Art Briefs

Alberto Giacometti has his first American one-man show in New York • FDR suggests remodeling the gingerbread ornamentation of the Library of Congress in a $1 million project.

Dance

School of American Ballet begins, with George Balanchine and Lincoln Kirstein; their first performance is a workshop of the new Balanchine *Serenade*. Ruth Page becomes principal dancer and director of the Chicago Grand Opera Company.

Charles Burchfield. *November Evening*, 1934. Oil. 32⅛ × 52″. *The Metropolitan Museum of Art, George A. Hearn Fund, 1934.*

Books

Fiction

Critics' Choice

Tender Is the Night, F. Scott Fitzgerald
A Cool Million, Nathanael West
Hacienda: A Story of Mexico, Katherine Anne Porter
The Daring Young Man on the Flying Trapeze, William Saroyan
Tropic of Cancer, Henry Miller
Appointment in Samarra, John O'Hara
The Young Manhood of Studs Lonigan, James T. Farrell
Call It Sleep, Henry Roth
The Postman Always Rings Twice, James M. Cain
🍃 *Joseph and His Brothers,* Thomas Mann
🍃 *I, Claudius,* Robert Graves

Best-Sellers

Anthony Adverse, Hervey Allen
Lamb in His Bosom, Caroline Miller
So Red the Rose, Stark Young
Good-Bye Mr. Chips, James Hilton
Within This Present, Margaret Ayer Barnes
Seven Gothic Tales, Isak Dinesen
Work of Art, Sinclair Lewis
Private Worlds, Phyllis Bottome
Mary Peters, Mary Ellen Chase
Oil for the Lamps of China, Alice Tisdale Hobart

Nonfiction

Critics' Choice

U.S. History: The People's Choice, Herbert Agar
Exile's Return, Malcolm Cowley
Art as Experience, John Dewey
Patterns of Culture, Ruth Benedict
The Ways of White Folks, Langston Hughes
The Robber Barons: The Great American Capitalists, Matthew Josephson
Hitler over Europe, Ernst Henry
Merchants of Death, H. C. Englebrecht
American Ballads and Folk Songs, J. Lomax

Best-Sellers

While Rome Burns, Alexander Woollcott
Life Begins at Forty, Walter B. Pitkin
Nijinsky, Romola Nijinsky
100,000,000 Guinea Pigs, A. Kallett, F. J. Schlink
The Native's Return, Louis Adamic
You Must Relax, Edmund Jacobson
The Life of Our Lord, Charles Dickens

Edna St. Vincent Millay. *D. Ouellette Collection.*

Brazilian Adventure, Peter Fleming
Forty-two Years in the White House, Ike Hoover

Poetry

Ezra Pound, *Eleven New Cantos, XXXI–XLI*
Edna St. Vincent Millay, *Wine from These Grapes*
Edwin Arlington Robinson, *Amaranth*
Laura Riding, *The Life of the Dead*
William Carlos Williams, *Collected Poems, 1921–1931*
🍃 W. H. Auden, *Poems*

Pulitzer Prizes

Now in November, Josephine Winslow Johnson (novel)
The Colonial Period of American History, Charles M. Andrews (U.S. history)
R. E. Lee, Douglas S. Freeman (biography)
Bright Ambush, Audrey Wurdemann (poetry)

Science and Technology

Ruth Benedict's *Patterns of Culture* explores the impact of culture as a cohesive ideological substrate.

Ladislas Von Meduna initiates chemical (Metrazol) convulsions as a treatment for schizophrenia.

Sodium pentothal, intravenous anesthesia, becomes widely used.

Dicumarol, an anticoagulant, is developed from clover.

🍃 Enrico Fermi pursues his work in Italy on the creation of new elements through the bombardment of uranium with neutrons.

🍃 Irène and Frédéric Joliot-Curie create the first man-made radioactive substance by bombarding aluminum with alpha particles that create radioactive phosphorus.

Nobel Prize

G. H. Whipple, George R. Minot, and W. P. Murphy win in physiology and medicine for work on liver therapy against anemia. Harold C. Urey wins in chemistry for the discovery of heavy hydrogen.

Sports

Baseball

Dizzy Dean (St. Louis, NL) predicts: "Me and Paul [his brother] will win 40–45 games"; they win 49; Dizzy wins 30.

In the All-Star game, Carl Hubbell (New York, NL) strikes out in succession Babe Ruth, Lou Gehrig, Jimmy Foxx, Al Simmons, and Joe Cronin.

Champions

Batting
Paul Waner (Pittsburgh, NL), .362
Lou Gehrig (New York, AL), .363

Pitching
Dizzy Dean (St. Louis, NL), 30–7
Lefty Gomez (New York, AL), 26–5
Home runs
Lou Gehrig (New York, AL), 49

Football

Beattie Feathers (Chicago Bears) is the first pro to rush for over 1,000 yards in a season. Other NFL season leaders are Arnie Herber (Green Bay), passing; Joe Carter (Philadelphia), receiving. Steve Owens, New York Giant coach, has his players wear sneakers on the icy turf in their upset championship win.

College All-Americans: Pug Lund (F), Minnesota; Don Hutson (E), Alabama. The Sugar Bowl is inaugurated on New Year's Day, 1935.

Bowls (Jan. 1, 1935)
Rose: Alabama 29–Stanford 13
Orange: Bucknell 26–Miami 0
Sugar: Tulane 20–Temple 14

Basketball

Ned Irish arranges a college doubleheader in Madison Square Garden between national and local powers, which popularizes the college game.

Other Sports

Golf: Babe Didrickson takes up golf; when asked, "Is there anything you don't play?" she replies, "Yeah, dolls."

Boxing: Maxie Baer KO's Primo Carnera in the eleventh for the heavyweight title; Carnera is down twelve times in eleven rounds.

Winners

World Series
St. Louis (NL) 4
Detroit (AL) 3
MVP
NL–Jerome Dean, St. Louis
AL–Gordon Cochrane, Detroit
NFL
New York 30–Chicago (Bears) 13
College Football
Michigan
College Basketball
Wyoming

Player of the Year
John Moir, Notre Dame
Stanley Cup
Chicago
U.S. Tennis Open
Men: Fred Perry
Women: Helen Hull Jacobs
USGA Open
Olin Dutra
Kentucky Derby
Cavalcade (M. Garner, jockey)

Fashion

For Women: Hair is pushed back across the head at a sharp angle, and hats, worn on one side of the head, look like record discs. Many women color and curl their hair like Harlow, wear red lipstick, rouge, and nail polish, and pencil in their brows. A new passion for hiking, sports, sunbathing, and even nudism, invites briefer sportswear. Bathing suits are slashed and backless, made of linen and Lastex yarn; described as "corset bathing suits," they mold the body as the woman walks out of the water. Designer news fills the magazines: the tailored look, Chanel's ready-to-wear collection, and the new surrealism in design. Chanel retains the easy skirt and jersey jacket for "understated" elegance (her term); Schiaparelli pursues "hard-edge chic" and fantasy, with prints designed by Dali and Cocteau, and buttons of huge fish, circus horses, and stars. Padded shoulders are even wider and covered with gold embroidery. The "little black dress" is new for the evening, as well as the long dinner suit in "shocking" colors: Patou's citron yellow, Schiaparelli's "shocking" blue and pink. New color combinations redefine day attire: brown and pink; prune and turquoise.

Other high-fashion notes: Silver fox broadtail, with muskrat for the more modest; Schiaparelli's and Mainbocher's box jackets.

Kaleidoscope

- The NRA banner of a bird and "We do our Part" is eventually displayed by 2.25 million firms with 22 million employees.
- The Civil Works Administration provides employment for 4 million people.
- The birth of the Dionne quintuplets in Ontario stirs international interest.
- The army takes over airmail delivery for a period, but numerous crashes lead to its return to private contractors.
- Food shopping patterns shift as consumers buy more red meats, fruits, green vegetables, and dairy products.
- Coca-Cola sales drop with the repeal of Prohibition. Wine companies, like Frank Schoonmaker's, begin operation but do poorly; Ernest and Julio Gallo invest $5,900 in a wine company.
- Cocktail lounges, most furnished with jukeboxes, are the only type of major new construction.
- Doubling up becomes prevalent, as grown children, in-laws, and parents share living space.
- Owing to the shortage of work, the five-day week becomes increasingly common.
- Many private golf courses are sold and become public links, as golf becomes less exclusively a sport of the wealthy.
- Estimates place Walter Lippmann's readership at 10 million in 200 newspapers.
- A *Literary Digest* poll reports that of six occupational groups (clergymen, businessmen, educators, lawyers, physicians, and bankers), all are pro-FDR except the bankers, where 52.4 percent are against the New Deal.
- Members of the Liberty League who oppose "that man" in the White House include Alfred Sloan of General Motors, the Du Ponts, Sewell Avery of Montgomery Ward, and Alfred E. Smith.
- Since the government pays high prices for gold, vast amounts accumulate at Fort Knox.
- A rocky island in San Francisco Bay becomes a maximum security prison, Alcatraz.
- Dillinger, "Baby Face" Nelson, "Pretty Boy" Floyd, Bonnie Parker and Clyde Barrows are all shot and killed during the year.

- After Clark Gable removes his shirt and reveals a naked chest in *It Happened One Night,* the male underwear business slumps.
- According to *Photoplay,* "Unmarried [Hollywood] Husbands and Wives" include Clark Gable and Carole Lombard, Paulette Goddard and Charles Chaplin, Gilbert Roland and Constance Bennett, Virginia Pine and George Raft, Barbara Stanwyck and Robert Taylor.
- The Hays Office, under pressure from the Catholic Legion of Decency, prescribes a code for motion pictures: no long kisses, double beds, naked babies, exposure of breasts, or suggestion of seduction or cohabitation; wrongdoing is not to be treated sympathetically.
- The Sears & Roebuck catalog begins to list contraceptive devices.
- "Little Orphan Annie," the comic strip, and its various spinoff products (e.g., rings) and endorsements (Ovaltine), gross $100,000.
- José Orozco's murals at Dartmouth College depicting capitalist persecution of the masses are not destroyed, despite a great deal of controversy.
- Within two months, 5 million people sign up for Father Coughlin's National Union for Social Justice, which advocates nationalization of banks.
- Huey Long presents his plan to the Senate to heavily tax the wealthy and distribute tax monies to the poor in order to make "Every Man a King."
- Francis Townsend, a California physician, proposes an old-age revolving pension plan based on a 2 percent tax that would provide $200 a month to all Americans over 60; they would be required to spend their stipend within the month, thus benefiting the economy.
- Novelist Upton Sinclair runs for governor in California on his End Poverty in California plan (EPIC).
- The migration to the West continues.
- In the Plains States, 300 million tons of soil blow away in the "black blizzard."

First Appearances: Snow goosebirds hatched, Eskimo chicken hatched, Mother-in-Law Day celebration (March 5, Amarillo, Texas), U.S. Information Service, pipeless organ, talking book for the blind, theater school offering a Ph.D. (Yale), washing machine for public use (Fort Worth, Texas), X ray of entire body in one-second exposure, paper underwear, launching of SS *Queen Mary,* Donald Duck, "Martha Dean," "Terry and the Pirates," "Li'l Abner," "Flash Gordon," "Jungle Jim," *Partisan Review,* Walgreen drugstores, Carvel, Seagram's Seven Royal Crown, Bard College, Black Mountain College, Hi-Fi (term for marketing records)

John Dillinger is killed by federal agents after seeing *Manhattan Melody* at the Biograph Theatre in Chicago. *D. Oulette Collection.*

1935

Facts and Figures

Economic Profile
  Dow-Jones: ↑ High 144–
    Low 96
  GNP: +9%
  Inflation: +1.0%
  Unemployment: 20.7%
Infant mortality/1,000: 57.1
Maternal mortality/1,000:
  56.8
Physicians in U.S.: 161,359
Hospital beds: 1,014,000
Used cars:
  1932 Pontiac: $325
  1932 Ford: $275
  1928 Buick: $65
Toys:
  Carpet sweeper: 24¢
  Typewriter: 98¢
  Doll in cradle: 98¢
Liquor:
  Cariola rum: $1.19 (pt.)
  Rock and Rye: 99¢ (pt.)
  Jameson Irish: $3.99 (⅘)
  Old Grand Dad: $2.99 (⅘)
  White Horse: $2.77 (pt.)

Deaths

Jane Addams, Alban Berg,
  Charles Demuth, Childe
  Hassam, Gaston Lachaise,
  T. E. Lawrence, Billy
  Mitchell, Wiley Post,
  Edwin Arlington Robinson,
  Will Rogers

In the News

SAAR VOTES 10–1 FOR UNION WITH GERMANY . . . FRED AND "MA" BARKER ARE KILLED BY G-MEN IN FLORIDA . . . GRIGORY ZINOVIEV, FORMER STALIN ASSOCIATE, IS FOUND GUILTY OF TREASON . . . SOIL CONSERVATION ACT IS PASSED . . . NATIONAL LABOR RELATIONS ACT PROVIDES FOR COLLECTIVE BARGAINING . . . WORKS PROGRESS ADMINISTRATION IS ORGANIZED . . . RURAL ELECTRIFICATION ACT IS PASSED . . . NATIONAL INDUSTRIAL RECOVERY ACT IS VOIDED BY SUPREME COURT . . . ADOLF HITLER DENOUNCES VERSAILLES TREATY AND DISARMAMENT . . . EMPLOYMENT RELIEF ACT ALLOWS GOVERNMENT TO PROVIDE JOBS . . . FEDERAL DOLE IS DISCONTINUED . . . INHERITANCE AND GIFT TAXES ARE ENACTED . . . THIRD COMMUNIST INTERNATIONAL SUPPORTS POPULAR FRONT GOVERNMENTS . . . BANKING ACT REORGANIZES FEDERAL RESERVE, FDIC IS CREATED . . . SHAH REZA PAHLAVI RENAMES PERSIA "IRAN" . . . HEINRICH HIMMLER BEGINS STATE BREEDING PROGRAM TO PRODUCE PERFECT ARYANS . . . HURRICANE KILLS 400 IN FLORIDA KEYS . . . FRANCE AND U.S.S.R. SIGN MUTUAL ASSISTANCE PACT . . . SOCIAL SECURITY ACT IS PASSED TO PROVIDE FOR THE AGED . . . HUEY LONG IS ASSASSINATED BY LOUISIANA PHYSICIAN . . . ITALY INVADES ETHIOPIA, LEAGUE OF NATIONS IMPOSES SANCTIONS . . . NUREMBERG LAWS ARE PASSED WITH DEATH PENALTY FOR INTERMARRIAGE . . . NEUTRALITY ACT PERMITS EMBARGO OF FOREIGN ARMS SHIPMENTS . . . JOHN L. LEWIS ORGANIZES CIO . . . DUTCH SCHULTZ IS VICTIM OF GANGLAND SLAYING . . . LEON BLUM, POPULAR FRONT CANDIDATE, IS ELECTED IN FRANCE.

Quotes

"The doctor says i hev got me thet sickness like Tom Prescott and thet is the reeson wy i am coughin sometime. . . . It is a terrible plague. . . . the doctor says i will be dead in about fore months."
— a West Virginia miner, a silicosis victim, quoted in Albert Maltz, *New Masses*

"The New Deal will bring them [the Communist party] within striking distance of the overthrow of the American form of government and the substitution therefore of a communist state."
— Arthur Sears Henning, *Chicago Tribune*

"Oh, I'm glad I've seen my Father—face to face!"
— Song at Harlem rally for Father Divine

"This may be the last presidential election America will have. The New Deal is to America what the early phase of Nazism was to Germany and the early phase of fascism to Italy."
— Mark Sullivan, *Buffalo Evening News*

"The editors of *Partisan Review* endorse this [Writer's] Congress . . . to accelerate the . . . establishment of a workers' government, [and] a new literature rooted in the dynamics of social development."
— *Partisan Review*

The "Kingfish," Senator Huey Long, and the "Radio Priest" Father Charles Coughlin, new opponents of President Roosevelt. *D. Ouellette Collection.*

"Four centuries of oppression, . . . hopes, . . . [and] bitterness . . . were rising to the surface. Yes, unconsciously [the young] . . . imputed to the brawny image of Joe Louis all the balked dreams of revenge . . . AND HE HAD WON! . . . Here's the real dynamite that Joe Louis uncovered!"
— Richard Wright

"The last temptation is the greatest treason: to do the right deed for the wrong reason."
— T. S. Eliot, *Murder in the Cathedral*

Ads

One fiddler you won't have to pay.
(Sanka Coffee)

Watch for your beer in this new container. You ought to have it soon. We're trying hard to catch up with the tremendous demand.
(Continental Can Co.)

All trails lead to ice-cold Coca-Cola.
(Coca-Cola)

Some Like It Cold.
(Heinz Consommé)

What makes the common cold so common?—Colds are no respecters of rank.
(Dixie Cups)

Museum of the City of New York.

Tortured in bed! Milly made a serious mistake. . . . She bought her husband pajamas with drawstrings, . . . "the rope" that ruins sleep.
(Faultless No-Belt Pajamas, Wilson Bros.)

Radio

Premieres

"Your Hit Parade"
"Backstage Wife," Vivian Fridell
"Vox Pop," Parks Johnson, Jerry Belcher
"Fibber McGee and Molly," Jim and Marian Jordan
"Dick Tracy," Matt Crowley
"Flash Gordon," Gale Gordon
"America's Town Meeting," George V. Denny, Jr.
"Cavalcade of America"
"The Helen Hayes Theatre"

Specials

Haile Selassie's plea for assistance against the invading Italians; Silver Jubilee celebration of King George V and Queen Mary's reign; first birthday party of the Dionne quintuplets

Of Note

Longest running shows include "Cities Service," "Concert" (Jessica Dragonette); "Major Bowes," "Midweek Hymn Sing," "A & P Gypsies," "Breen and DeRose," "H. V. Kaltenborn," "Betty Crocker Cooking Talk," "Cheerio" (inspirational talk with organ music).

New Catchphrases: ". . . the story of . . . what it means to be the wife of a famous Broadway star— dream sweetheart of a million other women ("Backstage Wife"); "You're a hard man, McGee [sound of crashing items from closet]" ("Fibber McGee and Molly")

Movies

Openings

Mutiny on the Bounty (Frank Lloyd), Clark Gable, Charles Laughton
Captain Blood (Michael Curtiz), Errol Flynn, Olivia de Havilland
The Informer (John Ford), Victor McLaglen, Preston Foster
Lives of a Bengal Lancer (Henry Hathaway), Gary Cooper, Franchot Tone
Les Miserables (Richard Boleslawski), Fredric March, Charles Laughton
A Midsummer Night's Dream (Max Reinhardt, William Dieterle), James Cagney, Mickey Rooney, Joe E. Brown
Naughty Marietta (W. S. Van Dyke), Nelson Eddy, Jeanette MacDonald
Ruggles of Red Gap (Leo McCarey), Charles Ruggles, Charles Laughton
Top Hat (Mark Sandrich), Fred Astaire, Ginger Rogers
Dangerous (Alfred E. Green), Bette Davis, Franchot Tone
Anna Karenina (Clarence Brown), Greta Garbo, Fredric March, Freddie Bartholomew, Maureen O'Sullivan
A Night at the Opera (Sam Wood), Marx Brothers
Bride of Frankenstein (James Whale), Elsa Lanchester, Boris Karloff
Becky Sharp (Rouben Mamoulian), Miriam Hopkins, Cedric Hardwicke, Pat Nixon

Ginger Rogers and Fred Astaire in *Top Hat*. "Can't act. Slightly bald. Can dance a little" was the verdict of Astaire's 1933 Hollywood screen test. *Movie Star News.*

The 39 Steps (Alfred Hitchcock), Robert Donat, Madeleine Carroll
She (Irving Pichel), Helen Gahagan, Randolph Scott
Magnificent Obsession (John M. Stahl), Irene Dunne, Robert Taylor
Crime and Punishment (Josef von Sternberg), Peter Lorre, Edward Arnold
Gold Diggers of 1935 (Busby Berkeley), Dick Powell, Alice Brady

Academy Awards

Best Picture: *Mutiny on the Bounty*
Best Director: John Ford (*The Informer*)
Best Actress: Bette Davis (*Dangerous*)
Best Actor: Victor McLaglen (*The Informer*)

Top Box-Office Stars

Shirley Temple, Will Rogers, Clark Gable, Fred Astaire and Ginger Rogers, Joan Crawford, Claudette Colbert, Dick Powell, Wallace Beery, Joe E. Brown, James Cagney

Popular Music

Hit Songs
"Begin the Beguine"
"The Music Goes 'Round and 'Round"
"East of the Sun and West of the Moon"
"It Ain't Necessarily So"
"I Got Plenty o' Nuthin' "
"Lovely to Look At"
"Red Sails in the Sunset"
"Stairway to the Stars"
"Summertime"
"These Foolish Things Remind Me of You"
"I Loves You, Porgy"
"You Are My Lucky Star"
"When I Grow Too Old to Dream"

Top Records
Cheek to Cheek (Fred Astaire); *I'm in the Mood for Love* (Frances Langford); *It's You I Adore* (Russ Morgan); *The Oregon Trail* (Ozzie Nelson); *Lullaby of Broadway* (Dick Powell); *Zing! Went the Strings of My Heart"* (Victor Young); *June in January* (Bing Crosby); *Footloose and Fancy Free* (Dorsey Brothers)

Jazz and Big Bands
The Savoy Ballroom, "the home of happy feet," in Harlem, presents Chick Webb and Teddy Hill. Benny Goodman, the "King of Swing," opens at the Palomar Ballroom, Los Angeles; his band includes Lionel Hampton, Gene Krupa, and Teddy Wilson. "Sweet bands," like Guy Lombardo's, compete with Goodman, the Dorseys, and Artie Shaw. Tommy and Jimmy Dorsey split up and form their own bands.

First recordings: Ella Fitzgerald, with Chick Webb; Billie Holiday, with Teddy Wilson

New Bands: Russ Morgan, Bob Crosby, New York; Count Basie, Kansas City

Theater

Broadway Openings

Plays
The Petrified Forest (Robert E. Sherwood), Leslie Howard, Humphrey Bogart, Peggy Conklin
Winterset (Maxwell Anderson), Margo, Burgess Meredith
Awake and Sing (Clifford Odets), Morris Carnovsky, Luther Adler, Stella Adler, John Garfield
The Old Maid (Zoe Akins), Judith Anderson, Helen Menken
Waiting for Lefty (Clifford Odets), Elia Kazan, Herbert Rattner, Paula Miller, Abner Bibberman
Till the Day I Die (Clifford Odets), Walter Coy, Elia Kazan, Alexander Kirkland, Lee J. Cobb
Paradise Lost (Clifford Odets), Morris Carnovsky, Stella Adler
Three Men on a Horse (John Cecil Holm, George Abbott), Shirley Booth, Sam Levene
Night of January 16 (Ayn Rand), Doris Nolan
Mulatto (Langston Hughes), Rose McClendon
Dead End (Sidney Kingsley), Marjorie Main, Dan Duryea, Martin Gabel, Sidney Lumet, Leo Gorcey
Victoria Regina (Laurence Housman), Helen Hayes

Musicals
At Home Abroad (Arthur Schwartz, Howard Dietz), Beatrice Lillie, Ethel Waters, Eleanor Powell, Reginald Gardner
Jubilee (Cole Porter), Mary Boland, Charles Walters, Montgomery Clift
Jumbo (Richard Rodgers, Lorenz Hart), Jimmy Durante, Bob Lawrence, Gloria Grafton
May Wine (Sigmund Romberg, Oscar Hammerstein II), Walter Slezak, Leo G. Carroll, Nancy McCord
Porgy and Bess (George Gershwin, Ira Gershwin), Todd Duncan, Anne Brown

Classics and Revivals On and Off Broadway
The Taming of the Shrew, Alfred Lunt, Lynn Fontanne; *Romeo and Juliet,* Katharine Cornell, Maurice Evans (U.S. debut), Ralph Richardson, Tyrone Power, Jr.; *Ghosts* (Ibsen), Nazimova; *Rain* (John Colton, Clemence Randolph), Tallulah Bankhead. *Founded:* American National Theatre and Academy (ANTA) by presidential charter (FDR)

Regional

Founded: Oregon Shakespeare Festival Association, Ashland, by Angus Bowmer; Federal Theatre Project organized under Hallie Flanagan

Pulitzer Prize
The Old Maid, Zoe Akins

Classical Music

Compositions

Roger Sessions, Violin Concerto
Edgard Varèse, Chamber Pieces
John Alden Carpenter, *Danza*
Walter Piston, Trio for Violin, Cello, and Piano;
    String Quartet no. 2
John Powell, *A Set of Three*
George Antheil, *Dreams*
Roy Harris, *Farewell to Pioneers*
Henry Cowell, *Sinister Resonance*
David Diamond, Partita for Oboe, Bassoon, and
    Piano
William Schuman, *Symphony no. 1 for Eighteen
    Instruments*

Important Events

18,000 musicians of all ranks are hired by the
government; the Federal Music Project also sponsors
thousands of concerts. The Composers Forum Lab
(organized by the Federal Music Project) opens in
New York with a program of Roy Harris's music.
Owing to the depression, the San Francisco
Orchestra almost goes bankrupt; Pierre Monteux is
appointed as musical director to attract larger
audiences. Arthur Schnabel, in seven consecutive
concerts at Carnegie Hall, plays all 32 Beethoven
sonatas.

Debuts: Emanuel Feuermann, Rosalyn Tureck

First Performances

Leo Sowerby, Concerto no. 2 for Violoncello and
Orchestra (New York); Roy Harris, *When Johnny
Comes Marching Home* (Minneapolis)

Opera

Metropolitan: Marjorie Lawrence, Kirsten Flagstad,
Die Walküre; Lotte Lehmann, Emmanuel List, *Der
Rosenkavalier;* Lotte Lehmann, *Tosca;* Lauritz
Melchior, Kirsten Flagstad, *Tristan und Isolde;*
Lawrence Tibbett, *Rigoletto.* Premieres: *In the
Pasha's Garden* (J. K. Seymour); *La serva padrona*
(G. B. Pergolesi, in Italian); gala farewell for Giulio
Gatti-Casazza

Chicago: Rosa Raisa, *La fiamma* (Respighi,
premiere); Lily Pons, *Lakmé*

Boston: *Porgy and Bess* (George Gershwin,
premiere)

Cleveland: *Lady Macbeth of the District of Mzensk*
(Shostakovitch, premiere)

San Francisco: Complete *Ring* (Kirsten Flagstad,
Elisabeth Rethberg, Friedrich Schorr, Emmanuel
List)

Philadelphia: *Iphigenie en Aulide* (C. W. Gluck,
premiere)

Music Notes

Pierre Monteux revives the San Francisco Orchestra
with $55,000 from municipal taxes and then concen-
trates on performing European music • Leopold
Stokowski retires • Otto Klemperer guest conducts
the New York Philharmonic • Igor Stravinsky leads
the Chicago • The Metropolitan Opera bans singers
from hiring claqueurs and hissers • Herbert
Witherspoon takes over management of the Met but
dies of a heart attack after six months; he is
succeeded by Edward Johnson.

Porgy and Bess, George Gershwin's transformation of
DuBose Heyward's novel. *Billy Rose Collection. The New
York Public Library at Lincoln Center. Astor, Lenox and
Tilden Foundations.*

Art _____

Painting

Joe Jones, *Threshing*
Arthur G. Dove, *Moon*
George Biddle, *Georgia Sweatshop*
Philip Evergood, *Railroad Men*
William Glackens, *The Soda Fountain*
William Gropper, *Senators*
Niles Spencer, *The Bird, Workmen*
Willem de Kooning, *Study of a Mural for a Project*
Paul Cadmus, *To the Lynching*
Frank A. Mechau paints *Dangers of the Mail* for the Post Office Department Building, Washington, D.C.

Sculpture

Chaim Gross, *Handlebar Riders, Strong Woman (Acrobat)*
Robert Laurent, *Kneeling Figure*
Alexander Archipenko, *Boxing*
Jo Davidson, *Dr. Albert Einstein*
Ibram Lassaw, *Sculpture*
Paul Manship, *Prometheus,* Rockefeller Center Fountain

Important Exhibitions

Museums

New York: *Metropolitan:* "Artistic Work of the Employees"; Bryson Burroughs memorial; Hogarth; Japanese costumes. *Museum of Modern Art:* African Negro art; Gaston Lachaise retrospective; George Caleb Bingham; Léger; Le Corbusier. *Whitney:* Abstract painting in America; genre painting from the nineteenth and twentieth centuries

Chicago: Rembrandt and his circle; Boudin, Léger

Architecture

Carl MacKley Public Housing Projects, Philadelphia (W. Pope Barney)
Triborough Bridge, New York (Aymar Embury II)
National Archives, Washington, D.C. (Cass Gilbert)
Corona Elementary School, Los Angeles (Richard Neutra)
Restoration of Williamsburg, Va. (Perry, Shaw, and Hepburn)

Threshing, Joe Jones, 1935. Oil on board. 36 × 48″. *The Metropolitan Museum of Art, George A. Hearn Fund, 1937.*

Dallas: Survey of the great masters

Toledo: French and Flemish primitives

Pittsburgh: Prizes are awarded to Hipolito Hidalgo de Caviedes, Burchfield, Vlaminck

Boston: Independent painters of nineteenth-century Paris

Art Briefs

Andrew Mellon donates $10 million and his $25 million art collection for the construction of the National Art Gallery in Washington, D.C., with the proviso that no gallery be named for him • John D. Rockefeller contributes $2.5 million for the construction of the Cloisters, the medieval branch of the Metropolitan Museum of Art • The Frick Gallery (New York) and the Wichita Museum open • The Federal Art project, under Holger Cahill, sponsors such artists as Jackson Pollock, Willem de Kooning, Arshile Gorky, and Raphael Soyer • Jacques Lipchitz has his first major show, in New York • "The Ten," a group of artists interested in abstractionism and expressionism, is founded.

Dance _____

George Balanchine and Lincoln Kirstein organize a touring company, the American Ballet. In two weeks at Adelphi College, New York, they perform seven Balanchine works; principal dancers include Tamara Geva, Eugene Loring, William Dollar, Leda Anchutina, and Ruthanna Boris. The Metropolitan Opera invites the ballet to be its permanent company.

Books

Fiction

Critics' Choice
Pylon, William Faulkner
Taps at Reveille, F. Scott Fitzgerald
Tortilla Flat, John Steinbeck
It Can't Happen Here, Sinclair Lewis
Somebody in Boots, Nelson Algren
Studs Lonigan (complete version), James T. Farrell
They Shoot Horses, Don't They, Horace McCoy
Paths of Glory, Humphrey Cobb
The Last Puritan, George Santayana
Bury the Dead, Irwin Shaw
Butterfield 8, John O'Hara

Best-Sellers
Green Light, Lloyd C. Douglas
Vein of Iron, Ellen Glasgow
Of Time and the River, Thomas Wolfe
Time Out of Mind, Rachel Field
Good-Bye, Mr. Chips, James Hilton
The Forty Days of Musa Dagh, Franz Werfel
Heaven's My Destination, Thornton Wilder
Lost Horizon, James Hilton
Come and Get It, Edna Ferber
Europa, Robert Briffault

Nonfiction

Critics' Choice
America Faces the Barricades, John L. Spivak
The Road to War, Walter Millis
The U.S., 1830–1850, Frederick Jackson Turner
Gay Reformer: Profits before Plenty under F.D.R., Mauritz A. Hallgren
The Green Hills of Africa, Ernest Hemingway
Jefferson and/or Mussolini, Ezra Pound
Black Reconstruction, W. E. B. Du Bois
Growing Up in New Guinea, Margaret Mead
My Country and My People, Lin Yutang
Proletarian Literature in the U.S., Granville Hicks
My Ten Years in a Quandary and How They Grew Up, Robert Benchley
Enjoyment of Laughter, Max Eastman
🔊 *The Two Sources of Morality and Religion*, Henri Bergson

Best-Sellers
North to the Orient, Anne Morrow Lindbergh
While Rome Burns, Alexander Woollcott

Life with Father, Clarence Day
Personal History, Vincent Sheean
Seven Pillars of Wisdom, T. E. Lawrence
Francis the First, Francis Hackett
Mary Queen of Scotland and the Isles, Stefan Zweig
Rats, Lice and History, Hans Zinsser
R. E. Lee, Douglas Southall Freeman
Skin Deep, M. C. Phillips

Poetry
Wallace Stevens, *Ideas of Order*
Lincoln Kirstein, *Low Ceiling*
Muriel Rukeyser, *Theory of Flight*
Marianne Moore, *Selected Poems*
Kenneth Fearing, *Poems*

Pulitzer Prizes
Honey in the Horn, Harold L. Davis (novel)
The Constitutional History of the U.S., Andrew C. McLaughlin (U.S. history)
The Thought and Character of William James, Ralph B. Perry (biography)
Strange Holiness, Robert P. Tristram Coffin (poetry)

Science and Technology

Du Pont chemist Wallace Hume Carothers creates nylon, the first completely synthetic fabric.

Wendell Stanley, at the Rockefeller Institute, isolates a virus (tobacco mosaic) in pure crystalline form, which demonstrates its proteinaceous nature.

Alcoholics Anonymous is organized in New York.

A federal hospital for narcotics addicts is opened in Lexington, Ky.

John Northrup isolates chymotrypsin from pancreatic juice.

The first wearable hearing aid, weighing 2½ pounds, is produced by A. Edwin Stevens.

Ergonovine is developed for obstetric use.

Robert Goddard continues his rocket experiments in New Mexico, achieving heights of 8,000 feet and supersonic speeds.

🔊 Aircraft-detecting radar is pioneered by Robert Watson Watt in England.

🔊 Clinical application of sulfa therapy, using Prontosil, takes place in Germany.

🔊 Henrik Dam discovers vitamin K.

Sports

Baseball

The first night baseball game is played in Cincinnati against Philadelphia; 22,422 attend.

Babe Ruth, traded to Boston (NL), hits three home runs in his last game and retires with lifetime records of 714 home runs, 5,793 total bases, and a .342 BA.

Rookie Wally Berger (Cincinnati, NL) leads his league with 34 home runs.

Champions

Batting
Arky Vaughan (Pittsburgh, NL), .385
Charles Myer (Washington, AL), .349

Pitching
Bill Lee (Chicago, NL), 20–6
Eldon Auker (Detroit, AL), 18–7

Home runs
Jimmy Foxx (Philadelphia, AL), 36
Hank Greenberg (Detroit, AL), 36

Football

The NFL college draft begins. Jay Berwanger, Chicago, is the first selection, by Philadelphia; Berwanger decides not to play pro ball.

Red Grange retires; Don Hutson (E), Green Bay, debuts.

The Heisman Trophy begins; Berwanger is the first winner.

NFL Season Leaders: Ed Danowski (New York), passing; Doug Russell (Chicago Cards), rushing; Todd Goodwin (New York), receiving.

College All-Americans: Sammy Baugh (Q), Texas Christian; Gaynell Tinsley (F), Louisiana State

Bowls (Jan. 1, 1936)

Rose: Stanford 7–Southern Methodist 0
Orange: Catholic 20–Mississippi 19
Sugar: Texas Christian 3–Louisiana State 2

Basketball

Hank Luisetti, Stanford star, originates the one-handed shot and breaks scoring records.

Other Sports

Horse Racing: Omaha, ridden by W. Saunders, wins the Triple Crown.

Boxing: James Braddock beats Maxie Baer for the heavyweight crown.

Tennis: Helen Hull Jacobs wins her third straight U.S. Open.

Winners

World Series
Detroit (AL) 4
Chicago (NL) 2

MVP
NL–Gabby Harnett, Chicago
AL–Henry Greenberg, Detroit

NFL
Detroit 26–New York 17

College Football
Minnesota

Heisman Trophy
Jay Berwanger, Chicago

College Basketball
New York University

Player of the Year
Leroy Edwards, Kentucky

Stanley Cup
Montreal (Maroons)

U.S. Tennis Open
Men: Wilmer Allison
Women: Helen Hull Jacobs

USGA Open
Sam Parks, Jr.

Kentucky Derby
Omaha (W. Saunders, jockey)

Fashion

For Women: A severe, though eclectic, military look is introduced with square, epaulette shoulders, low heels, plumed hats, and gauntlet gloves. Even Schiaparelli designs suits with a "tidy look" in his drummer-boy jackets. Evening wear contrasts: Greek or Indian dresses with heavy jewelry, extraordinary prints (of pigs, radishes, newspaper print). Hair is brushed to the top of the head in a mass of curls. Makeup emphasizes bone structure in a bold way. A red pencil lines the lips for very bright red shades; rouge is applied to earlobes and cheeks and over the eyes. Eyebrows are plucked to their thinnest, if not completely; false eyelashes are worn. Fingernails are scarlet and long; toenails, fashionable pink. Bra cup sizes (A–D) are introduced; net, woven fabrics, and zippers enter corsetry.

High-fashion note: Mainbocher's two-piece navy wool dress with lace cuffs and collar.

Kaleidoscope

- One out of four households is on relief; 750,000 farms have been foreclosed since 1930.
- The Civilian Conservation Corps (CCC) employs half a million young men in conservation projects for which they earn $40 a month.
- Direct relief is returned to the states as the WPA takes over work relief. A total of 8 million people build schools, libraries, bridges, roads, hospitals, and sewage systems.
- On the New Deal's "Black Monday," May 27, the Supreme Court voids the NIRA and condemns the president in the "Sick Chicken Case" begun by the Schechter brothers of Brooklyn.
- *Boondoggling* enters the national vocabulary when some critics call relief work busy work for the unemployed.
- Oklahoma, Texas, and Missouri are the leading places of origin of migrant families.
- FDR announces IRS figures: 0.1 percent of U.S. corporations own 52 percent of total corporate assets and earn 50 percent of all profits.
- William Randolph Hearst earns the highest salary in America, and Mae West, the second highest.
- Participation in group sports in public areas increases—swimming, golfing, and ice skating; there is also a marked increase in bicycling, skiing, and softball.
- The rhumba becomes popular.
- Bingo begins in movie houses and soon becomes popular with charity organizations.
- The 10¢ chain letter craze begins. Denver post office employees work into the night sorting hundreds of thousands of letters.
- Americans still spend $1,000 each day on buggy whips.
- The DC-3, with heated cabins and soundproofing, is the first reliable passenger plane able to go cross-country nonstop, in 15 hours.
- The Russian tourist agency, Intourist, advertises: "Travel dollars have not shrunk in the Soviet Union"; an estimated 30,000 travel to Russia.
- The average cost of advertising on radio is $360.80 per minute (NBC); the reduced rate is $262.91 per minute for a full hour.
- Instead of mailing Christmas cards, a Chicago printing salesman sends out a list of his favorite restaurants; he receives so many requests for copies, he goes into business: "Recommended by Duncan Hines."
- The Massachusetts Department of Mental Health reports that children from small families have a greater tendency to steal, and children from large families have a greater tendency to lie.
- Americans consume 50 million chickens a year and pay more for poultry than red meat.
- Theater audiences cry "Strike!" at the highly successful Clifford Odets's *Waiting for Lefty,* which asks that they pretend to be union members.
- The Federal Theatre Project under Hallie Flanagan

The administration completes Hoover Dam (formerly Boulder Dam) for flood control, irrigation, and electric power. *Library of Congress.*

presents 924 productions to more than 20 million people.
- Documentary prose-photography thrives, including the work of Margaret Bourke-White, Walker Evans, James Agee, Dorothea Lange, and Archibald MacLeish. The Rural Resettlement Administration (later, the Farm Security Administration), under Rexford G. Tugwell, photographs America's blighted land.
- WPA writers include Saul Bellow, John Cheever, Ralph Ellison, Chester Himes, Richard Wright, and Kenneth Rexroth.
- A senate committee investigates the munitions industry and its role in instigating American involvement in World War I; several popular books, like Walter Millis's *The Road to War,* indict the arms makers.
- New York attorney general Thomas Dewey convicts Lucky Luciano and 70 others of racketeering.
- Counterfeiting has increased 400 percent since the depression began.
- Huey Long's assassin is shot with 61 bullets by Long's bodyguards.
- With the enormous growth of Bernarr Macfadden's magazine empire (*True Confessions* sells 7,355,000 copies, an even greater number than *Collier's),* Macfadden considers running for president.

Fads: Monopoly (20 million sets sold in one week), the Irish Sweepstakes, pinball, bridge, bingo (in churches), gambling

First Appearances: Auto exceeding 300 m.p.h., woman stock exchange member, beer in cans, lie detector used in court, book series microfilmed, roller derby (Chicago), national skeet tournament (Indianapolis), Toyota, Richter scale for measuring earthquakes, Kodachrome for 16mm camera, RealLemon, Jolly Green Giant, Hayden Planetarium, Gallup Poll, hot meals served in the air, Shenandoah National Park (Virginia), SS *Normandie* in service crossing Atlantic

1936

In the News

DUST STORMS SWEEP THE MIDWEST . . . AGRICULTURAL ADJUSTMENT ACT IS STRUCK DOWN BY SUPREME COURT . . . GEORGE V OF BRITAIN DIES, EDWARD, PRINCE OF WALES, SUCCEEDS TO THE THRONE . . . SUPREME COURT UPHOLDS TENNESSEE VALLEY AUTHORITY . . . HITLER REPUDIATES LOCARNO TREATY, GERMAN TROOPS REENTER RHINELAND . . . MAJOR FLOODS HIT NORTHEAST U.S., MANY PEOPLE ARE HOMELESS OR DEAD . . . DEMOCRATS RENOMINATE FDR, GOP CHOOSES ALF LANDON . . . PANAMA TREATY ENDS U.S. PROTECTORATE . . . MINIMUM WAGE FOR WOMEN IS FOUND UNCONSTITUTIONAL . . . MUSSOLINI'S TROOPS TRIUMPH OVER ILL-EQUIPPED ETHIOPIANS . . . BRUNO HAUPTMANN IS ELECTROCUTED FOR LINDBERGH KIDNAPPING . . . 16-YEAR-OLD FAROUK BECOMES KING OF EGYPT . . . CIVIL WAR BEGINS IN SPAIN, FRANCISCO FRANCO AND EMILIO MOLA LEAD ARMY AGAINST THE REPUBLIC . . . GERMANY AND ITALY AID FRANCO . . . THOMAS DEWEY CONVICTS LUCKY LUCIANO, SENTENCED TO 30–50 YEARS . . . ANASTASIO SOMOZA LEADS COUP IN NICARAGUA . . . CHARLES LINDBERGH TOURS GERMANY ON HERMAN GOERING INVITATION . . . U.S. DECLARES NONINTERVENTION POLICY FOR SPAIN . . . STALIN BEGINS LARGE GOVERNMENT PURGE . . . ROME-BERLIN AXIS IS PROCLAIMED . . . SUPREME COURT INVALIDATES BITUMINOUS COAL CONSERVATION ACT . . . FDR IS REELECTED BY LANDSLIDE, ELECTORAL VOTE IS 523–8 . . . JAPAN AND GERMANY ANNOUNCE ANTI-COMINTERN PACT . . . PLANT WORKERS STAGE "SIT-DOWN" AT GENERAL MOTORS . . . EDWARD VIII ABDICATES FOR LOVE OF AMERICAN DIVORCÉE WALLIS WARFIELD SIMPSON.

Quotes _____

"The hand of Moscow backs the Communist leaders in America . . . [and] aims to support FDR. . . . I ask you to purge the man who claims to be a Democrat from the Democratic Party, and I mean Franklin Double-Crossing Roosevelt."

— Father Charles Coughlin

"For twelve years this nation was afflicted with hear-nothing, see-nothing, do-nothing government. Never before in our history have these forces been so united against one candidate as they stand today. They are unanimous in their hatred for me—and I welcome their hatred."

— FDR, final campaign speech

"This generation of Americans has a rendezvous with destiny."

— FDR

"Withering heat, rushing out of the furnace of the prairie dust bowl, blasted crops, sucked up rivers and lakes, and transformed the nation—from the Rockies to the Atlantic—into a vast simmering cauldron."

— *Newsweek*

"God and history will remember your judgment. It is us today. It will be you tomorrow."

— Ethiopian emperor Haile Selassie, appealing to the League of Nations for assistance

Despite his cheery campaign button, Alf Landon loses every state but Maine and Vermont. *Smithsonian Institution.*

"The Fifth Column will take Madrid."

— Gen. Emilio Mola

"They shall not pass."

— Spanish loyalist La Pasionara, Dolores Ibarruri

"I wanted to see New York . . . so I tried to see how fast I could do it in."

— Howard Hughes, on breaking cross-country flight record

"Suppose I'm not so cute when I grow up as I am now?"

— Shirley Temple

"I have found it impossible to carry the heavy burden of responsibility and to discharge my duties as King as I should wish to do, without the help and support of the woman I love."

— Edward VIII, abdication speech

"I regret that I have but one wife to lay down for my country."

— Apocryphal remark attributed to Ernest Simpson, as he and Wallis Warfield Simpson separate

Ads _____

Radio

Premieres
"The Kate Smith Show"
"John's Other Wife," Jimmy Scribner
"The Shadow," Robert Hardy Andrews
"Gangbusters," Phillips H. Lord
"Lux Radio Theatre," Cecil B. DeMille (host)
"We, the People," Gabriel Heatter
"Columbia Workshops" (experimental theater)
"Chase and Sanborn Hour," Edgar Bergen, Charlie
    McCarthy
"Professor Quiz," Craig Earl (first giveaway and quiz
    program)
"Pepper Young's Family," Curtis Arnall

Specials
Radio pickup from Nanking, China, on the
kidnapping of Chiang Kai-shek.

Of Note
The first question on "Professor Quiz" is "What is
the difference between a llama and lama?" • Favorite
programs include "Kate Smith," "Easy Aces,"
"Boake Carter," "Frances Langford and Dick
Powell," "Burns and Allen," "Helen Trent," "One
Man's Family," "Just Plain Bill," "Lux Radio
Theater" • Jack Benny and Fred Allen begin their
"feud"—a running gag on both shows—when Allen
insults Benny's violin playing.

New Catchphrases: "I'll clip ya! So help me, I'll
mow ya down" (Edgar Bergen and Charlie
McCarthy); "*(Marching feet, machine-gun fire, siren
wail)* . . . Calling all Americans to war on the
underworld!" ("Gangbusters"); "You have a friend
and adviser in John J. Anthony" ("The Goodwill
Hour"); "Several years ago in the Orient, [Lamont]
Cranston learned . . . the hypnotic power to cloud
men's minds so they cannot see him. . . . Who knows
what evil lurks in the hearts of men? The Shadow
knows! *(Laugh)*" ("The Shadow")

Movies

Openings
The Great Ziegfeld (Robert Z. Leonard), Luise
    Rainer, William Powell, Myrna Loy
Anthony Adverse (Mervyn LeRoy), Fredric March,
    Olivia de Havilland
Dodsworth (William Wyler), Walter Huston, Ruth
    Chatterton, David Niven
Romeo and Juliet (George Cukor), Leslie Howard,
    Norma Shearer, Basil Rathbone, John
    Barrymore
Libeled Lady (Jack Conway), Spencer Tracy, Myrna
    Loy, William Powell, Jean Harlow
Mr. Deeds Goes to Town (Frank Capra), Gary
    Cooper, Jean Arthur
San Francisco (W. S. Van Dyke), Clark Gable,
    Jeanette MacDonald, Spencer Tracy
A Tale of Two Cities (Jack Conway), Ronald Colman,
    Elizabeth Allan
The Story of Louis Pasteur (William Dieterle), Paul
    Muni
Three Smart Girls (Henry Koster), Deanna Durbin,
    Ray Milland
Modern Times (Charles Chaplin), Charles Chaplin,
    Paulette Goddard
Fury (Fritz Lang, U.S. debut), Spencer Tracy, Sylvia
    Sidney

Camille (George Cukor), Greta Garbo, Robert Taylor
These Three (William Wyler), Miriam Hopkins, Merle
    Oberon, Joel McCrea
The Ghost Goes West (René Clair), Robert Donat,
    Jean Parker
My Man Godfrey (Gregory La Cava), Carole
    Lombard, William Powell
Swingtime (George Stevens), Ginger Rogers, Fred
    Astaire

Academy Awards
Best Picture: *The Great Ziegfeld*
Best Director: Frank Capra (*Mr. Deeds Goes to
    Town*)
Best Actress: Luise Rainer (*The Great Ziegfeld*)
Best Actor: Paul Muni (*The Story of Louis Pasteur*)

Top Box-Office Stars
Shirley Temple, Clark Gable, Fred Astaire and
Ginger Rogers, Robert Taylor, Joe E. Brown, Dick
Powell, Joan Crawford, Claudette Colbert, Jeanette
MacDonald, Gary Cooper

Popular Music

Hit Songs
"I'm an Old Cow Hand"
"Is It True What They Say about Dixie?"
"I've Got You under My Skin"
"The Night Is Young and You're So Beautiful"
"Sing, Sing, Sing"
"Stompin' at the Savoy"
"There's a Small Hotel"
"W.P.A. Blues"
"Wiffenpoof Song"
"You've Gotta Eat Your Spinach, Baby"

Top Records
Let's Face the Music and Dance, Let Yourself Go, The Way You Look Tonight, and *Pick Yourself Up* (Fred Astaire); *Pennies from Heaven* (Bing Crosby); *In the Chapel in the Moonlight* (Ruth Etting) (Shep Fields); *No Regrets* (Billie Holiday); *Love Is Like a Cigarette* and *Welcome Stranger* (Eddy Duchin); *Indian Love Call* (Nelson Eddy, Jeanette MacDonald)

Jazz and Big Bands
Jo Jones and Buck Clayton join Count Basie; Mildred Bailey sings with the new Red Norvo band. Popular boogie-woogie piano includes Meade Lux Lewis, Pete Johnson, Albert Ammons, and Bob Zurke. Lester Young plays with the Count Basie combo in Chicago.

New Bands: Red Norvo; Woody Herman

Top Performers *(Downbeat):* Benny Goodman (soloist, big band); Ray Noble (sweet band); Eddie Lang, Pops Foster, Teddy Wilson, Gene Krupa, Tommy Dorsey, Bix Biederbecke (instrumentalists)

Theater

Broadway Openings

Plays
Idiot's Delight (Robert E. Sherwood), Alfred Lunt, Lynn Fontanne
Call It a Day (Dodie Smith), Gladys Cooper, Philip Merivale
Tovarich (Jacques Deval), John Halliday, Marta Abba
Stage Door (George S. Kaufman, Edna Ferber), Margaret Sullavan
You Can't Take It with You (Moss Hart, George S. Kaufman), Josephine Hull, Frank Conlan
Brother Rat (John Monks, Jr., Fred Finklehoff), Eddie Albert, Frank Albertson, José Ferrer
The Women (Clare Booth), Margalo Gillmore, Ilka Chase, Audrey Christie
Johnny Johnson (Paul Green), John Garfield, Elia Kazan, Luther Adler
The Postman Always Rings Twice (James M. Cain), Richard Barthelmess, Mary Philips
Ethan Frome (Owen Davis, Donald Davis), Pauline Lord, Ruth Gordon, Raymond Massey
The Wingless Victory (Maxwell Anderson), Katharine Cornell, Effie Shannon, Walter Abel
Tonight at 8:30 (Noel Coward), Noel Coward, Gertrude Lawrence
St. Helena (R. C. Sherriff, Jeanne de Casalis), Maurice Evans, Barry Sullivan
Night Must Fall (Emlyn Williams), May Whitty, Emlyn Williams

Musicals
George White's Scandals of 1936 (Ray Henderson, Jack Yellen), Rudy Vallee, Bert Lahr, Willie and Eugene Howard
On Your Toes (Richard Rodgers, Lorenz Hart), Tamara Geva, Ray Bolger, Monty Woolley, choreographed by George Balanchine
Red, Hot and Blue (Cole Porter), Ethel Merman, Jimmy Durante, Bob Hope
White Horse Inn (Ralph Benatsky, Irving Caesar), William Gaxton, Kitty Carlisle, Robert Halliday
Ziegfeld Follies of 1936 (Vernon Duke, Ira Gershwin), Fannie Brice, Bob Hope, Eve Arden, Josephine Baker

Classics and Revivals On and Off Broadway
St. Joan (George Bernard Shaw), Katharine Cornell, Maurice Evans, Tyrone Power, Jr.; *The Country Wife* (Wycherley), Ruth Gordon; *Cyrano de Bergerac* (Rostand), Walter Hampton; *Hamlet*, John Gielgud, Judith Anderson, Lillian Gish. *Founded:* The WPA, with *Chalk Dust, The Living Newspaper, Class of 1929, Macbeth*, Orson Welles; *Murder in the Cathedral* (T. S. Eliot), Harry Irvine

Regional

Cleveland: *Not for Children* (Elmer Rice), premiere

Pulitzer Prize
Idiot's Delight, Robert E. Sherwood

Classical Music

Compositions

Edgard Varèse, *Densité*
Aaron Copland, *El salon México*
Samuel Barber, Symphony no. 1, Adagio for Strings,
    String Quartet no. 1
Roy Harris, Quintet for Piano and Strings
Roger Sessions, String Quartet no. 1
Virgil Thomson, *The Plough that Broke the Plains*
John Alden Carpenter, Violin Concerto
Howard Hanson, Symphony no. 3
David Diamond, Psalm
William Schuman, String Quartet no. 1
Arnold Schoenberg (in U.S.), Violin Concerto

Important Events

The WPA Federal Music Program broadens to
support concert bands, chamber groups, and opera.
Lajos Shuk conducts the Buffalo Philharmonic in its
first concert, with Mischa Elman. Most frequently
performed international composers are Francesco
Malipiero, Georges Enesco, and Paul Hindemith. A
controversy is raised over whether orchestras should
have single or multiple conductors; the New York
Philharmonic has invited Arturo Toscanini, Wilhelm
Fürtwängler, Igor Stravinsky, Carlos Chávez, and
John Barbirolli, who becomes its permanent
conductor.

Debut: Gary Graffman, Robert Casadesus

First Performances

Chávez (conducting), *Sinfonia India* (New York);
Sergei Rachmaninoff, Symphony no. 3 (Philadelphia);
Roy Harris, Symphony no. 3 (Boston); Prelude and
Fugue for String Orchestra (Philadelphia); William
Schuman, Symphony no. 1 (New York); Samuel
Barber, Symphony no. 1 (Cleveland)

Opera

Metropolitan: Widespread efforts to popularize
opera include 25¢ to $3 tickets; the Opera Guild is
established to sponsor public talks and opera
publications; companies travel widely. Kerstin
Thorborg (debut), *Die Walküre; Tristan und Isolde;*
Bruna Castagna, *Il trovatore;* Dusolina Giannini,
Aïda; Gianni Schicchi (in English); Florence Easton's
farewell, *Die Walküre*

Chicago: *Jack and the Beanstalk* (Louis Gruenberg,
premiere); Helen Jepson, *Louise*

San Francisco: Mozart is introduced into the
repertory: *The Marriage of Figaro* (Elisabeth
Rethberg, Ezio Pinza); Fritz Reiner joins the
company to continue Wagner's *Ring* cycle from last
year.

Walker Evans's *Georgia* is
part of the pictorial record of
America gathered by the
Resettlement Administration
(RA) under Roy Stryker.
Library of Congress.

Art _____

Painting
Lyonel Feininger, *Church at Gelmeroda*
Arshile Gorky, *Aviation, Self-Portrait*
Adolph Gottlieb, *Sun Deck*
William Gropper, *Suburban Post in Winter*
Reginald Marsh, *Twenty-Cent Movie, End of the Fourteenth Street Crosstown Line*
Joe Jones, *American Farm*
John Steuart Curry, *Westward Migration, The Mississippi*
Raphael Soyer, *Office Girls, Artists on WPA*
Mark Tobey, *Broadway*
Ernest Leonard Blumenschein, *Jury for Trial of a Sheepherder for Murder*
Marsden Hartley, *The Old Bars*
Ben Shahn, *East Side Soap Box*

Sculpture
Alexander Calder, *Gibraltar*
Anna Hyatt Huntington, *Greyhounds Playing*
David Smith, *Head as Still Life, Growing Forms*
Alexander Archipenko, *Torso in Space*

Architecture
Hoover Dam, Boulder City, Nev. (U.S. Bureau of Reclamation)
Barclay-Vesey Building, New York (McKenzie, Vorhees, and Gmelin)
U.S. Supreme Court, Washington, D.C. (Cass Gilbert)
Designs are approved for the Jefferson Memorial, Washington, D.C. (John Russell Pope) and National Gallery, Washington, D.C. (Pope).

Dorothea Lange, *Migrant Mother. Library of Congress.*

Important Exhibitions

Museums

New York: *Metropolitan:* "Benjamin Franklin and his Circle"; Goya's drawings, Copley, La Farge. *Museum of Modern Art:* New horizons in American Art; Architecture of H. H. Richardson and his times; Cubism and abstract art; John Marin; "Fantastic Art, Dada and Surrealism" show includes Duchamp, Grosz, Moholy-Nagy, Seligmann, Tanguy. *Whitney:* "American Scene: WPA"

Chicago: Rembrandt; Mexican arts and crafts

Philadelphia: Degas

Boston: Art treasures of Japan

Art Briefs
Regional shows attract large audiences in Kansas City, Dallas, Buffalo, Syracuse, the Cumberland Valley, Pittsburgh, Chicago, Iowa, and Indiana; sales also revive • FDR publicly supports native art. • Government payments are $23.86 for a 15-hour week; 5,300 artists in 44 states paint 600 to 700 murals. William Baziotes and Mark Rothko join the WPA project • The influx of French art stirs little public interest, although Picasso, Matisse, Cézanne, Derain, and Vlaminck are widely shown in commercial galleries • American Abstract Artists is formed by Ilya Bolotowsky, Giorgio Cavallon, and Ibram Lassaw.

Dance _____

Lincoln Kirstein organizes a touring company, Ballet Caravan; Catherine Littlefield begins the Philadelphia Ballet Company.

Books _____

Fiction

Critics' Choice

The Crack-Up, F. Scott Fitzgerald
Absalom, Absalom! William Faulkner
The Big Money, John Dos Passos
Black Spring, Henry Miller
In Dubious Battle, John Steinbeck
House of Incest, Anaïs Nin
A World I Never Made, James T. Farrell
No Villain Need Be, Vardis Fisher
🍂 *Stories of Three Decades,* Thomas Mann

Best-Sellers

Gone with the Wind, Margaret Mitchell
The Last Puritan, George Santayana
Sparkenbroke, Charles Morgan
Drums along the Mohawk, Walter D. Edmonds
It Can't Happen Here, Sinclair Lewis
White Banners, Lloyd C. Douglas
Eyeless in Gaza, Aldous Huxley
The Thinking Reed, Rebecca West
The Hurricane, Charles Nordhoff, J. N. Hall
The Doctor, Mary Roberts Rinehart

Nonfiction

Critics' Choice

The Interpretation of History, Paul Tillich
The Geographical History of America, Gertrude Stein
The Higher Learning in America, Richard M. Hutchins
The Living Jefferson, James T. Adams
Hitler, Konrad Heiden
Hearst: Lord of San Simeon, O. Carlson, E. Sutherland Bates
Rich Land, Poor Land, Stuart Chase
The Family Encounters the Depression, Robert C. Angell
Homeless Men, Thomas Menchen
Mathematics for the Million, Lancelot Hogben
🍂 *General Theory of Employment, Interest and Money,* J. M. Keynes

Best-Sellers

Man the Unknown, Alexis Carrel
The Way of a Transgressor, Negley Farson
North to the Orient, Anne Morrow Lindbergh
Wake Up and Live! Dorothea Brande
Around the World in Eleven Years, Patience Abbe, Richard Abbe, Johnny Abbe

Live Alone and Like It, Marjorie Hills
I Write as I Please, Walter Duranty
An American Doctor's Odyssey, Victor Heiser
Life with Father, Clarence Day
Inside Europe, John Gunther

Poetry

T. S. Eliot, *Collected Poems*
Dorothy Parker, *Not So Deep as a Well*
Carl Sandburg, *The People, Yes*
Wallace Stevens, *Owl's Clover*
Marianne Moore, *The Pangolin and Other Verse*
Robert Penn Warren, *Thirty-Six Poems*
🍂 A. E. Housman, *More Poems*

Pulitzer Prizes

Gone with the Wind, Margaret Mitchell (novel)
The Flowering of New England, Van Wyck Brooks (U.S. history)
Hamilton Fish, Allan Nevins (biography)
A Further Range, Robert Frost (poetry)

Nobel Prize

Eugene O'Neill

Science and Technology _____

Dehydro-cortisone is the first adrenal cortex hormone to be isolated, by Edward C. Kendall.

Vitamin B, thiamine, is synthesized by Robert R. Williams.

Vitamin E is isolated by Herbert McLean Evans and Gladys Emerson.

Pharmaceutical firms develop sulfa drugs.

Alexis Carrel and Charles Lindbergh develop the first artificial heart.

Ernest O. Lawrence transmutes platinum into gold in the cyclotron.

The Douglas twin-engine DC-3, which can carry 21 passengers over 1,500 miles, begins production.

Boulder Dam, on the Colorado River, is completed; it creates the largest artificial reservoir in the world, 246 square miles, and provides power to 1.5 million people.

The cheap "baby" combine harvester is marketed by Allis Chalmers, facilitating small farm mechanization.

🍂 The first jet-powered flight is made by a Heinkel aircraft, based on Hans von Ohain's work.

🍂 The first successful helicopter flight is made.

Sports

Baseball

The first players elected to the Hall of Fame are Ty Cobb, Honus Wagner, Babe Ruth, Christy Mathewson, and Walter Johnson.
Joe DiMaggio (New York, AL) and Bob Feller (Cleveland, AL) debut; Feller strikes out 15 in his first game.

Champions

Batting	Pitching
Paul Waner (Pittsburgh, NL), .373	Carl Hubbell (New York, NL), 26–6
Luke Appling (Chicago, AL), .388	Monte Pearson (New York, AL), 19–7
	Home runs
	Lou Gehrig (New York, AL) 49

Football

NFL Season Leaders: Arnie Herber (Green Bay), passing; Tuffy Leemans (N.Y.), rushing; Don Hutson (Green Bay), receiving.

College All-Americans: Sammy Baugh (Q), Texas Christian; Clint Frank (B), Yale.
The Cotton Bowl, played at Dallas, Texas, is inaugurated on New Year's Day, 1937.

Bowls (Jan. 1, 1937)

Rose: Pittsburgh 21–Washington 0
Orange: Duquesne 13–Mississippi State 12
Cotton: Texas Christian 16–Marquette 6
Sugar: Santa Clara 21–Louisiana State 14

Basketball

The entire Renaissance Rens team is voted into the Basketball Hall of Fame; their overall record is 473–49.

Jesse Owens setting the broad jump record in the Berlin Olympics. *D. Ouellette Collection.*

Olympics

In the Berlin Olympics, the "Ebony Antelope," Jesse Owens, wins four gold medals (100m, 10.3s; 200m, 23.7s; broad jump, 26′ 3¹⁄₆₄″, a record; and 400m relay). Nine out of ten American blacks win gold medals. Hitler leaves the stadium before the awards are given. Other U.S. winners include Archie Williams (400m, 46.5s), John Woodruff (800m, 1:52.9s), Forest Towns (110m, 14.2s), Glenn Hardin (400 m.h., 52.4s), Cornelius Johnson (high jump, 6′ 7¹⁵⁄₁₆″), Earle Meadows (pole vault, 14′ 3¼″), Ken Carpenter (discus, 65′ 7²⁹⁄₆₄″), Glenn Morris (decathlon), Helen Stephens (100m, 11.5s).

Other Sports

Boxing: Max Schmeling defeats Joe Louis in 12 rounds; he says of Louis: "He fought like an amateur. This is no man who could ever be champion."

Winners

World Series	Player of the Year
New York (AL) 4	John Moir, Notre Dame
New York (NL) 2	*Stanley Cup*
MVP	Detroit
NL–Carl Hubbell, New York	*U.S. Tennis Open*
AL–Lou Gehrig, New York	Men: Fred Perry
NFL	Women: Alice Marble
Green Bay 21–Boston 6	*USGA Open*
College Football	Tony Manero
Minnesota	*Kentucky Derby*
Heisman Trophy	Bold Venture (I. Hanford, jockey)
Larry Kelley, Yale	
College Basketball	
Notre Dame	

Fashion

For Women: Enormously popular in the day is a plum or dark green wool tailored dress with long, tight sleeves and slightly bloused bodice; the dress gently flares to midcalf, has side pleats, and is worn with a wide leather belt. For evening, the black silk crepe with white silk overjacket is fashionable, along with the shiny, brown satin with its matching jacket and feather-trimmed sleeves. Formal wear ranges from short dresses in bright colors to gold lamé frocks with pressed pleats and short jackets.

Ferragamo designs the first evening wedge shoe in gold kid and red satin, but ankle boots of gold kid or embroidered velvet are also shown. The "bra" becomes a separate garment for the high and pointed look; falsies are marketed.

High-fashion notes: Schiaparelli's square bag and collarless coat with high sleeves; Molyneux's crescent brown calf pouch bag.

Kaleidoscope _____

Works Progress Administration site. During the year the WPA, under Harry Hopkins, provided employment to over 3 million. *Museum of the City of New York.*

- Dust storms denude large portions of the farmlands of Kansas, Oklahoma, Colorado, Nebraska, and the Dakotas.
- A Colorado farmland survey indicates that half of 6,000 farmhouses in one area have been abandoned.
- An ad for California's "All-Year Club" reads: "Warning! Come to California for a glorious vacation. Advise anyone not to come seeking employment."
- At its peak, the WPA Federal Art Project employs 3,500 artists, who in the next six years produce 4,500 murals, 19,000 sculptures, and 450,000 paintings. The WPA Federal Writers' Project employs 6,500; the Federal Music Project, 15,000 who, in 30 orchestras, play 225,000 programs.
- Joke: "St. Peter: We're a bit behind schedule today. God has an appointment with His psychiatrist. Recently He's started behaving like Franklin D. Roosevelt."
- Numerous federal parks and fish and game sanctuaries are set up by the National Park Service; 600,000 acres are added to state preserves.
- The Institute for Propaganda Analysis is set up in New York with a board that includes Charles Beard, Paul Douglas, and Robert Lynd.
- A *Fortune* article notes: "As for sex . . . the campus takes it more casually than it did ten years ago. . . . It is news that it is no longer news."
- A *Fortune* poll indicates that 67 percent favor birth control.
- Molly Dewson of the National Consumers League leads the fight for female federal patronage. More women postmasters are appointed.
- Josephine Baker introduces the conga to Broadway.
- According to *Life* magazine, one out of ten Americans is tattooed in whole or in part.
- At a premiere of *New Faces,* New York mayor S. Wilson Davis leaps out of his seat to demand the removal of a skit that caricatures Eleanor Roosevelt.
- David Sarnoff coaxes Arturo Toscanini out of retirement in Italy to lead a symphony orchestra for NBC; the finest musicians are gathered and perform in a special studio, 8H, at Rockefeller Center, New York.
- The Swing Music Concert in New York includes Bob Crosby, Tommy Dorsey, Stuff Smith, Red Norvo, Bunny Berigan, Glen Gray's Casa Loma Orchestra, groups from Paul Whiteman and Louis Armstrong, and Arthur (sic) Shaw's String Ensemble.
- Small jazz clubs spring up on 52nd Street, New York, with Stuff Smith and Jonah Jones at the Onyx and Wingy Malone at the Famous Door.
- Celebrity marriages include Paulette Goddard and Charles Chaplin, John Barrymore and Elaine Barrie, Mary Pickford and Buddy Rogers, Lily Pons and André Kostelanetz.
- Margaret Mitchell's *Gone with the Wind* sells a record 1 million copies in six months.

- Herbert LeRoy Hechler runs a trained flea circus on West 42nd Street, New York, where, for 30¢, spectators can watch, through magnifying glasses, fleas dance, juggle, walk a tightrope, stage a chariot race, and operate a carousel.
- Photography-related sales increase, owing to recent advances like the exposure meter and 35mm camera.
- Trailer sales peak; tourist camps for vacationing motorists are also popular.
- Seven million women pay more than $2 billion for 35,000,000 permanents.
- Ferdinand the Bull, Munro Leaf's fantasy about a pacifistic flower-loving bull, is a popular success.
- Sunflower buttons (the Kansas flower) appear throughout the counry in Alf Landon's campaign against FDR. Tiffany and Co. advertises a gold 19-petal sunflower pin with yellow diamonds for $815.
- German pro-Nazi Bund societies form as "Amerika-deutscher Volkbund," ostensibly devoted to social and athletic pursuits.
- Commemorative half-dollars are issued with the heads of P. T. Barnum, Stephen Foster, and Moses Cleveland (the city founder); three-cent Susan B. Anthony and Boulder Dam stamps are also issued.
- A revolt against progressive education is led by Robert M. Hutchins, president of the University of Chicago.
- The popular *Literary Digest* poll, correct since 1920, forecasts a Landon victory of 54 percent; the newer Gallup poll predicts that FDR will win.
- A sleeper berth from Newark to Los Angeles costs $150; the New York Fifth Avenue double-decker bus fare goes from 5¢ to 10¢.

First Appearances: Giant panda in U.S. (San Francisco), art course in fresco painting (Louisiana State University), newspaper microfilming current issues *(New York Herald Tribune),* old-age colony (Melville, N.Y.), photo-finish camera (electric eye) at racetrack, bicycle traffic court (Racine, Wisc.), screw-cap bottle with pour lip, sheet of postage stamps containing more than one variety, Presbyterian Church of America, Penguin books, Ford Foundation, *Life,* Chunky, knock-knock jokes, Goren point-counting system, Vitamin Plus (first vitamin pill), fluorescent tube, Tampax

1937

Facts and Figures

Economic Profile
  Dow-Jones: ↓ High 190–
    Low 118
  GNP: +9%
  Inflation: +1.5%
  Unemployment: 14.3%
Average salary: $1,250
  Teacher: $1,367
  Lawyer: $4,485
  Physician: $4,285
  Factory Worker: $1,376
I. Miller straparound sandal:
  $14.75
Tailored Woman wool and
  lamb coat: $95
Russek's velvet wraparound:
  $35
McCreery's fur coats, black
  pony, dyed lamb, leopard:
  $119
Bloomingdale's cashmere
  dress: $12.95
Mark Cross bag: $5–$16.50
Cocktails, double
  (Rockefeller Center): 25¢
Name-imprinted Christmas
  cards: $9.75 (for 100)
China porcelains: $1–$12

Deaths

J. M. Barrie, John
  Drinkwater, George
  Gershwin, Jean Harlow,
  Frank Billings Kellogg,
  Guglielmo Marconi,
  Maurice Ravel, John D.
  Rockefeller, Ernest
  Rutherford, Irving
  Thalberg, Edith Wharton.

In the News

SIT-DOWN STRIKES CLOSE 15 GENERAL MOTORS PLANTS . . . LEON TROTSKY ARRIVES IN MEXICO . . . HOWARD HUGHES FLIES FROM LOS ANGELES TO NEWARK IN RECORD 7 HOURS, 28 MINUTES, 5 SECONDS . . . NEVILLE CHAMBERLAIN APPEALS TO HITLER FOR COOPERATION IN PEACEKEEPING . . . HITLER REPUDIATES GERMAN WORLD WAR I GUILT . . . 13 PROMINENT DEFENDANTS ARE SENTENCED TO DEATH IN MOSCOW FOR TREASON . . . FDR ASKS CONGRESS FOR POWER TO REORGANIZE THE SUPREME COURT . . . NEW LAW ALLOWS SUPREME COURT JUSTICES TO RETIRE AT 70 WITH FULL PAY . . . U.S. STEEL AND WORKERS SETTLE FOR $5/DAY MINIMUM WAGE AND 40-HOUR WEEK . . . DIRIGIBLE "HINDENBERG" CRASHES AT LAKEHURST, N.J., 38 DIE . . . GERMAN EMBASSY PROTESTS FIORELLO LAGUARDIA'S ATTACKS ON HITLER . . . AMELIA EARHART, ON ROUND-THE-WORLD FLIGHT, VANISHES OVER PACIFIC . . . AFL LEADER WILLIAM GREEN CONDEMNS SIT-DOWN STRIKES, JOHN L. LEWIS ASSAILS GREEN . . . SUPREME COURT UPHOLDS MINIMUM WAGE LAW . . . WAGNER LABOR ACT IS DECLARED CONSTITUTIONAL . . . JOINT NEUTRALITY RESOLUTION OF CONGRESS FORBIDS WAR MATERIAL TRANSPORT TO BELLIGERENTS . . . DIVORCED WALLIS WARFIELD SIMPSON TO WED DUKE OF WINDSOR . . . SUPREME COURT UPHOLDS THE SOCIAL SECURITY ACT . . . FDR ASKS INVESTIGATION OF "IMMORAL" TAX EVASION BY THE WEALTHY . . . 7 SOVIET GENERALS, INCLUDING HERO TUKHACHEVSKY, ARE EXECUTED . . . CLARENCE NORRIS, SCOTTSBORO DEFENDANT, IS SENTENCED TO DEATH FOR THE THIRD TIME . . . SENATE VOTES DOWN COURT REORGANIZATION BILL . . . HUGO BLACK IS NOMINATED TO THE SUPREME COURT FOR THE WILLIS VAN DEVANTER SEAT . . . STOCK MARKET DECLINES SHARPLY.

Quotes _____

"I see one-third of a nation ill-housed, ill-clothed, ill-nourished."

— FDR, second inauguration

"No tin-hat brigade of goose-stepping vigilantes or Bible-babbling mob of blackguarding corporation-scoundrels will prevent the onward march of labor."
— John L. Lewis

"We'll never recognize the United Auto Workers Union or any other union."

— Henry Ford

"The major development in the General Motors strike is the sitdown. . . . It is a tactic which permits workers to halt production with a minimum of effort and a maximum of initial success—and it has management of all industry wondering how to stop it."

— *Business Week*

"Berlin does not hide its contempt for the democracies: 'stupid cows' Goebbels calls them. . . . Today it is Madrid. Tomorrow it will be Prague. How long before it knocks at our own doors?"
— I. F. Stone, *Nation*

"I am the law."
— Frank Hague, mayor of Jersey City

The Federal Arts Project strives to integrate "the arts with the daily life of the community." Above: a gas station in the Northeast U.S. *Library of Congress.*

"It is the people of Spain who have won already one of the great victories against fascism. How then can we, who profit by that victory, not claim the war as ours? How then can we refuse our help?"
— Archibald MacLeish

"When an epidemic of physical disease starts to spread, the community . . . joins in a quarantine . . . to protect the health of the community against the spread of the disease."

— FDR, on the fascist countries

"There are worse things than war. Cowardice, . . . treachery, . . . and simple selfishness."
— Ernest Hemingway

Ads _____

Radio

Premieres

"Stella Dallas," Anne Elstner
"The Guiding Light," Ed Prentiss, Sarajane Wells
"NBC Symphony," Arturo Toscanini
"Our Gal Sunday," Dorothy Lowell
"Grand Central Station," Jack Arthur
"Big Town," Edward G. Robinson
"Dr. Christian," Jean Hersholt
"Mr. Keen, Tracer of Lost Persons," Bennett
   Kilpack

Specials

John Barrymore in six Shakespeare plays; "Hamlet"
(Burgess Meredith, Walter Abel, Grace George)

Of Note

Mae West's sexy repartee with Charlie McCarthy on
the "Chase and Sanborn Hour" leads to an FCC
investigation • Popular quiz programs include
"Melody Puzzles," "Professor Quiz," "Spelling
Bee," and "Uncle Jim's Question Bee" • Most
popular comedians include Jack Benny, Edgar
Bergen and Charlie McCarthy, Burns and Allen,
Eddie Cantor, Fred Allen, Fibber McGee and Molly,
Joe Penner, Fannie Brice, George Jessel, Jack Oakie,
Jack Haley, Phil Baker, and Al Pearse and his gang.

New Catchphrases: "Can this girl from a mining
town in the West find happiness as the wife of a
wealthy and titled Englishman?" ("Our Gal
Sunday"); "Drawn by the magnetic force of the
fantastic metropolis, . . . great trains rush towards
. . . [the] gigantic stage on which are played a
thousand dramas daily!" ("Grand Central Station")

Movies

Openings

The Life of Emile Zola (William Dieterle), Paul Muni
The Awful Truth (Leo McCarey), Irene Dunne, Cary
   Grant
Captains Courageous (Victor Fleming), Freddie
   Bartholomew, Spencer Tracy, Lionel Barrymore
Dead End (William Wyler), Sylvia Sidney, Joel
   McCrea, Humphrey Bogart
The Good Earth (Sidney Franklin), Luise Rainer,
   Paul Muni
In Old Chicago (Henry King), Tyrone Power, Alice
   Faye, Don Ameche
Lost Horizon (Frank Capra), Ronald Colman, Sam
   Jaffe, Margo
Stage Door (Gregory LaCava), Katharine Hepburn,
   Ginger Rogers
A Star Is Born (William A. Wellman), Janet Gaynor,
   Fredric March
Nothing Sacred (William A. Wellman), Carole
   Lombard, Fredric March
Stella Dallas (King Vidor), Barbara Stanwyck, John
   Boles
Topper (Norman Z. McLeod), Cary Grant, Roland
   Young, Constance Bennett
Elephant Boy (Robert Flaherty, Zoltan Korda), Sabu,
   W. E. Holloway
One Hundred Men and a Girl (Henry Koster),
   Deanna Durbin, Leopold Stokowski and large
   orchestra

Warner Oland, in his
16th role as the B-
film detective-hero
Charlie Chan. *Movie
Star News.*

They Won't Forget (Mervyn LeRoy), Claude Rains,
   Allyn Joselyn, Lana Turner
You Only Live Once (Fritz Lang), Henry Fonda,
   Sylvia Sidney
La grande illusion (Jean Renoir), Jean Gabin, Eric
   von Stroheim

Academy Awards

Best Picture: *The Life of Emile Zola*
Best Director: Leo McCarey (*The Awful Truth*)
Best Actress: Luise Rainer (*The Good Earth*)
Best Actor: Spencer Tracy (*Captains Courageous*)

Top Box-Office Stars

Shirley Temple, Clark Gable, Robert Taylor, Bing
Crosby, William Powell, Jane Withers, Fred Astaire
and Ginger Rogers, Sonja Henie, Gary Cooper,
Myrna Loy

Popular Music

Hit Songs
"A Foggy Day"
"The Donkey Serenade"
"Harbor Lights"
"Nice Work if You Can Get It"
"Whistle while You Work"
"I've Got My Love to Keep Me Warm"
"Johnny One Note"
"The Lady Is a Tramp"
"My Funny Valentine"
"September in the Rain"
"Thanks for the Memory"
"In the Still of the Night"
"Where or When"

Top Records
Bei mir bist du Schoen (Andrew Sisters); *They Can't Take that Away from Me, They All Laughed, Let's Call the Whole Thing Off,* and *Shall We Dance?* (Fred Astaire); *Someone to Care for Me* (Deanna Durbin); *Ebb Tide* (Bunny Berigan); *Have You Met Miss Jones?* (Sammy Kaye); *Sweet Leilani* (Bing Crosby and Lani McIntire and His Hawaiians)

Jazz and Big Bands
Benny Goodman records *Sing, Sing, Sing.* Charlie Parker joins the Jay McShann Band. Mary Lou Williams plays with Andy Kirk's Kansas City Band in New York. Harry James plays with Benny Goodman.

First Recordings: George Shearing

New Bands: Glenn Miller, New York

Top Performers *(Downbeat):* Benny Goodman (soloist, big band); Hal Kemp (sweet band); Ella Fitzgerald (vocalist); Carmen Mastren, Bob Haggert, Teddy Wilson, Gene Krupa, Tommy Dorsey, Chu Berry, Harry James (instrumentalists)

Theater

Broadway Openings

Plays
High Tor (Maxwell Anderson), Burgess Meredith
Golden Boy (Clifford Odets), Luther Adler, Art Smith
Yes, My Darling Daughter (Mark Reed), Lucile Watson, Peggy Conklin
Having Wonderful Time (Arthur Rober), John Garfield
Room Service (John Murray, Allen Boretz), Eddie Albert, Betty Field, Sam Levene
The Star-Wagon (Maxwell Anderson), Lillian Gish, Burgess Meredith
Susan and God (Rachel Crothers), Gertrude Lawrence, Nancy Kelly
Amphitryon 38 (Jean Giraudoux), Alfred Lunt, Lynn Fontanne
Of Mice and Men (John Steinbeck), Broderick Crawford, Wallace Ford
French without Tears (Terence Rattigan), Frank Lawton
The Ghost of Yankee Doodle (Sidney Howard), Ethel Barrymore

Musicals
Babes in Arms (Richard Rodgers, Lorenz Hart), Mitzi Green, Ray Heatherton, Alfred Drake
Frederika (Franz Lehár), Helen Gleason, Dennis King, Ernest Truex
Horray for What! (Richard Arlen, E. Y. Harburg), Ed Wynn, Vivian Vance
I'd Rather Be Right (Richard Rodgers, Lorenz Hart), George M. Cohan
Pins and Needles (Harold Rome), International Ladies Garment Workers' Union (ILGWU), Millie Weitz, Ruth Rubinstein, Hy Goldstein
The Show Is On (Vernon Duke et al.), Bert Lahr, Beatrice Lillie, Reginald Gardner

Classics and Revivals On and Off Broadway
Julius Caesar, Orson Welles, Joseph Cotten, Martin Gabel; *Dr. Faustus* (Marlowe), Orson Welles; *Richard II,* (Maurice Evans); *Candida* (George Bernard Shaw), Katharine Cornell; *A Doll's House* (Ibsen), Ruth Gordon, Walter Slezak; *Othello,* Walter Huston. *Founded:* Playwrights' Company by Maxwell Anderson, S. N. Behrman, Sidney Howard, Elmer Rice, and Robert E. Sherwood

Pulitzer Prize
You Can't Take It with You, George S. Kaufman and Moss Hart

Classical Music

Compositions
Roy Harris, *Time Suite*, Symphony no. 3, String
    Quartet no. 3
Virgil Thomson, *The River, Filling Station*
Aaron Copland, *The Second Hurricane*
Ferde Grofé, *Broadway at Night, Symphony in Steel*
John Cage, *Construction in Metal*
Walter Piston, Symphony no. 1
William Schuman, Symphony no. 2, String Quartet
    no. 2, Choral Etude
John Powell, Symphony in A
Samuel Barber, First Essay for Orchestra
Arnold Schoenberg (in U.S.), String Quartet no. 4

Important Events
Robert Whitney conducts the first concert of the
Louisville Symphony Orchestra. Paul Hindemith
makes his first U.S. appearance, playing his Viola
Sonata at the Library of Congress. Artur Rubinstein,
at Carnegie Hall, premieres Stravinsky's
Petroushka's Suite, dedicated to Rubinstein. Well-
known composers writing for radio include Aaron
Copland ("Music for Radio"); Harris ("Time Suite");
William Grant Still ("Lenox Avenue"); Piston
("Concertino"); Howard Hanson (Symphony no. 3);
Henry Gruenberg ("Three Mansions"). Toscanini
signs with NBC to conduct the orchestra created for
him.

Guest Conductors: Pierre Monteux, Artur
Rodzinsky, and Arturo Toscanini, the New York
Philharmonic

Debut: Jorge Bolet, Julius Katchen

First Performances
Ernest Bloch, *A Voice in the Wilderness* (Los
Angeles); E. B. Hill, Symphony no. 3 (Boston); John
Alden Carpenter, Violin Concerto (Chicago); Daniel
Gregory Mason, *A Lincoln Symphony* (New York);
Marc Blitzstein, *The Cradle Will Rock* (New York)

Opera

Metropolitan: Bidú Sayão (debut), *Manon;* Sayão,
Helen Traubel (debut), *The Man without a Country*
(Walter Damrosch, premiere); Giovanni Martinelli,
Otello (first time since 1913); Kirsten Flagstad,
Elektra, Der Rosenkavalier; Zinka Milanov, *Il
trovatore*

Chicago: Jussi Bjoerling (American debut),
Rigoletto; Kirsten Flagstad, Lauritz Melchior,
Tristan und Isolde; Grace Moore, *Manon*

Philadelphia: Premieres: *Amelia Goes to the Ball*
(Gian Carlo Menotti); *Le pauvre Metelot* (Darius
Milhaud)

Music Notes
At the first outdoor concert at Tanglewood, Lenox,
Mass., rain pours during the first piece ("The Ride of
the Valkyries"); arrangements are made to build a
"shed." • A typical concert program consists of
Beethoven, Brahms, Wagner, or Strauss, with the
moderns Sibelius and Stravinsky; virtually no
unfamiliar compositions are played.

Already a legend as past conductor of La Scala and the
New York Philharmonic (and a passionate antifascist),
Arturo Toscanini is 70 when he begins his career with the
NBC Symphony Orchestra. *Library of Congress.*

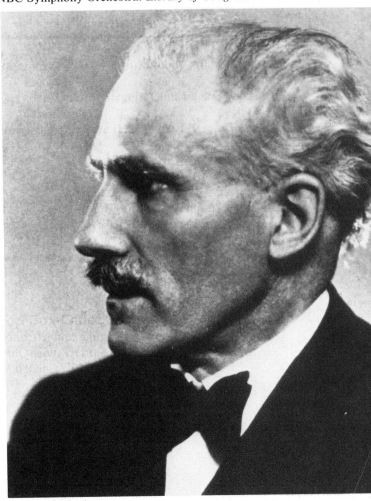

Art

Painting

Arnold Friedman, *Unemployable*

Peter Blume, *The Eternal City*

John Sloan, *Nude and Nine Apples*

Charles Burchfield, *Ice Glare, November Evening*

Ben Shahn, *West Virginia, 1937*

Willem de Kooning, *Untitled*

Jackson Pollock, *Untitled*

Arthur G. Dove, *Rise at the Full Moon*

Jack Levine, *The Feast of Pure Reason*

Philip Evergood, *The Story of Richmond*

Edwin Dickinson, *Composition with Still Life*

Sculpture

Paul Manship, *Night, Day, Time*

James Earle Fraser, *George Washington*

William Zorach, *Ben Franklin*

Lee Lawrie, *Atlas* (Rockefeller Center)

Naum Gabo, *Spheric Theme*

Alexander Archipenko, *Walking Woman*

John B. Flannagan, *Triumph of the Egg*

Architecture

Golden Gate Bridge, Oakland-San Francisco (Strauss, Ammann, Moisseff, and Derleth)

Kaufman House ("Falling Water"), Bear Run, Pa. (Frank Lloyd Wright)

Keck-Gottschalk-Keck Coop Apartment Building, Chicago (George F. Keck)

Trowbridge and Livingston win the design competition for the Oregon State Capitol Building, Salem.

Important Exhibitions

Museums

New York: *Metropolitan:* Renoir; "Sporting Prints and Painting"; Italian Renaissance prints and illustrative books; *Museum of Modern Art:* Van Gogh; Photography 1839–1937. *Whitney:* Gaston Lachaise memorial; Cleveland artists; "The Realists"

Philadelphia: French art; William Rush

Washington: *Corcoran:* Bicentennial prizes to Edward Hopper, Guy Pène du Bois, Francis Speight

Boston: Lithographs 1799–1937

Pittsburgh: Carnegie International First Prize won by Georges Braque

Art Briefs

Regional shows expand in Kansas City, Chicago, Cleveland, San Francisco, Pittsburgh, Denver, St. Louis, Milwaukee, and Seattle • The Washington Museum of Modern Art opens • The Solomon R. Guggenheim Museum for nonobjective art is planned • Gropius, Archipenko, Moholy-Nagy, and others open a new Bauhaus in a 25-room mansion in Chicago, donated by Marshall Field III • Major sales include Gauguin's *Tahiti* ($1,700), Corot's *Landscape with Bathers* ($9,000), Millet's *Shepherdess* ($3,700), Rembrandt's etching *Christ Healing the Sick* ($10,500), and Cézanne's *Bathers* ($110,000), purchased by the Philadelphia Museum.

Dance

The Mordkin Ballet opens in New York. Stravinsky visits the United States for the premiere of *Jeu de cartes* at the Metropolitan (Balanchine), with Lew Christensen and William Dollar.

Other Premieres

American Ballet: *La baiser de la fée* (Balanchine), Dollar; *Apollo* (Balanchine), Christensen. Martha Graham: *Letter to the World, Deep Song*

Dreams on a Washington, D.C., street. *Library of Congress.*

Books

Fiction
Critics' Choice
To Have and Have Not, Ernest Hemingway
Noon Wine, Katherine Anne Porter
The Sea of Grass, Conrad Richter
Their Eyes Were Watching God, Zora Neale Hurston
The Red Pony, John Steinbeck
Remembering Laughter, Wallace Stegner
They Came Like Swallows, William Maxwell
The Grandmothers, Glenway Westcott
The Seven Who Fled, Frederic Prokosch
Serenade, James M. Cain
&❧ *Bread and Wine*, Ignazio Silone

Best-Sellers
Gone with the Wind, Margaret Mitchell
Northwest Passage, Kenneth Roberts
The Citadel, A. J. Cronin
And So—Victoria, Vaughan Wilkins
Drums along the Mohawk, Walter D. Edmonds
The Years, Virginia Woolf
Theatre, W. Somerset Maugham
Of Mice and Men, John Steinbeck
The Rains Came, Louis Bromfield
We Are Not Alone, James Hilton
The Education of Hyman Kaplan, Leonard Q. Ross

Nonfiction
Critics' Choice
Bulwark of the Republic, Burton J. Kendrick
The Ultimate Power, Morris Ernst
Middletown in Transition, Robert S. and Mary M. Lynd
The Life and Death of a Spanish Town, Elliott Paul
The Realm of Truth, George Santayana
The Folklore of Capitalism, Thurman Arnold
An Artist in America, Thomas Hart Benton
You Have Seen Their Faces, Margaret Bourke-White, Erskine Caldwell
Beloved Friend, Catherine Drinker Bowen
In the American Jungle, 1925–1937, Waldo Frank
The Neurotic Personality of Our Time, Karen Horney
Let Your Mind Alone, James Thurber

Best-Sellers
How to Win Friends and Influence People, Dale Carnegie
An American Doctor's Odyssey, Victor Heiser
The Return to Religion, Henry C. Link
The Arts, Hendrik Willem Van Loon
Orchids on Your Budget, Marjorie Hollis
Present Indicative, Noel Coward
Life with Mother, Clarence Day
The Nile, Emil Ludwig
The Flowering of New England, Van Wyck Brooks
Mathematics for the Million, Lancelot Hogben

Poetry
Edna St. Vincent Millay, *Conversation at Midnight*
Robinson Jeffers, *Such Counsels You Gave to Me*
Ezra Pound, *The Fifth Decade of Cantos*
Wallace Stevens, *The Man with the Blue Guitar*
Louise Bogan, *The Sleeping Fury*
Richard Eberhart, *Reading the Spirit*
Sara Teasdale, *Collected Poems*
Archibald MacLeish, *The Fall of the City*
Allen Tate, *The Mediterranean*

Pulitzer Prizes
The Late George Apley, John P. Marquand (novel)
The Road to Reunion, 1865–1900, Paul H. Buck
Pedlar's Progress, Odell Shepard (U.S. history)
Andrew Jackson, Marquis James (history)
Cold Morning Sky, Marya Zaturenska (poetry)

Science and Technology

Johns Hopkins researchers release the first American report of successful treatment of bacterial infection with sulfanilamide.

Vitamin B is found to cure alcoholic neuritis.

Vitamin B_2 is isolated and analyzed and found to be nicotinic acid, an already known substance.

C. Bradley introduces amphetamines for the treatment of hyperactive children.

The structure of vitamin E is determined by Donald Fernholz.

Corticosterone, a second adrenal cortex hormonal substance, is isolated by Edward Kendall.

A prototype "antihistamine" is produced to treat allergic, or histamine, response to outward stimuli.

James Hillier and Albert Prebus build the first practical electron microscope.

AT&T completes the first coaxial cable for television hookups between New York and Philadelphia.

&❧ Hans Krebs postulates his "cycle" of oxidative phosphorylation, the basic process of cellular metabolism.

Nobel Prize
Clinton J. Davisson wins the prize in physics for work on the diffraction of electrons by crystals.

Sports ━━━━━━━━━━━━━━━━━━

Baseball

Carl Hubbell is beaten after a record 24-game streak extending over two seasons.

Cy Young, Nap Lajoie, and Tris Speaker are added to the Hall of Fame.

Champions ━━━━━━━━━━━━━━━━━━

Batting	*Pitching*
Ducky Medwick (St. Louis, NL), .374	Carl Hubbell (New York, NL), 22–8
Chuck Gehringer (Detroit, AL), .371	John Allen (New York, AL), 15–1
	Home runs
	Joe DiMaggio (New York, AL), 40

Football

Sammy Baugh (QB), Washington, debuts.

NFL Season Leaders: Sammy Baugh (Washington), passing; Cliff Battles (Washington), rushing; Don Hutson (Green Bay), receiving.

College All-Americans: Byron "Whizzer" White (B), Colorado; Marshall Goldberg (B), Pittsburgh; Clark Hinckle (G), Vanderbilt

Bowls (Jan. 1, 1938)

Rose: California 13– Alabama 0	Cotton: Rice 28– Colorado 0
Orange: Auburn 6– Michigan State 0	Sugar: Santa Clara 6– Louisiana State 0

Basketball

The National Basketball League, composed of neighboring midwestern teams, begins.

Hank Luisetti, Stanford, scores a record 50 points in one game.

Other Sports

Boxing: Joe Louis, 23, the "Brown Bomber," defeats James Braddock for the heavyweight title.

Winners ━━━━━━━━━━━━━━━━━━

World Series	*College Basketball*
New York (AL) 4	Stanford
New York (NL) 1	*Player of the Year*
MVP	Hank Luisetti, Stanford
NL–Joe Medwick, St. Louis	*Stanley Cup*
AL–Charles Gehringer, Detroit	Detroit
	U.S. Tennis Open
NFL	Men: Donald Budge
Washington 28	Women: Anita Lizana
Chicago 21	*USGA Open*
College Football	Ralph Guldahl
Pittsburgh	*Kentucky Derby*
Heisman Trophy	War Admiral (C. Kurtsinger, jockey)
Clint Frank, Yale	

Fashion ━━━━━━━━━━━━━━━━━━

For Women: The hourglass silhouette, with padded shoulders and small waist, gives way to a more tubular, natural shape with the new "uplift." Evening lengths remain long in wool fabrics; jewels are bulky and immense; Cartier clips of blackamoors' heads are copied everywhere. Bulky blue fox and silk jersey are also new. Veils return on hats. In makeup, Christian Berard introduces cyclamen rouge and deep blue lashes for blondes, and brown suntan rouge and pomegranate lips for brunettes.

High-fashion note: Strassner's white pullover, white wool slacks.

For men: For spring and summer: the single-breasted gabardine suit with patch pockets and

An ad displaying current fashion.

panama hat; for fall: the double-breasted dark blue suit with wide-cuffed trousers, padded square shoulders, double-pleated, high-waisted trousers. Vertical stripe suits, in two tones or with windowpane checks, are also new, as well as fabric blends of cotton and wool, nylon and silk, silk and wool. Neckwear is in deep tones, regimentals, polka dots, and tartans; socks are elasticized and have circular stripes.

Kaleidoscope ——————————

- The *Hindenburg,* the world's largest dirigible, carries 98 people and has 50 private cabins; its crash is witnessed by hundreds who have come to watch its triumphant landing.
- The massive Ohio River flood leaves 500,000 homeless.
- Despite torrential rains, the Tennessee River, with its TVA dams, does not overflow.
- A Gallup poll shows that 80 percent approve of relief through paid public work, as opposed to a dole.
- Controversy follows Hugo L. Black's appointment to the Supreme Court because of his youthful membership in the KKK.
- The United States is the world's greatest producer and consumer of spirits, with gin most in demand, followed by whiskey and rum.
- The AMA recognizes birth control advice as a legitimate professional concern.
- A *Fortune* poll reports that 50 percent of all college men and 25 percent of all college women have had premarital sexual relations; two-thirds of the women "would for true love."
- The Marijuana Taxation Act prohibits importation, sale, or possession, with heavy penalties for violators.
- The Miller-Tydings fair trade law is passed, allowing resale prices to be fixed by brand-name manufacturers.
- The UAW is recognized by General Motors as sole bargaining agent for its workers.
- Pierce-Arrow autos go out of business.
- Spinach growers erect a statue to Popeye in Wisconsin.
- Companies like American Radiator, Celotex, and Sears & Roebuck attempt prefabricated housing.
- According to *Vogue,* "It is no longer smart to be sleek, slick, and sexy but smart to be feminine . . . in a new calm way showing the body as a superb piece of sculpture."
- New writers in Hollywood include F. Scott Fitzgerald, Sidney Howard, Robert Sherwood, and Ernest Hemingway.
- Of the great silent movie comedians, only Charles Chaplin remains in Hollywood; others find that sound slows them up and retire (Buster Keaton, Harold Lloyd, and Harry Langdon).
- Among the many films on social themes are *They Won't Forget* (anti–mob violence), *Black Legion* (anti-KKK), *White Bondage* (on sharecroppers), *Make Way for Tomorrow* (on old age), and *Dead End* (about slums).
- Three thousand teenagers line up outside the Paramount Theater to see Benny Goodman.
- According to a Paramount poll, the top bands include Benny Goodman, Guy Lombardo, Shep Fields, Eddy Duchin, Tommy Dorsey, Horace Heidt, Fred Waring, and Sammy Kaye.
- A study indicates that people spend 4.5 hours daily listening to the radio.
- An Old Gold radio contest leads to greatly increased

FDR presenting the Harmon Trophy for outstanding aviator to the flamboyant industrialist-Hollywood playboy Howard Hughes. *Copyright* Washington Post. *Reprinted by permission of D.C. Public Library.*

usage of the New York Public Library.
- Bauhaus architect Walter Gropius becomes head of Harvard's Graduate School of Design; Marcel Breuer, also from Germany, joins him.
- Frank Lloyd Wright tells the International Congress of Architects in Moscow: "Vertical is vertigo in human life. The horizontal line is the lifeline of human kind."
- The restoration of Colonial Williamsburg, Va., is completed.
- Satin programs are distributed at the first NBC Symphony concert under Toscanini so that the rattling of paper will not disturb the maestro.
- John D. Rockefeller, dead at 98, leaves an estate estimated at $1 billion.
- Several thousand Americans join the Abraham Lincoln Brigade to fight with the Loyalists against the fascist-supported Franco forces; about 50 percent die in battle. Among the writers who go to Spain to report on the war are Dorothy Parker, Lillian Hellman, John Dos Passos, Ernest Hemingway, Malcolm Cowley, Josephine Herbst, and Upton Sinclair.
- United Steel agrees to terms with John L. Lewis without a strike, which greatly enhances Lewis's prestige.
- From September 1, 1936, to June 1, 1937, 484,711 workers have been involved in sit-down strikes.

First Appearances: Nylon, okapis (animals) imported in New York, National Cancer Institute, children's church (Milton, Mass.), Flag Day (June 14), Santa Claus school (Albion, N.Y.), trampoline, skywriting at night, Pepperidge Farm, Spam, sodium cyclamate, shopping cart, franchising (Howard Johnson), Lincoln Tunnel, Harlem River House

1938

Economic Profile
  Dow-Jones: ↑ High 156–
    Low 98
  GNP: −6%
  Inflation: −0.8%
  Unemployment: 19.0%
Balance of international
  payments: +$1.1 billion
Military on duty: 322,000
Voter participation:
  57% (1932)
  61% (1936)
Population with religious
  affiliation: 64 million
Children's clothing (Best &
  Co.):
  Corduroy overalls: $1.95
  Matching jacket: $3.95
  Wool slip-on sweater: $1.95
Children's shoes (Saks): $3
Chenille bedspread
  (Altman's): $3.95
Linen damask cloth (64″ ×
  84″): $7.95
Custom venetian blinds: 39¢
  (sq. ft.)
Lace net curtains: $1.79 (pr.)
Carpeting, broadloom: $3.39
  (sq. yd.)

Deaths

Karel Čapek, Fyodor
  Chaliapin, Gabriele
  D'Annunzio, Clarence
  Darrow, William Glackens,
  Edmund Husserl,
  Konstantin Stanislavsky,
  Owen Wister, Thomas
  Wolfe.

In the News

FDR ASKS FOR BUILDUP OF ARMY AND NAVY . . . SECOND AGRICULTURAL ADJUSTMENT ACT IS PASSED AND PROVIDES FOR EVER-NORMAL GRANARY . . . WINSTON CHURCHILL PROTESTS NEVILLE CHAMBERLAIN'S POLICIES OF APPEASEMENT . . . MUD SLIDES IN SOUTHERN CALIFORNIA KILL 144 . . . GERMANY INVADES AUSTRIA, PROCLAIMS ANSCHLUSS . . . SUDETEN GERMANS IN CZECHOSLOVAKIA "DEMAND" AUTONOMY . . . HERBERT HOOVER ADVISES AGAINST EUROPEAN ALLIANCES . . . HITLER VISITS MUSSOLINI IN ROME . . . NAVAL EXPANSION ACT OF 1938 IS PASSED, $1 BILLION ALLOCATED . . . HOUSE UN-AMERICAN ACTIVITIES COMMITTEE IS FORMED . . . WHEELER-LEA ACT PROVIDES CLOSER FOOD AND DRUG REGULATION . . . HOWARD HUGHES SETS ROUND-THE-WORLD FLYING RECORD, 3 DAYS, 19 HOURS, 8 MINUTES . . . "WRONG-WAY" CORRIGAN HEADS FOR CALIFORNIA, LANDS IN DUBLIN . . . FAIR LABOR STANDARDS ACT REGULATES MAXIMUM HOURS AND MINIMUM WAGES . . . FDR URGES ARBITRATION OF CZECH CRISIS . . . HITLER, CHAMBERLAIN, DALADIER, MUSSOLINI MEET IN MUNICH AND AGREE TO CEDE PART OF CZECHOSLOVAKIA TO GERMANY . . . POLES TAKE TESCHEN AREA FROM CZECHS . . . JAPANESE ADVANCE AND CAPTURE CANTON, MOVE ON HANKOW . . . MUSSOLINI PROCLAIMS LIBYA PART OF ITALY . . . HUNGARY ANNEXES SLOVAKIA FROM CZECHOSLOVAKIA . . . JEWISH SHOPS ARE SMASHED AND LOOTED THROUGHOUT GERMANY ON KRISTALNACHT, U.S. AMBASSADOR IS RECALLED FOR CONSULTATION . . . ANTHONY EDEN, ON NEW YORK RADIO, WARNS AMERICA OF FASCIST PERIL . . . FRANCO BEGINS MAJOR ASSAULT ON CATALONIA.

Quotes

"I sense a deep happiness that, despite the depression, Americans are happy at surviving under a democratic form of government."

— FDR

"It is intolerable at this moment to think of a large portion of our people exposed to the democratic hoards who threaten our people. I refer to Czechoslovakia!

— Adolf Hitler

"[This declaration] is symbolic of the desire of our two peoples never to go to war again."

— Joint document signed by Hitler and Chamberlain at Munich

"My friends, . . . there has come back from Germany peace with honor. I believe it is peace for our time."

— Neville Chamberlain

"It took the Big Four just five hours and twenty-five minutes here in Munich today to dispel the clouds of war and come to an agreement over the partition of Czechoslovakia. There is to be no European war, after all."

— William Shirer, CBS

Farmers with a recent loan from the Tenant Purchase Program. *Library of Congress.*

"[Let us be warned] against war or against alliances against fascists."

— Herbert Hoover

"The American people surely want to stay out of the next world war. . . . It may cost the blood of countless American boys."

— Charles A. Beard, defining *isolationism*

"I'm speaking from the roof of the Broadcasting Building, New York City. The bells you hear are ringing to warn the people to evacuate the city as the Martians approach."

— Announcer, "The War of the Worlds," Mercury Radio Theatre

Ads

"Just what does the word *Fascist* mean, Henry?"
(Webster's New International Dictionary)

What food these morsels be!
(*Heinz Fresh Cucumber Pickles*)

What do you do when you have a cold?
(*Ex-Lax*)

Avoid Washroom Infection.
(*Onliwon Towels*)

Thousands of girls today feel themselves unwanted. . . . Many seem to lack feminine allurement. They are too thin and angular. Their complexions may be blemished, lacking in natural bloom. . . . Blossom forth with new, enticing natural curves, new normal beauty of skin, new pep and ginger that often bring instant popularity.

(*Ironized Yeast*)

173

Radio

Premieres

"World News Roundup," William Shirer (London); Ansel Mowrer (Paris); Ed Murrow (Vienna); Bob Trout (Washington)

"Information, Please!" Clifton Fadiman (host), Oscar Levant, John Kieran, Franklin P. Adams

"Young Widder Brown," Florence Freeman

"The Green Hornet," Al Hodge

"The Mercury Theatre on the Air," Orson Welles

"Kay Kyser's Kollege of Musical Knowledge"

"Joyce Jordan, Girl Interne," Rita Johnson

Specials

"Air Raid" (Archibald MacLeish, with Orson Welles, Ray Collins)

Of Note

Most popular light, homey, or love-interest dramas include "Aunt Fanny," "Brent House," "County Seat," "Curtain Time," "Dog Heroes," "Dr. Christian" (Jean Hersholt), "First Nighter," "Grand Central Station," "Irene Rich," "Mary and Bob," "One Man's Family," "Princess Pat Players," "Second Husband" (Helen Mencken), "Those We Love," and "Wings for the Martins"

New Catchphrases: "Wake Up, America! It's time to stump the experts" ("Information Please!"); "Britt Reid, daring young publisher, matches wits with [the] underworld. . . . He hunts the biggest . . . of all game. Public enemies who try to destroy our America" ("The Green Hornet")

TV

Programs

Sidewalk interviews with passersby, Rockefeller Center, New York

Coverage of the suicide of John Warde, "the man on the ledge," who leaped from the seventeenth floor of the Hotel Gotham in N.Y.C. after 11 hours.

Movies

Openings

You Can't Take It with You (Frank Capra), James Stewart, Jean Arthur

The Adventures of Robin Hood (Michael Curtiz, William Keighley), Errol Flynn, Olivia de Havilland

Boys' Town (Norman Taurog), Spencer Tracy, Mickey Rooney

Jezebel (William Wyler), Bette Davis, Henry Fonda

Pygmalion (Anthony Asquith, Leslie Howard), Leslie Howard, Wendy Hiller

Test Pilot (Victor Fleming), Clark Gable, Myrna Loy, Spencer Tracy

Angels with Dirty Faces (Michael Curtiz), James Cagney, Pat O'Brien

Love Finds Andy Hardy (George B. Seitz), Mickey Rooney, Judy Garland

Algiers (John Cromwell), Charles Boyer, Hedy Lamarr (debut)

Marie Antoinette (W. S. Van Dyke), Norma Shearer, Tyrone Power

Blockade (William Dieterle), Madeleine Carroll, Henry Fonda

Bringing Up Baby (Howard Hawks), Katharine Hepburn, Cary Grant

Snow White and the Seven Dwarfs (Walt Disney)

The Baker's Wife (Marcel Pagnol), Raimu

The Lady Vanishes (Alfred Hitchcock), Michael Redgrave, Margaret Lockwood

Alexander Nevsky (Sergei Eisenstein), Nikolai Cherkassov

Academy Awards

Best Picture: *You Can't Take It with You*

Best Director: Frank Capra (*You Can't Take It with You*)

Best Actress: Bette Davis (*Jezebel*)

Best Actor: Spencer Tracy (*Boys' Town*)

Top Box-Office Stars

Shirley Temple, Clark Gable, Sonja Henie, Mickey Rooney, Spencer Tracy, Robert Taylor, Myrna Loy, Jane Withers, Alice Faye, Tyrone Power

Popular Music

Hit Songs
"Chiquita Banana"
"Falling in Love with Love"
"This Can't Be Love"
"They Say"
"You Must Have Been a Beautiful Baby"
"Get Out of Town"
"My Heart Belongs to Daddy"
"September Song"
"Jeepers Creepers"
"My Reverie"
"Spring Is Here"

Top Records
Love Walked In (Kenny Baker); *I Married an Angel* (Larry Clinton); *It's Wonderful* (Shep Fields); *Thanks for the Memory* and *Two Sleepy People* (Bob Hope and Shirley Ross); *You Go to My Head* (Kay Kyser); *Love in the Starlight* (Dorothy Lamour); *One O'Clock Jump* (Harry James); *Begin the Beguine* (Artie Shaw); *Jalousie* (Boston Pops, Arthur Fiedler); *Beer Barrel Polka* (Will Glahe); *A-Tisket, A-Tasket* (Chick Webb, Ella Fitzgerald); *Boogie Woogie* (Jimmy Dorsey)

Jazz and Big Bands
Benny Goodman gives his first Carnegie Hall concert.
The first John Hammond "From Spirituals to Swing" concert is given at Carnegie Hall with Count Basie and Joe Turner.
Billie Holiday joins Artie Shaw's band.

New Bands: Larry Clinton, Les Brown, Gene Krupa, all in New York

Top Performers (*Downbeat*): Benny Goodman (soloist); Artie Shaw (big band); Casa Loma (sweet band); Ella Fitzgerald (vocalist); Benny Heller, Bob Haggart, Bob Zurke, Jimmy Dorsey, Bud Freeman, Tommy Dorsey, Harry James (instrumentalists)

Raymond Massey. *Billy Rose Theatre Collection. The New York Public Library at Lincoln Center. Astor, Lenox and Tilden Foundations.*

Theater

Broadway Openings

Plays
Our Town (Thornton Wilder), Frank Craven, John Craven, Martha Scott
Bachelor Born (Ian Hay), Frederick Leister or Philip Tonge (alternating roles)
Shadow and Substance (Paul Vincent Carroll), Cedric Hardwicke, Sara Allgood
On Borrowed Time (Paul Osborn), Dudley Digges, Frank Conroy
Kiss the Boys Good-Bye (Clare Boothe), Helen Claire, Hugh Marlowe, Benay Venuta
Abe Lincoln in Illinois (Robert E. Sherwood), Raymond Massey, Muriel Kirkland
Missouri Legend (E. B. Ginty), Dorothy Gish, Dean Jagger, José Ferrer, Dan Duryea
Here Come the Clowns (Philip Barry), Eddie Dowling
Rocket to the Moon (Clifford Odets), Morris Carnovsky, Luther Adler

Musicals
The Boys from Syracuse (Richard Rodgers, Lorenz Hart), Teddy Hart, Jimmy Savo, Eddie Albert, Burl Ives
Hellzapoppin' (Sammy Fain), Olson and Johnson, Barte and Mann, Radio Rogues
I Married an Angel (Richard Rodgers, Lorenz Hart), Vera Zorina, Dennis King, Vivienne Segal
Knickerbocker Holiday (Kurt Weill), Walter Huston, Ray Middleton, Jeanne Madden
Leave It to Me (Cole Porter), William Gaxton, Victor Moore, Mary Martin, Sophie Tucker, Gene Kelly
The Three Waltzes (Johann Strauss, Sr. and Jr.), Kitty Carlisle, Michael Bartlett, Glenn Anders
The Cradle Will Rock (Marc Blitzstein), Will Geer

Classics and Revivals On and Off Broadway
Outward Bound (Sutton Vane), Laurette Taylor; *Hamlet* (Maurice Evans, in first full-length performance); *The Seagull* (Chekhov), Alfred Lunt, Lynn Fontanne. *Mercury Theatre: Heartbreak House* (George Bernard Shaw), Orson Welles, Vincent Price, Geraldine Fitzgerald; *Danton's Death* (Georg Buchner), Martin Gabel; *The Shoemaker's Holiday* (Dekker), Vincent Price, Joseph Cotten

Pulitzer Prize
Our Town, Thornton Wilder

Classical Music

Compositions

Aaron Copland, *An Outdoor Overture*
Arthur Shepherd, Symphony no. 2
Ernest Bloch, Violin Concerto
Elliott Carter, *Prelude, Fanfare, and Polka*
David Diamond, Elegy, Cello Concerto
Roy Harris, Symphony no. 3 in One Movement,
    Soliloquy and Dance
John Cage, *Bacchanale, Metamorphosis*

Important Events

The Federal Music Project employs 2,642 musicians in 38 orchestras. The Philadelphia Orchestra's Roy Harris concert is widely acclaimed. Eleanor Roosevelt heads the committee that sponsors Carnegie Hall's celebration concert for Moriz Rosenthal.

Major Recitals: Harold Bauer, Moriz Rosenthal, Josef Hofmann, Ignace Jan Paderewski

Debut: Rudolf Firkusny

First Performances

Stravinsky, *Dumbarton Oaks* (Washington, D.C.); Samuel Barber, Adagio for Strings (NBC); Bloch, Violin Concerto (Cleveland); Copland, *Billy the Kid* (Chicago); Walter Piston, Symphony no. 1, *The Incredible Flutist* (Boston); Samuel Barber, Essay for Orchestra (New York); William Schuman, Symphony no. 2 (New York); Milhaud, conducting and playing, Piano Concerto no. 1 (Minneapolis); Virgil Thomson, *Filling Station* (Hartford)

Shirley Temple, *Movie Star News.*

Opera

Metropolitan: Debuts: Risë Stevens, *Mignon;* Jussi Bjoerling, *La bohème;* Erich Leinsdorf, *Die Walküre.* Premieres: *Amelia Goes to the Ball* (Gian Carlo Menotti); *Beauty and the Beast* (Vittorio Giannini, on CBS)

Hartford, Conn.: *Knickerbocker Holiday* (Kurt Weill)

Chicago: Beniamino Gigli, Helen Jepson, *Martha;* Ezio Pinza, Jepson, *Faust*

San Francisco: Ebe Stignani (debut), Janine Micheau, *Pelléas et Mélisande;* Kerstin Thorborg, *Elektra;* Salvatore Baccaloni, *Don Pasquale*

Music Notes

Arturo Toscanini receives $4,000 per concert with the newly formed NBC Symphony • Harvard University awards Marian Anderson an honorary doctorate • Copland chairs the American Composers Alliance to promote "serious music" • The WPA sponsors a successful jazz *Mikado* • Serge Koussevitzy conducts Bach and Beethoven at the inaugural concert of the music shed, Tanglewood (Berkshire Festival).

Snow White and the Seven Dwarfs, Walt Disney's first feature length film, is an enormous success. "It made the nation smile," said critic Bosley Crowther. *Movie Star News.*

Art

Painting

Thomas Hart Benton, *Cradling Wheat, I Got a Gal on Sourwood Mountain, Rainy Day*
Willem de Kooning, *Pink Landscape*
Reginald Marsh, *Human Pool Tables*
Stuart Davis, *Swing Landscape*
Arshile Gorky, *Argula*
Peter Hurd, *Dry River*
John Steuart Curry, *Oklahoma Land Rush, Our Good Earth*
Joseph Stella, *Song of Barbados, Machina Naturale No. 13*
Jackson Pollock, *Composition with Figures and Banners, The Flame*
Yasuo Kuniyoshi, *I'm Tired*

Sculpture

Ibram Lassaw, *Sculpture in Steel*
José de Rivera, *Black and Red (Double Element)*
Burgoyne Diller, *Construction #16*
Heinz Warneke, *Mother and Child*
Isamu Noguchi, *News,* Associated Press Building, Rockefeller Center.
David Smith, *Amusement Park, Leda*
Placed at the N.Y. World's Fair: James Earle Fraser's *George Washington,* Paul Manship's *Time Groups,* and Leo Friedlander's *Four Freedoms*

Architecture

N.Y. World's Fair, Central Mall (William and Geoffrey Platt)
Kleinhan's Music Hall, Buffalo, N.Y. (Saarinen and Saarinen)
Taliesen West, near Scottsdale, Ariz. (Frank Lloyd Wright)
Resor House, Jackson Hole, Wyo. (Mies van der Rohe)
Gropius House, Lincoln, Mass. (Gropius and Breuer)

Important Exhibitions

Museums

New York: *Metropolitan:* 500 Years of Chinese bronzes; Egyptian styles in the Eastern Mediterranean; Tiepolo and his contemporaries. *Morgan:* French Art of ten centuries. *Museum of Modern Art:* Bauhaus art, U.S.A.; Frank Lloyd Wright; prints of Rouault; primitive art. *Whitney:* Art west of the Mississippi; memorials for Charles Demuth, William Glackens

Chicago: The two Tiepolos; Chicago artists; Giacometti

San Francisco: Fifteenth- and sixteenth-century Venetian painting

Philadelphia: Nineteenth-century art; Renoir; Benjamin West

Virginia: Inauguration of "American Painting Today" biennial, with prizes to Eugene Speicher and Henry Lee McFee

Boston: John Benson; Edmund Charles Tarbell; John Singleton Copley

Detroit: Italian Gothic and early Renaissance art

Buffalo: Artists of the Great Lakes

Traveling Show: "American Retrospective"—from Thomas Eakins to Thomas Hart Benton—through the United States and then Paris and London

Art Briefs

The Bauhaus group, transplanted from Germany to Chicago, disbands for lack of funds • The Cloisters opens • Arshile Gorky holds his first one-man show in New York • The Federal Art project employs 5,000; many decorate new federal buildings; John Steuart Curry is commissioned for the Topeka Capitol Building murals, Reginald Marsh for the N.Y. Customs House.

Dance

The National Ballet with the Ballet Caravan is organized, and the company makes a transcontinental tour. Willam Christensen becomes choreographer of the San Francisco Ballet and increases its repertoire to include full-length works, such as *Swan Lake*. The association of the American Ballet and Metropolitan Opera ends in acrimony and public controversy over artistic differences.

Premieres

Ballet Caravan: *Billy the Kid* (Eugene Loring), Loring, Lew Christensen, Todd Bolender; *Filling Station* (Christensen), Bolender

Chicago Grand Opera Ballet: *Frankie and Johnny* (Ruth Page, Bentley Stone)

Books

Fiction

Critics' Choice

The Fifth Column and the First Forty-nine Stories, Ernest Hemingway
The Unvanquished, William Faulkner
Uncle Tom's Children, Richard Wright
The Long Valley, John Steinbeck
No Star is Lost, James Farrell
The Fathers, Allan Tate
The King Was in His Counting House, James Branch Cabell
Laughter in the Dark, Vladimir Nabokov (trans. by author)
ɛ☙ *Homage to Catalonia*, George Orwell
ɛ☙ *Murphy*, Samuel Beckett

Best-Sellers

The Yearling, Marjorie Kinnan Rawlings
The Citadel, A. J. Cronin
My Son, My Son! Howard Spring
Rebecca, Daphne Du Maurier
Northwest Passage, Kenneth Roberts
All This, and Heaven Too, Rachel Field
The Rains Came, Louis Bromfield
And Tell of Time, Laura Krey
The Mortal Storm, Phyllis Bottome
Action at Aquila, Hervey Allen

Nonfiction

Critics' Choice

The World's Body, John Crowe Ransom
Understanding Poetry, Cleanth Brooks, Robert Penn Warren
Journey between Wars, John Dos Passos
The Tyranny of Words, Stuart Chase
The Culture of Cities, Lewis Mumford
Logic and the Theory of Inquiry, John Dewey
Tom Watson, Agrarian Rebel, C. Vann Woodward
Beyond Dark Hills, Jesse Stuart
The House That Hitler Built, Stephen H. Roberts
Red Star over China, Edgar Snow
Save America First, Jerome Frank
Man against Himself, Karl Menninger
Guide to Kulchur, Ezra Pound

Best-Sellers

The Importance of Living, Lin Yutang
How to Win Friends and Influence People, Dale Carnegie
Madame Curie, Eve Curie
Alone, Adm. Richard E. Byrd
Listen! The Wind, Anne Morrow Lindbergh
I'm a Stranger Here Myself, Ogden Nash
With Malice toward Some, Margaret Halsey
The Horse and Buggy Doctor, Arthur E. Hertzler
Benjamin Franklin, Carl Van Doren
Fanny Kemble, Margaret Armstrong

Poetry

William Carlos Williams, *Complete Collected Poems*
Archibald MacLeish, *Land of the Free—U.S.A.*
E. E. Cummings, *Collected Poems*
Kenneth Fearing, *Dead Reckoning*
Robinson Jeffers, *The Selected Poetry*
Delmore Schwartz, *In Dreams Begin Responsibilities*
Laura Riding, *Collected Poems*
ɛ☙ W. B. Yeats, *New Poems*

Pulitzer Prizes

The Yearling, Marjorie Kinnan Rawlings
A History of American Magazines, Frank Luther Mott (U.S. history)
Benjamin Franklin, Carl Van Doren (biography)
Selected Poems, John Gould Fletcher (poetry)

Nobel Prize

Pearl S. Buck

Science and Technology

Carl David Anderson discovers the meson—a particle 200 times the mass of an electron.
Chester F. Carlson produces the first xerographic print.
Teflon is developed by Joseph Plunkett at Du Pont.
Albert Doisy and Sidney Thayer isolate pure vitamin K.
Julius Lempert develops the fenestration operation to treat otosclerosis, a cause of deafness.
Reports indicate that Dilantin benefits epilepsy, eliminating the need for toxic bromide therapy.
Sulfonilamide is found to cure bruccellosis, a severe febrile illness.
Harold Cox grows typhus bacilli suitable for vaccine development in chick embryo yolk sacs.
ɛ☙ The Biro brothers, George and Ladislav, invent the ballpoint pen.
ɛ☙ U. Cerletti and L. Bini introduce electroconvulsive therapy, ECT or "shock," for the treatment of mental illness.

Sports

Baseball

Johnny Vandermeer (Cincinnati, NL) pitches back-to-back no-hitters against Boston and Brooklyn.
Bob Feller (Cleveland, AL) strikes out a record 18 in one game.

Champions

Batting
Ernie Lombardi (Cincinnati, NL), .342
Jimmy Foxx (Philadelphia, AL), .349

Pitching
Bill Lee (Chicago, NL), 22–9
Red Ruffing (New York, AL), 21–7
Home runs
Hank Greenberg (Detroit, AL), 58

Football

NFL Season Leaders: Ed Danowski (New York), passing; Byron White (Pittsburgh), rushing; Gaynell Tinsley (Chicago Cards), receiving.

College All-Americans: Parker Hall (B), Mississippi; Marshall Goldberg (B), Pittsburgh

Bowls (Jan. 1, 1939)
Rose: Southern California 7–Duke 3
Orange: Tennessee 17–Oklahoma 0
Cotton: St. Mary's (California) 20–Texas Tech 13
Sugar: Texas Christian 15–Carnegie Tech 7

Basketball

The Akron Goodyear Tires win the ABL title.
The National Invitation Tournament, at Madison Square Garden, is organized; it is the first national postseason tournament.

Other Sports

Boxing: Joe Louis knocks out Max Schmeling in the first round. Louis is hailed as "the first American to KO a Nazi."

Tennis: Ellsworth Vines and Fred Perry tour as pros and earn $34,000 each; Vines wins 48, and Perry 35. Helen Wills Moody wins her eighth Wimbledon title.

Winners

World Series
New York (AL) 4
Chicago (NL) 0
MVP
NL–Ernest Lombardi, Cincinatti
AL–James Foxx, Boston
NFL
New York 23–Green Bay 17
MVP
Mel Hein, New York
College Football
Texas Christian
Heisman Trophy
Davey O'Brien, Texas Christian

College Basketball
Temple
Player of the Year
Hank Luisetti, Stanford
Stanley Cup
Chicago
U.S. Tennis Open
Men: Donald Budge
Women: Alice Marble
USGA Open
Ralph Guldahl
Kentucky Derby
Lawrin (E. Arcaro, jockey)

Fashion

For Women: A varied elegance marks the year. The popular look is the modern pencil-thin silhouette—the black outfit and skunk jacket, hair piled on top of the head, an extravagant hat, and enormous amounts of artificial jewelry. In the evening, skin-tight molded dresses and short tailored jackets with paillettes or embroidery are worn. By spring, romantic styles are shown: full skirts in gay and sentimental patterns, tiny sailor hats trimmed with feathers and flowers, and clogs. Also new are the more formal strapless evening gowns. Hair is worn in a pageboy with side combs and bobby pins, or it is pushed off the ears or tied back in George Washington bows. Styles of 1890 and 1900 are revived for day and evening: big muffs, hoopskirts, leg-of-mutton sleeves. The smart color is cyclamen. Lipsticks and rouges have a bluish tint. Yellow red is out.

High-fashion note: Schiaparelli's print crepe dress

Bette Davis received her second Academy Award this year. *Movie Star News.*

Kaleidoscope

- H. V. Kaltenborn covers the Munich crisis with 85 broadcasts in 18 days, as intense interest is paid to the possibility of war in Europe.
- A Gallup poll indicates that 65 percent of the population approves of the Munich agreement with Germany.
- Orson Welles's radio show "The War of the Worlds" is so lifelike that people rush into the streets and cry out in fear of an extraterrestrial invasion.
- The newly formed House Un-American Activities Committee, under Martin Dies, receives more coverage than any other domestic news event; its investigations of the ACLU, Campfire Girls, and the WPA Federal Theatre Project raise great protests.
- The Ludlow Amendment, requiring a referendum before Congress can declare war except in the case of invasion, is defeated in the House by a narrow margin.
- Ten million are unemployed as the "second depression" worsens.
- The Fair Labor Standards law provides a 25¢-an-hour minimum wage, 44-hour work week, and time and a half for overtime; it abolishes child labor.
- The Civil Aeronautics Authority is created to regulate air traffic.
- Mae West's name is banned from mention on 130 licensed radio stations.
- The expensive search for stars for *Gone with the Wind* continues at a cost of $96,000.
- Foreign dances, such as the rhumba, tango, conga, and Lambeth walk, as well as community and group dances, gain in popularity.
- Elsa Maxwell becomes prominent as a Washington party hostess.
- Former New York speakeasies that become chic include the supper clubs El Morocco, Stork Club, and 21.
- Heiress Brenda Frazier makes her society debut, and the strapless gown becomes a national fad.
- As a promotional strategy, airlines offer wives free passage with their husbands, as female fear of flying is thought to be keeping air traffic down.

- Salvador Dali offers Harpo Marx a role in a surrealistic ballet.
- A container made of indestructible metal and containing photographic records and other examples of contemporary culture is buried in the New York World's Fair grounds; it is to be opened in 5,000 years.
- The Carnival of Swing at Randall's Island attracts 25,000 jitterbugs for five and three-quarters hours.
- To celebrate the 20th anniversary of the Armistice, Kate Smith revives "God Bless America," and it becomes a second national anthem.
- The Jefferson-head nickel goes into circulation.
- Thomas Mann settles in the United States.
- A "Thirty Dollars Every Thursday" movement is proposed that promises "ham and eggs" to all; it gains 1 million votes in a California referendum.
- The Oxford Movement promotes moral rearmament: "If men will be good, there will be no more wars."
- North Carolina initiates the first state-sponsored birth control clinics.
- As a result of federal activity, numerous highways are built, which in turn facilitate suburban expansion.
- The United States leads the world in candy production, which ranks sixth among food industries; 2 billion pounds are manufactured a year; 16 pounds are consumed per capita.
- "Wrong-Way Corrigan," refused a permit to fly across the Atlantic to Dublin, announces that he will fly to California; afterwards, he intentionally flies to Dublin and remarks, "Sorry, I flew the wrong way."

First Appearances: Society for the Preservation and Encouragement of Barber Shop Quartet Singing in America (Tulsa), cartoon school, chlorophyll (patent), Euthanasia Society, law requiring marriage license applicants to undergo medical tests, law requiring serological blood tests of pregnant women, nylon bristle filament for toothbrushes, woman of American descent to become a queen (King Zog of Albania's wife), March of Dimes

Russell Lee, *Travelling Evangelists. Library of Congress.*

FDR and his sons at Marblehead, Mass. *Smithsonian Institution.*

1939

Facts and Figures

Economic Profile
   Dow-Jones: − High 155–
      Low 121
   GNP: +7%
   Inflation: −0.6%
   Unemployment: 17.2%
Police expenditures, federal,
   state, local: $378 million
Persons arrested: 577,000
Executions: 160
Prisoners, federal, state:
   179,000
Juvenile court appearances:
   40,365
Average wages:
   62¢/hour
   $22.30/week
   $1,230/year
   $26/week (male)
   $15/week (female)
Billy Rose's Cafe Mañana,
   New York (dinner,
   entertainment): $1–$2.50
Yacht Club, New York
   (featuring Fats Waller):
   $1.50
Schiaparelli "grasshopper
   dress": $1.98
Horn and Hardart mince pie:
   35¢ (whole pie)
Glass coffee maker: $2.95

Deaths

Artur Bodanzky, Heywood
   Broun, Harvey Cushing,
   Havelock Ellis, Douglas
   Fairbanks, Sr., Ford
   Madox Ford, Sigmund
   Freud, William Butler
   Yeats.

In the News

FDR ASKS $535 MILLION FOR DEFENSE . . . GOLDEN GATE INTERNATIONAL EXPOSITION BEGINS IN SAN FRANCISCO . . . GERMANY INVADES CZECHOSLOVAKIA . . . U.S. RECALLS AMBASSADOR TO GERMANY . . . FRANCO TAKES MADRID, LOYALISTS SURRENDER . . . U.S. RECOGNIZES FRANCO GOVERNMENT . . . HATCH ACT PROHIBITS GOVERNMENT EMPLOYEES FROM POLITICKING . . . NEW YORK WORLD'S FAIR OPENS . . . HITLER AND MUSSOLINI SIGN 10-YEAR "PACT OF STEEL" . . . KING GEORGE VI VISITS U.S., IS TREATED TO HOT DOGS . . . PAN-AM DIXIE CLIPPER BEGINS FIRST REGULAR TRANSATLANTIC FLIGHTS TO LISBON . . . HOUSE UN-AMERICAN ACTIVITIES COMMITTEE CONTINUES TO INVESTIGATE FEDERAL THEATER PROJECT . . . GERMANY AND U.S.S.R. AGREE TO COMMERCE TREATY . . . GERMANY AND U.S.S.R. SIGN NONAGGRESSION PACT . . . GERMAN ARMIES INVADE POLAND IN LAND AND AIR ASSAULT . . . BRITAIN AND FRANCE DECLARE WAR ON GERMANY . . . POLAND SURRENDERS TO NAZI ARMIES . . . CHARLES LINDBERGH SPEAKS OUT AGAINST INTERVENTION . . . BRITAIN SENDS 150,000 TROOPS TO FRANCE . . . GERMANY AND U.S.S.R. DIVIDE POLAND AT ODER-NESSE LINE . . . FDR ORDERS U.S. PORTS AND WATERS CLOSED TO FOREIGN SUBMARINES . . . CONGRESS AMENDS NEUTRALITY ACT, BRITAIN AND FRANCE CAN BUY ARMS "CASH AND CARRY" . . . GERMANS SCUTTLE BATTLESHIP "GRAF SPEE" IN MONTEVIDEO . . . U.S.S.R. INVADES FINLAND.

Edward R. Murrow helps inform America about the European situation; his broadcast ends nightly with "Good night and good luck." *Billy Rose Theatre Collection. The New York Public Library at Lincoln Center. Astor, Lenox and Tilden Foundations.*

Quotes

"We are prepared to defend it [freedom]. Men are not prisoners of fate but prisoners of their own minds. They have within them the power to be free at any moment."

— FDR

"[Germany stands with Italy] against all hateful and incomprehensible attempts to restrict the justified will for living of our two peoples."

— Adolf Hitler

"Hitler and Mussolini jes' need a good whippin'."
— World War I hero Sgt. Alvin York

"It may be possible to set up a nuclear reaction in uranium by which vast amounts of power could be released. . . . This new phenomenon would also lead to the construction of . . . extremely powerful bombs of a new type."

— Albert Einstein, in a letter to FDR

"Force is the only language they understand, like bullies."

— FDR

"This nation will remain a neutral nation. . . . I have seen war and . . . I hate war. . . . I hope the United States will keep out of this war. I believe that is wise."

— FDR, fireside chat

"I cannot forecast to you the action of Russia. It is a riddle wrapped in a mystery inside an enigma."
— Winston Churchill

Clark Gable and Vivien Leigh in David O. Selznick's *Gone with the Wind,* the longest (3 hours, 42 minutes) and most expensive ($4.2 million) movie yet made and winner of 10 Academy Awards. *Movie Star News.*

"They were not farm men any more, but migrant men. . . . [Thought] and worry were not any more with rainfall, with wind and dust, with the thrust of the crops. Eyes watched tires, ears listened to clattering motors, and minds struggled with oil, with gasoline, with the thinning rubber between air and road. . . . A broken gear was a tragedy."
— John Steinbeck, *The Grapes of Wrath*

Ads

Radio

Premieres
"Kate Smith's Bandwagon"
"The Aldrich Family," Ezra Stone
"I Love a Mystery," Michael Raffetto
"The Colgate Sports Newsreel," Bill Stern
"Dr. I.Q. (the Mental Banker)," Lew Valentine
"The Milton Berle Show"
"Lil' Abner," John Hodiak
"Mr. District Attorney," Dwight Weist
"Young Doctor Malone," Alan Bunce

Specials
Edward R. Murrow broadcasts nightly from London.

Of Note
Popular journalists include Lowell Thomas, H. V. Kaltenborn, Drew Pearson, and Fulton Lewis, Jr.

New Catchphrases: Mrs. Aldrich: "Henry! Hen-ry Aldrich!" Henry: "Coming, Mother!" ("The Aldrich Family"); ". . . strange and fantastic stories . . . some legend, some hearsay, . . . but all so interesting" ("The Colgate Sports Newsreel"); "And it shall be my duty . . . not only to prosecute to the limit of the law all persons accused . . . but to defend with equal vigor the rights and privileges of all . . . citizens" ("Mr. District Attorney")

TV

Opening ceremonies of the New York World's Fair with FDR; the king and queen of England's arrival at the fair
First major league baseball game (Brooklyn Dodgers versus Cincinnati Reds)
Opening of *Gone with the Wind*

Dramas: "Mamba's Daughter," "Stage Door," "Dulcy"

Movies

Openings
Gone with the Wind (Victor Fleming), Clark Gable, Vivien Leigh, Leslie Howard, Olivia de Havilland
Dark Victory (Edmund Goulding), Bette Davis, George Brent, Humphrey Bogart, Ronald Reagan
Goodbye, Mr. Chips (Sam Wood), Robert Donat, Greer Garson
Mr. Smith Goes to Washington (Frank Capra), James Stewart, Jean Arthur
Ninotchka (Ernst Lubitsch), Greta Garbo, Melvyn Douglas
Destry Rides Again (George Marshall), Marlene Dietrich, Gary Cooper
Stagecoach (John Ford), John Wayne, Claire Trevor
The Wizard of Oz (Victor Fleming), Judy Garland, Frank Morgan, Ray Bolger, Bert Lahr, Jack Haley
Wuthering Heights (William Wyler), Laurence Olivier, Merle Oberon, David Niven
Babes in Arms (Busby Berkeley), Judy Garland, Mickey Rooney
The Women (George Cukor), Norma Shearer, Joan Crawford, Joan Fontaine, Rosalind Russell
The Hunchback of Notre Dame (William Dieterle), Maureen O'Hara, Charles Laughton
The Roaring Twenties (Raoul Walsh), James Cagney, Priscilla Lane, Humphrey Bogart
Gunga Din (George Stevens), Cary Grant, Douglas Fairbanks, Jr.
Jesse James (Henry King), Tyrone Power, Henry Fonda
Confessions of a Nazi Spy (Anatole Litvak), Edward G. Robinson, Francis Lederer
Pinocchio (Walt Disney)
Rules of the Game (Jean Renoir), Marcel Dalio, Nora Gregor

Academy Awards
Best Picture: *Gone with the Wind*
Best Director: Victor Fleming (*Gone with the Wind*)
Best Actress: Vivien Leigh (*Gone with the Wind*)
Best Actor: Robert Donat (*Goodbye, Mr. Chips*)
Special Award: Judy Garland (outstanding performance of a screen juvenile)

Top Box-Office Stars
Mickey Rooney, Tyrone Power, Spencer Tracy, Clark Gable, Shirley Temple, Bette Davis, Alice Faye, Errol Flynn, James Cagney, Sonja Henie

Popular Music

Hit Songs
"All the Things You Are"
"South of the Border"
"Frenesi"
"I Concentrate on You"
"I Didn't Know What Time It
  Was"
"I'll Never Smile Again"
"If I Didn't Care"
"My Prayer"
"Brazil"
"Ding-Dong! The Witch Is Dead"
"Tara's Theme"

Top Records
Oh Johnny, Oh (Orrin Tucker,
with Bonnie Baker); *Miss Thing*
(Count Basie): *Jazz Me Blues,*
Bunny Berigan; *It Don't Mean a
Thing* (Lionel Hampton); *Body
and Soul* (Coleman Hawkins);
Indiana (Earl Hines); *Some Like
It Hot* (Gene Krupa); *Little Brown
Jug, In the Mood,* and *Sunrise
Serenade* (Glenn Miller); *That
Silver-Haired Daddy of Mine*
(Gene Autry); *Ciribiribin* (Harry
James); *Over the Rainbow* (Judy
Garland); *Strange Fruit* (Billie
Holiday); *Tuxedo Junction*
(Erskine Hawkins); *Cherokee*
(Charlie Parker)

Jazz and Big Bands
Charlie Parker goes to New York
and plays at Monroe's Uptown
House. Charlie Christian joins
Benny Goodman. Jimmy Blanton,
Billy Strayhorn, and Ben Webster
join Duke Ellington. Sy Oliver
leaves Jimmy Lunceford to join
Tommy Dorsey; Billy Eckstine
joins Earl Hines.

New Bands: Teddy Wilson,
Harry James, Tony Pastor, Jack
Teagarden (all in New York)

Top Performers *(Downbeat):* Benny
Goodman (soloist, big band);
Tommy Dorsey (sweet band); Ella
Fitzgerald, Bing Crosby
(vocalists); Charlie Christian, Jess
Stacy, Gene Krupa, Coleman
Hawkins, Benny Goodman, Harry
James (instrumentalists)

Theater

Broadway Openings

Plays
Life with Father (Howard Lindsay, Russel Crouse),
  Howard Lindsay, Dorothy Stickney
The Little Foxes (Lillian Hellman), Tallulah
  Bankhead, Patricia Collinge, Charles Dingle,
  Dan Duryea
The Philadelphia Story (Philip Barry), Katharine
  Hepburn, Joseph Cotten, Van Heflin
No Time for Comedy (S. N. Behrman), Laurence
  Olivier, Katharine Cornell
The Man Who Came to Dinner (Moss Hart, George
  Kaufman), Monty Woolley, David Burns
The Time of Your Life (William Saroyan), Julie
  Hayden, Eddie Dowling
Skylark (Samson Raphaelson), Gertrude Lawrence
Mamba's Daughters (Dorothy and DuBose
  Heyward), Ethel Waters
The Gentle People (Irwin Shaw), Franchot Tone, Elia
  Kazan, Sylvia Sidney
Key Largo (Maxwell Anderson), Paul Muni
The White Steed (Paul Vincent Carroll), Barry
  Fitzgerald, Jessica Tandy
Mornings at Seven (Paul Osborn), Dorothy Gish,
  Effie Shannon

Musicals
Dubarry Was a Lady (Cole Porter, B. G. DeSylva),
  Ethel Merman, Bert Lahr, Betty Grable
George White's Scandals of 1939 (Sammy Fain, Jack
  Yellin) Willie and Eugene Howard, The Three
  Stooges, Ann Miller
One for the Money (Morgan Lewis), Nancy
  Hamilton, Alfred Drake, Gene Kelly, Keenan
  Wynn
Set to Music (Noel Coward), Beatrice Lillie, Richard
  Haydn
Stars in Your Eyes (Arthur Schwartz, Dorothy
  Fields), Ethel Merman, Jimmy Durante, Richard
  Carlson, Tamara Toumanova, Dan Dailey,
  Mildred Natwick
Too Many Girls (Richard Rodgers, Lorenz Hart),
  Marcy Wescott, Hal LeRoy, Eddie Bracken,
  Desi Arnaz, Van Johnson

Classics and Revivals On and Off Broadway
The Importance of Being Earnest (Oscar Wilde),
Clifton Webb, Estelle Winwood; *Henry IV, Part I,*
Maurice Evans

Pulitzer Prize
Abe Lincoln in Illinois, Robert E. Sherwood

Classical Music _____

Compositions
Roy Harris, Symphony no. 4
Walter Piston, Violin Concerto, Sonata for Violin and
    Piano
John Cage, *Imaginary Landscape*
Howard Hanson, Fantasy for String Orchestra
Aaron Copland, *The City, Sorcery and Science*
Elliott Carter, *Pocahontas*
Henry Cowell, *A Celtic Symphony*
William Schuman, *Prelude for Voices*
Roger Sessions, *Pages from a Diary*
Samuel Barber, Violin Concerto

Important Events
The World's Fair Festivals communicate the
"Brotherhood of Music" with numerous unusual
events, including the festivals of Norway, the Balkan
states, and Brazil (Heitor Villa-Lobos is a great
success); also of great interest is Arnold Bax's
Symphony no. 7; Georges Enesco as conductor of his
work at the Rumanian Pavilion, and Piston's Prelude
and Fugue, the only American work presented.
Boston holds a Festival of American Music with
Arthur Foote, George Gershwin, Virgil Thomson,
Hanson, Harris, and Schuman.
Béla Bartók plays *Contrasts* with Josef Szigeti and
Benny Goodman in New York.
Budget cuts reduce WPA programs; New York mayor
Fiorello La Guardia sponsors a symphony series of
single-composer concerts.

Major Recital: Josef and Rosina Lhévinne celebrate
40 years of piano partnership in a Carnegie Hall
program.

Marian Anderson
at the Lincoln
Memorial. She
stays in
Washington,
D.C., at a private
home because no
hotel will
accommodate
her. *Library of
Congress.*

Debuts: Leonard Rose, Gyorgy Sandor, Leonard
Pennario, William Masselos, Clifford Curzon

First Performances
Harris, Symphony no. 3 (Boston); Copland, Sextet
(New York); Schuman, *American Festival Overture*
(Boston); William Walton, Violin Concerto
(Cleveland); Ralph Vaughan Williams, *Five Variants
on Dives and Lazarus* (New York); Charles Ives,
Second Pianoforte Sonata (New York)

Opera

Metropolitan: Grace Moore, *Louise;* Herbert
Janssen, *Tannhaüser;* John Brownlee, Elisabeth
Rethberg, Ezio Pinza, Licia Albanese, *Der
Rosenkavalier;* John Charles Thomas, Helen Jepson,
Thaïs; Leonard Warren (debut), *Simon Boccanegra;*
44 of its 123 performances are of Wagner.

Martin Beck Theater, New York: *The Devil and
Daniel Webster* (Douglas Moore)

Dallas: Grace Moore, *Manon*

Chicago: Ezio Pinza, Rose Bampton, *Boris
Godunov;* Grace Moore, *Louise*

San Francisco: Marjorie Lawrence, Kirsten
Flagstad, *Die Walküre;* Jarmila Novotna, Lawrence
Tibbett, *La traviata*

Music Notes
Leopold Stokowski shocks audiences as he
rearranges the placement of the instruments.

Kate Smith, "the Songbird of the South." *Movie Star
News.*

Art

Painting

Edward Hopper, *Cape Cod Evening*

Thomas Hart Benton, *Threshing Wheat, Little Brown Jug*

Ben Shahn, *Jesus Exalted in Song, Handball*

John Steuart Curry, *The Tragic Prelude, The Homesteading*

Milton Avery, *The Dessert*

Philip Evergood, *Lily and the Sparrows*

Joseph Stella, *The Brooklyn Bridge*

Willem de Kooning, *Elegy, Portrait of Rudolph Burckhardt*

Lyonel Feininger, *San Francisco*

Grant Wood, *Parson Weems' Fable*

William Gropper's mural *Construction of the Dam* and Edgar Britton's *The Story of Petroleum* are placed in the Department of Interior, Washington, D.C.

Sculpture

Alexander Archipenko, *Moses*

José de Creeft, *The Cloud, Saturnia*

Isamu Noguchi, *Capital*

David Smith, *Medals for Dishonor: Bombing Civilian Populations*

Alexander Calder, *Lobster Trap and Fish Tail*

Calder's *Stabile* wins a major prize at the World's Fair.

Heinz Warneke's *Lewis and Clark* is placed at the Department of the Interior, Washington, D.C.

The last of Gutzon Borglum's presidents, Teddy Roosevelt, is unveiled on Mt. Rushmore.

Architecture

Johnson Wax Administration Building, Racine, Wisc. (Frank Lloyd Wright)

Hert Jacobs House, Middleton, Wisc. (Frank Lloyd Wright)

Black Mountain College project, North Carolina (Walter Gropius and Marcel Breuer)

The new Museum of Modern Art, on 53rd Street, New York, is completed (P. Goodwin and E. Stone).

Eliel and Eero Saarinen and Robert Swanson win the competition for the new Smithsonian Gallery of Art.

Mies van der Rohe begins work on the Illinois Institute of Technology, Chicago campus.

Important Exhibitions

Museums

New York: *Metropolitan:* "Life in America for 300 Years" (held concurrently with the fair); American pewterers; Augustan art; American daguerrotypes.

New York World's Fair: "Masterpieces of America and the World." *Museum of Modern Art:* Forty years of Picasso; "Art in Our Time"; Sheeler.

Chicago: Paintings of Bonnard, Vuillard; Picasso; ten best American watercolorists; San Francisco Golden Gate exhibit

Detroit: Pre-Columbian Art

Philadelphia: Blake; Flemish Art

Boston: Maillol, Despiau

San Francisco Golden Gate Exposition: Pacific cultures; contemporary art; masterworks of five centuries, including Botticelli's *Birth of Venus,* Raphael's *Madonna of the Chair,* and work by Michelangelo

Art Briefs

For the first time, European masterpieces travel on loan (for the New York World's Fair and San Francisco Exposition) • The Kress collection is added to the Mellon at the National Gallery, Washington, D.C. • 30 million people view art exhibitions at the World's Fair • The curtailment of the WPA Art Project is offset by commissions for the fair, the exposition, and new construction of public buildings in Washington, D.C. • After Hitler brands modern art "degenerate" and sells museum works at a Lucerne auction, many masterpieces pass into American museums and private collections • Important sales include Reynolds's *Lady Frances Warren* ($10,500); van Gogh's *Mlle. Ravoux* ($19,000); Cézanne's *Mme. Cézanne* ($27,500); Rouault's *The Clown* ($2,500); and Toulouse-Lautrec's *Femme dans le jardin* ($5,700).

Dance

Companies and stars emigrate to the United States: Massine's Ballet Russe with Alexandra Danilova, Alicia Markova, David Lichine, and Tamara Toumanova.

Premieres

Every Soul Is a Circus (Martha Graham); *Eight-Column Line* (Alwin Nikolais); the first American full-length *Coppelia* (Willam Christensen, San Francisco)

Books

Fiction

Critics' Choice
Wild Palms, William Faulkner
The Web and the Rock, Thomas Wolfe (posthumous)
Night Rider, Robert Penn Warren
Tommy Gallagher's Crusade, James T. Farrell
Adventures of a Young Man, John Dos Passos
Pale Horse, Pale Rider, Katherine Anne Porter
Tropic of Capricorn, Henry Miller
The Day of the Locust, Nathanael West
Children of God, Vardis Fisher
❧ *Finnegans Wake*, James Joyce

Best-Sellers
The Grapes of Wrath, John Steinbeck
All This, and Heaven Too, Rachel Field
Rebecca, Daphne Du Maurier
Wickford Point, John P. Marquand
Disputed Passage, Lloyd C. Douglas
The Yearling, Marjorie Kinnan Rawlings
Kitty Foyle, Christopher Morley
The Nazarene, Sholem Asch

Nonfiction

Critics' Choice
Thoreau, Henry Seidel Canby
Freedom and Culture, John Dewey
Heritage of America, Henry Steele Commager, Allan Nevins
Incredible Era, Samuel Hopkins Adams
After Seven Years, Raymond Moley
The Living Tradition: Change and America, Simeon Stransky
America in Mid-Passage, Charles and Mary Beard
Hereditary Fortunes, Gustavus Myers
Propaganda for War: The Campaign against American Neutrality, 1914–1917, H. C. Peterson et al.
❧ *The Knowledge of God and the Service of God*, Karl Barth

Best-Sellers
Days of Our Years, Pierre van Paassen
Reaching for the Stars, Nora Waln
Inside Asia, John Gunther
Autobiography with Letters, William Lyon Phelps
Wind, Sand, and Stars, Antoine de Saint-Exupéry
Mein Kampf, Adolf Hitler
A Peculiar Treasure, Edna Ferber
Not Peace But a Sword, Vincent Sheean
Listen! The Wind, Anne Morrow Lindbergh

Poetry
Robert Frost, *Collected Poems*
Edna St. Vincent Millay, *Huntsman, What Quarry?*
Robert P. Tristram Coffin, *Collected Poems*
Archibald MacLeish, *America Was Promises*
T. S. Eliot, *Old Possum's Book of Practical Cats*
Muriel Rukeyser, *A Turning Wind*

Pulitzer Prizes
The Grapes of Wrath, John Steinbeck (novel)
Abraham Lincoln: The War Years, Carl Sandburg (U.S. history)
Woodrow Wilson, Life and Letters, Vols. VII and VIII, Ray Stannard Baker (biography)
Collected Poems, Mark Van Doren (poetry)

Science and Technology

Newly emigrated Enrico Fermi and John R. Dunning, Columbia University, use the cyclotron to split uranium and obtain a huge energy release; Fermi suggests the idea of a "chain reaction."

Utilizing quantum theory, Linus Pauling postulates a resonance theory of chemical valence.

Karl Landsteiner and Alexander Weiner discover the Rh factor in blood.

Edward Doisy determines the chemical formula of vitamin K.

Studies accumulate indicating that sulfanilamide can treat many forms of coccal infection (for example, streptoccocal and gonococcal infections).

Heinz Hartmann's *Ego Psychology and the Problem of Adaptation* develops the importance of the ego, as opposed to the id, the previous emphasis of Freudian psychology.

Igor Sikorsky constructs and flies the first single rotor helicopter.

❧ Howard Florey and Ernest Chain concentrate penicillin and test it with success.

❧ Ernst Strassman and Otto Hahn set off a nuclear fission reaction by bombarding uranium with neutrons.

❧ Paul Miller develops DDT.

Nobel Prize
E. O. Lawrence wins the prize in physics for the development of the cyclotron.

Sports ───────────────────

Baseball

"You've been reading about my tough breaks for weeks now. But today I think I'm the luckiest man alive," says Lou Gehrig at his retirement ceremony at Yankee Stadium. Gehrig played 2,130 consecutive games since 1925, before becoming ill with amyotrophic lateral sclerosis.

Ted Williams (Boston, AL) debuts.

Cooperstown is established as the site of the Baseball Hall of Fame.

Champions ───────────────────

Batting
John Mize (St. Louis, NL), .349
Joe DiMaggio (New York, AL), .381

Pitching
Paul Derringer (Cincinnati, NL), 25–7
Lefty Grove (Boston, AL), 15–4

Home runs
Jimmy Foxx (Philadelphia, AL), 35

Football

NFL Season Leaders: Parker Hall (Cleveland Rams), passing; Bill Osmanski (Chicago Bears), rushing; Don Hutson (Green Bay), receiving

College All-Americans: Ken Kavanaugh (E), Louisiana State; John Kimbrough (Q), Texas A&M; Tom Harmon (B), Michigan

Bowls (Jan. 1, 1940)
Rose: Southern California 14– Tennessee 0
Orange: Georgia Tech 21–Missouri 7

Cotton: Clemson 6– Boston College 3
Sugar: Texas A&M 14– Tulane 13

Fashion ───────────────────

For Women: Suits become more "feminine"— pleated, flared, or straight—with tightly fitted jackets and gay blouses. Prime Minister Chamberlain's famous umbrella and hat become motifs in accessories and prints; snoods are popular. Hair is "Edwardian" or worn up in front, with the back hanging in a long mane of curls; the first permanent waves appear. In the summer, bare midriffs, flat sports sandals, Indian moccasins, and Carmen Miranda turbans are everywhere. Many winter dresses have fitted bodices for Mainbocher's new corset, which, laced up the back, makes front-page

Basketball

The first NCAA postseason championship tournament is played with teams from all over the country.

Other Sports

Tennis: Don Budge beats both Ellsworth Vines and Fred Perry on a pro tour.

Winners ───────────────────

World Series
New York (AL) 4
Cincinnati (AL) 0
MVP
NL–William Walters, Cincinnati
AL–Joe DiMaggio, New York
NFL
Green Bay 27–New York 0
MVP
Parker Hall, Cleveland
College Football
Texas A&M
Heisman Trophy
Niles Kinnick, Iowa

College Basketball
Oregon (NCAA)
Long Island University (NIT)
Player of the Year
Chester Jaworski, Rhode Island State
Stanley Cup
Boston
US Tennis Open
Men: Robert L. Riggs
Women: Alice Marble
USGA Open
Byron Nelson
Kentucky Derby
Johnstown (J. Stout, jockey)

Fashion model.

headlines. Smaller bras with circular seamed cups and stiffened inserts achieve the high-bosomed look. From Europe come "black-out" fashions: tailored suits, white hats and accesories, flashlights, and containers for gas masks.

High-fashion notes: Schiaparelli's patterned cardigan; Pinguet's reemphasis of the square shoulder ("the look" until Dior).

Kaleidoscope _____

- Eight million are unemployed.
- Newsreels, like the *March of Time,* gain in importance as worldwide events are documented.
- A Gallup poll indicates that 58 percent believe the United States will be drawn into war; 65 percent favor boycotting Germany.
- After the German attack on Poland and subsequent declarations of war, there is a quiet on the front, widely called the "Phony War."
- Barred from DAR-owned Constitution Hall, Marian Anderson gives an open-air concert before 75,000 people in Lincoln Memorial Park; the concert is sponsored, in part, by Secretary of State Harold Ickes and Eleanor Roosevelt.
- Two major expositions take place: (1) the New York World's Fair, "The World of Tomorrow," which holds exhibitions from almost every country (Germany does not participate) and is visited by 25 million, and (2) the Golden Gate Exposition, whose theme is "Recreation: Man's Gift from a Machine Age," built on a 400-acre man-made island in the center of San Francisco Bay.
- The sounds of King Tutankhamen's 22½″ trumpet of silver and gold, as well as his 19½″ copper trumpet, are heard on a world radio broadcast after their 3,297-year silence.
- Fifty percent of those polled select radio as the most reliable news media, 17 percent choose newspapers.
- *Reader's Digest,* whose circulation was 250,000 in 1930, is up to 8 million.
- Al Capone is released from prison but is severely ill with third-stage syphilis.
- Gangster Louis Lepke surrenders to columnist Walter Winchell, who hands him over to J. Edgar Hoover (whom Lepke prefers to New York district attorney Tom Dewey).
- Clara Adams is the first woman to fly around the world.
- The Social Security Act is amended to allow extended benefits to the aged and the widows, minors, and parents of a deceased person.
- Controversy arises over FDR's decision to appoint an envoy to the Vatican.

- Because of the war abroad, the Finns cease shipping cheese to the United States; Swiss production takes over.
- Sixty thousand German immigrants have arrived since 1933.
- Movie box-office receipts reach an all-time high and average out to $25 per family per year.
- Hollywood production code restrictions are lifted to enable Clark Gable, in *Gone with the Wind,* to say: "Frankly, my dear, I don't give a damn."
- The Federal Theatre Project is disbanded after accusations of Communist influence.
- In 1938, Columbia College seniors chose Madeleine Carroll as the woman with whom they would most like to be shipwrecked; their reason: her ability to speak French. This year they choose Hedy Lamarr and offer no reason.
- The largest production of chickens and turkeys in U.S. farm history is recorded.

College Fads: Swallowing goldfish (the record is 210), beetles, white mice, angleworms, phonograph records with salt and pepper—each followed by milk or soda; roller skating; knock-knock jokes; Chinese checkers; "skatarinas" (matching bloomers and circular skirts) and unisex clothes (baggy sweaters, saddle shoes, shirttails, jeans); the dances: chicken scratch, howdy-do, American promenade, palais glide, chestnut tree, boomps-a-daisy

Jive Language (from Gene Krupa): "Blowin' his plumbin'," "beating his skins," "spank the skin"

First Appearances: Billy Rose Aquacade, commercial manufacture of nylon yarn, anti–pinball machine legislation (Atlanta), air-conditioned auto (Packard), electric slicing knife, disposable can for dispensing under pressure (patent), transatlantic airmail service, marketing of nylon stockings

Far left: "George Washington" (James Farmer) and "The Mood of Time" (Paul Manship), at the New York World's Fair. *General Research Division. The New York Public Library. Astor, Lenox and Tilden Foundations.*

The king and queen of England visiting the U.S. *Manny Warman, Columbia University.*

Sailors decorating graves at Pearl Harbor. *Copyright* Washington Post. *Reprinted by permission of D.C. Public Library.*

THE *Forties*

Statistics

Vital
Population: 132,122,000
   Urban/Rural: 74/57
   Farm: 23.2%
Life expectancy
   Male: 60.8
   Female: 68.2
Births/1,000: 19.4
Marriages/1,000: 12.1
Divorces/1,000: 2.0
Deaths/1,000: 12.1
   per 100,000
      Heart: 485
      Cancer: 120
      Tuberculosis: 40
      Car accidents: 26.2

Economic
Unemployed: 8,120,000
GNP: $99.7 billion
Federal budget: $13.2 billion
National debt: $43.0 billion
Union membership: 8.1
   million
Strikes: 2,508
Prime rate: 0.6%
Car sales: 3,767,300
Average salary: $1,299

Social
Homicides/100,000: 6.3
Suicides/100,000: 14.4
Lynchings: 5
Labor force, male/female: 3/1
Social welfare: $8.80 billion
Public education: $2.34 billion
College degrees
   Bachelors'
      Male: 109,000
      Female: 77,000
   Doctorates
      Male: 2,861
      Female: 429
Attendance
   Movies (weekly): 80 million
   Baseball (yearly): 10.0
   million

Consumer
Consumer Price Index
   (1967 = 100): 42
Eggs: 33¢ (doz.)
Milk: 13¢ (qt.)
Bread: 8¢ (loaf)
Butter: 36¢ (lb.)
Bacon: 27¢ (lb.)
Round steak: 36¢ (lb.)
Oranges: 29¢ (doz.)
Coffee: 21¢ (lb.)

The first years of the decade were the darkest in modern times. A savage and militarily awesome German dictatorship conquered most of Western Europe and put England under furious aerial bombardment. Russia was invaded, and Moscow and Leningrad came under siege. A militarist government came to power in Japan, and on the infamous day of December 7, 1941, the Japanese launched a surprise air attack on the American naval base at Pearl Harbor, Hawaii, and then mounted swift, massive invasions throughout Southeast Asia, including the Philippines. Congress declared war, and U.S. "isolation" ended. As it turned out, the "bullies," as FDR called them, were no match for someone their own size, but proving this involved a great four-and-a-half-year struggle and all the men and material that America, harnessed to her full capacity, could produce.

Both at home and on the fronts, the war became a calling—loud, clear, and pure—and with the vast needs for swift production and manpower, employment ceased to be a problem. Large numbers enlisted: women worked in factories; dollar-a-year men went to Washington; baseball players, actors, and entertainers—people from every social stratum—signed up; labor and management agreed to keep peace; and even children, doing their share, collected scrap and helped plant the Victory Gardens that sprouted everywhere. With austerity a wartime necessity, consumer deprivation afforded a badge of honor. The desperate plight of the world, the malignant nature of the enemy, and the sneak attack had stirred a universal, idealistic commitment.

In 1942 came the first moments of victory, in North Africa and at Midway. Gigantic bombing raids began, and in 1943, the tide turned. The Russians beat the Germans into retreat. American and British forces took Sicily and began their way up the Italian peninsula. Guadalcanal was retaken. In 1944, the "great crusade" on the Continent fought ashore at Normandy, and the emancipation of Europe began. In the East, the Russians proceeded with equal speed. MacArthur returned to the Philippines, as he had promised, and the bloody Pacific island-hopping continued. All along, in both theaters, bombers from the great American arsenal filled the enemy skies.

Roosevelt, elected for a fourth time in 1944, did not live to see the final victory. In January 1945, the beloved president died, and when Arthur Godfrey, describing the funeral procession on radio, broke into tears, he echoed the sorrow of millions of his countrymen at the passing of a man who had led and comforted them through their most difficult trials.

Harry Truman, the feisty Missourian who succeeded FDR, accepted Germany's unconditional surrender in June 1945, before facing one of history's

epochal decisions. On August 6, he deployed a weapon secretly developed during the war at Roosevelt's directive; an atomic bomb was dropped on Hiroshima, Japan. Three days later, a second bomb was dropped on Nagasaki. Japan surrendered unconditionally, averting the possibility of a bloody invasion. A force of apocalyptic destructiveness had been demonstrated.

The postwar period was frenzied. Demobilization was rapid; in 1946, there were 35,000 discharges a day. Personal savings accumulated during wartime austerity sought an outlet, and a peacetime ethos of the pursuit of personal happiness replaced the wartime one of sacrifice. A mania developed for such consumer items as beef, ice cream, alcohol, cars, and toys; tickets for sporting events, theater, and travel were in short supply; housing was at a premium.

As workers sought higher wages and business higher profits, the relations between labor and management were strained. Massive strikes and inflation followed, and black markets developed; consumer goods remained in short supply while factories retooled for peacetime production. In the meantime, millions of veterans took advantage of the GI bill to educate themselves, start businesses, buy homes, and have families. Despite all the frenzy, fears that the depression would return proved unfounded, and the economy stabilized.

Throughout the decade, radio remained an important news and entertainment medium; some of its most popular shows included "Red Skelton," "Abbott and Costello," and "Lux Radio Theater." After the war, a new medium developed. Television, for twenty years an experimental toy, went into mass production, and large-scale programming began. Top programs starred ex-vaudevillian Uncle Miltie (Milton Berle), solemn Ed Sullivan, and congenial Arthur Godfrey, his friends and talent scouts. Popular "personalities" ranged from wrestler Gorgeous George to puppet Howdy Doody. At the end of the decade, Sid Caesar and Imogene Coca, as well as original drama showcases like "Studio One," explored the medium's potential.

Sports attendance soared beyond 1920s' levels. In football, the T-formation, validated by Sid Luckman in Chicago's 73–0 victory against Washington (1940), moved into prominence. The National Basketball Association (NBA) was formed, and George Mikan became the first of the dominating "big men." In baseball, Joe DiMaggio, Ted Williams, and Stan Musial returned from the service to stardom. The great baseball story of the decade, however, went beyond sports when Jackie Robinson became the first black in organized baseball. Robinson was subjected to abuse from bigots on and

Bob Hope and Bing Crosby ham it up on the golf course. Their "Road" pictures with Dorothy Lamour have been enormously successful. *Movie Star News.*

off the field, but his courage and dazzling talent gained him wide admiration, as it highlighted on a national stage the injustice of racial discrimination.

Among the great movies of the decade—and perhaps of all time—were *Citizen Kane, The Grapes of Wrath,* and *Casablanca,* as well as the revival favorites *The Maltese Falcon* and *Mildred Pierce.* Many patriotic war movies appeared, such as *Mrs. Miniver, The Purple Heart,* and *Guadalcanal Diary.* Betty Grable and Rita Hayworth were the sex symbols of the early decade, and their pinups were GI favorites; later on, Jane Russell, in a special undergarment designed by aircraft tycoon Howard Hughes, became prominent. Acting teams were also popular: in comedy, Abbott and Costello, and Hope and Crosby; for tough romance, Bogart and Bacall. After the war, a number of films explored social and previously taboo themes—*The Lost Weekend* (alcoholism), *Gentleman's Agreement* (anti-Semitism), *The Snake Pit* (mental illness), *Pinky* (racism), and *All the King's Men* (the abuse of political power). Perhaps the idealistic nature of the war encouraged a more open and urgent examination of moral problems on the home front.

This was the era when many big bands broke up and lead singers went out on their own. Frank Sinatra became a phenomenon as a bobby-sox idol. Bing Crosby's mellow voice and manner made him a top singer, as well as leading movie star. Other popular singers included Bob Eberle, Helen O'Connell, Ella Fitzgerald, Sarah Vaughan, and the Andrews sisters. War songs like "Praise the Lord and Pass the Ammunition" were hits, along with ballads like "As Time Goes By" and "My Foolish Heart," most of which told of the precariousness of love in wartime. "Bop" and "cool" succeeded swing in the forefront of jazz, and instrumentalists like Miles Davis and Thelonius Monk pursued their

experiments with harmony and improvisation.

In 1946, Dr. Spock's *The Common Sense Book of Baby and Child Care* appeared, to advise the many newcomers to the booming baby business. Dale Carnegie taught *How to Stop Worrying and Start Living,* and Rabbi Joshua Liebman advised on *Peace of Mind. Forever Amber,* a blockbuster in most cities, was banned in Boston, while Lloyd Douglas's tale of Christ's *Robe* sold out everywhere. Richard Wright's *Native Son* symbolically prophesied the fire to come; Saul Bellow debuted with *Dangling Man* and *The Victim,* both in his characteristic existential vein. French existentialism had a vogue in America, and writers like Jean-Paul Sartre and Albert Camus were much discussed in literary circles. Norman Mailer debuted with his realistic war novel *The Naked and the Dead.*

In the late forties, two American classics appeared on Broadway, Tennessee Williams's *A Streetcar Named Desire* and Arthur Miller's *Death of a Salesman.* Williams portrayed the fragility of romantic illusion, and Miller the tragic illusion of the American dream. For the musical stage, the new team of Rodgers and Hammerstein wrote *Oklahoma* and *South Pacific.* Painters like Jackson Pollock, Willem de Kooning, and Arshile Gorky worked in the new form of abstract expressionism. The music world saw the debuts of Leonard Bernstein, Richard Tucker, Jan Peerce, and Lorin Maazel (age 11), and premieres of Paul Hindemith, Béla Bartók, Arnold Schoenberg, and Igor Stravinsky, all now residing in the United States.

On the international scene, America determined not to isolate itself again, and the United States led in the formation of the United Nations, based on principles similar to the forsaken League of Nations. The Second World War had changed the order of

Victory gardening in New York City. *Library of Congress*

Supreme Allied Commander Dwight D. Eisenhower speaking to a soldier prior to Operation Overlord, the invasion of Nazi Europe. *Smithsonian Institution.*

Code name Trinity, the first atomic bomb, was exploded at Alamogordo Air Force Base, New Mexico, July 16, 1945. *Library of Congress.*

world power, and the former dominance of Western Europe was ended. When Britain turned out Winston Churchill in 1946 and gave independence to India, it was apparently ready to relinquish its world role. Once again, however, victory in a world war had not brought an easy peace, and the two remaining great powers, the United States and the USSR, though wartime allies, soon clashed over the fate of Berlin and West Germany, Poland and Czechoslovakia, China and Greece. Thus began, in Bernard Baruch's words, the "cold war."

America's involvement in world affairs went further. With severe economic conditions on the Continent and widespread food shortages, America took a number of steps. Large amounts of money and food were sent abroad. (Meatless Tuesdays and Eggless Thursdays were observed at home, because "children are starving in Europe.") Truman, now aided by previous isolationist leaders, also implemented Point Four, providing economic and arms assistance to rebellion-torn countries like Greece. This was followed by the Marshall Plan, which gave economic aid to Western Europe, including Germany. America thus became deeply committed to helping the "Free World" stay free from poverty and totalitarian forces.

At home, in 1946, the Republicans took Congress and then united against Truman's efforts to extend the New Deal reformation. Civil rights and housing legislation was vetoed; the Taft-Hartley Act

restricted labor. By 1948, everyone was certain that the Republicans would take the White House and that the president, opposed within his own party by Strom Thurmond's States' Righters and Henry Wallace's Progressive party, was headed for certain defeat. Truman's victory will undoubtedly remain one of the nation's great political upsets.

Conservative forces were, nevertheless, gaining in support, and with the advance of Communism abroad came fears of internal subversion. Loyalty became an issue, and President Truman ordered that federal employees be subjected to a loyalty check. Hollywood was investigated by the House Un-American Activities Committee (HUAC), and the clandestine blacklisting of entertainment and media figures began. A motif of the thirties, that the New Deal was merely a subterfuge for Communism, grew in credence. By the end of the decade, Czechoslovakia and China had fallen to Communist forces, and Russia had the bomb.

The decade closed with a trial that was viewed by many as a measure of the extent of Communist conspiracy, although others saw it as a right-wing persecution. Distinguished former New Dealer Alger Hiss was tried for perjury, for having denied under oath that he was a Russian spy; in January 1950, the jury convicted Hiss. Thus, while the nation was prosperous and at peace, its factories and families expanding, the forties closed on a disturbing and, to some, a menacing note.

1940

Economic Profile
- Dow-Jones: ↑ High 152– Low 113
- GNP: +10%
- Inflation: +0.4%
- Unemployment: 14.6%

Nash: $780

Packard: $907

Three-room apartment, New York City, E. 63d St.: $82 (monthly)

Eight-room townhouse, W. 77th St.: $2,600 (purchase price)

Gas range: $44.50

Chrome breakfast set: $25

Voss washing machine: $38

Noritake dinner set, 105-piece, gold encrusted: $54

Maple bedroom set: $49.88

Carpeting, wool: $3.88 (sq. yd.)

Wet mop: 89¢; dry mop: $1.49

Jumbo clothes hamper: $2.99

Ping-pong table: $18.98

Floor lamp: $9

Deaths

Mrs. Patrick Campbell, Neville Chamberlain, F. Scott Fitzgerald, Hamlin Garland, Emma Goldman, Paul Klee, Luisa Tetrazzini, Édouard Vuillard, Nathanael West.

In the News

FDR ASKS RECORD $1.8 BILLION FOR DEFENSE . . . WINSTON CHURCHILL REPLACES NEVILLE CHAMBERLAIN AS BRITISH P.M. . . . FINLAND AND USSR MAKE PEACE, FINNS CEDE TERRITORY . . . NAZIS INVADE DENMARK AND NORWAY, VIDKUN QUISLING IS INSTALLED AS HEAD OF NORWAY. . . . FDR APPEALS TO MUSSOLINI FOR HELP WITH PEACE . . . GERMAN ARMIES INVADE HOLLAND, BELGIUM, AND LUXEMBOURG IN LIGHTNING ATTACK . . . OFFICE OF EMERGENCY MANAGEMENT IS ESTABLISHED . . . AFL AND CIO PLEDGE WAR AID . . . 350,000 BRITISH TROOPS EVACUATE DUNKIRK IN SMALL BOATS . . . ITALY DECLARES WAR ON BRITAIN AND FRANCE, FDR DECRIES "STAB IN THE BACK" AND PLEDGES MATERIAL AID TO "OPPONENTS OF FORCE" . . . NAVAL SUPPLY ACT PROVIDES $1.5 BILLION, MILITARY SUPPLY ACT, $1.8 BILLION . . . GERMANS ENTER PARIS UNOPPOSED . . . FDR REJECTS GERMAN TERRITORIAL TRANSFERS . . . FRENCH SIGN ARMISTICE AT COMPIÈGNE, SITE OF WORLD WAR I TRIUMPH . . . JAPAN, ITALY, GERMANY SIGN 10-YEAR AXIS PACT . . . GERMANS COMMENCE DAILY AERIAL BOMBARDMENT OF ENGLAND, RAF FIGHTS BACK . . . FDR IS RENOMINATED FOR THIRD TERM, WENDELL WILLKIE IS GOP CANDIDATE . . . LEON TROTSKY IS ASSASSINATED BY RUSSIAN AGENT IN MEXICO . . . BRITISH NAVY SINKS FRENCH FLEET AT ORAN . . . U.S. GIVES BRITAIN 50 DESTROYERS UNDER LEND-LEASE BILL . . . FIRST PEACETIME DRAFT BEGINS . . . RUSSIA INVADES RUMANIA . . . TAX INCREASE IS VOTED . . . MILITARIST KONOYE BECOMES JAPANESE PREMIER, TOJO BECOMES WAR MINISTER . . . FDR WINS THIRD TERM WITH 27 MILLION, WILLKIE GAINS 22 MILLION . . . BRITISH DRIVE BACK ITALIANS IN NORTH AFRICA.

Quotes

"The three most important groups which have been pressing this country toward war are the British, the Jewish, and the Roosevelt administration."
— Charles Lindbergh

"I have said this before, but I shall say it again and again and again. Your boys are not going to be sent into any foreign wars."
— FDR

"France has been conquered and the sea power of Britain seems to be trembling in the balance. We may be next."
— Secretary of State Henry Stimson

"Never . . . was so much owed by so many to so few."
— Winston Churchill, on the RAF

"I have nothing to offer but blood, toil, tears and sweat."
— Winston Churchill

ON THE PRESIDENTIAL ELECTION
"The record of the New Deal is one of broken promises, contempt for free institutions and abuse of power" (Thomas Dewey). "Given four years more, the third-term candidate will lead you over the hills to the poorhouse" (Alfred E. Smith). "The reelection of [FDR] . . . will result in . . . war" (John L. Lewis). "I'm the cockiest fellow you ever saw. If you want to vote for me, fine. If you don't, go jump in the lake, and I'm still for you" (Wendell Willkie).

John Vachon, *Ozark Mountains, Missouri. Library of Congress.*

"Roosevelt will beat this Willkie just as bad as I'll beat Joe Louis the next time I catch up with the bum" (Boxer Tony Galento).

"I have a great stake in this country. My wife and I have given nine hostages to fortune. Our children and your children are more important than anything else in the world. . . . I believe Franklin Delano Roosevelt should be reelected president of the United States."
— Joseph P. Kennedy

Ads

Which [caricature] is Adolf? —There's a rumor that Hitler has a number of "doubles" all exactly like him—and all equally nasty! But it's a fact that FLAG margarine is exactly like butter—equally NICE and equally NOURISHING.
(Flag Margarine)

[They're] hunting the biggest game in the universe— the invisible atom. When the scientists successfully track it down and burst it wide open—they may be able to give us gold, . . . a cancer cure, or a rocket ship. . . . In man's long climb up from savagery, copper has been his best metal friend.
(Revere Copper and Brass)

Who is this man? He looks like an American. He dresses like an American. . . . But . . . he hates American democracy. He is a fifth columnist! Don't trust him!
(The League of Human Rights, Freedom and Democracy)

Their churches suffer pillage and burning. Our churches offer worship and learning.
("Appreciate America Day," Sunday, September 8)

PEACE OR WAR? Which will you choose? Should we fight for England? . . . Let's stop the Rush toward War! Let's make America Impregnable.
(America First Committee)

Radio

Premieres

"Quiz Kids," Joe Kelly and panelists under sixteen
years old
"Truth or Consequences," Ralph Edwards
"Beat the Band," The Incomparable Hildegarde
"Captain Midnight," Ed Prentiss
"Gene Autry's Melody Ranch"
"Portia Faces Life," Lucille Wall
"Crime Doctor," Ray Collins
"Superman," Clayton "Bud" Collyer

Top Ten

"Jack Benny," "Chase and Sanborn Hour," "Fibber
McGee and Molly," "Lux Radio Theater," "Bob
Hope," "Kate Smith Hour," "Major Bowes," "Kay
Kyser," "Aldrich Family," "One Man's Family"

Top Thriller Dramas: "Big Town" (Edward G.
Robinson), "Bishop and the Gargoyle," "City
Desk," "Crime Doctor," "Death Valley Days,"
"Famous Jury Trials," "Gangbusters," "I Love a
Mystery," "The Lone Ranger," "Mr. District
Attorney," "Mr. Keen," "The Shadow," and
"Sherlock Holmes"

Of Note

"Take It or Leave It," with Phil Baker and a top
prize of $64, popularizes the phrase, "the $64
question" • The first question on the "Quiz Kids" is:
"What would I be carrying home if I bought an
antimacassar, a dinghy, a sarong, and an apteryx?"

New Catchphrases: "Give me a little traveling
music, Harry" (Hildegarde); "Doctor Ordway will be
back in exactly forty-seven seconds with the solution
to tonight's case" ("Crime Doctor"); ". . . able to
leap tall buildings at a single bound! . . . It's a bird!
It's a plane! It's . . ." ("Superman").

TV

The first color broadcast takes place from the CBS
transmitter on the Chrysler Building, New York,
August 27.
The FCC grants the first state TV license to DuMont.
The Republican National Convention is telecast from
Philadelphia.

Movies

Openings

The Grapes of Wrath (John Ford), Henry Fonda,
Jane Darwell, John Carradine
Rebecca (Alfred Hitchcock), Joan Fontaine,
Laurence Olivier
The Great Dictator (Charles Chaplin), Charles
Chaplin, Jack Oakie, Paulette Goddard
The Letter (William Wyler), Bette Davis, Herbert
Marshall
The Philadelphia Story (George Cukor), Katharine
Hepburn, Cary Grant, James Stewart
Abe Lincoln in Illinois (John Cromwell), Raymond
Massey, Ruth Gordon
Fantasia, (Walt Disney)
Boom Town (Jack Conway), Spencer Tracy, Clark
Gable, Hedy Lamarr
The Bank Dick (Edward Cline), W. C. Fields
My Little Chickadee (Edward Cline), Mae West,
W. C. Fields
They Drive by Night (Raoul Walsh), George Raft, Ida
Lupino, Pat O'Brien
Waterloo Bridge (Mervyn LeRoy), Robert Taylor,
Vivien Leigh

The Great McGinty (Preston Sturges), Brian
Donlevy, Akim Tamiroff
The Thief of Bagdad (Michael Powell, Tim Whelan,
Ludwig Berger), Sabu, Conrad Veidt
Pride and Prejudice (Robert Z. Leonard), Laurence
Olivier, Greer Garson
Foreign Correspondent (Alfred Hitchcock), Joel
McCrea, Laraine Day
Road to Singapore (Victor Schertzinger), Bob Hope,
Bing Crosby, Dorothy Lamour

Academy Awards

Best Picture: *Rebecca*
Best Director: John Ford (*The Grapes of Wrath*)
Best Actress: Ginger Rogers (*Kitty Foyle*)
Best Actor: James Stewart (*The Philadelphia Story*)

Top Box-Office Stars

Mickey Rooney, Spencer Tracy, Clark Gable, Gene
Autry, Tyrone Power, James Cagney, Bing Crosby,
Wallace Beery, Bette Davis, Judy Garland

Popular Music

Hit Songs

"You Are My Sunshine"
"The Last Time I Saw Paris"
"When You Wish upon a Star"
"It's a Big, Wide Wonderful World"
"You Stepped out of a Dream"
"Cabin in the Sky"
"All or Nothing at All"
"Back in the Saddle Again"
"Pennsylvania 6–5000"
"Taking a Chance on Love"

Top Records

I'll Never Smile Again (Tommy Dorsey, Pied Pipers); *Beat Me, Daddy, Eight to the Bar* (Andrews Sisters); *Fools Rush In* (Mildred Bailey); *The Breeze and I* (Charlie Barnet); *I Hear a Rhapsody* (Jimmy Dorsey, Tommy Dorsey); *The Starlit Hour* (Ella Fitzgerald); *How High the Moon* (Benny Goodman); *Frenesi* (Artie Shaw); *The Nearness of You* (Dinah Shore); *Come Down to Earth, My Darling* (Fats Waller, Lawrence Welk); *Stardust* (Artie Shaw); *Concerto for Cootie* (Duke Ellington); *Perfidia* (Jimmy Dorsey); *Limehouse Blues* (Larry Clinton); *High Society* (Roy Eldridge); *Swing Time up in Harlem* (Tommy Dorsey)

Jazz and Big Bands

Harry James forms his own band and hires Frank Sinatra. *Bebop,* an onomatopoetic description of the new music, is coined. Lionel Hampton leaves Benny Goodman to form his own band. Minton's Playhouse, New York, introduces Dizzy Gillespie, Thelonious Monk, and Kenny Clark. Charlie Christian plays the electric guitar in Oklahoma City.

First Recording: King Cole Trio

Top Performers *(Downbeat):* Benny Goodman (soloist, big band); Glenn Miller (sweet band); Charlie Christian, Jess Stacy, Irving Fazola, Ziggy Elman, Ray Bauduc (instrumentalists); Helen O'Connell, Bing Crosby (vocalists)

Theater

Broadway Openings

Plays

The Corn Is Green (Emlyn Williams), Ethel Barrymore
My Sister Eileen (Joseph Fields, Jerome Chodorov), Shirley Booth, Morris Carnovsky, Jo Ann Sayers
The Male Animal (James Thurber, Elliott Nugent), Gene Tierney, Elliott Nugent
Ladies in Retirement (Reginald Denham, Edward Percy), Flora Robson
Love's Old Sweet Song (William Saroyan), Walter Huston, Jessie Royce Landis
My Dear Children (Catherine Turney, Jerry Horwin), John Barrymore
There Shall Be No Night (Robert E. Sherwood), Alfred Lunt, Lynn Fontanne, Montgomery Clift
The Fifth Column (Ernest Hemingway), Franchot Tone, Lenore Ulric
George Washington Slept Here (George S. Kaufman, Moss Hart), Ernest Truex, Dudley Digges

Musicals

Cabin in the Sky (Vernon Duke, John Latouche), Ethel Waters, Dooley Wilson, Rex Ingram, Todd Duncan
Hold on to Your Hats (Burton Lane, E. Y. Harburg), Al Jolson, Martha Raye, Jinx Falkenburg
Louisiana Purchase (Irving Berlin), Victor Moore, William Gaxton, Vera Zorina, Irene Bordoni
Panama Hattie (Cole Porter, B. G. DeSylva), Ethel Merman, James Dunn, Betty Hutton, June Allyson
Two for the Show (Morgan Lewis), Betty Hutton, Richard Haydn, Alfred Drake
Keep Off the Grass (James McHugh, Howard Dietz), Jimmy Durante, Ray Bolger, José Limón, Larry Adler, choreographed by George Balanchine
Pal Joey (Richard Rodgers, Lorenz Hart), Gene Kelly, June Havoc, Van Johnson

Classics and Revivals On and Off Broadway

Charley's Aunt (Brandon Thomas), José Ferrer, *Romeo and Juliet*, Laurence Olivier, Vivien Leigh; *Twelfth Night*, Helen Hayes, Maurice Evans; *Liliom* (Molnár), Ingrid Bergman, Burgess Meredith; *Juno and the Paycock* (Sean O'Casey), Barry Fitzgerald, Sara Allgood. *Founded:* The American Negro Company

Pulitzer Prize

The Time of Your Life, William Saroyan

Classical Music

Compositions
Samuel Barber, *A Stop Watch and an Ordnance Map*
Aaron Copland, *Quiet City, Of Mice and Men*
Paul Creston, Symphony no. 1
David Diamond, Concerto for Small Orchestra
Ulysses Kay, Ten Essays
Roy Harris, *Western Landscape, American Creed, Ode to Truth, Challenge.* String Quartet
Walter Piston, Chromatic Study for Organ
William Schuman, Secular Cantata no. 1

Important Events
An extraordinary amount of American music is performed throughout the country. In Rochester, José Iturbi conducts the Rochester Symphony in 40 American works. Also premiering contemporary and American work are John Barbirolli (Philadelphia), Leopold Stokowski and Eugene Ormandy (Philadelphia), Serge Koussevitsky (Boston), Frederick Stock (Chicago), Artur Rodzinsky (Cleveland), and Eugene Goossens (Cincinnati).

For the 50th anniversary of the Chicago Symphony, work is commissioned from Frederick Stock, John Carpenter, Roy Harris, Igor Stravinsky, and Darius Milhaud.

At the MoMA Carlos Chávez conducts the Mexican Orchestra in a concert of modern work, including *Xochipili-Macuilxochitl.*

Milhaud conducts for CBS *La cortège funèbre,* written shortly before the German occupation of France.

European refugees settle in the United States: Bruno Walter, Ignace Jan Paderewski, Fritz Kreisler, Paul Hindemith, Béla Bartók, Darius Milhaud, Arnold Schoenberg, Mario Castelnuovo-Tedesco, Igor Stravinsky, Kurt Weill; Sergei Rachmaninoff writes Piano Concerto no. 4, Stravinsky, Symphony in C major, Hindemith, *The Four Temperaments,* Symphony in E-flat Major, Harp Sonata, and Cello Concerto.

Stokowski forms the All-American Youth Orchestra

Henry Fonda and Jane Darwell in *The Grapes of Wrath,* the highly acclaimed film version of John Steinbeck's novel about migrant farmers. *Movie Star News.*

with members from every state. One hundred are selected from 15,000 tryouts. Formed to acknowledge "native American talent," the orchestra travels through South America and performs at Carnegie Hall.

Toscanini tours South America; NBC Symphony radio broadcasts also resume during the year.

Debuts: Abbey Simon, Joseph Szigeti

First Performances
Roger Sessions, Violin Concerto (Chicago); Arnold Schoenberg, Violin Concerto (Philadelphia); Chamber Symphony no. 2 (New York); Roy Harris, *Folk Song Symphony* (Cleveland); Walter Piston, Violin Concerto (Boston); Paul Creston, Concerto for Marimba and Orchestra (New York); William Grant Still, *And They Lynched Him on a Tree* (New York); John Carpenter, Symphony in C (Chicago); Béla Bartók, First Rhapsody (Washington, D.C.)

Opera

Metropolitan: Public donations exceed the necessary $1 million to purchase the company's new home. Performances include Kirsten Flagstad, Lauritz Melchior, Helen Traubel, *Siegfried;* Alexander Kipnis, *Parsifal;* Licia Albanese (debut) *La bohème;* Zinka Milanov, *Tosca;* Jennie Tourel, *Carmen;* Risë Stevens, *Der Rosenkavalier;* Lily Pons, Salvatore Baccaloni, *La fille du regiment;* Elisabeth Rethberg, John Brownlee, Ezio Pinza, Licia Albanese, *Figaro*

Chicago: Zinka Milanov, Giovanni Martinelli, *Aïda;* Kirsten Flagstad, Lauritz Melchior, *Tristan und Isolde*

San Francisco: Lotte Lehmann, Robert Weede, *Der Rosenkavalier;* John Brownlee, *La bohème*

Central City, Colo.: *The Bartered Bride*

Music Notes
Toscanini performs the original overture to *Aïda,* cut by Verdi from the opera • The appointment of the conductor Erich Leinsdorf, 27, to the Metropolitan Opera Company provokes threats from Kirsten Flagstad and Lauritz Melchior; publicity draws large audiences • Nervous Melchior puts on a warrior's helmet backwards in *Götterdämmerung.*

Art

Painting

Edward Hopper, *Gas*

Marsden Hartley, *Log Jam, Fishermen's Last Supper*

Loren MacIver, *Hopscotch*

Reginald Marsh, *New Dodgem, Swimming off West Washington Market*

Morris Graves, *Blind Bird*

Stuart Davis, *Hot Still-Scape for Six Colors*

Willem de Kooning, *Seated Woman*

Lyonel Feininger, *The River, Manhattan I*

Paul Cadmus, *Sailors and Floozies*

Ben Shahn, *Willis Avenue Bridge*

Edmund Archer, *Howard Patterson of the "Harlem Yankees"*

Morris Hirschfield, *Tiger*

Edward Laning paints four murals that trace the history of printing for the New York Public Library.

Sculpture

William Zorach, *Head of Christ*

Hugo Robus, *Girl Washing Her Hair*

Jacques Lipchitz, *Flight*

Alexander Calder, *Thirteen Spines, Black Beast*

Carl Milles, Aloe Fountain Plaza, St. Louis, Mo.

Architecture

Berkshire Music Shed, Tanglewood, Lenox, Mass. (Joseph Franz)

Workers' Village, New Kensington, Pa. (Gropius, Breuer)

Rockefeller Center is completed (Reinhard and Hofmeister, Hood and Fouilhoux, Corbett, Harrison and MacMurray)

Museum of Science and Industry, Chicago (Burnham)

Important Exhibitions

Museums

Latin American art travels across the United States.

New York: *Metropolitan:* The Art of the Jeweler; "Heads in Sculpture"; American watercolors. *Museum of Modern Art:* Visual and Nonvisual expressionism: "War Comes to the People"; Designs of Frank Lloyd Wright; Mexican art. *Iranian Institute:* 6,000 years of Iranian art

Chicago: 50 years of American art; Picasso; Amédée Ozenfant

San Francisco: Paintings of France since the Revolution

Boston: Arts of the Middle Ages, 1000–1400 A.D.; Giovanni Martino; Art of Argentina

Katharine Hepburn, in *The Philadelphia Story. Movie Star News.*

Detroit: "The Age of Impressionism and Objective Realism"

Toledo: Four centuries of Venetian Art

Los Angeles: Pre-Columbian Art

Individual Shows

John Marin, O'Keeffe (20 paintings of Hawaiian flora commissioned by the Dole Pineapple Company), Levi, Sheeler, Calder, Marc, MacIver, Avery, Davis, Moholy-Nagy, Feininger, Klee, Ozenfant, Kokoschka, Epstein, Vlaminck.

Art Briefs

Piet Mondrian joins the American Abstract Artists in New York • American artists boycott the Venice Biennale because of Italy's war declaration • More than 200 artists auction their work to provide bread for Finnish children • The Federal Art Project produces 1,125 murals, although the WPA is curtailed at the end of the year • Mrs. John D. Rockefeller donates 36 works to the Museum of Modern Art, including Maillol, Zorach, and Despiau sculptures for the museum garden • Charles Eames and Eero Saarinen win the Museum of Modern Art competition for "Organic Design in Home Furnishings" • The Department of Photography is established at the Museum of Modern Art.

Dance

Ballet Theatre, an outgrowth of the Mordkin Ballet, is founded by Lucia Chase and Richard Pleasant; its first season includes *Les sylphides, La fille mal gardée,* and *Jardin aux lilas* (Anthony Tudor). Dancers include Nora Kaye, Lucia Chase, Anton Dolin, William Dollar, Jerome Robbins, Alicia Alonso, Alicia Markova, Irina Baronova and Tudor.

Martha Graham: *El Penitente*

Books

Fiction

Critics' Choice
The Hamlet, William Faulkner
Sapphira and the Slave Girl, Willa Cather
You Can't Go Home Again, Thomas Wolfe (posthumous)
The Man Who Loved Children, Christina Stead
My Name Is Aram, William Saroyan
The Pilgrim Hawk, Glenway Wescott
The Heart Is a Lonely Hunter, Carson McCullers
Native Son, Richard Wright
The Ox-Bow Incident, Walter van Tilburg Clark
Darkness at Noon, Arthur Koestler
🔖 *The Power and the Glory*, Graham Greene

Best-Sellers
How Green Was My Valley, Richard Llewellyn
Kitty Foyle, Christopher Morley
Mrs. Miniver, Jan Struther
For Whom the Bell Tolls, Ernest Hemingway
The Nazarene, Sholem Asch
Stars on the Sea, F. van Wyck Mason
Oliver Wiswell, Kenneth Roberts
The Grapes of Wrath, John Steinbeck
Night in Bombay, Louis Bromfield
The Family, Nina Fedorova

Nonfiction

Critics' Choice
The Realm of Spirit, George Santayana
Since Yesterday, Frederick Lewis Allen
Race, Language and Culture, Franz Boas
Education for a Classless Society, James Bryant Conant
Dusk of Dawn, W. E. B. Du Bois
America Learns to Play, Foster Rhea Dulles
The President Makers, Matthew Josephson
John D. Rockefeller, Allan Nevins
To the Finland Station, Edmund Wilson
🔖 *How to Pay for the War*, J. M. Keynes
🔖 *The Interpretation of Personality*, C. G. Jung

Best-Sellers
I Married Adventure, Osa Johnson
How to Read a Book, Mortimer Adler
A Smattering of Ignorance, Oscar Levant
Country Squire in the White House, John T. Flynn
American White Paper, Joseph W. Alsop, Jr., and Robert Kintnor
New England: Indian Summer, Van Wyck Brooks
Land Below the Wind, Agnes Newton Keith
As I Remember Him, Hans Zinsser
Days of Our Years, Pierre van Paassen
Bet It's a Boy, Betty B. Blunt

Poetry
Robert Hayden, *Heartshape in the Dust*
E. E. Cummings, *50 Poems*
Edna St. Vincent Millay, *Make Bright the Arrows*
H. D., *Collected Poems*
Kenneth Rexroth, *In What Hour*
Muriel Rukeyser, *The Soul and Body of John Brown*
John Ciardi, *Homeward to America*
🔖 W. B. Yeats, *Last Poems and Plays* (posthumous)

Pulitzer Prizes
The Atlantic Migration, 1607–1860, Marcus Lee Hansen (U.S. history)
Jonathan Edwards, Ola Elizabeth Winslow (biography)
Sunderland Capture, Leonard Bacon (poetry)
No prize is awarded for the novel.

Science and Technology

More fissionable uranium 235 is isolated from the more stable uranium 238.
The University of California begins construction of a 4,900-ton cyclotron that produces mesons from atomic nuclei.
A new method of converting coal into organic chemicals useful for dyes, explosives, and medicines is developed at the California Institute of Technology.
The U.S. Air Force P-51 Mustang is designed.

Freeze drying is adapted for food preservation.
Hans Zinsser, at Harvard, announces a method to mass produce an antityphus vaccine.
Edwin Cohn separates blood plasma into globulin, albumin, and fibrin fractions.
Plasma is discovered to be a substitute for whole blood in transfusions.
Robert Gross performs the first successful surgery for congenital major blood vessel defect.
Karl Pabst designs the jeep.

Joe Louis, the youngest heavyweight champion in history, defends his title four times during the year. *Library of Congress.*

Sports

Other Sports

Horse Racing: Eight-year-old Seabiscuit becomes racing's all-time moneywinner. Gallahadion, the Kentucky Derby winner, goes off at 35–1.

Track and Field: Connie Warmerdam is the first to pole vault over 15 feet.

Boxing: Joe Louis KO's Arturo Godoy, who crouches in the ring like an ape and kisses him.

Car Racing: George Shaw wins his third Indianapolis 500.

Wimbledon, the Olympics, and Davis and Wightman Cups are called off because of the war.

Winners

World Series		College Basketball	
Cincinnati (NL) 4		Indiana (NCAA)	
Detroit (AL) 3		Colorado (NIT)	
MVP		*Player of the Year*	
NL–Frank McCormick, Cincinnati		George Glamack, North Carolina	
AL–Henry Greenberg, Detroit		*Stanley Cup*	
		New York	
NFL		*US Tennis Open*	
Chicago (Bears) 73–Washington 0		Men: Donald McNeill	
		Women: Alice Marble	
MVP		*USGA Open*	
Ace Parker, Brooklyn		W. Lawson Little, Jr.	
College Football		*Kentucky Derby*	
Minnesota		Gallahadion (C. Bierman, jockey)	
Heisman Trophy			
Tom Harmon, Michigan			

Baseball

Bob Feller (Cleveland, AL) pitches his first no-hitter, on opening day.

Champions

Batting	*Pitching*
Debs Garms (Pittsburgh, NL), .355	Fred Fitzsimmons (Brooklyn, NL), 15–2
Joe DiMaggio (New York, AL), .352	Lyn Rowe (Detroit, AL), 16–3
	Home runs
	John Mize (St. Louis, NL), 43

Football

"Students derive no special benefit from intercollegiate football," says the University of Chicago, as it withdraws from the Big Ten.

NFL Season Leaders: Sammy Baugh (Washington), passing; Don Looney (Philadelphia), rushing; and Don Hutson (Green Bay), passing.

College All-Americans: Frankie Albert (Q), Stanford; John Kimbrough (B), Texas A & M

College Bowls (Jan. 1, 1941)
Rose: Stanford 21–Nebraska 13
Orange: Mississippi State 14–Georgetown 7
Cotton: Texas A & M 13–Fordham 12
Sugar: Boston College 19–Tennessee 13

Fashion

For Women: With the occupation of France, the fashion center moves to New York. French "air force blue" becomes the popular color. Suit lapels are decorated with enamel shields in Ally colors; eagles appear on hatbands and purses. The times demand an emphasis on simplicity, economy, and practicality: short dresses, simple suits with pleated skirts; day dresses that can be worn at night with a muff or fur. New fashions include day dresses with aprons and pinafores and, at the other extreme, South Sea sarongs (after Dorothy Lamour) in colorful slinky crepes that expose the bare midriff and uplift bosom. Hair is worn to the shoulder with big curls, piled on top of the head with curls and pompadours, or curled into a sausage in the back. Lips are modeled like Crawford's "bow tie," in shades like "Regimented Red" (with matching polish); powder and rouge are applied over pancake makeup.

For Men: Fashions are marked by a new conservatism: the granite gray or blue striped suit; solid or red, blue, and white striped ties worn in Windsor knots; and spread-collared white, blue, or blue-white striped shirts. Rayon is introduced for wrinkleproof ties.

Kaleidoscope _____

- The speed and efficiency of the Nazi blitzkrieg, a sudden, combined air and tank assault, stuns America.
- The American movies *You Can't Take It with You* and *Going Places* are playing on the Champs Élysées as the Germans march through the Arc de Triomphe.
- FDR announces the buildup of a peacetime army; the Selective Service Training Act is passed, and 16,313,240 men receive registration cards for the first peacetime draft.
- Defense plants spring up throughout the United States with seven-day, round-the-clock workweeks.
- The Statue of Liberty stamp is issued with "For Defense" inscribed near the uplifted torch.
- Sheboygan, Wisconsin, votes to commence all concerts with "America" and "The Stars and Stripes Forever"; the second half will begin with "God Bless America" and "The Star Spangled Banner."
- Nickel jukeboxes appear in taverns, tearooms, variety stores, gas stations, restaurants, and barber shops; 16 records cost 50 cents; three minutes of silence is available for 5 cents.
- A *Downbeat* top singers poll includes Bing Crosby, Bob Eberle, Frank Sinatra, and James Rushing; "top girl singers" include Helen O'Connell, Dinah Shore, Billie Holiday, Mildred Bailey, Helen Forrest, and Martha Tilton.
- The popular Lindy Hop generates Saturday night social clubs; new dances include La Varsonviana; the rhumba peaks in popularity; Arthur Murray creates the "Americonga" and "Rhumba Reel."
- Artie Shaw, thought to be engaged to Betty Grable, marries Lana Turner, thought to be engaged to a Los Angeles attorney. Al Jolson and Ruby Keeler divorce.
- Newfangled supermarkets merchandise food differently; vegetables, for example, are available in bunches, rather than by the pound (carrots, 5 cents the bunch).
- McDonald's is started by Pasadena movie owners Richard and Maurice McDonald.
- The consumption of vermouth reaches a record high, 1,650,000 gallons.
- Radio news commentators include Boake Carter, Walter Winchell, Lowell Thomas, Fulton Lewis, Jr., Edward Morgan, Edward R. Murrow, and H. V. Kaltenborn (whose rolling *r*'s become an announcing style).
- In one of the auto industry's best years, the average car costs $1,200, a luxury car, $1,400; gasoline is 14 to 19 cents a gallon.
- John L. Lewis becomes a Republican.
- Albert Einstein becomes a U.S. citizen.
- The Pan American Yankee Clipper flies from New York to Lisbon in a record 18½ hours.
- When the New York El is torn down, the scrap is sold to Japan.
- The suspension bridge Galloping Gertie falls into Puget Sound.
- Bugs Bunny debuts in *O'Hare.*
- Procter and Gamble sues Lever Brothers for stealing

The Andrews Sisters popularize "Beat Me, Daddy (Eight to the Bar)." *Movie Star News.*

the "Ivory secret"; they settle for $10 million.
- The first Social Security checks total $75,844; the first recipient receives $22.54.
- A New York bill is signed that permits children to be absent from school for religious reasons.
- The NAACP denounces the army's policies of separate units for blacks and whites.
- A Syracuse University study reports that the word *I* is used every 53 words by Hitler, every 83 by Mussolini, and every 100 by FDR.
- The wartime shortage of Indian monkeys hinders medical research.
- FDR's gastronomic outline is as follows: he prefers seafood (terrapin), cheese, ice cream, and hot dogs; he enjoys one Scotch every afternoon and four old-fashioneds at banquets, and is a heavy smoker, his cigarette brand, Camels.
- News item: Hitler's Christmas cards are a photo of the *Winged Victory of Samothrace,* which the Germans took from the Louvre. His greeting is "Our Winged Victory."

First Appearances: Arnold bread, Morton salt, "Brenda Starr," cellophane wrap, cars with built-in running boards, safety wheel rims, fully air-conditioned store (Tiffany), commercial flight with pressurized cabins, photo of an albatross on U.S. coastal waters, photos of a sneeze, nonreflecting glass, odor absorber, chicken-feather plucker, cars with "torpedo" bodies, parachute wedding (New York, August 25), air raid shelter, synthetic rubber tire, public demonstration of stereo, synthetic tooth fillings. Patented: cigarettes with ads in invisible ink, ice bag shaped like a hat for headache sufferers, window alarm that catches a burglar at the window

1941

Facts and Figures

Economic Profile
- Dow-Jones:—High 133– Low 106
- GNP: +25%
- Inflation: +2.1%
- Unemployment: 9.9%

Median age, first marriage: Male: 24, Female: 21.5

Average household size: 3.16

Population over 65: 7%

Population under 10: 13%

Beer: 5¢

Soda: 49¢ (case)

Bokar coffee: 33¢ (2 lbs.)

Silver Crow gin: $1.14 (qt.)

Kentucky Straight whiskey: $1.59 (qt.)

Hiram Walker whiskey: $1.59 (qt.)

Veal: 13¢ (lb.)

Shrimp, frozen: 15¢ (lb.)

Chicken: 23¢ (lb.)

A&P salad dressing: 25¢ (qt.)

Above: FDR asking Congress to declare war, to which it assents 410 to 1 (Rep. Jeanette Rankin). *Library of Congress.*

Deaths

Sherwood Anderson, Frederick Banting, Henri Bergson, James Frazer, Charles Evans Hughes, James Joyce, Ignace Jan Paderewski, Joe Penner, Kaiser William II, Virginia Woolf.

In the News

OFFICE OF PRODUCTION MANAGEMENT IS CREATED . . . USO BEGINS . . . BRITISH ADVANCE IN AFRICA, GERMANS SEND ARMY UNDER ROMMEL . . . NATIONAL DEFENSE MEDIATION BOARD IS CREATED TO HANDLE STRIKES . . . NAZIS INVADE YUGOSLAVIA . . . NAZIS INVADE GREECE . . . 60,000 BRITISH TROOPS ARE SENT TO GREECE . . . OFFICE OF CIVIL DEFENSE IS CREATED . . . U.S. MERCHANT SHIP "ROBIN MOOR" IS SUNK BY NAZI SUB . . . FDR DECLARES STATE OF "LIMITED NATIONAL EMERGENCY" . . . FDR FREEZES AXIS FUNDS IN U.S. AND CLOSES CONSULATES . . . GERMANY INVADES RUSSIA . . . U.S. WILL GIVE RUSSIA $1 BILLION FOR LEND-LEASE . . . BRITAIN AND RUSSIA INVADE IRAN . . . FDR EMBARGOES OIL AND SCRAP METAL TO JAPAN . . . FDR AND CHURCHILL MEET IN NORTH ATLANTIC, DECLARE 8-POINT CHARTER FOR POSTWAR WORLD . . . SELECTIVE SERVICE IS EXTENDED TO 30 MONTHS . . . JAPANESE PREMIER KONOYE SAYS JAPAN WANTS PEACE . . . 100 DIE AS U.S. DESTROYER "REUBEN JAMES" IS SUNK OFF ICELAND . . . GERMANS REACH OUTSKIRTS OF LENINGRAD AND THREATEN MOSCOW . . . TOJO BECOMES JAPANESE PREMIER . . . JOHN L. LEWIS THREATENS COAL STRIKE, FDR INTERVENES . . . CALIFORNIA ANTI-OKIE LAW IS DECLARED UNCONSTITUTIONAL . . . FDR APPEALS TO HIROHITO FOR PEACE . . . JAPANESE ATTACK PEARL HARBOR, HAWAII, IN SURPRISE AIR ASSAULT, MASSIVE SHIP AND PLANE DAMAGE IS INFLICTED, JAPANESE ALSO ATTACK MANILA, SINGAPORE, AND HONG KONG . . . U.S. DECLARES WAR ON JAPAN . . . GERMANY AND ITALY DECLARE WAR ON U.S. . . . WAKE ISLAND AND GUAM FALL TO THE JAPANESE . . . DRAFT IS EXTENDED, MEN 18–65 MUST REGISTER, THOSE 20–44 MAY SERVE . . . $10 BILLION IS APPROPRIATED FOR DEFENSE . . . HONG KONG FALLS.

Quotes _____

"In the future days, which we seek to make secure, we look forward to a world grounded upon four essential freedoms: . . . speech . . . worship . . . freedom from want [and] . . . fear."

— FDR

"This decision [to aid Britain] is the end of any attempts at appeasement, . . . the end of compromise with tyranny and the forces of oppression."

— FDR

"This is a war warning. An aggressive move by Japan is expected within the next few days."
— Adm. Harold "Betty" Stark to Pacific Command, November 1941

"Yesterday, December 7, 1941—a date which will live in infamy—the United States of America was suddenly and deliberately attacked by naval and air forces of the Empire of Japan. . . . Very many American lives have been lost. Always will our whole nation remember the character of the onslaught against us. . . . No matter how long it may take to overcome this premeditated invasion, the American people in their righteous might will win through to absolute victory. We will not only defend ourselves to the uttermost but will make it very certain that this form of treachery shall never again endanger us. We will gain the inevitable triumph—so help us God. I ask that the Congress declare . . . a state of war."

— FDR

"[The final solution] will be killing with showers of carbon monoxide while bathing."

— Adolf Eichmann

Naval air station at Pearl Harbor, December 7, 1941. Three hours after the surprise attack, the Japanese declared war. *Official Navy Photograph. By permission of D.C. Public Library.*

Ads _____

Radio

Premieres

"Spirit of '41," John Charles Daly
"The Red Skelton Show"
"Armstrong Theater of Today"
"Inner Sanctum," Raymond Edward Johnson
"The Great Gildersleeve," Hal Peary
"Duffy's Tavern," Ed Gardner, Shirley Booth
"The Thin Man," Lester Damon

Most Popular Soap Operas: "Guiding Light,"
"Woman in White," "Road of Life," "Right to
Happiness" (all written by Irma Philips)

Of Note

An estimated world audience of 90 million people
listen to FDR on December 9 declare "We are going
to win the war and . . . the peace that follows" •
Popular reporters include Edward R. Murrow,
William L. Shirer, Albert Warner, and Bill Henry •
"Gangbusters" is canceled for fear it may instigate
crime.

New Catchphrases: "If I dood it, I gets a whipping"
(Red Skelton); ". . . where the elite meet to eat.
Archie, the manager, speaking" ("Duffy's Tavern";
Duffy never appeared); "Now it's time to close the
door of the Inner Sanctum. . . . *(Door squeaks shut)*
("Inner Sanctum")

TV

A 90-minute documentary on Pearl Harbor and the
national reaction reaches a record audience.
The first commercial: the Bulova Time Signal

Movies

Openings

How Green Was My Valley (John Ford), Walter
  Pidgeon, Maureen O'Hara
Citizen Kane (Orson Welles), Orson Welles, Joseph
  Cotten
Hold Back the Dawn (Mitchell Leisen), Charles
  Boyer, Olivia de Havilland
The Little Foxes (William Wyler), Bette Davis,
  Herbert Marshall
The Maltese Falcon (John Huston), Humphrey
  Bogart, Mary Astor, Peter Lorre
Sergeant York (Howard Hawks), Gary Cooper,
  Walter Brennan, Joan Leslie
Suspicion (Alfred Hitchcock), Cary Grant, Joan
  Fontaine
The Lady Eve (Preston Sturges), Barbara Stanwyck,
  Henry Fonda
Major Barbara (Gabriel Pascal), Wendy Hiller, Rex
  Harrison
The Shanghai Gesture (Josef von Sternberg), Gene
  Tierney, Victor Mature
Dumbo (Ben Springsteen)
Blood and Sand (Rouben Mamoulian), Tyrone
  Power, Nazimova, Linda Darnell
Dr. Jekyll and Mr. Hyde (Victor Fleming), Spencer
  Tracy, Ingrid Bergman
High Sierra (Raoul Walsh), Ida Lupino, Humphrey
  Bogart

Meet John Doe (Frank Capra), Gary Cooper,
  Barbara Stanwyck
Two-Faced Woman (George Cukor), Greta Garbo
  (her last film), Melvyn Douglas

Academy Awards

Best Picture: *How Green Was My Valley*
Best Director: John Ford (*How Green Was My
  Valley*)
Best Actress: Joan Fontaine (*Suspicion*)
Best Actor: Gary Cooper (*Sergeant York*)

Top Box-Office Stars

Mickey Rooney, Clark Gable, Abbott and Costello,
Bob Hope, Spencer Tracy, Gene Autry, Gary
Cooper, Bette Davis, James Cagney, Judy Garland

Stars of Tomorrow

Laraine Day, Rita Hayworth, Ruth Hussey, Robert
Preston, Ronald Reagan, John Payne, Jeffrey Lynn,
Ann Rutherford, Dennis Morgan, Jackie Cooper

Popular Music _____

Hit Songs
"Deep in the Heart of Texas"
"You Don't Know What Love Is"
"God Bless the Child"
"I'll Remember April"
"There! I've Said It Again"
"Jersey Bounce"
"How about You?"
"Waltzing Matilda"
"The Anniversary Waltz"

Top Records
Green Eyes (Jimmy Dorsey); *You Made Me Love You* (Harry James); *Racing with the Moon* (Vaughn Monroe); *By the Light of the Silvery Moon* (Ray Noble); *Blues in the Night* (Dinah Shore); *Dancing in the Dark* (Artie Shaw); *Flamingo* (Duke Ellington); *Buckle Down, Winsocki* (Benny Goodman); *This Love of Mine* (Stan Kenton); *Chattanooga Choo Choo* (Glenn Miller)

Jazz and Big Bands
Stan Kenton opens at the Rendezvous Ballroom, Balboa, California. Gil Evans joins the Claude Thornhill Orchestra. Peggy Lee, Cootie Williams, and Big Sid Catlett perform with Benny Goodman.

First Recording: Charlie Parker, with Jay McShann

Top Performers (*Downbeat*)**:** Harry James (soloist); Benny Goodman (big band); Glenn Miller (sweet band); Tex Beneke, Irving Fazola, J. C. Higginbotham, Ziggy Elman (instrumentalists); Helen O'Connell, Frank Sinatra (vocalists)

Theater _____

Broadway Openings

Plays
Watch on the Rhine (Lillian Hellman), Lucile Watson, Paul Lukas, Ann Blythe
Blithe Spirit (Noel Coward), Peggy Wood, Clifton Webb, Mildred Natwick
Arsenic and Old Lace (Joseph Kesselring), Josephine Hull, Boris Karloff
Native Son (Paul Green, Richard Wright), Canada Lee
Angel Street (Patrick Hamilton), Judith Evelyn, Vincent Price
Junior Miss (Jerome Chodorov, Joseph Fields), Francesca Bruning
Candle in the Wind (Maxwell Anderson), Helen Hayes
Clash by Night (Clifford Odets), Tallulah Bankhead, Joseph Schildkraut, Robert Ryan
Claudia (Rose Franken), Dorothy McGuire

Musicals
Best Foot Forward (Hugh Martin, Ralph Blane), June Allyson, Nancy Walker
Lady in the Dark (Kurt Weill, Ira Gershwin), Gertrude Lawrence, Victor Mature
Let's Face It (Cole Porter), Danny Kaye, Eve Arden, Vivian Vance, Nanette Fabray
Sons o' Fun (Sam E. Fain, Jack Yellen), Olsen and Johnson, Carmen Miranda, Ella Logan
Banjo Eyes (Vernon Duke, John Latouche), Eddie Cantor, June Clyde, Virginia Mayo

Classics and Revivals On and Off Broadway
Macbeth, Maurice Evans, Judith Anderson; *As You Like It,* Alfred Drake, Helen Craig; *Twelfth Night,* Beatrice Straight, Hurd Hatfield; *The Doctor's Dilemma* (George Bernard Shaw), Katharine Cornell, Raymond Massey; *Ah, Wilderness!* (Eugene O'Neill), Harry Carey. *Founded:* The Experimental Theatre of Dramatists by Antoinette Perry

Pulitzer Prize
There Shall Be No Night, Robert E. Sherwood

Clark Gable and Carole Lombard attend a Hollywood wedding shortly before her death. *Movie Star News.*

Classical Music

Compositions
Aaron Copland, Piano Sonata
Douglas Moore, *Village Music*
Walter Piston, *Sinfonietta*
William Schuman, Symphony no. 3, Symphony no. 4
John Alden Carpenter, *Song of Freedom*
Roy Harris, *Railroad Man's Ballad, From This
    Earth, Accelerator,* Violin Sonata
Leonard Bernstein, Symphony no. 1, Clarinet Sonata
Roger Sessions, *Montezuma*
Samuel Barber, Violin Concerto
David Diamond, Symphony no. 1
John Cage, *Double Music*

Important Events
For the conclusion of the Chicago Symphony's 50th anniversary, music performed includes Stravinsky's Symphony in C Major and Leo Sowerby's Symphony no. 3. Guest conductors are Leopold Stokowski, Bruno Walter, Artur Rodzinsky, Dimitri Mitropoulos, Eugene Goossens, Serge Koussevitzky, John Barbirolli, Walter Damrosch, Arturo Toscanini, and Fritz Busch, each for two weeks.
The League of Composers presents the work of the younger John Ayres Lessard, Emil Koehler, Donald Fuller, Norman Dello Joio, and Lukas Foss.

Debuts: Malcolm Frager, William Kapell

First Performances
Béla Bartók, Quartet no. 6, *Music for Strings, Percussion, and Celeste* (New York); Rachmaninoff, Symphonic Dances (Philadelphia); William Schuman, Symphony no. 3 (Boston); Aaron Copland, *Quiet City* (New York); Paul Hindemith, Cello Concerto (Boston); Symphony in E-flat (Seattle); Benjamin Britten, Sinfonia da Requiem (New York); Stravinsky, *Tango* (Philadelphia, Benny Goodman conducting): Ernest Bloch, *Baal Shem* (WPA Orchestra, New York); Virgil Thomson, Symphony no. 2 (Seattle); Samuel Barber, Concerto for Violin (Philadelphia); Robert Russell Bennett, *A Symphony in D for the Dodgers* (New York); Leo Sowerby, Symphony no. 3 (Chicago); Alfredo Casella, Symphony no. 3 (Chicago)

Opera

Metropolitan: Jan Peerce (debut), *La traviata, Rigoletto;* Astrid Varnay, *Siegfried;* Grace Moore, Ezio Pinza, *L'amore dei tre re;* Stella Roman, *Aïda;*

Joseph Cotten and Orson Welles in *Citizen Kane,* "boy wonder" Welles's first film, based on the life of William Randolph Hearst. Hearst tried to suppress the film. *Movie Star News.*

Helen Traubel, *Die Walküre;* Salvatore Baccaloni, *Il barbiere di Siviglia;* Elisabeth Rethberg, Lawrence Tibbett, Giovanni Martinelli, *Fidelio*

New Opera of New York: Organized to perform at modest costs and in English; *Così fan tutte* (premiere performance); scores commissioned are *Solomon and Balkis* (Randall Thompson); *No for an Answer* (Marc Blitzstein)

Boston: *Orfeo* (Claudio Monteverdi, the Malipiero version, premiere)

Chicago: Licia Albanese, Gladys Swarthout, *Carmen, Madama Butterfly*

San Francisco: *Simon Boccanegra;* Lily Pons, Salvatore Baccaloni, *La fille du regiment*

Music Notes
Albert Einstein plays the violin in a benefit concert for Refugee Children in England, in Princeton, N.J.

Art

Painting

Jackson Pollock, *Naked Man with Knife, Man, Bull, Bird, Birth*

Lyonel Feininger, *Tug*

Max Weber, *The Night Class*

Robert Motherwell, *The Little Spanish Prison*

Willem de Kooning, *The Wave*

Andrew Wyeth, *Farm at Broad Cove, Cushing, Maine*

Edward Hopper, *Nighthawks*

Stuart Davis, *New York under Gaslight*

Hyman Bloom, *The Bride*

Arshile Gorky, *Garden in Sochi*

Louis Guglielmi, *Terror in Brooklyn*

Morris Graves, *Bird in the Spirit*

Sculpture

Alexander Calder, *Mobile*

Peter Grippe, *The City #1, 1941*

Isamu Noguchi, *Contoured Playground*

Joseph Cornell, *Swiss Shoot-the-Chutes*

Carl Milles's figures are placed at the Cranbrook Academy Fountain, Bloomfield Hills, Mich.

Architecture

Federal housing communities, California, Texas (Richard Neutra)

Platt House, Portland, Oreg. (Pietro Belluschi)

Cranbrook Academy of Art, Bloomfield Hills, Mich. (Saarinen and Saarinen)

West Building, National Gallery of Art, Washington, D.C. (Pope, Eggers, and Higgins)

Important Exhibitions

Museums

New York: *Metropolitan:* "China Trade and Its Influences" (tours United States); Prints by six masters from the Warburg Collection; French prints after 1800; WPA exhibitions; Pages from early Korans; The art of Australia; French Painters from David to Toulouse-Lautrec. *Museum of Modern Art:* Miró, Dali, Grosz. *Brooklyn:* Paganism and Christianity in Egypt

Chicago: The first century of printmaking; 52nd exhibition of American paintings and sculpture; French paintings from David to Toulouse-Lautrec; Goya

Boston: Modern Mexican painters

Toledo: Spanish art

Niles Spencer, *Waterfront Mill*, 1941. Oil. 30 × 36". *The Metropolitan Museum of Art, Arthur H. Hearn Fund, 1942.*

San Francisco: Baroque Italian painting

Individual Shows

Goya (Chicago); Cassatt (Baltimore); Gorky (San Francisco); Grosz, Miró, Dali, Myers (New York); Grosz (Minneapolis); Weber (New York, Philadelphia, Washington, Chicago)

Art Briefs

Because of the war, the art capital moves from Paris to New York. Refugee artists in the United States include Léger, Lipchitz, Kisling, Mondrian, Tanguy, Masson, Tchelitchew, Chagall, Berman, Ozenfant, Zadkine, Moholy-Nagy, Dali, and Ernst • Kokoschka, called "most degenerate" by Hitler, holds the largest one-man show in the United States • The National Gallery in Washington, D.C., opens, the largest marble building in the world; it contains the Mellon, Kress, and Widener collections valued at $50 million.

Dance

At Nelson Rockefeller's request, Lincoln Kirstein and George Balanchine organize the American Ballet Caravan for a goodwill tour of Latin America; they premiere *Concerto Barocco* and *Ballet Imperial* (Balanchine), with Nicholas Magallanes and William Dollar. Alicia Markova and Anton Dolin organize the Jacob's Pillow International Dance Festival near Lee, Mass.

Other Premieres

Ballet Theatre: *Three Virgins and a Devil* (Agnes de Mille), de Mille, Lucia Chase; *Pas de Quatre* (Anton Dolin)

Martha Graham: *Letter to the World*

Doris Humphrey: *Song of the West*

Books

Fiction

Critics' Choice
The Last Tycoon, F. Scott Fitzgerald (posthumous)
Reflections in a Golden Eye, Carson McCullers
The Real Life of Sebastian Knight, Vladimir Nabokov
Fables, William Saroyan
The Hills Beyond, Thomas Wolfe (posthumous)
What Makes Sammy Run? Budd Schulberg
I'll Never Go There Any More, Jerome Weidman
Mildred Pierce, James Cain

Best-Sellers
The Keys of the Kingdom, A. J. Cronin
Random Harvest, James Hilton
This Above All, Eric Knight
The Sun Is My Undoing, Marguerite Steen
For Whom the Bell Tolls, Ernest Hemingway
Oliver Wiswell, Kenneth Roberts
H. M. Pulham, Esquire, John P. Marquand
Mr. and Mrs. Cugat, Isabel Scott Rorick
Windswept, Mary Ellen Chase
Saratoga Trunk, Edna Ferber

Nonfiction

Critics' Choice
Two-Way Passage, Louis Adamic
Twelve Million Black Voices, Richard Wright et al.
The New Critic, John Crowe Ransom
Let Us Now Praise Famous Men, James Agee, Walker Evans
A Philosophy of Literary Form, Kenneth Burke
The Mind of the South, C. F. Cash
Escape from Freedom, Erich Fromm
The Wound and the Bow, Edmund Wilson
Mythology, Edith Hamilton

Best-Sellers
Berlin Diary, William L. Shirer
The White Cliffs, Alice Duer Miller
Out of the Night, Jan Valtin
Inside Latin America, John Gunther
Blood, Sweat and Tears, Winston S. Churchill
You Can't Do Business with Hitler, Douglas Miller
Reading I've Liked, ed. Clifton Fadiman
Reveille in Washington, Margaret Leech
My Sister and I, Dirk van der Heide
Exit Laughing, Irvin S. Cobb

Poetry
Theodore Roethke, *Open House*
William Carlos Williams, *The Broken Span*
Edna St. Vincent Millay, *Collected Sonnets*
Louis Zukofsky, *55 Poems*
E. E. Cummings, *50 Poems*
Horace Gregory, *Poems 1930–1940*
Louise Bogan, *Poems and New Poems*
Robinson Jeffers, *Be Angry at the Sun*
Josephine Miles, *Poems on Several Occasions*

Pulitzer Prizes
In This Our Life, Ellen Glasgow (novel)
Reveille in Washington, Margaret Leech (U.S. history)
Crusader in Crinoline, Forrest Wilson (biography)
The Dust Which Is God, William Rose Benét

Science and Technology

Uranium and thorium are split into equal parts in the cyclotron at the University of California, Berkeley, by Glenn Seaborg and Emilio Segre.

At Berkeley, Glenn Seaborg and E. McMillan isolate plutonium, a fuel preferable to uranium for nuclear reactors.

The Manhattan Engineering District, a project to develop atomic energy for military purposes, is secretly authorized by FDR; scientists include Enrico Fermi, Leo Szilard, and Edward Teller.

RCA demonstrates a new simplified electron microscope that magnifies up to 100,000 times.

Successful treatment of pneumonia with sulfanilamide is reported by Dr. Norman Plummer.

The U.S. Indian Service reports that trachoma, a sight-destroying disease, can be cured by sulfanilamide.

Cardiac catheterization is developed by Dickinson Richards and André Cournaud.

Prevention of hemorrhage by vitamin K is announced by Dr. Henry Poncer, University of Illinois.

Standard Oil announces a new, simpler, and cheaper process of cracking oil.

The *American Medical Association Journal* describes the Sister Kenny massage method for treating infantile paralysis.

Sports ────────────────

Baseball

Ted Williams (Boston, AL) bats .400 until the last day of the season, plays despite this, and goes 6 for 9.

Joe DiMaggio (New York, AL) hits safely in 56 consecutive games; he gets 91 hits during a streak that ends in Cleveland.

Champions ─────────────

Batting	Pitching
Pete Reiser (Brooklyn, NL), .343	Elmer Riddle (Cincinnati, NL), 19–4
Ted Williams (Boston, AL), .406	Lefty Gomez (New York, AL), 15–5
	Home runs
	Ted Williams (Boston, AL), 37

Football

Elmer Layden is named NFL high commissioner.

NFL Season Leaders: Cecil Isbell (Green Bay), passing; Clarence Manders (Brooklyn), rushing; Don Hutson (Green Bay), receiving

College All-Americans: Frankie Albert (Q), Stanford; Bill Dudley (B), Virginia; Frank Sinkwich (B), Georgia

Bowls (Jan. 1, 1942)

Rose: Oregon 20–Duke 15
Orange: Georgia 40–Texas Christian 26
Cotton: Alabama 29–Texas A & M 21
Sugar: Fordham 2–Missouri 0

Other Sports

Horse Racing: Whirlaway, ridden by Eddie Arcaro, wins the Triple Crown.

Golf: Sam Snead wins the PGA tournament.

Winners ─────────────────

World Series	*College Basketball*
New York (AL) 4	Wisconsin (NCAA)
Brooklyn (NL) 1	Long Island University (NIT)
MVP	*Player of the Year*
NL–Adolph Camilli, Brooklyn	George Glamack, North Carolina
AL–Joe DiMaggio, New York	*Stanley Cup*
NFL	Boston
Chicago (Bears) 37–	*US Tennis Open*
New York 9	Men: Robert L. Riggs
MVP	Women: Sarah Palfrey Cooke
Don Hutson, Green Bay	*USGA Open*
College Football	Craig Wood
Minnesota	*Kentucky Derby*
Heisman Trophy	Whirlaway (E. Arcaro, jockey)
Bruce Smith, Minnesota	

Fashion ────────────────

For Women: Government regulations limit fabric lengths and banish pleats, more than one pocket, and trim. Civilian women follow the look of servicewomen with gray flannel suits, low-heeled shoes in polished leathers, the shoulder strap bag, and the beret or felt cloche hat. Hair is swept up and off the face, though sometimes decorated with bright little ribbon bows attached to combs and clips. At night, frilly dresses appear, along with short skirts of black crepe and long-sleeved blouses with deep décolletages. The satin evening suit is also worn with high-heeled ankle straps. With wool shortages, new fabrics are developed for new purposes: rayon and cotton stockings, cotton dresses for winter, trench and peacoats.

High-fashion note: Albouys's duster hats; the rayon crepe Molyneux dress with fuchsia sequined yoke and cyclamen sash

Joe DiMaggio, "the Yankee Clipper." *Library of Congress.*

Current fashion in clothing and cars. *Library of Congress*.

Kaleidoscope _____

- "Gentleman" Joe Louis, who defeats a contender a month, becomes a national hero.
- Eleven-year-old Lorin Maazel, who knows 22 symphonies by heart, leads the NBC Summer Symphony.
- "I'd have people buy the paintings and hang them in privies or anywhere anybody had time to look at 'em," says Thomas Hart Benton.
- St. John the Divine, the largest Gothic church in the world, opens in New York City; the Hoover Library on War, Peace and Revolution opens in Palo Alto, Calif.
- William Bishop, University of Michigan librarian, says the highly perishable nature of wood pulp threatens the preservation of documents; he suggests microfilm.
- Stalin toasts FDR at a ten-hour, seven-course dinner after the German invasion; there are 32 bottoms-up toasts in vodka and cognac.
- The Andrews sisters earn $5,000 a week—2 cents for each play of 8 million Decca records on jukeboxes.
- Liquidating some assets, William Randolph Hearst offers Gimbels and Saks part of his $50 million art collection for sale over their bargain counters; most works are bought by browsing housewives.
- The FDA seizes all heatless permanent wave preparations because they contain poisonous ammonia hydrogen sulfide.
- Pope Pius XII authorizes Roman Catholic bishops throughout the world to allow meat on Friday and omit certain fast days during the war.
- Yale, Harvard, and Princeton decide to cut their programs from four to three years by staying in session all year round.
- Claire Chennault organizes a group of American volunteers to fight in China, the Flying Tigers.
- Navy Secretary Frank Knox says that U.S. services were not "on the alert against the surprise air attack on Hawaii" and calls for a formal investigation.
- Pearl Harbor statistics: 1,500 civilians killed, 1,500 injured; 5 battleships sunk or beached (*Arizona, Oklahoma, California, Nevada, West Virginia*), 11 smaller ships destroyed, 3 ships damaged so as to be unusable; 177 planes destroyed; 91 navy officers killed, 20 wounded; 2,638 enlisted men dead, 636 wounded; 168 army men killed, 223 wounded, 26 missing.

- In his fifteenth fireside chat, FDR informs the nation that rationing will be necessary for full defense productivity; he adds: "Never before . . . has our American civilization been in such danger. . . . We must be the great arsenal of democracy."
- Thousands join the nation's industries that call for more workers; because of rising rents and the unavailability of building materials, many are forced to live in tents and tarpaper cities, raw-wood shacks, unused barns, garages, warehouses, and chicken coops.
- Major networks cancel broadcasts of their Berlin correspondents because of Nazi censorship.
- "Rosie the Riveter" (named after Rosina Bonavita) becomes the emblem of the American woman working in defense industries.
- After the opening of the Russian front, the peacetime draft is accelerated; "Uncle Sam Needs You" signs are posted in all public places.
- A Gallup Poll reveals that 60 percent of the public wants to aid Britain even if it risks war; 12 percent would go to war immediately.
- Goods shipped to England include Spam, a new kind of canned and processed meat, dehydrated meats, vegetables, and fruits; similar products begin to appear at home.
- With the shortage of certain metals, use of plastics increases; Philip Wrigley, in gum packaging, introduces cellophane in place of tinfoil; Lucky Strike substitutes a white and red bullseye logo for its green and red one, since green ink contains metal.
- With prices rising, FDR establishes the Office of Price Administration (OPA); priorities are set on civilian supplies: for example, spices, wine, palm oil, burlap, and tea are labeled nonessential.
- With the improvement in the economy, car sales soar; alcohol consumption also rises.
- Henry Ford, for the first time, agrees to negotiate with a union.
- Chrysler begins building the M-3 tank; GM, the B-25 bomber; Ford, Pratt Whitney engines.
- With soaring box office receipts Hollywood can barely produce films fast enough, and many westerns and grade B and C films are released.
- Greta Garbo, 36, retires after *Two-Faced Woman;* the film is banned in Rhode Island as "immoral."
- Charles Chaplin rejects the New York Film Critics' best male actor award because it implies competition.
- Cary Grant donates his entire salary, $137,500, from *The Man Who Came to Dinner* to British war relief.
- A *Photoplay* poll reports that the best figures in Hollywood belong to Betty Grable and Errol Flynn.

Fads: The saying "Kilroy was here," the congo, Lindy hop, and kangaroo jump

First Appearances: Rationing of silk stockings, Quonset huts, Merrill, Lynch, Pierce, Fenner, and Beane, furniture with plastic vinylite, Cheerios, Spice Island, Buitoni foods, paprika mill, municipally owned parking, Chemex coffee maker, "Sad Sack," health insurance clause in labor contract (ILGWU), heredity clinic, motion picture professorship (New York University)

1942

Ration coupon. *Smithsonian Institution.*

Deaths

John Barrymore, George M.
  Cohan, Michel Fokine,
  Condé Nast, Otis Skinner,
  Grant Wood.

In the News

MANILA FALLS, MACARTHUR RETREATS TO BATAAN . . . BURMA IS INVADED . . . SINGAPORE AND RANGOON FALL . . . FDR ASKS FOR 60,000 PLANES AND 45,000 TANKS . . . $58 BILLION BUDGET ALLOTS $52 BILLION FOR DEFENSE . . . WAR PRODUCTION BOARD IS ESTABLISHED . . . LATIN-AMERICAN TIES TO GERMANY AND ITALY ARE SEVERED . . . U.S. TROOPS LAND IN NORTHERN IRELAND . . . EMERGENCY PRICE CONTROL ACT IS PASSED . . . U.S. AND BRITAIN COMBINE CHIEFS OF STAFF . . . PRESIDENTIAL ORDER RELOCATES WEST COAST JAPANESE . . . JAPANESE WIN IN BATTLE OF JAVA SEA . . . MACARTHUR LEAVES PHILIPPINES FOR AUSTRALIA . . . WAR PRODUCTION BOARD STOPS ALL NONESSENTIAL BUILDING . . . JAPANESE TAKE SOLOMONS . . . BATAAN FALLS, WAINWRIGHT SURRENDERS . . . DOOLITTLE LEADS AIR RAID ON TOKYO . . . NAZIS BURN LIDICE IN REPRISAL FOR HEYDRICH ASSASSINATION . . . RAF RAIDS COLOGNE . . . JAPANESE SUFFER FIRST LOSSES IN CORAL SEA BATTLE . . . ROMMEL TAKES TOBRUK . . . WILLKIE RETURNS FROM OVERSEAS MISSION . . . COFFEE, SUGAR, AND GAS RATIONING BEGINS . . . GERMANS REACH STALINGRAD . . . NAVY WINS MAJOR BATTLE AT MIDWAY . . . JAPANESE OCCUPY ALEUTIANS . . . OFFICE OF STRATEGIC SERVICES FORMS . . . FDR AND CHURCHILL CONFER IN D.C. . . . SCRAP RUBBER DRIVE BEGINS . . . WACS, WAVES, SPARS RECRUIT . . . $25,000 SALARY CEILING IS INSTITUTED . . . MARINES LAND ON GUADALCANAL . . . ALLIES RAID DIEPPE AND SUFFER HEAVY LOSSES . . . MONTGOMERY'S TANKS SHATTER ROMMEL'S FORCES AT EL ALAMEIN . . . HALSEY DEFEATS JAPANESE IN SOLOMONS . . . WPA ENDS, GIVEN "HONORABLE DISCHARGE" . . . 400,000 U.S.-BRITISH FORCES UNDER EISENHOWER LAND IN NORTH AFRICA . . . 492 DIE IN COCOANUT GROVE FIRE, BOSTON.

Quotes _____

"This is a civilians' war—and as civilians, we must face the fury of our enemies, who have no respect for an 'open city' nor an unarmed opponent."
— N. Y. State Council of Defense

"Hard work isn't hard—it's a badge of courage. That 'old clothes look' doesn't matter. It's smart to be mended. . . . Conservation is a war weapon in the hands of every man, woman, and child."
— Office of Civilian Defense

"When we are dealing with the Caucasian race [in America], we have methods that will test . . . loyalty. But when we deal with the Japanese, we are in an entirely different field."
— California attorney general Earl Warren, on evacuating the Japanese to relocation camps

"Has the Gestapo come to America? Have we not risen in righteous anger at Hitler's mistreatment of the Jews? Then, is it not incongruous that citizen Americans of Japanese descent should be similarly mistreated and persecuted?"
— Miki Masoka, before the Tolan Committee, National Defense Migration Hearings

Library of Congress.

"We come among you to repulse the cruel invaders. . . . Help us where you are able. *Viva la France éternelle!*
— FDR, as U.S. troops invade French North Africa

"The President of the United States ordered me to break through the Japanese lines and proceed from Corregidor to Australia for the purpose of organizing the American offense against Japan. . . . I came through and I shall return."
— Gen. Douglas MacArthur

Smithsonian Institution.

Ads _____

Radio

Premieres
"Suspense," Joe Kearns
"Stage Door Canteen," Bert Lytell
"People Are Funny," Art Baker, Art Linkletter
"It Pays to be Ignorant," Tom Howard
"This Is War," Fredric March

Specials
"America Speaks to China," with Chinese journalist Yen Ying Yen (eight dramas by Pearl Buck translated and shortwaved to China)

Top Ten
"Chase and Sanborn Hour," "Jack Benny," "Fibber McGee and Molly," "Lux Radio Theater," "Aldrich Family," "Bob Hope," "Maxwell House Coffee Time," "Walter Winchell," "Kate Smith Hour," and "Fitch Bandwagon"

Of Note
Frances Langford, on "Command Performance," broadcasts, via 13 shortwave stations, song requests to U.S. troops throughout the world • "This Is War," written by famous authors and performed with extensive sound effects, is broadcast on the four major networks.

New Catchphrases: "Hey Abbott! I'm a ba-a-a-d boy" (Abbott and Costello); "It pays to be ignorant, To be dumb, to be dense, to be ignorant. / It pays to be ignorant, / Just like me!" ("It Pays to Be Ignorant" theme song)

TV

Training programs for air-raid wardens are televised.

Movies

Openings
Mrs. Miniver (William Wyler), Greer Garson, Walter Pidgeon
Casablanca (Michael Curtiz), Ingrid Bergman, Humphrey Bogart
The Magnificent Ambersons (Orson Welles), Tim Holt, Joseph Cotten, Anne Baxter, Dolores Costello Barrymore
Pride of the Yankees (Sam Wood), Gary Cooper, Teresa Wright
Random Harvest (Mervyn LeRoy), Ronald Colman, Greer Garson
Wake Island (John Farrow), Brian Donlevy, William Bendix
Yankee Doodle Dandy (Michael Curtiz), James Cagney, Walter Huston
Now, Voyager (Irving Rapper), Bette Davis, Paul Henreid
Tortilla Flat (Victor Fleming), Spencer Tracy, John Garfield, Hedy Lamarr
Woman of the Year (George Stevens), Spencer Tracy, Katharine Hepburn
In Which We Serve (Noel Coward, David Lean), Noel Coward, John Mills
To Be or Not to Be (Ernst Lubitsch), Jack Benny, Carole Lombard
Sullivan's Travels (Preston Sturges), Joel McCrea, Veronica Lake
Road to Morocco (David Butler), Bob Hope, Bing Crosby, Dorothy Lamour
The Battle of Midway (John Ford), documentary
Cat People (Jacques Tourneur), Simone Simon

Academy Awards
Best Picture: *Mrs. Miniver*
Best Director: William Wyler (*Mrs. Miniver*)
Best Actress: Greer Garson (*Mrs. Miniver*)
Best Actor: James Cagney (*Yankee Doodle Dandy*)

Top Box-Office Stars
Abbott and Costello, Clark Gable, Gary Cooper, Mickey Rooney, Bob Hope, James Cagney, Gene Autry, Betty Grable, Greer Garson, Spencer Tracy

Stars of Tomorrow
Van Heflin, Eddie Bracken, Jane Wyman, John Carroll, Alan Ladd, Lynn Bari, Nancy Kelly, Donna Reed, Betty Hutton, Teresa Wright

Popular Music ___

Hit Songs
"Don't Get Around Much
   Anymore"
"Praise the Lord and Pass the
   Ammunition!"
"Rosie, the Riveter"
"Serenade in Blue"
"Happiness Is a Thing Called Joe"
"In the Blue of Evening"
"I Left My Heart at the Stage
   Door Canteen"
"A String of Pearls"
"When the Lights Go on Again"
"We'll Meet Again"
"That Old Black Magic"
"You'd Be So Nice to Come
   Home To"
"This Is the Army, Mr. Jones"

Jitterbugging at a Washington, D.C., Elks' Club dance. *Library of Congress.*

Top Records
Don't Sit under the Apple Tree (Andrews Sisters); *White Christmas, Moonlight Becomes You* (Bing Crosby); *Sleepy Lagoon* (Xavier Cugat); *He Wears a Pair of Silver Wings* (Kate Smith); *Strip Polka* (Kay Kyser); *Why Don't You Do Right?* (Peggy Lee, Benny Goodman); *I've Got a Gal in Kalamazoo* (Glenn Miller); *Paper Doll* (Mills Brothers); *I Had the Craziest Dream* (Helen Forrest); *Der Fuehrer's Face* (Spike Jones)

Jazz and Big Bands
Max Roach joins Charlie Parker at Monroe's, New York. Swing bands become service bands.

Top Performers (*Downbeat):* Benny Goodman (soloist); Duke Ellington (big band); Tommy Dorsey (sweet band); Eddie Condon, Buddy Rich, Johnny Hodges, Tex Beneke, Pee Wee Russell, Roy Eldridge (instrumentalists); Helen Forrest, Frank Sinatra (vocalists)

Theater ___

Broadway Openings

Plays
The Skin of Our Teeth (Thornton Wilder), Tallulah Bankhead, Fredric March, Florence Eldridge, Montgomery Clift
The Eve of St. Mark (Maxwell Anderson), William Prince
Without Love (Philip Barry), Katharine Hepburn, Elliott Nugent
The Pirate (S. N. Behrman), Alfred Lunt, Lynn Fontanne, Estelle Winwood
Flare Path (Terence Rattigan), Alec Guinness, Nancy Kelly
The Morning Star (Emlyn Williams), Gregory Peck, Gladys Cooper

Musicals
By Jupiter (Richard Rodgers, Lorenz Hart), Benay Venuta, Ray Bolger, Constance Moore
Rosalinda (Johann Strauss, Paul Kerby), Dorothy Sarnoff, Gene Barry
Star and Garter (Irving Berlin et al., burlesque), Bobby Clark, Gypsy Rose Lee
This Is the Army (Irving Berlin), Ezra Stone, Irving Berlin, all-soldier cast

Irving Berlin's musical *This Is the Army,* with its all-army cast. *Billy Rose Theatre Collection. The New York Public Library at Lincoln Center. Astor, Lenox and Tilden Foundations.*

Classics and Revivals On and Off Broadway
The Three Sisters (Chekhov), Katharine Cornell, Judith Anderson, Ruth Gordon, Kirk Douglas; *Candida* (George Bernard Shaw), Katharine Cornell, Burgess Meredith, Raymond Massey, Mildred Natwick; *The Rivals* (Sheridan), Mary Boland, Walter Hampden

Pulitzer Prize
No prize is awarded.

Classical Music

Compositions

George Antheil, Symphony no. 4
Samuel Barber, Essay for Orchestra, no. 2
William Schuman, Secular Cantata no. 2, *A Free Song*
Roy Harris, Symphony no. 5, *American Ballads, Piano Concerto with Band,* Violin Sonata
Douglas Moore, Wind Quintet
Walter Piston, Quintet for Flute and Strings
Roger Sessions, Duo for Violin and Piano
Igor Stravinsky (in U.S.), *Dances Concertantes*

Important Events

The United States becomes the world music center and shelter for foreign musicians Bruno Walter, George Szell, Béla Bartók (Columbia University), Darius Milhaud (Mills College), Ernst Krenek (Vassar), Arnold Schoenberg (University of South Carolina), Paul Hindemith (Yale), Kurt Weill, and Ernest Toch.

Toscanini conducts the New York Philharmonic in six all-Beethoven concerts.

At NBC, Toscanini plays the music of American composers Paul Creston (*Choric Dance*), Morton Gould (*Lincoln Legend*), Charles Martin Loeffler (*Memories of My Childhood*), and George Gershwin (*Rhapsody in Blue,* with Earl Wild and Benny Goodman).

Shostakovitch's Symphony no. 7 gains world attention; it is sent to the United States on microfilm through enemy lines before its performance by Toscanini and the NBC Symphony.

American works to gain most attention during the year are William Schuman's Symphony no. 3 (Boston) and Symphony no. 4 (Cleveland).

Debut: Earl Wild

First Performances

Samuel Barber, Violin Concerto (Boston); Carlos Chávez, Piano Concerto (New York); John Cage, *Imaginary Landscape no. 3* (Chicago); Harl McDonald, *Bataan* (tribute to Douglas MacArthur, Washington); Paul Creston, *A Fanfare for Paratroopers* (Cincinnati); Darius Milhaud, *Fanfare de la liberté;* also commissioned by Cincinnati: *Lincoln Portrait* (Copland); *The Mayor La Guardia Waltzes* (Virgil Thomson); *Mark Twain* (Jerome Kern); Oscar Levant, playing his Concerto in One Movement (NBC radio); David Diamond, Symphony no. 1 (New York); Copland, *Statements* for Orchestra (New York)

Opera

Metropolitan: Helen Traubel, *Tristan und Isolde;* Eleanor Steber, *Le nozze di Figaro;* Leonard Warren, Astrid Varnay, Raoul Jobin, *The Island God* (Gian Carlo Menotti, George Szell, conducting, premiere); Lily Djanel, *Carmen*

New Opera Company, New York: *Solomon and Balkis* (Randall Thompson, premiere and on radio)

Chicago: *A Tree on the Plains* (Ernest Bacon); all-black *Aïda* (Chicago Negro Opera Guild)

Philadelphia: *Ramuntcho* (Deems Taylor, premiere)

Music Note

E. Power Biggs begins his Sunday morning organ recitals in Cambridge, Mass.; they are broadcast nationally and internationally by shortwave.

Weekend pass at the United Service Organization (USO). *Library of Congress.*

Art

Painting

Thomas Hart Benton, *July Hay and Negro Soldier, Invasion*

Marsden Hartley, *Evening Storm, Schoodic, Maine*

Ralston Crawford, *Elevators for the Bridge*

Edward Hopper, *Cobb's House, South Truro*

Isabel Bishop, *Card Game*

Stuart Davis, *Ursine Park*

Mark Tobey, *Threading Light, The Void Devouring the Gadget Era*

Arshile Gorky, *Bull in the Sun*

Yves Tanguy, *Slowly toward the North*

Pavel Tchelitchew, *Hide and Seek*

Jackson Pollock, *Moon Woman*

John Steuart Curry paints murals for the University of Wisconsin Law School and Kansas State Capitol Building.

Sculpture

Chaim Gross, *Acrobatic Dancers*

Theodore Roszak, *Vertical Composition*

Alexander Calder, *Constellation with Red Object*

Joseph Cornell, *Homage to the Romantic Ballet, A Pantry Ballet (for Jacques Offenbach)*

Jo Davidson, *Bust of Vice-President Wallace*

José de Creeft, *Himalaya*

Architecture

The Saarinens and Robert Swanson win the design competition for Wayne University, Detroit.

Church of Saints Peter and Paul, Pierre, S.D. (Barry Byrne)

Kramer Homes, Center Line, Mich. (Eliel and Eero Saarinen)

Packaged House System for General Panel Corporation (Gropius, Wachsmann)

Important Exhibitions

Numerous shows benefit war causes: "Dutch Masters" (for the Queen Wilhelmina Fund); El Greco (for Greek relief); Cézanne (for the Fighting French); Yasuo Kuniyoshi (United Chinese Relief); at the Metropolitan Museum of Art, "Artists for Victory"; at the Museum of Modern Art, the poster exhibit,

Corset display at R. H. Macy's. *Library of Congress.*

"Road to Victory (text by Carl Sandburg, photos by Lt. Comm. Edward Steichen).

Museums

New York: *Metropolitan:* Rembrandt; Gallatin posters of the nineties; "As Russia Saw Us in 1812"; "Originals of Renaissance in Fashion 1942." *Museum of Modern Art:* Eighteen artists from nine states; John Flannagan; Pavel Tchelitchew

Boston: Paul Revere

Chicago: Henri Rousseau; Grant Wood; "Hudson River School"

Baltimore: Age of the icon

Art Briefs

An important one-man show is held in New York by the little-known Marc Chagall • Yves Tanguy and others present "Artists in Exile" in New York • The "First Papers of Surrealism," with Robert Motherwell, David Hare, and William Baziotes, are exhibited at the Whitelaw Reid Mansion, New York • The Metropolitan Museum of Art leases a concrete and steel vault in which to store its treasures during wartime • Wendell Willkie brings 80 paintings and drawings from China to the Metropolitan for display • The Tennessee National Gallery of Art and Santa Barbara Museum of American Art open.

Dance

Michel Fokine restages *Petrouchka* for Ballet Theatre; he dies while working on *Helen of Troy*. George Balanchine stages an elephant ballet to Stravinsky for Ringling Brothers and Barnum and Bailey.

Ballet Theatre: *Pillar of Fire* (Antony Tudor, Arnold Schoenberg), Harold Laing, Nora Kaye; *Helen of Troy* (Fokine, David Lichine)

Ballet Russe de Monte Carlo: *Rodeo* (Agnes de Mille), de Mille

Books

Fiction

Critics' Choice

Go Down Moses, William Faulkner
Never Come Morning, Nelson Algren
The Just and the Unjust, James Gould Cozzens
Until the Day Break, Louis Bromfield
The Robber Bridegroom, Eudora Welty
The Unvanquished, Howard Fast
Valley of Decision, Marcia Davenport

Best-Sellers

The Song of Bernadette, Franz Werfel
The Moon Is Down, John Steinbeck

GI favorite pinup Betty Grable, whose legs are insured with Lloyds of London. *Movie Star News.*

Dragon Seed, Pearl S. Buck
And Now Tomorrow, Rachel Field
Drivin' Woman, Elizabeth Pickett
Windswept, Mary Ellen Chase
The Robe, Lloyd C. Douglas
The Keys of the Kingdom, A. J. Cronin
Kings Row, Henry Bellamann
The Sun Is My Undoing, Marguerite Steen

Nonfiction

Critics' Choice

Lee's Lieutenants, D. S. Freeman
Men on Bataan, John Hersey
The Managerial Revolution, James Burnham
Our Fighting Faith, James B. Conant
Storm over the Land, Carl Sandburg
Willard Gibbs, Muriel Rukeyser
On Native Grounds, Alfred Kazin
Generation of Vipers, Philip Wylie
Last Train from Berlin, Howard K. Smith
No Day of Triumph, J. Saunders Redding

Best-Sellers

See Here, Private Hargrove, Marion Hargrove
Mission to Moscow, Joseph E. Davies

Cross Creek, Marjorie Kinnan Rawlings
Victory through Air Power, Maj. Alexander O. de Seversky
Past Imperfect, Ilka Chase
They Were Expendable, W. L. White
Flight to Arras, Antoine de Saint-Exupéry
Washington Is Like That, W. M. Kiplinger
The Last Time I Saw Paris, Elliot Paul
Inside Latin America, John Gunther

Poetry

Wallace Stevens, *Parts of a World, Notes toward a Supreme Fiction*
John Berryman, *Poems*
Randall Jarrell, *Blood for a Stranger*
Kenneth Patchen, *The Teeth of the Lion*
J. V. Cunningham, *The Helmsman*

Pulitzer Prizes

Dragon's Teeth, Upton Sinclair (novel)
Paul Revere and the World He Lived In, Esther Forbes (U.S. history)
Admiral of the Ocean Sea, Samuel Eliot Morison (biography)
The Witness Tree, Robert Frost (poetry)

Science and Technology

The first safe self-sustaining nuclear chain reaction is accomplished by Enrico Fermi, Edward Teller, and Leo Szilard, at the University of Chicago.

Louis Fieser, at Harvard, develops napalm, a jellylike mixture of gasoline and palm oils that sticks to its target until it burns out.

Bazookas, shoulder-held rocket containers used as antitank weapons, are developed.

Radar comes into operational use.

A jet-propelled plane is tested by Bell Aircraft.

A synthetic morphinelike substance, demerol, said to be nonaddictive, is developed by Dr. David Climento, at Winthop Laboratories.

The vagotomy operation for the treatment of ulcers is introduced.

Radioactive iodine therapy is developed as an alternative to surgery for overactive thyroid.

Tubeless tires are successfully tested.

LORAN (Long-Range Air Navigation) goes into operation; it diagrams the air and sea like streets.

Sports ━━━━━━━━━━━━━━━━━━━━

Baseball
Stan Musial (St. Louis, NL) hits .315 in his first full
season.

Champions ━━━━━━━━━━━━━━

Batting
Ernie Lombardi (Cincinnati,
NL), .330
Ted Williams (Boston, AL),
.356

Pitching
John Beasley (St. Louis,
NL), 21–6
Ernie Bonham (New York,
AL), 21–5
Home runs
Ted Williams (Boston, AL),
36

Football
Don Hutson (E), Green Bay, sets an NFL season
scoring record, 138 points on 17 touchdowns.
Cecil Isbell (QB), Green Bay, is the first to pass for
2,000 yards in a season.

NFL Season Leaders: Cecil Isbell (Green Bay),
passing; Bill Dudley (Pittsburgh), rushing; Don
Hutson (Green Bay), receiving.

College All-Americans: Paul Governali (Q),
Columbia; Mike Holovak (B), Boston College.

Bowls (Jan. 1, 1943)
Rose: Georgia 9–UCLA 0
Orange: Alabama 37–Boston College 21
Cotton: Texas 14–Georgia Tech 7
Sugar: Tennessee 14–Tulsa 7

More than 350 colleges abandon football "for the
duration."

Hitler toilet paper. *Smithsonian Institution.*

Other Sports

Boxing: The heavyweight title is frozen as Joe Louis
enters the service.

Winners ━━━━━━━━━━━━━━

World Series
St. Louis (NL) 4
New York (AL) 1
MVP
NL–Morton Cooper, St.
Louis
AL–Joe Gordon, New York
NFL
Washington 14-Chicago
(Bears) 6
MVP
Don Hutson, Green Bay

College Football
Ohio State
Heisman Trophy
Frank Sinkwich, Georgia
College Basketball
West Virginia (NIT)
Stanford (NCAA)
Player of the Year
Stan Modzelewski, Rhode
Island State
Stanley Cup
Toronto
US Tennis Open
Men: Ted Shroeder
Women: Pauline Betz
Kentucky Derby
Shut Out (W. D. Wright,
jockey)

Fashion ━━━━━━━━━━━━━━━━━━

For Women: Emphasis remains on practical,
inconspicuous styles: wartime regulations allow for
little difference between high-style and inexpensive
clothing, apart from fabric. Suit jackets are cut with
peplums and with short, straight skirts. Striped wool
jersey middies appear over pleated wools; shirtwaists
are popular. What clothes lack in innovation they
gain in color, especially greens, pinks, and reds;
blouses, skirts, jackets, and snoods contrast in
brilliant color. Also new are ballet slippers with
winding ribbons, strapped and platform shoes, and
the enormously successful sling-back platform pump
with open toe. Jet is worn with everything, and short
satin evening skirts appear with lace blouses in a
variety of colors. The official regulations for
women's dress: no more than a two-inch hem, no
skirt more than 22 inches around, no more than one
patch pocket, no attached hoods or shawls, no coat
cuffs, no zippers or metal fastenings (wraparounds
instead), no silk stockings (cotton or rayon instead).
(Eyebrow pencil lines the naked leg to give the
illusion of hose.)

Kaleidoscope _____

- New Year's Day is proclaimed a National Day of Prayer; the president leads the nation "asking God's help in the days to come."
- Eligible for the draft are single men 18 to 35 and married men 18 to 26.
- Service flags hang in millions of windows, a star for each of the nation's 8 million sons in the service.
- The face of New York's Time Square changes: lights on Roseland, the Astor, and all high places are dimmed so that ships at sea are not betrayed to U-boats.
- Sales of women's trousers are five to ten times greater than last year.
- Willow Run, Detroit, becomes the fastest growing city in the United States, as thousands move there for defense work.
- The OPA stops all car and truck production; sugar, tire, and gas rationing begins: "A" stickers for cars used only for pleasure; "B," to drive to work; "C," to drive at work; "E," emergency vehicles.
- Boy Scouts salvage 150,000 tons of wastepaper; children receive 50 cents a pound per aluminum foil ball; Los Angeles contributes 6 tons of car tires to the nationwide rubber drive; Victory Book rallies are held throughout the country; 600,000 books are donated to the armed services through a New York Public Library two-week drive.
- One billion pounds of plastics are produced for use in everything from airplanes to hose nozzles; metal is replaced in every possible way.
- Of the vegetables consumed in the United States, 40 percent is grown in Victory Gardens; two-thirds of the crop had been grown by the Japanese-Americans now detained in camps.
- Over 900 translator-censors work in the New York Post Office examining foreign mail.
- Winston Churchill receives from his American admirers an extraordinary number of letters and gifts, including corncob pipes, a Shriner's hat, a set of Indian arrowheads, a turkey wishbone (the V-symbol), and a copy of George Washington's will.
- Soldiers at California's Camp Callan vote Rita Hayworth "proxy mother" for Mother's Day.
- Among those in the armed forces are Gene Autry, Richard Barthelmess, Jackie Coogan, Broderick Crawford, Douglas Fairbanks, Raymond Massey, Burgess Meredith, Robert Montgomery, Cesar Romero, James Stewart, Robert Stack, Spencer Tracy, Darryl Zanuck, Frank Capra, John Ford, and Hal Roach. Clark Gable enlists at 41.
- Eighty war movies are made.
- Carole Lombard and 20 others die in a TWA transport crash; she was on a tour selling War Bonds.
- The first open-air base hospital opens in Bataan.
- Songwriter Frank Loesser reads about a chaplain at Pearl Harbor who tells his congregation to "Praise the Lord and pass the ammunition. . . ."
- Billy Mitchell is posthumously restored to the rank of major general.

110,000 Japanese Americans are sent to "relocation" centers by executive order. *Library of Congress.*

- The Nobel Prize ceremonies, discontinued in Stockholm since 1939, take place at a dinner at the Waldorf Astoria, New York.
- Blacks complain of discrimination in the services, especially the navy.
- Thomas Mann joins the staff of the Library of Congress.
- Lew Ayres leaves Hollywood for a conscientious objectors' camp after his refusal to bear arms; his films are banned in 100 Chicago theaters; he later joins the army as a noncombatant.
- Dooley Wilson sings "As Time Goes By" in *Casablanca,* from the 1931 Broadway flop *Everybody's Welcome.*
- RCA Victor sprays gold over a recording of Glenn Miller's *Chattanooga Choo Choo* for having sold more than 1 million copies, the first "gold record."
- After the musicians' strike against the major record companies, Frank Sinatra leaves Tommy Dorsey to take his first club date at the Rio Bomba in New York and is highly successful.
- Hedda Hopper's contract with the *Chicago Tribune* and *New York News* syndicate challenges the queen of the gossipers, Louella Parsons.
- The romances of Mickey Rooney and Ava Gardner and Barbara Hutton and Cary Grant are highly publicized.
- Enrico Fermi secretly accomplishes a controlled nuclear fission reaction at the University of Chicago gym; in a coded message he informs FDR: "The Italian navigator has entered the new world."
- FDR has four sons on the front lines.
- A Japanese submarine fires about 25 shells at an oil refinery near Santa Barbara, California, the first attack on the American mainland.
- Reports of the deportation of Jews from Occupied Western Europe reach the United States.
- The Japanese execute three fliers captured during General Doolittle's raid on Tokyo.

First Appearances: Daylight Savings Time, three-cent "Win the War" stamp, nylon parachute, K rations packed by Wrigley Company, air raids and sirens, periodic blackout drills, zinc-coated pennies, Hunt Foods, Paine Webber, Jackson and Curtis, Dannon yogurt, Kellogg's Raisin Bran, *Yank* magazine

1943

Facts and Figures

Economic Profile
  Dow-Jones: ↑ High 146–
    Low 119
  GNP: +21%
  Inflation: +3.0%
  Unemployment: 1.9%
Daily newspapers: 2,043
Books published: 8,035
IRS collections: $22.5 billion
Airmail postage: 8¢
Postcard: 1¢
Rogers Peet boys' shoes:
  $5.45
Wanamaker men's shoes:
  $6.45
Tailored Woman alligator
  purse: $25
Dude ranch, New York State:
  $29 (week)
Maine resort: $6 (daily)
Two-gallon fish tank: 49¢
Guppies, snails: 5¢
Angel fish, tetras: 12¢
Talking doll: $5.95
Nelly Bee weaving set: $1.59

Deaths

Stephen Vincent Benét,
  George Washington
  Carver, Lorenz Hart,
  Marsden Hartley, Leslie
  Howard, Karl Landsteiner,
  Sergei Rachmaninoff,
  W. S. Van Dyke, Conrad
  Veidt, Beatrice Webb,
  Alexander Woollcott.

In the News

FDR AND CHURCHILL MEET AT CASABLANCA AND SET GOAL OF UNCONDITIONAL SURRENDER . . . DAYLIGHT BOMBING OF GERMANY BEGINS . . . JAPANESE COLLAPSE ON GUADALCANAL . . . FORCES UNDER PATTON RECAPTURE KASSERINE PASS, TUNISIA . . . FLYING FORTRESSES DESTROY 21 JAPANESE SHIPS IN BISMARCK SEA . . . POINT RATIONING SYSTEM IS SET . . . FREE FRENCH FORM UNDER DE GAULLE . . . AMERICAN FORCES TAKE TUNIS . . . U.S. RETAKES ATTU IN ALEUTIANS . . . GERMAN ARMIES IN NORTH AFRICA SURRENDER . . . NAZIS MASSACRE THOUSANDS IN WARSAW GHETTO UPRISING . . . "PAY AS YOU GO" INCOME TAX BEGINS, 20% IS WITHHELD . . . TROOPS QUELL DETROIT RACE RIOT, 34 DIE . . . RUSSIANS DESTROY GERMAN ARMY AT STALINGRAD . . . FDR ORDERS ICKES TO TAKE OVER MINES DURING STRIKE THREAT . . . ALLIES UNDER PATTON INVADE SICILY . . . SUPREME COURT RULES FLAG SALUTE OPTIONAL IN SCHOOL . . . ASSAULT ON SALERNO ESTABLISHES ITALIAN BEACHHEAD . . . NAPLES FALLS TO ALLIES . . . ITALY SURRENDERS UNCONDITIONALLY, MUSSOLINI ABDICATES . . . GERMANS RETREAT FROM CAUCASUS . . . CONGRESS FAVORS U.S. IN WORLD ORGANIZATION 360–29 . . . UNITED NATIONS RESCUE RELIEF ASSOCIATION IS FORMED . . . JAPANESE SUFFER WORST LOSSES TO DATE AT RABAUL . . . TARAWA IS TAKEN . . . AMERICANS LAND IN BOUGAINVILLE . . . STALIN AND FDR MEET AT TEHERAN . . . USSR AND CZECH EXILE GOVERNMENTS AGREE ON POSTWAR COLLABORATION . . . QUOTAS REPLACE CHINESE EXCLUSION IMMIGRATION LAW . . . IKE IS NAMED COMMANDER, ALLIED EUROPEAN FORCES . . . ALLIES POUND PAS DE CALAIS IN GIANT AIR RAID . . . GOVERNMENT SEIZES RAILROADS TO FORESTALL STRIKE.

Quotes

Yes, we have no Cassino
We have no Cassino today.
We have Aversa, Caserta, Mignano, Minturno
And dear old Napolii,
But, yes, we have no Cassino
We have no Cassino today.

— Popular GI song in Italy

STAMP OUT
Black Markets with your ration stamps.
Pay no more than legal prices.

— OPA

"Wear it up, wear it out, make it do, or do without."

— Home front saying

FIRST THING I SEE—in a MAN
  "His mouth" (Ellen Drew)
  "His dignity" (Dorothy Lamour)
  "His speaking voice" (Mary Martin)
  "His eyes" (Joan Fontaine)

—in a WOMAN
  "The general stance" (Tyrone Power)
  "The face" (Gary Cooper)
  "Her hands" (Brian Aherne)
  "It depends on the woman" (Bob Hope)

— *Photoplay*

U.S. Flying Fortresses bomb Stuttgart, Germany, one of many massive air raids on Axis military and industrial targets. *Library of Congress.*

"To American productivity, without which this war would have been lost."

— Joseph Stalin's toast at Teheran

"I know how easy it is . . . for a girl to be tempted to foresake her chastity . . . especially in these times when human life is uncertain, . . . especially still if the boy is in uniform. Our salvation . . . lies within us, in a hard-boiled code of wartime morals."

— Actress Bonita Granville

Ads

A High Honor for Your Daughter
"They're great believers in eugenics, these Nazis. They're strong for selective breeding. . . . Your daughter . . . well, if she's young and healthy, and strong, a Gauleiter with an eye for beauty may decide she is a perfect specimen."

(American Locomotive)

"It is not pleasant to have your peaceful life upset by . . . wartime restrictions. . . . It is not pleasant to die, either. . . . By your actions, . . . a certain number of men will die or they will come through alive. Sure as fate, you . . . [can] save the lives of some men who will otherwise die because you let the war last too long. . . . You cannot, in fairness to them, complain or waste or shirk . . . in the name of God and your fellow man.

(Citizens Service Corps)

Pass the Ammunition
Oldsmobile workers have been doing it for nearly two years. Backing up our fighting men with volume production of fire-power.

(Oldsmobile)

Even in wartime, free America still enjoys many "better things" which are not available to less fortunate peoples.

(P. Ballantine & Sons)

Well—Shut my Mouth
I shut my mouth on a Kleenex tissue
To give my lipstick that neat, natural look.
These days it's a crime to stain a towel.

(Kleenex)

Radio

Premieres

"The Dunninger Show," Joseph Dunninger
"Nick Carter, Master Detective," Lon Clark
"Perry Mason," Bartlett Robinson
"A Date with Judy," Dellie Ellis
"Meet Corliss Archer," Janet Waldo
"Theatre Guild on the Air," Lawrence Langner
"Blind Date," Arlene Francis
"The Buster Brown Gang," Ed McConnell
"Cisco Kid," Jackson Beck
"The Judy Canova Show"

Most Popular Variety Shows: "Army Hour" (from army camps), "Basin Street Chamber Music Society," "Bing Crosby," "Broadway Showtime," "Ed Sullivan Entertains," "Gay Nineties Revue," "Kate Smith Variety Show," "Meet Your Navy," "Paul Whiteman," "Stage Door Canteen," "This Is Fort Dix"

Most Popular Music Programs: "Cities Service," "Boston Symphony," "Cleveland Symphony," "Metropolitan Opera Auditions," "NBC Symphony Orchestra," "New York Philharmonic," "Salt Lake Tabernacle Choir, Stradivarius Orchestra," "Telephone Hour," "Voice of Firestone"

Of Note

Arguments intensify over the value of soap opera and of news editorializing • NBC is forced to sell its blue network, which later becomes ABC.

New Catchphrases: Pancho: "Cisco, the sheriff and hees posse . . . they are comeeng closer." Cisco: "This way, Pancho, *Vamonos*" ("Cisco Kid"); "Pardon me for talking in your face, Señorita" ("The Judy Canova Show").

Movies

Openings

The Ox-Bow Incident (William A. Wellman), Henry Fonda, Dana Andrews
For Whom the Bell Tolls (Sam Wood), Gary Cooper, Ingrid Bergman
The Human Comedy (Clarence Brown), Mickey Rooney, Frank Morgan
Madame Curie (Mervyn LeRoy), Greer Garson, Walter Pidgeon
The More the Merrier (Geroge Stevens), Jean Arthur, Joel McCrea
Stage Door Canteen (Frank Borzage), all-star cast
The Song of Bernadette (Henry King), Jennifer Jones, Charles Bickford
Watch on the Rhine (Herman Shumlin), Paul Lukas, Bette Davis
Five Graves to Cairo (Billy Wilder), Franchot Tone, Anne Baxter
Lassie Come Home (Fred M. Wilcox), Roddy McDowall, Donald Crisp
The Phantom of the Opera (Arthur Lubin), Nelson Eddy, Claude Rains
Air Force (Howard Hawks), John Garfield, Arthur Kennedy
I Walked with a Zombie (Jacques Tourneur), Frances Dee, Tim Conway
Guadalcanal Diary (Lewis Seiler), William Bendix, Lloyd Nolan, Preston Foster
Shadow of a Doubt (Alfred Hitchcock), Joseph Cotten, Teresa Wright
Ivan the Terrible (Sergei Eisenstein), N. Cherkassov

Whether Humphrey Bogart and Ingrid Bergman would go off together in the last scene of *Casablanca* was decided in the final shooting. *Movie Star News.*

Academy Awards

Best Picture: *Casablanca*
Best Director: Michael Curtiz (*Casablanca*)
Best Actress: Jennifer Jones (*The Song of Bernadette*)
Best Actor: Paul Lukas (*Watch on the Rhine*)

Top Box-Office Stars

Betty Grable, Bob Hope, Abbott and Costello, Bing Crosby, Gary Cooper, Greer Garson, Humphrey Bogart, James Cagney, Mickey Rooney, Clark Gable

Stars of Tomorrow

William Bendix, Philip Dorn, Susan Peters, Donald O'Connor, Anne Baxter, Van Johnson, Gene Kelly, Diana Barrymore, Gig Young, Alexis Smith

Popular Music

Hit Songs

"I Couldn't Sleep a Wink Last Night"
"Oh What a Beautiful Mornin' "
"Oklahoma"
"People Will Say We're in Love"
"Speak Low"
"The Surrey with the Fringe on Top"
"G.I. Jive"
"One for My Baby"
"As Time Goes By"

Top Records

You'll Never Know (Dick Haymes); *All or Nothing at All* (Harry James, Frank Sinatra); *Besamé Mucho* (Jimmy Dorsey, Kitty Kallen and Bob Eberle); *Pistol Packin' Mama* (Bing Crosby, Andrews Sisters); *I'll Be Home for Christmas* (Bing Crosby); *Boogie Woogie* (Tommy Dorsey); *Harlem Folk* (Stan Kenton); *Cross Your Heart* (Artie Shaw); *Furlough Fling* (Freddie Slack)

Jazz and Big Bands

The Earl Hines Bop Band includes Charlie Parker, Dizzie Gillespie, and Sarah Vaughan.

Duke Ellington gives his first Carnegie Hall concert, "Black, Brown, and Beige."
Art Tatum forms a trio with Tiny Grimes and Slam Stewart.
Dinah Washington joins Lionel Hampton's band.

Top Performers (*Downbeat*):

Benny Goodman (soloist, big band); Tommy Dorsey (sweet band); Eddie Condon, Artie Bernstein, Mel Powell, Gene Krupa, Vido Musso (instrumentalists); Jo Stafford, Frank Sinatra (vocalists)

Theater

Broadway Openings

Plays

The Voice of the Turtle (John Van Druten), Margaret Sullavan, Elliott Nugent, Audrey Christie
The Patriots (Sidney Kingsley), Raymond Edward Johnson, Cecil Humphreys, Madge Evans
Harriet (Florence Ryerson, Colin Clements), Helen Hayes
Kiss and Tell (F. Hugh Herbert), Joan Caulfield, Richard Widmark, Jessie Royce Landis
Tomorrow the World (James Gow, Arnaud d'Usseau), Ralph Bellamy, Shirley Booth
Get Away Old Man (William Saroyan), Richard Widmark, Glenn Anders

Musicals

Carmen Jones (Georges Bizet, Oscar Hammerstein II), Muriel Smith and Muriel Rohn alternating as Carmen; Luther Saxon and Napoleon Reed alternating as Joe; all-black cast
Oklahoma (Richard Rodgers, Oscar Hammerstein II), Alfred Drake, Joan Roberts, Celeste Holm, choreographed by Agnes de Mille
Something for the Boys (Cole Porter), Ethel Merman, Bill Johnson
Winged Victory (Sgt. David Rose, Moss Hart), all-soldier cast: Don Taylor, Barry Nelson, Peter Lind Hayes, Richard Travis, Ray Middleton

Ziegfeld Follies of 1943 (Ray Henderson, Jack Yellen), Milton Berle, Ilona Massey
One Touch of Venus (Kurt Weill, Ogden Nash), John Boles, Mary Martin

Classics and Revivals On and Off Broadway

Othello, Paul Robeson, José Ferrer, Uta Hagen, Margaret Webster; *Richard III*, George Coulouris, Uta Hagen. *Founded*: The New York City Center of Music and Drama by Jean Dalrymple

Regional

Cleveland: *You Touched Me* (Tennessee Williams and Donal Windham), premiere

Pulitzer Prize

The Skin of Our Teeth, Thornton Wilder

Classical Music

Compositions

Aaron Copland, Violin Sonata
Roy Harris, Cantata for Choir,
    Organ, and Brass, Mass
Douglas Moore, *In Memoriam*
Walter Piston, Symphony no. 2
Howard Hanson, Symphony no. 4
Ross Lee Finney, *Hymn, Fuguing
    and Holiday*
John Cage, *Amores*
William Schuman, *William Billings
    Overture,* Symphony for
    Strings, *Three Score Strings,*
    Symphony no. 5
Paul Hindemith (in U.S.),
    Symphonic Metamorphoses
Béla Bartók (in U.S.), Concerto
    for Orchestra

Important Events

Nineteen major orchestras give 1,398 performances
of 710 works by 242 composers. Most performed are
Tchaikovsky's Symphony no. 5, Wagner's *Die
Meistersinger* overture, and works by Beethoven,
Strauss, and Gershwin.

Othello, with Paul Robeson and Uta Hagen, has the longest
Broadway run of any Shakespeare play to date. *Billy Rose
Theatre Collection. The New York Public Library at
Lincoln Center. Astor, Lenox and Tilden Foundations.*

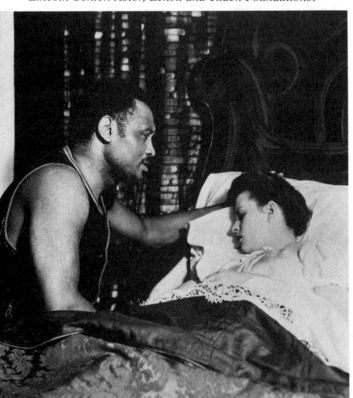

Bruno Walter conducts the uncut Bach *Passion
according to St. Matthew* at Carnegie Hall.
Eugene Istomin wins the Leventritt Award with the
Brahms Piano Concerto no. 2.

New Conductors: Karl Krueger at Detroit; Alfred
Wallenstein at Los Angeles; Erich Leinsdorf at
Cleveland

Premieres of Patriotic Music: Aaron Copland,
Fanfare for the Common Man; Robert Russell
Bennett, *The Four Freedoms* (based on FDR's
speech); Daniel Gregory Mason, *A Lincoln
Symphony;* Robert Palmer, *Lincoln Walks at
Midnight;* Bernard Rogers, *Invasion;* Samuel Barber,
Commando; William Schuman, *A Free Song and
Prayer in Time of War;* William Grant Still, *Plain
Song on America;* Ross Lee Finney, *Pole Star*

Debut: John Browning

First Performances

Roy Harris, Symphony no. 5 (Boston); Roger
Sessions, A Duo for Violin and Piano (Boston);
William Schuman, Symphony for Strings (Boston);
Concerto for Piano and Small Orchestra (New York);
Howard Hanson, Symphony no. 4 (Boston); Aaron
Copland, Sonata for Viola and Piano (New York);
Igor Stravinsky, *Dances Concertantes* (New York),
Ode (Boston)

Opera

Metropolitan: Alexander Kipnis, *Boris Godunov;*
Donald Dame, Patrice Munsel, *Mignon;* Zinka
Milanov, *Norma;* Farewell: Friedrich Schorr,
Siegfried; revivals: *Les contes d'Hoffmann; La forza
del destino*

Los Angeles: Kurt Baum, *Il trovatore*

Music Notes

Music is played regularly in U.S. factories to
stimulate war production • Shostakovich sells the
U.S. first performance rights to Symphony no. 8
(based on the Russian offensive) for $10,000 • With
news of Mussolini's fall, Toscanini conducts a gala
concert called *Victory Act I,* saving Acts II and III
for the downfall of the other Axis partners.

Art

Painting

Thomas Hart Benton, *Picnic*

Mark Rothko, *Sacrifice*

Arshile Gorky, *Virginia Landscape, Waterfall*

Robert Motherwell, *Pancho Villa, Dead and Alive, Surprise and Inspiration*

Jackson Pollock, *Pasiphaë, Search for a Symbol, The She-Wolf*

Mark Tobey, *Pacific Transition*

Loren MacIver, *Red Votive Lights*

Clyfford Still, *1943-A*

Bradley Walker Tomlin, *Burial*

Anna Mary ("Grandma") Moses, *The Thanksgiving Turkey*

Reginald Marsh, *Coney Island Beach, Number 1*

Piet Mondrian (in N.Y.), *Broadway Boogie Woogie*

Sculpture

Reuben Nakian, *Head of Marcel Duchamp*

Isamu Noguchi, *Monument to Heroes, Noodle, This Tortured Earth*

Theodore Roszak, *Vertical Construction*

Alexander Calder, *Morning Star*

Architecture

Willow Run Housing, Willow Run, Mich. (Eliel and Eero Saarinen, Robert F. Swanson)

Ford Motor Company Factory, Ypsilanti, Mich. (Albert Kahn)

John B. Nesbitt House, Brentwood, Calif. (Richard Neutra)

Important Exhibitions

Transportation difficulties created by the war curtail international exhibitions, with a resulting emphasis in the United States on native art and patriotic themes.

Museums

New York: *Metropolitan:* "Artists for Victory" continues; Contemporary American paintings from the University of Arizona; Modern Chinese paintings; "War Art"; "American Industry at War." *Metropolitan, Whitney:* "Front Line Paintings by War Correspondents." *Museum of Modern Art:* "Airways to Peace"; "Realistic and Magic Realists"; American Romantic painters. *Guggenheim:* Jackson Pollock. *Brooklyn:* Revival of "The Eight." *Whitney:* Gloria Vanderbilt Whitney Sculpture Memorial; Pollock; Calder Retrospective

Worcester: Eighteenth-century New England portraits

San Francisco: "Meet the Artist" (self-portraits)

Chicago: O'Keeffe, Hopper, Hartley, Watkins, Sheeler

Individual Shows

Pollock, I. Rice Pereira, Matta, Ruffino Tamayo

Art Briefs

Julius Rosenwald donates his rare print and drawing collection to the National Gallery • Forty-two paintings of J. P. Morgan are sold for $2 million.

Jackson Pollock, *Pasiphaë*, 1943. Oil. 56⅛ × 96″. *The Metropolitan Museum of Art, Purchase, 1982.*

Dance

Premieres

Ballet Theatre: *The Judgment of Paris* (Antony Tudor), Maria Karnilova, Hugh Laing, Tudor; *Dark Elegies* (Tudor), Laing, Nora Kaye, Tudor; *Romeo and Juliet* (Tudor), Alicia Markova, Laing; *Dim Lustre* (Tudor); Kaye, Laing

American Concert Ballet: *Mother Goose Suite* (Todd Bolender); *Concerto Barocco* (George Balanchine)

Martha Graham: *Deaths and Entrances*

Books

Fiction

Critics' Choice

The Way Some People Live, John Cheever
Gideon Planish, Sinclair Lewis
At Heaven's Gate, Robert Penn Warren
The Wide Net, Eudora Welty
Number One, John Dos Passos
The Big Rock Candy Mountain, Wallace Stegner
Wide Is the Gate, Upton Sinclair
Georgia Boy, Erskine Caldwell

Best-Sellers

The Robe, Lloyd C. Douglas
The Valley of Decision, Marcia Davenport
So Little Time, John P. Marquand
A Tree Grows in Brooklyn, Betty Smith
The Human Comedy, William Saroyan
Mrs. Parkington, Louis Bromfield
The Apostle, Sholem Asch
Hungry Hill, Daphne Du Maurier
The Forest and the Fort, Hervey Allen
The Song of Bernadette, Franz Werfel

Nonfiction

Critics' Choice

The Nature and Destiny of Man, Reinhold Niebuhr
Bound for Glory, Woody Guthrie
The Century of the Common Man, Henry Wallace
Thirty Seconds over Tokyo, Capt. Ted Lawson
My Native Land, Louis Adamic
The Infant and Child in the Culture of Today, Arnold L. Gesell
History of Bigotry in the United States, Gustavus Myers
God Is My Co-Pilot, Col. Robert L. Scott, Jr.
Seven Came Through, Capt. Eddie Rickenbacker
Total Peace, Ely Culbertson
🔖 *Being and Nothingness*, Jean-Paul Sartre
🔖 *Christianity and Democracy*, Jacques Maritain

Best-Sellers

Under Cover, John Roy Carlson
One World, Wendell L. Willkie
Journey among Warriors, Eve Curie
On Being a Real Person, Harry Emerson Fosdick
Guadalcanal Diary, Richard Tregaskis
Burma Surgeon, Lt. Col. Gordon Seagrave
Our Hearts Were Young and Gay, Cornelia Otis Skinner and Emily Kimbrough
U.S. Foreign Policy, Walter Lippmann
Here Is Your War, Ernie Pyle
See Here, Private Hargrove, Marion Hargrove

Poetry

T. S. Eliot, *Four Quartets*
Delmore Schwartz, *Genesis*
Kenneth Fearing, *Afternoon of a Pawnbroker*
Kenneth Patchen, *Cloth of the Tempest*
Weldon Kees, *The Last Man*

Pulitzer Prizes

Journey in the Dark, Martin Flavin (novel)
The Growth of American Thought, Merle Curti (U.S. history)
The American Leonardo: The Life of Samuel F. B. Morse, Carlton Mabee (biography)
Western Star, Stephen Vincent Benét (poetry)

Science and Technology

Selman Waksman discovers streptomycin and coins the term *antibiotic* for the actinomycete streptomyces griseus.
Sulfa is credited with an extraordinary reduction of U.S. Army fatalities.
Sulfathiazole is reported to prevent the venereal diseases gonorrhea and chancroid by army doctors James Loveless and William Denton.
A new painless method of childbirth, continuous caudal anesthesia, is described by Drs. Robert Hingson and Waldo Edwards.
Xylocaine, for local anesthesia, is developed.
Hepatitis is differentiated into two strains, A (short incubation) and B (long).

DDT is introduced in the United States and hailed as a boon to farmers.
The Lockheed Constellation becomes a military transport, the C-29; manufacture begins on the B-29 Superfortress.

Nobel Prize

Edward Doisy receives the prize in physiology and medicine for the discovery of the chemical structure of vitamin K. Otto Stern receives the prize in physics for the detection of the magnetic momentum of protons.

Sports

Baseball

Because of the war, spring training is held in the North for the first time.

Champions

Batting
Stan Musial (St. Louis, NL), .357
Luke Appling (Chicago, AL), .328

Pitching
Mort Cooper (St. Louis, NL), 21–8
Spud Chandler (New York, AL), 21–8

Home runs
Rudy York (Boston, AL), 34

Football

Sid Luckman, Chicago Bears, passes for 7 touchdowns against the New York Giants.

NFL Season Leaders: Sammy Baugh (Washington), passing; Bill Paschal (New York), running; Don Hutson (Green Bay), receiving.

College All-Americans: Otto Graham (Q), Northwestern; Alex Agase (G), Purdue

Bowls (Jan. 1, 1944)

Rose: Southern California 29–Washington 0
Orange: Louisiana State 19–Texas A & M 14
Cotton: Randolph Field 7–Texas 7
Sugar: Georgia Tech 20–Tulsa 18

Other Sports

Horse Racing: Count Fleet, ridden by Johnny Longden, wins the Triple Crown.

Winners

World Series
New York (AL) 4
St. Louis (NL) 1
MVP
NL–Stan Musial, St. Louis
AL–Spud Chandler, New York
NFL
Chicago (Bears) 41–Washington 21
MVP
Sid Luckman, Chicago Bears
College Football
Notre Dame

Heisman Trophy
Angelo Bertelli, Notre Dame
College Basketball
Wyoming (NCAA)
St. John's (NIT)
Player of the Year
George Senesky, St. Joseph
Stanley Cup
Detroit
US Tennis Open
Men: Joseph Hunt
Women: Pauline Betz
Kentucky Derby
Count Fleet (J. Longdon, jockey)

Fashion

For Women: Two silhouettes predominate: the slim, tubular look in knitted dresses or chemises with cinch belts, and the bulky look in box suits and coats with heavy, loose fabrics. Hair is neat, folded at the ear, netted at the back, twisted into braids, or pinned on top of the head. Small tight hats and snoods remain fashionable. Later, the "versatile suit," with nipped-in waist, short jacket, back hiked or pleated skirt, is popular. Women wear suits everywhere. Coats are long (the "officer's" style), or short (the "seaman's"). The fur-lined wool or canvas coat is new. Lounging teenage girls wear rolled-up jeans, sloppy shirttails, mixed shoes, and rag curlers.

For Men: Male teens are offered the "zoot suit," a long, one-button jacket with large padded shoulders, peaked lapels, and high-waisted trousers ballooning at the knees and gripping at the ankels, worn with knee-length key chains, broad-brimmed hats, and wide silk ties against striped or colored shirts. Older men reject mustaches because of their current, fascist associations.

Training women marines. The first, Oveta Culp Hobby, was sworn in by FDR. *Library of Congress.*

Kaleidoscope _____

- American planes make 64,000 sorties and drop 55,000 tons of bombs during the year.
- The American Jewish Congress reports that over 3 million Jews have been killed by the Nazis.
- Gen. George Patton strikes a GI being treated for shell shock; Patton is reprimanded and apologizes.
- Rubber, metal, tin, nylon, silk, and paper are collected for recycling. Kitchen fats are exchanged for ration points. Despite the 28-ounce allowance per week, meat consumption rises to 128.9 pounds per year. Butter is rationed at 4 ounces per week; cheese, 4 pounds per week; the sale of sliced bread is banned; flour, fish, canned goods, and coffee are rationed. Shoes are rationed at 3 pairs a year; new sneakers are unavailable because of the rubber shortage.
- With meat increasingly unavailable, Tuesdays and Fridays become "meatless days"; casseroles, fish, omelets, and soufflés become popular.
- Because alarm clock manufacture has ceased, thousands are late to work; 1.75 million "Victory model" clocks are ordered.
- With the paper shortage, few Christmas cards are available; women recycle their brown grocery bags.
- With the combined goods scarcity and improved economy, long lines develop at groceries, movies, bars, and restaurants; cabs are obliged to take as many passengers as they can carry; long-distance calls are limited to five minutes.
- The manpower shortage stimulates "pampering" of employees; music is piped into factories, and coffee breaks and suggestion boxes are instituted, as well as awards and fringe benefits. FDR orders a minimum 48-hour work week in war plants.
- Sonja Henie applies for $250,000 insurance on her remaining five pairs of ice skates, since skates are not being produced during wartime.
- An estimated 30,000 people riot at the Paramount Theater when Frank Sinatra appears.
- New pastimes for teens include the "slumber party," jalopies, the Saturday night soda shop (with jukebox and "messing around"), and "smooching" jargon; also popular are BMOC's, pep rallies, beach parties, and roller rinks; girls wear their boyfriends' parkas, knit argyles, and meet their dates at hamburger "joints."
- Dance tempos are either very fast or slow, for the fox trot, polka, rhumba, samba, waltz, jitterbug, and Lindy hop, along with their variations, the Jersey jump, flea hop, job walk, victory walk, and "Praise the Lord and Pass the Ammunition" dance.
- "Amos 'n' Andy" is canceled after 15 years and 4,000 consecutive radio shows. Campbell Soup, whose sales are cut in half by the tin shortage, can no longer afford to sponsor the show.
- One thousand special radio programs are sent to the troops, including Ann Sheridan preparing a steak dinner and Rita Hayworth singing in Spanish.
- The opening of Beethoven's Fifth Symphony becomes the Victory theme of the Allies; it is also the Morse code (. . .—) for the letter *V,* for *Victory.*

With her dedicated and vigorous public life, including a newspaper column, radio program, and tireless efforts for social reform, Eleanor Roosevelt sets a new style for the First Lady. Here she entertains Madame Chiang Kai-shek at the White House. *Library of Congress.*

- At a War Bond rally at Gimbels' basement, in New York, Jack Benny's $75 violin is bought for $1 million by Julius Klorten, president of Garcia Grande cigars, who shuns publicity following the purchase.
- Orson Welles marries Rita Hayworth, thought to be engaged to Victor Mature.
- Leslie Howard and 16 others are lost in an overseas airliner en route from Lisbon to England after being attacked by an enemy plane.
- A series of flag stamps is issued, honoring the countries overrun by Axis forces.
- Second-class mailings of *Esquire* are prohibited when the magazine is charged with being "lewd and lascivious."
- Ernie Pyle is the most widely read war correspondent, as he describes the ordinary GI's experiences in the war.
- As blacks move into the Detroit plants, racial tensions heighten; a riot develops when a black is killed for using a white swimming area.
- The AMA is found guilty of violating antitrust laws by preventing the activities of cooperative health groups.
- Marian Anderson's performance, January 7th, at Constitution Hall, Washington, D.C., breaks the DAR segregation policy.
- Bible sales increase 25 percent, and books on religious themes, like *The Robe* and *Song of Bernadette,* are popular.

First Appearances: Rent control, "converted" rice (Uncle Ben, Gordon Hariwell), women's fire department (Asheville, N.Y.), election law permitting 18-year-olds to vote (Georgia), Chicago subway

1944

Economic Profile
Dow-Jones: ↑ High 152–
Low 135
GNP: + 10%
Inflation: +0.9%
Unemployment: 1.2%
Expenditures:
Recreation: $5.4 billion
Spectator sports: $80
million
Golf courses: 409
Bowlers: 910,000
Arthur Rubinstein concert,
Carnegie Hall: $1.20–$3.60
Ice show: 75¢–$1.00
Ballet International: $1–$3.50
New York City Center: 90¢–
$2.40
Broadway show, top price: $3
Tabu: $18.50 (oz.)
Lily of France:
girdles: $9
bras: $1.85–$2.00

Deaths
Jean Giraudoux, Wassily
Kandinsky, Josef
Lhévinne, Aristide Maillol,
Edvard Munch, Lucien
Pissaro, Antoine de Saint-
Exupéry, Al Smith,
William Allen White,
Wendell Willkie.

In the News

EISENHOWER GOES TO ENGLAND . . . ALLIES LAND AT ANZIO, NEAR ROME . . . LENINGRAD IS RELIEVED . . . MARINES LAND ON KWAJALEIN . . . MASSIVE AIR ATTACK HITS JAPANESE BASE AT TRUK, 201 PLANES ARE DESTROYED, 17 U.S. AIRCRAFT LOST . . . ROUND THE CLOCK MASS AIR RAIDS STRIKE BERLIN . . . SUPREME COURT RULES COLOR CANNOT BE BAR TO PRIMARY VOTING . . . CASSINO IS CAPTURED . . . ROME IS TAKEN . . . D-DAY ALLIES LAUNCH A MASSIVE ASSAULT ON NORMANDY AND ESTABLISH BEACHHEAD . . . THOMAS DEWEY IS NOMINATED BY GOP, FDR IS NOMINATED FOR THE FOURTH TIME . . . U.S. SUPERFORTS BOMB JAPAN FOR THE FIRST TIME . . . 100,000 GERMAN SOLDIERS ARE CAPTURED AT MINSK . . . 402 JAPANESE PLANES ARE DOWNED IN BATTLE OF THE PHILIPPINE SEA . . . GI BILL OF RIGHTS IS PASSED . . . WORLD BANK IS CREATED AT BRETTON WOODS, N.H., CONFERENCE . . . OFFICERS' ATTEMPT TO ASSASSINATE HITLER FAILS . . . GUAM IS RECAPTURED . . . ALLIES BREAK OUT PAST ST. LO IN NORMANDY, GERMANS RETREAT . . . THIRD ARMY UNDER PATTON REACHES THE SEINE . . . ALLIES LAND IN SOUTH FRANCE . . . UN IS ESTABLISHED AT DUMBARTON OAKS, D.C. . . . RUMANIA SURRENDERS TO RUSSIA . . . PARIS IS LIBERATED . . . BRUSSELS IS LIBERATED . . . FDR AND CHURCHILL MEET AT QUEBEC . . . FIRST ARMY BREAKS THROUGH SIEGFRIED LINE . . . V-2 ROCKETS FALL ON LONDON . . . RUSSIA ENTERS HUNGARY AND YUGOSLAVIA . . . 300 JAPANESE PLANES ON FORMOSA ARE DESTROYED BY CARRIER-BASED PLANES . . . GENERAL MACARTHUR RETURNS, LANDS AT LEYTE GULF, PHILIPPINES, LARGE NAVAL VICTORY IS WON . . . FDR IS REELECTED, 25 MILLION TO 22 MILLION . . . GERMANS COUNTERATTACK, ARE DEFEATED AT BATTLE OF THE BULGE AS PATTON'S THIRD ARMY BRINGS RELIEF.

Quotes

"You are about to embark upon the Great Crusade, toward which we have striven these many months. The eyes of the world are upon you. The hopes and prayers of liberty-loving people everywhere march with you. . . . You will bring about the destruction of the German war machine, the elimination of Nazi tyranny over the oppressed peoples of Europe, and security for ourselves in a free world.

Your task will not be an easy one. Your enemy . . . will fight savagely.

But this is the year 1944! . . . The tide has turned! The free men of the world are marching together to Victory! . . . Let us beseech the blessing of Almighty God upon this great and noble undertaking."

— Dwight D. Eisenhower
to the Allied Expeditionary
Forces, before Normandy

D-Day, June 6: Allied troops landing at Normandy. *Library of Congress.*

"Men were sleeping on the sand, some of them sleeping forever. Men were floating in the water, but they didn't know they were in the water, for they were dead.

— Ernie Pyle, *Brave Men*

"I have returned. By the grace of Almighty God, our forces stand again on Philippine soil."

— Gen. Douglas MacArthur

"Good evening again to all the all-forgetting and forgotten men, the American fighting men of the South Pacific."

— Tokyo Rose

"We cannot have jobs and opportunities if we surrender our freedom to Government control. . . . We can have both opportunity and security within the framework of a free society."

— Thomas E. Dewey, presidential campaign address

"Truman? I never can remember that name."

— John W. Bricker, Dewey's running mate

"I've always voted for Roosevelt as President. My father always voted for Roosevelt as President."

— Bob Hope

Ads

Radio

Premieres

"Roy Rogers"
"Chesterfield Supper Club," Perry Como
"The Adventures of Ozzie and Harriet [Nelson]"
"The Danny Kaye Show"
"Ethel and Albert," Peg Lynch, Richard Widmark
"The FBI," Martin Blaine
"House Party," Art Linkletter
"Columbia Presents Corwin" (plays written, produced, directed by Norman Corwin)

Top Ten

"Bob Hope," "Fibber McGee and Molly," "Bing Crosby," "Edgar Bergen and Charlie McCarthy," "Joan Davis/Jack Haley," "Walter Winchell," "Radio Theatre," "Abbott and Costello," "Mr. District Attorney," "Eddie Cantor," "Jack Benny"

Most Popular Daytime Programs: "When a Girl Marries," "Aunt Jenny," "Life Can Be Beautiful," "Ma Perkins," "Romance of Helen Trent," "Kate Smith Show," "Big Sister," "Portia Faces Life," "Stella Dallas," "Young Widder Brown"

Of Note

"The FBI" begins with the march from *The Love of Three Oranges* • Evening programs consist of serial dramas (27.8 percent), audience participation shows (13.2 percent), news and talk shows (17.5 percent), popular and familiar music (18.2 percent), classical and semiclassical music (3.0 percent), and children's programs (2.1 percent).

TV

Premieres

"Missus Goes A'Shopping," Reed King
"At Home Show," Pacquito Anderson, Yul Brynner
"CBS News"

Movies

Openings

Going My Way (Leo McCarey), Bing Crosby, Barry Fitzgerald
Double Indemnity (Billy Wilder), Barbara Stanwyck, Fred MacMurray, Edward G. Robinson
Gaslight (George Cukor), Charles Boyer, Ingrid Bergman
The Purple Heart (Lewis Milestone), Dana Andrews, Richard Conte
Since You Went Away (John Cromwell), Claudette Colbert, Jennifer Jones, Joseph Cotten
Lifeboat (Alfred Hitchcock), Tallulah Bankhead, Walter Slezak, John Hodiak
Laura (Otto Preminger), Gene Tierney, Dana Andrews, Clifton Webb
None but the Lonely Heart (Clifford Odets), Cary Grant, Ethel Barrymore
Mr. Skeffington (Vincent Sherman), Bette Davis, Claude Rains
The Seventh Cross (Fred Zinnemann), Spencer Tracy, Signe Hasso
Dragon Seed (Jack Conway, Harold S. Bucquet), Katharine Hepburn, Walter Huston
Hail the Conquering Hero (Preston Sturges), Eddie Bracken, Ella Raines
Meet Me in St. Louis (Vincente Minnelli), Judy Garland, Margaret O'Brien
Destination Tokyo (Delmer Daves), Cary Grant, John Garfield
The Miracle of Morgan's Creek (Preston Sturges), Betty Hutton, Eddie Bracken
Up in Arms (Elliott Nugent), Danny Kaye, Dinah Shore
Cover Girl (Charles Vidor), Rita Hayworth, Gene Kelly

Academy Awards

Best Picture: *Going My Way*
Best Director: Leo McCarey (*Going My Way*)
Best Actress: Ingrid Bergman (*Gaslight*)
Best Actor: Bing Crosby (*Going My Way*)
Special Award: Margaret O'Brien (outstanding child actress)

Top Box-Office Stars

Bing Crosby, Gary Cooper, Bob Hope, Betty Grable, Spencer Tracy, Greer Garson, Humphrey Bogart, Abbott and Costello, Cary Grant, Bette Davis

Stars of Tomorrow

Sonny Tufts, James Craig, Gloria DeHaven, Roddy McDowall, June Allyson, Barry Fitzgerald, Marsha Hunt, Sydney Greenstreet, Turhan Bey, Helmut Dantine

Popular Music

Hit Songs
"Don't Fence Me In"
"Acc-cent-tchu-ate the Positive"
"I Should Care"
"I'll Walk Alone"
"Irresistible You"
"Long Ago and Far Away"
"Put the Blame on Mame"
"Spring Will Be a Little Late This
   Year"
"Dream"

Top Records
Tico-Tico (Andrews Sisters); *In the Middle of Nowhere* (Carmen Cavallaro); *Time Waits for No One* (Helen Forrest); *A Lovely Way to Spend an Evening* (Ink Spots); *This Heart of Mine* (Vaughn Monroe); *I Couldn't Sleep a Wink Last Night* (Frank Sinatra); *Tumbling Tumbleweeds* (Jo Stafford); *Rum and Coca-Cola* (Andrews Sisters); *Too-Ra-Loo-Ra-Loo-Rah* (Bing Crosby); *Cocktails for Two* (Spike Jones); *Moonlight in Vermont* (Billy Butterfield, Margaret Whiting). Country: *Smoke on the Water* (Red Foley); *I'm Wastin' My Tears on You* (Tex Ritter)

Jazz and Big Bands
Thelonious Monk's *Round Midnight* and Billie Holiday's *Record Man* gain wide attention.

First Recordings: Billy Eckstine's bop session with Dizzy Gillespie and Budd Johnson; Sarah Vaughan

Top Performers *(Downbeat):*
Benny Goodman (soloist); Duke Ellington (big band); Charlie Spivak (sweet band); Bob Haggart, Lester Young, Harry Carney, Buddy Rich, Mel Powell (instrumentalists); Dinah Shore, Bing Crosby (vocalists); Pied Pipers (vocal group)

Theater

Broadway Openings

Plays
Harvey (Mary Chase), Josephine Hull, Frank Fay
Anna Lucasta (Philip Yordan), Hilda Simms, Canada Lee
I Remember Mama (John Van Druten), Mady Christians, Oscar Homolka, Marlon Brando
Ten Little Indians (Agatha Christie), Estelle Winwood, Halliwell Hobbes
Jacobowsky and the Colonel (S. N. Behrman), Louis Calhern
The Late George Apley (John P. Marquand, George S. Kaufman), Leo G. Carroll, Janet Beecher
Over 21 (Ruth Gordon), Ruth Gordon
Catherine Was Great (Mae West), Mae West
The Searching Wind (Lillian Hellman), Cornelia Otis Skinner, Dennis King, Montgomery Clift
Pick-up Girl (Elsa Shelley), William Harrigan
A Bell for Adano (Paul Osborn), Margo, Fredric March
The Two Mrs. Carrolls (Martin Vale), Elisabeth Bergner

Musicals
Bloomer Girl (Harold Arlen, E. Y. Harburg), Celeste Holm, Joan McCracken, David Brooks, Dooley Wilson
Follow the Girls (Phil Charig et al.), Gertrude Niesen, Jackie Gleason
Mexican Hayride (Cole Porter), Bobby Clark, June Havoc
The Seven Lively Arts (Cole Porter), Beatrice Lillie, Bert Lahr, Dolores Gray, Benny Goodman Quintet
Song of Norway (Edvard Grieg, Robert Wright), Lawrence Brooks, Irra Petina
On the Town (Leonard Bernstein, Betty Comden, Adolph Green), Sono Osato, Nancy Walker, Betty Comden, Adolph Green
Sing Out, Sweet Land (many authors), Alfred Drake, Burl Ives

Classics and Revivals On and Off Broadway
The Cherry Orchard (Chekhov), Eva Le Gallienne, Joseph Schildkraut; *Othello*, Paul Robeson, José Ferrer. *Founded:* Equity Library Theatre by Sam Jaffe and George Freedley

Pulitzer Prize
No prize is awarded.

Classical Music

Compositions

John Cage, A Book of Music for Two Prepared
  Pianos
Aaron Copland, *Appalachian Spring*
Roger Sessions, Symphony no. 2
Samuel Barber, Symphony no. 2, *Capricorn*
  Concerto
Walter Piston, Fugue on a Victory Tune
Don Gilles, Symphony no. 5
Igor Stravinsky (in U.S.), Sonata for Two Pianos
Paul Hindemith (in U.S.), *Hérodiade*
Béla Bártok (in U.S.), Sonata for Unaccompanied
  Violin

Important Events

Serge Koussevitzky is reengaged at the Boston
Symphony; Artur Rodzinski takes over the New
York Philharmonic for two-thirds of the season,
followed by Bruno Walter, William Steinberg, and
Steinberg's assistant, Leonard Bernstein, 25, who
conducts on a few hours' notice to standing ovations.
Bernstein begins conducting the New York
Philharmonic and other orchestras regularly and
plays 14 world premieres, including his *Jeremiah
Symphony* and *Fancy Free*. George Szell receives
enormous acclamation as he conducts the Cleveland
Symphony Orchestra.

Debut: Leon Fleischer, Byron Janis

First Performances

Dmitri Shostakovich, Symphony no. 8 (New York);
Roy Harris, Symphony no. 6 (Boston); Paul
Hindemith, *Symphonic Metamorphoses on Themes
by Carl Maria von Weber* (New York); Arnold
Schoenberg, *Ode to Napoleon Buonaparte* (New
York), Piano Concerto no. 4 (NBC), Theme and
Variations in G minor (Boston); Samuel Barber,
Symphony no. 2 (Washington); Stravinsky
(conducting), *Four Norwegian Moods* (Boston);
William Schuman, *William Billings Overture* (New
York); Louis Gruenberg, Violin Concerto (New York,
for and with Jascha Heifetz).

Opera

Metropolitan: Celebration of Diamond Jubilee. Of
165 performances, most frequently produced are
*Mignon, La bohème, Carmen, La traviata, Tristan
und Isolde.* "Auditions of the Air" award ($1,000 and
Met contract): Regina Resnik. Performances: Resnik,
Il trovatore; Kerstin Thorborg, *Die Walküre;* Martial
Singher, *Pelléas et Mélisande, Aïda;* Emercy Darcy,
Parsifal; Patrice Munsel (debut), *Mignon*

National Negro Opera Co.: *La traviata,* Madison
Square Garden, New York, which then tours
Chicago, Pittsburgh, and Washington, D.C.

City Center, New York (first performance): *Tosca*

Chicago: Zinka Milanov, Kurt Baum, *Il trovatore;*
Jan Peerce, *Rigoletto;* Gladys Swarthout, Kurt
Baum, *Carmen*

San Francisco: Lily Djanel, Frederick Jagel,
Salomé; Salvatore Baccaloni, Vivian Della Chiesa,
Falstaff

Music Notes

After a year of inactivity, the Chicago Opera and
Detroit symphonies resume • William Grant Still wins
the $1,000 War Bond prize for *Jubilee Overture,*
which celebrates the Cincinnati Symphony
Orchestra's fiftieth anniversary.

Glenn Miller. Since 1939, everyone knew the "Miller
sound," with its penetrating tutti sax-section and lead
clarinet. *Movie Star News.*

Art

Painting

Milton Avery, *Mother and Child, Seated Girl with Dog*
Abraham Rattner, *The Emperor*
Arshile Gorky, *The Liver Is the Cock's Comb, Water of the Flowery Mill*
Reginald Marsh, *Bowery and Mell Street—Looking North*
Clyfford Still, *Jamais*
Lyonel Feininger, *Steamboat on the Yukon*
Mark Tobey, *Tundra*
I. Rice Pereira, *Green Depth*
Edward Hopper, *Morning in a City*
Jackson Pollock, *Gothic*
Robert Motherwell, *Mallarmé's Swan-C*
William Baziotes, *Cyclops*

Sculpture

Isamu Noguchi, *Bird's Nest*
William Zorach, *The Future Generation* (1942–44)
Peter Grippe, *Growth after Destruction*
David Hare, *The Magician's Game*

Architecture

Carver Court, Coatesville, Pa. (Howe, Stonorov, Kahn)
Municipal Asphalt Plant, New York (Kahn, Jacobs)

Important Exhibitions

Museums

New York: *Metropolitan:* "Naval Aviation in the Pacific"; Four masters of the Renaissance; 600 paintings (stored during the war); American battle paintings, 1776–1918. *Museum of Modern Art:* Hartley; Feininger; Renoir to the present: Modern Cuban painters; American snapshots; Twentieth-century Italian art. *Brooklyn:* One hundred paintings of Abraham Walkowitz (done by fellow artists). *Whitney:* Winslow Homer

Washington: American battle paintings, 1776–1918

Philadelphia: Thomas Eakins centennial

Cincinnati: Reconstructed 1913 Armory Show

Chicago: Art in the United Nations; "The Art of Posada"; Advertising art

Detroit: Romantic art

Arshile Gorky, *Water of the Flowery Mill*, 1944. Oil. 42½ × 48¾". *The Metropolitan Museum of Art, George A. Hearn Fund, 1956.*

Cleveland: Islamic art

Boston: Sporting art

Dayton: "The Church Tradition"

Art Briefs

Samuel Kress gives 90 more works to the National Gallery • Felix M. Warburg donates a house to the Jewish Theological Seminary for the Museum of Jewish Art, New York.

Dance

Premieres

Ballet Theatre: *Tally-Ho* (Agnes de Mille), Janet Reed, Anton Dolin; *Fancy Free* (Jerome Robbins, Leonard Bernstein), John Kriza, Erik Bruhn, Robbins; *Appalachian Spring* (Martha Graham, Aaron Copland), Graham (with designs by Isamu Noguchi); *Danses Concertantes* (George Balanchine)

San Francisco Ballet: The first full-length American *Nutcracker.*

Books

Fiction

Critics' Choice
The Dangling Man, Saul Bellow
The Leaning Tower, Katherine Anne Porter
Boston Adventure, Jean Stafford
The Lost Weekend, Charles Jackson
The Women on the Porch, Caroline Gordon
Avalanche, Kay Boyle
Under a Glass Bell, Anaïs Nin
Angels Can't Do Better, Peter de Vries
🝔 *Winter Tales*, Isak Dinesen

Best-Sellers
Strange Fruit, Lillian Smith
The Robe, Lloyd C. Douglas
A Tree Grows in Brooklyn, Betty Smith
Forever Amber, Kathleen Winsor
The Razor's Edge, W. Somerset Maugham
The Green Years, A. J. Cronin
Leave Her to Heaven, Ben Ames Williams
Green Dolphin Street, Elizabeth Goudge
A Bell for Adano, John Hersey
The Apostle, Sholem Asch

Nonfiction

Critics Choice
A Walk in the Sun, Harry P. M. Brown
U.S. War Aims, Walter Lippmann
The Road to Serfdom, Frederick A. Hayek
Invasion Diary, Richard Tregaskis
Bataan, Allison Ind
Many a Watchful Night, John Mason Brown
Air Gunner, Sgt. Bud Hutton, Sgt. Andy Rooney
An American Dilemma, Gunnar Myrdal
A Basic History of the United States, Charles and Mary Beard
The Public Schools and Spiritual Values, John Dewey
Social Darwinism in American Thought, Richard Hofstadter

Best-Sellers
I Never Left Home, Bob Hope
Brave Men, Ernie Pyle
Good Night, Sweet Prince, Gene Fowler
Under Cover, John Roy Carlson
Yankee from Olympus, Catherine Drinker Bowen
The Time for Decision, Sumner Welles
Here Is Your War, Ernie Pyle
Anna and the King of Siam, Margaret Landon
The Curtain Rises, Quentin Reynolds
Ten Years in Japan, Joseph C. Grew

Poetry
Robert Lowell, *Land of Unlikeness*
Kenneth Rexroth, *The Phoenix and the Turtle*
Muriel Rukeyser, *Beast in View*
E. E. Cummings, *1 × 1*
Allen Tate, *Winter Sea*
Stanley Kunitz, *Passport to War*
Maturya Zaturenska, *Golden Mirror*
🝔 W. H. Auden, *For the Time Being*

Pulitzer Prizes
A Bell for Adano, John Hersey (novel)
Unfinished Business, Stephen Bonsal (U.S. history)
George Bancroft: Brahmin Rebel, Russel Blaine Nye (biography)
V-Letter and Other Poems, Karl Shapiro (poetry)

Science and Technology

A mathematical "robot," a giant, automatic, sequence-controlled computer with a 50-foot panel of knobs, gears, and switches, is created at Harvard by Howard Aiken and IBM engineers.

Manufacturers of penicillin agree to pool their knowledge in order to speed production.

William Doering produces synthetic quinine from coal tar products.

Sister Kenny's methods of infantile paralysis treatment come under considerable debate.

DNA, the basic material of heredity, is isolated by Oswald Avery, Rockefeller Institute.

Aureomycin, the first broad-spectrum antibiotic, is extracted from soil.

The U.S. Army announces the development of a jet-propelled, propless plane.

The second atomic pile is built at Clinton, Tennessee, for the manufacture of plutonium for the atomic bomb.

🝔 The Germans develop the first true missile, the 1,600-pound V-2, with a 200-mile range; they also introduce the first operational jet fighter.

Nobel Prize
Joseph Erlanger and Herbert Gasser share the prize in physiology and medicine for work on nerve transmission. I. I. Rabi receives the prize in physics for work on the magnetic movements of atomic particles.

Sports

Baseball

Many retired major leaguers return to active play, since many young players are now in the service.

Champions

Batting	Pitching
Dixie Walker (Brooklyn, NL), .357	Ted Wilks (St. Louis, NL), 17–4
Lou Boudreau (Cleveland, AL), .327	Cecil Hughson (Boston, AL), 18–5
	Home runs
	Bill Nicholson (Chicago, NL), 33

Football

NFL Season Leaders: Frank Filchok (Washington), passing; Bill Paschal (New York), rushing; Don Hutson (Green Bay), receiving

College All-Americans: Felix "Doc" Blanchard (B), Glenn Davis (B), Army ("Mr. Inside and Mr. Outside"); Les Horvath (QB), Ohio State

Bowls (Jan. 1, 1945)
Rose: Southern California 25–Tennessee 0
Orange: Tulsa 26–Georgia Tech 12
Cotton: Oklahoma A & M 34–Texas Christian 0
Sugar: Duke 29–Alabama 26

Fashion

For Women: With fabrics still limited, three-quarter-length box coats and suits have false fronts; sleeveless dresses expose wide shoulders or have small shoulder caps. Chignons, as well as small pillbox hats and berets, draw attention to the face and makeup; the earring industry expands. Décolletage returns for both day and evening wear. The concept of "separates," or interchangeable clothes, enters the fashion world.

High-fashion note: Schiaparelli's hourglass black fur-lined wool coat with fur-trimmed buttons

For Men: War Production Board specifications, since 1942: 23¾" length for size 37 jacket; no waistcoat; trousers, 22" at the knee, 18½" at the bottom, 35" inseam for 32" waist; no cuffs, pleats, tucks, or overlapping waistbands.

Basketball

The NIT semifinal matches De Paul, with 6'9" George Mikan, and Oklahoma State, with 7' Bob Kurland, in a "Battle of the Giants." De Paul wins 41–38, but loses to St. Johns in the final.

Other Sports

Hockey: Maurice Richard (Montreal Canadiens) scores a record 50 goals in the 50-game season.

Winners

World Series	College Basketball
St. Louis (NL) 4	Utah (NCAA)
St. Louis (AL) 2	St. John's (NIT)
MVP	*Player of the Year*
NL–Martin Marion, St. Louis	George Mikan, De Paul
AL–Hal Newhouser, Detroit	*Stanley Cup*
NFL	Montreal
Green Bay 14–New York 7	*US Tennis Open*
MVP	Men: Sgt. Frank Parker
Frank Sinkwich, Detroit	Women: Pauline Betz
College Football	*Kentucky Derby*
Army	Pensive (C. McCreary, jockey)
Heisman Trophy	
Les Horvath, Ohio State	

World War II poster. *Smithsonian Institution.*

Kaleidoscope _____

- On D day, June 6, Operation Overlord, the Normandy invasion, is mounted by 6,939 naval vessels, 15,040 aircraft, and 156,000 troops. After two months, Normandy casualties number 16,434 dead, 76,535 wounded, 19,704 missing.
- Within five months of D day, the Allies take 637,544 prisoners.
- The War Refugee Board reveals the first details of mass murder at Birkenau and Auschwitz, estimating that 1.7 million have been killed there.
- With 3.5 million women working alongside 6 million men on assembly lines, production capacities change. Cargo ships are completed in 17 days, bombers in 13 days. For the working woman, slacks become, as Max Lerner puts it, a "badge of honor."
- Nearly half the steel, tin, and paper needed for the war are provided by people salvaging goods.
- Paper shortages stimulate publishers' experiments with soft-cover books.
- Because of a shortage of cheese and tomato sauce, pasta sales fall. Jello becomes a dessert substitute for canned fruit; baking powder sales fall with so many women on the work force; neighborhood groceries, rather than supermarkets, proliferate because of gas rationing and the consumer's greater spending power. Camel cigarettes, a GI favorite, are scarce.
- Seven laboratories refine and improve DDT, invaluable in reducing typhus and malaria; 350,000 pounds a month are sent to the military.
- Both women and men's fashions feature broad shoulders and pointed lapels, what many call the "football player" look.
- Horse racing is banned because of the war.
- Hollywood personalities still in the service include Clark Gable, James Stewart, Robert Taylor, Robert Montgomery, Mickey Rooney, Frank Capra, John Ford, William Wyler, and John Huston.
- "Stars for Dewey" include Ginger Rogers, Hedda Hopper, Cecil B. De Mille, Anne Baxter, Adolphe Menjou, and Leo G. Carroll. "For FDR" are Rita Hayworth, Olivia de Havilland, Katharine Hepburn, Orson Welles, Harpo Marx, Lana Turner, Walter Huston, and Fannie Brice.
- Some gossip columnists attribute Humphrey Bogart and Mayo "Sluggy" Methot's break up to his FDR support and her Dewey support.
- Paulette Goddard, the "Cheesecake Girl" of 1944, marries Air Force captain Burgess "Buzz" Meredith.
- Boston bans *Forever Amber* and *Strange Fruit,* the latter about the love between a white man and black woman.
- A New York judge finds *Lady Chatterley's Lover* obscene and orders to trial the publisher, Dial Press; a higher court reverses the decision.
- Bill Mauldin's cartoon "Willie & Joe," originally in *Yank* and *Stars and Stripes,* is picked up by the domestic press and achieves great acclaim.
- Hit song "Mairzy Doats" is written by Milton Drake after he listens to his small daughter's baby talk.

- The first jazz concert at the Metropolitan Opera House, New York, takes place, sponsored by *Esquire;* it features Coleman Hawkins, Louis Armstrong, Roy Eldridge, Jack Teagarden, Art Tatum, Lionel Hampton, Billie Holiday, and Mildred Bailey, among others.
- With many baseball players still in the service, college football becomes the number one sporting event.
- "Kilroy was here" graffiti moves out of public bathrooms to billboards, buildings, phone booths, and construction fences, mythologizing the valor of the GI.
- The worst disaster in theatrical history occurs in Hartford, Connecticut when, with the Barnum and Bailey Wallendas on a high wire, a fire begins and 168 people are killed.
- Maj. Glenn Miller is lost on a flight from England to Paris.
- Lt. John F. Kennedy receives the Navy and Marine Corps Medal for "extreme heroism" in rescuing two sailors after a Japanese destroyer cuts his PT boat in half.
- Richard Bong, 25, surpasses Eddie Rickenbacker's 26-year-old record by destroying his 27th Japanese aircraft.
- Maj. James Stewart, Eighth Air Force squadron commander and pilot leader of more than 20 B-24s on 11 missions over Germany, receives the Distinguished Flying Cross.
- Congress approves the appointment of the first five-star generals and five-star admirals.

First Appearances: Seabrook farms, Chiquita bananas, quadruplets delivered by cesarean section

Following the News on D-Day, Times Square, New York City. *Library of Congress.*

1945

Facts and Figures

Economic Profile
   Dow-Jones: ↑ High 195–
      Low 155
   GNP: 0%
   Inflation: +1.2%
   Unemployment: 1.9%
World War II Casualty
   Figures
   Americans
      16,354,000 in arms
      291,557 battle deaths
      113,842 other deaths
      670,846 wounded
   Russians: 7,500,000
   Germans: 2,900,000
   Chinese: 2,200,000
   Japanese: 1,500,000
   British: 398,000
   Italians: 300,000
   Jews: 6,000,000
   Total Deaths: 54,800,000

Above: Churchill, FDR, and
Stalin meet at Yalta, a resort
on the Russian Black Sea, to
plan the postwar world.
Library of Congress.

Deaths

Béla Bartók, Theodore
   Dreiser, Jerome Kern,
   David Lloyd George,
   Pietro Mascagni, John
   McCormack, Alla
   Nazimova, George Patton,
   Ernie Pyle, Paul Valéry,

In the News

RUSSIANS TAKE WARSAW, HUNGARY SURRENDERS . . . BATAAN IS RETAKEN, 500 POWs ARE FREED . . . 1,000-PLANE ARMADA BOMBS GERMANY . . . FDR, CHURCHILL, STALIN MEET AT YALTA TO MAKE POSTWAR PLANS . . . PRO-RUSSIAN GOVERNMENT IS INSTALLED IN RUMANIA . . . IWO JIMA IS CAPTURED, U.S. FLAG IS RAISED ON MT. SURIBACHI, 4,189 U.S. ARE DEAD, 20,000 JAPANESE . . . U.S. ARMY REACHES RHINE . . . BENEŠ FORMS CZECH GOVERNMENT . . . N.Y. PASSES ANTIDISCRIMINATION LAW . . . 325,000 GERMAN SOLDIERS SURRENDER IN RUHR . . . FDR DIES OF CEREBRAL HEMORRHAGE AT WARM SPRINGS, GEORGIA, THE NATION MOURNS . . . TRUMAN TAKES OFFICE . . . BUCHENWALD IS LIBERATED . . . RUSSIANS REACH BERLIN . . . MUSSOLINI AND MISTRESS ARE EXECUTED IN MILAN . . . GERMAN ARMIES IN ITALY SURRENDER . . . DOENITZ REPORTS HITLER'S SUICIDE . . . GERMANY SURRENDERS UNCONDITIONALLY . . . GERMANY IS DIVIDED INTO FOUR ZONES . . . OKINAWA IS TAKEN, 13,000 U.S. DEAD, 100,000 JAPANESE DEAD . . . FIRST ATOM BOMB IS TESTED IN NEW MEXICO . . . TRUMAN, CHURCHILL, STALIN MEET IN POTSDAM . . . RUSSIA DECLARES WAR ON JAPAN AND ENTERS MANCHURIA . . . LEAFLETS WARN JAPAN OF TERRIBLE DESTRUCTION . . . ATOM BOMB IS DROPPED ON HIROSHIMA, 189,000 CASUALTIES . . . ATOM BOMB IS DROPPED ON NAGASAKI . . . JAPANESE SURRENDER UNCONDITIONALLY . . . B-25 BOMBER CRASHES INTO EMPIRE STATE BUILDING, 13 DIE . . . BITUMINOUS COAL WORKERS STRIKE . . . GM AND FORD STRIKE . . . U.S., USSR OCCUPY KOREA . . . GANDHI AND NEHRU ASK BRITISH TO LEAVE INDIA . . . HO CHI MINH PUSHES FOR INDOCHINA INDEPENDENCE . . . ZIONISTS ASK THAT 1 MILLION JEWS GO TO PALESTINE . . . CHIANG KAI-SHEK AND MAO TSE-TUNG FORCES BEGIN FIGHTING . . . $6 BILLION IS VOTED IN TAX RELIEF . . . RATIONING ENDS.

Quotes

"I want a prayer to stop this rain. If we got a couple of clear days we could get in there and kill a couple of hundred thousand of those krauts."
— Gen. George Patton to his chaplain

"You begin to feel that you can't go on forever without being hurt. I feel that I have used up all my chances. And I hate it. I don't want to be killed."
— Ernie Pyle

"When he says he loves me he takes it about as seriously as his promises which he never keeps. . . . The weather is gorgeous and I, mistress of Germany's greatest man, have to sit at home and look at it through a window. If only I had a dog."
— from Eva Braun's diary

"We have learned lessons—at a fearful cost—and we shall profit by them. We have learned that we cannot live alone, at peace. . . . As Emerson said, . . . 'the only way to have a friend is to be one.'"   — FDR

"Have you ever seen stacks and piles of human bodies—200 to 300 in each pile, sprawled out, starved, beaten, and gassed to death?"
— Anonymous GI, on the liberation of Dachau

"Here were three greedy nations eager for loot and seeking greedily to advance their own self-interests by war, yet unable to agree on a strategic over-all plan for accomplishing a common objective."
— The Marshall Report

"Your city will be obliterated unless your government surrenders."
— Leaflets dropped on Hiroshima, August 5

Fierce battles on land and Kamikaze attacks at sea are occurring at Okinawa May 7th, as these GIs hear the news of V-E Day. *Copyright* Washington Post. *Reprinted by permission of D.C. Public Library.*

"Sixteen hours ago an American airplane dropped one bomb on Hiroshima . . . [with] more power than 20,000 tons of TNT. It is an atomic bomb. . . . If they do not now accept our terms, they may expect a rain of ruin from the sky the likes of which has never been seen on this earth."   — Harry S Truman

"A lightning flash covered the whole sky. . . . All green . . . perished."   — Witness, Hiroshima

Ads

Know what it's like to lie in a foxhole and hear the unearthly scream of "Banzai" in the night? How it feels to have your guts torn out by shrapnel? How you'd face the future with aluminum where a leg used to be? Or with your sight in the head of a dog? For God's sake, get back to work. . . . Buy more bonds. . . . Give more blood. Every little bit you do *is* important. *Remember, the shorter the war, the fewer American boys killed.*
(*Jones and Lamson Machine Co.*)

Something the Axis tanks don't have.
(*Quaker State Motor Oil*)

FREEDOM! Paper packages carried weapons to the Philippines.   (*Container Corp. of America*)

Home must be the greatest rehabilitation center of them all!
Vets—Belong to the 5220 Club: Unemployment pay, $20 for 52 Weeks.   (*Public service ad*)

—What You Can Do to Help the Returning Veteran
—Will He Be Changed?
—After two or three weeks he should be finished with talking, with oppressive remembering. If he still goes over the same stories, reveals the same emotions, you had best consult a psychiatrist. This condition is neurotic.   (*Good Housekeeping*)

Winged Victory—a new lipstick with matching nail polish.   (*Elizabeth Arden*)

Radio

Premieres
"Queen for a Day," Jack Bailey
"Arthur Godfrey Time"
"The Adventures of Topper," Roland Young
"Beulah," Marlin Hurt
"The Fat Man," Ed Begley, J. Scott Smart
"Meet Met at Parky's," Harry Einstein
"Bride and Groom" live weddings
"The Andrews Sisters Eight-to-the-Bar Ranch"
"The Second Mrs. Burton"
"This Is Your FBI," Frank Lovejoy, Stacy Harris

Favorite Programs: "One Man's Family" (soap opera), "Information Please!" (quiz), "Bob Hope" (entertainment/comedy), "Bing Crosby," "Dinah Shore" (singers), "Lowell Thomas" (commentator), "New York Philharmonic-Symphony"

Most Popular Serials: "Young Widder Brown," "Backstage Wife," "Guiding Light," "Helen Trent," "Ma Perkins," "Our Gal Sunday," "Portia Faces Life," "Right to Happiness," "Stella Dallas"

Of Note
During a newspaper deliverers' strike, New York mayor Fiorello La Guardia broadcasts the funnies.

TV

Premieres
"Here's [Henry] Morgan"
"The Singing Lady," Irene Wicker
"Ladies Be Seated," Johnny Olsen

Specials
Documentaries on V-E and V-J days; "Ring on Her Finger," unsponsored drama, 1 hour, 40 minutes (John Baragrey); Macy's first Thanksgiving Day Parade

Of Note
William Paley becomes chairman of the board at CBS • RCA's new camera, the image orthicon, has 100 times the sensitivity of the previous camera, developed in the 1920s.

Movies

Openings
The Lost Weekend (Billy Wilder), Ray Milland, Jane Wyman
Anchors Aweigh (George Sidney), Frank Sinatra, Gene Kelly
The Bells of St. Mary (Leo McCarey), Bing Crosby, Ingrid Bergman
Mildred Pierce (Michael Curtiz), Joan Crawford, Zachary Scott
Spellbound (Alfred Hitchcock), Ingrid Bergman, Gregory Peck
National Velvet (Clarence Brown), Mickey Rooney, Elizabeth Taylor
The Southerner (Jean Renoir), Zachary Scott
A Tree Grows in Brooklyn (Elia Kazan), Dorothy McGuire, James Dunn
The Story of GI Joe (William A. Wellman), Burgess Meredith, Robert Mitchum
The Picture of Dorian Gray (Albert Lewin), George Sanders, Hurd Hatfield
The House on 92nd Street (Henry Hathaway), William Eythe, Lloyd Nolan
They Were Expendable (John Ford), John Wayne, Robert Montgomery
The Body Snatcher (Robert Wise), Boris Karloff, Bela Lugosi
The Woman in the Window (Fritz Lang), Joan Bennett, Edward G. Robinson
Open City (Roberto Rossellini), A. Fabrizzi, Anna Magnani
Children of Paradise (Marcel Carne), Jean-Louis Barrault, Arletty

Academy Awards
Best Picture: *The Lost Weekend*
Best Director: Billy Wilder (*The Lost Weekend*)
Best Actress: Joan Crawford (*Mildred Pierce*)
Best Actor: Ray Milland (*The Lost Weekend*)
Special Award: Peggy Ann Garner (outstanding child actress)

Top Box-Office Stars
Bing Crosby, Van Johnson, Greer Garson, Betty Grable, Spencer Tracy, Humphrey Bogart, Gary Cooper, Bob Hope, Judy Garland, Margaret O'Brien, Roy Rogers

Stars of Tomorrow
Dane Clark, Jeanne Crain, Keenan Wynn, Peggy Ann Garner, Cornel Wilde, Tom Drake, Lon McCallister, Diana Lynn, Marilyn Maxwell, William Eythe

Popular Music

Hit Songs
"Cruising down the River"
"Autumn Serenade"
"I Love You for Sentimental Reasons"
"On the Atchison, Topeka and the Sante Fe"
"If I Loved You"
"It Might as Well Be Spring"
"Laura"
"Let It Snow!"
"June Is Bustin' Out All Over"
"Dig You Later-A-Hubba-Hubba-Hubba"
"It's a Grand Night for Singing"

Top Records

Albums: *The King Cole Trio* (King Cole Trio); *Songs of Norway* (original cast); *Glenn Miller* (Glenn Miller); *Carousel* (original cast); *Boogie Woogie* (Freddie Slack)

Singles: *I Fall in Love Too Easily, Am I Blue?* (Eugenie Bard with Mel Torme's Meltones); *The More I See You* (Carmen Cavallaro); *It's Been a Long, Long Time* (DeMarco Sisters); *This Heart of Mine* (Judy Garland); *Aren't You Glad You're You?* (Bing Crosby); *Put Your Dreams Away* (Frank Sinatra); *Sentimental Journey* (Les Brown, Doris Day); *Temptation* (Perry Como); *There, I've Said It Again* (Vaughn Monroe); *Cottage for Sale* (Billy Eckstine); *April Showers* (Al Jolson). Country: *At Mail Call Today* (Gene Autry); *Oklahoma Hills* (Jack Guthrie)

Jazz and Big Bands
Dizzy Gillespie tours with his first big band. Bop is at its peak. Miles Davis goes to New York to study at Juilliard. June Christy joins Stan Kenton; Charlie Shavers joins Tommy Dorsey.

First Recording: Dizzy Gillespie with Charlie Parker

New Bands: Ray Baudac, Billy Butterfield, Les Elgart, Dizzy Gillespie, Ted Heath

Top Performers (*Downbeat*): Benny Goodman (soloist); Woody Herman (big band); Tommy Dorsey (sweet band); Oscar Moore, Chubby Jackson, Dave Tough, Charlie Ventura, Buddy De Franco, Bill Harris (instrumentalists); Jo Stafford, Anita O'Day, Bing Crosby, Stuart Foster (vocalists); Pied Pipers (vocal group)

Theater

Broadway Openings

Plays
The Glass Menagerie (Tennessee Williams), Laurette Taylor, Julie Haydon, Eddie Dowling
State of the Union (Howard Lindsay, Russel Crouse), Ralph Bellamy, Ruth Hussey
The Hasty Heart (John Patrick), John Lund, Richard Basehart
Deep Are the Roots (Arnaud d'Usseau, James Gow), Barbara Bel Geddes
Dream Girl (Elmer Rice), Betty Field, Wendell Corey
He Touched Me (Tennessee Williams, Donald Windham), Montgomery Clift, Edmund Gwenn
Home of the Brave (Arthur Laurents), Eduard Franz
Foolish Notion (Philip Barry), Tallulah Bankhead, Donald Cook

Musicals
Are You with It? (Harry Revel, Arnold Horwitt), Joan Roberts, Johnny Downs, Dolores Gray
Carousel (Richard Rodgers, Oscar Hammerstein II), Jan Clayton, John Raitt

Laffing Room Only (Burton Lane), Olsen and Johnson, Betty Garrett
Up in Central Park (Sigmund Romberg, Dorothy Fields), Wilbur Evans, Maureen Cannon, Noah Beery
Dark of the Moon (Walter Hendl), Carol Stone, Richard Hart
The Day before Spring (Alan Jay Lerner, Frederick Loewe), Irene Manning, Bill Johnson

Classics and Revivals On and Off Broadway
Hamlet, Maurice Evans (GI version); *The Tempest*, Vera Zorina; *Pygmalion* (George Bernard Shaw), Gertrude Lawrence, Raymond Massey

Pulitzer Prize
Harvey, Mary Chase

Classical Music

Compositions
Walter Piston, Sonata for Violin and Harpsichord
Roy Harris, Piano Concerto no. 1
Samuel Barber, Cello Concerto
Norman Dello Joio, *Diversion of Angels*
Ross Lee Finney, *Pilgrim Psalms*
Béla Bartók (in U.S.), Piano Concerto no. 3, Viola Concerto
Arnold Schoenberg (in U.S.), *Prelude to a Genesis Suite*
Paul Hindemith (in U.S.), Piano Concerto
Igor Stravinsky (in U.S.), Symphony in Three Movements

First Performances
Stravinsky (conducting), *Scènes de Ballet* (New York); Bohuslav Martinů, Symphony no. 7 (Philadelphia); Leo Sowerby, *The Canticle of the Sun* (New York); Paul Creston, Symphony no. 2 (New York); Darius Milhaud (conducting), *La bal martiniquais* (New York). In Los Angeles, *Genesis for Narrator and Orchestra: Seven Pieces by Seven Composers* includes Arnold Schoenberg, Nathaniel Shilkret, Alexander Tansman, Darius Milhaud, Mario Castelnuovo-Tedesco, Ernest Toch, and Igor Stravinsky.

Opera

Metropolitan: Of 29 operas performed, most popular are *Die Meistersinger, Aïda, La bohème, Lucia di Lammermoor, Manon,* and *Don Giovanni.* Performances include Mimi Benzell, *Die Zauberflöte;* Jennie Tourel, *Il barbiere di Siviglia;* Richard Tucker (debut), *La Gioconda;* Risë Stevens, *Carmen;* Nadine Conner, *Faust.* Robert Merrill wins the radio auditions contest.

Chicago: Bidú Sayão, *La bohème;* in the company: Sayão, Zinka Milanov, Kerstin Thorborg, Helen Traubel, Jan Peerce

San Antonio: Grace Moore, *La bohème*

San Francisco: Licia Albanese, Salvatore Baccaloni, *L'heure espagnole;* Helen Traubel, Lauritz Melchior, *Tristan und Isolde, Die Walküre;* Lily Djanel, *Salomé*

Music Notes
The liberation of Europe is followed by the immediate restoration of musical activity • As a token of "global friendship," the State Symphony of Moscow performs a concert of Roy Harris, Wallingford Riegger, Samuel Barber, Élie Siegmeister, and George Gershwin • Numerous persons are investigated for suspected Nazi collaboration • War losses leave many orchestras with vacancies • William Schuman becomes president of Juilliard • The first Annual Festival of Contemporary American Music, at Columbia University, features David Diamond, Howard Hanson, Henry Brant, and Walter Piston.

Tommy Dorsey. *Movie Star News.*

Tennessee Williams's *The Glass Menagerie. Billy Rose Theatre Collection. The New York Library at Lincoln Center. Astor, Lenox and Tilden Foundations.*

1945

Art _____

Paintings
William Baziotes, *The Room*
Clyfford Still, *Number 6 (1945–46), Self-Portrait*
Walt Kuhn, *Young Clown*
Jackson Pollock, *Moon Woman Cuts the Circle, Totem Lesson II*
Arshile Gorky, *Diary of a Seducer*
Mark Rothko, *Baptismal Scene*
Reginald Marsh, *White Tower Hamburger*
Willem de Kooning, *Pink Angels*
Charles Sheeler, *Water*
Philip Guston, *Sentimental Moment*
Charles Burchfield, *Autumnal Fantasy*

Sculpture
Isamu Noguchi, *Kouros*
José de Creeft, *Rachmaninoff*
Alexander Calder, *Red Pyramid*
Herbert Ferber, *Three Legged Woman I*
David Smith, *Cockfight—Variation, The Rape*
Jacques Lipchitz, *Joy of Orpheus*

Architecture
Graduate Center, Harvard University, Cambridge (Walter Gropius)
Case Study, House 8, Pacific Palisades, Calif. (Charles Eames)
Frank Lloyd Wright completes the model for the Guggenheim Museum.

Important Exhibitions

Museums

New York: *Metropolitan:* Goya's prints and drawings; "The War against Japan"; "The Living Past of China"; "Costumes from the Forbidden City: Peking"; William Sidney Mount and his circle; Greek art (in the new permanent installation). *Museum of Modern Art:* Rouault, Stuart Davis. *Whitney:* Early American art

Chicago: Hudson River School

Boston: A thousand years of landscape art

Philadelphia: "The Philadelphia Story as Told by Philadelphia Press Artists": William Glackens, George Luks, Everett Shinn, John Sloan

Pittsburgh: "Painting in the U.S.," Philip Guston, first prize

Washington: *Corcoran:* Prizes are awarded to Reginald Marsh for *Strip Tease in New Jersey,*

Smithsonian Institution.

Malvin A. Zsissley for *Deer Isle, Maine,* and Isabel Bishop for *Two Girls Outdoors.*

Individual Shows
Klee, Kandinsky, Mondrian, Stuart Davis, Rouault, Miró (his first in the United States), Picasso, Matisse, and Bonnard.

Art Briefs
Auction rooms record the largest business in history; Parke-Bernet in New York sells $6 million of art; the top painting, Hals's *The Merry Lute Player,* brings $127,000 • Robert Niles wins first prize at the National Army Artists' Contest for *Between Trains* • Corporations like IBM, Pepsi-Cola, Encyclopædia Britannica, and Upjohn continue to support the arts.

Dance _____

Lucia Chase and Oliver Smith become codirectors of Ballet Theatre. Martha Graham signs for a world tour.

Premieres

Ballet Theatre: *Interplay* (Jerome Robbins), Janet Reed, Michael Kidd, John Kriza, Robbins; *Elegie* (George Balanchine); *Undertow* (Anthony Tudor), Hugh Laing, Nana Gollner; *The Firebird* (Adolf Bolm)

Ballet Russe de Monte Carlo: *Mozartiana* (Balanchine)

Books

Fiction

Critics' Choice

Cannery Row, John Steinbeck
The Friendly Persuasion, Jessamyn West
Apartment in Athens, Glenway Wescott
If He Hollers Let Him Go, Chester Himes
The Crack-Up, with Other Uncollected Pieces, F. Scott Fitzgerald (posthumous)
🔊 *Animal Farm*, George Orwell
🔊 *The Dwarf*, Pär Lagerkvist

Best-Sellers

Forever Amber, Kathleen Winsor
The Robe, Lloyd C. Douglas
The Black Rose, Thomas B. Costain
The White Tower, James Ramsey Ullman
Cass Timberlane, Sinclair Lewis
A Lion Is in the Streets, Adria Locke Langley
So Well Remembered, James Hilton
Captain from Castile, Samuel Shellabarger
Immortal Wife, Irving Stone
Earth and High Heaven, Gwethalyn Graham

Nonfiction

Critics' Choice

Atomic Energy for Military Purposes, Henry DeWolf Smyth
Race and Democratic Society, Franz Boaz (posthumous)
The American Language, (suppl. I), H. L. Mencken
Wars I Have Seen, Gertrude Stein
Japan and the Son of Heaven, Willard Price
Big Business in Democracy, James Truslow Adams
The Winning of the War in Europe and the Pacific, Gen. George C. Marshall
American Guerrilla in the Philippines, Ira Wolfert
Men under Stress, Lt. Col. Roy R. Grinker, Maj. John P. Spiegel
The Big Three: The United States, Britain and Russia, David J. Dallin
The Pattern of Soviet Power, Edgar Snow

Best-Sellers

Brave Men, Ernie Pyle
Dear Sir, Juliet Lowell
Up Front, Bill Mauldin
Black Boy, Richard Wright
Try and Stop Me, Bennett Cerf

Anything Can Happen, George and Helen Papashvily
General Marshall's Report, Gen. George C. Marshall
The Egg and I, Betty MacDonald
The Thurber Carnival, James Thurber
Pleasant Valley, Louis Bromfield

Poetry

Gwendolyn Brooks, *A Street in Bronzeville*
H. D., *Tribute to Angels*
Robert Frost, *A Masque of Reason*
Randall Jarrell, *Little Friend, Little Friend*
Kenneth Patchen, *An Astonishing Eye Looks Out of the Air*
John Crowe Ransom, *Selected Poems*
🔊 W. H. Auden, *The Collected Poems*

Pulitzer Prizes

The Age of Jackson, Arthur M. Schlesinger, Jr. (U.S. history)
Son of the Wilderness, Linnie Marsh Wolfe (biography)
No prizes are awarded for poetry or the novel.

Science and Technology

The first atomic bomb exploded in the Alamogordo, New Mexico, desert is a plutonium bomb; its power (equal to 20,000 tons of TNT) exceeds expectations.
Glenn Seaborg announces the discovery of two new elements, atomic numbers 95 and 96.
The method of administering penicillin orally is developed by Raymond Libby.
Successful treatment of scarlet fever with penicillin is reported.
The vitamin folic acid is discovered by American Cyanimid.
The navy reports a "complete cure" for cholera.

Dr. William Robbins reports the development of six new antibiotics: pleurotin, grisic acid, pleurin, irpexin, obtusin, and corticin; streptomycin, corticin, and pleurotin are marketed.
Helen Taussig and Alfred Blalock pioneer "blue baby" surgery.
A C-54 Douglas Skymaster goes around the world in a record 149 hours, 44 minutes.
A TWA Lockheed Constellation sets a New York–Paris record of 12 hours, 57 minutes.
Samuel Kramer, from the Pennsylvania Museum, discovers evidence of the 3000 B.C. Heroic Age of Sumer.

Sports

Baseball

A. B. "Happy" Chandler, former Kentucky senator, succeeds Kenesaw Landis as baseball commissioner with a seven-year contract at $50,000 a year.

Champions

Batting
  Phil Cavaretta (Chicago, NL), .355
  Snuffy Stirnweiss (New York, AL), .309

Pitching
  Harry Brecheen (St. Louis, NL), 15–4
  Hal Newhouser (Detroit, AL), 25–9
Home runs
  Tommy Holmes (Boston, NL), 28

Football

Bob Waterfield (QB), Los Angeles, debuts.

NFL Season Leaders: Sammy Baugh (Washington), passing; Steve Van Buren (Philadelphia), rushing; Don Hutson (Green Bay), receiving.

College All-Americans: Herman Wedemeyer (QB), St. Mary's; Bob Fenimore (B), Oklahoma A & M; Glenn Davis (B), Army; Felix "Doc" Blanchard (B), Army.

Bowls (Jan. 1, 1946)

Rose: Alabama 34–Southern California 13
Orange: Miami 13–Holy Cross 6
Sugar: Oklahoma A & M 33–St. Mary's 13
Cotton: Texas 40–Missouri 27

Basketball

In the NIT semifinal, Ernie Calverly, Rhode Island, ties the game at the buzzer with a 3/4 court shot; Rhode Island wins in overtime.

Winners

World Series
  Detroit (AL) 4–Chicago (NL) 3
MVP
  NL–Phil Cavaretta, Chicago
  AL–Hal Newhouser, Detroit
NFL
  Cleveland 15–Washington 14
MVP
  Bob Waterfield, Los Angeles
College Football
  Army
Heisman Trophy
  Felix Blanchard, Army

College Basketball
  Oklahoma A & M (NCAA)
  De Paul (NIT)
Player of the Year
  George Mikan, De Paul
Stanley Cup
  Toronto
US Tennis Open
  Men: Sgt. Frank Parker
  Women: Sarah Palfrey Cooke
Kentucky Derby
  Hoop Jr. (E. Arcaro, jockey)

Fashion

For Women: Ingenious designers deal with war regulations and the industry's need for change and style with "the rounded look." Dresses and suits are fitted at the midriff, neck, waist, and wrist; skirts bell over the stomach and thighs; large, felt, globe hats envelop the hair so the face and throat are again emphasized. Hair is worn in top and back knots with ribbons and bands of intertwined metal. Beachwear also gives the rounded look, especially bloomer shorts worn with breast bands. The new loose, shoulder-to-thigh cotton coat, the "cholo," appears. Flat shoes, like the new ballet slipper, and the low suede sandal with soft ankle band, are more popular than heeled styles. Also popular are gold neck bands, Zulu-like metal rings, gold chains, and the new belt with decals and a variety of decorative shapes. Cropped jeans and pants with stockings in the same rib (foreshadowing tights) are shown.

High-fashion note: Joffé's lampshade suit

Current fashion model. *Movie Star News.*

Kaleidoscope

V-E Day in an elementary school. *Copyright* Washington Post. *Reprinted permission D.C. Public Library.*

- The East Coast is alerted to the possibility of robot bomb attacks, and blackouts and brownouts intensify.
- Children continue to buy Defense Stamps weekly; schools give air raid drills; toys are scarce (there are no tricycles, bikes, sleds, skates, toy cars, mechanical or electric trains); girls write service boys whose names have been supplied by the USO.
- Thousands weep beside the train tracks and pay their last respects to FDR, as a train carries his body from Warm Springs, Georgia, to Washington.
- The 7th Army counterintelligence unit discovers Goering's $200 million art collection; the 101st Airborne Division puts it on display in the Bavarian village of Berchtesgaden.
- Ezra Pound, arrested near Geneva, is committed to a mental hospital in Washington, rather than tried for treason.
- William L. Laurence, *New York Times* science reporter, is permitted to join bombardier Maj. Thomas Ferebee and pilot Col. Paul Warfield Tibbets on the *Enola Gay* when the A-bomb is dropped on Hiroshima. Laurence's commentary is released a month later: "A giant ball of fire rose from the bowels of the earth. Then . . . a pillar of purple fire, 10,000 feet high, shooting skyward. . . . There came shooting out of the top a giant mushroom."
- The first Japanese envoys to Gen. Douglas MacArthur and Richard K. Sutherland in Manila arrive with half a dozen cartons of American cigarettes; the gifts are refused.
- Pablo Picasso welcomes GIs who tour Paris at the end of the war.
- Gas fuel rationing ends in August; by November, all items are available but sugar; the midnight curfew is lifted; the nationwide dimout is lifted; President Truman lights the National Community Christmas Tree at the White House for the first time since 1941.
- Penicillin, previously distributed to the armed forces, becomes more available to the civilian population.
- Former secretary of state Cordell Hull receives the Nobel Peace Prize.
- Audie Murphy returns home from North Africa, Italy, and France, the most decorated World War II hero; he is awarded 15 citations, including the Congressional Medal of Honor and high awards from both Belgium and France.
- Many families take their first vacations since Pearl Harbor; cabaret shows open in cities like Las Vegas, a by-product, in part, of the USO troop shows; motel construction increases.
- According to a Gallup poll, Greer Garson is America's most popular star.
- Gene Kelly and Fred Astaire dance together (the only time) in the film *Ziegfeld Follies.*
- Princess Elizabeth, 19, names Bing Crosby her favorite crooner.
- Frank Sinatra earns $13,500 a week, almost $1 million a year.
- Shirley Temple, 17, marries Air Force physical instructor John Agar; Judy Garland, 23, marries Vincente Minnelli, 38.
- The New York police commissioner resigns to preside over the radio show "Gangbusters."
- The bebop craze continues; the saying "Kilroy was here" remains popular.
- Truman is widely quoted for his sayings "The buck stops here" and "If you can't stand the heat, get out of the kitchen."
- The shortage of an estimated 4,660,000 homes forces many into makeshift arrangements that range from "doubling up" to living in autos.
- Women auto workers in Detroit, laid off because of returning war veterans, stage a march with posters such as "Stop Discrimination because of Sex."
- When Truman proposes his plan for peace and prosperity, some say it "out-Deals the New Deal."
- The Department of Agriculture reports that 20 million tons of food are needed to feed Europe.
- Nobel Laureate Irving Langmuir urges the establishment of a National Science Foundation in order to stay ahead of Russia in scientific progress.
- The Supreme Court affirms the right of each state to recognize or reject the Nevada divorce decree.
- The governor of Massachusetts signs a bill to end unofficial book censorship.
- A New York Court of Appeals voids the ban on *Esquire*'s second-class mail privileges.

First Appearances: Frozen orange juice, Flying Tiger airline; ballpoint pens on sale, aerosol spray insecticides, CARE (Cooperative for American Remittances to Europe), butane cigarette lighter, Tupperware, trademark "Coke" registered, long-lasting strawberry (University of California), Swanson and Sons' frozen chicken and turkey, an actor elected to Congress (Helen Gahagan Douglas), wax pencils, nonpictorial stamp (United Nations)

1946

Facts and Figures

Economic Profile
   Dow-Jones:—High 212–
      Low 165
   GNP: − 2%
   Inflation: +4.6%
   Unemployment: 3.9%
High school graduates
   entering college: 39%
4-year colleges: 1,304
Public/private schools: 10/1
Cartier victory pin, flag of
   rubies, diamonds,
   sapphires: $270–$750
Bergdorf Goodman or
   Bloomingdale's crepe and
   chiffon gown: $110
   Beaver or Persian lamb
      coat: $600
   Mink coat: $2,250
Neiman Marcus, Harzfeld, or
   Saks navy jersey bra: $7
Lily of France bra: $2 and up
I. Magnin fuchsia and purple
   robe: $29.75
Real-hair chignon: $18
Blue Grass perfume: $3.75
   and up
Tabu set of two lipsticks and
   vial: $2.50

Deaths

George Arliss, Robert
   Benchley, W. C. Fields,
   William S. Hart, Harry
   Hopkins, Damon Runyon,
   Gertrude Stein, Alfred
   Stieglitz, Booth
   Tarkington, H. G. Wells.

In the News

CIVIL WAR RAGES IN CHINA . . . SENATE ESTABLISHES ATOMIC ENERGY COMMISSION, DEAN ACHESON CHAIRMAN . . . AT FIRST UN MEETING, IN LONDON, NORWAY'S TRYGVE LIE IS ELECTED SECRETARY-GENERAL . . . 200,000 STRIKE AT GENERAL ELECTRIC . . . 750,000 STEELWORKERS STRIKE . . . JUAN PERON IS ELECTED PRESIDENT OF ARGENTINA . . . FAIR EMPLOYMENT PRACTICES ACT IS DEFEATED IN SENATE . . . BRITAIN AND FRANCE EVACUATE LEBANON . . . KOREAN PROVISIONAL GOVERNMENT IS SET UP, USSR TO CONTROL NORTH, U.S. TO CONTROL SOUTH . . . SECRETARY OF STATE JAMES BYRNES ADVISES TOUGH POLICY ON RUSSIAN AGGRESSION OR INFILTRATION . . . 400,000 COAL WORKERS STRIKE . . . TRUMAN ORDERS RAILROADS SEIZED IF WORKERS STRIKE . . . TRUMAN SEIZES COAL MINES . . . ATOM BOMB TEST IS HELD AT BIKINI ATOLL IN THE PACIFIC . . . PHILIPPINES ARE DECLARED INDEPENDENT . . . CONGRESSIONAL COMMITTEE ABSOLVES FDR OF BLAME FOR PEARL HARBOR . . . YUGOSLOVIA SHOOTS DOWN TWO U.S. PLANES, 5 ARE KILLED . . . U.S. AND USSR DISAGREE ON GERMANY AT PARIS PEACE CONFERENCE . . . 12 NAZIS ARE SENTENCED TO DEATH AT NUREMBERG, HERMAN GOERING COMMITS SUICIDE . . . HENRY WALLACE ATTACKS BYRNES ON HARSH POLICY TO USSR . . . TRUMAN ASKS WALLACE TO RESIGN . . . ALL WAGE AND PRICE CONTROLS, EXCEPT RENT AND SUGAR, ARE ABOLISHED, PRICES SOAR . . . REPUBLICANS MAKE MAJOR SENATE AND HOUSE GAINS . . . COMMUNIST PARTY GAINS PLURALITY IN FRENCH PARLIAMENT . . . U.N. ATOMIC ENERGY COMMISSION OUTLAWS A-BOMB . . . MACARTHUR PURGES JAPANESE ULTRANATIONALISTS, ORDERS WAR CRIMES TRIBUNAL.

Eisenhower travels briefly with his wartime comrade Winston Churchill, who tours the U.S. warning of world communism. *Library of Congress.*

"Across the motion picture screen moved, in light and shadow, what veteran war correspondents called the most terrible pictures of mass slaughter and torture they had ever seen—single corpses and small mountains of them, corpses lying still and corpses being carted away . . . corpses shrunk by starvation and . . . battered by boots or clubs."
— *Time,* on films of concentration camps shown during the Nuremberg trials

Subsequent reports . . . confirmed fears that this . . . election would not be free. . . . [The provisional government] employed widespread measures of coercion and intimidation. . . . The provisions of Yalta and Potsdam have not been fulfilled."
— State Department report on Poland

Quotes

"The general treaty known as the Kellogg-Briand Pact was binding on 63 nations, including Germany, Italy, Japan. After 1928, war was an illegal thing."
— Nuremberg Tribunal

Judge: For what reason were children murdered?
S.S. Officer Ohlendorf: The order was that the Jewish population should be totally exterminated.
Judge: Including the children?
Ohlendorf: Yes.
— Nuremberg trial testimony

"From Stettin in the Baltic to Trieste in the Adriatic, an iron curtain has descended across the Continent. . . . I am convinced there is nothing they so much admire as strength, and there is nothing for which they have less respect than weakness, especially military weakness."
— Former prime minister Winston Churchill, at Fulton, Mo.

"The danger of war is much less from communism than imperialism, whether it be of the U.S. or England."
— Secretary of Agriculture Henry Wallace, at Madison Square Garden

"If it is not possible . . . to keep Mr. Wallace . . . from speaking out on foreign affairs, then it would be a grave mistake . . . for me to continue in my office."
— Secretary of State James Byrnes

Ads

Beer belongs—enjoy it. In this home-loving land of ours, the kind of beverage Americans like . . . America's beverage of moderation.
(U.S. Brewers' Foundation)

Come home for the Holiday—but would there be time? Yes! The Airlines gain you time . . . time . . . time.
(Martin Aircraft)

Sight for Soaring Eyes
(TWA)

Everyone wants to save. Here's a truly timely aid in the food crisis.
(York Freezers)

Vogue—[for] the overwhelming minority.
(Vogue *Magazine*)

Modern life demands at least one man in seven to shave daily. For the one man in seven who shaves daily.
(Glider)

Even my husband says I'm a good driver now. . . . You'll make belittlers of women's driving eat their words now.
(Chevrolet)

Enough to make your hair curl.
(Best's Exclusive Lamp Curl)

I wanna give 'em away but Mrs. Muntz won't let me. She's crazy.
(Madman Muntz, Los Angeles used-car dealer)

Radio

Premieres

"Winner Take All," Bill Cullen
"Sam Spade," Howard Duff
"Meet the Press," Martha Rountree, Lawrence
   Spivak
"The Bing Crosby Show"
"Arthur Godfrey's Talent Scouts"
"Twenty Questions," Bill Slater

Most Popular Programs: "Jack Benny," "Fibber
McGee and Molly," "Bob Hope," "Fred Allen,"
"Radio Theater," "Amos 'n' Andy," "Walter
Winchell," "Red Skelton" "Screen Guild Players"

New Catchphrases: "[Is it] animal, vegetable, or
mineral? . . . larger or smaller than a breadbox?"
("Twenty Questions")

Movies

Openings

The Best Years of Our Lives (William Wyler), Fredric
   March, Myrna Loy, Dana Andrews, Harold
   Russell
The Big Sleep (Howard Hawks), Humphrey Bogart,
   Lauren Bacall
The Postman Always Rings Twice (Tay Garnett),
   John Garfield, Lana Turner
It's a Wonderful Life (Frank Capra), James Stewart,
   Donna Reed
The Razor's Edge (Edmund Goulding), Tyrone
   Power, Gene Tierney
The Yearling (Clarence Brown), Gregory Peck, Jane
   Wyman, Claude Jarman, Jr.
Brief Encounter (David Lean), Celia Johnson, Trevor
   Howard
Henry V (Laurence Olivier), Laurence Olivier,
   Robert Newton
The Killers (Robert Siodmak), Burt Lancaster, Ava
   Gardner
The Jolson Story (Alfred E. Green), Larry Parks,
   Evelyn Keyes
Gilda (Charles Vidor), Rita Hayworth, Glenn Ford
Duel in the Sun (King Vidor), Jennifer Jones,
   Gregory Peck
Song of the South (Harve Foster), Ruth Warrick,
   Bobby Driscoll
Notorious (Alfred Hitchcock), Cary Grant, Ingrid
   Bergman
The Blue Dahlia (George Marshall), Alan Ladd,
   Veronica Lake, William Bendix

TV

Premieres

"Small Fry Club," Bob Emery
"At Home with Tex [McCrary] and Jinx
   [Falkenburg]"
"Faraway Hill" (first TV soap opera), Flora
   Campbell
"You Are an Artist," John Gnagy
"See What You Know," Bennett Cerf
"Hour Glass," Helen Parris, first program with
   major sponsor (Standard Brands)

Of Note

The Joe Lewis versus Billy Conn fight is telecast on
June 19 • In September, large numbers of TV sets
become commercially available • Wrestling (with
Dennis James) airs three times weekly from Jamaica
Arena, N.Y.; popular wrestlers include Gorgeous
George, Haystack Calhoun, and Antonino Rocca,
who frequently wins with his "airplane spin."

Road to Utopia (Hal Walker), Bing Crosby, Bob
   Hope, Dorothy Lamour
My Darling Clementine (John Ford), Henry Fonda,
   Victor Mature, Linda Darnell
Shoeshine (Vittorio De Sica), Franco Interlenghi,
   Rinaldo Smordini

Academy Awards

Best Picture: *The Best Years of Our Lives*
Best Director: William Wyler (*The Best Years of Our
   Lives*)
Best Actress: Olivia de Havilland (*To Each His Own*)
Best Actor: Fredric March (*The Best Years of Our
   Lives*)
Special Awards: Laurence Olivier (actor, director,
   producer, *Henry V*); Claude Jarman, Jr.
   (outstanding child actor)

Top Box-Office Stars

Bing Crosby, Ingrid Bergman, Van Johnson, Gary
Cooper, Bob Hope, Humphrey Bogart, Greer
Garson, Margaret O'Brien, Betty Grable, Roy
Rogers

Stars of Tomorrow

Joan Leslie, Butch Jenkins, Zachary Scott, Don
DeFore, Mark Stevens, Eve Arden, Lizabeth Scott,
Dan Duryea, Yvonne DeCarlo, Robert Mitchum

Lana Turner, in *The Postman Always Rings Twice*. *Movie Star News.*

Popular Music

Top Records

Albums: *State Fair* (Dick Haymes); *Merry Christmas* (Bing Crosby); *The Voice of Frank Sinatra* (Frank Sinatra); *Dancing in the Dark* (Carmen Cavallaro); *The Ink Spots Album* (Ink Spots)

Singles: *Prisoner of Love* (Perry Como); *South America, Take It Away* (Bing Crosby, Andrews Sisters, Vic Schoen Orchestra); *Shoo-Fly Pie and Apple Pan Dowdy* (Stan Kenton, June Christy); *Hey! Ba-Ba-Re-Bop* (Tex Beneke); *Hampton's Sal* (Lionel Hampton); *Say It Isn't So* (Coleman Hawkins); *A Night in Tunisia* (Charlie Parker). Country: *You Will Have to Pay* (Tex Ritter); *Sioux City Sue* (Louis Jordan)

Jazz and Big Bands

Kai Winding and Shelly Manne join Stan Kenton. Red Norvo, with Woody Herman, introduces Stravinsky's *Ebony Concerto*. Eddie Condon opens a club in Greenwich Village, N.Y.

Top Performers (*Downbeat*)**:** Benny Goodman (soloist); Duke Ellington (band); Eddie Safranski, Vido Musso, Roy Eldridge, Bill Harris (instrumentalists); Peggy Lee, Frank Sinatra (vocalists)

Hit Songs

"Chiquita Banana"
"To Each His Own"
"Come Rain or Come Shine"
"Doin' What Comes Natur'lly"
"Full Moon and Empty Arms"
"I Got the Sun in the Morning"
"Zip-a-Dee-Do-Dah"
"Ole Buttermilk Sky"
"Now Is the Hour"
"Golden Earrings"
"Tenderly"
"There's No Business Like Show Business"
"They Say It's Wonderful"

Theater

Broadway Openings

Plays

The Iceman Cometh (Eugene O'Neill), James Barton, Dudley Digges
Joan of Lorraine (Maxwell Anderson), Ingrid Bergman
Another Part of the Forest (Lillian Hellman), Patricia Neal, Mildred Dunnock, Leo Genn
Born Yesterday (Garson Kanin), Judy Holliday (replacing Jean Arthur), Paul Douglas, Gary Merrill
O Mistress Mine (Terence Rattigan), Alfred Lunt, Lynn Fontanne
Present Laughter (Noel Coward), Clifton Webb
Years Ago (Ruth Gordon), Fredric March, Florence Eldridge
Antigone (Jean Anouilh), Katharine Cornell, Cedric Hardwicke
No Exit (Jean-Paul Sartre), Claude Dauphin, Annabella
Christopher Blake (Moss Hart), Richard Tyler, Shepperd Strudwick

Musicals

Annie Get Your Gun (Irving Berlin), Ethel Merman, Ray Middleton
Around the World in 80 Days (Cole Porter), Orson Welles
Call Me Mister (Harold Rome), Betty Garrett, Jules Munshin
Lute Song (Raymond Scott, Bernard Hanighen), Mary Martin
St. Louis Woman (Harold Arlen, Johnny Mercer), Ruby Hill, Rex Ingram, Pearl Bailey; all-black cast
Beggar's Holiday (Duke Ellington, John Latouche), Zero Mostel, Alfred Drake

Classics and Revivals On and Off Broadway

Candida (George Bernard Shaw), Marlon Brando, Katharine Cornell; *Lady Windermere's Fan* (Oscar Wilde), Cornelia Otis Skinner, Estelle Winwood; *The Playboy of the Western World* (John Synge), Burgess Meredith, Mildred Natwick; *The Duchess of Malfi* (Webster), Elisabeth Bergner, Canada Lee; Old Vic: *Oedipus, Henry IV, Parts I, II, Uncle Vanya* (Chekhov), *The Critic* (Sheridan), Laurence Olivier, Ralph Richardson, Margaret Leighton, Joyce Redman. *Founded:* American Repertory Theatre by Eva Le Gallienne, Margaret Webster, and Cheryl Crawford

Pulitzer Prize

State of the Union, Howard Lindsay and Russel Crouse

Classical Music ─────────────

Compositions

Roy Harris, Concerto for Two Pianos
Roger Sessions, Piano Sonata no. 2
Samuel Barber, *Medea*
Don Gillis, Symphony no. 5½, *Symphony for Fun*
Peter Mennin, Symphony no. 3
Ned Rorem, *Alleluia*
Ulysses Kay, Inventions for Piano
Walter Piston, Divertimento for Nine Instruments
John Cage, Sonatas and Interludes for Prepared
    Pianos
Robert Ward, *Jubilation*

Important Events

Postwar attendance at musical events breaks all records.
Beethoven is most frequently performed by the 21 major U.S. orchestras, followed by Tchaikovsky, Wagner, Mozart, Bach, and Mendelssohn, and, among the contemporaries, Richard Strauss and Aaron Copland.
Leonard Bernstein becomes director of symphony programs at New York City Center and conducts the New York City Symphony Orchestra without pay (1946–48). Artur Rodzinski returns to the New York Philharmonic Symphonic Society. Charles Munch conducts the Boston Symphony Orchestra.
Festivals resume throughout the country. The Berkshire premieres Benjamin Britten's *Peter Grimes* and Shostakovich's Symphony no. 9.

First Performances

Charles Ives, Symphony no. 3 (New York); Stravinsky, *Ebony Concerto* (New York); Stravinsky, conducting, Symphony in Three Movements (New York); Béla Bartók, Piano Concerto no. 3 (New York); Samuel Barber, Cello Concerto (Boston); Aaron Copland, Symphony no. 3 (Boston); Paul Hindemith, *When Lilacs Last in the Dooryard Bloom'd* (New York); Ernst Krenek, Piano Concerto no. 3 (Minneapolis); Darius Milhaud, Concerto for Clarinet and Orchestra (Washington); Arnold Schoenberg, *Genesis* (Los Angeles).

Opera

Metropolitan: Joel Berglund, *Tristan und Isolde, Die Meistersinger;* Raoul Jobin, *Lakmé;* Stella Roman, *La bohème;* Set Svanholm (debut) *Siegfried;* Ramon Vinay, *Otello;* premiere: *The Medium* (Gian Carlo Menotti); revival: *Il tabarro* (Puccini); company makes extensive tour of twelve countries.

City Center, New York: *Ariadne auf Naxos* (Richard Strauss, American premiere)

Chicago: Zinka Milanov, Kurt Baum, Leonard Warren, Italo Tajo, *Aïda;* Patrice Munsel, Richard Tucker, *Lucia di Lammermoor;* Helen Traubel, Set Svanholm, Blanche Thebom, *Tristan und Isolde;* premieres: *Amelia Goes to the Ball* (Gian Carlo Menotti) and *Emperor Jones* (Louis Gruenberg)

San Francisco: Risë Stevens, Eleanor Steber, *Carmen;* Set Svanholm, Astrid Varnay, *Lohengrin*

Dallas: *Bluebeard's Castle* (Béla Bartók, premiere, in English)

Nathan Milstein, Vladimir Horowitz, and Gregor Piatigorsky. *D. Ouellette Collection.*

Art

Paintings

Jackson Pollock, *Sounds in the Grass, Shimmering Substance*
Jack Levine, *Welcome Home*
Adolph Gottlieb, *Voyager's Return*
Mark Rothko, *Prehistoric Memories*
Dong Kingman, *The El and Snow*
Paul Cadmus, *Fantasia on a Theme by Dr. S.*
George Grosz, *Peace, II*
Willem de Kooning, *Queen of Hearts, Light in August*

Sculpture

Isamu Noguchi, glass and wood table

José de Rivera, *Yellow Block*
David Smith, *Spectre of Profit*
William Zorach, *The Artist's Daughter* (1930–46)
Chaim Gross, *Sisters*
Louise Nevelson, *Lovers II*

Architecture

Solar House, Kalamazoo, Mich. (George Fred Keck)
Plans are drawn for the Opera Pavillion, Cincinnati (William H. Tunke) and the UN Building (Wallace K. Harrison).

Important Exhibitions

Loans travel throughout the U.S.: from King George VI and the London Museum, Hogarth, Constable, Turner; from Standard Oil, "The Visual Story of Oil" (Joe Jones, Thomas Hart Benton).

Disabled veteran Harold Russell, with Dana Andrews and Fredric March, in *The Best Years of Our Lives,* which wins 8 Academy Awards. *Movie Star News.*

Museums

New York: *Metropolitan:* Diamond Jubilee displays include Michelangelo's *Madonna and Child* and Delacroix's *La Barricade* (from the Louvre); "The Taste of the '70s." *Museum of Modern Art:* Art of the South Seas; Fourteen Americans; Henry Moore and Marc Chagall retrospectives. *Whitney:* Pioneers of modern art (34 artists, including Marin, Stella, Weber, Hartley, Man Ray, Maurer); Current U.S. sculpture

Chicago: Chinese bronzes; George Bellows; Constable and Turner

Pittsburgh: Carnegie prizes are awarded to Karl Knath *(Gear),* Jack Levine *(Welcome Home),* and William Gropper *(Don Quixote, No. 1).*

Individual Shows

Inness, Robinson, Still

Art Briefs

A survey of museum directors on their favorite painters reports Hartley, first, followed by Kuniyoshi, Franklin C. Watkins, Marsh, Alexander Brook, Mattson, Burchfield, and Hopper • Billy Rose pays a record price ($75,000) for Rembrandt's *A Pilgrim at Prayer;* also sold this year are Cézanne's *Portrait of Mme. Cézanne* ($34,500); and Ryder's *Siegfried and the Rhine Maidens* ($23,500).

Dance

Ballet Society is organized by George Balanchine and Lincoln Kirstein to give subscription performances of new works.

Premieres

Ballet Theatre: *Facsimile* (Jerome Robbins), Nora Kaye, John Kriza

Ballet Society: *The Four Temperaments* (Balanchine, Hindemith), Tanaquil Le Clercq

Martha Graham: *Cave of the Heart*

Books

Fiction

Critics' Choice
The Bulwark, Theodore Dreiser
Thirty Stories, Kay Boyle
The Member of the Wedding, Carson McCullers
Delta Wedding, Eudora Welty
Focus, Arthur Miller
Mister Roberts, Thomas Heggen
The American, Howard Fast
Brewsie and Willie, Gertrude Stein
❦ *The Stranger*, Albert Camus

Best-Sellers
The King's General, Daphne Du Maurier
This Side of Innocence, Taylor Caldwell
The River Road, Frances Parkinson Keyes
The Miracle of the Bells, Russell Janney
The Hucksters, Frederic Wakeman
The Foxes of Harrow, Frank Yerby
Arch of Triumph, Erich Maria Remarque
The Snake Pit, Mary Jane Ward
B. F.'s Daughter, John P. Marquand

Nonfiction

Critics' Choice
Atomic Energy in Cosmic and Human Life, George Gamow
Manifesto for the Atomic Age, Virgil Jordan
Touched with Fire, ed. Mark De Wolfe
The Chrysanthemum and the Sword, Ruth Benedict
The Common Sense Book of Baby and Child Care, Benjamin Spock
Hiroshima, John Hersey
Problems of Men, John Dewey
War Reports, Henry Arnold, George Marshall, Ernest King
Thunder Out of China, Theodore White, Annalee Jacoby

Best-Sellers
The Egg and I, Betty MacDonald
Peace of Mind, Joshua L. Liebman
As He Saw It, Elliott Roosevelt
The Roosevelt I Knew, Frances Perkins
Last Chapter, Ernie Pyle
I Chose Freedom, Victor Kravchenko
The Anatomy of Peace, Emery Reves

Top Secret, Ralph Ingersoll

Poetry
Elizabeth Bishop, *North and South*
H. D., *Flowering of the Rod*
Robinson Jeffers, *Medea*
Kenneth Patchen, *Sleepers Awake*
William Carlos Williams, *Paterson, Book One*
Denise Levertov, *The Double Image*
Wallace Stevens, *Esthétique du Mal*
May Sarton, *The Bridge of Years*
❦ Dylan Thomas, *Deaths and Entrances*

Pulitzer Prizes
All the King's Men, Robert Penn Warren (novel)
Scientists against Time, James Phinney Baxter III (U.S. history)
The Autobiography of William Allen White, William Allen White (biography)
Lord Weary's Castle, Robert Lowell (poetry)

Science and Technology

"Printing" wiring circuits on ceramic furthers miniaturization of radios and other electronic equipment.

Eniac, the giant automated electronic computer, is further developed at Harvard to perform 1,000 times faster than humans.

The army makes the first radar contact with the moon, bouncing back a signal in 2.4 seconds.

Ernest O. Lawrence reports that the synchrotron, the new atom smasher, produces 300 million volts.

The first atomic pile for peaceful purposes is set up at Oak Ridge, Tennessee; plans for other facilities in Illinois and New York are announced.

The Mayo Clinic reports that streptomycin can check the advance of tuberculosis.

The University of Pennsylvania experiments with carbon 14, the first manmade radioactive substance to be used in medical research.

RCA markets an unbreakable disc of vinylite on which *Til Eulenspiegel* is recorded.

Harry Stack Sullivan, in *Conceptions of Modern Psychiatry*, develops his theory of the importance of interpersonal relations.

Nobel Prizes
The prize in chemistry is shared by James B. Sumner, for his research on enzymes, and Wendell Stanley and John Northrop, for their work on viruses. Percy W. Bridgman wins the award in physics, for his work on atmospheric pressure. Hermann J. Muller wins in physiology and medicine, for work on the effect of X rays on genes.

Sports

Baseball

Many stars return from the war.

Jackie Robinson, the first black player in organized baseball, stars for Montreal, a Brooklyn (NL) farm team.

Bob Feller (Cleveland) strikes out a record 348.

Warren Spahn (Boston, NL) and Yogi Berra (New York, AL) debut.

St. Louis (NL) beats Brooklyn (NL) in two out of three in the first pennant playoff.

Ted Williams goes four for four with two home runs in the All-Star game.

Champions

Batting	Pitching
Stan Musial (St. Louis, NL), .365	Howie Pollet (St. Louis, NL), 21–10
Mickey Vernon (Washington, AL), .353	Dave Ferris (Boston, AL), 25–6
	Home runs
	Hank Greenberg (Detroit, AL), 44

Football

The All-America Conference begins competition with the NFL. The Cleveland Browns beat the New York Yanks 14–7.

NFL Season Leaders: Bob Waterfield (Los Angeles), passing; Bill Dudley (Pittsburgh), rushing; Jim Benton (Los Angeles), receiving.

College All-Americans: John Lujack (QB), Notre Dame; Charles Trippi (B), Georgia; Glenn Davis (B), Army; Felix "Doc" Blanchard (B), Army

Bowls (Jan. 1, 1947)

Rose: Illinois 45–UCLA 14
Orange: Rice 9–Tennessee 8
Cotton: Arkansas 0–Louisiana 0
Sugar: Georgia 20–North Carolina 10

Basketball

The NBA is formed with 11 teams in major cities; Maurice Podoloff is president.

Other Sports

Boxing: Joe Louis knocks out Billy Conn in the eighth round at Yankee Stadium, New York; ringside seats are a record $100.

Golf: Ben Hogan, the top pro golfer, wins five tournaments and $42,566.

Horse Racing: Assault, ridden by W. Mehrtens, wins the Triple Crown.

Winners

World Series	College Basketball
St. Louis (NL) 4	Oklahoma A & M (NCAA)
Boston (AL) 3	Kentucky (NIT)
MVP	*Player of the Year*
NL–Stan Musial, St. Louis	Bob Kurland, Oklahoma
AL–Ted Williams, Boston	A & M
NFL	*Stanley Cup*
Chicago (Bears) 24–New	Montreal
York 14	*US Tennis Open*
MVP	Men: John Kramer
Bill Dudley, Chicago	Women: Pauline Betz
College Football	*USGA Open*
Notre Dame	Lloyd Mangrum
Heisman Trophy	*Kentucky Derby*
Glenn Davis, Army	Assault (W. Mehrtens, jockey)

Fashion

For Women: *Harper's Bazaar* reports five casual fashion trends: (1) shirtwaists worn with Civil War Phelps bags, (2) ginghams, which recall the frontier, (3) ballerina-length skirts, (4) overalls, (5) wool tights, hoods, and tightly belted coats. Most noticeable is the postwar trend toward femininity with emphasis on the natural, slightly idealized figure with no padding. Pastel day dresses have Peter Pan collars, full-gathered skirts, sashes, and ruffles. The "bellhop" suit is neat, tailored, buttoned, and tight. Wide-neck dinner dresses, which expose the shoulders and part of the back and chest, are willowy, in yards of fabric. Some have only one strap and an uneven hemline. Colors are faded pink, ice blue, yellow, and mauve. Hats are pleated or turbaned and trimmed with fine feathers; some match striped or patterned bags, blouses, and umbrellas. With nylons back again, shoes draw attention to the ankle and the arch and have slender high heels and ankle straps; cutouts above the toe expose even more foot to emphasize femininity.

High-fashion note: Hartnell's purple sheath; the Capezio ballet slipper

Kaleidoscope

- John D. Rockefeller donates $8.5 million for the construction of the UN headquarters along the East River, New York.
- Albert Einstein and a group of other nuclear scientists form the Emergency Committee of Atomic Science to advance the peaceful use of atomic energy.
- The August 31 issue of the *New Yorker* publishes John Hersey's *Hiroshima*.
- German physicists Otto Hahn and Werner Heisenberg claim they completed an "atomic energy machine" in Leipzig at the end of 1941, but lack of funds and facilities prohibited production of a bomb.
- Within a year of V-J Day, the American military goes from 11 to 1 million.
- A *New York Daily News* headline "PRICES SOAR, BUYERS SORE / STEERS JUMP OVER THE MOON" reflects the large accumulation of wartime capital and insufficient production of consumer goods; the cost of living is up 33 percent over 1941.
- Buying and vacation sprees occur; money is frequently paid under the counter for cars, apartments, and theater and sports tickets.
- The birth rate increases 20 percent over 1945.
- With sugar rationing over, ice-cream consumption takes on fad proportions.
- Bread consumption drops as flour and wheat are exported to Europe; flour whiteners are added for American consumers who dislike dark bread.
- The "Moscow mule" (vodka and ginger ale) is invented, and vodka sales increase.
- Fashion columnists report Louis Reard's "bikini" sensation in Paris.
- Auto innovations include the single unit of welded steel (Nash 600), wide windows (Studebaker Champion), and combined wood station wagon and passenger car (Chrysler Town and Country).
- The RCA 10-inch TV sells for $374, the Model T of television sets.
- More than half the top bands dissolve (Tommy Dorsey, Benny Goodman, Woody Herman, Les Brown, Benny Carter), and band vocalists strike out on their own (Dick Haymes, Doris Day, Perry Como).
- The DAR bars Eddie Condon's jazz band from Constitution Hall because of "the type of audience" it will attract.
- Mobster Bugsy Siegel and his gang open the Flamingo in Las Vegas, and building is widespread at the "entertainment capital of America."
- A syndicate that includes Bob Hope buys the Cleveland Indians.
- Ads for the movie *The Outlaw* read: "The Music Hall gets the Big Ones. What are the two great reasons for Jane Russell's rise to stardom?" Miss Russell wears a special uplift bra designed by Howard Hughes.
- Bing Crosby introduces transcribed, rather than live, programs on ABC; he earns $30,000 a week on the Philco radio show.
- Blacks vote for the first time in the Mississippi Democratic primary.

- The auction of FDR's stamp collection brings $211,000.
- Former secretary of state Henry Wallace becomes editor of the *New Republic*.
- Dr. Benjamin Spock's *The Common Sense Book of Baby and Child Care* is published; it was written while Spock was in the Navy Medical Corps in charge of severe disciplinary cases.
- Oklahoma City offers the first rapid public treatment of venereal diseases.
- United Airlines announces it has ordered jet planes for commercial purposes.
- The *AMA Journal* reports that the primary results of radiation disease suffered by Hiroshima and Nagasaki victims are disturbed liver function and suppression of the blood-formation system.
- A C-45 crashes into the 58th floor of a New York bank building; five are killed.
- *Life* reports (January 17) on the growing popularity of Jean-Paul Sartre's existentialism.

First Appearances: Estée Lauder, "Beautiful Hair" Breck ads, Sunshine biscuits, French's instant potatoes, electric blankets, FDR dime instead of the 1916 Mercury dime, DC-6 (Douglas Aircraft) for 70 passengers, 300 m.p.h., with cargo, Crosby compact car, autobank service, Lewyt vacuum cleaner, artificial snow, mobile telephone service, coin-operated TV, Fulbright awards, Tide, Timex watches, telephones on trains, automatic clothes dryers, *Family Circle, Scientific American, Holiday,* ektachrome color film, J. L. Hudson store (world's second largest, Detroit)

Jane Russell in *The Outlaw*. The film, first released in 1943 but withdrawn because of censorship controversy, is now released in defiance of the production code. *Movie Star News.*

1947

Facts and Figures

Economic Profile
  Dow-Jones:—High 184–
    Low 166
  GNP: +11%
  Inflation: +8.4%
  Unemployment: 3.9%
Average salary: $2,589
  Teacher: $2,261
  Lawyer: $7,437
  Physician: $10,700
  Factory Worker: $2,793
Samson folding table: $3.95
Bendix automatic washer:
  $239.50
Emerson AC-DC battery-
  operated, portable radio:
  $29.95
GE vacuum cleaner: $27.95
San Moritz Hotel, New York:
  $4.50 up
Hotel Commodore, San
  Francisco: $3 up
Copacabana, New York, Joe
  E. Lewis, star; three-
  course dinner: $2.50
Broadway theater: $1.20–
  $4.30
Pop records, Victor: 4/99¢

Deaths

Henry Ford, Mark Hellinger,
  Fiorello La Guardia, Ernst
  Lubitsch, Grace Moore,
  Max Planck, Damon
  Runyan, Laurette Taylor,
  Alfred North Whitehead.

In the News

GENERAL GEORGE MARSHALL BECOMES SECRETARY OF STATE . . .
U.S. CEASES MEDIATION OF CHINESE CIVIL WAR . . . COUNCIL OF
FOREIGN MINISTERS MEETS IN MOSCOW BUT FAILS TO AGREE . . .
TRUMAN ORDERS LOYALTY INVESTIGATION OF ALL FEDERAL
EMPLOYEES . . . BRITAIN PROPOSES PARTITION OF PALESTINE, ARABS
AND JEWS PROTEST . . . TELEPHONE COMPANY STRIKES NATIONWIDE
. . . TRUMAN ASSERTS DOCTRINE OF SUPPORT TO FREE PEOPLES, $400
MILLION IN AID TO GREECE AND TURKEY . . . FREIGHTER IN TEXAS
GULF EXPLODES, 500 ARE KILLED . . . SELECTIVE SERVICE ACT
EXPIRES . . . HENRY WALLACE ATTACKS U.S. "IMPERIALIST" POLICY
. . . MARSHALL PROPOSES PLAN TO HELP REBUILD EUROPE . . . $350
MILLION IS ALLOCATED TO WAR-RAVAGED COUNTRIES . . . $4
BILLION TAX REDUCTION IS PASSED . . . COAL MINES RETURN TO
PRIVATE OPERATION WITH LARGE WAGE HIKE . . . CONGRESS PASSES
TAFT-HARTLEY "EMPLOYER RIGHTS" ACT OVER TRUMAN VETO . . .
INDEPENDENCE OF INDIA IS PROCLAIMED WITH SEPARATE STATES FOR
HINDUS AND MOSLEMS, MASSIVE FIGHTING OCCURS . . . WILLIAM
ODUM SETS ROUND-THE-WORLD FLYING RECORD OF 73 HOURS IN
"REYNOLD'S BOMBSHELL" . . . PALESTINE QUESTION GOES TO UN
. . . HOUSE UN-AMERICAN ACTIVITIES COMMITTEE BEGINS HEARINGS
ON HOLLYWOOD COMMUNISTS . . . $540 MILLION FOR FRANCE,
HOLLAND, AND AUSTRIA IS APPROPRIATED . . . COMMUNISTS WIN IN
HUNGARIAN ELECTION . . . HUAC INDICTS 10 HOLLYWOOD FIGURES
FOR CONTEMPT . . . TAYLOR ACT PROHIBITS PUBLIC EMPLOYEE
STRIKES . . . JOHN L. LEWIS WITHDRAWS UNITED MINE WORKERS
FROM THE AFL . . . WALLACE ANNOUNCES CANDIDACY FOR
PRESIDENT.

Marlon Brando, as the brute Stanley Kowalski, alternately caresses and bellows for his "Stella," played by Kim Hunter (center) in *A Streetcar Named Desire*. Jessica Tandy, right, plays Blanche DuBois. *Billy Rose Theatre Collection. The New York Public Library at Lincoln Center. Astor, Lenox and Tilden Foundations.*

"[A woman must] accept herself fully as a woman [and] know . . . she is dependent on a man. There is no fantasy in her mind about being an independent woman, a contradiction in terms."
— Marynia Farnham and Ferdinand Lundberg, *Modern Woman*

"I have always depended on the kindness of strangers."
— Blanche DuBois, *A Streetcar Named Desire* (Tennessee Williams)

Quotes

"I believe that it must be the policy of the United States to support free peoples who are resisting attempted subjugation by armed minorities or by outside pressures."
— Truman Doctrine

"The people of America are highly concerned about whether . . . this is the opening wedge in taking over the job that Britain has done so well in the last 150 years."
— Sen. Arthur Vandenberg, on the Truman Doctrine

"Our policy is not directed against any country or doctrine, but against hunger, poverty, desperation and chaos. We of the United States are deeply conscious of our responsibilities in the world."
— George Marshall, in Harvard speech

ON THE IMPENDING HUAC MEETINGS:
"Before every free conscience in America is subpoenaed, please speak up."
—Judy Garland
"Are they going to scare us into silence?"
—Fredric March
"Once they get movies throttled, how long before we're told what we can say . . . into a radio microphone?"
—Frank Sinatra
"I'd like to see them all in Russia. . . . A taste of Russia would cure them [the Reds]."
—Adolphe Menjou
"You can't help smelling them [the Reds]."
—Rupert Hughes, novelist-screenwriter

Ads

TV

Premieres
"Kraft Television Theater" ("Double Door")
"World Series," New York Yankees–Brooklyn
    Dodgers
"Meet the Press," Larry Spivak, Martha Rountree
"Howdy Doody," "Buffalo Bob" Smith
"Juvenile Jury," Jack Barry
"Party Line"
"Mary Kay and Johnny," first situation comedy
"U.S. Congress," first coverage

Specials
"The Late George Apley" (Leo G. Carroll); Ilona
Massey entertaining the veterans at St. Albans Naval
Hospital on Christmas Day

Of Note
Newsletters and magazines such as *Counterattack*
list American entertainers with alleged Communist
ties • The dramatic rise in Kraft's Imperial Cheese
sales, advertised on the "Kraft Television Theater,"
demonstrates TV's marketing potential.

Radio

Premieres
"You Bet Your Life," Groucho Marx
"The Jack Paar Show"
"Lassie," Marvin Miller
"Strike It Rich," Todd Russell
"Candid Microphone," Allen Funt
"My Friend Irma," Marie Wilson
"Stop Me if You've Heard This One," Roger Bower
"You Are There," Don Hollenbeck

Movies

Openings
Gentleman's Agreement (Elia Kazan), Gregory Peck,
    Dorothy McGuire, John Garfield
Crossfire (Edward Dmytryk), Robert Ryan, Robert
    Mitchum
Great Expectations (David Lean), John Mills, Valerie
    Hobson, Alec Guinness
Miracle on 34th Street (George Seaton), Edmund
    Gwenn, John Payne, Maureen O'Hara
Body and Soul (Richard Rossen), John Garfield, Lilli
    Palmer
Life with Father (Michael Curtiz), William Powell,
    Irene Dunne
Mourning Becomes Electra (Dudley Nichols),
    Rosalind Russell, Leo Genn
Kiss of Death (Henry Hathaway), Victor Mature,
    Richard Widmark
The Egg and I (Chester Erskine), Claudette Colbert,
    Fred MacMurray, Marjorie Main
The Bachelor and the Bobbysoxer (Irving Reis), Cary
    Grant, Myrna Loy, Shirley Temple
Monsieur Verdoux (Charles Chaplin), Charles
    Chaplin, Martha Raye
The Ghost and Mrs. Muir (Joseph L. Mankiewicz),
    Gene Tierney, Rex Harrison
Black Narcissus (Michael Powell, Emeric
    Pressburger), Deborah Kerr, Flora Robson
Odd Man Out (Carol Reed), James Mason, Kathleen
    Ryan
Brute Force (Jules Dassin), Burt Lancaster, Hume
    Cronyn, Howard Duff

Academy Awards
Best Picture: *Gentleman's Agreement*
Best Director: Elia Kazan (*Gentleman's Agreement*)
Best Actress: Loretta Young (*The Farmer's
    Daughter*)
Best Actor: Ronald Colman (*A Double Life*)

Top Box-Office Stars
Bing Crosby, Betty Grable, Ingrid Bergman, Gary
Cooper, Humphrey Bogart, Bob Hope, Clark Gable,
Gregory Peck, Claudette Colbert, Alan Ladd

Stars of Tomorrow
Evelyn Keyes, Billy De Wolfe, Peter Lawford, Janis
Paige, Elizabeth Taylor, Claude Jarman, Jr., Janet
Blair, MacDonald Cary, Gail Russell, Richard Conte

Popular Music

Hit Songs

"Almost Like Being in Love"
"Chi-Baba Chi-Baba"
"Civilization (Bongo, Bongo, Bongo)"
"Mam'selle"
"Papa, Won't You Dance with Me?"
"Woody Woodpecker"
"Ballerina"
"A Fellow Needs a Girl"
"I'll Dance at Your Wedding"
"Open the Door, Richard"

Top Records

Albums: *Al Jolson Album* (Al Jolson); *All Time Favorites* (Harry James); *Dorothy Shay Sings* (Dorothy Shay); *Al Jolson Album—Vol. 2* (Al Jolson); *Glenn Miller Masterpieces—Vol. 2* (Glenn Miller)

Singles: *How Are Things in Glocca Morra / Treasure of Sierra Madre* (Buddy Clark); *That's My Desire* (Frankie Laine); *Peg o' My Heart / Fantasy Impromptu* (The Harmonicats); *But Beautiful You* (Tex Beneke); *Near You* (Francis Craig); *Confess* (Doris Day); *Everything I Have Is Yours* (Billy Eckstine); *I'm Looking over a Four-Leaf Clover* (Art Moonie); *Temptation* (Jo Stafford). Country: *It's a Sin* (Eddy Arnold); *Divorce Me C.O.D.* (Merle Travis)

Jazz and Big Bands

Louis Armstrong breaks up his big band and forms a sextet that includes Jack Teagarden and Barney Bigard; Woody Herman organizes the second "Herd."

Top Performers *(Downbeat):* Benny Goodman (soloist); Duke Ellington (band); Shelly Manne, Johnny Hodges, Oscar Moore, Eddie Safranski (instrumentalists); Nat "King" Cole (jazz group); Sarah Vaughan, Frank Sinatra (soloists)

Theater

Broadway Openings

Plays

A Streetcar Named Desire (Tennessee Williams), Marlon Brando, Jessica Tandy, Kim Hunter, Karl Malden
All My Sons (Arthur Miller), Ed Begley, Arthur Kennedy
The Heiress (Ruth Augustus Goetz), Wendy Hiller, Basil Rathbone
For Love or Money (F. Hugh Herbert), June Lockhart, Vicki Cummings
Command Decision (William Wister Haines), Paul Kelly, James Whitmore
The Winslow Boy (Terence Rattigan), Frank Allenby, Valerie White
John Loves Mary (Norman Krasna), William Prince, Nina Foch, Tom Ewell
An Inspector Calls (J. B. Priestley), Thomas Mitchell

Musicals

Allegro (Richard Rodgers, Oscar Hammerstein II), John Battles, Roberta Jonay
Barefoot Boy with Cheek (Sidney Lippman, Sylvia Dee), Nancy Walker, William Redfield, Red Buttons
Brigadoon (Alan Jay Lerner, Frederick Loewe), Marion Bell, David Brooks
Finian's Rainbow (Burton Lane, E. Y. Harburg), Ella Logan, David Wayne
High Button Shoes (Jule Styne, Sammy Cahn), Phil Silvers, Nanette Fabray, Helen Gallagher, Joey Faye
Street Scene (Kurt Weill, Langston Hughes), Norman Cordon, Anne Jeffreys, Hope Emerson

Classics and Revivals On and Off Broadway

Medea (Robinson Jeffers adaptation), Judith Anderson, Florence Reed, John Gielgud; *Man and Superman* (George Bernard Shaw), Maurice Evans; *Crime and Punishment* (Rodney Ackland), John Gielgud, Lillian Gish; *The Importance of Being Earnest* (Oscar Wilde), John Gielgud; *Antony and Cleopatra*, Katharine Cornell, Godfrey Tearle; *King Lear*, Donald Wolfit and Company. *Founded:* Actors Studio by Elia Kazan, Cheryl Crawford, and Robert Lewis

Regional

Founded: Theatre '47 (Margo Jones Theatre), Dallas, by Margot Jones: *Farther Off from Heaven* [*Dark at the Top of the Stairs*], William Inge, premiere; Alley Theatre, Houston, by Nina Vance

Pulitzer Prize

No prize is awarded.

Classical Music

Compositions
Henry Cowell, *Hymn and Fuguing Tune*
Walter Piston, Symphony no. 3, String Quartet no. 3
Leonard Bernstein, Symphony no. 2 *(Age of Anxiety)*
George Antheil, Symphony no. 5
Roy Harris, *Quest*
Samuel Barber, *Knoxville: Summer of 1915*
William Schuman, Violin Concerto
Milton Babbitt, Three Compositions for Piano
Alan Hovhaness, Symphony no. 8

Important Events
Widespread interest in music grows, as orchestras travel. The New York Philharmonic gives 28 concerts in 24 cities; the San Francisco Symphony tours with 56 concerts. Fritz Reiner takes the Pittsburgh to Mexico City, the first major U.S. orchestra in Mexico. The Metropolitan Opera gives 57 performances in 14 cities.
Artur Rodzinski resigns from the New York Philharmonic and signs with the Chicago.

Debut: Michael Rabin

First Performances
Roger Sessions, Symphony no. 2 (San Francisco); Paul Hindemith, *Symphonia Serena* (Dallas), Concerto for Piano and Orchestra (Cleveland); George Antheil, Concerto in D (Dallas); Erich Korngold, Violin Concerto (St. Louis); Heitor Villa-Lobos, conducting, *Bachianas Brasileiras* (New York); Don Gillis, Symphony no. 5½ (Boston).

Opera
Metropolitan: Ferruccio Tagliavini (debut), *La bohème;* Robert Merrill, *Il barbiere di Siviglia;* Astrid Varnay, *Die Walküre;* Jussi Bjoerling, *Roméo et Juliette;* Regina Resnik, *The Warrior* (Barnard Rogers, premiere)

New York: *The Medium, The Telephone* (Gian Carlo Menotti); *Street Scene* (Kurt Weill); *Trial of Lucullus* (Roger Sessions). Max Leavitt directs the Lemonade Opera Company in its first performance, *The Mother of Us All* (Virgil Thomson, Gertrude Stein); *The Cradle Will Rock* (Marc Blitzstein) is performed on Broadway.

Philadelphia: *Street Scene* (Kurt Weill, premiere)

Lenox, Mass.:   *Idomeneo* (Mozart, premiere)

Jascha Heifetz, who first gained recognition as a child prodigy. *Movie Star News.*

Chicago: *Amelia Goes to the Ball* (Gian Carlo Menotti); *The Emperor Jones* (Henry Gruenberg); Kirsten Flagstad, *Tristan und Isolde*

Central City, Colo.:   Regina Resnik, *Fidelio;* Leopold Simoneau, *Martha*

Music Notes
Margaret Truman makes her debut with the Detroit Symphony Orchestra • Pablo Casals vows to give no more public performances as long as Franco is in power • The National Symphony gives a series of "Hit Parade" concerts in Washington, and polls are held in hotel lobbies, groceries, and drugstores to determine public taste • $70,000 is raised in New York for the Palestine Philharmonic Symphony.

Art

Painting

Charles Sheeler, *Classic Still Life*
Stuart Davis, *Iris*
William Baziotes, *Dwarf*
Jackson Pollock, *War, Full Fathom Five*
Arshile Gorky, *The Betrothal II, Agony*
Stephen Greene, *The Deposition, The Burial*
Willem de Kooning, *Noon*
Robert Motherwell, *Western Air* (1946–47), *The Red Skirt*
Barnett Newman, *The Euclidean Abyss*
Hans Hofmann, *Ecstasy*

Sculpture

Theodore Roszak, *The Specter of Kitty Hawk*

Alexander Calder, *Little Red under Blue*
Mahonri Young, Mormon Memorial, Salt Lake City
Isamu Noguchi, *Kouros, Night Land*
José de Rivera, *Yellow Black*
William Zorach, *The Future Generation*

Architecture

Kauffmann House, Palm Springs, Calif. (Richard Neutra)
Robinson House, Williamstown, Mass. (Marcel Breuer)
Architect's House, New Canaan, Conn. (Philip Johnson)

Important Exhibitions

Museums

New York: *Metropolitan:* Costumes 1830–1912; Egyptian art; Far Eastern art; Survey of American art. *Museum of Modern Art:* Ben Shahn retrospective; Alfred Stieglitz memorial. *Whitney:* Painting in France 1939–47; Braque's "The Studio";

French contemporary paintings of artists under 49 years old

Chicago: Stieglitz collection of porcelain; Survey of abstract and surreal art

Baltimore: 1,000 Byzantine objects

Cleveland: Degas; Gold objects

Major Prizes: Zoltan Sapeshy (Carnegie); Steumpfig (Corcoran); Guston (National Academy of Design); Baziotes (Chicago Art Institute); Kallem (Pepsi-Cola)

Art Briefs

Jean Dubuffet holds his first New York one-man show • Chrysler joins the Encyclopædia Britannica, Pepsi-Cola, and Gimbels in the industrial patronage of the arts • The State Department recalls from Czechoslovakia 79 American paintings sent on a goodwill tour but used for Communist propaganda • The Bay Psalm Book of 1640, the first book printed in America, sells for $151,000.

Dance

Premieres

Ballet Theater: *Theme and Variations* (George Balanchine), Alicia Markova, Igor Youskevitch

Ballet Society: *The Seasons* (Merce Cunningham), Tanaquil Le Clercq

Gregory Peck and John Garfield in *Gentleman's Agreement,* with Peck posing as a Jew in order to investigate upper middle class anti-Semitism. *Movie Star News.*

Books

Fiction

Critics' Choice
The Victim, Saul Bellow
Bend Sinister, Vladimir Nabokov
The Harder They Fall, Budd Schulberg
Reflections in a Golden Eye, Carson McCullers
The Big Sky, A. B. Guthrie
End as a Man, Calder Willingham
Knock on Any Door, Willard Motley
The Middle of the Journey, Lionel Trilling
⤷ *The Diary of Anne Frank*, Anne Frank
⤷ *Dr. Faustus*, Thomas Mann

Best-Sellers
The Miracle of the Bells, Russell Janney
The Moneyman, Thomas B. Costain
Gentleman's Agreement, Laura Z. Hobson
Lydia Bailey, Kenneth Roberts
The Vixens, Frank Yerby
The Wayward Bus, John Steinbeck
House Divided, Ben Ames Williams
Kingsblood Royal, Sinclair Lewis
East Side, West Side, Marcia Davenport
Prince of Foxes, Samuel Shellabarger

Nonfiction

Critics' Choice
Ordeal of the Union, Allan Nevins
On Understanding Science, J. B. Conant
The Cold War, Walter Lippmann
American Memoir, Henry Seidel Canby
The Nuremberg Case, Robert H. Jackson
Command Decision, William Wister Haines
The Times of Melville and Whitman, Van Wyck Brooks
End of a Berlin Diary, William Shirer
The Well-Wrought Urn, Cleanth Brooks
Essay on Morals, Philip Wylie
History of Naval Operations in World War II, ed. Samuel Eliot Morison
Philosopher's Quest, Irwin Edman
Modern Woman: The Lost Sex, Ferdinand Lundberg, Marynia Farnham
⤷ *Existentialism*, Jean-Paul Sartre

Best-Sellers
Peace of Mind, Joshua L. Liebman
Information Please Almanac, 1947, ed. John Kieran
Inside U.S.A., John Gunther

A Study of History, Arnold J. Toynbee
Speaking Frankly, James F. Byrnes
Human Destiny, Pierre Lecomte du Noüy
The Egg and I, Betty MacDonald
The American Past, Roger Butterfield
Together, Katharine T. Marshall
The Fireside Book of Folk Songs, ed. Margaret Boni

Poetry
Wallace Stevens, *Transport to Summer*
Richard Wilbur, *The Beautiful Changes*
Conrad Aiken, *The Kid*
Robert Frost, *A Masque of Mercy*
Karl Shapiro, *Trials of a Poet*
Robert Duncan, *Heavenly City, Earthly City*

Pulitzer Prizes
Tales of the South Pacific, James A. Michener (fiction)
Across the Wide Missouri, Bernard De Voto (U.S. history)
Forgotten First Citizen: John Bigelow, Margaret Clapp (biography)
Age of Anxiety, W. H. Auden (poetry)

Science and Technology

Naval expeditions under Adm. Richard Byrd and Comdr. Finn Ronne explore Antarctica.
A United Airlines plane over Idaho reports "flying discs," "flat and round" and "larger than aircraft."
The Atomic Bomb Commission reports abnormalities in the offspring of bomb survivors.
Edwin Land announces the invention of a camera that develops and prints a picture in one minute.
A cure for schizophrenia through prefrontal lobotomy is announced by Spring Grove Hospital, Maryland.

The discovery of the anticoagulant heparin is reported.
⤷ Thor Heyerdal sets sail on a raft, the *Kon Tiki*, from Peru toward Tahiti.

Nobel Prize
Carl F. and Gerty Cori win the prize in physiology and medicine for the discovery of the catalytic metabolism of glycogen.

Sports

Baseball

Jackie Robinson (Brooklyn, NL) becomes the first black major league player and wins the Rookie of the Year Award.

Ralph Kiner (Pittsburgh, NL) hits eight home runs in four games.

In the World Series, Cookie Lavagetto (Brooklyn, NL) hits a double ending the no-hitter of Floyd Bevan (New York, AL) after 8⅔ innings and beats him 3–2.

Champions

Batting
  Harry Walker (St. Louis, Philadelphia, NL), .363
  Ted Williams (Boston, AL), .343
Pitching
  Larry Jansen (New York, NL), 21–5
  Allie Reynolds (New York, AL), 19–8

Home runs
  Ralph Kiner (Pittsburgh, NL), 51
  John Mize (St. Louis, NL), 51

Football

Charlie Trippi, Georgia tailback, signs with the NFL's Chicago Cardinals for a record $100,000 for four years.

NFL Season Leaders: Sammy Baugh (Washington), passing; Steve Van Buren (Philadelphia), rushing; Jim Keane (Chicago Bears), receiving.

College All-Americans: Chuck Bednarik (C), Pennsylvania; Doak Walker (B), Southern Methodist; John Lujack (QB), Notre Dame; Bob Chappuis (B), Michigan.

Bowls (Jan. 1, 1948)

Rose: Michigan 49–Southern California 0
Orange: Georgia Tech 20–Kansas 14
Cotton: Southern Methodist 13–Pennsylvania State 13
Sugar: Texas 27–Alabama 7

Other Sports

Boxing: Rocky Graziano KO's Tony Zale in the sixth for the middleweight title before a record indoor gate of $422,918. Sugar Ray Robinson wins the welterweight title.

Tennis: Jack Kramer and Bobby Riggs tour as pros and draw $248,000 for 89 appearances.

Winners

World Series
  New York (AL) 4
  Brooklyn (NL) 3
MVP
  NL–Robert Elliott, Boston
  AL–Joe DiMaggio, New York
NFL
  Chicago (Cards) 28–Philadelphia 21
College Football
  Notre Dame
Heisman Trophy
  John Lujack, Notre Dame

College Basketball
  Holy Cross (NCAA)
  Utah (NIT)
Player of the Year
  Gerald Tucker, Oklahoma
Stanley Cup
  Toronto
US Tennis Open
  Men: John Kramer
  Women: Louise Brough
USGA Open
  Lou Worsham
Kentucky Derby
  Jet Pilot (E. Guerin, jockey)

Fashion

For Women: Dior's "New Look" revolutionizes fashion history. The squarish straight skirt and flat hip look, popular for nearly a decade, is replaced by the swirling "feminine" dress, 12 inches from the floor with a natural shoulder and an entirely rounded look. Emphasis is on the hips, tiny waist, and pointed bosom. Some 450 Dior silks are copied by the thousands in $20 rayons. "New" also are suits and coats lengthened to the ankle, fitted jackets, and circle, often pegged, skirts. Complementing the round hips and small waists are spike heels with straps and "naked" sandals, all designed to emphasize the leg. To help accomplish the new look are boned girdles with waistbands and padded bras that flatten the midriff, cinch the waist, and point the breasts. Other innovations include the pillbox hat and beret, worn over one ear; fezzes with veils and feathers; V-neck and frothy blouses; the evening dress in pale blue, burgundy, green, cocoa, and brown taffeta or satin (although the strapless ball dress remains, worn with a tiara and long gloves above the elbow), espadrilles, long pearl chains, short pearl dog collars, and rhinestones. Flat ballet shoes remain very popular.

High-fashion note: Dior's first collection, February 12

Jackie Robinson, the first black in organized baseball. *Movie Star News.*

Kaleidoscope _____

- Oral Roberts gains a following as he claims healing through prayer and assistance from God.
- Publishing events include Mickey Spillane's sexy detective fiction, *I, the Jury,* Dr. Eustace Chesser's sexual manual *Love without Fear,* and Arnold Toynbee's study of the rise and fall of civilizations, *A Study of History.*
- The U.S. Motion Picture Association votes for stronger regulations against the glorification of crime on the screen; Communists are barred from holding office by the Screen Directors Guild.
- Gillette and Ford pay $65,000 to sponsor the first TV World Series; an estimated 3.7 million watch the Dodgers and Yankees on all three networks.
- Fleer's bubble gum blowing contests reach fad proportions.
- A fire destroys the $5 million Grace Lines pier 57 in New York; 144 firemen are injured.
- The United States is urged to study bacteriological warfare by the American Association of Scientific Workers.
- Kaiser-Frazier manufactures the first new make of car in more than 20 years, the 1947 Frazier.
- The GM-UAW settlement agrees to a cost-of-living raise for its workers, the first of its kind.
- The American Friends Service Committee wins the Nobel Peace Prize.
- Four million returning GI veterans take advantage of the GI bill and its broad opportunities for education, housing, and business.
- College enrollment rises to an all-time high of 6.1 million students.
- The first Pan American world service costs $1,700.
- A 25.8-inch snowfall paralyzes New York City for 16 hours.
- The KKK charter is revoked by the Georgia Supreme Court.
- New York bans Howard Fast's *Citizen Thomas Paine* from school libraries. Massachusetts rules *Forever Amber* not obscene.
- Soviets use repeated vetoes and boycott the UN Trusteeship Council with claims of "barbarous American imperialism."
- A new member is added to the president's cabinet to unify the army and navy commands—the "Secretary of Defense."
- Tax is reduced 10 percent on incomes of $10,000, 48 to 65 percent on incomes over $100,000.

First Appearances: Transit fares up from 5¢ to 10¢ (New York City), end of street cars (New York City), camera zoom lens demonstration, UN flag, Almond Joy, Redi Whip, Minute Maid Corp., Chun King, MSG as "Accent," Ajax, continuous coal-cutting machine, Everglades National Park, commercial tubeless auto tires, Sony, Cannes Film Festival, Edinburgh Festival, "Steve Canyon," Tony awards

- The Freedom Train, with 100 of the United States' greatest documents, tours America; the Friendship Train donates 200 carloads of food to France and Italy.
- "Let us not be deceived. Today we are in the midst of a *cold* war," says Bernard Baruch, in Columbia, South Carolina. Walter Lippmann publicizes the phrase.
- In an article signed "X" in *Foreign Affairs,* George Kennan proposes a policy of "containment" of Russia, which becomes the basis of U.S. policy.
- The CIA is authorized by Congress to counter Soviet espionage.
- A Hollywood blacklist of alleged Communist sympathizers includes 300 writers, directors, and actors.
- Jackie Robinson is refused hotel rooms in numerous cities and is abused verbally both on and off the field; he remarks: "I've got two cheeks."
- Seventeen children die from an overdose of Anabis, a tonsillitis treatment, now banned.
- "A sleeping sickness is spreading among the women of the land," remarks Fannie Hurst. "They are retrogressing into . . . that thing called Home."
- The American Meat Institute reports a turn from wartime casseroles to meat five nights a week.
- Pittsburgh begins a program to clean the smoky air.

1948

Facts and Figures

Economic Profile
Dow-Jones: – High 193–
    Low 165
GNP: +11%
Inflation: +5.2%
Unemployment: 3.8%
Balance of international
    payments: +$5.4 billion
Military on duty: 1,445,000
Voter participation: 63%
    (1940); 53% (1948)
Population with religious
    affiliation: 79 million
Buick Roadmaster: $2,900
DeSoto convertible: $2,500
Packard: $4,300
Rolls-Royce convertible:
    $18,500
Nash convertible: $3,100
Krum chocolate assortment:
    92¢ (lb.)
Schenley whiskey: $4.05 (⅘)
Margaret O'Brien "Memory
    Book" dress: $5
Best & Co. girls' shoes: $5

Deaths

Charles Beard, Ruth
    Benedict, Sergei
    Eisenstein, D. W. Griffith,
    Charles Evans Hughes,
    Rabbi Joshua Liebman,
    Fred Niblo, George
    Herman ("Babe") Ruth,
    Dame May Whitty, Orville
    Wright

In the News

TRUMAN ASKS VOLUNTARY RESTRAINT OF GAS AND OIL USE . . .
MUNDT ACT AUTHORIZES VOICE OF AMERICA . . . MAHATMA GANDHI
IS ASSASSINATED BY HINDU EXTREMIST . . . SUPREME COURT RULES
THAT STATE MONEY CANNOT BE USED FOR RELIGIOUS SCHOOLS . . .
COMMUNISTS GAIN ON CHIANG KAI-SHEK . . . 350,000 COAL MINERS
STRIKE, PENSION IS MAJOR ISSUE . . . TAX REDUCTION IS VOTED
OVER TRUMAN VETO . . . EUROPEAN RECOVERY PROGRAM
IMPLEMENTS MARSHALL PROGRAM, $5.3 BILLION IS APPROPRIATED
. . . RUSSIA CONDEMNS MARSHALL PLAN . . . RUSSIA BANS ALL
LAND TRAFFIC TO BERLIN, WEST AIRLIFTS SUPPLIES . . . UN PASSES
PALESTINE PARTITION PLAN, ISRAEL IS CREATED . . . EGYPT, SYRIA
AND TRANSJORDAN ATTACK ISRAEL . . . U.S. RECOGNIZES ISRAEL . . .
YUGOSLOVIA IS EXPELLED FROM COMINFORM . . . TRUMAN IS
NOMINATED BY DEMOCRATS, THOMAS DEWEY BY GOP, PROGRESSIVES
NOMINATE HENRY WALLACE . . . DIXIECRATS BOLT DEMOCRATIC
CONVENTION ON STATES' RIGHTS ISSUE AND NOMINATE STROM
THURMOND . . . HUAC FINDS SPY MICROFILM HIDDEN IN PUMPKIN
. . . DISPLACED PERSONS BILL IS PASSED, 205,000 ARE ADMITTED . . .
CHINESE COMMUNISTS DECLARE REPUBLIC IN NORTH CHINA . . .
TRUMAN CALLS SPECIAL SESSION OF CONGRESS AS COST OF LIVING
HITS ALL-TIME HIGH . . . 12 COMMUNIST PARTY LEADERS ARE
INDICTED FOR SMITH ACT VIOLATION . . . FEDERAL RESERVE IMPOSES
INSTALLMENT CURBS . . . RUSSIAN TEACHER JUMPS FROM SOVIET
EMBASSY WINDOW TO U.S. . . . SOVIETS CLOSE U.S. CONSULATES IN
MOSCOW, U.S. RECIPROCATES . . . 4 POWERS DISAGREE IN MOSCOW
OVER GERMAN ISSUE . . . TOJO AND 5 OTHERS HANG FOR WAR
CRIMES . . . TRUMAN DEFEATS DEWEY IN GIANT UPSET . . .
CARDINAL MINDSZENTY IS ARRESTED IN HUNGARY . . .

Quotes

Dewey's presidential victory was considered so certain that premature reports went to press. *Smithsonian Institution.*

President Harry S Truman. *Library of Congress.*

"Government will remain big, active, and expensive under President Thomas E. Dewey."
— *Wall Street Journal* (October)

"[The Truman civil rights plan] wants to reduce us to the status of a mongrel, inferior race, mixed in blood, our Anglo-Saxon heritage a mockery."
— Alabama governor F. Dixon, keynote speech, Dixiecrat convention

"I'll mow 'em down, Alben. I'll give 'em Hell."
— Truman to Vice-President Barkley (overheard)

"Republicans are . . . bloodsuckers with offices in Wall Street, princes of privilege, plunderers."
— Harry S Truman, "whistlestop" speech

"We're about as much in favor of Communism as J. Edgar Hoover."
— Bogart and Bacall

"I love your pictures and your directions. So if there's ever a small part for a little Swedish actress, please think of me."
— Letter to Roberto Rossellini from Ingrid Bergman

"A smart teenager thinks about how to start a conversation . . . [and] looks over . . . conversation starters, . . . like animals. [He might say] 'My dog has fleas—what'll I do?'"
— Edith Heal, *Teen Age Manual*

Ads

You can't baby a baby too much—whether she's 1, 21, or simply not telling.
—Give her Yolande Handmades.
(*Yolande Lingerie*)

Air Power is Peace Power—Lockheed
(*Lockheed Aircraft*)

One of America's Greatest Success Stories—Kaiser-Frazier
(*Kaiser-Frazier Automobile*)

High Blood Pressure . . . a fortunate warning.
(*Upjohn Pharmaceuticals*)

Railroads can't afford *not* to modernize!
(*Chesapeake and Ohio Lines*)

Which twin has the Toni?
(*Toni Permanents*)

Is fish really brain food?
(*American Cyanimid Corp.*)

It's in the bag.
(*Ballantine Beer*)

TV

Premieres
"The Morey Amsterdam Show," Art Carney, Jacqueline Susann
"Douglas Edwards and the News"
"Candid Camera," Allen Funt
"The Toast of the Town," Ed Sullivan
"Arthur Godfrey's Talent Scouts"
"The Milton Berle Show [Texaco Star Theater]"
"Studio One" ("The Storm," Margaret Sullavan)
"The Chesterfield Supper Club," Perry Como
"Philco Television Playhouse"
"The Bigelow Show," Paul Winchell and Jerry Mahoney
"Camel Newsreel Theater," John Cameron Swayze, first nightly news show

Specials
"Julius Caesar" (in modern dress, "Studio One"); "The NFL" (first regular pro sports event)

Emmy Awards
"Pantomine Quiz Time" (most popular); Shirley Dinsdale (personality); "The Necklace" on "Your Show Time" (TV-made film)

Radio

Premieres
"Life with Luigi," J. Carrol Naish
"Stop the Music," Bert Parks
"This Is Your Life," Ralph Edwards
"Our Miss Brooks," Eve Arden, Jeff Chandler
"My Favorite Husband," Lucille Ball, Gale Gordon

Most Popular Programs: "Walter Winchell," "Lux Radio Theater," "Arthur Godfrey," "Duffy's Tavern," "Phil Harris–Alice Faye"

Most Popular Comedy/Variety Shows: "Bing Crosby," "Dorothy Lamour," "Duffy's Tavern," "Jack Benny," "Fred Allen," "Fibber McGee and Molly," "George Burns and Gracie Allen"

Movies

Openings
Hamlet (Laurence Olivier), Laurence Olivier, Jean Simmons
Johnny Belinda (Jean Negulesco), Jane Wyman, Lew Ayres
The Red Shoes (Michael Powell, Emeric Pressburger), Moira Shearer, Marius Goring
The Snake Pit (Anatole Litvak), Olivia de Havilland
The Treasure of Sierre Madre (John Huston), Humphrey Bogart, Walter Huston
Sitting Pretty (Walter Lang), Clifton Webb, Robert Young, Maureen O'Hara
I Remember Mama (George Stevens), Irene Dunne, Barbara Bel Geddes
Sorry, Wrong Number (Anatole Litvak), Barbara Stanwyck, Burt Lancaster
Key Largo (John Huston), Humphrey Bogart, Lauren Bacall, Edward G. Robinson
The Naked City (Jules Dassin), Barry Fitzgerald, Howard Duff
Red River (Howard Hawks), John Wayne, Montgomery Clift, Joanne Dru
The Three Musketeers (George Sidney), Lana Turner, Gene Kelly
A Foreign Affair (Billy Wilder), Marlene Dietrich, Jean Arthur
Letter from an Unknown Woman (Max Ophuls), Joan Fontaine, Louis Jourdan
The Pirate (Vincente Minnelli), Judy Garland, Gene Kelly
Easter Parade (Charles Walters), Fred Astaire, Ann Miller, Judy Garland

Academy Awards
Best Picture: *Hamlet*
Best Director: John Huston (*The Treasure of Sierra Madre*)
Best Actress: Jane Wyman (*Johnny Belinda*)
Best Actor: Laurence Olivier (*Hamlet*)

Top Box-Office Stars
Bing Crosby, Betty Grable, Abbott and Costello, Gary Cooper, Bob Hope, Humphrey Bogart, Clark Gable, Cary Grant, Spencer Tracy, Ingrid Bergman

Stars of Tomorrow
Jane Powell, Cyd Charisse, Ann Blyth, Celeste Holm, Robert Ryan, Angela Lansbury, Jean Peters, Mona Freeman, Eleanor Parker, Doris Day

Popular Music

Hit Songs

"Buttons and Bows"
"It's a Most Unusual Day"
"A—You're Adorable"
"Cuanto le Gusta"
"So in Love"
"Mañana"
"Enjoy Yourself—It's Later than You Think"
"If I Had a Hammer"
"Baby, It's Cold Outside"
"On a Slow Boat to China"

Top Records

Albums: *Al Jolson, Vol. III* (Al Jolson); *Merry Christmas* (Bing Crosby); *A Sentimental Date with Perry Como* (Perry Como); *Down Memory Lane* (Vaughn Monroe); *A Presentation of Progressive Jazz* (Stan Kenton); *Busy Fingers* (Three Sons)

Singles: *Twelfth Street Rag* (Pee Wee Hunt); *Once in Love with Amy* (Ray Bolger); *Nature Boy* (Nat "King" Cole); *It's Magic* (Doris Day); *The Streets of Laredo* (Dennis Day); *My Happiness* (Ella Fitzgerald); *My Darling, My Darling* (Jo Stafford); *It's Too Soon to Know* (Dinah Washington); *Now Is the Hour* (Bing Crosby); *Lazy River* (Mills Brothers); *Because* (Perry Como); *The Fat Man* (Fats Domino). *Early Autumn* (Stan Getz);

Country: *Bouquet of Roses,* (Eddy Arnold); *Smoke, Smoke, Smoke that Cigarette* (Tex Williams)

Jazz and Big Bands

Stan Kenton gives a concert at the Hollywood Bowl. Earl Hines joins Louis Armstrong. Many of the 52d Street, New York, jazz clubs close.

Top Performers (*Downbeat*): Benny Goodman (soloist); Duke Ellington (band); Errol Garner, Shelly Manne, Flip Phillips, Charlie Shavers (instrumentalists); Charlie Ventura (jazz group); Sarah Vaughan, Billy Eckstine (vocalists)

Theater

Broadway Openings

Plays

Mister Roberts (Thomas Heggen, Joshua Logan), Henry Fonda, David Wayne, William Harrigan, Robert Keith
Anne of the Thousand Days (Maxwell Anderson), Rex Harrison, Joyce Redman
Edward, My Son (Robert Morley, Noel Langley), Robert Morley
The Madwoman of Chaillot (Jean Giraudoux), Estelle Winwood, Nydia Westman
Summer and Smoke (Tennessee Williams), Margaret Phillips, Tod Andrews
The Respectful Prostitute (Jean-Paul Sartre), Meg Mundy
Life with Mother (Howard Lindsay, Russel Crouse), Dorothy Stickney
Red Gloves (Jean-Paul Sartre), Charles Boyer
Goodbye, My Fancy (Fay Kanin), Madeleine Carroll, Conrad Nagel, Sam Wanamaker
The Silver Whistle (Robert McEnroe), José Ferrer

Musicals

Inside U.S.A. (Arthur Schwartz, Howard Dietz), Beatrice Lillie, Jack Haley
Look, Ma, I'm Dancin' (Hugh Martin), Nancy Walker, Harold Lang
Love Life (Kurt Weill, Alan Jay Lerner), Nanette Fabray, Ray Middleton
Magdalena (Heitor Villa-Lobos, Robert Wright, George Forrest), John Raitt, Irra Petina
Where's Charley? (Frank Loesser), Ray Bolger
Kiss Me, Kate (Cole Porter), Alfred Drake, Patricia Morison
Lend an Ear (Charles Gaynor), William Eythe, Carol Channing

Classics and Revivals On and Off Broadway

Private Lives (Noel Coward), Tallulah Bankhead; *The Play's the Thing* (Molnár), Faye Emerson, Louis Calhern; *Ghosts, Hedda Gabler* (Ibsen), Eva Le Gallienne; *Macbeth*, Michael Redgrave, Flora Robson; *John Bull's Other Island* (George Bernard Shaw), Michael MacLiammoir, Dublin Gate Theater

Pulitzer Prize

A Streetcar Named Desire, Tennessee Williams

Classical Music

Compositions
John Cage, Sonatas and Interludes
Howard Hanson, Piano Concerto
Walter Piston, Toccata for Orchestra, Suite no. 2
Milton Babbitt, Three Compositions for Piano,
    Composition for Twelve Instruments
Elliott Carter, Sonata for Cello
Roy Harris, Elegy and Paean for Viola and Orchestra
William Schuman, Symphony no. 6
Aaron Copland, Concerto for Clarinet and Strings,
    with harp and piano
Virgil Thomson, *Louisiana Story*

Important Events
A record number of festivals occur during the year,
as well as TV music specials (Toscanini and the NBC
Symphony performing Wagner; Eugene Ormandy
and the Philadelphia Symphony with "The
Classics").

Debuts: Alfred Brendel, Paul Badura-Skoda,
Raymond Lewenthal

First Performances
Rachmaninoff, Symphony in D minor (Philadelphia);
Samuel Barber, James Agee, *Knoxville: Summer of
1915;* Walter Piston, Symphony no. 3 (Boston);
David Diamond, Symphony no. 4 (Boston); Heitor
Villa-Lobos, *Mandu-Carara* (New York); Paul
Creston, Fantasy for Trombone and Orchestra (Los
Angeles); Wallingford Riegger, Symphony no. 3
(New York); Virgil Thomson, *The Seine at Night*
(Kansas City); George Antheil, Symphony no. 4
(Philadelphia); Norman Dello Joio, Three Symphonic
Dances (Pittsburgh); Harold Shapero, Symphony for
Classical Orchestra (Boston).

Opera

Metropolitan: Ferruccio Tagliavini, *L'elisir
d'amore; Peter Grimes* (Benjamin Britten)

New York City: *The Old Maid and the Thief* (Gian
Carlo Menotti, premiere)

Central City, Colo.:   Regina Resnik, *Die Fledermaus*

San Francisco: Ezio Pinza, *Boris Godunov* (Pinza's
last Boris); Tito Gobbi (debut) *Il barbiere di Siviglia*

Music Notes
As a promotional activity, the Buffalo Philharmonic
provides babysitters for season ticket holders •
Vincenzo Bellini's grandson, Ferruccio Burco, age 9,
makes his Carnegie Hall debut and conducts Wagner
and Beethoven.

Far left: Milton
Berle, "Mr.
Television." *Movie
Star News*.

The great
Shakespearean
Laurence Olivier
starred in and
directed *Hamlet*.
Movie Star News.

Art

Painting

Andrew Wyeth,
Christina's World
Hans Hofmann,
Construction
Willem de Kooning,
Woman
Clyfford Still, *1948-D,
World Tablet, Stamos*
Jackson Pollock,
*Composition No. 1,
November 1, 1948*
Mark Tobey, *Tropicalism*
Ben Shahn, *Miners'
Wives*
Edward Hopper,
Seven A.M.
Thomas Hart Benton,
Poker Night
Arshile Gorky, *The
Betrothed*
Lyonel Feininger, *The
Lake*
Barnett Newman, *Two
Edges*

Sculpture

Jacques Lipchitz,
Primordial Figure
(1947–48)

Alexander Calder,
Aspen, Snow Flurry
Richard Lippold,
Primordial Figure
Joseph Cornell, *Multiple
Cubes*
Seymour Lipton,
Imprisoned Figure

Architecture

Baker House,
Massachusetts
Institute of
Technology,
Cambridge (Alvar
Aalto)
Container Corporation of
America, Greensboro,
N.C. (Walter Gropius)
Graduate Housing Unit,
Harvard University,
Cambridge, Mass.
(Gropius)
The Saarinen design for
the Jefferson National
Expansion Memorial
in St. Louis wins
$40,000.

Important Exhibitions

Museums

New York: *Metropolitan:* French tapestries; World-famous masterpieces of painting from the Berlin museums; "From Casablanca to Calcutta" (costumes, fabrics). *Whitney:* Yasuo Kuniyoshi. *Museum of Modern Art:* Cole, Nadelman, Gabo-Pevsner

Boston: Japanese art; English watercolors; Kokoschka

Philadelphia: Matisse retrospective

Cleveland, Museum of Modern Art: Bonnard

Washington: Dutch Art

St. Louis: Max Beckmann

Art Briefs

The Des Moines Art Center (Saarinen) is built, the first museum construction since Pearl Harbor • Motherwell, Rothko, Hare, Baziotes, and Still found the Subjects of the Artist School in New York • Major sales include van der Weyden's *View of Delft* ($15,000) and Degas's pastel of Mary Cassatt ($4,000) • German masterpieces found by the U.S. Third Army in a salt mine near Merkers are sent on a tour of the United States; proceeds go to German children in the American zone.

Andrew Wyeth, *Christina's World*, 1948. Tempera. 32¼ × 47¾". *Collection, The Museum of Modern Art, New York.*

Dance

Ballet Society accepts New York City Center's offer of a home and becomes the New York City Ballet. In the company are Maria Tallchief, Tanaquil Le Clercq, Nicholas Magallanes, Francisco Moncion, Herbert Bliss, and Todd Bolender. Its first program consists of *Serenade, Orpheus,* and *Symphony in C,* all by Balanchine.
Alwin Nikolais becomes director of the New York Henry Street Playhouse.

Ballet Theater: *Fall River Legend* (Agnes de Mille), Nora Kaye, Lucia Chase, Sallie Wilson

Books

Fiction

Critics' Choice

Other Voices, Other Rooms, Truman Capote
Intruder in the Dust, William Faulkner
Remembrance Rock, Carl Sandburg
The City and the Pillar, Gore Vidal
Act of Love, Ira Wolfert
The Ides of March, Thornton Wilder
The World Is a Wedding, Delmore Schwartz
Circus in the Attic, Robert Penn Warren
🕭 *The Plague,* Albert Camus
🕭 *Cry, the Beloved Country,* Alan Paton

Best-Sellers

The Big Fisherman, Lloyd C. Douglas
The Naked and the Dead, Norman Mailer
Dinner at Antoine's, Frances Parkinson Keyes
The Bishop's Mantle, Agnes Sligh Turnbull
Tomorrow Will Be Better, Betty Smith
The Golden Hawk, Frank Yerby
Raintree County, Ross Lockridge, Jr.

Shannon's Way, A. J. Cronin
Pilgrim's Inn, Elizabeth Goudge
The Young Lions, Irwin Shaw

Nonfiction

Critics' Choice

The American Political Tradition, Richard Hofstadter
The Protestant Era, Paul Tillich
Jefferson, the Virginian, vol. 1, Dumas Malone
Our Plundered Planet, Fairfield Osborn
No Place to Hide, David Bradley
The Early Tales of the Atomic Age, Daniel Lang
The Price of Power, Hanson W. Baldwin
The United States and China, John King Fairbank
World Communism, Martin Ebon
The Nightmare of American Foreign Policy, Edgar Ansel Mowrer

Best-Sellers

Crusade in Europe, Dwight D. Eisenhower
How to Stop Worrying and Start Living, Dale Carnegie
Peace of Mind, Joshua L. Liebman
Sexual Behavior in the Human Male, A. C. Kinsey

Wine, Women and Words, Billy Rose
The Life and Times of the Shmoo, Al Capp
The Gathering Storm, Winston Churchill
Roosevelt and Hopkins, Robert E. Sherwood
A Guide to Confident Living, Norman Vincent Peale
The Plague and I, Betty MacDonald

Poetry

John Berryman, *The Dispossessed*
Theodore Roethke, *The Lost Sun*
Allen Tate, *Poems, 1922–1947*
Ezra Pound, *The Pisan Cantos*
Robinson Jeffers, *The Double Axe*
Randall Jarrell, *Losses*
William Carlos Williams, *Paterson,* Book Two

Pulitzer Prizes

Guard of Honor, James Gould Cozzens (fiction)
The Disruption of American Democracy, Roy F. Nichols (U.S. history)
Roosevelt and Hopkins, Robert E. Sherwood (biography)
Terror and Decorum, Peter Viereck (poetry)

Science and Technology

Captain Charles Yaeger breaks the sound barrier in a rocket-powered Bell X-1 at 35,000 feet.

Cmdr. Finn Ronne reports that Antarctica is a single continent, not two islands.

The world's largest reflector telescope, 200 inches, is dedicated at Mt. Palomar Observatory, California.

The University of Chicago and seven major corporations announce plans for cooperative atomic research for industrial use.

John Bardeen, William Shockley, and Walter Brattain of Bell Telephone Laboratories develop the transistor.

A new liquid hydrogen fuel for rockets is announced by H. L. Johnson, who says it will "send men to the moon."

Immunologist Bettina Carver, Pittsburgh, develops Rh hapten to save "Rh" babies.

The human poliomyelitis virus in concentrated form is isolated at the University of Minnesota.

Antibiotics aureomycin and chloromycetin are developed; vitamin B_{12}, the cure for pernicious anemia, is isolated.

Success with radiocobalt treatment of cancer is reported by the AEC.

Sports

Baseball

"Spahn and Sain and two days of rain" is the pennant-winning Boston Braves' motto. Cleveland beats Boston, 8–3, in the first American League pennant playoff tie.

Champions

Batting
Stan Musial (St. Louis, NL), .376
Ted Williams (Boston, AL), .369

Pitching
Harry Brecheen (St. Louis, NL), 20–9
Jack Kramer (Boston, AL), 18–5

Home runs
Ralph Kiner (Pittsburgh, NL), 40
John Mize (St. Louis, NL), 40

Football

NFL Season Leaders: Tommy Thompson (Philadelphia), passing; Steve Van Buren (Philadelphia) rushing; Tom Fears (Los Angeles), receiving.

College All-Americans: Charlie Justice (B), North Carolina; Chuck Bednarik (C), Pennsylvania; Jackie Jensen (B), California; Johnny Rauch (Q), Georgia.

Bowls (Jan. 1, 1949)
Rose: Northwestern 20–California 14
Orange: Texas 41–Georgia 28
Cotton: Southern Methodist 21–Oregon 13
Sugar: Oklahoma 14–North Carolina 6

Basketball

NBL star George Mikan signs with the BAA; four NBL teams then merge with the BAA, forming the NBA. The BAA champion is Baltimore, with Max Zaslofsky. The Harlem Globetrotters beat the NBL champs 61–59.

Olympics

In the 1948 Olympics at London, U.S. gold medal winners include Harrison Dillard (100m, 10.3s), Mel Patton (200m, 21.1s), Mal Whitfield (800m, 1:49.2), Willie Steele (broadjump, 25′8″), Guinn Smith (pole vault, 14′, 1¼″), Wilbur Thompson (16 lb. shot put, 56′2″), Bob Matthias (decathlon), Walter Ris (100m, swim, 57.3s). In the Winter Games at St. Moritz, Switzerland, Richard Button wins figure skating.

Other Sports

Horse Racing: Citation, ridden by Eddie Arcaro, wins the Triple Crown.

Golf: Ben Hogan wins the U.S. Open with a record 5 under par and is the top PGA money winner with $36,000.

Winners

World Series
Cleveland (AL) 4
Boston (NL) 2

MVP
NL–Stan Musial, St. Louis
AL–Lou Boudreau, Cleveland

NFL
Philadelphia 7–Chicago (Cards) 0

College Football
Michigan

Heisman Trophy
Doak Walker, Southern Methodist

College Basketball
Kentucky (NCAA)
St. Louis (NIT)

Player of the Year
Ed McCauley, St. Louis

Stanley Cup
Toronto

US Tennis Open
Men: Pancho Gonzales
Women: Margaret Osborne DuPont

USGA Open
Ben Hogan

Kentucky Derby
Citation (E. Arcaro, jockey)

Fashion

For Women: Dior's "New Look" continues, and jackets are even shorter and more fitted until they are rib tight; skirts are straight, except at the back. The tank coat is replaced by either the belted greatcoat or the fitted one with back fullness or pleats. Shoulder capes on coats are also fashionable. Many styles seem more interesting from the back and are called "going-away styles." At the end of the year, the empire gains attention, as well as the "lampshade" dress, with its body-glove-fit and immense flair at mid-thigh. Patent leather reappears in belts and bags; hair is shorter; gloves are wrist-length.

High-fashion note: Balenciaga's grass-green faille hat with black wings

For men: *Esquire* salutes the man of "self-confidence and good taste" with the "bold look." He initiates a revival of interest in men's fashion accessories: wide tie clasps, heavy gold key chains, bold striped ties, big buttons, and the coordination of hair coloring and clothing (brown hair with grey clothing, for example).

Kaleidoscope _____

- Inflation statistics include the following: a house costing $4,440 in 1939 is now $9,060; clothing is up 93 percent; food, 129 percent; home furnishings, 93.6 percent; rent, 12.2 percent; only gas and electricity are down, 4.8 percent.
- A Spokane butcher shop, responding to the meat shortage, advertises: "Choice Meats. The Management Will Accept Cash, First Mortgages, Bonds, and Good Jewelry."
- The bikini arrives on American beaches.
- Newly published Alfred Kinsey's *Sexual Behavior in the Human Male* reports the prevalence of sexual problems and indicates that 85 percent of those married have had premarital sex and 50 percent have been unfaithful.
- Isolationist Arthur Vandenberg defends the Marshall Plan as seeking "peace and stability . . . in a free world, . . . by economic rather than military means."
- McDonald's is franchised; the Baskin-Robbins chain begins.
- Fifty cities ban comic books dealing with crime or sex.
- A Nevada court declares prostitution legal in Reno.
- A Gallup poll reports the highest rate of belief in God in Brazil (96 percent); the lowest in France (66 percent); the American figure is 94 percent.

Hollywood beefcake. *Movie Star News.*

- *Cybernetics,* the study of information theory, is coined by MIT's Norbert Wiener.
- Five scientists are reported to be going blind as a result of their work with cyclotrons.
- To gain new literary perspectives, John Hopkins holds a symposium on criticism with John Crowe Ransom, Allen Tate, Herbert Read, André Gide, Benedetto Croce, and Richard Blackmur.
- Peter Goldmark of CBS invents a high-fidelity long-playing record that plays up to 45 minutes.
- The Supreme Court upholds the obscenity ban on Edmund Wilson's *Hecate County.*
- New York begins a fluoridation program for 50,000 children.
- With government supporting the well-balanced lunch, North Carolina children receive, for 5 cents, black-eyed peas, eggs, cheese, potatoes, a biscuit, milk, and a tangerine.
- Despite the financial success of his song "Nature Boy," Eben Ahbez continues to live in a Hollywood vacant lot on nuts and berries.
- Jack Benny sells his NBC radio program to CBS for a reported $2 to $3 million; the IRS then forces Benny to pay a 75 percent personal income tax, instead of 25 percent capital gains tax from the sale.
- Milton Berle's "Texaco Star Theatre" scores an 86.7 percent rating. The show's "Tell ya' what I'm gonna do" and Berle's "Duhh" gain popular usage.
- Truman orders racial equality in the armed forces; he also proposes antilynching and FEPC legislation, which Congress declines to act on.
- Eisenhower rejects Democratic efforts to draft him for president.
- Alger Hiss sues Whittaker Chambers for $75,000 for libel when Chambers accuses him of Communist party membership from 1934 to 1938; Hiss loses and is subsequently tried for perjury; the entire affair is dismissed by the president as a "red herring."
- On election eve, the Roper, Gallup, and Crossley polls predict a 5 to 15 percent Dewey victory.
- Patents are acquired for the vacuum leaf raker, fountain safety razor, suction ear muffs, metallic shoes, and "Adventure" bra with plastic prop-up snap-ins and uplift that won't wash out.

Fads: frozen foods, and chlorophyll gum, candies, and toothpaste

First Appearances: Garbage disposals, street lamp plastic lenses, nonglare headlights, heat-conducting windshields, Land Rover, Porsche sports car, Honda motorcycle, car air conditioner (for under dash), Salton Hottray, Nestlés Quik, Michelin radial tires, completely solar-heated house (Dover, Maine), Franklin 50¢ piece, World Health Organization, color newsreels, Scrabble, Dial soap, Korvette discount store, Nikon 35mm.

1949

Facts and Figures

Economic Profile
  Dow-Jones: ↑ High 200–
    Low 161
  GNP: 0%
  Inflation: −0.7%
  Unemployment: 5.9%
Police expenditures, federal,
  state, local: $724 million
Persons arrested: 792,000
Executions: 119
Prisoners, federal, state:
  163,700
Juvenile court cases: 45,775
Arnold Constable black or
  gray Persian lamb coat:
  $350
Boys' storm coat with
  mouton collar: $15.95
Zenith portable "tip top" dial
  radio: $39.95
Gladiolas: $1 (for 50)
Roses: $1.98 (for 25)
Red salmon: 59¢ (1 lb. can)
Del Monte asparagus: 35¢ (19
  oz.)
Cottage cheese: 13¢ (8 oz.)
Kraft's Velveeta: 30¢ (8 oz.)
Rib veal chops: 69¢ (lb.)

Deaths

Wallace Beery, Richard Dix,
James Forrestal, Maurice
Maeterlinck, Rev. Peter
Marshall, Bill Robinson,
Edward Stettinius, Richard
Strauss.

In the News _____

U.S. RECOGNIZES REPUBLIC OF KOREA HEADED BY SYNGMAN RHEE
. . . TRUMAN ANNOUNCES POINT FOUR . . . GEORGE MARSHALL
RESIGNS, DEAN ACHESON BECOMES SECRETARY OF STATE . . .
NATIONALIST CHINESE SUFFER SEVERE DEFEATS, CHIANG KAI-SHEK
RESIGNS . . . FRENCH SEND GRATITUDE TRAIN TO U.S. . . . U.S.
RECOGNIZES ISRAEL AND TRANSJORDAN . . . WHITTAKER CHAMBERS
ACCUSES ALGER HISS OF SPYING . . . XB-4 PLANE GOES CROSS-
COUNTRY IN 3 HOURS, 46 MINUTES . . . $16 MILLION IS
APPROPRIATED FOR PALESTINIAN REFUGEES . . . N.Y. LEGISLATURE
ORDERS COMMUNISTS DISMISSED FROM SCHOOLS . . . NORTH ATLANTIC
PACT IS SIGNED, NATO CREATED . . . THREE WESTERN ZONES OF
GERMANY MERGE . . . FRANCE RECOGNIZES BAO DAI AS HEAD OF
NONCOMMUNIST VIETNAM . . . BERLIN BLOCKADE IS LIFTED . . .
SIAM BECOMES THAILAND . . . BRITAIN RECOGNIZES EIRE AS
INDEPENDENT, NORTHERN IRELAND REMAINS IN UNITED KINGDOM
. . . LAST U.S. TROOPS LEAVE KOREA . . . APARTHEID BEGINS IN
SOUTH AFRICA . . . HOUSING ACT IS PASSED, PROVIDING FEDERAL
AID . . . COMMUNISTS DRIVE NATIONALISTS OFF MAINLAND TO
FORMOSA . . . STRATOCRUISER GOES COAST TO COAST IN 9 HOURS . . .
U.S. WHITE PAPER CONCLUDES THAT NATIONALISTS LOST CHINA
. . . 500,000 STEELWORKERS STRIKE . . . $29 MILLION IS VOTED FOR
YUGOSLOVIA . . . 11 COMMUNIST PARTY MEMBERS ARE CONVICTED OF
SMITH ACT VIOLATION . . . GREEK CIVIL WAR ENDS WITH
COMMUNIST REBELS DEFEATED . . . MUTUAL DEFENSE ASSISTANCE
ACT PROVIDES FUNDS FOR NATO . . . INDIA ADOPTS CONSTITUTION,
NEHRU VISITS U.S. AND ADDRESSES CONGRESS . . . U.S. EMBASSY IN
MANCHURIA IS ATTACKED . . .

Quotes

"In some crude sense, which no vulgarity, no humor, no overstatement can quite extinguish, the physicists have known sin, and this is a knowledge which they cannot lose."

— J. Robert Oppenheimer

Examiner: The Commission's information is also to the effect that you were attending Communist meetings at the time. Do you have any explanation?

Scientist: No, none. This just can't be true. May I ask, can it be found out who the person [accuser] is?

Examiner: I do not know at this time.

— Atomic Energy Commission hearing

"I believe the American people are entitled to be informed of all developments in the field of atomic energy. We have evidence that within recent weeks an atomic explosion occurred within the USSR."

— Charles Ross, presidential press secretary

"Here's the thing that is top secret. Our scientists . . . [since] Hiroshima and Nagasaki have been trying to make what is known as a superbomb, . . . a thousand times the effect of that terrible bomb. That's the secret, the big secret.

— Secretary of Defense Louis Johnson

"Past events . . . have no objective existence. . . . The past is whatever the records and memories agree upon. . . . The Party is in full control of all the records."

— George Orwell, *1984*

"Attention must be paid. . . . A small man can be just as exhausted as a great man."

— Arthur Miller, *Death of a Salesman*

"You eat it, usually sitting in a booth in a bare, plain restaurant, with a mural of Vesuvio on the wall, a jukebox, and a crowded bar. The customers are Italian families, Bohemians, lovers, and—if a college is nearby—students and faculty members."

— About the new "pizza," *Atlantic Monthly*

Ads

I dreamed I went shopping in my Maidenform bra.
(*Maidenform Bras*)

Darling, you don't need reins to be a dear.
(*Warner's Foundations*)

Escape from Seams! Nylon Nudes by Hanes.
(*Hanes Hoisery*)

Over three million Americans are heavy "social" drinkers—many are on their way to becoming confirmed alcoholics—helpless and lost. But this tragic fate can be largely averted if the sound practical advice given here reaches enough of them in time.

(*Woman's Home Companion*)

What chance TWINS?

If you are expecting the stork, the chances that he'll bring you twins may be greater than you think. One in eighty-nine. In any event, twins—or any new arrival . . . make it virtually important to see your PRUDENTIAL representative.

(*Prudential Life Insurance*)

Fervent Femininity in Four Fragrances—Plaintive, Tabu, Emir, 20 Carats

(*Dana*)

For your enchanted moment (and it may come any moment) only one lipstick will do!

(*Tangee*)

New! A lighter-bodied *cream* tonic . . . gives your hair that "clean-groomed look."

— *Vitalis*

Double protection against Under-Arm Perspiration and Odor!—Veto

(*Veto Deodorant*)

Model room in Bloomingdale's, New York. *Library of Congress.*

Radio

Premieres
"Martin Kane, Private Eye," William Gargan
"Dragnet," Jack Webb

TV

Premieres
"Mr. I. Magination," Paul Tripp
"Quiz Kids," Joe Kelly
"Original Amateur Hour," Ted Mack
"Arthur Godfrey and His Friends"
"Captain Video and His Video Rangers," Al Hodge
"The Fred Waring Show"
"Cavalcade of Stars," Jack Carter
"Hopalong Cassidy," William Boyd
"Mama," Peggy Wood
"The Goldbergs," Gertrude Berg
"Pantomime Quiz," Mike Stokey
"Kukla, Fran and Ollie," Fran Allison
"The Lone Ranger," Clayton Moore, Jay Silverheels

"Blind Date," Arlene Francis
"Crusade in Europe," first documentary
"These Are My Children," first daytime soap opera

Specials
"Kathy Fiscus Rescue [from a well]," "Nuremburg Trials," "Teleforum," "Crusade in Europe"

Emmy Awards
"Ed Wynn Show" (live); "Texaco Star Theatre" (kinescope): "Time for Beany" (children); "Life of Riley" (film for TV); "Wrestling, KTLA" (sports)

Of Note
Charlton Heston plays his first major role in "Battleship Bismarck" ("Studio One") • Milton Berle hosts the first telethon, 14 hours, for cancer research and raises $1 million • TV's first major weekly situation comedies begin with ". . . but most of all, I remember Mama" ("Mama") and "Yoo-hoo, Mrs. Bloom" ("The Goldbergs").

Movies

Openings
All the King's Men (Richard Rossen), Broderick Crawford, John Ireland, Mercedes McCambridge
Battleground (William A. Wellman), Van Johnson, John Hodiak
The Heiress (William Wyler), Olivia de Havilland, Montgomery Clift
A Letter to Three Wives (Joseph L. Mankiewicz), Linda Darnell, Ann Sothern, Kirk Douglas
Home of the Brave (Mark Robson), Lloyd Bridges, Frank Lovejoy, James Edwards
Twelve O'Clock High (Henry King), Gregory Peck, Dean Jagger, Gary Merrill
Champion (Stanley Kramer), Kirk Douglas, Arthur Kennedy
Sands of Iwo Jima (Allan Dwan), John Wayne, John Agar
Pinky (Elia Kazan), Jeanne Crain, Ethel Barrymore, Ethel Waters
My Foolish Heart (Mark Robson), Susan Hayward, Dana Andrews
White Heat (Raoul Walsh), James Cagney, Virginia Mayo
On the Town (Gene Kelly, Stanley Donen), Gene Kelly, Frank Sinatra, Betty Garrett
She Wore a Yellow Ribbon (John Ford), John Wayne, Joanne Dru
Little Women (Mervyn LeRoy), June Allyson, Elizabeth Taylor, Janet Leigh, Margaret O'Brien
Lost Boundaries (Alfred L. Werker), Mel Ferrer, Beatrice Pearson
Intruder in the Dust (Clarence Brown), David Brian
The Bicycle Thief (Vittorio De Sica), Lamberto Maggiorani
The Third Man (Carol Reed), Joseph Cotten, Trevor Howard, Orson Welles, Alida Valli

Academy Awards
Best Picture: *All the King's Men*
Best Director: Joseph L. Mankiewicz (*A Letter to Three Wives*)
Best Actress: Olivia de Havilland (*The Heiress*)
Best Actor: Broderick Crawford (*All the King's Men*)

Top Box-Office Stars
Bob Hope, Bing Crosby, Abbott and Costello, John Wayne, Gary Cooper, Cary Grant, Betty Grable, Esther Williams, Humphrey Bogart, Clark Gable

Stars of Tomorrow
Montgomery Clift, Kirk Douglas, Betty Garrett, Paul Douglas, Howard Duff, Pedro Armendariz, Dean Stockwell, Wanda Hendrix, Wendell Corey, Barbara Bel Geddes

Popular Music

Hit Songs
"Mona Lisa"
"Rudolph, the Red-Nosed
   Reindeer"
"Mule Train"
"Let's Take an Old-Fashioned
   Walk"
"Some Enchanted Evening"
"My Foolish Heart"
"Diamonds Are a Girl's Best
   Friend"
"The Cry of the Wild Goose"
"Ghost Riders in the Sky"
"Huckle-Buck"

Top Records

Albums: *Vaughn Monroe Sings*
(Vaughn Monroe); *Roses in
Rhythm* (Frankie Carle); *Words
and Music* (Soundtrack); *Kiss Me
Kate* (original cast); *South Pacific*
(original cast)

Singles: *Dear Hearts and Gentle
People* (Bing Crosby); *You're
Breaking My Heart* (Vic Damone);
That Lucky Old Sun (Frankie
Laine); *Baby, It's Cold Outside*
(Esther Williams, Ricardo
Montalban); *September in the
Rain* (George Shearing); Country:
Candy Kisses (George Morgan);
Lovesick Blues (Hank Williams)

Jazz and Big Bands
"Cool jazz" ("cultivated chamber
jazz") includes Miles Davis, Bill
Evans, Lee Konitz, Gerry
Mulligan, Modern Jazz Quartet
(John Lewis), Dave Brubeck, and
Lenny Tristano.
Miles Davis's nine-piece band
includes a tuba and French horn,
and soloists John Lewis, Gunther
Schuller, Max Roach, Gerry

Mulligan, Lee Konitz, and J. J.
Johnson.
The George Shearing Quintet is
organized; Milt Jackson joins
Woody Herman; Canadian Oscar
Peterson debuts in the United
States at Carnegie Hall; Birdland
opens in New York.

First Recordings: Lennie Tristano
with Lee Konitz; Dave Brubeck

Top Performers (*Downbeat*):
Woody Herman (band); George
Shearing (jazz group); Billy Bauer,
Oscar Peterson, Shelly Manne,
Charlie Parker, Serge Chaloff,
Howard McGhee
(instrumentalists); Sarah Vaughan,
Billy Eckstine (vocalists); Pied
Pipers (vocal group)

Theater

Broadway Openings

Plays
Death of a Salesman (Arthur Miller), Lee J. Cobb,
   Mildred Dunnock, Arthur Kennedy
Detective Story (Sidney Kingsley), Ralph Bellamy,
   Lee Grant
I Know My Love (S. N. Behrman), Alfred Lunt,
   Lynn Fontanne
Two Blind Mice (Samuel Spewack), Melvyn Douglas
Harlequinade (Terence Rattigan), Maurice Evans
The Browning Version (Terence Rattigan), Maurice
   Evans, Edna Best
The Big Knife (Clifford Odets), John Garfield

Musicals
South Pacific (Richard Rodgers, Oscar Hammerstein
   II), Mary Martin, Ezio Pinza, Juanita Hall
Gentlemen Prefer Blondes (Jule Styne, Leo Robin),
   Carol Channing
Lost in the Stars (Kurt Weill, Maxwell Anderson),
   Todd Duncan
Miss Liberty (Irving Berlin), Eddie Albert
Touch and Go (Jay Gorney, Jean and Walter Kerr),
   Kyle MacDonnell

Texas, Li'l Darlin' (Robert Dolan, Johnny Mercer),
   Kenny Delmar, Loring Smith

Classics and Revivals On and Off Broadway
Diamond Lil (Mae West), Mae West; *Caesar and
Cleopatra* (George Bernard Shaw), Cedric
Hardwicke, Lilli Palmer; *The Father* (Strindberg),
Raymond Massey, Grace Kelly; *Medea* (Euripides),
Judith Anderson; *Richard II*, Richard Whorf.
Founded: The Loft Players (Circle in the Square) by
Theodore Mann, José Quintero, Emile Stevens, and
Jason Wingreen; League of Off-Broadway Theatres
and Producers

Regional

Founded: Mummer's Theatre, Oklahoma City, by
Mack Scism

Pulitzer Prize
Death of a Salesman, Arthur Miller

Classical Music _____

Compositions
Samuel Barber, Piano Sonata
Wallingford Riegger, Music for Brass Choir
Walter Piston, Piano Quintet, Duo for Violin and
    Cello
Virgil Thomson, Cello Concerto
Ernest Bloch, *Scherzo Fantasque*

Important Events
Antal Dorati succeeds Dimitri Mitropoulos at
Minnesota; Charles Munch, Serge Koussevitzky in
Boston; Howard Mitchell, Hans Kindler, at the
National, in Washington. Leopold Stokowski and
Mitropoulos are appointed principal conductors of
the New York Philharmonic.
Musical organizations proliferate throughout the
United States. Texas has three major orchestras:
Dallas, Houston, and San Antonio.
Two hundred works are premiered at 500 concerts in
New York; the Chopin 100th anniversary is
celebrated throughout the country.

Debuts: Aldo Ciccolini, Gina Bachauer

First Performances
William Schuman, Symphony no. 6 (Dallas); Roy
Harris (conducting), *Kentucky Spring* (Louisville);
Leonard Bernstein (playing), Symphony no. 2 *(The
Age of Anxiety)* (Boston); Béla Bartók, Viola

For the second year Billy Eckstine is named "most popular
singer" by *Downbeat. Movie Star News.*

Bruno Walter's interpretations of Mozart and Mahler with
the New York Philharmonic gain wide critical and popular
success. *Movie Star News.*

Concerto (Minneapolis); David Diamond, *The
Enormous Room* (Cincinnati); Douglas Moore, *The
Emperor's New Clothes* (New York); Darius Milhaud,
Concerto for Marimba, Vibraphone (St. Louis);
Arnold Schoenberg, Phantasy for Violin (Los
Angeles); Paul Hindemith, Concerto for Organ,
Brass, Woodwinds (Boston)

Opera

Metropolitan: *Otello* is televised with backstage
interviews. Ljuba Welitsch (debut), *Salomé;* Bidú
Sayão, Giuseppe Di Stefano (debuts), *La traviata;*
Giuseppe Valdengo, *Simon Boccanegra;* Cloë Elmo,
Gianni Schicchi

City Opera, City Center, New York: *Troubled Island*
(William Grant Still, premiere); *The Love for Three
Oranges*

New Haven: *Regina* (Marc Blitzstein, premiere)

San Francisco: Kirsten Flagstad, Set Svanholm, *Die
Meistersinger;* Jussi Bjoerling and Licia Albanese,
Manon Lescaut

Music Notes
The Detroit Symphony calls off its season because its
members refuse a pay cut • Public protests continue
against many Germans as undesirables or aliens.

Art _____

Painting
Barnett Newman, *Abraham, Covenant, Concord, Onement III*
Stuart Davis, *The Paris Bit*
Willem de Kooning, *Ashville, Attic*
Robert Motherwell, *At Five in the Afternoon, The Voyage*
Robert Gwathmey, *Sowing*
Mark Rothko, *Number 24, Number 18*
Bradley Walker Tomlin, *Number 20, Number 5*
Clyfford Still, *Number 2*
Jackson Pollock, *Number 2*
Loren MacIver, *Venice*
Mark Tobey, *Universal Field*

Sculpture
Richard Lippold, *Variation No. 7: Full Moon*
Alexander Calder, *Pomegranate*
Herbert Ferber, *Portrait of Jackson Pollock II*
Isamu Noguchi, *Unknown Bird*
Ibram Lassaw, *Star Cradle*
Louise Bourgeois, *The Blind Leading the Blind, Installation*
The Lincoln Memorial Circle, at the approach to the Arlington Memorial Bridge, Washington, D.C. (Fraser, Friedlander)

Architecture
Glass House, New Canaan, Conn. (Philip Johnson)
Warren Tremaine House, Montecito, Calif. (Richard Neutra)
140 Maiden Lane project, San Francisco (Frank Lloyd Wright)
Promontory Apartments, Chicago (Mies van der Rohe)
Laboratory Tower for S. C. Johnson and Son, Racine, Wisc. (Frank Lloyd Wright)
Case Study House, Santa Monica, Calif. (Charles Eames)

Important Exhibitions
International exchanges of old and modern masters increases: 116 American artists are displayed in three Israeli museums; paintings from major Italian museums and eighteenth-century art from the Louvre visit various U.S. galleries.

Museums

New York: *Metropolitan:* Van Gogh, Michelangelo, Donatello; Art treasures of Iran; Nine Worthies tapestries and the Hunt of the Unicorn (Cloisters); Italian art. *Museum of Modern Art:* Braque retrospective; "Modern Art in the Modern World." *Whitney:* Juliana Force and American Art; Weber

Chicago: The woodcut through six centuries; Toulouse-Lautrec; "From Colony to Nation, 1650–1815"

Willem de Kooning, *Attic,* 1949. Oil, enamel, newspaper transfer on paper. 61⅞ × 81″. *The Metropolitan Museum of Art, jointly owned by the Metropolitan Museum of Art and Muriel Kallis Newman, in honor of her son, Glen David Steinberg. The Muriel Kallis Steinberg Newman Collection, 1982.*

Washington: *National:* Michelangelo's "David," Donatello's "San Lodovico"; Art Treasures from Vienna. *Corcoran:* "De Gustibus" (History of American taste)

Boston: Forty years of Canadian painting; Third National Ceramic Exhibition; Pompeiian silver (from the Louvre)

St. Louis: Mississippi panorama

Philadelphia: Third International Exhibit of Sculpture; Antique, engraved and Steuben glass

Pittsburgh: Carnegie International first prize to Max Beckmann *(Fisher Women);* second prize to Philip Evergood *(Leda)*

Art Briefs
Jean Arp has his first American show in New York • Because of the postwar European currency devaluation, U.S. sales accelerate: Degas's *L'école de ballet* ($25,000); Homer's *The Voice from the Cliffs* ($12,000); Renoir's *Young Bather* ($10,500).

Dance _____

Premieres
New York City Ballet: *The Firebird* (George Balanchine, Stravinsky), Maria Tallchief, Francisco Moncion, Patricia McBride

Of Interest
Sadler's Wells is acclaimed on its first visit to the Metropolitan with *Swan Lake* and *The Sleeping Beauty.* In the company are Margot Fonteyn, Frederick Ashton, Robert Helpmann, Moira Shearer, and Beryl Grey • Erik Bruhn joins Ballet Theatre.

Books

Fiction

Critics' Choice
Golden Apples, Eudora Welty
The Man with the Golden Arm, Nelson Algren
The Journey of Simon McKiever, Albert Maltz
The Sheltering Sky, Paul Bowles
The Track of the Cat, Walter Van Tilburg Clark
Knight's Gambit, William Faulkner
The Lottery, Shirley Jackson
The Cannibal, John Hawkes
🍂 *1984*, George Orwell

Best-Sellers
The Egyptian, Mika Waltari
The Big Fisherman, Lloyd C. Douglas
Mary, Sholem Asch
A Rage to Live, John O'Hara
Point of No Return, John P. Marquand
Dinner at Antoine's, Frances Parkinson Keyes
High Towers, Thomas B. Costain
Cutlass Empire, Van Wyck Mason
Pride's Castle, Frank Yerby
Father of the Bride, Edward Streeter

Nonfiction

Critics' Choice
American Freedom and Catholic Power, Paul Blanshard
Modern Arms and Free Men, Vannevar Bush
Situation in Asia, Owen Lattimore
The Negro in the United States, E. Franklin Frazier
Killers of the Dream, Lillian Smith
Mirror for Man, Clyde Kluckholn
The Universe and Dr. Einstein, Lincoln Barnett
This I Remember, Eleanor Roosevelt
Theory of Literature, Rene Wellek, Austin Warren
Faith and History, Reinhold Niebuhr
Ralph Waldo Emerson, Ralph L. Rusk

Best-Sellers
White Collar Zoo, Clare Barnes, Jr.
How to Win at Canasta, Oswald Jacoby
The Seven Storey Mountain, Thomas Merton
Home Sweet Zoo, Clare Barnes, Jr.
Cheaper by the Dozen, Frank B. Gilbreth, Jr., Ernestine G. Carey
The Greatest Story Ever Told, Fulton Oursler
Canasta, the Argentine Rummy Game, Ottilie H. Reilly
Canasta, Josephine Artayeta de Viel, Ralph Michael
Peace of Soul, Fulton J. Sheen
A Guide to Confident Living, Norman Vincent Peale

Poetry
Robert Frost, *Complete Poems*
Kenneth Fearing, *Stranger at Coney Island*
Louis Simpson, *The Arrivistes*
Muriel Rukeyser, *Orpheus*
Conrad Aiken, *Skylight One*
William Carlos Williams, *Paterson*, Book Three, *Selected Poems*

Pulitzer Prizes
The Way West, A. B. Guthrie, Jr. (fiction)
Art and Life in America, Oliver W. Larkin (U.S. history)
John Quincy Adams and the Foundations of American Foreign Policy, Samuel Flagg Bemis (biography)
Annie Allen, Gwendolyn Brooks (poetry)

Science and Technology

In his condensation theory of the solar system, Gérard Kuiper, University of Chicago, postulates that the planets were formed from a nebula of gas and dust rotating around the sun 3 billion years ago.

The U.S. Air Force ends its two-year investigation of flying saucer reports by denying the authenticity of UFOs.

A two-stage rocket soars to a record 250 miles at 5,000 m.p.h. above the White Sands Proving Grounds, N.M.

Willard Libby, University of Chicago, reports the use of carbon-14 to determine the age of objects.

The "breeder reactor," an atomic reactor that produces more energy than it uses, is developed.

"Binac" is demonstrated by John Mauch and J. Presper Eckert; it computes at 12,000 times the speed of the human brain.

Eight essential amino acids for humans are described.

The commercial production of ACTH, which stimulates the body to produce cortisone, begins.

The first use of the betatron to treat cancer occurs at the University of Illinois, Chicago.

🍂 The first atomic bomb tests begin in the USSR.

Nobel Prize
William Giauque wins the prize in chemistry for work in thermodynamics.

Sports

Baseball
Casey Stengel becomes New York Yankee manager. Happy Chandler declares amnesty for Mexican League jumpers; Danny Gardella sues and wins out of court.

Champions

Batting	Pitching
Jackie Robinson (Brooklyn, NL), .342	Preacher Roe (Brooklyn, NL), 15–6
George Kell (Detroit, AL), .345	Ellis Kinder (Boston, AL), 23–6
	Home runs
	Ralph Kiner (Pittsburgh, NL), 54

Football
The flanker is introduced by Clark Shaughnessy. The AAC and NFL merge, with Baltimore, Cleveland, and San Francisco joining 10 NFL teams.

NFL Season Leaders: Sammy Baugh (Washington), passing; Steve Van Buren (Philadelphia), rushing; Tom Fears (Los Angeles), receiver

College All-Americans: Doak Walker (B), Southern Methodist; Charlie Justice (B), North Carolina; Leon Hart (E), Notre Dame

Bowls (Jan. 1, 1950)
Rose: Ohio State 17–California 14

Orange: Santa Clara 21–Kentucky 13

Cotton: Rice 27–North Carolina 13

Sugar: Oklahoma 35–Louisiana State 0

Basketball
NBA All-Pro first team: George Mikan (Minneapolis), Joe Fulks (Philadelphia), Bob Davies (Rochester), Jim Pollard (Minneapolis), Max Zaslofsky (Chicago)

Kentucky wins its second straight NCAA title; its stars include Alex Groza, Ralph Beard, Wah Wah Jones.

Other Sports

Golf: Ben Hogan is seriously injured in a car accident.

Boxing: Jake La Motta KO's Marcel Cerdan for the middleweight title; Cerdan is killed in a plane crash while flying to America for a return match. Joe Louis retires. Ezzard Charles outpoints Joe Walcott for the heavyweight title.

Tennis: Pancho Gonzales turns pro and tours with Jack Kramer; they earn $250,000.

Winners

World Series	College Basketball
New York (AL) 4	Kentucky (NCAA)
Brooklyn (NL) 1	San Francisco (NIT)
MVP	*Player of the Year*
NL–Jackie Robinson, Brooklyn	Dante Lavelli, Yale
AL–Ted Williams, Boston	*Stanley Cup*
NFL	Toronto
Philadelphia 14–Los Angeles (Rams) 0	*US Tennis Open*
	Men: Pancho Gonzales
College Football	Women: Margaret Osborne DuPont
Notre Dame	*USGA Open*
Heisman Trophy	Cary Middlecoff
Leon Hart, Notre Dame	*Kentucky Derby*
	Ponder (S. Brooks, jockey)

Fashion

For Women: Dior, Schiaparelli, Fath, and others commute to New York and design for mass production. For evening, the chemise, beaded and fringed, is either strapless or has a slender shoulder strap. Day fashions include shirtwaists, tight skirts with panels of matching or contrasting fabrics, hip bows, tunic effects, overblouses, oval necklines, and the dropped shoulder line with large sleeves. Fabrics range from thick fleeces, tweeds, and chinchilla cloth to ribbed wools and silks. Nylon is increasingly popular. Accessories include long pearl ropes, dangling earrings, and pigskin, alligator, and even fur textures for bags, belts, gloves, and shoes.

High-fashion note: Hardy Amies's "princess" coat; McCardell's "monastic dress" with string criss-crossing at the midriff; mutation minks in colors like gold

For Men: A carryover from the military are light suits that hold their shape; also popular are the new nylon cord suits, seersuckers, and cotton, nylon, and rayon blends, which also permit a new boldness in dress and informality. Two-trouser suits in variations of gray, blue, tan, and brown are also stylish.

Kaleidoscope _____

- William Levitt converts a Long Island potato field into a prefabricated, "carbon copy," suburban community. For $60 a month and no down payment, one can buy a $7,990, four-room house with attic, outdoor barbecue, washing machine, and 12½-inch built-in TV set.
- For the first time, blacks are invited to the important social events at the Presidential Inaugural and stay at the same hotels as whites.
- Pro– and con–Alger Hiss factions provoke intense rivalries that frequently center on New and Fair Deal loyalties.
- Comedy teams in films are very popular: Hope and Crosby, Martin and Lewis, Abbott and Costello.
- Vaudeville returns to the Palace Theatre after 14 years.
- An enormous controversy occurs over the FBI loyalty checks of Atomic Energy Commission scientists; Enrico Fermi and the California Institute of Technology president question the FBI investigations of AEC researchers as a step toward a police state.
- A test tube with one ounce of uranium oxide, which is missing from an Illinois lab, sets off an intensive search; it is later recovered from wastes sent to Oak Ridge, Tennessee.
- San Diego experiences its first snowfall.
- Because of a water shortage, New Yorkers have bathless and shaveless days.
- The postwar baby boom levels off with 3.58 million live births.
- The AMA advocates voluntary medical care plans.
- The minimum wage rises from 40 cents to 75 cents an hour.
- A sharp decline in prices occurs until the fall: 5 cents for beer in New York, pie à la mode for a penny in Los Angeles.
- Because of the Communist takeover of China and Russia's development of the A-bomb, many fear an impending war with Russia.
- Rita Hayworth marries Prince Ali Khan.
- Phonograph records in three different speeds (33⅓, 45, 78) baffle listeners and cause sales to fall.

"I Remember Mama" (*above*) and "The Goldbergs" are TV's first two successful sitcoms. *Movie Star News.*

- The Polaroid Land camera, which produces a picture in 60 seconds, goes on sale for $89.75.
- The FCC ends an eight-year ban on radio editorializing but warns that stations must present all sides of controversial questions.
- The Nobel Prize for literature is withheld when the academy fails to choose among Winston Churchill, William Faulkner, Carl Sandburg, and Benedetto Croce.
- Dr. Ralph J. Bunche successfully guides negotiations for a truce in war-torn Palestine after UN mediator Folke Bernadotte is assassinated.
- Travel restrictions are relaxed with visas no longer necessary for many countries outside the Iron Curtain; travelers ship their cars to Europe for $375 and pay high gas prices of 60 cents a liter; hotel rates in Capri are $2.50 a day, including meals.
- In order to prove that growing old is nonsense, Bernarr Macfadden, 81, parachutes from a plane and, greeting his wife, 43, remarks that anyone using white flour could probably do it.

Fads: Gorgeous George, lady wrestlers, roller derbies, pyramid clubs, Canasta, décolletage and boned bras, bikinis, short straight hair, matching sweaters, mother-daughter matching playsuits, cowboy and Indian suits and toys, plastic erector sets, Toni permanents, Caesar salads

First Appearances: LP record catalog (by record shop owner William Schwann), bicycle rider crossing the continent in less than three weeks, lightweight plastic foam, inflatable vinyl products (boats), ripping needle for sewing machine, midget microphone, scented bras (by Love-E of Hollywood), O'Hare Airport (named), Volkswagen (in the United States), Radio Free Europe's news broadcasts behind the Iron Curtain, airmail post card, prepared cake mixes, Pillsbury "Bake-Offs," Sara Lee cheesecake, Revlon's "Fire and Ice," Silly Putty, vice president to marry in office (Alben Barkley)

Alger Hiss, Harvard '29, a member of the Washington social register and former New Deal administrator. Was he a Soviet spy? *Library of Congress.*

THE *Fifties*

President Eisenhower and his grandson. *Library of Congress.*

Statistics

Vital
Population: 149,188,000
  Urban/rural: 16/9
  Farm: 15.3%
Life expectancy
  Male: 65.6
  Female: 71.1
Births/1,000: 24.1
Marriages/1,000: 11.1
Divorces/1,000: 2.6
Deaths/1,000: 9.6
  per 100,000
    Heart: 502
    Cancer: 139
    Tuberculosis: 22
    Car accidents: 21.3

Economic
Unemployed: 3,288,000
GNP: $364.8 billion
Federal budget: $39.6 billion
National debt: $257.4 billion
Union membership: 14.8
  million
Strikes: 4,843
Prime rate: 1.5%
Car sales: 6,665,800
Average salary: $2,992

Social
Homicides/100,000: 5.3
Suicides/100,000: 11.4
Lynchings: 2
Labor force male/female: 5/2
Social welfare: $23.51 billion
Public education: $5.84 billion
College degrees
  Bachelors'
    Male: 328,000
    Female: 103,000
  Doctorates
    Male: 6,969
    Female: 714
Attendance
  Movies (weekly): 60 million
  Baseball (yearly): 17.6
    million

Consumer
Consumer Price Index
  (1967 = 100): 77.1
Eggs: 72¢ (doz.)
Milk: 21¢ (qt.)
Bread: 14¢ (loaf)
Butter: 60¢ (lb.)
Bacon: 64¢ (lb.)
Round steak: 94¢ (lb.)
Oranges: 52¢ (doz.)
Coffee: 55¢ (lb.)

The fifties were a time of conservative politics, economic prosperity, and above all, social conformity. From the tidy lawns of spreading split-level suburbs to the tidy minds of board rooms, club rooms, and bedrooms, "neat and trim" and "proper and prim" were "in." These attitudes, invariably associated with the period, may perhaps be explained as a response to the unsettling events at the beginning of the decade.

Czechoslovakia and China had just come under Communist rule and Russia had recently announced its A-bomb when Truman revealed in 1950 that the United States was developing an even more powerful nuclear weapon, the H-bomb. Such a disclosure exacerbated an already palpable fear about the cold war, and it became clear that a race for annihilating weapons was underway. Three other events of the same year further intensified national anxiety: Senator Joseph McCarthy claimed knowledge of Communists in the State Department, the Kefauver Committee exposed a widespread and powerful underworld, and North Korea invaded South Korea.

Truman was widely supported in his decision to send troops to Korea, and MacArthur's Inchon landings and subsequent campaign promised a quick victory. But Communist China entered the war in massive numbers, and a long, bloody, and disheartening stalemate developed. South Korea was largely under control, but the war continued alongside tortuous peace negotiations. When Truman dismissed MacArthur, who was eager to attack China proper, regardless of the risks, the nation rallied around the general, who later returned to the largest hero's welcome since Lindbergh.

Capitalizing on the nation's fear of Communist aggression at home and abroad, Joseph McCarthy moved the threat of Communist infiltration into everyone's backyard. In a time of relative helplessness against an alarming enemy abroad, combined with "egghead" thinking at home from "bleeding hearts," "do-gooders," and "fellow travelers," McCarthy claimed to know the enemies. His accusations, though never proved, mounted, and his general thesis of widespread Communist influence in government gained wide credibility. A suspiciousness enveloped American life, and scientists, diplomats, academics, and entertainers came under scrutiny, along with movies, television, and even classical literature and comic books. The 1951 treason convictions of Julius and Ethel Rosenberg confirmed for many the extent of Communist subversion, although for many others, the Rosenberg executions represented the persecution of the innocents. Their trial, the Kefauver hearings, the college basketball and West Point cheating scandals, as well as the subsequent revelations of questionable gifts accepted by

Truman's staff, gave further indication of the nation's weakened moral fiber. In 1952, the succession of five Democratic presidential victories came to an end.

Dwight Eisenhower swept into office on a campaign against Korea, Communism, and Corruption. He was a common-sense, down-to-earth man, a great military leader with a fatherly manner, who promised peace and prosperity. He vowed to take America down "the middle road," and with his victory, the quintessential fifties were set in gear. America returned to the business of business, and, as in the 1920s, businessmen were appointed to places of power in the government. Once again, material success assumed a place of reverence, and government's role as an agent of social reform was constrained.

In this climate of atomic anxiety, political paranoia, and moral self-doubt, most Americans looked to the time-honored virtues of home, church, and community. It was time to cultivate the gardens of ever-growing suburbia, to learn the new mambo steps, and to make every effort to find group acceptance as a sign of moral health and patriotism. There was a virtual revival of Victorian respectability and domesticity (marriage age and divorce rates fell) and of the pioneer sense of community (leagues of young baseball players and women voters proliferated). In a booming economy, corporate America offered many opportunities for those willing to conform—the organization men in their gray flannel suits and their wives who remained at home to bear children at the highest birthrate ever.

Female college attendance dropped well below twenties' levels. More than ever, the work world became the man's domain, as though the wish to enter it were abnormal. Women were offered the rewards of glittering new homes (stocked with new appliances), surrounded by other new homes, and the companionship of neighbors who might be potential ladies' club members, cobarbecuers, and cochauffeurs to and from the kids' piano and ballet classes. For those for whom this was not enough, there were the newly marketed tranquilizers whose sales were astonishing.

Uniform styles of dress and properly buttoned down attitudes concerning sexual mores helped assure acceptance. Stern undergarments like boned girdles and stiff, pointed, or padded bras helped confine the body, and styles like long, broad, crinolined skirts and Dior's A, H, and Y shapes helped conceal its natural shape. Buxomness, a display of femininity and maternal potential, was "in"—for perhaps the last time in this century.

Bible sales, like construction and babies, also boomed, and once again, not unlike the twenties, religion and success allied themselves. Best-sellers, such as the Reverend Norman Vincent Peale's *The*

Rock Hudson and Doris Day struggle over her chastity in *Pillow Talk*. Oscar Levant quips: "I knew Doris Day before she was a virgin." *Movie Star News*.

Power of Positive Thinking, confirmed that belief enhanced material well-being; the president made repeated references to the Almighty and reinforced the motto that the family that prays together stays together. Popular culture also provided reassurance and role models. Songs extolled "Love and Marriage" and were sung by wholesome stars like Pat Boone, Rosemary Clooney, Doris Day, and Perry Como. Hollywood began producing the big blockbusters like *Ben Hur* and *The Ten Commandments*. TV shows like "Father Knows Best" and "Leave It to Beaver" gave humorous demonstration that all was well in the well-run family. Lovable, dizzy Lucy, and lovable, capable Ricky even increased their tribe on the day of Ike's inauguration (both on and off the tube!). Popular fads like white bucks, crew cuts, hula hoops, and Davy Crockett paraphernalia were all manifestations of an endless wholesomeness.

The early fifties youth were unusual in the extent to which they assumed the mores of their elders; they also watched TV more hours than they attended school. As rock and Elvis became popular in the mid-fifties, the young people found their own music and language, and with money to spend, they became more highly defined than any other youth group in history. James Dean, the *Rebel without a Cause*,

became their alienated idol; the Beats also appeared. Interestingly, two fictional portrayals of teenagers, although decidedly different, became classics as well as best-sellers, Salinger's *The Catcher in the Rye* and Nabokov's *Lolita*.

Subtle dichotomies marked other areas of American culture. *The Seven-Year Itch, My Fair Lady, The Sound of Music,* and *Peter Pan* seem most representative of the fifties' stage, but *Waiting for Godot,* on Broadway, and the efflorescence of Off-Broadway theater of the absurd, indicated less cheerful sensibilities at work. Edward Albee's *Zoo Story,* which ends with the murder of an establishment man by an alienated youth, may well be seen as a coda of the decade. Films like the daring *From Here to Eternity,* and novels like *The Caine Mutiny, Bonjour Tristesse,* and *Marjorie Morningstar,* while cautioning the need to retain the accepted mores, bespoke a certain yearning among the middle class and youth for new rules. Two important nonfiction works expressed grave qualms. *The Lonely Crowd* described a society in which appearance and acceptance had replaced inner values as guidelines to life, and *The Affluent Society* decried the lack of public purpose in a society exalting accumulation. Self-doubt was more prominent in foreign films like *The Seventh Seal; Hiroshima, Mon Amour; Room at the Top;* and *La Dolce Vita;* all of which gained a devoted following.

In television, westerns were especially popular, but the fifties were also the Golden Age of serious and original drama, with shows like "Marty," "Patterns," and "Requiem for a Heavyweight" on regular programs such as "Playhouse 90" and "Philco Playhouse." An innovative kind of news reporting was represented by Edward R. Murrow, and television gained a new public role.

Many look back upon the fifties with distaste

Joseph Albers, *Homage to the Square: "With Rays"* 1959. Oil on masonite. 48⅛ × 48⅛". *The Metropolitan Museum of Art, Arthur H. Hearn Fund.*

J. Robert Oppenheimer, who questions the morality of the atomic weapons he helped to create. *Library of Congress*.

Elvis Presley's singing and body gyrations cause teenage hysteria and adult consternation. *Movie Star News*.

and call it an uncreative and unidealistic time. Among their evidence are the carbon-copy suburban housing developments and shopping areas of the period, as well as the boxlike apartment buildings and garishly decorated hotels in Miami and Las Vegas, 3-D movies, painting by number, grape and "sick" jokes, the invention of TV dinners, and gaudy fashion styles like pink ties and shirts with charcoal suits, felt skirts with sequined poodle appliques, and rhinestone-speckled, plastic shoes. Nixon's Checkers speech, endless speculations about flying saucers, and Christine Jorgensen's sex change, as well as the new phenomena of *Playboy* and Mickey Spillane fiction (which everyone pored over behind closed doors), are other emblems of the times.

Although there is still evidence of the "ticky-tacky" houses that dotted the nation, this was also the time when many of the magnificent glass and steel towers that characterize the American metropolis were built by architects like the Saarinens, Mies van der Rohe, Skidmore, Owings, and Merrill, and Philip Johnson. An aesthetic revolution continued with the abstract expressionists Jackson Pollock, Willem de Kooning, and Robert Motherwell. Great opera stars also came of age—Renata Tebaldi, Maria Callas, Richard Tucker—as well as the great choreographers George Balanchine and Jerome Robbins. Musical exchanges between the United States and the USSR introduced the American public to Richter,

Gilels, Oistrakh, and Rostropovich; attendance at symphony concerts reached record heights.

Among the personalities whose fascination has endured are Marilyn Monroe, the sensual, vulnerable child-woman in search of male protectors; Grace Kelly, the cool beauty who married a prince; and Elvis Presley, the talented musician whose uninhibited demeanor remains an influence today. The Salk and Sabin vaccines, which lifted forever the annual summer siege of polio, are perhaps the unequivocal stars of the period.

Throughout it all, imperative forces were at work. Those that forever changed American life include the 1954 ruling that segregated schools are not equal and Rosa Parks's 1955 refusal to go to the back of a Montgomery bus; images of black schoolchildren harangued by white parents in Little Rock remain indelible. In 1957, Russia fired a shot heard around the world when it launched its Sputnik. America's first efforts to match the USSR proved humiliating failures. As the decade ended and the economy slowed, TV quiz scandals gave rise to additional moral self-doubt, and America's continuing failures in space and the "missile gap" brought its scientific and military preeminence into question. As a chipper Khrushchev proclaimed "We will bury you" to a well-fed, well-clothed, and well-housed bourgeois nation, America wondered if it was on the right track.

1950

Facts and Figures

Economic Profile
Dow-Jones: ↑ High 235–
    Low 193
GNP: +13%
Inflation: +5.7%
Unemployment: 5.3%
Brick ranch home, Bayside
    Hills, N.Y., 2 bedrooms, 2
    baths: $12,900
Median price, nationally, for
    single-family home:
    $10,050 (at 4.09% interest)
Mink stole: $250
Stepladder: $3.44–$5.44
Mastercraft oil paint: $2.66
    (gal.)
12′ wide Congoleum: 69¢ (sq.
    yd.)
Sears 3-piece bedroom set:
    $49.98
Lionel trains, complete:
    $14.95
Toddling Twin dolls: $2.97
Slate blackboard, with drop
    lid, easel, rack: $4.98
Havana cruise, SS *Europe:*
    $135–$150 (8 days)
North American Airlines,
    New York–California: $88
    (round trip)

Invasion Beach at Inchon,
where MacArthur's surprise
landing leads to the recapture
of Seoul and the anticipation
of an early victory.
Department of the Navy.

Deaths

Walter Damrosch, Walter
    Huston, Emil Jannings, Al
    Jolson, Harold Laski,
    Vaslav Nijinsky, George
    Orwell, Eliel Saarinen,
    George Bernard Shaw,
    Kurt Weill

In the News

HOOVER AND TAFT CALL FOR PROTECTION OF FORMOSA . . . BRINKS EXPRESS IS HELD UP FOR RECORD $1.8 MILLION . . . BRITAIN RECOGNIZES COMMUNIST CHINA . . . TRUMAN BARS MILITARY AID TO FORMOSA . . . ALGER HISS IS FOUND GUILTY OF PERJURY . . . RACE RIOTS ERUPT IN JOHANNESBURG OVER NEW APARTHEID POLICY . . . CHINESE COMMUNISTS SEIZE U.S. CONSULATE, U.S. WITHDRAWS . . . TRUMAN TELLS AEC TO DEVELOP H-BOMB . . . RUSSIA AND CHINA SIGN 3-YEAR TREATY . . . BRITISH SCIENTIST KLAUS FUCHS IS FOUND GUILTY OF TREASON . . . RUSSIANS SHOOT DOWN UNARMED U.S. PLANE IN BALTIC FOR "SPYING" . . . NATO LEADERS AGREE ON 5-YEAR INTEGRATED DEFENSE PLAN . . . RUSSIA ANNOUNCES A-BOMB . . . POSTMASTER CUTS MAIL DELIVERY TO ONCE A DAY . . . KEFAUVER CRIME COMMISSION OPENS HEARINGS . . . GENERAL MOTORS–UNITED AUTOWORKERS PACT GRANTS PENSIONS . . . 15% OF FACULTY ARE DISCHARGED AT UNIVERSITY OF CALIFORNIA FOR FAILURE TO SIGN NONCOMMUNIST AFFIRMATION PLEDGE . . . NORTH KOREA INVADES SOUTH KOREA, U.S. GROUND FORCES ARE SENT, NAVY BLOCKADES COAST . . . SENATOR JOSEPH MCCARTHY CHARGES COMMUNIST INFILTRATION OF STATE DEPARTMENT . . . UN SECURITY COUNCIL AUTHORIZES UNIFIED UN COMMAND UNDER DOUGLAS MACARTHUR . . . TRUMAN SEIZES RAILROADS TO AVERT STRIKE . . . U.S. FORCES LAND AT INCHON IN MAJOR VICTORY . . . CHINESE COMMUNISTS INVADE TIBET . . . MCCARRAN'S INTERNAL SECURITY ACT PASSES OVER TRUMAN VETO . . . $500 THOUSAND IS VOTED FOR POINT FOUR ASSISTANCE . . . TRUMAN SAYS VICTORY IN KOREA STILL MEANS HANDS OFF ASIA . . . U.S. FORCES ADVANCE IN NORTH KOREA AND REACH YALU RIVER . . . COMMUNIST CHINESE ENTER WAR IN MASS NUMBERS, UN TROOPS ARE FORCED TO RETREAT.

Quotes

"The attack upon Korea makes it plain that Communism has passed beyond the use of subversion to conquer independent nations and will now use armed invasion and war. Accordingly, I have ordered the Seventh Fleet to prevent any attack on Formosa."

— Harry S Truman

"I have here in my hand a list of 205 names known to the Secretary of State as being members of the Communist party who nevertheless are still working and shaping the policy of the State Department.

— Sen. Joseph McCarthy (R-Wis.)

"I affirm my innocence."—Alger Hiss
"Disgusting."—Richard M. Nixon

Senator Estes Kefauver: You refuse to testify further?
Frank Costello: Mr. Senator, I want to think of my health first. When I testify, I want to testify truthfully, and my mind don't function.

— Kefauver committee hearings

"You goddamn bastards. I hope an atom bomb falls on every one of you."

— Bugsy Siegel's girlfriend, Virginia Hill Hauser, to Kefauver committee

"If the television craze continues with the present level of programs, we are destined to have a nation of morons."

— Boston University president Daniel Marsh

"We must accelerate obsolescence. . . . Basic utility cannot be the foundation of a prosperous apparel industry."

— B. E. Puckett, businessman

"I have just read your lousy review of Margaret's concert. . . . Some day I hope to meet you. When that happens, you'll need a new nose, a lot of beefsteak for black eyes, and perhaps a supporter below."

— Harry Truman to *Washington Post* critic Paul Hume

Margaret Truman, the president's daughter. The *Washington Daily News* ran her father's angry letter to *Washington Post* critic Paul Hume, who refused to print it. *Library of Congress.*

Ads

TV

Premieres
"Robert Montgomery Presents" ("The Letter")
"The Garry Moore Show"
"Your Hit Parade," Dorothy Collins, Snooky Lanson
"The Kate Smith Hour"
"Pulitzer Prize Playhouse"
"The Steve Allen Show"
"The Colgate Comedy Hour," Eddie Cantor, Dean Martin, Jerry Lewis, Fred Allen
"Your Show of Shows," Sid Caesar, Imogene Coca
"This Is Show Business," Clifton Fadiman, George S. Kaufman, Abe Burrows
"What's My Line?" John Daly, Dorothy Kilgallen, Bennett Cerf, Arlene Francis
"You Bet Your Life," Groucho Marx
"Beat the Clock," Bud Collyer
"Arthur Murray's Dance Party"
"The Stork Club," Peter Lind Hayes, Mary Healy
"The George Burns and Gracie Allen Show"
"The Jack Benny Program"
"Truth or Consequences," Ralph Edwards

Top Ten (Nielsen)
"Texaco Star Theater," "Fireside Theatre," "Philco TV Playhouse," "Your Show of Shows," "The Colgate Comedy Hour," "Gillette Cavalcade of Sports," "The Lone Ranger," "Arthur Godfrey's Talent Scouts," "Hopalong Cassidy," "Mama"

Specials
"Departure of Marines for Korea," "Arrival of Cruiser from Korea," "Vienna Philharmonic," "Marshall Plan," "What to Do during an A-Bomb Attack," "The Journey Back" (Edward R. Murrow)

Emmy Awards
"Pulitzer Prize Playhouse" (drama); "The Alan Young Show" (variety); "Time for Beany" (children); "Truth or Consequences" (game); Alan Young (actor, "The Alan Young Show"); Gertrude Berg (actress, "The Goldbergs"); Groucho Marx (personality)

Of Note
Eleanor Roosevelt begins a weekly forum with "What to Do with the Hydrogen Bomb?" • Bob Hope makes his debut on "Star Spangled Revue," the first major radio comedian on TV • "Broadway Open House," with Morey Amsterdam, Jerry Lester, and Dagmar, is the first late-night talk show • Paul Draper is dismissed from Ed Sullivan's show because of complaints concerning his leftist associations, the first public indication of blacklisting • For the first time, TV ratings match radio ratings • Radio superstars leave for TV.

Movies

Openings
All about Eve (Joseph L. Mankiewicz), Bette Davis, Anne Baxter, Celeste Holm, George Sanders
Born Yesterday (George Cukor), Judy Holliday, William Holden, Broderick Crawford
Father of the Bride (Vincente Minnelli), Elizabeth Taylor, Spencer Tracy, Joan Bennett
Sunset Boulevard (Billy Wilder), Gloria Swanson, William Holden, Erich von Stroheim
The Asphalt Jungle (John Huston), Sterling Hayden
Cyrano de Bergerac (Michael Gordon), José Ferrer
Harvey (Henry Koster), James Stewart, Josephine Hull, Peggy Dow
Adam's Rib (George Cukor), Katharine Hepburn, Spencer Tracy
The Men (Fred Zinnemann), Marlon Brando
Samson and Delilah (Cecil B. De Mille), Hedy Lamarr, Victor Mature
Cheaper by the Dozen (Walter Lang), Clifton Webb, Myrna Loy, Jeanne Crain
La Ronde (Max Ophuls), Simone Signoret, Jean-Louis Barrault, Danielle Darrieux
Bitter Rice (Giuseppe de Santis), Silvano Mangano, Vittorio Gassman
Kind Hearts and Coronets (Robert Hamer), Alec Guinness, Joan Greenwood
Los Olvidados (Luis Buñuel), Alfonso Méfia

Academy Awards
Best Picture: *All about Eve*
Best Director: Joseph L. Mankiewicz (*All about Eve*)
Best Actress: Judy Holliday (*Born Yesterday*)
Best Actor: José Ferrer (*Cyrano de Bergerac*)

Top Box-Office Stars
John Wayne, Bob Hope, Bing Crosby, Betty Grable, James Stewart, Abbott and Costello, Clifton Webb, Esther Williams, Spencer Tracy, Randolph Scott

Stars of Tomorrow
Dean Martin and Jerry Lewis, William Holden, Arlene Dahl, Ruth Roman, Vera-Ellen, John Lund, William Lundigan, Dean Jagger, Joanne Dru

Popular Music

Hit Songs
"Autumn Leaves"
"A Bushel and a Peck"
"Music! Music! Music!"
"It's So Nice to Have a Man around the House"
"Rag Mop"
"Tzena, Tzena, Tzena"
"La Vie en Rose"
"My Heart Cries for You"
"There's No Tomorrow"

Top Records

Albums: *Cinderella* (Ilene Woods); *Young Man with a Horn* (Harry James, Doris Day); *Three Little Words* (original cast); *Merry Christmas* (Bing Crosby)

Singles: *Goodnight Irene* (The Weavers); *It Isn't Fair* (Sammy Kaye); *Third Man Theme* (Anton Karas); *Mule Train* (Frankie Laine); *Mona Lisa* (Nat "King" Cole); *I Wanna Be Loved* (Andrews Sisters); *Twilight Time* (Three Suns); *Frosty, the Snow Man* (Gene Autry); *If I Knew You Were Coming I'd Have Baked a Cake* (Eileen Barton); *Be My Love* (Mario Lanza); *The Thing* (Phil Harris); *Tennessee Waltz* (Patti Page); *September in the Rain* (Lionel Hampton); *You Go to My Head* (Lee Konitz). Country: *Chattanooga Shoe Shine Boy* (Red Foley); *Long Gone Lonesome Blues* (Hank Williams)

Jazz and Big Bands
Stan Kenton organizes a 40-piece "Innovations in Modern Music Orchestra." Count Basie breaks up his big band and starts a septet; Dizzy Gillespie dismantles his big band. Horace Silver joins Stan Getz. The Red Norvo Trio includes Charles Mingus and Tal Farlow. Mahalia Jackson holds her first Carnegie Hall concert.

Top Performers (*Downbeat*): Stan Kenton (band); George Shearing (jazz group); Stan Getz, Serge Chaloff, Maynard Ferguson, Bill Harris, Terry Gibbs (instrumentalists); Sarah Vaughan, Billy Eckstine (vocalists); Mills Brothers (vocal group)

Theater

Broadway Openings

Plays
The Member of the Wedding (Carson McCullers), Julie Harris, Ethel Waters, Brandon De Wilde
Come Back, Little Sheba (William Inge), Stanley Blackmer, Shirley Booth
The Cocktail Party (T. S. Eliot), Alec Guinness, Cathleen Nesbitt
The Country Girl (Clifford Odets), Paul Kelly, Uta Hagen
Bell, Book, and Candle (John Van Druten), Rex Harrison, Lilli Palmer
The Happy Time (Samuel Taylor), Claude Dauphin, Eva Gabor
The Wisteria Trees (Joshua Logan), Helen Hayes
The Lady's Not for Burning (Christopher Fry), John Gielgud, Pamela Brown
The Innocents (William Archibald), Beatrice Straight

Musicals
Guys and Dolls (Frank Loesser), Robert Alda, Vivian Blaine, Sam Levene
Call Me Madam (Irving Berlin), Ethel Merman, Russell Nype, Paul Lukas
Peter Pan (Leonard Bernstein), Jean Arthur, Boris Karloff

Classics and Revivals On and Off Broadway
The Devil's Disciple (George Bernard Shaw), Maurice Evans; *As You Like It,* Katharine Hepburn; *The Tower beyond Tragedy* (Robinson Jeffers), Judith Anderson; *Twentieth Century* (Ben Hecht, Charles MacArthur), Gloria Swanson, José Ferrer. *Founded:* Arena Theater, Hotel Edison (first theater-in-the-round): *The Show Off,* Lee Tracy; *Julius Ceasar,* Basil Rathbone, Alfred Ryder; *Arms and the Man* (Shaw), Francis Lederer, Sam Wanamaker

Regional

Founded: Arena State Theatre, Washington, D.C., by Zelda and Thomas Fichandler, Edward Mangum

Alley, Houston: *Season with Ginger* [*Time Out for Ginger*] (Ronald Alexander)

Pulitzer Prize
South Pacific, Richard Rodgers, Oscar Hammerstein II, Joshua Logan

Tony Awards
The Cocktail Party, T. S. Eliot (play); *South Pacific,* Richard Rodgers, Oscar Hammerstein II, Joshua Logan (musical)

Classical Music ⎯⎯⎯⎯⎯

Compositions

Aaron Copland, *Twelve Poems of Emily Dickinson*
Norman Dello Joio, *Psalm of David*
John Cage, *Cartridge Music*
William Schuman, String Quartet no. 4
Walter Piston, Symphony no. 4
Douglas Moore, *Giants in the Earth*
Ross Lee Finney, String Quartet no. 6

Important Events

The bicentennial of Johann Sebastian Bach's death is celebrated throughout the world.
The Royal Philharmonic Orchestra, with Sir Thomas Beecham, tours the United States.
The Israeli Symphony, with Serge Koussevitsky, Eleanor de Carvalho, and Leonard Bernstein, tours 40 cities.
Robert, Gaby, and Jean Casadesus play the *Bach Concerto in C* arranged for three pianos and orchestra at Carnegie Hall.
Charles Munch pays tribute to Boston Symphony Hall's 50th anniversary by performing its original program, which included Handel's Organ Concerto no. 4 (now performed by E. Power Biggs).
Georges Enesco is violinist, pianist, and composer at the 60th-anniversary concert of his first appearance in New York.

Debuts: Claude Frank, Gerard Souzay, William Warfield

Lauren Bacall and Humphrey Bogart dining out. They met as costars of *To Have and Have Not* (1944). *Movie Star News.*

Metropolitan Opera impressario Rudolph Bing is gaining a reputation for his often stormy relationships with the company's prima donnas. *Movie Star News.*

First Performances

Paul Hindemith, conducting, Sinfonietta in E (Louisville); Francis Poulenc, playing, Piano Concerto (Boston); Paul Creston, Concerto for Piano and Orchestra (Washington, D.C.); Aaron Copland, Concerto for Clarinet, String Quartet, Harp and Piano (New York); Howard Hanson, Short Symphony (New York); Virgil Thomson, Concerto for Cello (Philadelphia); Samuel Barber, Piano Sonata (New York, Vladimir Horowitz)

Opera

Numerous chamber opera premieres include Norman Dello Joio's *The Triumph of Joan* (New York); Bernard Rogers's *The Veil,* and Lucas Foss's *The Jumping Frog* (Indiana University).

Metropolitan: Controversial Rudolf Bing is appointed; Bing plans for fewer singers and a smaller repertory. Roberta Peters (debut), *Don Giovanni;* Cesare Siepi, Lucine Amara (debuts), Robert Merrill, *Don Carlo;* Paul Schoeffler, *Die Meistersinger;* Erna Berger, *The Magic Flute;* Fedora Barbieri, *Il trovatore.* Kirsten Flagstad and Helen Traubel share honors as top Wagner sopranos.

San Francisco: Set Svanholm, Kirsten Flagstad, *Tristan und Isolde;* Renata Tebaldi, Mario del Monaco (debuts), *Aïda;* Kirsten Flagstad, *Parsifal*

Music Notes

Because of a financial deficit, the Philharmonic Symphony Society of New York plays on the stage of the Roxy Theater between movie shows, four times a day, for two weeks.

Art

Painting

Willem de Kooning, *Excavation, Woman I* (1950–1952)
Hans Hofmann, *Magenta and Blue*
Jackson Pollock, *Autumn Rhythm, One (Number 31, 1950)*
Franz Kline, *Chief*
Morris Graves, *Spring*
Mark Rothko, *Number 10, 1950*
George Tooker, *The Subway*
Barnett Newman, *Tundra, The Wild*
Bradley Walker Tomlin, *In Praise of Gertrude Stein*
Kurt Seligmann, *The Balcony, I*

Sculpture

Herbert Ferber, *He Is Not a Man*
Richard Lippold, *Variation within a Sphere, No. 10: The Sun*

Louise Bourgeois, *Sleeping Figure*
David Smith, *Blackburn: Song of an Irish Blacksmith, Twenty-Four Greek Ys*

Architecture

Bavington House, Norman, Okla. (Bruce Goff)
Christ Lutheran Church, Minneapolis (Saarinen and Saarinen)
Harvard Graduate Center, Cambridge, Mass. The Architects Collaborative [TAC].
Farnsworth House, Plano, Ill. (Mies van der Rohe)
UN Headquarters, New York (Harrison, Le Corbusier, Niemeyer, Markelius)
Construction begins on the Lever House, New York (Skidmore, Owings, and Merrill).

Important Exhibitions

Museums

New York: *Metropolitan:* Art treasures from the Vienna collection; "American Painting Today" (with works from a nationwide competition); "307 Paintings from 34 States"; Masterpieces of bronze; The world of silk. *Museum of Modern Art:* Klee, Demuth, Soutine retrospectives. *Whitney:* Hopper retrospective

Washington: *National:* Makers of history in Washington, 1800–1950; Art treasures from the Vienna collection. *Corcoran:* "American Processional 1492–1900"

Boston: American art (largest survey ever held, government-supported with $100,000); Iranian art; Hopper

Philadelphia: Diamond Jubilee—"Masterpieces in America"; 250 works from private collections: Angelico Crucifix to Picasso's *Three Musicians*

Cleveland: Hopper retrospective

Detroit: From David to Courbet

Richmond: Impressionism and postimpressionism

Venice Biennale: Marin, Gorky, Pollock, de Kooning, and Bloom represent the United States.

Art Briefs

The Metropolitan Museum of Art announces that its annual American show will include sculpture and alternate living painters and sculptors • Edvard Munch's work tours the United States • Major sales include Rembrandt's *Portrait of a Young Man* ($130,000) and *Portrait of a Student* ($135,000), Gilbert's full-length Washington portrait ($17,500), and Matisse's "Woman in Green" ($5,500) • Twenty-eight avant-garde artists issue a manifesto attacking the Metropolitan Museum of Art's aesthetic provincialism.

Dance

Ballet Theatre, New York City Ballet, Les Ballets Americains, and Martha Graham companies tour in Europe. Sadler's Wells, Ballets de Paris, and Marquis de Cuevas visit the United States.

Ballet Theatre celebrates its tenth anniversary. The company is renamed the American National Ballet Theatre and becomes the official company of the Metropolitan Opera. Dancers include Alicia Alonso, Nora Kaye, John Kriza, John Taras, Mary Ellen Moylan, and Igor Youskevitch. Jerome Robbins joins the New York City Ballet; the New York City Dance Theatre debuts with *The Moor's Pavanne* (José Limón).

Martha Graham dances *Judith* (William Schuman) in Louisville, Ky.; Sadler's Wells tour breaks box-office records.

Premieres

New York City Ballet: *The Age of Anxiety,* (Jerome Robbins, Leonard Bernstein), Tanaquil Le Clercq, Todd Bolender; *Illuminations* (Frederick Ashton), Nicholas Magallanes, Le Clercq, Melissa Hayden.

Books

Fiction

Critics' Choice

Collected Stories, William Faulkner
The Delicate Prey, Paul Bowles
Cast a Cold Eye, Mary McCarthy
The Family Moskat, Isaac Bashevis Singer
World Enough and Time, Robert Penn Warren
The Martian Chronicles, Ray Bradbury
The Town and the City, Jack Kerouac
The Trouble of One House, Brendan Gill
The Roman Spring of Mrs. Stone, Tennessee Williams

Best-Sellers

The Cardinal, Henry Morton Robinson
Joy Street, Frances Parkinson Keyes
Across the River and into the Trees, Ernest Hemingway
The Wall, John Hersey
Floodtide, Frank Yerby
The Adventurer, Mika Waltari
The Disenchanted, Budd Schulberg
Star Money, Kathleen Winsor
The Parasites, Daphne Du Maurier
Jubilee Trail, Gwen Bristow

Nonfiction

Critics' Choice

Decision in Germany, Lucius Clay
The Human Use of Human Beings, Norbert Wiener
Virgin Land, Henry Nash Smith
The American Mind, Henry Steele Commager
The Liberal Imagination, Lionel Trilling
A Rhetoric of Motives, Kenneth Burke
Classics and Commercials, Edmund Wilson
The Lonely Crowd, David Riesman, Jr., Reuel Denney, Nathan Glazer
Worlds in Collision, Immanuel Velikovsky
The Index of American Design, Edwin O. Christensen
Herman Melville, Newton Arvin

Best-Sellers

Betty Crocker's Picture Cook Book
The Baby
Look Younger, Live Longer, Gayelord Hauser
How I Raised Myself from Failure to Success in Selling, Frank Bettger
Kon-Tiki, Thor Heyerdahl
Your Dream Home, Hubbard Cobb
The Mature Mind, H. A. Overstreet
Bells on Their Toes, Frank Gilbreth, Jr., Ernestine Gilbreth Carey
Campus Zoo, Clare Barnes, Jr.
Mr. Jones, Meet the Master, Peter Marshall

Poetry

Wallace Stevens, *The Auroras of Autumn*
Robert Lowell, *Poems 1938–1949*
William Carlos Williams, *The Collected Later Poems*
Howard Nemerov, *Guide to the Ruins*
E. E. Cummings, *Xaïpe*
Delmore Schwartz, *Vaudeville for a Princess*
W. H. Auden, *Collected Shorter Poems 1930–1944*

Pulitzer Prizes

The Town, Conrad Richter (fiction)
The Old Northwest, Pioneer Period 1815–1840, vols. 1–2, R. Carlyle Buley (U.S. history)
John C. Calhoun: American Portrait, Margaret Louise Coit (biography)
Complete Poems, Carl Sandburg (poetry)

Science and Technology

Tritium, a hydrogen isotope and the basis for the new H-bomb, is discovered in ordinary water.

New elements Berkelium 97 and Californium 98 are created by the Berkeley cyclotron. The existence of subatomic "V" particles is confirmed.

On the basis of the La Jolla cave finds, George Carter, of Johns Hopkins, reports that man lived in North America 40,000 years ago.

Tromexan, an anticoagulant, is reported by Dr. Irving Wright to be a potential heart attack inhibitor.

Dr. Richard Lawler performs the first kidney transplant.

The first successful heart massage is performed at St. John's Hospital, Brooklyn, N.Y.

The first successful aorta transplant is performed on a fifty-seven-year-old man at Ford Hospital, Detroit.

B. J. Ludwig and E. C. Pich, of Wallace Labs, synthesize the tranquilizer meprobamate.

Nobel Prize

Philip S. Hench and Edward C. Kendall win the prize in physiology and medicine for their discoveries about the hormones of the adrenal cortex.

Sports

Baseball

Gil Hodges (Brooklyn, NL), hits four home runs in one game.

Connie Mack retires after fifty years as the Philadelphia A's manager.

The major leagues sign a $6 million TV contract for World Series rights, with benefits to go to the pension fund.

Champions

Batting	Pitching
Stan Musial (St. Louis, NL), .346	Sal Maglie (New York, NL), 18–4
William Goodman (Boston, AL), .354	Vic Raschi (New York, AL), 21–8
	Home runs
	Ralph Kiner (Pittsburgh, NL), 47

Football

The Cleveland Browns, of the old All-America Conference (AAC), win in the first year of the merged leagues.

NFL Season Leaders: Norm Van Brocklin (Los Angeles), passing; Marion Motley (Cleveland), rushing; Tom Fears (Los Angeles), passing

College All-Americans: Kyle Rote (B), Southern Methodist; Vic Janowicz (Q), Ohio State; Bill McColl (E), Stanford

Bowls (Jan. 1, 1951)

Rose: Michigan 14– California 6	Cotton: Tennessee 20– Texas 14
Orange: Clemson 15– Miami 14	Sugar: Kentucky 13– Oklahoma 6

Basketball

City College of New York wins the NCAA and the NIT, the first team to win both; Irwin Dambrot, Ed Roman, and Floyd Lane star.

NBA All-Pro First Team: George Mikan (Minneapolis), Jim Pollard (Minneapolis), Alex Groza (Indianapolis), Bob Davies (Rochester), Max Zaslofsky (Chicago)

Other Sports

Golf: In a comeback after his car accident, Ben Hogan wins the U.S. Open. Sam Snead is the PGA leader with $37,000 in winnings.

Boxing: Sugar Ray Robinson, middleweight champion, challenges Joey Maxim, light heavyweight champion, for his crown. Robinson is ahead on points but because of the heat can't come out for the 14th and loses by TKO.

Tennis: Gussie Moran's tennis outfit, including lace underwear, creates a stir on the pro circuit.

Winners

World Series	*College Basketball*
New York (AL) 4	C.C.N.Y. (NCAA, NIT)
Philadelphia (NL) 1	*Player of the Year*
MVP	Paul Arizin, Villanova
NL–Jim Konstanty, Philadelphia	*Stanley Cup*
AL–Phil Rizzuto, New York	Detroit
NFL	*US Tennis Open*
Cleveland 30–Los Angeles 28	Men: Arthur Larsen
College Football	Women: Margaret Osborne DuPont
Oklahoma	*USGA Open*
Heisman Trophy	Ben Hogan
Vic Janowicz, Ohio State	*Kentucky Derby*
NBA Championship	Middleground (W. Boland, jockey)
Minneapolis 4–Syracuse 2	

Fashion

For Women: The flapper revival at the beginning of the year is accompanied by more "wearable," "pretty," and "feminine" clothes: the belted chemise, sleeveless dresses, tailored suits, loose and fleecy topcoats. Velvet and velveteen are popular in ballgowns (with little jackets), suits, and dresses. Transparent fabrics, chiffons, and organdies in sherbet tones and white or gray tulle are worn at night with stoles in matching fabrics and patent leather shoes, bags, and belts. Most fashionable is the black/white combination, worn year round, with big, glittery rhinestone jewelry. Hair is longer, chignons are stylish, makeup is lighter, lips are pink and white, eyes are accented and elongated, eyebrows are natural.

High-fashion note: Balenciaga's belted jacket

Kaleidoscope

- Twelve live Russian sables are sent to the United States for breeding purposes in return for twelve U.S. minks; the sables arrive sterilized.
- Gen. Frank McConnell, at Fort Jackson, S.C., orders integration in the armed services following Truman's and the secretary of the army's directives.
- Bomb-shelter plans, like the government pamphlet *You Can Survive,* become widely available. Many leading scientists warn of Russia's race to achieve the H-bomb; Einstein and others argue that "general annihilation beckons."
- Blacklisting of performers with alleged Communist affiliations becomes widespread. CBS requires that a loyalty oath be signed; *Red Channels,* the "Report of Communist Influence in Radio and TV" lists Leonard Bernstein, Lee J. Cobb, Ben Grauer, Gypsy Rose Lee, Philip Loeb, Burgess Meredith, Arthur Miller, Zero Mostel, Pete Seeger, Howard K. Smith, and Orson Welles.
- Herblock coins the term *McCarthyism.*
- Thirty million people watch the Kefauver Commission crime hearings, which matches the World Series in TV ratings; one Chicago department store offers "10% off during Kefauver hours."
- Hallmark Greeting Cards buys reproduction rights for eighteen of Winston Churchill's canvases; he donates his stipend to Cambridge University.
- A Columbia University Press editor conducts a poll of librarians for the most boring books; the results are Bunyan's *Pilgrim's Progress,* Melville's *Moby Dick,* Milton's *Paradise Lost,* and Spenser's *Faerie Queene.*
- Americans consume 320 million pounds of potato chips annually and 750 million pounds of hotdogs; per capita consumption is 63.1 pounds of beef; 8.2 pounds of veal; 69.9 pounds of pork, and 3.9 pounds of lamb or mutton.
- At the 10,600 houses at Levittown, N.Y., rules mandate that grass be cut at least once a week and laundry washed on specific days.
- Polls indicate that President Truman's decisions to continue H-bomb research and to send the navy and air force to Korea have won him support from many who believe that America is finally taking a stand against Communism.
- The UN reports that half of the world's 800 million children are undernourished.
- A new low in illiteracy is recorded: 3.2 percent.
- A national survey reports that children spend 27 hours a week watching TV, three-fourths of an hour less than their weekly time in school.
- David Reisman's acclaimed *The Lonely Crowd* describes how rugged individualism has given way to the quest for peer group approval.
- After the Kefauver hearings, Young and Rubicam, one of the United States' largest advertising agencies, takes a full-page newspaper ad to express shock at "what's happened to public and private standards of morality."
- Congressman E. C. Johnson attacks the alleged immorality of film stars like Ingrid Bergman and Roberto Rossellini (who have conceived an out-of-wedlock child) and introduces a bill to license film producers and distributors.
- Jane Russell and Roy Rogers become born-again Christians. Miss Russell says of God: "He's a livin' doll."
- A *Downbeat* poll lists as the most popular male singers Billy Eckstine, Perry Como, Frankie Laine, Frank Sinatra, Louis Armstrong, and Mel Torme; female singers include Sarah Vaughan, Ella Fitzgerald, Doris Day, Kay Starr, Peggy Lee, Billie Holiday, Patti Page, Jo Stafford, and Fran Warren.
- A *Life* survey lists as the most popular teen idols Louisa May Alcott, Joe DiMaggio, Vera-Ellen, FDR, Lincoln, Roy Rogers, General MacArthur, Clara Barton, Doris Day, Sister Elizabeth Kenny, Babe Ruth, and Florence Nightingale.
- A Pan American flight from New York to London is recorded in 9 hours and 16 minutes.
- Flying saucers are sighted in Israel, Hong Kong, and Italy.
- UN diplomat Ralph J. Bunche receives the Nobel Peace Prize.
- Carol Fox, debutante daughter of a wealthy Chicago furniture manufacturer, founds the Chicago Lyric Theatre, goes to Europe, and lines up La Scala's Tito Gobbi, along with Guiseppe di Stefano, Giulietta Simionato, and Maria Callas.
- Without any evidence, Senator McCarthy names as the "top Russian espionage agent" Owen Lattimore of the State Department.
- "I do not intend to turn my back on Alger Hiss," says Dean Acheson, after his friend's conviction.
- Russian spy Klaus Fuchs says he had complete faith in Russian policy and no hesitation in giving away secrets.
- Russians, who have been boycotting the Security Council for five months, refuse Trygve Lie's invitation to return for the debate on Korea.

New Words and Usages: apartheid, captive audience, Cinerama, colorcast, dianetics, fusion bomb, H-bomb, integration, mambo, rat pack, spaceman, theater-in-the-round, triton bomb

Fads: Hopalong Cassidy outfits for children, along with toy guns, spurs, and boots; black molasses; Toni permanents; the mambo; square dancing; antihistamine pill popping

First Appearances: Learn-When-Sleeping machine, phototransistor, Sugar Pops, orlon, Miss Clairol, Smokey the Bear, Otis elevator with self-opening doors, Minute Rice, Sony tape recorders, syndicated "Peanuts," Diners Club, Corning Ware, cyclamates, Air Call (beepers), A. C. Nielsen Co. (rating service, formerly of C. E. Hooper)

1951

Economic Profile
   Dow-Jones: ↑ High 276–
      Low 238
   GNP: +15%
   Inflation: +0.7%
   Unemployment: 3.3%
Median age, first marriage:
   Male: 22.9
   Female: 20.4
Average household size: 3.37
Population over 65: 8%
Population under 10: 19%
Davega roller skates: $12.88
Metal skate case: $3.49
Skating skirt: $5.94
Jon Gnagy easel paint set:
   $4.95
Accordion: $14.95
Royal deluxe portable
   typewriter: $37.50
Viewmaster: $2.00; reels: $1
   (for 3)
Four-door Kaiser: $2,289.99
Avis Rent-a-car $6 (24 hours),
   8¢ (per mile)
Paper-Mate pocket pen: $1.69

Deaths

John Alden Carpenter,
   Dorothy Dix, Eddy
   Duchin, André Gide, Serge
   Koussevitzky, Willem
   Mengelberg, Maria
   Montez, Sigmund
   Romberg, Artur Schnabel,
   Arnold Schoenberg

In the News

CHINESE COMMUNISTS AND NORTH KOREANS RETAKE SEOUL AND INCHON . . . U.S. RESUMES ARMS SUPPLY TO CHINESE NATIONALISTS . . . TRUMAN SAYS RUSSIA SEEKS WORLD CONQUEST, ASKS CONGRESS FOR FULL MOBILIZATION AND WAGE-PRICE FREEZE . . . U.S. TESTS A-BOMB NEAR LAS VEGAS . . . UN RESOLUTION CONDEMNS CHINESE COMMUNIST AGGRESSION . . . PENN RAILROAD ACCIDENT IN N.J. KILLS 84 . . . RAIL STRIKE ENDS UNDER THREAT OF FIRINGS . . . U.S. WILL SEND 100,000 TROOPS TO EUROPE . . . LABOR BALKS AT 10% WAGE INCREASE LIMIT . . . 22D AMENDMENT TAKES EFFECT LIMITING THE PRESIDENT TO TWO TERMS . . . GENERAL OMAR BRADLEY ANNOUNCES THAT 250,000 GIS ARE NOW IN KOREA . . . J. EDGAR HOOVER WARNS THAT COMMUNISTS ARE GOING UNDERGROUND . . . ETHEL AND JULIUS ROSENBERG ARE FOUND GUILTY OF TREASON AND SENTENCED TO DEATH . . . GENERAL MACARTHUR URGES CROSSING THE YALU RIVER INTO CHINA . . . TRUMAN RELIEVES MACARTHUR, GIANT PARADE GREETS MACARTHUR IN NEW YORK . . . MOSSADEGH BECOMES PREMIER OF IRAN, PLANS TO NATIONALIZE OIL . . . THE DRAFT AGE IS LOWERED TO 18 . . . CHINESE COMMUNISTS ACCEPT U.S. PROPOSAL TO DISCUSS CEASE-FIRE . . . CEASE-FIRE TALKS BEGIN IN KAESONG . . . U.S. ASKS EGYPT TO OPEN SUEZ CANAL TO ISRAELIS . . . WASHINGTON ANNOUNCES SECOND SOVIET A-BOMB TEST . . . MUTUAL SECURITY ACT PROVIDES $7.5 BILLION FOR FOREIGN AID . . . CEASE-FIRE TALKS REOPEN IN PANMUNJOM . . . TRUMAN OFFERS "FOOLPROOF" DISARMAMENT PLAN . . . WEST GERMANY IS GRANTED SOVEREIGNTY . . . BRIEF CEASE-FIRE ENDS.

Gen. Douglas MacArthur's farewell address to a joint session of Congress. *Library of Congress.*

"We must . . . limit the war to Korea . . . to prevent a third World War. . . . General MacArthur did not agree with that policy. I have therefore considered it essential to relieve General MacArthur."
— Harry S Truman

"When you put on a uniform there are certain inhibitions which you accept."
— Gen. Dwight D. Eisenhower

"President Truman has given [the Communists] . . . just what they were after—MacArthur's scalp."
— Senator Richard M. Nixon

" 'Old soldiers never die; they just fade away.' And like the old soldier of that ballad, I now close my military career and just fade away—an old soldier who tried to do his duty as God gave him the light to see that duty. Good-bye."
— Gen. Douglas MacArthur

Ads _____

Quotes _____

"I saw a young kid of an outfielder I can't believe. He can run, hit to either field, and has a real good arm. Don't ask any questions. You've got to get this boy."
— New York Giants scout's report on Willie Mays

"One nice thing about television. You don't have to pick out where to look."
— *New Yorker* cartoon by Gardner Rea

"She has a favorite charity. . . . She belongs to the Arts and Literature Committee of the Women's Club, the DAR, and the Garden Club, . . . a charter member of the Wednesday Shakespeare Society."
— *Fortune* editorial, on the successful businessman's wife

"When you find an intellectual, you will probably find a Red."
— *Washington Confidential* (best-seller)

"I killed more people tonight than I have fingers on my hands. . . . I enjoyed every minute of it. . . . They were Commies. . . . They figure us all to be as soft as horse manure."
— Mike Hammer, *In a Lonely Night* by Mickey Spillane

Spencer Tracy. ("I've learned more about acting from watching Tracy than in any other way," says Laurence Olivier.) *Movie Star News.*

TV

Premieres
"The Cisco Kid," Duncan Renaldo
"Search for Tomorrow"
"Hallmark Hall of Fame," Sarah Churchill (host)
"Celanese Theater" ("Ah, Wilderness!")
"The Chevy Show Starring Dinah Shore"
"Treasury Men in Action," Walter Greaza
"See It Now," Edward R. Murrow
"Schlitz Playhouse of Stars" ("Not a Chance," Helen Hayes, David Niven)
"Wild Bill Hickok," Guy Madison, Andy Devine
"The Jack LaLanne Show"
"The Sam Levenson Show"
"Rocket Squad," Reed Hadley
"The Name's the Same," Robert Q. Lewis
"I Love Lucy," Lucille Ball, Desi Arnaz, Vivian Vance, William Frawley
"The Roy Rogers Show"
"The Red Skelton Show"
"Superman," George Reeves

Top Ten (Nielsen)
"Arthur Godfrey's Talent Scouts," "Texaco Star Theater," "I Love Lucy," "The Red Skelton Show," "The Colgate Comedy Hour," "Arthur Godfrey and His Friends," "Fireside Theatre," "Your Show of Shows," "The Jack Benny Show," "You Bet Your Life"

Emmy Awards
"Studio One" (drama); "The Red Skelton Show" (comedy); "Your Show of Shows" (variety); Sid Caesar (actor, "Your Show of Shows"); Imogene Coca (actress, "Your Show of Shows"); Senator Estes Kefauver (special achievement)

Of Note
The first commercial color broadcast takes place • The "eye" becomes CBS's logo • Many repeatedly "take the Fifth" on the Senate Crime Committee hearings chaired by Senator Estes Kefauver; underworld figures who appear include Joe Adonis, Frank Erickson, and Frank Costello (who allows only his hands to be televised) • "Amos 'n' Andy" is condemned by the NAACP for depicting "the Negro in a stereotyped and derogatory manner" • The Brooklyn and Golden Gate bridges appear simultaneously live on screen, as the coast-to-coast coaxial cable is completed ("See It Now").

Movies

Openings
An American in Paris (Vincente Minnelli), Gene Kelly, Leslie Caron, Oscar Levant
A Place in the Sun (George Stevens), Montgomery Clift, Elizabeth Taylor, Shelley Winters
Quo Vadis (Mervyn LeRoy), Robert Taylor, Deborah Kerr
A Streetcar Named Desire (Elia Kazan), Vivien Leigh, Marlon Brando, Kim Hunter
The African Queen (John Huston), Humphrey Bogart, Katharine Hepburn
Detective Story (William Wyler), Kirk Douglas, Eleanor Parker
David and Bathsheba (Henry King), Gregory Peck, Susan Hayward
Strangers on a Train (Alfred Hitchcock), Farley Granger, Robert Walker, Ruth Roman
Show Boat (George Sidney), Kathryn Grayson, Howard Keel, Ava Gardner
The Red Badge of Courage (John Huston), Audie Murphy, Bill Mauldin
The Great Caruso (Richard Thorpe), Mario Lanza, Ann Blyth, Dorothy Kirsten
Oliver Twist (David Lean), Alec Guinness, John Howard Davies
Cry, the Beloved Country (Zoltan Korda), Canada Lee, Sidney Poitier
The Lavender Hill Mob (Charles Crichton), Alec Guinness, Stanley Holloway
Rashomon (Akira Kurosawa), Toshiro Mifune

Academy Awards
Best Picture: *An American in Paris*
Best Director: George Stevens (*A Place in the Sun*)
Best Actress: Vivien Leigh (*A Streetcar Named Desire*)
Best Actor: Humphrey Bogart (*The African Queen*)

Top Box-Office Stars
John Wayne, Dean Martin and Jerry Lewis, Betty Grable, Abbott and Costello, Bing Crosby, Bob Hope, Randolph Scott, Gary Cooper, Doris Day, Spencer Tracy

Stars of Tomorrow
Howard Keel, Thelma Ritter, Shelley Winters, Frank Lovejoy, Debra Paget, David Brian, Piper Laurie, Gene Nelson, Dale Robertson, Corinne Calvet

Popular Music _____

Hit Songs
"Cold, Cold Heart"
"The Little White Cloud That
    Cried"
"Hello, Young Lovers"
"Mockin' Bird Hill"
"Jezebel"
"Shrimp Boats"
"Tell Me Why"
"In the Cool, Cool, Cool of the
    Evening"
"I Get Ideas"
"Unforgettable"

Top Records

Albums: *Guys and Dolls* (original cast); *Voice of the Xtabay* (Yma Sumac); *The Great Caruso* (Mario Lanza); *Showboat* (sound track); *Mario Lanza Sings Christmas Songs* (Mario Lanza)

Singles: *How High the Moon* (Les Paul, Mary Ford); *Loveliest Night of the Year* (Mario Lanza); *On Top of Old Smoky* (The Weavers); *I Apologize* (Billy Eckstine); *Because of You* (Tony Bennett); *Come On-a My House* (Rosemary Clooney); *Too Young* (Nat "King" Cole); *If* (Perry Como); *A Guy Is a Guy* (Doris Day); *The Syncopated Clock* (Leroy Anderson); *Aba Daba Honeymoon* (Debbie Reynolds); *Cry* (Johnnie Ray); *My Heart Cries for You* (Mitch Miller, Guy Mitchell). Country: *Shotgun Boogie* (Tennessee Ernie Ford); *I'm Movin' On* (Hank Snow)

Jazz and Big Bands
Dave Brubeck forms a quartet with Paul Desmond. Louis Bellson joins Duke Ellington.

First Recording: Sonny Rollins as leader

New Band: Count Basie reorganizes a big band.

Top Performers (*Downbeat*): Charlie Parker (soloist); Stan Kenton (band); George Shearing (jazz group); Stan Getz, Serge Chaloff, Buddy De Franco, Bill Harris, Maynard Ferguson (instrumentalists); Sarah Vaughan, Billy Eckstine (vocalists); Mills Brothers (vocal group)

Theater _____

Broadway Openings

Plays
The Rose Tattoo (Tennessee Williams), Maureen
    Stapleton, Eli Wallach
I Am a Camera (John Van Druten), Julie Harris,
    William Prince
Point of No Return (Paul Osborne), Henry Fonda,
    Leora Dana
The Moon Is Blue (F. Hugh Herbert), Barbara Bel
    Geddes, Donald Cook, Barry Nelson
Stalag 17 (Donald Bevin, Edmund Trzcinski), Robert
    Strauss, Harvey Lembeck
Gigi (Anita Loos), Audrey Hepburn
The Fourposter (Jan de Hartog), Jessica Tandy,
    Hume Cronyn
Darkness at Noon (Sidney Kingsley), Claude Rains,
    Kim Hunter
Billy Budd (Louis Coxe, Robert Chapman), Charles
    Nolte, Dennis King
The Autumn Garden (Lillian Hellman), Florence
    Eldridge, Fredric March
Barefoot in Athens (Maxwell Anderson), Barry Jones

Musicals
The King and I (Richard Rodgers, Oscar
    Hammerstein II), Gertrude Lawrence, Yul
    Brynner
Top Banana (Johnny Mercer), Phil Silvers

A Tree Grows in Brooklyn (Arthur Schwartz, Dorothy
    Fields), Shirley Booth, Johnny Johnston
Paint Your Wagon (Alan Jay Lerner, Frederick
    Loewe), James Barton, Olga San Juan

Classics and Revivals On and Off Broadway
Richard II, Maurice Evans; Reading of *Don Juan in Hell* (George Bernard Shaw), Charles Laughton, Charles Boyer, Cedric Hardwicke, Agnes Moorhead; *Caesar and Cleopatra, Antony and Cleopatra*, Laurence Olivier, Vivien Leigh; *Romeo and Juliet*, Olivia de Havilland, Jack Hawkins; *St. Joan* (Shaw), Uta Hagen, James Daly; *Peer Gynt* (Ibsen), John Garfield; *The Constant Wife* (W. Somerset Maugham), Katharine Cornell, Gladys George, Brian Aherne; *Diamond Lil* (Mae West), Mae West.
Founded: Circle in the Square (three-sided theater): *Dark of the Moon; Summer and Smoke*, Geraldine Fitzgerald

Pulitzer Prize
No prize is awarded.

Tony Awards
The Rose Tattoo, Tennessee Williams (play); *Guys and Dolls*, Frank Loesser (musical)

Classical Music _____

Compositions
Elliott Carter, String Quartet
Gail Kubik, Symphony Concertante
Morton Feldman, *Intersection I: Projections*
Walter Piston, String Quartet no. 4
Roger Sessions, Quartet no. 2
Roy Harris, Symphony no. 7
John Cage, *Imaginary Landscape* no. 4
Harold Shapero, Concerto for Orchestra
Aaron Copland, *Pied Piper*

Important Events
The 50th anniversary of Verdi's death is celebrated throughout the United States. Toscanini conducts the Requiem in New York.
Wanda Landowska records Bach's *Well-Tempered Clavier,* Book I.
Rudolf Serkin and Adolf and Hermann Busch perform at the first concert at the Marlboro Music School and Festival, Marlboro, Vermont.

Debut: Charles Rosen, Stephen Bishop-Kovacevich, Bruce Hungerford

First Performances
Charles Ives, Symphony no. 2 (New York), Symphony no. 4 (Minneapolis), Piano Concerto (Boston, with Lukas Foss, 29); Arthur Honegger, *Suite Archaique* (Louisville), Symphony no. 5

Imogene Coca and Sid Caesar in one of their satiric routines from "Your Show of Shows." Carl Reiner costars, and script writers include Mel Brooks, Neil Simon, Woody Allen, and Larry Gelbart. *Billy Rose Theatre Collection. The New York Public Library at Lincoln Center. Astor, Lenox and Tilden Foundations.*

Stuart Davis, *Owh! in San Pāo*, 1951. 52¼ × 41¾".
Whitney Museum of American Art, G. Clements.

(Boston); Roy Harris, *Cumberland* Concerto (Cincinnati)

Opera

NBC-TV Opera Theater: *Amahl and the Night Visitors* (Gian Carlo Menotti, premiere)

Columbia University: *Giants in the Earth* (Douglas Moore, premiere)

Metropolitan: Cesare Siepi, *Fidelio;* Patrice Munsel, *Die Fledermaus;* Kurt Baum, *Wozzeck;* Victoria de los Angeles (debut), *Faust;* Mario del Monaco, *Otello;* Nell Rankin, George London, *Aïda;* Roberta Peters, Leonard Warren, *Rigoletto*

New York City: *The Dybbuk* (David Tamkin); *The Four Ruffians* (Wolf-Ferrari), premieres

San Francisco: Lily Pons, Jan Peerce, *La traviata;* Dorothy Kirsten, Jussi Bjoerling, *Tosca*

Music Notes
Seven hundred orchestras play in the United States.

Art _____

Painting
Richard Pousette-Dart; *Chavade*
Clyfford Still, *Painting, 1951 Yellow, 1951-N*
Stuart Davis, *Owh! In San Pão*
Franz Kline, *Ninth Street*
Jackson Pollock, *Number 26, 27, Echo (Number 25, 1951)*
Ellsworth Kelly, *Colors for a Large Wall*
Barnett Newman, *Vir Heroicus Sublimis*
Fritz Glarner, *Relational Painting* (1949–51)
William Baziotes, *Sea Forms*
Adolph Gottlieb, *The Frozen Sounds, No. 1*
John Marin, *Sea Piece*

Sculpture
David Smith, *Australia, Cloak, Family Decision, Hudson River Landscape*
Seymour Lipton, *Cloak*
Theodore Roszak, *Maja*
José de Rivera, *Construction Blue and Black*

Marcel Duchamp, *Wedge of Chastity*

Architecture
Umbrella House, Aurora, Ill. (Bruce Goff)
860 Lake Shore Drive Apartments, Chicago (Mies van der Rohe)
General Motors Technical Research Center Auditorium, Detroit (Eero Saarinen)
First Unitarian Meeting House, Madison, Wisc. (Frank Lloyd Wright)
Wayfarers' Chapel, Palos Verdes, Calif. (Wright)
First Presbyterian Church, Cottage Grove, Ore. (Pietro Belluschi)
Charles Eames House, Santa Monica, Calif. (Eames)
Indian Chapel, University of Oklahoma (Eero Saarinen and Coe)

Important Exhibitions

Museums

New York: *Metropolitan:* 75th anniversary of the Art Students League; Eakins, LaFarge, Bellows, Chase; All-sculpture show. *Museum of Modern Art:* "Abstract Painting and Sculpture in America"; 100 works from 85 artists, 1913 to the present; Matisse retrospective. *Brooklyn:* "Italy at Work" (Crafts, industrial art since World War II)

Boston: Edward Jackson Holmes memorial exhibition of Persian art treasures of the Vienna collection; German expressionism

Chicago: Art of Vienna; Artists of Chicago; Munch; "Italy at Work"

Eugene O'Neill. *Billy Rose Theatre Collection. The New York Public Library at Lincoln Center. Astor, Lenox and Tilden Foundations.*

Washington: European paintings of the Gulbenkian collection; Audubon

Cleveland, San Francisco, Chicago: Matisse

Pittsburgh: Eight centuries of French painting 1100–1900

Baltimore, Yale: "Gertrude Stein as Collector and Writer"

Detroit, Toledo: "Artists in Italy 1830–1875"

Indiana, Dayton, Davenport: Art in Colonial Mexico

Individual Shows
Gorky (Whitney, Minneapolis, San Francisco); Lovis Corinth (Boston); Modigliani, Soutine, Lautrec (Cleveland); Tobey (San Francisco, Seattle, Whitney)

Art Briefs
The Metropolitan Museum of Art purchases a Leonardo drawing *Head of the Virgin* and expands and modernizes at a cost of $5,436,000 • At a Whitney show, $100 provides entrance and the purchase of one painting or sculpture • Top sales include Lautrec's print *Partie de Compagne* ($1,600), Delacroix's *Académie de Femme* ($10,500), Boucher's *Pastorale* ($13,000), and Watteau's *Feast of Pan* ($12,500) • The Houston Fine Arts Museum acquires a Carl Milles fountain.

Dance _____

Lew Christensen becomes director of the San Francisco Ballet; Nora Kaye, Diana Adams, and Hugh Laing move from Ballet Theatre to the New York City Ballet.

Premieres

New York City Ballet: *Cakewalk* (Ruthanna Boris); Tanaquil Le Clercq, Yvonne Mounsey; *The Cage* (Jerome Robbins, Stravinsky), Nora Kaye, Mounsey; *The Miraculous Mandarin* (Todd Bolender, Bartók), Melissa Hayden, Hugh Laing; *La Valse* (Balanchine), Le Clerq, Nicholas Magallanes, Francisco Moncion; *Swan Lake* (Balanchine)

Books

Fiction
Critics' Choice
The Morning Watch, James Agee
The Grass Harp, Truman Capote
Requiem for a Nun, William Faulkner
Notes on a Horse Thief, William Faulkner
The Beetle Leg, John Hawkes
Lie Down in Darkness, William Styron
Barbary Shore, Norman Mailer
The Ballad of the Sad Café, Carson McCullers
The Catcher in the Rye, J. D. Salinger
The Strange Children, Caroline Gordon
In the Absence of Angels, Hortense Calisher
❧ *The Masters*, C. P. Snow

Best-Sellers
From Here to Eternity, James Jones
The Caine Mutiny, Herman Wouk
Moses, Sholem Asch
The Cardinal, Henry Morton Robinson
A Woman Called Fancy, Frank Yerby
The Cruel Sea, Nicholas Monsarrat
Melville Goodwin, U.S.A., John P. Marquand
Return to Paradise, James A. Michener
The Foundling, Cardinal Francis B. Spellman
The Wanderer, Mika Waltari

Nonfiction
Critics' Choice
The Necessary Angel, Wallace Stevens
Life in America, Marshall B. Davidson
American Diplomacy, 1900–1950, George F. Kennan
The Far Side of Paradise, Arthur Mizener
Henry James, F. W. Dupee
White Collar, the American Middle Classes, C. Wright Mills
Jefferson and the Rights of Man, Dumas Malone
God and Man at Yale, William F. Buckley
The Origins of Totalitarianism, Hannah Arendt

Best-Sellers
Look Younger, Live Longer, Gayelord Hauser
Betty Crocker's Picture Cook Book
Washington Confidential, Jack Lait and Lee Mortimer
Better Homes and Gardens Handyman's Book
The Sea around Us, Rachel L. Carson
Pogo, Walt Kelly
The New Yorker Twenty-Fifth Anniversary Album
Kon-Tiki, Thor Heyerdahl

Poetry
Robert Lowell, *The Mills of the Kavanaughs*
Adrienne Rich, *A Change of World*
James Merrill, *First Poems*
William Carlos Williams, *Paterson, Book Four*
Randall Jarrell, *The Seven-League Crutches*
Theodore Roethke, *Praise to the End*

Pulitzer Prizes
The Caine Mutiny, Herman Wouk (fiction)
The Uprooted, Oscar Handlin (U.S. history)
Charles Evans Hughes, Merlo J. Pusey (biography)
Collected Poems (Marianne Moore)

Science and Technology

Scientists led by Edward Teller set off the first thermonuclear reaction.

Operation Greenhouse begins, a secret mission in the Pacific Islands believed to be related to hydrogen bomb testing.

The AEC completes its facility, called the "atomic apothecary," at Oak Ridge, Tenn., for processing radioisotopes for medical research.

Robert Leighton, at the California Institute of Technology, reports the discovery of the negative proton, a fundamental subatomic particle.

Remington Rand's UNIVAC is the first commercially produced, large-scale business computer; the first one is purchased by the U.S. Bureau of Census.

The U.S. Public Health Service reports that fluoridation of water greatly reduces tooth decay.

Antabuse, a drug that produces a powerful adverse reaction to alcohol, is marketed.

Carl Rogers, in *Client-Centered Therapy*, develops his nondirective approach.

Erik Erikson's *Childhood and Society* integrates psychoanalytical and anthropological studies.

❧ The "electrical artificial pacemaker" is developed in Canada.

Nobel Prize
Glenn T. Seaborg wins the prize in chemistry for the discovery of plutonium.

Sports

Baseball

Bobby Thomson hits a three-run home run in the bottom of the ninth off Ralph Branca to win the NL playoff for the New York Giants over the Brooklyn Dodgers; the Giants, managed by Leo Durocher had overcome a 13½ game deficit in the last two months.

Willie Mays (New York, NL) is the league rookie of the year.

Mickey Mantle (New York, AL) debuts; Joe DiMaggio (New York, AL) retires with a lifetime BA of .325 and 361 home runs.

Champions

Batting	Pitching
Stan Musial (St. Louis, NL), .355	Preacher Roe (Brooklyn, NL), 22–3
Ferris Fain (Philadelphia, AL), .344	Bob Feller (Cleveland, AL), 22–8
	Home runs
	Ralph Kiner (Pittsburgh, NL), 42

Football

Norm Van Brocklin (Los Angeles) passes for a record 554 yards in one game.

NFL Season Leaders: Bob Waterfield (Los Angeles), passing; Eddie Price (New York), rushing; Elroy Hirsh (Los Angeles), passing

College All-Americans: Hugh McElhenny (B), Washington; Babe Parilli (Q), Kentucky; Dick Kazmaier (B), Princeton

Bowls (Jan. 1, 1952)

Rose: Illinois 40–Stanford 7	Cotton: Kentucky 20–Texas Christian 7
Orange: Georgia Tech 14–Baylor 14	Sugar: Maryland 28–Tennessee 13

Basketball

Allegations of point-shaving involving City College of New York, Long Island University, Kentucky, and Bradley, all major national powers, shake college basketball.

NBA All-Pro First Team: George Mikan (Minneapolis), Alex Groza (Indianapolis), Ed McCauley (Boston), Bob Davies (Rochester), Ralph Beard (Indianapolis)

Other Sports

Boxing: Sugar Ray Robinson, welterweight

Bobby Thomson's home run, "the shot heard round the world."

champion, becomes a double titleholder when he beats middleweight champion Jake LaMotta in 13.

Winners

World Series	*College Basketball*
New York (AL) 4	Kentucky
New York (NL) 2	*Player of the Year*
MVP	Richard Groat, Duke
NL–Roy Campanella, Brooklyn	*Stanley Cup*
AL–Yogi Berra, New York	Toronto
NFL	*US Tennis Open*
Los Angeles 24–Cleveland 17	Men: Frank Sedgman
	Women: Maureen Connolly
College Football	*USGA Open*
Tennessee	Ben Hogan
Heisman Trophy	*Kentucky Derby*
Dick Kazmaier, Princeton	Count Turf (C. McCreary, jockey)
NBA Championship	
Rochester 4–New York 3	

Fashion

For Women: The look is youthful and pretty in (1) the full skirt and small waist magnified through bulky crinolines, and (2) the "feminine" suit with molded jacket, rounded waist and bosom, high lapel, and small round collar. Separates appear in a mix of colors; coats, both fitted and loose, have large collars and pockets. The high-waisted, beltless empire gains much attention, and Dior launches his "princess line" with dresses fitted through the midriff and unmarked waistline. Balenciaga goes on to indicate the waist with a loose bow or indented curve; he even drops the waistline to the hip, re-creating a new middy line. Pointed shoes with spike heels have occasional straps at the ankles. Two new markets grow, for (1) at-home wear, for the growing time spent with TV, and (2) the teenager who also demands her own look (from the square dancer in a spinning skirt to the girl who wears a pony tail and a strapless dress). Hair is sometimes shorter, brushed up and back; the "poodle" first appears.

High-fashion notes: Balenciaga's shantung charcoal suit, collarless yoke, coolie hat

Kaleidoscope ———————

- The 1939 dollar is now worth 59.3 cents; wartime inflation increases, and the sale of horsemeat triples in Portland; the New Jersey Telephone Company serves its employees whale pot roast; hoarding begins, and Macy's advertises: "Buy Nothing from Fear," although sales increase 25 percent.
- An estimated 3 million attend the MacArthur parade in New York City; six recordings of "Old Soldiers Never Die" appear, along with the MacArthur geranium, orchid, gladiola, and tea rose (which "needs no coddling or favor").
- Les Paul and Mary Ford perfect a method of superimposing their rendition of songs several times on a single record.
- Lyrics for "Come On-a My House" are written by William Saroyan on a bet by a relative.
- Margaret Sanger urges the development of an oral contraceptive.
- Monogram cancels a movie about Henry Wadsworth Longfellow, since Hiawatha, an Indian peacemaker, might be viewed as a Communist sympathizer.
- TV sponsors discover that dressing actors as doctors is good advertising.
- Ninety West Point cadets, including several football stars, are dismissed for cheating, although the Army coach remarks: "God help this country if we don't play football."
- It becomes public knowledge that Truman's assistant Harry Vaughn received a $520 deep freezer after World War II from a man who did business with the government.
- Korea becomes a battlefield of hills and valleys that gain designations such as Heartbreak Ridge, Sniper Ridge, Old Baldy, and The Punch Bowl.
- The North Koreans deliver a list of POWs that is 8,000 less than American figures.
- *Time* discontinues the "March of Time" newsreels after 16 years.
- The U.S. produces 350,000 pounds of streptomycin and 400,000 pounds of penicillin.
- Dorothy Stevens is discovered frozen stiff in a Chicago alley; she is thawed from a record low temperature of 64°.
- Hiroshima A-bomb survivor Shigeki Tanaha, 19, wins the Patriots Day Marathon in Boston.
- When Sioux City Memorial Park in Iowa refuses to bury John Rice, an American Indian who died in combat, Truman dispatches an air force plane to carry his family and his remains to Arlington National Cemetery.
- During National Music Week President Truman plays an impromptu concert on a piano made of materials from all the UN countries.
- Elizabeth Taylor and Conrad Hilton divorce; Janet Leigh and Tony Curtis marry.
- Milton Berle signs a 30-year contract in seven figures with NBC.
- Two-shows-a-day vaudeville is revived at the Palace; Judy Garland, booked for four weeks, plays 19.

Arthur Godfrey is the host of two of TV's top rated shows, as well as a popular radio program. *Billy Rose Theatre Collection. The New York Public Library at Lincoln Center. Astor, Lenox and Tilden Foundations.*

- Duke University researchers report that burned toast, strong tea, and milk of magnesia are universal antidotes for poisons of an unknown nature.
- The 5 cent phone call goes to 10 cents in New York and other large cities.
- "Don't tell my father we've been smoking," says a teenage Massachusetts girl who, with two babysitting friends, has stolen $18,000 and gone to New York on a shopping and sex spree.
- A Metropolitan Life Insurance Company report links fifteen pounds of overweight with early death.
- E. Merle Young, wife of a former RFC loan officer, receives a $9,540 mink coat from a company her husband did business with.
- Mrs. Blair Moody, wife of the Republican senator, wears a muskrat coat with its $381.25 price tag attached; mink farmers complain of an "unjust stigma."

First Appearances: Sugarless chewing gum, commercial electronic computer, dacron suits, pushbutton-controlled garage doors, hotels with all-foam rubber mattresses and pillows, telephone company answering service, college credit course in TV (Marquette), power steering (Chrysler), N.J. Turnpike, "Dennis, the Menace," Marimekko (textiles), Tropicana, Ore-Ida, Park's sausages, trading stamps (revival of S&H), orlon, infrared stoves, vibrating mattresses (300 times a minute), automatic gates for ranches and estates

1952

Facts and Figures

Economic Profile
- Dow-Jones:—High 252– Low 232
- GNP: +5%
- Inflation: +1.7%
- Unemployment: 3.0%

TV production: 6,096,000

AM radio stations: 2,355

Household telephones: 66%

Toll rate, New York–San Francisco: $2.50

Advertising expenditures: $7.7 billion

21″ Admiral console TV, radio, phonograph: $399.95

Folding TV table: $2.95

Pizza pie: 75¢ (large), 50¢ (small)

Complete Chinese dinner, House of Chan, New York: $1.50

Canaries: $9.95

Haig & Haig: $4.99 (⅘)

Fleischmann gin: $3.55 (qt.)

Body massager: $6.95

Vitatone: $9.95

Bulova watch: $27.50; Omega: $71.50

Deaths

John Dewey, John Garfield, Karen Horney, Sister Elizabeth Kenny, Hattie McDaniel, Maria Montessori, George Santayana, Chaim Weizmann.

In the News

IKE ANNOUNCES HE WILL ACCEPT NOMINATION IF DRAFTED . . . BRITISH AND EGYPTIANS CLASH AT SUEZ, 25 DIE . . . FRENCH BATTLE TUNISIAN NATIONALISTS, 50 DIE . . . GEORGE VI DIES, ELIZABETH II SUCCEEDS TO THE THRONE . . . GREECE AND TURKEY JOIN NATO . . . WINSTON CHURCHILL ANNOUNCES THAT BRITAIN HAS ATOM BOMB . . . GENERAL FULGENCIO BATISTA OUSTS ELECTED LEADERS IN CUBA . . . TRUMAN SAYS HE WILL NOT RUN AGAIN . . . TRUMAN ORDERS SEIZURE OF STEEL MILLS TO AVERT STRIKE . . . RUSSIA CALLS FOR ALL-GERMAN ELECTIONS . . . U.S. ENDS OCCUPATION OF JAPAN . . . SUPREME COURT RULES THAT STEEL TAKEOVER IS UNCONSTITUTIONAL . . . IKE IS NOMINATED BY GOP, DEMOCRATS NOMINATE ADLAI STEVENSON . . . IKE PROMISES TO GO TO KOREA IF ELECTED . . . GENERAL MOHAMMED NAGUIB SEIZES POWER IN EGYPT, FAROUK ABDICATES . . . HUSSEIN BECOMES KING OF JORDAN . . . IRANIAN PARLIAMENT GIVES MOSSADEGH DICTORIAL POWERS . . . EVA PERON DIES . . . 14 CALIFORNIA COMMUNISTS ARE CONVICTED UNDER SMITH ACT . . . STALIN AND CHOU EN-LAI CONFER IN MOSCOW OVER KOREA . . . MOSCOW DEMANDS RECALL OF AMBASSADOR GEORGE KENNAN FOR "INSULTS" . . . IKE WINS LARGE VICTORY, 33 MILLION TO 27 MILLION . . . ATOMIC ENERGY COMMISSION ANNOUNCES SUCCESS OF H-BOMB TESTS AT ENIWETOK ATOLL . . . EISENHOWER COMPLETES 3-DAY BATTLEFRONT TOUR . . . CHOU EN-LAI REJECTS U.S. PEACE PLAN.

The U.S. verifies "leaked" reports that it exploded a hydrogen bomb on Eniwetok Atoll, November 1st. *Library of Congress.*

Quotes _____

"I did get something, a gift, . . . a little cocker spaniel dog, . . . and our little girl, Trisha, the six-year-old, named it Checkers. . . . Pat and I have satisfaction that every dime that we've got is honestly ours. I should say this—that Pat doesn't have a mink coat, but she does have a respectable Republican cloth coat."

— Vice-presidential candidate Richard M. Nixon

"Our government makes no sense unless it is founded in a deeply felt religious faith and I don't care what it is."

— Dwight D. Eisenhower

"Some of us worship in churches, some in synagogues, some on golf courses."

— Adlai Stevenson

"Female card-holders are required to show their loyalty to the cause through indiscriminate intercourse where it will do the most good.

— *USA Confidential* by Lait and Mortimer, on the C.P.

"You can't fight Communism with perfume."

— Joseph McCarthy

"Adlai [is] the appeaser . . . who got his Ph.D. from Dean Acheson's College of Cowardly Communist Containment."

— Richard M. Nixon

"I cannot and will not cut my conscience to fit this year's fashions."

— Lillian Hellman, testifying before the House

"They'll wear toilet seats around their necks if you give 'em what they want to see."

— Bill Thomas, on 3-D glasses

"Late commuters, lost among identical rows of houses along identical street blocks, sometimes reported a sense of panic like bewildered children suddenly turned loose in a house of mirrors."

— P. Kimball, describing Levittown

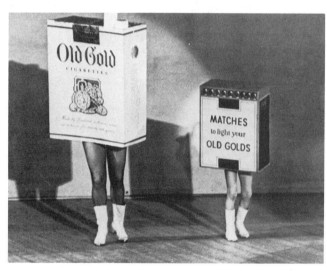

TV ad. *Movie Star News.*

Ads _____

America's Biggest Change
The Humble Diaper [is] . . . the greatest single fact in America's continued growth and prosperity. . . . The average American girl now marries at 20, has her first child at 22, . . . younger than ever before. . . . Victory goes to those who get there "fastest with the mostest," and MODERN ROMANCES gives you the answer with the "mostest of the firstest."

(Modern Romances)

Riddle: "What's college?"
"That's where girls who are above cooking and sewing go to meet a man they can spend their lives cooking and sewing for."

(Gimbel's ad for campus clothes)

STOP TRIPLE "O"
Stop Breath Odor
Stop Body Odor
Stop Other Personal Odors

(Ennds Chlorophyll Tablets)

Don't be an e.s.s.*
  Wear smart *seamless* stockings by Hanes
    *eternal seam straightener!

(Hanes)

Dancing pleats that won't sit out.

(Orlon)

Second honeymoon. . . . Bruce and Peggy Walden spent a priceless two-weeks in Britain for only $209 each.

(Come to Britain)

Korea, Communism, and Corruption
  [K_1C_2]

(GOP slogan)

TV

Premieres

"Arthur Godfrey Time"
"I've Got a Secret," Garry Moore
"The Jackie Gleason Show," Jackie Gleason, Art
        Carney, Audrey Meadows
"Death Valley Days," Stanley Andrews
"The Ernie Kovacs Show"
"The Today Show," Dave Garroway
"Dragnet," Jack Webb
"Mr. Peepers," Wally Cox
"Our Miss Brooks," Eve Arden, Gale Gordon
"The Adventures of Ozzie and Harriet [Nelson]"
"The Liberace Show"
"My Friend Irma," Marie Wilson
"This Is Your Life," Ralph Edwards
"My Little Margie," Gale Storm, Charles Farrell
"I Married Joan," Jim Backus, Joan Davis
"Omnibus," Alistair Cooke

"Texaco Star Theater," "The Buick Circus Hour,"
"The Colgate Comedy Hour," "Gangbusters," "You
Bet Your Life," "Fireside Theatre."

Specials

"Victory at Sea" (music by Richard Rodgers);
"President Truman's Tour of the White House"

Emmy Awards

"Robert Montgomery Presents" (drama); "I Love
Lucy" (situation comedy); "Your Show of Shows"
(variety); "Dragnet" (action); "Time for Beany"
(children); "What's My Line?" (game); "See It
Now" (public service); Jimmy Durante (comedian);
Lucille Ball (comedienne); Bishop Fulton J. Sheen
(personality)

Top Ten (Nielsen)

"I Love Lucy," "Arthur Godfrey's Talent Scouts,"
"Arthur Godfrey and His Friends," "Dragnet,"

Of Note

Walter Cronkite is CBS anchor at the Republican
National Convention • Atomic bomb explosions are
televised April 2 and May 1.

Movies

Openings

The Greatest Show on Earth (Cecil B. De Mille),
        Betty Hutton, Cornel Wilde, Charlton Heston
High Noon (Fred Zinnemann), Gary Cooper, Grace
        Kelly
Ivanhoe (Richard Thorpe), Robert Taylor, Elizabeth
        Taylor, George Sanders
Moulin Rouge (John Huston), José Ferrer, Colette
        Marchand, Zsa Zsa Gabor
The Quiet Man (John Ford), John Wayne, Maureen
        O'Hara
Five Fingers (Joseph L. Mankiewicz), James Mason,
        Danielle Darrieux, Michael Rennie
Viva Zapata! (Elia Kazan), Marlon Brando, Jean
        Peters, Anthony Quinn
The Member of the Wedding (Fred Zinnemann),
        Ethel Waters, Julie Harris, Brandon De Wilde
Singin' in the Rain (Gene Kelly, Stanley Donen),
        Gene Kelly, Debbie Reynolds, Donald O'Connor
Limelight (Charles Chaplin), Charles Chaplin, Claire
        Bloom, Buster Keaton
The Snows of Kilimanjaro (Henry King), Gregory
        Peck, Susan Hayward, Ava Gardner
Come Back, Little Sheba (Daniel Mann), Shirley
        Booth, Burt Lancaster
The Importance of Being Earnest (Anthony Asquith),
        Michael Redgrave, Edith Evans

Bend of the River (Anthony Mann), James Stewart,
        Arthur Kennedy
Forbidden Games (René Clement), Brigitte Fossey,
        Georges Poujouly
Umberto D (Vittorio de Sica), Carlo Battista

Academy Awards

Best Picture: *The Greatest Show on Earth*
Best Director: John Ford (*The Quiet Man*)
Best Actress: Shirley Booth (*Come Back, Little
        Sheba*)
Best Actor: Gary Cooper (*High Noon*)

Top Box-Office Stars

Dean Martin and Jerry Lewis, Gary Cooper, John
Wayne, Bing Crosby, Bob Hope, James Stewart,
Doris Day, Gregory Peck, Susan Hayward, Randolph
Scott

Stars of Tomorrow

Marilyn Monroe, Debbie Reynolds, Marge and
Gower Champion, Mitzi Gaynor, Kim Hunter, Rock
Hudson, Audie Murphy, David Wayne, Forrest
Tucker, Danny Thomas

Popular Music

Hit Songs
"Anywhere I Wander"
"Botch-a-Me"
"Don't Let the Stars Get in Your Eyes"
"High Noon"
"How Do You Speak to an Angel"
"Pretend"
"Your Cheatin' Heart"
"Somewhere along the Way"
"I Saw Mommy Kissing Santa Claus"

Top Records

Albums: *An American in Paris* (sound track); *I'll See You in My Dreams* (Doris Day); *With a Song in My Heart* (Jane Froman); *The Merry Widow* (original cast);

Because You're Mine (Mario Lanza)

Singles: *Blue Tango* (Leroy Anderson); *Wheel of Fortune* (Kay Starr); *You Belong to Me* (Jo Stafford); *Auf Widerseh'n* (Vera Lynn); *Tell Me Why* (Four Aces); *Till I Waltz Again with You* (Teresa Brewer); *Hold Me, Thrill Me, Kiss Me* (Karen Chandler); *Kiss of Fire* (Georgia Gibbs); *Why Don't You Believe Me?* (Joni James); *Lover* (Peggy Lee); *Glow Worm* (Mills Brothers); *Wish You Were Here* (Eddie Fisher). Country: *Wild Side of Life* (Hank Thompson); *Let Old Mother Nature Have Her Way* (Carl Smith)

Jazz and Big Bands
The Modern Jazz Quartet is organized; its *Vendôme* and *La Ronde* gain wide attention. Gerry Mulligan organizes a quartet without piano. Large jazz clubs, like Birdland, Box City, and the Royal Roost, present jazz without dancing; an interest in Latin American rhythms enters jazz, as in the music of Machito.

Top Performers (*Downbeat*): Louis Armstrong (soloist); Stan Kenton (band); George Shearing (jazz group); Les Paul, Gene Krupa, Harry Carney, Terry Gibbs, Art Van Damme (instrumentalists); Sarah Vaughan, Billy Eckstine (vocalists); Mills Brothers (vocal group)

Theater

Broadway Openings

Plays
The Shrike (Joseph Kramm), José Ferrer, Judith Evelyn
Mrs. McThing (Mary Chase), Helen Hayes, Brandon De Wilde
Dial "M" for Murder (Frederic Knott), Maurice Evans, Gusti Huber
The Seven-Year Itch (George Axelrod), Tom Ewell, Vanessa Brown
Venus Observed (Christopher Fry), Rex Harrison, Lilli Palmer
The Time of the Cuckoo (Arthur Laurents), Shirley Booth
The Deep Blue Sea (Terence Rattigan), Margaret Sullavan
Charles Dickens, readings and impersonations by Emlyn Williams

Musicals
Wish You Were Here (Harold Rome), Sheila Bond, Jack Cassidy
Two's Company (Vernon Duke, Ogden Nash), Bette Davis, David Burns
New Faces of 1952 (June Carroll, Arthur Siegal, et al.), Robert Clary, Carol Lawrence, Ronny Graham, Eartha Kitt, Alice Ghostley, Paul Lynde
An Evening with Beatrice Lillie

Classics and Revivals On and Off Broadway
Candida (George Bernard Shaw), Olivia de Havilland; *Anna Christie* (Eugene O'Neill), Celeste Holm, Kevin McCarthy; *Golden Boy* (Clifford Odets), John Garfield; *The Wild Duck* (Ibsen), Maurice Evans, Diana Lynn; *The Children's Hour* (Lillian Hellman), Patricia Neal, Kim Hunter; *The Millionairess* (George Bernard Shaw), Katharine Hepburn

Regional

Founded: Actor's Workshop, San Francisco, by Herbert Blau and Jules Irving

Pulitzer Prize
The Shrike, Joseph Kramm

Tony Awards
The Fourposter, Jan de Hartog (play): *The King and I,* Richard Rodgers, Oscar Hammerstein II (musical)

Classical Music ————————

Compositions
John Cage, *4'4*, Music for *Carillon, Imaginary
  Landscape,* no. 5
Elliott Carter, Sonata for Flute, Oboe, Cello, and
  Harp
Otto Luening, *Fantasy in Space, Low Speed,
  Invention*
Ned Rorem, *A Childhood Miracle*

Important Events
An unprecedented international exchange of
performers includes the Boston Symphony's tour of
Europe and participation in the Paris Festival of 20th-
Century Music; *Porgy and Bess* goes to Berlin,
Vienna, and London.
The most frequently performed composers by 31
leading orchestras are Beethoven, Mozart, Sibelius,
and Prokofiev; Gershwin and Barber are the most
frequently performed Americans.

First Performances
Roy Harris, Symphony no. 7 (Chicago); John Cage,
Water Music (New York); Paul Creston, Symphony
no. 4 (Washington); Gail Kubik, Symphony
Concertante (New York); Igor Stravinsky, Cantata
(Los Angeles, Stravinsky conducting); Boguslaw
Schaeffer, *Symphony pour un homme seul,
composed for tape recording machine* (Waltham,
Mass.); Ralph Vaughan Williams, Romance in D flat
for Harmonica, String Orchestra and Piano (New
York); Morton Gould, Concerto for Tap Dancer and
Orchestra (Rochester); Virgil Thomson, *Sea Piece
with Birds* (Dallas)

Gary Cooper and Grace Kelly in *High Noon*. Kelly's first
starring role is with this prototypical strong, silent hero.
Movie Star News.

Opera

Metropolitan: Rudolph Bing raises prices to $8
(evening) and $30 (opening) and brings in stage
directors Margaret Webster (*Aïda,* with Zinka
Milanov), Tyrone Guthrie *(Carmen),* and Alfred Lunt
(*Così fan tutte);* Kirsten Flagstad returns with
Alcestis. Set Svanholm, Hans Hotter, Elizabeth
Hoengen, Ljuba Welitsch, *Salomé;* Cesare Siepi,
Don Giovanni; Jerome Hines, *La forza del destino*

NBC-TV: *Billy Budd* (Benjamin Britten, premiere
from Covent Garden)

New York City: *Wozzeck, The Dybbuk, Bluebeard's
Castle* (premieres)

San Francisco: Nicola Rossi-Lemeni, *Mefistofele*

Music Notes
Conductor Manuel Rosenthal is fired from the Seattle
Symphony for living with a woman • Noah Greenberg
organizes the New York Pro Musica Antiqua.

Louis "Satchmo" Armstrong tours Europe with his All
Stars and becomes an international ambassador of
American jazz. *Movie Star News.*

Art

Painting

Willem de Kooning, *Woman I, Woman II*

Peter Blume, *Castle of Euryalus*

Helen Frankenthaler, *Mountains and Sea*

Ad Reinhardt, *Red Painting, No. 15*

Mark Rothko, *Black, Pink and Yellow over Orange*

Jackson Pollock, *Number 12, Convergence*

Barnett Newman, *Day One*

Andrew Wyeth, *April Wind*

Adolph Gottlieb, *Unstill Life, Frozen Sounds II*

Bradley Walker Tomlin, *Number 5*

Sculpture

David Hare, *Juggler* (1950–52)

Alexander Calder, *Sumac*

Jacques Lipchitz, *Sacrifice, II* (1948–52)

Ibram Lassaw, *Monoaros, Kwannon*

David Smith, *The Hero*

Joseph Cornell, *Dovecote*

Architecture

Alcoa Building, Pittsburgh (Harrison and Abramovitz)

Lever House, New York (Skidmore, Owings, and Merrill)

Hinds House, Los Angeles (Richard Neutra)

Important Exhibitions

International exchanges continue.

Museums

New York: *Metropolitan:* Cézanne, Rembrandt, da Vinci quincentenary anniversary. *Museum of Modern Art:* Fifteen American abstract painters and sculptors; "Rodin to the Present"; "Fauves and De Stijl from 1917 to 1927." *Whitney:* John Sloan Retrospective

Chicago: Cézanne, Rembrandt

Cleveland, Chicago, San Francisco: Matisse retrospective

Philadelphia: Twentieth-century sculpture

Boston: Kandinsky; Gropius; Charles Bain Hoyt memorial; Watercolors; Costume from the 18th to the 20th century; The Arts of England in the 18th century; Kandinsky

Detroit: Venice and the 18th century

Hartford: "2,000 Years of Tapestry Weaving"

Ed Sullivan, host of "The Toast of the Town." *Billy Rose Theatre Collection. The New York Public Library at Lincoln Center. Astor, Lenox and Tilden Foundations.*

Venice Biennale: Hopper, Kuniyoshi, Davis, Calder represent the United States.

Art Briefs

Rousseau's *Sleeping Gypsy*, Picasso's *Girl before a Mirror* and *Three Musicians*, Léger's *Three Women*, and Modigliani's *Stone Caryatid* are purchased for the Museum of Modern Art by Mrs. Simon Guggenheim • Private Paul Calle wins first prize for *Sad-Eyed Little Girl* in a worldwide army competition • Other major prizes include David Smith's *Beach Scene* (Chicago Art Institute), Lipchitz's *Prometheus Strangling the Vulture* (Pennsylvania Academy of Arts), and Calder's *Giraffe* (Venice International) • The International Graphic Arts Society is formed • Major sales include Corot's *l 'Odalisque sicilienne* ($17,500) and Pollaiuolo's *Battle of the Nudes* ($6,000).

Dance

New York City Ballet makes history with the longest continuous season on record, four months. The American Ballet Center is founded by Robert Joffrey, in New York City. Merce Cunningham forms his own company.

Premieres

New York City Ballet: *Harlequin Pas de Deux* (George Balanchine), Maria Tallchief, André Eglevsky; *Metamorphoses* (Balanchine), Tanaquil Le Clercq, Nicholas Magallanes, Todd Bolender; *Scotch Symphony* (Balanchine), Tallchief

Books

Fiction

Critics' Choice
Invisible Man, Ralph Ellison
The Natural, Bernard Malamud
The Groves of Academe, Mary McCarthy
The Catherine Wheel, Jean Stafford
Player Piano, Kurt Vonnegut
The Long March, William Styron
Wise Blood, Flannery O'Connor
The Works of Love, Wright Morris
Winds of Morning, H. L. Davis

Best-Sellers
The Silver Chalice, Thomas B. Costain
The Caine Mutiny, Herman Wouk
East of Eden, John Steinbeck
My Cousin Rachel, Daphne Du Maurier
Steamboat Gothic, Frances Parkinson Keyes
Giant, Edna Ferber
The Old Man and the Sea, Ernest Hemingway
The Saracen Blade, Frank Yerby

Nonfiction

Critics' Choice
Struggle for Europe, Chester Wilmot
The Confident Years: 1885–1915, Van Wyck Brooks
Poetry in Our Time, Babette Deutsch
Midcentury Journey, William Shirer
The Traitors, Allan Morehead
The Hidden History of the Korean War, I. F. Stone
Democracy and the Economic Challenge, R. M. MacIver
Faces in the Crowd, David Riesman, Nathan Glazer
Social History of Art, Arnold Hauser
A History of Jazz in America, Barry Ulanov
Discovery of the Civil War, Thomas Harry Williams
Christ and Culture, Reinhold Niebuhr

Best-Sellers
The Holy Bible: Revised Standard Version
A Man Called Peter, Catherine Marshall

U.S.A. Confidential, Jack Lait and Lee Mortimer
The Sea around Us, Rachel L. Carson
Tallulah, Tallulah Bankhead
The Power of Positive Thinking, Norman Vincent Peale
This I Believe, ed. Edward P. Morgan
This Is Ike, ed. Wilson Hicks
Witness, Whittaker Chambers

Poetry
T. S. Eliot, *The Complete Poems and Plays*
W. S. Merwin, *A Mask for Janus*
Adrienne Rich, *(Poems)*
Wallace Stevens, *Selected Poems*
Kenneth Rexroth, *The Dragon and the Unicorn*
Robert Creeley, *Le Fou*

Pulitzer Prize
The Old Man and the Sea, Ernest Hemingway (fiction)
The Era of Good Feeling, George Dangerfield (U.S. history)
Edmund Pendleton, 1721–1803, David J. Mays (biography)
Collected Poems, 1917–1952, Archibald MacLeish (poetry)

Science and Technology

Jonas Salk, 38, at the University of Pittsburgh, tests his vaccine against polio.

Gamma globulin is administered to 25,000 children in Utah, Texas, and Iowa, in an attempt to prevent polio.

The first mitral valve heart operation is performed by Dr. Forest Dewey Dodrill in Detroit.

The first plastic artificial heart valve is used on a patient at the Georgetown Medical Center.

John Gibbons develops the heart-lung machine to allow the separation of the heart from the circulatory system during surgery.

Chlorpromazine (Thorazine), reserpine, isoniazid, and tri-iodothyronine are developed.

RCA announces the development of bean-size transistors that can replace vacuum tubes.

William G. Pfann develops two techniques to purify silicon and germanium crystals, facilitating electronics research.

W. F. Libby, of the University of Chicago, dates Stonehenge to about 1842 B.C.

Astronomer Milton Humason, at Mt. Palomar, describes runaway stars as further support for the "expanding theory of the universe."

Linus Pauling and Robert Corey, at MIT, reveal the molecular structure of certain proteins.

At Edwards Air Force Base, California, an experimental D-558-2 Douglas skyrocket goes a record 70,000 feet in altitude; later, William Bridgeman goes to 72,300 feet.

Nobel Prize
Edward Mills Purcell and Felix Bloch win the prize in physics for work in the measurement of magnetic fields in atomic nuclei. Selman A. Waksman wins in physiology and medicine for the codiscovery of streptomycin.

Sports

Baseball

Walt Dropo (Boston, AL) gets 12 consecutive hits.

Champions

Batting
Stan Musial (St. Louis, NL), .335
Ferris Fain (Philadelphia, AL), .327
Pitching
Hoyt Wilhelm (New York, NL), 15–3

Bob Shantz (Philadelphia, AL), 24–7
Home runs
Ralph Kiner (Pittsburgh, NL), 37
Hank Sauer (Chicago, NL), 37

Football

Sammy Baugh, Washington, retires.

NFL Season Leaders: Norm Van Brocklin (Los Angeles), passing, Dan Towler (Los Angeles), rushing; Mac Speedie (Cleveland), receiving

College All-Americans: Paul Giel (B), Minnesota; Don Heinrich (Q), Washington; Johnny Lattner (B), Notre Dame

Bowls (Jan. 1, 1953)

Rose: Southern California 7– Wisconsin 0
Orange: Alabama 61– Syracuse 6

Cotton: Texas 16– Tennessee 0
Sugar: Georgia Tech 24– Mississippi 7

Basketball

NBA All-Pro First Team: Paul Arizin (Philadelphia), George Mikan (Minneapolis), Bob Cousy (Boston), Ed McCauley (Boston), Bob Davies (Rochester).

Olympics

In the Summer Games at Helsinki, U.S. winners include Lindig Rimigino (100m, 10.4s), Andy Stanfield (200m, 20.7s), Mal Whitfield (800m, 1:49.2), Harrison Dillard (110mh, 13.7s), Bob Richards (pole vault, 14′14″), Bob Mathias (decathlon). In the Winter Games at Oslo, Richard Button wins figure skating and Mrs. Andrea Mead Lawrence, giant slalom.

Other Sports

Boxing: Jersey Joe Walcott, 37, knocks out Ezzard Charles to become the oldest heavyweight champion to date.

Tennis: Australians Frank Sedgman and Ken McGregor beat the U.S. in Davis Cup play for the third straight time; Jack Kramer then signs them up as pros for a record $100,000 guaranteed minimum.

Winners

World Series
New York (AL) 4
Brooklyn 3
MVP
NL–Hank Sauer, Chicago
AL–Bobby Shantz, Philadelphia
NFL
Detroit 17–Cleveland 7
College Football
Michigan State
Heisman Trophy
Billy Vessels, Oklahoma
NBA Championship
Minneapolis 4–New York 3

College Basketball
Kansas
Player of the Year
Clyde Lovellette, Kansas
Stanley Cup
Detroit
US Tennis Open
Men: Frank Sedgman
Women: Maureen Connolly
USGA Open
Julius Boros
Kentucky Derby
Hill Gail (E. Arcaro, jockey)

Fashion

For Women: Numerous styles appear. One is toward a slimmer and softer look. The "siren sheath" is introduced for both day and evening, along with a coat that replaces the tent with a new "column" shape. The "sweater girl" returns in form-fitting clothing in stripes and plaids. At the same time, new permanent pleating processes bring forth the "morning glory" blouse with pleats, and big crinoline skirts are narrowed; elasticized belts and cummerbunds are relaxed. The silhouette gets bulky on top as the fitted jacket is replaced with a front, concave style. The accession of Queen Elizabeth revives Elizabethan fashions: collars, tiaras, and jeweled velvet dresses; the mink stole is extremely popular. Italian and Spanish fashions are stylish: the Italian mule sandal with a narrow instep band, shawls, hoop earrings, multiple strands of pearls and pearl bibs. "Mamie bangs," the "poodle" cut, and ponytails are everywhere. Sixty percent of the women who used to go to beauty shops stay home with recent developments in hair dyes and drying methods.

High-fashion notes: Jacques Heim's wrapped jersey blouse, tapered blue and green velvet pants and lilac cummerbunds; Dior's shantung dustcoat

Kaleidoscope

- "Eggheads of the world unite. You have nothing to lose but your yolks," says the Democratic presidential candidate, the intellectual and balding Adlai Stevenson.
- "The great problem of America today," says Dwight D. Eisenhower, "is to take that straight road down the middle."
- "Dum-De-Dum Dum . . . the story you are about to hear is true; only the names have been changed to protect the innocent," begins the enormously popular "Dragnet" with Jack Webb.
- George Jorgensen, 26, is surgically transformed into a woman (Christine) in Denmark.
- A priest, minister, and rabbi sanction the appearance of Lucille Ball's pregnancy on her TV show.
- Fifty-six million watch Nixon's speech on TV when he describes his mortgage loan, 1950 auto, and $4,000 life insurance policy; Eisenhower later praises Nixon's brave defense against improper gifts, and in response to Nixon's request for public support, post offices are flooded, 350 to 1, in favor of Nixon.
- Subversives are barred from teaching in public schools.
- Salt Lake City Colleen Hutchens is the first blonde in 13 years to win the Miss America contest; she is also the tallest (5′10″), the oldest (25), and the heaviest (143 pounds).
- The penny postcard becomes 2 cents.
- Leo Durocher, New York Giants manager, is fined and suspended for two days for "beanball pitching."
- A potato shortage sets black-market prices at $5 to $8 for a 100-pound bag; the ceiling price is $3.55.
- A. S. Rosenbach sells his 73-volume collection of Shakespeare folios and quartos for $1 million.
- The complete Torah is published in English for the first time.
- Thirty-seven-year-old *Birth of a Nation* is barred in Maryland as "morally bad and crime inciting."
- A *New York Times* study reveals that 90 percent of all university funding is distributed to the physical and biological sciences; 10 percent goes to the humanities.
- A poliomyelitis epidemic strikes more than 50,000.
- Physicist Arthur Robert's *Overture to the Dedication of a Nuclear Reactor,* inspired by atomic energy, is performed at Oak Ridge, Tenn.
- Ruth Simmons gains wide interest in her claim to be a reincarnation of the nineteenth-century Bridey Murphy.
- ILGWU members demonstrate in New York against the efforts of crime syndicates to enter their industry.
- Bank robber Willie "the Actor" Sutton is captured five years after he escaped from jail by tricking guards with a dummy of himself.
- Arnold Schuster, an ordinary citizen whose tip led to Willie Sutton's arrest, is shot and killed.
- A Louis Seltzer editorial in the *Cleveland Press* alluding to the need for religious belief is reprinted in 41 publications; Mickey Spillane turns to Jehovah Witnesses.

- Although never implemented, the Fort Worth Plan is the first to propose banning cars from a business district in order to create a pedestrian shopping mall.

New Words and Usages: Miniaturization, globalist, Manchurian fever, cool jazz, cronyism, hot rod, Pentagonese, poodle cut, stretch-out, telethon, drag, hack, panty raid, ponytail, printed circuit, psycholinguistics, teleprompter, whirlybird.

Fads: Flying saucer watching (and "man from Mars" theories), panty raids; "beanies" with propeller tops; chlorophyll (even in deodorants and dog food); collecting stamps, autographs, seals, and labels; needlework, gardening

First Appearances: "Saralee" black doll, mechanical lawn mower, 16mm home movie projector, cigarette with built-in lighter, midget adding machine, two-way radio cars, adjustable shower head, bowling alley automatic pin boy, revolving grocery check-outs, circular bed, plastic vinylite swimming pool, automatic food vending machines on trains, marketing of frozen bread, transistorized hearing aids, plastic lens for cataract patients, nylon stretch yarn, parachutist to make 124 jumps in one day, Cinerama, "Mad" comics, Kellogg's Sugar Frosted Flakes, Gleem, Kent filter tips, Holiday Inn (Memphis), BMW, Sony pocket-size transistor radio, No-Cal ginger ale, fiberglass

Casey Stengel (left), famous both as New York Yankees manager and rambling rhetorician ("stengelese"). *Movie Star News.*

1953

Facts and Figures

Economic Profile

Dow-Jones: ↑ High 293–
Low 255

GNP: +5%

Inflation: +0.6%

Unemployment: 2.9%

Korean Conflict

Total deaths: 54,246

Battle deaths: 33,629

Other deaths: 20,617

Wounded in action: 103,284

Daily newspapers: 2,009

Books published: 12,050

Airmail: 7¢ (oz.)

Postcard: 2¢

IRS total collections: $69.6
billion

Coronado Empire stove:
$99.95

Coronado refrigerator:
$199.95 (9 cubic ft.)

Revere pots (11-piece set):
$39.95

Dormeyer deep-fry cooker:
$19.50

Deaths

Hilaire Belloc, Raoul Dufy,
John Marin, Queen Mary,
Robert A. Millikan,
Eugene O'Neill, Sergei
Prokofiev, Robert Taft,
Jacques Thiabaud, Fred M.
Vinson, Jonathan
Wainwright.

In the News

TRUMAN ANNOUNCES THE DAWN OF HYDROGEN POWER, WARNS OF THE HORROR OF WARFARE . . . RUSSIA CLAIMS JEWISH DOCTORS CONSPIRED TO KILL STALIN . . . IKE, INAUGURATED, PLEDGES TO SEEK PEACE . . . STALIN DIES AT 72, GEORGI MALENKOV BECOMES SOVIET PREMIER . . . WAGE AND PRICE CONTROLS ARE ENDED . . . SWEDE DAG HAMMARSKJÖLD IS ELECTED UN SECRETARY GENERAL . . . CONRAD ADENAUER VISITS U.S. . . . BOTH SIDES IN KOREA AGREE TO EXCHANGE WOUNDED . . . HEALTH, EDUCATION AND WELFARE DEPARTMENT IS CREATED, OVETA CULP HOBBY IS FIRST SECRETARY . . . SYNGMAN RHEE ORDERS RELEASE OF 27,000 ANTICOMMUNIST NORTH KOREAN PRISONERS . . . TRUCE NEGOTIATIONS BEGIN AT PANMUNJOM . . . OFFSHORE OIL BILL GIVES TITLE TO STATES . . . EDMUND HILLARY AND TENZING NORKAY REACH PEAK OF MOUNT EVEREST . . . ELIZABETH IS CROWNED BRITISH QUEEN . . . ANTICOMMUNIST RIOTS IN EAST BERLIN ARE SUPPRESSED . . . 129 DIE IN AIR FORCE GLOBEMASTER CRASH, WORST AIR ACCIDENT IN HISTORY . . . JULIUS AND ETHEL ROSENBERG ARE ELECTROCUTED AT SING SING PRISON, N.Y. . . . COMMUNISTS LAUNCH HEAVY OFFENSIVE, ALLIES COUNTERATTACK . . . 100,000 EAST GERMANS DEFY THREATS AND ENTER THE WEST FOR FOOD PACKAGES . . . POW EXCHANGE BEGINS . . . MALENKOV DECLARES THAT RUSSIA HAS H-BOMB . . . ROYALIST UPRISING OVERTHROWS MOSSADEGH, SHAH TAKES IRANIAN THRONE . . . EARL WARREN IS NOMINATED CHIEF JUSTICE, SUPREME COURT . . . ATTORNEY GENERAL HERBERT BROWNELL CHARGES THAT TRUMAN PROMOTED SPY HARRY DEXTER WHITE, TRUMAN RIDICULES CHARGE . . . LAVRENTI BERIA, STALIN'S KGB HEAD, IS EXECUTED.

Quotes

"[In San Antonio] the main question is: Should books on the public library shelves whose authors are either identified as Communists or suspected of Communist sympathies be branded with a red stamp?"

— Stanley Walker, "Book Branding"

"The Soviet government deems it necessary to report that the United States has no monopoly in the production of the hydrogen bomb."

— Premier Georgi Malenkov

"What was good for our country was good for General Motors and vice versa."

— Secretary of Defense Charles Wilson

"A climate favorable to business has been substituted for the socialism of recent years."

— Secretary of Commerce Sinclair Weeks

THE WORLD DEMANDS
CLEMENCY FOR THE ROSENBERGS
FRENCH DEPUTIES SAY CLEMENCY
300 BRITISH SCIENTISTS SAY CLEMENCY
POPE PIUS SAYS CLEMENCY
2500 MINISTERS SAY CLEMENCY
RABBIS OF ISRAEL SAY CLEMENCY
— Poster on behalf of Ethel and Julius Rosenberg

Not One to Turn Your Back On

Anti-McCarthy cartoon. Albert Einstein, Harry Truman, and Milton Eisenhower are among those who attack McCarthy, as he and his cohorts continue to investigate Communist influence in the State Department, Army, Harvard, the media, and the Methodist Church. *Library of Congress.*

"America is so terribly grim in spite of all that material prosperity. . . . Compassion and the old neighborliness are gone, people stand by and do nothing when friends and neighbors are attacked, libeled and ruined."

— Charles Chaplin

"The smart woman will keep herself desirable. It is her duty to be feminine and desirable at all times in the eyes of the opposite sex."

— Leland Kirdel, *Coronet*

Ads

TV

Premieres

"You Are There," Walter Cronkite
"I Led Three Lives," Richard Carlson
"Person to Person," Edward R. Murrow
"Topper," Leo G. Carroll
"The Jack Paar Show"
"Romper Room," Gloria Flood
"The Tonight Show," Steve Allen
"Soupy Sales"
"General Electric Theater," Ronald Reagan (host)
"Coke Time with Eddie Fisher"
"Make Room for Daddy," Danny Thomas
"U.S. Steel Hour" ("P.O.W.," Gary Merrill, Richard Kiley)

Top Ten (Nielsen)

"I Love Lucy," "Dragnet," "Arthur Godfrey's Talent Scouts," "You Bet Your Life," "The Milton Berle Show," "Arthur Godfrey and His Friends," "Ford Theatre," "The Jackie Gleason Show," "Fireside Theatre," "The Colgate Comedy Hour"

Specials

"Marty" (Paddy Chayefsky, with Rod Steiger); "King Lear" (Orson Welles, TV debut); Coronation of Queen Elizabeth II

Emmy Awards

"U.S. Steel Hour" (drama); "I Love Lucy" (situation comedy); "Omnibus" (variety); "Dragnet" (action); "Kukla, Fran, and Ollie" (children); "Victory at Sea" (public affairs); Donald O'Connor (actor, "Colgate Comedy Hour"); Eve Arden (actress, "Our Miss Brooks"); Edward R. Murrow (personality)

Of Note

Ed Murrow uses film clips on "See It Now" to accuse Joe McCarthy of character assassination in the case of Lt. Milo Radulovich. McCarthy appears in rebuttal • Bob Hope hosts the first Academy Awards show • Marilyn Monroe makes her TV debut on "The Jack Benny Show" • Mary Martin and Ethel Merman celebrate Ford's 50th anniversary on both NBC and CBS.

Movies

Openings

From Here to Eternity (Fred Zinnemann), Burt Lancaster, Deborah Kerr, Montgomery Clift, Frank Sinatra
Stalag 17 (Billy Wilder), William Holden, Don Taylor, Otto Preminger
Roman Holiday (William Wyler), Gregory Peck, Audrey Hepburn
Julius Caesar (Joseph L. Mankiewicz), Louis Calhern, James Mason, Marlon Brando
The Bad and the Beautiful (Vincente Minnelli), Lana Turner, Kirk Douglas
The Robe (Henry Koster), Richard Burton, Jean Simmons (first Cinemascope)
Shane (George Stevens), Alan Ladd, Jean Arthur, Van Heflin, Brandon De Wilde
Lili (Charles Walters), Leslie Caron, Mel Ferrer
Mogambo (John Ford), Clark Gable, Ava Gardner, Grace Kelly
The Moon Is Blue (Otto Preminger), William Holden, David Niven, Maggie McNamara
Pickup on South Street (Sam Fuller), Richard Widmark, Jean Peters
The Captain's Paradise (Anthony Kimmins), Alec Guinness, Yvonne de Carlo
The Big Heat (Fritz Lang), Glenn Ford, Lee Marvin, Gloria Grahame, Alexander Scourby
The Band Wagon (Vincente Minnelli), Fred Astaire, Cyd Charisse, Jack Buchanan
Gentlemen Prefer Blondes (Howard Hawks), Jane Russell, Marilyn Monroe, Charles Coburn
Bwana Devil (Arch Oboler) Robert Stack, Barbara Britton (first 3-D)
Wages of Fear (Georges Clouzot), Yves Montand

Academy Awards

Best Picture: *From Here to Eternity*
Best Director: Fred Zinnemann (*From Here to Eternity*)
Best Actress: Audrey Hepburn (*Roman Holiday*)
Best Actor: William Holden (*Stalag 17*)

Top Box-Office Stars

Gary Cooper, Dean Martin and Jerry Lewis, John Wayne, Alan Ladd, Bing Crosby, Marilyn Monroe, James Stewart, Bob Hope, Susan Hayward, Randolph Scott

Stars of Tomorrow

Janet Leigh, Gloria Grahame, Tony Curtis, Terry Moore, Rosemary Clooney, Julie Adams, Robert Wagner, Scott Brady, Pier Angeli, Jack Palance

Popular Music

Hit Songs

"And This Is My Beloved"
"Baubles, Bangles and Beads"
"Hi-Lili, Hi-Lo"
"I Love Paris"
"My Love, My Love"
"Secret Love"
"Stranger in Paradise"
"That's Amore"
"You, You, You"
"Ebbtide"
"Ruby [Ruby Gentry]"

Top Records

Albums: *Hans Christian Andersen* (Danny Kaye); *Music for Lovers Only* (Jackie Gleason); *Music of Victor Herbert* (Mantovani); *Strauss Waltzes* (Mantovani); *Radio Bloopers* (Kermit Schafer)

Singles: *Crying in the Chapel* (June Valli); *Rags to Riches* (Tony Bennett); *Eh, Cumpari* (Julius La Rosa); *Song from Moulin Rouge* (Percy Faith); *Vaya con Dios* (Les Paul and Mary Ford); *Doggie in the Window* (Patti Page); *I'm Walking behind You* (Eddie Fisher); *Till I Waltz Again with You* (Teresa Brewer); *No Other Love, Don't Let the Stars Get in Your Eyes* (Perry Como). Country: *Kaw Liga* (Hank Williams); *It's Been So Long* (Webb Pierce)

Jazz and Big Bands

In the search for new sounds, Bud Shank, Frank Wess, and Herbie Mann introduce the flute; Count Basie, the Hammond organ; Oscar Pettiford, the cello.

New Band: The Dorsey Brothers are reunited.

Top Performers (*Downbeat*): Glenn Miller (soloist); Stan Kenton, Les Brown (bands); Dave Brubeck (jazz group); Les Paul, Ray Brown, Gerry Mulligan, Chet Baker, Don Elliott (instrumentalists); Ella Fitzgerald, Nat "King" Cole (vocalists); Four Freshmen (vocal group)

Theater

Broadway Openings

Plays

The Teahouse of the August Moon (John Patrick), David Wayne, John Forsythe, Larry Gates
Picnic (William Inge), Ralph Meeker, Janice Rule, Paul Newman, Kim Stanley, Eileen Heckart, Arthur O'Connell
The Solid Gold Cadillac (Howard Teichmann, George S. Kaufman), Josephine Hull, Loring Smith
Tea and Sympathy (Robert Anderson), Deborah Kerr, John Kerr
The Crucible (Arthur Miller), Walter Hampden, Beatrice Straight, Arthur Kennedy, E. G. Marshall
Camino Real (Tennessee Williams), Eli Wallach, Frank Silvera, Jo Van Fleet, Martin Balsam
John Brown's Body (Stephen Vincent Benét), Raymond Massey, Tyrone Power, Judith Anderson
Sabrina Fair (Samuel Taylor), Margaret Sullavan, Joseph Cotten
The Love of Four Colonels (Peter Ustinov), Lilli Palmer, Rex Harrison

Musicals

Kismet (Alexander Borodin, Robert Wright, George Forest), Alfred Drake, Joan Diener, Richard Kiley
Wonderful Town (Leonard Bernstein, Betty Comden, Adolph Green), Rosalind Russell, Edith Adams

Can-Can (Cole Porter), Gwen Verdon, Lilo, Peter Cookson, Hans Conried
Hazel Flagg (Jule Styne, Bob Hilliard), Helen Gallagher
Me and Juliet (Richard Rodgers, Oscar Hammerstein II), Isabel Bigley, Joan McCracken
Comedy in Music with Victor Borge
John Murray Anderson's Almanac (Richard Adler, Jerry Ross), Harry Belafonte, Orson Bean, Polly Bergen
Porgy and Bess (George and Ira Gershwin, revival) Leontyne Price, Cab Calloway

Classics and Revivals On and Off Broadway

The Misalliance (George Bernard Shaw), Richard Kiley, Roddy McDowall. *Founded:* Phoenix Theatre by T. Edward Hambleton and Norris Houghton: *Richard III* (José Ferrer), *The Merchant of Venice* (Luther Adler)

Pulitzer Prize

Picnic, William Inge

Tony Awards

The Crucible, Arthur Miller (play); *Wonderful Town,* Leonard Bernstein, Betty Comden, Adolph Green (musical)

William "Count" Basie was first associated with Fats Waller, Walter Page, and Bennie Moten before his debut with his own group at the Reno Club in Kansas City. *Movie Star News.*

Ella Fitzgerald, *Downbeat's* most popular singer this year and from 1937 to 1939, when she took over the late Chick Webb's band. *Movie Star News.*

Compositions

Chou Wen-chung, *All in the Spring Wind*
Earle Brown, *Folio, 25 Pages—for 1 to 25 Pianos*
Quincy Porter, Concerto for Two Pianos and Orchestra
Alan Hovhaness, *Triptych*
Stefan Wolpe, *Enactment* for Three Pianos
Arthur Berger, *Ideas of Order*
John Cage, *Music for Piano—"4–84 to 1–84 Pianists"*
George Antheil, *Capital of the World*
Roger Sessions, Sonata for Solo Violin

Important Events

In addition to a $200,000 grant to the New York City Center, the Rockefeller Foundation gives $400,000 to the Louisville Philharmonic Society to encourage the performance, composition, and recording of contemporary music.
Of 4,000 performances of 900 works by 30 orchestras, European compositions dominate. Most frequently performed Americans are Aaron Copland, George Gershwin, Samuel Barber, Virgil Thomson, Paul Creston, and Gian Carlo Menotti.

Debut: Phillippe Entremont

Deborah Kerr and Burt Lancaster in *From Here to Eternity;* their passionate beach scene shocks audiences. *Movie Star News.*

Classical Music _____

First Performances

Roy Harris, Piano Concerto no. 2 (Louisville); Ernest Bloch, *Suite Hebraïque* (Chicago); Henry Cowell, Symphony no. 8 (Wilmington); Peter Mennin, Symphony no. 6 (Louisville); Darius Milhaud, *Christophe Columbe* (New York, in opera form)

Opera

Metropolitan: Hilde Gueden, *The Rake's Progress* (Stravinsky, premiere); Irmgard Seefried (debut), *Le nozze de Figaro;* Theodor Uppman, *Pelléas et Mélisande;* Cesare Siepi/George London, *Boris Godunov;* Victoria de los Angeles, Jussi Bjoerling, Robert Merrill, conductor Pierre Monteux (debut), *Faust*

New York City: *The Trial* (Von Einem, premiere)

Cincinnati: *Taming of the Shrew* (Vittorio Giannini)

Hartford: *The Mighty Casey* (William Schuman, premiere)

Dayton: *The Miracle of Saint Nicholas* (Benjamin Britten, premiere)

Central City, Colo.: *The Merry Wives of Windsor* (Giannini, premiere)

San Francisco: Giulietta Simionato, *Il barbiere di Siviglia;* Inge Borkh, *Elektra;* Cesare Valetti, *Werther* (Massenet)

Art

Painting
I. Rice Pereira, *Spirit of Air*

Jackson Pollock, *Portrait and a Dream, Ocean Grayness*

Richard Lindner, *The Meeting*

Jack Levine, *Gangster Funeral* (1952–53)

Willem de Kooning, *Woman and Bicycle, Woman VI*

Mark Tobey, *Edge of August*

Stuart Davis, *Something on the Eight Ball*

Barnett Newman, *Onement No. 6*

Josef Albers, *Homage to the Square*

Franz Kline, *New York*

Sam Francis, *Big Red*

Ad Reinhardt, *Blue Painting*

Moses Soyer, *Girl in Orange Sweater*

Jose Vela Zanetti completes a 20-yard mural for the UN Headquarters Building in New York.

Sculpture
Joseph Cornell, *Hôtel du Nord*

Louise Bourgeois, *Garden at Night*

David Smith, *Tanktotem II*

Seymour Lipton, *Sanctuary*

Architecture
General Motors Building, Warren, Mich. (Saarinen and Saarinen)

Private House, Madison, Wis. (James Dressler)

North Carolina State Fair Building, Raleigh (Nowicki and Dietrich)

Ford Rotunda, Dearborn, Mich. (Buckminster Fuller)

Mini-Earth Sphere Geoscope, Cornell University, Ithaca, N.Y. (Fuller)

Corning Glass Center, Corning, N.Y. (Harrison, Abramovitz, and Abbe)

David Smith, *Tanktotem II*, 1953. Steel and bronze 49½ × 80½". *The Metropolitan Museum of Art, Fletcher Fund, 1953.*

Important Exhibitions
Major visiting shows include De Stijl (from Amsterdam) and Japanese paintings and sculpture (sponsored by the Japanese government).

New York: *Metropolitan:* American painting from 1754–1954; "From the Land of the Bible"; Watercolors contest and show: Ivan Le Lorraine Albright, Claude Bentley, Charles Burchfield, John Marin; Japanese painting and sculpture. *Museum of Modern Art:* "The Juxtaposition of the Traditional and Modern" (in the newly opened sculpture garden). *Guggenheim:* Foundations of abstractionism; Living architecture

Washington: *Corcoran:* First prize to Abraham Rattner

Boston: Early American Jewish portraits and silver; Japanese paintings and sculpture

Chicago: International exhibition of contemporary drawings of 12 countries; Léger; Japanese paintings and sculpture; Jean Metzinger

San Francisco: Ward Lockwood retrospective; Léger

Cleveland: Rouault

Art Briefs
Forty-four painters and sculptors compose the *Reality* manifesto attacking the Museum of Modern Art and nonobjective art; the Museum defends "the moderns." Frank Lloyd Wright attacks the international style • Auction prices are lower than in recent years: Manet's *Mme. Jeanne Martin*, $28,000; Degas's *Laundress Carrying Linen*, $10,500

Dance

New York City Ballet: A record-breaking 12 new productions are mounted, including *Fanfare* (Jerome Robbins) and *Afternoon of a Faun* (Robbins), Kay Mazzo.

San Francisco: *Con Amore* (Lew Christensen); *Creatures of Beethoven* (Christensen)

Alwin Nikolais: *Masks, Props, and Mobiles*

Books

Fiction

Critics' Choice

The Adventures of Augie March, Saul Bellow
The Enormous Radio and Other Stories, John Cheever
The Deep Sleep, Wright Morris
Plexus, Henry Miller
Nine Stories, J. D. Salinger
Children Are Bored on Sunday, Jean Stafford
The Outsider, Richard Wright
Junkie, William Burroughs
The Stones of the House, Theodore Morrison
Go Tell It on the Mountain, James Baldwin
The Bridges at Toko Ri, James Michener
🐦 *The Erasers*, Alain Robbe-Grillet

Best-Sellers

The Robe, Lloyd C. Douglas
The Silver Chalice, Thomas B. Costain
Désirée, Annemarie Selinko
Battle Cry, Leon M. Uris
From Here to Eternity, James Jones
The High and the Mighty, Ernest K. Gann
Beyond This Place, A. J. Cronin
Time and Time Again, James Hilton

Nonfiction

Critics' Choice

Science and Human Behavior, B. F. Skinner
Shame and Glory of the Intellectuals, Peter Viereck
The Conservative Mind, Russell Kirk
The Challenge to American Foreign Policy, John Jay McCloy
The Natural Superiority of Women, Ashley Montague
The Interpersonal Theory of Psychiatry, Harry Stack Sullivan
Modern Science and Modern Man, James Bryant Conant
In Search of Theater, Eric Bentley
Poetry and the Age, Randall Jarrell
The New England Mind, Roger Williams, Perry Miller
🐦 *The Hedgehog and the Fox*, Isaiah Berlin

Best-Sellers

The Holy Bible: Revised Standard Version
The Power of Positive Thinking, Norman Vincent Peale
Sexual Behavior in the Human Female, Alfred C. Kinsey
Angel Unaware, Dale Evans Rogers

Life Is Worth Living, Fulton J. Sheen
A Man Called Peter, Catherine Marshall
The Greatest Faith Ever Known, Fulton Oursler, G. A. O. Armstrong
How to Play Your Best Golf, Tommy Armour
A House Is Not a Home, Polly Adler

Poetry

John Ashbery, *Turandot and Other Poems*
Richard Eberhart, *Undercliff: Poems 1946–1963*
Conrad Aiken, *Collected Poems*
Karl Shapiro, *Poems 1940–1953*
Wallace Stevens, *Selected Poems*
Robert Penn Warren, *Brother to Dragons*
Archibald MacLeish, *This Music Crept by Me upon the Waters*
May Sarton, *The Land of Silence*

Pulitzer Prizes

No prize is awarded in fiction.
A Stillness at Appomattox, Bruce Catton (U.S. history)
The Spirit of St. Louis, Charles A. Lindbergh (autobiography)
The Waking: Poems 1933–1953, Theodore Roethke (poetry)

Science and Technology

Francis Crick and James Watson solve the structure of DNA, the basic unit of heredity, with their double helix model.

The Salk vaccine is formally certified to prevent infantile paralysis; Salk says mass inoculations can begin.

The first successful open-heart surgery is performed at Jefferson Medical College, Philadelphia.

R. Bunge, at the University of Iowa, describes his work with artificial insemination using semen preserved by freezing.

Dr. Alfred Kinsey's *Sexual Behavior in the Human Female* concludes that women have less sex drive than men and engage in less forbidden sexual activity.

Oxytocin, the uterine contracting hormone, is synthesized.

Charles Yaeger goes a record 1,600 m.p.h. in a Bell X-1A at Edwards Air Force Base, California.

The atomic nucleus is shown to be twice as dense and smaller than previously believed.

University of Chicago archeologists unearth a 10,000-year-old Indian village at Prairie du Rocher, Ill.

The first atomic shell is fired at the Nevada Training Grounds.

Nobel Prize

Fritz A. Lipmann wins in physiology and medicine for his studies of living cells.

Sports

Baseball

The Boston Braves are permitted by the NL to move to Milwaukee, the first franchise shift in the century.

The New York Yankees under Casey Stengel win a record fifth straight pennant and World Series.

Champions

Batting	Pitching
Mickey Vernon (Washington, AL), .337	Carl Erskine (Brooklyn, NL), 20–6
Carl Furillo (Brooklyn, NL), .344	Ed Lopat (New York, AL), 16–4
	Home runs
	Ed Matthews (Milwaukee, NL), 47

Football

Lou Groza (Cleveland) kicks a record 23 field goals; Burt Rechichar (San Francisco) kicks a record 56-yard field goal.

NFL Season Leaders: Otto Graham (Cleveland), passing; Joe Perry (San Francisco), rushing; Pete Pihos (Philadelphia), receiving.

College All-Americans: J. C. Caroline (B), Illinois; Paul Cameron (B), UCLA; Matt Hazeltine (G), California.

Bowls (Jan. 1, 1954)

Rose: Michigan State 28–UCLA 20	Cotton: Rice 28–Alabama 6
Orange: Oklahoma 7–Maryland 0	Sugar: Georgia Tech 42–West Virginia 19

Basketball

NBA All-Pro First Team: Neil Johnston (Philadelphia), George Mikan (Minneapolis), Bob Cousy (Boston), Ed McCauley (Boston), Adolph Schayes (Syracuse)

Other Sports

Boxing: Rocky Marciano knocks out Joe Walcott in the 13th for the heavyweight title.

Golf: Ben Hogan wins the Masters, U.S. Open, and British Open.

Racing: Bill Vukovich wins the Indianapolis 500.

Winners

World Series	*College Basketball*
New York (AL) 4	Indiana
Brooklyn (NL) 2	*Player of the Year*
MVP	Robert Houbregs,
NL–Roy Campanella, Brooklyn	Washington
AL–Al Rosen, Cleveland	*Stanley Cup*
NFL	Montreal
Detroit 16–Cleveland 10	*US Tennis Open*
College Football	Men: Tony Trabert
Maryland	Women: Maureen Connolly
Heisman Trophy	*USGA Open*
John Lattner, Notre Dame	Ben Hogan
NBA Championship	*Kentucky Derby*
Minneapolis 4–New York 1	Dark Star (H. Moreno, jockey)

Fashion

For Women: A mood of elegance and "femininity" is emphasized. Hair, waistlines, and hems become shorter. The semifitted suit with brief, narrow jacket is cinched at the waist and worn with a full, gathered skirt. The form-fitting sheath is also softened as widened or slashed necklines appear and are filled in with scarves or jewelry. Narrow skirts gain huge pockets. Dior moves the hemline to nearly 16 inches and reintroduces the low hip style. A new sophistication characterizes sportswear: sweaters are trimmed and even jeweled; slacks taper to the ankle or are molded to the leg in "toreador" pants.

Interesting accessories include hoop earrings, jeweled heels on plain shoes, and multipatterned scarves, which are worn with almost everything. The "poodle" hairdo gives way to the Italian "pixie," short and layered or casually pushed forward onto the face. Evening makeup includes new liquid rouges, foundations, heavy powder, dark brown eyeshadow, penciled eyebrows and eyelines, and pale, nearly white lipstick.

High-fashion note: Dior's skirt, 15½ inches off the ground

Kaleidoscope

- Citizen groups in Central, New Mexico, halt the filming of the controversial *Salt of the Earth,* which has been produced with alleged Communist screenwriters and actors.
- The Screen Actors Guild adopts a by-law banning Communists from membership.
- Senator Joseph McCarthy announces that he has arranged for the Greeks to stop trading at Soviet ports.
- Charlie Chaplin says he finds it "virtually impossible" to continue work in the United States owing to "vicious propaganda" by powerful reactionary groups; once in Europe, he gives up his reentry permit.
- Vice President Richard Nixon attends a Boy Scout jamboree of 50,000 near his hometown in Newport Beach, California, and demonstrates how to scramble eggs.
- A member of the Indiana State Textbook Committee charges that "there is a Communist directive in education now to stress the story of Robin Hood . . . because he robbed the rich and gave to the poor."
- A jury acquits Yvonne Chevallier of shooting her husband, Pierre, mayor of New Orleans and newly appointed cabinet member, after he requested a divorce to marry his mistress.
- The gold in Fort Knox is counted and found to accord with records: $30,442,415,581.70.
- Rectifying an 1803 oversight, the House Interior Committee votes to admit Ohio to the Union.
- Senator Wayne Morse's 22-hour, 26-minute Senate speech, opposing a bill to return offshore oil reserves to their individual states, is unsuccessful.
- Air Force pilots report chasing clusters of red, white, and green lights over northern Japan, a report similar to recent UFO sightings in the United States and elsewhere.
- Easter egg rolling is revived at the White House.
- Thirty million attend performances of classical music, 15 million major league baseball; 7,250,000 children and young adults take music lessions.
- Arthur Godfrey fires Julius La Rosa on the air because La Rosa "lacks humility"; the public sympathizes with La Rosa.
- Actress June Havoc renounces her career to enter a Roman Catholic convent; six months later, she returns to Hollywood.
- Lucille Ball and Desi Arnaz sign TV's biggest contract ($8 million) to continue "I Love Lucy" for 30 months; the birth of their baby occurs on the show on the same day as in real life.
- Elvis Presley pays four dollars to cut "My Happiness" in Memphis for his mother's birthday.
- His career still at a low, Frank Sinatra takes the role of Maggio in *From Here to Eternity.*
- New sexual jargon includes baseball terms like "first base" and "home run."
- The comic book market expands to 650 titles; Scrabble also becomes a fad.

Christine Jorgensen elicits wide public interest after her sex change from George, achieved last year in Denmark by a combination of surgical and hormonal techniques. *Library of Congress.*

- The New York Fifth Avenue double-decker bus goes out of service.
- General Motors introduces the Chevrolet Corvette, the first plastic laminated fiberglass sports car, for $3,250.
- A correlation is indicated between coronary heart disease and diets high in animal fats.
- Oleo heir Minot (Mickey) Frazier is sentenced to three to six years on charges of running a ring of high-priced call girls.
- "Eight millionaires and a plumber" is a description given Ike's cabinet, the plumber a reference to Martin Durkin, head of a plumber's union and now secretary of labor.
- McCarthy staff members Roy Cohn and David Schine make an 18-day European trip to determine subversion in U.S. overseas programs; librarians are ordered to remove books by "Communists, fellow travelers, and the like."

New Words and Usages: Main Man, drag strip, name-dropper, bit, cookout, countdown, discount house, doublethink, egghead, girlie magazine, jet stream, metalinguistics, split-level, 3-D

First Appearances: DC-7 propeller plane, Japan Airlines, Sugar Smacks, bottled Schweppes quinine water, Irish Coffee, White Rose Redi-Tea, underground freezer storage (Kansas City, Mo.), *TV Guide, Playboy,* L & M cigarettes, Tareyton filter tips, 3-D Cinerama in stereo and wide screen, tufted plastic carpeting, 3-D newspaper ad (Waukesha, Wis.), aluminum-faced building (Alcoa, Pittsburgh), burglar alarm operated by ultrasonic or radio waves, element 100, 3-D cartoon and movies (*Melody, Bwana Devil, House of Wax*)

1954

In the News

FOUR SUPERPOWERS MEET AT BERLIN CONFERENCE . . . MOLOTOV PROPOSES A UNIFIED NEUTRAL GERMANY, DULLES REFUSES . . . MCCARTHY PROBE OF ARMY BEGINS . . . GAMAL ABDEL NASSER BECOMES PREMIER OF EGYPT . . . FIVE U.S. CONGRESSMEN ARE SHOT BY PUERTO RICAN NATIONALISTS . . . LARGEST THERMONUCLEAR BLAST OCCURS AT BIKINI ATOLL . . . ARMY CHARGES THAT MCCARTHY AND ROY COHN SOUGHT FAVORS FOR PRIVATE DAVID SCHINE . . . SOVIETS PROPOSE JOINING NATO AS PART OF GENERAL PEACE TREATY . . . ADMIRAL LEWIS STRAUSS SAYS H-BOMB CAN DESTROY CITY OF ANY SIZE . . . SUPREME COURT UPHOLDS INTERNAL SECURITY ACT . . . SENATE HEARINGS ON ARMY-MCCARTHY DISPUTE BEGIN . . . FRENCH FORTRESS AT DIEN BIEN PHU, VIETNAM, FALLS, THE ENTIRE GARRISON IS CAPTURED . . . SURGEON SAM SHEPPARD IS ACCUSED OF WIFE'S MURDER . . . SUPREME COURT RULES THAT RACIAL SEGREGATION IN PUBLIC SCHOOLS IS UNCONSTITUTIONAL . . . CHOU EN-LAI AND MENDES-FRANCE AGREE ON INDOCHINA SETTLEMENT . . . GENERAL MOTORS ANNOUNCES $1 BILLION EXPANSION . . . AEC VOTES 4–1 TO DENY SECURITY CLEARANCE TO J. ROBERT OPPENHEIMER . . . VIETNAM IS DIVIDED AT 17TH PARALLEL, PENDING THE 1956 ELECTION . . . HEAVY RIOTING OCCURS IN MOROCCO . . . HOLLAND ENDS UNION WITH INDONESIA . . . IKE SIGNS ESPIONAGE AND SABOTAGE ACT . . . BRITISH AGREE TO RETURN SUEZ CANAL TO EGYPT IN 1956 . . . DEMOCRATS GAIN IN HOUSE AND SENATE . . . U.S. SIGNS MUTUAL DEFENSE TREATY WITH NATIONALIST CHINA . . . SENATE VOTES TO CONDEMN MCCARTHY FOR CONTEMPT OF SENATE.

Quotes

WELCH: . . . You were asked for something different from the thing that hung on Schine's wall?

JULIANA: I never knew what hung on Schine's wall. . . .

WELCH: Did you think this [picture] came from a pixie? . . .

MCCARTHY *(interrupting):* Will counsel for my benefit define—I think he might be an expert on that—what a pixie is?

WELCH: Yes. I should say, Mr. Senator, that a pixie is a close relative of a fairy.
— Army-McCarthy hearings

"Have you left no sense of decency?"
— Joseph Welch to Senator Joseph McCarthy

"The doctrine of 'separate but equal' has no place [in public education]. . . . Separate facilities are inherently unequal."
— Supreme Court Decision, *Brown* v. *Board of Education of Topeka*

"[The U.S. needs a] deterrent of massive retaliatory power, . . . a great capacity to retaliate instantly by means and at times of our own choosing."
— Secretary of State John Foster Dulles

Ads

In 13,000 B.C. smart women wore nothing. In 1954 A.D. smart women wear nothing but seamless stockings by Hanes.
(Hanes Hosiery)

I feel I've got nothing on . . . when I'm in a Scandale by True Balance.
(True Balance Undergarments)

Looking for trouble? Wear "See Red" . . . the maddening new lipstick color. . . . And careful—don't start anything you can't finish.
(Max Factor)

Suddenly, everyone's drinking vodka.
(Smirnoff)

Now you can eat the sweets you like . . . and stop worrying about cavities.
(Ipana)

Here's spaghetti sauce with meat—the way Italians make it.
(Franco-American canned spaghetti)

"The average American male stands five feet nine inches . . . 158 pounds, prefers brunettes, baseball, beefsteak, and French fried potatoes, and thinks the ability to run a home smoothly and efficiently is the most important quality in a wife. [The average American woman] . . . is five feet four, weighs 132, [and] can't stand an unshaven face."
— *Reader's Digest*

"College women in general have greater difficulty in marrying. . . . Men still want wives who will bolster their egos rather than detract from them."
— Paul H. Landis, *Your Marriage and Family Living*

(Left) Howdy Doody and "Buffalo Bob" Smith, who first aired in 1947, remain a popular afternoon babysitter. *Billy Rose Theatre Collection. The New York Public Library at Lincoln Center. Astor, Lenox and Tilden Foundations.*

(Right) Lucille Ball (and her husband Desi Arnaz) in "I Love Lucy" move CBS ratings ahead of NBC for the first time. *Billy Rose Theatre Collection. The New York Public Library at Lincoln Center. Astor, Lenox and Tilden Foundations.*

How to Keep Warm in a Turkish Bath One way is to set fire to a library. The Turks tried it in 642 A.D. when . . . the Caliph Omar burned the world's greatest library at Alexandria using its precious manuscripts to heat the Turkish baths. Knowledge is a precious commodity, easily lost through man's indifference or carelessness.
(Rand McNally)

Many Happy Returns.
(IBM Electric Typewriters)

TV

Premieres

"Father Knows Best," Robert Young, Jane Wyatt
"Private Secretary," Ann Sothern
"The Jimmy Durante Show"
"People Are Funny," Art Linkletter
"Disneyland/Walt Disney"
"Lassie," George Cleveland
"The Secret Storm"
"The George Gobel Show"
"Producer's Showcase" ("State of the Union," Nina
    Foch, Joseph Cotten, Margaret Sullavan)
"The Loretta Young Show"
"Stop the Music," Bert Parks

Top Ten (Nielsen)

"I Love Lucy," "The Jackie Gleason Show,"
"Dragnet," "You Bet Your Life," "The Toast of the
Town," "Disneyland," "The Jack Benny Show,"
"The Martha Raye Show," "The George Gobel
Show," "Ford Theatre"

Specials

"Twelve Angry Men" (Robert Cummings); "Babes in
Toyland" (Jack E. Leonard, Wally Cox); "Crime in
the Streets" (Reginald Rose, with John Cassavetes);
"Naughty Marietta" (Alfred Drake, Patrice Munsel);
"Macbeth" (Judith Anderson); "Christmas Carol"
(Fredric March); "Visit to a Small Planet" (Gore
Vidal); "The Petrified Forest" (Humphrey Bogart,
Henry Fonda, Lauren Bacall); "Scenes from South
Pacific" (Mary Martin, Ezio Pinza); "McCarthy
Hearings"; "Satins and Spurs" (Betty Hutton)

Emmy Awards

"U.S. Steel Hour" (drama); "Make Room for
Daddy" (situation comedy); "Disneyland" (variety);
"Stories of the Century" (action); "Lassie"
(children); "This Is Your Life" (game); Danny
Thomas (actor, "Make Room for Daddy"); Loretta
Young (actress, "The Loretta Young Show"); John
Daly (news); George Gobel (personality)

Movies

Openings

On the Waterfront (Elia Kazan), Marlon Brando,
    Karl Malden, Eva Marie Saint, Lee J. Cobb
The Country Girl (George Seaton), Bing Crosby,
    Grace Kelly, William Holden
The Caine Mutiny (Edward Dmytryk), Humphrey
    Bogart, Van Johnson, José Ferrer
Seven Brides for Seven Brothers (Stanley Donen),
    Howard Keel, Jane Powell
Three Coins in the Fountain (Jean Negulesco),
    Clifton Webb, Dorothy McGuire, Jean Peters,
    Louis Jourdan, Rossano Brazzi
Rear Window (Alfred Hitchcock), James Stewart,
    Grace Kelly
Sabrina (Billy Wilder), Humphrey Bogart, Audrey
    Hepburn, William Holden
A Star Is Born (George Cukor), Judy Garland, James
    Mason
The Barefoot Contessa (Joseph L. Mankiewicz), Ava
    Gardner, Humphrey Bogart
Bad Day at Black Rock (John Sturges), Spencer
    Tracy, Robert Ryan
Dial M for Murder (Alfred Hitchcock), Ray Milland,
    Grace Kelly
La Strada (Federico Fellini), Giulietta Masina,
    Anthony Quinn
Mr. Hulot's Holiday (Jacques Tati), Jacques Tati
The Wild One (Laslo Benedek), Marlon Brando

Beat the Devil (John Huston), Humphrey Bogart,
    Jennifer Jones, Gina Lollobrigida
Doctor in the House (Ralph Thomas), Dirk Bogarde,
    Kenneth More
Pather Panchali (Satyajit Ray), Subir Banerji
Diabolique (Henri-Georges Clouzot), Simone
    Signoret, Veral Clouzot
The Seven Samurai (Akira Kurosawa), Toshiro
    Mifune

Academy Awards

Best Picture: *On the Waterfront*
Best Director: Elia Kazan *(On the Waterfront)*
Best Actress: Grace Kelly *(The Country Girl)*
Best Actor: Marlon Brando *(On the Waterfront)*

Top Box-Office Stars

John Wayne, Dean Martin and Jerry Lewis, Gary
Cooper, James Stewart, Marilyn Monroe, Alan Ladd,
William Holden, Bing Crosby, Jane Wyman, Marlon
Brando

Stars of Tomorrow

Audrey Hepburn, Maggie McNamara, Grace Kelly,
Richard Burton, Pat Crowley, Guy Madison, Suzan
Ball, Elaine Stewart, Aldo Ray, Cameron Mitchell

Popular Music

Hit Songs

"The Man That Got Away"
"Three Coins in the Fountain"
"Teach Me Tonight"
"Young and Foolish"
"Hernando's Hideaway"
"Cara Mia"
"If I Give My Heart to You"
"Mambo Italiano"
"Steam Heat"
"Papa Loves Mambo"
"Shake, Rattle, and Roll"
"Let Me Go, Lover"

Top Records

Albums: *Music for Lovers Only* (Jackie Gleason); *Selections from "The Glenn Miller Story"* (Glenn Miller); *The Student Prince* (Mario Lanza); *Songs for Young Lovers* (Frank Sinatra); *Music, Martinis, and Memories* (Jackie Gleason)

Singles: *Sh-boom* (Chords, Crew Cuts); *Rock around the Clock* (Bill Haley and the Comets, best-selling single to date); *Little Things Mean a Lot* (Kitty Kallen); *Hey, There* (Rosemary Clooney); *Wanted* (Perry Como); *Oh! My Pa-Pa* (Eddie Fisher); *Young at Heart* (Frank Sinatra). Country: *I Don't Hurt Anymore* (Hank Snow); *More and More* (Webb Pierce)

Jazz and Big Bands

J. J. Johnson and Kai Winding form a trombone-duo-lead quartet. Joe Williams joins Count Basie. The Miles Davis quintet includes John Coltrane; Art Blakey's Jazz Messengers include Horace Silver and Kenny Dorham. Hard bop, or "soul jazz," "gospel jazz," and "funky jazz," gain a following in reaction to the cool style. Sonny Rollins's *Oleo* gains wide interest. The Newport Jazz Festival begins.

Top Performers (*Downbeat*): Stan Kenton (soloist); Kenton, Les Brown (bands); Dave Brubeck (jazz group); Johnny Smith, Ray Brown, Shelly Manne, Charlie Parker, Chet Baker (instrumentalists); Ella Fitzgerald, Frank Sinatra (vocalists); Four Freshman (vocal group)

Theater

Broadway Openings

Plays

The Caine Mutiny Court Martial (Herman Wouk), Henry Fonda, John Hodiak, Lloyd Nolan
The Bad Seed (Maxwell Anderson), Nancy Kelly, Patty McCormack, Eileen Heckart
Witness for the Prosecution (Agatha Christie), Patricia Jessel, Frances L. Sullivan
Ondine (Jean Giraudoux), Audrey Hepburn, Mel Ferrer
Anastasia (Marcelle Maurette), Viveca Lindfors, Eugenie Leontovich
The Rainmaker (N. Richard Nash), Geraldine Page, Darren McGavin
The Immoralist (Ruth and Augustus Goetz), Geraldine Page, Louis Jourdan, James Dean
The Flowering Peach (Clifford Odets), Menasha Skulnik, Janice Rule
The Confidential Clerk (T. S. Eliot), Ina Claire, Douglas Watson, Claude Rains, Joan Greenwood

Musicals

The Pajama Game (Richard Adler, Jerry Ross), John Raitt, Janis Paige, Eddie Foy, Jr., Carol Haney
The Boy Friend, (Sandy Wilson), Julie Andrews
Fanny (Harold Rome), Ezio Pinza, Walter Slezak, Florence Henderson
Peter Pan (Mark Charlap, Carolyn Leigh), Mary Martin, Cyril Ritchard
The Golden Apple (Jerome Moross, John Latouche), Kay Ballard
The Threepenny Opera (Kurt Weill, Marc Blitzstein), Lotte Lenya, Scott Merrill

Classics and Revivals On and Off Broadway

A Midsummer Night's Dream, Stanley Hollaway, Robert Helpmann, Moira Shearer; *What Every Woman Knows* (James Barrie), Helen Hayes; *The Seagull* (Chekhov), Judith Evelyn, George Voskovic, Maureen Stapleton, Montgomery Clift

Regional

Founded: Milwaukee Repertory Theater Company by Mary John and Charles McCallum; the Front Street Theatre of Memphis; the Dallas Theater Center by Paul Baker

Pulitzer Prize

The Teahouse of the August Moon, John Patrick

Tony Awards

The Teahouse of the August Moon, John Patrick (play); *Kismet*, Alexander Borodin, Robert Wright, George Forest (musical)

Classical Music _____

Compositions
Edgard Varèse, *Déserts*
Ralph Shapey, Concerto for Clarinet with Six
    Instruments
Walter Piston, Symphony no. 5
Wallingford Riegger, Variations for Piano and
    Orchestra
Samuel Barber, *Souvenirs*

Important Events
Toscanini retires; Fritz Reiner spends his first year
with the Chicago Symphony; Enrique Jorda conducts
the San Francisco, Josef Krips, the Buffalo.
International exchanges continue: the
Concertgebouw travels through the United States.
Most frequently performed modern European
composers are Prokofiev, Stravinsky, and Bártok;
most frequently performed Americans include
Barber, Copland, Piston, and Gould.

Debuts: Mieczyslaw Horszowski, Andre Watts

First Performances
Stravinsky, Septet (Dumbarton Oaks); *Three Songs
for William Shakespeare, Four Russian Peasant
Songs, In Memoriam: Dylan Thomas* (Los Angeles);
Roy Harris, Symphonic Fantasy (Pittsburgh);
Charles Ives, *Washington's Birthday* (New York);
Alan Hovhaness, Piano Concerto no. 5 (New York);
Ernst Krenek, Cello Concerto (Los Angeles); Ernest
Bloch, *War no. 4* (Lenox, Mass.); David Diamond,
Ahavah (Washington, D.C., to celebrate the 300th

Watts Tower, Los Angeles. *Roger Whitehouse.*

Niccola Rosi-Lemeni and Maria Callas in *Norma*. Callas,
who became a public personality because of her
tempestuous personality and her love affair with Aristotle
Onassis, turns down an offer from the Metropolitan and
makes her American debut in Chicago. *Chicago Lyric
Opera.*

anniversary of the first Jew in America); Samuel
Barber, *Prayers of Kierkegaard* (Boston); Walter
Piston, Fantasy for English Horn, Strings, and Harp
(Boston); Ernest Bloch, Concerto Grosso no. 2
(Boston)

Opera

Metropolitan: Nicola Rossi-Lemeni, *Boris
Godunov;* Ettore Bastianini, *Aïda;* Richard Tucker,
Andrea Chenier

New York City: *The Tender Land* (Aaron Copland),
The Saint of Bleecker Street (Gian Carlo Menotti);
The Trial (Gottfried Von Einem), premieres

Chicago: Carol Fox founds the Lyric Opera, with
Lawrence V. Kelly and Nicola Rescigno. "Calling
Card" performance of *Don Giovanni;* Maria Callas
(debut), *Norma, Lucia di Lammermoor;* Leopold
Simoneau, Tito Gobbi, *Il barbiere di Siviglia*

San Francisco: *The Portuguese Inn* (Cherubini,
premiere); *Joan of Arc at the Stake* (Arthur
Honegger, first full production); *Carmina Burana*
(Carl Orff, premiere)

Music Notes
For their 100th anniversary Steinway & Sons sponsor
a charity concert at Carnegie Hall with dozens of
pianists performing together: one Chopin Polonaise is
played on ten pianos • Paul Hindemith receives the
distinguished Sibel Award ($35,000).

Art

Painting

Jackson Pollock, *White Light*
Mark Tobey, *Canals*
William Baziotes, *Congo, Flame*
Jasper Johns, *Flag*
Franz Kline, *Third Avenue*
Mark Rothko, *Earth and Green*
Edward Hopper, *Morning Sun*
Robert Motherwell, *Elegy to the Spanish Republic* (1953–54)
Robert Rauschenberg, *Charlene, Collection*
Stuart Davis, *Colonial Cubism*
Charles Sheeler, *Architectural Cadences*
Grace Hartigan, *Grand Street Brides*
Philip Guston, *Painting*

Sculpture

Sam Rodia, *Watts Towers* (1921–54)
Milton Hebald, *Convalescent Returns*
Reuben Nakian, *The Emperor's Bedroom*
The Iwo Jima Monument is dedicated at Washington, D. C.

Architecture

Oasis House, Ojai, Calif. (Richard Neutra)
First United Methodist Church, Midland, Mich. (Alden B. Dow)
Manufacturer's Hanover Bank, New York (Skidmore, Owings, and Merrill)
Bubble Prefab Houses, Hobe Sound, Fla. (Eliot Noyes)

Cincinnati: The Peale painters

San Francisco: Dufy

Minneapolis: Reality and fantasy

New Orleans: Sesquicentennial of Louisiana Purchase: 22 Louisiana Works

Chicago: Three expatriates: Sargent, Whistler, Cassatt; "Designer-Craftsmen, U.S.A"; Masterpieces of religious art

Venice Biennale: de Kooning, Shahn, Lachaise, Smith, Lassaw represent the United States

Art Briefs

The Metropolitan Museum of Art opens 44 renovated galleries with 700 masterpieces from the 13th to the 20th century • Major sales include Matisse's *Odalisque* ($75,000), which sold in 1930 for $25,000; Cézanne's *Baigneurs et Baigneuses* ($10,000); Grant Wood's charcoal study for *Daughters of the American Revolution* ($2,800).

Important Exhibitions

Museums

New York: *Metropolitan:* "Art 1754–1954" (to celebrate Columbia University's bicentennial); The Lehman collection; Masterpieces of Pre-Columbian gold; Ancient art of the Andes; Art of three expatriates—Sargent, Whistler, Cassatt; Dutch painting. *Museum of Modern Art:* Spencer retrospective; Vuillard; 25th-anniversary retrospective of modern art. *Whitney:* Grosz retrospective. *Guggenheim:* "Young European Painters," "Younger American Painters"

Toledo: Dutch painting

Boston: American arts of the 18th and early 19th centuries; Masterpieces from ancient civilizations; John Marin memorial

Philadelphia: The newly acquired Walter Arensberg collection; van Gogh

Indianapolis: Mannerism

Dance

Paul Taylor forms his own company.
The Robert Joffrey Ballet debuts with *Pas des déesses, Le Bal Masques*; the 25th anniversary of Diaghilev's death is commemorated throughout the ballet world.

Premieres

New York City Ballet: *Western Symphony* (George Balanchine), Diana Adams, Jacques d'Amboise; *Opus 34, Nutcracker, Ivesiana* (Balanchine), Adams, Francisco Moncion

Alvin Ailey: *House of Flowers*

Martha Graham: *Night Journey*

Ballet Theatre: *A Streetcar Named Desire* (Valerie Bettis)

Books

Fiction

Critics' Choice

The Goose on the Grave, John Hawkes

The Bird's Nest, Shirley Jackson

A Spy in the House of Love, Anaïs Nin

The Ponder Heart, Eudora Welty

The Dollmaker, Harriette Arnow

Cress Delahanty, Jessamyn West

The Tunnel of Love, Peter De Vries

🦢 *The Fellowship of the Ring*, J. R. R. Tolkien

🦢 *Lord of the Flies*, William Golding

Best-Sellers

Not as a Stranger, Morton Thompson

Mary Anne, Daphne Du Maurier

Love Is Eternal, Irving Stone

The Royal Box, Frances Parkinson Keyes

The Egyptian, Mika Waltari

No Time for Sergeants, Mac Hyman

Sweet Thursday, John Steinbeck

The View from Pompey's Head, Hamilton Basso

Never Victorious, Never Defeated, Taylor Caldwell

Benton's Row, Frank Yerby

Nonfiction

Critics' Choice

The Verbal Icon, Monroe C. Beardsley, W. K. Wimsatt

A Child of the Century, Ben Hecht

Realities of American Foreign Policy, George F. Kennan

The China Tangle, Herbert Feis

Call to Greatness, Adlai E. Stevenson

The American Presidency, Sidney Hyman

The Future of Architecture, Frank Lloyd Wright

Individualism Reconsidered, David Reisman

Freedom, Loyalty, Dissent, Henry Steele Commager

McCarthy and His Enemies, William F. Buckley, L. Brent Bozell

McCarthy and the Communists, James Rorty, Moshe Decter

Best-Sellers

The Holy Bible: Revised Standard Version

The Power of Positive Thinking, Norman Vincent Peale

Better Homes and Gardens New Cook Book

Betty Crocker's Good and Easy Cook Book

The Tumult and the Shouting, Grantland Rice

I'll Cry Tomorrow, Lillian Roth, Gerold Frank, Mike Connolly

The Prayers of Peter Marshall, ed. Catherine Marshall

This I Believe, 2d, ed., Raymond Swing

But We Were Born Free, Elmer Davis

Poetry

Louise Bogan, *Collected Poems 1923–1953*

E. E. Cummings, *Poems 1923–1954*

Robinson Jeffers, *Hungerfield and Other Poems*

W. S. Merwin, *The Dancing Bears*

William Carlos Williams, *The Desert Music and Other Poems*

Anthony Hecht, *A Summoning of Stones*

Weldon Kees, *Poems 1947–1954*

Leonie Adams, *Collected Poems*

Pulitzer Prizes

A Fable, William Faulkner (fiction)

Great River, the Rio Grande in North American History, Paul Horgan (U.S. history)

The Taft Story, William S. White (biography)

Collected Poems, Wallace Stevens

Nobel Prize

Ernest Hemingway

Science and Technology

Jonas Salk begins inoculation of schoolchildren in Pittsburgh; 900,000 children are eventually vaccinated nationwide.

A kidney transplant patient survives a record five months.

Vincent Du Vigneaud synthesizes two important pituitary hormones, oxytocin and vasopressin.

More resilient hybrid wheats are developed, based on wheat genetics work by Ernest Sears.

An electronic analog computer capable of mathematical logic is demonstrated at Princeton.

Bell Telephone Labs develop a solar battery.

The Boeing 707, the first jet-powered transport, is tested.

The first atomic-powered submarine, USS *Nautilis*, is commissioned at Groton, Conn.

An atomic-powered railway locomotive is developed at Utah University.

Nobel Prize

John F. Enders, Thomas H. Weller, and Frederick C. Robbins share the prize in physiology and medicine for their work in the cultivation of a polio virus.

Linus C. Pauling wins in chemistry for the study of forces holding together protein and other molecules.

Sports

Baseball

The Cleveland Indians win a record 111 games led by pitchers Bob Lemon, Early Wynn, Mike Garcia and Bob Feller.

Henry Aaron (Milwaukee-NL) debuts.

Stan Musial (St. Louis, NL) hits a record five home runs in a doubleheader.

Joe Adcock (Milwaukee, NL) hits four home runs and a double in one game.

Champions

Batting	Pitching
Willie Mays (New York, NL), .345	John Antonelli (New York, NL), 21–7
Bob Avila (Cleveland, AL), .341	Sandy Consuegra (Chicago, AL), 16–3
	Home runs
	Ted Kluszewski (Cincinnati, NL), 49

Football

Adrian Burk (Philadelphia) throws a record-tying seven touchdown passes in one game.

NFL Season Leaders: Norm Van Brocklin (Los Angeles), passing; Joe Perry (San Francisco), rushing; Pete Pihos (Philadelphia), receiving.

College All-Americans: Ralph Guglielmo (B), Notre Dame; Howard Cassady (B), Ohio State; Alan Ameche (B), Wisconsin.

Bowls (Jan. 1, 1955)

Rose: Ohio State 20– Southern California 7	Cotton: Georgia Tech 14–Arkansas 6
Orange: Duke 34– Nebraska 7	Sugar: Navy 21– Mississippi 0

Basketball

The NBA institutes the 24-second clock.

NBA All-Pro First Team: Neil Johnston (Philadelphia), Bob Cousy (Boston), Ed Macauley (Boston), George Mikan (Minneapolis), Ray Felix (Baltimore)

Other Sports

Running: Roger Bannister, of England, runs the mile in 3:59.4, the first under four minutes.

Racing: Bill Vukovich wins his second straight Indianapolis 500.

Tennis: Pancho Gonzales makes a comeback and defeats Pancho Segura and Frank Sedgman in round-robin matches.

Winners

World Series	*College Basketball*
New York (NL) 4	Kentucky
Cleveland (AL) 0	*Player of the Year*
MVP	Tom Gola, LaSalle
NL–Willie Mays, New York	*Stanley Cup*
AL–Yogi Berra, New York	Detroit
NFL	*US Tennis Open*
Cleveland 56–Detroit 10	Men: Tony Trabert
College Football	Women: Doris Hart
Ohio State	*USGA Open*
Heisman Trophy	Ed Furgol
Alan Ameche, Wisconsin	*Kentucky Derby*
NBA Championship	Determine (R. York,
Minneapolis 4–Syracuse 3	jockey)

Fashion

For Women: If Dior gave women curves in 1947, this year he rescinded them. The new look is the "H" with deemphasized bosom (necessitating a new lingerie line) and a straighter, longer silhouette, accented at the hips with low belts, sashes, and cuffs. The "costume ensemble" is also new: matched or blended dresses and coats, suits and overblouses. Jackets of various lengths include the long "skyscraper" worn with the hip-length pullover. Coats are flared from the shoulder, in ¾ or ⅞ lengths. The jumper is also popular, along with shorter slacks, again worn with sweaters that fall over the hip. A new interest appears in furs — sable, fox, leopard, and mink (for trim and full wear)—and the rope necklace of various beads and stones, as well as pearls. Of note, a silken shimmer covers most fabrics, even textured and flecked materials. Synthetics, like "miracle orlon," are enormously successful. The most popular casual clothes are the shirtwaist, worn with wide cinched belt, the off-the-shoulder top with ¾-length slacks, Bermuda shorts, and hooded shirts.

High-fashion notes: Dior's H-line; Balenciaga's "semi-fit" (close in front, straight in back)

Kaleidoscope ──────────

Senator Joseph McCarthy attacks the democratic party for "20 years of treason." *Library of Congress.*

- President Eisenhower modifies the Pledge of Allegiance from "one nation indivisible" to "one nation, under God, indivisible."
- The Supreme Court declares that membership in the Communist party is sufficient grounds for deportation of aliens.
- Televised Army-McCarthy hearings make Army counsel Joseph Welch a popular hero; McCarthy's repeated interruptions "point of order" and "Mr. chairman, Mr. chairman" cost him public support.
- "This is no time for men who oppose Senator McCarthy's methods to keep silent," says Edward R. Murrow on his prime-time "See It Now" show.
- Seventy-eight percent of Americans polled think it important to report to the FBI relatives or acquaintances suspected as Communists.
- Alan Freed, paid $75,000 a year, plays what he calls "rock 'n' roll" on radio station WINS, which becomes number one in only a few months.
- The first color TV sets are marketed for $1,000 (RCA).
- The Toledo Water Commission notes strange intervals of increased usage and discovers they coincide with TV commercials.
- Twenty million horror books are sold a month; there are more "deaths" portrayed on TV than occurred (of Americans) in the Korean War.
- A noticeable interest develops in group membership and mass culture; industrial workers, farmers, and businessmen join organizations in record numbers.
- One in ten households is headed by women, who number 21 million in the nation's 64 million workers.
- Although he is attacked by critics, Wladziu Valentino Liberace becomes a TV sensation with his candelabras, soft lights, and wide smiles.
- Jimmy Durante's famed nose is injured as it is accidentally caught under pianist Liberace's piano during a TV rehearsal.
- J. Robert Oppenheimer becomes controversial when the AEC calls him "loyal" but a "security risk" and guilty of "lack of enthusiasm."
- A record $3,135,000,000 is spent in new construction.
- Gas prices rise from 21 cents (1944) to 29 cents.
- The AEC thermonuclear tests at Bikini Atoll wound 31 Americans, 236 natives, and 23 Japanese fishermen. The United States offers an $800,000 indemnity.
- The AEC denies charges that its experiments were responsible for the death of 1,000 sheep in Utah.
- The Tobacco Industry Research Committee reports there is "no proof . . . that cigarette smoking is a cause of lung cancer."
- The public is alerted to the dangers of radioactive wastes.
- The Davy Crockett episodes on TV's "Disneyland" initiate a national mania for Davy Crockett products.
- Elvis Presley makes his first commercial recording and signs with RCA to promote "Elvis, the Pelvis."
- San Francisco's City Lights Bookshop becomes a gathering place for the beat generation and poets like Allen Ginsberg and Lawrence Ferlinghetti.
- The raccoon look describes the heavy eye makeup that "beat" girls wear; 10 million cakes of Max Factor pancake makeup are sold.
- There are 154 Americans with annual incomes of over $1 million (513 in 1929).
- Marilyn Monroe and Joe DiMaggio are married on January 14; they file for divorce October 5.
- A Gallup Poll reports that a family of four can live on $60 a week and that 94 percent of the population believes in God.
- Salvador Dali sues Mrs. William Woodward for $7,000, "the value of his services"; she walked away from her portrait "scared," as though she were "walking away from a monster."
- Miltown and Equanil, brands of the tranquilizer meprobamate, are marketed; sales are high.
- Mississippi voters approve a constitutional amendment to abolish public schools if there is no other way to avoid segregation.
- For the first time a senator is elected by write-in vote: Strom Thurmond, South Carolina.

New Words and Usages: Cat music, massive retaliation, desegregation, windfall profit, crazy pants, do-it-yourself, dragster, fall-out, goof, hard sell, hotline, hairy, greaser, hip, togetherness, cool (acceptable), bread (money)

Fads: Felt skirts with poodle appliques, "grape" jokes, the mambo, the "creep," raffles, bingo, "droodles," panty raids, roller skating marathons, flattops and crew cuts, the "ducktail" haircut.

First Appearances: Gas turbine car and bus, verified bridge hand, in which each player is dealt a perfect hand, automatic toll collector (Garden State Parkway, N.J.), newspaper vending machine, electric computers in business, Fontainebleau (Miami, Fla.); Ohrbach's (34th St., New York), Statler-Hilton Hotels, Inc., Studebaker-Packard Corp., Mercedes 300 SL with fuel injection, New York's Chemical Bank; cha-cha, U.S. Air Force Academy, Shakey's Pizza Parlors, Veterans' Day (replacing Armistice Day), F-100 Supersabre (supersonic fighter), Trix, Frozen TV brand dinners (turkey, sweet potatoes, peas), breath-inhaler alcoholism detector, check cashing with ID camera, vacation houseboy (light), wrist radio, language translating machine, Levi's faded blue denims, "Marmeduke"

1955

Facts and Figures

Economic Profile
  Dow-Jones: ↑ High 488–
    Low 391
  GNP: +9%
  Inflation: −0.3%
  Unemployment: 4.4%
Infant mortality/1,000: 26.0
Maternal mortality/10,000:
  4.1
Physicians in U.S.: 214,000
Dentists in U.S.: 95,000
Hospital beds: 1,604,000
Air France, New York–Nice:
  $520 (round trip)
National Airlines, New York–
  Havana: $176.50 (round
  trip)
Budapest String Quartet
  (Kaufman auditorium, New
  York City): $2–3
New York City Center: $3.60
LP records: $3.98
Annie Oakley cowgirl outfit:
  $4.90
"Morgan" stuffed animal:
  $2.95
English bike: $47.50
Croquet set: $12.98
Gimbel's professional ice
  skates: $17.95

Deaths

Theda Bara, Lionel
  Barrymore, Albert
  Einstein, Enrico Fermi,
  Alexander Fleming,
  Cordell Hull, Fernand
  Léger, Thomas Mann,
  Carmen Miranda, Charlie
  Parker

In the News

CONGRESS AUTHORIZES PRESIDENT TO USE FORCE TO DEFEND FORMOSA . . . U.S. BEGINS AID TO INDOCHINA WITH $216 MILLION . . . NIKITA KHRUSHCHEV BECOMES PARTY SECRETARY, MALENKOV IS OUSTED FOR "DEVIATION" . . . WEST GERMANY ENTERS NATO . . . 8 EASTERN EUROPEAN COUNTRIES SIGN WARSAW TREATY OF MUTUAL DEFENSE . . . IKE SAYS A-BOMB WOULD BE EMPLOYED IN WAR . . . SUPREME COURT ORDERS SCHOOL SEGREGATION TO END "IN REASONABLE TIME" . . . AFRO-ASIAN CONFERENCE MEETS AT BANDUNG . . . BIG FOUR MEET IN GENEVA, IKE PROPOSES MUTUAL AERIAL RECONNAISSANCE . . . CHINESE ANNOUNCE RELEASE OF 11 U.S. AIRMEN . . . REVOLTS CONTINUE IN MOROCCO AND ALGERIA, 2,200 DIE . . . GENERAL MOTORS SPLITS 3 FOR 1 . . . WEST GERMANY AND RUSSIA AGREE TO DIPLOMATIC RELATIONS . . . MILITARY OUSTS JUAN PERON IN ARGENTINA . . . IKE SUFFERS HEART ATTACK IN COLORADO, MARKET PLUNGES $14 BILLION . . . UN VOTES TO TAKE UP ALGERIA, FRANCE WALKS OUT . . . BAO DAI IS OUSTED, SOUTH VIETNAM PROCLAIMS REPUBLIC . . . JAMES DEAN, 24, DIES IN CAR CRASH . . . ISRAEL ATTACKS SYRIA IN RETALIATION FOR SHELLING . . . FORD FOUNDATION TO GIVE $500 MILLION TO COLLEGES . . . INTERSTATE COMMERCE COMMISSION BANS SEGREGATION ON INTERSTATE TRAINS AND BUSES . . . AFL AND CIO MERGE, GEORGE MEANY BECOMES PRESIDENT . . . KHRUSHCHEV CRITICIZES AERIAL INSPECTION PLAN AND ATTACKS COLONIALISM.

Quotes _____

"It's nice to be included in people's fantasies, but you also like to be accepted for your own sake."
— Marilyn Monroe

"Ah just act the way ah feel."
— Elvis Presley

"Sincerity is the quality that comes through on television."
— Richard M. Nixon

"Recognition of the Supreme Being is the first, the most basic, expression of Americanism. Without God, there could be no American form of government, nor American way of life."
— Dwight D. Eisenhower

"The south stands at Armageddon. . . . We cannot make the slightest concession to the enemy in this dark and lamentable hour of struggle. There is no more difference in compromising the integrity of race on the playing field than in doing so in the classroom."
— Governor Marvin Griffin, Georgia, on the Supreme Court *Brown* decision (1954)

Ads _____

He was a first-name kind of guy. He was everybody's kind of guy. . . . He was God's kind of guy.
(*film* A Man Called Peter)

Boys and Girls! Join the Davy Crockett Club at Bullock's Downtown—To qualify for the Davy Crockett Club, you need courage and common sense, an adventurous spirit and the will to succeed. Come to Bullock's . . . and get your . . . badge at no cost."
(*Bullock's Department Store, Los Angeles*)

Is there an angel in the house?—Give her a fabulous cherry colored nylon tricot gown.
(*Kayser*)

Our doubts are traitors,
And make us lose the good we oft might win,
  By fearing to attempt.—Shakespeare, *Measure for Measure*
(*Container Corp. of America*)

How you gonna keep 'em away from the farm after they've seen this machine?
(*New Departure Ball Bearings*)

Jackie Gleason, Art Carney, Audrey Meadows, and Joyce Randolph in "The Honeymooners." "The Great One," Gleason, signs for 78 episodes but decides to stop after 39. *Movie Star News*.

Popular singer Eddie Fisher and popular actress Debbie Reynolds form what fan magazines call "a perfect union."

James Dean and Natalie Wood in *Rebel without a Cause*. Dean also stars in *East of Eden*. In both, he plays a sensitive young man not understood by parental figures. *Movie Star News*.

More Jobs Through Science
(*Union Carbide and Carbon*)

TV

Premieres

"The Lawrence Welk Show"
"The $64,000 Question," Hal March
"The Millionaire," Marvin Miller
"The Alcoa Hour"
"Gunsmoke," James Arness (first adult western)
"The Honeymooners," Jackie Gleason, Art Carney, Audrey Meadows, Joyce Randolph
"You'll Never Get Rich [Sergeant Bilko]," Phil Silvers
"The Life and Legend of Wyatt Earp," Hugh O'Brien
"Alfred Hitchcock Presents"
"Captain Kangaroo," Bob Keeshan
"The Mickey Mouse Club," The Mouseketeers, Annette Funicello

Top Ten (Nielsen)

"The $64,000 Question," "I Love Lucy," "The Ed Sullivan Show," "Disneyland," "The Jack Benny Show," "December Bride," "You Bet Your Life," "Dragnet," "The Millionaire," "I've Got a Secret"

Specials

"Patterns" (Rod Serling, with Ed Begley, Richard Kiley); "A Catered Affair" (Paddy Chayefsky); "Our Town" (musical, Frank Sinatra, Paul Newman, Eva Marie Saint); "The Caine Mutiny Court Martial" (Lloyd Nolan); "A-Bomb Test Coverage"; "Davy Crockett and the River Pirates" on "Disneyland"; "Promenade" (Tyrone Power, Judy Holliday, Janet Blair); "Tosca" (Leontyne Price); "She Stoops to Conquer" (Michael Redgrave)

Emmy Awards

"Producer's Showcase" (drama); "Phil Silvers' You'll Never Get Rich" (comedy); "Ed Sullivan Show" (variety); "Disneyland" (action); "Lassie" (children); "The $64,000 Question" (game); Phil Silvers (actor, "You'll Never Get Rich"); Lucille Ball (actress, "I Love Lucy"); Edward R. Murrow (news)

Of Note

CBS passes NBC to become number one for the first time • "The Honeymooners" ends after 39 episodes.

Movies

Openings

Marty (Delbert Mann), Ernest Borgnine, Betsy Blair
The Rose Tattoo (Daniel Mann), Burt Lancaster, Anna Magnani
East of Eden (Elia Kazan), James Dean, Julie Harris
Rebel without a Cause (Nicholas Ray), James Dean, Sal Mineo, Natalie Wood
To Catch a Thief (Alfred Hitchcock), Cary Grant, Grace Kelly
The Blackboard Jungle (Richard Brooks), Glenn Ford, Sidney Poitier, Vic Morrow
Love Is a Many-Splendored Thing (Henry King), Jennifer Jones, William Holden
Mister Roberts (John Ford, Mervyn LeRoy), Henry Fonda, James Cagney, Jack Lemmon
Picnic (Joshua Logan), William Holden, Kim Novak
Love Me or Leave Me (Charles Vidor), James Cagney, Doris Day
The Man with the Golden Arm (Otto Preminger), Frank Sinatra, Eleanor Parker
I'll Cry Tomorrow (Daniel Mann), Susan Hayward
Guys and Dolls (Joseph L. Mankiewicz), Marlon Brando, Jean Simmons
The Bridges at Toko-Ri (Mark Robson), William Holden, Grace Kelly
Oklahoma! (Fred Zinnemann), Gordon McRae, Shirley Jones
The Night of the Hunter (Charles Laughton), Robert Mitchum, Lillian Gish
It's Always Fair Weather (Stanley Donen, Gene Kelly), Grace Kelly, Dan Dailey, Cyd Charisse
Smiles of a Summer Night (Ingmar Bergman), Ulla Jacobsson, Eva Dahlbeck

Academy Awards

Best Picture: *Marty*
Best Director: Delbert Mann (*Marty*)
Best Actress: Anna Magnani (*The Rose Tattoo*)
Best Actor: Ernest Borgnine (*Marty*)

Top Box-Office Stars

James Stewart, Grace Kelly, John Wayne, William Holden, Gary Cooper, Marlon Brando, Dean Martin and Jerry Lewis, Humphrey Bogart, June Allyson, Clark Gable

Stars of Tomorrow

Jack Lemmon, Tab Hunter, Dorothy Malone, Kim Novak, Ernest Borgnine, James Dean, Anne Francis, Richard Egan, Eva Marie Saint, Russ Tamblyn

Popular Music

Hit Songs

"The Ballad of Davy Crockett"
"Dance with Me, Henry"
"Cherry Pink and Apple Blossom
   White"
"Domani"
"Whatever Lola Wants"
"Cry Me a River"
"Love and Marriage"
"Love Is a Many-Splendored
   Thing"
"Moments to Remember"

Top Records

Albums: *Crazy Otto* (Crazy
Otto); *Starring Sammy Davis, Jr.*
(Sammy Davis, Jr.); *Lonesome
Echo* (Jackie Gleason); *Love Me
or Leave Me* (Doris Day)

Singles: *The Yellow Rose of
Texas* (Mitch Miller); *Sixteen Tons*
(Tennessee Ernie Ford); *Tweedle
Dee* (Georgia Gibbs); *Mr.
Sandman* (Chordettes); *Ain't It a
Shame* (Fats Domino); *Maybelline*
(Chuck Berry); *Earth Angel*
(Penguins); *I've Got a Woman*
(Ray Charles); *Unchained Melody*
(Roy Hamilton); *Everyday* (Count
Basie); *Only You* (The Platters).
Country: *Loose Talk* (Carl Smith);
Cattle Call (Eddy Arnold)

Jazz and Big Bands

First Recordings: Cannonball
Adderley

Top Performers (*Downbeat*):
Charlie Parker (soloist); Count
Basie, Les Brown (bands);
Modern Jazz Quartet (jazz group);
Erroll Garner, Max Roach, Paul
Desmond, Milt Jackson, Stan
Getz, Gerry Mulligan, J. J.
Johnson, Miles Davis
(instrumentalists); Ella Fitzgerald,
Frank Sinatra, Joe Williams
(vocalists); Four Freshmen (vocal
group).

Theater

Broadway Openings

Plays

Cat on a Hot Tin Roof (Tennessee Williams), Barbara
   Bel Geddes, Burl Ives, Pat Hingle, Mildred
   Dunnock
Inherit the Wind (Jerome Lawrence, Robert E. Lee),
   Ed Begley, Paul Muni, Tony Randall
The Lark (Jean Anouilh), Boris Karloff, Julie Harris,
   Christopher Plummer
Tiger at the Gates (Jean Giraudoux), Michael
   Redgrave, Leueen MacGrath, Leo Ciceri
The Matchmaker (Thornton Wilder), Robert Morse,
   Arthur Hill, Ruth Gordon, Eileen Herlie
Bus Stop (William Inge), Kim Stanley, Albert Salmi
The Diary of Anne Frank (Frances Goodrich, Albert
   Hackett), Joseph Schildkraut, Susan Strasberg
No Time for Sergeants (Ira Levin), Andy Griffith,
   Roddy McDowall
The Desperate Hours (Joseph Hayes), Paul Newman,
   George Grizzard, Karl Malden
A View from the Bridge (Arthur Miller), Van Heflin,
   Jack Warden, Eileen Heckart
The Chalk Garden (Enid Bagnold), Gladys Cooper,
   Siobhan McKenna
A Hatful of Rain (Michael V. Gasso), Ben Gazzara,
   Anthony Franciosa, Shelley Winters
The Dark Is Light Enough (Christopher Fry), Tyrone
   Power, Katharine Cornell, Christopher Plummer

Musicals

Damn Yankees (Richard Adler, Jerry Ross), Gwen
   Verdon, Stephen Douglass, Ray Walston

Plain and Fancy (Albert Hague, Arnold B. Horwitt),
   Shirl Conway, Richard Derr
Silk Stockings (Cole Porter), Hildegarde Neff, Don
   Ameche

Classics and Revivals On and Off Broadway
The Skin of Our Teeth (Thornton Wilder), Helen
Hayes, Mary Martin, George Abbott; *Six Characters
in Search of an Author* (Luigi Pirandello), Kurt
Kasznar

Regional

Founded: American Shakespeare Theatre,
Stratford, Conn., by Lawrence Langner: *Julius
Caesar, The Tempest,* Raymond Massey, Jack
Palance, Roddy McDowall, Christopher Plummer,
Fritz Weaver; Second City, Chicago

Dallas Theater Center: *Hamlet,* Burgess Meredith

Pulitzer Prize
Cat on a Hot Tin Roof, Tennessee Williams

Tony Awards
The Desperate Hours, Joseph Hayes (play); *The
Pajama Game,* Richard Adler, Jerry Ross (musical)

Classical Music

Compositions

Ross Lee Finney, Quartet
Ernest Toch, Symphony no. 3
Milton Babbitt, Two Sonnets
John Cage, Music for Piano
H. Owen Reed, *Michigan Dream*

Debuts: Glenn Gould, Emil Gilels, Lorin Hollander, David Oistrakh, Alicia de Larrocha, Geza Anda

First Performances

Walter Piston, Symphony no. 5 (Boston); Edgard Varèse, *Déserts* (Bennington, Vt.); Heitor Villa-Lobos, Symphony no. 18 (Philadelphia), Cello Concerto (New York); Howard Hanson, Symphony no. 5, *Sinfonia Sacra* (Philadelphia); Leonard Bernstein, Serenade (Boston); Arthur Honegger, *A Christmas Cantata* (Boston); Roy Harris, *Symphonic Epigram* (New York); Sergei Prokofiev, Suite of Waltzes (Cincinnati); Darius Milhaud, Symphony no. 8.

Opera

Porgy and Bess is the first American opera to be performed at La Scala. Lukas Foss's *Gruffelkin* is commissioned for TV.

Metropolitan: Marian Anderson (debut), *Un Ballo in Maschera;* Renata Tebaldi (debut), *Otello,* Risë Stevens, *Orfeo ed Euridice;* Richard Tucker, Roberta Peters, Zinka Milanov, Marian Anderson, Leonard Warren, *Un ballo in Maschera; Arabella* (Richard Strauss, premiere)

New York City: *The Golden Slippers* (Tchaikovsky), *Troilus and Cressida* (William Walton)

Indiana University: *The Ruby* (Norman Dello Joio, premiere)

Florida State University: *Susannah* (Carlisle Floyd, premiere)

Chicago: Maria Callas, *I Puritani;* Renata Tebaldi, *Aïda;* triple bills: *Il tabarro, Il ballo delle ingrate, The Merry Widow,* and *Cavalleria rusticana, Lord Byron's Love Letter,* and *Revanche.*

San Francisco: Robert Weede, Inge Borkh, *Macbeth;* Elisabeth Schwarzkopf, Licia Albanese, Cesare Siepi, *Don Giovanni*

Music Notes

Eugene Ormandy and the Philadelphia Symphony Orchestra is officially sent abroad to exemplify the breadth of American culture • The Berlin Philharmonic gives its first concert in Washington, D.C., as the State Department rejects protests of musicians' unions that von Karajan is an ex-Nazi.

Nat "King" Cole. From Montgomery, Alabama, Cole is the first jazz-grounded male voice since Louis Armstrong to gain world wide fame. *Movie Star News.*

Glenn Gould, famous for his brilliant interpretations of Bach and his keyboard mannerisms, such as reduced use of pedal and a nearly horizontal piano posture. *Movie Star News.*

Art

Painting
Morris Graves, *Flight of Plover*
Robert Rauschenberg, *Satellite*
Larry Rivers, *Double Portrait of Birdie*
Hans Hofmann, *Exuberance*
Jasper Johns, *Flag, Target with Four Faces*
Robert Motherwell, *Je t'aime, IIA*
Philip Guston, *The Room* (1954–55)
William Baziotes, *The Beach, Pompeii*
Helen Frankenthaler, *Blue Territory*

Sculpture
Louise Nevelson, *Black Majesty*
Richard Stankiewicz, *Gross Bathers, Kabuki Dancer*
Sidney Gordin, *Construction, No. 10*

Louise Bourgeois, *One and Others*
Raoul Hague, *Sawkill Walnut*

Architecture
Connecticut General Life Insurance Company Building, Bloomfield, Conn. (Skidmore, Owings, and Merrill)
Socony-Mobil Building, New York (Harrison and Abramovitz)
H. C. Price Tower, Bartlesville, Okla. (Frank Lloyd Wright)
MIT Chapel, Kresge Auditorium (Eero Saarinen)
Under construction: $17 million Walt Disney Amusement Park, Anaheim, Calif.; $35 million New York Coliseum; $18 million Los Angeles County Courthouse.

Important Exhibitions
Loan shows include over 100 Goyas from Spain (at the National, Metropolitan, San Francisco, Los Angeles, Boston); 70 Dutch paintings of the 17th century and French drawings from the Louvre (at the Metropolitan and Toledo).

Museums

New York: *Metropolitan:* The Comédié Française and the theatre in France; Art of the Hebrew tradition; Persian and Assyrian art. *Museum of Modern Art:* 22 contemporary Europeans; Tanguy; de Chirico. *Whitney:* 35 contemporary Americans; Levine and Bloom. *Guggenheim:* Giacometti; Brancusi retrospective

Washington: Renaissance prints by Lucan van Leyden; Austrian drawings and prints; German drawings of five centuries

Chicago: French drawings from the 14th to the 19th century; Japanese prints

National, Cleveland, San Francisco, Fogg: German old masters

Los Angeles, San Francisco: Renoir

Cleveland: Chinese landscapes

Boston: Matisse bronzes and drawings; Sport in art

Pasadena: The blue four: Jawlensky, Kandinsky, Klee, Feininger

Art Briefs
Edward Steichen assembles "The Family of Man" show at the Museum of Modern Art • Major sales include Soutine's *The Old Mill near Cannes* ($20,500) and Cézanne's *The Water Can* ($19,000).

Dance

Chicago Opera Ballet debuts, founded by Ruth Page; New York City Ballet tours Europe; Ballet Theatre visits South America; Sadler's Wells, Royal Danish, and several Spanish companies tour the United States.

Premieres

New York City Ballet: *Pas de Dix* (George Balanchine), Maria Tallchief, André Eglevsky

George Balanchine, distinguished for his modern productions and the famous statement: "Ballet is woman." Balanchine was married to Tamara Geva, Vera Zorina, Maria Tallchief, and Tanaquil LeClerq. *Library of Congress.*

Books

Fiction

Critics' Choice

The Recognitions, William Gaddis
The Deer Park, Norman Mailer
A Charmed Life, Mary McCarthy
Lolita, Vladimir Nabokov
A Good Man Is Hard to Find, Flannery O'Connor
Satan in Goray, Isaac Bashevis Singer
Band of Angels, Robert Penn Warren
The Simple Truth, Elizabeth Hardwick
Sincerely, Willis Wayde, John P. Marquand
☙ *Cards of Identity*, Nigel Dennis

Best-Sellers

Marjorie Morningstar, Herman Wouk
Auntie Mame, Patrick Dennis
Andersonville, MacKinlay Kantor
Bonjour Tristesse, Françoise Sagan
The Man in the Gray Flannel Suit, Sloan Wilson
Something of Value, Robert Ruark
Not as a Stranger, Morton Thompson
No Time for Sergeants, Mac Hyman
The Tontine, Thomas B. Costain
Ten North Frederick, John O'Hara

Nonfiction

Critics' Choice

The Scrolls from the Dead Sea, Edmund Wilson
The Armed Vision, Stanley Edgar Hyman
A Democrat Looks at His Party, Dean Acheson
The African Giant, Stuart Cloete
Notes of a Native Son, James Baldwin
The Life and Work of Sigmund Freud, Ernest Jones
Dylan Thomas in America, John Malcolm Brinnin
An End to Innocence, Leslie Fiedler
The Strange Career of Jim Crow, C. Vann Woodward
Black Power, Richard Wright
American in Italy, Herbert Kubly

Best-Sellers

Gift from the Sea, Anne Morrow Lindbergh
The Power of Positive Thinking, Norman Vincent Peale
The Family of Man, Edward Steichen
A Man Called Peter, Catherine Marshall
How to Live 365 Days a Year, John A. Schindler
Better Homes and Gardens Diet Book

The Secret of Happiness, Billy Graham
Why Johnny Can't Read, Rudolf Flesch
Inside Africa, John Gunther
Year of Decisions, Harry S Truman

Poetry

W. H. Auden, *The Shield of Achilles*
Gregory Corso, *The Vestal Lady on Brattle*
Adrienne Rich, *The Diamond Cutters and Other Poems*
A. R. Ammons, *Ommateum*
Howard Nemerov, *The Salt Garden*
William Carlos Williams, *Journey to Love*
Lawrence Ferlinghetti, *Pictures of a Gone World*

Pulitzer Prizes

Andersonville, MacKinlay Kantor (fiction)
The Age of Reform; From Bryan to FDR, Richard Hofstadter (U.S. history)
Benjamin Henry Latrobe, Talbot F. Hamlin (biography)
Poems: North and South—A Cold Spring, Elizabeth Bishop (poetry)

Science and Technology

Retrolental fibroplasia, which causes childhood blindness, is associated with high doses of oxygen usually given premature babies.

An oral contraceptive ("the pill") made of a progesterone-type substance is discovered by Gregory Pincus.

The steroid prednisone is introduced.

Thorazine and reserpine are found effective for severe mental illness.

Albert Sabin, at the University of Cincinnati, says he believes a live virus anti-polio vaccine to be more effective than the dead one (Salk's).

RNA- and DNA-like molecules are synthesized by Severo Ochoa of New York University.

Experiments with "anti-protons" that annihilate protons on contact are reported.

The AEC reports that fallout from last year's H-bomb tests at Bikini will affect human life in a 7,000-square-mile area.

The U.S. Army announces that German rocket pioneer Herman Oberth will join 100 others in missile research at Redstone Arsenal, Alabama.

Nobel Prize

Polykarp Kusch and Willis E. Lamb, Jr., win the prize in physics for atomic measurements. Vincent Du Vigneaud wins in chemistry for work on pituitary hormones.

Sports

Baseball

The Brooklyn Dodgers win the first ten games of the season and go on to win their first World Series, over the Yankees.

Champions

Batting
  Richie Ashburn (Philadelphia, NL), .338
  Al Kaline (Detroit, AL), .340

Pitching
  Don Newcombe (Brooklyn, NL), 20–5
  Tommy Byrne (New York, AL), 16–5
Home runs
  Willie Mays (New York, NL), 51

Football

Otto Graham (QB), Cleveland, retires.
Johnny Unitas (QB), Baltimore, a free agent pickup, debuts.

NFL Season Leaders: Otto Graham (Cleveland), passing; Alan Ameche (Baltimore), rushing; Pete Pihos (Philadelphia), receiving

College All-Americans: Tommy McDonald (B), Oklahoma; Paul Hornung (B), Notre Dame

Bowls (Jan. 1, 1956)

Rose: Michigan State 17–UCLA 14
Orange: Oklahoma 20–Maryland 6
Cotton: Georgia Tech 7–Pittsburgh 0
Sugar: Mississippi 14–Texas Christian 13

Basketball

NBA All-Pro First Team: Neil Johnston (Philadelphia), Paul Arizin (Philadelphia), Bob Cousy (Boston), Bob Pettit (Milwaukee), Larry Foust (Fort Wayne)

Other Sports

Horse Racing: Nashua, ridden by Willie Hartack, wins the Preakness and Belmont.

Boxing: Sugar Ray Robinson comes out of retirement to knock out Bobo Olson and win the middleweight title for the third time.

Winners

World Series
  Brooklyn (NL) 4
  New York (AL) 3
MVP
  NL–Roy Campanella, Brooklyn
  AL–Yogi Berra, New York
NFL
  Cleveland 38–Los Angeles 14
MVP
  Harlon Hill, Chicago Bears
College Football
  Oklahoma
Heisman Trophy
  Howard Cassady, Ohio State

NBA Championship
  Syracuse 4–Fort Wayne 3
College Basketball
  San Francisco
Player of the Year
  Bill Russell, San Francisco
Stanley Cup
  Detroit
US Tennis Open
  Men: Tony Trabert
  Women: Doris Hart
USGA Open
  Jack Fleck
Kentucky Derby
  Swaps (W. Shoemaker, jockey)

Fashion

For Women: Twenties' "siren simplicity" combines with the French empire style to create an unusual blend of willowy and youthful sexiness. The sheath is semifitted and beltless, and it emphasizes a long bodice and high bosom; hips remain rounded. Dior and Balenciaga introduce the Oriental tunic and semifitted coat and jacket worn with a straight tube dress or narrow skirt. Sari silks and Indian/Persian brocades and silks also appear in unusual color combinations: pink-orange, green-peacock blue, red-black. Jeweled jackets also gain popularity. For more formal wear, long evening gowns return with long, tight sleeves, high fronts, and low backs; the World War I wrap-around dance dress also returns. The market for at-home fashions grows: tapered satin, velvet, brocade pants with decorative sweaters or satin tops. Brilliant colors are everywhere, especially reds, emerald greens, and sapphire blues. College girls wear black leotards, tweed jumpers, camel-hair and gray coats; blazers appear in new, boldly contrasting stripes.

High-fashion notes: Balenciaga's black tunic with black fox collar and shoulder "flying panel"; Dior's A-line

For Men: The continental influence begins to be felt in sports clothes—cotton jersey pullovers, bateau necklines, lower cut, more flexible shoes, and moccasin slip-ons.

Kaleidoscope ————

An H-bomb shelter in Garden City, Long Island. *Library of Congress.*

- Revlon buys "The $64,000 Question" and begins TV's big quiz era. Marine Corps Captain Richard S. McCutchen wins $64,000 by identifying the seven courses served King George and his guests in 1939; Joyce Brothers wins $64,000 but then misses on Sugar Ray Robinson's welterweight victory.
- Weekly church attendance is 49 million adults, half the total adult population.
- Wayne Morse, of Oregon, is the first senator to move from one party to another when he becomes a Democrat.
- Construction of suburban shopping centers and motels increases.
- Over 3.8 million people play golf on approximately 5,000 courses.
- Altman's department store, in New York, sells mink-handled can openers; a Beverly Hills shop offers 14k gold charge cards.
- Ira Hayes, Pima Indian and one of the six who raised the flag on Iwo Jima, dies of exposure and alcoholism.
- After an eight-month marriage, stripteaser Anita Manville wins a $400,000 settlement from Tommy Manville; she was his ninth wife.
- Richard J. Daley becomes mayor of Chicago.
- HEW Secretary Oveta Culp Hobby opposes free distribution of the Salk vaccine to poor children as "socialized medicine . . . by the back door."
- Twenty-five women scarred in the Hiroshima A-bomb blast arrive in New York for free plastic surgery.
- Walter Winchell tips audiences that Pentepec Oil is a good stock; those who follow his advice lose 21 percent.
- Eddie Fisher and Debbie Reynolds marry.
- Dior, Fath, Lanvin, and Patou sue U.S. manufacturers for "dress piracy."
- The U.S. Information Agency changes its address from 1778 to 1776 Pennsylvania Avenue.
- A campaign is launched to cultivate European interest in American culture and lessen the publicity of American scandals. The State Department sends to France Judith Anderson in *Medea, Oklahoma, The Skin of Our Teeth;* Balanchine and the New York City Ballet; Eugene Ormandy and the Philadelphia Orchestra; and an exhibit of 50 years in American art.
- "Pop art" gains attention with Robert Rauschenberg's *Bed,* which incorporates a real pillow and quilt on a stretcher, along with other objects and design materials.
- At its peak *Confidential* magazine has a circulation of 4.5 million readers.
- The population explosion creates a shortage of 120,000 teachers and 300,000 schoolrooms.
- "Smog," or "poisoned air," becomes a public concern.
- J. Edgar Hoover turns down mayor Wagner's $25,000-a-year offer to be New York City police commissioner.
- Textron American is incorporated as the first business conglomerate.

- The first TV presidential press conference occurs on January 19.
- The minimum wage goes up from 75 cents to $1.
- Richard Byrd is greeted by pickets in Dallas that read: "Little America [Antarctica] Needs the Little Woman" in response to his comment: "No woman has ever set foot on Little America, . . . the most silent and peaceful place in the world."
- Jackie Gleason applies to the U.S. Patent Office for "And away we go."

New Words and Usages: Automated, certified mail, junk mail, rock-and-roll, A-line, atomic rain, Thorazine, church key, cue card, one-take, bombed, stoned, isolation booth, blast off, har-dee-har, passion pit, Third World

Fads: Davy Crockett hats, books, and T-shirts; pink shirts; charcoal gray suits; mooning; raccoon coats; stuffing people into a car; pizza (replacing hamburger snacks); the new games of Chuggedy Chug, Annie-Oakley, Uncle Wiggley, Chutes and Ladders; Tutti-Frutti; Maybelline; driving around

First Appearances: Ten-story display ad on Times Square, plastic containers for shipping, polyglot typewriters, Disneyland (Anaheim, Calif.), army male nurse (E. L. T. Lyon), woman flying faster than the speed of sound (Jacqueline Cochran), sun-powered auto demonstration, auto seat belt safety law (Illinois), solar-heated and radiator-cooled house (Phoenix), element 101, electric stove for home use, commercial telephone using electricity generated by the sun's rays, Nieman-Marcus (Houston), Merengue (dance), Eden Roc (Miami Beach, Fla.), Crest, Gorton's Fish Sticks, Special K, Colonel Sanders' Kentucky Fried Chicken, New York alternate side of the street parking, Ford Thunderbird (two-seater), Karmann-Ghia, Long Island Expressway, Tappan Zee Bridge, "Ann Landers Says," "Dondi," Chase Manhattan Bank, First National City Bank, Sperry-Rand, H & R Block, Dreyfus Fund, *National Review, Village Voice,* Whirlpool, roll-on deodorant, Revlon "no-smear" Lanolite lipstick

1956

In the News

AUTHERINE LUCY, FIRST BLACK AT UNIVERSITY OF ALABAMA, IS SUSPENDED AFTER RIOTS . . . KHRUSHCHEV, AT 20TH PARTY CONGRESS, ASSAILS STALIN AS TERRORIST, EGOTIST, AND MURDERER . . . 11 BLACKS ARE ARRESTED DURING MONTGOMERY BUS BOYCOTT . . . SIX MARINE RECRUITS ARE DROWNED DURING A MARCH AT PARRIS ISLAND, S.C. . . . MOROCCO GAINS INDEPENDENCE . . . NGO DIEM IS ELECTED PRESIDENT OF SOUTH VIETNAM . . . TUNISIA GAINS INDEPENDENCE . . . GRACE KELLY MARRIES PRINCE RAINIER OF MONACO . . . KHRUSHCHEV SAYS RUSSIA WILL PRODUCE AN ICBM . . . COLUMNIST VICTOR RIESEL IS BLINDED BY ACID ATTACK . . . ADLAI STEVENSON IS RENOMINATED BY DEMOCRATS, IKE BY GOP . . . IKE UNDERGOES SURGERY FOR ILEITIS . . . BRITAIN LEAVES SUEZ AFTER 74 YEARS . . . UNITED DC-7 AND TWA SUPERCONSTELLATION CRASH OVER GRAND CANYON, 128 DIE . . . U.S. AND BRITAIN WITHDRAW ASWAN DAM AID FROM EGYPT . . . "ANDREA DORIA" SINKS AFTER COLLISION WITH "STOCKHOLM," 50 ARE DEAD, 1,652 ARE SAVED . . . SALK VACCINE GOES ON THE OPEN MARKET . . . 33-DAY STEEL STRIKE ENDS . . . NATIONAL GUARD IS CALLED OUT FOR ANTI-BLACK RIOTING AT CLINTON, TENNESSEE, HIGH SCHOOL . . . LABOR RIOTS ARE QUELLED IN POLAND, KHRUSHCHEV ATTACKS LIBERALIZATION . . . ANTI-SOVIET DEMONSTRATIONS IN HUNGARY ARE SUPPRESSED, HUNGARIANS REVOLT . . . EGYPT AND ISRAEL CLASH, GAZA STRIP FALLS TO ISRAEL . . . SOVIET FORCES CRUSH HUNGARIAN REVOLT . . . IKE WINS LANDSLIDE VICTORY, 36 MILLION TO 26 MILLION . . . FRENCH AND BRITISH LAND IN SUEZ, ISRAEL TAKES SINAI, IKE URGES THAT ALL WITHDRAW . . . U.S. EMERGENCY FORCE IS SENT TO SINAI . . . BUS SEGREGATION IN MONTGOMERY, ALABAMA, ENDS.

Senator Estes Kefauver, campaigning for the presidential nomination in a popular style of the day. *Copyright Washington Post. Reprinted courtesy D.C. Library.*

Quotes

"History is on our side. We will bury you!"
— Nikita Khrushchev, to Western ambassadors at Kremlin reception

"Of all the accomplishments of the American woman, the one she brings off with the most spectacular success is having babies."
— *Life* magazine

"[The U.S. and USSR] are like two scorpions in a bottle, each capable of killing the other but only at the risk of his own life. . . . The atomic clock ticks faster and faster."
— J. Robert Oppenheimer

"Nonviolence is the most potent technique for oppressed people. Unearned suffering is redemptive."
— Martin Luther King, Jr.

"I intend to continue not to be angry or bear ill will to anyone."
— Autherine Lucy, expelled from the University of Alabama

"Many unconsciously wondered if they deserved better conditions. Their minds were so conditioned to segregation that they submissively adjusted to things as they were. This is the ultimate tragedy of segregation."
— Martin Luther King, Jr.

"The ability to get to the verge without getting into war is the necessary art."
— Secretary of State John Foster Dulles, on "brinkmanship"

Nobel Peace Prize winner and Harvard government professor Ralph Bunche and Democratic nominee for president Adlai Stevenson at a breakfast meeting. *Library of Congress.*

Ads

TV

Premieres

"As the World Turns"
"The Edge of Night"
"NBC News—Huntley-Brinkley"
"The Price Is Right," Bill Cullen
"The $64,000 Challenge," Sonny Fox
"Playhouse 90" ("Requiem for a Heavyweight," Jack Palance, Ed Wynn)
"Twenty-One," Jack Barry
"Tic Tac Dough," Jay Jackson
"The Steve Allen Show"

Top Ten (Nielsen)

"I Love Lucy," "The Ed Sullivan Show," "General Electric Theater," "The $64,000 Question," "December Bride," "Alfred Hitchcock Presents," "I've Got a Secret," "Gunsmoke," "The Perry Como Show," "The Jack Benny Show"

Specials

"The Plot to Kill Stalin" (Melvyn Douglas); "Charley's Aunt" (Art Carney); "Tragedy in a Temporary Town" (Reginald Rose); "A Night to Remember" (George Roy Hill); "Composing, Conducting" (Leonard Bernstein); "Born Yesterday" (Paul Douglas, Mary Martin); "High Tor" (Julie Andrews, Bing Crosby); Grace Kelly–Prince Rainier wedding

Emmy Awards

"Requiem for a Heavyweight" (program); "Phil Silvers Show," "Caesar's Hour" (series); "See It Now" (public service); Robert Young, (actor, "Father Knows Best"); Loretta Young (actress, "The Loretta Young Show"); Perry Como, Dinah Shore (personality)

Of Note

"Hillbilly singer" Elvis Presley debuts on "Stage Door," hosted by the Dorsey Brothers • The first of the pre-1948 film sales is made, and *The Wizard of Oz,* with Judy Garland, and *Richard III,* with Laurence Olivier, are aired.

Movies

Openings

Around the World in Eighty Days (Lindsay Anderson), David Niven, Shirley MacLaine, Cantinflas
The King and I (Walter Lang), Yul Brynner, Deborah Kerr
War and Peace (King Vidor), Audrey Hepburn, Mel Ferrer, Henry Fonda
Giant (George Stevens), Rock Hudson, James Dean, Elizabeth Taylor
Friendly Persuasion (William Wyler), Gary Cooper, Dorothy McGuire, Anthony Perkins
The Ten Commandments (Cecil B. De Mille), Charlton Heston, Yul Brynner, Anne Baxter
Lust for Life (Vincente Minnelli), Kirk Douglas, Anthony Quinn
Anastasia (Anatole Litvak), Ingrid Bergman, Yul Brynner
Baby Doll (Elia Kazan), Carroll Baker, Eli Wallach
Love Me Tender (Robert D. Webb), Elvis Presley
Bus Stop (Joshua Logan), Marilyn Monroe, Don Murray
The Searchers (John Ford), John Wayne, Natalie Wood, Jeffrey Hunter
High Society (Charles Walters), Frank Sinatra, Louis Armstrong, Bing Crosby, Grace Kelly
Invasion of the Body Snatchers (Donald Siegel), Dana Wynter, Kevin McCarthy
The Seventh Seal (Ingmar Bergman), Max von Sydow, Bibi Andersson
Rififi (Jules Dassin), Jean Servais, Carl Mohner

Academy Awards

Best Picture: *Around the World in Eighty Days*
Best Director: George Stevens (*Giant*)
Best Actress: Ingrid Bergman (*Anastasia*)
Best Actor: Yul Brynner (*The King and I*)

Top Box Office Stars

William Holden, John Wayne, James Stewart, Burt Lancaster, Glenn Ford, Martin and Lewis, Gary Cooper, Marilyn Monroe, Kim Novak, Frank Sinatra

Stars of Tomorrow

Rod Steiger, Jeffrey Hunter, Natalie Wood, Dana Wynter, Tim Hovey, Yul Brynner, George Nader, Joan Collins, Sheree North, Sal Mineo

Popular Music

Hit Songs
"Blue Suede Shoes"
"Friendly Persuasion"
"Hound Dog"
"Love Me Tender"
"Mack the Knife"
"Mr. Wonderful"
"My Prayer"
"The Party's Over"
"Too Close for Comfort"
"You're Sensational"

Top Records

Albums: *Oklahoma* (sound track); *Belafonte* (Harry Belafonte); *Elvis Presley* (Elvis Presley); *My Fair Lady* (original cast); *Calpyso* (Harry Belafonte); *Elvis* (Elvis Presley); *The Eddy Duchin Story* (sound track); *The King and I* (sound track)

Singles: *Que Sera, Sera* (Doris Day); *Moonglow* (Morris Stoloff); *Hot Diggity* (Perry Como); *Wonderful, Wonderful* (Johnny Mathis); *The Great Pretender* (The Platters); *Why Do Fools Fall in Love?* (Teenagers with Frankie Lyman); *On the Street Where You Live* (Vic Damone); *Heartbreak Hotel* (Elvis Presley); *Standing on the Corner* (Four Lads). Country: *Singing the Blues* (Marty Robbins); *Crazy Arms* (Ray Price)

Jazz and Big Bands
Horace Silver forms his own quartet. The first U.S. government–sponsored jazz tour travels to the Near and Middle East.

Top Performers (*Downbeat*): Duke Ellington (soloist); Count Basie, Les Brown (bands); Modern Jazz Quartet (jazz group); Stan Getz, J. J. Johnson, Dizzy Gillespie, Milt Jackson, Bud Shank (instrumentalists); Ella Fitzgerald, Frank Sinatra (vocalists); Four Freshmen (vocal group)

Theater

Broadway Openings

Plays
Middle of the Night (Paddy Chayefsky), Edward G. Robinson, Gena Rowlands
Waiting for Godot (Samuel Beckett), Bert Lahr, E. G. Marshall, Alvin Epstein, Kurt Kasznar
Long Day's Journey into Night (Eugene O'Neill), Fredric March, Florence Eldridge, Bradford Dillman, Katharine Ross, Jason Robards, Jr.
Separate Tables (Terence Rattigan), Margaret Leighton, Eric Portman
The Great Sebastians (Howard Lindsay, Russel Crouse), Alfred Lunt, Lynn Fontanne
Auntie Mame (Jerome Lawrence, Robert E. Lee), Rosalind Russell, Peggy Cass

Musicals
My Fair Lady (Alan Jay Lerner, Frederick Loewe), Julie Andrews, Rex Harrison
The Most Happy Fella (Frank Loesser), Robert Weede, Jo Sullivan, Art Lund
Mr. Wonderful (Jerry Bock), Sammy Davis, Jr. and Sr., Chita Rivera
Li'l Abner (Gene de Paul, Johnny Mercer), Peter Palmer, Edie Adams, Julie Newmar
Bells Are Ringing (Jule Styne, Betty Comden, Adolph Green), Judy Holliday, Sydney Chaplin
Candide (Leonard Bernstein, Richard Wilbur), Robert Rounseville, Barbara Cook

Classics and Revivals On and Off Broadway
King Lear, Orson Welles; *Major Barbara* (George Bernard Shaw), Eli Wallach, Burgess Meredith, Glynis Johns, Charles Laughton; *Saint Joan* (Shaw), Siobhan McKenna; *Troilus and Cressida*, Claire Bloom, Rosemary Harris, John Neville

Regional

American Shakespeare Festival: *King John*, Mildred Dunnock, Arnold Moss; *Measure for Measure*, Moss, Nina Foch; *The Taming of the Shrew*, Foch, Pernell Roberts

Actor's Workshop, San Francisco: *Mother Courage* (Bertolt Brecht), American premiere

Coconut Grove Playhouse, Miami: *Waiting for Godot* (Samuel Beckett, directed by Alan Schneider), Bert Lahr, Alvin Epstein, American premiere

Pulitzer Prize
The Diary of Anne Frank, Frances Goodrich, Albert Hackett

Tony Awards
The Diary of Anne Frank, Frances Goodrich, Albert Hackett (play); *Damn Yankees*, Richard Adler, Jerry Ross (musical)

Classical Music

Compositions

Hugo Weisgall, *Six.Characters in Search of an Author, The Stranger*
Elliott Carter, *Narrations* for Orchestra
Norman Dello Joio, *Mediations on Ecclesiastes*
Vladimir Ussachevsky, A Piece for Tape Recorder
William Schuman, *New England Triptych*
George Rochberg, Sinfonia Fantasy
Igor Stravinsky, *Canticum sacrum*
Lejarin Hiller and L. M. Isaacson, *Illiac* Suite (computer composition)

Important Events

Musical celebrations include Sibelius's 90th birthday; the 50th anniversary of Artur Rubinstein's American debut, the 25th of Lily Pons's Metropolitan debut, and the much-celebrated Mozart bicentennial. Eduard Van Beinum becomes musical director of the Los Angeles Philharmonic.
International exchanges reach a peak: in the United States, the Berlin Philharmonic (Herbert von Karajan); Vienna Philharmonic; Salzburg Mozart Orchestra; Emil Gilels; David Oistrakh; and Mstislav Rostropovich. Americans abroad include Jan Peerce, Isaac Stern, the New Orleans Orchestra, Los Angeles Philharmonic, Juilliard String Quartet, and Robert Shaw Chorale; the Boston Symphony visits the USSR. To celebrate its 50th anniversary, Juilliard commissions work for six concerts from Roger Sessions (Piano Concerto); Peter Mennin (Cello Concerto); David Diamond (*Diaphony*); Roy Harris (*Festival Folk Fantasy*); Walter Piston (Symphony no. 5); and a William Bergsma opera. Artur Rubinstein plays the complete Beethoven and Brahms piano concerti at Carnegie Hall.

First Performances

Heitor Villa-Lobos, conducting, Symphony no. 11 (Boston); Miklós Rósza, Violin Concerto (Dallas); Paul Creston, Symphony no. 5 (Washington, D.C.); Gail Kubik, Symphony no. 2 (Louisville); Norman Dello Joio, *The Trial at Rouen* (NBC Opera); Carlos Chávez, Symphony no. 3 (New York); Darius Milhaud, Symphony no. 7 (Chicago); Ned Rorem, Symphony no. 2 (La Jolla, Calif.); Ernest Toch, Symphony no. 3 (Pittsburgh); Samuel Barber, *The School for Scandal* (New York); Charles Ives, *Robert Browning* (New York); Rolf Libermann, *The School for Wives* (Louisville)

Opera

Metropolitan: Maria Callas's debut in *Norma* grosses a record $75,510.50. Other performances include Mattiwilda Dobbs, *Rigoletto;* Carlo Bergonzi, *Aïda;* Richard Tucker, Renata Tebaldi, *Tosca;* Lisa Della Casa, *Der Rosenkavalier.*

New York City: *The Tempest* (Frank Martin, premiere); *The Moon* (Carl Orff, premiere)

Chicago: Eleanor Steber, *La fanciulla del West;* Inge Borkh, Martha Lipton, Ramon Vinay, *Salomé;* Borkh, Birgit Nilsson, *Die Walküre;* Renata Tebaldi, Jussi Bjoerling, *Tosca*

San Francisco: Debuts: Leonie Rysanek, *Die Walküre;* Boris Christoff, *Boris Godunov;* Eileen Farrell, *Il trovatore*

Central City, Colo.: Beverly Sills (debut), "The Ballad of Baby Doe" (Douglas Moore)

Julie Andrews and Rex Harrison in *My Fair Lady.*

Below: *Waiting for Godot.* Billy Rose Theatre Collection. The New York Public Library at Lincoln Center. Astor, Lenox and Tilden Foundations.

Art

Painting

Georgia O'Keeffe, *Patio with Cloud*

George Tooker, *Government Bureau*

Helen Frankenthaler, *Eden*

Larry Rivers, *George Washington Crossing the Delaware*

Mark Rothko, *Orange and Yellow*

Adolph Gottlieb, *Unstill Life III*

Stuart Davis, *Colonial Cubism*

Franz Kline, *Mahoning*

Philip Guston, *Dial*

Sculpture

Ibram Lassaw, *Procession*

David Smith, *Tanktotem V, Five Spring, History of LeRoy Borton*

Joseph Cornell, *Homage to Blériot*

Louise Nevelson, *First Personage, Royal Voyage*

Leonard Baskin, *Man with a Dead Bird*

Theodore Roszak, *Sea Sentinel*

Important Exhibitions

Museums

New York: *Metropolitan:* British painting 1800–1950; Costumes and decorative arts of Japan; Feininger, Kuhn, Kuniyoshi, Marin, Nordfeldt; Asian artists in crystal. *Museum of Modern Art:* Kirchner; Nolde. *Whitney:* Burchfield; Graves. *Guggenheim:* Brancusi

Kurt Kaznar, E.G. Marshall, Alvin Epstein, and Bert Lahr in *Waiting for Godot,* Samuel Beckett's existential query into friendship, loneliness, and the passage of time. *Billy Rose Theatre Collection. The New York Public Library at Lincoln Center. Astor, Lenox and Tilden Foundations.*

Herbert Ferber, *Sun Wheel*

Architecture

John Olin Library, Washington University, St. Louis (John Hejduk)

Navy Chapel, Miramar, Calif. (Richard Neutra)

Kneses Tifeth Israel Synagogue, Port Chester, N.Y. (Philip Johnson)

Brandeis University Chapel, Waltham, Mass. (Harrison and Abramovitz)

St. Louis Airport (Harrison and Abramovitz)

Crown Hall, Illinois Institute of Technology (Mies van der Rohe)

Graf House, Dallas (Edward Durell Stone)

Frank Lloyd Wright exhibits a design for a mile-high skyscraper, 528 stories.

Chicago: "Louis Sullivan and the Architecture of Free Enterprise"; Toulouse-Lautrec; Design in Scandinavia

Washington: The Kress collection; contemporary German prints; "A Century and a Half of Painting in Argentina"

Boston: Sargent's Boston; German prints; Burchfield watercolors

Minneapolis: Kirchner; Nolde

Houston: "Caribbean International"

Venice Biennale: "[46] American Artists Paint the City," including Marin, Hopper, Davis, Pollock

Art Briefs

"Modern Art in the U.S.," which includes works by Pollock, de Kooning, Rothko, and Kline, is sent by the Museum of Modern Art to the Tate Gallery, London • The National Gallery celebrates its 15th birthday with a "World Masterpieces Show," which 2,250,000 people visit • A canvas purchased in Chicago for $450 is discovered to be a Leonardo valued at $1 million • Frank Lloyd Wright begins construction on the new Guggenheim Museum, New York.

Dance

Jerome Robbins starts his own company, Ballets U.S.A.; Sadler's Wells's *Sleeping Beauty,* on TV, is viewed by 30 million people.

Premieres

New York City Ballet: *Divertimento, No. 15* (George Balanchine, for the Mozart celebration), Diana Adams, Melissa Hayden, Yvonne Mounsey, Nicholas Magallanes; *Allegro Brillante* (Balanchine), Maria Tallchief, Magallanes; *The Still Point* (Bolender), Hayden, Jacques d'Amboise

Alwin Nikolais: *Kaleidoscope*

Paul Taylor: *Three Epitaphs*

Books

Fiction

Critics' Choice

The Floating Opera, John Barth
Seize the Day, Saul Bellow
The Long March, William Styron
The Field of Vision, Wright Morris
Further Fables for Our Time, James Thurber
Comfort Me with Apples, Peter De Vries
Bang the Drum Slowly, Mark Harris
A Walk on the Wild Side, Nelson Algren
The Presence of Grace, J. F. Powers
Giovanni's Room, James Baldwin

Best-Sellers

Don't Go Near the Water, William Brinkley
The Last Hurrah, Edwin O'Connor
Peyton Place, Grace Metalious
Auntie Mame, Patrick Dennis
Eloise, Kay Thompson
Andersonville, MacKinlay Kantor
A Certain Smile, Françoise Sagan
The Mandarins, Simone de Beauvoir
The Tribe That Lost Its Head, Nicholas Monsarrat
Boon Island, Kenneth Roberts

Nonfiction

Critics' Choice

Testament of a Liberal, Albert Guérard
The Meaning of Yalta, John F. Snell
The Permanent Purge: Politics in Soviet Totalitarianism, Zbigniew Brezinski
Conservatism in America, Clinton Rossiter
The Power Elite, C. Wright Mills
The Art of Loving, Erich Fromm
Form and Idea in Modern Theatre, John Gassner
The Case for Modern Man, Charles Frankel
Freud and the Crisis of Our Culture, Lionel Trilling
Eros and Civilization, Herbert Marcuse
The Crucial Decade: America 1945–1955, Eric F. Goldman
American Politics in a Revolutionary World, Chester Bowles

Best-Sellers

Arthritis and Common Sense, Dan Dale Alexander
Webster's New World Dictionary of the English Language, Concise ed., ed. David B. Guralnik
Betty Crocker's Picture Cook Book
Etiquette, Frances Benton
Better Homes and Gardens Barbecue Book
The Search for Bridey Murphy, Morey Bernstein
Love or Perish, Smiley Blanton
The Nun's Story, Kathryn Hulme
How to Live 365 Days a Year, John A. Schindler
Better Homes and Gardens Decorating Book

Poetry

Donald Hall, *Exiles and Marriages*
John Ashbery, *Some Trees*
John Berryman, *Homage to Mistress Bradstreet*
Marianne Moore, *Like a Bulwark*
Elizabeth Bishop, *Poems*
Allen Ginsberg, *Howl*

Pulitzer Prizes

No prize is awarded in fiction.
Russia Leaves the War, George F. Kennan (U.S. history)
Profiles in Courage, John F. Kennedy (biography)
Things of This World, Richard Wilbur (poetry)

Science and Technology

Albert Sabin announces the development of three types of oral polio vaccine, which, together, will produce long-term immunity.

Techniques of hemodialysis, blood purification on an artificial kidney machine, are pioneered.

Wendell Stanley, at the University of California, reports the chemical creation of a virus capable of reproduction.

The DNA molecule is photographed.

The "neutrino," a particle of no electrical charge, is observed at Los Alamos.

The first photos of the birth of stars are taken.

The first American test rocket for sending a manmade satellite into orbit ascends 125 miles at 4,000 m.p.h.

James Pritchard, of the Chicago Divinity School, unearths biblical Gibeon, where the "sun stood still."

Nobel Prize

John Bardeen, Walter Brattain, and William Shockley win the prize in physics for work in the development of the electronic transistor. D. W. Richards, Jr., and André Cournand win in physiology and medicine for work in treating heart disease.

Sports

Baseball

Don Larsen (New York, AL) pitches the first perfect game in a World Series. The Cy Young Award, honoring the best major league pitcher, begins; Don Newcombe (Brooklyn, NL) is the first winner.

Champions

Batting	Pitching
Hank Aaron (Milwaukee, NL), .328	Don Newcombe (Brooklyn, NL), 27–7
Mickey Mantle (New York, AL), .340	Whitey Ford (New York, AL), 19–6
	Home runs
	Mickey Mantle (New York, AL), 52

Football

NFL Season Leaders: Ed Brown (Chicago), passing; Rick Casares (Chicago), rushing; Billy Wilson (San Francisco), receiving

College All-Americans: Jim Brown (B), Syracuse; Ron Kramer (E), Michigan; Alex Karras (G), Iowa

Bowls (Jan. 1, 1957)

Rose: Iowa 35–Oregon State 19	Cotton: Texas Christian 28–Syracuse 27
Orange: Colorado 27–Clemson 21	Sugar: Baylor 13–Tennessee 7

Basketball

Bill Russell, Boston, debuts.

NBA All-Pro First Team: Bob Pettit (St. Louis), Paul Arizin (Philadelphia), Neil Johnston (Philadelphia), Bill Cousy, Bill Sharman (Boston)

Olympics

At the Melbourne Summer Games, U.S. winners include Bobby Morrow (100m, 10.5s and 200m, 20.6s.), Glenn Davis (400mh, 50.1s.), Charley Dumas (high jump, 6'11¼"), Parry O'Brien (16 lb. shotput, 60'11"), Al Oerter (discus, 184'11"), Harold Connolly (16 lb. hammer, 207'3½"), Milton Campbell (decathlon), Patricia McCormick (diving, 2). In the Winter Games at Cortina D'Ampezzo, Italy, Tenley Albright wins figure skating.

Other Sports

Winners

World Series	*NBA Championship*
New York (AL) 4	Philadelphia 4–Fort
Brooklyn (NL) 3	Wayne 1
MVP	*MVP*
NL–Don Newcombe, Brooklyn	Bob Pettit, St. Louis
AL–Mickey Mantle, New York	*College Basketball* San Francisco
NFL	*Player of the Year*
New York 47–Chicago Bears 7	Bill Russell, San Francisco
MVP	*Stanley Cup* Montreal
Frank Gifford, New York	*US Tennis Open*
College Football Oklahoma	Men: Ken Rosewall Women: Shirley Fry
Heisman Trophy	*USGA Open* Cary Middlecoff
Paul Hornung, Notre Dame	*Kentucky Derby* Needles (D. Erb, jockey)

Fashion

For Women: *My Fair Lady* and late Edwardian decor influence fashion. Emphasis is on both flowing and clinging fabrics, ribbons, and feathers; the long-legged figure is created through long drapery, a high waistline, and sashes or belts under the bosom. Bloused backs and low-backed bodices give a "slouch" to the profile. Hair is swept up in a pompadour or chignon; capes and big hats become popular.

High-fashion notes: Dior's sac dress, the PVC (vinyl-coated raincoat); Chanel's quilted shoulder bag with intertwined gold metal, Rose Marie Reid's elasticized swimsuit with wide shorts and contrasting color trim at the top

For Men: Many boys wear crew cuts ("flattops") and "fabulous" dirty, white bucks, pants and bermudas with buckles on the back. Unlike these boys—"bananas," "weenies," and "yo-yos"—the "greasers," "skids," and "rocks" wear ducktail haircuts, black leather jackets, and T-shirts. The college boy chooses either the button-down "ivy" look or pegged pants, padded shoulders, and the newly popular and colorful Hawaiian shirts. Madison Avenue will soon be filled with young men in gray flannel suits, pink shirts, skinny bow or pink and black striped ties.

Kaleidoscope —————

- Ed Sullivan vows never to allow Elvis Presley's vulgar performance on his TV show; he later pays Presley $50,000 for three appearances; the last is televised only from the waist up.
- Boston religious leaders urge the banning of rock 'n' roll; a Connecticut psychiatrist calls rock a "communicable disease."
- William Whyte describes how corporations force their officers to toe the company line in his popular *The Organization Man*.
- Increasing numbers of lower-middle-class people move to the suburbs; colleges actively recruit from the middle classes.
- Eleanor Roosevelt receives the First Woman of Valor award.
- Clark Gable and Yul Brynner refuse to play Stalin in a projected movie.
- Mickey Hargitay, Mr. Universe, is KO'ed during a press conference in Mae West's dressing room.
- Artur Rubinstein calls Neil Sedaka the best high school pianist he has heard and gives him a Juilliard scholarship.
- Marilyn Monroe and Arthur Miller marry on June 29; she wears a sweater and skirt; he, a blue linen suit, white shirt, and no tie; on July 2, a rabbi performs a religious ceremony.
- European autos gain popularity, such as the Volkswagen, TR-2, Jaguar, Ferrari, Hillman Minx, Saab, Mercedes, Citroen, and Fiat.
- Golda Myerson, former Milwaukee schoolteacher, becomes the Israeli prime minister and accepts Premier Ben-Gurion's suggestion that she hebraize her name to Meir.
- Jean Seberg, daughter of an Iowa druggist, is selected from 18,000 applicants to play Joan of Arc in a movie.
- Disc jockey Jean Shepperd promotes as "turbulent" and "tempestuous" a nonexistent book, "I Libertine," which a month later he and Theodore Sturgeon write.
- The ex-Mrs. Adlai Stevenson, Ellen Borden, announces that she will vote for Eisenhower.
- Nat "King" Cole is knocked down by six white men on a Birmingham, Alabama, stage because they protest his appearance.
- Audiences find movies so expensive ($2 in New York, $1.50 in Los Angeles) that they stay home and watch TV.
- Seventeen recordings of "The Ballad of Davy Crockett" are made; Estes Kefauver campaigns in a coonskin cap.
- Harry Belafonte's "Jamaica Farewell" begins a widespread interest in calypso.
- The last Union veteran of the Civil War, Albert Woolson, dies; he was a drummer boy at seventeen.
- Oxford University confers the doctorate of civil law honorary degree on Harricum Truman.
- Eleven percent of all cars sold are station wagons; airlines carry as many passengers as railroads.
- Drive-in theaters multiply to 7,000 in number.
- "The sum and substance of it all is that God and I are

Arthur Miller and Marilyn Monroe, who met while she was studying acting in New York with Lee and Paula Strasberg. *Movie Star News*.

tired of men taking advantage of women," says Beatrice Adams, who runs her car over her 300-pound boyfriend several times until a passerby rips out the car's ignition wires.
- Procter & Gamble produces disposable Pampers after it discovers that women change babies' diapers 25 billion times a year.
- Ford Motor Company goes public and sells over 10 million shares ($650 million) to over 250,000 investors.
- Jackie Collins sells 500,000 copies of *James Dean Returns,* presumably dictated by the dead star; bits from his death car sell from $20; people can sit behind the wheel for 25 cents.
- For the first time since 1848, neither branch of Congress is won by the party of the elected president.
- Seventy-seven percent of college-educated women marry; 41 percent work part time, 17 percent full time.

New Words and Usages: Fuzz, the most, the greatest, cop-out, put-on, headshrinker, hero sandwich, lay-off pay

Fads: Wearing a "steady's" ring on a gold necklace, Captain Midnight decoders, Elvis Presley products

First Appearances: Bert and Harry Piel (Bob and Ray), Betty Furness and Westinghouse, Julia Mead and Lincoln-Mercury, gorilla born in captivity, Midas Muffler shop, Comet, Raid, Salem cigarettes, La Leche League, Imperial margarine, circular school building (Kankakee, Ill.), circular office building (Los Angeles), motto of the United States ("In God We Trust") authorized, motion picture actor on stamp (Gene Kelly), woman ordained as minister in Presbyterian church (M. E. Tower, Syracuse, N.Y.), all-steel convertible top (Ford), hair-splitting by .001 inch drill

1957

In the News

ANTHONY EDEN RESIGNS OVER SUEZ DEBACLE, HAROLD MACMILLAN IS NEW BRITISH P.M. . . . NEW YORK "MAD BOMBER" IS ARRESTED . . . ISRAEL LEAVES EGYPTIAN TERRITORY, UN EMERGENCY FORCE TAKES OVER . . . EISENHOWER DOCTRINE IS STATED, TO HELP INDEPENDENT COUNTRIES IN THE MIDEAST . . . BRITAIN BECOMES H-BOMB POWER AT CHRISTMAS ISLAND . . . TEAMSTER DAVE BECK IS EXPELLED FROM AFL-CIO FOR MISUSE OF FUNDS . . . U.S. AGREES ON LOAN TO POLAND . . . USSR WILL AID SYRIA . . . GEORGI MALENKOV IS OUSTED FROM POLITBURO FOR "ANTIPARTY ACTIVITIES" . . . RUSSIA REJECTS AERIAL INSPECTION . . . IKE PROPOSES TWO-YEAR TEST BAN . . . USSR ANNOUNCES SUCCESSFUL INTERCONTINENTAL BALLISTIC MISSILE TEST . . . MCCLELLAN COMMITTEE DENOUNCES JIMMY HOFFA AND TEAMSTERS UNION . . . REVEREND BILLY GRAHAM DRAWS 92,000 AT YANKEE STADIUM . . . ARKANSAS NATIONAL GUARD BLOCKS BLACK HIGH SCHOOL STUDENTS IN LITTLE ROCK . . . IKE SENDS FEDERAL TROOPS TO STOP "MOB RULE" IN LITTLE ROCK . . . SPUTNIK I, FIRST SPACE SATELLITE, IS LAUNCHED BY RUSSIA . . . HOFFA BECOMES PRESIDENT OF TEAMSTERS . . . SPUTNIK II, WITH DOG LAIKA, GOES INTO ORBIT . . . EDWARD TELLER URGES STRONGER BOMBER BASE DEFENSE . . . POLICE RAID MAFIA MEETING AT APPALACHIN, N.Y. . . . U.S. SATELLITE EXPLODES AT CAPE CANAVERAL, FLORIDA . . . FIRST U.S. ATLAS ICBM IS TESTED.

Deaths

Dennis Brain, Constantin Brancusi, Richard E. Byrd, Jimmy Dorsey, Joseph McCarthy, Ezio Pinza, Jean Sibelius, Arturo Toscanini, Erich von Stroheim.

Rock 'n' Roll, a teenage "fad" that is not passing. *Library of Congress*.

"The first artificial earth satellite in the world . . . was successfully launched in the USSR. . . . The new socialist society turns even the most daring of man's dreams into reality."
— Tass, the Soviet news agency

"[Sputnik is] a hunk of iron anybody could launch."
— Rear Adm. Lawson Bennett

"The balance of terror is more and more the foundation of peace."
— *Le Monde* editorial

"Everything I have is hers—and brother, that's plenty."
— Mike Todd, 54, newly married to Elizabeth Taylor, 24

Ads

New technique helps Los Alamos scientists take a sharp look at shock waves. . . . If you are a scientist or engineer of superior qualifications, interested in a creative atmosphere with a minimum of administrative detail, . . . write for an illustrated brochure.
(Los Alamos Scientific Lab, Los Alamos, N.M.)

College Dean Discovers Delicious New Casserole Made with Carnation Milk!
(Carnation Evaporated Milk)

Martini drinkers are divided into two glasses! says Ernie Kovacs. But the on the rocks faction is growing.
(Heublein Cocktails)

The road isn't built that can make it breathe hard!
(Chevrolet)

Quotes

"[This drive-in church] . . . with its loudspeakers set among the trees, provides an extra spiritual dimension, brought on by the sun, pines and the birds."
— Announcement of the Presbyterian Drive-in Church, Florida

"I like Charlie. He's the only man in the administration who doesn't talk about God."
— Reporter's comment on Secretary of Defense Charles Wilson

"The American satellite ought to be called Civil Servant. It won't work and you can't fire it."
— Popular joke

The Edsel, named after Henry Ford's son, one of the all-time manufacturing flops. *Library of Congress*.

Italian actress Sophia Loren is promoted as the new sex goddess. *Movie Star News*.

Keep the curves where they count.
(Sealtest Skim Milk)

Winstons taste good like a cigarette should.
(Winston Cigarettes)

TV

Premieres
"Mike Wallace Interviews"
"Tales of Wells Fargo," Dale Robertson
"Perry Mason," Raymond Burr
"Have Gun, Will Travel," Richard Boone
"Wagon Train," Robert Horton, Ward Bond
"To Tell the Truth," Bud Collyer
"Bat Masterson," Gene Barry
"The Pat Boone Show"
"Leave It to Beaver," Jerry Mathers, Hugh Beaumont
"Maverick," James Garner, Jack Kelly
"Bachelor Father," John Forsythe
"American Bandstand," Dick Clark

Top Ten (Nielsen)
"Gunsmoke," "The Danny Thomas Show," "Tales of Wells Fargo," "Have Gun, Will Travel," "I've Got a Secret," "The Life and Legend of Wyatt Earp," "General Electric Theater," "The Restless Gun," "December Bride," "You Bet Your Life"

Specials
"The Comedian" (Rod Serling); "The Miracle Worker" (William Gibson, with Teresa Wright); "The Helen Morgan Story" (Polly Bergen); "Oedipus the King" (Christopher Plummer, William Shatner); "Annie Get Your Gun" (John Raitt, Mary Martin); "Face the Nation" (interview with Khrushchev in Moscow); Senate Rackets Investigation (Senator John F. Kennedy, Counsel Robert Kennedy)

Emmy Awards
"Gunsmoke" (drama); "Phil Silvers Show" (comedy); Robert Young (actor), Jane Wyatt (actress), "Father Knows Best"; Jack Benny, Dinah Shore (personality)

Of Note
Important TV directors include John Frankenheimer, George Roy Hill, and Arthur Penn • Five of the top ten shows are Westerns • Jack Paar replaces Steve Allen on "The Tonight Show" • Video tape comes into general use, anticipating the end of live television.

Movies

Openings
The Bridge on the River Kwai (David Lean), William Holden, Alec Guinness
The Three Faces of Eve (Nunnally Johnson), Joanne Woodward, Lee J. Cobb, Vince Edwards
Peyton Place (Mark Robson), Lana Turner, Diane Varsi, Hope Lange
Sayonara (Joshua Logan), Marlon Brando, Red Buttons, Miyoshi Umeki
Twelve Angry Men (Sidney Lumet), Henry Fonda, Martin Balsam
Witness for the Prosecution (Billy Wilder), Marlene Dietrich, Charles Laughton, Tyrone Power
The Prince and the Showgirl (Laurence Olivier), Laurence Olivier, Marilyn Monroe
Silk Stockings (Rouben Mamoulian), Fred Astaire, Cyd Charisse
Love in the Afternoon (Billy Wilder), Gary Cooper, Audrey Hepburn
Les Girls (George Cukor), Gene Kelly, Kay Kendall
St. Joan (Otto Preminger), Jean Seberg
Paths of Glory (Stanley Kubrick), Kirk Douglas, Adolph Menjou
A Face in the Crowd (Elia Kazan), Andy Griffith, Patricia Neal, Anthony Franciosa
And God Created Woman (Roger Vadim), Brigitte Bardot
Wild Strawberries (Ingmar Bergman), Victor Sjöström, Ingrid Thulin

Academy Awards
Best Picture: *The Bridge on the River Kwai*
Best Director: David Lean (*The Bridge on the River Kwai*)
Best Actress: Joanne Woodward (*The Three Faces of Eve*)
Best Actor: Alec Guinness (*The Bridge on the River Kwai*)

Top Box-Office Stars
Rock Hudson, John Wayne, Pat Boone, Elvis Presley, Frank Sinatra, Gary Cooper, William Holden, James Stewart, Jerry Lewis, Yul Brynner

Stars of Tomorrow
Anthony Perkins, Sophia Loren, Jayne Mansfield, Don Murray, Carroll Baker, Martha Hyer, Elvis Presley, Anita Ekberg, Paul Newman, John Kerr

Popular Music

Hit Songs
"All Shook Up!"
"An Affair to Remember"
"All the Way"
"April Love"
"A White Sport Coat—and a Pink Carnation"
"Chances Are"
"Fascination"
"I'm Gonna Sit Right Down and Write Myself a Letter"
"Jailhouse Rock"
"Maria"

Top Records

Albums: *Love Is the Thing* (Nat "King" Cole); *Around the World in 80 Days* (sound track); *Loving You* (Elvis Presley); *Elvis' Christmas Album* (Elvis Presley); *Merry Christmas* (Bing Crosby)

Singles: *Diana* (Paul Anka); *Banana Boat Song* (Harry Belafonte); *Bye, Bye Love* (Everly Brothers); *Tammy* (Debbie Reynolds); *Blueberry Hill* (Fats Domino); *Love Letters in the Sand* (Pat Boone); *Lucille* (Little Richard). Country: *Gone* (Ferlin Husky); *Whole Lot of Shaking Going On* (Jerry Lee Lewis)

Jazz and Big Bands
Sonny Rollins forms his own combo. The School of Jazz is founded at Music Inn, Lenox, Massachusetts. Gunther Schuller coins "Third Stream," referring to the combination of jazz with European classical music forms, exemplified by the Modern Jazz Quartet; Charlie Mingus, in reaction to the style, moves to freer, open-ended, improvisational forms.

First Recordings: Miles Davis with Gil Evans; Shelly Manne with André Previn (jazz renditions of Broadway musicals); Ray Charles

Top Performers (*Downbeat*): Benny Goodman (soloist); Count Basie, Les Brown (bands); Modern Jazz Quartet (jazz group); Barney Kessel, Ray Brown, Errol Garner, Jimmy Giuffre, Miles Davis, Herbie Mann (instrumentalists); Ella Fitzgerald, Frank Sinatra (vocalists); Hi-Lo's (vocal group)

Theater

Broadway Openings

Plays
Look Homeward, Angel (Ketti Frings), Anthony Perkins, Jo Van Fleet, Hugh Griffith
The Dark at the Top of the Stairs (William Inge), Pat Hingle, Eileen Heckart, Teresa Wright
Romanoff and Juliet (Peter Ustinov), Peter Ustinov
Look Back in Anger (John Osborne), Alan Bates, Mary Ure, Kenneth Haigh
Time Remembered (Jean Anouilh), Susan Strasberg, Helen Hayes, Richard Burton
Visit to a Small Planet (Gore Vidal), Cyril Ritchard
A Clearing in the Woods (Arthur Laurents), Kim Stanley
The Waltz of the Toreadors (Jean Anouilh), Ralph Richardson, Mildred Natwick, Betty Field
Nude with Violin (Noel Coward), Noel Coward
Compulsion (Meyer Levin), Roddy McDowall, Dean Stockwell, Barbara Loden
A Moon for the Misbegotten (Eugene O'Neill), Wendy Hiller, Franchot Tone, Cyril Cusack
Orpheus Descending (Tennessee Williams), Maureen Stapleton, Cliff Robertson

Musicals
West Side Story (Leonard Bernstein, Stephen Sondheim), Carol Lawrence, Larry Kert, Chita Rivera
The Music Man (Meredith Willson), Robert Preston, Barbara Cook, David Burns
Ziegfeld Follies (Sammy Fain et al.), Beatrice Lillie, Billy De Wolfe (the last *Ziegfeld*)

Classics and Revivals On and Off Broadway
Mary Stuart (Friedrich Schiller), Irene Worth; *The Lady's Not for Burning* (Christopher Fry)

Regional

Founded: Charles Playhouse, Boston, by Murray Sugrue

American Shakespeare Festival: *Much Ado about Nothing*, Alfred Drake, Katharine Hepburn; *Othello*, Drake; *The Merchant of Venice*, Hepburn, Morris Carnovsky

Pulitzer Prize
Long Day's Journey into Night, Eugene O'Neill

Tony Awards
Long Day's Journey into Night, Eugene O'Neill (play); *My Fair Lady*, Alan Jay Lerner, Frederick Loewe (musical)

The Modern Jazz Quartet, with its "cerebral" style, manipulating classical forms within a jazz context, tours the British Isles with 88 performances in 4 months.

Classical Music

Compositions

Aaron Copland, Piano Fantasy
Gunther Schuller, *Transformation*
David Diamond, *The World of Paul Klee*
John Cage, Piano Concerto
Roger Sessions, Symphony no. 3
Walter Piston, Concerto for Viola

Important Events

A ten-day Festival of American Music takes place in Brussels.
Igor Stravinsky's 75th birthday is celebrated in Los Angeles with the premiere of *Agon* and *Canticum sacrum.*
The Philharmonic-Symphony Orchestra of New York changes its name to the New York Philharmonic; Leonard Bernstein becomes musical director.
A 44-story, vermillion-colored office building is proposed as the replacement for Carnegie Hall, scheduled to be razed August 7.
Most frequently performed symphonies are of Beethoven and Mozart; most performed American moderns are Samuel Barber, William Schuman, George Gershwin; most performed European moderns: Paul Hindemith, Ralph Vaughan Williams

Debuts: Daniel Barenboim, Lynn Harrell

First Performances

Charles Ives, Symphony no. 2 (New York); Roger Sessions, Symphony no. 3 (Boston); William Walton, Concerto for Cello and Orchestra (Boston, Gregor Piatigorsky, performing); Walter Piston, Symphony no. 4 (Minneapolis); Morton Gould, *Jekyll and Hyde Variations* (New York); Ernst Bacon, *Great River* (Dallas); Arthur Honegger, Symphony no. 5 and no. 6 (Boston); Gian Carlo Menotti, *Apocalypse* (Pittsburgh); Gian Francesco Malipiero, Sinfonia-Cantata (New York); Howard Hanson, *The Song of Democracy* (Philadelphia); Wallingford Riegger, Symphony no. 4 (University of Illinois); Lukas Foss, *Psalms* (New York); Morton Gould, *Declaration* (Washington, D.C.); Paul Creston, *Lydian Ode* (Wichita)

Opera

NBC Opera: *War and Peace* (Sergei Prokofiev)

Metropolitan: Renata Tebaldi, *La traviata;* Wolfgang Windgassen, Martha Mödl, *Das Rheingold;* George London, Lucine Amara, Martha Lipton, Richard Tucker, *Eugene Onègin;* Zinka Milanov, *Ernani;* premiere: *La périchole* (Jacques Offenbach). The complete *Ring* returns after six years.

Central City, Colo.: Cornell MacNeil, *Rigoletto*

Chicago: Giulietta Simionato, *Mignon;* Tito Gobbi, Renata Tebaldi, Mario del Monaco, *Andrea Chenier;* Maria Tallchief dances in *La Gioconda.*

San Francisco: *Dialogues of the Carmelites* (Francis Poulenc, premiere); Dorothy Kirsten, Eileen Farrell, Jussi Bjoerling, *Manon Lescaut*

Santa Fe: *The Rake's Progress* (Igor Stravinsky)

Art

Painting

Mark Rothko, *Black over
Reds, Red, White and
Brown*
Adolph Gottlieb, *Blast I*
Mark Tobey, *New Life
(Resurrection)*
Philip Guston, *The
Clock, Painter's City*
William Baziotes, *Red
Landscape*
Clyfford Still, *D No. 1*
Andrew Wyeth, *Brown
Swiss*
Robert Rauschenberg,
*Painting with Red
Letter "S"*
Richard Diebenkorn, *Girl
Looking at Landscape*
Ellsworth Kelly, *New
York, New York*
Helen Frankenthaler,
Jacob's Ladder

Sculpture

Seymour Lipton, *Pioneer*
Reuben Nakian, *The
Burning Walls of Troy*

Important Exhibitions

Museums

New York: *Metropolitan:* Paintings from the New
São Paulo, Brazil, Museum from the 18th to the 20th
centuries; "Children in Style"; Greek vases; Rodin
and French sculpture. *Museum of Modern Art:*
Pollock; Smith; 20th-century German art; Chagall;
Matta. *Guggenheim:* Duchamp, Duchamp-Villon,
Jacques Villon; Mondrian

Museum of Modern Art, Chicago, Philadelphia:
Picasso—75th anniversary, 328 works

Boston: Monet; Jan Cox; Feininger; New England
miniatures; William Blake; Tessai; Venetian villas

Chicago: Monet; 60th annual show—Artists of
Chicago and vicinity; Japanese stencils; African
sculpture; Midwest designer-craftsmen

Cleveland: "The Venetian Tradition from the 16th
Century to the Present"

Robert Motherwell, *Elegy
to the Spanish Republic,
1957*. Oil on canvas, 70 ×
7'6¼". The Museum of
Modern Art, given
anonymously.

Alexander Calder, *Black,
White and 10 Red*
Calder's *.125,1957* is
installed in the new
International Arrivals
Building, Idlewild
Airport, N.Y.

Architecture

Old Orchard Shopping
Center, Skokie, Ill.
(Loebl, Schlossman,
Bennett and Dart)
Connecticut General Life
Insurance Company
Building, Bloomfield,
Conn. (Skidmore,
Owings, and Merrill)
Skidmore, Owings, and
Merrill present their
design for the Air
Force Academy,
Colorado Springs.

Minneapolis: Rare Print Exhibition; Davis; Matta

Baltimore: 4,000 works of Modern art

National: Bellows; American primitives; 100 years
of American architecture; Masterpieces of Korean art

Art Briefs

The New York Public Library sells 10 paintings for
$169,000, including Gainsborough's *Woody
Landscape* ($20,500) and Turner's *A Scene on the
French Coast* ($56,000) • Record sales include
Renoir's *La Serre* ($200,000) • Oil tanker magnate
Stavros Niarchos buys 58 paintings for $3–4 million
from Edward G. Robinson and his wife in their
divorce settlement. Works include El Greco's
Deposition, Cézanne's *Eternal Woman*, and Renoir's
Two Sisters.

Dance

American Ballet Theatre (name changed from Ballet
Theatre) encourages young choreographers and
experimental performances: 15 new works, like
Sebastian (Agnes de Mille), are performed without
orchestral accompaniment or new scenery; dancers
wear practice clothes.
Margot Fonteyn and Michael Somes dance
Cinderella with the Royal Ballet for TV.

Premieres

New York City Ballet: *Square Dance* (George
Balanchine), Patricia Wilde, Nicholas Magallanes;
Agon (Balanchine, Stravinsky), Diana Adams,
Melissa Hayden

Books

Fiction

Critics' Choice

The Short Reign of Pippin IV, John Steinbeck
The Wapshot Chronicle, John Cheever
The Town, William Faulkner
On the Road, Jack Kerouac
The Assistant, Bernard Malamud
Love among the Cannibals, Wright Morris
63: Dream Stories, James Purdy
Gimpel the Fool, Isaac Bashevis Singer
Stories, Jean Stafford
ઐ *Justine*, Lawrence Durrell

Best-Sellers

By Love Possessed, James Gould Cozzens
Peyton Place, Grace Metalious
Compulsion, Meyer Levin
Rally Round the Flag, Boys! Max Shulman
Blue Camellia, Frances Parkinson Keyes
Eloise in Paris, Kay Thompson
The Scapegoat, Daphne Du Maurier
On the Beach, Nevil Shute
Below the Salt, Thomas B. Costain
Atlas Shrugged, Ayn Rand

Nonfiction

Critics' Choice

The Function of Criticism, Yvor Winters
Anatomy of Criticism, Northrop Frye
The Crisis of the Old Order, 1919–1933, Arthur Schlesinger, Jr.
The Price of Power: America since 1945, Herbert Agar
America as a Civilization, Max Lerner
Theodore Roosevelt and the Rise of America to World Power, Howard K. Beale
The Hidden Persuaders, Vance Packard
The Roots of American Communism, Theodore Draper
Memoirs of a Revolution, Dwight MacDonald
Day of Infamy, Walter Lord
The Road to Miltown, or Under the Spreading Atrophe, S. J. Perelman
Syntactic Structures, Noam Chomsky

Best-Sellers

Kids Say the Darndest Things! Art Linkletter
The FBI Story, Don Whitehead
Stay Alive All Your Life, Norman Vincent Peale
To Live Again, Catherine Marshall
Better Homes and Gardens Flower Arranging
Where Did You Go? Out. What Did You Do? Nothing, Robert Paul Smith
Baruch: My Own Story, Bernard M. Baruch
Please Don't Eat the Daisies, Jean Kerr
The American Heritage Book of Great Historic Places
The Day Christ Died, Jim Bishop

Poetry

Denise Levertov, *Here and Now*
Theodore Roethke, *The Exorcism*
Richard Wilbur, *Poems 1943–1956*
Wallace Stevens, *Opus Posthumous*
Robert Hillyer, *The Relic*
James Wright, *The Green Wall*
ઐ Nellie Sachs, *And No One Knows How to Go On*

Pulitzer Prizes

A Death in the Family, James Agee (posthumous, fiction)
Banks and Politics in America—from the Revolution to the Civil War, Bray Hammond (U.S. history)
George Washington, Douglas Southall Freeman (biography)
Promises: Poems 1954–56, Robert Penn Warren (poetry)

Science and Technology

The U.S. Thor ICBM is successfully tested.

An intended U.S. earth satellite, the six-foot Viking blows up at the launching pad at Cape Canaveral, Florida.

Maj. John Glenn sets a new transcontinental record in a Navy BV-1P Voight Crusader—3 hours, 23 minutes, 8.4 seconds.

Despite record admissions, the number of long-term patients in mental hospitals decreases significantly as new medicines reduce lengths of stay.

Anticoagulants are shown to aid stroke victims by reducing permanent damage.

Darvon, a new pain killer, is marketed.

ઐ The USSR launches a 180-pound satellite, Sputnik I, into orbit around the earth; it also launches a second satellite, Sputnik II (carrying an Eskimo dog), to study conditions for a living organism in space.

ઐ Soviets successfully test an intercontinental ballistic missile.

Sports _____

Baseball

After the season, the Brooklyn Dodgers and New York Giants move to Los Angeles and San Francisco.

Warren Spahn (Milwaukee) wins the Cy Young Award.

Jackie Robinson retires.

Champions _____

Batting	Pitching
Stan Musial (St. Louis, NL), .351	Bob Buhl (Milwaukee, NL) 18–7
Ted Williams (Boston, AL), .388	Tom Sturdivant (New York, AL), 16–6
	Dick Donovan (Chicago, AL), 16–6
	Home runs
	Henry Aaron (Milwaukee, NL), 44

Football

Jim Brown (Cleveland), a rookie, gains a league-leading 942 yards rushing, including a record 237 in one game.

Other NFL Season Leaders: Tom O'Connell (Cleveland), passing; Ray Berry (Baltimore), receiving

College All-Americans: King Hill (B), Rice; John Crow (B), Texas A & M; Lou Michaels (T), Kentucky

Bowls (Jan. 1, 1958)

Rose: Ohio State 10–Oregon 7

Orange: Oklahoma 48–Duke 21

Cotton: Navy 20–Rice 7

Sugar: Mississippi 39–Texas 7

Jim Brown, former Syracuse star, debuts with the Cleveland Browns. *Pro Football Hall of Fame.*

Basketball

NBA All-Pro First Team: Paul Arizin (Philadelphia), Bob Pettit (St. Louis), Dolph Schayes (Syracuse), George Yardley (Fort Wayne), Bob Cousy (Boston), Bill Sharman (Boston)

Other Sports

Tennis: Australian Lew Hoad turns pro for a record offer of $125,000 guaranteed.

Boxing: Sugar Ray Robinson wins the middleweight title for the fourth time, beating Gene Fullmer.

Winners _____

World Series	*MVP*
Milwaukee (NL) 4	Bob Cousy, Boston
New York (AL) 3	*College Basketball*
MVP	North Carolina
NL–Henry Aaron, Milwaukee	*Player of the Year*
AL–Mickey Mantle, New York	Len Rosenbluth, North Carolina
NFL	*Stanley Cup*
Detroit 59–Cleveland 14	Montreal
MVP	*US Tennis Open*
John Unitas, Baltimore	Men: Mal Anderson
College Football	Women: Althea Gibson
Auburn	*USGA Open*
Heisman Trophy	Dick Mayer
John Crow, Texas A & M	*Kentucky Derby*
NBA Championship	Iron Liege (W. Hartack, jockey)
Boston 4–St. Louis 1	

Fashion _____

For Women: In the search for a new look, Balenciaga and Givenchy create the sack silhouette with sheath beneath, a combination of loose overdress of transparent fabric on top of a form-fitting dress. Generally, the look is slim, and necklines are revealing. Coat shapes expand, and large cape collars stand away from the face and neck. Rounded at the waist and swept wide at the hem, these bulky coats and suits appear in orange, yellow, red, brilliant blue, and emerald green. Fancy shoes with pointed toes and buckles are popular. The silk dress with bubble skirt, rounded neck, and ¾-length tight sleeves is high style for evening. Long dresses in royal blue and green silks and satins have deep V necklines and uneven trails.

For Men: Change in men's style since the depression has been slow and subtle. Dramatic this year, however, are the small glen plaids for suits and the huge plaids for sport jackets; four, not six, buttons; oriental raw silks; the Hapi coat; and fake furs. Synthetics in pastels also make news, as well as the increasingly fashionable ascot and paisley prints for handkerchiefs, scarves, and ties.

On "The $64,000 Question" contestants enter an "isolation booth" to avoid audience prompting. *Library of Congress.*

- Columbia College professor Charles Van Doren, 30, becomes a national hero, winning $129,000 on TV's quiz show "Twenty-One"; he loses on the question "Who is the king of Belgium?" Van Doren receives many letters praising him as a role model in contrast to Elvis Presley.
- Allen Ginsberg's *Howl,* seized by the police as obscene, brings a great deal of attention to the Beat movement; a judge later releases the book.
- Average wages for a factory production worker are $2.08 an hour, or $82.00 a week.
- The first civil rights legislation since 1872 passes, despite Strom Thurmond's (Dem., S.C.) record 24-hour, 18-minute filibuster.
- The 16-year search for the Mad Bomber of New York City, who planted 32 homemade bombs, ends with the arrest of an electric company ex-employee.
- Mobsters fill the headlines: Frank Costello is shot in a New York apartment; Frank Scalice is shot at a peach stand in the Bronx; Albert Anastasia, "Lord High Executioner" of Murder, Inc., is shot in the barber shop of New York's Park Sheraton Hotel.
- The Cadillac Eldorado Brougham has on its dashboard a lipstick, vanity case, and four gold cups.
- Montgomery Ward's catalog includes a Shetland pony for $300 and a Great Dane for $120.
- The Supreme Court rules that Congress can only investigate matters related to potential legislation, rather than for the purposes of exposé.
- Khrushchev muses that Soviet Sputniks are "lonely . . . waiting for American satellites to join them in space."
- Philip Morris, aware that its brown cigarette package will not sell on color TV, invests $250,000 to develop a colorful package.
- The recreational fishing industry grows, as 21 million people spend $2 billion on the sport.
- Briefly popular are whiskey-flavored toothpaste and radarlike fishing poles; one in three women goes regularly to a beauty shop, many for apricot- or silver-colored hair.

Kaleidoscope _____

- The United Nations Emergency Force is the first multinational peacekeeping force in history.
- Industry begins supporting education; in the fall, the first of the 556 National Merit Scholars go to 160 colleges.
- Volkswagen sells 200,000 Beetles.
- A replica of the Mayflower goes from England to Plymouth Rock in 54 days.
- The yearly per capita consumption of margarine overtakes that of butter, 8.6 pounds to 8.3 pounds.
- An intensive study of birth control with pills is begun in Puerto Rico.
- Edward Teller, Ernest O. Lawrence, and others report that radioactive fallout from H-bomb detonations has been reduced by 95 percent and is "negligible."
- Twelve leading scientists warn of fallout concentrated in the northern hemisphere beneath the high-altitude jet stream. Linus Pauling also states that 10,000 persons are dying or have died of leukemia because of nuclear weapons testing.
- The Massachusetts governor reverses the 1692 witchcraft convictions of six Salem women.
- *Fortune* names Paul Getty the richest American; his real estate is estimated at $1 billion.
- Humphrey Bogart, dies, after reportedly saying to his wife, Lauren Bacall, "Goodbye, kid."
- Animal lovers throughout the world protest Russia's use of an animal (Laika) in flight.
- The VD rate increases from 122,000 to 126,000, the first increase since 1948.
- Ford introduces a new model, the Edsel.
- The Everly Brothers' "Wake Up Little Susie" is banned in Boston; a Columbia University psychiatrist compares rock dancing to the medieval St. Vitus plague where victims were unable to stop dancing.

New Words and Usages: Asian flu, Common Market, Sputnik, meter maid, factsheet, subliminal projection, total theater, bird dog, shook up, funky

Fads: Crinolines, poodle haircuts, saddle shoes, girls wearing their boyfriends' varsity sweaters, silly putty, Slinky, raccoon coats (from the leftover Davy Crockett raccoon materials), Dick Clark's "American Bandstand" with the bunny hop, hula hoops, bowling, frisbees, Bloody Mary jokes, Daisy Mae, Dog Patch outfits, sack dresses

First Appearances: Commercial building heated by the sun (Albuquerque), charting of Northwest Passage, element 102, pocket-size transistor (Sony), installment sales law, car with retractable hardtop (Ford), Zysser vegetable steamer, animal insurance, marketing of electric typewriter, Union Carbide Corp., Gulf and Western, Newport, Americana (Florida), Gino's

1958

Economic Profile

Dow-Jones: ↑ High 583–
Low 451

GNP: 0%

Inflation: +1.9%

Unemployment: 6.8%

Balance of international
payments: +$5.8 billion

Military on duty: 2,600,000

Voter participation: 63%
(1952), 61% (1956)

Population with religious
affiliation: 109 million

Oldsmobile: $2,933

Renault: $1,345

Simca: $1,775

Wheel alignment: $7.50

Emerson 7½ amp, 115-volt
air conditioner: $128

Air France, New York–Paris:
$489.60 (round trip,
economy class)

Delta, New York–Houston:
$66.65

Harvard tuition: $1,250

Blue jeans: $3.75

Macy's rhinestone-decorated
silk shoes: $19.94

Deaths

Claire L. Chennault, Ronald
Colman, Christian Dior,
Robert Donat, W. C.
Handy, Ernest O.
Lawrence, Louis B.
Mayer, Tyrone Power,
Mike Todd, Ralph Vaughan
Williams.

In the News

TWO INTERMEDIATE-RANGE BALLISTIC MISSILE SQUADRONS ARE FORMED UNDER THE STRATEGIC AIR COMMAND . . . BULGANIN ASKS FOR SUMMIT, IKE AGREES . . . IKE WARNS AGAINST WAGE AND PRICE INCREASES . . . U.S. AND USSR AGREE TO CULTURAL EXCHANGES . . . EXPLORER I, FIRST U.S. SATELLITE, IS LAUNCHED FROM CAPE CANAVERAL . . . TRUMAN BLAMES RECESSION ON IKE . . . UNITED ARAB REPUBLIC IS FORMED BY EGYPT AND SYRIA . . . IRAQ AND JORDAN UNITE . . . RIOTS AGAINST PRESIDENT CHAMOUN TEAR BEIRUT . . . IKE ASKS FOR ON-SITE INSPECTION . . . RIGHTISTS SEIZE POWER IN ALGERIA, ASK DE GAULLE TO FORM NEW FRENCH GOVERNMENT . . . VICE PRESIDENT NIXON IS STONED IN CARACAS WHILE ON GOODWILL TOUR . . . ONE-AND-A-HALF-TON SPUTNIK III ORBITS . . . LAST TROOPS LEAVE ARKANSAS . . . DE GAULLE BECOMES FRENCH PREMIER . . . FREE HUNGARY LEADER, IMRE NAGY, IS EXECUTED . . . ALASKA IS ADMITTED TO THE UNION . . . IKE ORDERS THE MARINES TO LEBANON TO SAFEGUARD ITS INDEPENDENCE . . . MAO TSE-TUNG AND KHRUSHCHEV PARLEY IN PEKING . . . IKE ORDERS ONE-YEAR TEST BAN . . . CHINESE BOMBARD QUEMOY AND MATSU ISLANDS OFF CHINA COAST . . . SEVENTH FLEET SUPPLIES QUEMOY, CHINESE HOLD FIRE . . . PRESIDENT'S CHIEF AIDE SHERMAN ADAMS RESIGNS OVER ALLEGED BRIBE OF VICUNA COAT . . . PIONEER ROCKET GOES UP 7,300 MILES . . . POPE PIUS XII DIES, POPE JOHN XXIII IS ELECTED . . . BORIS PASTERNAK REFUSES NOBEL PRIZE . . . CASTRO—LED REBELS SEIZE PROVINCIAL CAPITAL IN CUBA.

Quotes

"The Strip" in Las Vegas. The gambling center is a rapid growth industry. *Roger Whitehouse.*

"In the field of marketing, . . . the trend toward selling [has] reached something of a nadir with the unveiling . . . of so-called subliminal projection. That is the technique designed to flash messages past our conscious guard."

— Vance Packard

"If the public wants to lower its standard of living by driving a cheap crowded car, we'll make it."
— Anonymous General Motors Executive

Ads

"The schools are in terrible shape. . . . What has long been an ignored material problem, Sputnik has made a recognized crisis. [The] spartan Soviet system is producing many students better equipped to cope with the technicalities of the Space Age."
— *Life* editorial

"[The Russian sputnik is] an outer-space raspberry to a decade of American pretensions that the American way of life is a gilt-edge guarantee of our national security."

— Clare Boothe Luce

"In their mauve and cerise, air-conditioned, power-steered and power-braked automobiles, . . . [people] pass through cities that are badly paved, made hideous by blighted buildings, billboards, . . . decaying refuse. Is this, indeed, American genius?"
— John Kenneth Galbraith

"Is That All There Is?" remains Peggy Lee's theme song; she began her career with Benny Goodman. *Movie Star News.*

TV

Premieres
"The Donna Reed Show"
"Naked City," John McIntire
"77 Sunset Strip," Efrem Zimbalist, Jr., Edd "Kookie" Byrnes
"Peter Gunn," Craig Stevens
"Dr. Joyce Brothers"
"The Rifleman," Chuck Connors
"Wanted: Dead or Alive," Steve McQueen
"The Lawman," John Russell
"Concentration," Hugh Downs
"Open End," David Susskind

Top Ten (Nielsen)
"Gunsmoke," "Wagon Train," "Have Gun, Will Travel," "The Danny Thomas Show," "Maverick," "Tales of Wells Fargo," "The Real McCoys," "I've Got a Secret," "The Life and Legend of Wyatt Earp"

Specials
"Days of Wine and Roses" (Piper Laurie, Cliff Robertson); "Little Moon of Alban" (James Costigan, with Christopher Plummer, Julie Harris); "The Old Man" (Horton Foote); Leonard Bernstein and the New York Philharmonic; "Face of Red China"; "Little Women" (Margaret O'Brien, Risë Stevens, Florence Henderson)

Emmy Awards
"An Evening with Fred Astaire" (program); "Playhouse 90," "Alcoa-Goodyear" (drama); "Jack Benny Show" (comedy); "Dinah Shore—Chevy Show" (variety); "Maverick" (western); "Omnibus" (public service); "What's My Line?" (game); Raymond Burr (actor, "Perry Mason"); Loretta Young (actress, "The Loretta Young Show")

Of Note
"A Turkey for the President" stars Ronald Reagan and Nancy Davis on the G.E. Theater, Thanksgiving Day • ABC tries out prime-time news with John Daly for 15 minutes at 10:30 P.M., but popular response is poor.

Movies

Openings
Gigi (Vincente Minnelli), Louis Jourdan, Leslie Caron, Maurice Chevalier
Separate Tables (Delbert Mann), Deborah Kerr, Burt Lancaster, David Niven, Rita Hayworth
Auntie Mame (Morton DaCosta), Rosalind Russell, Forrest Tucker
Cat on a Hot Tin Roof (Richard Brooks), Paul Newman, Elizabeth Taylor, Burl Ives
The Defiant Ones (Stanley Kramer), Sidney Poitier, Tony Curtis
The Inn of the Sixth Happiness (Mark Robson), Ingrid Bergman, Curt Jurgens
Some Came Running (Vincente Minnelli), Frank Sinatra, Shirley MacLaine, Dean Martin
Lonelyhearts (Vincent J. Donehue), Montgomery Clift, Myrna Loy, Robert Ryan
The Young Lions (Edward Dmytryk), Montgomery Clift, Marlon Brando, Dean Martin
The Goddess (John Cromwell), Kim Stanley, Lloyd Bridges
South Pacific (Joshua Logan), Mitzi Gaynor, Rossano Brazzi
Touch of Evil (Orson Welles), Charleton Heston, Orson Welles
Vertigo (Alfred Hitchcock), James Stewart, Kim Novak
The Magician (Ingmar Bergman), Max von Sydow, Ingrid Thulin

Academy Awards
Best Picture: *Gigi*
Best Director: Vincente Minnelli (*Gigi*)
Best Actress: Susan Hayward (*I Want to Live*)
Best Actor: David Niven (*Separate Tables*)

Top Box-Office Stars
Glenn Ford, Elizabeth Taylor, Jerry Lewis, Marlon Brando, Rock Hudson, William Holden, Brigitte Bardot, Yul Brynner, James Stewart, Frank Sinatra

Stars of Tomorrow
Red Buttons, Diane Varsi, Andy Griffith, Anthony Franciosa, Hope Lange, Brigitte Bardot, Burl Ives, Mickey Shaughnessy, Russ Tamblyn

Popular Music

Hit Songs
"All I Have to Do Is Dream"
"Bird Dog"
"A Certain Smile"
"Gigi"
"Pink Shoe Laces"
"Tears on My Pillow"
"Tom Dooley"
"Chanson d'amour"
"Nel blu dipinto di blu (Volare)"
"The Purple People Eater"

Top Records

Albums: *Ricky* (Ricky Nelson); *Come Fly with Me* (Frank Sinatra); *The Music Man* (original cast); *South Pacific* (sound track); *Johnny's Greatest Hits* (Johnny Mathis); *The Kingston Trio*

Singles: *Catch a Falling Star* (Perry Como); *He's Got the Whole World in His Hands* (Laurie London); *Twilight Time* (Platters); *Lollipop* (Chordettes); *Who's Sorry Now?* (Connie Francis); *Tea for Two Cha Cha* (Tommy Dorsey); *Fever* (Peggy Lee); *Hard-Headed Woman* (Elvis Presley). Country: *Ballad of a Teenage Queen* (Johnny Cash); *Blue Boy* (Jim Reeves)

Grammy Awards
Nel blu dipinto di blu (Volare), Domenico Modugno (record); *The Music from "Peter Gunn,"* Henry Mancini (album); "Nel blu dipinto di blu" (song)

Jazz and Big Bands
The Monterey, California, Jazz Festival takes place.
Lambert, Hendricks & Ross are organized; Ella Fitzgerald and Duke Ellington give a concert at Carnegie Hall.
Miles Davis's *Milestones* experiments with modal improvisation.

Top Performers (*Downbeat*): Count Basie (soloist, big band); Les Brown (dance band); Modern Jazz Quartet (jazz quartet); Oscar Peterson, Shelly Manne, Paul Desmond, Tony Scott, Milt Jackson, Herbie Mann, Art Van Damme (instrumentalists); Ella Fitzgerald, Frank Sinatra (vocalists); Four Freshmen (vocal group)

Theater

Broadway Openings

Plays
J. B. (Archibald MacLeish), Pat Hingle, Christopher Plummer, Raymond Massey
Two for the Seesaw (William Gibson), Henry Fonda, Anne Bancroft
Sunrise at Campobello (Dore Schary), Ralph Bellamy
A Touch of the Poet (Eugene O'Neill), Kim Stanley, Eric Portman, Helen Hayes, Betty Field
The Pleasure of His Company (Samuel Taylor), Cyril Ritchard, Cornelia Otis Skinner
The Marriage-Go-Round (Leslie Stephens), Charles Boyer, Claudette Colbert, Julie Newmar
The Visit (Friedrich Dürrenmatt), Alfred Lunt, Lynn Fontanne, Eric Porter
Ages of Man (Shakespeare scenes and sonnets), John Gielgud
The Disenchanted (Bud Schulberg, Harvey Breit), Rosemary Harris, George Grizzard, Jason Robards, Jr.
The Cold Wind and the Warm (S. N. Behrman), Eli Wallach, Maureen Stapleton
Epitaph for George Dillon (John Osborne, Anthony Creighton), Eileen Herlie, Robert Stephens
The Entertainer (John Osborne), Laurence Olivier, Joan Plowright

Musicals
Flower Drum Song (Richard Rodgers, Oscar Hammerstein II), Pat Suzuki, Juanita Hall, Larry Blyden
A Party with Betty Comden and Adolph Green
La Plume de Ma Tante (Gerard Calvi), Robert Dhéry, Colette Brosset

Classics and Revivals On and Off Broadway
Old Vic: *Hamlet, Twelfth Night, Garden District* (Tennessee Williams); *Blood Wedding* (Garcia Lorca); *Endgame* (Samuel Beckett); *Family Reunion* (T. S. Eliot), Lillian Gish, Florence Reed, Fritz Weaver; *Ivanov* (Chekhov); *The Quare Fellow* (Brendan Behan); *Ulysses in Nighttown* (Oliver Saylor), Zero Mostel; *The Chairs*, Eli Wallach, and *The Lesson* (Eugene Ionesco), Joan Plowright, Wallach; *The Infernal Machine* (Jean Cocteau), Claude Dauphin

Pulitzer Prize
Look Homeward, Angel, Ketti Frings

Tony Awards
Sunrise at Campobello, Dore Schary (play); *The Music Man*, Meredith Willson (musical)

Classical Music _____

Compositions
Edgard Varèse, *Poème electronique*
John Cage, *Fontana Mix*
Salvatore Martirano, *0,0,0,0, that Shakespeherian Rag*
Roger Sessions, Symphony no. 4
George Rochberg, Symphony no. 2
John La Montaine, Concerto for Piano and Orchestra

Important Events
Touring orchestras include the New York Philharmonic to South and Central America, and the Philadelphia to the USSR, Romania, and Poland.
Four composers are invited to the USSR: Roger Sessions, Peter Mennin, Roy Harris, and Ulysses Kay.
Benno Moiseiwitsch plays the three Rachmaninoff concerti with the Symphony of the Air, at Carnegie Hall.
Harvey Lavan Cliburn, Jr. (Van Cliburn), 23, wins first prize in the International Tchaikovsky Piano Competition and gains instant fame, including a ticker tape parade in New York.

Debuts: Leonid Kogan, Vladimir Ashkenazy

First Performances
Roger Sessions, Symphony no. 3 (Boston); Deems Taylor, *The Dragon* (New York); Gian Carlo Menotti, Piano Concerto (Cleveland); Paul Creston, *Pre-Classic Suite* (New Orleans); Henry Humphreys, *The Waste Land of T. S. Eliot* (Cincinnati)

Opera

Metropolitan: During this 75th anniversary year, there are 240 performances; Inge Borkh (debut), *Salomé;* Borkh, Nicolai Gedda, *Cavalleria rusticana, I pagliacci;* Antonietta Stella, *Madama Butterfly;* Eleanor Steber, *Vanessa* (Samuel Barber, premiere); Rudolph Bing cancels Maria Callas in *Macbeth,* which is rescheduled with Leonie Rysanek (debut).

New York City: *The Silent Woman* (Richard Strauss), *Good Soldier Schweik* (Robert Kurka), premieres

Boston: Opera Group of Boston founded by Sarah Caldwell; *The Voyage to the Moon* (Offenbach)

Chicago: Birgit Nilsson, *Turandot;* William Wildermann, *Tristan und Isolde;* Tito Gobbi, *Falstaff*

San Francisco: *Medée* (Cherubini, premiere)

San Antonio: Lily Pons, *Lakmé*

Santa Fe: *Capriccio* (Richard Struass, premiere)

Music Notes
Pablo Casals's appearance at the UN General Assembly on UN Day, for the first time in over twenty years, is considered a symbol of the "exchange of peace through music" • Paul Robeson returns to New York after eleven years • President Truman and Jack Benny play in a benefit performance with the Kansas City Philharmonic.

Far left: Frank Lloyd Wright's innovative Solomon R. Guggenheim Museum. *Roger Whitehouse.*

Texan Van Cliburn is the first American to win the International Tchaikovsky Competition in Moscow. He studied with Rosina Lhévinne at Juilliard and made his debut with the Houston Symphony when he was 13. *Movie Star News.*

Art

Painting

Sam Francis, *Blue on a Point*

Philip Guston, *Passage*

Jan Müller, *Jacob's Ladder*

Abraham Rattner, *Song of Esther*

Morris Louis, *Russet*

Hans Hofmann, *Bird Cage—Variation II, Moloch*

Franz Kline, *King Oliver, Requiem, Siegfried*

Willem de Kooning, *Woman and Bicycle*

Jasper Johns, *Three Flags*

Mark Rothko, *Four Darks in Red, Red, Brown and Black*

Robert Motherwell, *Iberia No. 18*

Sculpture

Seymour Lipton, *Sorcerer*

Reuben Nakian, *The Rape of Lucrece*

Louise Nevelson, *Sky Cathedral*

George Rickey, *Omaggio a Bernini*

Naum Gabo, *Linear Construction in Space, Number 4*

Architecture

Solomon R. Guggenheim Museum, New York (Frank Lloyd Wright)

Main Library, Palo Alto, Calif. (Edward Durell Stone)

Seagram Building, New York (Mies van der Rohe, Philip Johnson)

Exterior, Museum of Fine Arts, Houston (Mies van der Rohe)

Four Seasons Restaurant, New York (Philip Johnson)

Inland Steel Building, Chicago (Skidmore, Owings and Merrill)

McGregor Memorial Center, Wayne State University, Detroit (Minoru Yamasaki)

Roofless Church, New Harmony, Ind. (Philip Johnson, Jacques Lipchitz)

Union Tank Car Co. Quarter Sphere Dome, Baton Rouge, La. (Buckminster Fuller)

Important Exhibitions

"Masterpieces of Korean Art" travels to Washington, Boston, and New York.

Museums

New York: *Metropolitan:* American art from Copley to O'Keeffe; Paintings by Sir Winston Churchill; "A Century of City Views"; Prints by Callot and Daumier; Paintings from colonial times to today; Korean art. *Museum of Modern Art:* 70th Anniversary of Chagall; Seurat; Modigliani; Arp. *Whitney:* "Nature in Abstraction"

Boston: Scenic painters and draughtsmen of 18th century Venice; Daumier; Primitive arts; Maillol's bronzes and drawings; Korean art

Washington: Photographs by Alfred Stieglitz; 150 Dutch drawings; Homer; Illuminated manuscripts; "The Fantastic, the Occult, and the Bizarre"; Blake's engravings; Korean art

Chicago: Seurat; Gris; Umberto Boccioni; Animals in Pre-Columbian art

Kansas City: Japanese art of the Edo period

Houston: The four Guardis; 18th century Venetian masters

Art Briefs

A workman is killed and 31 are injured in a fire at the Museum of Modern Art; works by Monet, Rivers, Tchelitchew, and others are damaged; the current exhibit, "U.S.A.: 1958—5,000 Works," is moved to the Madison Square Garden basement • Rothko begins his first commission, the monumental paintings for the Four Seasons Restaurant in New York • Major sales include Van Gogh's *Public Gardens at Arles* ($369,600), Manet's *La Rue de Berne* ($316,400), Renoir's *La Pensée* ($201,600), and Cézanne's *Garçon au Gilet Rouge* ($616,000, the highest price ever paid for a single painting at auction, by art dealer Georges Keller).

Dance

Alvin Ailey forms the American Dance Theater; the Moscow Moiseyev Dance Company tours with enormous success.

Premieres

New York City Ballet: *Stars and Stripes* (George Balanchine), Melissa Hayden, Jacques d'Amboise

Ballets U.S.A.: *New York Export: Op. Jazz* (Jerome Robbins)

San Francisco: *Beauty and the Beast* (Lew Christensen)

Merce Cunningham: *Antic Meet* (John Cage)

Martha Graham: *Clytemnestra*

Martha Graham and Bertram Ross: *Night Journey*

Books

Fiction

Critics' Choice

The End of the Road, John Barth
Breakfast at Tiffany's, Truman Capote
The Housebreaker of Shady Hill, John Cheever
The Violated, Vance Bourjaily
The Sundial, Shirley Jackson
The Subterraneans, Jack Kerouac
The Magic Barrel, Bernard Malamud
The Dharma Bums, Jack Kerouac
Home from the Hill, William Humphrey
Mrs. Bridge, Evan Connell

Best-Sellers

Doctor Zhivago, Boris Pasternak
Anatomy of a Murder, Robert Traver
Lolita, Vladimir Nabokov
Around the World with Auntie Mame, Patrick Dennis
From the Terrace, John O'Hara
Eloise at Christmastime, Kay Thompson
Ice Palace, Edna Ferber
The Enemy Camp, Jerome Weidman

Nonfiction

Critics' Choice

The Democratic Vista, Richard Chase
More in Anger, Marya Mannes
Irrational Man, William Barrett
Eisenhower, Captive Hero, Marquis Childs
The Shook-Up Generation, Harrison E. Salisbury
The Affluent Society, John Kenneth Galbraith
Russia, the Atom and the West, George F. Kennan
Our Nuclear Future, Edward Teller, Albert L. Latter
Mistress to an Age: A Life of Madame de Staël, J. Christopher Herold
🍃 *The Theatre and Its Double*, Antonin Artaud
🍃 *Structural Anthropology*, Claude Lévi-Strauss

Best-Sellers

Kids Say the Darndest Things! Art Linkletter
'Twixt Twelve and Twenty, Pat Boone
Only in America, Harry Golden
Masters of Deceit, J. Edgar Hoover
Please Don't Eat the Daisies, Jean Kerr

Better Homes and Gardens Salad Book
The New Testament in Modern English
Aku-Aku, Thor Heyerdahl
Dear Abby, Abigail Van Buren
Inside Russia Today, John Gunther

Poetry

William Meredith, *The Open Sea and Other Poems*
William Carlos Williams, *Paterson, Book V*
Karl Shapiro, *Poems of a Jew*
E. E. Cummings, *95 Poems*
Muriel Rukeyser, *Body of Waking*
William Jay Smith, *Poems 1947–1957*
Lawrence Ferlinghetti, *A Coney Island of the Mind*
Theodore Roethke, *Words for the Wind*
Gregory Corso, *Gasoline*

Pulitzer Prizes

The Travels of Jamie McPheeters, Robert Lewis Taylor (fiction)
The Republican Era: 1869–1901, Leonard D. White, with Jean Schneider (U.S. history)
Woodrow Wilson, Arthur Walworth (biography)
Selected Poems, 1928–1958, Stanley Kunitz (poetry)

Science and Technology

Integrated circuitry is invented; Jack Kilby describes the "monolithic idea," the basis of the microchip.

Stereo records are introduced by EMI and Decca.

John Enders develops a measles vaccine.

Joseph Wolpe in *Psychotherapy by Reciprocal Inhibition* develops a behavioral approach.

Explorer I, weighing 30.8 pounds, is launched by the army.

The navy fails for the sixth time to orbit Vanguard II.

The air force launches the heaviest U.S. missile to date, 8,750 pounds.

NASA is organized to unify and develop U.S. nonmilitary space efforts; it announces a space program, Project Mercury, with the goals of a man in space in two years, a man on the moon in six to ten years, and the exploration of Mars in ten to fifteen years.

James Van Allen describes two belts of cosmic radiation around the earth.

The first regular domestic jet service, from New York to Miami, begins.

Ultrasound for examination of the fetus during pregnancy is pioneered.

🍃 USSR orbits Sputnik III, weighing 2,925.53 pounds.

Nobel Prize

Sharing the prize in physiology and medicine are Joshua Lederberg, for work on genetic mechanisms, and George W. Beadle and Edward L. Tatum, for work on the genetic transmission of hereditary characteristics.

Sports

Basketball

NBA All-Pro First Team: George Yardley (Detroit), Dolph Schayes (Syracuse), Bob Pettit (St. Louis), Bob Cousy (Boston), Bill Sharman (Boston)

Other Sports

Golf: Arnold Palmer is the PGA's top money-winner with $42,607.

Tennis: Pancho Gonzales beats Lew Hoad on the pro tour.

Winners

World Series		MVP	
New York (AL) 4		Bill Russell, Boston	
Milwaukee (NL) 3		*College Basketball*	
MVP		Kentucky	
NL–Ernie Banks, Chicago		*Player of the Year*	
AL–Jackie Jensen, Boston		Elgin Baylor, Seattle	
NFL		*Stanley Cup*	
Baltimore 23		Montreal	
New York 17 (OT)		*US Tennis Open*	
MVP		Men: Ashley Cooper	
Jim Brown, Cleveland		Women: Althea Gibson	
College Football		*USGA Open*	
Louisiana State University		Tommy Bolt	
Heisman Trophy		*Kentucky Derby*	
Pete Dawkins, Army		Tim Tam (I. Valenzuela,	
NBA Championship		jockey)	
St. Louis 4–Boston 2			

Jack Kerouac, spokesman of "the beat generation," whose San Francisco "subterraneans" are "hip without being slick, intelligent without being corny, . . . [and] very Christlike." *Courtesy Grove Press.*

Baseball

Stan Musial (St. Louis, NL) gets his 3,000th hit.
Bob Turley wins the Cy Young Award.

Champions

Batting
Richie Ashburn (Philadelphia, NL), .350
Ted Williams (Boston, AL), .328

Pitching
Warren Spahn (Milwaukee, NL), 22–11

Lew Burdette (Milwaukee, NL), 20–10
Bob Turley (New York, NL), 21–7

Home runs
Ernie Banks (Chicago, NL), 47

Football

Jim Brown (Cleveland) gains a record 1,527 yards rushing.
Johnny Unitas (Q) stars in Baltimore's sudden-death overtime victory over New York in the NFL playoff, the first title game televised coast to coast.

NFL Season Leaders: Eddie LeBaron (Washington), passing; Ray Berry (Baltimore), receiving

College All-Americans: Billy Cannon (B), LSU; Pete Dawkins (B), Army; Buddy Dial (E), Rice.

Bowls (Jan. 1, 1959)

Rose: Iowa 38–California 12
Orange: Oklahoma 21–Syracuse 6

Cotton: Air Force 0–Texas Christian 0
Sugar: Louisiana State 7–Clemson 0

Fashion

For Women: The "chemise," "trapeze," and "empire" are ruby red, red-violet, lavender, orange, yellow, emerald, and fuchsia. The "shift," or sack dress, also strives for popularity. Nonfunctional dress decorations include big buttons, patch pockets, fringes, bows, sashes, and buckles. The trapeze, often called "a half-opened umbrella," is short-lived. Mohair is new, along with paisley and patterned wool knits; the new polished cottons are worn in the evening. Shoes are round or square, with thin heels; pumps have low straps and stitching (some have jeweled trim). In addition to beads in all colors and large pins, a rage grows for pearl drop earrings and gold hearts, and they are often worn together. The raccoon and loden coat are popular.

High-fashion notes: Yves St. Laurent's trapeze for Dior; Dior's 2d "demi-longeur"; Balenciaga's chemise; Cardin's blouse-backed jacket

Kaleidoscope _____

- Five months after Sputnik, *Life*'s series "Crisis in Education" focuses on major U.S. educational problems, including poor curricula, overcrowding of classrooms, poorly paid teachers, and lack of proper professional attention to substantive matters.
- For the 11th year, Eleanor Roosevelt is first on the "Most Admired Woman" list; Queen Elizabeth is second.
- John Kenneth Galbraith, in *The Affluent Society,* describes the materialism and conformity that characterize the United States and argues for a redistribution of income to end the poverty of public services.
- Paul Robeson, denied a passport for eight years because of his leftist affiliations, is allowed to tour abroad.
- Elvis Presley is inducted into the army on March 24 as no. 53310761.
- The Kingston Trio's "Tom Dooley" begins the folk music vogue.
- Colorado and Kansas are overrun by grasshoppers.
- Eisenhower tries but is unable to issue a "posthumous pardon" to O. Henry, who started writing fiction when jailed for an $854.08 embezzlement from an Austin, Texas, bank.
- Los Angeles Dodgers Roy Campanella fractures two back vertebrae and is paralyzed from the shoulders down.
- Lana Turner's 14-year-old daughter, Cheryl Crane, fatally stabs her mother's boyfriend, Johnny Stompanato, which the court rules "justifiable homocide."
- Approximately 250,000 attend the Jehovah's Witnessess's Convention at Yankee Stadium.
- Treason charges against Ezra Pound are dropped because he is "not competent" to stand trial.
- College tuition doubles since 1940 and is expected to double again by 1970; the average cost is $1,300 a year.
- A survey indicates that 40 percent of college students admit to cheating, many with no regrets.

In "Alfred Hitchcock Presents" stars like Barbara Bel Geddes, Gary Merrill, and Brian Keith make multiple appearances. *Billy Rose Theatre Collection. The New York Public Library at Lincoln Center. Astor, Lenox and Tilden Foundations.*

Harry Belafonte's renditions of "Scarlet Ribbons" and "Shenandoah" are becoming classics. *Movie Star News.*

- Brigitte Bardot becomes the new sex symbol.
- Jack Webb marries Miss America 1952, Jackie Loughery.
- The paperback edition of *Lolita* sells a million copies.
- A nationwide scandal involves a number of quiz shows giving answers beforehand; 12 of 20 contestants who won between $500 and $220,500 plead guilty but receive suspended sentences because of their "humiliation."
- City College of New York student Herbert Stempel, who won $49,500 on "Twenty One," claims that he was forced to lose to Charles Van Doren, "a guy that had a fancy name, Ivy League education, parents all his life."
- Nathan Leopold, jailed with Richard Loeb (who was killed in prison) for their 1924 kidnapping, is paroled.
- SANE is formed with 25,000 members.
- The food additive amendment prohibits the use of any substance that induces cancer in animals or people.
- The Elizabeth Taylor, Eddie Fisher, and Debbie Reynolds love triangle is widely publicized.
- The construction of a nuclear power plant at Bodega Head, California, is stopped by court action of environmental groups.

New Words and Usages: Beatniks, DNA, lunar probe, action-painting, carry-out, moon dust, news satellite, reentry, sex kitten, sick joke, trapeze dress

Fads: Waterskiing, British bobbies' capes

First Appearances: Privately owned atomic reactor, solid state electronic computer, bifocal contact lens, presidential pension, two-way moving sidewalk, John Birch Society, Grammy award, Chevrolet Impala, Green Giant canned beans, Sweet 'n Low, Cocoa Puffs, Cocoa Krispies, Pizza Hut (Kansas City), Synanon, acupuncture (in United States), Bankamericard, American Express, UPI, National Defense Education Act

1959

Economic Profile
  Dow-Jones: ↑ High 679–
    Low 574
  GNP: +8%
  Inflation: +0.7%
  Unemployment: 5.5%
Police expenditures, federal,
  state, local: $1.9 billion
Persons arrested: 2,613,000
Executions: 49
Prisoners, federal and state:
  207,400
Juvenile court: 63,038
Castro convertible king-size
  sofa: $199.75
Caribbean cruise: $355 (15
  days, 7 ports)
Greyhound, New York–
  Florida: $87.74 (9 days)
Willoughby's Bell & Howell
  8mm moving picture
  camera: $19–$48
Hi-fi tape recorder: $49.95
Macy's "trapeze suit in
  transition": $59.95
Rogers Peet young men's
  tropical suit: $38.50
  Summer sport coat:
    $14.95–$19.95

Deaths

George Antheil, Ethel
  Barrymore, Ernest Bloch,
  Raymond Chandler, Lou
  Costello, Cecil B.
  De Mille, Errol Flynn,
  George C. Marshall, Mel
  Ott, Tyrone Power, Frank
  Lloyd Wright.

In the News

FIDEL CASTRO TAKES HAVANA, BATISTA FLEES . . . POPE JOHN CALLS FOR ECUMENICAL COUNCIL . . . KHRUSHCHEV BOASTS OF SOVIET MILITARY SUPERIORITY . . . NORFOLK, VIRGINIA, SCHOOLS INTEGRATE . . . CYPRUS IS GIVEN INDEPENDENCE BY BRITAIN . . . CASTRO VISITS U.S. AND IS WARMLY RECEIVED . . . HAWAII BECOMES THE 50TH STATE . . . KAMBA TRIBES IN TIBET FIGHT CHINESE, DALAI LAMA SEEKS ASYLUM . . . IKE CALLS FOR ON-SITE MISSILE INSPECTION AND IS AGAIN REJECTED . . . UNITED ARAB REPUBLIC HALTS ISRAELI CARGO IN SUEZ CANAL . . . MONKEYS ABEL AND BAKER ARE RECOVERED AFTER ORBIT . . . RUSSIANS FIRE 4,400-POUND PAYLOAD INTO SPACE WITH TWO DOGS AND A RABBIT . . . 500,000 STEELWORKERS STRIKE . . . CUBAN PRESIDENT URRUTIA RESIGNS, ALLEGING COMMUNIST CONTROL . . . NIXON, ON RUSSIAN T.V., DEFENDS U.S. AND ASKS THAT RUSSIANS IMPROVE . . . INDIA CHARGES THAT CHINA SEIZED BORDER TERRITORY . . . LAOS ASKS FOR U.S. AID AGAINST NORTH VIETNAM AGGRESSION . . . EISENHOWER AND KHRUSHCHEV MEET AT CAMP DAVID . . . KHRUSHCHEV TOURS THE U.S. . . . CHARLES VAN DOREN ADMITS HIS T.V. QUIZ ROLE WAS FIXED . . . LUNIK II HITS THE MOON . . . HUNGARIAN LEADER JANOS KADAR SAYS RUSSIAN TROOPS WILL STAY AS LONG AS NECESSARY . . . IKE WILL TAKE 22,370-MILE GOODWILL TOUR.

Quotes _____

"It is necessary to provide every person in the U.S. with a shelter."
— Edward Teller, "father" of the H-bomb

"The immediate cause of World War III is the preparation of it."
— C. Wright Mills

"Let us never forget that there can be no second place in a contest with Russia and there can be no second chance if we lose."
— Adm. H. G. Rickover

"America when will we end the human war?
  Go F—— yourself with your atomic bomb"
— Allen Ginsberg, *Howl*, 2d ed.

"I am not willing to accept the idea that there are no Communists left in this country. I think if we lift enough rocks we'll find some."
— Sen. Barry Goldwater (R, Ariz.)

"We have beaten you to the moon, but you have beaten us in sausage making."
— Nikita S. Khrushchev in Des Moines

"Probably we will never be able to determine the psychic havoc of the concentration camp and the atomic bomb. One is Hip or one is Square, . . . one is a rebel or one conforms."
— Norman Mailer, "The White Negro"

The Mercury Seven, test pilots selected by NASA. *Courtesy NASA.*

"It got to the point where there were just too many quiz shows. Ratings began to drop. . . . Some producers turned to rigging. . . . They just couldn't afford to lose their sponsors."
— Hal March, host, "The $64,000 Question"

"[The producer] instructed me on how to answer the questions. . . . He gave me a script to memorize. . . . I would give almost anything I have to reverse the course of my life in the last three years."
— Charles Van Doren

Ads _____

TV

Premieres
"Rawhide," Clint Eastwood
"The G. E. College Bowl"
"The Bell Telephone Hour"
"The Many Loves of Dobie Gillis," Dwayne Hickman
"The Untouchables," Robert Stack
"Bonanza," Lorne Green, Dan Blocker, Pernell Roberts, Michael Landon
"The Late Show"
"The Twilight Zone," Rod Serling

Top Ten (Nielsen)
"Gunsmoke," "Wagon Train," "Have Gun, Will Travel," "The Danny Thomas Show," "The Red Skelton Show," "Father Knows Best," "77 Sunset Strip," "The Price Is Right," "Wanted: Dead or Alive," "Perry Mason"

Specials
"The Turn of the Screw" (Ingrid Bergman); "The Moon and Sixpence" (Laurence Olivier); "Biography of a Missile" (Ed Murrow, Fred Friendly); "Ethan Frome" (Julie Harris); "Give My Regards to Broadway" (Jimmy Durante, Ray Bolger); "The Violent World of Sam Huff"; "Twentieth Century" (Walter Cronkite, host)

Emmy Awards
"Playhouse 90" (drama); "Art Carney Special" (comedy); "Fabulous Fifties" (variety); "Huckleberry Hound" (children); Robert Stack (actor, "The Untouchables"); Jane Wyatt (actress, "Father Knows Best"); Rod Serling (writing achievement)

Of Note
Ed Murrow interviews Fidel Castro, who is wearing pajamas, on "Person to Person" • George Reeves, star of "Superman," commits suicide.

Movies

Openings
Ben-Hur (William Wyler), Charlton Heston, Stephen Boyd
Anatomy of a Murder (Otto Preminger), James Stewart, Lee Remick, Ben Gazzara
The Nun's Story (Fred Zinnemann), Audrey Hepburn, Peter Finch
Room at the Top (Jack Clayton), Laurence Harvey, Simone Signoret
Some Like It Hot (Billy Wilder), Tony Curtis, Marilyn Monroe, Jack Lemmon
Pillow Talk (Michael Gordon), Doris Day, Rock Hudson, Tony Randall
Suddenly, Last Summer (Joseph L. Mankiewicz), Elizabeth Taylor, Katharine Hepburn, Montgomery Clift
Imitation of Life (Douglas Sirk), Lana Turner, Juanita Moore, John Gavin
North by Nothwest (Alfred Hitchcock), Cary Grant, Eva Marie Saint, James Mason
On the Beach (Stanley Kramer), Gregory Peck, Ava Gardner, Fred Astaire
The Best of Everything (Jean Negulesco), Hope Lange, Suzy Parker, Joan Crawford, Louis Jourdan
Gidget (Paul Wendkos), Sandra Dee, Cliff Robertson
Rio Bravo (Howard Hawks), John Wayne, Dean Martin, Ricky Nelson

Hiroshima, Mon Amour (Alain Resnais), Eiji Okada
The 400 Blows (François Truffaut), Jean-Pierre Leaud
La Dolce Vita (Federico Fellini), Marcello Mastroianni, Anita Ekberg, Anouk Aimée
Breathless (Jean-Luc Godard), Jean-Paul Belmondo, Jean Seberg
Black Orpheus (Marcel Camus), Breno Mello, Marpessa Dawn

Academy Awards
Best Picture: *Ben-Hur*
Best Director: William Wyler *(Ben-Hur)*
Best Actress: Simone Signoret *(Room at the Top)*
Best Actor: Charlton Heston *(Ben-Hur)*

Top Box-Office Stars
Rock Hudson, Cary Grant, James Stewart, Doris Day, Debbie Reynolds, Glenn Ford, Frank Sinatra, John Wayne, Jerry Lewis, Susan Hayward

Stars of Tomorrow
Sandra Dee, Ricky Nelson, James Garner, Curt Jurgens, Lee Remick, John Saxon, Sidney Poitier, Ernie Kovacs, Kathryn Grant, Carolyn Jones

Popular Music

Hit Songs
"Everything's Coming up Roses"
"Personality"
"Put Your Head on My Shoulder"
"The Sound of Music"
"I'm Just a Lonely Boy"
"Small World"
"Do-Re-Mi"
"Franky"
"Kookie, Kookie"

Top Records

Albums: *Flower Drum Song* (original cast); *Peter Gunn* (Henry Mancini); *The Kingston Trio at Large* (Kingston Trio); *Heavenly* (Johnny Mathis); *Film Encores* (Mantovani)

Singles: *Mack the Knife* (Bobby Darin); *I Loves You Porgy* (Nina Simone); *Misty* (Johnny Mathis); *Tiger* (Fabian); *What'd I Say?* (Ray Charles); *A Teenager in Love* (Dion and the Belmonts); *What a Difference a Day Makes* (Dinah Washington). Country: *Battle of New Orleans* (Johnny Horton); *Three Bells* (Browns)

Grammy Awards
Mack the Knife, Bobby Darin (record); *Come Dance with Me,* Frank Sinatra (album); "Battle of New Orleans," Jimmy Driftwood (song)

Jazz and Big Bands
Ornette Coleman's *The Shape of Jazz to Come* gains wide attention; Coleman's arrival in New York stirs the greatest controversy since Dizzy Gillespie's and Charlie Parker's in 1944. Miles Davis and John Coltrane, in *Kind of Blue,* create "free jazz."

Top Performers (*Downbeat*): Lester Young (soloist); Count Basie, Les Brown (bands); Dave Brubeck (jazz group); Stan Getz, Gerry Mulligan, Tony Scott, J. J. Johnson, Miles Davis (instrumentalists); Ella Fitzgerald, Frank Sinatra (vocalists); Lambert, Hendricks and Ross (vocal group)

Theater

Broadway Openings

Plays
A Raisin in the Sun (Lorraine Hansberry), Claudia McNeil, Sidney Poitier
The Miracle Worker (William Gibson), Anne Bancroft, Patty Duke
The Tenth Man (Paddy Chayefsky), George Voskovec, Lou Jacobi, Jack Gilford
Five Finger Exercise (Peter Shaffer), Jessica Tandy, Michael Bryant, Brian Bedford
A Majority of One (Leonard Spigelgass), Cedric Hardwicke, Gertrude Berg
Sweet Bird of Youth (Tennessee Williams), Geraldine Page, Paul Newman
The Andersonville Trial (Saul Levitt), George C. Scott, Herbert Berghof, Albert Dekker
Rashomon (Fay and Michael Kanin), Rod Steiger, Claire Bloom
Mark Twain Tonight, Hal Holbrook

Musicals
Fiorello! (Jerry Bock, Sheldon Harnick), Tom Bosley, Patricia Wilson, Howard da Silva
The Sound of Music (Richard Rodgers, Oscar Hammerstein II), Mary Martin, Theodore Bikel, Kurt Kazner

Once upon a Mattress (Mary Rodgers, Marshall Barer), Carol Burnett
Gypsy (Jule Styne, Stephen Sondheim), Ethel Merman, Jack Klugman, Sandra Church
Take Me Along (Robert Merrill), Jackie Gleason, Walter Pidgeon, Eileen Herlie, Robert Morse
At the Drop of a Hat, played and written by Michael Flanders, Donald Swann

Classics and Revivals On and Off Broadway
Much Ado about Nothing, Margaret Leighton, Maurice Evans; *Heartbreak House* (George Bernard Shaw), Maurice Evans, Pamela Brown; *The Connection* (Jack Gelber), Leonard Hicks, Ira Lewis; *The Zoo Story* (Edward Albee), George Maharis; *The Balcony* (Jean Genet), Nancy Marchand

Regional

Founded: Dallas Theater Center by Robert D. Stecker, Sr., and Beatrice Handel

Pulitzer Prize
J. B., Archibald MacLeish

Tony Awards
J. B., Archibald MacLeish (play); *Redhead,* Albert Hague, Dorothy Fields (musical)

Classical Music

Compositions

Walter Piston, Concerto for Piano and Orchestra
William Schuman, *Three Moods*
David Diamond, Symphony no. 7
Ralph Shapey, Violin Concerto
Virgil Thomson, *Collected Poems*
Wallingford Riegger, Variations for Violin and Orchestra
Elliott Carter, Second String Quartet
Gian Carlo Menotti / Samuel Barber, *A Hand of Bridge*
Gunther Schuller, Concertino, *Conversations*

Important Events

Celebrations include the tercentenary of Purcell's birth, the bicentennial of Handel's death, the sesquicentenary of Haydn's death, and the sesquincentennial of Mendelssohn's birth.
Mischa Elman, celebrating his fifty years of performance, presents a gala concert (New York).
The New York Philharmonic, under the auspices of Eisenhower's International Program for Cultural Presentations, gives 50 concerts in 17 countries, including its first performance in Russia since the revolution (*Rites of Spring* and *The Age of Anxiety*).
Closer international relations between the United States and USSR are also marked by visits in the United States of Dmitri Shostakovich, Tikhon Khrennikov, Dmitri Kabelevsky, Konstantin Dankevitch, and Fikret Amirov.
Pablo Casals leads the Third Festival in San Juan.
Maria Callas and Van Cliburn perform to capacity audiences at the Philadelphia Academy of Music ($100 a ticket).
Jaime Laredo wins the Belgian International Prize and debuts at Carnegie Hall.

First Performances

Paul Hindemith, *Pittsburgh Symphony* (commissioned for the city's birthday); Bohuslav Martinů, *Parables* (Boston); Walter Piston, *Three New England Sketches* (Worcester, Mass.); George Rochberg, Symphony no. 2 (Cleveland); Paul Creston, *Janus* (Denver); Howard Hanson, *Summer Seascape* (New Orleans); John Vincent, *Symphonic Poem after Descartes* (Philadelphia); Ned Rorem, Symphony no. 3 (New York)

Opera

Metropolitan: Eleanor Steber, Hermann Uhde, *Wozzeck* (Alban Berg, premiere); Giulietta Simionato (debut), *Il trovatore;* Cornell MacNeil (debut), *Rigoletto;* Renata Tebaldi, Mario del Monaco, George London, *Tosca;* Birgit Nilsson, *Tristan und Isolde*

New York City: *Six Characters in Search of an Author* (Hugo Weisgall, premiere)

Chicago: Leontyne Price, *Thaïs;* Sylvia Fisher, Gre Brouwenstijn (debuts), *Jenůfa;* Christa Ludwig, *Così fan tutte*

San Francisco: Sena Jurinac, *Madama Butterfly; Die Frau ohne Schatten* (Richard Strauss, American premiere)

Music Notes

Columbia and Princeton universities receive $175,000 from the Rockefeller Foundation to establish an electronic music center.

Far left: Tennessee Williams, author of *Sweet Bird of Youth. Billy Rose Theatre Collection. The New York Public Library at Lincoln Center. Astor, Lenox and Tilden Foundations.*

Sidney Poitier in the Broadway production of *A Raisin in the Sun,* Lorraine Hansberry's play about the aspirations of a black family. *Billy Rose Theatre Collection. The New York Public Library at Lincoln Center. Astor, Lenox and Tilden Foundations.*

Art

Painting

Adolph Gottlieb, *Brink*
Franz Kline, *Orange and Black Wall, Dahlia,*
Jasper Johns, *Numbers in Color* (1958–59)
Hans Hofmann, *Cathedral*
Larry Rivers, *The Last Civil War Veteran*
Frank Stella, *The Marriage of Reason and Squalor*
Willem de Kooning, *Merritt Parkway*
Morris Louis, *Blue Veil* (1958–59), *Saraband*
Stuart Davis, *The Paris Bit*
Ellsworth Kelly, *Gate, Running White*
Josef Albers, *Homage to the Square: With Rays*
Kenneth Noland, *Virginia Site*

Sculpture

Alexander Calder, *Big Red, Black Widow*
Isamu Noguchi, *Integral*
Richard Lippold, *Variation No. 7: Full Moon*

Louise Nevelson, *Dawn's Wedding Feast, Sky Columns— Presences*
John Chamberlain, *Wildroot*
Peter Voulkos, *Little Big Horn*

Architecture

Beth Sholom Synagogue, Elkins Park, Penn. (Frank Lloyd Wright)
Kalita Humphreys Theatre, Dallas (Frank Lloyd Wright)
Concordia Senior College, Fort Wayne, Ind. (Eero Saarinen)
Time-Life Building, New York (Harrison, Abramovitz, Harris)
Hockey Rink, Yale University, New Haven, Conn. (Eero Saarinen)
Stanford University Medical Center, Palo Alto, Calif. (Edward Durell Stone)
Asia House, New York (Philip Johnson)

Bolshoi Ballet. *Movie Star News.*

The Bolshoi Theatre Ballet of Moscow performs to record audiences with Galina Ulanova in *Romeo and Juliet;* other dancers include Maya Plisetskaya,

Important Exhibitions

Museums

New York: *Metropolitan:* French drawings from American collections; Homer and Gauguin retrospectives; Ceramic international exhibition. *Museum of Modern Art:* 20th-century design; Miró retrospective; The new American painting; Recent U.S. sculpture; "New Talent": David Hayes, Ronni Solbert, among others. *Whitney:* American sculpture, including Hopper, Zorach, Weber, O'Keeffe, Calder, Smith, Lipton

Chicago: Lithographs by Max Kahn; Contemporary Swedish fabrics; Rare Dutch drawings; Claude Bentley drawings; Homer and Gauguin retrospectives

Washington, Cleveland, Chicago, San Francisco: 150 Dutch paintings from the 15th to the 20th century

Washington: Impressionist and postimpressionist painting (on loan from private collections)

Toledo, Minneapolis: Poussin

Cincinnati: Robert Lehmann's American art collection

Baltimore: "The Age of Elegance: The Rococo"

Art Briefs

The Solomon R. Guggenheim Museum, New York City, opens • A Gilbert Stuart portrait of Thomas Jefferson is discovered • Van Gogh's *Park of the Hospital at Saint Rémy* sells for $74,000.

Dance

Raissa Struchkova, and Vladimir Levashev. Jerome Robbins's Ballets U.S.A. creates a sensation in Europe.

Premieres

New York City Ballet: *Episodes* (Martha Graham, George Balanchine), Graham, Sallie Wilson

San Francisco: *Danses Concertantes* (Lew Christensen, Stravinsky)

Alwin Nikolais, *Totem*

Books

Fiction

Critics' Choice

Malcolm, James Purdy
Goodbye Columbus and Five Short Stories, Philip Roth
The Poorhouse Fair, John Updike
The Sirens of Titan, Kurt Vonnegut
Henderson, the Rain King, Saul Bellow
The Mansion, William Faulkner
The Haunting of Hill House, Shirley Jackson
The Little Disturbances of Man, Grace Paley
The Empire City, Paul Goodman
The Naked Lunch, William Burroughs
&. *A Change of Heart*, Michel Butor

Best-Sellers

Exodus, Leon Uris
Doctor Zhivago, Boris Pasternak
Hawaii, James Michener
Advise and Consent, Allen Drury
Lady Chatterley's Lover, D. H. Lawrence
The Ugly American, William J. Lederer, Eugene L. Burdick
Lolita, Vladimir Nabokov
Poor No More, Robert Ruark
Mrs. 'Arris Goes to Paris, Paul Gallico
Dear and Glorious Physician, Taylor Caldwell

Nonfiction

Critics' Choice

Education and Freedom, Hyman Rickover
The American High School Today, James Bryant Conant
The Americans: The Colonial Experience, Daniel Boorstein
Advertisements for Myself, Norman Mailer
Life against Death. Norman O. Brown
The Question of Hamlet, Harry Levin
The Tragedy of American Diplomacy, William Appleman Williams
The Coming of the New Deal, Arthur Schlesinger, Jr.
The House of Intellect, Jacques Barzun
The Civil War: A Narrative, Shelby Foote
A History of Western Morals, Crane Brinton
James Joyce, Richard Ellmann
&. *The Two Cultures*, C. P. Snow
&. *The Phenomenon of Man*, Pierre Teilhard de Chardin

Best-Sellers

'Twixt Twelve and Twenty, Pat Boone
Folk Medicine, D. C. Jarvis
For 2¢ Plain, Harry Golden

The Status Seekers, Vance Packard
Act One, Moss Hart
Charley Weaver's Letters from Mamma, Cliff Arquette
The General Foods Kitchens Cookbook
Only in America, Harry Golden
Mine Enemy Grows Older, Alexander King
Elements of Style, William Strunk, Jr., E. B. White

Poetry

Robert Lowell, *Life Studies*
E. E. Cummings, *100 Selected Poems*
James Wright, *Saint Judas*
Robert Duncan, *Selected Poems, 1942–1950*
Jack Kerouac, *Mexico City Blues*
David Wagoner, *A Place to Stand*

Pulitzer Prizes

Advise and Consent, Allen Drury (fiction)
In the Days of McKinley, Margaret Leech (U.S. history)
John Paul Jones, Samuel Eliot Morison (biography)
Heart's Needle, William Snodgrass (poetry)

Science and Technology

Louis Leakey discovers the skull of Australopithecus (man-ape), 1.78 million years old, in the Olduvai Gorge, Tanganyika.
The Pioneer IV space probe passes the moon and heads into orbit around the sun.
The navy successfully orbits a Vanguard satellite, which will be the first weather station in space.
The navy develops a radar system to monitor Soviet nuclear tests and rocket launchings.
The red-eye, a heat-seeking missile, is developed.
Hypnosis, as a medical aid, is sanctioned by the AMA.

DNA isolated from a cancer-causing virus is found to cause cancer on its own.
&. Soviet Lunik II becomes the first man-made object to strike the moon; Lunik III takes the first photos of the moon's hidden side.

Nobel Prize

Emilio Segrè and Owen Chamberlain win the prize in physics for demonstrating the existence of the anti-proton. Severo Ochoa and Arthur Kornberg win in physiology and medicine for work on chromosomes.

Sports

Baseball

Harvey Haddix (St. Louis, NL) pitches 12 perfect innings against Milwaukee before giving up a hit in the 13th inning.
Rocky Colavito (Cleveland, AL) hits four home runs in one game.
Early Wynn (Chicago, AL) wins the Cy Young Award.

Champions

Batting
Henry Aaron (Milwaukee, NL), .355
Harvey Kuenn (Detroit, AL), .353

Pitching
Elroy Face (Pittsburgh, NL), 18–1
Robert Shaw (Chicago, AL), 18–6

Home runs
Ed Matthews (Milwaukee, NL), 46

Football

The American Football League is organized by Lamar Hunt with eight teams.
Vince Lombardi becomes Green Bay coach.

NFL Season Leaders: Charles Conerly (NY), passing; Jim Brown (Cleveland), rushing, 1,329 yards; Ray Berry (Baltimore), receiving.

College All-Americans: Bill Carpenter (E), Army; Charley Flowers (B), Mississippi; Billy Cannon (B), Louisiana State; Maxie Baughan (C), Georgia Tech

Bowls (Jan. 1, 1960)

Rose: Washington 44– Wisconsin 8
Orange: Georgia 14– Missouri 0
Cotton: Syracuse 23– Texas 14
Sugar: Mississippi 21– Louisiana State 0

Basketball

Wilt Chamberlain (Philadelphia) debuts.

NBA All-Pro First Team: Bob Pettit (St. Louis), Elgin Baylor (Minneapolis), Bill Russell (Boston), Bob Cousy (Boston), Bill Sharman (Boston)

Other Sports

Hockey: The Montreal Canadiens win their third straight Stanley Cup.

Winners

World Series
Los Angeles (NL) 4
Chicago (AL) 2
MVP
NL–Ernie Banks, Chicago
AL–Nelson Fox, Chicago
NFL
Baltimore 31–New York 16
MVP
Charles Conerly, New York
College Football
Louisiana State, Syracuse
Heisman Trophy
Billy Cannon, Louisiana State University
NBA Championship
Boston 4–Minneapolis 0

MVP
Bob Pettit, St. Louis
College Basketball
California
Player of the Year
Oscar Robertson, Cincinnati
Stanley Cup
Montreal
US Tennis Open
Men: Neale Fraser
Women: Maria Bueno
USGA Open
Bill Casper, Jr.
Kentucky Derby
Tommy Lee (W. Shoemaker, jockey)

Fashion

For Women: College girls wear brass button blazers, chesterfields, reversible or belted fur-trimmed coats, straight skirts with a dirndl fullness at the hip, and pleated skirts. Leotards with sleeveless jumpers are especially popular with massive jewelry or multiple strands of necklaces, along with tartans, madras plaids, and leather ensembles. Soft boots of tight, hugging, light suede appear. Shirtwaists remain a favorite, but more stylish dresses redefine the waistline in fitted styles in muted taupes, blues, black-white, blue-orange, and blue, the color of the year. At night the black cocktail dress with plunging neckline appears. A medium heel with rounded toe replaces spike heels.

High-fashion notes: Givenchy's soft jacket and cuffed skirt; Balenciaga and Givenchy's loose sleeve, and high neck blouse over slim skirt

For Men: The Continental look challenges the Ivy look, and pattern becomes predominant with richer fabrics and offbeat colors. Cuffless pants are more form fitting, and although still three-buttoned, jackets are narrower and shorter, with square shoulders and side vents; lapels are semipeaked, and pockets slant backward. Vests appear in different fabrics and colors, along with spread-collar shirts and silk, figure-decorated ties. Shoes are slimmer, with pointed toes.

Kaleidoscope _____

- A *Look* magazine poll on moral attitudes reports a moral relativity based on group acceptance: one should do whatever he wants as long as it would be accepted by the neighbors.
- TV quiz shows remain under investigation; in House hearings, producers Jack Barry and Dan Enright and contestant Charles Van Doren admit to "controls." Disc jockeys also come under investigation for accepting "payola."
- Letters to NBC are 5 to 1 against the firing of Charles Van Doren, hired by the network as an announcer; Columbia College students also rally to protest Van Doren's dismissal.
- After rigorous testing, the "Mercury Seven" astronauts are chosen: John Glenn, Scott Carpenter, Virgil Grissom, Gordon Cooper, Walter Schirra, Donald Slayton, and Alan Shepard.
- Eighty-six percent of the population owns a TV; the average person watches it 42 hours a week.
- Perry Como signs a $25 million contract with Kraft Foods.
- To combat TV's popularity, Hollywood makes more racy films like *Pillow Talk, Some Like It Hot, North by Northwest,* and *Anatomy of a Murder.*
- The government experiments with programs for bright students; languages are introduced in grade school; early college admissions are encouraged.
- Japanese-Americans whose citizenship was surrendered during the war gain restitution.
- Nixon and Khrushchev debate in the kitchen of a model home at the U.S. National Exhibition in Moscow.
- On Khrushchev's visit to Washington, he comments to CIA director Allen Dulles: "I believe we get the same reports—and probably from the same people."
- Oklahoma finally repeals Prohibition, which came with statehood in 1907.
- The Lincoln penny is redesigned with the Lincoln Memorial on one side.
- At the American National Exhibition in Moscow, Rep. Frances E. Walters (D, Pa.) associates many of the 67 artists on display with "communist fronts and causes"; Eisenhower stands by the artists, who include Andrew Wyeth, Ben Shahn, Robert Motherwell, Willem de Kooning, and Jackson Pollock.
- Modern art is declared duty free by a bill signed into law.
- After a USSR nuclear testing period, reports are released of a 300 percent increase in atmospheric radioactivity in the eastern United States.
- A contaminated-cranberries scare around Thanksgiving frightens millions of Americans.
- General Motors redesigns its cars with larger portholes and more chrome; small cars, like the Falcon, become popular; the Lark is introduced. Cadillac is designed with a large expanse of rear glass, a "jeweled" rear grill, pointed fins, "cruise control" heating units, electric door locks, and air conditioning.

Jonas Salk, inventor of the first polio vaccine. *Copyright* Washington Post. *Reprinted by permission of D.C. Public Library.*

The Chrysler has swivel seats, electric mirrors, and automatic headlight dimmers.
- The total of deaths from auto accidents in the U.S. surpasses the total of American deaths in war.
- The average car costs $1,180 ($1,300 in 1939).
- Rock and roll stars Buddy Holly, Ritchie Valens, and the Big Bopper are killed in a plane crash.
- Dell pays a record $265,000 for the paperback rights to *Return to Peyton Place.*
- Khrushchev is denied entrance to Disneyland because security cannot be guaranteed.
- Eisenhower is welcomed by millions in India and hailed as the "Prince of Peace."
- In *Life against Death,* a psychoanalytic interpretation of history, Norman O. Brown argues for "polymorphous perversity," a return to intuition and rejection of rationality.

Fads: Go-karting; black leotards; do-it-yourself sports (boating, bowling); western paraphernalia, like toy guns; parachute jumping as a sport

New Words and Usages: A gas, cut out, get with it, gung ho, joint, head, make the scene, a groove, bugged, chick

First Appearances: Transparent plastic bags for clothing, weather station, movies with scent (*Behind the Great Wall*), nuclear merchant ship (*Savannah*)

THE *Sixties*

"Think of the time we're living through. Both of us young, with health, and two wonderful children—and to live through all this." Jacqueline Kennedy. *Library of Congress.*

Statistics

Vital
Population: 177,830,000
 Urban/rural: 125/54
 Farm: 8.7%
Life expectancy
 Male: 66.6
 Female: 73.1
Births/1,000: 23.7
Marriages/1,000: 8.5
Divorces/1,000: 2.2
Deaths/1,000: 9.5
 per 100,000
 Heart: 522
 Cancer: 149
 Tuberculosis: 6
 Car accidents: 21.3

Economic
Unemployed: 3,852,000
GNP: $503.7 billion
Federal budget: $92.3 billion
National debt: $286.3 billion
Union membership: 17.5
 million
Strikes: 3,333
Prime rate: 3.9%
Car sales: 6,674,200
Average salary: $4,743

Social
Homicides/100,000: 4.7
Suicides/100,000: 10.6
Lynchings: 0
Labor force male/female:
 49/23
Social welfare: $52.3 billion
Public education: $15.6 billion
College degrees
 Bachelors'
 Male: 253,000
 Female: 157,000
 Doctorates
 Male: 8,801
 Female: 1,028
Attendance
 Movies (weekly): 40 million
 Baseball (yearly): 20.3
 million

Consumer
Consumer Price Index
 (1967 = 100): 88.7
Eggs: 58¢ (doz.)
Milk: 26¢ (qt.)
Bread: 20¢ (loaf)
Butter: 75¢ (lb.)
Bacon: 66¢ (lb.)
Round steak: $1.06 (lb.)
Oranges: 75¢ (doz.)
Coffee: 75¢ (lb.)

The sixties were a time of momentous social movements and sweeping legislation, of remarkable space achievements and tragic assassinations, a time during which the longest war and most active antiwar protest in American history took place. Although the economy prospered, a social and political idealism challenged the materialistic values and conformity of the fifties with an energy that effected changes throughout the American scene. The youth movement, with its assault on authority ("the establishment"), gained an influence that was unprecedented in American history.

The decade began with a new type of leadership. John Kennedy—young, handsome, Harvard educated, wealthy, and Catholic—won broad public acclaim on the first televised presidential debate. By the barest popular majority, the dashing knight of Camelot defeated Richard Nixon to succeed the fatherly Dwight Eisenhower. Kennedy faltered at the Bay of Pigs but demonstrated his capability in the Cuban missile crisis. He built conventional forces, accelerated the production of atomic missiles, cut taxes to stimulate the economy, and embarked on a massive space program; he also established the Peace Corps and proposed civil rights legislation. Kennedy brought to the presidency a youthful, sophisticated, and widely admired style. His wife, Jacqueline, possessed a vibrant beauty and caché that also elicited voguish emulation. By 1963, the country was alive and hopeful, although, on the domestic scene, few changes had yet been made.

The day of Kennedy's assassination, much like December 7, 1941, is one of the few days of national import on which most Americans alive at the time can trace their whereabouts. The tragic, senseless death of a man in the prime of life who embodied so much of the American ideal of intelligence, power, and generosity of spirit was taken by the grieving nation as evidence of a violent, dark side to the national character, of a spiritual viciousness that underlay the country's material well being.

Indeed, there did remain an intolerable shame in American life—the persistent denial of rights and subjection to humiliating indignities of blacks. Starting in the late fifties, increasing numbers of civil rights advocates had begun to challenge racial bigotry in the laws and mores of the land. In the early sixties, a major assault was mounted: blacks and some white supporters sat in at segregated lunch counters, boycotted segregated buses, sought to integrate white colleges, and organized marches on southern towns for voting rights. Their efforts were often brutally opposed, and the struggle was bloody. Their unifying force, nevertheless, was one of those great leaders that just causes sometimes find. Espousing the Gandhian ideology of nonviolent civil disobedience, Martin Luther King led many of the

marches, and his courage and brilliant power of expression gave an irresistible moral and spiritual impetus to the undeniable justice of his message. More than 250,000 at the 1963 Washington, D.C., civil rights march heard his "I have a dream" speech. In JFK's successor, Lyndon Johnson, Dr. King found an ally who would propose the legislation to codify the rights for which he fought. The civil rights bill of 1964 and the Voting Rights Act of 1965 made blacks at least equal before the law. That Congress passed these bills and other Johnson "Great Society" legislation, like Medicare and the poverty program, indicated, perhaps, that America yearned to fulfill its basic ideals and that material well-being alone was not sufficient; government had a responsibility for social change.

Much of the remaining decade involved youthful revolt against the establishment. Although Johnson had campaigned and won a giant victory as a champion of peace and social progress, he began sending combat troops to Vietnam in 1965. Many young people, already involved in the civil rights movement, saw the war as a further example of imperialistic might and materialist greed. As the "best and the brightest" of the administration pursued the war with increasing troop requirements and military power, a widening gap grew between a government that promised victory "around the corner" for a just cause and an increasing portion of the public that saw wanton destruction and defeat in a dubious or immoral war. America's lasting involvement in Vietnam undoubtedly gave energy and a broad base of adult support to the rebel youth and their cause.

The manifestations of antiestablishment sentiments were diverse, and they filtered through much of society. Dress and grooming changes were most visible. Hairstyles, especially for men, grew longer and wilder; beards and mustaches became popular. Women's skirts rose to mid-thigh, and bras were discarded. A casual unisex style favored faded jeans and decorated T-shirts. Large numbers of young people, many from middle-class backgrounds, "dropped out." Called "hippies," they advocated "alternate life-styles," "doing your own thing," and being "laid back." They proposed "turning on" and "making love, not war." Drug use increased, especially marijuana and LSD ("acid"), as a vehicle to more authentic experience ("trips"). Some went to live together in "communes"; others espoused meditation, Zen, astrology, and cult religions. Many sought to evade the draft by remaining in school or leaving the country. They adored the Beatles and later turned to "acid rock," practiced by such groups as the Rolling Stones, Big Brother with Janis Joplin, Jimi Hendrix, Grateful Dead, and Jefferson Airplane. Bob Dylan's and Joan Baez's folk lyrics vocalized

Martin Luther King with Lyndon Johnson, as the president signs the Voting Rights Act. Johnson, in proposing the bill, uses the civil rights motto "We Shall Overcome." *LBJ Library.*

their credo: "The Times They Are a-Changin'." They danced with uninhibited sensuality in discos with light shows and psychedelic posters. Late in the decade, they gathered, in astonishing numbers, at public concerts to celebrate their values and community.

College campuses became a major site of demonstration. Initially focused in forums such as teach-ins and marches, protest later took the form of militant sit-ins (for example, at Columbia University) or armed occupation (Cornell), and many colleges and universities were forced to close down temporarily. Students later demanded the right to assess faculty, determine curriculum, and monitor university policy. They gathered off-campus as well, their most electrifying demonstration the 1967 March on the Pentagon celebrated in Norman Mailer's *Armies of the Night.*

The black movement also changed from the passive resistance of Martin Luther King to the "black power" of Stokely Carmichael. The initial unity of the civil rights movement fragmented, as groups such as SNIC, CORE, and the Black Panthers espoused a more militant black posture, ranging from an emphasis on black identity ("Black is Beautiful") to black separatism. From Watts to Harlem, ghetto riots resulted in numerous deaths and widespread property destruction.

The Supreme Court, headed by Earl Warren, issued rulings that led to major social change. Those that prohibited school prayer, assured legal counsel for the poor, limited censorship of sexual material, and increased the rights of the accused were among the most far-reaching.

Changes were evident elsewhere in American life. Pop artists, like Robert Rauschenberg, Roy Lichtenstein, Andy Warhol, and Jasper Johns, blurred the distinction between popular and high culture. "Camp" did the same. "Happenings" expressed a wish for a more spontaneous, less conventionally structured art form, as in the sculptured forms of Edward Kienholz or the music of John Cage; the Moog synthesizer produced an entirely new sound. Writers such as Truman Capote (*In Cold Blood*), Norman Mailer, and Tom Wolfe, blurred the distinction between fact and fiction. Postmoderns like John Barth, Donald Barthelme, and Robert Coover challenged the sanctity of language as a viable expression of perception and communication.

More traditional in form, works like Joseph Heller's *Catch-22* and Ken Kesey's *One Flew over the Cuckoo's Nest* portrayed as heroes the victims of what they envisioned as a basically insane, inhuman, authoritarian system. A vigorous black literature condemned a racist white society, ranging from James Baldwin's warning *The Fire Next Time* to Eldridge Cleaver's savage denunciation *Soul on Ice.* Conventional attitudes about women came under attack as Betty Friedan condemned the "feminine mystique" of the woman as housewife and mother in a male-dominated culture that subjugates women to male needs. Masters and Johnson demonstrated the myth of vaginal orgasm. Rachel Carson in *The Silent Spring* indicted industry for poisoning the environment; in *Unsafe at Any Speed,* Ralph Nader attacked the automakers and government for callous disregard of highway safety. (Nader, like Friedan and Baldwin, gathered large, idealistic followings.) Enovid, the first marketed oral contraceptive, enhanced the ease of sexual liberation, and institutes like Esalen presented opportunities for freedom from social and sexual convention.

A number of films also expressed the unique sixties sensibility—*Dr. Strangelove, The Graduate, Bob and Carol and Ted and Alice,* and *Easy Rider. Who's Afraid of Virginia Woolf?* violated accepted movie standards in its language and subject matter and was responsible for a new film code. In the late sixties, the legitimate stage, as well as movies, began to routinely portray the previously taboo. *Hair, Oh! Calcutta!,* and *I Am Curious (Yellow)* contained nudity, simulated and real sex, and unrestricted language. Among other emblems of the times were the epic of onanism *Portnoy's Complaint,* topless bathing suits, the Truth in Packaging law, Valium, go-go girls, and the list of rare and endangered species.

Although protest may have been the leading edge of the sixties, it was not, as Nixon's election was to indicate, everyone's "bag." With a booming economy, many Americans were not involved in

The Beatles revolutionize American song and hairstyles. Their first hit is "I Want to Hold Your Hand."

Neil Armstrong and Buzz Aldrin plant the American flag on the moon, July 20, 1969. *Courtesy NASA.*

protest, and they pursued less rebellious life-styles. Rural sit-coms like "The Beverly Hillbillies" and "Green Acres" topped the TV ratings, along with detective fare like "Kojak" and spy spoofs like "The Man from U.N.C.L.E." Films like Sean Connery's James Bond series enjoyed great popularity, as did Julie Andrews flying about as *Mary Poppins*. Barbra Streisand became a superstar, and her frizzed look and eclectic dress style were much copied. Neil Simon began his Broadway career with *Barefoot in the Park,* and Charles Shultz's *Peanuts* books sold widely. *Valley of the Dolls* (about show biz pill popping) and *The Godfather* were the enormous sellers, and *The Games People Play,* the top self-help book of the decade. The art and music worlds of the sixties produced some of the most interesting works in American cultural history; in sculpture alone were the great works of David Smith, Reuben Nakian, Louise Nevelson, Eva Hesse, George Segal, and Richard Lippold. In sports a new pro-football league, the AFL, challenged the NFL, and eventually the two merged to create a sensational new championship game to rival the World Series, the Super Bowl. Sports superstars included Joe Namath, Willie Mays, Sandy Koufax, Bill Russell, Wilt Chamberlain, and Cassius Clay.

When the North Vietnamese mounted their Tet offensive in 1968, many believed that despite 500,000 combat troops in Vietnam, the United States was still far from victory. After antiwar candidate Eugene McCarthy showed strongly in the New Hampshire primary, LBJ announced that he would not seek reelection, and Robert Kennedy entered the race. With student rebellions sweeping the world from Mexico to France to Japan, 1968 may well be seen as

the apotheosis of the sixties; Martin Luther King, Jr. was assassinated, and widespread rioting followed; Robert Kennedy, like his brother John, was assassinated; protesters led by the Youth International Party (yippies), clashed with Chicago mayor Richard Daley's police and turned the Democratic Convention into a battlefield.

Although the presidential election was close, Richard Nixon, appealing to the "silent majority," won. Committed to "peace with honor," he nonetheless called for, and in 1969 began, troop withdrawal. He established a lottery system for the draft, hoping to undercut student rebellion. While 1969 was the year that 500,000 young people gathered at Woodstock for a free concert, the public tide that was already turning against youth was further strengthened by two highly publicized crimes, the Manson family murders and a killing at a Rolling Stones concert. Adult sympathy for protest had centered on the young people's ideals, but these two events appeared to lend credence to the Nixon-Agnew indictment of the "permissivists."

Indeed, 1969 was also the year of a great establishment triumph. Space accomplishments had multiplied during the decade, and while some condemned the space program as pyramid building, most of the public watched with intense interest as men with "the right stuff," like Neil Armstrong, Buzz Aldrin, and Michael Collins, made increasingly complex journeys into space. On July 20, 1969, 700 million throughout the world witnessed, via television, an American plant the first step on the moon—a happening to forever fire the imagination of human possibility.

1960

Facts and Figures

Economic Profile
Dow-Jones: — High 685–
   Low 566
GNP: +4%
Inflation: +1.4%
Unemployment: 5.5%
GE spray iron: $21.95
Toastmaster electric toaster:
   $34.95
Waring blender: $39.95
Universal coffee maker:
   $29.95
Philco portable TV (17"):
   $139.95
A&P:
   Swordfish steaks: 59¢ (lb.)
   Codfish: 39¢ (lb.)
   Veal shoulder: 69¢ (lb.)
   Bottom or top round roast:
      77¢ (lb.)
   Brussels sprouts: 19¢ (pint)
   Chicken of the Sea white-
      meat tuna: 39¢
Apartments, New York City:
   Park Ave., 65th St., 5
      rooms, 2 baths: $500
   140–150 E. 56th St., 2½–4
      rooms: from $165
   Central Park West, 8
      rooms, view: $425

Deaths

Jussi Bjoerling, Oscar
   Hammerstein II, Clara
   Haskell, Aly Khan, Dimitri
   Mitropoulos, Boris
   Pasternak, Emily Post,
   Margaret Sullavan,
   Lawrence Tibbett.

In the News

IKE SAYS ATLAS ICBM CAN GO 5,000 MILES . . . KHRUSHCHEV CLAIMS SOVIET ICBM GOES 7,762 MILES . . . BLACKS SIT IN AT GREENSBORO, NORTH CAROLINA, LUNCH COUNTER . . . FRENCH TEST FIRST A-BOMB IN SAHARA . . . CASTRO AND RUSSIANS SIGN ECONOMIC AGREEMENT . . . SOUTH AFRICAN POLICE KILL 92 BLACKS DURING DEMONSTRATION AT SHARPEVILLE . . . CIVIL RIGHTS ACT PROVIDES VOTING REFEREES . . . CHINESE COMMUNISTS ATTACK MODERN REVISIONISM IN FIRST RIFT WITH MOSCOW . . . U-2 RECONNAISSANCE JET, WITH PILOT GARY POWERS, IS SHOT DOWN OVER RUSSIA . . . MURDERER-WRITER CARYL CHESSMAN IS EXECUTED, INTERNATIONAL PROTESTS OCCUR . . . BRITISH PRINCESS MARGARET AND PHOTOGRAPHER TONY ARMSTRONG-JONES MARRY . . . KHRUSHCHEV, IN PARIS, DENOUNCES U.S. OVER POWERS INCIDENT, SUMMIT IS CALLED OFF . . . ATLAS ICBM GOES 9,000 MILES . . . ISRAELIS KIDNAP ADOLF EICHMANN FROM ARGENTINA TO JERUSALEM . . . IKE POSTPONES VISIT TO JAPAN BECAUSE OF ANTI-U.S. DEMONSTRATIONS . . . BELGIAN CONGO BECOMES INDEPENDENT . . . IKE CUTS CUBAN SUGAR QUOTA AND THREATENS COMMUNISTS IN WESTERN HEMISPHERE, KHRUSHCHEV THREATENS RETALIATION . . . JOHN F. KENNEDY WINS DEMOCRATIC NOMINATION, NIXON WINS GOP . . . UN FORCES ARE SENT TO CONGO TO RESTORE PEACE . . . CUBA EXPROPRIATES U.S. ASSETS . . . GARY POWERS IS SENTENCED TO 70 YEARS IN MOSCOW . . . CONGO PRESIDENT KASAVUBU EJECTS LEFTIST PREMIER LUMUMBA . . . KHRUSHCHEV AT U.N. POUNDS SHOE IN ANGER . . . DE GAULLE ANNOUNCES SELF-RULE AND REFERENDUM FOR INDEPENDENCE IN ALGERIA . . . KENNEDY WINS NARROW VICTORY BY 112,881, DEMOCRATS SWEEP CONGRESS . . . TWO WHITE PUBLIC SCHOOLS IN NEW ORLEANS ARE FIRST TO INTEGRATE . . . TWO AIRLINERS COLLIDE OVER STATEN ISLAND, 134 DIE.

Quotes

We've grown unbelievably prosperous, and we maunder along in a stupor of fat."

— Eric Goldman

"The politics of the Fifties were . . . the politics of fatigue . . . [and student] apathy probably unexampled in history. . . . [We chose] to invest not in people but in things."

— Arthur Schlesinger, Jr., "The Mood in Politics"

"We don't expect to live in [these houses] . . . very long. Some of the junior executives expect to become seniors . . . and a lot of us will be transferred all over the U.S. . . . We want to be sure there is a good re-sale value."

— Deerfield, Illinois, couple agitating against black occupancy

"Our society is an immense stamping ground for the careless production of underdeveloped and malformed human beings . . . [not] concerned with moral issues, with serious purposes, or with human dignity."

— Robert Heilbroner

"[Nixon] never told the truth in his life."

— Harry S Truman

"Our Secretary of Defense now frankly concedes that . . . the Soviet Union . . . will have a three-to-one superiority in the intercontinental ballistic missile."

— John F. Kennedy

"The Democrats were going to nominate a man who, no matter how serious his political dedication might be, was indisputably and willy-nilly going to be seen as a great box-office actor, and the consequences of that were staggering."

— Norman Mailer, "Superman Comes to the Supermarket"

"[We need] a new generation of leadership—new men to cope with new problems and new opportunities."

— John F. Kennedy

Ads

One thing leads to another. Babies just like mother used to make. But . . . young adults make them faster than ever. . . . These growing families buy by the gallon. . . . You see them throng shopping centers and [we] got them first.

(Redbook)

Stop right now and forget everything you ever knew about being a blonde. Up to now you could never be any of these delicate blondes.

(Clairol)

Here's the new white hexachlorophene paste with the cool clean refreshing minty taste. It's the one that kills decay germs best of all leading brands.

(Ipana)

No hits and misses. No dibs, dabs, and splatters.

(5-Day Deodorant Pads)

Around the world, the same standard of excellence you have learned to expect—250 branch offices, 14 manufacturing plants, 33,000 employees.

(IBM Machines)

I'M VOTING FOR NIXON
NO GIVE AWAYS!
Remember Yalta?
NO APOLOGIES!
Remember the Summit?
NO PIE IN THE SKY!
Remember it's YOUR Money
Jack will play Poker with

Pro-Nixon button. An October Gallup poll calls the race too close to call. *Smithsonian Institution.*

Small wonder.

(Volkswagen)

Nothing else you use so often does so much yet costs so little. And the more you use it the more valuable it becomes.

(Bell Telephone)

Don't spread the cold. . . . Spread the word.

(Coldene Cold Tablets)

A homemade product, juvenile delinquency can be stopped at home.

(Public Service Ad)

TV

Premieres

"Route 66," George Maharis, Martin Milner
"Sing Along with Mitch"
"My Three Sons," Fred MacMurray
"The Flintstones" (first prime-time cartoon)
"The Andy Griffith Show"
"The Bob Newhart Show"
"Saturday Night at the Movies"
"Eyewitness to History," Charles Kuralt
"Face the Nation," Stuart Movins

Top Ten (Nielsen)

"Gunsmoke," "Wagon Train," "Have Gun, Will Travel," "The Andy Griffith Show," "The Real McCoys," "Rawhide," "Candid Camera," "The Untouchables," "The Price Is Right," "The Jack Benny Show"

Specials

"The Nixon-Kennedy Debate," "Winston Churchill: The Valiant Years," "Aaron Copland's Birthday Party," "Leonard Bernstein and the New York Philharmonic," "Harvest of Shame" (Fred Friendly, David Lowe, Edward R. Murrow), "Astaire Time," "Macbeth" (Maurice Evans, Judith Anderson), "Interview with Nikita Khrushchev" (David Susskind)

Emmy Awards

"Macbeth" (program and drama); "Jack Benny Show" (comedy); "Astaire Time" (variety); Raymond Burr (actor, "Perry Mason"); Barbara Stanwyck (actress, "The Barbara Stanwyck Show"); "Huntley-Brinkley Report" (news)

Of Note

"Howdy Doody" ends after 13 years and 2,343 episodes, as Clarabell, the silent clown, finally speaks: "Goodnight, kids" • CBS's unsponsored coverage of the winter Olympic Games draws unexpectedly high ratings.

Movies

Openings

The Apartment (Billy Wilder), Jack Lemmon, Shirley MacLaine, Fred MacMurray
The Alamo (John Wayne), John Wayne, Richard Widmark, Laurence Harvey
Elmer Gantry (Richard Brooks), Burt Lancaster, Jean Simmons
Never on Sunday (Jules Dassin), Melina Mercouri, Jules Dassin
Psycho (Alfred Hitchcock), Anthony Perkins, Janet Leigh
Inherit the Wind (Stanley Kramer), Spencer Tracy, Fredric March, Gene Kelly
Spartacus (Stanley Kubrick), Kirk Douglas, Laurence Olivier, Jean Simmons
Exodus (Otto Preminger), Paul Newman, Eva Marie Saint, Sal Mineo
Butterfield 8 (Daniel Mann), Elizabeth Taylor, Laurence Harvey
The Fugitive Kind (Sidney Lumet), Marlon Brando, Anna Magnani, Joanne Woodward
The Magnificent Seven (John Sturges), Yul Brynner, Steve McQueen, Eli Wallach
Where the Boys Are (Henry Levin), George Hamilton, Yvette Mimieux
The Virgin Spring (Ingmar Bergman), Max von Sydow, Birgitta Valberg
L'Avventura (Michelangelo Antonioni), Monica Vitti, Gagride Ferzetti
Big Deal on Madonna Street (Mario Monicelli), Vittorio Gassman, Marcello Mastroianni

Academy Awards

Best Picture: *The Apartment*
Best Director: Billy Wilder (*The Apartment*)
Best Actress: Elizabeth Taylor (*Butterfield 8*)
Best Actor: Burt Lancaster (*Elmer Gantry*)

Top Box-Office Stars

Doris Day, Rock Hudson, Cary Grant, Elizabeth Taylor, Debbie Reynolds, Tony Curtis, Sandra Dee, Frank Sinatra, Jack Lemmon, John Wayne

Stars of Tomorrow

Jane Fonda, Stephen Boyd, John Gavin, Susan Kohner, Troy Donahue, Angie Dickinson, Tuesday Weld, Fabian, James Darren, George Hamilton

Art Blakey. *Movie Star News.*

Popular Music

Top Records

Albums: *The Sound of Music* (original cast); *Persuasive Percussion* (Terry Snyder and the All Stars); *Nice 'n' Easy* (Frank Sinatra)

Singles: *The Twist* (Chubby Checker); *Georgia on My Mind* (Ray Charles); *It's Now or Never* (Elvis Presley); *Everybody's Somebody's Fool* (Connie Francis); *Where or When* (Dion and the Belmonts); *Puppy Love* (Paul Anka); *Let It Be Me* (Everly Brothers); *I Want to Be Wanted* (Brenda Lee); *Handy Man* (Jimmy Jones); *Ramona* (The Blue Diamonds). Country: *He'll Have to Go* (Jim Reeves)

Grammy Awards

Theme from "A Summer Place," Percy Faith (record); *The Button-Down Mind of Bob Newhart,* Bob Newhart (album); "Theme from *Exodus*" (song)

Jazz and Big Bands

Dave Brubeck continues his experiments with irregular meter in *Time Out;* Ornette Coleman makes "Free Jazz" with free group improvisation and the use of African instruments.
Joe Williams leaves Count Basie; John Coltrane leaves Miles Davis to form his own quartet and records *Meditations.*
A riot occurs at the Newport Jazz Festival.

Top Performers *(Downbeat):* Dizzy Gillespie (soloist); Count Basie, Les Brown (bands); Modern Jazz Quartet (jazz group); Cannonball Adderley, John Coltrane, Buddy DeFranco, Milt Jackson, Herbie Mann (instrumentalists); Ella Fitzgerald, Frank Sinatra (vocalists); Lambert, Hendricks and Ross (vocal group)

Hit Songs

"Alley Oop"
"Are You Lonesome To-Night"
"Chain Gang"
"If Ever I Would Leave You"
"Never on Sunday"
"Theme from 'The Apartment' "
"Tracy's Theme"
"You Talk Too Much"
"Itsy Bitsy Teenie Weenie Yellow Polka Dot Bikini"

Theater

Broadway Openings

Plays

All the Way Home (Tad Mosel), Lillian Gish, Colleen Dewhurst, Arthur Hill
Toys in the Attic (Lillian Hellman), Jason Robards, Jr., Maureen Stapleton, Irene Worth
A Taste of Honey (Shelagh Delaney), Joan Plowright, Angela Lansbury, Billy Dee Williams
Becket (Jean Anouilh), Laurence Olivier, Anthony Quinn
The Best Man (Gore Vidal), Melvyn Douglas, Frank Lovejoy, Lee Tracy
A Thurber Carnival (James Thurber), Tom Ewell, Peggy Cass, Paul Ford
Period of Adjustment (Tennessee Williams), James Daly, Barbara Baxley, Robert Webber
Advise and Consent (Loring Mandel), Richard Kiley, Ed Begley, Chester Morris
The Hostage (Brendan Behan), Alfred Lynch
An Evening with Mike Nichols and Elaine May
Duel of Angels (Jean Giraudoux), Vivien Leigh, Mary Ure

Little Moon of Alban (James Costigan), Robert Redford, Julie Harris, John Justin

Musicals

Irma La Douce (Marguerite Monnot, Julian More, et al.), Keith Mitchell, Elizabeth Seal, Clive Revill
Do Re Mi (Jule Styne, Betty Comden, Adolph Green), Nancy Walker, Phil Silvers
The Fantasticks (Harvey Schmidt, Tom Jones), Jerry Orbach (to be longest running musical in history)
Bye, Bye Birdie (Charles Strouse, Lee Adams), Dick Van Dyke, Chita Rivera, Dick Gautier
Camelot (Frederick Leowe, Alan Jay Lerner), Robert Goulet, Julie Andrews, Richard Burton
The Unsinkable Molly Brown (Meredith Willson), Tammy Grimes, Harve Presnell

Classics and Revivals On and Off Broadway

Krapp's Last Tape (Samuel Beckett), Donald Davis; *Women of Trachis* (Sophocles), Judith Malina; *The Prodigal* (Jack Richardson). *Founded:* Repertory Theatre of Lincoln Center with directors Robert Whitehead and Elia Kazan; APA by Ellis Raab

Theater (cont.)

Regional

Founded: Cincinnati Playhouse in the Park by Brook Jones

Actor's Workshop, San Francisco: *The Birthday Party* (Harold Pinter); *Saint's Day* (John Whiting), premieres

Pulitzer Prize

Fiorello: George Abbott, Jerry Bock, Sheldon Harnick, Jerome Weidman

Tony Awards

The Miracle Worker, William Gibson (play); *Fiorello!* George Abbott, Jerry Bock, Sheldon Harnick, Jerome Weidman, and *The Sound of Music,* Richard Rodgers, Oscar Hammerstein II (musical)

Classical Music

Compositions

Elliott Carter, String Quartet no. 2
Walter Piston, Symphony no. 7
George Perle, Three Movements for Orchestra
Irving Fine, *V-Alcestis*
Paul Creston, Violin Concerto
Milton Babbitt, Composition for Tenor and Six Instruments
Aaron Copland, Nonet for Strings
John Cage, *Theatre Piece*
Lukas Foss, *Time Cycle*

Important Events

Anniversaries celebrated throughout the world include the 250th birthday of Pergolesi, 150th of Chopin and Schumann, and 100th of Mahler. Pierre Monteux and Fritz Kreisler are 85; Aaron Copland is 60; Wallingford Riegger is 75. Musical exchanges are numerous: the Israeli Philharmonic and Moscow State symphonies visit the United States. Emil Gilels plays an all-Tchaikovsky concert, New York; Copland, Foss, and Byron Janis visit the USSR. A growing number of festivals present avant-garde "serialism" and electronic pieces. Malcolm Frager, 25, wins the Queen Elisabeth International Music Competition in Brussels after premiering Marcel Poot's Piano Concerto. Sviatoslav Richter tours the United States. At Eugene Ormandy's request, Leopold Stokowski returns, after 19 years, to conduct the Philadelphia Orchestra; he introduces Shirley Verrett, in de Falla's *El amor brujo*.

Conductors in New Locations: Stanislaw Skrowaczewski replaces Antal Dorati in Minneapolis; Georg Solti goes to Los Angeles; John Barbirolli goes to Houston.

First Performances: William Schuman, Symphony no. 7 (Boston); Roger Sessions, Symphony no. 4 (Minneapolis); Walter Piston, Concerto no. 2 for Violin (Pittsburgh); Paul Hindemith, Sinfonietta in E Major (Minneapolis); Samuel Barber, *Toccata Festiva* (Philadelphia), *A Hand of Bridge* (Boston).

Opera

Metropolitan: Anselmo Colzani (debut), *Simon Boccanegra;* Jon Vickers (debut), *I pagliacci;* Leonie Rysanek, Cesare Siepi, Rosalind Elias, Cornell MacNeil, *Nabucco;* Eileen Farrell (debut), *Alcestis;* Hermann Prey, *Tannhaüser*. During *La forza* Leonard Warren dies on stage.

New York City: *The Inspector General* (Werner Egk, premiere)

Dallas: Joan Sutherland (debut), *Alcina;* Sutherland, Giuseppi Taddei, Elisabeth Schwarzkopf, *Don Giovanni*

Chicago: Renata Scotto (debut), Richard Tucker, *La bohème;* Renata Tebaldi, *Fedora* (Giordano); Jon Vickers, Birgit Nilsson, *Die Walküre*

San Francisco: Marilyn Horne, Geraint Evans, *Wozzeck*

Music Notes

Isaac Stern leads a campaign to save Carnegie Hall from destruction; New York City takes title and gives the hall to a nonprofit organization to run • Harold Schonberg replaces Howard Taubman as *New York Times* music critic.

Art

Painting

Willem de Kooning, *Door to the River, A Tree in Naples*

Kenneth Noland, *Provence, Whirl*

Frank Stella, *Marquis de Portago*

Sam Francis, *Middle Blue, No. 5*

Edward Hopper, *Second-Story Sunlight*

Robert Indiana, *Moon*

Philip Evergood, *Virginia in the Grotto*

Adolph Gottlieb, *Circular*

Jasper Johns, *Light Bulb*

Morris Louis, *Beta Lambda*

Sculpture

Louise Nevelson, *Sky Cathedral*

Mark di Suvero, *Hankchampion*

Architecture

T.W.A. Terminal, John F. Kennedy Airport, New York (Eero Saarinen)

Union Carbide Building, New York City (Skidmore, Owings, and Merrill)

Climatron, St. Louis, Mo. (Murphy and Mackay)

Colonnades Apartments, Newark, N.J. (Mies van der Rohe)

IBM Watson Research, Yorktown Heights, N.Y. (Edward Durell Stone)

Gateway Center, Pittsburgh (Harrison and Abramovitz)

First Presbyterian Church, Stamford, Conn. (Harrison and Abramovitz)

Important Exhibitions

Museums

New York: *Metropolitan:* "Ancient Art: Sumerian, Mesopotamian, Phoenician, Egyptian, Etruscan, and Roman Works"; 18th-century design; The arts of Denmark. *Museum of Modern Art:* "Monet: Seasons and Moments"; "New Images of Man"; 16 Americans; Art nouveau

Washington: Haniwa—Japanese Burial Mound Figures (sent by the Japanese government to commemorate the centennial of U.S.-Japanese diplomatic relations); Daumier

Detroit: "Masterpieces of Flemish Art—Van Eyck to Bosch"

Chicago: Corot; Japan's modern prints; Primitive art; Prints by Lasansky, Harold Altman, Rembrandt, and Ensor; Corot

Boston: Buddhist sculpture from Gandhara; Courbet; Feininger and Prendergast memorials; Corot

Philadelphia: Cassatt; Courbet; Corot

Robert Rauschenberg, *Summer Rental, Number 2*, 1960. Oil on canvas, 70 × 54". Collection of Whitney Museum of American Art. Gift of the Friends of the Whitney Museum of American Art.

Dallas: Magritte

Venice Biennale: Kline, Guston, and Hofmann represent the United States.

Art Briefs

An unprecedented number of galleries opens throughout the country, with numerous museums under construction • Levels of bidding at auctions soar • The first large-scale American sculpture exhibit is held in Paris; it includes Nevelson and Lassaw • Major sales include Cézanne's *Paysan en blouse bleue* ($406,000) and *Apples* ($200,000), and Braque's *The Violin* ($145,000).

Dance

The American Ballet Theatre is the first U.S. company to tour the USSR; Maria Tallchief and Toni Lander join the company.

Premieres

Alvin Ailey: *Revelations*

American Ballet Theatre: *Lady from the Sea* (Birgit Cullberg), Nora Kaye

New York City Ballet: *Monumentum pro Gesualdo* (Balanchine, Stravinsky), Diana Adams, Conrad Ludlow; *Liebeslieder Waltzer* (Balanchine), Adams

Martha Graham: *Acrobats of God*

San Francisco: *Con Amore* (Lew Christensen)

Books

Fiction

Critics' Choice

The Sot-Weed Factor, John Barth
The Waters of Kronos, Conrad Richter
The Magician of Lublin, Isaac Bashevis Singer
Set This House on Fire, William Styron
Rabbit, Run, John Updike
The Magic Christian, Terry Southern
The Violent Bear It Away, Flannery O'Connor
The Ferguson Affair, Ross MacDonald
❧ *The Affair,* C. P. Snow

Best-Sellers

Advise and Consent, Allen Drury
Hawaii, James A. Michener
The Leopard, Giuseppe di Lampedusa
The Chapman Report, Irving Wallace
Ourselves to Know, John O'Hara
The Constant Image, Marcia Davenport
Sermons and Soda-Water, John O'Hara

Nonfiction

Critics' Choice

Human Nature and the Human Condition, Joseph Wood Krutch
Love and Death in the American Novel, Leslie Fiedler
Grant Moves South, Bruce Catton
The Politics of Upheaval, Arthur M. Schlesinger, Jr.
Victory in the Pacific, 1945, Samuel Eliot Morison
The End of Ideology, Daniel Bell
The Liberal House, John Kenneth Galbraith
The Stages of Economic Growth, Eugene Rostow
Dictionary of American Slang, ed. Harold Wentworth, Stuart Berg Flexner
The Papers of Benjamin Franklin, ed. L. W. Larabee, W. J. Bell
Growing Up Absurd, Paul Goodman
Listen Yankee: The Revolution in Cuba, C. Wright Mills
Rococo to Cubism in Art and Literature, Wylie Sypher

Best-Sellers

Folk Medicine, D. C. Jarvis
The General Foods Kitchens Cookbook
May This House Be Safe from Tigers, Alexander King
Better Homes and Gardens Dessert Book

The Rise and Fall of the Third Reich, William L. Shirer
The Conscience of a Conservative, Barry Goldwater

Poetry

James Dickey, *Into the Stone and Other Poems*
Kenneth Koch, *Ko: or, A Season on Earth*
W. H. Auden, *Homage to Clio*
Randall Jarrell, *The Woman at the Washington Zoo*
W. S. Merwin, *The Drunk in the Furnace*
Anne Sexton, *To Bedlam and Part Way Back*
Denise Levertov, *With Eyes at the Back of Our Heads*
Charles Olson, *The Maximus Poems*
Gregory Corso, *The Happy Birthday of Death*

Pulitzer Prizes

To Kill a Mockingbird, Harper Lee (fiction)
Between War and Peace: The Potsdam Conference, Herbert Feis (U.S. history)
Charles Sumner and the Coming of the Civil War, David Donald (biography)
Times Three: Selected Verse from Three Decades, Phyllis McGinley (poetry)

Science and Technology

The laser (light amplification caused by stimulated emission of radiation) is created by Theodore Maiman.
Nick Holonyak invents the digital display for pocket calculators and electronic watches.
The first robot to imitate the grasping human hand is employed in a nuclear plant.
Echo I is launched, the world's first communications satellite.
The world's first weather satellite, Tiros I, is launched.
Robert Burns Woodward and German Martin Strell independently synthesize chlorophyll.

Drs. A. Jefferson and D. Gordon use ultrasound to diagnose brain damage.
Several new synthetic penicillins are developed, including cephalosporin, effective against penicillin-resistant organisms.

Nobel Prize

D. A. Glaser wins the prize in physics for the invention of the bubble chamber for the study of subatomic particles. Willard F. Libby wins in chemistry for the atomic time clock to estimate the age of objects by measuring their radioactivity.

Sports _____

Baseball

The Cy Young Award winner is Vernon Law
(Pittsburgh, NL).

Champions _____

Batting	Pitching
Pete Runnels (Boston, AL), .320	Ernie Broglio (St. Louis, NL), 21–9
Dick Groat (Pittsburgh, NL), .325	Jim Coates (New York, AL), 13–3
	Home runs
	Ernie Banks (Chicago, NL), 41

Football

Pete Rozelle becomes NFL commissioner.
Paul Hornung (Green Bay) scores a record 176
points. The AFL plays its first season; Houston beats
Los Angeles 24–16 before 32,183 spectators; the
winning player's share is $1,025.

NFL Season Leaders: Milt Plum (Cleveland),
passing; Jim Brown (Cleveland), rushing; Ray Berry
(Baltimore), receiving. **AFL Season Leaders:** Jack
Kemp (Los Angeles), passing; Abner Haynes
(Dallas), rushing; Lionel Taylor (Denver), receiving

College All-Americans: Mike Ditka (E) Pittsburgh,
Bob Lilly (T) Texas Christian, Bill Kilmer (UCLA)

Bowls (Jan. 1, 1961)

Rose: Washington 17–Minnesota 7	Cotton: Duke 7–Arkansas 6
Orange: Missouri 21–Navy 14	Sugar: Mississippi 14–Rice 6

Basketball

NBA All-Pro First Team: Bob Pettit (St. Louis),
Elgin Baylor (Minneapolis), Wilt Chamberlain
(Philadelphia), Bob Cousy (Boston), Oscar Robertson
(Cincinnati)

Olympics

At Rome, American gold medal winners include
Rafer Johnson (decathlon, 8,392 pts.), Cassius Clay
(light heavyweight boxing), Wilma Rudolph (100,
11.0s. and 200m, 24.0s.), Ralph Boston (broad jump,
26'7¾"), Don Bragg (pole vault, 15'5⅛"), Al Oerter
(discus, 184'1"). In the Winter Games at Squaw
Valley, California, Carol Heiss and David Jennings
win figure skating. The United States wins ice
hockey.

Other Sports

Boxing: Floyd Patterson knocks out Ingemar
Johansson in the fifth, becoming the first
heavyweight to regain his crown.

Golf: Jack Nicklaus, 20, is second to Arnold Palmer
in the U.S. Open.

Winners _____

World Series	*MVP*
Pittsburgh (NL) 4	Wilt Chamberlain,
New York (AL) 3	Philadelphia
MVP	*College Basketball*
NL–Richard Groat,	Ohio State
Pittsburgh	*Player of the Year*
AL–Roger Maris, New	Oscar Robertson,
York	Cincinnati
NFL	*Stanley Cup*
Philadelphia 17–Green Bay	Montreal
13	*US Tennis Open*
MVP	Men: Neal Fraser
Norm Van Brocklin, Los	Women: Darlene Hard
Angeles	*USGA Open*
College Football	Arnold Palmer
Minnesota	*Kentucky Derby*
Heisman Trophy	Venetian Way (W. Hartack,
Joe Bellino, Navy	jockey)
NBA Championship	
Boston 4–St. Louis 3	

Fashion _____

For Women: Mrs. Kennedy becomes the model of
good style in the empire-waist coat and dress, the
slim dirndl or elongated skirt that ends in a tapered
hem, the loose blouse worn with braided sash belt,
and the rich and patterned fabrics. Popular hair
styling involves the bouffant or "fluid bang." The
college set wears abstract expressionist designs in
colors of the harvest or stained glass. Coeds
especially favor culottes, skirts above the knee, and
knickers. Also "really in" are the bikini and chemise.

*High-fashion notes: Norrell's culottes; Thocolette's
topless Liberty Lawn nightdress; Chanel's rough
white tweed suit bound with navy braid; Gernreich's
cutaway diamond swimsuit*

For Men: Continental and British influences appear
in (1) bold prints, plaids, stripes, and checks for sport
jackets and topcoats, and (2) shirt colors in muted
olives, golds, heathers, blue, and grape.

Kaleidoscope

- Enovid 10, the first oral contraceptive, is marketed at 55 cents a pill.
- Eisenhower summarizes the progress of his presidency as including a 15 percent increase in average family income, 20 percent in real wages, 25 percent in output of goods, and more housing and school construction than ever before.
- Daniel Bell, describing the 1950s' sense of unity and moderation, publishes *The End of Ideology.* Herman Kahn's *On Thermonuclear War* discusses how, with careful planning, only 20 to 30 million Americans will be killed in a nuclear attack.
- Following the Greensboro, N.C., incident when four blacks sit down at a white lunch counter, 70,000 blacks and whites hold sit-ins in more than 100 cities.
- Brooklyn singer Barbra Streisand wins a Thursday night talent contest at a small Greenwich Village club with "A Sleepin' Bee."
- Berry Gordy borrows $800 and starts Motown Records.
- Ebbets Field, former home of the Brooklyn Dodgers, is demolished to become an apartment project site.
- The number of women over 14 in the work force increases from 25 percent in 1940 to 34 percent.
- The census shows large population gains in Nevada, Florida, Alaska, Arizona, and California.
- An estimated 850,000 "war baby" freshmen enter college, bringing total enrollment to 4 million; emergency living quarters are set up in dorm lounges, hotels, and trailer camps.
- Recognizing the new youth power, Pepsi-Cola begins a "For those who think young" campaign.
- John F. Kennedy, Jr., is born on November 25 by cesarean delivery.
- Aluminum cans for food and beverages are manufactured, although 95 percent of all soft drinks and 50 percent of all beer are sold in reusable bottles (reused 40 to 50 times).
- Lucille Ball and Desi Arnaz file for divorce.
- Ernest Evans, playing on Fats Domino's name, becomes Chubby Checker.
- Hollywood continues its permissive trend with films on so-called adult themes, such as *Butterfield 8.*
- The New York Circuit Court of Appeals moves that *Lady Chatterley's Lover* is not obscene.
- A new style that marks home furnishing includes the fusion of different period or national styles with unusual woods like African zebra wood.
- The year's most publicized joke results from NBC's censorship of Jack Paar's story of a WC mistaken for a wayside chapel. Paar is cut off the air for tasteless humor.
- Americans consume 73% fewer potatoes but 25% more fish, poultry, and meat, and 50% more citrus and tomato than in 1940.
- According to a *Downbeat* pool, the most popular male jazz singers are Frank Sinatra, Joe Williams, Mel Torme, Ray Charles, Jon Hendricks, Johnny Mathis, Jimmy Rushing, Bill Henderson, and Nat "King"

"The Flintstones," often compared to "The Honeymooners," is an animated sitcom intended for adult audiences. *Movie Star News.*

Cole; the most popular females are Ella Fitzgerald, Sarah Vaughan, Anita O'Day, Nina Simone, Annie Ross, Peggy Lee, June Christy, Chris Connor, and Dinah Shore.
- The largest TV audience to date, 75 million, watches the first Kennedy-Nixon debate.
- A record number of Broadway shows with distinguished stars fail; the stars include Bette Davis, Lucille Ball, Jack Lemmon, Henry Fonda, Charlton Heston, and John Wayne.
- The Museum of Modern Art, in New York, hosts Swiss Jean Tinguely's *Happening,* a self-destroying mechanical contraption 23 by 27 feet driven by 15 motors and consisting of 80 wheels, a bathtub, toy wagon, and junk objects; it makes musical sounds as it self-destroys.
- The year's most popular hobbies include science kits, rocket models, and plastic car sets; a survey reports that the most popular cartoons are "Peanuts," "Li'l Abner," and "Pogo."

Fads: Comedy records, talkathons, "Ken" (Barbie doll's friend), folk singing in coffee houses

New Words and Usages: Anchorman, bluegrass, compact car, sit-in, American Football League, area rug, balloon satellite, beehive hairdo, cosmonaut, laser, wild card rule, freedom rider

First Appearances: Bulova Accutron, Librium, Xerox 914 copier, felt-tip pen, underseas park (Reef Reserve, Fla.), artificial tanning creams, astroturf, Avron (rayon), soul music ("Spanish Harlem," Ben E. King), law to reduce auto fumes (California), OPEC meeting

1961

Facts and Figures

Economic Profile
- Dow-Jones: ↑ High 734– Low 610
- GNP: +3%
- Inflation: +1.9%
- Unemployment: 6.7%

Median age, first marriage: Male: 22.8 Female: 20.3

Average household size: 3.34

Population over 65: 9%

Population under 10: 21%

Kinney Rent-a-Car, compact: $119 a month

Sam Goody hi-fi package (Garrard, Harman, Kardon): $498

Abercrombie & Fitch:
- Fly rod outfit: $49.95
- Menabone plates: $25 (for 4)

Schirmer's soprano (13″) recorder: $4.50

Black Angus Christmas dinner, 8-course: $3.75

Albert's all-the-sirloin-you-can-eat: $2.65

Carnegie Hall, Christmas eve concert: 50¢

Broadway musical, top: $8.60

Longchamps, New Year's Eve: $5–$6

Deaths

Sir Thomas Beecham, Ty Cobb, Gary Cooper, Marion Davies, Joan Davis, Lee De Forest, Carl Jung, George S. Kaufman, Chico Marx, Richard Wright.

In the News

U.S. SEVERS DIPLOMATIC RELATIONS WITH CUBA . . . FRENCH APPROVE DE GAULLE'S ALGERIA REFERENDUM . . . KENNEDY, AT INAUGURATION, CALLS FOR "GRAND, GLOBAL ALLIANCE FOR PROGRESS" . . . PATRICE LUMUMBA IS KILLED BY "HOSTILE TRIBESMEN," USSR BLAMES U.S. . . . 29 ELECTRIC EQUIPMENT MANUFACTURERS ARE CONVICTED OF PRICE FIXING . . . KENNEDY CREATES THE PEACE CORPS . . . DEAN RUSK URGES FREE NATIONS TO AID THREATENED SOUTHEAST ASIAN COUNTRIES . . . WARSAW PACT NATIONS CALL NATO "HOTBED OF DANGER" . . . ADOLF EICHMANN GOES ON TRIAL IN JERUSALEM . . . RUSSIANS SEND FIRST MAN INTO SPACE . . . ANTI-CASTRO CUBANS FAIL IN ASSAULT AT BAY OF PIGS . . . FIRST U.S. MANNED FLIGHT, WITH ALAN SHEPARD, STAYS IN SPACE FOR 15 MINUTES . . . JFK URGES ACCELERATED SPACE PROGRAM . . . KENNEDY AND KHRUSHCHEV MEET AT VIENNA SUMMIT . . . EAST GERMANS BUILD BERLIN WALL, TENSIONS RISE . . . FREEDOM RIDERS ARE ATTACKED BY MOBS IN BIRMINGHAM, ALABAMA . . . MARTIAL LAW IS DECLARED IN MONTGOMERY, ALABAMA, AFTER ANTIBLACK VIOLENCE . . . KENNEDY ORDERS REAPPRAISAL OF U.S. MILITARY POWER . . . RAFAEL TRUJILLO, DOMINICAN DICTATOR, IS ASSASSINATED . . . ERNEST HEMINGWAY DIES OF SELF-INFLICTED GUNSHOT . . . SECOND SOVIET MANNED FLIGHT LASTS 25 HOURS . . . RUSSIA WILL RESUME NUCLEAR TESTING . . . KENNEDY ORDERS U.S. RESUMPTION OF N-TESTS . . . JFK ADVISES THE "PRUDENT FAMILY" TO HAVE BOMB SHELTER . . . NONALIGNED NATIONS MEET IN YUGOSLAVIA . . . JFK ASKS TARIFF LIBERALIZATION.

Quotes _____

"I invite you to sit down in front of your television sets . . . and stay there. You will see a vast wasteland—a procession of game shows, violence, audience participation shows, formula comedies about totally unbelievable families . . . blood and thunder . . . mayhem, violence, sadism, murder . . . and, endlessly, commercials—many screaming, cajoling, and offending."
— FCC Chairman Newton N. Minow

"What our time needs is mystery. . . . There is a hex on us, the specters in books, the authority of the past; and to exorcise these ghosts is the great work of magical self-liberation. . . . What education does is to put a series of filters over your awareness so that year by year . . . you experience less and less."
— Norman O. Brown

"[We will] pay any price, bear any burden, meet any hardship, support any friend, oppose any foe, to assure the survival and the success of liberty."
— John F. Kennedy

"Orr was crazy and he could be grounded. All he had to do was ask: and as soon as he did he would no longer be crazy and would have to fly more missions. Or be crazy to fly more missions and sane if he didn't, but if he was sane he had to fly them. If he flew them he was crazy, didn't have to; but if he didn't want to he was sane and had to."
— Joseph Heller, *Catch-22*

President John F. Kennedy. At his inauguration he says: "We observe today not a victory of a party but a celebration of freedom. . . . Ask not what your country can do for you; ask what you can do for your country." *Library of Congress*.

"I believe this nation should commit itself to achieving the goal, before this decade is out, of landing a man on the moon and returning him safely to earth."
— John F. Kennedy

"Of a power leading from its strength and pride / Of young ambition eager to be tried, / Firm in our beliefs without dismay, / In any game the nations want to play, / A golden age of poetry and power / Of which this noonday's the beginning hour."
— Robert Frost, "For John F. Kennedy," on his inauguration

Ads _____

TV

Premieres

"The Mike Douglas Show"
"Dr. Kildare," Richard Chamberlain
"The Defenders," E. G. Marshall
"Ben Casey," Vince Edwards
"Hazel," Shirley Booth
"Password," Allen Ludden
"Wide World of Sports," Jim McKay
"The Dick Van Dyke Show"
"The Lucy Show," Lucille Ball, Vivian Vance

Top Ten (Nielsen)

"Wagon Train," "Bonanza," "Gunsmoke," "Hazel," "Perry Mason," "The Red Skelton Show," "The Andy Griffith Show," "The Danny Thomas Show," "Dr. Kildare," "Candid Camera"

Specials

"Victoria Regina" (Julie Harris); "Vincent van Gogh—A Self-Portrait"; "Judy Garland Show"; "Biography of a Bookie Joint" (Jay McMullen)

Emmy Awards

"Victoria Regina" (program); "The Defenders" (drama); "Bob Newhart Show" (comedy); "Garry Moore Show" (variety); "New York Philharmonic—Young People's Concert with Leonard Bernstein" (children); E. G. Marshall (actor, "The Defenders"); Shirley Booth (actress, "Hazel"); "Huntley-Brinkley Report" (news)

Movies

Openings

West Side Story (Jerome Robbins, Robert Wise), Natalie Wood, Rita Moreno, Richard Beymer
The Guns of Navarone (John Lee Thompson), Gregory Peck, David Niven, Anthony Quinn
The Hustler (Robert Rossen), Paul Newman, Piper Laurie, George C. Scott
Judgment at Nuremberg (Stanley Kramer), Spencer Tracy, Burt Lancaster, Judy Garland, Maximilian Schell
The Mark (Guy Green), Stuart Whitman, Rod Steiger, Maria Schell
Two Women (Vittorio De Sica), Sophia Loren, Raf Vallone, Jean-Paul Belmondo
Breakfast at Tiffany's (Blake Edwards), Audrey Hepburn, George Peppard
Splendor in the Grass (Elia Kazan), Natalie Wood, Warren Beatty
One-Eyed Jacks (Marlon Brando), Marlon Brando, Karl Malden
A Raisin in the Sun (Daniel Petrie), Sidney Poitier, Diana Sands
The Misfits (John Huston), Clark Gable, Marilyn Monroe, Montgomery Clift
Through a Glass Darkly (Ingmar Bergman), Harriet Andersson, Max von Sydow, Gunner Bjornstrand
Last Year at Marienbad (Alain Resnais), Delphine Seyrig
Saturday Night and Sunday Morning (Karel Reisz), Albert Finney, Rachel Roberts
Viridiana (Luis Buñuel), Fernando Rey, Sylvia Pinal
Divorce—Italian Style (Pietro Germi), Marcello Mastroianni, Daniela Rocca

Paul Newman, who studied at Kenyon College and the Yale School of Drama, stars in *The Hustler*. *Movie Star News*.

Academy Awards

Best Picture: *West Side Story*
Best Director: Robert Wise and Jerome Robbins (*West Side Story*)
Best Actress: Sophia Loren (*Two Women*)
Best Actor: Maximilian Schell (*Judgment at Nuremberg*)

Top Box-Office Stars

Elizabeth Taylor, Rock Hudson, Doris Day, John Wayne, Cary Grant, Sandra Dee, Jerry Lewis, William Holden, Tony Curtis, Elvis Presley

Stars of Tomorrow

Hayley Mills, Nancy Kwan, Horst Buchholtz, Carol Lynley, Delores Hart, Paula Prentiss, Jim Hutton, Juliet Prowse, Connie Stevens, Warren Beatty

Popular Music

Hit Songs
"Big Bad John"
"Dum Dum"
"Exodus"
"Michael—Row the Boat Ashore"
"Moon River"
"Pocketful of Miracles"
"Wimoweh"
"Tossin' and Turnin' "
"I Fall to Pieces"
"Runaway"

Top Records

Albums: *The Button-Down Mind Strikes Back* (Bob Newhart); *Wonderland by Night* (Bert Kaempfert); *Exodus* (sound track); *Calcutta* (Lawrence Welk), *Judy at Carnegie Hall* (Judy Garland)

Singles: *Don't Be Cruel / It's Now or Never* (Elvis Presley); *My Heart Has a Mind of Its Own / Where the Boys Are* (Connie Francis); *I Want to Be Wanted* (Brenda Lee); *Tonight, My Love, Tonight / Summer's Gone* (Paul Anka); *Cryin'* (Roy Orbison); *My True Story* (Jive Five); *Tossin' and Turnin'* (Bobby Lewis); *I Fall to Pieces* (Patsy Cline). Country: *Wings of a Dove* (Ferlin Husky); *Hello Wall Street* (Faron Young)

Grammy Awards
Moon River, Henry Mancini (record); *Judy at Carnegie Hall,* Judy Garland (album); "Moon River" (song)

Jazz and Big Bands
Stan Getz's quartet includes Scott LaFaro, Lem Winchester, and Booker Little.

Top Performers *(Downbeat):* Billie Holiday (soloist); Count Basie (band); Modern Jazz Quartet (jazz group); Wes Montgomery, Ray Brown, Max Roach, Cannonball Adderley, John Coltrane (instrumentalists); Ella Fitzgerald, Frank Sinatra (vocalists); Lambert, Hendricks, and Ross (vocal group)

Theater

Broadway Openings

Plays
A Man for All Seasons (Robert Bolt), Paul Scofield
The Night of the Iguana (Tennessee Williams), Margaret Leighton, Alan Webb, Patrick O'Neill
Mary, Mary (Jean Kerr), Barbara Bel Geddes, Barry Nelson
A Far Country (Henry Denker), Sam Wanamaker, Lili Darvas, Patrick O'Neil, Kim Stanley
The Caretaker (Harold Pinter), Alan Bates, Donald Pleasence, Robert Shaw
Gideon (Paddy Chayefsky), Fredric March, George Segal, Douglas Campbell
Rhinoceros (Eugene Ionesco), Zero Mostel, Eli Wallach, Anne Jackson
Come Blow Your Horn (Neil Simon), Hal March
Ross (Terence Rattigan), John Mills
A Shot in the Dark (Harry Kurnitz), Julie Harris, William Shatner, Walter Matthau
Purlie Victorious (Ossie Davis), Ruby Dee, Ossie Davis, Alan Alda, Godfrey Cambridge
The Complaisant Lover (Graham Greene), Michael Redgrave, Googie Withers

Musicals
How to Succeed in Business without Really Trying (Frank Loesser), Robert Morse, Rudy Vallee
Carnival (Bob Merrill), Jerry Orbach, Anna Maria Alberghetti

Milk and Honey (Jerry Herman), Mimi Benzell, Robert Weede, Molly Picon
From the Second City (William Mathieu, revue), Alan Arkin, Barbara Harris
An Evening with Yves Montand, Yves Montand

Classics and Revivals On and Off Broadway
The American Dream (Edward Albee); *The Death of Bessie Smith* (Albee); *Under Milk Wood* (Dylan Thomas); *The Hostage* (Brendan Behan); *Happy Days* (Beckett); *The Blacks* (Jean Genet), James Earl Jones; *The Automobile Graveyard* (Fernando Arrabal). *Founded:* Judson Poets' Theater by Al Carmines

Regional

Actor's Workshop, San Francisco: *Serjeant Musgrave's Dance* (John Arden), premiere

Arena Stage, Washington, D.C.: *The Caucasian Chalk Circle* (Bertolt Brecht, directed by Alan Schneider), American premiere

Pulitzer Prize
All the Way Home, Tad Mosel

Tony Awards
Becket, Jean Anouilh (play); *Bye, Bye Birdie,* Charles Strouse, Lee Adams (musical)

Classical Music

Compositions

Earle Brown, *Available Forms II*
Roy Harris, *Canticle of the Sun*
Milton Babbitt, *Composition for Synthesizer, Vision and Prayer*
Morton Feldman, *Durations*
Ralph Shapey, *Incantations*
Karl Korte, Symphony no. 2
Robert Ashley, *Public Opinion Descends upon the Demonstrators*
Robert Ward, *The Crucible*

Important Events

Celebrations include the 150th anniversary of the birth, and 75th anniversary of the death, of Liszt. Pablo Casals, 84, Alexander Schneider, and Miezeslaw Horszowski play Mendelssohn, Schumann, and Couperin at a White House state dinner, November 13.
Sviatoslav Richter plays six concerts at Carnegie Hall; Artur Rubinstein, 75, gives a "Great Recitals" series—10 concerts in 40 days—and decides not to retire.
Van Cliburn performs and conducts the Prokofiev Piano Concerto no. 3 at Carnegie Hall's "Tribute to Dimitri Mitropoulos."
The lost recordings of Dinu Lipatti are recovered.
The Boston Symphony travels to the Far East.

First Performances

Walter Piston, Symphony no. 7 (Philadelphia), *Symphonic Prelude* (Cleveland); Francis Poulenc, *Gloria* (Boston); Elliott Carter, Double Concerto for Harpsichord, Piano, and Two Chamber Orchestras (New York); David Diamond, Symphony no. 8 (New York); Easley Blackwood, Symphony no. 2 (Cleveland); Henry Cowell, Symphony no. 14 (Washington, D.C.); Roy Harris, *Give Me the Splendid Silent Sun* (Washington, D.C.)

Opera

Grace Bumbry sings in *Tannhäuser* at the Wagner Festival, Bayreuth, under the direction of Wagner's grandson Wieland Wagner.

Metropolitan: A labor controversy between management and orchestra almost cancels the season; JFK asks Secretary of Labor Arthur Goldberg to intervene; Leopold Stokowski, on crutches because of a broken leg, leads *Turandot*. Joan Sutherland (debut), *Lucia di Lammermoor;*

Quote by President Kennedy: "We must regard artistic achievement and action as an integral part of our free society." *CBS Records.*

Leontyne Price, Franco Corelli (debuts), *Il trovatore;* Galina Vishnevskaya (debut), *Aïda;* Franco Corelli, Birgit Nilsson, *Turandot;* Price, Richard Tucker, Anselmo Colzani, *La fanciulla del West*

New York City: *The Wings of the Dove* (Douglas Moore, premiere)

Dallas: Denise Duval (debut), *Thaïs*

Chicago: Joan Sutherland, *Lucia di Lammermoor* (Teatro Massimo, Palermo production) Boris Christoff, *Mefistofele;* Jon Vickers, Birgit Nilsson, *Fidelio; The Harvest* (Vittorio Giannini, premiere)

San Francisco: *Blood Moon* (Norman Dello Joio, premiere)

Music Notes

Modern works most performed include Samuel Barber's Adagio for Strings; Benjamin Britten's *Young Person's Guide to the Orchestra;* Debussy's *La Mer;* Hindemith's *Symphonic Metamorphoses on Themes by Weber;* Prokofiev's *Classical Symphony,* Piano Concerto no. 1 and Violin Concerto no. 2; Ravel's *Second Suite from Daphnis and Chloe* and *La valse;* and Stravinsky's *Firebird Suite.*

Art

Painting
Larry Rivers, *Parts of the Face*

Andrew Wyeth, *Distant Thunder*

Robert Indiana, *Eat/Die, The American Dream I*

Robert Rauschenberg, *Black Market, First Landing Jump*

James Rosenquist, *Waves* (1960–61)

Jim Dine, *Hair*

Cy Twombley, *The Italians*

Robert Motherwell, *Elegy to the Spanish Republic*

Frank Stella, *New Madrid*

Tom Wesselmann, *Still-Life No. 14*

Jasper Johns, *Device, First Landing Jump*

Sculpture
John Chamberlain, *Mr. Press*

Leonard Baskin, *Seated Birdman*

George Segal, *The Man*

Sitting at the Table

David Smith, *Zig IV, Zig III*

Naum Gabo, *Linear Construction No. 4*

Architecture
Assembly Hall, University of Illinois (Harrison and Abramovitz)

Willow Creek Apartments, Palo Alto, Calif. (John C. Warnecke)

Alfred Newton Richards Medical Research Building, University of Pennsylvania (Louis I. Kahn)

Crown Zellerbach, San Francisco (Hertzka and Knowles, Skidmore, Owings, and Merrill)

New York Equitable Building, Chase Manhattan Bank, First National City Bank, New York (Skidmore, Owings, and Merrill)

Important Exhibitions
Shows include "Chinese Treasures" and "Italian Drawings: Masterpieces of Five Centuries" and "34 Objects from King Tutankhamen's Tomb," which begins in Washington, D.C.

Museums

New York: *Metropolitan:* The Arts of Thailand; "The Splendid Century: French 17th-Century Art"; "Italian Drawings"; "Chinese Treasures"; "Musical Instruments of Five Continents." *Museum of Modern Art:* Rothko; Max Ernst retrospective; Steichen; "The Art of Assemblage"; Norbert Kricke. *Guggenheim:* Arensberg and Gallatin collections (Duchamp's "Nude Descending a Staircase, No. 2"). *Brooklyn:* Egyptian sculpture of the Late Period, 700 B.C.–A.D. 100

Washington: The Civil War; Ingres; "34 Objects from King Tutankhamen's Tomb"; "Italian Drawings"; "The Splendid Century: French 17th-Century Art"; Eakins retrospective

Worcester: Roman portrait sculpture

Boston: "Latin America—New Departures"; "Italian Drawings"; Modigliani; Art of Thailand; Art of Peru; "Chinese Treasures"

Chicago: The arts of Denmark; Contemporary Spanish Painting; Sculptures of Africa; "Dinner with the Presidents"; "Chinese Treasures"; "Max Ernst"; "Italian Drawings"

Chicago, Cleveland: Japanese decorative arts

Pittsburgh: Carnegie International Prize to Alberto Giacometti

Individual Shows
Ryder (Corcoran); Modigliani (Los Angeles); Hartley (Cincinnati, Minneapolis, St. Louis, Portland, New York); Magritte (Dallas); Ernst (New York, Chicago); Rothko (New York); Kuhn (Cincinnati)

Art Briefs
André Breton and Marcel Duchamp organize "Surrealist Intrusion in the Enchanters' Domain," a show that travels through the United States • Philip Johnson's Amon Carter Museum of Western Art opens in Fort Worth, Texas • An unprecendented wave of thefts occurs, including ten Picassos and numerous works by Léger, Miró, and Dufy • Rembrandt's *Artistotle Contemplating the Bust of Homer* is sold to the Metropolitan Museum of Art for a record $2.3 million.

Dance

Russian Rudolf Nureyev asks for political asylum in Paris.

Premieres

American Ballet Theatre: *Moon Reindeer* (Birgit Cullberg); *Etudes* (Harold Lander), Toni Lander, Bruce Marks, Royes Fernandez

New York City Ballet: *Donizetti Variations*

Books

Fiction

Critics' Choice
The Moviegoer, Walker Percy
Seduction of the Minotaur, Anaïs Nin
Catch-22, Joseph Heller
Children Is All, James Purdy
The Spinoza of Market Street, Isaac Bashevis Singer
Tell Me a Riddle, Tillie Olsen
A New Life, Bernard Malamud
Canary in a Cathouse, Kurt Vonnegut
Some People, Places and Things, John Cheever
🕮 *Riders in the Chariot*, Patrick White
🕮 *A House for Mr. Biswas*, V. S. Naipaul

Best-Sellers
The Agony and the Ecstasy, Irving Stone
Franny and Zooey, J. D. Salinger
To Kill a Mockingbird, Harper Lee
Mila 18, Leon Uris
The Carpetbaggers, Harold Robbins
Tropic of Cancer, Henry Miller
Winnie Ille Pu, trans. Alexander Lenard
Daughter of Silence, Morris West
The Winter of Our Discontent, John Steinbeck

Nonfiction

Critics' Choice
Russia and the West under Lenin and Stalin, George F. Kennan
Soviet Foreign Policy after Stalin, David J. Dallin
The Necessity for Choice, Henry A. Kissinger
The Death and Life of Great American Cities, Jane Jacobs
The Predicament of Democratic Man, Edmund Cahn
The Price of Liberty, Alan Barth
The City in History, Lewis Mumford
The Coming Fury, Bruce Catton
The Death of Tragedy, George Steiner
Nobody Knows My Name, James Baldwin
The Myth of Mental Illness, Thomas Szasz

Best-Sellers
The New English Bible: The New Testament
The Rise and Fall of the Third Reich, William L. Shirer
Better Homes and Gardens Sewing Book
Casserole Cook Book
A Nation of Sheep, William Lederer
Better Homes and Gardens Nutrition for Your Family

The Making of the President, 1960, Theodore H. White
Calories Don't Count, Dr. Herman Taller
Betty Crocker's New Picture Cook Book: New Edition
Ring of Bright Water, Gavin Maxwell

Poetry
Richard Wilbur, *Advice to a Prophet*
Charles Olson, *The Distances: Poems*
Allen Ginsberg, *Kaddish, and Other Poems, 1958–60*
Langston Hughes, *Mama*
Lawrence Ferlinghetti, *Starting from San Francisco*
Robert Frost, *Dedication: The Gift Outright*
Robert Lowell, *Imitations*
May Sarton, *Cloud, Stone, Sun, Vine*

Pulitzer Prizes
The Edge of Sadness, Edwin O'Connor (fiction)
The Triumphant Empire, Thunder-Clouds Gather in the West, Lawrence H. Gipson (U.S. history)
Poems, Alan Dugan
No prize is awarded in biography.

Science and Technology

Alan B. Shepard, on the Freedom 7, becomes the first American in space on a suborbital flight, which lasts 15 minutes.

The U.S. Air Force sends a chimpanzee, Enos, on two 17,500-mile revolutions around the earth in 3 hours, 21 minutes.

High-voltage electron beam welding becomes available so silicon chips can be better incorporated into integrated chips.

Jack Lippes produces an inert plastic contraceptive, the intrauterine device (IUD).

Antirhesus serum is administered to Rh-negative mothers to reduce the harmful antibodies produced during pregnancy.

🕮 Russian Yuri Gagarin becomes the first man to travel in space, orbiting in a 6-ton satellite for 1 hour, 48 minutes.

🕮 Russia's G. S. Titov orbits 17 times.

Nobel Prize
Robert Hofstadter wins the prize in physics for work on the shape and size of the atomic nucleus. Georg von Békésy wins in physiology and medicine for work on the cochlea. Melvin Calvin wins in chemistry for establishing the chemical steps during photosynthesis.

Sports ━━━━━━━━━━━━━━━

Baseball

Roger Maris (New York, AL) hits 61 home runs in the newly expanded 162-game season. Commissioner Ford Frick decides on an asterisk to distinguish Maris's record from Babe Ruth's; Maris hit 59 in the first 154 games.

Willie Mays (San Francisco, NL) hits 4 home runs in one game.

The American League expands to ten teams with Los Angeles and Washington.

The Cy Young Award is won by Whitey Ford.

Champions ━━━━━━━━━━━━━━━

Batting	Pitching
Roberto Clemente (Pittsburgh, NL), .351	John Podres (Los Angeles, AL), 18–5
Norm Cash (Detroit, AL), .361	Whitey Ford (New York, AL), 25–4
	Home runs
	Mickey Mantle (New York, AL), 54

Football

The NFL championship game at Green Bay draws its first million-dollar gate; the winner's share is a record $5,195.

Canton, Ohio is chosen as the site for the Pro Football Hall of Fame.

NFL Season Leaders: Milt Plum (Cleveland), passing; Jim Brown (Cleveland), rushing; James Phillips (Los Angeles), receiving

AFL Season Leaders: George Blanda (Houston), passing; Billy Cannon (Houston); Lionel Taylor (Denver), receiving

College All-Americans: Ernie Davis (B), Syracuse; Merlin Olsen (T), Utah State; Sandy Stephens (B), Minnesota

Bowls (Jan. 1, 1962)

Rose: Minnesota 21–UCLA 3

Orange: Louisiana State 25–Colorado 7

Cotton: Texas 12–Mississippi 7

Sugar: Alabama 10–Arkansas 3

Basketball

NBA All-Pro First Team: Wilt Chamberlain (Philadelphia), Elgin Baylor (Minneapolis), Oscar Robertson (Cincinnati), Bob Pettit (St. Louis), Jack Twyman (Cincinnati)

Winners ━━━━━━━━━━━━━━━

World Series	*MVP*
New York (AL) 4	Bill Russell, Boston
Cincinnati (NL) 1	*College Basketball*
MVP	Cincinnati
NL–Frank Robinson, Cincinnati	*Player of the Year*
AL–Roger Maris, New York	Jerry Lucas, Ohio State
NFL	*Stanley Cup*
Green Bay 37–New York 0	Chicago
MVP	*US Tennis Open*
Y.A. Tittle, New York	Men: Roy Emerson
College Football	Women: Darlene Hard
Alabama	*USGA Open*
Heisman Trophy	Gene Littler
Ernie Davis, Syracuse	*Kentucky Derby*
NBA Championship	Carry Back (J. Sellers, jockey)
Boston 4–St. Louis 1	

Fashion ━━━━━━━━━━━━━━━

For Women: Gloves and hats gain a new importance, especially Mrs. Kennedy's pillbox, the cloche, and the high, rounded styles. Hair is teased into the "beehive," following Mrs. Kennedy, Princess Margaret, and Brigitte Bardot. The biggest news of the year is the "Little Nothing" dinner and evening dress—slender, low-bloused, and simple. Fashion appears to be moving away from the ornate and formal. Suits, coats, and dress fabrics are, in addition, textured and ridged in coral reds, oranges, greens, blues, and off-whites. The simple pump and low square shoe in the stacked and medium heel are also popular. Large costume jewelry includes bright

Audrey Hepburn and George Peppard in *Breakfast at Tiffany's*, the film version of Truman Capote's novella. *Movie Star News.*

beads and stones in irregular shapes, heavy, ornate earrings, and the year's fashionable jet.

High-fashion notes: Norell's "little black dress"; Madame Gres's draped jersey; revival of old furs, such as curly lamb, fox, and raccoon

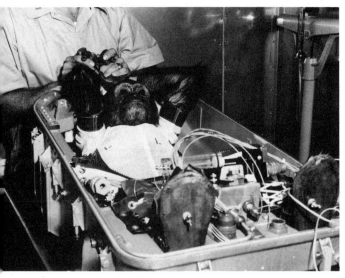

Enos preparing for flight. The chimp looks content as he prepares to circle the earth in space. *Courtesy NASA.*

- President Kennedy calls for "broad participation in exercise" by all Americans.
- Timothy Leary and Richard Alpert are fired from Harvard for using undergraduates in their research experiments; they create the International Foundation for International Freedom (IF-IF), publish *Psychedelic Review,* and prescribe that individuals can be free only through hallucinogenic drugs.
- CORE organizes Freedom Rides to integrate buses, trains, and terminals.
- The ICC bans segregation on all interstate facilities.
- Henry Miller's long-banned *Tropic of Cancer* is published in the United States; many cities censor it.
- The twist craze begins.
- Le Club, the first disco in the United States, opens in New York.
- Ray Kroc borrows $2.7 million, buys out the McDonald brothers, organizes 200 stands, and begins the McDonald's empire.
- Four thousand servicemen are sent to Vietnam as "advisers."
- JFK sign a law making airplane hijacking punishable by death.
- The Civil War Centennial celebration begins.
- The minimum wage rises from $1 to $1.25.
- Michael Rockefeller, the New York governor's son, is lost at sea off the coast of New Guinea.
- An updated version of the *Merriam-Webster Dictionary* takes a more permissive view of language and arouses the ire of purists.
- Reading specialists prefer the phonetic to the whole-word method of reading instruction, which is said to have caused reading retardation in 35 percent of the youth population.
- JFK signs a bill reducing the amount of duty-free goods that may be brought back to the United States from $500 to $100.
- Civil Defense officials distribute 22 million copies of the pamphlet *Family Fallout Shelter.*
- Eisenhower, in his farewell address, warns that the

Kaleidoscope _____

immense civilian arms industry and military establishment have "grave implications for the very structure of our society."
- A university poll reports that 72 percent of elementary and high school teachers approve of corporal punishment as a disciplinary measure.
- A Gallup Poll indicates that 74 percent of the teens interviewed believe in God; 58 percent plan to go to college. Of the 16-to-21 year-old girls interviewed, almost all expect to be married by age 22, and most want four children.
- The Supremes sign a four-year contract with Motown.
- Robert Zimmerman (Bobby Dylan), 20, begins singing in a Greenwich Village nightclub; he gets his first recording opportunity as a backup harmonica player.
- Clark Gable dies at the conclusion of filming *The Misfits.*
- JFK appoints a committee to study the status of women.

Fads: Guitars, yo-yos, rocking chairs

New Words and Usages: Microsurgery, new wave, Peace Corps, troika, third stream, high rise, New Frontier, go ape, soul, zonked

First Appearances: Woman appointed as personal physician to the president (J. G. Travell), vending machine with fresh flowers, First National Bank Certificates of Deposit (New York), IBM Selectric, self-wringing mops, freezers with front door, IBM golf ball, electric toothbrush, Coffee-mate, Total, Country corn flakes, Green Giant vegetables in pouch with butter sauce, Century City (Los Angeles), Haleakala National Park (Hawaii)

The Beat Poets: Peter Orlovsky, William Burroughs, Allen Ginsberg, Alan Ansen, Gregory Corso, Paul Bowles, and Ian Sommerville. *Courtesy Allen Ginsberg.*

1962

Facts and Figures

Economic Profile
  Dow Jones: ↑ High 767–
    Low 723
  GNP: +7%
  Inflation: +0.4%
  Unemployment: 5.5%
TV production: 6,047,000
AM radio stations: 5,710
Household telephones: 80%
Toll rate: New York–San
    Francisco: $2
Advertising expenditures:
    $12.3 billion
Van Cleef & Arpels 18k leaf
    pin: $115
Black Starr & Gorham
    diamond circle pin, on
    platinum: $660–$1975
Tiffany sapphire-centered
    cuff links, 14k: $35;
    matching tie bar: $19
Perfumes:
    Shalimar: $25 (1 oz.)
    Replique: $30 (2 oz.)
    Joy: $50 (1 oz.)
I. W. Harper bourbon:
    $6.70 (⅘)
Taster's Choice Scotch:
    $6.59 (⅘)
Four Roses: $6 (qt.)

Above: Lt. Col. John Glenn
and Atlas VI, the first
manned orbital launch on
the Freedom 7, makes 3
orbits and is picked up at
sea by a force of 24 ships,
126 aircraft, and 26,000
personnel. *Courtesy NASA.*

Deaths

Niels Bohr, Arthur Compton,
  William Faulkner, Kirsten
  Flagstad, Moss Hart, Ernie
  Kovacs, Charles Laughton,
  Eleanor Roosevelt, James
  Thurber, Bruno Walter.

In the News

KENNEDY EMBARGOES TRADE WITH CUBA, CASTRO DECRIES U.S. IMPERIALISM . . . U.S. REMOVES TANK FORCE FROM BERLIN WALL . . . U-2 PILOT GARY POWERS IS TRADED FOR SOVIET SPY RUDOLF ABEL . . . JOHN GLENN ORBITS EARTH THREE TIMES . . . SUPREME COURT RULES FEDERAL GOVERNMENT CAN OVERSEE STATE LEGISLATURE DISTRICTING . . . NEW ORLEANS ARCHBISHOP ORDERS ALL CATHOLIC SCHOOLS DESEGREGATED . . . U.S. RESUMES ATMOSPHERIC NUCLEAR TESTING AT CHRISTMAS ISLAND . . . BAY OF PIGS PRISONERS ARE RANSOMED FOR $2.5 MILLION . . . RANGER IV SPACECRAFT HITS THE MOON . . . STOCK MARKET PLUNGES, $20 BILLION IS LOST IN ONE DAY, LARGEST DROP SINCE 1929 . . . ADOLF EICHMANN IS HANGED IN JERUSALEM . . . SUPREME COURT RULES AGAINST OFFICIAL PRAYER IN PUBLIC SCHOOLS . . . BOEING 707 CRASHES IN PARIS, 130 DIE, THE WORST SINGLE PLANE DISASTER TO DATE . . . ALGERIA VOTES FOR INDEPENDENCE, 5.98 MILLION TO 16,000 . . . RUSSIA RESUMES ATMOSPHERIC TESTS IN ARCTIC . . . MARILYN MONROE DIES OF OVERDOSE . . . TWO RUSSIANS ORBIT SEPARATELY . . . DE GAULLE ESCAPES ASSASSINATION ATTEMPT IN PARIS . . . SOVIETS ANNOUNCE ARMS AND TECHNOLOGY FOR CUBA, KHRUSHCHEV WARNS U.S. NOT TO INTERFERE . . . ROSS BARNETT, MISSISSIPPI GOVERNOR, BARS BLACK, JAMES MEREDITH, FROM UNIVERSITY OF MISSISSIPPI, KENNEDY SENDS FEDERAL TROOPS . . . CHINA ATTACKS INDIA OVER DISPUTED BORDER . . . ADLAI STEVENSON IN UN ACCUSES USSR OF PLACING MISSILES IN CUBA . . . JFK ANNOUNCES AIR AND SEA QUARANTINE OF CUBA, U.S. INTERCEPTS CUBA-BOUND SOVIET TANKER . . . RUSSIA AGREES TO DISMANTLE CUBAN MISSILES . . . KENNEDY ORDERS END OF SEGREGATION IN FEDERAL HOUSING . . . INDIA ANNOUNCES CHINESE WITHDRAWAL.

Demonstrations against segregation occur throughout the south. *National Archives.*

"There are tens of millions of Americans who are beyond the welfare state. Taken as a whole there is a culture of poverty . . . bad health, poor housing, low levels of aspiration and high levels of mental distress. Twenty per cent of a nation, some 32,000,000."
— Michael Harrington, *The Culture of Poverty*

"We may be the last generation in the experiment with living."
— Tom Hayden, announcing the birth of SDS, Students for a Democratic Society

"Man does not live by ratings alone."
— Newton Minow, chairman, Federal Communications Commission

Quotes

"The medium *is* the message."
— Marshall McLuhan, *The Gutenberg Galaxy*

"As I leave you I want you to know—just think how much you're going to be losing: you won't have Nixon to kick around anymore, because, gentlemen, this is my last press conference."
— Richard M. Nixon, after losing to Pat Brown in the California gubernatorial race.

"I made two mistakes during my first year. One was Cuba. The other was letting it be known that I read as much as I do."
— John F. Kennedy

"Esteemed Mr. President . . .
I understand very well your anxiety. . . . In order to liquidate with greater speed the dangerous conflict, . . . the Soviet government . . . has issued an order for the dismantling of weapons, which you describe as 'offensive,' their crating, and return to the Soviet Union. . . . The UN may verify the dismantling. . . .
Respectfully yours,
Nikita Khrushchev"

"Heeeeeere's Johnny."
— "The Tonight Show," as Johnny Carson begins, October 1

"It was quite a day. I don't know what you can say about a day when you see four beautiful sunsets. . . . This is a little unusual, I think."
— Col. John Glenn

Ads

Your client is a poor, rejected stepchild, whose best friends are dwarfs. Can you insure her against poisoned apples?
(Continental Insurance Co.)

My son, the pilot.
(El Al Airlines)

Has anyone given you a handful of emeralds? . . . Does traffic stop when you arrive in Paris? No? Then start wearing the fragrance that can take you places.
(Yardley)

Why be color-blind? . . . This fall more than ⅔ of nighttime programming will be in color.
(NBC)

Dr. Spock is worried. If you've been raising a family on Dr. Spock's books you know he doesn't worry easily.
(National Committee for SANE Nuclear Policy)

TV

Premieres

"The Virginian" (first 90-minute western), James Drury

"The Andy Williams Show"

"The Beverly Hillbillies," Buddy Ebsen

"Combat," Vic Morrow

"McHale's Navy," Ernest Borgnine

"The Merv Griffin Show"

"The Tonight Show Starring Johnny Carson"

Top Ten (Nielsen)

"The Beverly Hillbillies," "Candid Camera," "The Red Skelton Show," "Bonanza," "The Lucy Show," "The Andy Griffith Show," "Ben Casey," "The Danny Thomas Show," "The Dick Van Dyke Show"

Specials

Barbara Walters's report on Mrs. Kennedy's goodwill tour of India, "The Today Show" (her first major on-the-air assignment); "Julie [Andrews] and Carol [Burnett] at Carnegie Hall"; "The Tunnel" (Piers Anderson, Berlin news correspondent); "The Political Obituary of Richard Nixon" (Howard K. Smith)

Emmy Awards

"The Tunnel" (program); "The Defenders" (drama); "The Dick Van Dyke Show" (comedy); "The Andy Williams Show" (variety); "Walt Disney's Wonderful World of Color" (children); "G.E. College Bowl" (game); E. G. Marshall (actor, "The Defenders"); Shirley Booth (actress, "Hazel").

Of Note

Walter Cronkite replaces Douglas Edwards on the CBS "Evening News" • Benny "Kid" Paret dies in a boxing match with Emile Griffith on ABC's "Fight of the Week" • The bill requiring UHF capabilities on all TV sets greatly aids educational and other nonnetwork TV.

Movies

Openings

Lawrence of Arabia (David Lean), Peter O'Toole, Omar Sharif, Alec Guinness, Anthony Quinn, Jose Ferrer

The Longest Day (Andrew Marton, Ken Annakin, Bernhard Wicki), John Wayne, Henry Fonda, Robert Ryan

To Kill a Mockingbird (Robert Mulligan), Gregory Peck, Mary Badham, Brock Peters

The Miracle Worker (Arthur Penn), Anne Bancroft, Patty Duke

Birdman of Alcatraz (John Frankenheimer), Burt Lancaster, Karl Malden

Days of Wine and Roses (Blake Edwards), Lee Remick, Jack Lemmon

Whatever Happened to Baby Jane? (Robert Aldrich), Bette Davis, Joan Crawford

Long Day's Journey into Night (Sidney Lumet), Katharine Hepburn, Ralph Richardson, Jason Robards, Jr., Dean Stockwell

Sweet Bird of Youth (Richard Brooks), Paul Newman, Geraldine Page

The Manchurian Candidate (John Frankenheimer), Frank Sinatra, Janet Leigh, Laurence Harvey

Jules and Jim (François Truffaut), Oskar Werner, Jeanne Moreau

Lolita (Stanley Kubrick), James Mason, Shelley Winters, Sue Lyon, Peter Sellers

Freud (John Huston), Montgomery Clift, Susannah York

The Chapman Report (George Cukor), Shelley Winters, Efrem Zimbalist, Jr.

The Counterfeit Traitor (George Seaton), William Holden, Lilli Palmer

The Four Horsemen of the Apocalypse (Vincente Minnelli), Glenn Ford, Ingrid Thulin

Dr. No (Terence Young), Sean Connery, Ursula Andress (first James Bond film)

Advise and Consent (Otto Preminger), Henry Fonda, Charles Laughton

Academy Awards

Best Picture: *Lawrence of Arabia*

Best Director: David Lean (*Lawrence of Arabia*)

Best Actress: Anne Bancroft (*The Miracle Worker*)

Best Actor: Gregory Peck (*To Kill a Mockingbird*)

Top Box-Office Stars

Doris Day, Rock Hudson, Cary Grant, John Wayne, Elvis Presley, Elizabeth Taylor, Jerry Lewis, Frank Sinatra, Sandra Dee, Burt Lancaster

Stars of Tomorrow

Bobby Darin, Ann-Margret, Richard Beymer, Suzanne Pleshette, Capucine, George Peppard, James MacArthur, Peter Falk, Michael Callan, Yvette Mimieux

Popular Music

Hit Songs
"Shout! Shout! (Knock Yourself Out)"
"The Sweetest Sounds"
"Days of Wine and Roses"
"I Left My Heart in San Francisco"
"Walk on By"
"What Kind of Fool Am I?"
"Fly Me to the Moon"
"As Long as He Needs Me"
"Go Away Little Girl"

Top Records

Albums: *Holiday Sing along with Mitch* (Mitch Miller); *Breakfast at Tiffany's* (Henry Mancini); *West Side Story* (sound track); *Modern Sounds in Country and Western Music* (Ray Charles); *Peter, Paul and Mary* (Peter, Paul and Mary)

Singles: *Stranger on the Shore* (Acker Bilk); *I Can't Stop Loving You* (Ray Charles); *Mashed Potato Time* (Dee Dee Sharp); *Roses Are Red* (Bobby Vinton); *Johnny Angel* (Shelley Fabares); *Loco-Motion* (Little Eva); *Soldier Boy* (Shirelles); *Breaking Up Is Hard to Do* (Neil Sedaka); *Where Have All the Flowers Gone?* (Kingston Trio); *Hey! Baby* (Bruce Channel). Country: *Wolverton Mountain* (Claude King); *Mama Sang a Song* (Bill Anderson)

Grammy Awards
I Left My Heart in San Francisco, Tony Bennett (record, album); "What Kind of Fool Am I?" Anthony Newley (song)

Jazz and Big Bands
Archie Shepp leaves Cecil Taylor to form the Shepp-Dixon Quartet. The government sends Benny Goodman to the USSR on a cultural exchange program; his band includes Zoot Sims, Joe Newman, Teddy Wilson, and Victor Feldman.
Stan Getz, Charlie Byrd, Joao Gilberto, and Antonio Carlos Jobim continue to popularize the bossanova.

Top Performers *(Downbeat):* Miles Davis (soloist); Duke Ellington, Count Basie (band); Dave Brubeck (jazz group); Wes Montgomery, Max Roach, Cannonball Adderley, Stan Getz (instrumentalists); Ella Fitzgerald, Frank Sinatra (vocalists); Lambert, Hendricks and Ross (vocal group)

Theater

Broadway Openings

Plays
Who's Afraid of Virginia Woolf? (Edward Albee), Uta Hagen, Arthur Hill, George Grizzard
A Thousand Clowns (Herb Gardner), Jason Robards, Jr., Sandy Dennis
Never Too Late (Sumner Arthur Long), Paul Ford, Maureen O'Sullivan, Orson Bean
Tchin-Tchin (Sidney Michaels), Margaret Leighton, Anthony Quinn

Musicals
Stop the World—I Want to Get Off (Leslie Bricusse, Anthony Newley), Anthony Newley
I Can Get It for You Wholesale (Harold Rome), Elliott Gould, Barbra Streisand, Lillian Roth
A Funny Thing Happened on the Way to the Forum (Stephen Sondheim), Zero Mostel, Jack Gilford
Little Me (Neil Simon, Cy Coleman, Carolyn Leigh), Sid Caesar, Virginia Martin
No Strings (Richard Rodgers), Diahann Carroll, Richard Kiley
Beyond the Fringe, written and performed by Dudley Moore, Peter Cook, Jonathan Miller,

Classics and Revivals On and Off Broadway
Oh Dad, Poor Dad, Mamma's Hung You in the Closet and I'm Feelin' So Sad (Arthur Kopit), Barbara Harris, Jo Van Fleet; *The Collection* (Harold Pinter); *The Dumb Waiter* (Harold Pinter); *Brecht on Brecht*, Viveca Lindfors, George Voskovec; *Plays for Bleeker Street* (Thornton Wilder); *Romeo and Juliet*, John Stride, Joanna Dunham, directed by Franco Zeffirelli. *Founded:* La Mama E.T.C. (Experimental Theatre Club) by Ellen Stewart

Regional
Ford Foundation makes the largest grant to date: $2.1 million to the Alley Theatre (Houston), among others.

Pulitzer Prize
How to Succeed in Business without Really Trying, Frank Loesser

Tony Awards
A Man for All Seasons, Robert Bolt (play); *How to Succeed in Business without Really Trying*, Frank Loesser (musical)

Artur Rubinstein, who made his U.S. debut in 1906, continues to give concerts despite frequent considerations of retirement. *Move Star News*.

Compositions

Samuel Barber, Piano Concerto, no. 1, Cello Sonata
Charles Whittenberg, Fantasy
Earle Brown, *Available Forms II*
Walter Piston, *Lincoln Center*, String Quartet no. 5
David Diamond, Nonet
Ross Finney, *Still Are New Worlds*

Important Events

Birthday celebrations include the centennial for Claude Debussy and Frederick Delius; 80th for Zoltán Kodály and Gian Francesco Malipiero; 65th for Henry Cowell, Virgil Thomson, and Howard Hanson.
Igor Stravinsky celebrates his 80th birthday with numerous tours, including his first to the USSR in 48 years; he conducts *Oedipus Rex* (Washington, D.C.); CBS televises the premiere of *Noah and the Flood;* Kennedy honors him at a White House dinner.
Philharmonic Hall, the first completed building at Lincoln Center, New York, opens September 23, and dominates the musical year. Leonard Bernstein conducts the New York Philharmonic at the Inaugural Concert, broadcast on TV and radio: "Gloria," from Beethoven's *Missa Solemnis;* first movement, Mahler, Symphony no. 8; Ralph Vaughan Williams, *Serenade to Music;* Aaron Copland, *Connotations for Orchestra* (commissioned). Because of acoustical problems with the hall, Bernstein asks Daniel Pinkham to write *Catacoustical Measures* with every possible orchestral sonority; Bernstein later performs it at a Young People's Concert.
The American Symphony debuts with Leopold Stokowski, 80, at Carnegie Hall.
The Robert Shaw Chorale performs Bach's *B Minor Mass* in Moscow.

Classical Music

New Appointments: Jean Martinon at the Chicago Symphony; Erich Leinsdorf, the Boston Symphony; Josef Krips, the San Francisco Orchestra; Otto Klemperer returns after 20 years to New York to conduct the Philharmonic; William Schuman becomes president of Lincoln Center for the Performing Arts.

Visiting Orchestras: Concertgebouw, Leningrad, National French.

Debuts: Peter Serkin, Igor Oistrakh, Jean-Marie Darré, Stern-Rose-Istomin trio

First Performances

William Schuman, Symphony no. 8 (New York); Roy Harris, Symphony no. 8 (San Francisco); Darius Milhaud, Symphony no. 12 (San Francisco); Abraham Ellstein, *The Golem* (New York); George Antheil, *Cabeza de Vaca* (CBS-TV, New York); Henry Cowell, Symphony no. 15 (New York); Paul Creston, Piano Concerto (New York); Carlisle Floyd, *The Passion of Jonathan Wade* (New York); Pablo Casals, *El Pesebre* (San Francisco); David Diamond, Symphony no. 7 (Philadelphia), Symphony no. 8 (New York); Alexei Haieff, Symphony no. 3 (New York); Walter Piston, Violin Concerto no. 2 (New York)

Opera

Metropolitan: Longest season in history: Joan Sutherland, *La sonnambula;* Renata Tebaldi, *Adriana Lecouvreur;* Anneliese Rothenberger, Hertha Toepper, *Der Rosenkavalier* (directed by Lotte Lehmann); James McCracken, Renata Tebaldi, *Otello;* Judith Raskin (debut), *Le nozze di Figaro*

Boston: Beverly Sills, *Manon*

Chicago: Boris Christoff, dancers Sonia Arova and Rudolf Nureyev, *Prince Igor; Orfeo ed Euridice* (production of the Royal Opera House, Covent Garden)

San Francisco: *Le rossignol* (in Russian, Stravinsky); *Joan at the Stake* (Arthur Honegger)

Fort Worth: Placido Domingo (debut), Lily Pons (last time in role), *Lucia di Lammermoer*

Aspen: *The Pearl Fishers* (Georges Bizet)

Art _____

Paintings

Robert Indiana, *American Gas Works* (1961–62), *Star*

Andy Warhol, *Four Campbell's Soup Cans, 100 Cans, Green Coca-Cola Bottles, Gold Marilyn Monroe*

Josef Albers, *Homage to the Square*

Robert Rauschenberg, *Ace*

James Rosenquist, *Marilyn Monroe, I*

Jack Youngerman, *Anajo, Black, Red and White*

Edward Hopper, *New York Office*

Hans Hofmann, *Memoria in Aeternum*

Jules Olitski, *Cleopatra Flesh*

Roy Lichtenstein, *Flatten—Sand Fleas!*

Sculpture

Tony Smith, *Cigarette, Die*

Claes Oldenburg, *Two Cheeseburgers with Everything (Dual Hamburgers)*

Robert Morris, *I-Box*

Raoul Hague, *Sculpture in Walnut*

John Chamberlain, *Velvet White, Dolores James*

Marisol, *The Family*

George Segal, *The Bus Driver*

Lee Bontecou, *Untitled*

Isamu Noguchi, *Shrine of Aphrodite*

David Smith, *Voltri XVII, XIX*

Mark DiSuvero, *Blue Arch for Matisse*

Architecture

T.W.A. Terminal, Idlewild Airport (Mies van der Rohe)

Fine Arts Center, Howard University, Washington, D.C. (Le Corbusier)

"Century 21," Science Pavilion, Seattle World's Fair (Minoru Yamasaki)

Philharmonic Hall, Lincoln Center, New York (Harrison and Abramovitz)

Dulles International Airport Terminal Building, Chantilly, Va. (Eero Saarinen)

Air Force Academy, Colorado Springs, Colo. (Skidmore, Owings, and Merrill)

Marin County Civic Center, San Rafael, Calif. (Frank Lloyd Wright)

Greek Orthodox Church, Milwaukee (Frank Lloyd Wright, posthumous)

Important Exhibitions

Rare objects from King Tutankhamen's tomb tour the United States for a second year, sent by the Cairo Museum to raise funds to preserve the Nile temples threatened by flood. "Treasures of Versailles" tours Chicago, Toledo, San Francisco, and Los Angeles.

Museums

New York: *Metropolitan:* 141 drawings purchased in 1961 (Poussin, Delacroix, David, Rubens, Bruegel); Rowland's England; Drawings and watercolors from British collections. *Museum of Modern Art:* Dubuffet, Redon, Moreau, Rodolphe Bresdin; José Orozco drawings; "Recent Painting: U.S.A." *Whitney:* 30th-anniversary celebration: "American Art of Our Century"; "Geometric Abstraction in America." *Morgan:* Chinese paintings from the collection of John M. Crawford, Jr.

Chicago: Eakins; Redon-Moreau-Bresdin; Dubuffet retrospective; Chinese art treasures; Last works of Matisse

Washington: Samuel H. Kress and Andrew Myer collection; 16 German abstract artists; Eakins

Pittsburgh: Carnegie International Awards—Mark Tobey, Jules Olitski, Adolph Gottlieb, Ellsworth Kelly

Venice Biennale: Louise Nevelson, Loren MacIver, Jan Müller, Dimitri Hadzi, and Arshile Gorky represent the United States.

Art Briefs

Henry Moore has his first one-man show in eight years, at the Knoedler Gallery, New York • Leonardo da Vinci's *Mona Lisa* arrives in New York on December 19 for the Metropolitan Museum of Art's exhibit • The Dallas Museum of Fine Arts purchases Wyeth's *That Gentleman* for $58,000, the highest price ever paid by a museum to a living American artist • The National Museum of Sports Show in New York, "Fine Arts in Sports," is highly successful.

Dance _____

Rudolf Nureyev makes his American debut in the grand pas de deux from *Don Quixote* (Ruth Page's Chicago Opera Ballet), at the Brooklyn Academy. Rebecca Harkness makes a major financial contribution to the Joffrey.

Premieres

New York City Ballet: *A Midsummer Night's Dream* (George Balanchine), Melissa Hayden, Edward Villella, Arthur Mitchell

Paul Taylor: *Aureole.* **Alvin Ailey:** *Hermit Songs, Feast of Ashes.* **Martha Graham:** *Phaedra*

Books

Fiction

Critics' Choice
Pale Fire, Vladimir Nabokov
One Flew over the Cuckoo's Nest, Ken Kesey
Letting Go, Philip Roth
Another Country, James Baldwin
Stern, Bruce Jay Friedman
Big Sur, Jack Kerouac
Pigeon Feathers, John Updike
Eleven Kinds of Loneliness, Richard Yates
🐎 *Labyrinths, Ficciones*, Jorge Luis Borges
🐎 *The Tin Drum*, Günter Grass

Best-Sellers
Ship of Fools, Katherine Anne Porter
Dearly Beloved, Anne Morrow Lindbergh
A Shade of Difference, Allen Drury
Youngblood Hawke, Herman Wouk
Franny and Zooey, J. D. Salinger
Fail-Safe, Eugene Burdick, Harvey Wheeler
Seven Days in May, Fletcher Knebel, Charles W. Bailey II
The Prize, Irving Wallace
The Agony and the Ecstasy, Irving Stone

Nonfiction

Critics' Choice
Thinking about the Unthinkable, Herman Kahn
The Structure of Scientific Revolutions, T.S. Kuhn
The Paradoxes of Freedom, Sidney Hook
Silent Spring, Rachel Carson
Six Crises, Richard M. Nixon
Mark Twain's Letters from the Earth, ed. Bernard De Voto
Patriotic Gore, Edmund Wilson
The Legacy of Hiroshima, Edward Teller
A Sad Heart at the Supermarket, Randall Jarrell
Theatre of the Absurd, Martin Esslin
🐎 *The Gutenberg Galaxy*, Marshall McLuhan

Best-Sellers
Calories Don't Count, Dr. Herman Taller
The New English Bible: The New Testament
Happiness Is a Warm Puppy, Charles M. Schulz
The Joy of Cooking: New Edition, Irma S. Rombauer, Marion Rombauer Becker
My Life in Court, Louis Nizer
The Rothschilds, Frederic Morton
Sex and the Single Girl, Helen Gurley Brown

Travels with Charley, John Steinbeck

Poetry
Robert Frost, *In the Clearing*
Sylvia Plath, *The Colossus and Other Poems*
Anne Sexton, *All My Pretty Ones*
Brother Antoninus, *The Hazards of Holiness*
Kenneth Koch, *Thank You and Other Poems*
Howard Nemerov, *The Next Room of the Dream*
James Merrill, *Water Street*
William Stafford, *Traveling through the Dark*
Robert Bly, *Silence in the Snowy Fields*
🐎 Yevgeny Yevtushenko, *Selected Poems*

Pulitzer Prizes
The Reivers, William Faulkner (fiction)
Washington, Village and Capital, 1800–1878, Constance M. Green (U.S. history)
The Guns of August, Barbara Tuchman (nonfiction)
Henry James: The Middle Years, Henry James: The Conquest of London, Leon Edel (biography)
Pictures from Brueghel, William Carlos William (poetry)

Nobel Prize
John Steinbeck

Science and Technology

John Glenn, on the Friendship VII mission, becomes the first American to orbit the earth; later in the year, Scott Carpenter orbits three times, and Walter Schirra, six times.

Mariner II is the first successful interplanetary probe; it passes Venus in 109 days and confirms that with temperatures of 800° to 2000° F., Venus is inhospitable to life.

Ranger IV makes the first lunar impact, but picture taking fails.

Telstar is launched, initiating transatlantic TV broadcasts of 20 minutes' duration at one time.

Bell Labs directs a laser beam at the moon's surface and 2½ seconds later receives its reflection.

The MOS (metal odide semicondenser) integrated circuit is perfected by RCA scientists; it allows increased circuit information on a chip.

The first industrial robot is marketed by Unimation.

Digital markets a minicomputer for $15,000.

The Braille system of printing and writing is applied to the typewriter.

🐎 Pavel Popovich and Andrian Nikolayev make the first simultaneous space flights.

Nobel Prize
James D. Watson wins the prize in medicine and physiology for work on the molecular structure of DNA.

Sports

Baseball

Maury Wills (Los Angeles, NL) steals 104 bases, breaking Ty Cobb's 1915 record of 96.

Sandy Koufax (Los Angeles, NL) strikes out 18 men in a nine-inning game.

Jackie Robinson is the first black inducted into the Hall of Fame.

The National League expands to ten teams with the Houston Colts and New York Mets; the Mets under Casey Stengel lose a record 120 games.

Don Drysdale (Los Angeles, NL) wins the Cy Young Award.

Champions

Batting
Tommy Davis (Los Angeles, NL), .346
Pete Runnels (Washington, AL), .326
Pitching
Bob Purkey (Cincinnati, NL), 23–5
Ray Herbert (Chicago, AL), 20–9
Home runs
Willie Mays (San Francisco, NL), 49

Football

NFL Season Leaders: Bart Starr (Green Bay), passing; Jim Taylor (Green Bay), rushing; Bobby Mitchell (Washington), receiving; Taylor gains 1,474 yards. **AFL Season Leaders:** Len Dawson (Kansas City), passing; Cookie Gilchrist (Buffalo), rushing; Lionel Taylor (Denver) receiving.
College All-Americans: Jerry Stovall (B), Louisiana State; Lee Roy Jordan (C) Alabama

Bowls (Jan. 1, 1963)

Rose: Southern California 42–Wisconsin 37
Orange: Alabama 17–Oklahoma 0
Cotton: Louisiana State 13–Texas 0
Sugar: Mississippi 17–Arkansas 13

Basketball

Wilt Chamberlain (Philadelphia) scores 100 points in an NBA game, as Philadelphia beats New York 169–147.

NBA All-Pro Team: Bob Pettit (St. Louis), Elgin Baylor (Los Angeles), Wilt Chamberlain (Philadelphia), Jerry West (Los Angeles), Oscar Robertson (Cincinnati)

Other Sports

Tennis: Rod Laver wins the Grand Slam, all four major tournaments.

Golf: Jack Nicklaus wins his first major tournament, beating Arnold Palmer in overtime in the U.S. Open.

Horse Racing: Kelso is named Horse of the Year for the third straight year.

Winners

World Series
New York (AL) 4
San Francisco (NL) 3
MVP
NL–Maury Wills, Los Angeles
AL–Mickey Mantle, New York
NFL Championship
Green Bay 16–New York 7
MVP
Jim Taylor, Green Bay
College Football
Southern California
Heisman Trophy
Terry Baker, Oregon State
NBA Championship
Boston 4–Los Angeles 3
MVP
Bill Russell, Boston
College Basketball
Cincinnati
Player of the Year
Paul Hogue, Cincinnati
Stanley Cup
Toronto
US Tennis Open
Men: Rod Laver
Women: Margaret Smith
USGA Open
Jack Nicklaus
Kentucky Derby
Decidedly (W. Hartack, jockey)

Fashion

For Women: International styles and films contribute to an eclectic and casual vogue. One popular mix includes the Basque sheepherder coat, Wild West cowboy boots and bandanas, blue jeans, sheriff jackets, suspenders, and the combination of odd jackets, suede shirts, skirts, vests, pants, and Breton middies. "Breen" (brown/green) is fashionable in hooded jacketlike sweaters of thick mohair; the crocheted or flat turtleneck pullover is also popular. Generally, the silhouette is less abstract and more anatomical, the bosom the fashion focus. From *Last Year at Marienbad* comes short straight hair pushed behind the ear and swept across the forehead. From *Breakfast at Tiffany's,* and also the style set by Mrs. Kennedy, comes the high-bosomed look in coats, suits, and dresses, as well as the "princess" dress, which discards sleeves and belt, and the long, slim evening dress. Also fashionable are widespread color contrasts with black accents, influenced by the Picasso show.

High-fashion note: Gernreich's wool tank and topless swimsuit

Kaleidoscope _____

Mary Tyler Moore and Dick Van Dyke, in "The Dick Van Dyke Show." Carl Reiner created this sitcom, which ranked 80th during its first season. *Movie Star News*.

- "I'll say it again, I've said it before / Archie Moore will fall in four" and "He knocks them all out in the round he'll call / And that's why he's called the greatest of all" are examples of Cassius Marcellus Clay's poetry.
- After Decca and other recording companies turn him down, Brian Epstein convinces George Martin at EMI to sign the Beatles for 1 cent per side and 10 cents per song album.
- *My Fair Lady* closes after 2,717 performances, the longest running musical in Broadway history.
- Bobby Kennedy, on TV, asks: "Are we to say to the world that this is the land of the free except for the Negroes?"
- SNCC (Students' Nonviolent Coordinating Committee) organizes the "freedom ballot" and registers black voters in Georgia, Mississippi, and Alabama.
- President Kennedy awards Dr. Frances O. Kelsey of the Federal Drug Administration the Gold Medal of Distinguished Public Service for his "rigorous demands" to clear the market of birth-defects-producing thalidomide.
- Scientist Linus Pauling wins the Nobel Peace Prize.
- JFK instructs U.S. troops in Vietnam to protect themselves if fired upon but to understand that they are "not combat troops in the generally understood sense of the word."
- As they film *Cleopatra,* Richard Burton and Elizabeth Taylor pursue a romance that makes worldwide headlines.
- Richard Avedon's photograph of high-fashion model Christina Paolozzi, nude in a full-page color ad in *Harper's Bazaar,* causes a furor.
- The United States and USSR sign a two-year agreement to expand cultural, scientific, technical, and educational exchanges.
- JFK awards poet Robert Frost, on his 88th birthday, a special medal voted by Congress.
- Benny Goodman plays a jazz concert at Red Army Sports Palace in Moscow, which Khrushchev attends unexpectedly; the crowds and Khrushchev are highly responsive.
- Ralph Ginzberg's conviction for pornography is upheld by the Supreme Court; he has applied for bulk-mail privileges from cities with such names as Intercourse, Climax, and Blue Balls.
- Over $2.5 million is found in an abandoned 1947 Plymouth in Jersey City, N.J. The IRS files an immediate claim for $3.4 million from its owner, a 50-ish former newsboy and numbers runner.
- Horror movies like *Premature Burial* and *Tales of Terror* make a comeback; they offer audiences a violence TV cannot provide and are inexpensive to produce.
- Erle Stanley Gardner, author of the Perry Mason mysteries, announces a major archeological find of prehistoric cave paintings in California.
- With auto sales running high, the Big Three emphasis is on longer, heavier, and more powerful cars.
- Eleanor Roosevelt wins a Gallup Poll for the "Most Admired Woman" for the thirteenth time.
- When the United States decides to resume nuclear testing, a major problem is "Where?"
- "We're eyeball to eyeball and I think the other fellow just blinked," comments Dean Rusk when Soviet vessels turn back from the U.S. quarantine.
- Paul Guilhard, 30, an Agence Presse reporter covering James Meredith's admission to the University of Mississippi, is fatally shot in the back; his last dispatch is: "The Civil War never came to an end."
- Tom Hayden's "Port Huron Statement" pledges SDS to the New Left and places particular emphasis on the university as an agency of social change.
- An advertising company promoting Brahms, Beethoven, and Bach faces on sweatshirts sues a competitor who brings out a similar item at a lower cost; it claims copyright infringement.
- Hulda Clark, 14 and the daughter of a black laborer, is given a $2,000 scholarship to a Moscow boarding school and air fare by Madame Khrushchev.
- Van Kemp bakes a 25,000-pound cake for the Seattle World's Fair.
- Rachel Carson, in *Silent Spring,* indicates that over 500 new chemicals are entering our bodies because of widespread insecticide usage.
- JFK contributes his presidential salary to charity.

Fads: JFK coloring books, worry beads

New Words and Usages: Splashdown, bank (as verb), status report, corner back, join-in, weather girl, mono, moononaut, unword

First Appearances: Diet Rite; Tab; powdered orange juice; child's molded car seat with seatbelt; "The Incredible Hulk"; Polaroid color film; national monuments: homes of (1) Abraham Lincoln (Lincoln City, Ind.), (2) Alexander Hamilton (New York City), and (3) Theodore Roosevelt (three in New York state); Esalen Institute encounter group (Big Sur, Calif.); merged Pennsylvania and New York Railroad; E. J. Korvette on 5th Avenue, New York City; K Mart; Petrified National Park (Arizona); Baxter State Park (Maine); Americana Hotel (New York City); "We Shall Overcome" copyright by Guy Carawan; Electronic Data Systems; Lear Jet Corp.; COMSAT (Communications Satellite Corp.)

1963

Facts and Figures

Economic Profile
  Dow-Jones:—High 767–
    Low 646
  GNP: +5%
  Inflation: +1.7%
  Unemployment: 5.7%
Daily newspapers: 1,974
Books published: 25,784
Airmail postage: 8¢
Postcard: 4¢
IRS total collections: $105.9
  billion
Shoes:
  Hush Puppies: $8.75–$9.95
  Baker leather pumps: $7.99
  Chandler's golden mesh:
    $12.99
Bloomingdale's sleeveless
  silk dress: $59.95
Macy's suede coat, zip-out
  pile lining: $84.97
A&S eight-button leather
  gloves: $8.79
Balenciaga scarf: $20
Jack Winter stretch pants:
  $13
Lord & Taylor leather bag:
  $36–$60
Hammacher Schlemmer foot
  scraper: $5.95

Above: after the
assassination of John F.
Kennedy, Lyndon Baines
Johnson takes the oath of
office aboard Air Force I.
Library of Congress.

Deaths

Richard Barthelmess, Jean
  Cocteau, W. E. B.
  Du Bois, Robert Frost,
  Paul Hindemith, Rogers
  Hornsby, Aldous Huxley,
  Estes Kefauver, Clifford
  Odets, Dick Powell, Monty
  Woolley.

In the News

KENNEDY ASKS $13.5 BILLION TAX CUT TO STIMULATE ECONOMY
. . . DISARMAMENT CONFERENCE MEETS AT GENEVA . . .
KHRUSHCHEV SAYS DE-STALINIZATION ALLOWS NO INDIVIDUAL
LIBERTY . . . SUPREME COURT RULES THAT STATES MUST PROVIDE
FREE LEGAL COUNSEL FOR THE POOR . . . NEW YORK NEWSPAPER
STRIKE ENDS AFTER 114 DAYS . . . MOSCOW AND WASHINGTON
ESTABLISH HOT LINE . . . SUBMARINE "THRESHER" SINKS WITH 129
ABOARD . . . MASS BLACK ANTISEGREGATION DEMONSTRATION
OCCURS IN BIRMINGHAM, ALABAMA, 1,000 ARE ARRESTED . . .
BLACKS RIOT AFTER BIRMINGHAM HEADQUARTERS ARE BOMBED, JFK
SENDS TROOPS . . . ASTRONAUT GORDON COOPER CIRCLES THE EARTH
TWICE . . . POPE JOHN XXIII DIES, POPE PAUL VI IS ELECTED . . .
FEDERAL NATIONAL GUARD HELPS TWO BLACKS TO ENROLL AT
UNIVERSITY OF ALABAMA . . . RUSSIA REJECTS CHINESE POSITION AND
SAYS NUCLEAR WAR MUST BE AVERTED . . . USSR AND U.S.
AGREE TO NUCLEAR TEST BAN IN AIR, ATMOSPHERE, AND WATER
. . . U.S. EMBARGOES ARMS TO SOUTH AFRICA . . . 250,000 MARCH
FOR CIVIL RIGHTS IN WASHINGTON, D.C. . . . PUBLIC SCHOOLS IN
SOUTH CAROLINA AND LOUISIANA INTEGRATE . . . BOMB EXPLOSION
KILLS FOUR GIRLS AT BLACK CHURCH IN BIRMINGHAM . . . $250
MILLION OF WHEAT FOR RUSSIA IS AUTHORIZED . . . RUSSIA DELAYS
WEST BERLIN CONVOY . . . NGO DIEM IS ASSASSINATED IN SOUTH
VIETNAM . . . JFK IS ASSASSINATED IN DALLAS . . . LEE HARVEY
OSWALD IS ARRESTED . . . LYNDON BAINES JOHNSON TAKES OFFICE,
THE NATION MOURNS KENNEDY . . . OSWALD IS KILLED BY TEXAN
JACK RUBY DURING LIVE NEWS COVERAGE . . . ZANZIBAR AND
KENYA BECOME INDEPENDENT . . . 500,000 WEST BERLINERS VISIT
EAST BERLIN ON HOLIDAY SPECIAL.

Quotes

"Before the Pilgrims landed at Plymouth, we were here. Before the pen of Jefferson etched across the pages of history the majestic words of the Declaration of Independence, we were here. If the inexpressible cruelties of slavery cannot stop us, the oppression we now face will surely fail.
— Martin Luther King, Jr., from a Birmingham jail

"I have a dream that one day this nation will rise up and live out the true meaning of its creed . . . that all men are created equal. I have a dream that my four little children will one day live in a nation where they will not be judged by the color of their skin but by the content of their character. I have a dream today. And if America is to be a great nation, this must become true. So let freedom ring. From the prodigious hilltops of New Hampshire, let freedom ring. From the heightening Alleghenies of Pennsylvania, let freedom ring. But not only that; let freedom ring from Stone Mountain of Georgia. Let freedom ring from every hill and molehill of Mississippi. And when this happens, when we let it ring, we will speed that day when all of God's children, black men and white men, Jews and Gentiles, Protestants and Catholics, will be able to join hands and sing in the words of the old Negro spiritual:
    'Free at last, free at last,
    Thank God Almighty, we're free at last.' "
— Martin Luther King, Jr., speech in Washington, D.C.

"She was very worried about a civilization which produced those five policemen standing on the Negro woman's neck in Birmingham."
— James Baldwin, citing Lorraine Hansberry

"I am called Baldwin because I was sold by my African tribe and kidnappd out of it into the hands of a white Christian named Baldwin, who forced me to

The "March on Washington for Jobs and Freedom," at which Martin Luther King, Jr., gives his "I have a dream" speech. *National Archives.*

kneel at the foot of the cross. . . . God gave Noah the rainbow sign, no more water, the fire next time!"
— James Baldwin, *The Fire Next Time*

"America wept tonight not alone for its dead young President, but for itself. . . . Somehow the worst prevailed over the best. . . . Some strain of madness and violence had destroyed the highest symbol of law and order."
— James Reston

"He died as a soldier under fire, doing his duty in the service of his country."
— Charles de Gaulle

"We are in this country . . . watchmen on the walls of freedom. . . . We ask, therefore, that we may be worthy of our power and responsibility, . . . that we may achieve the ancient vision of peace on earth, goodwill toward men."
— JFK's speech planned for November 22

Ads

Author James Baldwin, active in the civil rights movement, calls for "the unconditional freedom of the Negro." *Courtesy Sedat Pakay.*

Premieres
"The Fugitive," David Janssen
"Bob Hope Presents the Chrysler Theater"
"The Patty Duke Show"
"My Favorite Martian," Bill Bixby
"Petticoat Junction," Bea Benaderet
"Let's Make a Deal," Monty Hall
"General Hospital"
"The Saint," Roger Moore

TV

Top Ten (Nielsen)
"The Beverly Hillbillies," "Bonanza," "The Dick Van Dyke Show," "Petticoat Junction," "The Andy Griffith Show," "The Lucy Show," "Candid Camera," "The Ed Sullivan Show," "The Danny Thomas Show," "My Favorite Martian"

Specials
"The Making of the President, 1960"; "Abe Lincoln in Illinois" (Jason Robards, Jr.); "One Day in the Life of Ivan Denisovich"; "Cuba: The Bay of Pigs, The Missile Crisis"; "Elizabeth Taylor in London"

Emmy Awards
"The Defenders" (drama); "Dick Van Dyke Show" (comedy); "Danny Kaye Show" (variety); "Discovery '63–'64" (children); "Huntley-Brinkley Report" (news); Dick Van Dyke (actor, "The Dick Van Dyke Show"); Mary Tyler Moore (actress, "The Dick Van Dyke Show")

Of Note
Julia Child, on "The French Chef," becomes NET's first star.

Movies

Openings
Tom Jones (Tony Richardson), Albert Finney, Susannah York, Hugh Griffith
Cleopatra (Joseph L. Mankiewicz), Elizabeth Taylor, Rex Harrison, Richard Burton
How the West Was Won (John Ford, Henry Hathaway, George Marshall), Gregory Peck, Henry Fonda, James Stewart, Debbie Reynolds
Lilies of the Field (Ralph Nelson), Sidney Poitier, Lilia Skala
8 ½ (Federico Fellini), Marcello Mastroianni, Anouk Aimée
Hud (Martin Ritt), Paul Newman, Patricia Neal, Melvyn Douglas, Brandon De Wilde
It's a Mad, Mad, Mad, Mad World (Stanley Kramer), Sid Caesar, Buddy Hackett, Mickey Rooney
All the Way Home (Alex Segal), Robert Preston, Jean Simmons
The Birds (Alfred Hitchcock), Rod Taylor, Jessica Tandy, Tippi Hedren
Charade (Stanley Donen), Cary Grant, Audrey Hepburn, Walter Matthau
The Ugly American (George Englund), Marlon Brando, Eiji Okada

America, America (Elia Kazan), Stathis Giallelis
The Trial (Orson Welles), Anthony Perkins, Orson Welles
Irma La Douce (Billy Wilder), Shirley MacLaine, Jack Lemmon

Academy Awards
Best Picture: *Tom Jones*
Best Director: Tony Richardson (*Tom Jones*)
Best Actress: Patricia Neal (*Hud*)
Best Actor: Sidney Poitier (*Lilies of the Field*)

Top Box-Office Stars
Doris Day, John Wayne, Rock Hudson, Jack Lemmon, Cary Grant, Elizabeth Taylor, Elvis Presley, Sandra Dee, Paul Newman, Jerry Lewis

Stars of Tomorrow
George Chakiris, Peter Fonda, Stella Stevens, Diane McBain, Pamela Tiffin, Pat Wayne, Dorothy Provine, Barbara Eden, Ursula Andress, Tony Bill

Popular Music

Hit Songs

"Wipeout"
"Call Me Irresponsible"
"If I Had a Hammer"
"More"
"Puff (the Magic Dragon)"
"Da Doo Ron Ron"
"The Times They Are A-
    Changin' "
"Dominique"

Top Records

Albums: *My Son, the Celebrity*
(Allan Sherman); *Jazz Samba*
(Stan Getz, Charlie Byrd); *Days of
Wine and Roses* (Andy Williams);
*Little Stevie Wonder, the 12-Year-
Old Genius* (Stevie Wonder);
Blowin' in the Wind (Peter, Paul
and Mary).

Singles: *Sugar Shack* (Jimmy
Gilmer and the Fireballs); *Surfin'
U.S.A.* (Beach Boys); *The End of
the World* (Skeeter Davis);
Rhythm of the Rain (Cascades);
He's So Fine (Chiffons); *Blowin'
in the Wind* (Peter, Paul and
Mary); *Heatwave* (Martha and the
Vandellas); *Fingertips* (Little
Stevie Wonder). Country: *Don't
Let Me Cross Over* (Carl Butler);
Love's Gonna Live Here (Buck
Owens)

Grammy Awards

The Days of Wine and Roses,
    Henry Mancini (record, song);
The Barbra Streisand Album
    (album)

Jazz and Big Bands

Jazz, both traditional and more
progressive, is widely written
about as an art form.
Don Ellis tours with his jazz
"happenings."
New York City's jazz clubs begin
closing, and the Lower East Side
replaces Greenwich Village for
avant-garde jazz.

Top Performers *(Downbeat):*
Thelonius Monk (soloist); Duke
Ellington, Count Basie (bands);
Dave Brubeck (jazz group);
Charlie Byrd, Ray Brown, Joe
Morello, Roland Kirk, Jimmy
Smith (instrumentalists); Ella
Fitzgerald, Ray Charles
(vocalists); Lambert, Hendricks,
and Ross (vocal group)

Theater

Broadway Openings

Plays

Barefoot in the Park (Neil Simon), Robert Redford,
    Elizabeth Ashley, Kurt Kasznar, Mildred
    Natwick
Enter Laughing (Joseph Stein), Vivian Blaine, Alan
    Arkin, Sylvia Sidney
A Case of Libel (Henry Denker), Sidney Blackmer,
    Van Heflin
Nobody Loves an Albatross (Ronald Alexander),
    Robert Preston
Luther (John Osborne), Albert Finney
Ballad of the Sad Café (Edward Albee), Colleen
    Dewhurst, Michael Dunn
Mother Courage and Her Children (Bertolt Brecht),
    Anne Bancroft
The Milk Train Doesn't Stop Here Anymore
    (Tennessee Williams), Mildred Dunnock
The Private Eye (Peter Shaffer), Barry Foster
One Flew over the Cuckoo's Nest (Dale Wasserman),
    Gene Wilder, Kirk Douglas
The Rehearsal (Jean Anouilh), Keith Michell, Alan
    Badel

Musicals

Oliver! (Lionel Bart), Clive Revill, Bruce Pochnik,
    Georgia Brown
She Loves Me (Jerry Bock, Sheldon Harnick), Jack
    Cassidy, Barbara Baxley, Barbara Cook, Daniel
    Massey
110 in the Shade (Harvey Schmidt, Tom Jones),
    Robert Horton, Inga Swenson
Tovarich (Lee Pockriss, Anne Crosswell), Vivien
    Leigh, Jean Pierre Aumont

Classics and Revivals On and Off Broadway

School for Scandal (Sheridan), Ralph Richardson,
John Gielgud, Geraldine McEvan; *Desire under the
Elms* (Eugene O'Neill), George C. Scott, Colleen
Dewhurst; *Strange Interlude* (O'Neill), Geraldine
Page, Ben Gazzara, Pat Hingle, Franchot Tone, Jane
Fonda; *A Month in the Country* (Turgenev), Celeste
Holm; *Too True to Be Good* (George Bernard Shaw),
David Wayne, Cyril Ritchard, Glynis Johns, Ray
Middleton, Eileen Heckart, Robert Preston, Lillian
Gish; *The Trojan Women* (Euripides), Mildred
Dunnock, Carrie Nye; *The Bald Soprano, The
Lesson* (Eugene Ionesco); *In White America* (Martin
B. Duberman); *The Maids* (Jean Genet), Lee Grant

Regional

Founded: Minnesota Theatre Company (Guthrie
Theater), Minneapolis, by Sir Tyrone Guthrie, Peter

Theater (cont.)

Ziesler, Oliver Rea: *Hamlet, The Miser, The Three Sisters, Death of a Salesman,* Hume Cronyn, Jessica Tandy, George Grizzard, Rita Gam, Zoë Caldwell; Seattle Repertory Theatre by Stuart Vaughan; Center Stage, Baltimore

Boston Theatre Company: *The Knack* (Ann Jellicoe)

Arena Stage, Washington, D.C.: *The Devils* (John Whiting), Joan Van Ark, Ned Beatty, Hurd Hatfield, René Auberjonois, Anthony Zerbe, premiere

Pulitzer Prize
No prize is awarded.

Le Guichet (The box office), by Alexander Calder, at Lincoln Center for the Performing Arts. *Marjorie Cox.*

Tony Awards
Who's Afraid of Virginia Woolf, Edward Albee (play), *A Funny Thing Happened on the Way to the Forum,* Stephen Sondheim (musical)

Classical Music

Compositions
Roy Harris, *Epilogue to Profiles in Courage: JFK, Salute to Death*
Roger Reynolds, *The Emperor of Ice Cream*
Lukas Foss, *Echoi*
Leonard Bernstein, Symphony no. 3 *(Kaddish)*
Roger Shapey, Brass Quintet, String Quartet no. 6
Lejaren Hiller, *Computer Cantata*

Important Events
Celebrations include the sesquicentennial birthdays of Wagner and Verdi.
The International Festival of Visiting Orchestras opens at Carnegie Hall with the Royal Philharmonic of London (Sir Malcolm Sargent); participating are the Hamburg, Hague, Leningrad, and National French Orchestras.
The most celebrated composition of the year is Benjamin Britten's *War Requiem.*
Of the works played by 262 orchestras, 812 were composed before 1899, 357 between 1900 and 1955, and 574 between 1955 and 1963. The Prelude to Wagner's *Die Meistersinger* is most performed, as well as an excerpt from *Lohengrin,* Beethoven's Symphony no. 5 and his Overtures; also, the symphonies of Mozart, Brahms, and Tchaikovsky.

Conductors in New Locations: Lukas Foss takes over the Denver; Jean Martinon goes to Chicago; Eleazar de Carvalho, to St. Louis.

Debut: Itzhak Perlman

First Performances
Roy Harris, Symphony no. 9 (Philadelphia); Benjamin Lees, Violin Concerto; (Boston); Samuel Barber, *Andromache's Farewell* (New York); Francis Poulenc, *Sept répons des ténébres* (New York); Paul Hindemith, Concerto for Organ and Orchestra (New York); Alan Hovhanness, Symphony no. 17 (Cleveland); Howard Hanson, *Song of Human Rights* (text includes excerpts from JFK's Inaugural Address, Washington, D.C.).

Opera

Premieres
Labyrinth (Gian Carlo Menotti, NBC-TV); *Death of the Bishop of Brindisi* (Menotti, Cincinnati); *Highway No. 1, U.S.A.* (William Grant Still, Miami); *Gentlemen, Be Seated!* (Jerome Moross, New York); *The Sojourner and Mollie Sinclair* (Carlisle Floyd, Raleigh, N.C.); *The Long Christmas Dinner* (Paul Hindemith, New York)

Metropolitan: George Shirley, *Madama Butterfly;* Joan Sutherland, *La sonnambula;* Régine Crespin, Herta Topper, *Der Rosenkavalier;* James McCracken, *Otello;* Raina Kabaivanska, *Don Carlo;* Eileen Farrell, Franco Corelli, *Andrea Chénier;* Leonard Bernstein debuts, conducting *Eugene Onègin;* Lorin Maazel, *Don Giovanni*

Chicago: Jon Vickers, Régine Crespin, *Un ballo in maschera;* Vickers, Sena Jurinac, *Otello*

Dallas: *L'incoronazione di Poppea* (Monteverdi, American premiere)

San Francisco: *Lulu* (Alban Berg, American premiere); Regina Resnik, *The Queen of Spades*

Art

Painting

Andy Warhol, *Mona Lisa*

Roy Lichtenstein, *Okay Hot Shot, Okay, Wham!, Drowning Girl*

Larry Rivers, *Dutch Masters and Cigars II*

Helen Frankenthaler, *Blue Atmosphere*

Richard Lindner, *The Actor*

Jack Levine, *Witches' Sabbath*

Ellsworth Kelly, *Red, Blue, Green*

Jasper Johns, *Map, Periscope (Hart Crane)*

Jim Dine, *Walking Dream with a Four-Foot Clamp*

Tom Wesselmann, *Great American Nude No. 44, Still-Life No. 34*

Sculpture

David Smith, *Zig VII, Cubi XVII, Cubi I, Voltron XVIII*

Reuben Nakian, *Leda and the Swan*

Richard Lippold, *Orpheus and Apollo* (Philharmonic Hall, New York)

Herbert Ferber, *Homage to Piranesi II*

Edward Kienholz, *Back Seat Dodge*

George Segal, *Cinema*

Claes Oldenburg, *Bedroom Ensemble*

Lippold's sculptures are placed in the Pan American Building, New York.

Architecture

Sheldon Memorial Art Gallery, University of Nebraska, Lincoln (Philip Johnson)

Yale School of Art and Architecture (Paul Rudolph)

Carpenter Center for Visual Arts, Harvard University, Cambridge, Mass. (Le Corbusier)

Science Library, Lake Forest College, Illinois (Perkins and Will)

University of California, Music Building, Santa Barbara, and Macgowan Hall, Los Angeles (Charles Luckman)

College of Education, Wayne State University, Detroit (Minoru Yamasaki)

Teneco Building, Houston (Skidmore, Owings, and Merrill)

O'Hare Centralized Terminal Building, Chicago (C. F. Murphy)

Important Exhibitions

Museums

New York: *Metropolitan: Mona Lisa* (on loan); "Treasure from the Mannean Land"; American art. *Museum of Modern Art:* Nolde memorial; Hofmann retrospective; "Americans 1963"; Sculpture of Rodin and Medardo Rosso. *Guggenheim:* Francis Bacon; Kandinsky retrospect

Whitney: "The Decade of the Armory Show"

Philadelphia: "A World of Flowers: Masterpieces of Flower Paintings and Fruit"; Breughel, von Huysum, Manet, Degas, Matisse; Clyfford Still

Guggenheim, Los Angeles, Ann Arbor, Minneapolis: "6 Artists and the Object" (first pop art show)

Washington: Turner; *Mona Lisa* (on loan)

Virginia Museum of Fine Arts: Mellon collection from 1700 to 1950

Boston: "She Walks in Splendor: Great Costumes 1550–1950"

Minneapolis: "The Nabis and Their Circle"

Boston, Toledo, Cleveland, San Francisco: "Barbizon Revisited—Millet, Dupré, Rousseau, Corot

Utica, N.Y.: 320 works from the 1913 Armory show

Art Briefs

Major sales include Rembrandt's *The Merry Lute Player* ($600,000) and *Portrait of a Young Girl* ($260,000), and Wyeth's *Her Room* ($65,000) • The highest purchase price at a Sears & Roebuck show hosted by Vincent Price is $750 for a Chagall lithograph • University of Mississippi professor G. Ray Kerciu is arrested for desecrating a Confederate flag in his painting *America the Beautiful,* inspired by desegregation riots on campus.

Dance

Willam Christensen goes from San Francisco to Salt Lake City and founds Ballet West.

The Pennsylvania Ballet develops from Barbara Weisberger's Philadelphia school.

Premieres

New York City Ballet: *Movements for Piano and Orchestra* (George Balanchine), Susan Farrell, Jacques D'Amboise; *Bugaku* (Balanchine)

Paul Taylor: *Scudorama*

Alwin Nikolais: *Imago*

Books

Fiction

Critics' Choice
V, Thomas Pynchon
The Centaur, John Updike
The Bell Jar, Sylvia Plath
Idiot's First, Bernard Malamud
Textures of Life, Hortense
  Calisher
Names and Faces of Heroes,
  Reynolds Price
Cat's Cradle, Kurt Vonnegut
The Island, Robert Creeley
🔊 *One Day in the Life of Ivan
  Denisovich*, Alexander
  Solzhenitsyn

Best-Sellers
The Shoes of the Fisherman,
  Morris L. West
The Group, Mary McCarthy
*Raise High the Roof Beam,
  Carpenters, and Seymour—An
  Introduction*, J. D. Salinger
Caravans, James A. Michener
Elizabeth Appleton, John O'Hara
Grandmother and the Priests,
  Taylor Caldwell
City of Night, John Rechy
The Glass-Blowers, Daphne Du
  Maurier
The Sand Pebbles, Richard
  McKenna

Nonfiction

Critics' Choice
*Eichmann in Jerusalem: A Report
  on the Banality of Evil*, Hannah
  Arendt
*The Rise of the West: A History of
  Human Community*, William H.
  McNeill
The Great Ascent, Robert
  Heilbroner
The Feminine Mystique, Betty
  Friedan
Prospect for the West, J. William
  Fulbright
The American Way of Death,
  Jessica Mitford
The Fire Next Time, James
  Baldwin
John F. Kennedy, President, Hugh
  Sidey
The Deadlock of Democracy,
  James McGregor Burns
*The American Economic
  Republic*, Adolf A. Berle
Beyond the Melting Pot, Nathan
  Glazer, Daniel P. Moynihan
*John Keats: The Making of a
  Poet*, Aileen Ward
Man-Made America, Christopher
  Tunnard, Boris Pushkarev

Best-Sellers
Happiness Is a Warm Puppy,
  Charles M. Schulz

*Security Is a Thumb and a
  Blanket*, Charles M. Schulz
J.F.K.: The Man and the Myth,
  Victor Lasky
*Profiles in Courage: Inaugural
  Edition*, John F. Kennedy
O Ye Jigs & Juleps!, Virginia Cary
  Hudson
*Better Homes and Gardens Bread
  Cook Book*
The Pillsbury Family Cookbook
I Owe Russia $1200, Bob Hope
Heloise's Housekeeping Hints

Poetry
James Wright, *The Bough Will Not
  Break*
E. E. Cummings, *73 Poems*
Conrad Aiken, *The Morning Song
  of Lord Zero*
W. S. Merwin, *The Moving Target*
James Merrill, *The Thousand and
  Second Night*
Adrienne Rich, *Snapshots of a
  Daughter-in-Law*

Pulitzer Prizes
No prize is awarded in fiction.
*Puritan Village: The Formation of
  a New England Town*, Sumner
  Chilton Powell (U.S. history)
*Anti-Intellectualism in American
  Life*, Richard Hofstadter
  (nonfiction)
John Keats, Walter Jackson Bate
  (biography)
At the End of the Open Road,
  Louis Simpson (poetry)

Science and Technology

The laser is developed for retinal operations.
F. D. Moore and T. E. Starzl perform the first liver
  transplant.
J. D. Hardy performs the first human lung transplant.
The FDA declares cancer "cures" Krebiozen and
  laetrile to be worthless.
Roche Labs introduces the tranquilizer Valium.
The electrical hospital "watchdog" is developed to
  record up to twelve postoperative patients' body
  functions.
Gordon Cooper, on the Faith 7 mission, makes 22
  orbits and orients manually for reentry.
The Minuteman ICBM is declared combat-ready; its
weight is 70,000 pounds, speed capability 15,000
  m.p.h., and range, 6,300 miles.
A Polaris missile is launched from a submarine.
The first commercial nuclear reactor, at the Jersey
  Central Power Company, becomes operational.
🔊 Phillips introduces the compact cassette.
🔊 Russian Valentina Tereshkova becomes the first
  woman in space.

Nobel Prize
E. P. Wigner wins the prize in physics for work in
nuclear and theoretical physics. Maris Goppert-
Mayer and J. H. D. Henson win for discoveries in
the shell structure of atomic nuclei.

Sports _____

Baseball

Sandy Koufax (Los Angeles, NL) pitches his second no-hitter, strikes out 306 in the season, and strikes out 15 in a World Series game.

Stan Musial retires; his lifetime totals include an NL record 3,630 hits, 475 homers, and a .330 BA.

Sandy Koufax (Los Angeles, NL) wins the Cy Young Award.

Champions _____

Batting	
Tommy Davis (Los Angeles, NL), .326	Angeles, NL), 16–3
	Whitey Ford (New York, AL), 24–5
Carl Yastrzemski (Boston, AL), .321	*Home runs*
Pitching	Henry Aaron (Milwaukee, NL), 44
Ron Perranoski (Los	Willie McCovey (San Francisco, NL), 44

Football

Don Shula becomes Baltimore Colt coach and Weeb Ewbank becomes New York Jet coach.

The Supreme Court turns down the AFL antitrust suit.

The Pro Football Hall of Fame begins; original selections include Sammy Baugh, Earl Clarke, Red Grange, George Halas, Wilbur Henry, Cal Hubbard, Don Hutson, Curly Lambeau, Bronko Nagurski, Ernie Nevers, and Jim Thorpe.

Paul Hornung (Green Bay) and Alex Karras (Detroit) are suspended one year for betting on games.

Jim Brown (Cleveland) gains a record 1,863 yards; Y. A. Tittle (New York) throws a record 36 TD passes.

NFL Season Leaders: Y.A. Tittle (New York), passing; Bobby Joe Conrad (St. Louis), receiving.

AFL Season Leaders: Tobin Rote (San Diego), passing; Clem Daniels (Oakland), rushing; Lionel Taylor (Denver), receiving

Cassius Clay (Muhammad Ali) and Howard Cosell. Cosell's "Tell-It-Like-It-Is" interviews alter the style of sports reporting. *Movie Star News.*

College All-Americans: Roger Staubach (QB), Navy; Dick Butkus (C), Illinois; Gale Sayers (B), Kansas; Carl Eller (T), Minnesota

Bowls (Jan. 1, 1964)

Rose: Illinois 17–Washington 7

Orange: Nebraska 13–Auburn 7

Cotton: Texas 28–Navy 6

Sugar: Alabama 12–Mississippi 7

Basketball

NBA All-Pro First Team: Bill Russell (Boston), Elgin Baylor (Los Angeles), Oscar Robertson (Cincinnati), Bob Pettit (St. Louis), Jerry West (Los Angeles)

Other Sports

Winners _____

World Series	*NBA Championship*
Los Angeles (NL) 4	Boston 4–Los Angeles 2
New York (AL) 3	*MVP*
MVP	Bill Russell, Boston
NL–Sandy Koufax, Los Angeles	*College Basketball*
AL–Elston Howard, New York	Loyola, Chicago
	Player of the Year
NFL	Art Heyman, Duke
Chicago Bears 14–New York 10	*Stanley Cup*
MVP	Toronto
Y. A. Tittle, New York	*US Tennis Open*
Jim Brown, Cleveland	Men: Rafael Osuna
College Football	Women: Maria Bueno
Texas	*USGA Open*
Heisman Trophy	Julius Boros
Roger Staubach, Navy	*Kentucky Derby*
	Chateaugay (B. Baeza, jockey)

Fashion _____

For Women: The sleeveless dress virtually disappears, and the "offbeat look" sweeps through fashion in layered outfits of various textures and styles. Boots reach over woolen tights and the thigh. Saint Laurent taps the Robin Hood and Joan of Arc look. Desired bulk is, in part, accomplished through turtlenecks and decorative scarves worn with collared shirts, all of which go beneath V-neck cardigans. Chunky tweed jackets and trench coats borrow men's styling. The offbeat look includes blouses modeled after the peasant smock shirt with double stitching, low-slung pants, fishnet stockings, sporty oxfords, white kid boots, thirties' open-back T-strap sandals, and sport watches. The woman who affects the hearty outdoor look moves easily from bulky textures to willowy silks and skinny coats. For the more mature woman, travel coordinates, by Norrell, include woolen slacks, jerkins, skirts, capes, and coats. Evening wear is more beautiful than ever with brocade theater suits and full-length tailored coats.

High-fashion note: Dior's evening chemise with flounces and low back

Kaleidoscope

- Joseph M. Valachi publicly identifies the chiefs of organized crime on a televised Senate hearing.
- Eighty-one Teamster officials are indicted, and 58 convicted, by Attorney General Robert Kennedy.
- JFK, visiting the Berlin wall, says, "Ich bin ein Berliner."
- Bayard Rustin and A. Philip Randolph, black president of the Union of Sleeping Car Porters, organize the March on Washington for Jobs and Freedom, at which Martin Luther King delivers his "I have a dream" speech.
- Police chief Bull Connor of Birmingham uses police dogs, fire hoses, and cattle prods on Martin Luther King and the marching schoolchildren and adults in Birmingham.
- A Gallup Poll shows Nelson Rockefeller's fall in popularity after his divorce and remarriage to a divorcée.
- Betty Friedan, in *The Feminine Mystique,* attacks the myth of the happy homemaker.
- The Zapruder film, an amateur movie of the JFK assassination, shows Texas governor John Connally being shot 1.8 seconds after the president and leads to controversy over whether the same bullet hit both men; this lends support to the possibility of a conspiracy.
- California passes New York as the most populous state.
- The Beatles have their first big success, "I Want to Hold Your Hand"; the group includes John Lennon, 23, Paul McCartney, 22, George Harrison, 20, and Ringo Starr, 24.
- "Hootenanies"—group folk concerts with audience participation—gain in popularity, especially with Joan Baez and Bobby Dylan.
- Although unemployment is at 6.1 percent, U.S. factory workers earn more than $100 a week, their highest earnings in history.
- On June 10, congressional legislation guarantees equal pay for equal work.

Birmingham, Alabama's police force confronting civil rights marchers. *Courtesy Dr. Archie Allen.*

Eleanor Roosevelt and Helen Keller meet during the Year of the Woman. *Copyright* Washington Post. *Reprinted by permission of D.C. Public Library.*

- Illegitimate births among teenage mothers are up 150 percent since 1940.
- Frank Sinatra, Jr., is kidnapped at Lake Tahoe and released unhurt in Los Angeles after his father pays a $240,000 ransom. The FBI arrests three suspects two days later and recovers most of the money.
- Two fatal botulism cases are tied to canned tuna fish.
- Julia Child prepares Boeuf Bourguignon on TV, beginning the popularization of French food through cooking demonstrations.
- New Hampshire passes a sweepstakes bill authorizing government-operated lotteries for educational programs.
- Fourteen thousand are arrested in 75 southern cities during civil rights demonstrations.
- "South Vietnam is on its way to victory," United States ambassador Fred Nolting writes, as Diem's campaign against the Buddhists continues.
- Sarah Lawrence graduate Hope Cooke marries Crown Prince Palden Thondup Namgyal of Sikkim; he becomes maharajah when his father dies at the end of the year.
- Fifty girls each week apply to *Playboy* to be "Playmate of the Month."

New Words and Usages: Beatlemania, rat fink, fake out

First Appearances: Kodak Instamatic camera with film cartridge, New York Hilton, Weight Watchers, Trimline phone, commercial service of push-button telephones (Carnegie and Greensburg, Pa.), illuminated nine-hole regulation golf course (Sewell, N.J.), international postcard, John F. Kennedy Airport (Idlewild), gerenuk born in U.S. (Bronx Zoo), the "Amazing Spider Man"

1964

Facts and Figures

Economic Profile
- Dow-Jones: ↑ High 891–Low 776
- GNP: +7%
- Inflation: +1.2%
- Unemployment: 5.2%

Expenditures:
- Recreation: $24.5 billion
- Spectator sports: $365 million
- European travel: $1.25 billion

Golf courses: 1,005
Bowlers: 7,496,000
Bloomingdale's pima cotton shirts for men: $5.95
Imported lisle hose: $2.50
Brooks Brothers:
- Tweed sport jackets for boys: $30–$39
- Flannel wool blazer: $29.50

Browning Shetland crew-neck sweater: $12.95
Oldsmobile: $3,495
Volkswagen: $1,695
Chevrolet (rental): $99 (per month)
Cadillac (rental); $159 (per month)
Hitachi tape recorder: $99
Lafayette classical Spanish guitar: $29.95

Deaths

Gracie Allen, Stuart Davis, Ian Fleming, Herbert Hoover, Alan Ladd, Douglas MacArthur, Harpo Marx, W. Somerset Maugham, Pierre Monteux, Jawaharlal Nehru, Cole Porter, Edith Sitwell, Norbert Weiner.

In the News

LBJ Calls for an End to Poverty and Racial Discrimination . . . Riots Occur in Panama Canal Zone over Display of American Flag . . . Supreme Court Rules That Congressional Districts Must Be Equal . . . James Hoffa Is Sentenced to Eight Years for Jury Rigging . . . Jack Ruby Is Sentenced to Death for Lee Harvey Oswald's Murder . . . Ian Smith, White Supremacist, Will Head Rhodesia . . . Khrushchev and Nasser Hail First Stage of Aswan Dam . . . 24th Amendment, Prohibiting Poll Tax, Passes . . . Civil Rights Act of 1964 Passes, Forbidding Public, Employment, and Union Discrimination . . . GOP Nominates Barry Goldwater for President, Democrats Nominate LBJ . . . Harlem and Brooklyn Blacks Riot, 141 Are Injured . . . Ranger VII Transmits Photos of Moon . . . FBI Finds Bodies of Three Slain Civil Rights Workers in Philadelphia, Mississippi . . . U.S. Planes Bomb North Vietnam after Attack on U.S. Destroyer in the Gulf of Tonkin, the Senate Votes Resolution of U.S. Support . . . $947 Million Is Voted for Antipoverty Program, Job Training, Domestic Peace Corps . . . Blacks in Philadelphia, Pa., Riot over Police Brutality, 248 Are Injured . . . Warren Commission Report Concludes That Oswald Acted Alone in Kennedy Assassination . . . At Cairo, 47 Nonaligned Nations Denounce the U.S. . . . Martin Luther King Wins Nobel Peace Prize . . . Khrushchev Is Removed, Leonid Brezhnev and Aleksei Kosygin Take Over . . . China Explodes Its First A-Bomb . . . LBJ Wins Landslide Victory, 43 Million to 27 Million . . . Ecumenical Council Exonerates Jews of Christ's Death . . . Supreme Court Upholds the Civil Rights Act.

EXTREMISM IN THE DEFENSE
OF LIBERTY IS NO VICE;
MODERATION IN THE PURSUIT
OF JUSTICE IS NO VIRTUE
**GOLDWATER
IN '64**

Campaign button for Barry Goldwater with
the presidential candidate's famous dictum.
Smithsonian Institution.

"I'm the only President you've got."
— Lyndon B. Johnson

"I don't see an American dream; . . . I see an
American nightmare. . . . Three hundred and ten
years we worked in this country without a dime in
return."

— Malcolm X

"Why does integration have to begin with *our*
children?"

— Anonymous (quoted in *New York Times*)

Quotes

"Camp is the answer to the problem: how to be a
dandy in an age of mass culture. Camp asserts . . .
there is a good taste of bad taste . . . [for example]
The *Enquirer* . . . 'Swan Lake' . . . Shoedsack's
'King Kong' . . . Jayne Mansfield . . . Victor Mature
. . . Bette Davis . . . Art Nouveau."
— Susan Sontag, "Notes on Camp"

"[Pop art is] the use of commercial art as a subject
matter in painting. . . . It was hard to get a painting
that was despicable enough so that no one would
hang it. . . . The one thing everyone hated was
commercial art; apparently they didn't hate that
enough either."
— Roy Lichtenstein

"In the electronic age, we wear all mankind as our
skin."
— Marshall McLuhan, *Understanding Media*

"By continuously embracing technologies we relate
ourselves to them. . . . That is why we must, to use
them at all, serve these objects as gods or minor
religions."

— Marshall McLuhan

Ads

Trichinosis, encephalitis, scarlet fever, amoebiasis,
jungle rot.
We think you'll find them more challenging than the
sniffles.

(Peace Corps)

I quit school when I were sixteen.

(Public Service Ad)

Act your age—today is Election Day. If you're over
21, make sure you vote.

(Public Service Ad)

Does it make sense to jump out of a warm bed into a
cold cereal?

(Quaker Oats)

Only 1 out of 25 men is color blind. The other 24 just
dress that way.

(Mohara Suits)

167 days of foggy, foggy dew can't claim all the credit
for beautiful English complexions.

(Elizabeth Arden)

Peter Sellers as a former Nazi missile expert in Stanley
Kubrick's *Dr. Strangelove, or How I Learned to Stop
Worrying and Love the Bomb. Movie Star News.*

TV

Premieres

"The Man from U.N.C.L.E.," Robert Vaughn, David McCallum

"Flipper," Brian Kelly

"Gomer Pyle, U.S.M.C.," Jim Nabors

"Daniel Boone," Fess Parker

"Jeopardy"

"Peyton Place," Mia Farrow, Ed Nelson

"Bewitched," Elizabeth Montgomery

"Mr. Magoo"

"Gilligan's Island," Jim Backus, Alan Hale, Jr.

"The Munsters," Yvonne De Carlo, Al Lewis

"The Addams Family," John Astin, Carolyn Jones

Top Ten (Nielsen)

"Bonanza," "Bewitched," "Gomer Pyle, U.S.M.C.," "The Andy Griffith Show," "The Fugitive," "The Red Skelton Show," "The Dick Van Dyke Show," "The Lucy Show," "Peyton Place II," "Combat"

Specials

"The Magnificent Yankee" (Alfred Lunt, Lynn Fontanne); "My Name Is Barbra" (Barbra Streisand); "The Decision to Drop the Bomb" (NBC White Paper); "What Is Sonata Form?" (New York Philharmonic Young People's Concert with Leonard Bernstein); "Profiles in Courage"

Emmy Awards

"Dick Van Dyke Show" (program); "I, Leonardo da Vinci," "The Louvre" (documentaries); Leonard Bernstein, Dick Van Dyke (performers)

Of Note

An American version of the British "That Was the Week That Was," with Elliot Read, Henry Morgan, and David Frost, initiates a biting form of topical political satire on prime-time TV • Owing to its great success, "Peyton Place" is aired twice weekly in prime time.

Movies

Openings

My Fair Lady (George Cukor), Audrey Hepburn, Rex Harrison

Becket (Peter Glenville), Richard Burton, Peter O'Toole, John Gielgud

Dr. Strangelove (Stanley Kubrick), Peter Sellers, George C. Scott

Mary Poppins (Robert Stevenson), Julie Andrews, Dick Van Dyke

Zorba the Greek (Michael Cacoyannis), Anthony Quinn, Alan Bates, Lila Kedrova

The Pumpkin Eater (Jack Clayton), Anne Bancroft, Peter Finch, James Mason

Seven Days in May (John Frankenheimer), Burt Lancaster, Kirk Douglas, Fredric March

Hush, Hush, Sweet Charlotte (Robert B. Aldrich), Bette Davis, Olivia de Havilland

A Hard Day's Night (Richard Lester), Beatles

The Pink Panther (Blake Edwards), Peter Sellers, David Niven, Capucine

The Americanization of Emily (Arthur Hiller), James Garner, Julie Andrews

Cheyenne Autumn (John Ford), Richard Widmark, Carroll Baker

The Umbrellas of Cherbourg (Jacques Demy), Catherine Deneuve

Woman in the Dunes (Hiroshi Teshigahara), Eiji Okada, Kyoko Kishida

The Servant (Joseph Losey), Dirk Bogarde, James Fox, Sarah Miles

From Russia with Love (Terence Young), Sean Connery, Daniela Bianchi, Lotte Lenya

Goldfinger (Guy Hamilton), Sean Connery, Honor Blackman

The Gospel According to St. Matthew (Pier Paolo Pasolini), Enrique Irazoqui

Academy Awards

Best Picture: *My Fair Lady*

Best Director: George Cukor (*My Fair Lady*)

Best Actress: Julie Andrews (*Mary Poppins*)

Best Actor: Rex Harrison (*My Fair Lady*)

Top Box-Office Stars

Doris Day, Jack Lemmon, Rock Hudson, John Wayne, Cary Grant, Elvis Presley, Shirley MacLaine, Ann-Margret, Paul Newman, Richard Burton

Stars of Tomorrow

Elke Sommer, Annette Funicello, Susannah York, Elizabeth Ashley, Stefanie Powers, Harve Presnell, Dean Jones, Keir Dullea, Nancy Sinatra, Joey Heatherton

Popular Music

Hit Songs
"Chim Chim Cher-ee"
"I Want to Hold Your Hand"
"Downtown"
"People"
"Pink Panther Theme"
"Walk on By"
"We'll Sing in the Sunshine"
"King of the Road"

Top Records

Albums: *Hello Dolly!* (original cast); *Honey in the Horn* (Al Hirt); *The Barbra Streisand Album, West Side Story* (sound track); *The Second Barbra Streisand Album; Meet the Beatles*

Singles: *She Loves You* (Beatles); *Baby, I Need Your Loving* (Four Tops); *Oh, Pretty Woman* (Roy Orbison); *Hello Dolly!* (Louis Armstrong); *I Get Around* (Beach Boys); *Everybody Loves Somebody* (Dean Martin); *Baby Love* (Supremes); *A Hard Day's Night* (Beatles); *Leader of the Pack* (Shangri-La). Country: *Understand Your Man* (Johnny Cash); *Dang Me* (Roger Miller)

Grammy Awards
The Girl from Ipanema, Stan Getz, Astrud Gilberto (record); *Getz / Gilberto* (album); "Hello Dolly!" (song)

Jazz and Big Bands
Successful concerts include those of Charlie Mingus, Earl Hines, Cecil Taylor, Jimmy Giuffre, Paul Bley, and Rod Levill; Andrew Hill and Charles Lloyd attract much attention.
Frank Zappa introduces jazz into rock with The Mothers of Invention.

Top Performers *(Downbeat):* Eric Dolphy (soloist); Duke Ellington, Count Basie (bands); Dave Brubeck (jazz group); Jim Hall, Charlie Mingus, Bill Evans (instrumentalists); Ella Fitzgerald, Ray Charles (vocalists); Double Six (vocal group)

Theater

Broadway Openings
Plays
The Subject Was Roses (Frank D. Gilroy), Martin Sheen, Jack Albertson, Irene Dailey
Dylan (Sidney Michaels), Alec Guinness, Kate Reid
Any Wednesday (Muriel Resnik), Sandy Dennis, Gene Hackman, Rosemary Murphy
Luv (Murray Schisgal), Eli Wallach, Anne Jackson, Alan Arkin
The Owl and the Pussycat (Bill Manhoff), Diana Sands, Alan Alda
The Deputy (Rolf Hochhuth), Emlyn Williams, Jeremy Brett
Tiny Alice (Edward Albee), John Gielgud, Irene Worth
The Sign in Sidney Brustein's Window (Lorraine Hansberry), Rita Moreno, Gabriel Dell
The Physicists (Friedrich Dürrenmatt), Jessica Tandy, George Voskovec, Hume Cronyn
Blues for Mr. Charlie (James Baldwin), Al Freeman, Jr., Rip Torn, Diana Sands
After the Fall (Arthur Miller), Barbara Loden, Jason Robards, Jr.
Incident at Vichy (Arthur Miller), David Wayne, Hal Holbrook

Musicals
Hello Dolly! (Jerry Herman), Carol Channing, David Burns, Charles Nelson Reilly
Fiddler on the Roof (Jerry Bock, Sheldon Harnick), Zero Mostel, Maria Karnilova
Funny Girl (Jule Styne), Barbra Streisand, Sydney Chaplin
Golden Boy (Charles Strouse, Lee Adams), Sammy Davis, Jr.

Classics and Revivals On and Off Broadway
Hamlet, Richard Burton; *The Slave, The Toilet* (LeRoi Jones), Jaime Sanchez; *Othello*, James Earl Jones; *A Slight Ache, The Room, The Lover* (Harold Pinter); *The Old Glory* (Robert Lowell); *Three Sisters* (Chekhov), Geraldine Page, Kim Stanley, Shirley Knight; *The Blood Knot* (Athol Fugard), James Earl Jones; *The New Tenant, Victims of Duty* (Eugene Ionesco); Royal Shakespeare: *King Lear* (Paul Scofield), *Comedy of Errors. Founded:* The American Place Theatre by Wynn Handman and Sidney Lanier

Regional
Founded: Eugene O'Neill Memorial Theater, Waterford, Conn., by George C. White; Hartford Stage Company by Jacques Cartier; Actors Theatre of Louisville, by Richard Block, Ewel Cornett; Trinity Square Repertory, Providence, R.I., by Adrian Hall

Minnesota Theatre Company: *Henry V, St. Joan, Volpone*, George Grizzard, Ed Flanders

Pulitzer Prize No prize is awarded.

Tony Awards
Luther, John Osborne (play), *Hello Dolly!* Jerry Herman (musical)

Classical Music

Compositions
Milton Babbitt, *Philomel*
Ferde Grofé, *World's Fair Suite*
Roy Harris, *Horn of Plenty*
William Schuman, Symphony no. 7
Leo Sowerby, Symphony no. 5
John Cage, *Atlas Elipticales*
Henry Brant, *Voyage Four*
Charles Wuorinen, Piano Variations

Important Events
Interest grows in electronic music: the Ojai Festival, California, includes *Ensembles for Synthesizer* (Milton Babbitt); Duo for Clarinet and Recorded Clarinet (William O. Smith); and *Rhythm Studies Performed on Perforated Piano* (John Powell). The Festival of Chamber Music, Library of Congress, includes *In Time of Daffodil* (Riccardo Malipiero); *Amaryllis* (William Schuman); String Septet (Darius Milhaud); *Four Psalms* (Howard Hanson); String Sextet (Walter Piston); and *The Feast of Love* (Virgil Thomson).
Jascha Heifetz and Gregor Piatigorsky give three chamber music and concerto concerts, New York; Artur Rubinstein gives three major concerts, New York.
The Los Angeles Music Center for the Performing Arts opens: the Los Angeles Philharmonic with Zubin Mehta, 28, conductor, gives a week of concerts, including *American Festival Overture* (William Schuman); Beethoven Violin Concerto and Symphony no. 9, and *Le sacre du printemps* (Igor Stravinsky).

Debut: John Ogdon

Newcomer Régine Crespin, with Richard Tucker, one of the Metropolitan's leading tenors since 1945, in *Tosca*. *Chicago Lyric Opera: David H. Fishman.*

First Performances
Leonard Bernstein, Third Symphony (*Kaddish*), Boston; Carlos Chávez, Symphony no. 6 (New York); Peter Mennin, Symphony no. 7 (Cleveland); Roger Sessions, Symphony no. 5 (Philadelphia); Quincy Porter, Symphony no. 2 (Louisville); Lukas Foss, *Elytres* (Los Angeles); Henry Cowell, Concerto for Koto and Orchestra (Philadelphia); Igor Stravinsky, *Elegy for JFK* (Los Angeles)

Opera

Metropolitan: Roberta Peters, George London, *The Last Savage* (Gian Carlo Menotti, premiere); Joan Sutherland, *Lucia di Lammermoor;* Rita Gorr, Jess Thomas, *Samson et Delila;* Gabriella Tucci, Regina Resnik, Anselmo Colzani, *Falstaff;* Elisabeth Schwarzkopf (debut), *Der Rosenkavalier;* Donald Gramm (debut), *Ariadne auf Naxos*

New York City: *Natalia Petrovna* (Lee Hoiby, premiere)

Boston: Joan Sutherland, *I Puritani; Lulu*

Philadelphia: Renata Tebaldi returns to the stage in *La bohème;* Joan Sutherland, *La traviata*

Chicago: Fiorenza Cossotto, *La favorita;* Irmgard Seefried, Regine Crespin, *Ariadne auf Naxos*

Santa Fe: *Daphne* (Richard Strauss)

San Francisco: *Der Freischütz, Susanna*

Fiddler on the Roof, the highly successful musical based on Sholem Aleichem's stories of Jewish life in Russia. *Billy Rose Theatre Collection. The New York Public Library at Lincoln Center. Astor, Lenox and Tilden Foundations.*

Art

Painting

Jasper Johns, *Field Painting, Studio*
Agnes Martin, *The Tree*
Ad Reinhardt, *Abstract Painting*
Kenneth Noland, *Tropical Zone, Prime Course*
Frank Stella, *Ifafa II, Fez*
Jack Youngerman, *Black, Yellow, Red*
Jim Dine, *Double Self-Portrait (The Green Line)*
Robert Rauschenberg, *Retroactive*
Andy Warhol, *Brillo Boxes*

Sculpture

David Smith, *Cubi XVIII, Cubi XIX*
Louise Nevelson, *Black Cord, Silent Music I*
George Segal, *Woman in a Doorway I*
Edward Kienholz, *The Birthday*
Jasper Johns, *Painted Bronze II (Ale Cans)*
Alexander Calder designs sculpture for the Federal Center, Chicago.

Architecture

Verrazano-Narrows Bridge, New York (Ammann, Hermann)
New York World's Fair, New York Pavilion (Philip Johnson)
Kline Science Tower, Yale University, New Haven, Conn. (Philip Johnson)
Chicago Federal Center, United States Courthouse, Federal Office Building, Post Office, Chicago (Mies van der Rohe)
Venturi House, Philadelphia (Venturi and Rausch)
Gallery of Modern Art, New York (Edward Durell Stone)
New York State Theater, Lincoln Center, New York (Harrison and Johnson)
Green Center for the Earth Sciences, M.I.T., Cambridge (I.M. Pei)

Important Exhibitions

Museums

New York: *Metropolitan:* "The World's Fairs— Architectures of Fantasy." *Gallery of Modern Art:* Tchelitchew; The Pre-Raphaelites. *Museum of Modern Art:* Sculpture retrospective; Hofmann; Bonnard. *Whitney:* Joseph Stella and Hopper retrospectives. *Guggenheim:* Francis Bacon Retrospective

Chicago: Albright; Chinese art of the Ming and Ch'ing dynasties

Richmond: Elizabethan art (to celebrate Shakespeare's 400th birthday); Dutch 17th-century paintings

Baltimore: 250 works from 1914

Washington: *Corcoran:* John Singer Sargent; Contemporary Japanese painting. *National:* Turner; 7,000 years of Persian art

Cleveland, Brooklyn, Kansas City, Houston, San Francisco: Turner—80 watercolors

Art Briefs

Michelangelo's *Pièta* is displayed at the New York World's Fair (Vatican Pavilion) • The Museum of Modern Art in New York opens two new wings and expands the sculpture garden; the first permanent photo gallery is installed • Chagall completes a stained-glass memorial panel to Dag Hammarskjöld for the UN Building, New York • Mark Rothko completes murals for a Houston interdenominational chapel later named the Rothko Chapel • Major prizes of the year are awarded to painters Rauschenberg, Motherwell, and Kelly, and architects David, Georges, Conway, and McCullough.

Dance

The Boston Ballet is founded by E. Virginia Williams. Rebecca Harkness and Robert Joffrey separate because of conflicting artistic policies; she forms the Harkness Ballet. The New York City Ballet opens in the new New York State Theater, Lincoln Center. The Ford Foundation gives $7.7 million to the company.

Premieres

New York City Ballet: *Tarantella* (George Balanchine), Patricia McBride, Edward Villella; *Irish Fantasy* (Jacques D'Amboise)

Merce Cunningham: *Event Number One*

Books _____

Fiction

Critics' Choice

Because I Was Flesh, Edward Dahlberg
Second Skin, John Hawkes
Julian, Gore Vidal
Come Back, Dr. Caligari, Donald Barthelme
Cabot Wright Begins, James Purdy
Little Big Man, Thomas Berger
The Wapshot Scandal, John Cheever
Teeth, Dying and Other Matters, Richard G. Stern
Last Exit to Brooklyn, Hubert Selby
❧ *The Interrogation*, J. G. Le Clézio

Best-Sellers

The Spy Who Came in from the Cold, John Le Carré
Candy, Terry Southern, Mason Hoffenberg
Herzog, Saul Bellow
Armageddon, Leon Uris
The Man, Irving Wallace
The Rector of Justin, Louis Auchincloss
The Martyred, Richard E. Kim
You Only Live Twice, Ian Fleming

Nonfiction

Critics' Choice

Waiting for the End, Leslie Fiedler
Crowell's Handbook of Classical Literature, Lillian Feder
Understanding Media, Marshall McLuhan
Science: The Glorious Entertainment, Jacques Barzun
The Games People Play, Eric Berne
Experiment, Willie Lee Rose
The End of Alliance, Ronald Steel
The Theatre of Revolt, Robert Brustein
Of Poetry and Power: A Tribute to John F. Kennedy, ed. Pierre Salinger, Sander Vanocur
The Warren Commission Report
God and Golem, Inc., Norbert Wiener
The Life of Lenin, Louis Fischer
The Oysters of Locmariaquer, Eleanor Clark
❧ *The Wretched of the Earth*, Franz Fanon

Best-Sellers

Four Days, American Heritage, United Press International
I Need All the Friends I Can Get, Charles M. Schulz
Profiles in Courage: Memorial Edition, John F. Kennedy
In His Own Write, John Lennon
Christmas Is Together-Time, Charles M. Schulz
A Day in the Life of President Kennedy, Jim Bishop
The Kennedy Wit, Bill Adler
A Moveable Feast, Ernest Hemingway

Poetry

Robert Lowell, *For the Union Dead*
Theodore Roethke, *The Far Field* (posthumous)
Karl Shapiro, *The Bourgeois Poet*
Charles Olson, *Signature to Petition on Ten Pound Island*
James Dickey, *Helmets, Two Poems of the Air*
Richard Eberhart, *The Quarry*
Ted Berrigan, *The Sonnets*
J. V. Cunningham, *To What Strangers, What Welcome*

Pulitzer Prizes

Collected Stories of Katherine Anne Porter, Katherine Anne Porter (fiction)
The Greenback Era, Irwin Unger (U.S. history)
O Strange New World, Howard Mumford (nonfiction)
Henry Adams, 3 vols., Ernest Samuels (biography)
77 Dream Songs, John Berryman (poetry)

Science and Technology _____

A total of 4,316 high-resolution photos of the moon's surface are taken by Ranger VII.

IBM introduces chips into its 360 system; it also demonstrates a word processor that stores, corrects, and retypes.

Motions of an orbiting satellite are visualized by an IBM 7090 digital computer.

The fundamental subatomic particle, omega-minis, is discovered.

Home dialysis for kidney patients is introduced in the United States and England.

Dr. Michael DeBakey replaces a section of the aorta with Dacron.

The U.S. Surgeon General links cigarette smoking and cancer.

The "battered-child syndrome" is described.

Methadone is developed as a means of rehabilitating heroin users by Vincent Dole and Marie Nyswander.

The Verrazano-Narrows Bridge, in New York, opens, the world's largest single-span suspension bridge.

❧ A new strain of "miracle" rice, suitable for tropical cultivation, is developed.

Nobel Prize

Dr. Konrad Bloch wins the prize in physiology and medicine for work on the relationship between heart disease and cholesterol. C. H. Townes wins in physics for work on high-intensity radiation.

Sports

Baseball

Dean Chance (Los Angeles, AL) pitches a record 11 shutouts. He also wins the Cy Young Award.

Champions

Batting
Roberto Clemente (Pittsburgh, NL), .339
Tony Oliva (Minnesota, AL), .323
Pitching
Sandy Koufax (Los Angeles, NL), 19–5
Wally Bunker (Baltimore, AL), 19–5
Home runs
Harmon Killebrew (Minneapolis, AL), 49

Football

Jim Brown (Cleveland) ties Don Hutson's career record of 105 touchdowns.

NFL Season Leaders: Bart Starr (Green Bay), passing; Jim Brown (Cleveland), rushing; John Morris (Chicago), receiving. **AFL Season Leaders:** Len Dawson (Kansas City), passing; Cookie Gilchrist (Buffalo), rushing; Charlie Hennigan (Houston) receiving

College All-Americans: Gale Sayers (B), Kansas; Jerry Rhome (QB), Tulsa; Dick Butkus (LB), Illinois

Bowls (Jan. 1, 1965)

Rose: Michigan 34–Oregon State 7
Orange: Texas 21–Alabama 17
Cotton: Arkansas 10–Nebraska 7
Sugar: Louisiana State 13–Syracuse 10

Basketball

NBA All-Pro First Team: Wilt Chamberlain (Philadelphia), Oscar Robertson (Cincinnati), Bob Pettit (St. Louis), Walt Bellamy (Baltimore), Jerry West (Los Angeles)

Olympics

In the Summer Games at Tokyo, Don Schollander wins four gold medals in swimming (100m, 400m, two relays). Other U.S. winners include Robert Hayes (100m, 10.0s.); Henry Carr (200m, 20.35s.); Michael Larrabee (400m, 45.1s.); Robert Schul (5000m, 13:48.8); Walter Mills (10,000m, 28.24.4); Fred Hansen (pole vault, 16′8¾′′); Dallas Long (shot put, 66′8¼′′); Al Oerter (discus, 200′1½′′); Wyomia Tyus (100m, 11.4s.); Edith McGuire (200m, 23.0s.); Virginia Duenkel (swimming, 400m, 4:43.3); Joseph Frazier (HW boxing). In the Winter Games at Innsbruck, Austria, R. Terrance McDermott wins the 500m.

Other Sports

Boxing: Cassius Clay, an 8–1 underdog, beats Sonny Liston in seven rounds for the heavyweight title before 8,200 in Miami.

Running: Seventeen-year old Jim Ryun runs the mile in 3:50.0.

Winners

World Series
St. Louis (NL) 4
New York (AL) 3
MVP
NL–Ken Boyer, St. Louis
AL–Brooks Robinson, Baltimore
NFL
Cleveland 27–Baltimore 0
MVP
Len Moore, Baltimore
College Football
Alabama
Heisman Trophy
John Huarte, Notre Dame
NBA Championship
Boston 4–San Francisco 1
MVP
Oscar Robertson, Cincinnati
College Basketball
UCLA
Player of the Year
Walt Hazzard, UCLA
Stanley Cup
Toronto
US Tennis Open
Men: Roy Emerson
Women: Maria Bueno
USGA Open
Ken Venturi
Kentucky Derby
Northern Dancer (W. Hartack, jockey)

Fashion

For Women: Colored or textured tights give the body a sculpted look. Bold blocks of strongly contrasting color and pattern, in sharp outlines and with colored borders, echo pop art. Barbra Streisand's "eclectic look" shares fashion honors with that of the more traditionally elegant Mrs. Kennedy and the Duchess of Windsor. Mary Quant and Sally Triffin's "mod" emphasizes "the nude look" (Gernreich's topless tank has already appeared). The body stocking is a great success, along with transparent sports blouses and décolletages that reach both the navel and the base of the spine. Courrèges pursues the opposite fashion extreme with tops that cover all except the face and hands and are worn with narrow pipe-stem pants. Generally, the "superfeminine look" replaces the sporty one, with accents from North Africa, and the Middle and Far East. Long hair is pulled back into designer scarves; the raincoat becomes ubiquitous.

High-fashion notes: Picciu's draped and folded pants from Bali, India, and Africa; Cashin's evening sportswear; Ferraud's see-throughs

Kaleidoscope _____

The New York World's Fair. *Museum of the City of New York.*

- A controversial LBJ TV ad portrays a little girl picking daisies, an atomic explosion, and the statement: "These are the stakes."
- "Go-go" girls on raised platforms in "discos" set the dance pace to the frug, swim, watusi, dog, children, and monkey. A San Francisco bar introduces topless go-go girls on June 19; on September 3, they go bottomless.
- Marshall McLuhan popularizes his belief that "the medium is the message," that the experience of seeing and hearing, rather than content, matters.
- The Hell's Angels receive a great deal of publicity with their huge Harley-Davidson motorcycles, colored and unwashed clothing (like sleeveless vests), helmets, huge sunglasses, and tattoos.
- The largest mass arrest of student demonstrators includes 732 sit-ins at Sproul Hall at the University of California (Berkeley), led by Mario Savio, Bettina Aptheker, and Jack Weinberg.
- The Warren Commission, finding no conspiracy in JFK's assassination, issues a paperback report 80 hours after its conclusions are made.
- Some 464,000 black students boycott the New York public schools to end, through busing, de facto segregation.
- Lester Maddox closes his Atlanta restaurant, Pickwick, rather than serve blacks; he had previously distributed pickax handles to anyone willing to cudgel entering blacks.
- Martin Luther King donates most of his $54,600 Nobel Peace Prize to the civil rights movement.
- James Chaney, Andrew Goodman, and Michael Schwerner are murdered, along with 12 others, after SNCC's Freedom Summer; the FBI arrests 21, including Sheriff Lawrence Rainey of Neshoba County, Mississippi.
- Ten thousand await the Beatles at JFK Airport: the group gets $2,400 for its Ed Sullivan appearance, and, later, a record $150,000 in Kansas City; "Can't Buy Me Love" has the biggest advance sale to date.
- Rudy Gernreich's topless bathing suit begins the no-bra fad.
- Over 250 million paperback books are sold.
- Movies have their most successful year since TV began.
- Elizabeth Taylor divorces Eddie Fisher and marries Richard Burton 10 days later.
- As evidence of his thriftiness, LBJ goes around the White House turning off lights.
- LBJ promises not "to send American boys 9 or 10,000 miles away from home to do what Asian boys should do for themselves."
- LBJ appoints Sargent Shriver head of the Office of Economic Opportunity in the "national war on poverty"; he is to coordinate the Job Corps, Neighborhood Youth Corps, VISTA, Head Start, and other organizations.
- The surgeon general's reports linking cigarettes and cancer lead the Federal Trade Commission to require that cigarette packages carry health warnings.
- A record 276 million gallons of alcohol is consumed, averaging 1.45 gallons per capita; bourbon is the largest-selling whiskey.
- Thieves, led by Murph the Surf, are caught after stealing rare stones from the Museum of Natural History in New York, including the world's largest sapphire, the 565-carat Star of India.
- The motto of the New York World's Fair is "Peace through Understanding"; 27 million attend, less than anticipated.
- Cigarette advertising is halted in magazines, sports programs, and college papers, and on radio stations.
- Michelangelo's *Pièta,* on loan from St. Peters for the New York World's Fair, arrives in a special waterproof, floatable crate designed to free itself from a sinking ship.
- An outraged public reads about an indifferent public on the occasion of Kitty Genovese's assault: many neighbors watched but no one phoned the police until after she was beaten to death.
- Police capture the suspected "Boston Strangler," Albert Henry De Salvo.
- "In your heart you know he might [push the button]" is one takeoff on Barry Goldwater's campaign slogan "In your heart you know he's right."

Fads: Beatles items, the Prince Valiant hairdo, GI Joe dolls

First Appearances: Films shown on airplanes, Ford Mustang, Awake, Pop-Tarts, Lucky Charms, Dole fresh pineapple, Dynel, rivets removed from Levi Straus blue jean pockets, Carlton, Reverend Ike (Frederick J. Eikeronkoetter), Klear, zip codes, Canyonlands National Park (Utah), Campobello International Park, Brunswick Island, freeze-dried coffee (Maxim), artificial leather (Corfam), electronic voting machines, elliptical-shaped office building, geodesic dome, Washington's Capital Beltway, self-service post office (Wheaton, Md.), bridge player to earn a lifetime total of 8,000 points (Oswald Jacoby), picture-phone service (New York, Chicago), presidential election in which votes are tallied electronically, Allan and Midge dolls (to go with Barbie and Ken), Kennedy half dollar, *Crawdaddy* (first rock magazine), Robert Moog synthesizer

1965

Facts and Figures

Economic Profile
  Dow-Jones: ↑ High 969–
    Low 867
  GNP: +8%
  Inflation: +1.6%
  Unemployment: 4.5%
Infant mortality/1,000: 24.7
Maternal mortality/10,000:
  3.2
Physicians in U.S.: 297,000
Dentists in U.S.: 109,000
Hospital beds: 1,703,000
New York City apartments:
  5th Ave. (60s), 6-room
    duplex: $575
  Broadway, 72nd St., 2
    bedrooms: $200
  Park West Village, 2
    bedrooms, with view of
    Central park: $239
Help wanted (*New York
  Times*):
  Receptionist: $65–$80
  Clerk-typist: $70–$90
  TV programmer: $125
  IBM key punch: $65–$90
  Dental assistant: $150

Deaths

Bernard Baruch, Clara Bow,
Winston Churchill, Nat
"King" Cole, T. S. Eliot,
Felix Frankfurter, Judy
Holliday, Stan Laurel,
Georgi Rimsky-Korsakov,
Edward R. Murrow,
Helena Rubinstein, Albert
Schweitzer, Adlai E.
Stevenson

In the News

LBJ PLEDGES TO SUPPORT SOUTH VIETNAM AND TO BUILD "THE GREAT SOCIETY" . . . FIRST U.S. COMBAT TROOPS LAND IN VIETNAM . . . MALCOLM X IS ASSASSINATED IN HARLEM . . . $1.4 BILLION IS APPROPRIATED FOR APPALACHIA . . . SOVIET COSMONAUT LEONOV IS THE FIRST MAN TO FLOAT IN SPACE . . . 3,200 MAKE A 54-MILE "FREEDOM MARCH" FROM SELMA TO MONTGOMERY, ALABAMA, MARCHER VIOLA LIUZZO IS MURDERED . . . GEMINI MAKES THE FIRST TWO-MAN U.S. ORBIT . . . TERRORIST BOMB DEVASTATES U.S. SAIGON EMBASSY . . . LBJ OFFERS NORTH VIETNAM UNCONDITIONAL PEACE AND $1 BILLION FOR RECONSTRUCTION . . . CIVIL WAR BREAKS OUT IN DOMINICAN REPUBLIC, JOHNSON SENDS TROOPS . . . 100,000 ON 100 CAMPUSES ATTEND NATIONAL TEACH-IN ON VIETNAM . . . BOMBING OF NORTH VIETNAM RESUMES AS HO CHI MINH REJECTS LBJ OFFER . . . ED WHITE TAKES A RECORD 20-MINUTE WALK FROM GEMINI IV . . . SUPREME COURT STRIKES DOWN COMPULSORY ANTI–BIRTH CONTROL LAWS . . . MARINER FLIES PAST MARS AND TRANSMITS PHOTOS . . . MEDICARE BILL PASSES . . . VOTING RIGHTS ACT OF 1965 PASSES . . . 34 DIE IN WATTS GHETTO RIOTS . . . MAO CALLS FOR REVOLUTIONARY WARS IN DEVELOPING NATIONS . . . OAS PEACE PLAN FOR DOMINICAN REPUBLIC IS ACCEPTED . . . FRANCE LEAVES NATO . . . HUD IS CREATED . . . INDONESIAN ARMY CRUSHES COMMUNIST COUP AND BEGINS ERADICATION . . . $2.3 BILLION HIGHER EDUCATION ACT IS PASSED . . . RHODESIA DECLARES INDEPENDENCE OF BRITAIN, BRITISH P.M. WILSON ORDERS SANCTIONS . . . 25,000 IN WASHINGTON, D.C., MARCH TO PROTEST WAR . . . LBJ STOPS BOMBING AND OFFERS PEACE . . . VIETNAM: U.S. TROOP STRENGTH, 190,000; U.S. DEAD, 1,350; WOUNDED, 5,300; ENEMY DEAD, 34,585.

Antiwar march. Protest accelerates at home, alongside military buildup in Vietnam. *Photographer: Richard Hofmeister.*

"The Vietcong are going to collapse within weeks."
— National Security Adviser Walt Rostow

"This is a theatre of assault. The play that will split the heavens will be called THE DESTRUCTION OF AMERICA. The heroes will be Crazy Horse, Denmark Vesey, Patrice Lumumba."
— Leroi Jones, "The Revolutionary Theatre"

"Once it was power that created style. But now high styles come from low places, from people who have no power, . . . who are marginal, who carve out worlds for themselves in the nether depths, in tainted 'undergrounds.' "
— Tom Wolfe, "Girl of the Year"

"We like books that have a lot of *dreck* in them, matter which presents itself as not wholly relevant . . . but which, carefully attended to, can supply a 'sense' of what is going on."
— Donald Barthelme, *Snow White*

Quotes

"Let us march on segregated schools. Let us march on poverty. Let us march on ballot boxes, until the Wallaces of our nation tremble away in silence. My people, my people, listen! The battle is in our hands."
— Martin Luther King, Jr., en route from Selma to Montgomery

"At times, history and fate meet at a single time in a single place to shape a turning point in man's unending search for freedom. So it was at Lexington and Concord. So it was a century ago at Appomattox. So it was last week at Selma."
— President Lyndon Johnson

Vietnam: Orange Beach, South of Danang. In the first year ground troops are sent to Vietnam, LBJ declares "the people of South Vietnam have chosen to resist aggression from the north. The U.S. has taken its place beside them." *U.S. Navy Department.*

Ads

TV

Premieres

"Days of Our Lives"
"Green Acres," Eva Gabor, Eddie Albert
"Run for Your Life," Ben Gazzara
"The Dean Martin Show"
"The Wild, Wild West," Robert Conrad, Ross Martin
"Get Smart," Don Adams, Barbara Feldon
"The Big Valley," Barbara Stanwyck
"I Dream of Jeannie," Barbara Eden
"The FBI," Efrem Zimbalist, Jr.
"F Troop," Forrest Tucker, Larry Storch
"Hogan's Heroes," Werner Klemperer, Bob Crane
"The Avengers," Patrick Macnee, Diana Rigg
"I Spy," Robert Culp, Bill Cosby

Top Ten (Nielsen)

"Bonanza," "Gomer Pyle, U.S.M.C.," "The Lucy Show," "The Red Skelton Hour," "Batman," "The Andy Griffith Show," "Bewitched," "The Beverly Hillbillies," "Hogan's Heroes," "Green Acres"

Specials

"Ages of Man"; "Frank Sinatra: A Man and His Music"; "A Charlie Brown Christmas"; "Inherit the Wind" (Melvyn Douglas, Ed Begley); "Eagle in a Cage" (Trevor Howard, James Daly); "Senate Hearings on Viet Nam" (NBC)

Emmy Awards

"The Fugitive" (drama); "The Dick Van Dyke Show" (comedy); "Andy Williams Show" (variety); Bill Cosby (actor, "I Spy"); Dick Van Dyke (comedic actor, "The Dick Van Dyke Show"); Barbara Stanwyck (actress, "The Big Valley"); Mary Tyler Moore (comedic actress, "The Dick Van Dyke Show")

Of Note

NBC is the first network to present early evening, 30-minute news • Forty new shows, the highest number in TV history, appear in the fall • For the first time, all the top shows are in color.

Movies

Openings

The Sound of Music (Robert Wise), Julie Andrews, Christopher Plummer, Eleanor Parker
The Collector (William Wyler), Terence Stamp, Samantha Eggar
Cat Ballou (Elliot Silverstein), Jane Fonda, Lee Marvin
The Spy Who Came in from the Cold (Martin Ritt), Richard Burton, Claire Bloom
Othello (Stuart Burge), Laurence Olivier, Frank Finlay, Maggie Smith
The Pawnbroker (Sidney Lumet), Rod Steiger, Geraldine Fitzgerald
Juliet of the Spirits (Federico Fellini), Giulietta Masina, Sandra Milo, Sylva Koscina
Darling (John Schlesinger), Julie Christie, Dirk Bogarde, Laurence Harvey
Dr. Zhivago (David Lean), Julie Christie, Omar Sharif, Tom Courtenay, Alex Guinness
A Thousand Clowns (Fred Coe), Jason Robards, Barbara Harris
Ship of Fools (Stanley Kramer), Simone Signoret, Oskar Werner, Vivien Leigh, Lee Marvin
To Die in Madrid (documentary), narrated by John Gielgud
Help! (Richard Lester), The Beatles
Alphaville (Jean-Luc Godard), Eddie Constantine, Anna Karina
The Agony and the Ecstasy (Carol Reed), Charlton Heston, Rex Harrison
The Ipcress File (Stanley T. Furie), Michael Caine, Nigel Green
The Shop on Main Street (Jan Kadar, Elmar Klos), Ida Kaminska, Josef Kroner

Academy Awards

Best Picture: *The Sound of Music*
Best Director: Robert Wise (*The Sound of Music*)
Best Actress: Julie Christie (*Darling*)
Best Actor: Lee Marvin (*Cat Ballou*)

Top Box-Office Stars

Sean Connery, John Wayne, Doris Day, Julie Andrews, Jack Lemmon, Elvis Presley, Cary Grant, James Stewart, Elizabeth Taylor, Richard Burton

Stars of Tomorrow

Rosemary Forsythe, Michael Anderson, Jr., Michael Parks, Michael Caine, Mary Ann Mobley, Jocelyn Lane, Mia Farrow, Julie Christie, Richard Johnson, Senta Berger

Popular Music

Hit Songs

"Crying in the Chapel"
"Goldfinger"
"It's Not Unusual"
"Help!"
"Like a Rolling Stone"
"Look of Love"
"Mr. Tambourine Man"
"Mrs. Brown, You've Got a
    Lovely Daughter"
"Red Roses for a Blue Lady"
"The Shadow of Your Smile"
"What the World Needs Now Is
    Love"
"Stop! In the Name of Love"

Top Records

Albums: *Roustabout* (Elvis Presley); *Beatles '65* (Beatles); *Mary Poppins* (sound track); *Goldfinger* (sound track); *Out of Our Heads* (Rolling Stones)

Singles: *Wooly Bully* (Sam the Sham and the Pharaohs); *I Can't Help Myself* (Four Tops); *(I Can't Get No) Satisfaction* (Rolling Stones); *King of the Road* (Roger Miller); *What's New Pussycat?* (Tom Jones); *Ferry Cross the Mersey* (Gerry and the Pacemakers); *I Got You Babe* (Sonny and Cher); *Downtown* (Petula Clark). Country: *Is It Really Over?* (Jim Reeves); *Make the World Go Away* (Eddy Arnold)

Grammy Awards

A Taste of Honey, Herb Alpert and the Tijuana Brass (record); *September of My Years,* Frank Sinatra (album); "The Shadow of Your Smile" (song)

Jazz and Big Bands

Maynard Ferguson and Lionel Hampton break up their big bands and form small combos.

New Bands: Stan Kenton and the Los Angeles Neophonic Orchestra; Don Ellis, the Hindustani Jazz Sestet

Top Performers (*Downbeat*): John Coltrane (soloist); Duke Ellington, Count Basie (bands); Dave Brubeck (jazz group); Jim Hall, Charles Mingus, Bill Evans, J. J. Johnson (instrumentalists); Ella Fitzgerald, Frank Sinatra (vocalists); Double Six (vocal group)

Theater

Broadway Openings

Plays

The Persecution and Assassination of Marat as Performed by the Inmates of the Asylum at Charenton under the Direction of the Marquis de Sade (Peter Weiss), Patrick Magee, Glenda Jackson, Ian Richardson

The Odd Couple (Neil Simon), Art Carney, Walter Matthau

Cactus Flower (Abe Burrows), Lauren Bacall, Barry Nelson

Generation (William Good Hart), Henry Fonda

The Royal Hunt of the Sun (Peter Shaffer), Christopher Plummer, George Rose

Inadmissible Evidence (John Osborne), Nicol Williamson

The Right Honourable Gentleman (Michael Dyne), Charles D. Gray

The Amen Corner (James Baldwin), Bea Richards

Entertaining Mr. Sloane (Joe Orton), Dudley Sutton

The Devils (John Whiting), Anne Bancroft, Jason Robards

Musicals

Man of La Mancha (Mitch Leigh, Joe Darion), Richard Kiley, Joan Diener

Do I Hear a Waltz? (Richard Rodgers, Stephen Sondheim), Elizabeth Allen, Sergio Franchi

The Roar of the Grease Paint—the Smell of the Crowd (Leslie Bricusse, Anthony Newley), Cyril Ritchard, Anthony Newley

On a Clear Day You Can See Forever (Burton Lane, Alan Jay Lerner), John Cullum, Barbara Harris

Flora, the Red Menace (John Kander, Fred Ebb), Liza Minnelli, Bob Dishy

Classics and Revivals On and Off Broadway

Hogan's Goat (William Alfred), Faye Dunaway, Cliff Gorman; *A View from the Bridge* (Arthur Miller), Robert Duvall, Jon Voight; *Happy Days* (Samuel Beckett), Ruth White; *The Zoo Story* (Edward Albee); *Baal* (Bertolt Brecht); *An Evening's Frost* (Donald Hall), Will Geer; *Danton's Death* (Buechner); *The Condemned of Altona* (Jean-Paul Sartre); *The Caucasian Chalk Circle* (Brecht); *Happy Ending, Day of Absence* (Douglas Turner Ward), Robert Hooks. *Founded:* Roundabout Theatre by Gene Feist

Regional

Founded: Philadelphia Theatre of the Living Arts by André Gregory; Long Wharf, New Haven, by Jon Jory and Harlan Kleiman; American Conservatory Theatre (A.C.T.), Pittsburgh, by William Ball; Studio Arena, Buffalo, by Neal Du Broch

Theater (cont.)

Alley, Houston: *The Effect of Gamma Rays on Man-in-the-Moon Marigolds* (Paul Zindel), premiere

Theatre Company of Boston: *Live Like Pigs* (John Arden), premiere

Goodman, Chicago: *The Ballad of the Sad Café* (Edward Albee); *Anna Karenina* (adapted by Eugenie Leontovich, James Goodwin), premieres

Minneapolis Theatre Company: *Richard III*, Jessica Tandy, Hume Cronyn; *The Way of the World*, Zoë Caldwell, Tandy, Ed Flanders; *The Caucasian Chalk Circle*, Flanders, Caldwell

Pulitzer Prize

The Subject Was Roses, Frank D. Gilroy

Tony Awards

The Subject Was Roses, Frank D. Gilroy (play), *Fiddler on the Roof*, Jerry Bock, Sheldon Harnick

Classical Music

Compositions
Gunther Schuller, Symphony no. 1
Roy Harris, Symphony no. 10
Roger Sessions, Piano Sonata no. 3
Walter Piston, Symphony no. 8
George Rochberg, *Music for the Magic Theater*
Charles Wuorinen, *Orchestral and Electronic Exchanges*
Karl Korte, String Quartet no. 2

Important Events
Vladimir Horowitz returns to the concert stage (Carnegie) after 12 years and plays the Bach-Busoni Chromatic Fantasy and Fugue and Schumann *Kinderscenen.*
The Rockefeller Foundation, Ford Foundation, and National Council on the Arts make unprecedented contributions to the musical arts.
Leonard Bernstein, after his sabbatical, begins a two-year survey of 20th-century music with the New York Philharmonic.
The Chicago Symphony Orchestra, for its 75th birthday, commissions works from Gunther Schuller, Jean Martinon, and performs world premieres of Stravinsky's *Variations* and *T. S. Eliot in Memoriam.* Numerous avant-garde concerts, as in Buffalo and Washington, D.C., premiere Luis Escobar, Robert Evett, Carlos Chávez, Ezra Laderman, Walter Piston, Armando Krieger, and Bernal Flores.

Acclaimed Concerts: The Berlin Philharmonic, with Herbert von Karajan, plays a Beethoven cycle in five concerts (New York). Wilhelm Kempff's U.S. debut includes Beethoven's last four sonatas; the New York Philharmonic performs a Bruckner cycle. The touring Munich Bach Choir and Orchestra present, in one week, the St. Matthew Passion, St. John Passion, B-minor Mass, and Christmas Oratorio.

Debuts: Jacqueline Du Pré, James Oliver Buswell, Rolf Smedvig

First Performances
Benjamin Britten, *Voices for Today* (for UN anniversary, New York); Walter Piston, Symphony no. 8 (Boston); Charles Ives, Symphony no. 4 (Washington, D.C.); Easley Blackwood, Symphony no. 3 (Chicago); Roy Harris, *Abraham Lincoln Symphony* (Long Beach, Calif.); Gustav Mahler, Symphony no. 10 (Philadelphia)

Opera

Metropolitan: Montserrat Caballé (debut), *Faust;* Renata Tebaldi, Anna Moffo, Regina Resnik, *Carmen;* Mirella Freni, *La bohème;* Grace Bumbry (debut), *Don Carlo;* Martina Arroyo, *Madama Butterfly;* Nicolai Ghiaurov (debut), *Faust, Don Carlo*

New York City: *Lizzie Borden* (Jack Beeson), *The Flaming Angel* (Sergei Prokofiev), *Miss Julie* (Ned Rorem), premieres

Kansas City: Evelyn Lear, *Julius Caesar*

Boston: *Intolleranza* (Luigi Nono, American premiere); *Boris Godunov* (original version)

Santa Fe: *The King Stag* (Hans Werner Henze); *The Nose* (Shostakovich)

Dallas: Montserrat Caballé, *La traviata*

Chicago: Nicolai Ghiaurov, *Mefistofele;* Grace Bumbry, Jon Vickers, *Samson et Dalila;* Leontyne Price, *Aïda;* double bill: Teresa Berganza, Alfredo Kraus, *L'heure espagnole* and *Carmina Burana;* Geraint Evans, *Wozzeck*

San Francisco: *La forza del destino, Don Giovanni, Un ballo in maschera,* each with Leontyne Price

Art _____

Painting

Frank Stella, *Empress of India*

Jim Dine, *Double Isometric Self-Portrait*

Jules Olitski, *Prince Patutsky Command*

Andy Warhol, *Campbell's Tomato Soup*

Roy Lichtenstein, *Little Big Painting*

Marc Chagall designs murals for the Metropolitan Opera House, New York.

Sculpture

Robert Arneson, *Typewriter*

Donald Judd, *Untitled*

Richard Tuttle, *The Fountain*

Tony Smith, *Generation*

Edward Kienholz, *The Friendly Grey Computer—Star Gauge Model #54, The Beanery*

Carl Andre, *Crib, Coin, and Compound*

Henry Moore's *Reclining Figure* as well as Alexander Calder's *Stabile,* are placed at Lincoln Center, New York.

Eero Saarinen's 630-foot concrete and steel Gateway Arch is installed in St. Louis.

Architecture

Salk Institute for Biological Studies, La Jolla, Ill. (Louis I. Kahn)

CBS Building, New York (Eero Saarinen)

Smith House, Darien, Conn. (Richard Meier)

At Lincoln Center, New York: Vivian Beaumont Theater (Harrison and Saarinen); Library, Museum of the Performing Arts (Harrison and Skidmore, Owings and Merrill)

Woodrow Wilson School, Princeton University, Princeton, N.J. (Minoru Yamasaki)

Medical Center, New Haven, Conn. (Perkins and Will)

Henry Miller, whose sexually explicit 1930s novels were banned in the U.S. but have since become popular sellers. *Photographer: Cedric Wright. Courtesy Grove Press.*

Important Exhibitions

Museums

New York: *Metropolitan:* Indian sculpture; American painting from Copley to Johns. *Museum of Modern Art:* Giacometti and Magritte retrospectives; Beckmann. *Guggenheim:* Baziotes memorial

Washington: Copley, Terbrugghen; Watercolorists

Pittsburgh: *Carnegie International:* 400 works from 30 nations; Awards to Kelly (United States); Pasmore (Great Britain), Soulages, Arp (France), Chilida, Saura (Spain)

Detroit: Art of Italy, 1600–1700

Art Briefs

The National Council for the Arts is founded • Shows expand and travel: The Museum of Modern Art's "The Responsive Eye" (op art) travels across the United States and includes Smith, Poons, Davis, Dorazio, Riley, Neal, Kelly, Goodyear, Anuszkiewicz, Reinhardt, and Noland • Sculpture has an unprecedented renaissance; works invite more active spectator participation • Exhibitions of color and music and the special uses of lighting have wide success • Rembrandt's portrait of his son Titus sells for $2,234,000 to Norton Simon.

Richard Kiley in *Man of La Mancha,* a musical based on Cervantes's *Don Quixote. Billy Rose Theatre Collection. The New York Public Library at Lincoln Center. Astor, Lenox and Tilden Foundations.*

Dance _____

Premieres

American Ballet Theatre: *Les Noces* (Jerome Robbins); *The Four Marys; The Wind and the Mountains* (Agnes de Mille); *Tank Dive* (Twyla Tharp)

New York City Ballet: *Don Quixote* (George Balanchine), Richard Rapp, Suzanne Farrell; *Harlequinade* (Balanchine), Patricia McBride; Edward Villella

Books

Fiction

Critics' Choice

Going to Meet the Man, James Baldwin
The Painted Bird, Jerzy Kosinski
Everything that Rises Must Converge, Flannery O'Connor
God Bless You, Mr. Rosewater, Kurt Vonnegut
Thirteen Stories, Eudora Welty
Dune, Frank Herbert
An American Dream, Norman Mailer
Miss MacIntosh, My Darling, Marguerite Young
At Play in the Fields of the Lord, Peter Matthiessen
🛥 *The Clown*, Heinrich Böll

Best-Sellers

The Source, James A. Michener
Up the Down Staircase, Bel Kaufman
Herzog, Saul Bellow
The Looking Glass War, John Le Carré
The Green Berets, Robin Moore
Those Who Love, Irving Stone
The Man with the Golden Gun, Ian Fleming
Hotel, Arthur Hailey

Nonfiction

Critics' Choice

The Troubled Partnership, Henry A. Kissinger
The Making of a Quagmire, David Halberstam
Letters to Anaïs Nin, Henry Miller
Manchild in the Promised Land, Claude Brown
The Autobiography of Malcolm X
The Kandy-Colored, Tangerine-flake Stream-line Baby, Tom Wolfe
The Psychedelic Reader, Timothy Leary
The Americans: The National Experience, Daniel Boorstein
Starting Out in the Thirties, Alfred Kazin
Paris Journal (1944–1965), Janet Flanner

Best-Sellers

How to Be a Jewish Mother, Dan Greenburg
A Gift of Prophecy, Ruth Montgomery
Games People Play, Eric Berne, M.D.
World Aflame, Billy Graham
Happiness Is a Dry Martini, Johnny Carson

Markings, Dag Hammarskjöld
My Shadow Ran Fast, Bill Sands
Kennedy, Theodore C. Sorensen
The Making of the President, 1964, Theodore H. White

Poetry

Randall Jarrell, *The Lost World*
James Dickey, *Buckdancer's Choice*
Elizabeth Bishop, *Questions of Travel*
Robert Lowell, *Selected Poems*
Sylvia Plath, *Ariel, Uncollected Poems*
Amiri Baraka (Leroi Jones), *The Dead Lecturer*
🛥 Salvatore Quasimodo, *Selected Poems*

Pulitzer Prizes

Collected Stories, Katharine Anne Porter (fiction)
The Life of the Mind in America, Perry Miller (U.S. history)
A Thousand Days: John F. Kennedy in the White House, Arthur M. Schlesinger, Jr. (biography)
Selected Poems, Richard Eberhart (poems)

Science and Technology

Mariner IV transmits 21 photos of Mars.

The world's first commercial satellite, Early Bird, is put into orbit by COMSAT; it relays transatlantic telephone and TV.

Virgil Grissom and John Young, the first U.S. two-man crew, use the orbital maneuvering system on the Gemini III mission.

Edward White walks in space and uses a personal propulsion system on his mission with James McDivitt (on Gemini IV).

Gordon Cooper and Charles Conrad, on Gemini V, make 120 orbits in eight days, demonstrating the human physiologic feasibility of a lunar mission.

Frank Borman and James Lovell make 206 orbits on Gemini VII.

Walter Shirra and Thomas Stafford, on Gemini VIA, accomplish the first docking in space and come within six feet of Gemini VII.

Minuscule integrated circuits on a semiconductor material, silicon, are marketed.

The discovery of "blue galaxies" lends support to the big-bang theory of creation.

Nobel Prize

Richard P. Feynman and Julian S. Schwinger win the prize in physics for work in quantum electrodynamics. Robert B. Woodward wins in chemistry for research on the synthesizing of complicated organic compounds.

Sports ────────────────────────────────

Baseball

Sandy Koufax (Los Angeles, NL) strikes out a
record 382, pitches a perfect game (1–0 over
Chicago), and wins his second Cy Young Award.
Willie Mays (San Francisco, NL) hits 52 home runs,
a record-tying 17 in one month.
Casey Stengel retires.
Warren Spahn retires with 363 wins, a record for a
lefthander.

Champions ────────────────────

Batting
  Roberto Clemente
  (Pittsburgh, NL), .329
  Tony Oliva (Minnesota,
  AL), .321
Pitching
  Sandy Koufax (Los

Angeles, NL), 26–5
Wally Bunker (Baltimore,
AL), 19–5
Home runs
  Willie Mays (San Francisco,
  NL), 52

Football

Joe Namath, Alabama quarterback, is drafted by the
AFL's New York Jets and signed for a record
$400,000 bonus.
Gayle Sayers (Chicago) scores a record 22 TD's,
including 6 in one game to tie Ernie Nevers's record.
NFL attendance is a record 4.6 million, AFL's, 1.7
million.

NFL Season Leaders: Rudy Bukich (Chicago),
passing; Jim Brown (Cleveland), rushing; Dave Parks
(San Francisco), receiving. **AFL Season
Leaders:** Len Dawson (Kansas City), passing; Paul
Lowe (San Diego), rushing; Lionel Taylor (Denver),
receiving

College All-Americans: Tom Nobis (G), Texas;
Howard Twilley (E), Tulsa; George Webster (DB),
Michigan State; Bob Griese (QB), Purdue

Bowls (Jan. 1, 1966)

Rose: UCLA 14–
  Michigan State 12
Orange: Alabama 39–
  Nebraska 28

Cotton: Louisiana State
  14–Arkansas 7
Sugar: Missouri 20–
  Florida 18

Basketball

NBA All-Pro First Team: Bill Russell (Boston),
Elgin Baylor (Los Angeles), Oscar Robertson
(Cincinnati), Jerry Lucas (Cincinnati), Jerry West
(Los Angeles)

Other Sports

Boxing: Underdog heavyweight champion Cassius
Clay knocks out Sonny Liston in one round at
Lewiston, Maine.

Winners ────────────────────

World Series
  Los Angeles (NL) 4
  Minnesota (AL) 3
MVP
  NL–Willie Mays, San
  Francisco
  AL–Zoilo Versalles,
  Minnesota
NFL
  Green Bay 23–Cleveland 12
MVP
  Jim Brown, Cleveland
College Football
  Michigan State (UPI)
  Alabama (AP)
Heisman Trophy
  Mike Garrett, Southern
  California

NBA Championship
  Boston 4–Los Angeles 1
MVP
  Bill Russell, Boston
College Basketball
  UCLA
Player of the Year
  Bill Bradley, Princeton
Stanley Cup
  Montreal
US Tennis Open
  Men: Manuel Santana
  Women: Margaret Smith
USGA Open
  Gary Player
Kentucky Derby
  Lucky Debonair (W.
  Shoemaker, jockey)

Fashion ────────────────────────────────

For Women: Popular are op art fabrics in swirling,
eye-teasing designs, along with black and white
contrasting patterns, like checkerboard prints. Saint
Laurent's "Mondrian" chemise is enormously
successful. Lengths extend from above the knee to
the ankle. Leotards attenuate "the leggy look." The
"nothing-under" effect for see-through blouses and
cut-out fabrics is accomplished with "invisible
lingerie" by Gertrude Seperak and Warner. Ankle-to-
shoulder underwear is available for slacks and tights.
Peekaboo fashions extend from midriff tops to cut-
out shoes and hats. Popular day fabrics include
suede, suede cloth, and crocheted yarn. In the
evening, firmer silks, satins, and gabardines replace
more traditional chiffons and crepes. Summer
innovations include huge, round goggles, canoe-
shaped, white, mid-calf, kid boots, and Cole's one-
piece Lycra swimsuit, which plunges to the navel
with a mesh V.

*High-fashion note: The ultra short skirt by John
Bates, Courrèges*

Kaleidoscope

- Unemployment is the lowest in 8 years, 4.2 percent.
- The first teach-in is held March 2 at the University of Michigan; the largest is held at Berkeley, where 12,000 hear Dr. Benjamin Spock, Norman Mailer, I. F. Stone, and Senator Ernest Gruening, among others.
- "Flower Power" is coined by Allen Ginsberg at a Berkeley antiwar rally.
- The Medicaid rider to the Medicare bill provides funds to states for care of the poor.
- Studies show that American cities are becoming progressively more dangerous with public services increasingly less adequate; New York City has a water shortage and blackout during the year.
- In *The Psychedelic Reader* Harvard professor Timothy Leary advises: "Drop out, turn on, tune in."
- Students carry Viet Cong and North Vietnam flags in demonstrations and chant: "Hey, hey, LBJ, how many kids did you kill today?"
- The Voting Rights Act, eliminating literacy tests and authorizing federal supervision of voting procedures, stimulates an increase in black voting registration from 29 percent to 52 percent.
- "Clad" coins eliminate 90 percent of the silver in dollars, half dollars, quarters, and dimes.
- Since the Vietnam conflict is a guerrilla war, battle reports emphasize casualties ("body counts") and political progress, rather than decisive battles or territorial gains.
- Vietnam news reportage familiarizes the nation with places like Danang, Cam Ranh Bay, and Bien Hoa, sites of major U.S. installations, as well as combat zones like the Mekong Delta, Dakto, and Pleiku.
- Over $60 million is spent for prescription drugs to lose weight, twice the amount spent in 1960.
- More than 70 percent of the world's orchestras reside in the United States, 1,401 (600 in 1939).
- Pope Paul visits New York to address the UN; he speaks for peace: "No more war, war never again."
- Ralph Nader, who has left his job with the Department of Labor, intensifies his crusade for consumer protection; *Unsafe at Any Speed,* concerning auto safety, is published.
- The Clean Air Act allows for federal regulation of auto emissions; the Water Quality Act requires that states set antipollution standards for interstate waters.
- A group planning to destroy the Washington Monument, Statue of Liberty, and Liberty Bell is arrested.
- Quaker Norman Morrison immolates himself on the steps of the Pentagon.
- Congress passes a bill making it an offense to mutilate or destroy a draft card; the penalty is set at $10,000 or five years in jail.
- Robert Lowell's refusal to attend the White House Festival of the Arts because he is "dismayed" at foreign policy is widely publicized; the president later comments: "Some of them insulted me by staying away and some of them insulted me by coming."

- Of 2,560 cadets at the Air Force Academy, 105 resign for cheating on exams.
- The first singles community is built in Los Angeles.
- The birth rate falls to 19 per 1,000 people, the lowest since 1940.
- Sheriff Jim Clark of Selma, Alabama, leads an attack with tear gas and clubs against civil rights marchers led by Martin Luther King.
- Fourteen thousand National Guardsmen are called out at Watts, a black ghetto in South Los Angeles; 34 die, 4,000 are arrested, and the area is in ashes after five days.
- The truth in packaging bill is written to standardize weights in packaged goods.
- César Chavez's 25-day fast convinces the Brown Power militants to align themselves with his nonviolent strike against the grape growers; shoppers boycott table grapes in sympathy.
- The word *soul* replaces *rhythm and blues* on hit charts.
- Ads for men's colognes and face lotions increase eightfold since 1960, and body-building ads virtually disappear.
- The Beatles and Elvis Presley meet in Bel Air, California.
- The Supreme Court eliminates state and local film censorship.
- The Grateful Dead begin in San Francisco, their name taken from an Oxford English Dictionary notation on the burial of Egyptian pharaohs.
- The Fillmore, in San Francisco, begins rock concerts; the first stars Jefferson Airplane and Grateful Dead.
- At Lady Bird's urging, Congress appropriates funds to beautify U.S. highways and remove their large number of billboards.

Fads: I Ching, macrobiotic foods, body painting, trivia contests, computer dating, disposable paper dresses, James Bond toys

New Words and Usages: Camp, campy, computerize, degradable, discotheque, electronic music, hardware, kook, op art, printout, program, quark, skateboard, crash, dude, do your own thing, groupie, no way, old lady, old man, rap, vibes, straight

First Appearances: Miniskirt (Mary Quant), International Society for Krishna Consciousness (Hare Krishna, by A. C. Bhaktivedanta), domed stadium (Astrodome), Bravo, Diet Pepsi, Apple Jacks, Cranapple, Avis Rent-a-Car acquired by ITT, all-news radio station (New York), master skyscraper antenna (Empire State Building, New York), American Stock Exchange women members (J. M. Walsh, P. K. S. Peterson, New York), Sony home video tape recorder

1966

Facts and Figures

Economic Profile
  Dow-Jones: ↓ High 950–
    Low 744
  GNP: +9%
  Inflation: +2.7%
  Unemployment: 3.8%
Urban/rural population:
  126/54
Male/female ratio: 88/91
High school graduates
  entering college: 25%
Four-year colleges: 1,608
Public/private schools: 7/1
TWA, New York–Las Vegas:
  $230.50 (8 days, 7 nights)
TWA, 4 weeks in Israel: $535
American Flyer bicycle: $110
Zale's diamond engagement
  and wedding ring outfit:
  $297
Meat, fish (lb.):
  Veal rib chop or roast: 79¢
  Swift butterball turkey: 45¢
  Bay scallops: 95¢
  Swordfish, frozen: 69¢
  King Crab legs or claws:
    89¢

Deaths

Gertrude Berg, Lenny Bruce,
Montgomery Clift, Walt
Disney, S. S. Kresge, Billy
Rose, Delmore Schwartz,
Sophie Tucker, Evelyn
Waugh, Clifton Webb, Ed
Wynn.

In the News

ROBERT WEAVER IS APPOINTED SECRETARY OF HUD, THE FIRST BLACK IN CABINET . . . B-52 AND JET TANKER COLLIDE, 7 CREW DIE, 4 H-BOMBS ARE LOST, 3 ARE RECOVERED . . . JOHNSON ASKS $4 BILLION MORE FOR DEFENSE, $3 BILLION FOR THE GREAT SOCIETY . . . JOHNSON AND SOUTH VIETNAM LEADER KY MEET AND ISSUE DECLARATION OF HONOLULU . . . BOMBING OF NORTH VIETNAM IS RESUMED . . . OPERATION WHITE WING SUCCEEDS IN QUANG NGAT . . . RUSSIA MAKES FIRST SOFT MOON LANDING . . . SUHARTO TAKES OVER IN INDONESIA . . . LBJ ASKS $1 BILLION FAMINE AID FOR INDIA . . . STOKELY CARMICHAEL IS ELECTED HEAD OF STUDENT NONVIOLENT COORDINATING COMMITTEE . . . LOST H-BOMB IS FOUND OFF SPANISH COAST . . . STUDENTS DEMONSTRATE NATIONWIDE AGAINST THE WAR . . . SURVEYER MAKES FIRST U.S. SOFT LANDING ON THE MOON . . . SUPREME COURT RULES ON RIGHTS OF ACCUSED IN MIRANDA CASE . . . MICHAEL COLLINS AND JOHN W. YOUNG DOCK AND WALK IN SPACE AT A RECORD 474 MILES . . . SNIPER ON TOWER IN TEXAS SHOOTS 45, KILLS 12 AND SELF . . . 8 NURSES ARE SLAIN IN CHICAGO DORMITORY . . . AIRLINE STRIKE ENDS AFTER 43 DAYS . . . GEMINI GOES TO RECORD 850-MILE ALTITUDE . . . LBJ MAKES 26,000-MILE FAR EAST TOUR . . . UN AMBASSADOR ARTHUR GOLDBERG PLEDGES U.S. FORCE REDUCTION IF NORTH VIETNAM ASSENTS . . . COMMUNIST CHINA TESTS INTERCONTINENTAL BALLISTIC MISSILE . . . REPUBLICANS GAIN IN CONGRESSIONAL ELECTIONS . . . VIETNAM: U.S. TROOP STRENGTH, 400,000; U.S. DEAD, 6,358; ENEMY DEAD, 77,115.

Quotes

"Their symbol is the black panther, a bold, beautiful animal, representing the strength and dignity of black demands today."
> — Stokely Carmichael, describing a new party in Loundes County, Alabama

"We have stopped losing the war."
> — General William Westmoreland

"[We seek]" to confront with concrete action the conditions which now prevent women from enjoying equality of opportunity and freedom of choice which is their right as individual Americans and as human beings."
> — NOW manifesto

"If you want to join the New York intellectual establishment, . . . all you've got to do is make the right friends and then attack them, claim that the establishment doesn't exist and that everyone in it is brilliant, and denounce the mass media while they are lionizing you."
> — Victor S. Navasky

"I noticed that mannequins in windows were smiling and Elizabeth Taylor from an enormous poster advertising the film *Cleopatra* several times gestured for me to come to her."
> — Report of psychedelic drug experience in R. Masters and J. Houston, *The Varieties of Psychedelic Experience*

"Just when you think you're getting famous, somebody comes along and makes you look like a warm-up act for amateur night. . . . Pope Paul VI [for example, just arrived]. Talk about advance PR— I mean for centuries."
> — Andy Warhol, *Popism*

"We came, therefore (and with many Western thinkers before us), to suspect civilization may be overvalued."
> — Gary Snyder

"The mad truth: the boundary between sanity and insanity is a false one. . . . The proper posture is to listen and learn from lunatics as in former times."
> — Norman O. Brown, *Love's Body*

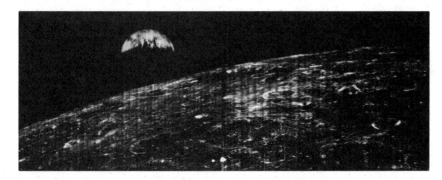

The first view of the earth from the vicinity of the moon is taken by Lunar Orbiter 1. *Courtesy NASA.*

Ads

Burma-Shave
so creamy it's almost fattening.
> *(Burma-Shave)*

Maybe you need a nice relaxing hobby out in the sun—Big A.
> *(Aqueduct Race Track)*

If you want good food *and* atmosphere, we suggest you take a little something home from one of our retail shops.
> *(Horn and Hardart)*

Governor Rockefeller spends 45% [of his] budget on education. Too bad kids can't vote.
> *(Political Ad)*

The mainspring in a Bulova is made to last 256 years or 146 leather straps—whichever comes first.
> *(Bulova Watches)*

SMARTEE:
They thought of putting T-shirts on girls.
> *(Smartee Shirts)*

If you want to impress someone, put him on your Black list.
> *(Johnny Walker Black)*

TV

Premieres

"The Newlywed Game," Bob Eubanks
"Mission: Impossible," Martin Landau, Barbara Bain, Peter Graves
"The Hollywood Squares," Peter Marshall
"Batman," Adam West
"Family Affair," Brian Keith
"Star Trek," William Shatner, Leonard Nimoy
"The Monkees," David Jones
"That Girl," Marlo Thomas
"Felony Squad," Howard Duff
"The Dating Game," Jim Lange
"The Smothers Brothers Comedy Hour"

Top Ten (Nielsen)

"Bonanza," "The Red Skelton Hour," "The Andy Griffith Show," "The Lucy Show," "The Jackie Gleason Show," "Green Acres," "Daktari," "Bewitched," "The Beverly Hillbillies," "Gomer Pyle, U.S.M.C."

Specials

"Death of a Salesman" (Lee J. Cobb); "Barefoot in Athens" (Peter Ustinov); "Anastasia" (Lynn Fontanne, Julie Harris); "The Glass Menagerie"

(Shirley Booth); "China: The Roots of Madness" (Theodore White); "Organized Crime in America" (NBC); "The Homosexuals" (CBS); "A Christmas Memory" (Geraldine Page); "Bob Hope's Christmas Tour of the GI Bases"; "Ages of Man" (John Gielgud)

Emmy Awards

"Mission: Impossible" (drama); "The Monkees" (comedy); "Andy Williams Show" (variety); "Jack and the Beanstalk" (children); Bill Cosby (actor, "I Spy"); Don Adams (comedic actor, "Get Smart"); Barbara Bain (actress, "Mission: Impossible"); Lucille Ball (comedic actress, "The Lucy Show")

Of Note

Movies in prime time increase to five evenings a week • ABC's "Scope" joins "Vietnam Weekly Review" (NBC) and "Vietnam Perspective" (CBS), as coverage of the war intensifies • "The Bridge on the River Kwai" receives a 60 percent rating, the most popular movie shown on TV to date; network interest in high-cost, quality, made-for-TV movies also increases.

Movies

Openings

A Man for All Seasons (Fred Zinnemann), Paul Scofield, Robert Shaw
Who's Afraid of Virginia Woolf? (Mike Nichols), Richard Burton, Elizabeth Taylor, George Segal, Sandy Dennis
The Professionals (Richard Brooks), Burt Lancaster, Lee Marvin, Claudia Cardinale
Georgy Girl (Silvio Narizzano), Lynn Redgrave, Alan Bates, James Mason
Morgan! (Karel Reisz), Vanessa Redgrave, David Warner
Closely Watched Trains (Jiri Menzel), Vaclav Neckar, Jitka Bendova
Khartoum (Basil Dearden), Charlton Heston, Laurence Olivier
Blow-up (Michelangelo Antonioni), Vanessa Redgrave, David Hemmings
Fahrenheit 451 (François Truffaut), Oskar Werner, Julie Christie
Harper (Jack Smight), Paul Newman, Lauren Bacall, Arthur Hill
Madame X (David Lowell Rich), Lana Turner, John Forsythe, Ricardo Montalban

La guerre est fini (Alain Resnais), Yves Montand, Ingrid Thulin, Genevieve Bujold
Alfie (Lewis Gilbert), Michael Caine, Shelley Winters

Academy Awards

Best Picture: *A Man for All Seasons*
Best Director: Fred Zinnemann (*A Man for All Seasons*)
Best Actress: Elizabeth Taylor (*Who's Afraid of Virginia Woolf?*)
Best Actor: Paul Scofield (*A Man for All Seasons*)

Top Box-Office Stars

Julie Andrews, Sean Connery, Elizabeth Taylor, Jack Lemmon, Richard Burton, Cary Grant, John Wayne, Doris Day, Paul Newman, Elvis Presley

Stars of Tomorrow

Elizabeth Hartman, George Segal, Alan Arkin, Raquel Welch, Geraldine Chaplin, Guy Stockwell, Robert Redford, Beverly Adams, Sandy Dennis, Chad Everett

Popular Music

Hit Songs
"The Ballad of the Green Berets"
"Born Free"
"Good Vibrations"
"The Impossible Dream"
"Sunny"
"What Now, My Love"
"Winchester Cathedral"
"Alfie"
"The Sounds of Silence"
"Georgy Girl"

Top Records

Albums: *Rubber Soul* (Beatles); *Going Places* (Herb Alpert and the Tijuana Brass); *If You Can Believe Your Eyes and Ears* (Mamas and the Papas); *Doctor Zhivago* (sound track); *The Monkees* (Monkees)

Singles: *Strangers in the Night* (Frank Sinatra); *These Boots Are Made for Walking* (Nancy Sinatra); *Last Train to Clarksville* (Monkees); *Yellow Submarine, Eleanor Rigby* (Beatles); *Scarborough Fair* (Simon and Garfunkel); *Rainy Day Women #12 and 35* (Bob Dylan); *Cherish* (Association); *You're My Soul and Inspiration* (Righteous Brothers); *Reach Out and I'll Be There* (Four Tops); *Monday, Monday* (Mamas and the Papas). Country: *Almost Persuaded* (David Houston); *Giddy Up Go* (Red Sovino)

Grammy Awards
Strangers in the Night, Frank Sinatra (record); *Sinatra: A Man and His Music* (album); "Michelle" (song)

Jazz and Big Bands
Don Ellis's *Synthesis* attempts to fuse jazz and raga.

Top Performers *(Downbeat):* Ornette Coleman (soloist); Duke Ellington (band); Miles Davis (jazz group); Wes Montgomery, Ray Brown, Oscar Peterson, Elvin Jones, Paul Desmond (instrumentalists); Ella Fitzgerald, Frank Sinatra (vocalists); Double Six (vocal group); Ornette Coleman, *At the Golden Circle, Vol. I* (album)

Theater

Broadway Openings

Plays
Wait until Dark (Frederick Knott), Lee Remick
The Investigation (Peter Weiss), Richard Castellano
Don't Drink the Water (Woody Allen), Lou Jacobi
The Star-Spangled Girl (Neil Simon), Anthony Perkins, Richard Benjamin, Connie Stevens
A Delicate Balance (Edward Albee), Jessica Tandy, Hume Cronyn, Rosemary Murphy
America Hurrah (Jean-Claude Van Itallie), Ruth White, Bill Macy
Malcolm (Edward Albee, James Purdy), Estelle Parsons, Ruth White, John Heffernan
The Lion in Winter (James Goldman), Robert Preston, Rosemary Harris
Philadelphia, Here I Come! (Brian Friel), Patrick Bedford, Donal Donnelly
The Killing of Sister George (Frank Marcus), Beryl Reid, Eileen Atkins
Slapstick Tragedy (Tennessee Williams), Kate Reid, Margaret Leighton, Zoë Caldwell

Musicals
Cabaret (John Kander, Fred Ebb), Jill Haworth, Joel Grey, Lotte Lenya, Bert Convy
Viet-Rock (Megan Terry), Seth Allen
Sweet Charity (Cy Coleman, Dorothy Fields), Gwen Verdon, Helen Gallagher, John McMartin
Mame (Jerry Herman), Angela Lansbury, Beatrice Arthur
The Apple Tree (Jerry Bock, Sheldon Harnick), Barbara Harris, Alan Alda, Larry Blyden
I Do! I Do! (Harvey Schmidt, Tom Jones), Mary Martin, Robert Preston

Classics and Revivals On and Off Broadway
Galileo (Bertolt Brecht), Anthony Quayle; *School for Scandal* (Sheridan), Helen Hayes, Ellis Rabb, Rosemary Harris; *Serjeant Musgrave's Dance* (John Arden), Dustin Hoffman; *Ivanov* (Chekhov), John Gielgud, Vivien Leigh, Claire Bloom; *The Kitchen* (Arnold Wesker), Sylvia Miles

Regional

Founded: Repertory Theatre, New Orleans, by the National Endowment for the Humanities; Theatre Atlanta; Ypsilanti Greek Festival: *Oresteia,* Judith Anderson; *The Birds,* Bert Lahr

Pulitzer Prize   No prize is awarded.

Tony Awards
Marat/Sade, Peter Weiss (play), *Man of La Mancha,* Mitch Leigh, Joe Darion (musical)

Classical Music ⎯⎯⎯⎯⎯

Compositions
Salvatore Martirano, Ballad
Roger Reynolds, *Blind Men*
David Saturen, Sonata for Clarinet and Piano
Walter Piston, Variations for Cello and Orchestra
Roger Sessions, Symphony no. 6, Six Pieces for
    Cello
Leon Kirchner, Quartet no. 3
Earl Brown, *Modules 1 and 2*

Important Events
New York hosts the Igor Stravinsky Festival, Lincoln
Center; the David Diamond Concert at the New York
Philharmonic, with the first performance of the
Symphony no. 5 for Piano and Orchestra; Arturo
Benedetti Michelangeli's return to the stage after
fifteen years; Jascha Heifetz's first solo recital in ten
years, and the Heifetz and Gregor Piatigorsky series
of four chamber concerts.
Leonard Bernstein announces his plan to retire from
the New York Philharmonic; his two-year survey of
symphonic music includes all of Sibelius's and
Nielsen's symphonies, both celebrated for their 100th
birthday.

Debuts: Martha Argerich, Radu Lupu

First Performances
Roger Sessions, "Psalm 140" (Boston), Symphony
no. 6 (Newark); Virgil Thomson, Fantasy (Kansas
City); Ulysses Kay, *Markings* (Rochester); Paul
Creston, *Variations* (La Jolla, Calif.); Henry Cowell,
Hymn and Fuguing Tune no. 16 (New York); Igor
Stravinsky, *Requiem Canticles* (Princeton, N.J.);
Douglas Moore, *Carry Nation* (University of Kansas,
commissioned for university centennial); Busoni,
Piano Concerto (New York)

Elizabeth Taylor and Richard Burton in the uncensored
movie adaptation of Edward Albee's *Who's Afraid of
Virginia Woolf? Movie Star News.*

CBS Records.

Opera

Metropolitan: After a gala performance at the old
Met, with excerpts from 23 operas, the new Met, at
Lincoln Center for the Performing Arts, opens with
the world premiere of *Antony and Cleopatra* (Samuel
Barber) with an all-American cast: Leontyne Price,
Justino Diaz; the top price is $250; other productions
for the season include Walter Berry (debut), Christa
Ludwig, Leonie Rysanek, *Die Frau ohne Schatten;*
Birgit Nilsson, Rysanek, *Elektra;* Zinka Milanov,
Andrea Chenier

New York City Opera: Opening at the New York
State Theatre—Beverly Sills, Norman Treigle, *Don
Rodrigo* (Alberto Ginastera, premiere)

Fort Worth: Beverly Sills: *I pagliacci; Die schöne
Galatea* (Suppé)

Boston: *Moses und Aron* (Schoenberg, American
premiere); Placido Domingo, Beverly Sills, *Hippolyte
et Aricie* (Rameau, American premiere)

Chicago: Alfredo Kraus, *The Pearl Fishers; Angel
of Fire;* Nicolai Ghiaurov, *Boris Godunov*

San Francisco: Evelyn Lear, *Lulu*

Music Notes
The touring company of the Met disbands because of
rising costs • The Jesse H. Jones Hall for the
Performing Arts, Houston, opens with the world
premiere of Alan Hovhaness's *Ode to the Temple of
Sound.*

Art

Paintings

Ad Reinhardt, *Black Painting* (1960–66)

Barnett Newman, *Who's Afraid of Red, Yellow, Blue I* (1966–67)

Allan D'Arcangelo, *Proposition No. 9*

Richard Lindner, *Checkmate*

Kenneth Noland, *Par Transit*

Philip Pearlstein, *Woman Reclining on Couch*

Roy Lichtenstein, *Yellow and Red Brushstrokes*

Willem de Kooning, *Woman Acabonic*

Sculpture

Eva Hesse, *Hang Up*

Louise Nevelson, *Atmosphere and Environment*

Reuben Nakian, *Hiroshima*

Chryssa, *Variations on the Ampersand*

Robert Indiana, *Love*

Mark di Suvero, *Elohim Adonai*

Edward Kienholz, *The State Hospital*

Sol LeWitt, *B-258, Open Modular Cube*

Lucas Samaras, *Mirror Room*

Carl Andre, *Lever, Sanbornville III*

Robert Smithson, *Alogon*

Alexander Calder, *Totems*

Architecture

School of Social Service Administration, University of Chicago (Mies van der Rohe)

Whitney Museum of American Art, 945 Madison Avenue, New York City (Marcel Breuer)

University Plaza, New York City (I. M. Pei)

Metropolitan Opera House, New York City (Wallace K. Harrison)

Johnson Museum, New Canaan, Conn. (Philip Johnson)

Charles Gwathmey Residence and Studio, Amagansett, N.Y. (Charles Gwathmey)

Richard J. Daley Center, Chicago (C. F. Murphy; Skidmore, Owings, and Merrill)

Construction begins on the World Trade Center, New York City (Yamasaki, Roth).

Important Exhibitions

Museums

New York: *Metropolitan:* 3,000 years of Chinese metalwork; "200 Years of Watercolors." *Museum of Modern Art:* Motherwell, Turner retrospectives; Magritte. *Whitney:* Davis; "7 Decades—Cross Currents in Modern Art: 277 Major Modern Artists." *Guggenheim:* Munch; Gauguin

Chicago: Manet; Great works from the Polish collection

Philadelphia: Manet; Mondrian retrospective; "The Older Tradition"

Washington: Art treasures of Turkey; Chinese art objects

San Francisco, Toledo, Boston: Rembrandt

Art Briefs

Popular interest grows in the avant-garde—"Nine Evenings, Theatre and Engineerings," in New York, combines several forms of "happenings": John Cage, Robert Whitman, Robert Rauschenberg, Andy Warhol, Roy Lichtenstein; the ideal is an environment of sensory saturation. Minimalist shows gain interest, along with "object" art, "primary structures," and "kinetic sculpture." The Guggenheim's "systemic painting" show displays shaped and multiple canvases and modular paintings. Edward Kienholz's *The Beanery,* with its taped sound effects and cooking smells, gains much attention • The National Gallery in Washington, D.C., purchases a $4\frac{1}{8}$-by-$5\frac{5}{8}$-inch painting, *St. George and the Dragon,* by Rogier van der Weyden for $616,000. Brancusi's "Bird in Space" sells for $140,000 • Chagall's *Le Triomphe de la Musique* is installed at the Metropolitan Opera House, New York.

Dance

The Joffrey Ballet moves to New York's City Center; Bruce Marks joins Willam Christensen at Ballet West, Salt Lake City.

Premieres

New York City Ballet: *Variations* (George Balanchine), Suzanne Farrell; *Brahms-Schoenberg Quartet* (Balanchine), Edward Villella, Suzanne Farrell, Jacques D'Amboise, Melissa Hayden

American Ballet Theatre: *Ricarcare, Sargasso* (Glen Tetley), Sallie Wilson

Books ━━━━━━━━━━━━━━━━━━━━━━━━

Fiction

Critics' Choice

The Crying of Lot 49, Thomas Pynchon
Giles Goat-Boy, John Barth
Up above the World, Paul Bowles
Nothing Ever Breaks Except the Heart, Kay Boyle
A Christmas Memory, Truman Capote
The Last Gentleman, Walker Percy
Been Down So Long It Looks like Up to Me, Richard Fariña
The Origin of the Brunists, Robert Coover
Criers and Kibitzers, Kibitzers and Criers, Stanley Elkin
The Diary of a Rapist, Evan S. Connell, Jr.
Omensetter's Luck, William Gass
🐌 *Hopscotch*, Julio Cortázar

Best-Sellers

Valley of the Dolls, Jacqueline Susann
The Adventurers, Harold Robbins
The Secret of Santa Vittoria, Robert Crichton
Capable of Honor, Allen Drury
The Double Image, Helen MacInnes
The Fixer, Bernard Malamud
Tell No Man, Adela Rogers St. Johns
Tai-Pan, James Clavell
The Embezzler, Louis Auchincloss
All in the Family, Edwin O'Connor

Nonfiction

Critics' Choice

Against Interpretation, Susan Sontag
Freedom in the Modern World, Herbert J. Miller
The Report on the Warren Report
The Social Novel at the End of an Era, Warren French
Cannibals and Christians, Norman Mailer
La Vida, Oscar Lewis
Inquest: The Warren Commission, Edward Jay Epstein
The Enlightenment, Peter Gay
Papa Hemingway, A. E. Hotchner
The Proud Tower, Barbara Tuchman
🐌 *Quotations of Chairman Mao*
🐌 *On Aggression*, Konrad Lorenz

Best-Sellers

How to Avoid Probate, Norman F. Dacey
Human Sexual Response, William Howard Masters, Virginia E. Johnson
In Cold Blood, Truman Capote
Games People Play, Eric Berne, M.D.
A Thousand Days, Arthur M. Schlesinger, Jr.
Everything But Money, Sam Levenson
The Random House Dictionary of the English Language
Rush to Judgment, Mark Lane
The Last Battle, Cornelius Ryan
Phyllis Diller's Housekeeping Hints, Phyllis Diller

Poetry

John Ashbery, *Rivers and Mountains*
Robert Creeley, *Poems 1950–1965*
Adrienne Rich, *Necessities of Life*
May Sarton, *A Private Mythology*
James Merrill, *Nights and Days*
🐌 Andrei Voznesensky, *Anti-World*

Pulitzer Prizes

The Fixer, Bernard Malamud (fiction)
Exploration and Empire, William H. Goetzmann (U.S. history)
The Problem of Slavery in Western Culture, David Brion Davis (nonfiction)
Mr. Clemens and Mark Twain, Justin Kaplan (biography)
Live or Die, Anne Sexton (poetry)

Science and Technology ━━━━━━━━━━━━━

Har Gobind Khorana completes the deciphering of the DNA code.

The FDA concludes that there are no adequate scientific reasons to declare "the pill" unsafe, in reply to concern over blood clots.

Biodegradable liquid detergents are produced to reduce pollution.

Astronauts who walk in space include Eugene Cernan (Gemini IX), Michael Collins (Gemini X), Richard Gordon (Gemini XI), and Buzz Aldrin (Gemini XII).

Gemini XIII, manned by Neil Armstrong and David Scott, is the first dual launch in space to dock with a target rocket, Agena.

Surveyor I achieves a soft lunar landing in the Ocean of Storms.

Sealab II, with a crew led by astronaut Scott Carpenter, spends 45 days under the sea to test survival problems.

Nobel Prize

The prize in physiology and medicine is shared by Charles Brenton Huggins, for work on the hormone treatment of cancer of the prostate, and Francis P. Rous, for work on tumor-producing viruses. Robert S. Mulliken wins in chemistry for his work on the bond that holds atoms together in molecules.

Sports

Baseball

The Major League Players Association is formed.
Frank Robinson (Baltimore, AL) becomes the first player to win an MVP award in each league.
Sandy Koufax (Los Angeles, NL) wins a record third Cy Young Award and retires.

Coach Vince Lombardi: "Winning isn't everything. It's the only thing." *Football Hall of Fame.*

Champions

Batting
Matty Alou (Pittsburgh, NL), .342
Frank Robinson (Baltimore, AL), .326
Pitching
Juan Marichal (San Francisco, NL), 25–6
Mudcat Grant (Minnesota, AL), 21–5
Home runs
Henry Aaron (Atlanta, AL), 44

Football

The Green Bay Packers, under Vince Lombardi, win a record third straight NFL title.
The NFL and AFL announce their plan to merge in 1970 and to begin a championship series.
Jim Brown (Cleveland) retires with a career rushing record of 12,312 yards.

NFL Season Leaders: Bart Starr (Green Bay), passing; Gale Sayers (Chicago), rushing; Charles Taylor (Washington), receiving
AFL Season Leaders: Len Dawson (Kansas City), passing; Jim Nance (Boston), rushing; Lance Alworth (San Diego), receiving

College All-Americans: Ray Perkins (E), Alabama; Mel Farr (B), UCLA; Nick Eddy (B), Notre Dame

Bowls (Jan. 1, 1967)
Rose: Purdue 14– Southern California 13
Orange: Florida 27– Georgia Tech 12
Cotton: Georgia 24– Southern Methodist 9
Sugar: Alabama 34– Nebraska 7

Winners

World Series
Baltimore (AL) 4
Los Angeles (NL) 0
MVP
NL–Roberto Clemente, Pittsburgh
AL–Frank Robinson, Baltimore
Sugar Bowl I (Jan. 1967)
Green Bay 35–Kansas City 10
MVP
Bart Starr, Green Bay
College Football
Notre Dame
Heisman Trophy
Steve Spurrier, Auburn

NBA Championship
Boston 4–Los Angeles 3
MVP
Wilt Chamberlain, Philadelphia
College Basketball
Texas Western
Player of the Year
Cazzie Russell, Michigan
Stanley Cup
Montreal
US Tennis Open
Men: Fred Stolle
Women: Maria Bueno
USGA Open
Billy Casper
Kentucky Derby
Kauai King (D. Brumfield, jockey)

Basketball

NBA All-Pro First Team: Rick Barry (San Francisco), Jerry Lucas (Cincinnati), Wilt Chamberlain (Philadelphia), Jerry West (Los Angeles), Oscar Robertson (Cincinnati)

Other Sports

Boxing: Cassius Clay becomes a Muslim and changes his name to Muhammed Ali; he makes five successful title defenses.

Running: Jim Ryun runs the half-mile in a record 1:44.9; he also runs 3:51.3 and 3:51.1 miles.

Fashion

For Women: Emphasis is on "femininity," despite the Carnaby or English mod look: short shirts, T-shirt dresses with chin-high necklines and turtlenecks, scarves, and headbands. Coats include the tent, the straight, slim style, and the military coat with epaulettes and brass buttons. Long, straight hair and op art glasses complete the look, which also includes low-slung bell bottoms, wide belt or hip-riding miniskirts five to six inches above the knee, and daytime pantsuits of twill and bright tartans. With the growing interest in surfing, the two-piece bathing suit replaces the bikini. Harem pants, wide trousers with matching tops, and elaborate jumpsuits are worn all year around. Mia Farrow's hair, cut to the scalp, sets a style, along with tiny pearl stud earrings.

High-fashion note: Mary Quant's midi

For Men: Men begin to devote as much money and time to their hair as women, with permanent waves, hair coloring, transplants, and replacements. It is no longer fashionable for a man to look as if he has just had a haircut.

Kaleidoscope _____

- "Black Power" is introduced into the civil rights movement, clarifying the rift between the pacifist followers of Martin Luther King, SCLC, and the militants following Stokely Carmichael, SNCC, and Floyd McKissick, CORE.
- March 25–27 are International Days of Protest against the war in Vietnam in seven American and seven foreign cities.
- Senator William Fulbright, at Johns Hopkins University, attacks the administration for its foreign policy, condemning those who "feel qualified to play God."
- Much attention is paid to the controversial elite combat unit in Vietnam, the Green Berets.
- Blanket student deferments are abolished; draft calls reach 50,000 a month.
- "Can you pass the acid test?" is author Ken Kesey's motto at the San Francisco Trips Festival, an acid-rock, multimedia happening of rock, light shows, and acid dropping, which begins the "San Francisco Sound."
- A new style of dance hall, like the Fillmore in San Francisco, replaces discos with strobe lights, liquid color blobs, glow paint, and psychedelic posters.
- The publication of the Catholic edition of the Bible in the Revised Standard Version is considered a milestone in the mid-century ecumenical movement.
- Roman Catholic bishops rule that except during Lent, American Catholics may eat meat on Friday.
- The Clean Waters Restoration Act allocates funds for preventing river and air pollution.
- The Traffic Safety Act, long urged by Ralph Nader, provides for auto safety standards and recalls.
- James Roche, General Motors president, apologizes for spying into Ralph Nader's private life after he cited the GM Corvair as dangerous; Nader sues Roche and two private detectives and settles out of court for $500,000.
- César Chavez's National Farm Workers Union, in its strike against grape growers, is recognized as the bargaining agent for farm workers.
- James Meredith is shot walking from Memphis to Jackson; the walk is then joined by Dick Gregory, Martin Luther King, Floyd B. McKissick (CORE), and Stokely Carmichael (SNCC).
- The social event of the year is Truman Capote's New York Plaza Hotel party to celebrate *In Cold Blood*'s success.
- John Lindsay faces his first crisis the day he becomes New York City mayor—the city's first "official" transit strike; an estimated 850,000 cars enter Manhattan in a single day.
- Virginia Masters and William Johnson's *Human Sexual Response* asserts, among other things, that women possess at least as much sexual energy as men and enjoy a variety of sexual responses, including multiple orgasms.
- The National Association of Broadcasters instructs all disc jockeys to screen all records for hidden (drug) or obscene meanings.
- *Time* magazine's "Man of the Year" is actually a group: the "Twenty-Five and Under . . . Generation."
- At what is presumably the last performance at the old Metropolitan Opera House, a five-hour gala evening ends with the audience and performers joining hands and singing "Auld Lang Syne"; the gold curtain is cut into small patches and packaged with a souvenir recording.
- *Who's Afraid of Virginia Woolf?* is a landmark film whose shocking language receives the new seal "suggested for mature audiences"; the new production code is voluntarily accepted by the studios.
- Beginning the conglomerate takeover of the big film studios, Gulf and Western absorbs Paramount; Kinney National Service takes over Warner and Seven Arts. The big studios make TV films as well.
- Per capita consumption of processed potato chips rises from 6.3 pounds a year (1958) to 14.2 pounds a year.
- A nationwide sports poll tallies 59 million bikers, 40 million boaters and volleyball players, 36 million fishers and campers, and 2 million tennis players.
- Because of the smog, California imposes standards on car exhausts, to take effect in 1969.
- A study reports that food prices are higher in the poorer rather than the more affluent neighborhoods.
- The President's Commission on Food Marketing reports that consumers pay 29 percent more for nationally advertised brands than high-quality local brands.
- Jimi Hendrix helps popularize the electric guitar.
- "Batman" airs twice weekly and becomes a national fad. Batman's adversaries include the Archer (Art Carney), the Penguin (Burgess Meredith), and the Joker (Cesar Romero).

Fads: Monkee items, underground newspapers, Batman accessories, Ouija boards, astrology, Tarot cards

New Words and Usages: Abort, big-bang theory, bowser bag, cable TV, chip, flashcube, glitch, commune, flower children, psychedelic, acid rock, mind blowing, zap, go-go, gypsy cab, hawk, hippy, interface, intrauterine device, loop, LSD, miniskirt, mod, pop, Third World

First Appearances: Medicare ID card (presented to Harry Truman, Jan. 20), sandwich grill toaster, tape cartridges, stereo cassette decks, NOW, Bank Americard, Interbank Card, Laker Airways, Product 19, Taster's Choice, BacOs, Maxwell's Plum (New York), Guadelupe National Park (Texas), Fifth Avenue (New York) as one-way south-bound street, Madison Avenue (New York) as one-way northbound street, Chicago Civic Center, UN Plaza, Random House acquired by RCA, lyrics on record albums, Rare and Endangered Species List (Department of the Interior)

1967

Facts and Figures

Economic Profile
Dow-Jones: ↑ High 943–
   Low 786
GNP: +5%
Inflation: +2.8%
Unemployment: 3.8%
Average salary: $6,230
   Teacher: $6,605
   Physician: $34,600
   Factory worker: $6,880
Bonwit Teller Bengal lizard
   bags: $75–$90
Altman's trench coat: $26–
   $110
A&S African cotton tent
   dress: $30
"Teddy-Bra" slip: $7
Alexander's cashmere
   sweater: $12.99
Sloane's Afskar rug: $268
   (12' by 8')
   Tabriz rug, used: $548 (12'
   by 9')
   Cambridge upholstered
   chair: $159
Altman's upholstered sofa:
   $439–$569
Ironstone, 93-piece set:
   $39.99

Deaths

Dan Duryea, Mischa Elman,
   Geraldine Farrar, Dorothy
   Gish, Fannie Hurst, Vivien
   Leigh, Thomas Merton,
   Ramon Novarro, Basil
   Rathbone, Upton Sinclair,
   Robert Taylor, Spencer
   Tracy.

In the News

ROGER CHAFFEE, VIRGIL GRISSOM, AND EDWARD WHITE ARE KILLED IN APOLLO TEST LAUNCH FIRE . . . KOSYGIN MEETS POPE PAUL . . . U.S. BOMBERS RAID HANOI . . . HO CHI MINH LETTERS REJECT LBJ PEACE PROPOSAL . . . ARMY JUNTA SEIZES POWER IN GREECE . . . SVETLANA ALLILUYEVA, STALIN'S DAUGHTER, DEFECTS TO WEST . . . SOVIET COSMONAUT KOMAROV DIES IN REENTRY . . . NASSER DEMANDS WITHDRAWAL OF UN FORCES IN SINAI, SECRETARY-GENERAL U THANT COMPLIES . . . UN APPOINTS COMMISSION ON SOUTHWEST AFRICA, NOW CLAIMED BY SOUTH AFRICA . . . NASSER CLOSES AQABA GULF TO ISRAELI SHIPS . . . EAST NIGERIA CLAIMS INDEPENDENCE AS BIAFRA . . . ISRAEL SMASHES ARABS, TAKES SINAI, GAZA, OLD JERUSALEM, GOLAN HEIGHTS, AND WEST BANK IN SIX DAYS . . . THURGOOD MARSHALL IS FIRST BLACK APPOINTED TO SUPREME COURT . . . COMMUNIST CHINA ANNOUNCES IT HAS H-BOMB . . . JOHNSON AND KOSYGIN TALK AT GLASSBORO, N.J. . . . NEWARK BLACK RIOTS END AFTER SIX DAYS WITH 26 DEAD . . . DETROIT BLACK RIOTS END AFTER 8 DAYS, 43 ARE DEAD . . . DE GAULLE, ON CANADA VISIT, CALLS FOR "QUÉBEC LIBRE" . . . CAMBRIDGE RIOTS FOLLOW STOKELY CARMICHAEL SPEECH . . . U.S. TROOP LEVEL IN VIETNAM REACHES 525,000 . . . RED GUARDS SACK BRITISH COMPOUND IN PEKING . . . U.S. AND USSR PRESENT ANTI–NUCLEAR PROLIFERATION TREATY TO GENERAL DISARMAMENT CONFERENCE . . . U.S. ANNOUNCES ANTI–BALLISTIC MISSILE DEFENSE PLAN AGAINST CHINESE ATTACK . . . BOLIVIA CONFIRMS CAPTURE AND DEATH OF CHE GUEVARA . . . ANTIWAR PROTESTERS MAKE NIGHT MARCH ON PENTAGON . . . EXPO '67 OPENS IN MONTREAL . . . CHRISTIAAN BARNARD PERFORMS FIRST HEART TRANSPLANT . . . VIETNAM: U.S. DEAD, 15,997.

Vietnam: near the Bassac River. National Security Advisor Walt Rostow states that "Victory is just around the corner." *Department of the Navy.*

"I don't have no personal quarrel with those Viet Congs."

— Muhammad Ali

"We believe that all men somehow possess a divine potentiality. . . . We reject the tired dualism that seeks God and human potentialities in denying the joys of the senses."

— George B. Leonard, Esalen

"There [in Haight-Ashbury], in a daily street-fair atmosphere, upwards of 15,000 unbonded girls and boys interact in a tribal love-seeking, free-winging, acid-based society, where if you are a hippie and you have a dime, you can put it in a parking meter and lie down in the street for an hour's sunshine."

— Warren Hinckle, *Social History of the Hippies*

Ads

If enough people would stop smoking and start drinking, we could get out of ashtrays and into vermouth.

(Cinzano)

The Other Pill
(One-a-Day Multiple Vitamins Plus Iron)

It's sort of a souped-down Ferrari.

(Volvo)

Come to the Central Park Zoo Cafeteria. Let the animals watch you eat for a change.

(Central Park Zoo)

If your son is old enough to shave, he's old enough to get syphilis.

(WINS Radio)

Quotes

"I have tried to show that contemporary society is a repressive society in all its aspects, that even the comfort and the prosperity, the alleged political and moral freedom, are utilized for repressive ends."

— Herbert Marcuse

"If I could turn you on, if I could drive you out of your wretched mind, if I could tell you, I would let you know."

— R. D. Laing, *Politics of Experience*

" 'An investigation into Sex' is now offered at Dartmouth. 'Analogues to the LSD Experience' can now be studied at Penn. 'Guerilla Warfare' is being examined by DePauw students. Stanford undergraduates are studying 'American Youth in Revolt,' and 'The Origins and Meaning of Black Power' is a course at Brooklyn College. Has higher education finally caught up with the times?"

— Ralph Keyes, "The Free Universities"

"Batman." *Movie Star News.*

Wishful Thinning

(Enhance, by Lily of France)

Betcha can't eat just one.

(Lay's Potato Chips)

446

TV

Premieres
"Mannix," Mike Connors
"Judd for the Defense," Carl Betz
"The David Susskind Show"
"N.Y.P.D.," Jack Warden, Robert Hooks
"The Flying Nun," Sally Field
"The Carol Burnett Show," Carol Burnett, Vicki
　　Lawrence, Tim Conway, Harvey Korman
"Ironside," Raymond Burr
"The Phil Donahue Show"

Top Ten (Nielsen)
"The Andy Griffith Show," "The Lucy Show,"
"Gomer Pyle, U.S.M.C.," "Gunsmoke," "Family
Affair," "Bonanza," "The Red Skelton Show," "The
Dean Martin Show," "The Jackie Gleason Show,"
"Saturday Night at the Movies"

Specials
"Elizabeth the Queen" (Dame Judith Anderson); "St.
Joan" (Genevieve Bujold); "The Crucible" (Colleen
Dewhurst); "Do Not Go Gentle into That Good
Night" (Melvyn Douglas); "Crisis in the Cities"
(NET); "Eric Hoffer: The Passionate State of Mind"

Emmy Awards
"Mission: Impossible" (drama); "Get Smart"
(comedy); "He's Your Dog, Charlie Brown"
(children); Bill Cosby (Actor, "I Spy"); Don Adams
(comedic actor, "Get Smart"); Barbara Bain (actress,
"Mission: Impossible"); Lucille Ball (comedic
actress, "The Lucy Show")

Of Note
Both CBS and NBC televise the Super Bowl • The
Public Broadcasting Act, which funds public TV, is a
great aid for educational TV.

Movies

Openings
In the Heat of the Night (Norman Jewison), Sidney
　　Poitier, Rod Steiger
Bonnie and Clyde (Arthur Penn), Warren Beatty,
　　Faye Dunaway
The Graduate (Mike Nichols), Dustin Hoffman,
　　Anne Bancroft, Katharine Ross
Guess Who's Coming to Dinner (Stanley Kramer),
　　Spencer Tracy, Sidney Poitier, Katharine
　　Hepburn
In Cold Blood (Richard Brooks), Robert Blake, Scott
　　Wilson, John Forsythe, Paul Stewart
Cool Hand Luke (Stuart Rosenberg), Paul Newman,
　　George Kennedy
The Dirty Dozen (Robert Aldrich), Lee Marvin,
　　Ernest Borgnine, Charles Bronson
Barefoot in the Park (Gene Saks), Robert Redford,
　　Jane Fonda
Two for the Road (Stanley Donen), Audrey Hepburn,
　　Albert Finney
Elvira Madigan (Bo Widerberg), Pia Degermark,
　　Thommy Berggren
Accident (Joseph Losey), Dirk Bogarde, Stanley
　　Baker
The Battle of Algiers (Gillo Pontecorvo), Yacef
　　Saadi, Jean Martin
The Night of the Generals (Anatole Litvak), Peter
　　O'Toole, Omar Sharif, Tom Courtenay
Persona (Ingmar Bergman), Bibi Andersson, Liv
　　Ullmann

Reflections in a Golden Eye (John Huston), Elizabeth
　　Taylor, Marlon Brando
Belle de Jour (Luis Buñuel), Catherine Deneuve,
　　Jean Sorel

Academy Awards
Best Picture: *In the Heat of the Night*
Best Director: Mike Nichols (*The Graduate*)
Best Actress: Katharine Hepburn (*Guess Who's
　　Coming to Dinner*)
Best Actor: Rod Steiger (*In the Heat of the Night*)

Top Box-Office Stars
Julie Andrews, Lee Marvin, Paul Newman, Sean
Connery, Elizabeth Taylor, Sidney Poitier, John
Wayne, Richard Burton, Steve McQueen

Stars of Tomorrow
Lynn Redgrave, Faye Dunaway, James Caan, John
Phillip Law, Michele Lee, Michael Sarrazin, Sharon
Tate, Michael York, Hywell Bennett, David
Hemmings

Popular Music _____

Hit Songs
"A Natural Woman"
"Soul Man"
"I Never Loved a Man"
"Make Me Yours"
"I Was Made to Love Her"
"Penny Lane"
"By the Time I Get to Phoenix"
"Cabaret"
"Can't Take My Eyes off You"
"It Must Be Him"

Top Records

Albums: *More of the Monkees; Diana Ross and the Supremes' Greatest Hits; Sounds Like* (Herb Alpert and the Tijuana Brass)

Singles: *To Sir with Love* (Lulu); *The Letter* (Box Tops); *San Francisco (Wear Some Flowers in Your Hair)* (Scott McKenzie); *The Beat Goes On* (Sonny and Cher); *Light My Fire* (Doors); *I'm a Believer* (Monkees); *Lucy in the Sky with Diamonds* (Beatles); *Windy* (Association); *Jimmy Mack* (Martha and the Vandellas). Country: *There Goes My Everything* (Jack Greene)

Grammy Awards
Up, Up and Away, 5th Dimension (record); *Sgt. Pepper's Lonely Hearts Club Band,* Beatles (album); "Up, Up and Away" (song)

Jazz and Big Bands
Charles Lloyd records *Forest Flower* with a basso ostinato.

Top Performers *(Downbeat):* Charles Lloyd (soloist); Duke Ellington (band); Miles Davis (jazz group); Wes Montgomery, Ray Brown, Buddy Rich, Stan Getz (instrumentalists); Ella Fitzgerald, Lou Rawls (vocalists); Beatles (vocal group); *Miles [Davis] Smiles* (album)

Theater _____

Broadway Openings

Plays
The Homecoming (Harold Pinter), Vivien Merchant, Ian Holm, Paul Rogers
The Birthday Party (Harold Pinter), Ruth White, Ed Flanders, James Patterson
Rosencrantz and Guildenstern Are Dead (Tom Stoppard), Brian Murray, John Wood
Black Comedy (Peter Shaffer), Geraldine Page, Michael Crawford, Lynn Redgrave
There's a Girl in My Soup (Terence Frisby), Gig Young, Barbara Ferris
You Know I Can't Hear You When the Water's Running (Robert Anderson), Martin Balsam, Eileen Heckart, George Grizzard
More Stately Mansions (Eugene O'Neill), Ingrid Bergman, Colleen Dewhurst, Arthur Hill
Little Murders (Jules Feiffer), Elliott Gould, Barbara Cook

Musicals
How Now, Dow Jones (Elmer Bernstein, Carolyn Leigh) Anthony Roberts, Brenda Vaccaro
Hallelujah, Baby! (Jule Styne, Betty Comden, Adolph Green), Leslie Uggams, Robert Hooks
You're a Good Man, Charlie Brown (Clark Gesner), Gary Burghoff, Reva Rose
Judy Garland at the Palace

Classics and Revivals On and Off Broadway
The Little Foxes (Lillian Hellman), Margaret Leighton, E. G. Marshall, Anne Bancroft, George C. Scott; *Scuba Duba* (Bruce Jay Friedman), Jerry Orbach; *Macbird* (Barbara Garson), Cleavon Little, Stacy Keach, William Devane; *Fortune and Men's Eyes* (John Herbert); *Iphigenia in Aulis* (Euripides), Irene Papas; *The Ceremony of Innocence* (Ronald Ribman), Sandy Duncan, Donald Madden. Founded: CSC (Classic Stage Company) by Christopher Martin, Harris Laskawy, and Kathryn Wyman.

Regional

Founded: Mark Taper Forum, Los Angeles, by Gordon Davidson: *The Sorrows of Frederick* (Romulus Linney), premiere; Center Theatre Group (Dal Manson), Los Angeles: *More Stately Mansions* (Eugene O'Neill), Ingrid Bergman, Arthur Hill, Colleen Dewhurst, premiere; *The Happy Time* (John Kander and Fred Ebb), Robert Goulet, premiere
Arena Stage, Washington, D.C.: *The Great White Hope* (Howard Sackler), James Earl Jones, Jane Alexander, premiere
Minneapolis: *The House of Atreus* (John Lewin's adaptation of *The Oresteia*)
A.C.T., San Francisco: Three versions of *Hamlet*

Pulitzer Prize
A Delicate Balance, Edward Albee

Tony Awards
The Homecoming, Harold Pinter (play), *Cabaret,* John Kander, Fred Ebb (musical)

Classical Music ———————————

Compositions
Walter Piston, Clarinet Concerto
David Diamond, Violin Concerto no. 3
Roger Sessions, Symphony no. 7
Lukas Foss, Cello Concerto
William Albright, *Tic*
George Crumb, "Echoes of Time and the River"

Important Events
For the New York Philharmonic's 125th anniversary, Leonard Bernstein repeats its inaugural program (1842), which includes Beethoven, Weber, Rossini, Mozart, Hummel, and Kalliwoda. For the remainder of the season, each concert presents at least one work that the orchestra premiered or commissioned. Zubin Mehta and the Los Angeles Philharmonic begin a world tour.
Celebrating their 40th year on the stage are Vladimir Horowitz, Robert Goldsand, and Yehudi Menuhin.
In its first U.S. appearance, La Scala performs Verdi's Requiem at Carnegie Hall.
Mstislav Rostropovich and the London Symphony play eight concerts in 18 days.
Dietrich Fischer-Dieskau sings three lieder concerts of Shumann, Schubert, and Beethoven (New York). Other highly acclaimed New York recitals are by Jacqueline du Pré, Lily Kraus (Mozart's 25 solo piano concerti), and Rostropovich with Galina Vishnevskaya.

The House of Atreus, the first regional theater production to tour the country. *Minneapolis Theatre Company.*

Contemporary music festivals proliferate from New York and Cleveland to Dallas and Seattle; the Third International Webern Festival is held in Buffalo, N.Y.
Robert Shaw becomes director of the Atlanta Symphony.

Debuts: Kyung-Wha Chung, Alexis Weissenberg

First Performances
Webern, Three Pieces for Orchestra (Philadelphia); Krzysztof Penderecki, *St. Luke Passion* (Chicago); Elliott Carter, Piano Concerto (Boston); Morton Subotnick, *An Electronic Christmas* (New York); Walter Piston, Variations for Cello and Orchestra (New York); Paul Creston, *Chthonic Ode* (Detroit); Alan Hovhannes, *The Holy City* (Portland, Me.), *To Vishnu* (New York); Lalo Schifrin, *The Rise and Fall of the Third Reich* (Hollywood); Aaron Copland, *Inscape* (Ann Arbor, Mich.)

Opera

Metropolitan: Evelyn Lear, Marie Collier, *Mourning Becomes Elektra* (Marvin Levy, premiere); Grace Bumbry, *Carmen;* Jon Vickers, *Peter Grimes;* Pilar Lorengar, Teresa Berganza (debut), *Le nozze di Figaro;* Marc Chagall sets are used for *Die Zauberflöte.*

City Center: *The Servant of Two Masters* (Vittorio Giannini, premiere)

Washington, D.C.: *Bomarzo* (Alberto Ginastera)

Chicago: Season canceled because of labor disputes

San Francisco: Luciano Pavarotti, *La bohème;* Irene Dalis, *Tristan und Isolde*

Boston: *Voyage to the Moon* (in modern style at the White House for LBJ and Turkish president); double bill: *Bluebeard's Castle* and *The Miraculous Mandarin* (Béla Bartók)

Santa Fe: House burns down after *Cardillac.*

Music Notes
Owing to deficits, the Met raises its ticket prices to a maximum $15.50.

Art _____

Painting

Kenneth Noland, *Wild Indigo, Via Blues*

Alfred Leslie, *Notan Study for the Killing of Frank O'Hara, Alfred Leslie*

Tom Wesselmann, *Great American Nude, No. 98*

James Rosenquist, *U-Haul It*

Ellsworth Kelly, *Spectrum III*

Jules Olitski, *High a Yellow*

Andrew Wyeth, *The Apron*

Helen Frankenthaler, *Guiding Red*

Sculpture

George Segal, *Portrait of Sidney Janis with Mondrian*

Claes Oldenburg, *Giant Soft Fan* (1966–67)

Richard Tuttle, *Gray Extended Seven*

Carl Andre, *Cuts*

Donald Judd, *Untitled*

Barnett Newman, *Broken Obelisk*

Lucas Samaras, *Corridor*

Bruce Nauman, *From Hand to Mouth*

Important Exhibitions

"The Art of India and Nepal" tours the United States.

The year is dominated by retrospectives, theme shows, and sculpture. Retrospectives include Ingres, Gilbert, Smart (Washington); Hogarth (Richmond); Degas (Philadelphia); Manet (Chicago, Philadelphia); The Peale family (Detroit, Utica); Wyeth (Whitney); Pollock (Museum of Modern Art); Klee (Guggenheim); and Léger (Chicago).

Protest shows include "Angry Artists against the War in Vietnam," a week-long demonstration with D'Arcangelo, di Suvero, Rosenquist, Golub, and Greene; "Protest and Hope": New School works by Indiana, Levine, Segal, and Shahn.

Picasso's abstract steel sculpture is placed at the Richard J. Daley Center, Chicago.

Architecture

Hanselmann House, Ft. Wayne, Ind. (Michael Graves)

Stuhr Museum, Grand Island, Neb. (Edward Durell Stone)

Bell Tower, St. John's Abbey Church, Collegeville, Minn. (Marcel Breuer)

Ford Foundation, New York (Roche and Dinkeloo)

National Center for Atmospheric Research, Boulder, Colo. (I. M. Pei)

Gulf Life Tower, Jacksonville, Fla. (Welton Becket)

Sante Fe Opera House, Sante Fe, N.M. (McHugh and Kidder)

Marina City, Chicago (Bertrand Goldberg)

Hyatt Regency Hotel, Atlanta, Ga. (John Portman)

First Unitarian Church, Rochester (Louis I. Kahn)

George Segal, *Portrait of Sidney Janis with Mondrian Painting* 1967. Plaster figure with Mondrian's *Composition*, 1933, on an easel; figure, 66″ high; easel 67″ high. *The Sidney and Harriet Janis Collection. Gift to the Museum of Modern Art, New York.*

As the "sculpture renaissance" continues, numerous avant-garde shows are held (Guggenheim, Washington, Los Angeles, Minneapolis). Various exhibits travel through the United States: environmental projects, serial ideas, mass production techniques, and minimalism.

Shows on experimental work include polyurethane pieces, colored plastics, electromagnetics, plexiglass reliefs, rearranged modules: Piero Gilardi, John Chamberlain, Dan Flavin, David Weinrib, Craig Kauffman, Robert Morris, Isamu Noguchi, along with the enormous projects of Sol LeWitt, and Claes Oldenburg.

Art Briefs

Five and a half tons of Picasso sculpture arrive at the Museum of Modern Art for the exhibition October 11–January 1 • Sidney Janis donates his $2 million collection to the Museum of Modern Art • Thomas P. F. Hoving becomes director of the Metropolitan Museum of Art • The United States joins the world in efforts to save the art treasures damaged by the flood in Florence, Italy • Support for technical experiments extend from organizations such as AT&T, IBM, and AFL-CIO to EAT (Experiments in Art and Technology) • The National Gallery purchases Leonardo da Vinci's *Ginevra dei Benci* from the prince of Liechtenstein for $5–6 million, the highest price ever paid for a painting; it also receives $20 million from the Andrew Mellon family • Monet's *La Terasse à Saint-Adresse,* purchased in 1926 for $11,000, sells for $1.4 million.

Dance _____

Premieres

American Ballet Theatre: *Las Hermanas, Concerto* (Kenneth Macmillan)

New York City Ballet: *Jewels* (George Balanchine), Violette Verdy, Patricia McBride, Suzanne Farrell

Eliot Feld: *At Midnight, Harbinger*

Alwin Nikolais: *Triptych*

Books

Fiction
Critics' Choice
The Manor, Isaac Bashevis Singer
When She Was Good, Philip Roth
Stop Time, Frank Conroy
Snow White, Donald Barthelme
Why Are We in Vietnam?, Norman Mailer
Fathers, Herbert Gold
A Garden of Earthly Delights, Joyce Carol Oates
A Bad Man, Stanley Elkin
Trout Fishing in America, Richard Brautigan
Hall of Mirrors, Robert Stone

Best-Sellers
The Arrangement, Elia Kazan
The Confessions of Nat Turner, William Styron
The Chosen, Chaim Potok
Topaz, Leon Uris
Christy, Catherine Marshall
The Eighth Day, Thornton Wilder
Rosemary's Baby, Ira Levin
The Plot, Irving Wallace
The Gabriel Hounds, Mary Stewart
The Exhibitionist, Henry Sutton

Nonfiction
Critics' Choice
The Fabulators, Robert Scholes
Hell's Angels, Hunter S. Thompson
Selected Essays, William Troy
The New Industrial State, John Kenneth Galbraith
Death at an Early Age, Jonathan Kozol
Like a Conquered Province: The Moral Ambiguity of America, Paul Goodman
The Temper of Our Time, Eric Hoffer
F. Scott Fitzgerald: The Last Laocoön, Robert Sklar
The Naked Ape, Desmond Morris
❧ *Twenty Letters to a Friend*, Svetlana Alliluyeva
❧ *Writing Degree Zero*, Roland Barthes
❧ *The Medium Is the Massage*, Marshall McLuhan, Quentin Fiore

Best-Sellers
Death of a President, William Manchester
Misery Is a Blind Date, Johnny Carson
Games People Play, Eric Berne, M.D.
A Modern Priest Looks at His Out-Dated Church, Father James Kavanaugh
Everything But Money, Sam Levenson
Our Crowd, Stephen Birmingham
Phyllis Diller's Marriage Manual
Stanyan Street (poetry), Rod McKuen
Edgar Cayce—The Sleeping Prophet, Jess Stearn
Better Homes and Gardens Favorite Ways in Chicken

Poetry
Howard Nemerov, *The Blue Swallows*
W. S. Merwin, *The Lice*
Robert Bly, *The Light around the Body*
Elizabeth Bishop, *Selected Poems*
Denise Levertov, *The Sorrow Dance*
Marianne Moore, *Complete Poems*

Pulitzer Prizes
The Confessions of Nat Turner, William Styron (fiction)
The Ideological Origins of the American Revolution, Bernard Bailyn (U.S. history)
Rousseau and Revolution, William and Ariel Durant (nonfiction)
Memoirs 1925–1950, George F. Kennan (biography)
The Hard Hours, Anthony Hecht (poetry)

Science and Technology

Rene Favaloro, at the Cleveland Clinic, develops the coronary bypass operation.

A connection between a cholesterol-lowering diet and reduced incidence of heart disease is shown in the report of a five-year study on 412 men.

The structure of the enzyme ribonuclease (RNA) is discovered.

R. M. Dolby develops a system for eliminating background hiss in audio recordings.

Multiple Independent Reentry Vehicles (MIRV) are developed, permitting many separate missiles from one launch.

The laser range finder is developed.

Pioneer VIII is launched to investigate and monitor interplanetary phenomena at diverse points in space throughout the solar system.

Lunar Orbiter V is launched to obtain a complete photo mapping of the lunar surface.

Biosatellite II is the first successful United States satellite for bioscientific research.

E. Hay and Y. Yellott build a solar house with ponds of water on the roof to act as insulation.

❧ Dr. Christiaan Barnard performs the first heart transplant in Capetown, South Africa; the patient, Lewis Washansky, lives 18 days.

Nobel Prize
Hans A. Bethe wins the prize in physics for work on the energy production of stars. H. K. Hartline, George Wald, and Ragnar Granit win in physiology and medicine for work on the human eye.

Sports

Baseball

The Boston Red Sox go from ninth place, last season, to the pennant; Carl Yastrzemski leads the league with .326, 121 RBIs, and 44 home runs (triple crown).

Cy Young Awards go to Mike McCormick (San Francisco, NL) and Jim Lonborg (Boston, AL).

Champions

Batting
  Roberto Clemente (Pittsburgh, NL), .357
  Carl Yastrzemski (Boston, AL), .326
Pitching
  Richard Hughes (St. Louis, NL), 16–6
  Sonny Siebert (Cleveland, AL), 16–8
Home runs
  Frank Robinson (Baltimore, AL), 49

Football

The first interleague championship, called the Super Bowl, is played January 15 at Los Angeles; the score is Green Bay 35–Kansas City 10.

Lou Groza retires with a record 1,349 points.

Raymond Berry retires with a record 631 receptions.

NFL Season Leaders: Sonny Jurgensen (Washington), passing; Leroy Kelley (Cleveland), rushing; Charles Taylor (Washington), receiving

AFL Season Leaders: Darryl Lamonica (Oakland), passing; Jim Nance (Boston), rushing; George Sauer (New York Jets), receiving

Bowls (Jan. 1, 1968)

Rose: Southern California 14–Indiana 3
Orange: Oklahoma 26–Tennessee 24
Cotton: Texas A & M 20–Alabama 16
Sugar: Louisiana State 20–Wyoming 13

College All-Americans: O. J. Simpson (B), Southern California; Larry Csonka (B), Syracuse; Ted Hendricks (DE), Miami

Basketball

The Philadelphia 76'ers post a record 68–13 season led by Wilt Chamberlain, 24.1 p.p.g., 24 r.p.g. The ABA begins; stars include Connie Hawkins, Roger Brown, and Mel Daniels.

NBA All-Pro First Team: Rick Barry (San Francisco), Elgin Baylor (Los Angeles), Wilt Chamberlain (Philadelphia), Jerry West (Los Angeles), Oscar Robertson (Cincinnati)

Other Sports

Winners

World Series
  St. Louis (NL) 4
  Boston (AL) 3
MVP
  NL–Orlando Cepeda, San Francisco
  AL–Carl Yastrzemski, Boston
Super Bowl II (Jan. 1968)
  Green Bay 33–Oakland 14
MVP
  John Unitas, Baltimore
College Football
  Southern California
Heisman Trophy
  Gary Beban, UCLA
NBA Championship
  Philadelphia 4–San Francisco 2

MVP
  Wilt Chamberlain, Philadelphia
College Basketball
  UCLA
Player of the Year
  Lew Alcindor, UCLA
Stanley Cup
  Toronto
US Tennis Open
  Men: John Newcombe
  Women: Billie Jean King
USGA Open
  Jack Nicklaus
Kentucky Derby
  Proud Clarion (R. Ussery, jockey)

Fashion

For Men: A revolution occurs in men's wear: color is at its most unrestrained; coordinates are carefully matched. Jackets are double-breasted in plaids, tattersall, cavalry twill, and whipcord; citified tweeds are used for all styles. Turtlenecks join both formal and casual wear, along with colored or boldly striped shirts with spread collars and French cuffs. Soft, square-toed leather shoes, hand-sewn slip-ons, and saddle stitching are popular.

For Women: Fashion model Twiggy arrives in New York in March with short skirts, boots, pin-striped jumpsuits, and the boldest contrasting colors yet. The maxi is worn over the mini; white wool tents, velvet knickers and jeweled, embroidered, sequined, and lace fabrics appear. Underwear no longer hides body shape. Made of laces, net, and marquisette, it reveals and controls the natural shape. Bras, almost invisible in wear, are wire and padding free. Gernreich coordinates mini slips and mini bras; stockings are virtually replaced by tights.

High-fashion note: Deliss's linen and lace peasant dress, pleated and embroidered

Kaleidoscope _____

- Colorado leads in the liberalization of abortion laws.
- Estimates report 50,000–100,000 hippies in the San Francisco area: "Haight is Love" is a popular slogan; 1,000 psychedelic bands play in the area.
- The Esalen Institute in northern California ("Third Force Psychiatry") practices a gestalt therapy that encourages people to act out their dreams, role play, and take nude hot baths together; it grosses $1 million and is followed by T-groups throughout the United States.
- Secretary of Defense Robert McNamara becomes World Bank president after resigning his office.
- Army physician Captain Harold Levy refuses to train Green Berets in the treatment of skin disease on the grounds that they commit war crimes and are "killers of women and children"; he is court-martialed and sent to Fort Leavenworth Prison.
- U.S. troop levels in Vietnam pass 475,000, exceeding the total troop strength in Korea; U.S. total bombing tonnage, 1,630,000, exceeds that of World War II.
- "Pacification," "strategic revolutionary development," and "strategic hamlets" are key concepts in American efforts to control the countryside.
- Muhammad Ali, heavyweight champion, is denied conscientious objector status; after refusing induction into the army, he is arrested, given a five-year sentence, and fined $10,000; ring authorities have already removed his title.
- A black, Carl Stokes, is elected mayor of Cleveland.
- Over 700,000 people march in a Fifth Avenue parade against the war.
- Norman Mailer mythologizes the October 21 March on the Pentagon in *Armies of the Night;* Dr. Benjamin Spock, Paul Goodman, Philip Hirschkop, Robert Lowell, Noam Chomsky, and Dwight McDonald are prominent figures in both.
- Black leader Rap Brown says of the ghetto riots: "Violence is as American as cherry pie," and adds, they are "a dress rehearsal for revolution."
- The Supreme Court rules unconstitutional state laws against interracial marriage.
- The National Student Association reveals that it has secretly been receiving CIA funds.
- Coed dorms open at numerous colleges across the country.
- Violence in movies escalates in such films as *Bonnie and Clyde, The Dirty Dozen,* and *In Cold Blood;* a landmark interracial film is *Guess Who's Coming to Dinner.*
- The final TV episode of "The Fugitive," when the killer is caught and the innocent David Janssen hero is vindicated, is advertised as "the day the running stopped"; it draws over a 50 percent rating.
- Record albums begin to outsell singles; *Sgt. Pepper* introduces electronic rock.
- The first rock festival is held at Monterey, Calif., with Grateful Dead and Big Brother and the Holding Company (Janis Joplin).

Dustin Hoffman and Anne Bancroft (as Mrs. Robinson) in *The Graduate,* a story of the alienation of educated youth in a materialistic society. *Movie Star News.*

- The world's largest outdoor Monopoly game, 550 by 470 feet, is played at Juniata College, Huntington, Pa.
- Lynda Bird Johnson marries Marine Captain Charles Robb in the White House.
- George Lincoln Rockwell, president of the U.S. Nazi party, is shot to death.
- Annual beef consumption, per capita, is 105.6 pounds, up from 99 pounds in 1960.
- Pillsbury buys Burger King.
- The U.S. population has doubled since 1917; college enrollment has almost doubled since 1960 (6,963,687, from 3,570,000).
- Operation Match, a two-year-old computer dating corporation, reports that 130,000 of its 5 million clients have married.
- James Garrison, New Orleans district attorney, claims he has solved the JFK assassination and arrests Clay Shaw, a retired businessman for conspiracy; Shaw is acquitted.
- Journalist Bernard Fall is killed in Vietnam by a land mine.
- The *New York Times* Sunday magazine publishes an article by General Maxwell Taylor entitled "The Cause in Vietnam Is Being Won."

Fads: Jogging, Mickey Mouse watches, protest buttons, Finnish saunas, psychedelic art

New Words and Usages: Guru, hangup, blow your cool, narc, kicky, beautiful, head shop, shades, ballsy, peacenik, boondocks, Spirit of Glassboro

First Appearances: "Be-In" (Golden Gate Park, San Francisco), combination knife–can opener, UHF-VHF combination, laser surgery operating theater (Cincinnati), general who rose from draftee (K. L. Ware), Zen Buddist monastery (Tassajara Springs, Calif.), horse motel (Marshfield, Mo.), wine museum (Hammondsport, N.Y.) large-type weekly (*New York Times),* electric fishing reel, Hertz acquired by RCA, Hilton Hotels International acquired by TWA, compact microwave (Amana), Holt, Rinehart & Winston acquired by CBS, Phoenix House, airmail postcard commemorative (Charlotte Amalie, Virgin Islands)

1968

Facts and Figures

Economic Profile

Dow-Jones: ↑ High 985–
Low 825
GNP: +8%
Inflation: +4.2%
Unemployment: 3.6%
Balance of international
payments: +$1.5 billion
Military on duty: 3,548,000
Voter participation: 64%
(1960), 61% (1968)
Population with religious
affiliation: 128 million
Zenith 20″ color TV: $399.95
Sunbeam cannister vacuum:
$49.95
Allen carpet: $5.88–$9.88 (sq.
yd.)
Chrysler: $2,249
Plymouth: $2,049
Toyota: $1,666
Chock Full O'Nuts:
Coffee, milk, orange juice:
15¢
Sandwich (chicken salad,
nutted cheese): 35¢
Frankfurter: 25¢
Beefburger: 45¢
Whole wheat doughnut:
10¢
Coconut layer cake,
huckleberry pie: 25¢

Deaths

John Coltrane, Nelson Eddy,
Woody Guthrie, Langston
Hughes, Jayne Mansfield,
Ann Sheridan, Alice B.
Toklas, Paul Whiteman.

In the News

ALEXANDER DUBCEK IS ELECTED CZECH LEADER . . . NORTH KOREA SEIZES USS "PUEBLO" AND CREW . . . VIET CONG BEGIN TET OFFENSIVE ON SAIGON, HUE, AND OTHER MAJOR CITIES, SAIGON EMBASSY IS INVADED . . . HUE IS RECAPTURED . . . EUGENE MCCARTHY GIVES LBJ CLOSE RACE IN NEW HAMPSHIRE DEMOCRATIC PRIMARY . . . ROBERT KENNEDY DECLARES PRESIDENTIAL CANDIDACY . . . JOHNSON ANNOUNCES PARTIAL HALT IN BOMBING AND DECLARES HE WILL NOT RUN AGAIN . . . MARTIN LUTHER KING, JR. IS ASSASSINATED IN MEMPHIS, MASSIVE RIOTING ERUPTS IN 125 CITIES, 46 ARE KILLED . . . "OPERATION COMPLETE VICTORY" IS LAUNCHED WITH 100,000 TROOPS . . . THE 1968 CIVIL RIGHTS ACT PASSES . . . COLUMBIA UNIVERSITY IS OCCUPIED BY STUDENT REBELS . . . U.S. AND NORTH VIETNAM SCHEDULE PARIS PEACE TALKS . . . FRENCH STUDENTS CLASH WITH POLICE . . . ROBERT KENNEDY IS ASSASSINATED IN CALIFORNIA, ALLEGED KILLER SIRHAN SIRHAN IS ARRESTED ON THE SPOT . . . JAMES EARL RAY, ALLEGED MARTIN LUTHER KING ASSASSIN, IS ARRESTED . . . CREIGHTON ABRAMS REPLACES WESTMORELAND AS VIETNAM COMMANDER . . . INCOME TAX SURCHARGE IS PASSED . . . JOHNSON AND SOUTH VIETNAMESE THIEU MEET IN HONOLULU . . . GOP NOMINATES RICHARD NIXON . . . USSR INVADES CZECHOSLOVAKIA . . . 200,000 MEXICAN STUDENTS DEMONSTRATE . . . YIPPIES LEAD MAJOR RIOTS AT DEMOCRATIC CONVENTION IN CHICAGO, HUBERT HUMPHREY IS NOMINATED . . . JACKIE KENNEDY WEDS ARISTOTLE ONASSIS . . . JOHNSON CALLS FOR BOMBING HALT . . . NIXON IS ELECTED BY MARGIN OF 500,000 . . . U.S. "ADMITS GUILT" AND NORTH KOREA RELEASES "PUEBLO" CREW . . . ASTRONAUTS CIRCLE MOON TEN TIMES . . . VIETNAM: U.S. TROOP STRENGTH, 540,000; U.S. DEAD, 30,857; ENEMY DEAD, 422,979.

Martin Luther King is assassinated April 4th. *Copyright* Washington Post. *Reprinted by permission of D.C. Public Library.*

Students take over the president's office at Columbia University. *L. Strong.*

"We've got some difficult days ahead. But it really doesn't matter with me now. Because I've been to the mountain top. Like anybody, I would like to live a long life, [but] I've seen the Promised Land. I may not get there with you, [but] we as a people will get [there]. . . . So I'm happy tonight. I'm not fearing any man. Mine eyes have seen the glory of the coming of the Lord."
— Martin Luther King, Jr., in Memphis, shortly before his assassination

"I shall not seek, and I will not accept, the nomination of my party for another term as your President" (Lyndon Baines Johnson). "I don't know quite what to say" (Bobby Kennedy). "I went and had another drink" (Everett Dirksen). "THANKS, LBJ" (Youths outside the White House). "Congratulations. It was the best thing you could possibly have given up for Lent" (Unidentified photographer).
(all cited in *Time*)

Quotes

"I know some of you have been through defeats, as I have, and had your hearts broken. It has been said that great philosophy is not won without defeat. But a great philosophy is always won without fear."
— Richard M. Nixon

"[Those] phony intellectuals . . . don't understand what we mean by hard work and patriotism. . . . If you've seen one ghetto area, you've seen them all."
— Spiro T. Agnew

"We are at a crisis point in the history of American education and probably in that of the Western world."
— Richard Hofstadter, Columbia University professor

"The youth rebellion is a worldwide phenomenon that has not been seen before in history. I do not believe they will calm down and be ad execs at thirty as the Establishment would like us to believe."
— William Burroughs

"Shoot to kill."
— Chicago mayor Richard Daley

"Slave catchers, slave owners, murderers, butchers, oppressors—the white heroes have acquired new names."
— Eldridge Cleaver, *Soul on Ice*

"No girl child born today should responsibly be brought up to be a housewife. Too much has been made of defining human personality and destiny in terms of the sex organs. After all, we share the human brain."
— Betty Friedan

Ads

TV

Premieres

"It Takes a Thief," Robert Wagner
"The Dick Cavett Show"
"The Mod Squad," Peggy Lipton, Michael Cole, Clarence Williams III
"Rowan and Martin's Laugh-In"
"The Ghost and Mrs. Muir," Hope Lange, Edward Mulhare
"Hawaii Five-O," Jack Lord
"The Prisoner," Patrick McGoohan
"60 Minutes," Harry Reasoner, Mike Wallace
"Adam-12," Martin Milner
"Mayberry R.F.D.," Ken Berry
"Here's Lucy," Lucille Ball
"Julia," Diahann Carroll

Top Ten (Nielsen)

"Rowan and Martin's Laugh-In," "Gomer Pyle, U.S.M.C.," "Bonanza," "Mayberry R.F.D.," "Family Affair," "Gunsmoke," "Julia," "The Dean Martin Show," "Here's Lucy," "The Beverly Hillbillies"

Specials

"Hunger in the United States" (Martin Carr); "Police after Chicago" (John Laurence); "Martin Luther King;" "Man Who Dances: Edward Villella"; "Teacher, Teacher" (Billy Schulman); "Vladimir Horowitz: A Television Concert at Carnegie Hall"

Emmy Awards

"NET Playhouse" (drama); "Get Smart" (comedy); "Rowan and Martin's Laugh-In" (variety); "Mister Rogers' Neighborhood" (children); Carl Betz (actor, "Judd for the Defense"); Don Adams (comedic actor, "Get Smart"); Barbara Bain (actress, "Mission: Impossible")

Of Note

"Rowan and Martin" regulars include Goldie Hawn, Lily Tomlin, Eileen Brennan, Richard Dawson, and Judy Carne • Fifteen-minute soap operas ("Search for Tomorrow," "The Guiding Light") expand to half an hour • CBS cuts the successful Smothers Brothers after they publicly attack the network for censorship of Joan Baez.

Movies

Openings

Oliver! (Carol Reed), Ron Moody, Oliver Reed, Shani Wallis, Mark Lester
Funny Girl (William Wyler), Barbra Streisand, Omar Sharif
The Lion in Winter (Anthony Harvey), Peter O'Toole, Katharine Hepburn
Rachel, Rachel (Paul Newman), Joanne Woodward, Estelle Parsons, Kate Harrington
Romeo and Juliet (Franco Zeffirelli), Olivia Hussey, Leonard Whiting
2001: A Space Odyssey (Stanley Kubrick), Keir Dullea, Gary Lockwood
Charly (Ralph Nelson), Cliff Robertson, Claire Bloom
Faces (John Cassavetes), John Marley, Gena Rowlands
The Producers (Mel Brooks), Zero Mostel, Gene Wilder
Rosemary's Baby (Roman Polanski), Mia Farrow, John Cassavetes, Ruth Gordon
The Thomas Crown Affair (Norman Jewison), Steve McQueen, Faye Dunaway
Barbarella (Roger Vadim), Jane Fonda
Pretty Poison (Noel Black), Anthony Perkins, Tuesday Weld
Yellow Submarine (George Duning), animation with music by the Beatles

Planet of the Apes (Franklin Schaffner), Charlton Heston, Roddy McDowall
Charlie Bubbles (Albert Finney), Albert Finney, Liza Minnelli
Petulia (Richard Lester), Julie Christie, George C. Scott, Richard Chamberlain

Academy Awards

Best Picture: *Oliver!*
Best Director: Carol Reed (*Oliver!*)
Best Actress: Katharine Hepburn (*The Lion in Winter*) and Barbra Streisand (*Funny Girl*)
Best Actor: Cliff Robertson (*Charly*)

Top Box-Office Stars

Sidney Poitier, Paul Newman, Julie Andrews, John Wayne, Clint Eastwood, Dean Martin, Steve McQueen, Jack Lemmon, Lee Marvin, Elizabeth Taylor

Stars of Tomorrow

Dustin Hoffman, Katharine Ross, Katharine Houghton, Estelle Parsons, Judy Geeson, Robert Drivas, Robert Blake, Jim Brown, Gayle Hunnicut, Carol White

Popular Music

Hit Songs
"Folsom Prison Blues"
"Sunshine of Your Love"
"The Windmills of Your Mind"
"Galveston"
"Spinning Wheel"
"Blond on Blond"
"Lady Madonna"
"Do Your Own Thing"

Top Records

Albums: *Magical Mystery Tour* (Beatles); *Bookends* (Simon and Garfunkel); *Cheap Thrills* (Big Brother and the Holding Company); *The Beatles* (Beatles); *The Graduate* (sound track)

Singles: *(Sittin' on) The Dock of the Bay* (Otis Redding); *Little Green Apples* (O. C. Smith); *Stoned Soul Picnic* (5th Dimension); *Does Your Mama Know about Me?* (B. Taylor/Vancouvers); *This Guy's in Love with You* (Herb Alpert); *Slip Away* (Clarence Carter); *Love Is Blue* (Paul Mauriat); *Midnight Confessions* (Grass Roots); *Love Child* (Diana Ross and the Supremes). Country: *Honey* (Bobby Goldsboro); *Fist City* (Loretta Lynn)

Grammy Awards
Mrs. Robinson, Simon and Garfunkel (record); *By the Time I Get to Phoenix,* Glen Campbell (album); "Little Green Apples" (song)

Jazz and Big Bands
Walter Carlos uses the Moog synthesizer in *Switched-on Bach.*

Top Performers (*Downbeat*): Gary Burton (soloist); Duke Ellington (band): Miles Davis (jazz group); Kenny Burrell, Richard Davis, Herbie Hancock, Elvin Jones, Cannonball Adderley, Pee Wee Russell (instrumentalists); Ella Fitzgerald, Ray Charles (vocalists); Beatles (vocal group); Don Ellis, *Electric Bath* (album)

Theater

Broadway Openings

Plays
The Great White Hope (Howard Sackler), James Earl Jones, Jane Alexander
The Prime of Miss Jean Brodie (Jay Allen), Zoë Caldwell
Loot (Joe Orton), George Rose
The Seven Descents of Myrtle (Tennessee Williams), Harry Guardino, Estelle Parsons
The Man in the Glass Booth (Robert Shaw), Donald Pleasence
Plaza Suite (Neil Simon), Maureen Stapleton, George C. Scott
The Price (Arthur Miller), Arthur Kennedy, Pat Hingle, Kate Reid
A Day in the Death of Joe Egg (Peter Nichols), Elizabeth Hubbard, Albert Finney
We Bombed in New Haven (Joseph Heller), Jason Robards, Diana Sands
Forty Carats (Jay Allen), Julie Harris
I Never Sang for My Father (Robert Anderson), Hal Holbrook, Lillian Gish, Teresa Wright
Lovers (Brian Friel), Art Carney

Musicals
Promises, Promises (Burt Bacharach, Hal David), Jerry Orbach, Jill O'Hara
George M! (George M. Cohan), Joel Grey
Hair (Galt MacDermot, James Rado, revised version), James Rado, Gerome Ragni
Zorba (John Kander, Fred Ebb), Herschel Bernardi, Maria Karnilova
Jacques Brel Is Alive and Well and Living in Paris (Jacques Brel), Ellie Stone, Mort Shuman
Dames at Sea (Jim Wise, Robin Miller), Bernadette Peters
Marlene Dietrich, program of songs

Classics and Revivals On and Off Broadway
The Boys in the Band (Mart Crowley), Cliff Gorman, Laurence Luckinbill; *The Basement* (Harold Pinter); *King Lear,* Lee J. Cobb; *In the Matter of J. Robert Oppenheimer* (Heinar Kipphardt), Joseph Wiseman; *Futz* (Rochelle Owens), Sally Kirkland; *No Place to Be Somebody* (Charles Gordone), Ron O'Neal; Living Theater: *Frankenstein, Paradise Now* (Julian Beck, Judith Malina). *Founded:* Negro Ensemble, with *The Song of the Lusitanian Bogey* (Peter Weiss), American premiere

Regional

Founded: Atlanta Repertory Theatre opens with John Dryden's masque *King Arthur*

Theater (cont.)

Mark Taper, Los Angeles: *In the Matter of J. Robert Oppenheimer* (Heinar Kipphardt); *The Golden Fleece* (A. R. Gurney), premieres

Long Wharf, New Haven: *A Whistle in the Dark* (Thomas Murphy), premiere

Studio Arena, Buffalo: *Box, Quotations from Chairman Mao Tse-Tung* (Edward Albee), premieres

Trinity Square Repertory, Providence: *Years of the Locust* (Norman Holland), premiere

Theater Atlanta: *Red, White and Maddox* (Jay Broad and Don Tucker), premiere

Dallas Theater Center: *The Latent Heterosexual*

Hair, a musical about a draftee's experiences with the flower children. *Billy Rose Theatre Collection. The New York Public Library. Astor, Lenox and Tilden Foundations.*

(Paddy Chayefsky, directed by Burgess Meredith), Zero Mostel, premiere

Goodman, Chicago: *Othello,* James Earl Jones

Pulitzer Prize
No prize is awarded.

Tony Awards
Rosencrantz and Guildenstern Are Dead, Tom Stoppard (play), *Hallelujah, Baby!,* Jule Styne, Betty Comden, Adolph Green (musical)

Classical Music

Compositions
Howard Hanson, Symphony no. 6
Roger Sessions, Symphony no. 8
Roy Harris, Concerto for Amplified Piano, Brass, and Percussion
Karl Korte, Symphony no. 3
Michael Colgrass, *The Earth's a Baked Apple*
Charles Whittenberg, *Games of Fire*
Karel Huse, String Quartet no. 3

Important Events
Numerous electronic music festivals include the Buffalo with Lukas Foss, John Cage, and Iannis Xenakis.
The New York Philharmonic premieres thirteen symphonies, including the composers Richard Rodney Bennett, Roberto Gerhard, Howard Hanson, Nicolas Nabokov, and Roger Sessions.

New Appointments: Seiji Ozawa, San Francisco; William Steinberg, Boston; George Szell, New York Philharmonic

Debut: Maurizio Pollini

First Performances
Roy Harris, Symphony no. 11 (New York); Benjamin Lees, Piano Concerto no. 2 (Boston); Ulysses Kay, Symphony (Macomb, Ill.); Dave Brubeck, *Oratorio* (Cincinnati); Paul Creston, Concerto for Two Pianos (New Orleans); Philip Glass, *Piece in the Shape of a Square* (New York)

Opera

Metropolitan: *Das Rheingold* (Herbert von Karajan, Salzburg production); Luciano Pavarotti (debut), *La bohème;* Teresa Zylis-Gara, *Don Giovanni;* Shirley Verrett (debut), *Carmen;* Birgit Nilsson, *Elektra;* Montserrat Caballé, Richard Tucker, Sherrill Milnes, *Luisa Miller;* Martti Talvela (debut), *Don Carlo*

New York City: Beverly Sills, *Manon; Nine Rivers from Jordan* (Hugo Weisgall)

Santa Fe: *Die Jakobsleiter*

Chicago: Elena Suliotis, *Norma;* Tito Gobbi, *Falstaff;* Renata Tebaldi, *Manon Lescaut*

San Francisco: Anja Silja (debut), *Salome;* Régine Crespin, *Les Troyens;* premieres: *Fra Diavolo* (Daniel Auber); *Royal Palace* (Kurt Weill)

Music Notes
The $13 million Atlanta Memorial Arts Center opens with the premiere of *King Arthur* (Purcell). Also opening are the Blossom Music Center, between Cleveland and Akron, Ohio; the Santa Fe Opera; San Antonio Theater for the Performing Arts; Powell House, St. Louis; Jackson, Mississippi, Music Hall; and Garden State Arts Center (New Jersey).

Art

Painting

Frank Stella, *Hatra II, Sinjerli-Variation IV*
Romare Bearden, *Eastern Barn*
Ellsworth Kelly, *Yellow Black, Green Blue*
Marisol, *Portrait of Sidney Janis Selling Portrait of Sidney Janis by Marisol*
Chuck Close, *Self-Portrait*
Robert Mangold, *½ W Series*

Sculpture

Robert Smithson, *Non-site (Palisades—Edgewater, N.J.)*
Walter De Maria, *Dirt Room, Mile Long Drawing*
Carl Andre, *Joint*
Robert Morris, *Earthworks*
Claes Oldenburg, *Toilet—Hard Model, Soft Toilet*
Richard Serra, *Splashing*
Eva Hesse, *Repetition 19, III*

Christo, *The Museum of Modern Art Packed*
Michael Heizer, *Isolated Man/Circumflex*
Dan Flavin, *Untitled (to the "innovator" of Wheeling Peachblow)*

Architecture

General Motors Building, New York (Edward Durell Stone)
Lake Point Tower, Chicago (Shipporeit and Heinrich)
Xerox Square Building, Rochester, N.Y. (Welton Becket)
One Main Place, Dallas (Skidmore, Owings, and Merrill)
Department of Housing and Urban Development, Washington, D.C. (Marcel Breuer)
Juilliard School of Music, Lincoln Center, New York (Harrison & Belluschi)

Mark Rothko, standing before one of his paintings shortly before his death. *Courtesy Sedat Pakay.*

Brooklyn, Richmond, San Francisco: "The Triumph of Realism"

Buffalo: "Plus by Minus": The constructivist tradition from Malevich to Minimalism

Venice Biennale: Dickinson, Nakian, Gallo, Grooms represent the U.S.

Other Avant-Garde Shows: "Foundings"—Rauschenberg; "Machine Art" (Museum of Modern Art); "Options" (Metropolitan, Chicago); "Object and Image," with the use of light and kinetic materials (Whitney)

Art Briefs

The Egyptian Temple of Dendur, rescued from the rising Nile, arrives at the Metropolitan Museum of Art in 661 crates • Renoir's *Le Pont des Arts* sells for $1,550,000.

Important Exhibitions

"Negro Art" originates in Minnesota and travels throughout the United States; also touring are "New Primitive Paintings" (from Los Angeles) and "Painting in France 1900–1967" (organized by the French government), which travels to New York, Washington, Boston, Chicago, and Detroit. Important retrospectives include Noguchi, Ray, Arp, Smith, Lipchitz, Kollwitz, and Feeley.

Museums

New York: *Metropolitan:* The Great Age of the Fresco—from Giotto to Pontormo. *Museum of Modern Art:* "The Art of the Real: O'Keeffe, Kelly, Smith"; "Dada, Surrealism and their Heritage"; Word and Image (posters)

Dance

George Balanchine revives *Slaughter on Tenth Avenue* from *On Your Toes* with Suzanne Farrell and Arthur Mitchell

Premieres

American Ballet Theater: *Giselle* (David Blair); *Coppélia* (Enrique Martinez)

Merce Cunningham: *Rainforest* (for which Andy Warhol fills the stage with rectangular silver balloons)

New York City Ballet: *Metastaseis and Pithoprakta* (George Balanchine)

Books

Fiction

Critics' Choice

The Universal Baseball Association, Robert Coover
Up, Ronald Sukenick
Expensive People, Joyce Carol Oates
Mosby's Memoirs, Saul Bellow
Lost in the Funhouse, John Barth
Stranger in a Strange Land, Robert A. Heinlein
In the Heart of the Heart of the Country, William H. Gass
Steps, Jerzy Kosinski
The Seance and Other Stories, Isaac Bashevis Singer

Best-Sellers

Airport, Arthur Hailey
Couples, John Updike
The Salzburg Connection, Helen MacInness
A Small Town in Germany, John Le Carré
Testimony of Two Men, Taylor Caldwell
Preserve and Protect, Allen Drury
Myra Breckenridge, Gore Vidal

Nonfiction

Critics' Choice

Soul on Ice, Eldridge Cleaver
The Electric Kool-Aid Acid Test, Tom Wolfe
The Double Helix, James D. Watson
While Six Million Died, Arthur J. Morse
Death in Life: Survivors of Hiroshima, Robert Jay Lifton
Slouching towards Bethlehem, Joan Didion
The Whole Earth Catalog, Stewart Brand
Making It, Norman Podhoretz
The Algiers Motel Incident, John Hersey
36 Children, Herbert R. Kohl
❧ *The Visible and the Invisible*, Maurice Merleau-Ponty
❧ *The Teachings of Don Juan: A Yaqui Way of Knowledge*, Carlos Castaneda

Best-Sellers

Random House Dictionary of the English Language, ed. Laurence Urdang
Listen to the Warm (poetry), Rod McKuen
Between Parent and Child, Haim G. Ginott
Lonesome Cities (poetry), Rod McKuen
The Doctor's Quick Weight Loss Diet, Erwin M. Stillman, Samm Sinclair Baker
The Money Game, Adam Smith
Stanyon Street (poetry), Rod McKuen
The Weight Watcher's Cook Book, Jean Nidetch

Poetry

Gwendolyn Brooks, *In the Mecca*
W. D. Snodgrass, *After Experience: Poems and Translations*
Allan Ginsberg, *T.V. Baby Poems, Planet News*
John Berryman, *His Toy, His Dream, His Rest: 308 Dream Songs*
Diane Wakoski, *Inside the Blood Factory*
Richard Brautigan, *The Pill Versus the Springhill Mine Disaster*
Nikki Giovanni, *Black Judgment*
Philip Levine, *Not This Pig*

Pulitzer Prizes

House Made of Dawn, N. Scott Momaday (fiction)
Origins of the Fifth Amendment, Leonard W. Levy (U.S. history)
Armies of the Night, Norman Mailer (nonfiction)
So Human an Animal, Dr. René Jules Dubos (nonfiction)
Of Being Numerous, George Oppen (poetry)

Science and Technology

ILLIAC is developed; it performs 39 million computations per second.

New, fast-growing crops bring about a worldwide "green revolution."

The largest reservoir of petroleum in North America is discovered on Alaska's North Slope.

Pulsars, radio waves emitted by neutron stars, are discovered.

An asteroid, Icarus, comes within 395,000 miles of the earth.

Amniocentesis, a technique for investigating amniotic fluid early in pregnancy for genetic disorders, is developed.

Dr. Denton Cooley performs the first U.S. heart transplant and gives a 47-year-old a 15-year-old's heart.

The first Poseidon, a submarine-launched strategic missile, is fired from Cape Kennedy.

Apollo VII, manned by Walter Shirra, Donald Eisale, and Walter Cunningham, performs eight successful propulsion firings and transmits seven live TV sessions with its crew.

❧ Dr. Christiaan Barnard performs a heart transplant on Philip Blaiberg, who survives 18 months.

Nobel Prize

Luis W. Alvarez wins the prize in physics for work on subatomic particles. R. W. Holley, H. G. Khorana, and M. W. Nirenberg win in physiology and medicine for work on the genetic code. Lars Onsager wins in chemistry for work in thermodynamics.

Sports

Baseball

Denny McLain (Detroit, AL) is the first since Dizzy Dean in 1934 to win 30 games.

Don Drysdale (Los Angeles, NL) pitches a record 58⅔ consecutive scoreless innings.

Bob Gibson has a record low ERA of 1.12.

Frank Howard (Washington) hits a record 10 home runs in six games; Luis Tiant (Cleveland) strikes out 19 in a 10-inning game and Don Wilson (Houston, NL) 18 in 9.

The Cy Young Award is won by Bob Gibson (St. Louis, NL) and Denny McLain (Detroit, AL).

Champions

Batting	*Pitching*
Pete Rose (Cincinnati, NL), .335	Bill Blass (Pittsburgh, NL), 18–6
Carl Yastrzemski (Boston, AL), .301	Denny McLain (Detroit, AL) 31–6
	Home runs
	Frank Howard (Washington, AL), 44

Football

The first combined NFL–AFL draft is held.

Johnny Unitas (Baltimore) becomes the all-time passing leader with 2,261 completions for 33,340 yards and 252 touchdowns.

George Halas retires as Chicago Bears coach.

NFL Season Leaders: Earl Morrall (Baltimore), passing; Leroy Kelley (Cleveland), rushing; Clifton McNeil (San Francisco), receiving

AFL Season Leaders: Len Dawson (Kansas City), passing; Paul Robinson (Cincinnati), rushing; Lance Alworth (San Diego), receiving

College All-Americans: Terry Hanratty (Q), Notre Dame; Roger Wehrli (DB), Missouri; Ted Kwalick (E), Pennsylvania State

Olympics

The Summer Games are held in Mexico City. American gold medal winners include James Hines (100m, 9.9s.), Tommy Smith (20m, 19.8s.), Lee Evans (400m, 43.8s.), Willie Davenport (110mh, 13.3s.), Dick Fosbury (high jump, 7'4¼"), Bob Beamon (broad jump, 29'2½"), Randy Matson (shot put, 67'4¾"), Al Oerter (200'1¼"), William Toomey (decathlon, 8,193 points), Wyomia Tyus (100m, 11.0s.), George Foreman (heavyweight boxing), Debby Meyer (3 in swimming), Michael Burton (2 in swimming). Two athletes give the black power salute on the winners' stand.

Peggy Fleming wins women's figure skating at the Winter Games at Grenoble, France.

Winners

World Series	*MVP*
Detroit (AL) 4	Wilt Chamberlain, Philadelphia
St. Louis (NL) 3	*College Basketball*
MVP	UCLA
NL–Bob Gibson, St. Louis	*Player of the Year*
AL–Dennis McLain, Detroit	Lew Alcindor, UCLA
Super Bowl III (Jan. 1969)	*Stanley Cup*
New York (Jets) 16–	Toronto
Baltimore 7	*US Tennis Open*
MVP	Men: Arthur Ashe
Earl Morrall, Baltimore	Women: Margaret Smith Court
College Football	*USGA Open*
Ohio State	Lee Trevino
Heisman Trophy	*Kentucky Derby*
O. J. Simpson, Southern California	Dancer's Image (R. Ussery, jockey)
NBA Championship	
Boston 4–Los Angeles 2	

Fashion

For Women: A "do-your-own-thing" attitude prevails in a year of contrasts and contradictions, but styles are generally more feminine while flamboyant. Pants of all fabrics are worn for every occasion by women of all ages, with shirt jackets, long white sweaters, hip-length vests, and multiple chains. Jumpers and sweater-tunics are also worn over pants with large and unusual buckled belts. Scarves, sashes, pendants, and chains accompany everything. Leather appears in dresses and vests. The stylish look begins with a belted leather skirt and turtleneck with matching tights, novelty rings on all five fingers, long scarves, and the safari pouch bag.

High-fashion notes: Valentino's stockings; Anne Klein's navy blazer, white skirt, and gray flannel pants; the Afro and corn-row hairdos

For Men: Bolder plaids and bigger tattersalls appear, along with new colors—cobalt blue, shocking pink, emerald green, and fire-engine red. Blazers are white with blue trim and are worn with shirts in blazing colors, decorative scarves, belts, chains, and pendants. Ties, infrequently worn, become increasingly wider.

Kaleidoscope _____

- Following the assassinations of Martin Luther King and Robert Kennedy, Sears & Roebuck removes toy guns from its Christmas catalog and orders its 815 stores to cease advertising them; this is followed by stores throughout the country.
- Riots occur in over 100 cities following Martin Luther King's assassination; 46 die (41 blacks) and 21,000 federal and 34,000 state troops are called out, the largest military civil emergency force in modern times.
- The Poor People's Campaign, led by the Reverend Ralph Abernathy, arrives in Resurrection City, Washington, a 15-acre meadow between the Lincoln and Washington monuments that houses the poor blacks, Indians, Mexican, and Appalachian whites.
- On the nightly TV news the nation watches the Saigon chief of police calmly shoot a prisoner in the head.
- Polls in February indicate that only 35 percent support LBJ's policies.
- Yale College admits women.
- Film courses become popular at universities.
- Black Studies programs are developed at many universities.
- Black militancy increases on campuses; the president of San Francisco State resigns as black instructors urge black students to bring guns on campus.
- Protesting the war, Daniel Berrigan, Jesuit priest-writer, his brother, Phil, and seven other priests enter the Maryland Selective Service offices and burn hundreds of 1-A classification records.
- Protesting an off-campus gym and the university's ties to the Institute for Defense Analysis, Columbia University students seize President Grayson Kirk's office and hold three hostages.
- Student protest leaders at the Democratic Convention in Chicago include Abbie Hoffman and Jerry Rubin of the Youth International Party, Tom Hayden of SDS, and Bobby Seale and David Dillinger.
- Four permanent three-day weekends—Washington's Birthday, Memorial Day, Columbus Day, and Veterans' Day—are created by shifting the holidays to Monday.
- Vietnam casualties exceed Korean War totals.
- Occupational and graduate school deferments are cut back.
- Nixon's 43.4 percent victory is the lowest presidential margin since 1912.
- Violent crimes are up 57 percent since 1960.
- "Come tiptoe through the tulips," sings new cult hero Tiny Tim, in orange socks and plaid shirt.
- John Lennon and Yoko Ono's nude record album cover is banned.
- There is a marked increase in college courses in Oriental theology, religion, sorcery, witchcraft, Zen, and Oriental magic; *I Ching* sales (Princeton University Press) go from 1,000 a year to 50,000.
- Rock ballrooms include the Fillmore (San Francisco), Fillmore East (New York), Boston Tea Party (Boston), and Kinetic Playground (Chicago).
- Valerie Solanos, a bit player in Andy Warhol's movies, shoots Warhol; he dictates a novel while recuperating; she is also founder of SCUM (Society for Cutting Up Men).
- Off-off-Broadway's *Hair,* billed as "the first tribal-love-rock musical," sets a fad and is followed by numerous productions with nudity, sexuality and antiestablishment values, such as *Futz* (New York) and *Big-Time Buck White* (Los Angeles).
- Judith Malina and Julian Beck tour *Paradise Now* (the new improvisational "living theater"), which protests drug laws and clothing; they are arrested fifteen times.
- The AMA formulates a new standard of death, "brain death."
- Celibacy of the priesthood becomes an issue in the Catholic church; Pope Paul VI's ban on contraception is also challenged by 800 U.S. theologians.
- The New York Hilton rents rooms on a travelers' one-day hour plan; $12 for the first three hours and $3, each hour after.
- Jackie Onassis's wedding gift from Aristotle Onassis is a large ruby ring surrounded by large diamonds and matching earrings, valued at $1.2 million.
- A nine-day sanitation strike hits New York City.
- Twenty thousand are added monthly to New York's welfare rolls; one-fourth of the city's budget goes to welfare.
- IBM stocks split, up from $320, 20 months ago, to $667.50. One hundred shares purchased in 1914 ($2,750) are now 59,320 shares valued at more than $20 million.
- A Florida heiress leaves $450,000 to 150 stray dogs.
- Feminists picket the Miss America Contest and drop girdles and bras in trash cans.
- Joe Namath buys a mink coat.
- In April, following the Vietnamese Tet offensive, General Westmoreland states, "We have never been in a better relative position."
- The Vietnam war becomes the longest war in U.S. history.

First Appearances: Mobile coronary-care ambulance (St. Vincent's Hospital, New York), woman on the "Ten Most Wanted" list (Ruth Eisemann-Schier), professional school exclusively for training circus clowns (Venice, Fla.), North Cascades National Park (Washington State), Redwood National Park, investigations into "Chinese Restaurant Syndrome," Zero Population Growth Inc., "Zap" (underground comic book), Little, Brown acquired by Time, Inc., enzyme detergents, Sheraton Hotels acquired by ITT, *Queen Elizabeth II,* direct service, New York–USSR (Pan American, Aeroflot), *New York* magazine, book set into type completely by electronic composition, Bureau of Customs receipts totaling over $3 billion, legislation permitting postage stamps to be illustrated in color, water bed filtration system (East Chicago, Ind.), Clinique fragrance-free makeup

1969

Economic Profile
  Dow-Jones: ↓ High 952–
    Low 769
  GNP: +7%
  Inflation: +5.7%
  Unemployment: 3.5%
Police expenditures, federal,
  state, local: $4.4 billion
Persons arrested: 5,577,000
Executions: 0
Prisoners, federal and state:
  196,000
Juvenile court: 69,669
SS France, Caribbean: $240
  (2 wks.)
Willoughby Yashica zoom
  moving picture camera: $79
Henri Bendel bikini,
  matching robe, nylon and
  Lycra: $90
Saks 5th Ave. leotard, brass
  buttons: $40
Halston terry wrap, Indian
  print muffler: $130
Bill Blass "silco" brown knit:
  $100
Calvin Klein gray wool skirt,
  tube, with slit: $165
Diane von Furstenberg
  cotton midi dress, elastic
  waist, Bloomingdale's and
  Neiman Marcus: $100

Above: American flag on the
moon. *Courtesy NASA.*

Deaths

Maureen Connolly, Dwight
  D. Eisenhower, Walter
  Gropius, Walter Hagen,
  Sonja Henie, Boris
  Karloff, Joseph P.
  Kennedy, Jack Kerouac,
  John L. Lewis, Drew
  Pearson, Thelma Ritter.

In the News

HENRY CABOT LODGE IS APPOINTED CHIEF NEGOTIATOR IN PARIS . . . GIANT OIL SLICK CONTAMINATES SANTA BARBARA COAST . . . VIETNAMIZATION POLICY OF WAR IS INITIATED . . . RUSSIA AND CHINA CLASH ON BORDER, 31 SOVIETS ARE KILLED . . . JAMES EARL RAY PLEADS GUILTY TO MARTIN LUTHER KING, JR.'S MURDER AND IS SENTENCED TO 99 YEARS . . . SENATE RATIFIES ANTI–NUCLEAR PROLIFERATION TREATY . . . NIXON ASKS FUNDS FOR ABM AROUND MISSILE BASES . . . POLICE REMOVE 400 HARVARD UNIVERSITY SIT-INS . . . SOVIETS REPLACE ALEXANDER DUBCEK WITH GUSTAV HUSAK . . . SIRHAN SIRHAN IS CONVICTED OF ROBERT KENNEDY'S MURDER . . . NIGERIA CAPTURES BIAFRA HEADQUARTERS . . . DE GAULLE RESIGNS AFTER ELECTION DEFEAT . . . NIXON APPOINTS WARREN BURGER CHIEF JUSTICE, SUPREME COURT . . . TED KENNEDY ADMITS TO PART IN CHAPPAQUIDDICK DEATH OF MARY JO KOPECHNE . . . ASTRONAUT NEIL ARMSTRONG IS THE FIRST MAN TO WALK ON THE MOON . . . BRITAIN BEGINS AIRLIFTING TROOPS TO IRELAND AS VIOLENCE INCREASES . . . JUNTA OVERTHROWS LIBYAN KING IDRIS . . . NIXON ANNOUNCES REMOVAL OF 25,000 MORE TROOPS . . . HIPPIE CULT LEADER CHARLES MANSON AND "FAMILY" ARE CHARGED WITH MURDERS OF PREGNANT SHARON TATE POLANSKI AND THREE OTHERS . . . MANY PARTICIPATE IN VIETNAM MORATORIUM DAY . . . STUDENTS HOLD MASS RALLIES IN JAPAN . . . SENATE VETOES CLEMENT HAYNESWORTH SUPREME COURT NOMINATION . . . FRED HAMPTON, BLACK PANTHER LEADER, IS KILLED IN CHICAGO POLICE RAID . . . LIEUTENANT WILLIAM CALLEY TO BE TRIED FOR MY LAI MASSACRE . . . FIRST DRAFT LOTTERY IS HELD . . . VIETNAM: U.S. TROOP STRENGTH, 484,000; U.S. DEAD, 39,893; WOUNDED, 250,000; MISSING, 1,400; ENEMY DEAD, 568,989.

Quotes _____

"Houston, Tranquility Base here. The Eagle has landed. . . . I'm at the foot of the ladder. I'm going to step off the LM now. That's one small step for man, one giant step for mankind. The surface is fine and powdery. I can kick it up with my toe. . . . It's different but it's very pretty out here."
— Neil Armstrong, landing on the moon

"READ THIS BOOK STONED
The Youth International Revolution will begin with a mass breakdown of authority. . . . Tribes of long hairs, blacks, armed women, workers, peasants and students will take over. . . . The White House will become one big commune. . . . The Pentagon will be replaced with an LSD experimental farm. . . . To steal from the rich is a sacred and religious act."
— Jerry Rubin, *Do It*

"[The protesters are] a vocal minority. The great silent majority support us."
— Richard M. Nixon

"Drugs, crime, campus revolution, racial discord, draft resistance . . . on every hand we find old standards violated, old values discarded, old principles ignored. [This threatens] the fundamental values, the process by which a civilization maintains its continuity."
— Richard M. Nixon

Left: Janis Joplin, famed for her hoarse voice, stamping feet, and "hooker clothes" (her description), drinks Southern Comfort while she performs. *Movie Star News*.

"A spirit of national masochism prevails encouraged by an effete core of impudent snobs who characterize themselves as intellectuals, . . . instant analysis and querulous criticism . . . [by] a tiny enclosed fraternity of privileged men [the media]. . . . [Americans want] a cry of alarm to penetrate the cacophony of seditious drivel."
— Spiro Agnew

"[The counterculture stands against] the final consolidation of a technocratic totalitarianism in which we shall find ourself ingeniously adapted to an existence wholly estranged from anything that has ever made the life of man an interesting adventure."
— Theodore Roszak, *The Making of a Counterculture*

Ads _____

TV

Premieres

"The David Frost Show"
"The Brady Bunch," Florence Henderson, Robert
    Reed
"The Johnny Cash Show"
"Hee Haw," Buck Owens, Roy Clark
"This Is Tom Jones"
"Marcus Welby, M.D.," Robert Young, James Brolin
"Medical Center," Chad Everett
"The Bold Ones," John Saxon, David Hartman,
    E. G. Marshall, Burl Ives, Joseph Campanella
"The Bill Cosby Show"

Top Ten (Nielsen)

"Rowan and Martin's Laugh-In," "Gunsmoke,"
"Bonanza," "Mayberry R.F.D.," "Family Affair,"
"Here's Lucy," "The Red Skelton Hour," "Marcus
Welby, M.D.," "Walt Disney's Wonderful World of
Color," "The Doris Day Show"

Specials

"The Forsyte Saga"; "The Sound of Burt
Bacharach"; "Model Hippie" (Huntley-Brinkley);
"The Desert Whales" ("The Undersea World of
Jacques Cousteau"); "An Investigation of Drug
Addiction—Odyssey House" (Huntley-Brinkley);
"Apollo: A Journey to the Moon"; "Silent Night,
Lonely Night" (Robert Anderson); "Solar Eclipse: A
Darkness at Noon"; "Man on the Moon: The Epic
Journey of Apollo XI" (Walter Cronkite); "Artur
Rubinstein"

Emmy Awards

"Marcus Welby, M.D." (drama); "My World and
Welcome to It" (comedy); "The David Frost Show"
(variety); "Sesame Street" (children); Robert Young
(actor, "Marcus Welby, M.D."); William Windom
(comedic actor, "My World and Welcome to It");
Susan Hampshire (actress, "The Forsyte Saga");
Hope Lange, (comedic actress, "The Ghost and Mrs.
Muir")

Of Note

CBS's "Morning News" is the first hour-long daily
news show • Doctor shows increase • Ninety-five
percent of all homes have TV sets; 40 percent are
color TVs • The first-year lineup for PBS includes
"The Forsyte Saga" and "Sesame Street."

Movies

Openings

Midnight Cowboy (John Schlesinger), Dustin
    Hoffman, Jon Voight
Butch Cassidy and the Sundance Kid (George Roy
    Hill), Paul Newman, Robert Redford
Hello, Dolly! (Gene Kelly), Barbra Streisand, Walter
    Matthau
Z (Costa-Gavras), Yves Montand, Irene Pappas,
    Jean-Louis Trintignant
Alice's Restaurant (Arthur Penn), Arlo Guthrie, Pat
    Quinn, James Broderick
They Shoot Horses, Don't They (Sydney Pollack),
    Jane Fonda, Michael Sarrazin, Gig Young
The Sterile Cuckoo (Alan Pakula), Liza Minnelli,
    Wendell Burton
Bob and Carol and Ted and Alice (Paul Mazursky),
    Natalie Wood, Robert Culp, Dyan Cannon,
    Elliott Gould
Easy Rider (Dennis Hopper), Peter Fonda, Jack
    Nicholson, Dennis Hopper
Goodbye Columbus (Larry Peerce), Richard
    Benjamin, Ali MacGraw
The Damned (Luchino Visconti), Dirk Bogarde,
    Ingrid Thulin
The Wild Bunch (Sam Peckinpah), William Holden,
    Ernest Borgnine, Robert Ryan
Medium Cool (Haskell Wexler), Robert Foster,
    Verna Bloom
True Grit (Henry Hathaway), John Wayne, Glen
    Campbell, Kim Darby
I am Curious (Yellow) (Vilgot Sjoman), Lena Nyman,
    Peter Lindgren
My Night at Maud's (Eric Rohmer), Jean-Louis
    Trintignant, Françoise Fabian

Academy Awards

Best Picture: *Midnight Cowboy*
Best Director: John Schlesinger (*Midnight Cowboy*)
Best Actress: Maggie Smith (*The Prime of Miss Jean
    Brodie*)
Best Actor: John Wayne (*True Grit*)

Top Box-Office Stars

Paul Newman, John Wayne, Steve McQueen, Dustin
Hoffman, Clint Eastwood, Sidney Poitier, Lee
Marvin, Jack Lemmon, Katharine Hepburn, Barbra
Streisand

Stars of Tomorrow

Jon Voight, Kim Darby, Glen Campbell, Richard
Benjamin, Mark Lester, Olivia Hussey, Leonard
Whiting, Ali MacGraw, Barbara Hershey, Alan Alda

Popular Music

Hit Songs
"Good Morning Starshine"
"Hair"
"I've Got to Be Me"
"Lay Lady Lay"
"Get Back"
"It's Your Thing"
"Oh Happy Day"
"Honky Tonk Women"
"Sugar Baby"
"Crimson and Clover"
"Love (Can Make You Happy)"

Top Records

Albums: *Hair* (original cast); *Abbey Road* (Beatles); *Blood, Sweat and Tears* (Blood, Sweat and Tears); *Led Zeppelin II* (Led Zeppelin); *Green River* (Creedence Clearwater Revival)

Singles: *Sugar, Sugar* (Archies); *Everyday People* (Sly and the Family Stone); *Aquarius / Let the Sun Shine In* (5th Dimension); *Give Peace a Chance* (John Lennon and the Plastic Ono Band); *I'll Never Fall in Love Again* (Tom Jones); *Spinning Wheel* (Blood, Sweat and Tears); *Yester-Me, Yester-You, Yesterday* (Stevie Wonder); *Raindrops Keep Falling on My Head* (B. J. Thomas); *Leaving on a Jet Plane* (Peter, Paul and Mary); *I Can't Get Next to You* (Temptations). Country: *All I Have to Offer You* (Charley Pride); *Wichita Lineman* (Glen Campbell)

Grammy Awards
Aquarius / Let the Sun Shine In, 5th Dimension (record); *Blood, Sweat and Tears* (album); "Games People Play" (song)

Jazz and Big Bands
Miles Davis's *In a Silent Way* integrates rock and jazz. Archie Shepp plays with African musicians in *Jazz Meets Arabia*.

Top Performers (*Downbeat*): Miles Davis, Ornette Coleman (soloists); Duke Ellington (band); Miles Davis (jazz group); Stan Getz, Gerry Mulligan, Jimmy Hamilton, J. J. Johnson, Gary Burton, Herbie Mann (instrumentalists); Ella Fitzgerald, Ray Charles (vocalists); Blood, Sweat and Tears (vocal group); Miles Davis, *Filles de Kilimanjaro* (album)

Theater

Broadway Openings

Plays
Hadrian VII (Peter Luke), Alec McCowen
Play It Again, Sam (Woody Allen), Woody Allen, Diane Keaton, Anthony Roberts
Butterflies Are Free (Leonard Gershe), Blythe Danner, Keir Dullea, Eileen Heckart
Indians (Arthur Kopit), Stacy Keach, Sam Waterston
A Patriot for Me (John Osborne), Maximilian Schell
Last of the Red Hot Lovers (Neil Simon), James Coco, Linda Lavin
Ceremonies in Dark Old Men (Lonnie Elder), Billy Dee Williams
No Place to Be Somebody, (Charles Gordone), Ron O'Neal

Musicals
1776 (Sherman Edwards), William Daniels, Ken Howard, Howard da Silva
Oh! Calcutta (devised by Kenneth Tynan and various contributors, first nude musical)
Coco (André Previn, Alan Jay Lerner), Katharine Hepburn (musical debut), René Auberjonois
Dear World (Jerry Herman), Angela Lansbury, Milo O'Shea

Classics and Revivals, On and Off Broadway
Ché (Lennox Raphael); *Hamlet*, one version, Nichol Williamson; another, Ellis Rabb; *To Be Young, Gifted, and Black* (Lorraine Hansberry); *The Front Page* (Ben Hecht, Charles MacArthur), Bert Convy; *Our Town* (Thornton Wilder), Henry Fonda; *Private Lives* (Noel Coward), Tammy Grimes, Brian Bedford. *Founded:* Circle Repertory Company by Lanford Wilson, Marshall W. Mason, Rob Thirkield, and Tanya Berezin

Regional

Arena Stage, Washington, D.C.: *Indians* (Arthur Kopit), Stacy Keach, premiere

Charles Playhouse, Boston: *The Indian Wants the Bronx* (Israel Horovitz), premiere

A.C.T., San Francisco: *Glory! Hallelujah!* (Anna Marie Barlow), premiere; *The Architect and the Emperor of Assyria* (Fernando Arrabal), American premiere

Pulitzer Prize
The Great White Hope, Howard Sackler

Tony Awards
The Great White Hope, Howard Sackler (play), *1776*, Sherman Edwards (musical)

Classical Music

Compositions

Roy Harris, Symphony no. 12
Samuel Barber, *Despite and Still*
William Schuman, *In Praise of Shahn*
Earl Brown, *Modules 3*
John Cage, *Cheap Imitation, HPSCHD*
Charles Wuorinen, *Time's Encomium*

Important Events

Byron Janis performs two Chopin waltzes that he discovered in 1967 in Yvelines.

Rising costs threaten the musical world. The Met closes for three months over a strike; the Atlanta Opera closes; the Cincinnati and Indiana orchestras merge; a proposal is considered for merging the Buffalo and Rochester orchestras; Washington's National Symphony strikes. Five major orchestras (Boston, Chicago, Cleveland, New York, and Philadelphia) and 77 others meet to apply for assistance from the National Endowment for the Arts.

To stimulate concertgoers, a variety of programs is devised: Leonard Bernstein and Leopold Stokowski present a concert of Bach, rock, and the Moog synthesizer; Rosalyn Tureck plays Bach on the Moog; Seattle Opera: *Fidelio* with junk-sculpture sets; Kansas City: "Love-In" (ballet with baroque orchestra, rock, and amplified instruments); Fresno Philharmonic: "The Electric Eye": concert and light show; Lorin Hollander: the Baldwin electronic amplified concert grand.

Debut: Garrick Ohlsson, Ursula Oppens

First Performances

Luciano Berio, *Sinfonia,* with Swingle Singers and electronic harpsichord and organ (New York); William Schuman, "To Thee Old Cause [Martin Luther King]" (New York); Alberto Ginastera, Piano Concerto no. 2 (Indianapolis); Carlos Chávez, conducting, *Fuego Olimpico* (New York); Gian Carlo Menotti, Triple Concerto (New York); Peter Mennin, *Pied Piper of Hamlin* (Cincinnati, Mayor John Lindsay of New York narrating); Dmitri Shostakovich, Symphony no. 12 (Oregon); Leo Smit, Piano Concerto (Kansas City)

Opera

Metropolitan: Leonie Rysanek, Régine Crespin, Christa Ludwig, *Der Rosenkavalier;* Ludwig, Walter Berry, *Die Frau ohne Schatten;* Geraint Evans, *Wozzeck;* Jon Vickers, *Peter Grimes;* Renato Bruson, *Lucia di Lammermoor;* Marilyn Horne (debut), *Norma*

New York City: *Mefistofele* (Boito), first staging in New York in 40 years

Washington, D.C.: *Comte Ory, The Turn of the Screw*

Santa Fe: *Help! Help! The Globolinks* (Gian Carlo Menotti, premiere)

Chicago: Nicolai Ghiaurov, *Khovanshchina; El amor brujo* (Falla); The *Ring* cycle begins.

San Francisco: *Götterdämerung; Christopher Columbus* (Darius Milhaud, premiere)

Music Notes

Leonard Bernstein ends his tenure as conductor of the New York Philharmonic with Mahler's Symphony no. 3 • Other shifts in conductors include Pierre Boulez, New York; Georg Solti, Chicago; Thomas Schippers, Cincinnati; Antonio de Almeida, Houston; and Antal Dorati, National • The Juilliard School opens at Lincoln Center for the Performing Arts.

Vladimir Horowitz, legendary for his dazzling technique and unique interpretations, continues to perform and record.

Art

Paintings

James Rosenquist, *Horse Blinders* (1968–69)

Brice Marden, *Point*

Philip Pearlstein, *Nude Seated on Green Drape*

Helen Frankenthaler, *Commune*

Malcolm Bailey, *Hold, Separate but Equal*

Chuck Close, *Phil*

Cy Twombley, *Untitled*

Frank Stella, *Abra Variation I*

Michael Heizer, *Double Negative*

Robert Smithson, *First Mirror Displacement*

Nancy Graves, *Camel VI, Camel VII, Camel VIII*

Sol LeWitt, *Serial Project No. I (ABCD)*

Robert Morris, *37 Pieces of Work*

Sculpture

Carl Andre, *144 Pieces of Lead*

Dan Flavin, *An Artificial Barrier of Green Fluorescent Light (to Trudie and Enno Develing)*

Richard Serra, *House of Cards*

Architecture

Oakland Museum, Oakland, Calif. (Roche and Dinkeloo)

City Hall, Boston (Kallmann, McKinnell and Knowles)

Rotating House, Wilton, Conn. (Richard T. Foster)

John Hancock Center, Boston (I. M. Pei)

Important Exhibitions

Winslow Homer Show travels to 14 cities.

Museums

New York: *Metropolitan:* Primitive art; New York painting and sculpture, 1940 to the present; "Harlem on My Mind"; Florentine Baroque art; Stained glass and illuminated manuscripts of the Middle Ages (Cloisters); Jules Olitski. *Museum of Modern Art:* de Kooning, Kandinsky, Oldenburg. *Guggenheim:* Peggy Guggenheim's Picassos, Giacomettis, Légers, among others; David Smith retrospective

Washington: 19th-century American painting; William Sidney Mount; Turner

Chicago, Boston: The old masters; Rembrandt

Philadelphia: Mexican art from the 16th century to the present; Comic strips and American art

Chicago: Moholy-Nagy

Illinois Institute of Technology: German Bauhaus (over 2,500 objects)

Leonard Bernstein, the first native-born director of the New York Philharmonic, sometimes conducts so strenuously that he must be carried off the podium. *Movie Star News.*

Milwaukee: "New Realism": Jack Beal, Gabriel Laderman, Robert Bechtle, Philip Pearlstein, Sidney Tillim, Alfred Leslie, Wayne Thiebaud

Art Briefs

Robert Lehman bequeaths 3,000 works valued at over $100 million to the Metropolitan Museum of Art • Nelson Rockefeller donates his primitive collection to the Metropolitan, for which a new wing is to be built • James Michener gives his American collection to the University of Texas • New museums include the Everson Museum of Art (Syracuse) and Des Moines Art Center • The Museum of Modern Art purchases the Gertrude Stein collection for $6 million • Other major sales include Bierstadt's *Emigrants Crossing the Plains, Sunset* ($115,000), and Rembrandt's *Self-Portrait* ($1,159,200).

Dance

Eliot Feld forms his own company to stage his own works; Jerome Robbins rejoins the New York City Ballet.

Premieres

New York City Ballet: *Dances at a Gathering* (Jerome Robbins), Allegra Kent, Patricia McBride, Violette Verdy, John Clifford

Alvin Ailey: *Masakela Language*

Books

Fiction

Critics' Choice
Them, Joyce Carol Oates
Pictures of Fidelman: An Exhibition, Bernard Malamud
Slaughterhouse-Five, Kurt Vonnegut
Bullet Park, John Cheever
Going Down Fast, Marge Piercy
Tell Me That You Love Me, Junie Moon, Marjorie Kellogg
Pricksongs and Descants, Robert Coover
Going Places, Leonard Michaels

Best-Sellers
Portnoy's Complaint, Philip Roth
The Godfather, Mario Puzo
The Love Machine, Jacqueline Susann
The Inheritors, Jerome Robbins
The Andromeda Strain, Michael Crichton
The Seven Minutes, Irving Wallace
Naked Came the Stranger, Penelope Ashe
Ada, or Ardor, Vladimir Nabokov

Nonfiction

Critics' Choice
Ernest Hemingway, Carlos Baker
Living Room War, Michael Arlen
I Know Why the Caged Bird Sings, Maya Angelou
The Establishment Is Alive and Well in Washington, Art Buchwald
The Making of the President, 1968, Theodore H. White
The Burden of Southern History, C. Vann Woodward
The Children of the Dream, Bruno Bettelheim
The Valachi Papers, Peter Maas
The Kingdom and the Power, Gay Talese
On Death and Dying, Elizabeth Kubler-Ross
The 900 Days: The Siege of Leningrad, Harrison Salisbury
The Trial of Dr. Spock, Jessica Mitford

Best-Sellers
American Heritage Dictionary of the English Language, ed. William Morris
The Peter Principle, Laurence J. Peter, Raymond Hull
The Graham Kerr Cookbook
In Someone's Shadow (poetry), Rod McKuen
Between Parent and Teenager, Dr. Haim Ginott
The Selling of the President, 1968, Joe McGinniss
My Life and Prophecies, Jeanne Dixon with Rene Noorbergen

Poetry
Robert Lowell, *Notebooks 1967–68*
Kenneth Koch, *The Pleasures of Peace*
Amiri Baraka, *Black Magic: Poetry 1961–1967*
Donald Hall, *The Alligator Bride*
Richard Wilbur, *Waking to Sleep*
Elizabeth Bishop, *The Complete Poems*
W. H. Auden, *City without Walls*

Pulitzer Prizes
Collected Stories, Jean Stafford (fiction)
Present at the Creation, Dean Acheson (U.S. history)
Gandhi's Truth, Erik H. Erikson (nonfiction)
Huey Long, T. Harry Williams (biography)
Untitled Subjects, Richard Howard (poetry)

Science and Technology

Apollo X, manned by Eugene Cernan, James Young, and Thomas Stafford, evaluates lunar module performance in the lunar environment.

Apollo XI, manned by Neil Armstrong, Buzz Aldrin, and Michael Collins, is the first lunar landing mission. Armstrong walks on the moon on July 20; he and Aldrin collect 9 pounds, 12 ounces of rock and soil. They remain on the moon 21 hours, 31 minutes.

Apollo XII, manned by Charles Conrad, Richard Gordon, and Alan Bean, lands on the moon; EVA time is 15 hours, 30 minutes; it returns with samples of the lunar surface.

A magnetic device that stores information on tiny "bubbles" that can be retrieved within 100 microseconds is developed; hundreds of thousands of bubbles can be placed on a single microchip.

A scanning electron microscope is developed that permits stereoscopic images of thicker specimens.

Rubella (German measles) vaccine is made available

The chemical structure of antibodies is discovered.

The FDA removes cyclamates from the market.

DDT usage in residential areas is banned.

The first commercial 747 goes into service.

The Concorde makes its first trans-U.S. flight, from Seattle to New York.

❧ A human egg is fertilized out of the mother's body in Cambridge, England.

Nobel Prize
M. Gell-Mann wins the prize in physics for his theory of elementary particles. Max Delbruck, Alfred Hershey, and Salvador Luria win in physiology and medicine for work on the genetic structure of viruses.

Sports

Baseball

Bowie Kuhn becomes commissioner.

Each major leagues is split into two divisions, with pennant playoffs.

Denny McLain (Detroit, AL) wins his second straight Cy Young Award. Tom Seaver (New York, NL) also wins the award.

The New York Mets (NL) are the first expansion team to win the pennant.

Champions

Batting
Pete Rose (Cincinnati, NL), .348
Rod Carew (Minnesota, AL), .332

Pitching
Tom Seaver (New York, NL), 25–7

Jim Palmer (Baltimore, AL), 16–4

Home runs
Harmon Killebrew (Minnesota, AL), 49

Football

The 17-point underdog New York Jets, led by Joe Namath (QB), who promises a victory, upset the Baltimore Colts, 16–7, to become the first AFL Super Bowl winner.

Johnny Unitas is named Player of the Decade.

Vince Lombardi leaves Green Bay for Washington.

NFL Season Leaders: Sonny Jurgensen (Washington), passing; Gale Sayers (Chicago), rushing; Danny Abramowicz (New Orleans), receiving. **AFL Season Leaders:** Greg Cook (Cincinnati), passing; Dickie Post (San Diego), rushing; Lance Alworth (San Diego), receiving

College All-Americans: Mike Phipps (Q), Purdue; Mike McCoy (T), Notre Dame

Bowls (Jan. 1, 1970)

Rose: Southern California 10–Michigan 3
Orange: Pennsylvania State 10–Missouri 3

Cotton: Texas 21–Notre Dame 7
Sugar: Mississippi 27–Arkansas 22

Basketball

UCLA, with Lew Alcindor at center, wins its third straight NCAA tournament.

Bill Russell, in his last season, leads Boston to a 4–3 play-off win over Wilt Chamberlain and Los Angeles; it is the Celtics' 11th title in 12 years.

NBA All-Pro First Team: Billy Cunningham (Philadelphia), Elgin Baylor (Los Angeles), Wes Unseld (Baltimore), Earl Monroe (Baltimore), Oscar Robertson (Cincinnati)

Winners

World Series
New York (NL) 4
Baltimore (AL) 1
MVP
NL–Willie McCovey, San Francisco
AL–Harmon Killebrew, Minnesota
Super Bowl IV (Jan. 1970)
Kansas City 23–Minnesota 7
MVP
Roman Gabriel, Los Angeles
College Football
Texas
Heisman Trophy
Steve Owens, Oklahoma

NBA Championship
Boston 4–Los Angeles 3
MVP
Wes Unseld, Baltimore
College Basketball
UCLA
Player of the Year
Lew Alcindor, UCLA
Stanley Cup
Montreal
US Tennis Open
Men: Rod Laver
Women: Margaret Smith Court
USGA Open
Orville Moody
Kentucky Derby
Majestic Prince (W. Hartack, jockey)

Fashion

For Women: Contributing to the eclectic look are (1) the unisex revolution in jackets, vests, and other apparel, (2) the thirties' "Bonnie and Clyde" look, (3) "gypsy" fashions, (4) the Gibson Girl hairdo, and (5) art deco touches in belts, bags, jewelry, and fabrics. Basic are body-hugging and layered clothes: shirts, trousers, and dresses in clinging crepes, knit jersey, silk chiffons, velvets, and the hip-length sweaters or long blazers that fit over both ripple-pleated skirts and straight cuffed pants. The summer brings forth midriff blouses with Dietrich pants or Gable shorts, clogs, and wide-strapped, clunky platforms. Everything appears in faded, murky colors and thirties' "wallpaper prints." The Gibson girl haircut frames the face in a soufflelike puff with the hair pulled to the crown in a tiny knot, tendrils framing the face in a soft, sexy way. Hair is colored only for highlights.

High-fashion note: Cerutti's unisex look

For Men: The indented waist, longer jacket vest, cuffed trousers, and wider lapels and shoulders recall the thirties. Shirts, in huge stripes, prints, and weaves, hug the body; collars are higher, with longer points. Ties, 3½ to 5 inches wide, are patterned and worn with striped shirts and suits. Long hair is styled with conditioners, hair dyes, and sprays at salons.

Joe Namath. Three days before the Super Bowl, he says: "I think we'll win it; in fact, I'll guarantee it." *Movie Star News*.

Kaleidoscope _____

- The FBI is exposed for tapping Martin Luther King's phones, following an LBJ order for "national security."
- Nixon proposes a federally maintained income minimum.
- After weeks of debate, the United States and Vietnam delegates agree on the shape of the table to be used when South Vietnam and the National Liberation Front join the peace talks.
- A total of 448 universities have strikes or are forced to close; student demands broaden to include revision of admissions policies and reorganization of entire academic programs.
- Billboards appear with signs such as "Keep America Clean. Take a Bath" and "Get a Haircut."
- John Lennon and Yoko Ono marry.
- Jackie and Aristotle Onassis reportedly spend $20 million their first year together, a rate of $384,000 a week.
- Police raid a Greenwich Village, New York, gay bar after which a march takes place; the Gay Liberation Front later participates in the Hiroshima Day March, the first homosexual participation in a peace march as a separate constituency.
- Dr. Benjamin Spock's conviction for encouraging draft evasion is reversed by a U.S. court of appeal.
- Writers Norman Mailer and Jimmy Breslin run for mayor on a platform to make New York City the 51st state; their intention is to stop the state government from taking all of the city's tax money.
- *I am Curious (Yellow)* begins a series of "cultural" skin-flicks; it is exhibited after several court battles and depicts frontal nudity and simulated intercourse.
- The "Smothers Brothers Comedy Hour" is canceled because the show has not been submitted to prescreening, for "mindless" censorship, as one spokesman describes it.
- Harold Robbins receives a $2.5 million advance for *The Inheritors*.
- Rock concerts proliferate as the Rolling Stones, the Who, Joan Baez, Ravi Shankar, Jimi Hendrix, and the Jefferson Airplane draw record audiences: 100,000 at Atlanta, 150,000 at Dallas, and an estimated 400,000 to 500,000 at Woodstock.
- An estimated 300,000 attend a free Rolling Stones concert at the Altamont Music Festival in San Francisco. The Stones hire the Hell's Angels as their own security guards and the Angels stab to death a

boy who tries to reach the stage; the Stones are singing "Sympathy for the Devil."
- Richard Schechner's *Dionysus 69* introduces group participation into the theater: each night a girl from the audience is selected to be made love to on stage; many plays of "communal celebration" follow, such as *Sweet Eros* and *Ché*.
- Richard Burton buys Elizabeth Taylor a 69.42-carat diamond from Cartier; its price is not revealed, although Cartier says it paid $1,050,000 for it the day before and has now "made a profit."
- Bobby Seale is ordered bound and gagged by Judge Julius Hoffmann when Seale repeatedly disrupts the Chicago Eight trial.
- Ted Kennedy's long delay in reporting Mary Jo Kopechne's drowning elicits widespread questioning of his character.
- Many universities make ROTC voluntary or abolish it; Defense Department contracts with universities drop from 400 to 200.
- A group of black students armed with machine guns take over a building at Cornell University; they leave after negotiations with the administration.
- "Hip, Hip, Hippocrates. . . . Up with the service, down with the fees," shout demonstrators at an AMA meeting.
- The addition of MSG to commercially prepared infant food is halted as studies indicate damage to the hypothalamus.
- A copy of the first printing of the Declaration of Independence sells for $404,000.
- On his 70th birthday, Duke Ellington is presented the Medal of Freedom by President Nixon.

Fads: Underground newspapers *(Berkeley Barb, L. A. Free Press, East Village Other)*, dune buggies

New Words and Usages: Downs, uppers, command module, lunar module, mini beard, "-wise" (fashionwise, careerwise), crunch, hair weaving, headhunter, noise pollution, hunk, total

First Appearances: Army war college women graduates; medals of army, navy, air force presented to one person at the same time (L. L. Lemnitrev), city commissioner who is a former Miss America (Bess Meyerson, New York City), transatlantic solo rowboat (January 20–July 19, Canary Islands to Florida), senator to become movie actor (Everett Dirksen, *The Monitors*), *Penthouse*, Frosted Mini-Wheats, bank to install automatic teller (Chemical, New York), vasectomy outpatient service (Margaret Sanger Research Bureau, New York), postage stamp to depict living American (moon issue, Neil Armstrong), harness race track to handle more than $300 million in bets (Yonkers), ship to pass both ways through the Northwest Passage

Nixon's farewell. *Congressional Library.*

Statistics

Vital

Population: 204,879,000
  Urban/rural: 149/54
  Farm: 4.8%
Life expectancy
  Male: 67.1
  Female: 74.8
Births/1,000: 18.4
Marriages/1,000: 10.6
Divorces/1,000: 3.5
Deaths/1,000: 9.5
  per 100,000
    Heart: 521
    Cancer: 163
    Tuberculosis: 3
    Car accidents: 26.9

Economic

Unemployed: 4,088,000
GNP: $977.1 billion
Federal budget: $197.2 billion
National debt: $382 billion
Union membership: 20.7
  million
Strikes: 5,716
Prime rate: 7.7%
Car sales: 6,546,800
Average salary: $7,564

Social

Homicides/100,000: 8.3
Suicides/100,000: 11.6
Percent below poverty level:
  12.6
Labor force, male/female: 27/
  16
Social welfare: $145.9 billion
Public education: $40.7 billion
College degrees
  Bachelors'
    Male: 484,000
    Female: 343,000
  Doctorates
    Male: 22,890
    Female: 3,976
Attendance
  Movies (weekly): 18 million
  Baseball (yearly): 28.9
    million

Consumer

Consumer Price Index
  (1967 = 100): 116.3
Eggs: 61¢ (doz.)
Milk: 33¢ (qt.)
Bread: 24¢ (loaf)
Butter: 87¢ (lb.)
Bacon: 95¢ (lb.)
Round steak: $1.30 (lb.)
Oranges: 86¢ (doz.)
Coffee: 91¢ (lb.)

The seventies witnessed many unprecedented events in American life—the first peacetime gas shortage, the first lost war, and the first president to resign. It is perhaps no wonder that self-doubt clouded the nation's bicentennial, and many questioned whether the era of American preeminence was passing. Close inspection of the social fabric, however, provides a more auspicious view.

The decade began with a tragic event when, during an antiwar rally at Kent State University, Ohio National Guardsmen opened fire and killed four students. Nationwide protest followed, and it appeared that the unrest of the late sixties was to continue. A more hopeful period ensued, however, as Nixon wound down the war and prepared to swallow the bitter pill of peace without victory. The president also took far-reaching initiatives in foreign affairs. Long a vaunted anticommunist, he and his shuttling minister, Henry Kissinger, made friendly overtures to Red China. Nixon, in addition, developed a policy of détente with Russia and eventually exchanged visits with Russian premier Leonid Brezhnev; in 1972, the first major postwar arms agreement, the Strategic Arms Limitation Treaty (SALT), was signed.

Elected in 1972 by a landslide that rivaled FDR's in 1936, and at the pinnacle of his roller-coaster public life, Nixon soon plummeted to scandal and ignominy. The Senate Watergate committee, chaired by Sam Ervin, pursued an investigation of the preelection break-in at Democratic Committee headquarters, and an extraordinary tale of suspense and intrigue unfolded. White House and other party underlings confessed and implicated their superiors, and the cover-up question arose. As Howard Baker succinctly put it: what did the president know, and when did he know it? All varieties of the shabby abuse of power came to light, from an "enemies list" of administration opponents targeted for IRS hassling and the employment of clandestine teams of "plumbers" for illicit break-ins to the president's predilection for secretly taping White House conversations and his typically obscene language. In due course, the president's counsel, John Dean, implicated Nixon, who then fired his chief aides, H. R. Haldeman and John Erlichman; Nixon later fired Archibald Cox, his own appointee as Watergate prosecutor. Finally, after battling the Supreme Court, Nixon agreed to release his secret tapes, and their publication sealed his fate. With the president's criminal complicity widely accepted, a House committee in 1974 voted articles of impeachment. During this time, Vice President Spiro Agnew resigned over corruption charges, and Gerald Ford was appointed vice president. Nixon, then facing an impeachment trial, elected to resign, and Ford became America's first appointed president; Ford's

first official act was to pardon his disgraced predecessor. Continuing Senate investigations subsequently revealed dubious practices of both the FBI and CIA.

The country was shocked at the extent of its leaders' moral turpitude, and the immediate post-Vietnam War period, concurrent with Watergate, contributed to the national disillusionment. When, in 1975, North Vietnam occupied Saigon, a final American tally recorded over fifty thousand soldiers dead and more than 6 million veterans of the lost war. An unclarified sense of defeat and moral disaffection troubled many. Returning soldiers experienced great difficulties reintegrating into society. Most were greeted with ambivalence, in contrast to the glory and honor bestowed on veterans of previous wars. Perhaps in recognition of the widespread popular skepticism about the war's validity, Ford, in a limited way, and later Jimmy Carter, unconditionally, offered amnesty to those who had exiled themselves to avoid the draft. Throughout the decade, popular books and movies continued to question the nature and meaning of America's involvement in the war, including *The Best and the Brightest, Fire in the Lake, Coming Home, The Deer Hunter,* and *Apocalypse Now.*

Between Vietnam and Watergate, the most cynical of Americans lost faith in the integrity and judgment of the national leadership. In the meantime, the economy suffered, as inflation and recession ("stagflation") combined in an unprecedented manner. Then, in 1973, the nation's lifeline, its oil supply, became imperiled when OPEC, an organization of Third World oil producers, embargoed oil exports in response to America's posture toward the Arab-Israeli war. The erosion of America's might, as well as its moral prestige, seemed evident.

In 1976, America elected a little-known, born-again Christian from the Deep South, Jimmy Carter, who advocated human rights and promised executive candor. During his administration, however, the country's economic problems grew worse, and double-digit inflation and soaring interest rates (the "great inflation") devalued the dollar both at home and abroad. Gold prices jumped, and banks began to advertise borrowing as a means of hedging against inflation. Pan Am advised: "Live Today. Tomorrow Will Cost More."

Central to the crisis was the ever-increasing cost of oil, as OPEC relentlessly manipulated supply and increased prices of crude. The economy, in general, fared poorly, and basic industries like automaking and steel suffered enormous losses; Chrysler required a government loan to prevent bankruptcy. Other problems mounted. Crime, especially among the young, reached record heights; college enrollments fell; an accident at the Three Mile Island nuclear plant increased fears of a poisoned environment.

Carter's foreign policy, in the beginning, showed great promise. He negotiated the Panama Canal treaties and was instrumental in helping Egypt and Israel reach accord at Camp David. It was, however, in foreign affairs that America suffered its most severe humiliation as a world power. America's staunch ally, the shah of Iran, was overthrown by a theocratic revolution that installed a religious fanatic, the Ayatollah Khomeini, as ruler. In late 1979, the new Iranian government imprisoned forty-six Americans in the U.S. embassy, leaving America and its president to wring their hands and tie yellow ribbons.

There is another story to be told of this decade, but it is a more subtle one. It tells of the gradual integration of many of the ideals of the sixties into the mainstream of American consciousness. To the extent that these supported equality, diversity, and the individual's right to a private determination of social, moral, sexual, and spiritual beliefs, the history of the seventies takes on a brighter aspect.

Despite controversies over busing and affirmative action, and the persistence of racial bigotry and economic disadvantage, the ideals and legislation of the civil rights movement gained significant acceptance during the seventies. Segregation was officially eliminated, and blacks were free to vote everywhere. In southern towns, as well as northern cities, more blacks than ever entered political life and gained office, from Carl Stokes of Cleveland to Thomas Bradley of Los Angeles. Even sports reflected a responsible change in attitude, as blacks who had played in the early Negro baseball leagues were elected to the Major League Hall of Fame. Movies and television shows, like "The Jeffersons" and "Sanford and Son," began to portray blacks as role models and ordinary people, rather than as stereotypes and victims. *Roots*, Alex Haley's epic of black American history, became a blockbuster best-seller and, when dramatized on TV for seven nights later in the decade, drew all-time record audiences. Perhaps the black struggle for freedom had become an American, not just a black, story. Needless to say, ingrained prejudice still remained in many areas of society, but the principle of equality was taking hold. Children raised during this decade probably lacked the color line distinctions that surrounded their parents as recently as twenty years before.

The ideal of female equality also became further amalgamated into the national consciousness. Despite the failure of sufficient states to ratify the ERA—a great setback to many—numerous positive changes took place. A federal law forbidding discrimination based on gender was passed. More women went to medical, law, and business schools, and more women worked and demanded and received dignified treatment. The growth of child care helped women to work and parent at the same time. Early in the decade, Gloria Steinem's *Ms.* magazine got underway, and a number of important feminist books reached a wide audience, telling of *Sexual Politics, The Female Eunuch, Our Bodies, Ourselves,* and *Against Our Will.* Women gained a sense of community with one another, and new role models were visible. Barbara Jordan became the first woman and first black to give the keynote address at a presidential convention; Barbara Walters became the first female major network anchor. As women's roles expanded, male roles also became more flexible. Men were encouraged to be more sensitive; the emergence of the witty but insecure Woody Allen as a romantic hero in *Annie Hall,* the sophisticated romance of the decade, further defined changing role models. Other films like *Kramer vs. Kramer* addressed the dilemma of parents fulfilling their identities and still sharing in the raising of children. Probably the most controversial and far-reaching event concerning individual rights was the 1973 Supreme Court ruling on first-trimester abortion.

During the seventies, ethnic uniqueness also became a source of enrichment, rather than embarrassment, as Hispanics, Chicanos, American Indians, and Italians celebrated their heritage. *Bury My Heart at Wounded Knee,* Dee Brown's work on Indian history, was a best-seller, and "Chico and the Man," a popular TV show. Although not without problems, laws were passed supporting bilingual education.

Other issues, like the future of the environment—the danger of its exhaustion as well as the reality of its pollution—entered the mainstream of national awareness. The oil crisis jolted the public into a recognition of the limits of the earth's natural resources, and public attention focused on smaller, gas-efficient cars. Environmental concerns also prompted numerous industrial regulations geared toward reducing toxic waste in the air and water. An expanding health food industry promised uncontaminated ("natural") foods.

There was also a trend toward self-awareness, self-improvement, and self-fulfillment. Part of this was expressed in the explosive interest in exercise (especially running), health foods and gourmet cuisine, and psychologically oriented self-help books like *I'm O.K., You're O.K., Be Your Own Best Friend,* and *Your Erroneous Zones,* along with the many assertiveness-training manuals like *Looking Out for #1.* Later age at marriage and lower birth and higher divorce rates were perhaps also evidence of greater freedom of individual choice and self-awareness, as were books like *Fear of Flying* and

Passages. The growth of singles' communities and activities, as well as the marketing of singles' products, also indicated new life-styles.

It was during this time that the nation grew better able to own up to its Archie Bunkers. Norman Lear virtually elevated the sit-com into an art form by exaggerating realistic human foibles whereby his audience could laugh at itself and confront genuine social issues. A new candor was also evident in television movies, which portrayed subjects like interracial love affairs and homosexuality. Movies portrayed a more realistic and open attitude toward sex as a natural and mutual expression of romantic and/or erotic feelings, rather than as the reward women give scheming men as the prize for marriage in the way the earlier, coy, and tortured Doris Day–Rock Hudson films had portrayed it.

The new openness toward sexuality became widespread. *Last Tango in Paris,* an X-rated movie, starred a major box-office actor, Marlon Brando. *Deep Throat,* a hard-core porno film, played at posh neighborhood theaters. Two graphic self-help books, *Everything You Always Wanted to Know about Sex* and *The Joy of Sex,* became best-sellers, along with *The Sensuous Man* and *The Sensuous Woman. Open Marriage,* which advocated shelving sexual fidelity, had a vogue, and *Carnal Knowledge,* a film about this very subject, was well received. Jane Fonda, in many ways the female star of the decade, won an Oscar for her realistic portrayal of a prostitute. In an allied vein, streaking (running nude in public) became a fad.

Of course, as with all social change, there was resistance. Marabel Morgan's best-selling *Total Woman* advocated a more submissive female role. Clint Eastwood's emergence as the number one box-office star indicated the persistence of more or less traditional macho role models. The return among youth to the materialistic concerns of "getting on" and "getting ahead" indicated the sway of tradition. Adam Smith's *The Money Game* and Sylvia Porter's *The Money Book* also reflected this trend, as did the return to preppie clothes late in the decade.

Also in the seventies, Saul Bellow won the Nobel prize in literature, and E. L. Doctorow's critically acclaimed *Ragtime* received a record paperback advance. Three film directors were so successful as to virtually displace actors as Hollywood stars: George Lucas *(Star Wars),* Francis Ford Coppola *(The Godfather),* and Steven Spielberg *(Jaws).* In the world of opera, Beverly Sills became a leading personality; in ballet, many new companies flourished, and dancers such as Rudolf Nureyev and Mikhail Baryshnikov gained enormous popularity. Major popular music personalities and groups included Diana Ross, Elton John, Chicago, Earth, Wind and Fire, and Peter Frampton; there was a

Beverly Sills, who was "Bubbles" on radio at age 3, becomes general director of the New York City Opera in 1979. *Ian Howarth.*

renewed interest in country and jazz. Regional theater expanded, initiating shows like *Crimes of the Heart* and *Children of a Lesser God.* On Broadway, innovative musicals included *Jesus Christ Superstar* and *A Chorus Line.* Dominant sports figures were Henry Aaron, Kareem Abdul-Jabbar, O. J. Simpson, and Muhammad Ali. Interestingly, the sports world reflected the new role changes in its own good-natured way. New York Jets quarterback Joe Namath, for example, advertised mink coats and pantyhose. A huge television audience watched the battles between aging, self-proclaimed male chauvinist tennis star Bobby Riggs and the two current women champions, Margaret Smith Court and Billie Jean King. The sex symbols of the decade were Charlie's Angel detective Farrah Fawcett-Majors and the laconic he-man Burt Reynolds. In the trial of the decade, heiress Patty Hearst, kidnapped by a small terrorist group, was later found guilty of joining her captors in bank robbery. In another sequela of the sixties, nine hundred religious cult members committed suicide at their pastor's direction.

Finally, alongside America's political and economic trials and its social and cultural transfigurations, the seventies witnessed another phenomenon—the dawning of the Microchip Age. From calculators and digital electronics to personal computers, Atari, and video arcade games, computer technology became part of everyone's awareness. Genetic engineering, test-tube babies, and the experimental space shuttle seemed to give further reality to sci-fi fantasies. The children who flocked three and four times to see the movie *Star Wars,* making it the greatest box-office hit of all time, themselves demonstrated an addictive interest in the new computer gadgetry. In fact, a technological revolution, and with it perhaps yet another industrial revolution, was in the making, promising vast, exciting, but uncertain changes whose tale those Star Wars children, and their children, will tell.

1970

In the News

U.S. AND CHINA RESUME TALKS IN WARSAW . . . SENATE CURBS DE FACTO SCHOOL SEGREGATION . . . CHICAGO 7 ARE ACQUITTED OF CONSPIRACY TO RIOT, 5 ARE FOUND GUILTY OF LESSER CHARGES . . . SOUTH CAROLINA WHITES STORM BUSES TO PREVENT INTEGRATION . . . NUCLEAR NONPROLIFERATION TREATY GOES INTO EFFECT . . . ARMY ACCUSES GEN. SAMUEL KOSTER OF SUPPRESSING INFORMATION ABOUT MY LAI CIVILIAN MASSACRE . . .. SENATE REJECTS SUPREME COURT NOMINEE CARSWELL OVER RACIST BACKGROUND . . . 2D ROUND OF STRATEGIC ARMS LIMITATION TREATY TALKS BEGINS . . . NIXON PLEDGES TO BRING 150,000 TROOPS BACK IN THE NEXT YEAR . . . NATION CELEBRATES EARTH DAY . . . NIXON ADMITS SENDING TROOPS INTO CAMBODIAN SANCTUARIES, STUDENTS PROTEST ACROSS THE COUNTRY . . . FOUR STUDENTS ARE KILLED AT KENT STATE UNIVERSITY WHEN NATIONAL GUARD OPENS FIRE . . . TWO STUDENTS ARE KILLED IN JACKSON STATE DEMONSTRATION . . . MAO CALLS FOR WORLD REVOLUTION . . . STOCKS RISE 32.04 ON RECORD DAY . . . PENN CENTRAL ASKS FOR BANKRUPTCY REORGANIZATION . . . NIXON ASKS VOTE FOR 18-YEAR-OLDS . . . NEW YORK ABORTION LAW TAKES EFFECT, THE MOST LIBERAL IN U.S. . . . 747 JUMBO JET WITH 379 ABOARD IS HIJACKED TO CUBA . . . FOUR NEW YORK–BOUND AIRLINERS ARE HIJACKED IN EUROPE, 300 HOSTAGES ARE HELD IN JORDANIAN DESERT . . . KING HUSSEIN CRUSHES PALESTINIAN REVOLT IN JORDAN . . . EGYPTIAN RULER NASSER DIES OF HEART ATTACK, VICE PRESIDENT ANWAR SADAT TAKES OVER . . . 200,000 ARE KILLED IN EAST PAKISTAN CYCLONE TIDAL WAVE . . . U.S. FAILS IN ATTEMPT TO FREE NORTH VIETNAM POW'S . . . VIETNAM: U.S. TROOP STRENGTH, 343,700; U.S. DEAD 44,241; WOUNDED, 293,529; ENEMY DEAD, 687,648.

Woodstock, the film of the 1969 rock festival dubbed by Abbie Hoffman "Woodstock Nation." *Movie Star News.*

"The senate must not remain silent now while the President uses the armed forces of the United States to fight an undeclared and undisclosed war in Laos."
— Senator William Fulbright (D-Ark.)

"We are not a weak people. We are a strong people. America has never been defeated in the proud, 199-year history of this country and we shall not be defeated in Vietnam. . . . We will not be humiliated. The world's most powerful nation [will not act] like a pitiful, helpless giant."
— Richard M. Nixon, on the bombing of Cambodia

"Unnecessary, unwarranted, and inexcusable."
— Scranton Report, on the Kent State shootings

"Pablum for the permissivists."
— Spiro Agnew, on the Scranton Report

Quotes

"Youth in its protest must be heard."
— Secretary of the Interior Walter Hickel

"I know that probably most of you think I'm an S.O.B., but I want you to know I understand just how you feel."
— Nixon, to student demonstrators

"The issue of race has been too much talked about. . . . We may need a period in which Negro progress continues and racial rhetoric fades, . . . [a policy of] benign neglect."
— Daniel Moynihan

"This is not a bedroom war. This is a political movement."
— Betty Friedan, on women's rights

Feminist Betty Friedan leads a nationwide women's demonstration on the occasion of the 50th anniversary of women's suffrage. *Philippe Halsman.*

Ads

TV

Premieres

"The Flip Wilson Show"
"Monday Night Football," Howard Cosell, Don Meredith
"The Odd Couple," Jack Klugman, Tony Randall
"The Mary Tyler Moore Show," Ed Asner, Valerie Harper
"The Partridge Family," Shirley Jones
"The Don Knotts Show"
"All My Children"
"Flipper"

Top Ten (Nielsen)

"Marcus Welby, M.D.," "The Flip Wilson Show," "Here's Lucy," "Ironside," "Gunsmoke," "ABC Movie of the Week," "Hawaii Five-O," "Medical Center," "Bonanza," "The F.B.I."

Specials

"The Andersonville Trial" (Jack Cassidy); "My Sweet Charlie" (Al Freeman, Patty Duke); "The Price" (George C. Scott, Colleen Dewhurst); "The Neon Ceiling" (Gig Young, Lee Grant); "David Copperfield" (Sir Laurence Olivier); "Civilisation" (Sir Kenneth Clark); "The World of Charlie Company" (CBS); "LBJ: The Decision to Halt the Bombing"; "VD: A Plague on Our Houses" (Frank Field); "Hamlet" (Richard Chamberlain)

Emmy Awards

"The Senator—The Bold Ones" (drama); "All in the Family" (comedy, premiered 1/71); "The Flip Wilson Show" (variety); "Sesame Street" (children); Hal Holbrook (actor, "The Senator"); Jack Klugman (comedic actor, "The Odd Couple"); Susan Hampshire (actress, "The First Churchills"); Jean Stapleton (comedic actress, "All in the Family")

Of Note

PBS takes over NET • Despite network complaints, Nixon refuses to distribute advance copies of his speeches in order to forestall "instant analysis" • Thirty-three percent of the TV audience watches ABC's "Monday Night Football," the first prime-time football event.

Movies

Openings

Patton (Franklin J. Schaffner), George C. Scott, Karl Malden
Airport (George Seaton), Burt Lancaster, Dean Martin, Helen Hayes
Five Easy Pieces (Bob Rafelson), Jack Nicholson, Karen Black
Love Story (Arthur Hiller), Ali MacGraw, Ryan O'Neal
*M*A*S*H* (Robert Altman), Elliott Gould, Donald Sutherland, Sally Kellerman
Women in Love (Ken Russell), Alan Bates, Glenda Jackson
Diary of a Mad Housewife (Frank Perry), Richard Benjamin, Carrie Snodgress
Lovers and Other Strangers (Cy Howard), Gig Young, Richard Castello, Beatrice Arthur
Satyricon (Federico Fellini), Martin Potter, Hiram Keller
Tora! Tora! Tora! (Richard Fleischer, Toshio Masuda, Kinji Fukasada), Jason Robards, Martin Balsam
Husbands (John Cassavetes), John Cassavetes, Ben Gazzara, Peter Falk
Gimme Shelter (David Maysles, Albert Maysles, Charlotte Zwerin), Mick Jagger, Charlie Watts, Melvin Belli
The Wild Child (François Truffaut), François Truffaut, Jean-Pierre Cargol, Jean Daste
Woodstock (Michael Wadleigh), Jimi Hendrix, Joan Baez, Joe Cocker, Arlo Guthrie
The Boys in the Band (William Friedkin), Cliff Gorman, Laurence Luckinbill
Little Big Man (Arthur Penn), Dustin Hoffman, Faye Dunaway, Martin Balsam
Ryan's Daughter (David Lean), Robert Mitchum, Sarah Miles, John Mills

Academy Awards

Best Picture: *Patton*
Best Director: Franklin Schaffner (*Patton*)
Best Actress: Glenda Jackson (*Women in Love*)
Best Actor: George C. Scott (*Patton*) (declined)

Top Box-Office Stars

Paul Newman, Clint Eastwood, Steve McQueen, John Wayne, Elliott Gould, Dustin Hoffman, Lee Marvin, Jack Lemmon, Barbra Streisand, Walter Matthau

Stars of Tomorrow

Donald Sutherland, Liza Minnelli, Goldie Hawn, Jack Nicholson, Genevieve Bujold, Dyan Cannon, Marlo Thomas, Beau Bridges, Sharon Farrell, Peter Boyle

Popular Music

Hit Songs
"We've Only Just Begun"
"Do the Funky Chicken"
"I'll Be There"
"I Like Your Lovin' "
"Psychedelic Shack"
"Signed, Sealed, Delivered I'm Yours"
"Love on a Two Way Street"
"The Love You Save"

Top Records

Albums: *Bridge over Troubled Water* (Simon and Garfunkel); *Cosmo's Factory* (Creedence Clearwater Revival); *Abraxas* (Santana); *McCartney* (Paul McCartney); *Woodstock* (Sound track)

Singles: "*(They Long to Be) Close to You*" (Carpenters); *American Woman / No Sugar Tonight* (Guess Who); *War* (Edwin Starr); *Ain't No Mountain High Enough* (Diana Ross); *Let It Be* (Beatles); *Get Ready* (Rare Earth); *Everything Is Beautiful* (Ray Stevens); *Rainy Night in Georgia* (Brook Benton). Country: *Wonder Could I Live There Anymore* (Charlie Pride); *Baby, Baby* (David Houston)

Grammy Awards
Bridge over Troubled Water, Simon and Garfunkel (record, album, song)

Jazz and Big Bands
Top Performers (*Downbeat*): Miles Davis, Jimi Hendrix (soloists); Duke Ellington (band); Miles Davis (jazz group); Rahsaan Roland Kirk, Wayne Shorter (instrumentalists); Ella Fitzgerald, Leon Thomas (vocalists); Frank Zappa (rock/blues musician); Blood, Sweat, and Tears (vocal group); Miles Davis, *Bitches Brew;* Blood, Sweat, and Tears, *B.S. & T3* (albums)

Theater

Broadway Openings

Plays
Child's Play (Robert Marasco), Pat Hingle, Fritz Weaver
Conduct Unbecoming (Barrie England), Paul Jones, Jeremy Clyde
Sleuth (Anthony Shaffer), Anthony Quayle, Keith Baxter
Borstal Boy (Brendan Behan), Niall Tolbin, Frank Grimes
Home (David Storey), Ralph Richardson, John Gielgud
The Gingerbread Lady (Neil Simon), Maureen Stapleton

Musicals
Purlie (Gary Geld, Peter Udell), Melba Moore, Cleavon Little, John Heffernan
Applause (Charles Strouse, Lee Adams), Lauren Bacall, Len Cariou, Penny Fuller
Company (Stephen Sondheim), Elaine Stritch, Dean Jones
Two by Two (Richard Rodgers, Martin Charnin), Danny Kaye
The Rothschilds (Jerry Boch, Sheldon Harnick), Hal Linden
The Me Nobody Knows (Gary Friedman, Will Holt), Melanie Henderson, Laura Michaels, Irene Cara
Bob and Ray, The Two and Only, written and performed by Bob Elliott, Ray Goulding

Classics, Revivals, and Off-Broadway Premieres
The Effect of Gamma Rays on Man-in-the-Moon Marigolds (Paul Zindel), Sada Thompson; *Steambath* (Bruce Jay Friedman), Anthony Perkins; *Happy Birthday, Wanda June* (Kurt Vonnegut, Jr.), Marsha Mason, Kevin McCarthy; *Colette* (Elinor Jones), Zoë Caldwell; *Emlyn Williams as Charles Dickens; Landscape, Silence* (Harold Pinter); *The Good Woman of Setzuan* (Bertolt Brecht), Colleen Dewhurst; *Jack McGowan in the Works of Beckett; The Basic Training of Pavlo Hummel* (David Rabe), William Atherton; *Harvey* (Mary Chase), Helen Hayes, James Stewart; *The White House Murder Case* (Jules Feiffer); *What the Butler Saw* (Joe Orton), Laurence Luckinbill; *Boesman and Lena* (Athol Fugard), James Earl Jones, Ruby Dee. *Founded:* Manhattan Theatre Club

Regional
Long Wharf, New Haven: *Country People* (Gorky); *A Place without Doors* (Marguerite Duras); *Yegor Bulichov* (Gorky), Martha Schlamme, Morris Carnovsky, American premieres

Seattle Repertory Theatre: *Richard III,* Richard Chamberlain

Mark Taper Forum, Los Angeles: *A Dream on Monkey Mountain* (Derek Wolcott), *Crystal and Fox* (Brian Friel); *Murderous Angels* (Conor Cruise O'Brien), premieres

Theater (cont.)

Dallas Theater Center: *The Night Thoreau Spent in Jail* (Jerome Lawrence, Robert E. Lee), premiere

Studio Arena, Buffalo: *Scenes from American Life* (A. R. Gurney), premiere

Pulitzer Prize
No Place to Be Somebody, Charles Gordone

Tony Awards
Borstal Boy, Brendan Behan (play); *Applause,* Charles Strouse, Lee Adams (musical)

Ralph Richardson and John Gielgud in *Home. Billy Rose Theatre Collection. The New York Public Library at Lincoln Center Astor, Lenox and Tilden Foundations.*

Classical Music

Compositions
Roger Sessions, Rhapsody, *When Lilacs Last in the Dooryard Bloom'd*
Walter Piston, Fantasia for Violin
Philip Glass, *Music with Changing Parts*
David Saturen, *Ternaria* for Organ and Orchestra
Steve Reich, Four Organs
George Crumb, *Ancient Voices of Children*
Ulysses Kay, *The Capitoline Venus*
Charles Wuorinen, *Time's Encomium*

Important Events
Beethoven's 200th birthday is celebrated throughout the country. Rudolf Serkin, Daniel Barenboim, and Claude Frank perform in the two-week Casals Festival. In New York, Barenboim plays the complete piano sonatas; Stern-Istomin-Rose play the complete piano trios; the Juilliard and Guarneri perform the quartets.
For Copland's 70th birthday, the composer leads the New York Philharmonic in his most famous works. At the MacDowell Colony, Isaac Stern and Leonard Bernstein perform *Aaron's Canon;* William Warfield sings "Old American Songs."
Garrick Ohlsson, 22, wins the Eighth International Chopin Festival in Warsaw.

Debut: Israela Margalit

First Performances
William Walton, Improvisations on an Impromptu of Benjamin Britten (San Francisco); Dmitri Shostakovich, Symphony no. 13 (Philadelphia); Elliott Carter, Concerto for Orchestra (New York); Charles Ives, *The Yale-Princeton Football Game* (New York); Hans Werner Henze, Symphony no. 6 (New York); Norman Dello Joio, *Mass* (Chicago); Karlheinz Stockhausen, *Carré* (Minneapolis); William Schuman, *In Praise of Shahn* (New York)

Opera

Metropolitan: Joan Sutherland, Marilyn Horne (debut), *Norma;* Franco Corelli, Grace Bumbry in Zeffirelli production of *Cavalleria rusticana;* Richard Tucker, Lucine Amara, Sherrill Milnes in Zeffirelli's *I pagliacci;* Martina Arroyo, Milnes, *Ernani;* Grace Bumbry, *Orfeo ed Euridice;* Placido Domingo, Cornell MacNeil, *La traviata;* Gabriel Bacquier, *Les contes d'Hoffmann*

Boston: *Good Soldier Schweik* (Robert Kurka); Beverly Sills, *Daughter of the Regiment*

Minneapolis: *17 Days and 4 Minutes* (Werner Egk)

Chicago: Theodor Uppman, *Billy Budd* (Benjamin Britten, premiere); Birgit Nilsson, *Turandot;* Marilyn Horne, *L'Italiana in Algieri* (Rossini)

San Francisco: Completes four-year *Ring* cycle; Geraint Evans, *Falstaff*

Music Notes
Unconventional efforts to enlarge audiences continue throughout the United States • The Los Angeles Philharmonic tries to enlarge its audience with "Contemporary '70–20th Century Music: How It Was, How It Is," a fusion of the classics and rock • On national TV: *Switched-On Symphony* (classical/rock).

Art _____

Painting

Philip Pearlstein, *Two Female Nudes with Red Drape*

Philip Guston, *Courtroom, Cellar*

Jim Dine, *Twenty Hearts*

Vija Celmins, *Ocean Image*

Richard Hamilton, *Kent State*

Red Grooms, *The Discount Store*

Alice Neel, *Andy Warhol*

Alfred Leslie, *Act and Portrait* (1968–70)

Dorothea Rockburne, *A, C and D from Group/ And*

Romare Bearden, *Patchwork Quilt*

Wayne Thiebaud, *Still Life with Bowl*

Sculpture

Robert Smithson, *Spiral Jetty*

Jackie Ferrara, *Untitled*

Eva Hesse, *Untitled (Seven Poles)*

Architecture

John Hancock Center, Chicago (Skidmore, Owings and Merrill)

Central Library, University of California, San Diego (William L. Pereira)

Knights of Columbus Building, New Haven, Conn. (Roche and Dinkeloo)

Mailman Clinic, Miami (Ferendino, Grafton, Spillis and Candela)

John F. Kennedy Memorial, Dallas (Philip Johnson)

Hyatt House, Chicago (Portman, Grafton, Spillis)

Outdoor Theatre, Santa Fe, N.M. (Paolo Soleri)

Sculpture Museum, New Canaan, Conn. (Philip Johnson)

Buckminster Fuller. *Movie Star News*.

San Francisco, Washington, Detroit, Whitney: "The Reality of Appearance": William Harnett, J. F. Peto, John Haberle

Washington: Robert Morris retrospective; Selections from the Nathan Cummings collection

Detroit: Robert Morris retrospective

Art Briefs

The U.S. Pavilion at the Japan World's Fair ignores traditionalism; prominent is Andy Warhol's *Rain Curtain* • Artists join in political and social protest such as "The New York Artists' Strike against Racism, Sexism, Repression, War"; numerous shows collect funds for antiwar political candidates • Jacques Lipchitz begins large-scale commissions for the Municipal Plaza in Philadelphia and Columbia University • The University of Wisconsin opens a $3.5 million Elvehjem Art Center; other museums open at the University of California (Berkeley) and SUNY (Purchase) • Major sales include Cézanne's *Study of His Father* ($1.5 million) and Andy Warhol's *Campbell Soup Can with Peeling Label* ($60,000).

Important Exhibitions

Museums

New York: *Metropolitan:* Before Cortès; Sculpture of Middle America; "The Year 1200"; New York Painting and Sculpture (Pollock, Calder, Rauschenberg); 19th-Century America; Masterpieces of Painting from the Boston Museum of Fine Arts. *Museum of Modern Art:* Stella, Archipenko, Oldenburg retrospectives; Hector Guimard. *Whitney:* Nineteenth-century trompe l'oeil; "The Reality of Appearance"; "New Realism": William Bailey, Jack Beal, John Clarke, Alfred Leslie, Wayne Thiebaud

Boston: Afro-American artists—Alvin Loving, Bill Rivers, Jack White, Norman Lewis, "New York and Boston"

Chicago: Brancusi retrospective

Dance _____

Natalia Makarova joins the American Ballet Theatre and debuts in *Giselle*.

Alvin Ailey tours North Africa prior to visiting the USSR on a cultural exchange program.

Premieres

American Ballet Theatre: Thirtieth anniversary, *The River* (Alvin Ailey, Duke Ellington)

New York City Ballet: *Who Cares?* (George Balanchine), Patricia McBride, Jacques d'Amboise; *In the Night* (Jerome Robbins)

Joffrey: *Trinity* (Gerald Arpino)

National Ballet of Washington: *Cinderella* (Ben Stevenson)

Books

Fiction

Critics' Choice
Mr. Sammler's Planet, Saul Bellow
Islands in the Stream, Ernest Hemingway (posthumous)
Jeremy's Version, James Purdy
The Estate, A Friend of Kafka, Isaac Bashevis Singer
Bech: A Book, John Updike
The Perfectionist, Gail Godwin
Standing Fast, Harvey Swados
Going All the Way, Dan Wakefield
The Stunt Man, Paul Brodeur
❧ *One Hundred Years of Solitude*, Gabriel García Márquez

Best-Sellers
Love Story, Erich Segal
The French Lieutenant's Woman, John Fowles
Deliverance, James Dickey
Great Lion of God, Taylor Caldwell
The Crystal Cave, Mary Stewart
The Gang That Couldn't Shoot Straight, Jimmy Breslin
Travels with My Aunt, Graham Greene
God Is an Englishman, R. F. Delderfield
The Secret Woman, Victoria Holt
Calico Palace, Gwen Bristow

Nonfiction

Critics' Choice
Jefferson and the Presidency: First Term, 1801–1805, Dumas Malone
Sexual Politics, Kate Millett
On Violence, Hannah Arendt
Future Shock, Alvin Toffler
George Washington and the New Nation, James T. Flexner
Science in the British Colonies of America, Raymond Phineas Stearns
Hard Times: An Oral History of the Great Depression, Studs Terkel
Nixon Agonistes, Garry Wills
My Lai 4, Seymour M. Hersh
The Game of Nations, Miles Copeland
Cocteau, Francis Steegmuller
The End of the American Era, Andrew Hacker
The Limits of Intervention, Townsend Hoopes
The Greening of America, Charles Reich

Best-Sellers
Everything You Always Wanted to Know about Sex but Were Afraid to Ask, David Reuben
The New English Bible
The Sensuous Woman, "J"
American Heritage Dictionary of the English Language, ed. William Morris

Up the Organization, Robert Townsend
Ball Four, Jim Bouton
Zelda, Nancy Milford
Inside the Third Reich, Albert Speer
Body Language, Julius Fast
Human Sexual Inadequacy, William Masters, Virginia E. Johnson

Poetry
Robert Creeley, *The Finger: Poems 1966–1969*
Nikki Giovanni, *Black Talk / Black Judgement*
John Berryman, *Love and Fame*
Robert Lowell, *Notebook 1967–1968*
Don Lee, *Walk the Way of the New World*
James Dickey: *The Eye-Beaters, Blood, Victory, Madness, Buckhead, and Mercy*
Philip Levine, *5 Detroits*

Pulitzer Prizes
No prize is awarded in fiction.
Roosevelt: The Soldier of Freedom, James McGregor Burns (U.S. history)
The Rising Sun, John Toland (nonfiction)
Robert Frost: The Years of Triumph, 1915–1938, Lawrance Thompson (biography)
The Carrier of Ladders, W. S. Merwin (poetry)

Science and Technology

University of Wisconsin scientists, led by Har Gobind Khorana, perform the first complete synthesis of a gene.

The IBM Model 145 is the first mainframe computer to use monolithic semiconductor circuits for the entire main memory.

The floppy disc, a computer storage record, is introduced by the IBM 3740.

The FDA approves Lithium for the treatment of manic-depression and L-DOPA for the treatment of Parkinson's disease.

The FDA warns that "the pill" can cause blood clots.

The first known survivor from rabies is a six-year-old who is treated with vigorous supportive measures.

Lasers are used to improve bombing accuracy.

Nobel Prize
Julius Axelrod wins the prize in physiology and medicine for work on human nerve impulse transmission.

Sports

Baseball

Curt Flood (St. Louis, NL) sues the major leagues for contractual freedom and loses.

Hank Aaron (Atlanta, NL) and Willie Mays (San Francisco, NL) both get their 3,000th hit.

Jim Bunning (Philadelphia, NL) becomes the first pitcher to win 100 games in each league.

Tom Seaver (New York, NL) strikes out 19 men in a nine-inning game, the last 10 in a row.

The Cy Young awards go to Bob Gibson (St. Louis, NL) and Jim Perry (Minnesota, AL).

Champions

Batting
Rico Carty (Atlanta, NL), .366
Alex Johnson (California, AL), .329
Pitching

Bob Gibson (St. Louis, NL), 23–7
Miguel Cuellar (Baltimore, AL), 23–8
Home runs
Johnny Bench (Cincinnati, NL), 45

Football

The NFL and AFL merge into the NFL with an NFC and AFC.

NFC Season Leaders: John Brodie (San Francisco), passing; Larry Brown (Washington), rushing; Dick Gordon (Chicago), passing

AFC Season Leaders: Darryl Lamonica (Oakland), passing; Floyd Little (Denver), rushing; Fred Biletnikof (Oakland), receiving

College All-Americans: Joe Theisman (Q), Notre Dame; Jim Stillwagon (MG), Ohio State; Jack Ham (LB), Penn State

Bowls (Jan. 1, 1971)

Rose: Stanford 27–Ohio State 17
Orange: Nebraska 17–Louisiana State 12

Cotton: Notre Dame 24–Texas 11
Sugar: Tennessee 24–Air Force 13

Basketball

NBA All-Pro Team: Billy Cunningham (Philadelphia), Connie Hawkins (Phoenix), Willis Reed (New York), Jerry West (Los Angeles), Walt Frazier (New York)

Other Sports

Hockey: Bobby Orr, 23, Boston Bruins, scores 120 points, a record for a defenseman.

Boxing: Muhammad Ali returns to boxing with a third round TKO over Jerry Quarry.

Winners

World Series
Baltimore (AL) 4
Cincinnati (NL) 1
MVP
NL–Johnny Bench, Cincinnati
AL–Boog Powell, Baltimore
Super Bowl V (Jan. 1971)
Baltimore 16–Dallas 13
MVP
John Brodie, San Francisco
College Football
Texas (UPI)
Nebraska (AP)
Heisman Trophy
Jim Plunkett, Stanford
NBA Championship
New York 4–Los Angeles 3

MVP
Willis Reed, New York
College Basketball
UCLA
Player of the Year
Pete Maravich, Louisiana State
Stanley Cup
Boston
US Tennis Open
Men: Ken Rosewall
Women: Margaret Smith Court
USGA Open
Tony Jacklin
Kentucky Derby
Dust Commander (M. Manganello, jockey)

Fashion

For Women: Freedom in fashion is unprecedented: skirts are all lengths; pants are worn for any occasion; young people shop in army-navy surplus stores and thrift shops for the eclectic look; the thirties' influence is still felt. The slow demise of the mini appears as the polo dress and slithering look take over. The "midi" shows up in early spring at mid-calf lengths in denims, ginghams, and cinch-waist skirts. Heavy wool skirts are slit or buttoned, and dark stockings and boots are worn with everything. Long trench coats of canvas, leather, vinyl, and poplin are also worn over everything; men dislike the midi (64 percent), and during the controversy, pants and pant-sets prevail for all occasions and jobs; they appear in every shape, fabric, and design: straight-legged, to midcalf (gaucho), knickers, jumpsuits, blue jeans, in velvets with tunics. Anything ethnic or folksy is also fashionable, especially the Indian/Eastern Indian peasant look: cross stitching, feathers, fringes, deerskin, and beaded headbands. Cosmetics become "pure"; hair teasing is out; the Afro is chic for both blacks and whites; makeup is natural and subtle, with blush used to give a healthy, shining look; more makeup is used to give a less made-up look.

High-fashion notes: Blass's Persian embroidery, gaucho hat and Zhivago boots; de la Renta's "steppe" look.

Kaleidoscope ⎯⎯⎯⎯⎯⎯

Mr. and Mrs. David Bowie, who favor futuristic costumes. *Movie Star News.*

- A bomb is planted in the math building at the University of Wisconsin as a protest against war research; a student working late is killed.
- A Greenwich Village townhouse in New York is destroyed by an explosion in what is believed to be a "bomb factory" of a radical group known as the Weathermen; three bodies are found.
- Nearly 100,000 students demonstrate in Washington; Nixon, unable to sleep, goes to the Lincoln Memorial before dawn to address them.
- Six construction workers are arrested after they attack 70 students carrying antiwar posters at Pace College in New York. Union leader Peter Brennan presents Nixon with an honorary hard hat.
- Nixon orders the Scranton committee to gather information about campus unrest; the committee reports a counterculture dedicated to "humanity, equality, and the sacredness of life."
- Agricultural scientist Norman Borlaug wins the Nobel Peace Prize.
- At demonstrations celebrating the 50th anniversary of the Nineteenth Amendment, sample placards read: "REPENT MALE CHAUVINISTS, YOUR WORLD IS COMING TO AN END," "DON'T COOK DINNER TONIGHT—STARVE A RAT TODAY,"and "DON'T IRON WHILE THE STRIKE IS HOT."
- Environmentalists and ecologists sponsor Earth Day (April 22), a national teach-in to publicize the problems of the environment.
- The amount of collected urban garbage, per capita, has risen from 2.75 pounds per day (1920) to 5 pounds per day.
- As boots become a fad, Golo Footwear sells 100,000 $30 patent leather boots in two months.
- An estimated 69,000 abortions are performed in the first six months after the New York state abortion law takes effect.
- The smallest ratio of men to women in history is recorded: 94.8 to 100.
- The National Research Council tells expectant mothers not to restrict weight gain; 20 to 25 pounds is desirable.
- Construction at "Acrosanti," Cords Junction, Arizona, begins for a ten-acre, ecologically sound environment for 3,000 people in 25-story buildings.
- Alexander Calder designs 74 feet of sidewalk on Madison Avenue, New York, in front of the Karl Perls Gallery.
- Slogans for the three major TV stations reflect current usage: "It's Happening on NBC!" "Let's Get it Together on ABC," and "We're Putting It All Together on CBS."
- "Let It Be," "Jesus Christ Superstar," and "Spirit in the Sky" mark the religious trend in rock music.
- Allstate Insurance Company offers to cut rates as much as 20 percent if manufacturers will improve the resistance of their bumpers to low-speed crash damage.
- The FDA orders a massive recall of canned tuna for possible mercury poisoning.

- An independent postal service replaces the U.S. Post Office.
- The Supreme Court rules that if necessary, trial judges may bind, gag, jail, or expel from court unruly defendants.
- Jane Alpert, convicted of bombing "military and war-related corporate buildings" in New York, breaks bail and goes underground.
- Financier Robert Vesco arranges a loan to save Bernie Cornfeld's International Overseas Services.
- With Howard Hughes in seclusion in the Bahamas, legal maneuverings over the control of his vast financial empire begin.
- Pop rock folk documentaries such as "Gimme Shelter" and "Woodstock" become a new genre.
- Health food sales rise to $3 billion.
- Vassar College becomes coed.
- The Bureau of Census reports that 143,000 unmarried couples live together (17,000 in 1960); a *New York Times* survey estimates that there are 2,000 communes in the United States.

Fads: Wigs, Mickey Mouse watches, sweatshirts

New Words and Usages: Fortran, ergonomics, psycho-technology, blahs, fast-food, head shop, hype, megafamily, Oreo, plastic (credit), ripoff, sexploitation, T-group, marathon group, sensitivity training, encounter group, Jesus people, hassle, putdown, trash, preppie, radical chic

First Appearances: Quadraphonic sound and records, commercial videophone, Gray Panthers, safety tops on drugs and dangerous products like turpentine, electronic editing terminal for newspapers, 30 cents New York City subway fare (20 cents since 1966), commissioned women generals, nun in the air force, cabinet member to serve in four different capacities (Elliot Richardson), no-fault divorce law (California), no-fault auto insurance (Massachusetts), lottery with $1 million top prize (New York City), European king buried in United States (Peter Karageorgevich), Boeing 747 transatlantic service (Pan American), ambulatory surgical facility independently operated (Surgicenter, Phoenix), woman jockey to ride in the Kentucky Derby (Diane Crump), strike of postal employees

1971

In the News

PRIEST DANIEL BERRIGAN IS CHARGED WITH CONSPIRACY TO KIDNAP HENRY KISSINGER . . . ROBERT BYRD OUSTS TED KENNEDY AS SENATE MAJORITY WHIP . . . IDI AMIN BECOMES UGANDA RULER . . . APOLLO XIV LANDS ON MOON . . . TREATY IS SIGNED TO KEEP NUKES OFF OCEAN FLOOR . . . BOMB DAMAGES SENATE FLOOR . . . CHARLES MANSON AND HIS "FAMILY" ARE SENTENCED TO DEATH . . . LIEUTENANT WILLIAM CALLEY IS FOUND GUILTY IN MY LAI MASSACRE . . . SOCIALIST SALVADOR ALLENDE WINS CHILE ELECTION . . . FIRST LEGALIZED OFF-TRACK BETTING BEGINS IN N.Y. . . . CHOU EN-LAI WELCOMES U.S. PING PONG TEAM . . . "NEW YORK TIMES" PUBLISHES PENTAGON PAPERS, DANIEL ELLSBERG IS ARRESTED FOR THEIR DISCLOSURE . . . SUPREME COURT UPHOLDS BUSING FOR DESEGREGATION . . . 200,000 RALLY AGAINST VIETNAM WAR IN WASHINGTON, D.C. . . . SUPREME COURT SAYS THAT JURIES CAN PASS DEATH SENTENCE . . . NIXON INSTITUTES WAGE AND PRICE CONTROLS . . . BRITAIN WILL ENTER COMMON MARKET . . . NIXON ENDS 21-YEAR TRADE EMBARGO ON CHINA . . . PRISONERS RIOT AT ATTICA, 10 HOSTAGES AND 39 CONVICTS DIE AS TALKS FAIL . . . HUNGARIAN CARDINAL MINDSZENTY IS EXILED TO ROME . . . SHAH CELEBRATES PERSIA'S 2500TH ANNIVERSARY . . . UN VOTES TO SEAT PEKING . . . U.S. WILL SELL $136 MILLION IN LIVESTOCK TO USSR . . . 45,000 MORE TROOPS ARE RECALLED FROM VIETNAM . . . INDIA AND PAKISTAN FIGHT IN EAST PAKISTAN, U.S. BRANDS INDIA AGGRESSOR . . . AIR ATTACKS ON NORTH VIETNAM INCREASE . . . 26TH AMENDMENT IS PASSED, LOWERING THE VOTING AGE TO 18 . . . NIXON ANNOUNCES HE WILL VISIT CHINA . . . NIXON SEVERS GOLD-DOLLAR TIE AND ASKS TAX CUT, STOCK MARKET LEAPS RECORD 32.93 . . . VIETNAM: U.S. TROOP STRENGTH, 152,000; U.S. DEAD, 45,543.

Feminist and editor of *Ms.* magazine, Gloria Steinem. *Courtesy of* Ms.

"I've suffered more as a woman than as a black."
— Shirley Chisholm

"Eliminating the patriarchal and racist base of the existing social system requires a revolution, not a reform."
— *Ms.* magazine, first issue

"A woman's liberty and right to privacy may include the right to remove an unwanted child."
— Gerhard Gesell, federal judge

"Let me make one thing perfectly clear. I wouldn't want to wake up next to a lady pipefitter."
— Richard M. Nixon (quoted in *Ms.*)

"Send me your poor, your deadbeats, your filthy . . . all of them free to live together in peace and harmony in their little, separate sections where they feel safe, and break your head if you go in there."
— Archie Bunker, "All in the Family"

Quotes

"We are men. We are not beasts. We only want to live."
— Attica inmates

"There was the whole rule of law to consider . . . the whole fabric of society."
— Governor Nelson Rockefeller, on Attica

"It is indisputably clear . . . that the Justice Department was simply wrong as a matter of law in advising that [Muhammad] Ali's beliefs were not religiously based and were not sincerely held."
— Supreme Court ruling

"The Constitution is larger than the executive branch."
— Daniel Ellsberg

"Every senator in this chamber is partly responsible for sending 50,000 young Americans to an early grave."
— Senator George McGovern (D-S. Dak.)

Jack Klugman and Tony Randall in "The Odd Couple": "Can two divorced men share an apartment without driving each other crazy?" *Movie Star News.*

Ads

I can't believe I ate the whole thing!
(Alka Seltzer)

Should a Tough Man Make a Tender Turkey?
(Frank Perdue Poultry)

In a 45 m.p.h. crash, the average head hits the average windshield with a force of over a ton.—We want you to live.
(Mobil)

Your wife deserves something sexy for Christmas. So do you.
(Dreyer and Meyer Nightgowns)

99% of all babies are born with perfect feet. Too bad they don't stay that way.
(Jumping Jacks)

What the well undressed man is wearing this year.
(Jockey International Shorts)

Clap
In Minnesota, it's not applause. Dial out VD. (612) 339–7055
(Public Service Ad)

TV

Premieres

"All in the Family," Carroll O'Connor, Jean Stapleton

"The Sonny and Cher Comedy Hour"

"Owen Marshall, Counselor at Law," Arthur Hill, Lee Majors

"Columbo," Peter Falk

"Cannon," William Conrad

"McMillan and Wife," Susan St. James, Rock Hudson

Top Ten (Nielsen)

"All in the Family," "The Flip Wilson Show," "Marcus Welby, M.D.," "Gunsmoke," "ABC Movie of the Week," "Sanford and Son," "Mannix," "Funny Face," "Adam 12," "The Mary Tyler Moore Show"

Specials

"Brian's Song" (James Caan, Lou Gossett); "The Selling of the Pentagon" (Peter Davis); "Elizabeth R"; "Beethoven's Birthday: A Celebration in Vienna with Leonard Bernstein"; "Look Homeward, Angel" (Ben Edwards); "The Pentagon Papers" (PBS); "The China Trip" (ABC); "The Homecoming"; "The Six Wives of Henry VIII"

Emmy Awards

"Elizabeth R" (drama); "All in the Family" (comedy); "The Carol Burnett Show" (variety); "Sesame Street" (children); Peter Falk (actor, "Columbo"); Carroll O'Connor (comedic actor, "All in the Family"); Glenda Jackson (actress, "Elizabeth R"); Jean Stapleton (comedic actress, "All in the Family")

Of Note

After much debate, the three major networks agree to limit prime time to 8:00–11:00 P.M. • John Chancellor becomes solo anchor on NBC nightly news.

Movies

Openings

The French Connection (William Friedkin), Gene Hackman, Fernando Rey, Roy Scheider

A Clockwork Orange (Stanley Kubrick), Malcolm McDowell, Patrick Magee

The Last Picture Show (Peter Bogdanovich), Timothy Bottoms, Jeff Bridges, Ben Johnson, Cloris Leachman, Ellen Burstyn, Eileen Brennan

Sunday, Bloody Sunday (John Schlesinger), Peter Finch, Glenda Jackson

The Hospital (Arthur Hiller), George C. Scott, Diana Rigg

McCabe and Mrs. Miller (Robert Altman), Julie Christie, Warren Beatty

The Go-Between (Joseph Losey), Julie Christie, Alan Bates

Carnal Knowledge (Mike Nichols), Jack Nicholson, Candice Bergen, Arthur Garfunkel, Ann-Margret

The Garden of the Finzi-Continis (Vittorio De Sica), Dominique Sanda

Summer of '42 (Robert Mulligan), Jennifer O'Neill, Gary Grimes

Diamonds Are Forever (Guy Hamilton), Sean Connery, Jill St. John

Klute (Alan J. Pakula), Jane Fonda, Donald Sutherland

Shaft (Gordon Parks), Richard Roundtree, Moses Gunn

Bananas (Woody Allen), Woody Allen, Louise Lasser

Dirty Harry (Don Siegel), Clint Eastwood, Harry Guardino

Harold and Maude (Hal Ashby), Ruth Gordon, Bud Cort

Academy Awards

Best Picture: *The French Connection*

Best Director: William Friedkin (*The French Connection*)

Best Actress: Jane Fonda (*Klute*)

Best Actor: Gene Hackman (*The French Connection*)

Top Box-Office Stars

John Wayne, Clint Eastwood, Paul Newman, Steve McQueen, George C. Scott, Dustin Hoffman, Walter Matthau, Ali MacGraw, Sean Connery, Lee Marvin

Stars of Tomorrow

Jennifer O'Neill, Karen Black, Gary Grimes, Sally Kellerman, Arthur Garfunkel, Bruce Davison, Richard Roundtree, Deborah Winters, Jane Alexander, Rosalind Cash

Popular Music

Hit Songs
"How Can You Mend a Broken Heart?"
"Rainy Days and Mondays"
"Joy to the World"
"Maggie May"
"One Bad Apple"
"Got to Be There"
"Theme from *Shaft*"
"Ain't No Sunshine"

Top Records

Albums: *All Things Must Pass* (George Harrison); *Jesus Christ Superstar* (various artists); *Pearl* (Janis Joplin); *Tapestry* (Carole King); *Santana* (Santana)

Singles: *Family Affair* (Sly and the Family Stone); *Got to Be There* (Michael Jackson); *All I Ever Need Is You* (Sonny and Cher); *It's Too Late* (Carole King); *She's a Lady* (Tom Jones); *That's the Way I've Always Heard It Should Be* (Carly Simon); *Every Picture Tells a Story* (Rod Stewart); *Take Me Home, Country Roads* (John Denver with Fat City); *Go Away Little Girl* (Donny Osmond). Country: *Rose Garden* (Lynn Anderson); *Help Me Make It through the Night* (Sammi Smith)

Grammy Awards
It's Too Late, Carole King (record); *Tapestry,* Carole King (album); "You've Got a Friend," Carole King (song)

Jazz and Big Bands
T.T.T. (Twelve Tone Tune) is recorded by Bill Evans.

Top Performers *(Downbeat):* Miles Davis, Charles Mingus (soloists); Duke Ellington (band); Miles Davis (jazz group); Kenny Burrell, Richard Davis, Herbie Hancock, Buddy Rich, Cannonball Adderley (instrumentalists); Roberta Flack, Leon Thomas (vocalists); Frank Zappa (rock/blues musician); Blood Sweat, and Tears (vocal group); Weather Report, (album)

Theater

Broadway Openings

Plays
The Prisoner of Second Avenue (Neil Simon), Lee Grant, Peter Falk
Twigs (George Furth), Sada Thompson
Lenny (Julian Barry), Cliff Gorman, Joe Silver
And Miss Reardon Drinks a Little (Paul Zindel), Estelle Parsons, Julie Harris, Nancy Marchand
Abelard and Heloise (Ronald Millar), Keith Mitchell, Diana Rigg
How the Other Half Loves (Alan Ayckbourn), Phil Silvers, Sandy Dennis
Old Times (Harold Pinter), Robert Shaw, Mary Ure, Rosemary Harris
All Over (Edward Albee), Jessica Tandy, Colleen Dewhurst, George Voskovec, Betty Field
The Philanthropist (Christopher Hampton), Alec McCowen

Musicals
Follies (Stephen Sondheim), Alexis Smith, Dorothy Collins, Gene Nelson, Yvonne DeCarlo
No, No, Nanette (Vincent Youmans, revival), Ruby Keeler, Helen Gallagher, Patsy Kelly, Jack Gilford
Jesus Christ Superstar (Andrew Lloyd Webber, Tim Rice), Jeff Fenholt, Ben Vereen
Ain't Supposed to Die a Natural Death (Melvin Van Peebles), Carl Gordon, Barbara Alston

Two Gentlemen of Verona (Galt MacDermot, John Guare), Raul Julia, Clifton Davis, Jonelle Allen
Godspell (Stephen Schwartz), David Haskell

Classics, Revivals, and Off-Broadway Premieres
The Trial of the Catonsville Nine (Daniel Berrigan), Sam Waterston, Michael Moriarty; *A Doll's House* (Ibsen), Claire Bloom; *Hamlet,* Judith Anderson (as Hamlet); *Hedda Gabler* (Ibsen), Claire Bloom, Donald Madden; *Othello,* James Earl Jones; *Waiting for Godot* (Samuel Beckett), Tom Ewell; *Long Day's Journey into Night* (Eugene O'Neill), Robert Ryan, Stacy Keach, Geraldine Fitzgerald; *School for Wives* (Molière, Richard Wilbur), Brian Bedford; *Sticks and Bones* (David Rabe), Tom Aldredge; *The House of Blue Leaves* (John Guare), William Atherton, Anne Meara

Regional

Long Wharf, New Haven: *Solitaire, Double Solitaire* (Robert Anderson), Martha Schlamme

Ivanhoe, Chicago: *Out Cry* (Tennessee Williams)

Arena Stage, Washington, D.C.: *The Ruling Class*

Theater (cont.)

(Peter Barnes); *Moonchildren* (Michael Weller), premieres

Washington Theatre Club, D.C.: *The Web and the Rock* (Dolores Sutton), premiere

Mark Taper Forum, Los Angeles: *The National Health* (Peter Nichols); *The Trial of the Catonsville Nine* (Daniel Berrigan), Beau Bridges, James Daly, Peter Strauss, Anthony Zerbe, premieres

Yale Repertory Theatre: *Where Has Tommy Flowers Gone* (Terrence McNally) Henry Winkler, premiere

Classical Music

Compositions
Roger Sessions, Concerto for Viola and Cello
Aaron Copland, Duo for Flute and Piano
Peter Mennin, Sinfonia for Orchestra
Karl Korte, *Remembrances* (for Flute and Tape)
Lawrence Moss, *Auditions*
George Crumb, *Songs, Drones and Refrains of Death*
Mario Davidovsky, *Synchronisms,* no. 6
Jacob Druckman, *Windows*

Important Events
The John F. Kennedy Center for the Performing Arts, Washington, D.C., opens with a variety of concerts: Leonard Bernstein's *Mass,* with 200 participants, jazz and taped material, and the Alvin Ailey Dance Company; the National Symphony (Antal Dorati) and the premiere of Alberto Ginastera's *Beatrix Cenci.* During the year the varied programs include Beverly Sills, *Ariodante, Candide,* Eugene Istomin–Isaac Stern–Leonard Rose, and the Fifth Dimension.
Pierre Boulez becomes director of the New York Philharmonic and performs the avant-garde; he conducts the Juilliard Ensemble in "New and Newer Music." Boulez plans "preconcerts," recitals for subscription holders.
Alexander Schneider celebrates the New School's (New York) 40th anniversary with Pinchas Zukerman and Peter Serkin.
For Roger Sessions's 75th birthday, Virgil Thomson and the New York Philharmonic premiere *Nativity* and perform *The Mother of Us All.*

Other New Facilities: Heinz Hall for the Performing Arts (Pittsburgh); University of Michigan Power Center for the Performing Arts; Wolf Trap Farm Park, Vienna, Va.

Leading opera stars Joan Sutherland and Marilyn Horne in *Semiramide. Chicago Lyric Opera.*

Debut: Pinchas Zukerman, Yo-Yo Ma

First Performances
Ingolf Dahl, Saxophone Concerto (New York); Dmitri Shostakovich, Symphony no. 4; Lalo Schifrin, *Pulsations* (Los Angeles); Pablo Casals, 94, conducting, *Hymn to the United Nations* (UN); Samuel Barber, *The Lovers* (Philadelphia)

Opera

Metropolitan: Rudolph Bing retires after 22 years of managing the company and is knighted by Queen Elizabeth. Goeran Gentele replaces him and dies in December; Schuyler G. Chapin takes over. James Levine debuts, conducting *Tosca.* Birgit Nilsson, Jess Thomas, *Tristan und Isolde;* Luigi Alva, *L'elisir d'amore;* Adriana Maliponte (debut), *La bohème;* Stuart Burrows (debut), *Don Giovanni;* William Dooley, *Fidelio*

Boston: Beverly Sills, *Norma*

Minneapolis: *The Mother of Us All; Faust Counter Faust* (H. Wesley Balk)

St. Paul: *Summer and Smoke* (Lee Hoiby)

Santa Fe: *Yerma* (Heitor Villa-Lobos, premiere)

Chicago: Joan Sutherland, Marilyn Horne, *Semiramide*

San Francisco: Christa Ludwig, *Der Rosenkavalier*

Art

Painting

Helen Frankenthaler, *Chairman of the Board*
Audrey Flack, *Macarena of Miracles*
Al Held, *Black Nile III*
Jack Tworkov, *Partitions*
Richard Estes, *Helena's Florist*
Richard Artschwager, *Doors*
Red Grooms, *Mr. and Mrs. Rembrandt*
Jasper Johns, *Decoy*
Ellsworth Kelly, *Chatham XI, Blue, Yellow*
Richard Diebenkorn, *Ocean Park, N. 36*

Sculpture

Mark di Suvero, *Il Ook*
Robert Morris, *Observatory*
Claes Oldenburg, *Three Way Plug, Scale A (Soft), Prototype in Blue*
Alexander Calder, *Animobiles*
Lynda Benglis, *For Darkness: Situation and Circumstance*
Michael Heizer, *Adze Dispersal*
Hammarskjöld Plaza, United Nations, New York (Alexander Liberman)
Welded steel construction, Seagram Building, New York (Louise Nevelson)

Architecture

Cleo Rodgers Memorial Library, Columbia, Ind. (I. M. Pei)
Bank of America, San Francisco (Wurster and Associates)
Hyatt-Regency Hotel, San Francisco (John C. Portman)
New Haven Pre-Fab Housing (Paul Rudolph)
John F. Kennedy Center for the Performing Arts, Washington, D.C. (Edward Durell Stone)
Lyndon Baines Johnson Library, Austin, Texas (Skidmore, Owings and Merrill)
Mummer's Theater, Oklahoma City, Okla. (John Johnson)
National Airlines Terminal, J. F. Kennedy Airport, New York (I. M. Pei)

Important Exhibitions

Albrecht Dürer's 500th birthday and Picasso's 90th birthday prompt shows throughout the United States. The Marin and Sloan centennial shows travel widely.

Museums

New York: *Metropolitan:* "The Cubist Epoch"; Joseph Cornell; "Arts from the Rooftops of Asia"; Dürer; "Greek and Roman Art: Triumphs and Tribulations." *Museum of Modern Art:* "The Collections of Gertrude Stein and Her Family"; Marin Centennial; Retrospectives: Philip Johnson, Kevin Roche, Paul Rudolph. *Whitney:* O'Keeffe, Eakins

Philadelphia: "The Multiple": Duchamp, Warhol, Oldenburg, Vasarely

Washington: Cézanne; Ingres; Sloan centennial

Boston: Zen painting and calligraphy; "Earth, Air, Water, Fire: Elements of Art" (live show)

Baltimore, San Francisco: Matisse

Minneapolis: Dutch masters

Chicago, San Francisco: Vuillard

Art Briefs

Avant-garde exhibitions include various "confrontation shows," the new "street" and "wall" artists, the "new realists," the minimalists, and pop. The Guggenheim Museum in New York sponsors a show of kinetic sculpture as a metaphor for the creative process • The Salvador Dali Museum in Cleveland opens • The Whitney's "Contemporary Black Artists in America" becomes controversial because of the museum's lack of a black curator; eight well-known artists reply to the article "Why Have There Been No Great Women Artists?" and a long public controversy follows. The Whitney and Brooklyn museums hold shows of women artists. The Museum of Modern Art sponsors "The Artist as Adversary" • The Metropolitan Museum of Art pays a record $5,544,000 for a Velasquez portrait.

Dance

The American Ballet Theatre is named the official company of the John F. Kennedy Center for the Performing Arts.
Dance Company of Harlem is founded by Arthur Mitchell and Karel Shook.
The Joffrey dances at Filene Center, Wolf Trap Farm Park, the first national park for the performing arts.

Premieres

New York City Ballet: *The Goldberg Variations* (Jerome Robbins), Gelsey Kirkland, Peter Martins

Joffrey: *Feast of Ashes* (Alvin Ailey)

National Ballet of Washington: *The Sleeping Beauty* (Marius Petipa, full-length version), Margot Fonteyn

Alvin Ailey: *Cry* (Alvin Ailey, Alice Coltrane, Laura Nyro), Judith Jamison; *Flowers* (Ailey, Big Brother and the Holding Company, Janis Joplin), Lynn Seymour

Books

Fiction
Critics' Choice
Blood Oranges, John Hawkes
City Life, Donald Barthelme
Being There, Jerzy Kosinski
The Tenants, Bernard Malamud
Birds of America, Mary McCarthy
Love in the Ruins, Walker Percy
The Pagan Rabbi and Other Stories, Cynthia Ozick
Fire Sermon, Wright Morris
Grendel, John Gardner
The Death and Life of Harry Goth, D. Keith Mano
The Complete Stories, Flannery O'Connor
&. *Maurice*, E. M. Forster (posthumous)

Best-Sellers
Wheels, Arthur Hailey
The Exorcist, William Peter Blatty
The Passions of the Mind, Irving Stone
The Day of the Jackal, Frederick Forsyth
The Betsy, Harold Robbins
The Winds of War, Herman Wouk
The Drifters, James Michener
The Other, Thomas Tryon
Rabbit Redux, John Updike

Nonfiction
Critics' Choice
Steal This Book, Abbie Hoffman
Ordeal of the Union, vols. 7, 8, Allan Nevins
Living on the Earth, Alicia Bay Laurel
The Female Eunuch, Germaine Greer
The Memoirs of Chief Ned Fox, Ned Fox
Fiction and the Figures of Life, William H. Gass
The Classic Style: Haydn, Mozart, Beethoven, Charles Rosen
The European Discovery of America, Samuel Eliot Morison
The Prisoner of Sex, Norman Mailer
Beyond Freedom and Dignity, B. F. Skinner
Roots of Involvement: The U.S. in Asia 1784–1971, Marvin Kalb, Elie Abel

Best-Sellers
The Sensuous Man, "M"
Bury My Heart at Wounded Knee, Dee Brown
Better Homes and Gardens Blender Cook Book
I'm O.K., You're O.K., Thomas Harris
Any Woman Can! David Reuben
Inside the Third Reich, Albert Speer
Honor Thy Father, Gay Talese
Fields of Wonder (poetry), Rod McKuen

Poetry
Anne Sexton, *Transformations*
Erica Jong, *Fruits and Vegetables*
Adrienne Rich, *The Will to Change: Poems 1968–1970*
A. R. Ammons, *Briefings: Poems Small and Easy*
David Shapiro, *A Man Holding an Acoustic Panel*
Diane Wakoski, *The Motorcycle Betrayal Poems*
Frank O'Hara, *The Collected Poems*
&. Ted Hughes, *Crow*

Pulitzer Prizes
Angle of Repose, Wallace Stegner (fiction)
Neither Black nor White: Slavery and Race Relations in Brazil and the United States, Carl N. Degler (U.S. history)
Stilwell and the American Experience in China, 1911–1945, Barbara W. Tuchman (nonfiction)
Eleanor and Franklin, Joseph P. Lash (biography)
Collected Poems, James Wright (poetry)

Science and Technology

Intel of California introduces the microprocessor, the "computer on a chip."
Illiac IV can handle 200 million instructions per second.
Direct dialing begins between New York and London.
Choh Hao Li, at the University of California, synthesizes the growth hormone, somatrotropin, for the treatment of pituitary dwarfism in children.
The USPHS no longer advises smallpox vaccination.
Diethylstilbesterol (DES), used since the 1930s to prevent miscarriage, is found to be carcinogenic for children of those pregnancies.
Interest in acupuncture revives.
The world's largest proton accelerator is built at Batavia, Illinois.
Apollo XIV, manned by Alan Shepard, Allen Roosa, and Edgar Mitchell, explores the moon's surface.
Apollo XV, manned by David Scott, Alfred Worden, and James Irwin, utilizes the lunar roving vehicle, spends 18 hours EVA time, and gathers 180 pounds of samples.
Mariner IX orbits Mars.
&. The diamond-bladed scalpel is developed for eye microsurgery.

Nobel Prize
Earl Sutherland wins in chemistry for work on the enzyme cyclic AMP.

Sports

Baseball

A special commission is formed to select Negro League players for the Baseball Hall of Fame.

The Supreme Court upholds baseball's "unique exemption" from antitrust laws.

Willie Mays scores his 1,950th run.

Rookie Vida Blue (Oakland, AL) wins the MVP and Cy Young Awards.

Ferguson Jenkins (Chicago, NL) also wins the Cy Young award.

Champions

Batting
Joe Torre (St. Louis, NL), .363
Tony Oliva (Minnesota, AL), .337
Pitching
Don Gullet (Cincinnati, NL), 16–6

Steve McNally (Baltimore, AL), 21–5
Home runs
Willie Stargell (Pittsburgh, NL), 48

Football

Joe Kapp begins an antitrust suit against the NFL.

NFC Season Leaders: Roger Staubach (Dallas), passing; John Brockington (Green Bay), rushing; Bob Tucker (New York Giants), receiving
AFC Season Leaders: Bob Griese (Miami), passing; Floyd Little (Denver), rushing; Fred Biletnikof (Oakland), receiving

College All-Americans: Gregg Pruitt (B), Oklahoma; Ed Marinaro (B), Cornell; Lydell Mitchell (B), Penn State

Bowls (Jan. 1, 1972)

Rose: Stanford 13–Michigan 12
Orange: Nebraska 38–Alabama 6

Cotton: Penn State 30–Texas 6
Sugar: Oklahoma 40–Auburn 22

Basketball

NBA All-Pro First Team: John Havlicek (Boston), Billy Cunningham (Philadelphia), Lew Alcindor (Milwaukee), Jerry West (Los Angeles), Dave Bing (Detroit)
ABA All-Pro First Team: Roger Brown (Indiana), Rick Barry (NY), Mel Daniels (Indiana), Mack Calvin (Floridians), Charlie Scott (Virginia)

Other Sports

Boxing: The Muhammad Ali–Joe Frazier fight draws the largest gate ever, with closed-circuit TV; Frazier wins in 15, and each earns $3.5 million.

Golf: Jack Nicklaus wins a record $244,000 on the pro tour. Ken Rosewall is the World Championship Tennis (WCT) champion.

Winners

World Series
Pittsburgh (NL) 4
Baltimore (AL) 3
MVP
NL–Joe Torre, St. Louis
AL–Vida Blue, Oakland
Super Bowl VI (Jan. 1972)
Dallas 24–Miami 3
MVP
Bob Griese, Miami
College Football
Nebraska
Heisman Trophy
Pat Sullivan, Auburn
NBA Championship
Milwaukee 4–Baltimore 0

MVP
Lew Alcindor, Milwaukee
College Basketball
UCLA
Player of the Year
Sidney Wicks, UCLA
Stanley Cup
Montreal
US Tennis Open
Men: Stan Smith
Women: Billie Jean King
USGA Open
Lee Trevino
Kentucky Derby
Canonero II (G. Avila, jockey)

Fashion

For Women: Hot pants save the day for the controversial midi, now used as a cover-up. No longer "drab and dowdy," it is slashed thigh high in front or on the side, revealing a sleek, booted, bare, or stockinged leg. Pants are suspendered and cuffed, worn below a bare midriff with a knit, velvet, or brocade vest and a number of varied accessories. Tie-dye shirts, slinky sweaters, halters, open-laced sandals, high and low boots, all in many colors, add to the wardrobe, Denim dungarees turn fashionable with do-it-yourself patches, butterflies, stars, and macramé belts. T-shirts are hand-painted with Disneyland pictures, but anything goes in front and back. The "military look" also becomes popular, with shoulder patches on coats, and insignias on everything from hot pants to bikinis. A nostalgia for the forties is apparent in wedgies and platform shoes, chubby jackets, and fake furs, the ¾-length pinstripe coat, herringbone tweeds, and striped skirts. Pants are pleated at the waist, worn with blouses flowing to the elbow or waist in soft, clinging fabrics with deep V necklines. Hems fall to about the knee. Hair is both long and short, cut to the shoulder but layered above in the shag or gypsy cut; teasing and spraying are out.

High-fashion notes: Syndica's layers of bubble-knit sweaters; Ungaro's hot pants

Kaleidoscope _____

- The *New York Times* publishes the first installment of "The Pentagon Papers" June 13, a secret (classified) history of American involvement in Vietnam since World War II.
- Seventy-five percent of those polled oppose the publication of "The Pentagon Papers"; 15 percent want to know more about "government secrecy."
- Attorney General John Mitchell denounces the federal courts for restricting his wiretapping privileges.
- The Supreme Court mandates busing as a means of school desegregation where no acceptable alternative is offered.
- President Nixon revives the Subversive Activities Control Board.
- Returning Vietnam veterans have an increasingly difficult time adjusting to a public that, according to a Harris Poll, considers them "suckers" for risking their lives "in the wrong place, at the wrong time."
- The Supreme Court rules that qualification for conscientious-objector status necessitates opposing all wars, not just Vietnam.
- Two thousand Vietnam veterans protest the war by throwing away their medals on the steps of the Capitol.
- The National Cancer Act is passed to provide $1.5 billion a year for research; the president has urged an all-out attempt to find a cure.
- The Senate votes down funding for an American supersonic transport, which leaves the field to the British-French Concorde.
- Nixon vetoes Congress's approval of the Child Development Act, which would authorize federal funding of child-care centers.
- A Yankelovich poll indicates that 34 percent of the general population believes marriage is obsolete, up from 24 percent in 1969.
- *Gourmet* magazine circulation doubles since 1967 to 550,000, and the fancy food industry rapidly expands.
- The Boston Women's Health Collective attacks the myth of the female vaginal orgasm and of lesbianism as a perversion.
- Mick and Bianca Jagger marry, and also become parents; Margaret Sinclair, 22, and Canadian prime minister Pierre Trudeau marry.
- A survey of upper-class women at a major eastern college indicates that 18 percent would stop working if they became mothers, compared with 59 percent in 1943.
- George Harrison appears in the Benefit for Bangladesh concert at Madison Square Garden.
- Diana Ross begins a solo career; the Beatles break up.
- Many traditional barbers go out of business or become hair stylists.
- Three-fourths of all moviegoers are under 30.
- Sears reprints its 1903, 1908, and 1927 catalogs after its 1902 edition sells 400,000 copies.
- William Reinquist becomes the fourth Nixon appointee to the Supreme Court.
- Ralph Nader contends that $1 billion is spent yearly

English model Twiggy, in *The Boyfriend;* her slender frame inspires a vogue. *Movie Star News.*

on worthless drugs and fraudulent home repairs.
- *Scientific American* devotes its September issue to "Energy and Power" and warns that the United States will face critical shortages by the year 2000.
- The FDA warns against mercury-tainted swordfish.
- Cigarette advertising is banned from TV.
- Beef consumption per capita rises from 113 pounds to 128.5 pounds.
- The nickel candy bar goes to 6 cents and 7 cents; Wrigley's gum is 10 cents for seven sticks (5 cents since 1893).
- Alleged Mafia leader Joseph Colombo organizes the Italo-American Unity Day in New York; at the parade, he is shot and left brain dead.
- *Look* magazine ceases publication.
- Billie Jean King becomes the first woman athlete to earn $100,000 in one year.

Fads: Gourmet foods, jogging, tote bags, directors' chairs

New Words and Usages: Think tank, demo, lib, body language, gross out, hot line, hot pants, right on, sexism, up front, workaholic

First Appearances: College with tuition based on family income (Beloit, Wisc.), the Jesus Movement, OTB, RMG (New York City), snowmobiles, EST, dunebuggies, *Family Circle* acquired by *New York Times,* Park Lane Hotel (New York City), ice skater to cover 100 miles in less than 6 hours, state litter legislation (Ore.), auto-train to transport passengers and their autos on the same train, road paved with glasphalt (Omaha, Neb.), public school built in conjunction with apartment house (Bronx, N.Y.), technical school for American Indians (Albuquerque, N.M.), state law banning sex discrimination (Wash.).

1972

Deaths

John Berryman, William
  Boyd, Maurice Chevalier,
  Brian Donlevy, Rudolph
  Friml, Gil Hodges, George
  Sanders, Helen Traubel,
  Harry S Truman, Walter
  Winchell.

In the News

U.S. AND USSR TO POOL MEDICAL RESEARCH . . . ALABAMA GOVERNOR GEORGE WALLACE ENTERS DEMOCRATIC PRIMARIES . . . ATTORNEY GENERAL JOHN MITCHELL RESIGNS, WILL HEAD COMMITTEE TO REELECT THE PRESIDENT . . . NIXON CONFERS WITH MAO IN CHINA . . . U.S. SUSPENDS PARIS TALKS . . . NORTH VIETNAM LAUNCHES MAJOR EASTER OFFENSIVE . . . CHARLIE CHAPLIN RETURNS TO U.S. AFTER 20 YEARS ABROAD . . . U.S. BOMBS HAIPHONG FOR THE FIRST TIME SINCE 1968 . . . J. EDGAR HOOVER DIES . . . U.S. MINES HAIPHONG HARBOR . . . WALLACE IS SHOT IN LAUREL, MD., AND PARALYZED . . . NIXON AND BREZHNEV SIGN TWO SALT AGREEMENTS . . . ANGELA DAVIS IS ACQUITTED OF MURDER IN CALIFORNIA . . . SOCIAL SECURITY IS INCREASED 20% . . . U.S. WILL SELL USSR $750 MILLION IN GRAIN . . . DEMOCRATS NOMINATE GEORGE MCGOVERN FOR PRESIDENT AND THOMAS EAGLETON FOR VICE PRESIDENT . . . SADAT EXPELS SOVIETS . . . EAGLETON REVEALS HOSPITALIZATION FOR DEPRESSION, IS REPLACED BY SARGENT SHRIVER . . . SENATE APPROVES SALT . . . LAST U.S. GROUND TROOPS LEAVE VIETNAM . . . 11 ISRAELIS ARE KILLED BY PALESTINIAN TERRORISTS AT MUNICH OLYMPICS . . . AGRICULTURE SECRETARY EARL BUTZ DENIES THAT GRAIN SALE LEAK LED TO WINDFALL PROFITS . . . BREAK-IN OCCURS AT DEMOCRATIC HEADQUARTERS IN WATERGATE BUILDING, FIVE ARE CAUGHT . . . KISSINGER AND LE DUC THO TALK IN PARIS . . . NORTH VIETNAM ACCEPTS CEASE-FIRE, THIEU REJECTS PLAN . . . "WASHINGTON POST" CONNECTS WATERGATE WITH COMMITTEE TO REELECT THE PRESIDENT . . . NIXON WINS LANDSLIDE VICTORY, 47 MILLION TO 29 MILLION, DEMOCRATS KEEP CONGRESS . . . DOW JONES TOPS 1,000 . . . U.S. RESUMES BOMBING OF HANOI AND HAIPHONG.

Quotes

"What really hurts is if you try to cover it up. . . . I can categorically say that no one on the present White House staff, no one in this administration, presently employed, was involved in this very bizarre incident."
— Richard M. Nixon, on the Watergate break-in

"I'm not going to comment on a third-rate burglary attempt."
— Ron Ziegler, press secretary

"All that crap, you're putting it in the paper? It's all been denied. [*Washington Post* publisher] Katie Graham's gonna get her tit caught in a big fat wringer if that's published."
— John Mitchell

"I love my husband very much, but I'm not going to stand for all those dirty things that go on. . . . They threw me down on the bed—five men did it—and stuck a needle in my behind. . . . They're afraid of my honesty. . . . Yes, Martha's honesty."
— Martha Mitchell

"Once the toothpaste is out of the tube, it's hard to get it back in."
— H. R. Haldeman, presidential aide

"I'm 1000% for Tom Eagleton, and I have no intention of dropping him from the ticket."
— Senator George McGovern

Chou En Lai: "What do you think of the wall?"
Richard Nixon: "I think you would have to conclude that this is a great wall."
— Exchange during President Nixon's trip to China

"Everywhere new hopes are rising for a world no longer overshadowed by fear, and want and war."
— Richard M. Nixon, on the SALT signing

"You are only as good as the people you dress."
— Halston

Ads

Have you ever had a bad time in Levi's?
(Levi's)

What this commercial is trying to sell you won't make your breath any sweeter, your clothes any whiter or your acid indigestion any better. It'll just make you more human.
Support the Arts for your [own] sake.
(Business Committee for the Arts)

Women: Stand up for your right to sit down at dinner time.
(Salton Hottray)

Most women hear better than men, so when she screams turn down the sound what she really means is turn down the damn distortion because the distortion is driving her bananas.
(Marantz Stereo)

Play it again, Sam.
(New York State Lottery)

With a Timme fake you can have a beautiful tiger, and he can have his.
(Timme Fake Furs)

Consumer advocate, lawyer, and author Ralph Nader. *Movie Star News.*

Vacation is a world where there are no locks on the doors or the mind or the body.
(Club Med)

The rich need Volvos too.
(Volvo)

I'd like to teach the world to sing in perfect harmony, / I'd like to buy the world a Coke and keep it company. It's the Real Thing.
(Coca-Cola)

TV

Premieres
"Sanford and Son," Redd Fox, Demond Wilson

"The Streets of San Francisco," Karl Malden, Michael Douglas

"Maude," Beatrice Arthur

"M*A*S*H," Alan Alda, Wayne Rogers, Loretta Swit, McLean Stevenson

"The Joker's Wild," Jack Barry

"Kung Fu," David Carradine

"The Bob Newhart Show"

"The Waltons," Michael Learned, Ralph Waite, Richard Thomas

Top Ten (Nielsen)
"All in the Family," "Sanford and Son," "Hawaii Five-O," "Maude," "Bridget Loves Bernie," "The NBC Sunday Mystery Movie," "The Mary Tyler Moore Show," "Gunsmoke," "The Wonderful World of Disney," "Ironside"

Specials
"Long Day's Journey into Night" (Laurence Olivier); " 'Sleeping Beauty': Bernstein in London"; "The Marcus-Nelson Murders" (Telly Savalas); "A War of Children" (James Costigan); "Singer Presents Liza"; "The U.S./Soviet Wheat Deal: Is There a Scandal?" (Walter Cronkite); "The Watergate Affair" (CBS); "The Great American Dream Machine"

Emmy Awards
"The Waltons" (drama); "All in the Family" (comedy); "The Julie Andrews Hour" (variety); Richard Thomas (actor, "The Waltons"); Jack Klugman (comedic actor, "The Odd Couple"); Michael Learned (actress, "The Waltons"); Mary Tyler Moore (comedic actress, "The Mary Tyler Moore Show")

Of Note
Time/Life HBO, subscription cable TV, begins with a National Hockey League contest and the film "Sometimes a Great Notion" • Controversy builds when mid-life "Maude" becomes pregnant and decides, after much soul-searching, to have an abortion • "That Certain Summer," with Hal Holbrook and Martin Sheen, is an early TV drama on male homosexuality.

Movies

Openings
The Godfather (Francis Ford Coppola), Marlon Brando, Al Pacino, James Caan, Robert Duvall

Cabaret (Bob Fosse), Liza Minnelli, Michael York, Joel Grey

Deliverance (John Boorman), Jon Voight, Burt Reynolds

Sounder (Martin Ritt), Cicely Tyson, Paul Winfield, Kevin Hooks

Sleuth (Joseph L. Mankiewicz), Laurence Olivier, Michael Caine

The Ruling Class (Peter Medak), Peter O'Toole, Harry Andrews

Lady Sings the Blues (Sidney J. Furie), Diana Ross, Billy Dee Williams, Richard Pryor

The Heartbreak Kid (Elaine May), Charles Grodin, Cybill Shepherd

The Candidate (Michael Ritchie), Robert Redford, Melvyn Douglas, Peter Boyle

The Discreet Charm of the Bourgeoisie (Luis Buñuel), Fernando Rey, Delphine Seyrig

The Poseidon Adventure (Ronald Neame), Gene Hackman, Ernest Borgnine, Shelley Winters

Cries and Whispers (Ingmar Bergman), Harriet Andersson, Ingrid Thulin, Liv Ullmann

Play It Again, Sam (Herbert Ross), Woody Allen, Diane Keaton, Tony Roberts

Last Tango in Paris (Bernardo Bertolucci), Marlon Brando, Maria Schneider

Deep Throat, Linda Lovelace, Harry Reems

Academy Awards
Best Picture: *The Godfather*

Best Director: Bob Fosse (*Cabaret*)

Best Actress: Liza Minnelli (*Cabaret*)

Best Actor: Marlon Brando (*The Godfather*)

Top Box-Office Stars
Clint Eastwood, Ryan O'Neal, Steve McQueen, Burt Reynolds, Robert Redford, Barbra Streisand, Paul Newman, Charles Bronson, John Wayne, Marlon Brando

Stars of Tomorrow
Al Pacino, Edward Albert, Jeff Bridges, Joel Grey, Sandy Duncan, Timothy Bottoms, Madeline Kahn, Cybill Shepherd, Malcolm McDowell, Ron O'Neal

Popular Music

Hit Songs

"Let's Stay Together"
"I'd Like to Teach the World to
　Sing"
"Oh Girl"
"Lean on Me"
"Where Is the Love?"
"Alone Again (Naturally)"
"Anticipation"
"Last Night I Didn't Get to Sleep
　at All"
"I'll Take You There"

Top Records

Albums: *Music* (Carole King);
American Pie (Don McLean);
Chicago V (Chicago); *First Take*
(Roberta Flack); *America*
(America); *Honky Chateau* (Elton
John)

Singles: *The First Time Ever I
Saw Your Face* (Roberta Flack);
Candy Man (Sammy Davis, Jr.); *If
Loving You Is Wrong* (Luther
Ingram); *Rocket Man* (Elton
John); *Morning Has Broken* (Cat
Stevens); *Without You* (Nilsson); *I
Gotcha* (Joe Tex); *Baby Don't Get
Hooked on Me* (Mac Davis).
Country: *The Happiest Girl in the
Whole U.S.A.* (Donna Fargo); *All
His Children* (Charlie Pride)

Grammy Awards

*The First Time Ever I Saw Your
Face,* Roberta Flack (record);
The Concert for Bangla Desh,
George Harrison et al. (album);
"The First Time Ever I Saw
Your Face" (song)

Jazz and Big Bands

The main part of the Newport
Jazz Festival moves to New York
City.

Top Performers *(Downbeat):*
Ornette Coleman (soloist); Thad
Jones and Mel Lewis (band);
Weather Report (jazz group);
Kenny Burrell, Richard Davis,
Herbie Hancock, Hubert Laws,
Wayne Shorter (instrumentalists):
Roberta Flack, Leon Thomas
(vocalists); Frank Zappa (rock/
blues musician); Blood, Sweat,
and Tears (vocal group);
Mahavishnu Orchestra, *Inner
Mounting Flame* (album)

Theater

Broadway Openings

Plays

The Sunshine Boys (Neil Simon), Jack Albertson,
　Sam Levene
The Last of Mrs. Lincoln (James Prideaux), Julie
　Harris
Butley (Simon Gray), Alan Bates
Vivat! Vivat Regina! (Robert Bolt), Claire Bloom,
　Eileen Atkins
Moon Children (Michael Weller), James Woods,
　Kevin Conway, Edward Herrmann
6 Rms Riv Vu (Bob Randall), Jerry Orbach, Jane
　Alexander
Night Watch (Lucille Fletcher), Joan Hackett, Len
　Cariou
The Creation of the World and Other Business
　(Arthur Miller), Zoë Caldwell, George Grizzard

Musicals

Grease (Jim Jacobs, Warren Casey), Barry Bostwick,
　Carole Demas
Pippin (Stephen Schwartz), Ben Vereen, John
　Rubinstein, Jill Clayburgh
Sugar (Jule Styne, Bob Merrill), Tony Roberts,
　Elaine Joyce, Robert Morse, Cyril Ritchard

Classics, Revivals, and Off-Broadway
　　Premieres

The Country Girl (Clifford Odets), Jason Robards,
Maureen Stapleton, George Grizzard; *Captain
Brassbound's Conversion* (George Bernard Shaw),

Ingrid Bergman; *Mourning Becomes Electra* (Eugene
O'Neill), Colleen Dewhurst; *That Championship
Season* (Jason Miller), Michael McGuire, Walter
McGinn; *Don't Bother Me I Can't Cope* (Micki
Grant); *Small Craft Warnings* (Tennessee Williams),
The Great God Brown (Eugene O'Neill), Patrick
Macnee, Jordan Christopher; *Much Ado about
Nothing,* Sam Waterston, Kathleen Widdoes; *The
Real Inspector Hound, After Magritte* (Tom
Stoppard), Carrie Nye. Founded: The Acting
Company by John Houseman and Margot Harley;
Negro Ensemble Company: *The River Niger* (Joseph
A. Walker), Douglas Turner Ward, premiere

Regional

Long Wharf, New Haven: *The Changing Room*
(David Storey), premiere

Cleveland: *A Yard of Sun* (Christopher Fry),
directed by José Ferrer, premiere

A.C.T., San Francisco: *The Mystery Cycles* (Nagle
Jackson)

Pulitzer Prize

No prize is awarded.

Tony Awards

Sticks and Bones, David Rabe (play), *Two Gentlemen
of Verona,* Galt MacDermot, John Guare (musical)

Classical Music ———————————

Compositions

Elliott Carter, String Quartet, no. 3
Aaron Copland, Three Latin-American Sketches
George Rochberg, String Quartet no. 3,
    Electrikaleidoscope
Lukas Foss, *Cave of the Winds*
Earle Brown, *Time Spans, Sign Sounds*

Important Events

New facilities include Philharmonic Hall, Miami;
Eastman Theater (renovated), Rochester, N.Y.;
Indiana University $11.3 million Musical Arts
Theater; and the University of Cincinnati Patricia
Corbett Pavillion.
Centennials of Ralph Vaughan Williams and
Alexander Scriabin are celebrated.
Interesting concerts include a musical marathon of
sixteen pianists at Carnegie Hall, at which Czerny's
Overture to Rossini's *Semiramide* is performed on
eight pianos, and John Philip Sousa's *Stars and
Stripes,* on ten; the Bach Aria Group celebrates its
25th anniversary with a cantata aria series; the J. F.
Kennedy Center performs 31 concerts in a 12-day
series with "The Old and the New" (a survey of
Italian Baroque to modern music).
Murray Perahia is the first American to win the
Leeds International Pianoforte Competition.

Debuts: Eugene Fodor, Radu Lupu, Vladimir
Pleshakov

First Performances

Jacob Druckman, *Windows* (Chicago); Olivier
Messiaen, *La transfiguration de notre seigneur,*

Jésus-Christ (Washington, D.C.); John La Montaine,
Wilderness Journal (Washington, D.C.); Oscar
Morawetz, *From the Diary of Anne Frank* (New
York)

Opera

Metropolitan: Final new Bing productions: Teresa
Zylis-Gara, James McCracken, *Otello;* Marilyn
Horne, James McCracken, *Carmen* (Leonard
Bernstein, conducting); Montserrat Caballé, *Don
Carlo;* Joan Sutherland, *Norma;* Sherrill Milnes,
Sutherland, Luciano Pavarotti, *Rigoletto;* Anja Silja
(debut), *Fidelio*

New York City: Beverly Sills, *Maria Stuarda;* Sills,
Norman Treigle, *Les contes d'Hoffmann*

Atlanta: *Treemonisha* (Scott Joplin, premiere)

Seattle: *Black Widow* (Thomas Pasatieri)

Chicago: *I due Foscari* (Verdi)

San Francisco: Regina Resnik, *The Visit*

Boston: Régine Crespin, *Les Troyens* (first U.S.
complete staging)

Music Notes

On January 26, bombs explode in Sol Hurok's offices
in protest against the importation of Russian artists; a
receptionist is killed.

Cicely Tyson wins an Academy Award nomination for her
role in *Sounder,* about black sharecroppers during the
depression. *Movie Star News.*

Jackie Winsor,
Bound Logs, 1972–
1973. Wood and
hemp, 114 × 29 ×
18". *Collection of
Whitney Museum of
American Art. Gift
of the Howard and
Jean Lipman
Foundation, Inc.*

Art

Painting
Robert Mangold, *Incomplete Circle No. 2*
Andrew Wyeth, *Bale*
Richard Serra, *Untitled*
Thomas Hart Benton, *Turn of the Century Joplin*
Jules Olitski, *Willemite's Vision*
Brice Marden, *Star (for Patti Smith)*
Adja Yunkers, *The Pinned-Up Woman*

Sculpture
Tony Smith, *Gracehoper*
H. C. Westermann, *American Death Ship on the Equator*
Sylvia Stone, *Another Place*
Jackie Winsor, *Bound Logs, Bound Square*

Architecture
Kimball Art Museum, Fort Worth, Texas (Louis I. Kahn)
One Shell Plaza, Houston (Skidmore, Owings & Merrill)
Graduate School of Design, Harvard University, Cambridge, Mass. (Andrews, Anderson, Baldwin)
College Life Insurance Company, Indianapolis (Roche and Dinkeloo)
One Liberty Plaza, New York (Skidmore, Owings and Merrill)
Pennsylvania Mutual Life Insurance Company building, Philadelphia (Romaldo Giurgola)
Federal Reserve Bank, Minneapolis (Gunnar Birkerts)
Crown Center, Kansas City, Mo. (Edward Larrabee Barnes)
Omni Coliseum, Atlanta, (Thompson, Ventulett and Stainbeck)

Important Exhibitions
Exhibits of Soviet arts and crafts, as well as Mexican decorative arts, tour the United States. Numerous American Indian and Eskimo art shows also tour.

Museums

New York: *Metropolitan:* Chinese calligraphy; Lipchitz. *Museum of Modern Art:* Modern European sculpture; Matisse; The 90th birthday of Picasso is celebrated with a show of 84 paintings, 69 works of sculpture. *Guggenheim:* Mondrian centennial; Rodin. *Cultural Center:* Giorgio de Chirico retrospective.

Boston: Ancient art of the Americas

Washington: National parks and the American landscape

Minneapolis, Toledo: Dutch masterpieces of the 18th century; Matisse

Los Angeles: Gericault; The American West

Buffalo: Nostalgia for the fifties: Pollock, de Kooning, Gorky, Guston, Still, Kline, Motherwell, Rothko, Frankenthaler

Cleveland: Caravaggio and his followers

Art Briefs
Accused of discrimination against women and blacks, the Whitney devotes its 40th Annual to both groups • Women artists become active in (1) workshops with Kate Millet and Yoko Ono, (2) the New York Interart Center, and (3) "Dream-Space" in Los Angeles • James Rosenquist gains a great deal of attention with *F-111,* 86 feet long • A 1914 living room of Frank Lloyd Wright, from Wayzata, Minnesota, is installed in the Metropolitan Museum of Art • Moore's *Reclining Figure* is auctioned for $260,000 • The Norton Simon Foundation pays a record $3 million for Zubarán's *Still Life* • Headline news reports that Michelangelo's *Pièta* in St. Peter's basilica has been badly damaged by a deranged man with a 12-pound hammer • Christo's $700,000 *Orange Valley Curtain,* made of parachute cloth, is torn to ribbons by a wind storm at Rifle Gap, Colo.

Dance

Ballet attendance increases 500 percent since 1905, with dance performances increasing 600 percent. At the New York State Theatre celebration of Stravinsky's birthday (he would have been 90), Balanchine stages nine ballets to Stravinsky's music, including *Duo Concertante, Pulcinella,* and the Violin Concerto.
Benjamin Harkarvy becomes co-artistic director of the Pennsylvania Ballet.

Premieres

New York City Ballet: *Watermill* (Jerome Robbins), Edward Villella

Boston Ballet: *Les Sylphides,* Liliana Cosi

Ballet of the 20th Century: *Nijinsky Clown of God* (Maurice Béjart), Jorge Donn

Twyla Tharp: *Raggedy Dances* (Scott Joplin, Mozart), *The Bix Pieces*

Alvin Ailey: *The Lark Ascending*

Books

Fiction

Critics' Choice

Chimera, John Barth
The Breast, Philip Roth
The Western Coast, Paula Fox
I Am Elijah Thrush, James Purdy
Mumbo-Jumbo, Ishmael Reed
Fredi and Shirl and the Kid, Richard Elman
Augustus, John Williams
The Sunlight Dialogues, John Gardner

Best-Sellers

Jonathan Livingston Seagull, Richard Bach
August 1914, Alexander Solzhenitsyn
The Odessa File, Frederick Forsyth
The Day of the Jackal, Frederick Forsyth
The Word, Irving Wallace
The Winds of War, Herman Wouk
Captains and the Kings, Taylor Caldwell
Two from Galilee, Marjorie Holmes
My Name Is Asher Lev, Chaim Potok
Semi-Tough, Dan Jenkins

Nonfiction

Critics' Choice

Who Pushed Humpty Dumpty? Donald Barr
The New 100 Years War, Georgie Geyer
The Closing Circle, Barry Commoner
The Children of Pride, Robert Manson Myers
The New Chastity, Midge Dechter
Papers on the War, Daniel Ellsberg
The Boys of Summer, Roger Kahn
The United States and the Origins of the Cold War 1941–1947, John Lewis Gaddis
Eleanor: The Years Alone, Joseph P. Lash
A Study in Suicide, A. Alvarez
Intuition, R. Buckminster Fuller
George Washington: Anguish and Farewell (1793–1799), James Thomas Flexner

Best-Sellers

The Living Bible, Kenneth Taylor
I'm O.K., You're O.K., Thomas Harris
Open Marriage, Nena O'Neill, George O'Neill
Harry S Truman, Margaret Truman
Dr. Atkins' Diet Revolution, Robert A. Atkins
Better Homes and Gardens Menu Cook Book
The Peter Prescription, Laurence J. Peter
A World Beyond, Ruth Montgomery
Journey to Ixtlan, Carlos Castaneda
Better Homes and Gardens Low-Calorie Desserts

Poetry

John Berryman, *Delusions, Etc.*
James Merrill, *Braving the Elements*
Howard Nemerov, *Gnomes and Occasions*
A. R. Ammons, *Collected Poems, 1951–1971*
Sylvia Plath, *Winter Trees*
James Tate, *Absences*
Nikki Giovanni, *My House*
John Ashbery, *Three Poems*

Pulitzer Prizes

The Optimist's Daughter, Eudora Welty (fiction)
People of Paradox: An Inquiry Concerning the Origin of American Civilization, Michael Kammen (U.S. history)
Fire in the Lake: The Vietnamese and the Americans in Vietnam, Frances FitzGerald (nonfiction)
Children of Crisis, vols. 1 and 2, Robert Coles (nonfiction)
Luce and His Empire, W. A. Swanberg (biography)
Up Country, Maxine Kumin (poetry)

Science and Technology

Genetic engineering, biochemical methods of joining genes, is developed.

The sites of DNA production on genes are discovered.

Hexachlorophene is ordered off the market by the FDA; it causes brain lesions in monkeys and is suspect in several newborn deaths.

Storage software is marketed by IBM.

Einstein's prediction of a time difference in a moving clock is validated.

Pioneer X is launched to explore the nature of the asteroid belt and Jupiter.

Apollo XVII is the sixth and last currently planned lunar landing; manned by Eugene Cernan, Ronald Evans, and Harrison Schmitt, it returns with 250 pounds of samples.

A brainscanner is introduced (in England), which provides cross sectional X rays; the technique is called Computerized Axial Tomography, CAT.

Nobel Prize

John Bardeen, Leon N. Cooper, and John R. Schrieffer win in physics for work on the theory of superconductivity. G. M. Edelman wins in physiology and medicine for work on antibodies. C. B. Anfinsen, Stanford Moore, and William H. Stein win in chemistry, for research on enzymes.

Sports ────────────

Baseball

The Players Association strike delays the season's opening 13 days, the first major sports strike.

Roberto Clemente (Pittsburgh, NL) gets his 3,000th hit in his last at-bat of the season. In December, he dies in a plane crash while taking part in the Nicaragua earthquake relief effort.

The Cy Young awards go to Steve Carlton (Philadelphia, NL) and Gaylord Perry (Cleveland, AL).

Champions ────────────

Batting
  Billy Williams (Chicago, NL), .333
  Rod Carew (Minnesota, AL), .318
Pitching
  Gary Nolan (Cincinnati, NL), 15–5
  Catfish Hunter (Oakland, AL), 21–7
Home runs
  Johnny Bench (Cincinnati, NL), 40

Football

The undefeated Miami Dolphins win a record 17 straight games; Larry Czonka and Mercury Morris both rush over 1,000 yards.

NFC Season Leaders: Fran Tarkenton (Minnesota), passing; Larry Brown (Washington), rushing; Harold Jackson (Philadelphia) receiving

College All-Americans: Randy Gradishar (LB), Penn State; John Hannah (G), Alabama; Otis Armstrong (B), Purdue

Bowls (Jan. 1, 1973)

Rose: Southern California 42–Ohio State 19
Orange: Nebraska 40–Notre Dame 6
Cotton: Texas 17–Alabama 13
Sugar: Oklahoma 14–Penn State 0

Basketball

NBA All-Pro First Team: John Havlicek (Boston), Spencer Haywood (Seattle), Kareem Abdul-Jabbar (Milwaukee), Walt Frazier (New York), Gail Goodrich (Los Angeles)

ABA Stars: Don Issel (Kentucky), Rick Barry (New York), Artis Gilmore (Kentucky), Dan Freeman (Dallas)

Olympics

At Munich, Arab terrorists seize Israeli Olympians as hostages, and eleven die in an attempt to free them. Swimmer Mark Spitz wins a record seven gold medals. Other American winners include Vincent Matthews (400m, 44.6s). Frank Shorter (marathon, 2:12:19.7), and Melissa Belote (2 in swimming). The USSR beats the United States in basketball for the first time on a disputed continuation of the game, after the United States had originally won. In the Winter Games at Sapporo, Japan, Anne Henning (500m, 42.3s.), Diane Holum (1500m, 2:20.8), and Barbara Cochran (slalom) win.

Winners ────────────

World Series
  Oakland (AL) 4
  Cincinnati (NL) 3
MVP
  NL–Johnny Bench, Cincinnati
  AL–Dick Allen, Chicago
Super Bowl VII (Jan. 1973)
  Miami 14–Washington 7
MVP
  Larry Brown, Washington
College Football
  Southern California
Heisman Trophy
  Johnny Rodgers, Oklahoma
NBA Championship
  Los Angeles 4–New York 1

MVP
  Kareem Abdul-Jabbar, Milwaukee
College Basketball
  UCLA
Player of the Year
  Bill Walton
Stanley Cup
  Boston
US Tennis Open
  Men: Ille Nastase
  Women: Billie Jean King
USGA Open
  Jack Nicklaus
Kentucky Derby
  Riva Ridge (R. Turcotte, jockey)

Fashion ────────────

For Women: Despite hot pants in mini lengths, it is width, rather than length, that makes the news: tent coats, beltless chemises, bat-wing sleeves, and evening caftans. Influencing style is the president's visit to China, after which lacquer-red colors, silk evening pajamas, and lotus and patterned gowns appear. The London King Tutankhamen exhibit prompts colorful Nile prints. Pants are replaced by beltless chemises and two-piece sweater dresses; "natural" and "organic" makeups gain a following.

High-fashion notes: Peretti's ivory egg pendant; Dior's cuffed trousers; Ruffin's T-shirt dress of polyester jersey; wooden combs for the Afro/natural hairdo; Cartier's tank watch

For Men: The male "peacock revolution" (*Esquire*) is at a peak with straight hip huggers or flared and cuffed bell bottoms. Men of all ages wear large herringbones and suits in colorful prints, heavy wools in lumber jacket plaids, the Hudson Bay blanket coat, and in spring, the twenties off-white suit. There is also an interesting display of chest hair. The British "bobby" coat in navy blue melton with silver buttons and whistle becomes popular for both men and women, an example of the unisex clothing revolution.

Kaleidoscope _____

- The budget of the Law Enforcement Assistance Administration goes from $63 million to $700 million.
- In a 5-to-4 decision, the Supreme Court rules that capital punishment is "cruel and unusual punishment," pending further legislation from the states.
- A black political convention is organized in Gary, Ind., at which New York representative Shirley Chisholm announces her candidacy for president.
- The number of fast-food establishments increases to 6,784 (3,418, in 1967; 1,120, in 1958).
- High-rated TV "Bridget Loves Bernie" is canceled because religious groups object to its intermarriage (Catholic-Jewish) situation. The stars marry in real life.
- David Bowie introduces "glitter rock."
- The Rolling Stones earn $4 million in a 30-city tour and appear before 750,000 people.
- The first graphically erotic movie with a major star opens— *Last Tango in Paris,* with Marlon Brando.
- Porno films find a wide audience and include *Deep Throat* and an X-rated cartoon, *Fritz the Cat;* sex-oriented radio programs also become popular (Bill Ballance, KGBS, Los Angeles).
- After 3,242 performances, *Fiddler on the Roof* closes, the longest running show in Broadway history.
- China sends a pair of giant pandas to Washington.
- Bobby Fisher beats Boris Spassky and becomes the first American world chess champion.
- McGraw-Hill proudly announces the publication of a long-awaited Howard Hughes autobiography; the book turns out to be a fraud perpetrated by Clifford Irving, who has received a $750,000 advance.
- Frank Sinatra is subpoened by a House committee on crime and indignantly denies all Mafia connections: "I'm not a second-class citizen," he states; "Let's get that straight."
- Mafia boss Joey Gallo is shot during a birthday party at Umberto's Clam House in New York; 26 flower-decked limosines serve in his funeral cortege.

Henry Kissinger, U.S. representative to the Paris peace talks, at the Playboy Club, Chicago. *Courtesy Morton Tanner.*

"M*A*S*H" begins with low TV ratings, but CBS gives it time to build an audience. *Movie Star News.*

- The Massachusetts Supreme Court rules unconstitutional the law prohibiting the sale of contraceptives to single persons.
- Jack Anderson accuses Acting Attorney General R. Kleindienst of settling an ITT antitrust case for a $400,000 contribution to the GOP convention.
- Congress passes Title IX, which entitles women to participate equally in all areas of sports.
- Published annual salaries include the following: Julia Child ("French Chef," $13,000), Walter Cronkite (CBS, $250,000), Hugh Hefner (*Playboy,* $303,847), Tom Seaver (New York Mets, $120,000), Harold S. Geneen (ITT, $382,494), Thomas Watson, Jr. (IBM, $413,735); Gaspare Greco (subway pretzel vendor, $2,600), Sue Long (second-grade private-school teacher, $7,500).
- Items in the Watergate burglars' possession include: one AWOL bag, 39 rolls of film, two spotlight bulbs and clamps, one extension cord, one small battery, one screwdriver, one roll of black tape, one piece of white plastic, four sponges, and one pair of needle-nose pliers.

Fads: Health food, acupuncture, pinball, Jesus freaks, TM (transcendental meditation)

First Appearances: Walter Pollution Control Act, Washington, D.C., Metro, bank to provide motion pictures for its customers waiting in line (Chemical, New York), corporation to have more than 3 million stockholders (AT&T), electric power using municipal refuse as a boiler fuel (Union Electric, St. Louis, Mo.), acupuncture treatment center (New York), statewide noise-control legislation (New Jersey), block of four postage stamps combined in 1 design in which each stamp is an entity (Cape Hatteras National Seashore stamps), pictorial postal card, Polaroid SC-70, pocket calculators, electronic lock and key system with plastic card

1973

Facts and Figures

Economic Profile
Dow-Jones: ↓ High 1051–
   Low 788
GNP: +12%
Inflation: +7.6%
Unemployment: 4.9%
Daily newspapers: 1,750
Books published: 38,000
Airmail postage: 10¢ (oz.)
Postcard: 5¢
IRS total collections: $195
   billion
Plummer, stemmed, on-the-
   rocks glasses: $10 (for 8)
Bloomingdale's parsons-style
   table: $99–$179
Chivari chair: $39–$45
Sloane leather and chrome
   chair: $329
American Shakespeare
   Theatre (Connecticut):
   $4.50–$8.50
Broadway theaters: $4–$9
Richter's jade snuff bottles:
   $10
Audi: $3,900
Rolls-Royce: $29,700

The great red spot on Jupiter,
the photo taken by Pioneer
10, launched in 1972.
Courtesy NASA.

Deaths

W. H. Auden, David Ben-
   Gurion, Pearl S. Buck,
   Pablo Casals, Noel
   Coward, John Ford, Betty
   Grable, Lyndon Baines
   Johnson, Pablo Picasso,
   Edward G. Robinson,
   Robert Ryan.

In the News

U.S. SUSPENDS ALL ACTIVITIES OVER NORTH VIETNAM . . . MARCOS DECLARES INDEFINITE MARTIAL LAW IN PHILIPPINES . . . SUPREME COURT RULES ALL FIRST-TRIMESTER ANTIABORTION LAWS UNCONSTITUTIONAL . . . KISSINGER AND LE DUC THO AGREE TO CEASE-FIRE . . . DEFENSE SECRETARY LAIRD SAYS DRAFT WILL END . . . U.S. AND CUBA SIGN ANTIHIJACK PACT . . . MCCORD LETTER TO JUDGE JOHN SIRICA IMPLICATES COMMITTEE TO REELECT THE PRESIDENT . . . MILITANT INDIANS SEIZE HOSTAGES AT WOUNDED KNEE, S.D. . . . LAST U.S. COMBAT TROOPS LEAVE VIETNAM . . . ERVIN SENATE COMMITTEE BEGINS WATERGATE HEARINGS . . . JOHN DEAN, PRESIDENTIAL COUNSEL, IMPLICATES THE PRESIDENT . . . NIXON ADMITS MAJOR WATERGATE RESPONSIBILITY AND ANNOUNCES RESIGNATION OF HALDEMAN AND EHRLICHMAN . . . MITCHELL AND STANS ARE INDICTED . . . ALL CHARGES AGAINST DANIEL ELLSBERG ARE DROPPED . . . ARCHIBALD COX IS APPOINTED SPECIAL WATERGATE PROSECUTOR . . . BRANDT AND BREZHNEV SIGN 10-YEAR PACT . . . MONARCHY IS ABOLISHED IN GREECE, DEMOCRACY IS ESTABLISHED . . . NIXON'S SECRET TAPING SYSTEM IS REVEALED . . . LAST PRICE CONTROLS ARE LIFTED . . . SIRICA ORDERS TAPE RELEASE, NIXON REFUSES . . . JUAN PERON IS ELECTED PRESIDENT OF ARGENTINA . . . SALVADOR ALLENDE TAKES HIS LIFE AS CHILEAN MILITARY OVERTHROWS HIM . . . SYRIA AND EGYPT ATTACK ISRAEL ON YOM KIPPUR . . . AGNEW RESIGNS, PLEADING "NOLO CONTENDERE" TO CORRUPTION CHARGES . . . GERALD FORD IS APPOINTED V.P. . . . OPEC IMPOSES OIL EMBARGO . . . NIXON DISMISSES COX OVER WEEKEND . . . ISRAEL RETAKES SINAI, GOLAN, NEGEV . . . CEASE-FIRE IS AGREED TO IN MIDEAST . . . ALASKAN PIPELINE IS AUTHORIZED . . . MILITARY RETAKES POWER IN GREECE.

Senate Watergate Committee: standing (left to right)—Lowell Weicker (R-Conn.), Daniel Inouye (D-Hawaii), Herman Talmadge (D-Ga.), Edward Gurney (R-Fla.); seated (left to right)—Howard Baker (R-Tenn.), Sam Ervin (D-So. Car.). *U.S. Senate.*

"Every tree in the forest will fall."
— James McCord, accused Watergate burglar

"I'll probably do better in the next four years, having gone through a few crises in the White House. I confront tough problems without flapping. Actually, I have a reputation for being the coolest person in the room. I've trained myself to be that."
— Richard M. Nixon

"The burglers who broke into the Democratic National Committee were in effect breaking into the home of every American."
— Senator Sam Ervin (D-N. Car.)

"There can be no whitewash at the White House."
— Richard M. Nixon

Quotes

"Lee took the blame. 'It was all my fault,' he said to Pickett's troops. That's quite different from some people I know."
— Senator Sam Ervin

". . . a beauty contest."
— Spiro Agnew, on the Ervin committee

"We have a cancer within, close to the presidency, that is growing."
— John Dean to Richard M. Nixon

"People have got to know whether or not their President is a crook. Well, I'm not a crook."
— Richard M. Nixon

"I have had to speak against the President of the United States."
— John W. Dean

"I was hoping you fellows wouldn't ask me about that."
— Alexander Butterfield, about the White House taping system

"Under the doctrine of separation of powers, . . . the President is not subject to questioning by another branch of government."
— Richard M. Nixon

"Executive poppycock."
— Senator Sam Ervin

"It's beginning to be like the Teapot Dome. There's a smell to it; let's get rid of the smell."
— Senator Barry Goldwater (R-Ariz.)

Ads

TV

Premieres
"Barnaby Jones," Buddy Ebsen
"Kojak," Telly Savalas
"Police Story," Ed Asner
"The Young and the Restless"
"The Six-Million-Dollar Man," Lee Majors

Top Ten (Nielsen)
"All in the Family," "The Waltons," "Sanford and Son," "M*A*S*H," "Hawaii Five-O," "Maude," "Kojak," "The Sonny and Cher Comedy Hour," "The Mary Tyler Moore Show," "Cannon"

Specials
"Marlo Thomas and Friends in Free to Be . . . You and Me"; "The Autobiography of Miss Jane Pittman" (Cicely Tyson); "Pueblo" (Hal Holbrook): "The Merchant of Venice" (Laurence Olivier); "The Execution of Private Slovik" (Martin Sheen); "A Case of Rape" (Elizabeth Montgomery); "Watergate: The White House Transcripts" (CBS); "Watergate Coverage" (PBS); "America's Nerve Gas Arsenal" (NBC); "Solzhenitsyn" (CBS); "Steambath" (Bruce Jay Friedman); "QB VII" (Anthony Hopkins)

Emmy Awards
"Upstairs, Downstairs" (drama); "M*A*S*H" (comedy); "The Carol Burnett Show" (variety); "A Charlie Brown Thanksgiving" (children); Telly Savalas (actor, "Kojak"); Alan Alda (comedic actor, "M*A*S*H"); Michael Learned (actress, "The Waltons"); Mary Tyler Moore (comedic actress, "The Mary Tyler Moore Show")

Of Note
Particularly popular are shows about families like "The Waltons" • 50 percent of the new programs are on law and order.

Movies

Openings
The Sting (George Roy Hill), Paul Newman, Robert Redford, Robert Shaw
American Graffiti (George Lucas), Richard Dreyfuss, Ronny Howard
The Exorcist (William Friedkin), Ellen Burstyn, Max Von Sydow, Linda Blair
Mean Streets (Martin Scorsese), Robert De Niro, Harvey Keitel
Sleeper (Woody Allen), Woody Allen, Diane Keaton
Save the Tiger (John G. Avildsen), Jack Lemmon, Jack Gilford
The Last Detail (Hal Ashby), Jack Nicholson, Otis Young, Randy Quaid
Serpico (Sidney Lumet), Al Pacino, John Randolph
A Touch of Class (Melvin Frank), George Segal, Glenda Jackson
The Way We Were (Sydney Pollack), Barbra Streisand, Robert Redford
The Paper Chase (James Bridges), Timothy Bottoms, John Houseman, Lindsay Wagner
Bang the Drum Slowly (John Hancock), Michael Moriarty, Robert De Niro, Vincent Gardenia
Scenes from a Marriage (Ingmar Bergman), Liv Ullmann, Erland Josephson
Day for Night (François Truffaut), François Truffaut, Jacqueline Bisset, Valentina Cortese
Blume in Love (Paul Mazursky), George Segal, Susan Anspach, Kris Kristofferson

Produced on a "Head Start" grant and aimed at teaching letters and numbers to ghetto preschoolers, Jim Henson's "Sesame Street" continues its great success. *Billy Rose Theatre Collection. The New York Public Library at Lincoln Center. Astor, Lenox and Tilden Foundations.*

Academy Awards
Best Picture: *The Sting*
Best Director: George Roy Hill (*The Sting*)
Best Actress: Glenda Jackson (*A Touch of Class*)
Best Actor: Jack Lemmon (*Save the Tiger*)

Top Box-Office Stars
Clint Eastwood, Ryan O'Neal, Steve McQueen, Burt Reynolds, Robert Redford, Barbra Streisand, Paul Newman, Charles Bronson, John Wayne, Marlon Brando

Stars of Tomorrow
Diana Ross, Michael Moriarty, Marsha Mason, Joe Don Baker, Jeannie Berlin, Candy Clark, Robert De Niro, Jan-Michael Vincent, Tatum O'Neal

Popular Music

Hit Songs

"Tie a Yellow Ribbon"
"Delta Dawn"
"Let's Get It On"
"Me and Mrs. Jones"
"Bad, Bad Leroy Brown"
"Why Me?"
"Rocky Mountain High"
"Natural High"
"Could It Be I'm Falling in Love?"

Top Records

Albums: *Goodbye Yellow Brick Road* (Elton John); *No Secrets* (Carly Simon); *Living in the Material World* (George Harrison); *Chicago VI* (Chicago); *Brothers and Sisters* (Allman Brothers Band); *Goat's Head Soup* (Rolling Stones)

Singles: *Killing Me Softly with His Song* (Roberta Flack); *You Are the Sunshine of My Life* (Stevie Wonder); *Touch Me in the Morning* (Diana Ross); *You're So Vain* (Carly Simon); *Crocodile Rock* (Elton John); *Will It Go Round in Circles?* (Billy Preston); *My Love* (Paul McCartney and Wings); *We're an American Band* (Grand Funk Railroad); *The Night the Lights Went Out in Georgia* (Vicki Lawrence). Country: *Behind Closed Doors* (Kenny O'Dell/Charlie Rich); *Till I Get It Right* (Tammy Wynette)

Grammy Awards

Killing Me Softly with His Song, Roberta Flack (record); *Innervisions,* Stevie Wonder (album); "Killing Me Softly with His Song," Roberta Flack (song)

Jazz and Big Bands

The New York Jazz Festival features swing musicians Benny Goodman, Gene Krupa, Lionel Hampton, and Slam Stewart.

Top Performers (*Downbeat*): Chick Corea (soloist); Thad Jones and Mel Lewis (band); Weather Report (jazz group); John McLaughlin, Ron Carter, Gary Burton, Billy Cobham, Freddie Hubbard (instrumentalists); Roberta Flack, Leon Thomas (vocalists); Stevie Wonder (rock/blues musician); Mahavishnu Orchestra (vocal group); Mahavishnu Orchestra, *Birds of Fire* (album)

Theater

Broadway Openings

Plays

The Changing Room (David Storey), John Lithgow
The Jockey Club Stakes (William Douglas Home), Wilfred Hyde-White
Finishing Touches (Jean Kerr), Barbara Bel Geddes
Crown Matrimonial (Royce Ryton), Eileen Herlie, George Grizzard
Veronica's Room (Ira Levin), Arthur Kennedy, Eileen Heckart
The Good Doctor (Neil Simon), Christopher Plummer, Marsha Mason
Out Cry (Tennessee Williams), Michael York, Cara Duff-MacCormick
Hot L Baltimore (Lanford Wilson), Trish Hawkins, Judd Hirsch
The River Niger (Joseph A. Walker), Douglas Turner Ward, Les Roberts

Musicals

A Little Night Music (Stephen Sondheim), Glynis Johns, Len Cariou, Hermione Gingold
Seesaw (Cy Coleman, Dorothy Fields), Michele Lee, Ken Howard, Tommy Tune
Raisin (Judd Woldin, Robert Brittan), Virginia Capers, Joe Morton

Good Evening, revue written and performed by Peter Cook, Dudley Moore
The Tooth of Crime (Performance Group, Sam Shepard), Stephen Borst

Classics, Revivals, and Off-Broadway Premieres

A Moon for the Misbegotten (Eugene O'Neill), Colleen Dewhurst, Jason Robards; *Uncle Vanya* (Chekhov), George C. Scott, Nicol Williamson, Julie Christie, Lillian Gish; *A Streetcar Named Desire* (Tennessee Williams), Rosemary Harris; *Henry IV* (Pirandello), Rex Harrison; *The Iceman Cometh* (O'Neill), James Earl Jones; *The Contractor* (David Storey), Kevin O'Connor, George Taylor; *The Women* (Clare Boothe Luce), Dorothy Loudon, Myrna Loy, Kim Hunter, Rhonda Fleming; *Medea* (Euripides), Irene Papas; *When You Comin' Back, Red Ryder?* (Mark Medoff), Brad Dourif

Regional

Arena Stage, Washington, D.C.: Takes *Inherit the Wind* and *Our Town* to the Soviet Union, sponsored by the U.S. Department of State; *Raisin* (Robert Brittan, Judd Woldin); *A Public Prosecuter Is Sick of It All* (Max Frisch), premieres; *Bartholomew Fair* (Ben Jonson), American premiere

Theater (cont.)

Goodman, Chicago: *The Freedom of the City* (Brian Friel), premiere

Long Wharf, New Haven: *Forget-Me-Not Lane* (Peter Nichols); *The Widowing of Mrs. Holroyd* (D. H. Lawrence); *The Contractor* (David Storey), premieres

Minneapolis Theatre Company: *Cyrano* (musical by

Anthony Burgess, Michael J. Lewis), Christopher Plummer

Pulitzer Prize
That Championship Season, Jason Miller

Tony Awards
That Championship Season, Jason Miller (play), *A Little Night Music,* Stephen Sondheim (musical)

Classical Music

Compositions
Donald Martino, *Notturno*
Virgil Thomson, *Cantata based on Nonsense Rhymes*
Peter Mennin, Symphony no. 8
Walter Piston, *Fantasy*
William Schuman, *A Story of Orpheus,* Concerto on Old English Rounds for Viola, Female Chorus, and Orchestra

Important Events
Gregor Piatigorsky is honored on his 70th birthday at Lincoln Center; Sol Hurok on his 85th (with vignettes by his star performers at the Met); John Cage, on his 60th birthday, is the subject of several retrospectives (New York, Boston).
Symphony of the New World presents "Black Week"; the New York Philharmonic gives Haydn and Stravinsky retrospectives.
The Philadelphia Orchestra is the first to tour the People's Republic of China.

Debut: Elmar Oliveira, Ida Levin

First Performances
Leonardo Balada, *Steel Symphony* (Pittsburgh); Arne Norheim, *Greeting* for Orchestra (Los Angeles); Louis Ballard, *Devil's Promenade* (Tulsa); Marvin David Levy, *Masada* (Washington, D.C.); Luciano Berio, Concerto for Two Pianos and Orchestra (New York)

Opera

Metropolitan: Nicolai Gedda, Raina Kabaivanska, *Pique Dame* (Tchaikovsky, in Russian); Montserrat Caballé, *Norma;* Shirley Verrett, Christa Ludwig, Jon Vickers, *Les Troyens;* Marilyn Horne, *L'Italiana in Algeri;* Clamma Dale, Hilda Harris, *Four Saints in Three Acts;* Carlo Cossutta (debut), *Norma;* Teresa

Kubiak (debut), *Pique Dame;* "Opera at the Forum" begins (three short operas)

New York City: Beverly Sills, *Anna Bolena; The Young Lord* (Sarah Caldwell, conducting), with Rudolf Bing as Sir Edgar

Houston: William Dooley, Donald Gramm, John Alexander, *Don Carlos* (1867, 4½-hour version)

New Orleans: Carol Neblett, *Thaïs*

Boston: *Don Carlos* (in original Paris version of 1867); Emmett Kelly, Sr., Mary Costa, James Atherton, *The Bartered Bride; Mahagonny*

Santa Fe: *Melusine* (Reimann, premiere); Alan Titus, Regina Resnik, *Owen Wingrave* (Benjamin Britten)

Chicago: Montserrat Caballé, *Maria Stuarda;* Luciano Pavarotti, Ileana Cotrubas, *La bohème*

San Francisco: Jess Thomas, *Peter Grimes*

Music Notes
At the Norton Lectures, at Harvard, Leonard Bernstein draws a parallel between the structure of music and language • The New York Philharmonic institutes "Rug Concerts," where seats are removed and the audience sits on the floor and stage pillows • The Santa Fe Chamber Music Festival begins • Music and politics clash before Nixon's inauguration as (1) members of the New York Philharmonic Orchestra refuse to perform for a president whose politics they "deplore," (2) Charlton Heston reads portions of the Declaration of Independence against a musical background, and (3) Leonard Bernstein conducts *Mass in Time of War* at a "Counterconcert."

Art

Paintings
Jim Dine, *Untitled Tool Series*
Richard Artschwager, *Interior*
Jasper Johns, *Two Flags*
James Bishop, *Untitled, No. 2*
Andy Warhol, *Mao*
Al Held, *South Southwest*
Frank Stella, *Targowica*
Sam Francis, *Untitled #7*
David Hockney, *The Weather Series: Sun*

Sculpture
Robert Rauschenberg, *Untitled*
Donald Judd, *Untitled*
Christopher Wilmarth, *My Divider*
Brice Marden, *Grove Group, I*

Robert Smithson, *Amarillo Ramp*

Architecture
Frank House study, Cornwall, Conn. (Peter Eisenman)
Boston Public Library Wing (Philip Johnson, John Burgee)
Murray Lincoln Center, University of Massachusetts, Amherst (Marcel Breuer)
American Institute of Architects, Washington, D.C. (The Architects Collaborative)
IDS Center, Minneapolis (Johnson, Burgee)
88 Pine Street Building, New York (I. M. Pei)

Important Exhibitions
The United States hosts shows from the Soviet Union, China, India, and Japan, including "Impressionists and Post-Impressionists from the USSR," 41 paintings from the Hermitage and Pushkin museums.

Museums

New York: *Metropolitan:* American realism: Sargent, Robinson, Hassam, Chase; 125 photograhic works of Man Ray; Frank Lloyd Wright; Japanese work, 2700 B.C.–19th century. *Museum of Modern Art:* Ellsworth Kelly; Miró; Duchamp; Matisse's sculpture: "Collage and the Photo Image." *Guggenheim:* Miró, Dubuffet. *Whitney:* Nineteenth-century America. *Asia House:* Works, 1520–1900.

Chicago: Renoir; "Multitudinous uses of Gold"; The arts and crafts movement in America; Nineteenth-century America

Indianapolis: Religion in American art

Avant-garde Shows: Abstract art: Jules Olitski (Boston, Whitney); Morris Louis, Larry Poons (New York); Ellsworth Kelly, Philip Woffard (Washington)

Group Shows: "Women Choose Women: Unmanly Art" (New York Cultural Center); "The Art Heritage of Puerto Rico" (Museo del Barrio and Metropolitan Museum of Art); "United Graffiti Artists" (Razor Alley, New York); "The Art of Maximum Security Prisoners" (National Gallery); "Fakes and Forgeries" (Minneapolis)

Art Briefs
Several museums open in California, including the Desert Museum in Palm Springs. In Texas, museums open at Fort Worth, Corpus Christi, and Amarillo • Artrain begins, organized by the Michigan Council on the Arts and the NEA; it is a six-railroad-car traveling museum show that visits remote communities in the Rocky Mountain states • The Salvador Dali Holographic Room opens at M. Knoedler, in New York • The Metropolitan's "de-accessioning" controversy continues • The Italian government questions the Metropolitan's 1972, $1,000 purchase of the calyx krater by Euphronios, valued at $1 million • Japanese collectors and dealers buy a great many Western works, including Kuniyoshi's *Little Joe with Cow* ($220,000) and Stuart Davis's *Hot Still-Scape for Six Colors* ($175,000) • Major sales include Georgia O'Keeffe's *Poppies* ($120,000) and Jasper Johns's *Double White Map* ($240,000). Jackson Pollock's *Blue Poles* sells to the National Museum of Australia for $2 million, the highest price ever paid for an American painting.

Dance

A Los Angeles company is formed by John Clifford of the New York City Ballet; Michael Smuin leaves the American Ballet Theatre to join the San Francisco Ballet.

Premieres/Important Productions

New York City Ballet: *Cortège Hongrois* (George Balanchine), for retiring Melissa Hayden, Jacques d'Amboise; *An Evening's Waltzes* (Jerome Robbins), Patricia McBride, Jean-Pierre Bonnefous, John Clifford; Sara Leland, Bart Cook

American Ballet Theatre: *Tales of Hoffmann* (Peter Darrell, full length), for Cynthia Gregory

Joffrey: *The Dream* (Sir Frederick Ashton); *Deuce Coupe* (Twyla Tharp, Beach Boys)

Alvin Ailey: *Hidden Rites*

Books

Fiction

Critics' Choice

Gravity's Rainbow, Thomas Pynchon

Ninety-two in the Shade, Thomas McGuane

People Will Always Be Kind, Wilfred Sheed

Do with Me What You Will, Joyce Carol Oates

Rembrandt's Hat, Bernard Malamud

Theophilus North, Thornton Wilder

Nickel Mountain, John Gardner

Best-Sellers

Jonathan Livingston Seagull, Richard Bach

Once Is Not Enough, Jacqueline Susann

Breakfast of Champions, Kurt Vonnegut, Jr.

The Odessa File, Frederick Forsyth

Burr, Gore Vidal

Evening in Byzantium, Irwin Shaw

The Matlock Paper, Robert Ludlum

The Billion Dollar Sure Thing, Paul E. Erdman

The Honorary Consul, Graham Greene

Nonfiction

Critics' Choice

The Best and the Brightest, David Halberstam

Franklin D. Roosevelt: Launching the New Deal, Frank Freidel

Pentimento, Lillian Hellman

A Second Flowering, Malcolm Cowley

Sincerity and Authenticity, Lionel Trilling

The Anxiety of Influence, Harold Bloom

The New Left and the Origins of the Cold War, Robert James Maddox

Deeper into Movies, Pauline Kael

The World of Nations, Christopher Lasch

Economics and the Public Purpose, John Kenneth Galbraith

The Living Presidency, Emmet John Hughes

Marilyn, Norman Mailer

Bright Book of Life, Alfred Kazin

The Briar Patch, Murray Kempton

Life: The Unfinished Experiment, S. E. Luria

Best-Sellers

The Living Bible, Kenneth Taylor

Dr. Atkins' Diet Revolution, Robert C. Atkins

I'm O.K., You're O.K., Thomas Harris

The Joy of Sex, Alex Comfort

Weight Watchers Program Cookbook, Jean Nidetch

How to Be Your Own Best Friend, Mildred Newman et al.

The Art of Walt Disney, Christopher Finch

Alistair Cooke's America, Alistair Cooke

Sybil, Flora R. Schreiber

Poetry

Robert Bly, *Sleepers Joining Hands*

Allen Ginsberg, *The Fall of America*

Muriel Rukeyser, *Breaking Open*

W. S. Merwin, *Writings to an Unfinished Accompaniment*

Alice Walker, *Revolutionary Petunias and Other Poems*

Adrienne Rich, *Diving into the Wreck*

૨૦ Czselaw Milosz, *Selected Poems*

Pulitzer Prizes

No prize is awarded in fiction.

The Americans: The Democratic Experience, vol. 3, Daniel Boorstin (U.S. history)

The Denial of Death, Ernest Becker (nonfiction)

O'Neill, Son and Artist, Louis Sheaffer (biography)

The Dolphin, Robert Lowell (poetry)

Science and Technology

Pioneer X approaches closer to Jupiter and shows the planet and its great red spot in significant detail.

The first manned Skylab launch is accomplished with Charles Conrad, Joseph Kerwin, and Paul Weitz as crew. They spend 28 days in space and conduct medical experiments related to manned space flight.

The second manned Skylab launch, with Alan Bean, Owen K. Garriott, and Jack Lousma, continues medical experiments; the mission spends 59½ days in space.

A computerized brain scanner (CAT) is marketed.

Heinz Kohut's *Analysis of the Self* challenges psychoanalytic theory by emphasizing self-worth rather than instinctual drives.

The multiple accurate reentry vehicle is developed (MARV), which permits accurate multiple missile guidance.

A cigarette-pack-size electronic brain-wave reader is developed that can detect and signal lapses in concentration.

Nuclear Magnetic Resonance (NMR) is developed; it measures the absorption of radio waves in a magnetic field to distinguish healthy from diseased tissue.

Nobel Prize

Ivar Giaever wins the prize in physics for work in miniature electronics.

Sports ━━━━━━━━━━━━━━━━━━

Baseball

Arbitrator Peter Seitz rules, in the Andy Messersmith case, that after one season without a contract, a player is a free agent.

The AL begins allowing the designated hitter.

Nolan Ryan (California, AL) pitches two no-hitters and strikes out a record 393.

Tom Seaver (New York, NL) and Jim Palmer (Baltimore, AL) receive the Cy Young awards.

Champions ━━━━━━━━━━━━━

Batting	Catfish Hunter (Oakland,
Pete Rose (Cincinnati, NL),	AL), 21–5
.338	*Home runs*
Rod Carew (Minnesota,	Willie Stargell (Pittsburgh,
AL), .350	NL), 44
Pitching	
Tommy John (Los Angeles,	
NL), 16–7	

Football

O. J. Simpson (Buffalo, AFC) rushes for a record 2,003 yards.

Congress prohibits TV blackouts for sold-out games.

NFC Season Leaders: Roman Gabriel (Philadelphia), passing; John Brockington (Green Bay), rushing; Harold Carmichael (Philadelphia), receiving

AFC Season Leaders: Ken Anderson (Cincinnati), passing; Fred Willis (Houston), receiving

College All-Americans: Lynn Swann (E), Southern California; Roosevelt Leaks (B), Texas; Lucius Selmon (L), Oklahoma

Bowls (Jan. 1, 1974)

Rose: Ohio State 42–	Cotton: Nebraska 19–
Southern California 21	Texas 3
Orange: Penn State 16–	Sugar: Notre Dame 24–
Louisiana State 9	Alabama 23

Basketball

NBA All-Pro First Team: John Havlicek (Boston), Spencer Haywood (Seattle), Kareem Abdul-Jabbar (Milwaukee), Nate Archibald (Kansas City, Omaha), Jerry West (Los Angeles)

ABA All-Pro First Team: Billy Cunningham (Carolina), Julius Erving (Virginia), Artis Gilmore (Kentucky), James Jones (Utah), Warren Jabali (Denver)

Other Sports

Tennis: Long-retired tennis star Bobby Riggs beats current star Margaret Smith Court on Mother's Day in a $10,000 winner-take-all match. Later, Billie Jean King beats Bobby Riggs in the Astrodome in a $100,000 match; 30,000 attend and 40 million watch on TV. She arrives by elephant; he, by rickshaw.

Golf: Jack Nicklaus wins his 14th major tournament, one more than Bobby Jones.

Winners ━━━━━━━━━━━━━

World Series	*MVP*
Oakland (AL) 4	Dave Cowens, Boston
New York (NL) 3	*College Basketball*
MVP	UCLA
NL–Pete Rose, Cincinnati	*Player of the Year*
AL–Reggie Jackson,	Bill Walton, UCLA
Oakland	*Stanley Cup*
Super Bowl VIII (Jan. 1974)	Montreal
Miami 24–Minnesota 7	*US Tennis Open*
MVP	Men: John Newcombe
O. J. Simpson, Buffalo	Women: Margaret Smith
College Football	Court
Alabama (UPI)	*USGA Open*
Notre Dame (AP)	Johnny Miller
Heisman Trophy	*Kentucky Derby*
John Cappeletti, Penn State	Secretariat (R. Turcotte,
NBA Championship	jockey)
New York 4–Los Angeles 3	

Fashion ━━━━━━━━━━━━━━━━

For Men: "The look" is easy, bright, and youthful, the Mark Spitz look: loosely brushed black hair, dark mustache, slim figure—elegant but casual—the decorative sport shirt over jeans or hiphuggers, the knit turtleneck with flared slacks, the textured sports shirt with collar outside the jacket. The shift to "casual" even extends to business: not only do sleeveless sweaters replace the vest but print shirts and patterned jackets and ties are also prominent. Shirts appear in every print, including polka dots; white shirts are a rarity. Any variety of dot, plaid, and solid color is used for bow and wide ties. The "Great Gatsby" look, with white hat, shoes, open shirt, wide pants, and slim jacket, is stylish. Shoes get bolder, in cream with bright red bands, or they copy the twenties' golfing style with flopping tongue; the "chunky" shoe is also very popular. T-shirts are decorated with names or cartoon characters.

For Children: With the casual look and jeans and underwear-type T-shirts decorated with names of children or odd animals, for the first time, rich and poor kids look alike.

High-fashion note: Biba's sequined dress and matching skull cap

Kaleidoscope

- Questionable government activities alluded to during the Watergate hearings include an administration "enemies list" of journalists, businessmen, politicians, and others (like Barbra Streisand and Joe Namath), who might be subjected to IRS harassment.
- After Archibald Cox is fired during the "Saturday Night Massacre," more than 250,000 telegrams arrive at the White House denouncing the president; crowds march there day and night.
- Nine hundred delegates to the AFL-CIO convention in Florida adopt a resolution asking for Nixon's impeachment.
- Eighty-four congressmen in the House sponsor 22 bills calling for impeachment.
- Long gas lines are seen throughout the nation during the OPEC embargo.
- Fuel prices since 1964 have risen at an annual rate of 3.7 percent; OPEC raises the price for crude oil 300 percent during the last four months of the year.
- The Nobel Peace Prize is awarded to Henry Kissinger and North Vietnamese Le Duc Tho, who refuses it.
- Screening of airline passengers to prevent hijacking begins.
- Oregon is the first state to decriminalize marijuana.
- There is a rise of interest in pentecostal and charismatic religions, as well as in Eastern movements such as Hare Krishna, yoga, Zen, Tibetan Buddhism, and I Ching.
- Michael Novak, in *The Rise of the Unmeltable Ethnics* defines the revival of ethnicity ("Kiss me, I'm Italian") as a rejection of American white, Anglo-Saxon, Protestant domination and a return to old values like loyalty.
- It is estimated that one out of three meals is consumed out of the house (one in eight in 1965).
- Vodka outsells whiskey for the first time.
- The median sale price of a single-family house is $28,900, up from $20,000 in 1968.
- A *Playboy* survey indicates that sexual liberalism is now the dominant ideal but that highly organized standards of love, marriage, and family remain.
- The popular PBS show "An American Family" focuses on the disintegration of a family ("Oh, we're mad at each other all the time," says the father, Bill Loud) and reflects the increasing divorce rate, nearly double since 1966.
- Elvis gives Priscilla $750,000 in their divorce settlement.
- The Supreme Court rules that employment ads cannot specify gender.
- The American Psychiatric Association revises its categorization of homosexuality; it is no longer considered a mental disorder.
- The Supreme Court establishes a narrower definition of pornography and allows the use of local, not national, standards to define what is obscene.
- New young Hollywood directors include George Lucas, Peter Bogdanovich, and Martin Scorsese; new male screen heroes include Robert De Niro, Martin Sheen, and Al Pacino.

Singer Barbra Streisand, whose look set a vogue, and top male box office star Robert Redford in *The Way We Were*. *Movie Star News*.

- Fifty rock stars earn $2–6 million a year.
- Most single records are country and western.
- The *Washington Post* wins a Pulitzer for its Watergate investigative reporting by Bob Woodward and Carl Bernstein.
- The FDA standardizes nutritive information on food labels, which lists such items as calories and grams of protein, fat, and carbohydrates.
- According to a Gallup Poll, 25 percent of all consumers (50 million people) participate in boycotts against food inflation; groups, like Operation Pocketbook, form and set up pickets ("NUTS TO BUTZ," "NIX-ON BEEF").
- Charles Revson signs Lauren Hutton, 28, for a record-breaking $200,000 as exclusive model for his Ultima II eye makeup and skin creams.
- "Pet rocks," which become a fad, are said to be an ironic testimony to the individual's power over his environment.
- An estimated 600,000 attend the Watkins Glen Rock Music Festival to hear the Grateful Dead and Allman Brothers.
- Because there are so many art thefts, Interpol publishes the first "Most Wanted Paintings" list.
- "I'm a Ford, not a Lincoln," says the new vice president, Gerald Ford.

Fads: CB radios, martial arts, backgammon

New Words and Usages: Skylab, spacelab, space shuttle, juggernaut, biofeedback, interface, consensus of opinion, doomster, ego trip, let it all hang out, time frame, nouvelle cuisine

First Appearances: Balloon flight powered by solar energy (Statesville, N.C.), college belly dancing course (University of Texas, Arlington), college to offer athletic scholarship to women (University of Miami, Coral Gables), woman prison guard in maximum security prison for men (Iowa State Penitentiary), state highway metric-distance-marker system (Ohio), vote recorded by electronic means in the House of Representatives, twilight zoo (Highland Park, Pittsburgh), floating international currencies

1974

Facts and Figures

Economic Profile
Dow-Jones: ↓ High 950–Low 590
GNP: +8%
Inflation: +13.9%
Unemployment: 5.6%

Expenditures
Recreation: $42 billion
Spectator sports: $550 million
European travel: $3.2 billion

Number of bowlers: 7,900,000

The String bathing suit: $15.99

Arnold Constable furs
sable: $6,999–$8,599
lynx: $3,999
red fox jacket: $329

Saks 5th Ave. jersey floral dress: $54

Bonwit Teller long jacket and pants, polyester: $68

Brooks Brothers "346" gabardine suit: $190

Bellini cotton stripe suit: $200

Balmain tattersall shirt, white collar, cuffs: $35

Jaeger lightweight flannel trousers: $55

Oscar de la Renta gabardine no-vent jacket: $185

Phone Butler answering machine: $99.95

Richard Nixon's resignation speech. *Congressional Library.*

Deaths

Bud Abbott, Jack Benny, Walter Brennan, Dizzy Dean, Duke Ellington, Chet Huntley, Charles Lindbergh, Walter Lippmann, Ed Sullivan, Jacqueline Susann, Earl Warren.

In the News

55-Mile-per-Hour Speed Limit Is Enacted . . . Nixon Rejects Ervin Subpoena . . . 18½-Minute Nixon Tape Gap Is Exposed . . . Israel and Egypt Sign Troop Disengagement Accord . . . Mao Launches Cultural Revolution . . . Heiress Patty Hearst Is Kidnapped by Symbionese Liberation Army . . . House Votes 410–4 to Investigate the President . . . Solzhenitsyn Is Deported from Russia . . . Grand Jury Indicts President's Aides Haldeman, Ehrlichman, Colson . . . Turkish DC-10 Jet Crashes, 346 Die . . . OPEC Oil Embargo Ends . . . Kissinger and Brezhnev Meet in Moscow . . . Nixon Agrees to Pay $432,000 in Back Taxes . . . Portuguese Army Seizes Power to End Dictatorial Rule . . . Nixon Will Make Public 2,100 Pages of Tapes . . . Brandt Resigns in Spy Scandal, Helmut Schmidt Is New German P.M. . . . Palestinian Terrorists Seize School in Maalot, 21 Children Die . . . India Announces It Has A-Bomb . . . Nixon and Brezhnev Hold Summit, 10-Year Economic Pact Is Signed . . . Juan Peron Dies, His Wife Isabel Takes Over . . . Turkey Invades Cyprus . . . Civilian Government Returns in Greece . . . House Judiciary Approves Bill of Impeachment . . . Ehrlichman Is Sentenced 1½–5 Years for Ellsberg Civil Rights Violation . . . John Dean Pleads Guilty, Is Sentenced 1–4 Years . . . Nixon Admits "Serious Act of Omission" . . . President Resigns . . . Ford Is Sworn in as President . . . Nelson Rockefeller Is Appointed Vice President . . . Ford Gives Nixon Absolute Pardon . . . Ethiopian Emperor Haile Selassie Is Deposed by Army Coup . . . President Offers "Earned Clemency" to Draft Evaders . . . Democrats Increase Majority in Mid-Term Elections . . . PLO Is Given Observer Status at UN . . . Oil Is Found in Mexico.

Quotes

"Don't lie to them to the extent to say 'No involvement,' but just say this is a comedy of errors, without getting into it; the President believes that it is going to open the whole Bay of Pigs thing up again. . . . I know these people. . . . When they detect weakness somewhere, they would not hesitate to harden their position. If they want to put me behind bars, let them."

— Richard M. Nixon on tape

"The question is: What did the President know, and when did he know it?"

— Senator Howard Baker (R-Tenn.)

"There are only so many lies you can take, and now there has been one too many. Nixon should get his ass out of the White House today."

— Senator Barry Goldwater (R-Ariz.)

"Whatever we learn or conclude, let us now proceed with such care and decency and thoroughness and honor that the vast majority of the American people, and their children after them, will say: 'This was the right course. There was no other way.'"

— Peter Rodino, chairman, House Judiciary Committee on Impeachment

"Richard M. Nixon has acted in a manner contrary to his trust as President and subversive of constitutional government. . . . Wherefore Richard M. Nixon by such conduct warrants impeachment and trial and removal from office."

— House Judiciary Committee

"[I am, in the words of Teddy Roosevelt,] the man in the arena whose face is marred by dust and sweat and blood, who at the best knows in the end the triumphs of high achievement and with the worst fails, at least fails while daring greatly."

— Richard M. Nixon, on leaving the presidency

"I, Gerald Ford, President of the United States, . . . do grant a full, free, and absolute pardon unto Richard Nixon for all offenses against the United States."

— Gerald Ford

"[This nation is becoming] a nation of hamburger stands, a country stripped of industrial capacity and meaningful work, . . . a service economy, . . . a nation of citizens busily buying and selling cheeseburgers and rootbeer floats."

— AFL-CIO Public Statement

"[Two million dollars worth of food to] all people with welfare cards, social security pension cards, food stamps, medical cards, parole or probation papers, and jail or bail release slips."

— Symbionese Liberation Army ransom demand for Patty Hearst

White House counsel John Dean gives testimony incriminating the president. *U.S. Senate.*

Ads

Live today. Tomorrow will cost more.

(Pan Am)

If you can't decide between a Shepherd, a Setter, or a Poodle, get them all. . . . Adopt a mutt.

(ASPCA)

Have a child. It's as beautiful as having a baby.

(New York State Board of Adoption)

Einstein's Theory of Relativity: give strangers the same price you give relatives.

(Einstein-Moomjy Carpets)

Our readers knew Henry [Kissinger] was getting married before Henry did.

(National Enquirer)

Equal Pay / Equal Time

(Bulova Accutron, for Men and Women)

If gas pains persist, try Volkswagen.

(Volkswagen)

We sell more cars than Ford, Chrysler, Chevrolet, and Buick combined.

(Matchbox Toy Cars)

TV

Premieres

"The Rockford Files," James Garner

"Tony Orlando and Dawn"

"Happy Days," Henry Winkler, Ron Howard

"Good Times," Esther Rolle, Jimmy Walker

"$25,000 Pyramid," Bill Cullen

"Monty Python's Flying Circus"

"Rhoda," Valerie Harper

"Little House on the Prairie," Michael Landon

"Chico and the Man," Freddie Prinze, Jack Albertson

"Police Woman," Angie Dickinson

Top Ten (Nielsen)

"All in the Family," "Sanford and Son," "Chico and the Man," "The Jeffersons" (premiered 1/75), "M*A*S*H," "Rhoda," "Good Times," "The Waltons," "Maude," "Hawaii Five-O"

Specials

"Love among the Ruins" (Laurence Olivier, Katharine Hepburn); "Queen of the Stardust Ballroom" (Jean Stapleton, Charles Durning); "The Missiles of October" (William Devane); "The American Film Institute Salute to James Cagney"; "Profile in Music: Beverly Sills"; "An Evening with John Denver"

Emmy Awards

"Upstairs, Downstairs" (drama): "The Mary Tyler Moore Show" (comedy); "The Carol Burnett Show" (variety); "Yes, Virginia, There Is a Santa Claus" (children); Jim McKay (sportscaster); Robert Blake (actor, "Baretta," premiered 1/75); Tony Randall (comedic actor, "The Odd Couple"), Jean Marsh (actress, "Upstairs, Downstairs"); Valerie Harper (comedic actress, "Rhoda")

Of Note

NBC pays a record $10 million for the movie *The Godfather* and will charge $225,000 per minute for commercials during its airing • "J.J." (Jimmy Walker), on "Good Times," coins a new catchphrase: "Dyn-o-mite."

Movies

Openings

The Godfather, Part II (Francis Ford Coppola), Al Pacino, Robert De Niro, Diane Keaton, Robert Duvall

Alice Doesn't Live Here Anymore (Martin Scorsese), Ellen Burstyn, Kris Kristofferson

Chinatown (Roman Polanski), Jack Nicholson, Faye Dunaway

The Conversation (Francis Ford Coppola), Gene Hackman, Allen Garfield

Lenny (Bob Fosse), Dustin Hoffman, Valerie Perrine

The Towering Inferno (John Guillermin), Steve McQueen, Paul Newman

Harry and Tonto (Paul Mazursky), Art Carney, Ellen Burstyn

Murder on the Orient Express (Sidney Lumet), Albert Finney, Ingrid Bergman, Lauren Bacall

Blazing Saddles (Mel Brooks), Cleavon Little, Gene Wilder, Madeline Kahn, Mel Brooks

Young Frankenstein (Mel Brooks), Gene Wilder, Peter Boyle, Madeline Kahn

Badlands (Terrence Malick), Martin Sheen, Sissy Spacek

That's Entertainment (Jack Haley, Jr.), Fred Astaire, Judy Garland, Gene Kelly

Andy Warhol's Frankenstein (Paul Morrissey), Joe Dallesandro, Monique Van Vooren

The Pedestrian (Maximilian Schell), Maximilian Schell, Mary Tamar

Amarcord (Federico Fellini), Puppela Maggio, Magali Noel

The Great Gatsby (Jack Clayton), Robert Redford, Mia Farrow, Sam Waterston

Death Wish (Michael Winner), Charles Bronson, Vincent Gardenia, Hope Lange

Academy Awards

Best Picture: *The Godfather, Part II*

Best Director: Francis Ford Coppola (*The Godfather, Part II*)

Best Actress: Ellen Burstyn (*Alice Doesn't Live Here Anymore*)

Best Actor: Art Carney (*Harry and Tonto*)

Top Box-Office Stars

Robert Redford, Clint Eastwood, Paul Newman, Barbra Streisand, Steve McQueen, Burt Reynolds, Charles Bronson, Jack Nicholson, Al Pacino, John Wayne

Stars of Tomorrow

Valerie Perrine, Richard Dreyfuss, Randy Quaid, Deborah Raffin, Joseph Bottoms, Ron Howard, Sam Waterston, Linda Blair, Keith Carradine, Steven Warner

Popular Music

Hit Songs

"Seasons in the Sun"
"The Most Beautiful Girl"
"The Streak"
"The Entertainer"
"Please, Mister Postman"
"Mandy"
"Top of the World"
"Just You and Me"

Top Records

Albums: *Elton John—Greatest Hits* (Elton John); *You Don't Mess around with Him* (Jim Croce); *The Sting* (Sound track); *Planet Waves* (Bob Dylan); *Band on the Run* (Paul McCartney and Wings); *461 Ocean Boulevard* (Eric Clapton)

Singles: *The Way We Were* (Barbra Streisand); *Cats in the Cradle* (Harry Chapin); *Love's Theme* (Love Unlimited Orchestra); *(You're) Having My Baby* (Paul Anka); *If You Love Me* (Olivia Newton-John); *Feel Like Makin' Love* (Roberta Flack); *Come and Get Your Love* (Redbone); *Dancing Machine* (Jackson Five); *The Loco-Motion* (Grand Funk Railroad); *Bennie and the Jets* (Elton John). Country: *I Will Always Love You* (Dolly Parton); *A Very Special Love Song* (Charlie Rich)

Grammy Awards

I Honestly Love You, Olivia Newton-John (record); *Fulfillingness' First Finale*, Stevie Wonder (album); "The Way We Were" (song)

Jazz and Big Bands

Rick Ulman records *Hillbilly Jazz*. Jazz hits the big charts again with John McLaughlin, Freddy Hubbard, Donald Byrd, Herbie Hancock, Keith Jarrett, and Mahavishnu.

Top Performers (*Downbeat*): Herbie Hancock (soloist), Thad Jones and Mel Lewis (band); Weather Report (jazz group); John McLaughlin, Ron Carter, Stanley Clarke, McCoy Tyner, Garnett Brown, Airto Moreira, Jean-Luc Ponty (instrumentalists); Flora Purim, Stevie Wonder (vocalists); Pointer Sisters (vocal group); Weather Report, *Mysterious Traveller*, Stevie Wonder, *Fulfillingness' First Finale* (albums)

Theater

Broadway Openings

Plays

Equus (Peter Shaffer), Anthony Hopkins, Peter Firth
Noel Coward in Two Keys (Noel Coward), Anne Baxter, Hume Cronyn, Jessica Tandy
My Fat Friend (Charles Laurence), Lynn Redgrave, George Rose
Jumpers (Tom Stoppard), Brian Bedford, Jill Clayburgh
Absurd Person Singular (Alan Ayckbourn), Richard Kiley, Geraldine Page, Sandy Dennis
The National Health (Peter Nichols), Rita Moreno, Leonard Frey
In Praise of Love (Terence Rattigan), Rex Harrison, Julie Harris, Martin Gabel
Sizwe Banzi Is Dead / The Island (Athol Fugard), John Kani, Winston Ntshona

Musicals

Lorelei (Jule Styne, Leo Robin), Carol Channing, Dody Goodman
The Magic Show (Stephen Schwartz), Doug Henning
Mack and Mabel (Jerry Herman), Robert Preston, Bernadette Peters
Over Here! (Richard and Robert Sherman), Janie Sell, Andrews Sisters

Classics, Revivals, and Off-Broadway Premieres

Ulysses in Nighttown (Majorie Barkentin), Zero Mostel, Fionnuala Flanagan; *Cat on a Hot Tin Roof* (Tennessee Williams), Elizabeth Ashley, Keir Dullea; *Scapino* (Molière), Jim Dale; *As You Like It* (all-male cast); Henry Fonda as Clarence Darrow; *The Wager* (Mark Medoff), Kristoffer Tabori; *The Dance of Death* (Strindberg), Robert Shaw, Zoë Caldwell; *A Doll's House* (Ibsen), Liv Ullmann; *The Sea Horse* (Edward Moore); *Sherlock Holmes* (Arthur Conan Doyle, William Gillette), John Wood

Regional

Founded: St. Nicholas Theater, Chicago, by William H. Macy, David Mamet, Patricia Cox, and Stephen Schachter

Mark Taper Forum, Los Angeles: *Savages* (Christopher Hampton), premiere

Stage Arena, Washington, D.C.: *Zalmen, or the Madness of God* (Elie Wiesel), premiere

Theater (cont.)

Dallas Theater Center: *A Texas Trilogy: The Last Meeting of the Knights of the White Magnolia, Lu Ann Hampton Laverty Oberlander, The Oldest Living Graduate* (Preston Jones)

Yale Repertory: *The Tubs (The Ritz)* (Terrence McNally), premiere

Goodman, Chicago: *The Sea* (Edward Bond), premiere

Long Wharf, New Haven: *Sizwe Banzi Is Dead* (Athol Fugard), premiere

Classical Music

Compositions
Dominick Argento, *From the Diary of Virginia Woolf*
Milton Babbitt, *Reflections*
George Rochberg, *Imago Mundi*
Elliott Carter, Violin and Piano Duo, Brass Quintet
Walter Piston, Concerto for String Quartet and
    Orchestra
Milton Feldman, Instruments I, Voice and
    Instruments II

Important Events
Numerous festivals celebrate the Arnold Schoenberg and Charles Ives centennials.
The New York Philharmonic continues its unusual programming with such works as Robert Schumann's Scenes from Goethe's *Faust,* Aaron Copland's *Connotations,* and the premieres of Aribert Reimann's *Cycle* for Baritone, Alberto Ginastera's *Serenata,* and Marvin Levy's *In Memoriam, W. H. Auden.*
The Chicago and Los Angeles symphonies visit twelve European cities; the Cleveland tours Japan.
Virgil Fox performs on the new $200,000 Rodgers electric organ (Carnegie Hall) with a concert of Bach, Dupré, Louis Vierne, and César Frank.
Vladimir Horowitz, at the Met, in his first concert in six years, plays Clementi, Schumann, Chopin, and Scriabin; proceeds go to the opera company. Maria Callas and Giuseppe di Stefano participate in other Met benefits.

Debut: Myung-Whun Chung

First Performances
Alberto Ginastera, String Quartet no. 3 (Dallas); Richard Rodney Bennett, Concerto for Orchestra (Denver); Sir Michael Tippett, Symphony no. 3 (Boston); Philip Glass, Music in 12 Parts (New York)

Pulitzer Prize
No prize is awarded.

Tony Awards
The River Niger, Joseph A. Walker (play), *Raisin,* Judd Woldin, Robert Brittan (musical)

Sarah Caldwell often produces, as well as directs and conducts, operas at the Opera Company of Boston. *Copyright* Washington Post. *Reprinted courtesy of D.C. Public Library.*

Opera

Metropolitan: Peter Pears (debut), *Death in Venice* (Benjamin Britten); Maureen Forrester, *Das Rheingold;* Kiri Te Kanawa (debut), *Otello;* double bill: *Bluebeard's Castle* and *Gianni Schicchi;* Montserrat Caballé, Nicolai Gedda / Placido Domingo, *I vespri siciliani*

New York State: Beverly Sills in all three Donizetti "English Queen" operas: *Maria Stuarda, Roberto Devereaux, Anna Bolena;* Sills, *I Puritani*

Boston: Donald Gramm, John Moulson, Arlene Saunders, *War and Peace* (Prokofiev, American premiere, performed at Wolf Trap, Washington, D.C.)

Chicago: Jon Vickers, *Peter Grimes*

Houston: Richard Stilwell, Frederica von Stade, John Reardon, *The Seagull* (Thomas Pasatieri)

Santa Fe: *Lulu*

Washington, D.C.: Frederica von Stade, Richard Stilwell, *Il ritorno d'Ulisse in patria* (Monteverdi)

San Francisco: Leontyne Price, *Manon Lescaut;* John Sutherland, *Esclarmonde*

Art

Paintings

Fairfield Porter, *The Cliffs of Isle au Haut*

Chuck Close, *Robert/ 104,072*

Richard Estes, *Woolworth's America*

Frank Stella, *Pratfall, York Factory*

Richard Artschwager, *Rockefeller Center*

Ralph Goings, *McDonald Pickup*

Helen Frankenthaler, *Savage Breeze*

Sculpture

Lynda Benglis, *Victor*

Carl Andre, *Decks*

Joel Shapiro, *Untitled (house on shelf)*

Richard Serra, *Ollantoyambo*

Robert Morris, *Labyrinth*

Michael Heizer, *The City, Complex One*

Calder's *Universe* is installed in the Sears Tower, Chicago.

Architecture

J. Paul Getty Museum, Malibu, Calif. (Langdon and Wilson)

Air and Space Museum, Washington, D.C. (Hellmuth, Obata, Kassabaum)

Sears Tower, Chicago (Skidmore, Owings and Merrill), world's tallest building (1,450 feet)

Roche and Dinkeloo design a downtown plan for Denver; the revitalization of Burlington Square, Vermont, is designed by Mies van der Rohe and Freeman-French-Freeman.

Important Exhibitions

Museums

New York: *Metropolitan:* Medieval tapestries; "A Centenary of Impressionism"; American Indian art. *Museum of Modern Art:* Miró, Duchamp. *Whitney:* Pop art, organized by Lawrence Alloway: Johns's flag paintings, Warhol's soup cans, Ramos's Batmen, Lichtenstein's comic strip frames. *Guggenheim:* Retrospective of 200 works of Giacometti

Philadelphia: Achievement of women in the arts; Duchamp

Washington: "American Self-Portraits": West, Copley, Whistler, Sargent, Eakins, Shahn, Warhol

Minneapolis: Willem de Kooning drawings and sculptures

Richmond, Whitney, San Francisco: The flowering of American folk art, 1776–1876.

Art Briefs

Numerous museums open, including the J. Paul Getty Museum in Malibu, Calif.; the Hirschhorn Museum and Sculpture Garden, Washington, D.C.; the Newberger Modern Museum (State University of New York, Purchase); the Walters, in Baltimore, builds a $4 million wing • Major sales include Willem de Kooning's *Woman V* ($850,000, the highest price ever paid a living artist; the painting brought $30,000 in 1955), Brancusi's *La Negresse* ($750,000), and Dali's *Resurrection of the Flesh* ($240,000).

Andy Warhol, in front of one of his paintings. *Courtesy Sedat Pakay.*

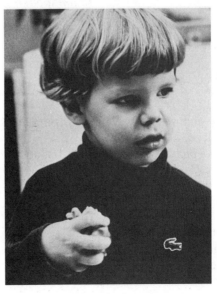

Designer clothing becomes fashionable for children.

Books

Fiction

Critics' Choice

Look at the Harlequins, Vladimir Nabokov
The War between the Tates, Alison Lurie
The Shadow Knows, Diane Johnson
Enormous Changes at the Last Minute, Grace Paley
The Hair of Harold Roux, Thomas Williams
The Last Days of Louisiana Red, Ishmael Reed
The Odd Woman, Gail Godwin
The House of the Solitary Maggot, James Purdy
Fear of Flying, Erica Jong
The King and India, John Gardner
Guilty Pleasures, Donald Barthelme
Dog Soldiers, Robert Stone
Sula, Toni Morrison

Best-Sellers

Centennial, James A. Michener
Watership Down, Richard Adams
Jaws, Peter Benchley
Tinker, Tailor, Soldier, Spy, John le Carré
Something Happened, Joseph Heller
The Dogs of War, Frederick Forsyth
The Pirate, Harold J. Robbins

The Seven-Per-Cent Solution, John H. Watson, M.D.
The Fan Club, Irving Wallace

Nonfiction

Critics' Choice

Time on the Cross, Robert Fogel, Stanley L. Engerman
Seduction and Betrayal, Elizabeth Hardwick
From Reverence to Rape, Molly Haskell
Flying, Kate Millet
Kissinger, Marvin and Bernard Kalb
The Diary of Anaïs Nin
The Real America, Ben Wattenberg
A Bridge Too Far, Cornelius Ryan
The Lives of a Cell, Lewis Thomas
Zen and the Art of Motorcycle Maintenance, Robert M. Pirsig
Choosing Our Language, Michael Novak
Marcel Proust, Roger Shattuck
The Life of Emily Dickinson, Richard Sewall

Best-Sellers

The Total Woman, Marabel Morgan
All the President's Men, Carl Bernstein and Bob Woodward
Plain Speaking: An Oral Biography of Harry S Truman, Merle Miller
More Joy: A Lovemaking

Companion to the Joy of Sex, ed. Alex Comfort
Alistair Cooke's America, Alistair Cooke
Tales of Power, Carlos A. Castaneda
You Can Profit from a Monetary Crisis, Harry Browne
All Things Bright and Beautiful, James Herriot
The Bermuda Triangle, Charles Berlitz, with J. Manson Valentine
The Memory Book, Harry Lorayne, Jerry Lucas

Poetry

Anne Sexton, *The Death Notebooks*
Robert Creeley, *Sitting Here*
W. H. Auden, *Thank You, Fog: Last Poems* (posthumous)
Marilyn Hacker, *Presentation Piece*
James Merrill, *The Yellow Pages: 59 Poems*

Pulitzer Prizes

The Killer Angels, Michael Shaara (fiction)
Jefferson and His Time, Dumas Malone (U.S. history)
Pilgrim at Tinker Creek, Annie Dillard (nonfiction)
The Power Broker: Robert Moses and the Fall of New York, Robert A. Caro (biography)
Turtle Island, Gary Synder (poetry)

Science and Technology

Mariner X's fly-by pictures show Venus surrounded by a shell of haze.
Pioneer II transmits pictures of Jupiter that include its large moon, Callisto.
Ultrasound diagnostic techniques are developed.
A new particle "J" or "psi" is discovered.
An air force SR-71 jet flies from New York to London in 1 hour, 55 minutes.
The National Academy of Science calls a halt to research in genetic engineering, pending safer techniques.

🙠 A USSR space probe lands on Mars and detects more water vapor than previously observed.
🙠 Great Britain, France, China, and India conduct nuclear tests.

Nobel Prize

Paul Jon Flory wins the prize in chemistry for his experiments with polymers. George E. Palade and Christian de Duve win in physiology and medicine for studies on the inner workings of living cells.

Sports

Baseball

Henry Aaron (Atlanta, NL) hits his 715th home run, off Al Downing, breaking Babe Ruth's lifetime record.

Lou Brock (St. Louis, NL) steals a record 118 bases.

Nolan Ryan (California, AL) strikes out a record-tying 19 in one game and also pitches his third no-hitter and wins the Cy Young Award.

Mike Marshall (Los Angeles, NL) appears in a record 106 games and also wins the Cy Young Award.

Champions

Batting	Angeles, NL), 20–6
Ralph Garr (Atlanta, NL), .353	Miguel Cuellar (Baltimore, AL), 22–10
Rod Carew (Minnesota, AL), .364	*Home runs*
Pitching	Mike Schmidt (Philadelphia, NL), 36
Andy Messersmith (Los	

Football

Kickoffs are moved to the 35-yard line in the NFL.

NFL Season Leaders: Sonny Jurgensen (Washington), passing; Larry McCutcheon (Los Angeles), rushing; Charlie Young (Philadelphia), receiving

AFC Season Leaders: Ken Anderson (Cincinnati), passing; Otis Armstrong (Denver), rushing; Lydell Mitchell (Baltimore), receiving

College All-Americans: Steve Bartkowski (Q), California; Randy White (L), Maryland; Joe Washington (RB), Oklahoma

Bowls (Jan. 1, 1975)

Rose: Southern California 18–Ohio State 17	Cotton: Penn State 41– Baylor 20
Orange: Notre Dame 13– Alabama 11	Sugar: Nebraska 13– Florida 10

Basketball

NBA All-Pro First Team: John Havlicek (Boston), Rick Barry (Golden State), Kareem Abdul-Jabbar (Milwaukee), Walt Frazier (New York), Gail Goodrich (Los Angeles)

ABA All-Pro First Team: Julius Erving (New York), George McGinnis (Indiana), Artis Gilmore (Kentucky), Jimmy Jones (Utah), Mack Calvin (Carolina)

Other Sports

Boxing: Muhammad Ali, using "rope-a-dope" tactics, knocks out George Foreman, in the eighth round, in Zaire.

Tennis: John Newcombe is the World Championship Tennis (WCT) champion.

Winners

World Series	*MVP*
Oakland (AL) 4	Kareem Abdul-Jabbar,
Los Angeles (NL) 1	Milwaukee
MVP	*College Basketball*
NL–Steve Garvey, Los Angeles	North Carolina State
AL–Jeff Burroughs, Texas	*Player of the Year*
Super Bowl IX (Jan. 1975)	David Thompson, North Carolina State
Pittsburgh 16–Minnesota 7	*Stanley Cup*
MVP	Philadelphia
Ken Stabler, Oakland	*US Tennis Open*
College Football	Men: Jimmy Connors
Southern California (UPI)	Women: Billie Jean King
Oklahoma (AP)	*USGA Open*
Heisman Trophy	Hale Irwin
Archie Griffin, Ohio State	*Kentucky Derby*
NBA Championship	Cannonade (A. Cordero,
Boston 4–Milwaukee 3	jockey)

Fashion

For Women: Fashion is marked by both the "covered" and "uncovered" look: (1) the string bikini, two soft, clinging, fabric postage stamps held together by string ties at the hip, and (2) the blanketed look with wide capes, along with coats and skirts that fall below the knee to mid and low calf and loose blouses. A nostalgia for the twenties and thirties also characterizes the year, with art deco revived in silver accessories and geometric prints. T-shirt graphics include comic characters and historical, musical, and contemporary personalities; screen-print dresses have color reproductions of Rolls-Royces and heroes of the twenties and thirties. Victorian camisoles are worn on top of skirts; garter belts, twenties' teddy lingerie (loose pants with one-piece camisole tops) are also worn. Ethnic clothing includes Russian-style tunics that are side-buttoned and belted, and pants that tuck into ankle boots, Chinese worker shirts, pants, and quilted vests. Capes become fashionable again.

High-fashion notes: St. Laurent's "Steppes look"; Missone's knit stripes and zigzags; Lagerfeld's smocks atop midis; Valentino's long, pleated knits; Biba's naughty thirties' look; Hermès's envelop bag

Kaleidoscope ───────────

- The nation witnesses the House Judiciary Committee roll-call vote, 27–11, on the first article of impeachment (obstruction of justice) against the president; 28–10 on the second (abuse of power); and 21–17 on the third (violation of congressional subpoena).
- Director William Colby admits that the CIA has thousands of illegally obtained secret files on various Americans.
- White House associates who leave the administration because of Watergate include Robert Haldeman, John Ehrlichman, John Dean, Charles Colson, John Mitchell, Jeb Stuart Magruder, Gordon Strachen, Herbert Porter, John Caulfield, Anthony Ulasewicz, Howard Hunt, Maurice Stans, Robert Mardian, Donald Segretti, Herbert Kalmbach, L. Patrick Gray, and Dwight Chapin.
- After Gerald Ford gives Richard Nixon his "full" and "absolute" pardon, his popularity drops from 72 percent to 49 percent.
- The Equal Opportunity Act forbids discrimination based on sex or marital status.
- The number of Vietnam veterans totals 6,558,000.
- Forty-two nuclear plants are operable, 56 are under construction, 101 have been ordered, 14 are in the planning stage.
- An antitrust suit is brought against AT&T, Western Electric, and Bell Labs.
- Because of gasoline shortages, daylight savings time is observed year around to save fuel.
- Car sales are down 35 percent from 1973; home construction is down 40 percent.
- Thousands bare their buttocks in the year's streaking fad: 1,543 at the University of Georgia boast the largest number; hundreds at Texas Tech stay naked for hours; streaking also marks major academic, cultural, and sports gatherings, including the Academy Awards.
- Philippe Petit dances along a one-inch wire strung between the twin towers of the World Trade Center, New York, 1,350 feet high; Petit gets a job as high-wire man with Barnum and Bailey.
- Frank Sinatra makes news as he calls the press "bums" and women "broads" and "hookers."
- Newlyweds of the year include Henry and Nancy Kissinger and singer Sly of the Family Stone and Kathy; the latter marry at Madison Square Garden before a record audience.
- AT&T, the world's largest private employer, bans discrimination against homosexuals.
- Four Episcopal bishops defy church law and ordain 11 women as priests.
- During court-ordered busing in Boston, Louise Day Hicks leads a group called Restore Our Alienated Rights (ROAR) to halt integration; rioting follows.
- The public is warned of the environmental carcinogen polyvinyl chloride used in plastic containers.
- Lt. William Calley, convicted for his role in the My Lai massacre, is paroled.

"All in the Family," the Norman Lear-Bud Yorkin production with Jean Stapleton and Carroll O'Connor, continues as Number 1 for the third year. *Movie Star News.*

- Soul music moves into discos; in addition to the renewed interest in jazz, ragtime is revived.
- CBGB, New York, introduces Blondie, the Ramones, and Talking Heads, among other glitter-backlash groups.
- Evel Knievel fails to launch across the Idaho Snake River in his Sky-Cycle X-2, and riots and stampedes follow.
- The "singles" industry is estimated at $40 billion.
- Gay Gaer Luce helps found SAGE, Senior Actualization and Growth Exploitation, bringing greater attention to "gray power," senior citizens who comprise 10 percent of the population.
- The biggest money-making films are all-star disaster movies like *Towering Inferno* and *Earthquake* and films of supernatural violence like *The Exorcist*.
- Although a disgruntled artist sprays "KILL YES ALL" on Picasso's *Guernica*, in the Museum of Modern Art, the painting is undamaged.

New Words and Usages: Nuke, yen, stonewalling, striking, scientism

First Appearances: An avowed homosexual elected to state office (Elaine Noble, Boston), girls allowed into the Little League, bachelor's degree awarded by a recognized institution without requiring a single college credit (N. E. France, SUNY, Albany), woman mayor of a major city (J. G. Hayes, San Jose, Calif.), woman police officer killed in the line of duty (G. A. Cobb), pressure-sensitive adhesive postage stamp

1975

In the News

H. R. Haldeman, John Ehrlichman, and John Mitchell Are Convicted of Conspiracy . . . President Ford Announces Recession Policy . . . House Democrats Remove Three Chairmen in Successful Challenge to Seniority System . . . Ford Signs $22.8 Billion Tax Cut . . . U.S. Air Force Plane with Vietnamese Orphans Crashes, 200 Are Killed . . . Ford Officially Ends American Role in Vietnam . . . Saigon Falls to North Vietnam, Thousands Flee by Boat . . . Unemployment Reaches 8.9%, Highest Since 1941 . . . Marines Rescue 39 from USS "Mayaguez," Seized by Cambodia . . . Cambodian Khmer Rouge Evacuate Populace from Cities, Massive Death Toll Is Feared . . . Indira Gandhi Declares State of Emergency and Arrests Opponents . . . Apollo-Soyez Link-Up Mission Is Launched . . . 35 East and West Nations Meet in Helsinki, Accords on Human Rights Are Declared . . . Teamster Leader Jimmy Hoffa Disappears, Foul Play Is Suspected . . . Voting Rights Act Is Extended Seven Years . . . Israel and Egypt Sign Sinai Interim Agreement . . . Lynette Fromme, Manson Family Member, Is Arrested for Pointing Gun at President . . . Patty Hearst Is Arrested by FBI . . . Ford Escapes Shot Fired by Sara Jane Moore . . . U.S. and Russia Agree on Five-Year Grain Export Plan . . . OPEC Increases Oil Prices 10% . . . Portuguese Leave Angola . . . Spanish Dictator Francisco Franco Dies . . . Ford Rejects Federal Bailout of N.Y.C. . . . Arab Terrorists Seize Hostages at OPEC Meetings in Vienna . . . CIA Acknowledges Plots to Kill Undesirable Heads of State . . . Bomb at La Guardia Airport, N.Y.C., Kills 11.

Quotes —————————————

"Today, accountants look like Shakespearean actors, space salesmen look like art directors, hair stylists wear short hair, clothes designers dress conservatively, . . . an orthodontist comes on like a cowboy. . . . Everybody's into reverse role-playing."
— John Weitz, fashion designer

"A total woman caters to her man's special quirks, whether it be in salads, sex, or sports."
— Marabel Morgan, *The Total Woman*

"FORD TO CITY: DROP DEAD"
— *New York Daily News* headline

"I don't know of any foreign leader that was ever assassinated by the CIA. . . . There were always discussions of everything . . . things that may not be acceptable to the American people."
— Richard Helms, former CIA director

"In addition to the inflation, we have stagnating productivity. People don't work the way they used to."
— Arthur Burns, chairman, Federal Reserve

"[The lesson of Vietnam is] we must throw off the cumbersome mantle of world policeman and limit our readiness to areas where our interests are truly in danger."
— Senator Edward Kennedy (D-Mass.)

President Gerald Ford, the first appointed president. *Library of Congress.*

"The United States is no longer in a position to take on warmongering adventures. . . . Only fifteen years ago, the United States was very powerful—but no more."
— Fidel Castro

"Though we are no longer predominant, we are inescapably a leader."
— Henry Kissinger

Ads —————————————

The Arabs have the oil.
America has the corn.
(*CPC International Corn Products*)

"Some of my favorite performers are horses."
(*Frank Sinatra for Off-Track Betting*)

When it comes to buying an engagement ring, don't let love get in the way.
(*Fortunoff*)

Send yourself across the country in four minutes or less.
(*Xerox Telecopier*)

If you forget to have your children vaccinated, you could be reminded of it the rest of your life.
(*Metropolitan Life Insurance Company*)

Warren Beatty, in *Shampoo*, portrays a womanizing hairdresser. *Movie Star News.*

Perform a death-defying act. Have your blood pressure checked.
(*American Heart Association*)

Due to a lack of funds, there will be a shortage of justice this year.
(*Give to the Legal Aid Society*)

TV

Premieres
"A.M. America"
"Robert MacNeil Report"
"Baretta," Robert Blake
"S.W.A.T.," Steve Forrest
"The Jeffersons," Isabel Sanford, Sherman Hemsley
"Barney Miller," Hal Linden
"Starsky and Hutch," David Soul, Paul Michael Glaser
"One Day at a Time," Bonnie Franklin
"Phyllis," Cloris Leachman
"NBC's Saturday Night Live," Chevy Chase, John Belushi, Gilda Radner, Dan Akroyd
"Welcome Back, Kotter," Gabriel Kaplan, John Travolta

Top Ten (Nielsen)
"All in the Family," "Rich Man, Poor Man," "Laverne and Shirley," "Maude," "The Bionic Woman," "Phyllis," "Sanford and Son," "Rhoda," "The Six-Million-Dollar Man," "ABC Monday Night Movie"

Specials
"Eleanor and Franklin" (Edward Herrmann, Jane Alexander); "A Moon for the Misbegotten" (Jason Robards); "Rich Man, Poor Man" (Nick Nolte, Peter Strauss); "The Adams Chronicles" (George Grizzard); "Vietnam: A War That Is Finished"; "7,382 Days in Vietnam"; "Vietnam: Lessons Learned, Prices Paid"

Emmy Awards
"Policy Story" (drama); "The Mary Tyler Moore Show" (comedy); "NBC's Saturday Night Live" (variety); "You're a Good Sport, Charlie Brown" (children); Jim McKay (sports personality); Peter Falk (actor, "Columbo"); Jack Albertson (comedic actor, "Chico and the Man"); Michael Learned, (actress, "The Waltons"); Mary Tyler Moore (comedic actress, "The Mary Tyler Moore Show")

Of Note
Situation comedy peaks with shows such as "All in the Family," "M*A*S*H," "The Mary Tyler Moore Show," "The Odd Couple," "Barney Miller," "Rhoda," and "Chico and the Man" • As a result of protests over TV violence and sex, as well as subsequent FCC pressure, the networks agree to establish 8:00–9:00 P.M. as the "family hour."

Movies

Openings
One Flew over the Cuckoo's Nest (Milos Forman), Jack Nicholson, Louise Fletcher
Barry Lyndon (Stanley Kubrick), Ryan O'Neal, Marisa Berenson
Dog Day Afternoon (Sidney Lumet), Al Pacino, John Cazale, James Broderick, Charles Durning
Jaws (Steven Spielberg), Roy Scheider, Robert Shaw, Richard Dreyfuss
Nashville (Robert Altman), Karen Black, Ronee Blakley, Keith Carradine
Shampoo (Hal Ashby), Warren Beatty, Julie Christie, Goldie Hawn, Lee Grant, Jack Warden
The Story of Adele H. (François Truffaut), Isabelle Adjani, Bruce Robinson
Hester Street (Joan Micklin Silver), Steve Keats, Carol Kane
The Man Who Would Be King (John Huston), Michael Caine, Sean Connery
Monty Python and the Holy Grail (Terry Gilliam, Terry Jones), Graham Chapman, John Cleese, Terry Gilliam, Eric Idle, Terry Jones
Swept Away (Lina Wertmuller), Mariangela Melato, Giancarlo Giannini
Three Days of the Condor (Sydney Pollack), Robert Redford, Faye Dunaway
Tommy (Ken Russell), Roger Daltrey, Ann-Margret, Oliver Reed, Elton John
Seven Beauties (Lina Wertmuller), Giancarlo Giannini, Shirley Stoler

Academy Awards
Best Picture: *One Flew over the Cuckoo's Nest*
Best Director: Milos Forman (*One Flew over the Cuckoo's Nest*)
Best Actress: Louise Fletcher (*One Flew over the Cuckoo's Nest*)
Best Actor: Jack Nicholson (*One Flew over the Cuckoo's Nest*)

Top Box-Office Stars
Robert Redford, Barbra Streisand, Al Pacino, Charles Bronson, Paul Newman, Clint Eastwood, Burt Reynolds, Woody Allen, Steve McQueen, Gene Hackman

Stars of Tomorrow
Stockard Channing, Bo Svenson, Susan Blakely, William Atherton, Brad Dourif, Bo Hopkins, Conny Van Dyke, Ronee Blakley, Paul Le Mat

Popular Music

Hit Songs
"Rhinestone Cowboy"
"Fame"
"Best of My Love"
"Laughter in the Rain"
"The Hustle"
"Have You Never Been Mellow?"
"One of These Nights"
"Jive Talkin' "
"Black Water"

Top Records

Albums: *Captain Fantastic & the Brown Dirt Cowboy* (Elton John); *Physical Graffiti* (Led Zeppelin); *Chicago X—Chicago's Greatest Hits* (Chicago); *Red Octopus* (Jefferson Starship); *Rock of the Westies* (Elton John)

Singles: *Philadelphia Freedom* (Elton John); *Before the Next Teardrop Falls* (Freddy Fender); *My Eyes Adored You* (Frankie Valli)*: Shining Star* (Earth, Wind and Fire); *Thank God I'm a Country Boy* (John Denver); *You're No Good* (Linda Ronstadt). Country: *San Antonio Stroll* (Tanya Tucker); *A Legend in My Time* (Ronnie Milsap)

Grammy Awards
Love Will Keep Us Together, Captain and Tennille (record); *Still Crazy after All These Years,* Paul Simon (album); "Send in the Clowns" (song)

Jazz and Big Bands
Electronic keyboard instruments gain in popularity with one-man bands: Herbie Hancock, Chick Corea.

Popular mainstream performers include Cecil Taylor, Bill Evans, Dizzy Gillespie, Miles Davis, Gerry Mulligan, Oscar Peterson, and Jim Hall.

Top Performers *(Downbeat):* McCoy Tyner (soloist); Thad Jones and Mel Lewis (band); Weather Report (jazz group); Joe Pass, Phil Woods, Bill Watrous (instrumentalists); Flora Purim, Stevie Wonder (vocalists); Pointer Sisters (vocal group); Earth, Wind and Fire (rock/blues group); Weather Report, *Tale Spinnin'*, Jeff Beck, *Blow by Blow* (albums)

Theater

Broadway Openings
Plays
Seascape (Edward Albee), Deborah Kerr, Frank Langella
Travesties (Tom Stoppard), John Wood
Same Time, Next Year (Bernard Slade), Ellen Burstyn, Charles Grodin
The Ritz (Terrence McNally), Rita Moreno, Jack Weston, F. Murray Abraham
The Norman Conquests (Alan Ayckbourn), Barry Nelson, Ken Howard, Estelle Parsons, Richard Benjamin, Paula Prentiss
Habeas Corpus (Alan Bennett), Alan Bennett, Donald Sinden

Musicals
The Wiz (Charlie Smalls), Stephanie Mills
Shenandoah (Peter Udell, Gary Geld), John Cullum
Chicago (John Kander, Fred Ebb), Gwen Verdon, Jerry Orbach, Chita Rivera
A Chorus Line (Edward Kleban, Marvin Hamlisch), Donna McKechnie, Ann Reinking, choreographed by Michael Bennett

Classics, Revivals, and Off-Broadway Premieres
A Doll's House (Ibsen), Liv Ullmann; *Private Lives* (Noel Coward), Maggie Smith, Brian Bedford; *The Misanthrope* (Molière), Diana Rigg, Alec McCowen; *Hamlet,* Sam Waterston; *All God's Chillun Got Wings* (Eugene O'Neill), Trish Van Devere; *Death of a Salesman* (Arthur Miller), George C. Scott, Teresa Wright; *Sweet Bird of Youth* (Tennessee Williams), Christopher Walken, Irene Worth; *The Constant Wife* (W. Somerset Maugham), Ingrid Bergman; *The Skin of Our Teeth* (Thornton Wilder), Elizabeth Ashley, Alfred Drake; *Trelawny of the Wells* (Pinero), John Lithgow, Meryl Streep; *The Devils* (John Whiting), Anne Bancroft, Jason Robards

Regional
Goodman, Chicago: *American Buffalo* (David Mamet), premiere

Long Wharf, New Haven: *Ah, Wilderness!* (Eugene O'Neill), Teresa Wright, Geraldine Fitzgerald, Paul Rudd, revival

Mark Taper Forum, Los Angeles: *The Shadow Box* (Michael Cristofer), premiere

Pulitzer Prize
Seascape, Edward Albee

Tony Awards
Equus, Peter Shaffer (play), *The Wiz,* Charlie Smalls (musical)

Classical Music _____

Compositions
Ned Rorem, *Air Music*
John Cage, *Etudes Australes*
George Rochberg, Piano Quintet, Violin Concerto
Roy Harris, Symphony no. 14
Roger Sessions, Three Choruses on Biblical Texts
Leonard Bernstein, Seven Dances and Suite no. 1
    from *Dybbuck*
Morton Feldman, *Piano and Orchestra*
Floyd Carlisle, *Flower and Hawk*
Garrett List, Process #1, #2

Important Events
Birthday celebrations include Strauss's 150th,
Britten's and Ravel's 100th, and Copland's 75th.

New Appointments: Mstislav Rostropovitch
(National) and André Previn (Pittsburgh)

Debut: Emanuel Ax

First Performances
Dominick Argento, *From the Diary of Virginia Woolf*
(Minneapolis); Elliott Carter, Duo for Violin and
Piano (New York); Michael Colgrass,
Concertmasters (Detroit); Henry Brant, *Homage to
Ives* (Denver); Eric Stokes, *Continental Harp and
Band Report* (Minneapolis); Alberto Ginastera
Turbae ad Passionem Gregioranam (Philadelphia);
Lewis Weingarden, Piano Concerto (Denver); George
Rochberg, Piano Concerto (Pittsburgh)

A Chorus Line, Michael Bennett's musical psychodrama
concerning the hardships of show business. *Movie Star
News.*

Rudolf
Nureyev.
*Movie Star
News.*

Opera

Metropolitan: James Levine is appointed musical
director; Anthony Bliss becomes executive director.
Beverly Sills (debut), *Siege of Corinth; Ring* cycle is
completed after seven years (in the von Karajan,
Salzburg productions), with Birgit Nilsson, Mignon
Dunn, Berit Lindholm (debut), Maureen Forrester,
Thomas Stewart, Jess Thomas, Ragnar Ulfung;
Teresa Kubiak, *Un ballo in maschera;* Régine
Crespin, *Carmen; Boris Godunov* (based on two
original versions)

New York City: Beverly Sills, *Daughter of the
Regiment*

Dallas: Beverly Sills, *Lucrezia Borgia;* Marilyn
Horne, *Rinaldo*

Houston: *Treemonisha*

Chicago: Ileana Cotrubas, Richard Stilwell, *Orfeo
ed Euridice;* Nicholai Ghiaurov, *Don Quichotte;*
Carlo Cossutta, Gilda Cruz-Romo, *Otello*

Boston: Jon Vickers, Donald Gramm, John
Reardon, Patricia Wells, *Benvenuto Cellini* (Berlioz,
American premiere)

Seattle: Complete *Ring* (once in German, once in
English)

Music Notes
On its first visit to the United States, the Moscow
Bolshoi Opera performs six operas • James Dixon
conducts the University of Iowa Symphony in
Aleksandr Scriabin's *Prometheus,* which features a
laser apparatus that renders the visualization of color
that Scriabin envisioned.

Art

Paintings

Richard Estes, *Central Savings*

Jasper Johns, *Scent*

Bill Beckley, *Hot and Cold Faucets with Drain*

Frank Stella, *Grodno (1–7)*

Willem de Kooning, *Whose Name Was Writ in Water*

Sculpture

Carl Andre, *Twenty-Ninth Copper Cardinal*

Lynda Benglis, *Bravo 2*

Louise Nevelson, *Transparent Horizon*

Jackie Winsor, *Fifty-five*

Larry Le Va, *Center Points and Lengths (through Tangents)*

Richard Serra, *Sight Point*

Claes Oldenburg, *Geometric Mouse—Scale A*

Scott Burtain, *Bronze Chair*

Sheila Hicks, *Communications Labyrinth*

Alexander Calder's *Flying Colors of the United States* is installed at Braniff International.

Architecture

Herbert F. Johnson Museum, Cornell University (I. M. Pei)

Best Products Showroom, Houston (Site, Inc.)

Penzoil Plaza, Houston (Philip Johnson, John Burgee)

"Decade 80" Solar House, Tucson (Cooper Development Association)

INA Tower, Philadelphia (Mitchell, Guirgola)

Franklin Court, Philadelphia (Venturi and Rauch)

Crystal Court, IDS Center, Minneapolis (Philip Johnson)

Design competition for 1,000 housing units, Roosevelt Island, New York City, Philip Johnson in charge

Important Exhibitions

Museums

Visiting the Metropolitan, Philadelphia, and Detroit museums: "French Painting 1774–1830: From David to Delacroix"; also touring: "Archeological Finds of the People's Republic of China"; "Master Paintings from the Hermitage and State Russian Museums"; "King Tutankhamen's Treasures"

New York: *Metropolitan:* Scythian Ancient Treasures; "The Impressionist Epoch." *Whitney:* "The Flowering of American Folk Art"; Sheldon Peck; Mark di Suvero retrospective. *Whitney, Hirshhorn:* Elie Nadelman retrospective. *Guggenheim:* Max Ernst retrospective

Boston: *Institute of Fine Arts:* "Boston Celebrations: Jubilee Projects for the Bicentennial"

Washington, D.C.: *John F. Kennedy Center:* "Art Now, '75 Cartoon Festival" (first U.S. comprehensive comic art show)

Cleveland, Los Angeles, Metropolitan: Chinese paintings from the Arthur M. Sackler collection

San Francisco: *Palace of Legion of Honor:* De Young; "Rainbow Show." *Museum of Modern Art:* Benefit on theme of artists' soapbox derby with five nudes, pumpernickel sports car

Chicago: Monet

Art Briefs

The Metropolitan sponsors a rare one-man show of Francis Bacon • Bicentennial celebrations begin and include an exhibition of Calder's red, white, and blue flagship sculpture • The Metropolitan sends an exhibition of 19th- and 20th-century realistic art to the Hermitage and Pushkin museums • Paul Gauguin's *Hina Maruru* sells for $950,000.

Dance

The Bolshoi Ballet visits the United States after almost ten years. Rudolf Nureyev dances with the Martha Graham and Murray Louis modern dance companies. Bicentennial celebrations begin, such as Alvin Ailey's *The Mooche* and *Night Creature*.

Premieres/Important Productions

American Ballet Theatre: For its 35th anniversary gala—*The Sleeping Beauty* (Anton Dolin); *Pillar of Fire, Fancy Free, Three Virgins and a Devil, Raymonda,* and the premiere of *The Leaves Are Falling* (Anthony Tudor, Dvorak)

New York City Ballet: *Homage à Ravel—six new works,* including *Gaspard de la Nuit, Daphnis and Chloe, Tzigane* (Balanchine, Taras, Robbins)

San Francisco: *Shinju* (Michael Smuin); *Romeo and Juliet* (Smuin, full length)

Joffrey: *Deuce Coupe* (Twyla Tharp)

Martha Graham: *The Scarlet Letter*

Of Interest

Valery Panov and Galina Panova dance in *Lady and Hooligan* and *The Corsair* • Nureyev and Dame Margot Fonteyn dance with Martha Graham in *Lucifer* for her 50th anniversary gala.

Books

Fiction

Critics' Choice

A Month of Sundays, John Updike
The Dead Father, Donald Barthelme
Cockpit, Jerzy Kosinski
The Underground Woman, Kay Boyle
J R, William Gaddis
Tyrants Destroyed and Other Stories, Vladimir Nabokov
I Would Have Saved Them If I Could, Leonard Michaels
Beyond the Bedroom Wall, Larry Woiwode
A Dove of the East and Other Stories, Mark Helprin

Best-Sellers

Ragtime, E. L. Doctorow
The Moneylenders, Arthur Hailey
Curtain, Agatha Christie
Looking for Mister Goodbar, Judith Rossner
The Choirboys, Joseph Wambaugh
The Eagle Has Landed, Jack Higgins
The Great Train Robbery, Michael Crichton
Shōgun, James Clavell

Nonfiction

Critics' Choice

Anarchy, State, and Utopia, Robert Nozick
Sociobiology, Edward O. Wilson
The War against the Jews, 1933–1945, Lucy Davidowicz
Synergetics, Buckminster Fuller
Against Our Will: Men, Women and Rape, Susan Brownmiller
A Time to Die, Tom Wicker
The Courage to Create, Rollo May
Before the Fall, William Safire
Thinking about Crime, James Q. Wilson
The Great Railway Bazaar, Paul Theroux
Fathers and Children, Michael Rogin
A Century of Struggle, Eleanor Flexner
American Slavery, American Freedom, Edmund S. Morgan
The Great War and Modern Memory, Paul Fussell
Passage to Ararat, Michael J. Arlen
The Problem of Slavery in the Age of Revolution, David Brion Davis

Best-Sellers

Angels: God's Secret Agents, Billy Graham
Winning through Intimidation, Robert Ringer
TM, Harold H. Bloomfield
The Ascent of Man, Jacob Bronowski
Sylvia Porter's Money Book, Sylvia Porter
Total Fitness in 30 Minutes a Week, Laurence E. Morehouse, Leonard Gross

Poetry

Anne Sexton, *The Awful Rowing toward God*
Nikki Giovanni, *The Women and the Men*
A. R. Ammons, *Diversifications*
Galway Kinnell, *The Avenue Bearing the Initial of Christ into the New World*
Denise Levertov, *The Freeing of the Dust*
William Meredith, *Hazard, the Painter*

Pulitzer Prizes

Humboldt's Gift, Saul Bellow (fiction)
Lamy of Santa Fe, Paul Horgan (U.S. history)
Why Survive? Being Old in America, Robert N. Butler (nonfiction)
Edith Wharton: A Biography R. W. B. Lewis (biography)
Self-Portrait in a Convex Mirror, John Ashbery (poetry)

Science and Technology

Apollo 18 and the USSR's Soyuz 19 dock in space, perform experiments together, and indicate the possibility of space rescue.

A telephone transmission device is developed to analyze a distant patient's heartbeat.

EMI develops a scanner that takes cross-sectional X-rays through any part of the body.

The highly controversial DES is approved for limited use, such as "morning-after" contraception.

The Heimlich Maneuver, for people who choke on food, is approved.

Leading scientists try to formulate safety precautions for genetic engineering at the Asilomar (California) Conference.

Discovered in Texas, a pterosaur fossil with a 51-foot wing span offers evidence of the largest known flying animal.

🦋 Encephalin, "the brain's own opiate," is isolated, leading to further research in the production of a natural analgesic without addictive properties.

🦋 Atari/Sears of Japan produces the first low-priced integrated circuits for TV games.

Nobel Prize

James Brainwater wins in physics for demonstrating that the atomic nucleus is asymmetrical. David Baltimore, Howard M. Temin, and Renato Dulbecco win in physiology and medicine for work on the interaction between tumor viruses and the genetic material of the cell.

Sports

Baseball

Newly declared free agent Catfish Hunter signs a record $2.85 million contract with New York Yankee owner George Steinbrenner.

Cincinnati's "Big Red Machine" wins 108 games, the most won by any team in the National League since 1906, when Chicago won 116.

Fred Lynn (Boston, AL) is the first player to win Rookie of the Year and MVP in the same season.

A record TV audience of 75.9 million watches the seventh game of the World Series.

The Cy Young awards are won by Tom Seaver (New York, NL) and Jim Palmer (Baltimore, NL).

Champions

Batting
Bill Madlock (Chicago, NL), .354
Rod Carew (Minnesota, AL), .359
Pitching
Don Gullett (Cincinnati, NL), 15–4
Mike Torrez (Baltimore, AL), 20–9
Home runs
Mike Schmidt (Philadelphia, NL), 38

Football

Archie Griffin (Ohio State) is the first player to win a second Heisman Trophy.

Oklahoma's 37-game unbeaten streak is ended.

NFL Season Leaders: Fran Tarkenton (Minnesota), passing; Jim Otis (St. Louis), rushing; Chuck Foreman (Minnesota), receiving

AFC Season Leaders: Ken Anderson (Cincinnati), passing; O. J. Simpson (Buffalo), rushing, 1,827 yards; Reggie Rucker (Cleveland), receiving

College All-Americans: Tony Dorsett (B), Pittsburgh; Ricky Bell (B), Southern California.

Bowls (Jan. 1, 1976)

Rose: UCLA 23–Ohio State 10
Orange: Oklahoma 14–Michigan 6
Cotton: Arkansas 31–Georgia 10
Sugar: Alabama 13–Penn State 6

Basketball

NBA All-Pro First Team: John Havlicek (Boston), Rick Barry (Golden State), Kareem Abdul-Jabbar (Milwaukee), Walt Frazier (New York), Gail Goodrich (Los Angeles)

Other Sports

Boxing: In the "Thrilla in Manila," Muhammad Ali beats Joe Frazier by a TKO in the 15th round to regain the title.

Golf: Jack Nicklaus wins the Masters and PGA, misses the U.S. Open by two and the British Masters by one; he has won 16 majors.

Soccer: The New York Cosmos soccer team signs Brazilian star Pelé to a $1 million contract.

Tennis: Arthur Ashe wins Wimbledon and is the leading money winner with $325,000.

Horse racing: Unbeaten three-year-old Ruffian breaks an ankle and must be destroyed.

Winners

World Series
Cincinnati (NL) 4
Boston (AL) 3
MVP
NL–Joe Morgan, Cincinnati
AL–Fred Lynn, Boston
Super Bowl X (Jan. 1976)
Pittsburgh 21–Dallas 17
MVP
Fran Tarkenton, Minnesota
College Football
Oklahoma
Heisman Trophy
Archie Griffin, Ohio State
NBA Championship
Golden State 4–Washington 0

MVP
Bob McAdoo, Buffalo
College Basketball
UCLA
Player of the Year
David Thompson, North Carolina State
Stanley Cup
Philadelphia
US Tennis Open
Men: Manuel Orantes
Women: Chris Evert
USGA Open
Lou Graham
Kentucky Derby
Foolish Pleasure (J. Vasquez, jockey)

Fashion

For Women: East and West meet in the ethnic and layered look: from Britain come the Sherlock Holmes cape, Norfolk jacket, and tartan kilt; from China, the velvet gown, cossack coat, pants tucked in boots-style, and hats with ear flaps; from France, skin-tight jeans rolled at the knee with boots. Also popular are khaki and blue fatigues and jumpsuits, along with wide-shouldered pinafore dresses and other early American dress styles (for the bicentennial) with prim, high necks, fitted bodices, and gathered skirts. The T-shirt fad continues.

For Men: The casual look dominates: leisure suits with large patch pockets, worn with open shirts (collars extended over the lapels), or sweaters, scarves, ascots, and string ties. Women's designers, like Halston, turn to men's wear.

High-fashion notes: For Women—the Louis Vuitton duffle bag; Dorothy Bis's sweater coat. For Men—the St. Laurent fitted, double-breasted, "banker-gangster" suit

Kaleidoscope

- When Apollo 18 and USSR Soyez dock in space, the astronauts celebrate with a dinner of borscht, turkey, and lamb.
- A national opinion survey indicates that 69 percent of the population believes that "over the last 10 years, this country's leaders have consistently lied to the people"; public confidence in physicians drops from 73 percent (1966) to 42 percent; in big business, 55 percent to 16 percent.
- Attorney General Edward Levi confirms that J. Edgar Hoover kept files on the private lives of prominent people, including presidents and congressmen.
- Former CIA director Richard Helmes divulges CIA sponsorship of the assassination of foreign leaders—the attempt, for example, to enlist the Mafia's aid in killing Castro. One plot involved poisoned pens; another, poisoned cigars.
- The so-called typical nuclear family, with working father, housewife, and two children, represents only 7 percent of the population; average family size is 3.43 (in 1970, 3.58; in 1920, 4.3).
- Harvard changes its 5 to 2 male-female admissions policy to equal admissions.
- Vandalism and violence increase in public schools; homicides increase nearly 20 percent, rapes and robberies, 40 percent; since 1965, crimes against students escalate 3,000 percent and against teachers 7,000 percent.
- Despite the International Women's Year, efforts to pass statewide ERAs in New York and New Jersey suffer defeat.
- The Atomic Energy Commission is dissolved.
- A Massachusetts physician is convicted of manslaughter by a Boston jury for aborting a fetus and is sentenced to a year on probation.
- California and New York doctors publicize their enormous malpractice insurance increases by withholding all but emergency services; premiums have increased 93.5 percent in New York since last year.
- The Supreme Court rules that the mentally ill cannot be hospitalized against their will unless they are dangerous to themselves or others.
- A New Jersey superior court denies the petition of Karen Ann Quinlan's parents, which asks to remove her life support systems; she has suffered irreversible brain damage after an overdose of alcohol and tranquilizers.
- New York City, under threat of default, is bailed out by union pension funds, which buy Municipal Assistance Corporation bonds; MAC is headed by Felix Rohatyn.
- Governor James Rhodes and the Ohio National Guard are acquitted of all claims against them in the Kent State deaths of 1971.
- Joanne Little is declared "not guilty" of stabbing a white prison guard who tried to rape her.
- Rape laws are changed in nine states, narrowing the amount of corroborative evidence necessary for conviction and also restricting the trial questions permitted regarding the victim's past sex life.
- Sixty-nine cents shops replace 5 and 10 cents stores.
- The Rolling Stones tour grosses $13 million; Elton John signs a record contract for $8 million; Stevie Wonder later signs for $13 million; Bruce Springsteen appears on both *Time* and *Newsweek* covers.
- New dances include the hustle, bump, and robot.
- *Penthouse* sales surpass *Playboy*'s.
- Bantam pays a record $1,850,000 for the paperback rights to E. L. Doctorow's *Ragtime*.
- The Brewers' Society reports that Americans consume an average of 151 pints of beer per year, 11.5 pints of wine, and 9.1 pints of spirits.
- Studies indicate a decrease in heart attack deaths because of better diet, exercise, and decreased smoking.
- Many big cities are hit by strikes, including San Francisco (police), Charleston, West Virginia, and Chicago (teachers), and New York (sanitation workers).
- Chrysler, followed by other auto companies, offers rebates to counter record low sales.
- The first bulletproof fashion collection for men and women is manufactured.
- Vice President Nelson Rockefeller buys a bed designed by Max Ernst for $35,000.
- Charleston, S.C., passes a law requiring horse owners to diaper their animals.

Fads: Pie throwing, dance marathons, skateboards, mood rings, Spiderman

New Words and Usages: Fireperson, chairperson

First Appearances: Whooping crane born in captivity (Laurel, Md.), commencement exercises within a prison (Jackson, Mich.), black chief justice of a federal court (J. B. Parsons, Illinois), hotel for dogs, (Kennilworth, New York City); state finding unconstitutional the ban against girls competing with boys in athletics on a state basis (Pa.), ski carousel, individuals permitted to buy gold (since 1933), word processing equipment, digital records, women's bank (New York City), Swingline multiple-shot-fastening staple gun, disposable razor, Altair home computer kit, electronic watch (Commodore), doll that "grows," American canonized by the Catholic church (Elizabeth Seton), nonstick chewing gum for denture wearers (Wrigley), satellite TV cable, videocassette recorders (VCR, Betamax), computerized supermarket checkout, Pulitzer prize for cartoon ("Doonesbury"), legislation enabling women to attend Annapolis, West Point, and the Air Force Academy, advertisement for tampons on TV

1976

Facts and Figures

Economic Profile
- Dow-Jones: ↑ High 1004– Low 858
- GNP: +10%
- Inflation: +8.7%
- Unemployment: 8.3%

Entering college students: 31%

Four-year colleges: 1,913

Public/private schools: 7.5/1

VW Rabbit: $3,499

Plymouth Cordoba: $4,899

Cadillac Seville: $13,442

Puma "Clydes": $21.95

Rossignol ski sets: $99–$229

Vacation packages:
- Hawaii from Chicago (8 days, American Airlines): $329
- Mexico from Denver (8 days, Mexicana): $119–$139
- Disneyland from New York (8 days, Eastern): $206

House, Pine Hill, N.J. (former home of Al Capone): $180,000

Veterans' mortgage rates, Milwaukee: 7.¾%

Deaths

Busby Berkeley, Benjamin Britten, Alexander Calder, Agatha Christie, André Malraux, Sal Mineo, Walter Piston, Lily Pons, Paul Robeson, Rosalind Russell.

In the News

CHINESE PREMIER CHOU EN-LAI DIES . . . SPAIN ANNOUNCES PLAN FOR DEMOCRACY . . . FORD ANNOUNCES REORGANIZATION OF U.S. INTELLIGENCE SERVICES . . . PORTUGAL ESTABLISHES DEMOCRACY . . . LOCKHEED BRIBE OF JAPANESE IS EXPOSED . . . PATTY HEARST IS FOUND GUILTY OF BANK ROBBERY . . . LEBANESE CIVIL WAR ERUPTS, SYRIAN TROOPS MOVE IN . . . SUPREME COURT ALLOWS REMOVAL OF KAREN QUINLAN'S LIFE SUPPORT SYSTEMS . . . NIXON SAYS KISSINGER AIDES' PHONES WERE TAPPED . . . FRENCH PRESIDENT GISCARD D'ESTAING ADDRESSES CONGRESS, ASKS FOR "CONFIDENCE IN US" . . . CONCORDE BEGINS REGULAR TRANSATLANTIC SERVICE . . . U.S. AND USSR SIGN UNDERGROUND NUCLEAR LIMITATIONS TREATY . . . SUPREME COURT RULES THAT CAPITAL PUNISHMENT IS CONSTITUTIONAL . . . VIETNAM IS REUNIFIED, HANOI IS NAMED CAPITAL, SAIGON IS RENAMED HO CHI MINH CITY . . . ISRAELI COMMANDOS RAID ENTEBBE AIRPORT, UGANDA, AND FREE 103 HOSTAGES . . . DEMOCRATS NOMINATE JIMMY CARTER FOR PRESIDENT, FORD IS NOMINATED BY GOP . . . RHODESIAN P.M. IAN SMITH ACCEPTS PLAN TO TRANSFER POWER TO BLACKS . . . 26 CHILDREN ON SCHOOL BUS ARE KIDNAPPED AND LATER FREED IN CHOWCHILLA, CALIF. . . . VIKING I LANDS ON MARS, SENDS BACK PHOTOS . . . FORD, ON TV DEBATE, DENIES RUSSIA'S POWER OVER POLES . . . U.S. AND IRAN SIGN $10 BILLION ARMS SALE . . . CHILEAN EXILE ORLANDO ATELIER IS ASSASSINATED IN WASHINGTON, D.C. . . . MAO TSE-TUNG DIES . . . SECRETARY OF AGRICULTURE EARL BUTZ RESIGNS OVER ALLEGED RACIST REMARK . . . CARTER WINS PRESIDENCY, 40.8 MILLION TO 39.1 MILLION, DEMOCRATS RETAIN CONGRESS . . . SEPARATISTS GAIN LARGE VICTORY IN QUEBEC . . . OPEC ANNOUNCES 5%–10% OIL PRICE HIKE.

President Jimmy Carter and his family. "I'll never tell a lie," Mr. Carter promises. *Library of Congress.*

Quotes

"I speak to you as a direct descendant from George III. . . . It seems to me that Independence Day, the Fouth of July, should be celebrated in both our countries. . . . Let Freedom Ring."
— Queen Elizabeth II, presenting a new liberty bell

"It's the Me-Decade."
— Tom Wolfe, *New York* magazine

"[This is a time of] hedonism, . . . narcissism, . . . cult of the self."
— Christopher Lasch, *New York Review of Books*

"What we succeeded in doing in the Sixties was in dealing with the constitutional issue of rights. We've won that battle. . . . [Now] we're dealing with real equality."
— James Farmer, former head, CORE

"I've got a momma who joined the Peace Corps and went to India when she was sixty-eight. I've got one sister [Ruth], who's a Holy Roller preacher, another sister [Gloria], who . . . rides a motorcycle. So that makes me the only sane person in the family."
— Jimmy Carter

"Governor Reagan and I have one thing in common. We both played football. . . . I played for Michigan. He played for Warner Brothers."
— Gerald Ford

"That word would be 'faith.' "
— Jimmy Carter's one-word summary of his campaign

"I have looked upon a lot of women with lust. I've committed adultery in my heart many times."
— Jimmy Carter, *Playboy* interview

"In his heart, he knows your wife."
— Bumper sticker, following Jimmy Carter's *Playboy* interview

"I can't type, I can't file, I can't even answer the phone."
— Elizabeth Ray, secretary to Congressman Wayne Hayes

"For some reason, self-doubt appears to thrive in our Bicentennial year."
— Arthur Schlesinger, Jr.

Ads

TV

Premieres

"The Muppet Show," Jim Henson
"Quincy, M.E.," Jack Klugman
"The Gong Show," Chuck Barris
"Mary Hartman, Mary Hartman," Louise Lasser
"The Bionic Woman," Lindsay Wagner
"Laverne and Shirley," Cindy Williams, Penny Marshall
"Donny and Marie [Osmond]"
"Charlie's Angels," Jaclyn Smith, Farrah Fawcett-Majors, Kate Jackson
"Alice," Linda Lavin
"Wonder Woman," Lynda Carter

Top Ten (Nielsen)

"Happy Days," "Laverne and Shirley," "ABC Monday Night Movie," "M*A*S*H," "Charlie's Angels," "The Big Event," "The Six-Million-Dollar Man," "ABC Sunday Night Movie," "Baretta," "One Day at a Time"

Specials

"Sybil"; "Rich Man, Poor Man, Book II"; "American Ballet Theatre: 'Swan Lake' " ("Live from Lincoln Center"); "Eleanor and Franklin: The White House Years" (Edward Herrmann, Jane Alexander); "Arthur Rubinstein at 90"; "Jesus of Nazareth" (Franco Zeffirelli)

Emmy Awards

"Upstairs, Downstairs" (drama); "The Mary Tyler Moore Show" (comedy); "Van Dyke and Company" (variety); "Ballet Shoes, Parts I and II, Piccadilly Circus" (children); James Garner (actor, "The Rockford Files"); Carroll O'Connor (comedic actor, "All in the Family"); Lindsay Wagner (actress, "The Bionic Woman"); Beatrice Arthur (comedic actress, "Maude")

Of Note

There are 20 police–private eye shows • Showtime becomes the second major pay-cable TV network • The film *Gone with the Wind* draws the highest ratings to date • The Gerald Ford–Jimmy Carter debate is the first presidential campaign debate since Nixon and Kennedy's in 1960 • Barbara Walters signs a 5-year, $1 million-a-year contract with ABC as co-anchor with Harry Reasoner • ABC, under Fred Silverman's guidance, becomes number one in ratings, after many years of CBS dominance.

Movies

Openings

Rocky (John G. Avildsen), Sylvester Stallone, Talia Shire, Burgess Meredith
All the President's Men (Alan J. Pakula), Dustin Hoffman, Robert Redford, Jason Robards
Bound for Glory (Hal Ashby), David Carradine, Melinda Dillon, Ronny Cox, Gail Strickland
Network (Sidney Lumet), Faye Dunaway, William Holden, Peter Finch
Taxi Driver (Martin Scorsese), Robert De Niro, Harvey Keitel, Cybill Shepherd
Carrie (Brian De Palma), Sissy Spacek, Piper Laurie
Marathon Man (John Schlesinger), Dustin Hoffman, Laurence Olivier, Roy Scheider
The Sailor Who Fell from Grace with the Sea (Lewis John Carlino), Sara Miles, Kris Kristofferson
The Front (Martin Ritt), Woody Allen, Zero Mostel
King Kong (John Guillermin), Jeff Bridges, Jessica Lange, Charles Grodin
A Star Is Born (Frank Pierson), Barbra Streisand, Kris Kristofferson
The Omen (Richard Donner), Gregory Peck, Lee Remick
Harlan County, U.S.A. (Barbara Kipple), documentary
The Bad News Bears (Michael Ritchie), Walter Matthau, Tatum O'Neal
The Man Who Fell to Earth (Nicolas Roeg), David Bowie, Rip Torn
The Memory of Justice (Marcel Ophuls), documentary
Cousin, Cousine (Jean-Charles Tacchelia), Marie-Christine Barrault, Victor Lanoux

Academy Awards

Best Picture: *Rocky*
Best Director: John G. Avildsen (*Rocky*)
Best Actress: Faye Dunaway (*Network*)
Best Actor: Peter Finch (*Network*)

Top Box-Office Stars

Robert Redford, Jack Nicholson, Dustin Hoffman, Clint Eastwood, Mel Brooks, Burt Reynolds, Al Pacino, Tatum O'Neal, Woody Allen, Charles Bronson

Stars of Tomorrow

Sylvester Stallone, Talia Shire, Jessica Lange, Sissy Spacek, Robby Benson, Sam Elliott, Margaux Hemingway, Susan Sarandon, Ellen Greene

Popular Music

Hit Songs

"Silly Love Songs"
"Don't Go Breaking My Heart"
"Play that Funky Music"
"A Fifth of Beethoven"
"(Shake, Shake, Shake) Shake Your Booty"
"Breaking Up Is Hard to Do"
"Love Is Alive"
"Sara Smile"
"Get Closer"

Top Records

Albums: *Songs in the Key of Life* (Stevie Wonder); *Peter Frampton Comes Alive!* (Peter Frampton); *Desire* (Bob Dylan); *Their Greatest Hits 1971–1975* (Eagles); *Black and Blue* (Rolling Stones); *Gratitude* (Earth, Wind and Fire)

Singles: *Disco Lady* (Johnnie Taylor); *December 1963* (Four Seasons); *Kiss and Say Goodbye* (Manhattans); *50 Ways to Leave Your Lover* (Paul Simon); *I Write the Songs* (Barry Manilow); *Love Hangover* (Diana Ross); *Lonely Night* (Captain and Tennille). Country: *Stranger* (Johnny Duncan); *If I Had to Do It All Over Again* (Roy Clark)

Grammy Awards

The Masquerade, George Benson (record); *Songs in the Key of Life,* Stevie Wonder (album); "I Write the Songs" (song)

Jazz and Big Bands

Bob Marley and the Wailers popularize reggae ("Rastaman Vibration").

Popular Performers: Carlos Santana, Cal Tjader, Eddie Palmieri, Ray Barretto, Johnny Pachecho, Tito Puente, Willie Colon

Popular Jazz-Rock-Blues Groups: Weather Report, Mahavishnu Orchestra, Blood, Sweat, and Tears, Chicago; the avant-garde: Keith Jarrett, Roswell Rud and Jazz Composers Orchestra, Gato Barbieri; space jazz: Lonnie Liston Smith, "Astral Traveling"; African jazz: Dollar Brand "Sangoma"; the revival of old sounds: National Jazz Ensemble (Chuck Israel).

Top Performers *(Downbeat):* McCoy Tyner (soloist); Thad Jones and Mel Lewis (band); Weather Report (jazz group); Chick Corea, George Benson, Wayne Shorter, Phil Woods, Sonny Rollins, Gerry Mulligan, Bill Watrous, Freddie Hubbard, Airto Moreira (instrumentalists); Flora Purim, Mel Torme (vocalists); Pointer Sisters (vocal group); Weather Report, *Black Market,* McCoy Tyner, *Trident* (albums)

Theater

Broadway Openings

Plays

A Matter of Gravity (Enid Bagnold), Katharine Hepburn
The Belle of Amherst (William Luce), Julie Harris
California Suite (Neil Simon), Barbara Barrie, George Grizzard, Tammy Grimes, Jack Weston
Texas Trilogy (Preston Jones), Diane Ladd
The Comedians (Trevor Griffins), John Lithgow, Jonathan Pryce, Milo O'Shea
Days in the Trees (Marguerite Duras), Madeleine Renard, in French; Mildred Dunnock, in English
No Man's Land (Harold Pinter), Ralph Richardson, John Gielgud
Poor Murderers (Pavel Kahout), Maria Schell, Laurence Luckinbill
The Innocents (William Archibald), Claire Bloom, Pauline Flanagan
Sly Fox (Larry Gelbart), George C. Scott, Robert Preston, Jack Gilford
The Heiress (Ruth Augustus Goetz), Richard Kiley, Jane Alexander
Knock Knock (Jules Feiffer), Lynn Redgrave, John Heffernan, Charles Durning

Musicals

Pacific Overtures (Stephen Sondheim), Mako, Yuki Shimodo, Sab Shimono
Bubbling Brown Sugar (various authors), Avon Long, Josephine Premice
Your Arms Too Short to Box with God (Alex Bradford), Delores Hall, William Hardy, Jr.

Classics, Revivals, and Off-Broadway Premieres

The Old Glory (Robert Lowell), Roscoe Lee Browne; *The Lady from the Sea* (Ibsen), Vanessa Redgrave, Pat Hingle; *Who's Afraid of Virginia Woolf?* (Edward Albee), Ben Gazzara, Colleen Dewhurst; *Mrs. Warren's Profession* (George Bernard Shaw), Ruth Gordon; *For Colored Girls Who Have Considered Suicide When the Rainbow Is Enuf* (Ntozake Shange), Trazana Beverley; *American Buffalo* (David Mamet), Michael Egen; *Long Day's Journey into Night* (Eugene O'Neill), Zoë Caldwell, Jason Robards, Michael Moriarty, Kevin Conway

Regional

Arena Stage, Washington, D.C., is the first company outside New York to win a Tony Award.

Theater (cont.)

Long Wharf, New Haven: *Streamers* (David Rabe), premiere

Pulitzer Prize
A Chorus Line, Edward Kleban, Marvin Hamlisch

Tony Awards
Travesties, Tom Stoppard (play); *A Chorus Line*, Edward Kleban, Marvin Hamlisch (musical)

Classical Music

Compositions
Richard Wernick, *Visions of Terror and Wonder*
Karl Korte, Concerto for Piano and Winds
Gian Carlo Menotti, *Landscapes and Remembrances, First Symphony*
Don Gillis, *The Secret History of the Birth of the Nation*
Vivian Fine, *Romantic Ode; Meeting for Equal Rights 1866*
William Schuman, *Concerto on Old English Rounds; The Young Dead Soldiers*
Morton Feldman, *Voices and Instruments*

Important Events
Avery Fisher Hall at Lincoln Center reopens, after acoustical adjustments, with a month of Mahler and a nine-day festival of 20th-century music performed by Juilliard and the New York Philharmonic.
The Kennedy Center in Washington, D.C., presents a year-long Bicentennial Parade of American Music, sponsored by a $200,000 grant from Exxon.
Lorin Maazel conducts the Cleveland in programs devoted to individual modern composers Boris Blacher, Luciano Berio, and Raymond Premru.
On the event of its 85th birthday, Carnegie Hall raises over a million dollars at a concert at which Isaac Stern, Yehudi Menuhin, Mstislav Rostropovitch, Dietrich Fischer-Dieskau, Leonard Bernstein, and Vladimir Horowitz perform and together sing the Hallelujah chorus from Handel's *Messiah*.
Artur Rubinstein, 89, gives a 70th-anniversary concert at Carnegie Hall.

New Appointments: Seiji Ozawa, Boston (full time); Eduardo Mata, Dallas; Edo de Waart, San Francisco

Debuts: Ken Noda, Lazar Berman, James Galway

First Performances
Mario Davidorsky, Synchronism 7 (New York); John Cage, *Renga, Apartment House 1776* (Boston); Lukas Foss, Folk Song (Baltimore); Roy Harris, Symphony no. 14 (Washington); Ned Rorem, *Air Music* (Cincinnati); Ross Lee Finney, Violin Concerto, (Dallas); William Bolcom, Piano Concerto (Seattle); Michael Colgrass, *New People* (Minneapolis)

Opera

Metropolitan: Sarah Caldwell (debut), Beverly Sills, Stuart Burrows, Ingvar Wixell, *La traviata;* Renata Scotto, Shirley Verrett, Luciano Pavarotti, *Il trovatore;* Joan Sutherland, *Esclarmonde;* Giuseppe Giacomini, Ezio Flagello, *La forza del destino*

New York State: Beverly Sills, Donald Gramm, Samuel Ramey, *Il barbiere di Siviglia* (Sarah Caldwell, conducting)

Chicago: Nicolai Ghiaurov, *Khovanshchina* (Mussorgsky); Richard Gill, William Dooley, Alan Titus, Klara Barlow, *The Love for Three Oranges*

Boston: Donald Gramm, Brent Ellis, Phyllis Bryn-Julson, *Montezuma* (Roger Sessions, American premiere)

Santa Fe: *The Mother of Us All* (Virgil Thomson)

Dallas: Alfredo Kraus, *Les contes d'Hoffmann*

Houston: *Bilby's Doll* (Carlisle Floyd, premiere)

Minnesota: *The Voyage of Edgar Allan Poe* (Dominick Argento, premiere)

Baltimore: Richard Stilwell, *Ines de Castro* (Thomas Pasatieri, premiere). Visiting for the Bicentennial: Paris Opera (*Le nozze di Figaro*), La Scala (Strehler's *Macbeth; La Cenerentola*)

Music Notes
Philip Glass's *Einstein on the Beach* is performed in numerous European cities and in New York • Particular attention to women musicians includes a "Meet the Woman Composer" series of 11 concerts in New York and premieres of works by Jean Eichelberger-Ivey (Baltimore) and Marga Richter (Tucson) • The Festival Institute at Round Top, Texas, begins • Artur Rubinstein receives the Medal of Freedom from Gerald Ford.

Art

Paintings

Jasper Johns, *Corpse and Mirror, End Paper*

Jim Dine, *Four Robes Existing in This Vale of Tears*

Chuck Close, *Linda no. 6646*

Red Grooms, *Ruckus Manhattan*

Philip Guston, *Wharf: Source*

Frank Stella, *Wake Island Rail*

Lee Krasner, *Present Perfect*

Isabel Bishop, *Recess #3*

William Jensen, *Heaven, Earth*

Willem de Kooning, *Untitled VI*

Sculpture

Christo, *Running Fence*

Duane Hanson, *Couple with Shopping Bags*

Jackie Winsor, *Cement Piece, #1 Rope*

Claes Oldenburg, *Inverted Q*

Sol LeWitt, *Lines to Points on a Grid*

Architecture

Occupational Health Center, Columbia, Ind. (Holzman, Pfeiffer)

Richardson-Merrell Headquarters, Wilton, Conn. (Roche and Dinkeloo)

Liberty Bell Pavilion, Living History Center, Philadelphia (Mitchell, Giurgola)

Columbus East High School, Indiana (Mitchell, Giurgola)

Important Exhibitions

For the bicentennial, the Prado sends a collection of Spanish paintings that tours the United States. The King Tutankhamen Treasures exhibition begins its tour to New York, Chicago, Los Angeles, New Orleans, Oakland, and Seattle.

Museums

New York: *Metropolitan:* "The Two Worlds of Andrew Wyeth: Kuerners and Olsons." *Museum of Modern Art:* "Fauvism and Its Affinities" (travels to San Francisco, Fort Worth); Retrospective: André Masson. *Whitney:* 200 Years of American Sculpture

Yale: "American Art 1750–1800 toward Independence"

Philadelphia: "Three Centuries of American Art" (the largest bicentennial show)

National: "The Age of Jefferson"; "The European Vision of America" (also at Cleveland)

Worcester: "The Early Republic: Consolidation of Revolutionary Goals"

Sol LeWitt, *Lines to Points on a Grid,* 1976. Six-inch pencil grid and white chalk on four black walls. *Collection of Whitney Museum of American Art. Gift of the Gilman Foundation, Inc.*

Chicago: Ecclesiastical vestments from the 11th–20th centuries

Art Briefs

Much attention is given to the disposition of Mark Rothko's multimillion-dollar estate • A Rembrandt portrait at the Boston Museum, valued at $1–2 million, is stolen, adding to an estimated $1 billion of stolen or smuggled art in the United States • Major sales include Gauguin's *Nature Morte à l'estampe Japonaise* ($1.4 million) and a marble bust of Ben Franklin by Jean-Antoine Houdon ($310,000).

Dance

Bruce Marks becomes artistic director of Ballet West, Salt Lake City.

Premieres/Important Productions

American Ballet Theatre: *Push Comes to Shove* (Twyla Tharp); *Le sacre du printemps* (Glen Tetley); *The Nutcracker* (Mikhail Baryshnikov), *La Bayadère* (Natalia Makarova); *Other Dances* (Jerome Robbins); dancing in the company are Baryshnikov, Makarova, Erik Bruhn, Fernando Bujones, Gelsey Kirkland, Ivan Nagy, Carla Fracci, Alicia Alonso, Marcia Haydee, Lynn Seymour.

New York City Ballet: *Union Jack* (Balanchine); *Chaconne* (Balanchine); *Calcium Light Night* (Peter Martins)

Alvin Ailey: *Pas de Duke* (Ailey, Duke Ellington), Baryshnikov, Judith Jamison

Paul Taylor: *Cloven Kingdom*

Saul Bellow. *Thomas Victor.*

Books

Fiction

Critics' Choice

The Public Burning, Robert Coover
Kinflicks, Lisa Alther
Meridian, Alice Walker
Lovers and Tyrants, Francine du Plessix Gray
Will You Please Be Quiet, Please?, Raymond Carver
Searching for Caleb, Anne Tyler
Ordinary People, Judith Guest
Chilly Scenes of Winter, Ann Beattie
The Spectator Bird, Wallace E. Stegner
❧ *Autumn of the Patriarch*, Gabriel García Márquez

Best-Sellers

Trinity, Leon Uris
Sleeping Murder, Agatha Christie
Dolores, Jacqueline Susann
The Deep, Peter Benchley
1876, Gore Vidal
Slapstick or Lonesome No More! Kurt Vonnegut, Jr.

Nonfiction

Critics' Choice

Born on the Fourth of July, Ron Kovic
The Uses of Enchantment, Bruno Bettelheim
World of Our Fathers, Irving Howe
The Black Family in Slavery and Freedom 1750–1925, Herbert Gutman
Friendly Fire, C. D. B. Bryan
Lyndon Johnson and the American Dream, Doris Kearns
The Survivor, Terrence Des Pres
The Woman Warrior, Maxine Hong Kingston
The Russians, Hedrick Smith
Plagues and People, William McNeill
The Time of Illusion, Jonathan Schell
Norman Thomas: The Last Idealist, W. A. Swanberg

Best-Sellers

The Final Days, Bob Woodward, Carl Bernstein
Roots, Alex Haley
Your Erroneous Zones, Dr. Wayne W. Dyer
Passages, Gail Sheehy
Born Again, Charles W. Colson

The Grass Is Always Greener over the Septic Tank, Erma Bombeck
Blind Ambition: The White House Years, John Dean
The Hite Report: A Nationwide Study of Female Sexuality, Shere Hite

Poetry

Robert Lowell, *Selected Poems*
James Dickey, *The Zodiac*
Muriel Rukeyser, *The Gates*
Richard Eberhart, *Collected Poems, 1930–76*
Philip Levine, *The Names of the Lost*

Pulitzer Prizes

No prize is awarded in fiction.
The Impending Crisis: 1841–1861, David M. Potter (U.S. history) (posthumous)
Beautiful Swimmers, William W. Warner (nonfiction)
A Prince of Our Disorder, John E. Mack (biography)
Divine Comedies, James Merrill (poetry)

Nobel Prize

Saul Bellow

Science and Technology

Viking I makes a successful soft landing on Mars and returns photos of a rusty brown landscape with rocky desert and pink sky; its findings indicate the presence of nitrogen in Mars's atmosphere.

The Pershing IA ground-to-ground guided missile system permits firing from an unsurveyed site.

The Navy tests Tomahawk, a sea-launched cruise missile (SLCM) with a high-explosive warhead.

The Air-Launched Cruise Missile (ALCM) system is developed to intentionally confuse the distinctions between tactical or strategic and conventional or nuclear weapons.

Cimetidine (Tagamet) is marketed for peptic ulcers; it prevents the secretion of excessive acid.

A swine flu virus is cultured for mass inoculation to avoid a recurrence of the 1918–19 epidemic.

U.S. and Soviet surgeons implant artificial hearts in calves, the first joint project to develop an artificial heart for human beings.

Richard Leakey discovers the most complete homo erectus skull (like Peking man) to date, in Kenya; its estimated age is 1.5 million years.

❧ British scientists develop PGE, a prostaglandin, which prevents blood clotting.

Nobel Prize

Burton Richter and Samuel C. C. Ting win in physics for the discovery of the J and psi subatomic particles. Baruch S. Blumberg and D. Carleton Gajdusek win in physiology and medicine for their work on infectious disease. William N. Lipscom wins in chemistry for work on the structure and bonding mechanism of boranes.

Sports

Baseball

Players and owners negotiate a contract allowing for free agency for players with more than six years of service; after the season Reggie Jackson signs for a record $2.9 million for five years.

Pitcher Mark "The Bird" Fydrich (Detroit, AL) wins Rookie of the Year and excites fans with antics such as talking to the baseball.

Henry Aaron retires with a career total of 755 home runs.

The Cy Young awards are won by Randy Jones (San Diego, NL) and Jim Palmer (Baltimore, AL).

Champions

Batting

Bill Madlock (Chicago, NL), .339	NL), 20–7
George Brett (Kansas City, AL), .333	Bill Campbell (Minnesota, AL), 17–5
Pitching	*Home runs*
Steve Carlton (Philadelphia,	Mike Schmidt (Philadelphia, NL), 38

Football

O. J. Simpson (Buffalo) signs a record $2.9 million, three-year pact; he also rushes for a single-game record of 273 yards. Rocky Bleier and Franco Harris each gain over 1,000 yards rushing for Pittsburgh.

NFC Season Leaders: Fran Tarkenton (Minnesota), passing; Walter Payton (Chicago), rushing; Drew Pearson (Dallas), receiving

AFC Season Leaders: Ken Stabler (Oakland), passing; O. J. Simpson (Buffalo), rushing, 1,503 yards; MacArthur Lane (Kansas City), receiving

College All-Americans: Rob Lyttle (B), Michigan; Tommy Kramer (Q), Rice; Ricky Bell (B), Southern California

Bowls (Jan. 1, 1977)

Rose: Southern California 14–Michigan 6	Cotton: Houston 30–Maryland 21
Orange: Ohio State 27–Colorado 10	Sugar: Pittsburgh 27–Georgia 3

Basketball

Four ABA teams—Denver, Indiana, New York, San Antonio—merge with the NBA after the season. An NBA playoff game goes to triple overtime: Boston 128–Phoenix 126.

NBA All-Pro First Team: Rick Barry (Golden State), George McGinnis (Philadelphia), Kareem Abdul-Jabbar (Los Angeles), Nate Archibald (Kansas City), Pete Maravich (New Orleans)

ABA All-Pro First Team: Julius Erving (New York), Billy Knight (Indiana), Artis Gilmore (Kentucky), James Silas (San Antonio), Ralph Simpson (Denver)

Olympics

At the Summer Games in Montreal, security, of foremost concern, costs over $100 million. U.S. winners include John Nabor (4 in swimming), Edwin Moses (400 mh, 47.64s.). Arnie Robinson (broad jump, 27'4.7"), Bruce Jenner (decathlon, 8,618 pts.), Mac Wilkins (discus, 221'5.4"), Ray Leonard (LW boxing), Michael Spinks (MW boxing), and Leon Spinks (HW boxing). In the Winter Games at Innsbruck, Austria, winners are Dorothy Hamill (figure skating), Peter Mueller (1,000m, 1:19.32), and Sheila Young (500m, 42.7s.).

Other Sports

Boxing: Muhammad Ali fights a Japanese wrestler to a draw in a highly publicized match.

Tennis: Transexual René Richards is barred from the U.S. Open, as players demand chromosomal sex determination.

Winners

World Series	*MVP*
Cincinnati (NL) 4	Kareem Abdul-Jabbar, Los
New York (AL) 0	Angeles
MVP	*College Basketball*
NL–Joe Morgan, Cincinnati	Indiana
AL–Thurman Munson, New York	*Player of the Year*
Super Bowl XI (Jan. 1977)	Adrian Dantley, Notre Dame
Oakland 32–Minnesota 14	*Stanley Cup*
MVP	Montreal
Bert Jones, Baltimore	*US Tennis Open:*
College Football	Men: Bjorn Borg
Pittsburgh	Women: Chris Evert
Heisman Trophy	*USGA Open*
Tony Dorsett, Pittsburgh	Jerry Pate
NBA Championship	*Kentucky Derby*
Boston 4–Phoenix 2	Bold Forbes (A. Cordero, jockey)

Fashion

For Women: Split-pea-colored loden coats regain popularity and are worn with knit mufflers and wide-brim hats, along with a variety of pants (particularly harem or culotte), tube skirts and tunics, caftans, and long blouses. The layered and bulky look remains, but fabrics are lighter (in silk and cashmere); checked pants are often matched with striped tunics, shirts, and scarves. Large smocks, big capes, and large, loose blazers fit over a variety of skirts—dirndls and culottes, or pleated, gypsy, flared, tube, or wraparound styles. The tailored look is also popular in gabardines and Harris tweeds. Bags are either businesslike or rugged, in canvas, pigskin, or buckskin. Lapel pins, link bracelets, hoop earrings, and tiny, widely separated diamonds on gold chains are stylish accessories. Dorothy Hamill popularizes a short brush-and-bang haircut.

For Men: Men begin to show an interest in traditional, conservative styles. Vests, windbreakers, peacoats, and classical pullovers regain attention.

High-fashion notes: Halston's strapless dress; Mollie Parnis's peasant cotton

Kaleidoscope

- Bicentennial festivities include a reenactment of a Revolutionary War battle in Western Springs, Illinois; a reenactment of the Minutemen battling the British on Lexington Green; "Operation Sail" in New York City, with 16 of the world's tallest old windjammers and thousands of other ships; and the Freedom Train, traveling over 17,000 miles to 80 cities, with 12 cars of Americana exhibitions.
- In the preelection presidential debate with Gerald Ford, Jimmy Carter defines a new economic barometer, the "misery index," the sum of the unemployment and inflation rates, which he views as an excessive 12.4.
- The Supreme Court rules that employers are not required to give paid maternity leave.
- FBI chief Clarence Kelly apologizes publicly for bureau excesses, such as the Martin Luther King and Black Panther surveillances.
- Amy Carter, nine, attends a predominantly black Washington public school.
- Renowned lawyer F. Lee Bailey defends Patty Hearst, daughter of publisher William Randolph Hearst, with expert witnesses such as psychiatrist Robert J. Lifton who claim she was "brainwashed."
- The *Encyclopaedia Britannica* reports that roughly 15 percent of American adults are functional illiterates, unable to read an average newspaper or write a simple letter.
- Numerous will forgeries appear claiming the estate of Howard Hughes, who apparently left no will.
- President Ford orders a major inoculation campaign against a projected swine flu epidemic (which does not occur).
- With the repeal of the Fair Trade law, manufacturers can no longer fix retail prices; this is anticipated to save consumers $2 billion through discount shopping.
- The arrest rate for women since 1964 has risen three times faster than the rate for men.
- Sales of bran cereals increase 20 percent and of high-fiber bread 30 percent, as consumers respond to widely published medical studies reporting health benefits from high-fiber diets.
- Daniel Schorr is suspended from CBS after he gives the *Village Voice* newspaper a House Intelligence Committee report on alleged illegal CIA activities.
- California is the first state to legalize "living wills," the right of the terminally ill to decree their own deaths.
- Legionnaire's disease, from a bacterium of unknown origin, fatally strikes 34 at an American Legion convention in Philadelphia.
- Two amateur electronics enthusiasts develop the Apple computer in a California garage.
- In his revised *Baby and Child Care,* Dr. Benjamin Spock redefines the sex roles: "The father's responsibility is as great as the mother's," he writes.
- Richard Nixon is disbarred in New York State.
- Former president and Mrs. Nixon visit China, where they are warmly welcomed.
- Cars, like the Cadillac Seville, are reduced in weight and size; production of the Eldorado, the last U.S. convertible model, ceases.
- Average SAT scores drop to 472 in math and 435 in English (501 and 480 in 1968).
- Shirley Temple Black becomes the U.S. State Department chief of protocol.
- Barbara Jordan becomes the first woman and first black to deliver a convention keynote speech at the Democratic convention.
- One out of five children now lives in a one-parent home; three out of five marriages end in divorce.

Fads: Mattress stacking, Farrah Fawcett-Majors posters

First Appearances: Rhodes scholarship to a woman, six-star general (George Washington, posthumously), woman president of *Harvard Law Review,* women in NASA training program for astronauts, electronic sewing machine (Singer), commercial supersonic airline service (Concorde), protoplasts (animal and plant cells combined), underground school (Artesia, N.M.)

1977

Facts and Figures

Economic Profile
  Dow-Jones: ↓ High 999–
    Low 800
  GNP: +11%
  Inflation: +11.0%
  Unemployment: 7.6%
Infant mortality/1,000: 16.1
Maternal mortality/10,000:
  12.8
Physicians: 393,700
Dentists: 107,000
Hospital beds: 1,466,000
Herman's sporting
  equipment:
  Adidas finalist tennis
    shoes: $12.99
  Butchart Nicholls golf
    shoes: $19.99
  Whitely trim ride exercise
    bike: $54.99
Billard 115-lb. barbell set:
  $24.99
Hudson vitamin C, 250 mg.:
  $4.09 (250)
Megavitamin B complex:
  $5.75–$13.20 (250)
Radio Shack CB: $59.99–
  $159.95
Cuisinart: $224.99
Tiffany 15-inch chain, 14
  diamonds: $395

Deaths

Maria Callas, Charles
  Chaplin, Joan Crawford,
  Bing Crosby, Anthony
  Eden, Guy Lombardo,
  Groucho Marx, Vladimir
  Nabokov, Anaïs Nin, Elvis
  Presley, Leopold
  Stokowski.

Anti-Shah Demonstration.
Copyright Washington Post.
Reprinted courtesy of D.C.
Public Library.

In the News

GARY GILMORE IS KILLED BY FIRING SQUAD, THE FIRST U.S. EXECUTION IN 10 YEARS . . . CARTER GRANTS UNCONDITIONAL AMNESTY TO VIETNAM DRAFT EVADERS . . . CARTER LIFTS ALL TRAVEL BANS TO CUBA, VIETNAM, NORTH KOREA, AND CAMBODIA . . . INDIRA GANDHI IS DEFEATED AND RESIGNS . . . SENATE APPROVES RIGOROUS CODE OF SENATE ETHICS, LIMITS SENATORS' OUTSIDE INCOME . . . 570 DIE AS TWO 747'S COLLIDE IN CANARY ISLANDS . . . MARTIN LUTHER KING'S ASSASSIN, JAMES EARL RAY, IS RECAPTURED AFTER PRISON ESCAPE . . . EGYPTIAN LEADER ANWAR SADAT VISITS CARTER . . . CARTER SAYS B-1 BOMBER IS UNNECESSARY . . . MENACHEM BEGIN IS ELECTED ISRAELI PREMIER . . . LEON JAWORSKI IS NAMED "KOREAGATE" PROSECUTOR TO INVESTIGATE BRIBES BY U.S. CORPORATIONS . . . DEPT. OF ENERGY IS CREATED . . . "SON OF SAM" KILLER IS ARRESTED IN N.Y.C. . . . BERT LANCE, BUDGET DIRECTOR, RESIGNS OVER ISSUE OF BANKING PRACTICES . . . UNEMPLOYMENT FALLS TO 7% . . . ALI BHUTTO, FORMER PAKISTANI P.M., IS ARRESTED FOR MURDER . . . U.S. AND PANAMA SIGN CANAL ZONE TREATIES . . . SHAH OF IRAN VISITS WHITE HOUSE DESPITE PROTEST DEMONSTRATIONS . . . EGYPTIAN PRESIDENT ANWAR SADAT VISITS JERUSALEM . . . ISRAELI PREMIER MENACHEM BEGIN VISITS EGYPT.

Quotes

"Ring the bells for your sons. Tell them that those wars were the last of wars and the end of sorrows."
— Anwar Sadat

"The time of the flight between Cairo and Jerusalem is short . . . [but] the distance between them . . . until yesterday, quite large. . . . Sadat passed this distance with heartfelt courage. . . . We, the Jews, know how to appreciate this courage."
— Menachem Begin

"We need a better family life to make us better servants of the people. So those of you living in sin, I hope you get married. And those of you who have left your spouses, go back home."
— Jimmy Carter

"Which of you is going to step up and put me out to pasture?"
— John Wayne, to Congressional Committee on Aging

"For the first time in our history, a small group of nations controlling a scarce resource [oil] could, over time, be tempted to pressure us into foreign policy decisions not dictated by our national interests."
— Henry Kissinger

"Society cannot continue to live on oil and gas. Those fossil fuels represent nature's savings accounts which took billions of years to form."
— Buckminster Fuller

"The massive failure in basic skills—particularly reading and writing—is nothing short of scandalous."
— Fred M. Hechinger, editor, *New York Times*

"We don't so much want to see a female Einstein become an assistant professor. We want a woman schlemiel to get promoted as quickly as a male schlemiel."
— Bella Abzug

"I think Gerald Ford will be remembered as a man who bumped his head, had a wonderful wife, and left Americans more at peace with themselves and the rest of the world than at any time since it became a world power."
— Senator Daniel Moynihan (D-N.Y.)

"You can always find something on the evening news to take your mind off life."
— "Mary Hartman, Mary Hartman"

Woody Allen and Diane Keaton in *Annie Hall*, a romantic comedy about the difficulties of relating to oneself and others in a modern, urban environment. *Movie Star News.*

Ads

Last night I did two things I've never done before. One was wearing Geminesse.
(Geminesse Perfume)

Skim milk does not come from skinny cows.
(Alba)

This country needs more air-conditioning repairmen, not more English professors.
(IC, International Correspondence Schools)

Try walking into Merrill Lynch and asking for Mr. Lynch.
(Goldberg-Pollen)

We will sell no wine before its time.
(Paul Masson)

One of Soviet Georgia's senior citizens thought Dannon was an excellent yogurt. She ought to know. She's been eating yogurt for 137 years.
(Dannon)

If you choose the wrong executor for your estate, you might as well take it with you.
(Putnam Trust)

If man were meant to fly, God would have lowered the fares.
(American Coach Lines)

TV

Premieres
"Family Feud," Richard Dawson
"The Dick Cavett Show"
"Three's Company," Suzanne Somers, John Ritter
"Eight Is Enough," Dick Van Patten
"Chips," Erik Estrada
"Soap," Robert Mandan
"Lou Grant," Edward Asner
"The Love Boat," Gavin MacLeod

Top Ten (Nielsen)
"Laverne and Shirley," "Happy Days," "Three's Company," "60 Minutes," "Charlie's Angels," "All in the Family," "Little House on the Prairie," "Alice," "M*A*S*H," "One Day at a Time"

Specials
"Roots" (Ben Vereen, Cicely Tyson, Lloyd Bridges, LeVar Burton, Maya Angelou); "Holocaust"; "The Body Human"; "I, Claudius"; "American Ballet Theatre's 'Giselle' "; Bette Midler: Ol' Red Hair Is Back"; "The Great Whales: National Geographic"; "The Gathering"; Interview with Anwar Sadat and Menachem Begin (Walter Cronkite); Interviews with Richard Nixon (David Frost)

Emmy Awards
"The Rockford Files" (drama); "All in the Family" (comedy); "The Muppet Show" (variety); "Hollywood Is Grinch Night" (children); Ed Asner (actor, "Lou Grant"); Carroll O'Connor (comedic actor, "All in the Family"); Sada Thompson (actress, "Family"); Jean Stapleton (comedic actress, "All in the Family")

Of Note
"Roots" draws the largest audience in TV history, 130 million people; "Holocaust" draws 120 million.

Movies

Openings
Annie Hall (Woody Allen), Woody Allen, Diane Keaton
The Goodbye Girl (Herbert Ross) Richard Dreyfuss, Marsha Mason
Julia (Fred Zinnemann), Jane Fonda, Vanessa Redgrave, Jason Robards
Star Wars (George Lucas), Mark Hamill, Harrison Ford, Carrie Fisher
The Turning Point (Herbert Ross), Anne Bancroft, Shirley MacLaine, Mikhail Baryshnikov
Close Encounters of the Third Kind (Steven Spielberg), Richard Dreyfuss, François Truffaut, Teri Garr
The Late Show (Robert Benton), Art Carney, Lily Tomlin
Looking for Mr. Goodbar (Richard Brooks), Diane Keaton, Richard Kiley, Tuesday Weld
Saturday Night Fever (John Badham), John Travolta, Karen Lynn Gorney, Donna Pescow
Providence (Alain Resnais), Ellen Burstyn, Dirk Bogarde, John Gielgud
Oh, God! (Carl Reiner), George Burns, John Denver, Teri Garr
Pumping Iron (George Butler, Robert Fiore), Arnold Schwarzenegger
That Obscure Object of Desire (Luis Buñuel), Fernando Rey, Carole Bouquet
Madame Rosa (Moshe Mizrahi), Simone Signoret, Claude Dauphin
Handle with Care (Jonathan Demme), Ann Wedgeworth, Paul Le Mat
Stroszek (Werner Herzog), Bruno S., Eva Mattes, Clemens Scheitz

Academy Awards
Best Picture; *Annie Hall*
Best Director: Woody Allen (*Annie Hall*)
Best Actress: Diane Keaton (*Annie Hall*)
Best Actor: Richard Dreyfuss (*The Goodbye Girl*)

Top Box-Office Stars
Sylvester Stallone, Barbra Streisand, Clint Eastwood, Burt Reynolds, Robert Redford, Woody Allen, Mel Brooks, Al Pacino, Diane Keaton, Robert De Niro

Stars of Tomorrow
John Travolta, Karen Lynn Gorney, Michael Ontkean, Mark Hamill, Harrison Ford, Carrie Fisher, Kathleen Quinlan, Peter Firth, Richard Gere, Melinda Dillon

Popular Music _____

Hit Songs
"Tonight's the Night"
"Nobody Does It Better"
"Theme from 'Rocky' (Gonna Fly Now)"
"I Like Dreamin' "
"Don't Leave Me This Way"
"Feels Like the First Time"
"Star Wars (Main Title)"
"Couldn't Get It Right"
"Torn between Two Lovers"

Top Records
Albums: *Rumours* (Fleetwood Mac); *A Star Is Born* (Barbra Streisand, Kris Kristofferson); *Simple Dreams* (Linda Ronstadt); *Wings over America* (Wings); *Barry Manilow/Live* (Barry Manilow)

Singles: *I Just Want To be Your Everything* (Andy Gibb); *Best of My Love* (Emotions); *Angel in Your Arms* (Hot); *Handy Man* (James Taylor); *I Wish* (Stevie Wonder); *You're My World* (Helen Reddy); *(Your Love Has Lifted Me) Higher and Higher* (Rita Coolidge); *I'm Your Boogie Man* (K. C. and the Sunshine Band). Country: *Heaven's Just a Sin Away* (Kendalls); *Lucille* (Kenny Rogers)

Grammy Awards
Hotel California, Eagles (record); *Rumours,* Fleetwood Mac (album); "You Light Up My Life" (song)

Jazz and Big Bands
Scott Hamilton, on tenor sax, gains attention with his revival of swing.

"Second Generation of Fusion Jazz" includes Spyro Gyra, Seawind, Auracle, Caldera.

Top Performers *(Downbeat)*: McCoy Tyner (soloist); Thad Jones/Mel Lewis (band); Weather Report (jazz group); Dexter Gordon, Jean-Luc Ponty, Rahsaan Roland Kirk, Hubert Laws, Joe Pass, Anthony Braxton, Phil Woods (instrumentalists); Flora Purim, Al Jarreau (vocalists); Earth, Wind and Fire (vocal group); Weather Report, *Heavy Weather* (album)

Theater _____

Broadway Openings
Plays
Chapter Two (Neil Simon), Judd Hirsch, Anita Gillette
The Gin Game (D. L. Coburn), Hume Cronyn, Jessica Tandy
Dirty Linen/New-Found-Land (Tom Stoppard), Stephen D. Newman, Remak Ramsay
Gemini (Albert Innaurato), Danny Aiello
Golda (William Gibson), Anne Bancroft
Vieux Carré (Tennessee Williams), Sylvia Sidney
Miss Margarida's Way (Roberto Athayde), Estelle Parsons
Otherwise Engaged (Simon Gray), Tom Courtenay
American Buffalo (David Mamet), Robert Duvall, John Savage
The Shadow Box (Michael Christofer), Laurence Luckinbill
Dracula (Hamilton Deane, John L. Balderston), Frank Langella

Musicals
Annie (Charles Strouse, Martin Charnin), Andrea McArdle, Dorothy Loudon, Reid Shelton
The Act (John Kander, Fred Ebb), Liza Minnelli, Barry Nelson
Side by Side by Sondheim (Stephen Sondheim et al.) Millicent Martin, Julie N. McKenzie, David Kernan
Beatlemania (John Lennon, Paul McCartney, George Harrison, Ron Rabinowitz et al.), Mitch Weissman
The King and I (Richard Rodgers, Oscar Hammerstein II, revival), Yul Brynner

Classics, Revivals, and Off-Broadway Premieres
A Life in the Theatre (David Mamet), Ellis Rabb, Peter Evans; *A Touch of the Poet* (Eugene O'Neill), Geraldine Fitzgerald, Jason Robards, Milo O'Shea; *Agamemnon* (Aeschylus), Gloria Foster, Earle Hyman; *The Cherry Orchard* (Chekhov), Irene Worth, George Voskovec; *St. Joan* (George Bernard Shaw), Lynn Redgrave; *Tartuffe* (Molière), John Wood, Tammy Grimes; *Caesar and Cleopatra* (Shaw), Rex Harrison, Elizabeth Ashley; *The Basic Training of Pavlo Hummel* (David Rabe), Al Pacino; *Anna Christie,* (O'Neill), Liv Ullmann; *The Three Sisters* (Chekhov), Rosemary Harris, Tovah Feldshuh, Ellen Burstyn

Regional
Goodman, Chicago: *The Sport of My Mad Mother* (Ann Jellicoe); *A Life in The Theatre* (David Mamet), premieres

Actors Theater of Louisville: *Getting Out* (Marsha Norman); *The Gin Game* (D. L. Coburn); *Whose Life Is It Anyway?* (Brian Clark, joint production with Folger Theatre Group); premieres

Theater (cont.)

Pulitzer Prize
The Shadow Box, Michael Cristofer

Tony Awards
The Shadow Box, Michael Cristofer (play); *Annie,* Charles Strouse, Martin Charnin (musical)

Classical Music

Compositions
Michael Colgrass, *Déjà Vu* for Percussion Quartet and Orchestra
George Crumb, *Star Child*
Harold Faberman, *War Cry*
Ralph Shapey, *The Covenant*
Lou Harrison, *Serenade*
Garrett List, *Slugging Rocks*
Ned Rorem, Six Songs, *Romeo and Juliet*
Elliott Schwartz, Chamber Concerto III

Important Events
Numerous festivals include the 150th anniversary of Beethoven's death and the New York Philharmonic's Celebration of Black Composers series. Charleston, S.C., hosts the new Spoleto Festival U.S.A., which opens with *Pique Dame* (Magda Olivero).
For the first time, Congress appropriates the full budget request of the National Endowment of the Arts, $123.5 million (in 1969, $8 million).

New Appointments: Antal Dorati, Detroit; Mstislav Rostropovich, National; John Nelson, Indianapolis; Leonard Slatkin, New Orleans Philharmonic

Debut: Thomas Lorango

First Performances
David Del Tredici, *Final Alice* (performed by six orchestras); Elliott Carter, A Symphony of Three Orchestras (New York); Jacob Druckman, *Chiaroscuro* (Cleveland); Toru Takemitsu, *Quatrain* (Boston); Sir Michael Tippett, Symphony no. 4 (Chicago); Dominick Argento, *In Praise of Music* (Minnesota)

Opera
PBS broadcasts four operas live from the Met, one from the New York City Opera, and five from the Vienna and La Scala companies.

Metropolitan: Marilyn Horne, *Le prophète;* Régine Crespin, Shirley Verrett, *Dialogues des Carmelites;* Leontyne Price, Placido Domingo, Cornell MacNeil, Martti Talvela, *La forza del destino;* Elena Obraztsova, Guy Chauvet, *Samson et Dalila;* Marius Rintzler, Yvonne Minton, *Der Rosenkavalier*

New York City: *Henderson, the Rain King* (Leon Kirchner, premiere); *The Voice of Ariadne* (Thea Musgrave, premiere)

San Francisco: Eric Tappy, *Idomeneo;* Leontyne Price, *Ariadne auf Naxos;* Montserrat Caballé, Luciano Pavarotti, *Turandot*

Houston: *Tancredi* (Rossini, revised and cut edition); *Of Mice and Men*

Boston: *Russlan and Ludmilla* (Glinka, American premiere)

Santa Fe: *The Italian Straw Hat* (Nino Rota, premiere)

Chicago: *Idomeneo;* "Maria Callas Tribute"

San Antonio: *Rienzi*

Roots, taken from Alex Haley's current best-seller, "remakes the TV world" (*Variety*) with its saga of black history beginning with Kunte Kinte, an African hunter brought to the colonies as a slave. *Movie Star News.*

Star Wars. This sci-fi epic rapidly earns the highest box office receipts in history. Many children see it more than once—or twice. *Movie Star News.*

Art

Painting

Agnes Martin, *Untitled No. 11, No. 12*
Audrey Flack, *Marilyn*
Richard Estes, *Ansonia*
Ellsworth Kelly, *Blue Panel I*
Philip Guston, *Cabal*
Nicholas Africano, *The Cruel Discussion*
Red Grooms, *Quick Elysées*
Frank Stella, *Sinjerli Variations, Steller's Albatross*

Sculpture

Dan Flavin, *Untitled (for Robert with Fond Regards)*
Louise Nevelson, *Mrs. N's Place*
Luccio Pozzi, *Four Windows*
Alice Aycock, *Studies*

Architecture

World Trade Center, New York City (Minoru Yamasaki, Emery Roth)
Faneuil Hall Marketplace, Boston (restoration design, Benjamin Thompson)
Yale University Center for British Art, New Haven (Louis I. Kahn)
Citicorp Center, New York (Hugh Stubbins)
Thanksgiving Square, Dallas (Johnson, Burgee)
Renaissance Center, Detroit (John Portman)
Lehman Wing, Metropolitan Museum (Roche and Dinkeloo)
Cesar Pelli is commissioned, with Gruen Associates, for the addition to the Museum of Modern Art.

Important Exhibitions

Museums

New York: *Metropolitan:* Celtic art; Islamic, Egyptian art; Thracian art treasures; Russian costumes. *Whitney:* "Turn of the Century America"; Retrospective: Richard Diebenkorn

Washington, D.C.: Henri Matisse's paper cut-outs. *Smithsonian:* "A Nation of Nations" (on exhibit until 1981)

Boston: Winslow Homer

Houston, Boston: Nineteenth-century French art

Yale: Paul Mellon collection of British paintings: Constable, Reynolds, Gainsborough

St. Petersburg, Fla.: "Art of European Glass 1600–1800"

Cleveland: Japanese screens

Richard Estes, *Ansonia* 1977. Oil on canvas. 48 × 60″. *Collection of Whitney Museum of American Art. Gift of Frances and Sydney Lewis.*

Los Angeles: Sixty-two Chinese jade carvings

Los Angeles, Carnegie Institute, University of Texas (Austin), Brooklyn: Women artists 1550–1950

Art Briefs

Thomas Hoving leaves the Metropolitan after ten years; the building facade is redesigned; the sidewalk and fountains are modernized • Sales: Van Gogh: *La fin de la journée* ($880,000); Renoir, *Baigneuse Couchée* ($600,000).

Dance

Rudolf Nureyev dances *Pierrot Lunaire* (Glen Tetley) and other ballets on Broadway.

Premieres/Important Productions

American Ballet Theatre: *The Firebird* (Michel Fokine), Natalia Makarova

New York City Ballet: *Vienna Waltzes* (George Balanchine); *Bournonville Divertissements* (Bournonville, Stanley Williams)

Joffrey: *Les Patineurs* (Ashton), Christian Holder

Merce Cunningham: *Images*

Books

Fiction
Critics' Choice
Falconer, John Cheever
The Professor of Desire, Philip Roth
True Confessions, John Gregory Dunne
Song of Solomon, Toni Morrison
Torch Song, Anne Roiphe
A Book of Common Prayer, Joan Didion
Lancelot, Walker Percy
In the Future Perfect, Walter Abish
The Women's Room, Marilyn French

Best-Sellers
The Silmarillion, J. R. R. Tolkien
The Thorn Birds, Colleen McCullough
Illusions, Richard Bach
The Honourable Schoolboy, John le Carré
Oliver's Story, Erich Segal
Dreams Die First, Harold Robbins
Beggarman, Thief, Irwin Shaw
How to Save Your Own Life, Erica Jong
Delta of Venus: Erotica, Anaïs Nin
Daniel Martin, John Fowles

Nonfiction
Critics' Choice
Gates of Eden, Morris Dickstein
Origins, Richard E. Leakey, Roger Lewin
A Rumor of War, Philip Caputo
Dispatches, Michael Herr
Coming into the Country, John A. McPhee
The Age of Uncertainty, John Kenneth Galbraith
The Path between the Seas: The Creation of the Panama Canal, 1870–1914, David McCullough
Ontogeny and Phylogeny, Stephen Jay Gould
The Origin of Consciousness in the Breakdown of the Bicameral Mind, Julian Jaynes
Convention, Richard Reeves
The Economic Transformation of America, Robert Heilbroner, Aaron Singer
On Photography, Susan Sontag
Winners and Losers: Battles, Retreats, Gains, Losses and Ruin from a Long War, Gloria Emerson

Best-Sellers
Roots, Alex Haley
Looking Out for #1, Robert Ringer
All Things Wise and Wonderful, James Herriot
Your Erroneous Zones, Dr. Wayne W. Dyer
The Book of Lists, David Wallechinsky
The Possible Dream: A Candid Look at Amway, Charles Paul Conn
The Dragons of Eden: Speculations on the Evolution of Human Intelligence, Carl Sagan
The Second Ring of Power, Carlos Castaneda
The Grass Is Always Greener over the Septic Tank, Erma Bombeck
The Amityville Horror, Jay Anson

Poetry
Kenneth Koch, *The Duplications*
John Berryman, *Henry's Fate and Other Poems, 1967–1972* (posthumous)
Robert Lowell, *Day by Day* (posthumous)
John Ashbery, *Houseboat Days*
A. R. Ammons, *The Snow Poems*
Hayden Carruth, *Brothers, I Loved You All*
W. S. Merwin, *The Compass Flower*

Pulitzer Prizes
Elbow Room, James Alan McPherson (fiction)
The Invisible Hand: The Managerial Revolution in American Business, Alfred D. Chandler, Jr. (U.S. history)
The Dragons of Eden, Carl Sagan (nonfiction)
Samuel Johnson, W. Jackson Bate (biography)
The Collected Poems, Howard Nemerov (poetry)

Science and Technology

The first fusion reactions by laser are achieved.

The neutron bomb is developed, which, through neutron radiation, destroys population but leaves property intact.

A U.S. space shuttle, Enterprise, makes its first gliding test flight after being carried on the back of a Boeing 747.

Voyagers I and II are launched to explore Jupiter, Saturn, and Uranus.

A study reports that alcohol consumed during pregnancy may injure the fetus.

Charles I. Reford and Richard J. Whitley, at the University of Alabama, develop a drug (ara-A) to treat the viral disease herpes encephalitis.

Solomon Snyder, at Johns Hopkins, traces brain pathways where endorphins (natural tranquilizers) act.

❧ The Japanese car industry employs 7,000 robots for painting, welding, and assembly.

Nobel Prize
Rosalyn S. Yalow, Roger C. L. Guillemin, and Andrew V. Schally win in physiology and medicine for work on the role of hormones in body chemistry.

Sports ▬▬▬▬▬▬▬▬▬▬▬▬▬▬

Baseball

Many stars sign free-agent contracts, including Rollie Fingers, Gary Matthews, Dave Cash, and Don Gullett.

Reggie Jackson (New York, AL) hits three home runs in successive at-bats in the final game of the World Series.

Nolan Ryan strikes out 341, a record fifth time over 300.

"Billy Martin should win the Nobel Peace Prize for winning this season," says Reggie Jackson.

The Cy Young awards are won by Steve Carlton (Philadelphia, NL) and Sparky Lyle (New York, AL).

Champions ▬▬▬▬▬▬▬▬▬▬▬

Batting	*Pitching*
Dave Parker (Pittsburgh, NL), .338	John Candeleria (Pittsburgh, NL), 20–5
Rod Carew (Minnesota, AL), .388	Paul Splitorff (Kansas City, AL), 16–6
	Home runs
	George Foster (Cincinnati, NL), 52

Football

Walter Payton, Chicago, sets a single-game rushing record of 275.

NFC Season Leaders: Roger Staubach (Dallas), passing; Walter Payton (Chicago), rushing; Ahmad Rashad (Minnesota), receiving

AFL Season Leaders: Bob Griese (Miami), passing; Mark Van Eeghen (Oakland), rushing; Lydell Mitchell (Baltimore), receiving

College All-Americans: Joe Montana (Q), Notre Dame; Earl Campbell (B), Texas; Terry Miller (B), Oklahoma

Bowls (Jan. 1, 1978)

Rose: Washington 27–Michigan 20	Cotton: Notre Dame 38–Texas 7
Orange: Arkansas 31–Oklahoma 6	Sugar: Alabama 35–Ohio State 6

Basketball

Al McGuire, Marquette, wins the NCAA in his last season of coaching.

NBA All-Pro First Team: Elvin Hayes (Washington), David Thompson (Denver), Kareem Abdul-Jabbar (Los Angeles), Pete Maravich (New Orleans), Paul Westphal (Phoenix)

Other Sports

Car Racing: A. J. Foyt wins the Indianapolis 500 a record fourth time.

Horse Racing: Seventeen-year-old jockey Steve Cauthen earns a record $6.1 million in purses with 487 wins.

Tennis: Jimmy Connors is the leading pro tennis money winner with $822,656.

Winners ▬▬▬▬▬▬▬▬▬▬▬

World Series	*MVP*
New York (AL) 4	Bill Walton, Portland
Los Angeles (NL) 2	*College Basketball*
MVP	Marquette
NL–George Foster, Cincinnati	*Player of the Year*
AL–Rod Carew, Minnesota	Marques Johnson, UCLA
Super Bowl XII (played Jan. 1978)	*Stanley Cup*
Dallas 27–Denver 10	Montreal
MVP	*US Tennis Open*
Walter Payton, Chicago	Men: Guillermo Vilas
College Football	Women: Chris Evert
Notre Dame	*USGA Open*
Heisman Trophy	Hubert Greene
Earl Campbell, Texas	*Kentucky Derby*
NBA Championship	Seattle Slew (J. Cruguet, jockey)
Portland 4–Philadelphia 2	

Fashion ▬▬▬▬▬▬▬▬▬▬▬▬

For Men: The return to conservatism is marked by narrow, silk challis ties with small patterns and oxford and broadcloth shirts (no longer tapered) in tattersall and solids with small button-down collars. Also popular are pin-stripe and herringbone double-breasted suits with narrow lapels, soft shoulders, and straight, uncuffed trousers. The layered look characterizes casual dress in tweeds and textured fabrics, suede and leather elbow patches, vests, and classic V-neck pullovers. Specific fabrics create the traditional and country look: Harris, Donegal, and Shetland tweeds, corduroy, twill, flannel, camel hair, and cashmere. Soft leather, high-polished shoes with tassels or stitching are popular, along with wing tips and a variety of loafers, moccasins, and low boots. Limited accessories are in keeping with the new understated look: little jewelry (a small collar pin, watch, and ID bracelet) and narrow belts, in soft leathers with decorative buckles.

High-fashion notes: John Weitz's pin stripe and glen plaid suits, blue blazer, and tan cavalry twill pants

Kaleidoscope

Farah Fawcett, whose posters are best-sellers, plays one of three braless female detectives on "Charlie's Angels"; "jiggling" (an ABC executive's term) leads to high ratings. *Movie Star News.*

- The Supreme Court rules that the spanking of schoolchildren by teachers is constitutional.
- Three first ladies—Rosalynn Carter, Betty Ford, and Lady Bird Johnson—attend the National Women's Conference in Houston.
- Twenty-six-year-old George Willig scales the side of New York's World Trade Center tower, 1,350 feet high, and is fined $1.10 for each story.
- The *New York Times* reports on the CIA's program to develop mind control techniques.
- Larry Flint resigns as publisher of *Hustler* when he becomes a born-again Christian, under the guidance of Ruth Carter Stapleton, the president's sister.
- A parking ticket leads to the arrest of David Berkowitz, "Son of Sam" killer, so named after a dog that, he says, instructed him to kill.
- Two million Elvis Presley records sell within a day of his death; Presley's funeral costs $47,000.
- The Supreme Court rules that states do not have to use Medicaid funds for elective abortion.
- Freddie Prinze, 22 and star of the hit TV show "Chico and the Man," commits suicide.
- Forty-five million people watch the highest rated TV interview in history—Richard Nixon's appearance on David Frost's program—for which Nixon receives $600,000 and 10 percent of the show's profits.
- CBS anchor Walter Cronkite acts as an intermediary between Anwar Sadat and Menachem Begin in arranging their meeting in Israel.
- A study at Princeton University reveals that 6.8 million married couples have elected surgical contraception (3.8 million women, 3 million men).
- Sales of smoke detectors surpass 8 million.
- Singer Connie Francis is awarded $1,475,000 from the Howard Johnson motel chain after she is raped; she charged that she was not provided a safe and secure room.
- Widespread looting occurs during a blackout in New York and Westchester that affects 9 million people.
- The FDA bans Red No. 2 additive in foods, drugs, and cosmetics, and Red No. 4 in maraschino cherries; Yellow No. 5 is indicated to be a potential allergen.
- International tourism breaks records, despite the rise in hotel rates abroad; especially popular are Venice, London, and Paris.
- The Supreme Court reverses a New York law that prohibits the distribution of contraceptives to minors.
- Spencer Sacco receives a proclamation in Boston from Massachusetts governor Michael Dukakis that states that his grandfather, Nicola Sacco, and Bartolomeo Vanzetti were improperly tried for murder in 1927; both were executed.
- A California judge grants temporary custody to the parents of several young adults ("Moonies") said to be under the brainwashing influence of the Rev. Sun Myung Moon's Unification church.
- "Go back to oranges and leave the other fruits alone" reads one placard outside a Kansas City auditorium the day of Anita Bryant's concert appearance. Bryant campaigns to repeal a Dade County ordinance outlawing discrimination against homosexuals in housing and employment.
- The number of imported cars breaks all records with sales of 1.5 million.
- Because of soaring prices, consumers boycott coffee.
- CB radios achieve record sales as 25 million anonymous callers create a new language and make new friends.
- Over 400,000 teenage abortions are performed, a third of the total in the United States; 21 percent of the pregnant unmarried teens give birth and 87 percent of these keep their children.
- Cheryl Tiegs, the world's highest paid model, earns $1,000 a day.
- Billy Carter, the president's brother, endorses Billy Beer.
- Jimmy Carter, in a cardigan sweater, begins his fireside chats.
- "Li'l Abner" ceases publication.
- J. R. R. Tolkien's *Silmarillion* sells a record 1,056,696 copies in the first three months after its publication.

Fads: Roller disco; mopeds, food processors (20 brands), TV recorders, T-shirts, cheese, health foods, bottled water, poster saloons

First Appearances: Presidential call-in, lethal-drug capital punishment authorized (Oklahoma), killer whale born in captivity, no-brand generic products (Chicago), "Supercall" (electronic line judge for tennis play decisions), public automatic blood pressure machines, pocket TV ($300), Life Achievement Academy Award (Bette Davis), parade with music from transistor radios (Steamwood, Ill.), woman referee for heavyweight championship fight (Eva Shain, Ali vs. Shavers, New York City); American male saint (J. N. Neumann)

1978

In the News

37 Israelis Are Slain in PLO Raid on Haifa Bus . . . Carter Defers Neutron Bomb . . . Second Canal Treaty Is Ratified, Canal Will Go to Panama in 1999 . . . South Korean Airliner Is Forced Down in Russia, 2 Are Killed, 110 Survive . . . Body of Aldo Moro, Italian Leader Kidnapped by Terrorists, Is Found in Rome . . . "Bugs" Are Discovered in U.S. Embassy in Moscow . . . U.S. Recalls Ambassador to Chile over Letelier Murder . . . Supreme Court Rules Against Reverse Discrimination in Allan Bakke Case . . . 100,000 March in Washington, D.C., for the ERA . . . Antishah Riots Spread in Iran . . . Pope Paul VI Dies, John Paul I Is Elected . . . Camp David Talks End in Accord between Sadat and Begin . . . John Paul I Dies, Polish Cardinal Is Named Pope John Paul II . . . Wall Posters Criticizing Mao Appear in Peking . . . Ethiopia and Russia Sign Friendship Treaty . . . GOP Gains in Congress, Democrats Keep Control . . . 900 American Cult Members Commit Suicide in Guyana, Representative Ryan and 4 Others Are Slain . . . Pioneer Venus II Enters Venus Atmosphere . . . OPEC Raises Prices 14% . . . City of Cleveland Defaults . . . Strikes Paralyze Iran . . . Inflation Rate: 12.4%; Prime Rate: 12%.

Deaths

Edgar Bergen, Charles Boyer, Dan Dailey, Hubert Humphrey, Aram Khachaturian, Margaret Mead, Golda Meir, Norman Rockwell, William Steinberg, Gene Tunney.

Quotes

"Hurry, my children, hurry. They will start parachuting out of the air. They'll torture our children. Lay down your life with dignity. Let's get gone. Let's get gone."
— Reverend Jim Jones, People's Temple, Guyana

"We trust the Shah to maintain stability in Iran, to continue with the democratic process, and also to continue the progressive change in the Iranian social-economic structure."
— Jimmy Carter

"With credit, you can buy everything you can't afford."
— Edith Bunker, "All in the Family"

Billie Jean King, many-time U.S. Open and Wimbleton champion, has helped popularize women's tennis. *Copyright* Washington Post. *Reprinted courtesy of D.C. Public Library.*

The president's intensive conversations with both Begin and Sadat at Camp David help them to reach accord. *Jimmy Carter Library.*

"ERA would nullify any laws that make any distinction between men and women. When the good Lord created the earth, he didn't have the advice of Gloria Steinem or Bella Abzug."
— Sam Ervin

"The country is fed up with radical causes . . . the unisex movement . . . the departure from basics, decency, from the philosophy of the monogamous home."
— Jerry Falwell

"My esteem in this country has gone up substantially. It is very nice now [that] when people wave at me, they use all their fingers."
— Jimmy Carter

Ads

TV

Premieres
"The Incredible Hulk," Bill Bixby, Lou Ferrigno
"Fantasy Island," Ricardo Montalban, Herve Villechaize
"Dallas," Larry Hagman, Barbara Bel Geddes
"WKRP in Cincinnati," Loni Anderson
"Diff'rent Strokes," Gary Coleman, Conrad Bain
"Mork and Mindy," Robin Williams, Pam Dawber
"20/20," Hugh Downs
"Vegas," Robert Urich
"Taxi," Judd Hirsch

Top Ten (Nielsen)
"Laverne and Shirley," "Three's Company," "Mork and Mindy," "Happy Days," "Angie," "60 Minutes," "M*A*S*H," "The Ropers," "All in the Family," "Taxi"

Specials
"Balanchine IV, Dance in America"; "Friendly Fire"; "The Jericho Mile"; "Who Are the De Bolts—and Where Did They Get Nineteen Kids?" "Live from Lincoln Center with Luciano Pavarotti and Joan Sutherland"; "Strangers: The Story of a Mother and Daughter" (Bette Davis)

Diana Ross, Motown recording star, who began in the sixties with the Supremes. *Movie Star News.*

Emmy Awards
"Lou Grant" (drama); "Taxi" (comedy); "Christmas Eve on Sesame Street" (children); "The Tonight Show Starring Johnny Carson" (special class); Ron Leibman (actor, "Kaz"); Carroll O'Connor (comedic actor, "All in the Family"); Mariette Hartley (actress, "The Incredible Hulk"); Ruth Gordon (comedic actress, "Taxi")

Of Note
Fred Silverman, former CBS executive who brought ABC to a number one rating, moves to NBC as president.

Movies

Openings
The Deer Hunter (Michael Cimino), Robert De Niro, Meryl Streep, Christopher Walken
Coming Home (Hal Ashby), Jane Fonda, Jon Voight, Bruce Dern
Midnight Express (Alan Parker), Brad Davis, John Hurt, Randy Quaid
An Unmarried Woman (Paul Mazursky), Jill Clayburgh, Alan Bates, Michael Murphy
Interiors (Woody Allen), E. G. Marshall, Geraldine Page, Maureen Stapleton, Diane Keaton
Autumn Sonata (Ingmar Bergman), Ingrid Bergman, Liv Ullmann
Get Out Your Handkerchiefs (Bertrand Blier), Gerard Depardieu, Patrick Dewaere
Foul Play (Colin Higgins), Goldie Hawn, Chevy Chase
Grease (Randal Kleiser), John Travolta, Olivia Newton-John
Superman (Richard Donner), Christopher Reeve, Marlon Brando, Gene Hackman
Pretty Baby (Louis Malle), Keith Carradine, Brooke Shields, Susan Sarandon

National Lampoon's Animal House (John Landis), Tim Matheson, John Belushi, Donald Sutherland, Tom Hulce
Days of Heaven (Terence Malick), Sam Shepard, Linda Manz, Richard Gere
La Cage aux Folles (Edouard Molinaro), Ugo Tognazzi, Michel Serrault, Michel Galabru

Academy Awards
Best Picture: *The Deer Hunter*
Best Director: Michael Cimino (*The Deer Hunter*)
Best Actress: Jane Fonda (*Coming Home*)
Best Actor: Jon Voight (*Coming Home*)

Top Box-Office Stars
Burt Reynolds, John Travolta, Richard Dreyfuss, Warren Beatty, Clint Eastwood, Woody Allen, Diane Keaton, Jane Fonda, Peter Sellers, Barbra Streisand

Stars of Tomorrow
Christopher Reeve, John Belushi, Brad Davis, Amy Irving, John Savage, Brooke Adams, Gary Busey, Brooke Shields, Harry Hamlin, Tim Matheson

Popular Music

Hit Songs
"Night Fever"
"Stayin' Alive"
"I Go Crazy"
"Love Is Thicker than Water"
"Boogie Oogie Oogie"
"Three Times a Lady"
"Miss You"
"With a Little Luck"

Top Records

Albums: *Saturday Night Fever* (Sound track); *Grease* (Sound track); *52nd Street* (Billy Joel); *Some Girls* (Rolling Stones); *Don't Look Back* (Boston); *Live and More* (Donna Summer)

Singles: *Shadow Dancing* (Andy Gibb); *Kiss You All Over* (Exile); *How Deep Is Your Love* (Bee Gees); *Baby Come Back* (Player); *If I Can't Have You* (Yvonne Elliman); *Feels So Good* (Chuck Mangione); *Last Dance* (Donna Summer); *Our Love* (Natalie Cole). Country: *Mammas Don't Let Your Babies Grow Up to Be Cowboys / I Can Get Off on You* (Waylon Jennings and Willie Nelson); *Sleeping Single in a Double Bed* (Barbara Mandrell)

Grammy Awards
Just the Way You Are, Billy Joel (record); *Saturday Night Fever*, Bee Gees (album); "Just the Way You Are" (song)

Jazz and Big Bands

Top Performers *(Downbeat):* Dexter Gordon (soloist); Toshiko Akiyoshi and Lew Tabackin (band); Weather Report (jazz group); Elvin Jones, Ron Carter, Jaco Pastorius, Woody Shaw, Wayne Shorter, Jimmy Smith, Airto Moreira (instrumentalists); Al Jarreau, Flora Purim (vocalists); Woody Shaw, *Rosewood* (album)

Theater

Broadway Openings

Plays
Tribute (Bernard Slade), Jack Lemmon
First Monday in October (Jerome Lawrence, Robert E. Lee), Henry Fonda, Jane Alexander
The Kingfisher (William Douglas Home), Claudette Colbert, Rex Harrison
Deathtrap (Ira Levin), John Wood, Marian Seldes
The Crucifer of Blood (Paul Giovanni), Glenn Close, Paxton Whitehead

Musicals
Ballroom (Billy Goldenberg, Alan and Marilyn Bergman), Dorothy Loudon, Vincent Gardenia
The Best Little Whorehouse in Texas (Carol Hall), Carlin Glynn, Henderson Forsythe
Ain't Misbehavin' (Fats Waller, revue), Nell Carter, Andre De Shields
On the 20th Century (Betty Comden, Adolph Green, Cy Coleman), John Collum, Kevin Kline, Madeline Kahn
Dancin' (numerous authors), Ann Reinking, choreographed by Bob Fosse
Eubie! (Eubie Blake, Nobel Sissle, et al.), Gregory Hines

Classics, Revivals, and Off-Broadway Premieres
Da (Hugh Leonard), Barnard Hughes; *13 Rue de l'Amour* (Feydeau), Louis Jourdan, Patricia Elliott; *Buried Child* (Sam Shepard), Jacqueline Brookes; *Once in a Lifetime* (Moss Hart, George S. Kaufman), John Lithgow; *Man and Superman* (Shaw), George Grizzard; *The Inspector General* (Gogol), Theodore Bikel; *5th of July* (Lanford Wilson), William Hurt; *Getting Out* (Marsha Norman); *Molly* (Simon Gray), Tammy Grimes; *St. Mark's Gospel*, Alec McCowen; *Taming of the Shrew*, Meryl Streep, Raul Julia; *The Show-off* (George Kelly), Paul Rudd

Regional

Mark Taper Forum, Los Angeles: *Zoot Suit* (Luis Valdez), premiere

Alley, Houston: *Echelon* (Mikhail Raschin), directed by Soviet Galina Volchek, with American actors, American premiere

Actors Theater, Louisville: *Crimes of the Heart* (Beth Henley), premiere

Pulitzer Prize
The Gin Game, D. L. Coburn

Tony Awards
Da, Hugh Leonard (play), *Ain't Misbehavin'*, Fats Waller (musical)

Classical Music _____

Compositions

Joseph Schwantner, *Aftertones of Infinity*
John Cage, *Etudes Borealis, Freeman Etudes*
Morton Feldman, *Neither: Spring of Chosroes*
Charles Wuorinen, *Fast Fantasy*
Morton Subotnik, *Game Room, Wild Beasts*
Milton Babbitt, *A Solo Requiem*
Ezra Laderman, Piano Concerto
William Kraft, *Andirivieni*

Important Events

The year's celebrations include the 150th anniversary of the death of Schubert (with national tours by Andre Watts, Charles Treger, and others), and the 50th of Janáček. Horowitz, for the 50th anniversary of his U.S. debut, performs the Rachmaninoff Piano Concerto, no. 3 in New York and the White House. Andrés Segovia, on the 50th anniversary of his New York debut, gives his first performance with an orchestra in 25 years (Avery Fisher Hall, New York). Leonard Bernstein's 60th birthday is commemorated by the National Symphony at Wolf Trap Farm Park; Roy Harris, on his 80th birthday, is honored at his hometown, Chandler, Okla.

New Appointments: Zubin Mehta, New York Philharmonic; Carlo Maria Giulini, Los Angeles; Eduardo Mata, Dallas

Debuts: Youri Egorov, Dylan Jenson, Mark Kaplan

Pulitzer Prize winner Carl Sagan. *Copyright* Washington Post. *Reprinted courtesy of D.C. Library.*

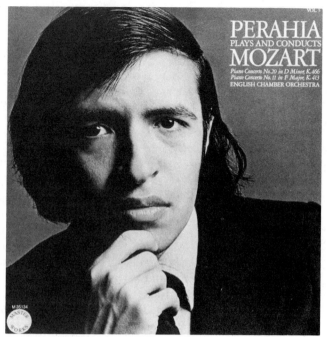

CBS records.

First Performances

Gene Gutche, *Helios Kenetic* (Miami); Krzysztof Penderecki, Violin Concerto (Minneapolis); Percy Grainger, *Free Music, no. 1* (Oakland); Pierre Boulez, *Notations* (New York); Karlheinz Stockhausen, *Sirius* (Houston); William Kraft, Tuba Concerto (Los Angeles); Ralph Shapey, *O Jerusalem* (Pittsburgh)

Opera

Metropolitan: *Don Pasquale;* Maria Ewing, Jerome Hines, *Dialogues of the Carmelites;* Richard Stilwell, Peter Pears, *Billy Budd;* Jon Vickers, *Peter Grimes;* Beverly Sills, Sherrill Milnes, *Thaïs*

Houston: Marilyn Horne, Joan Carden (debut), *Tancredi* (with long-lost, 80-bar "tragic finale"); Donald Gramm, *Falstaff* (in English)

Chicago: Arnold Moss, William Stone, *Paradise Lost* (premiere, Krzysztof Penderecki)

Washington, D.C.: *Poro* (Handel, premiere)

Virginia: *Mary, Queen of Scots* (Thea Musgrave, premiere)

Temple University, Philadelphia: *Every Good Boy Deserves Favor* (André Previn, Tom Stoppard, premiere)

San Francisco: Placido Domingo, *Elegy for Young Lovers* (Hans Werner Henze)

Art

Painting

Willem de Kooning, *Untitled III*

Jennifer Bartlett, *Summer Lost at Night (for Tom Hess)*

Philip Guston, *Tomb, The Ladder*

Roy Lichtenstein, *Razzmatazz*

Susan Rothenberg, *For the Light*

Alice Neel, *Geoffrey Hendricks and Brian*

Ralph Goings, *Still Life with Sugars*

Audrey Flack, *Bounty*

Elizabeth Murray, *Children Meeting*

Sculpture

Louise Bourgeois, *Confrontation, Structure III—Three Floors*

Duane Hanson, *Woman Reading a Paperback*

William Tucker, *Arc*

Richard Long, *Cornish Stone Circle*

Alexander Calder's 980-pound aluminum mobile is placed in the National Gallery.

Isamu Noguchi's 36-foot portal is placed in the Justice Center, Cleveland.

Architecture

East Building, National Gallery of Art, Washington, D.C. (I. M. Pei)

Dallas City Hall, Dallas (Pei)

Moorehead Cultural Bridge, Fargo (Michael Graves)

Purchase Campus, State University of New York (Edward Larrabee Barnes)

Roy Lichtenstein, *Stepping Out*, 1978. Oil and magna on canvas. 86 × 70″. *The Metropolitan Museum of Art. Purchase, Lila Acheson Fund, Inc. Gift, Arthur Hoppock Hearn Fund, Stephen C. Swid, The Bernhill Fund, Walter Bareiss, and Louise Smith Gifts, 1980.*

Clint Eastwood, who gained movie fame as a star of "spaghetti westerns" in the sixties, remains a top box office attraction and often directs his own films. *Movie Star News.*

Important Exhibitions

"Pompeii 79 A.D." opens in Boston, Chicago, Dallas, and New York. The Pei Wing of the National Gallery opens with "The Splendor of Dresden," which goes to the Metropolitan and San Francisco.

Museums

New York: *Metropolitan:* "Monet's Years at Giverny"; "The Arts under Napoleon"

Guggenheim, Houston, Minneapolis, Los Angeles: Mark Rothko retrospective

Minneapolis, Washington, D.C. (National): "Noguchi's Imaginary Landscapes"

Washington, D.C.: *Hirschhorn:* "The 'Noble Buyer': John Quinn, Patron of the Avant-Garde." *National:* "Aspects of 20th Century Art"; American art at mid-century

Fort Worth: "Stella since 1970"

Art Briefs

The two-year King Tutankhamen show collects $5 million for the Cairo Museum • Nelson Rockefeller invests $4 million in a mail-order business of high quality reproductions of works from his collection • The J. Paul Getty Museum, Malibu, will receive $50 million a year under Getty's will to purchase works • Three Gutenberg Bibles are sold within three months, one for $2.2 million.

Books

Fiction

Critics' Choice

Shosha, Isaac Bashevis Singer
Picture Palace, Paul Theroux
The World According to Garp, John Irving
Final Payments, Mary Gordon
Going after Cacciato, Tim O'Brien
The Coup, John Updike
Natural Shocks, Richard G. Stern
Whistle, James Jones
Airships, Barry Hannah
Detour, Michael Brodsky

Best-Sellers

Chesapeake, James A. Michener
War and Remembrance, Herman Wouk
Fools Die, Mario Puzo
Bloodlines, Sidney Sheldon
Scruples, Judith Krantz
Evergreen, Belva Plain
Illusions, Richard Bach
The Holcroft Covenant, Robert Ludlum
Second Generation, Howard Fast
Eye of the Needle, Ken Follett

Nonfiction

Critics' Choice

The World within the Word, William Gass
American Caesar, William Manchester
On Moral Fiction, John Gardner
Inventing America, Garry Wills
The Snow Leopard, Peter Matthiessen
Lying: Moral Choice in Public and Private Life, Sissela Bok
Perjury: The Hiss-Chambers Case, Allen Weinstein
My Mother / Myself, Nancy Friday
Robert Kennedy and His Times, Arthur Schlesinger, Jr.
Intellectual Life in the Colonial South 1585–1763, Robert Beale Davis
The Rise of American Philosophy, Bruce Kuklick
Modern Art, Meyer Schapiro

Best-Sellers

If Life Is a Bowl of Cherries— What Am I Doing in the Pits? Erma Bombeck
Gnomes, Wil Huygen, with illustrations by Rien Poortvliet
The Complete Book of Running, James Fixx
Mommie Dearest, Christina Crawford
The Memoirs of Richard Nixon, Richard Nixon
A Distant Mirror, Barbara W. Tuchman
Faeries, Brian Froud, Alan Lee
In Search of History, Theodore H. White

Poetry

Maya Angelou, *And Still I Rise*
Anthony Hecht, *Millions of Strange Shadows*
Adrienne Rich, *The Dream of a Common Language*
John Hollander, *Spectral Emanations*
James Merrill, *Mirabell: Books of Numbers*
Peter Davidson, ed., *Hello, Darkness: The Collected Poems of L. E. Sissman*

Pulitzer Prizes

The Stories of John Cheever, John Cheever (fiction)
The Dred Scott Case, Don E. Fehrenbacher (U.S. history)
On Human Nature, Edward O. Wilson (nonfiction)
Days of Sorrow and Pain: Leo Baeck and the Berlin Jews, Leonard Baker (biography)
Now and Then, Robert Penn Warren (poetry)

Nobel Prize

Isaac Bashevis Singer

Science and Technology

The drug Anturane is discovered to reduce, by 50 percent, sudden death following heart attack.

A study of longshoremen shows that the risk of fatal heart attack is cut in half by physical labor.

A balloon compression method of opening arteries is developed.

Elective induced labor in pregnancy is banned because of the side effects of oxytocin.

Recombinant, self-replicating DNA is used to program E. choli bacteria to make insulin.

Stanford physicist William Fairbank questions whether "free" quarks exist only in combinations as subatomic particles or in isolation.

NASA's Seasat I satellite collects information on 95 percent of the world's oceans (70 percent of the total surface) every 36 hours.

Plate techtonics research shows a "Siberian connection"—a piece of North America joined to Asia 1.5 million years ago.

- Louise Brown, the first test-tube baby, is born in Oldham, England, after a fertilized egg is implanted in her mother's womb.
- Ultrasound techniques are developed in London to view the fetus through the mother's abdomen.
- Canadian researchers propose that aspirin reduces the chance of stroke.

Nobel Prize

Arno Penzias and Robert W. Wilson win in physics for work in cosmic microwave radiation. Daniel Nathans and Hamilton Smith win in physiology and medicine for their work in restriction enzymes and molecular genetics.

Sports _____

Baseball

Pete Rose sets an NL consecutive-game hitting
streak record of 44.

New York (AL) beats Boston (AL), 5–4, on Bucky
Dent's home run in the AL-East playoff.

The Cy Young awards are won by Gaylord Perry
(San Diego, NL) and Ron Guidry (New York,
AL).

Champions _____

Batting	Pitching
Dave Parker (Pittsburgh, NL), .334	Gaylord Perry (San Diego, NL), 21–6
Rod Carew (Minnesota, AL), .333	Ron Guidry (New York, AL), 25–3
	Home runs
	Jim Rice (Boston, NL), 46

Football

NFC Season Leaders: Roger Staubach (Dallas),
passing; Walter Payton (Chicago), rushing; Ricky
Young (Minnesota), receiving

AFC Season Leaders: Terry Bradshaw (Pittsburgh),
passing; Earl Campbell (Houston), rushing; Steve
Largent (Seattle), receiving

College All-Americans: Chuck Fusina (Q), Penn
State; Joe Montana (Q), Notre Dame; Rick Leach
(Q), Michigan

Bowls (Jan. 1, 1979)

Rose: Washington 27– Michigan 20	Cotton: Notre Dame 35– Houston 34
Orange: Oklahoma 31– Nebraska 24	Sugar: Alabama 14–Penn State 7

Basketball

NBA All-Pro First Team: Leonard Robinson (New
Orleans), Julius Erving (Philadelphia), Bill Walton
(Portland), George Gervin (San Antonio), David
Thompson (Denver)

Other Sports

Soccer: North American Soccer League attendance
rises 50 percent to 5.3 million.

Boxing: Leon Spinks, 24, former Olympic
champion, decisions Muhammad Ali for the
heavyweight title; Ali later regains the crown before
70,000 who pay $7 million.

Horse Racing: Affirmed, ridden by Steve Cauthen,
wins the triple crown; Alydar is second in all three
races. In the Marlboro Cup, Seattle Slew beats
Affirmed in the first match between triple crown
winners.

Tennis: Top money winners are Bjorn Borg
($691,886) and Martina Navratilova ($500,757).

Winners _____

World Series	*MVP*
New York (AL) 4	Bill Walton, Portland
Los Angeles (NL) 3	*College Basketball*
MVP	North Carolina
NL–Dave Parker, Pittsburgh	*Player of the Year*
AL–Jim Rice, Boston	Phil Ford, North Carolina
Super Bowl XIII (Jan. 1979)	*Stanley Cup*
Pittsburgh 35–Dallas 31	Philadelphia
MVP	*US Tennis Open*
Earl Campbell, Houston	Men: Jimmy Connors
College Football	Women: Chris Evert
Alabama	*USGA Open*
Heisman Trophy	Andy North
Billy Sims, Oklahoma	*Kentucky Derby*
NBA Championship	Affirmed (S. Cauthen, jockey)
Washington 4–Seattle 2	

Fashion _____

For Women: The exercise rage provides a new
market for sportswear: T-shirts (with Mickey
Mouses, for Mickey's 50th birthday), jogging outfits,
bright terry-cloth fabrics, bloomers, and a variety of
matching sports shoes. Jeans, even when ripped to
the calf or mid-thigh, are coordinated with fancy
tops, such as silk blouses and beaded cardigans, and
are worn with a diversity of belt styles. Shorter boots
reach only to the ankle or mid-calf and have a low
heel. Denim gains even more popularity, now in
blousons and jackets. For the evening, the forties
style is revived in the broad-shouldered and slim-
hipped silhouette (the "Joan Crawford" look, now
called the "Joe Namath look"), black satins, high
heels, large jeweled accessories, and vivid makeup
(bright pinks, reds, purples on lips, fingers, and
toes).

*High-fashion notes: Perry Ellis's slouch coat; Bill
Blass's red silk and satin draped skirt and jacket*

Kaleidoscope _____

- Forty-seven percent of the adult population exercises daily or "almost daily" (up from 24 percent in 1961); 30 million play tennis (20 million in 1973); 3 million, racquetball (50,000 in 1970); one person in nine runs.
- Betty Ford announces that she has entered a treatment program for alcohol and pill addiction.
- The Karen Silkwood estate is awarded $10 million damages by a jury that finds she was poisoned by plutonium.
- Nelson Rockefeller dies of a heart attack in the apartment of one of his female assistants.
- The Mormons ordain their first black priest.
- The legal retirement age is raised to 70.
- NASA selects 35 new astronauts, including 6 women and 3 blacks.
- The Bee Gees' *Saturday Night Fever* album sells a record 12 million copies.
- A Soviet satellite, Cosmo 954, crashes in the Canadian wilderness by accident; the United States is forewarned by the Russians.
- Fifty percent of all shoe sales are sneakers; sales soar to 200 million.
- Unmarried couples living together number 1,137,000 (523,000 in 1970).
- The baseball commissioner's ban of female reporters in locker rooms is set aside by a federal judge.
- A Salem, Oregon, jury acquits John Rideout of raping his wife.
- A "Singles Expo" in California provides seminars on "Finding that Perfect Mate"; it also provides exhibits of singles products, like soup for one; there is a 60 percent increase in people living alone, 23 percent of the population.
- Alex Haley's *Roots* is followed by a growing interest in genealogy.
- Competing in the New York City marathon are 9,875 runners; 8,748 complete the 26 miles.
- Howard Jarvis, 75, becomes a national hero by organizing the petition to put Proposition 13 (reducing state property tax 57 percent) on the California June ballot; it passes.
- The Harvard University faculty votes 182–65 to return to a more structured undergraduate curriculum, thereby moving away from the more "relevant" one with greater options established during the 1960s.
- The USDA and FDA warn of the danger of nitrites in processed and cured meat products, saying that sodium nitrite may cause cancer.
- Attracted by seemingly unlimited employment and housing possibilities, more than 1,000 families move to Dallas each month.
- By mid-June, passengers have 18 different fares to choose from when flying from New York to London.
- Following a study of recidivism, the New York City police begin to arrest wife beaters.

- Nine Lives' (cat food) Morris dies in Chicago at the age of 17.
- U.S. and Egyptian researchers analyze the hair of a mummy in King Tutankhamen's tomb and identify King Tut's grandmother.
- The first American-made Volkswagen comes off the assembly line at New Stanton, Pa.
- Statewide limitations on indoor smoking are passed in Iowa and New Jersey.
- James Fixx earns $930,000 as *The Complete Book of Running* sells 620,000 copies.
- Some of TV's top salaries are paid to Johnny Carson ($4 million), James Garner ($1,700,000), Henry Winkler ($990,000), and Valerie Harper ($660,000).
- Bjorn Borg earns $50,000 for advertising headbands and Tuborg beer; $200,000 for endorsing Fila clothing; $100,000, Bancroft rackets; $2,000, VS gut; $50,000, Tretorn shoes; and $25,000, Scandinavian Airlines (on a shoulder patch).

Fads: Biorhythm, college toga parties

First Appearances: 45 RPM picture disc records, woman commemorated on a circulating coin (Susan B. Anthony dollar), pen with erasable ink (Eraser Mate), postage stamp to honor a black woman (Harriet Tubman), legalized gambling in N.J. (Atlantic City), slot machine payoff of $275,000 (Las Vegas), Garfield cartoon, "Battlestar Galactica," 2XL, Merlin, Master Mind, pocket math game calculator, microchip technology in washing machines, federal deregulation of airlines

Kareem Abdul-Jabbar continues as the dominant pro basketball player of the decade. *Copyright* Washington Post. *Reprinted courtesy of D.C. Public Library.*

1979

Deaths

Mamie Eisenhower, Arthur
Fiedler, Roy Harris,
Emmett Kelly, Leonide
Massine, Thurman
Munson, Merle Oberon,
Mary Pickford, Richard
Rodgers, Jean Seberg,
Bishop Fulton Sheen, John
Wayne.

In the News

U.S. AND CHINA ESTABLISH DIPLOMATIC RELATIONS, FORMAL TIES WITH TAIWAN ARE SEVERED . . . VIETNAM TAKES OVER CAMBODIA . . . SHAH LEAVES IRAN FOR "VACATION" . . . AYATOLLAH KHOMEINI RETURNS TO IRAN FROM FRANCE . . . CHINA INVADES VIETNAM . . . VOYAGER I SENDS PHOTOS OF JUPITER . . . ACCIDENT AT THREE MILE ISLAND, PA., NUCLEAR PLANT THREATENS AREA . . . MARGARET THATCHER IS ELECTED, FIRST WOMAN BRITISH P.M. . . . CARTER DECONTROLS DOMESTIC OIL . . . U.S. AND RUSSIA ANNOUNCE COMPLETION OF SALT II AGREEMENT . . . DC-10 CRASHES IN CHICAGO, 274 ARE DEAD, ALL DC-10 FLIGHTS ARE HALTED . . . FIRST BLACK GOVERNMENT IS ELECTED IN RHODESIA . . . SOMOZA FLEES NICARAGUA, SANDINISTAS TAKE POWER . . . OPEC ANNOUNCES FURTHER OIL PRICE RAISE, 50% IN ONE YEAR . . . CARTER PROCLAIMS "MORAL EQUIVALENT OF WAR" ON OIL USAGE . . . CARTER DOUBLES INDOCHINA REFUGEE QUOTA TO 14,000 PER MONTH . . . PRESIDENT RESHUFFLES CABINET, JOSEPH CALIFANO AND JAMES SCHLESINGER LEAVE . . . U.N. AMBASSADOR ANDREW YOUNG RESIGNS AFTER HIS MEETING WITH PLO IS REVEALED . . . LORD MOUNTBATTEN IS ASSASSINATED BY IRA IN IRELAND . . . PIONEER XI RETURNS PHOTOS OF SATURN . . . CARTER PROPOSES MX MISSILES ON RACETRACK PLAN . . . SHAH COMES TO N.Y. FOR GALL BLADDER SURGERY . . . STUDENTS SEIZE U.S. EMBASSY IN IRAN, 62 AMERICANS ARE HELD HOSTAGE . . . $1.5 BILLION FEDERAL BAILOUT LOAN TO CHRYSLER IS APPROVED . . . RUSSIA INVADES AFGHANISTAN . . . GOLD REACHES A RECORD $524 PER OUNCE, UP FROM $223 IN 1978 . . . INFLATION: 13.3%; PRIME RATE: 15.75%.

Ronald Reagan, the former movie star and governor of California, and his wife Nancy. Reagan seeks the Republican nomination for president. *Courtesy Sedat Pakay.*

"[This] is the first day of the government of God."
— Ayatollah Khomeini

"My initial reaction was to do something. [But] none of us would want to do anything that would worsen the danger in which our fellow citizens have been placed."
— Jimmy Carter, following seizure of the hostages

"If one works for years at becoming a pitiful, helpless giant, one might just succeed."
— Former Secretary of Energy James Schlesinger

Quotes

"The poor . . . are your brothers and sisters in Christ. You must never be content to leave them just crumbs from the feast."
— Pope John Paul II, at Yankee Stadium

"Are we going to guarantee businessmen against their own incompetence?"
— Senator William Proxmire (D-Wis.), on the Chrysler bail-out

"The defeat of the Equal Rights Amendment is the greatest victory for women's rights since the woman's suffrage movement of 1920."
— Phyllis Schlafly

"No More Iranian Students Will be Permitted on These Premises Until the Hostages Are Released."
— Bordello sign near Reno

"Shouldn't we stop worrying whether someone likes us and decide once again we're going to be respected in the world?"
— Ronald Reagan

"For the average American, the message is clear. Liberalism is no longer the answer. It is the problem."
— Ronald Reagan

"The craze for genealogy . . . is connected with the epidemic for divorce. . . . If we can't figure out who our living relatives are, then maybe we'll have more luck with the dead ones."
— Jane Howard, *Families*

Ads

TV

Premieres

"Benson," Robert Guillaume
"Archie Bunker's Place," Carroll O'Connor, Martin Balsam
"Real People," Fred Willard
"The Dukes of Hazzard," Tom Wopat, John Schneider
"The Facts of Life," Charlotte Rae
"Trapper John, M. D.," Pernell Roberts, Gregory Harrison
"Knots Landing," Joan Van Ark, Michele Lee
"Hart to Hart," Robert Wagner, Stefanie Powers

Top Ten (Nielsen)

"60 Minutes," "Three's Company," "That's Incredible," "Alice," "M*A*S*H," "Dallas," "Flo," "The Jeffersons," "The Dukes of Hazzard," "One Day at a Time"

Specials

"The Miracle Worker" (Patty Duke Astin, Melissa Gilbert); "Every Little Movement" (Shirley MacLaine); "IBM Presents Baryshnikov on Broadway"; "Live from Studio 8H: A Tribute to Toscanini"; "The Body Human: The Magic Sense"; "Fred Astaire: Change Partners and Dance"; "Edward and Mrs. Simpson"; "Roots: The Next Generation" (Marlon Brando, James Earl Jones); "Blind Ambition" (Martin Sheen, Rip Torn); "Attica" (Marvin J. Chomsky); "Guyana Tragedy" (Powers Boothe)

Emmy Awards

"Lou Grant" (drama); "Taxi" (comedy); "IBM Presents Baryshnikov on Broadway" (variety or music); "The Body Human" (informational); "A Tribute to Toscanini" (classical); Ed Asner (actor, "Lou Grant"); Richard Mulligan (comedic actor, "Soap"); Barbara Bel Geddes (actress, "Dallas"); Cathryn Damon (comedic actress, "Soap")

Of Note

ABC begins a nightly report, "The Iran Crisis: America Held Hostage," with Frank Reynolds and Ted Koppel.

Movies

Openings

Kramer vs. Kramer (Robert Benton), Dustin Hoffman, Meryl Streep
All that Jazz (Bob Fosse), Roy Scheider
Apocalypse Now (Francis Ford Coppola), Marlon Brando, Robert Duvall, Martin Sheen
Breaking Away (Peter Yates), Dennis Christopher, Paul Dooley, Barbara Barrie
Norma Rae (Martin Ritt), Sally Field, Ron Leibman, Beau Bridges
Manhattan (Woody Allen), Woody Allen, Diane Keaton, Mariel Hemingway
The China Syndrome (James Bridges), Jane Fonda, Jack Lemmon, Michael Douglas
10 (Blake Edwards), Dudley Moore, Julie Andrews, Bo Derek
Being There (Hal Ashby), Peter Sellers, Shirley MacLaine, Melvyn Douglas
The Rose (Mark Rydell), Bette Midler, Alan Bates
The Black Stallion (D. Carroll Ballard), Kelly Reno, Mickey Rooney, Teri Garr
Fedora (Billy Wilder), William Holden, Marthe Keller, José Ferrer
Hair (Milos Forman), John Savage, Treat Williams
The Marriage of Maria Braun (Rainer Werner Fassbinder), Hanna Schygulla
Star Trek—The Motion Picture (Robert Wise), Leonard Nimoy, William Shatner

Kramer vs. Kramer, with Meryl Streep and Dustin Hoffman, wins five Academy Awards. *Movie Star News.*

Monty Python's Life of Brian (Terry Jones), John Cleese, Terry Gilliam
The Muppet Movie (James Frawley), Jim Henson and the Muppets

Academy Awards

Best Picture: *Kramer vs. Kramer*
Best Director: Robert Benton (*Kramer vs. Kramer*)
Best Actress: Sally Field (*Norma Rae*)
Best Actor: Dustin Hoffman (*Kramer vs. Kramer*)

Top Box-Office Stars

Burt Reynolds, Clint Eastwood, Jane Fonda, Woody Allen, Barbra Streisand, Sylvester Stallone, John Travolta, Jill Clayburgh, Roger Moore, Mel Brooks

Stars of Tomorrow

Bo Derek, Dennis Christopher, Treat Williams, Michael O'Keefe, Lisa Eichhorn, Sigourney Weaver, Chris Makepeace, Ricky Schroder, Karen Allen, Mary Steenburgen

Popular Music _____

Hit Songs
"Le Freak"
"I Will Survive"
"Reunited"
"Hot Stuff"
"Sad Eyes"
"Too Much Heaven"
"My Life"
"Mama Can't Buy You Love"

Top Records

Albums: *Bad Girls* (Donna Summer); *Barbra Streisand's Greatest Hits, vol. 2* (Barbra Streisand); *The Long Run* (Eagles); *Breakfast in America* (Supertramp); *Spirits Having Flown* (Bee Gees); *Minute by Minute* (Doobie Brothers)

Singles: *My Sharona* (Knack); *Bad Girls* (Donna Summer); *Da Ya Think I'm Sexy* (Rod Stewart); *Y.M.C.A.* (Village People); *Ring My Bell* (Anita Ward); *Makin' It* (David Naughton); *Fire* (Pointer Sisters); *A Little More Love* (Olivia Newton-John). Country: *Amanda* (Waylon Jennings); *Every Which Way but Loose* (Eddie Rabbitt)

Grammy Awards
What a Fool Believes, Doobie Brothers (record); *52nd Street*, Billy Joel (album); "What a Fool Believes" (song)

Jazz and Big Bands

Top Performers (*Downbeat*): Charles Mingus (soloist); Toshiko Akiyoshi/Lew Tabackin (band); Weather Report (jazz group); Phil Woods, Hubert Laws, McCoy Tyner, Jaco Pastorius, Gary Burton, Chick Corea, Tony Williams (instrumentalists), Al Jarreau, Sarah Vaughan (vocalists); Steely Dan (vocal group); Joni Mitchell, *Mingus* (album)

Theater _____

Broadway Openings
Plays
The Elephant Man (Bernard Pomerance), Philip Anglim, Carole Shelley, Kevin Conway
Wings (Arthur Kopit), Constance Cummings
Bedroom Farce (Alan Ayckbourn), Michael Gough
Whose Life Is It Anyway? (Brian Clark), Tom Conti, Jean Marsh
On Golden Pond (Ernest Thompson), Frances Sternhagen, Tom Aldredge
Loose Ends (Michael Weller), Kevin Kline, Roxanne Hart
Spokesong (Stewart Parker), John Lithgow, Virginia Vestoff
Romantic Comedy (Bernard Slade), Mia Farrow, Anthony Perkins
Night and Day (Tom Stoppard), Maggie Smith
Bent (Martin Sherman), Richard Gere
Strider: The Story of a Horse (Mark Rozorsky), Gerald Hiken
Knockout (Louis La Russa), Danny Aiello

Musicals
Sweeney Todd (Stephen Sondheim), Angela Lansbury, Len Cariou
I Remember Mama (Richard Rodgers, Martin Charnin), Liv Ullmann
Sugar Babies (Ralph C. Allen, Harry Rigby), Mickey Rooney, Ann Miller
Whoopee! (Gus Kahn, Walter Donaldson), Bob Allen, Charles Repole
Evita (Andrew Lloyd Weber, Tim Rice), Patti LuPone, Bob Gunton
They're Playing Our Song (Marvin Hamlisch, Carole Bayer Sager), Robert Klein, Lucie Arnaz
Every Good Boy Deserves Favour (André Previn, Tom Stoppard), René Auberjonois, Eli Wallach

Classics, Revivals, and Off-Broadway Premieres
Happy Days (Samuel Beckett), George Voskovec, Irene Worth; *Talley's Folly* (Lanford Wilson), Judd Hirsch, Trish Hawkins: *Hamlet*, William Hurt; *A Month in the Country* (Turgenev), Tammy Grimes, Farley Granger; *Gertrude Stein* (Marty Martin), Pat Carroll; *A Lovely Sunday for Creve Coeur* (Tennessee Williams), Shirley Knight; *Richard III*, Al Pacino; *Drinks before Dinner* (E. L. Doctorow), Christopher Plummer; *The Art of Dining* (Tina Horne), Dianne Wiest, George Guidall; *The Human Voice* (Cocteau), Liv Ullmann; *Taken in Marriage* (Thomas Babe), Colleen Dewhurst, Meryl Streep; *The Inspector General* (Gogol), Theodore Bikel

Regional
Goodman, Chicago: *Death and the King's Horseman* (Wole Soyinka), premiere

Mark Taper Forum, Los Angeles: *Children of a Lesser God* (Mark Medoff), premiere

Theater (cont.)

Arena, Washington, D.C.: *Loose Ends* (Michael Weller), premiere

Pulitzer Prize
Buried Child, Sam Shepard

Tony Awards
The Elephant Man, Bernard Pomerance (play), *Sweeney Todd,* Stephen Sondheim (musical)

Classical Music _____

Compositions
David Del Tredici, *In Memory of a Summer Day*
George Rochberg, Three String Quartets
Gunther Schuller, Sonata Serenata
Marvin Feinsmith, *Isaiah* Symphony
William Bolcomb, Second Sonata for Violin and
    Piano
Samuel Barber, Oboe Concerto
James Tenney, Harmonium #4; Saxony #2

Important Events
A total of 1,470 symphony orchestras perform before 25 million people.

Elliott Carter's 70th birthday is celebrated with numerous performances of *Syringa;* California honors Carter with a day named after him. Ernst Krenek is honored in an eight-day festival in Santa Barbara.

Beverly Sills, 50, retires from the stage: Gian Carlo Menotti writes a farewell opera in her honor, *La Loca,* premiered in San Diego.

A great deal of concertizing occurs abroad. After the first cultural pact, the Boston Symphony becomes the first U.S. orchestra to tour China. Eugene Istomin is the first American to concertize in Egypt. Numerous Russian émigrés give highly acclaimed recitals: Youri Egorov, Bella Davidovich, Gidon Kremer.

Retirements: Eugene Ormandy, Philadelphia Orchestra (after 44 years); Maurice Abravanel, Utah (32 years); Lorin Maazel, Cleveland (10 years)

New Appointments: Neville Marriner, Minnesota; Michael Gielen, Cincinnati; Leonard Slatkin, St. Louis; Julius Rudel, Buffalo; Pinchas Zukerman, St. Paul Chamber Orchestra

Debuts: Carmit Zori, Gennadi Rozhdestvensky

First Performances
William Schuman, Symphony no. 10 (Minneapolis); Jacob Druckman, *Aureole* (New York); Earl Kim, Violin Concerto (New York): Morton Subotnik, *Place* (Portland); Henry Brant, Antiphonal Responses (Oakland): Barbara Kolb, *Grisaille* (Portland); Alan Hovhaness, Symphony no. 36 for Solo Flute and Orchestra (Washington, D.C.); Easley Blackwood, Symphony no. 4 (Chicago)

Opera
Metropolitan: Birgit Nilsson returns with a gala concert; Placido Domingo, Gilda Cruz-Romo, *Otello* (PBS, televised); Teresa Zylis-Gara, Tatyana Troyanos, Kurt Moll (debut), *Tannhaüser;* Teresa Stratas, Nicolai Gedda, Martti Talvela, Jon Vickers, *The Bartered Bride;* Vasile Moldoveanu, *Don Carlo;* Astrid Varnay, *The Rise and Fall of the City of Mahagonny; Der Rosenkavalier*

New York City: Rita Shane, *Miss Havisham's Fire* (Dominick Argento, premiere). Sills becomes director on July 1.

Chicago: Richard Gill, Bill Dooley, *The Love for Three Oranges;* Jon Vickers, *Tristan und Isolde*

Boston: *The Ice Break* (Sir Michael Tippett, premiere); *Madama Butterfly* (original version, Puccini)

Santa Fe: *Lulu* (Alban Berg, premiere in English)

San Francisco: *A Winter's Tale* (John Harbison, premiere); *Mary, Queen of Scots* (Thea Musgrave)

Virginia: *A Christmas Carol* (Musgrave, premiere)

Aspen: *Houdini* (Peter Schat)

Spoleto: *The Desperate Husband* (Domenico Cimarosa)

Music Notes
The tour of the Moscow Philharmonic in the United States is canceled after the defections of the Bolshoi Ballet stars • AT&T begins the Bell System American Orchestras on Tour program with $10 million; major orchestras tour the United States; NEA increases aid to orchestras by $1.6 million ($10.8 million for 120 grants) • The Pierpont Morgan Library purchases the holograph manuscript of Mozart's Symphony in D major for an undisclosed price • 100,000 attend a memorial concert in Boston for Arthur Fiedler.

Art

Paintings

Robert Rauschenberg; *Barge*
Richard Diebenkorn, *Ocean Park 105*
Ellsworth Kelly, *Diagonal with Curve 9*
Susan Rothenberg, *Pontiac*
Frank Stella, *Guadalupe Island, Kastüra*
Jim Dine, *Jerusalem Nights, In the Harem*
Ida Applebroog, *Sure, I'm Sure*
Jack Beal, *The Harvest*
Hans Haacke, *Thank You, Paine Webber*
Julian Schnabel, *Procession for Jean Vigo*

Alice Adams, *Three Arches*
Christopher Wilmarth, *The Whole Soul Summed Up, Insert Myself within Your Story*
Vito Acconci, *The People Machine*

Architecture

Boettcher Concert Hall, Denver (Holzman, Pfeiffer)
Deere West Building, Moline, Ill. (Roche and Dinkeloo)
John F. Kennedy Library, Boston (I. M. Pei)

Sculpture

Richard Serra, *Left Corner Rectangles*

Important Exhibitions

"From Leonardo to Titian" (from the USSR) tours Washington, New York, Detroit, and Los Angeles; also touring is "5,000 years of Korean Art."

Museums

New York: *Metropolitan:* Greek Art of the Aegean Islands; Costumes and designs of ballets. *Museum of Modern Art:* Klee. *Guggenheim:* Matisse retrospective; "The Planar Dimension: Europe 1912–1932. *Whitney:* "William Carlos Williams and the American Scene 1920–1930"; George Segal retrospective; "Traditionalism and Modernism in American Art, 1900–1930"

Brooklyn, Philadelphia, Detroit: "Victorian High Renaissance"; "The Second High Empire: Art in France under Napoleon III"

Washington: *National:* Munch; "Berenson and the Connoisseurship of Italian Painting"

Chicago: Toulouse-Lautrec (100th anniversary), 109 paintings; 16th-century Roman drawings from the Louvre

Isamu Noguchi, *Unidentified Object,* 1979. Black basalt. 11½ × 7'. *Noguchi Foundation Inc. Permission granted by the artist.*

Los Angeles: "Daumier in Retrospect, 1808–1879"

Madison, Seattle, Minneapolis: Art of Norway

Art Briefs

The Museum of Modern Art plans for a gigantic Picasso retrospective • Controversy develops over the removal of Gilbert Stuart's portraits of Martha and George Washington from the Boston Atheneum and their placement in the National Gallery.

Dance

Bolshoi principals Alexander Godunov and Leonid and Valentina Kozlov defect to the United States; Mikhail Baryshnikov returns to ABT as director.

Premieres/Important Productions

American Ballet Theatre: *The Tiller in the Fields* (Anthony Tudor); a labor dispute continues for two months.

New York City Ballet: *The Four Seasons* (Jerome Robbins); abridged *Apollo* for Baryshnikov; *Opus 19* (Jerome Robbins); *Sonate di Scarlatti* (Peter Martins); George Balanchine's illness halts productions.

Joffrey: Financial difficulties limit premieres, although Rudolf Nureyev is guest artist; the company does *Homage to Diaghilev, L'apres-midi d'un faune* (Nureyev).

Books

Fiction
Critics' Choice
Letters, John Barth
Mulligan Stew, Gilbert Sorrentino
Dubin's Lives, Bernard Malamud
Great Days, Donald Barthelme
Good as Gold, Joseph Heller
The Ghost Writer, Philip Roth
Black Tickets, Jayne Anne Phillips

Best-Sellers
The Matarese Circle, Robert Ludlum
Sophie's Choice, William Styron
Overload, Arthur Hailey
Memories of Another Day, Harold Robbins
Jailbird, Kurt Vonnegut
The Dead Zone, Stephen King
The Last Enchantment, Mary Stewart
The Establishment, Howard Fast
The Third World War: August 1985, Gen. Sir John Hackett et al.
Smiley's People, John le Carré

Nonfiction
Critics' Choice
The Powers That Be, David Halberstam
Truth in History, Oscar Handlin
The Medusa and the Snail, Lewis Thomas
The Right Stuff, Tom Wolfe
African Calliope, Edward Hoagland
The Culture of Narcissism, Christopher Lasch
Sideshow: Nixon and the Destruction of Cambodia, William Shawcross
Anatomy of an Illness, Norman Cousins
The Nature of Mass Poverty, John Kenneth Galbraith
The White Album, Joan Didion
Close to Home, Ellen Goodman
Franklin D. Roosevelt and American Foreign Policy, 1932–1945, Robert Dallek
The Gnostic Gospels, Elaine Pagels

Best-Sellers
Aunt Erma's Cope Book, Erma Bombeck
The Complete Scarsdale Medical Diet, Herman Tarnower, M.D., Samm Sinclair Baker
How to Prosper during the Coming Bad Years, Howard J. Ruff
Cruel Shoes, Steve Martin
The Pritikin Program for Diet and Exercise, Nathan Pritikin, Patrick McGrady, Jr.
White House Years, Henry Kissinger
Lauren Bacall by Myself, Lauren Bacall
The Brethren: Inside the Supreme Court, Bob Woodward, Scott Armstrong
Restoring the American Dream, Robert J. Ringer

Poetry
Denise Levertov, *Life in the Forest*
John Hollander, *Blue Wine*
Louis Zukofsky, *A*
David Wagoner, *In Broken Country*
John Ashbery, *As We Know*
Irving Feldman, *New and Selected Poems*

Pulitzer Prizes
The Executioner's Song, Norman Mailer (fiction)
Been in the Storm So Long: The Aftermath of Slavery, Leon F. Litwack (U.S. history)
Gödel, Esher, Bach: An Eternal Golden Braid, Douglas R. Hofstadter (nonfiction)
The Rise of Theodore Roosevelt, Edmund Morris (biography)
Selected Poems, Donald Justice (poetry)

Science and Technology

Viking I discovers a thin, flat ring of particles around Jupiter.

Pioneer 11 reaches Saturn and reports that its rings are made up of ice-covered rocks; it is blue with bright bands near its North Pole.

Voyager I and II explore Jupiter's moons; they reveal that Io, the innermost moon, is the most volcanically active body discovered thus far in the solar system.

A fusion reactor at Princeton achieves a temperature of 60 million degrees F.

A microelectronic "syringe driver" is developed.

A new artificial kidney machine for dialysis is developed that can be carried in an attaché case.

Controlling mild hypertension is found to greatly reduce the incidence of heart attack.

Replantation surgery increases, incorporating many techniques learned from the Chinese.

A more effective, less painful six-shot rabies vaccine is developed.

Research into the use of interferon (a body protein) in the treatment of cancer is pioneered.

Work begins on robots able to "see"; they are programmed with "visual" coded memory.

Nobel Prize
Steven Weinberg and Sheldon L. Glashow win in physics for work on radioactive decay in atomic nuclei. Allan McLeod Cormack wins in physiology and medicine for developing the CAT scan. Herbert C. Brown wins in chemistry for work in developing substances that facilitate difficult chemical reactions.

Sports

Baseball

Lou Brock (St. Louis, NL) and Carl Yastrzemski (Boston, AL) get their 3,000th hit, making a total of 15 players to accomplish this.

Willie Stargell wins the MVP awards of the season's playoffs and World Series.

Thurman Munson (New York, AL), catcher, dies when his private plane crashes.

The Cy Young awards go to Bruce Sutter (Chicago, NL) and Mike Flanagan (Baltimore, AL).

Champions

Batting	Pitching
Keith Hernandez (St. Louis, NL), .344	Tom Seaver (Cincinnati, NL), 16–6
Fred Lynn (Boston, AL), .333	Mike Caldwell (Milwaukee, AL), 16–6
	Home runs
	Dave Kingman (Chicago, NL), 48

Football

O. J. Simpson, Buffalo, retires with 11,236 yards rushing, second only to Jim Brown's 12,312.

Dan Fouts, San Diego, passes for a record 4,082 yards.

NFC Season Leaders: Roger Staubach (Dallas), passing; Walter Payton (Chicago), rushing; Ahmad Rashad (Minnesota), receiving

AFC Season Leaders: Dan Fouts (San Diego), passing; Earl Campbell (Houston), rushing; Joe Washington (Baltimore), receiving

College All-Americans: Billy Sims (B), Oklahoma; Jim Richter (C), North Carolina State

Bowls (Jan. 1, 1980)

Rose: Southern California 17–Ohio State 16	Cotton: Houston 17–Nebraska 14
Orange: Oklahoma 24–Florida State 7	Sugar: Alabama 24–Arkansas 0

Basketball

Ann Meyers becomes the first woman to sign an NBA contract ($50,000), with Indiana; she does not play during the season.

NBA All-Pro First Team: Marques Johnson (Milwaukee), Elvin Hayes (Washington), Moses Malone (Houston), George Gervin (San Antonio), Paul Westphal (Phoenix)

Other Sports

Boxing: Muhammad Ali "officially" retires; his record is 56 (37 KOs)–3–0; he has earned an estimated $50 million. Undefeated Sugar Ray Leonard defeats Wilfredo Benitez for the welterweight title.

Hockey: Montreal wins its fourth consecutive Stanley Cup; the WHA merges with the NHL.

Golf: Tom Watson wins a record $462,636; Nancy Lopez wins a women's record $197,489.

Tennis: Both Bjorn Borg and John McEnroe exceed $1 million in earnings; Borg wins a modern record fourth straight Wimbleton.

Winners

World Series	*NBA Championship*
Pittsburgh (NL) 4	Seattle 4–Washington 1
Baltimore (AL) 3	*MVP*
MVP	Moses Malone, Houston
AL–Don Baylor, Baltimore	*College Basketball*
NL–Keith Hernandez, St. Louis, Willie Stargell, Pittsburgh	Michigan State
	Player of the Year
Super Bowl XIV (Jan. 1980)	Larry Bird, Indiana State
Pittsburgh 31–Los Angeles 19	*Stanley Cup*
	Montreal
MVP	*US Tennis Open*
Earl Campbell, Houston	Men: John McEnroe
College Football	Women: Tracy Austin
Alabama	*USGA Open*
Heisman Trophy	Hale Irwin
Charles White, Southern California	*Kentucky Derby*
	Spectacular Bid (R. Franklin, jockey)

Fashion

For Women: High inflation and the energy crisis precipitate more traditional styles and less radical silhouette changes. Emphasis is on accessories, like blouses, camisoles, and jackets, that can expand the wardrobe. Interest in ethnic styles diminishes, and more popular, for day, are slim slit skirts worn with belted sweaters, and broad-shouldered suits worn with spike-heeled shoes. Soft silk blouses grow in popularity, along with black velvet jackets and plaid skirts and tartans. Pants take on a roomy pajama look. New to the fashion scene are disco clothes, like body suits and wraparound skirts, but tight jeans remain ubiquitous. Popular accessories (and investments) are gold chains, earrings, and bangles, as well as tiny diamond earrings.

High-fashion notes: Halston's sequined and "skin" lace chemise; Trigère's black chiffon gown with Chinese motif

Kaleidoscope —————

- Over 315,000 microcomputers are sold (172,000 in 1978).
- Health food sales reach $1.6 billion ($140 million in 1970).
- John Mitchell is freed from prison, the last Watergate convict; 25 people served 25 days to 53 months.
- The Supreme Court rules that "husbands-only" alimony laws are unconstitutional.
- The *Reader's Digest* plans to condense the revised standard version of the Bible by omitting repetitions and genealogies.
- Jane Fonda and Tom Hayden tour 50 cities to speak out against nuclear power.
- Patty Hearst's sentence is commuted to 22 months, and she leaves prison.
- California is the first state to initiate gas rationing via alternate-day purchasing; many states follow.
- With 3,243 performances, *Grease* passes *Fiddler on the Roof* as the longest playing Broadway show.
- Record sales drop from 4.3 billion in 1978 to 3.5 billion, the first major decline in many years.
- Chrysler Corporation's annual losses are $1.1 billion, the largest in U.S. corporate history.
- Massachusetts joins six other states to raise the legal drinking age from 18 to 20.
- A *New York Times* poll reports that 55 percent of the population sees nothing wrong with premarital sex, over double the statistic in 1969.
- Marlon Brando, Steve McQueen, Clint Eastwood, Burt Reynolds, and Robert Redford command $3 million per film.
- Eleven people are trampled to death rushing for seats at a Cincinnati concert by the Who.
- An amendment to the 1964 Civil Rights law says that employers with disability plans must provide disability for pregnancy.
- A California court awards Michelle Triola $104,000 in her "palimony" suit against Lee Marvin; she had asked for half of Marvin's $3.6 million earnings during the time they lived together.
- Jane Margaret Byrne becomes Chicago's first female mayor when she defeats Mayor Michael A. Bilandic,

Alfalfa sandwiches, one of the stock products in the expanding health food industry. *Copyright* Washington Post. *Reprinted courtesy of D.C. Library.*

Punk rock star Deborah Harry ("Blondie"), former beautician and *Playboy* bunny, sings "Heart of Glass." *Movie Star News.*

who had previously fired her as consumer affairs commissioner.

- The Supreme Court reverses a Massachusetts law requiring unmarried minors to obtain their parents' or a judge's permission for an abortion.
- Following the Three Mile Island accident, antinuclear rallies are held throughout the country.
- Numerous brands of hair dryers are recalled because of suspected harmful amounts of asbestos.
- Risks International, Inc., computes an up-to-the-minute data log of terrorist acts throughout the world and sells it to firms whose executives might be threatened by terrorists.
- Fifty-year-old Treasury bills worth $80,000 float through the air in Cleveland when a building is demolished; the bills are gathered by passersby.
- *U.S. Trust* reports that 520,000 Americans are millionaires, 1 in every 424.
- The divorce rate increases 69 percent since 1968, with the median duration of marriage 6.6 years; 40 percent of the children born during the decade will spend some time in a single-parent household, 90 percent headed by the mother.
- Judith Krantz receives a record $3.2 million advance for the paperback rights to *Princess Daisy*.
- A sociological study reports that clothing with designer labels, T-shirts with slogans, and bumper stickers with such mottoes as "I'd rather be fishing" express a wish for connection with other people.

Fads: Electronic games like Chess Challenger, backgammon, bridge, Microvision, Speak and Spell, Little Professor

First Appearances: Video digital sound disc, electronic blackboard, "tera" pocket calculator (connecting to company computer by three-way radio), throwaway toothbrushes, U.S. ambassador to the People's Republic of China (Leonard Woodcock), "Drabble" cartoon (in *Seventeen* magazine), nitrite-free hot dogs, railroad train operated exclusively by women (Port Washington, N.Y., to Penn Station), highest purchase price for a comic book (Marvel Comic, no. 1, $43,000), Cracker Jack ice cream bars, rocket vehicle to break the sound barrier on land (Stan Barrett, Edwards Air Force Base), woman commander of naval ship on regular patrol (Beverly Kelley)